W9-CSI-060

W. & Thurs
1-4:00
office hrs.
Tues Dec 12
4-6

Adolescent Psychology

Adolescent

Frontispiece Key

(See frontispiece, p. iii)

1. Mike, age 14
2. Kyle, age 17
3. Louis, age 17
4. Candace, age 15
5. Mike, age 15
6. Cara, age 19
7. Penny, age 15
8. Niki, age 14
9. Joni, age 13
10. Tito, age 14
11. Amelia, age 15
12. Sheilah, age 13

Psychology

a contemporary view

Linda Nielsen
Wake Forest University

HOLT, RINEHART AND WINSTON
New York Chicago San Francisco Philadelphia
Montreal Toronto London Sydney
Tokyo Mexico City Rio de Janeiro Madrid

Publisher: **Robert Woodbury**
Acquiring Editor: **Susan Meyers**
Developmental Editor: **Kate Morgan**
Managing Editor: **Kathy Nevils**
Project Editors: **Arlene Katz, Catherine Buckner**
Production Manager: **Pat Sarcuni**
Art Director: **Gloria Gentile**
Text Design: **William Gray**
Cover Design: **Gloria Gentile**

Library of Congress Cataloging-in-Publication Data

Nielsen, Linda.
Adolescent psychology.

Bibliography: p.
Includes index.
1. Adolescent psychology. I. Title.
BF724.N53 1987 155.5 86-11997

ISBN 0-03-070493-6

Copyright © by 1987 by Holt, Rinehart and Winston, Inc.
All rights reserved. No part of this publication may be reproduced or transmitted in any form or by any means, electronic or mechanical, including photocopy, recording or any information storage and retrieval system, without permission in writing from the publisher.
Requests for permission to make copies of any part of the work should be mailed to: Permissions, Holt, Rinehart and Winston, Inc., 111 Fifth Avenue, New York, New York 10003
Printed in the United States of America
Published simultaneously in Canada

7 8 9 016 9 8 7 6 5 4 3 2

Holt, Rinehart and Winston
The Dryden Press
Saunders College Publishing

CREDITS

Chapter 1 *pp. 6, 8, 9* The Bettman Archive, Inc. *p. 16* Ken Heymann
(Continued on p. 745)

To my friend

who knows there are no guarantees, not even for those who promise to keep mud off the carpet.

About the Author

Linda Nielsen has written extensively about adolescents and adolescent psychology. Her other publications include *How to Motivate Adolescents: A Guide for Parents, Teachers, and Counselors* (Prentice-Hall, 1982); *Understanding Sex Roles and Moving Beyond* (with C. White, U.S. Department of Education, 1979), and numerous articles and textbook chapters. A high school teacher for five years and an educational psychologist for ten years, Dr. Nielsen currently teaches at Wake Forest University and conducts workshops for counselors, parents, and teachers. Her work with public schools and federal research projects has included delinquent, learning-disabled, and unmotivated adolescents. She was the winner of the 1980 author's award from the U.S. Center for Women Scholars and a post-doctoral fellowship in 1981 from the American Association of University Women. She is a member of the American Psychological Association.

Preface

To the instructor

Given all the books you've already reviewed and the time you've invested designing a course around your present text, why consider adopting another adolescent psychology text? Having asked myself this question each time a newly published textbook finds its way into the stack on my desk, I now find myself, as an author, wanting to answer this question as candidly and succinctly as possible for you.

In my search for the ideal textbook, I become frustrated by the same dogged dilemmas. The first is a tug-of-war between wanting my students to be captivated by the reading and simultaneously wanting them to be introduced to the most thorough, challenging scholarship available. Unfortunately, the texts that provide the most careful examinations of the research are the ones my students find the most boring. When I've adopted books of this ilk, I'm confronted with laments: "I don't see the relevance or the practicality of this material"; "I'm having a hard time figuring out what the author is trying to say." Taking the most "scholarly" texts further to task, my students have also subjected me to a lecture on how the most talented scholars should be capable of presenting the data and theories in an engaging and pragmatic manner. Under these circumstances, I wind up defending my choice of books by inviting my students to "work with your classmates in devising practical applications and in discovering the relevance of these data and theories."

Safely ensconced in the privacy of my office, however, I've taken my students' criticisms to heart and adopted the second type of text—the book that students find more engaging and more pragmatic. As in any worthy tug-of-war, however, while I too find myself more entertained by these books and while I applaud their more applied approach to adolescent psychology, I feel uneasy with several aspects of the scholarship. In examining the text's references, I find inadequacies in terms of quantity, recency, breadth, and diversity of perspective. Having counted the number of citations from the 1970s and the number referring exclusively to college samples, I end up supplementing the text with a host of readings from the 1980s and from the burgeoning field of research on early adolescence.

More troublesome still, despite which of the two types of texts I adopt, I've encountered three other problems. First, there are too few attempts to teach students to evaluate the relative merit of various studies, to recognize the contradictions and inconsistencies in the data, or to identify significant methodological shortcomings. Consequently, I've found myself cringing when students discuss teenage pregnancy on the basis of the data displayed on a brightly colored, full-page table entitled "Causes of adolescent pregnancy"—data derived from a 1975 correlational study with a nonrandom sample of 100 white, college freshmen volunteers. In a text's effort to interpret and to summarize data for students, I've been left with the gnawing feeling that too often the data have been oversimplified by ignoring the contradictory data and by failing to note the methodological flaws that plague even the most compelling studies.

Second, I have been unable to find a thorough presentation of the data or the contemporary issues relevant to female adolescents or youths from minority cultures. Given that almost half of the adolescent population is female and that nearly one-fifth are members of minority cultures, I am compelled to modify a text's conclusions and inferences by presenting the recent data and issues through lectures and supplementary readings—a time-consuming task that neither my students nor I particularly relish. Realizing that we have advanced beyond mere "consciousness raising" in regard to racism and sexism, I've been seeking a more rigorous, contemporary examination of the empirical research and theoretical issues related to female and minority youth.

Third, as a teacher who aspires to be "inspiring" and "engaging" (well, at least occasionally!), I want a text whose instructor's manual contributes to my teaching skills and whose pedagogical aids benefit my least successful students. I also want a fresh supply of provocative questions for class discussions and challenging test questions that distinguish between those students who truly comprehend the material and those who have merely skimmed the text and are "good guessers" on multiple-choice items. Finally, given the range of my students' abilities, I need a text whose study aids and writing style make the book appropriate for my most advanced students, as well as for their classmates whose poor study skills or whose unfamiliarity with psychology impede their understanding of the text.

Having shared my concerns with you, let me briefly describe my own attempts to create an adolescent psychology text that meets my own criteria. Each of my chapters is based primarily on data from the 1980s and focuses on adolescents between the ages of 13 and 18, rather than on college-aged youth. I invite you to examine the references in terms of their quantity, their currency, and the variety that they represent in terms of adolescents' race, sex, and socioeconomic status. I especially encourage you to examine Chapter 5 on sex-role development and Chapter 6 on adolescents from minority cultures, in terms of their thoroughness and empirical rigor.

In addition, each chapter describes many of the shortcomings, the discrepancies, and the unresolved controversies in the existing data. By explaining the advantages and disadvantages of various types of research in Chapter 1 and by highlighting the methodological aspects of specific studies throughout the text, such as nonrandom sampling and correlational designs, I am encouraging students to interpret statistics and research with more care and sophistication. Although my strategy may exacerbate the discomfort of students who are seeking an unwavering, "correct" answer to pressing social problems, such as delinquency and teenage pregnancy, I think it engenders a more mature understanding of the complexities involved in research and a more tolerant attitude in regard to the well-intentioned yet naive accusation that "somebody ought to do something about those deplorable situations."

I am also committed to motivating college students and to demonstrating the pragmatic value of our empirical research and theories. Consequently, each of my chapters offers a multitude of specific examples and practical applications of theories, data, and issues. To diminish the chance of your students asking "so what?" after having read a chapter, the questions for discussion and debate and the self-administered quizzes in each chapter ask for a personal examination of controversies, such as providing abortion and contraception for minors, offering death-education classes in our schools, establishing schools for gay adolescents, eliminating curricular tracking in U.S. education, and permitting students with AIDS to attend public school. The chapters' quizzes and questions require students to apply seemingly abstract theories and concepts to their interactions with adolescents, as well as to their own adolescent and adult life.

Moreover, I've included recent news articles and writings by adolescents themselves, which breathe life into otherwise impersonal, lifeless data. To provoke your students' curiosity, these materials have been set aside from the text in specially highlighted boxed inserts. For example, your students will find adolescents' own descriptions of being bisexual, of coping with a parent's death, of becoming a teenage parent, of adjusting to their parents' divorce, of living in a biracial family, of discovering incest within their family, of losing their virginity, and attempting suicide. I have also taken care to include contemporary topics that directly affect college students themselves, such as herpes, the cervical sponge, PMS, math anxiety, anorexia, interracial dating, and rape.

Finally, the text offers a number of features designed to enhance your students' understanding of the material: instructional objectives, a detailed outline of the chapter, a list of key terms that are then highlighted in the text, a set of review questions, and a glossary. In addition, when research concerning a particular topic is presented in a chapter, it is placed within the context of the theories introduced in Chapter 1, rather than as a series of isolated empirical findings. This pedagogical strategy provides students with a continuity between the chapters and fosters their understanding of the different theoretical approaches to adolescent psychology, which may have seemed abstract at the beginning of the text.

In conjunction with these features, the instructor's manual offers additional strategies for increasing students' understanding and for enlivening the time you spend together in class: topics for research projects, annotated bibliographies of supplementary readings, relevant audiovisual aids, suggested speakers from the community, possible lecture topics, and class activities other than lectures and seminars, which other instructors have employed with their college students. I have also suggested ways in which the tables, boxed inserts, and photographs in the text can be incorporated into your lectures and class activities. Moreover, in order to hone your students' abilities in interpreting data cautiously, the manual provides exercises that require students to examine the strengths and weaknesses of particular studies and statistics. A file of multiple-choice and essay questions is also provided for each chapter.

In closing, I feel simultaneously frustrated and satisfied. The seemingly endless deluge of newly published data, which challenge our once-revered theories and our supposed "conclusions" about adolescence, remind me that, even as this book goes to press, it is already outdated. In striving to be current, I am already part of the past; in striving to be comprehensive, I am still confined by the limitations of time, personal energy, and manuscript length; in trying to be objective, I am nonetheless influenced, as are we all, by my own personal past and present. These reservations about my own work notwithstanding, I am convinced that this book can provoke your students' passions, hone their critical thinking, deepen their understanding of adolescence, debunk many of the myths surrounding today's adolescents, and leave you with the satisfaction of having presented material that is both engaging and intellectually demanding.

To the student

Would you like to be 14 again? If given the option of supervising either adolescents or younger children for a weekend, which would you choose? Would you be more likely to write an article entitled "The adolescent years: A survival guide for parents" or "Adolescence: Time of love and laughter"? Your answers to such questions depend both on the nature of your own adolescent experiences and on the accuracy of your information about adolescents. Obviously, neither you nor I have the power to alter your adolescence. We do, however, have the power to examine the validity of your assumptions about the adolescent period of life and to scrutinize your convictions about the adolescents of today and of yesteryear.

With this power in mind, my primary objective in writing this book is to introduce you to the most recent data and the most prevalent controversies in the field of adolescent psychology. In so doing, I am hoping simultaneously to alter many of your images of adolescents and to reinforce some of the feelings and opinions that you presently cannot defend with statistical data or empirical research.

Because we all tend to generalize (and sometimes to proselytize!) on the basis of our own personal experiences, a number of myths and misperceptions regarding adolescence continue to thrive, despite the absence of empirical or statistical support. Indeed, I have found it frustrating and sometimes poignantly touching that my own students so often defend their opinions by citing their own personal experiences in total disregard of the data from national surveys or from carefully designed experimental research. With reams of data and statistics in hand, I am often trying to jar students into understanding that their personal experiences do not necessarily reflect the realities of most other Americans: ''Just because the earth looks flat from your view out of this window, are you willing to discount the photographic and navigational data that disprove your personal vision of reality?'' Understanding the difficulties involved, I nonetheless invite you to give your most careful consideration to the data and theories that contradict your personal experiences and that challenge some of your most heart-felt convictions—a feat which, in and of itself, will require considerable selflessness and a certain kind of courage on your part.

My second aspiration is to engage you in an examination of your own adolescence—to recognize its impact upon your present life and to appreciate the differences between your own adolescence and that of thousands of other young people in our society. In pursuit of this goal, I have provided questions with each chapter to provoke discussions about your adolescence and to heighten your awareness of the diversity within our society's adolescent population. If your instructor does not allot time in class for discussing these questions, I hope you will share them with friends and relatives as a way of better understanding yourself and others. In addition, I invite you to attend with care to the voices of adolescents that appear in the chapters' boxed inserts—voices that speak poignantly and powerfully to those willing to listen.

Finally, as you embark on this study of adolescent psychology, your attention will probably wander to an aspect of the course that can arouse considerable anxiety—your grade. Confronted wih a 700-page book, you may be asking, as do most of my students, ''How do I know what information should receive most of my attention? How should I prepare myself for the tests?'' Having heard too many students lament, ''I studied but it sure didn't show in my grade,'' I have tried to discern the differences between the study habits of students who do well on tests and those who do poorly. As a consequence, I have provided special features throughout my book to guide you in preparation for your exams.

First, each chapter is prefaced by a detailed outline, a statement of the main objectives, and a list of technical terms and concepts. These concepts are further highlighted in the chapter by italics. Some terms in the text are in boldface print and are briefly defined in the glossary at the end of the book. Before beginning to read a chapter, examine the outline, the list of concepts, and the objectives. Most important, read the questions at the end of the chapter at least twice *before* you begin reading. As you read, attend carefully to the explanations of the highlighted terms, take notes on the material relevant to the study questions, and read the boxed inserts and tables carefully, when instructed to do so in the textual passages. After having completed the reading, define each of the concepts listed at the outset and write your answers to the chapter's questions.

If my advice doesn't appeal to you, there are several sure-fire methods for maximizing the chances that your instructor's tests will frustrate you. First, read several chapters of the book at a time and then quickly survey the questions at the end of each chapter. Second, rather than reading the chapter carefully, rely on the glossary's brief definitions to give you an understanding of the terms and concepts. Third, consider the tables, the figures, and the boxed inserts to be irrelevant "fillers" and ignore them. Fourth, without reading the chapter yourself, divvy up the study questions among your friends, so that each of you has to read only those segments of the chapter relevant to your assigned questions. Then get together and swap answers. Finally, skip all the sections of a chapter that treat topics that you have already studied in another course. "Studying" in this manner will almost inevitably yield interesting test results.

My hope is that, having finished my book, you'll decide to keep it as a permanent part of your personal library, rather than rushing back to the bookstore in hopes of a sizable refund. In any event, I'd value your recommendations for improving the text, as well as your comments regarding what you found most provocative or most entertaining. I invite you to write to me at my university address—Box 7266, Wake Forest University, Winston-Salem, NC, 27109.

Acknowledgments

Despite the technological marvels that have contributed to the production of this book—word processors, micro-waved hot coffee, a copying machine that draws me a picture when its paper tray needs feeding—I am most grateful for the human marvels whose work and advice are reflected in this final manuscript. Although I admit to never quite having overcome the anxiety associated with reading my reviewers' critiques, I thank each of them for the candor of their criticisms, the specificity of their suggestions, and the unselfishness of their encouragement: Georgia Babladelis, California State University, Hayward; Gerald Bachman, The University of Michigan; John Childers, East Carolina University; Maxine Clark, Wake Forest University; Patrick DeBoli, Nassau Community College; Elizabeth Douvan, The University of Michigan; Joyce Epstein, The Johns Hopkins University; Mark Grabe, University of North Dakota; Elizabeth Henry, Old Dominion University; Martin Hoffman, The University of Michigan; Rene Klinzing, University of Delaware; Richard McCarbery, Lorian County Community College; David Matteson, Governor's State University; Harold Perkins, Shippensburg University; W. Ray Rhine, University of Missouri; Lee Ross, Frostburg State College; Diane Scott-Jones, North Carolina State University; Wilbur Scoville, University of Wisconsin at Oshkosh; Cathleen Smith, Portland State University; Glenn Weisfield, Wayne State University; Melvin Zelnick, The Johns Hopkins University.

On many evenings when the writing was particularly burdensome, I found myself rereading the commentaries from my reviewer Margaret Malmberg at Lake Superior State College. Her red-penned suggestions in the margins of almost every page, her provocative questions, her humorous asides, and her generous applause soothed and revitalized me time and again. Without yet having heard her voice or seen her face, I somehow feel that we have become more than just distant acquaintances.

I am also indebted to Ruth Anne Clarke whose captivating photographs of adolescents and children grace many pages of this text. Her works arouse the emotions and evoke the questions that are too often lost amidst the data and statistics. And, needless to say, without my editor, Kate Morgan, my work could not have come to fruition—an understatement that anyone associated with producing a book can appreciate.

Finally, I appreciate the unselfish encouragement and the unrestrained enthusiasm of my friends: Betsy, who wishes that young people could be helped to see the world without illusions and to love it nevertheless; Alan, who wishes that the child in us could eventually feel worthy; and Carol, who wishes that she and I could someday see ourselves through eyes other than those of the adolescent girl who never felt quite lovely, or quite smart, or quite lovable enough.

July 1986 L. Nielsen

Contents

2 Adolescent physical development 35

8 *Adolescents and their families* 333

Adolescent Psychology

Chapter Outline

A Historical View of Adolescence
Theoretical Perspectives on Adolescence
Biological Theories of Adolescence
Sociological and Anthropological Theories of Adolescence
Psychoanalytic Theories of Adolescence
Cognitive-Developmental Views of Adolescence
Behavioral and Social Learning Theories
A Synthesis of Theories
Conducting Research on Adolescence
Descriptive Research
Correlational Research
Experimental Research
Conclusion

Goals and Objectives

This chapter is designed to enable you to:

- *Discuss the historical development of the concept of adolescence*
- *Delineate the major differences among the various theoretical perspectives on adolescence*
- *Enumerate the distinctions between descriptive, experimental, and correlational research*
- *Explain the benefits of the various types of research designs employed in the study of adolescence*
- *Identify in various types of research the methodological shortcomings that might lead to misinterpretation of the data regarding adolescents*

Concepts and Terminology

stage theories
neo-Freudian
continuous developmental view
recapitulation
Skinnerian psychology
organismic model
phylogeny versus ontogeny
biosocial perspective
dialectical view
social learning theory
cognitive developmental theories
Piagetian theory
discontinuous cultures
operational definitions
descriptive research
sequential design
cross-sectional design
cohort group
random sample
random selection
independent variable
confounding variable
life-span approach
behaviorism
correlation coefficient
experimental research
experimental mortality
longitudinal design
statistically significant
inverse correlation
random assignment
dependent variable

1 Adolescence: Theories and Research

"Leave me the hell alone, you old lop-eared heifer!" And so began my relationship with six-foot, 200-pound Joe Romines, who at the age of 18 indignantly refused my requests for him to complete just one of the exercises on short vowel sounds that I had so proudly designed for the class. As those early winter months passed with Joe and his classmates, I came to understand that "far" was what caused things to burn, that "Jews are people who don't believe in God," and that "using coca-cola after sex will keep you from getting pregnant." I was to be continually perplexed by students like the tow-headed Troy Meyers who year after year signed up for my reading classes, despite having told me several times to "go to hell" in front of the whole class—but only when he had become frustrated with the "silent *e*'s" or when his stepfather had given him another black eye. How was I to explain to myself why, during his senior year, Troy—who had by then become infamous for his delinquency and encounters with the police—still carried in his wallet a complimentary letter that I had written about him to his mother four years earlier?

Believing that love and empathy were essentially what my adolescent clients and students needed, I spent hours listening to their woeful tales and reassuring them that I cared about their well-being. Yet the impact of my efforts seemed to me both unpredictable and inexplicable, for each time I suceeded in convincing one sexually active student to use contraceptives or in preventing one frustrated student from dropping out of school, I failed in convincing two others. Baffled by the seemingly unpredictable and sometimes serendipitous outcomes of my work with adolescents, I resigned from my teaching and counseling job and embarked on the formal study of psychology, which I hoped would enhance my effectiveness with adolescents.

For personal or vocational reasons of your own, you have decided to undertake a similar journey—one that will begin with our glancing back into the early part of the twentieth century, when the concept of adolescence was in its infancy. Without examining the ways in which adolescence, as we now know it, is distinct from adolescence as it has traditionally been perceived, we are unable to appreciate fully the dramatic transformations that have occurred. Moreover, in our quest for a more accurate and more complete understanding of contemporary adolescents, we must examine the five approaches that have traditionally been employed to study and to hypothesize about young people. Although this chapter will present only a brief overview of these theoretical approaches, subsequent chapters will elaborate upon each in detail as it applies to the myriad issues involved in adolescent development.

Finally, our journey into the empirical and theoretical data of adolescent psychology requires that we equip ourselves with some rudimentary information regarding the manner in which research is conducted. Accordingly, this chapter examines the relative shortcomings and benefits of the various kinds of research employed by the researchers whose findings underlie our present knowledge about adolescents.

Whether you intend to apply the information in this text to your own interactions with adolescents or to achieve greater insight into your own adolescence, it is my hope that the adolescents' own commentaries and the cartoons in these chapters will evoke your emotions and lend a special dimension to the empirical and theoretical data.

A HISTORICAL VIEW OF ADOLESCENCE

Derived from the Latin verb *adolescere,* the literal meaning of "adolescence" is apparent: "to grow to maturity." An intriguing question, however, is how did the concept of a special period of human development known as adolescence come into being? How valid are our notions about this period of life? Is there any truth to the humorous definitions of adolescence: "the period when Humpty Dumpty is replaced by hanky panky"; "the awkward age when a child is too old to say something cute and too young to say something sensible"; "the period of time spent as if it were the last fling at life rather than a preparation for it"; "that period when the young feel their parents should be told the facts of life" (Brussell, 1970).

The concept of adolescence as a period of life distinct from childhood or adulthood has some roots in writings from the far distant past. For example, Plato (1952) wrote that males under the age of 18 should not be permitted to drink, because "fire must not be poured on fire." Likewise, Aristotle (1941) conceived of the young as distinct from their elders: "Of bodily desires it is the sexual to which they [the young] are most disposed to give way and in regard to sexual desire they exercise no self-restraint."

Yet despite the existence of such historical commentary on the young, the concept of adolescence is a relatively recent development. The concept of a period of the life cycle known as adolescence seems to have developed only during the nineteenth century (Demos & Demos, 1979). Moreover, it is only in recent decades that both the social significance and the psychological development of adolescents have assumed their present importance. Even as recently as the 1970s, only 48 percent of U.S. universities offered undergraduate courses in adolescent development, while only a meager 26 percent offered graduate

If you had to have been an adolescent at any other time in history, which period would you choose?

courses. Furthermore, during the 1950s and 1960s fewer than 2 percent of the published research articles on human behavior included adolescent subjects (L'Abate, 1971).

The leading historian of adolescence, Joseph Kett, explains that our modern perception of adolescence as a distinct period of life has developed only recently in conjunction with changes in our society's educational system and labor market (1977). In the eighteenth century in the United States, formal schooling was limited almost exclusively to male children from upper-class families, the only members of society who were preparing themselves for professional occupations. Furthermore, since school attendance was not compulsory, young people between the ages of 12 and 17 seldom congregated in groups, which would have enabled them to form a subculture distinct from that of their elders. Indeed, most young people in the past grew up in agricultural communities where age segregation was atypical. Working alongside their elders, children grew into adolescence in a society where one's participation in work did not mark the advent of adulthood, as it does in our present social structure. In contrast to our own highly technical urban environment, in a predominantly agrarian society most adolescents interacted with both younger and older members of the community and passed relatively unobtrusively from their roles as children into their roles as workers and parents.

Although the percentage of teenage people was higher in 1890 than at any other period in our country's history, these nineteenth-century youths were not perceived as "adolescents" in the contemporary sense (see Figure 1.1). Several factors coalesce to account for this lack of identification as members of a specific age group. In addition to the ramifications of living in an agricultural society, adolescents developed physically at a later age than today's young people. Pubescence, literally meaning "development of hair," did not occur as early in life as it does today. In sum, as Kett comments, "If adolescence is defined as the period after puberty during which a young person is institutionally segregated from casual contacts with a broad range of adults, then it can scarcely be said to have existed at all, even for those young people who attended school beyond age 14" (1977, p. 36).

After the 1860s the period of life now known as adolescence underwent a dramatic redefinition as a consequence of two events: compulsory education and industrialization (Kett, 1977). Between 1852 and 1918 all states enacted compulsory education laws. As a result, while only about a third of the young people between 14 and 17 were enrolled in school in 1920, enrollment has hovered near 90 percent since 1960. To account for such phenomenal growth in school attendance, it must be noted that the unavailability of jobs during the Great Depression and the fact that our industrialized society needed young workers with more formal education to perform technological jobs encouraged adolescents to remain in school. Once valued for their labor on the family farm, adolescents became less necessary in the labor market as the society became more technologically advanced. The creation of restrictive child-labor laws reflected the country's new attitudes toward adolescents in the labor market. Thus, over time, adolescence was gradually delineated as a period distinct from childhood or adulthood—a period in which the young were assembled in large numbers on a daily basis for a formal education.

One factor contributing to the dramatic changes affecting adolescents and our evolving views of this developmental period is the transformation that has occurred in the size and composition of elementary and secondary schools during the past three decades (Elder, 1980). Between the 1930s and the 1960s the average size of a high school more than doubled, increasing from approximately 700 to 1,600 students. During the 1950s the average high school located in a suburb with more than 10,000 residents rose to an enrollment of more than 1,000 students. In cities like Chicago and New York this figure sometimes climbed to and still remains above 3,000. The far-ranging implications of this educational phenomenon are addressed in books of the period, such as *The Lonely Crowd* published in 1950, *The Social System of the High School* in 1957, and *The Adolescent Society* in 1961, all of which highlighted the growing importance of the adolescent's peer group and the segregation that had occurred between young and old (Elder, 1980).

Another factor that has focused increasing attention on adolescents was the unparalleled demographic change during the 1960s. Born to parents after the end of World War II, members of the "baby boom" generation reached adolescence during the 1960s. As is significantly illustrated in Figure 1.1, individuals between the ages of 14 and 24 increased by an unprecedented 52 percent between 1960 and 1970. Not unexpectedly, given their high percentage in the population in comparison to previous decades, adolescents captured the attention of industries and retailers. Members of the business community were anxious to sell them the records, cosmetics, clothes, movies, athletic equipment, and other commodities that the young, both increasingly numerous and more affluent, could potentially purchase. Similarly, as a function of growing numbers, problems like drug use, out-of-wedlock pregnancies, delinquency, and political dissent became more apparent as the adolescent population grew dramatically in proportion to the adult population. In summary, this proportional increase in relative numbers contributed to both social scientists' interests in and the general public's attention to the needs and behavior of adolescents (Elder, 1980).

By recognizing and appreciating the recent development of the concept of adolescence, we can more fully comprehend the basis for the current confusions and contradictions that appear in the literature. As we shall see, the collection of empirical data concerning adolescence has lagged behind the development of theories about the period of adolescence. Thus, our views of adolescents have been influenced more by conceptions of adolescence than by empirical descriptions of adolescents' behavior.

Figure 1.1

Secular trends in population aging and school enrollment

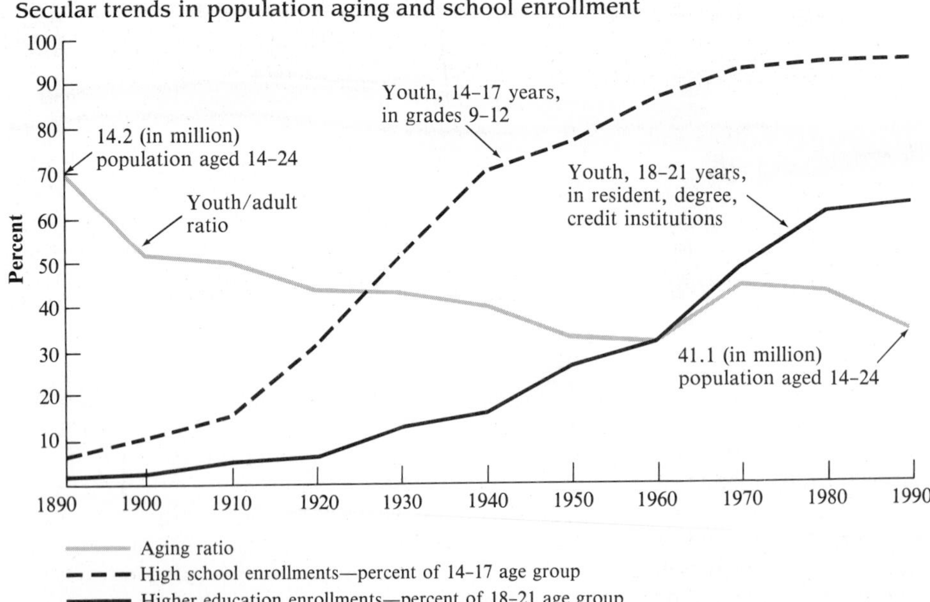

Source: Projections of education statistics. Washington, D.C.: National Center for Education Statistics, 1976, p. 18.

Do you smile at what you see here? Which of your own adolescent customs and fashions do you now find amusing or embarrassing?

THEORETICAL PERSPECTIVES ON ADOLESCENCE

Not only is the development of the concept of adolescence relatively recent, but researchers have adopted different theoretical perspectives with regard to the study of adolescent behavior. As Table 1.1 demonstrates, these theoretical views can be categorized as biological, psychoanaltyic, cognitive-developmental, sociological-anthropological, and social learning or behavioral (Muuss, 1975).

Each theoretical perspective can be compared and evaluated in terms of certain criteria that contribute to its value. First, we can judge a theory by its ability to explain a large range of seemingly unrelated phenomena or behavior. In this

Table 1.1

Theoretical Perspectives on Adolescence

Organismic Theorists	*Environmental Theorists*
Biological Views	*Sociological-Anthropological*
Stanley Hall	Kingsley Davis
Arnold Gesell	Ruth Benedict
Ernst Kretschner	Margaret Mead
William Sheldon	August Hollingshead
Psychoanalytic Views	Robert Havighurst
Sigmund Freud	*Social Learning-Behavioral Views*
Anna Freud	B. F. Skinner
Karen Horney	Walter Mischel
Erik Erikson	Albert Bandura
Peter Blos	John Dollard
James Marcia	Neal Miller
Cognitive-Developmental Views	J. B. Rotter
Jean Piaget	
David Elkind	
Lawrence Kohlberg	
Carol Gilligan	

regard, the broader the scope, the more attractive the theory. Thus, one might ask, does the theory account for a number of the actions and feelings that we witness in adolescents or is it too limited in scope? For example, the psychoanalytic concepts regarding the ego's development and individuation during adolescence are perceived as broad constructs, since they are used to explain adolescents' behavior toward their parents as well as their behavior toward their peers.

A second criterion for a theory's evaluation is elegance or parsimony. Thus, a carefully developed theory must not only be broad in scope but must avoid offering so many theoretical constructs that it appears unorganized and unwieldy. Since one of the advantages of constructing theories is to simplify data, the theory itself needs to be parsimonious. In this regard, the behavioral psychologists are seen to be quite parsimonious, for they attempt to explain adolescents' conduct and attitudes primarily in terms of a relatively few constructs, which are quite straightforward: reinforcement, punishment, and modeling.

In addition to a broad scope and a propensity for parsimony, a theory's value is enhanced if it demonstrates its ability to predict adolescents' behavior rather than to merely explain behavior retrospectively. For example, a theory that can successfully predict how a new strategy for preventing delinquency will affect adolescents' behavior is more beneficial than one that attempts to explain why students have been committing delinquent acts. Finally, and perhaps most importantly, the best theories are those that can be empirically verified. Empirical verification is predicated on **operational definitions,** meaning that a concept is defined in terms of specific, observable measures, around which testable hypotheses can be constructed. In this regard, psychoanalytic terms like "ego" and "id" fail to meet the criteria for operational definitions, since they cannot be observed, measured, or empirically tested. In contrast, behavioral psychologists are noted for casting all concepts in operational terms that permit empirical verification. For example, "being sociable" might be defined operationally as "speaking voluntarily in new social situations and being the first to initiate conversations with strangers."

Throughout this text the various theories of adolescence will be examined in relation to their degree of generalizability, their predictive validity, and their capability for empirical verification. Each theoretical perspective will also be discussed in terms of its research techniques, methodological shortcomings, and practical utility in helping adolescents with specific problems like delinquency and academic failure. Tables 1.1 and 1.2 present only a small sample of researchers whose conceptual differences and theoretical approaches will be discussed in subsequent chapters. On the basis of the data presented, you will see that no theoretical model of adolescence is totally consistent with the available empirical evidence. While each contributes to our understanding of adolescent development, none is complete or consistent enough to warrant our disregarding the others.

The following brief introduction to theoretical models underscores the presence of broad theoretical disagreements among current researchers in regard to several questions germane to the study of adolescence: What are the essential goals or tasks of adolescence? Are adolescents' attitudes and behavior primarily controlled by environmental, cognitive, psychological, or physiological variables? To what extent are adolescents' behaviors influenced by their past and by their genetic endowment? Is adolescence a distinct stage of human development or part of a gradual, continuous cycle without discriminable stages or critical periods? Is adolescence typically a period of relatively moderate pains and pleasures that accompany us throughout life, or is it a period of upheaval unparalleled by any other in our lives?

Questions like these serve as the basis for the disputes among the various

Table 1.2

Stage Theorists' Views of Human Development

Cognitive: Jean Piaget	*Psychoanalytic: Sigmund Freud*	*Neo-Freudian: Erik Erikson*	*Biological: Stanley Hall*
Childhood			
Sensorimotor	Oral	Trust/mistrust	Animalistic
Preoperational	Anal	Autonomy/doubt	
Concrete operations	Phallic	Initiative/guilt	Primitive
	Latent	Industry/inferiority	
Adolescence			
Formal operations	Genital	Identity/confusion	Savage
Adulthood			
		Intimacy/isolation	
		Generativity/stagnation	
		Integrity/despair	

theoretical perspectives on adolescence. Moreover, the major theoretical views on adolescence can be categorized along two dimensions. First, one may ask, is the theory primarily organismic or environmental? Second, one may ascertain whether the theory espouses a stage approach or a continuous developmental approach. Given this classification scheme, each theory may be categorized on the basis of its position on each of these two bipolar dimensions. For example, according to the **organismic model,** processes within the individual rather than factors in the environment are the primary forces underlying human development. As endorsers of this perspective, some cognitive-developmental psychologists contend that an adolescent's increasingly sophisticated moral reasoning is primarily a function of the youngster's internal cognitive growth, a phenomenon that reduces egocentric thinking and increases abstract reasoning. In contrast, a behavioral psychologist would argue that moral reasoning is primarily dependent upon the exigencies of the external environment—how an adolescent has been rewarded and punished, both in the past and in the present, by people or through experience.

Theories that are representative of the organismic model can either endorse the stage approach to human development or contend that human growth is continuous. **Stage theories** maintain that adolescence is one of the many distinct stages in life during which specific types of development occur in a relatively predictable fashion. From the stage-theory perspective, specific developmental stages are considered both universal and invariant. Thus, although most stage theorists agree that environmental events do influence and modify an individual's behavior, they argue that environmental theorists exaggerate the power of external events and underestimate the role of cognitive, physiological, and psychological processes. Consequently, stage theorists contend that if adolescents are to advance to higher stages as adults, they must successfully complete the stages accompanying infancy and childhood and master the tasks associated with the 12–20 stage. As you will see in succeeding chapters, most organismic theorists view themselves and are viewed by others as stage theorists.

Within the organismic model, stage theorists can assume a biological, a psychoanalytic, or a cognitive perspective on adolescence (see Table 1.2). Thus, Jean Piaget, Sigmund Freud, Erik Erikson, and Stanley Hall are all stage theorists. As we shall see, however, for Piaget the stages are based on cognitive development, for Freud and Erikson the stages are predicated on psychological development, and for Hall the stages are a function of biological development. Nevertheless, despite their different perspectives concerning the bases for the stages, these theories share the common premise that human development occurs in distinct, invariant, universal stages.

In contrast to stage theories, theories predicated upon the environmental model do not perceive adolescence as a distinct stage of development (Muuss, 1975). Endorsing the *continuous developmental view,* environmental theorists do not perceive adolescence as an invariant, sequential stage of life, whose outcome depends on the individual's having developed specific skills in earlier stages. Rather, development is perceived as a gradual, continuous process, without stages that differ qualitatively from one another. Environmentalists refute the assumption that adolescence is an experience shared universally by the inhabitants of our planet because of their common cognitive, psychological, or physiological stages of development.

Although no current theory of adolescence denies the influence of either organismic or environmental factors, the environmental perspective emphasizes the importance of factors external to the adolescent, while the organismic approach emphasizes the individual's internal processes. The following introduction to the various theories of adolescence will further illuminate these differences between organismic and environmental theorists.

Biological Theories of Adolescence

According to the biological or **biosocial perspective,** adolescent behavior is primarily a consequence of the physiological changes that accompany puberty. An oversimplified, humorous version of this view might be described as the "raging hormones" view of adolescence: Once Mother Nature takes over and changes a person physiologically from a child into an adolescent, the youngster's behavior is in her hands.

Exemplified by the theory of psychologist Stanley Hall (1904), often acclaimed as the "father of adolescence," biological views dominated the field of adolescent psychology during the early part of the century. Strikingly, in his theory of *recapitulation* Hall asserted that our individual development reflects the development of the human species throughout its entire evolution. Just as the earliest human inhabitants of our planet lived in ways that modern society considers primitive or animallike, so do infants and young children behave in animalistic ways.

According to Hall, since children are dominated by instinct and are beyond the bounds of environmental influence, they are in the "animal" stage of development. Later, at the onset of adolescence, an evolutionary mechanism makes it possible for the individual to behave in more sophisticated, although still primitive, ways. Furthermore, as time progresses, the adolescent's susceptibility to environmental influences makes adolescents more manageable and somewhat more "civilized" than children. During this transitional period from primitive to civilized behavior, Hall assumed that all adolescents experience an extended period of upheaval, rebellion, and suffering. It was through such pronouncements that Stanley Hall established the long-standing assumption that adolescence is inevitably and unalterably a stage of "storm and stress" dictated by nature's physiological control over hormones and physical growth. In spite of the lack of empirical support for this position, many people still hold this view of adolescents today.

Given the fact that Hall believed that the experiences of the human species *(phylogeny)* had become part of the genetic structure of individuals *(ontogeny)*, his recapitulation theory is viewed as the source of the famous line, "Ontogeny recapitulates phylogeny." Nevertheless, although Hall viewed adolescence as the period between "savagery" and "civilization," he optimistically believed that young people who are properly encouraged by environmental influences can eventually constitute an elite that will create a better society through the evolutionary process. Although an advocate of Charles Darwin's ideologies regarding evolution, Hall considered environmental factors as important as biological ones during the period of adolescence. Hence, his theory was biosocial in terms of conceding the importance of both biological and environmental influences during adolescence.

Although the empirical evidence that has accumulated since Hall's time discredits many of his strictest biological conceptions, biologically oriented theories are by no means extinct in the contemporary literature on adolescence. To the contrary, no other period of life, with the exception of specific events such as postpartum and menopause in the lives of women, continues to receive as much attention as adolescence among researchers trying to link biological change to human behavior. Despite the fact that the scant amount of available empirical research is generally either inconclusive or refutes the link between adolescent behavior and biological causes, the biosocial model continues to attract attention. Adolescents' behavior is still frequently attributed to biological factors associated with puberty, although empirical research on the relationship between the physiological and psychological aspects of adolescence is scant, with the exception of studies on the effects of early and late maturation. For example, as traditionally presented within the psychodynamic model, physical maturation has typically been viewed as the impetus underlying the social and psychological changes of adolescence (Peterson & Taylor, 1980).

One explanation for the tenacity of biological viewpoints has been offered by experts like Anne Peterson and Brandon Taylor (1980, p.117): "In our society at least, we may have been overestimating the significance of biological factors because of the difficulty of dealing with some problems associated with adolescence." Unable to explain certain phenomena like delinquency that appear relatively immutable, we resort to biological explanations.

Despite the criticisms leveled against it, the biological perspective continues to exert its influence on our study of adolescent behavior and to fan the fires of controversy in the ranks of psychoanalytic, cognitive, and behavioristic psychologists. In subsequent chapters the relevance of biosocial perspectives will become more clear in regard to questions such as: Does the age at which a girl starts to menstruate influence her heterosexual behavior? How do adolescents who become physically mature at an early age differ from those who mature later? How do the hormones estrogen and testosterone affect male and female behavior? Do delinquents and aggressive youths differ in certain biological respects from their peers? Are the differences in adolescents' IQ scores primarily the consequence of genetic endowment or of environmental influences?

Sociological and Anthropological Theories of Adolescence

Although biological theories dominated the field of adolescent psychology in the early 1900s, their premises have been challenged and often discredited by sociological and anthropological theorists. In contrast to biological approaches to adolescent behavior, sociological and anthropological approaches stress the importance of cultural influences. Comparing adolescents in different cultures, in different periods of history, and in different socioeconomic situations within a culture has demonstrated the impact that social structures and cultural mores have on adolescents' behavior and attitudes. Some of the earliest illustrations of this view are found in the work of Ruth Benedict, Margaret Mead, and Kingsley Davis (see Table 1.1).

In his 1940 treatise on the etiology of parent-youth conflicts, the sociologist Kingsley Davis (1941) argued that modern society changes so rapidly that each new generation experiences a social milieu almost totally distinct from its predecessor. In socializing and interacting with their children, Davis noted, parents naturally rely upon the experiences relevant to their own generation. Since, however, these experiences are now relatively irrelevant to their progeny in a more modern society, a certain amount of conflict must inevitably arise between the young and their elders.

From a similar perspective, cultural anthropologist Ruth Benedict (1934) argued that different societies impose on the young their own unique expectations and social roles, which create distinct, not universal, adolescent experiences. According to Benedict, adolescents' behavior primarily reflects whether they are living in a *continuous* or a *discontinuous culture.* In continuous cultures the young are expected to work from childhood throughout adulthood with a gradual increase in responsibilities with age. There are no dramatic transitions during adolescence and no strict lines of demarcation separating the young and old in this regard. Furthermore, children are permitted to be dominant over others within their areas of expertise, rather than relegated to positions of submissiveness to all adults, as is the case in discontinuous cultures. In addition, within continuous cultures, children and adolescents are allowed to express their sexuality as they are growing up, rather than being expected to restrict sexual experimentation to their adult years, as is expected in discontinuous cultures. Given these differences, U.S. culture is considered to be more discontinuous than continuous in its tone and expectations.

A contemporary of Benedict's, Margaret Mead, also acknowledged the culture's role in defining adolescence. In her classic study, *Coming of Age in Samoa,* Mead (1961) noted that Samoan adolescents did not experience the emotional distress associated with U.S. adolescence. Mead attributed these differences to the fact that Samoans did not expect adolescence to be a critical period for making economic, social, sexual, and vocational decisions. She further noted that Samoans did not present the young with conflicting, hypocritical standards of sexual morality, a practice that creates anxiety and confusion among youths in the United States. In sum, the work of Mead and Benedict represented the anthropological perspective that adolescent behavior is primarily determined by cultural influences, rather than by biological or psychological factors that are a universal and invariant part of human growth.

As an adjunct to the anthropological perspective, the sociological view of adolescence was ably presented in Hollingshead's *Elmstown's Youth*—a 1949 study of U.S. young people in a quiet midwestern town. Hollingshead's research focus was on the changing status and new roles associated with physical growth during adolescence. His data showed that adolescence is influenced more by external social forces, such as socioeconomic status, than by internal biological forces. Although this study may seem less than noteworthy, given our relatively compatible contemporary views of adolescence, Hollingshead's research was instrumental in helping to change the prevailing early view of adolescence as a universal and uniformly stressful period controlled by biological forces.

Some time later Robert Havighurst (1952, 1972) elaborated on Hollingshead's findings by conducting longitudinal research on children and adolescents from various social classes. Havighurst's results further supported the sociological view: Social class is strongly related to a person's adolescent experiences and to his or her adolescent and adult behavior. Confirming much of the recent data, which will be presented in succeeding chapters, Havighurst found that chil-

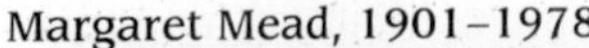

Margaret Mead, 1901–1978

dren from lower-income families are more likely to quit school, to behave aggressively, to become delinquent, to marry early, and to experience stress during adolescence than children from wealthier backgrounds.

Havighurst also expanded biological perspectives by describing the developmental tasks that he believed were central to achieving a personal identity throughout a lifetime. These tasks represent the interplay of physical maturation and the expectations for normal development that are compatible with our culture's particular standards. According to the proponents of Havighurst's view, adolescents who successfully master these tasks have established the essential bases for their adult identity. Although Havighurst describes tasks for every period of life, he proposed eight for the adolescent years, which are described in Box 1.1. Note that the first four tasks, which assume central importance during early adolescence, are more dependent upon physical maturity and biological changes than are the other tasks that typify later adolescence.

The sociological and anthropological perspectives espoused by theorists like Havighurst, Hollingshead, Mead, and Benedict challenge the traditional notions of adolescence as a period dominated exclusively by biological forces. In addition to these challenges to the biological theorists, still others are presented by the psychoanalytic approaches to adolescence.

Psychoanalytic Theories of Adolescence

Like sociological and anthropological perspectives, the psychoanalytic approach contends that forces other than the physiological changes of puberty are primarily responsible for behavior that distinguishes adolescence from other periods of life (Adelson & Doehrman, 1980). Unilke the environmentalists, however, psychoanalytic theorists attribute adolescents' behavior primarily to internal, psychological struggles related to their achieving independence from their parents. While Sigmund Freud and his daughter Anna are surely the most renowned psychoanalytic theorists, other respected theorists like Peter Blos and Erik Erikson have contributed much to the study of contemporary adolescence (Blos, 1962; Erikson, 1968; Freud, 1953; A. Freud, 1958).

According to the psychoanalytic viewpoint, one can understand the adolescent's life in depth only by having a sufficient understanding of that adolescent's personal past. Within this context, behavior that superficially appears to be motivated by environmental factors is often found to be related to the individual's past, with a particular relevance attached to previous interactions within one's own family. More specifically, the psychodynamic approach has traditionally maintained that internal drives and the inevitably resulting psychological conflicts are at the core of adolescent development. Thus, a primary task of adolescence involves controlling the expression of these internal drives that, if unbridled, would result in unacceptable behavior.

In her definitive account of the psychodynamics of adolescence in 1958, Anna Freud underscored the point that the increased desires of the instincts during adolescence are accompanied by defense mechanisms intended to keep these instincts under control. Adolescent behavior appears particularly unusual because it is a manifestation of this internal battle. As Chapter 4 will explain, the conflict has been described as one waged by the id against the ego and superego.

In addition to learning to control their instinctual urges, adolescents have the task of overcoming their childhood attachments to parents. According to psychodynamic theory, this process is called **individuation,** and its successful completion is seen to be necessary before young people can form their own identities or develop healthy heterosexual relationships. From the psychodynamic perspective, there must be a shift from reliance on parents to appreciation of peers; hence, the growing importance of the peer group is viewed as a healthy and inevitable aspect of individuation. Although other theoretical approaches consider the family as one of the most important influences on adolescents, in the psychodynamic model family interactions are central to the adolescent

1.1 A Closer Look

Havighurst's Developmental Tasks of Adolescence

Task One: Acquiring More Mature Social Skills

Prior to adolescence most friendships are formed with members of the same sex. During early adolescence the young begin to interact with the opposite sex within the security of group settings where members of the same sex are present. As they become more confident in their social skills, the young are also gaining the cognitive abilities that permit a more complete understanding of social roles and friendships. Heterosexual relationships thus become more frequent and more intimate as adolescents age.

Task Two: Achieving a Masculine or Feminine Sex Role

The maturational changes of puberty exacerbate the physical differences between males and females. In addition, the culture encourages each sex to assume specified social, sexual, and vocational roles. Consequently, adolescence becomes a time for either adopting, rejecting, or modifying cultural expectations regarding male and female behavior and attitudes.

Task Three: Accepting the Changes in One's Body, Using the Body Effectively, and Accepting One's Own Physique

In a culture that often exaggerates the value of physical appearance, adolescents whose bodies fail to fit our culture's expectations of "beauty" confront the difficult tasks of learning to value themselves physically. For the fortunate ones whose bodies conform to our society's notions of beauty, the task is limited to brief periods of time when the body's rapid growth may make its owner feel awkward, ungainly, and unattractive. If adolescents are able to accept themselves physically without being overly critical, their anxieties about physical appearance should diminish considerably by the end of adolescence.

Task Four: Achieving Emotional Independence from Parents and Other Adults

Increased social skills and physical maturation motivate adolescents to be less reliance on adults. Although their desires for independence are culturally sanctioned in the sense that all children must eventually become self-reliant, adolescents often expect to be granted independence before their elders feel they are emotionally, intellectually, or socially prepared. Parents must relinquish their former roles as protectors of dependent children and the family must establish new relationships reflecting the adolescent's increasing self-reliance. Understandably, the successful completion of this developmental task often creates conflict between young and old.

Task Five: Preparing for Sex, Marriage, and Parenthood

As physical maturation is completed and emotional attachments to the opposite sex become more intimate, older adolescents must develop ideologies and behavior that allow them to incorporate aspects of sexuality into their lives. This involves developing realistic attitudes about sex, love, marriage, and parenthood and casting aside many mythical beliefs that were part of early adolescence.

Task Six: Selecting and Preparing for an Occupation

As older adolescents advance toward independence from their parents, they confront the inevitable questions related to financial self-reliance. These include whether or not to continue one's education beyond high school, what vocation to pursue, and how to overcome whatever obstacles may lie in the path of accomplishing these vocational goals. In the case of girls in contemporary society, this task may now also involve deciding whether or not to postpone marriage for a career, deciding whether to have children in one's early twenties or to postpone motherhood until the thirties, and deciding whether to pursue a profession that might somehow interfere with men's perceptions of her social desirability.

Task Seven: Developing a Personal Ideology and Ethical Standards

As cognitive growth enables older adolescents to think more abstractly and less egotistically than younger people, questions related to morality, religion, philosophy, and politics are more likely to arise. Through their interactions with people outside their own families and their observations of the world around them, older adolescents often come to question their elders' ethical standards and to experiment with other beliefs. This experimentation may involve joining religious sects, becoming active in political parties, or interacting with people from other cultures whose views challenge their own. By accepting, rejecting, or modifying the beliefs that they readily accepted as younger children, older adolescents are confronted with the task of developing their own ethical standards and philosophies of life.

Task Eight: Assuming Membership in the Larger Community

As independence from parents and other elders grows, older adolescents must learn to recognize their roles and responsibilities to a community beyond the school, neighborhood, or family. Rather than defining themselves exclusively through their roles in the school and family, young adults learn to derive self-satisfaction and identity from their roles within the community.

SOURCE: R. Havighurst, *Developmental tasks and education*. New York: David McKay, 1972.

Sigmund Freud, 1856–1939

experience. Indeed, among the most crucial tasks of adolescence are those that involve overcoming sexual and emotional attachments to parents. Furthermore, it is recognized that as a family attempts to come to terms with a youngster's increasing independence, both adolescent and parents will occasionally regress to behavior characteristic of earlier periods in their lives. As a consequence, adolescence can evoke unresolved parent-child conflicts from a parent's own youth.

For both Freud and his followers, often referred to as **neo-Freudians,** the development of an independent identity is viewed as a task delegated to the psychological construct referred to as the "ego." One of the chief contributions of Erik Erikson and James Marcia has been to describe the various stages through which adolescents may pass in developing their identities (Erikson, 1968; Marcia, 1980). As conceived by these neo-Freudian psychologists, a primary purpose of adolescence is to permit young people to experiment with various ideologies, vocational roles, and social identities. Adolescents who use this period of life for such experimentation and who become individuated from their parents form independent identities. Others, less fortunate either remain in a state of identity confusion or adopt an identity prematurely. These aspects of ego development will be carefully examined in Chapter 4 and Chapter 11.

Cognitive-Developmental Views of Adolescence

Although psychoanalytic and cognitive-developmental theories of adolescence are similar in that they both represent the organismic perspective, their many differences will become apparent in Chapters 3 and 4. Most renowned among the cognitive or developmental theorists is Jean Piaget, an eminent scholar whose *developmental-stage theory* has provided the basis for the work

Jean Piaget, 1896–1980

of contemporary researchers like David Elkind and Lawrence Kohlberg. Given the heuristic nature of Piaget's work, a brief description of Piaget's **cognitive theories** will serve to highlight the differences between the cognitive and psychoanalytic viewpoints (Piaget, 1971).

As a stage theorist, Piaget contends that adolescence is a qualitatively unique period of life, set apart from childhood by the individual's expanding cognitive abilities. While one is experiencing the joys and lessons of childhood, the individual's abilities to reason abstractly, to develop moral principles on a sophisticated level, and to empathize with others are restricted by his or her cognitive abilities. During adolescence, however, our cognitive abilities presumably advance from what is known as the **concrete operational** level of reasoning to the more advanced stage known as **formal operational** thought. According to cognitive psychologists, this cognitive advance is responsible for the many new behaviors and attitudes that accompany adolescence: the ability to think less egocentrically, to reason abstractly, to formulate and test hypotheses, to assume the perspective of another person, to recognize incongruities and hypocrisy, to behave less self-consciously, to recognize the motivations underlying other people's behavior, and to appreciate wit and satire. Given the importance of these new skills, additional attention will be directed to them in Chapter 3 and Chapter 4.

In sum, cognitive developmentalists differ from other organismic theorists in that they emphasize the importance of the cognitive stage in determining an individual's behavior and attitudes. From the cognitive-developmental perspective, whether in the social, moral, vocational, academic, sexual, religious, or political domain, it is the adolescent's thinking ability—not the psychodynamics of the relationship with parents, not the stage of ego development, and not the culture's influences—that exerts the strongest influence.

Behavioral and Social Learning Theories

Although social learning theorists and behaviorists do not couch their theories in terms of an explicit "theory of adolescence," their principles of learning are both critical and relevant to our understanding of adolescence. As future chapters will demonstrate, the social learning and behavioral psychologists have contributed many of the most pragmatic and most successful strategies for therapists, teachers, and parents who relate to adolescents. Having critiqued the literature on child and adolescent development, Muuss (1975) concludes that social learning theorists are responsible for some of the most influential research in the field.

Behaviorism, or the behavioral approach includes both the radical behavioral theory, generated by the controversial psychologist B. F. Skinner, and the modifications of the behavioral perspective known as **social learning theories,** exemplified by researchers like Walter Mischel and Albert Bandura (see Table 1.1). From Skinner's strictly behaviorisitc approach, human behavior and attitudes depend primarily on the reinforcement and the punishment that an individual receives from other people or from actual consequences of experiences in the environment (Skinner, 1953). Within this operationally oriented context, the adolescent's behavior and attitudes are not attributed to unobservable, abstract constructs, such as Piaget's cognitive stages, Erikson's stages of ego development, or Freud's notions about the id, ego, and superego. Instead, according to **Skinnerian psychologists,** the attitudes and actions of people at all ages are primarily determined by the positive or negative consequences that follow their behavior in particular types of situations. From the Skinnerian perspective, conduct or attitudes that are rewarded are likely to be repeated, while those that are punished or ignored are going to be abandoned.

Expanding upon these behavioristic or Skinnerian views, social learning theorists contend that our behavior is also influenced by the models—both live and vicarious—we observe in our daily activities. For example, some research shows that children who are exposed to violent television programs behave more aggressively thereafter than those exposed to nonviolent programs (Mischel, 1981). Social learning theorists acknowledge, however, that internal cognitive factors and interpretive overlays, such as the individual's idiosyncratic expectations and selective perceptions, interact with the rewards, punishments, and modeling. Hence, consistently predicting any single adolescent's behavior in a particular situation is a difficult if not an impossible task.

Despite these distinctions between strictly Skinnerian and social learning theorists, both focus on the relationship between the adolescent's behavior and the environmental antecedents and consequences, rather than relying upon inferred motives or the creation of hypothetical constructs like the ego to explain human behavior and attitudes. As future chapters will demonstrate, the social learning and behavioral approaches have to date proven themselves to be the most empirical of all adolescent theories in terms of being able to provide operational definitions, testable hypotheses, and replicable results. Nevertheless, you will see that these empirically based positions are not without their critics, and further, that each theoretical perspective has contributed to our understanding of contemporary adolescents.

A Synthesis of Theories

During recent decades the life-span approach to human development has become increasingly popular (Baldwin, 1980; Baltes & Reese, 1984). Rather than viewing change as a phenomenon characteristic solely of childhood and adolescence, theorists endorsing this position examine change as an inevitable process that occurs throughout adult life as well. In so doing, some *life-span* theorists are suggesting that human development may be discontinuous, a stance that endorses the position that the theories applicable to understanding behavior during one period of our lives may be relatively less important for understanding behavior in another period. For example, a discontinuous view might maintain that biological theories may be more applicable to explaining behavior during infancy and childhood than to explaining the behavior of adolescents or adults. In addition to its focus upon the unique characteristics of particular developmental periods, the discontinuous view deemphasizes the universal aspects of human development. Instead, the discontinuous view aligns itself more closely with the cross-cultural evidence, which reveals vast discrepencies in adolescent behavior throughout the world.

This contemporary life-span approach has been described as a *transactional, contextual, or dialectical view* of human development, because it attempts to synthesize both the organismic and environmental perspectives (Baldwin,

1980). From the life-span theorists' frame of reference, an adolescent's behavior is a consequence of the exchange between internal factors, such as cognitive development, and environmental factors, such as reinforcement. Thus, the adolescent is both acting upon and being acted upon by the environment. In attempting to synthesize the various viewpoints on adolescence, it has been suggested that theoreticians develop a common, neutral language that would permit a more effective method for comparing theories (Baldwin, 1980). Once this linguistic obstacle is overcome, a more complete and accurate understanding of adolescence will hopefully emerge.

CONDUCTING RESEARCH ON ADOLESCENCE

The research on which our present understanding of adolescence is predicated can be categorized as descriptive, correlational, or experimental (Achenbach, 1978). In each of these three forms of research, the factor that is being measured is referred to as the **dependent variable,** while the experimental treatment or the characteristic that distinguishes one group from the other is called the **independent variable.** A single study may have more than one dependent or independent variable. For instance, in a descriptive study comparing the IQ scores of males and females and of blacks and whites, the dependent variable is the IQ test score and the two independent variables are sex and race. Yet, in an experimental study in which adolescents were given an IQ test, then subjected to a six-week training program intended to raise their scores, and subsequently retested on the IQ test, the dependent variable is the IQ test and the independent variable is the training program.

Of utmost importance in interpreting the results of experimental or descriptive studies is whether the groups of adolescents being studied are representative samples of the population to which the results are going to be generalized. A representative or **random sample** is one in which particular characteristics of the subjects, such as age, socioeconomic status, race, or academic achievement, are similar to the characteristics of the group to whom the results will be generalized. Under conditions in which the sample is representative, the people from whom the data have been collected must possess characteristics similar to those of the people to whom the study's conclusions are to be generalized. In brief, without representative samples the interpretation of the results is highly limited. For example, it would be a mistake to conclude that all female adolescents have problems communicating with their mothers on the basis of findings from a study that had employed a sample of white seventh-grade girls from low socioeconomic backgrounds. The results of this particular study should be generalized only to other white seventh-grade girls from similar backgrounds. Although a mistake that is more frequent than is generally acknowledged, applying a study's conclusions to people who differ from the sample is totally inappropriate.

In general, the larger a study's sample size, the more likely the group is to be representative and the findings to be generalizable to a large segment of the entire population. Particularly in cases where there is evidence to suggest that a particular characteristic, such as age, sex, race, or income, could have a considerable influence on the dependent variable, these traits need to be represented randomly in the study's sample. As you evaluate the research presented in this text, as well as the data from general publications and professional journals, your appreciation of the importance of representative sampling will immeasurably aid your assessment of the limits of a study's generalizability.

Descriptive Research

Descriptive research on adolescence presents data from the past or present without trying to establish any causal relationships. The researcher's purpose is to describe adolescents' behavior or attitudes by conducting surveys or personal interviews, by administering standardized tests, or by comparing historical information with similar data in the present. For example, the Gallup public-opinion polls, which survey thousands of adolescents and adults each year on a variety of topics, do not permit assertions about the causes of adolescents' behavior or attitudes. At best, descriptive data can provide hypotheses concerning causative factors. Other forms of research, however, are subsequently employed to test the validity of hypotheses related to cause-and-effect relationships.

Correlational Research

Correlational research is also descriptive. Its purpose, however, extends beyond merely describing data. In a correlational study the researcher is trying to establish whether or not a *statistically significant* relationship or correlation exists between two or more variables. For example, in regard to an adolescent's behavior and religious attitudes, a researcher could apply correlational statistics to a number of questions: Is there a significant relationship between an adolescent's age, race, sex, or socioeconomic class and church attendance or type of religious affiliation? Is there a significant correlation between adolescents' sexual activity, drinking, or drug use and their religious values?

Correlational statistics yield a number called a **correlation coefficient,** which permits us to determine whether the relationship between the variables is strong enough to conclude that it did not occur by chance. The coefficients range from .01 to 1.00 and are accompanied by either a positive (+) or a negative (−) sign. The further the coefficient is from .0, the stronger or more statistically significant is the relationship between the variables. That is, if a correlation coefficient of +.80 is obtained between an adolescent's age and church attendance and a coefficient of +.20 is obtained between socioeconomic class and church attendance, we conclude that the relationship between age and attendance is stronger than that between income and attendance. The closer the correlation is to −1.00 or to +1.00, the more likely it is that the relationship between the two variables has not occurred by chance. Consequently, our confidence in the relationship between the two variables increases as the values of the correlation coefficients move closer to +1.00 or −1.00.

A negative sign in front of the coefficient indicates that the two variables are **inversely** or **negatively correlated.** In other words, while there is a relationship between the variables, an increase in one variable is related to a decrease in the other. As is the case with a positive correlation, the closer to the whole number, in this case a −1.00, the stronger the correlation between the variables.

Thus, a coefficient of −.80 between church attendance and an adolescent's socioeconomic status would indicate a strong but inverse relationship between the two variables: As income increases, church attendance decreases.

Unfortunately, correlational research is too frequently misinterpreted and misquoted as evidence of causality. Since correlational data will be cited repeatedly throughout this text, understanding the distinction between correlational and experimental research is of utmost importance. Correlational studies do not imply that one factor has "caused" the other to increase or decrease. For instance, a researcher who finds a correlation of −.98 between an adolescent's grades and the number of cigarettes he or she smokes each day would be committing a heinous error to assert that "cigarette smoking causes poor grades." All that we can reasonably conclude is that smoking is inversely related to good grades. In this hypothetical situation, further investigation might show that the heavy smokers are also those whose parents have the least education, whose own lives are filled with the most stress, whose self-confidence and IQ scores are lowest, and whose diets are the least healthy. Deciding which of these variables might be causing poor grades is the goal of experimental research and is a task that lies beyond the bounds of correlational studies.

Both correlational and descriptive research are sometimes conducted in order to identify differences between adolescents of different ages. To do so, the researcher uses a **cross-sectional design.** In cross-sectional research adolescents from two or more different age groups are used in the sample and measured at the same point in time on whatever dependent variable the researcher has chosen. For instance, a researcher may administer a self-concept test to a sample of 100 eighth-graders, 100 tenth-graders, and 100 college freshmen during a single month in a given year in order to describe self-concept scores at varying ages of adolescence. If, however, we find that the college freshmen have the highest self-concept scores and the eighth-graders have the lowest, we cannot conclude that self-concept scores increase with age. Why not?

The reason is that cross-sectional research permits us to describe the differences among adolescents of different ages but does not allow us to conclude anything about the impact of the aging process on the dependent variable. This limitation exists because in order to determine the impact of aging upon a dependent measure such as self-concept scores, we would have to repeatedly measure people from the same cohort group across time. A **cohort group** is a group of people born during the same year. As might be expected, members of a cohort share social and historical events as they occur during a particular period of their lives and thus have significant experiences in common that shape their personalities and attitudes. Because modern society is continually changing and because historical events can have a dramatic impact on the way people view themselves and others, people who are from the same cohort are much more likely to be alike than those born in different years.

For example, let's assume we want to determine whether self-esteem increases or decreases with age. If we compare the self-concept scores of a group of 14-year-olds who experienced childhood during a period of national war, rampant epidemics, and economic depression to the self-concept scores of 20-year-olds who experienced childhood during a period of national peace, health, and prosperity, we would be in error to conclude that the 20-year-olds' higher scores meant that self-esteem increases with age. Confounding the interpretation of the results of the study is the fact that the two groups' self-esteem could very well have been affected by the type of society in which they spent their childhood, rather than by the process of aging. Unfortunately, the cross-sectional research design does not permit these two possible explanations to be tested separately.

In order to overcome some of the limitations associated with cross-sectional research, **longitudinal studies** can be conducted. In these studies adolescents from the same cohort groups are measured periodically throughout a span of years on a particular dependent variable or variables. For instance, we could administer a self-concept test to eighth-graders and retest them once a year thereafter until they graduated from high school. Since the subjects are from the same cohort, we have eliminated one confounding variable that might have caused us to misinterpret our results.

Unfortunately, longitudinal research also has its limitations. First, the results can be generalized only to adolescents from that particular cohort group and not to those born in other years. Second, measuring the same people repeatedly may alter their behavior or responses. Finally, some subjects drop out of the study over the years, a phenomenon known as *experimental mortality.*

A **sequential design** can help compensate for some of these shortcomings. In a sequential design, data from at least two cross-sections of two longitudinal studies are used. Thus, there are at least two cohorts represented in the research and at least two separate times of measurement on the dependent variable. The greater sophistication of the research design permits us to make a number of comparisons to better determine how the process of aging is truly affecting an adolescent's behavior or attitudes as they are measured on the dependent variable.

Throughout this text you should take special note of studies that are designated as having used a sequential design. These studies are especially beneficial in helping us discover the extent to which cohort differences, aging, and significantly shared societal events, which may alter a youngster's responses at the moment of measurement, are affecting the dependent variable.

Experimental Research

In order to identify the causes of adolescents' behavior or attitudes, researchers must rely on the third type of data collection—**experimental research** studies. In attempting to establish cause-and-effect relationships, a carefully designed experimental study attempts to eliminate as many confounding variables as possible in order to strengthen the validity and generalizability of the results. **Confounding variables** are those factors, other than the treatment itself, that might account for a change in the subjects' attitudes or behaviors. To minimize these confounding variables, most well-designed experimental studies compare data from a control group, which has not received a particular treatment, with data from the experimental group which did receive the treatment.

For example, assume that we are in the midst of conducting a six-week program intended to change adolescents' attitudes toward drug abuse. Having administered a test to assess our subjects' attitudes at the outset, we are hoping to find a significant change when we readminister the attitudes test at the end of our program. Tragically, in the midst of our six-week drug program, one of the school's most popular students dies from a drug overdose. Without a control group, even if our statistical analyses showed that the adolescents' attitudes toward drug abuse had changed significantly, the assertion that our treatment caused the change could be contested on the grounds that the classmate's death was actually responsible for the change in our subjects' attitudes. If, however, we have been foresightful enough to provide a control group against which the results of our experiment can be compared, the classmate's death can no longer be considered a confounding variable, because the tragedy would have theoretically affected students in both the control group and the experimental group. Therefore, if the statistical comparisons demonstrate that the attitudes of students in the six-week program have significantly changed, while those in the control group have remained unchanged, our data have not been confounded by the student's death.

Although the ways to reduce all possible confounding variables are too extensive for a discussion in this text, both *random selection* of subjects for inclusion in the study and *random assignment* of subjects to the treatment or no-treatment condition serve to eliminate certain confounding variables. If we randomly select the students in our study from the school's entire population and then randomly assign them to either the control or the experimental group, we have made it possible to generalize our results to adolescents who share similar characteristics with the students in our school. We have also eliminated certain confounding variables related to environmental influences. For example, if during the course of our study, the television networks sponsor a series of public service ads on contraception, aimed at adolescent viewers, our having used random selection and random assignment in our study reduces the chances that the ads will affect our dependent variable. This is the case because the viewers of the ads are likely to be approximately equally distributed across both groups in our experiment.

It is extremely important to note the difference between an experimental and a correlational study. Although people often incorrectly assume that correlational data "prove" cause-and-effect relationships, this is an egregious misinterpretation of the data. Only experimental studies can establish causality, and even then, the study must be designed in such a way that the confounding variables are reduced. For example, assume we want to determine whether we can increase adolescents' use of contraceptives through a four-week sex education course. A correlational study might alert us to a possible causal relationship by showing that there is a correlation of +.76 between using contraceptives and having received reliable information about conception and birth control. In order to demonstrate causality, however, we would have to design an experimental study. One example of such an experimental study would require that we collect data from a control group of students who do not undergo the four-week program and compare their contraceptive use before and after the four weeks to that of the students who take the course.

Although descriptive and correlation research studies are valuable in furthering our understanding of adolescence, only experimental studies can enhance our understanding of causality. Experimental studies differ, however, in the degree to which the researcher has controlled for the various confounding variables. For example, while one experimental study will have randomly selected adolescents and will then have randomly assigned them to a control group, another study will have neither a random sample nor a control group.

With these understandings in mind, the studies cited throughout this text typically include information about the distinguishing factors, such as the characteristics of the adolescents in the sample, the type of research design employed, and the presence of a control group. In combination with the information in this chapter, such information is intended to increase your capacity for evaluating the data critically and for generalizing a study's findings to the appropriate groups of adolescents. It is my hope that your interpretation of the empirical data and the degree of confidence you place in the findings of any particular study will be significantly influenced by your awareness of the relative strengths and weaknesses of descriptive, correlational, and experimental research.

Conclusion

Having begun this chapter with an explanation of the reasons underlying my initial involvement in adolescent psychology, let me now conclude with similar tales regarding the role of empirical research and theory. Convinced that a knowledge of the empirical data and theory would enhance my relationships with adolescents, I embarked on my studies, as do all graduate students, with the intent of being both scholarly and open-minded. While I enthusiastically spent the next several years in school, becoming more familiar with the empirical data on adolescence, I remained totally oblivious to the fact that I was committing several fundamental errors—errors which, in my years of college teaching, I have observed repeatedly in the comments and in the writing of my own graduate and undergraduate students.

First, in failing to apply my knowledge of research and statistics consistently as a graduate student, I inadvertently presumed that the results of most studies in prestigious journals deserved equal merit and equal consideration. I attended too little to what seemed to me at the time the less significant "details" of a study, such as the research design and the representativeness of the sample. In this regard, therefore, I have tried within this text to devote additional attention to those studies that are most compelling and noteworthy in terms of their methodology. However, given my desire to acquaint you with as much research as possible and my decision to emphasize the practical applications of the empirical and theoretical data, you are inevitably left with the responsibility for independently evaluating many of the studies cited throughout the remaining chapters. Hopefully, you will continue to draw upon the information in this first chapter as you embark upon your independent evaluation of the research.

Given the independence you have now been accorded, my second shortcoming as a former student will perhaps appear all the more relevant. Having spent several years teaching and counseling adolescents, I was naively confident that my personal experiences were the nexus for my understanding of adolescents. While still able to join other graduate students in academic debates over the relative merits of various theories and empirical studies, I nonetheless tended to discount, to deemphasize, or to discredit data that contradicted either my own experiences as an adolescent or my own interactions with adolescents as a teacher and counselor. In other words, I found it difficult to put aside the "fact" that the earth is flat because that is exactly how it appeared from my window, and to accept the "fact" offered by satellites and navigators that the earth is pear-shaped.

As evidenced by my scores on written exams, I could examine data and theories that contradicted or were not part of my personal experiences on an abstract and intellectual level. I continued to gravitate, however, toward data that supported my own preconceived views of adolescents. My first method of discounting data that contradicted my personal feelings, convictions, and ideologies was to compare the data to my own personal experience: "Well, I never knew an adolescent who felt that way"; "Nobody I ever knew behaved like that"; "I really don't think things could be that bad on the basis of what I've seen and heard." Although such comparisons were not, in and of themselves, reprehensible or illogical, I had grossly inflated the validity of convictions derived exclusively from firsthand experiences—convictions based upon my having taught fewer than 2,000 of the 22 million adolescents in the United States—notions based on working with adolescents from only two racial groups in one region of a very large country—views based on my own life as an adolescent whose socioeconomic background alone gave her little in common with most of the country's youths.

My second method for discounting data that failed to support my views was considerably more sophisticated than the first. Armed with the knowledge of statistics and research that supposedly insured objectivity, I would subject certain studies to far more thorough scrutiny than others. Although honestly unaware of my behavior at the time, I nonetheless imposed stricter standards of scholarship in evaluating the studies whose conclusions were in least accord with my own. Unfortunately, it was inevitably easier for me to recognize the methodological shortcomings and to question the underlying premises of data or theory that contradicted my visions of adolescence or of related social issues. Despite my best intentions, I seldom approached the various studies with equal objectivity, equal willingness to scrutinize the results, and equal proclivity to lay aside my own feelings about the matter at hand.

Although I was once convinced that my own behavior as a student of adolescent psychology was atypical, my years as a college teacher have persuaded me that both my cohorts and my students share—to greater or lesser degrees—my own difficulties in regard to encountering empirical data. Moreover, I myself continue to struggle against the inadvertent oversights, the ethnocentricity, the lack of objectivity, or the overreliance on the validity of my personal experiences. It is my hope that in reading this text you will encounter theories and empirical data that will arouse discomfort, surprise, and on occasion, anger. It is my further hope that, when such feelings arise, you will accept the challenge of scrutinizing data that confirm your own experiences and convictions as carefully as data that dispute them.

Questions for Discussion and Review

Basic Concepts and Terminology

1. How has the concept of adolescence developed historically?
2. In what major ways do the biological, sociological, psychoanalytic, cognitive, and behavioral theories differ with regard to adolescence?

3. How do organismic and environmental theories of adolescence differ? What, if anything, do they share in common?
4. What are the limitations and advantages of each of the three research designs discussed in this chapter? Which appear the easiest to conduct and why?
5. How do descriptive, correlational, and experimental studies differ in terms of their purpose, limitations, and relevance to the study of adolescence? Which kinds of research questions can each legitimately answer?
6. Give a specific example and definition for each of the terms listed in the overview of this chapter. Then explain why each needs consideration in our study of adolescence.
7. How are stage theories distinct from environmental theories, and which famous theoreticians represent each view?
8. Considering both their sign and their numerical value, how are correlation coefficients to be interpreted?

Questions for Discussion and Debate

1. How relevant is Havighurst's description of developmental tasks for today's adolescents? What are the potential consequences associated with failing to complete each of these developmental tasks during adolescence?
2. Which theoretical perspective do you feel most adequately explains your own adolescent development? Least adequately? Why?
3. Forced to align yourself with only one of the five theoretical perspectives on adolescence, which would you choose? Why?
4. How would you design the best possible descriptive study and the most convincing experimental study to answer a question of your choice regarding adolescents' behavior? Consider the importance of your research design and the presence of confounding variables in each of your studies.
5. Find a correlational study and an experimental study in a recent journal on adolescence and discuss the merits and limitations of each.
6. Given the information on conducting research, how have you formerly misinterpreted data relevant to the study of adolescent behavior?
7. Given the fact that the meaning of adolescence differs from culture to culture, what changes would you recommend be made with regard to our own culture's expectation of adolescents?
8. Is the concept of adolescence still evolving? What constancies might remain by the year 2050?
9. What significant aspects of adolescence are not presently addressed by any of the theories to date?
10. Why have you embarked upon this study of adolescent psychology? What experiences in your past and present influenced your decision? What do you hope to have gained as a consequence of completing this course? What kinds of interactions with your fellow students or your professor might help you achieve these goals?

REFERENCES

Achenbach, T. *Research in developmental psychology.* New York: Free Press, 1978.

Adelson, J., & Doehrman, M. The psychodynamic approach to adolescence. In J. Adelson (ed.), *Handbook of adolescent psychology.* New York: Wiley, 1980. Pp. 99–117.

Aristotle. Ethica Nicomachea. In R. McKeon (ed.), *The basic works of Aristotle.* New York: Random House, 1941.

Baldwin, A. *Theories of child development.* New York: Wiley, 1980.

Baltes, P., & Reese, H. The life span perspective in developmental psychology. In M. Bornstein & M. Lamb (eds.), *Developmental psychology: An advanced textbook.* Hillsdale, N.J.: Lawrence Erlbaum, 1984. Pp. 493–531.

Benedict, R. *Patterns of culture.* Boston: Houghton Mifflin, 1934.

Blos, P. *On adolescence.* New York: Free Press, 1962.

Brussell, E. *Dictionary of quotable quotes.* Englewood Cliffs, N.J.: Prentice-Hall, 1970.

Davis, K. The sociology of parent-youth conflict. *Amercian Sociological Review,* 1941, *5,* 523–525.

Demos, J. & Demos, V. Adolescence in historical perspective. *Journal of Marriage and the Family,* 1979, *31,* 632–628.

Elder, G. Adolescence in historical perspective. In J. Adelson (ed.), *Handbook of adolescent psychology.* New York: Wiley, 1980. Pp. 3–46.

Erickson, E. *Identity: Youth and crisis.* New York: Norton, 1968.

Freud, A. *Adolescence: Psychoanalytic study of the child.* New York: International Universities Press, 1958.

Freud, S. *A general introduction to psychoanalysis.* New York: Permabooks, 1953.

Hall, S. *Adolescence: Its psychology and its relations to physiology, anthropology, sociology, sex, crime, religion and education.* Englewood Cliffs, N.J.: Prentice-Hall, 1904, 1905.

Havighurst, R. *Developmental tasks and education.* New York: McKay, 1952.

Havighurst, R. *Developmental tasks and education.* New York: David McKay, 1972.

Hollingshead, A. *Elmstown's youth.* New York: Wiley, 1949.

Kett, J. *Rites of passage: Adolescence in America 1790 to the present.* New York: Basic Books, 1977.

L'Abate, L. The status of adolescent psychology. *Developmental Psychology,* 1971, *4,* 201–205.

Marcia, J. Identity in adolescence. In J. Adelson (ed.), *Handbook of adolescent psychology.* New York: Wiley, 1980. Pp. 159–188.

Mead, M. *Coming of age in Samoa.* New York: Morrow, 1961.

Mischel, W. *Introduction to personality.* New York: Holt, Rinehart and Winston, 1981.

Muuss, R. *Theories of adolescence.* New York: Random House, 1975.

Peterson, A., & Taylor, B. The biological approach to adolescence. In J. Adelson (ed.), *Handbook of adolescent psychology.* New York: Wiley, 1980. Pp. 117–159.

Piaget, J. The theory of stages in cognitive development. In D. Green (ed.), *Measurement and Piaget.* New York: McGraw-Hill, 1971.

Plato. *The dialogues of Plato.* New York: Oxford University Press, 1952.

Skinner, B. F. *Science and human behavior.* New York: Free Press, 1953.

Chapter Outline

Puberty: What, When, and Why?
Physical Transformations
The Sequence of Growth
The Head and Face
Height
Muscle Tissue
Adipose Tissue
Basal Metabolism Rate
Breast Development
Male Reproductive System
Female Reproductive System
Abnormal Development of the Reproductive System
Issues Related to Adolescent Physical Development
Early and Late Maturation
Physical Appearance and Personality
Food, Nutrition, and Dieting
The Advantages and Disadvantages of Sports
Air Pollution
Adolescent Diseases
Acne
Diabetes
Epilepsy
Cancer
Anemia
Sickle-Cell Anemia
Conclusion

Goals and Objectives

This chapter is designed to enable you to:

- *Describe the physical changes that occur during adolescence*
- *Explain the factors that influence adolescent growth and appearance*
- *Examine the physiological and developmental difference between males and females*
- *Explore adolescents' reactions to their physical changes*
- *Identify some common adolescent diseases and genetic abnormalities*
- *Discuss the advantages and disadvantages of organized sports*
- *Consider the impact of air pollution, diet, exercise, hormones, and early maturation on adolescent behavior*
- *Examine the relationship between appearance and personality*

Concepts and Terminology

gonadotrophins
adipose tissue
amenorrhea
menorrhagia
dysmenorrhea
anovulatory
PMS
atherosclerosis
cholesterol
protein loading
progesterone
allergen
endorphins
gonads
vas deferens
seminal vesicles
prostate gland
ectomorph
mesomorph
endomorph
mammary glands
areola
shaft
foreskin
testicles
scrotum
seminal fluid
vasectomy
nocturnal emissions
Klinefelter's syndrome
Turner's syndrome
petit and grand mal seizures
basal metabolism rate
skin-fold test
isles of insular
macrobiotic diet
hypothalamus
sickle cell
Hodgkin's disease
cervix
urethra
prepuce
Fallopian tubes
uterus
ovulation
estrogen
os
tubal ligation
G spot
semen
clitoris
labia
vagina
hymen
placenta
leukemia
mucus

2 Adolescent Physical Development

PUBERTY: WHAT, WHEN, AND WHY?

Between the ages of 9 and 16 it happens to everyone—puberty begins. Literally meaning "to be covered in fine hair," the word is derived from the Latin verb *pubescere,* which means "to grow hairy or mossy." In a more contemporary context, the term "puberty" has come to signify the period of life during which a young person becomes physically capable of sexual reproduction. Given the dramatic rise in hormonal levels, which are responsible for the adolescent's sexual maturity, it is not surprising that researchers have devoted considerable attention to the impact that adolescents' hormones might have on their moods and behavior, as Box 2.1 indicates. Although such research will inevitably expand our understanding of the relationship between human behavior and physiological factors, the present chapter will be limited to an exploration of the actual physiological transformations that accompany adolescence.

Puberty technically begins when the part of the upper brain stem known as the **hypothalamus** signals the pituitary gland to release the hormones known as **gonadotrophins.** Heralded as the "master gland" in our endocrine system, the pituitary releases the gonadotrophins into the adolescent's body during sleep, a year or so before any of the physical changes associated with puberty actually become apparent (Schowalter & Anyan, 1981). These gonadotrophins cause the ovaries and testes, glands that are referred to as the **gonads,** to increase their production of estrogen and androgen. Consequently, the ovaries increase their production of estrogen sixfold, and the testes produce 20 times the amount of testosterone formerly present in a boy's body (Higham, 1980). When released in sufficient amounts, **testosterone** increases muscle mass, body hair, and size of the vocal cords. Similarly, the elevated estrogen levels in a girl's body are accompanied by such changes as breast development, menstruation,

A Closer Look 2.1 

The Impact of Hormones on Adolescents' Behavior

Are the dramatic increases in hormone levels that accompany puberty responsible for changes in adolescents' emotions and behavior? Preliminary findings from a correlational study being conducted at the National Institutes of Mental Health suggest that the answer may be yes.

In an effort to examine the impact of hormones on adolescent moods and behavior, psychologists are monitoring the hormone levels, physical development, and behavior of 108 adolescent boys and girls. While monitoring the youngsters' gonadotrophins, sex steroids, and adrenal androgens, the researchers are simultaneously gathering data on the adolescents' moods, self-image, behavior, social and academic activities, and physical competence. One of the most consistent findings thus far is that, for boys, obsessive-compulsive, delinquent, and hyperactive behaviors are associated with higher levels of adrenal androgens, in combination with lower levels of sex steroids. For girls, lower adrenal androgen levels are associated with such problems as depressive withdrawal and delinquent behavior. For both sexes, higher sex steroid and lower gonadotrophin levels are related to self-ratings of competence. As a consequence, early hormonal maturation is associated with better adjustment than hormonal maturation later in adolescence.

A second finding is that the correlation between hormone levels and adjustment are stronger and more consistent for boys than for girls. The researchers have hypothesized that this difference might be occurring because girls' hormone levels tend to fluctuate more dramatically on a daily basis during the menstrual cycle, thereby making it more difficult to obtain accurate hormonal measurements. The lower correlations between girls' hormones and their behavior might also be the consequence of biological differences between the sexes in areas other than the hormonal. The researchers have also recognized that the differences could be related to the fact that males and females are socialized to behave differently and that this sex-role socialization exerts more influence over their behavior than do hormones.

In addition to gathering data on the correlations between youths' hormone levels and their behavior throughout adolescence, the researchers will also be examining how different types of interactions between adolescents and their parents affect children's adjustment and behavior during puberty.

SOURCE: E. Nottelmann et al., Gonadal and adrenal hormone correlates of adjustment in early adolescence. In R. Lerner and T. Foch (eds.), *Biological-psychosocial interactions in early adolescence: A life-span perspective.* Hillsdale, N.J.: Erlbaum, 1986.

and extra adipose tissue around the hips and abdomen, resulting in the loss of her younger boyish figure.

From birth, both the male's and the female's body produce androgen and estrogen. The distinction between the sexes is that during adolescence a boy's androgen level becomes 20–60 percent higher than a girl's, while her estrogen level becomes 2–30 percent higher than his. Although the level of estrogen varies with a female's age and with the phase of her menstrual cycle, the ovaries produce both estrogen and androgen throughout her lifetime. Interestingly, however, it has not yet been determined whether the estrogen in a male's body is produced by the testes or whether the male body somehow converts testosterone into estrogen. Nevertheless, the two hormones that influence masculine or feminine appearance are produced by the bodies of both sexes (Higham, 1980).

The obvious physical differences among adolescents of the same chronological age underscore an endocrinological fact: The hypothalamus does not relay the message to release gonadotrophins at the same time in each adolescent's life. Some 11-year-olds' bodies are responding to the commands of the hypothalamus, while some 15-year-olds have not yet begun to respond to the hormonal changes within them. The factors that activate the hypothalamus are still undetermined. According to some theorists, the hypothalamus monitors the adolescent's body weight and releases the necessary hormones when the body is heavy enough (Frisch, 1984). This hypothesis would explain why youngsters in richer communities, where nutritional and medical benefits increase their weight, reach puberty before children from poorer communities (Katchadorian, 1977; Tanner, 1962). Further corroborative evidence shows that girls whose body weight drops below a certain level stop menstruating (Frisch, 1984). Despite the evidence suggesting a relationship between messages from the hypothalamus and weight, most biologists still contend that an adolescent's weight is a response to—not the cause of—the hypothalamus' activity (Peterson & Taylor, 1980).

In addition to the activity of the hypothalamus, puberty appears to be affected by certain environmental factors. For example, adolescents living in higher altitudes and those from small families mature earlier than those in lower altitudes and those from large families (Beau, Baker, & Haas, 1977; Malina, 1979). Children who are malnourished, emotionally deprived during infancy, or financially impoverished also mature more slowly (Katchadorian, 1977; Tanner, 1962). Two facts suggest that seasonal changes may somehow influence puberty: Fewer girls start to menstruate in the spring than in any other season, and most adolescents grow tallest during the springtime and gain the most weight during the autumn (Katchadorian, 1977; Zacharias, Rand, & Wintman, 1976). Although environment seems to influence certain aspects of puberty, genetic endowment still asserts primary control over when and how quickly a youngster will mature. In sum, if a 10-year-old girl is curious about how quickly she will mature, her most reliable predictor is her own mother's pattern during adolescence. In general, adolescents whose parents are tall and thin mature more slowly than those whose parents are shorter and stockier (Katchadorian, 1977).

Over the last century the age of puberty has steadily decreased, although the trend is now abating. The average U.S. boy now begins puberty around the age of 12 and completes his growth by 19. Most girls mature about two years earlier than boys, beginning around the age of 11 and reaching the end of growth around the age of 17. The height spurt starts in most girls between 9.5 and 14.5 years and between 10.5 and 16 years for boys. Pubic hair generally appears around 11 in girls and 12 in boys. By the end of the teenage years, most males and females have entirely completed the growth that has transformed them physiologically from children to adults (Katchadorian, 1977; Tanner, 1962).

PHYSICAL TRANSFORMATIONS

The Sequence of Growth

Although the age at which puberty begins differs among adolescents, the sequence of physiological changes is relatively predictable (Faust, 1977). Most adolescent girls develop pubic hair before their breasts develop and thereafter experience rapid growth in weight and height. Menstruation and the growth of other body hair generally occur last in the growth sequence. Most adolescent boys first experience enlargement of the penis and testicles, followed by the growth of pubic hair, voice changes, and a rapid spurt in height and weight. A boy's facial and underarm hair develop last in the growth sequence, because these areas have the highest tolerance for testosterone.

The fact that boys produce more testosterone and less estrogen than girls accounts for a number of differences between the sexes, which manifest themselves during adolescence (Katchadorian, 1977; Tanner, 1962). Testosterone is responsible for boys' hairier bodies, their higher ratio of muscle to fat tissue, and their larger number of sweat glands. Although a girl's voice undergoes some change during adolescence, as her vocal cords grow, a boy's vocal cords nearly double in length, thus causing his voice to drop nearly an octave. Similarly, blood volume and lung size increase more significantly in boys than in girls during adolescence. This larger blood volume permits most boys to exchange oxygen more efficiently than girls. Before puberty a girl's shoulders are proportionately larger than a boy's, in comparison to the size of the hips; but during adolescence this ratio of shoulder to hip size reverses—boys' shoulders grow larger than their hips, while girls' grow smaller. As information later in this

A Closer Look 2.2 

How Much Is a Body Worth?

If an adolescent looks like a million bucks, there is a logical reason. That's just about what a human body is worth on today's market. Using a chemical supply catalog, Daniel Sadoff, a University of Washington animal researcher, determined the value of every marketable substance in a normal 150-pound body. The body's 10,200 units of the clotting agent prothrombin would sell for $30,600. One pint of blood containing about 30 grams of albumin is worth $945. The total market value of a body is close to one million dollars, according to Dr. Sadoff.

chapter will demonstrate, however, these differences do not mean that boys are necessarily stronger or more athletically talented than girls.

The Head and Face

Both male and female adolescents undergo a host of other physical alterations. The lymphatic tissues, which increase in size throughout childhood, begin to decrease during adolescence. This shrinkage in the tissues of the tonsils and adenoids accounts for adolescents' "growing out of" the allergic reactions, colds, and sore throats that so often plague them during childhood. Unfortunately this gain is offset by a new loss—the loss of vision. Rapid changes in the eye between the ages of 11 and 14 often produce myopia or short-sightedness, which diminishes a youngster's long-range vision. As a consequence many young adolescents who have had perfect vision during childhood suddenly need glasses.

Another change accompanying adolescence is the loss of a childlike face. As the hairline recedes and the facial bones grow in such a way that the nose and chin become more prominent, the adolescent's face assumes its permanent adult features. The one feature of the head that changes relatively little during adolescence is the brain. Having attained 90 percent of its weight by the time we're 5 and 95 percent by the time we're 10, it grows little during our adolescence (Katchadorian, 1977; Tanner, 1962).

Height

Familiar questions from our own adolescence are reminders that most of us are concerned over our weight and height during the years of most rapid growth: How tall am I going to be? Will I ever gain weight or will I look like a scarecrow forever? Why do I still have all this "baby fat" when everyone else looks so muscular and lean? Why do I feel that I'm all hands and feet? How come my legs are so long compared to my arms?

These questions reflect the confusing but relatively predictable pattern that the human body follows as it matures. Both adolescents who fear that their body's awkward appearance is permanent and those who hope that adolescence will somehow magically bestow an entirely new body upon them are in error. Because the body grows at different rates throughout the course of a given year and because certain parts of the body grow faster than others, adolescents may sometimes feel ungainly. Such anxieties might be relieved if adolescents were acquainted with several physiological realities: Legs grow to their full length before arms, and hands and feet reach their full size before arms and legs. Because human beings grow tallest in the spring and gain the most weight during the autumn, adolescents may feel especially lanky and skinny during the summers, when their bodies have not yet added the weight that corresponds more closely to their height. These uneven patterns of growth inevitably make some adolescents feel physically awkward, but the assumption that adolescence causes graceful human beings to suddenly become clumsy oafs is unfounded. People who are uncoordinated and clumsy during adolescence were uncoordinated and clumsy as children (Katchadorian, 1977).

Another consoling or perhaps disconsoling fact is that an individual will generally have the same basic body type after adolescence as before. In other words, the short, stocky 9-year-old is generally going to be a short, stocky 20-year-old, and the girl who is taller and skinnier than her peers in the third grade is still likely to be taller and skinnier than her peers in the twelfth grade. Furthermore, despite what adolescents look like at the moment, they are likely to resemble their parents in terms of weight and height by the end of puberty. Youngsters who wonder how tall or how heavy they will be as adults should simply look at their own parents. Although there are exceptions to this rule, genetics generally dictate our adult height and weight (Katchadorian, 1977; Tanner, 1962).

Between the ages of 11 and 17 most males and females grow taller by about 11 inches (Katchadorian, 1977; Tanner, 1962). During the fastest year of growth a youngster grows three to five inches in height, and by the end of adolescence most boys are about five inches taller than girls. The average U.S. female grows to be about 5′ 5″ tall, while the average boy grows to be about 5′ 10″. Although in the 1890s only 5 percent of the boys grew taller than six feet, nearly 25 percent of today's boys will exceed six feet (Gallagher, 1960; Hammill, 1977). In trying to predict children's adult height, we can assume that they will be about 20 percent taller at the end of puberty than at the beginning. More accurate predictions can be gleaned from X-rays, which demonstrate how far the bones have progressed in their process of calcification. From X-rays of the hand and wrist, a specialist can determine skeletal or "bone age" and thereby estimate the amount of additional height the adolescent can expect.

Muscle Tissue

Although height usually increases by only about 20 percent during adolescence, weight may actually double (Katchadorian, 1977; Tanner, 1962). By the end of adolescence most boys weigh about 25 pounds more than girls. Besides the additional weight of the organs, bones, and blood, boys generally outweigh girls because of their higher proportion of muscle to fat tissue. The average boy's muscle tissue doubles during adolescence, while a girl's increases by only 50 percent. During childhood about 16 percent of a boy's or a girl's weight is accounted for by fat tissue, but by the end of adolescence, only about 12 percent of a boy's body is fat tissue, in contrast to 20–25 percent of a girl's. Because muscle tissue weighs more than fat tissue, the average male is heavier than a female. As the data in Box 2.3 demonstrate, if a male and female both weigh 120 pounds, only 14 pounds of his weight is fat, compared to 28 pounds of hers.

The ramifications of these gender differences are both fascinating and controversial: How can adolescent girls compete athletically with boys, since they don't have equal muscle tissue? Is one sex any better suited than the other for specific types of activities, like long-distance swimming and running? Should girls abstain from rigorous physical activity or contact sports with boys? Why encourage girls to develop their muscles like boys?

Addressing such questions, physiologists have accumulated considerable evidence refuting traditional assumptions about the differences between males' and females' physical abilities (Katchadorian, 1977; Peterson & Taylor, 1980). For example, the notion that adolescent boys are better suited than girls for

Box 2.3 A Closer Look

The Body's Composition

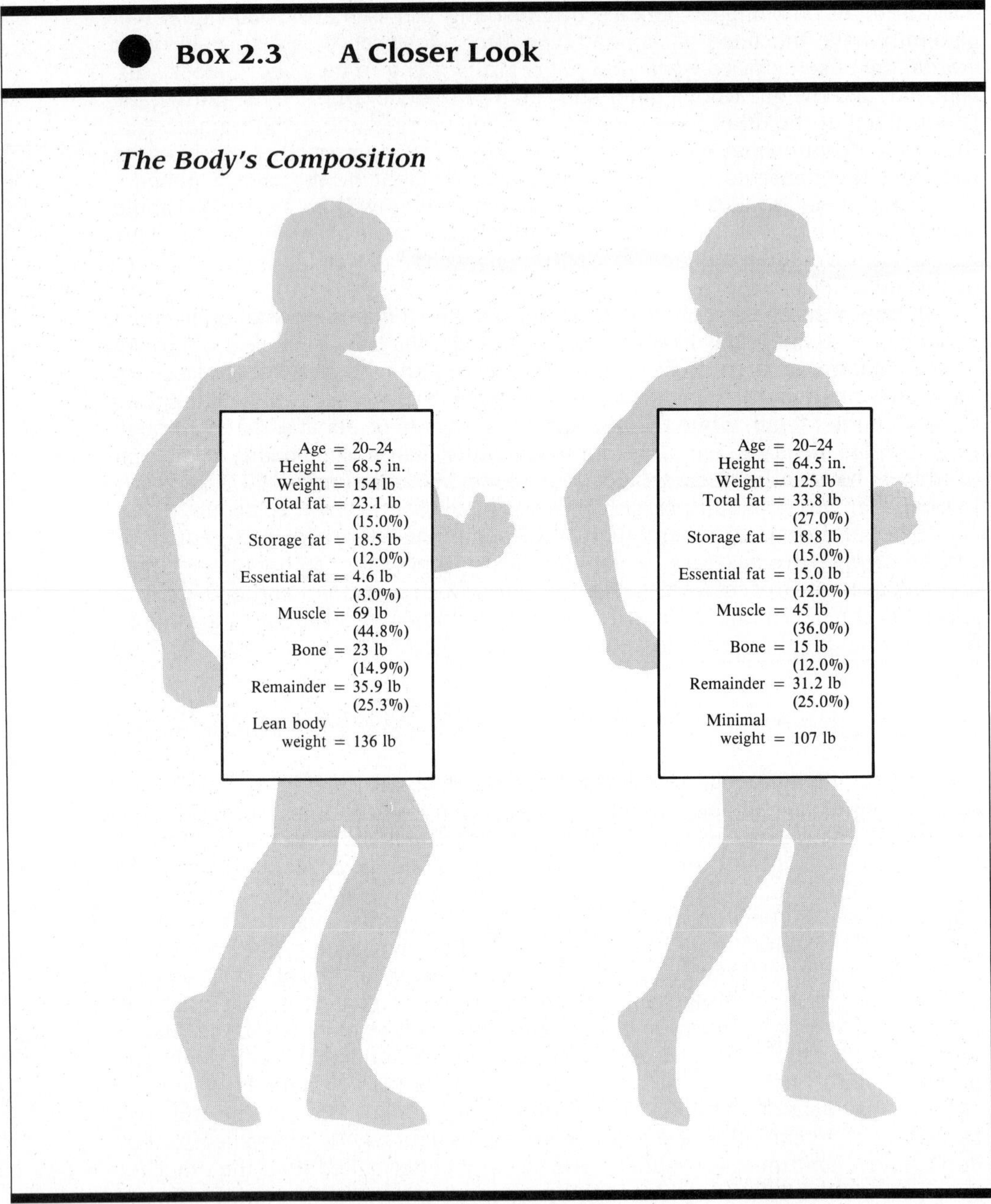

sports and strenuous physical tasks is overly simplistic when the overlapping abilities of the sexes are considered. First, there are enough small, overweight, or poorly exercised males and enough large, muscular, well-conditioned girls to undermine gross generalizations about strength solely on the basis of a youngster's sex. Second, recent evidence suggests that when adolescent boys and girls exercise alike, their percentages of body fat become much more similar. Unfortunately, reliable comparisons of males' and females' athletic and physical potential are difficult, due to the fact that girls have traditionally been discouraged from exercising as rigorously or as frequently as boys and are, as a consequence, generally less physically fit. Nevertheless, some physiologists have proposed that as the discrepancies in physical exercise between the sexes diminish, the percentage of muscle and fat tissue and the physical abilities of males and females will become more similar (Kaplan, 1979; Peterson & Taylor, 1980).

Indeed, empirical data already lend support to this contention (Kaplan, 1979; Marshall, 1981; Ogelsby, 1978). For example, athletic girls have higher oxygen intake, more stamina, more strength, and a lower percentage of body fat than unathletic boys. In addition, girls are generally more loose-jointed than boys, which enables them to perform certain physical tasks more easily, such as touching the floor with the palms of the hand. (Unfortunately, wearing high-heeled shoes contracts the heel muscles and necessitates special stretching exercises to reinstate the muscles to their more naturally limber state.) Furthermore, a girl's lighter bones, smaller shoulders, and additional adipose tissue are assets in activities like long-distance running and swimming. As the information in Box 2.4 demonstrates, many erroneous assumptions about females' physical abilities are slowly falling by the wayside.

Data on females' physical potential, however, should not be misconstrued to mean that the physiological differences between the sexes have no impact whatsoever on the motor performance of adolescent males and females. For

Are You Sure? 2.4 

Myths about Females and Physical Exercise

If a female adolescent seeks your counsel on physical exercise, which of the following beliefs would you endorse?

1. If girls lift weights, they will develop muscles as large as boys'.
2. Jogging causes the breasts and facial muscles to sag.
3. Exercising decreases the size of the breasts.
4. Rigorous exercises aggravate menstrual cramps.
5. A girl is incapable of performing as well athletically during her period as she can before or after menstruation.
6. Being injured on the chest during sports causes permanent damage to a girl's breast tissue.
7. A girl's reproductive organs are more vulnerable to athletic injuries than a boy's.
8. Girls are less well-equipped physically than boys to cope with high temperatures or humidity.
9. Rigorous athletic competition during adolescence creates complications in pregnancy and childbirth later in a girl's life.
10. Girls have less stamina and muscle power relative to their size than boys.

Answers: All of the above are false.

SOURCES: J. Marshall, *The sports doctor's fitness book for women.* New York: Delacorte, 1981; S. Twin, *Out of the bleachers: Writings on women and sports.* New York: McGraw-Hill, 1979.

example, an analysis of 176 studies revealed that since most adolescent boys are larger and have a higher percentage of muscle tissue than their female peers, they generally have a biological advantage in motor skills that depend on size and muscle strength. Moreover, after the onset of puberty, a girl and boy who engage in similar amounts of exercise will not develop the same muscular appearance, because the male's body has less fat tissue covering the muscles and because muscle mass is partially dependent on the higher level of testosterone in the boy's body. Prior to puberty, however, the differences in male and female motor performance appear to be socially induced by parents, peers, teachers, and coaches. In other words, the studies suggest that if boys and girls were subjected to equal expectations and equal opportunities, their physical performances would be similar before puberty, and the differences in their performance would be less exaggerated during adolescence (Thomas & French, 1985).

Adipose Tissue

Adolescents often become confused about the relationship between the fat and muscle tissues in their bodies, as Box 2.5 illustrates. This confusion provokes a number of naive questions: How can I get rid of all the fat inside my body? Why aren't I losing weight now that I am exercising more? How much food do I need to eat each day so I can gain some weight? Why is my tummy still fat, even though I've lost ten pounds? Why is my best friend skinnier than I am, when she eats so much more? Why don't I feel stronger, even though I made my muscles bigger through special training? Questions like these reflect adolescents' lack of information about their fat and muscle tissues.

Purposes of Fat Despite our derogatory comments about adipose tissue, fat is essential for our health and survival. Everyone's body contains three kinds of fat or **adipose tissue:** essential fat, subcutaneous fat, and storage fat. The essential fat protectively covers our nerves, organs, and cells. Lying just underneath the skin, subcutaneous fat envelops the entire body, protecting us from extremes of heat and cold. Storage fat is distributed around the abdomen, thighs, hips, and underarms.

During adolescence girls develop more storage fat than boys, causing them to lose their "boyish" childhood bodies as this adipose tissue distributes itself around the hips, thighs, upper arms, abdomen, and breasts. No matter how much weight a girl loses, these parts of her body remain fleshier and fuller than a boy's because of this different distribution of adipose tissue. This extra adipose tissue does not, however, mean that girls are "fat" and need to diet. Unfortunately, too many adolescent girls expect their bodies to look straight and lean like a ten-year-old's or a boy's body; thus the adolescent girl's primary complaint about her body is that it's "too fat" (Gunn & Peterson, 1984; Heuneman, 1974; Offer, Ostrov, & Howard, 1981). As the data in Chapter 14 will demonstrate, girls with this false perception of "fatness" are prime candidates for anorexia nervosa—a psychological disorder in which a girl's refusal to eat enough food can become life threatening (Bruch, 1978). In less extreme forms, the adolescent girl's perception of herself as too fat can lead to other unhealthy habits, such as dangerous diets and diet pills, which will be examined later in this chapter.

Although some adolescent boys also consider themselves too fat, they more

Are You Sure? 2.5

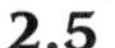

Physical Exercise: Facts and Fairy Tales

How accurately could you answer adolescents' questions about physical exercise? To assess your knowledge, determine which of the following statements are false:

1. You need to lose weight before you start to exercise.
2. Exercise makes you hungry afterwards.
3. Some diets cause you to lose muscles instead of fat.
4. Exercise raises your basal metabolic rate.
5. Exercise can improve your posture, relieve menstrual cramps, and decrease your need for sleep.
6. There is a possibility that exercise early in life restricts the total number of fat cells or will alter their size.
7. The fatter and more out of shape you are, the more slowly you should exercise in the beginning.
8. Exercise is more effective than a diet for losing fat quickly.
9. If you stay busy all day long, you do not need to exercise.
10. The best fitness program is to exercise 60 minutes daily three days a week instead of 20 minutes every day.
11. The best way to determine the benefit of an exercise for your heart is to take your pulse afterwards.
12. Exercising can make you look skinnier without your losing any weight.
13. Your body burns calories more quickly in the hours after you exercise than if you had not exercised at all.
14. Your muscles get as much benefit from 15 minutes of jogging as from two hours of tennis.
15. Two vigorous 6-minute exercises burn up more fat than one slow, continuous 12-minute exercise.

Answers: All are true except 1, 2, 9, 10, and 15.

commonly complain about their lack of musculature (Heunemann, 1974; Offer, Ostrov & Howard, 1981). The boy's adipose tissue typically accumulates around his abdomen rather than on his hips, breasts, and thighs. Consequently, too much adipose tissue causes a "pot-bellied" look. Like girls, boys sometimes mistakingly assume that they have too much fat tissue. Although the most popular way of determining whether an adolescent is too fat is to compare his or her weight to standardized charts, this method is far less reliable than more recent methods for measuring fat and muscle tissue (see Table 2.1).

Measuring Fat Tissue What does it mean to say that a youngster "lost weight"? Many people erroneously assume that if an adolescent loses ten pounds, he or she has lost ten pounds of fat tissue, though this is not the case. For example, let's suppose Juan notices after his four-mile run on a hot afternoon that he weighs five pounds less than before he jogged. Likewise, Susan notices that in the week before menstruation she weighs four pounds more than

Table 2.1

Desirable Weights for Designated Heights and Body Builds, for Persons 20 to 30 Years Old

	Weight in Pounds (without Clothing)		
Height (without Shoes)	*Small Frame*	*Medium Frame*	*Large Frame*
Men			
5 feet 3 inches	118	129	141
5 feet 4 inches	122	133	145
5 feet 5 inches	126	137	149
5 feet 6 inches	130	142	155
5 feet 7 inches	134	147	161
5 feet 8 inches	139	151	166
5 feet 9 inches	143	155	170
5 feet 10 inches	147	159	174
5 feet 11 inches	150	163	178
6 feet	154	167	183
6 feet 1 inch	158	171	188
6 feet 2 inches	162	175	192
6 feet 3 inches	165	178	195
Women			
5 feet	100	109	118
5 feet 1 inch	104	112	121
5 feet 2 inches	107	115	125
5 feet 3 inches	110	118	128
5 feet 4 inches	113	122	132
5 feet 5 inches	116	125	135
5 feet 6 inches	120	129	139
5 feet 7 inches	123	132	142
5 feet 8 inches	126	136	146
5 feet 9 inches	130	140	151
5 feet 10 inches	133	144	156
5 feet 11 inches	137	148	161
6 feet	141	152	166

SOURCE: U.S. Department of Agriculture. *Food and your weight.* Washington, D.C.: U.S. Department of Agriculture, 1973.

during the week following her period. Despite what their scales show, neither Juan nor Susan has lost or gained any fat. In these two examples the scales are measuring the amount of water in the adolescent's body. When Juan runs several miles on hot afternoons, his body sweats profusely by releasing pints of water stored in his tissues. For every pint of water that Juan sweats, he loses about one pound on the scales (Bailey, 1978). If he weighs five pounds less after his run, he has lost about five pints of water, not fat, and will regain this weight once he replenishes his liquids.

Typically, boys lose more weight than girls after rigorous exercise, because their sweat glands release more water than girls' (Marshall, 1981). So if Susan isn't sweating as much as Juan after her four-mile run, don't assume that she hasn't exerted just as much effort or received just as much exercise! In addition, her weight will probably change more than Juan's from week to week, no matter what she eats or how she exercises, depending on her menstrual cycle. Prior to and during menstruation most girls retain more liquids in their tissues and weigh more than at other phases of their cycle. Once again, weight on the scales has changed, but the percentage of fat or muscle in the adolescent's body remains unaltered.

There is one other reason why adolescents should not rely on the bathroom scales to determine how fat or muscular they are. Consider this situation: Samantha decides to build up her arm and leg muscles and to get rid of some fat by lifting weights. After six weeks of lifting, she's angry because her weight has increased by four pounds and she presumes the exercises have made her fatter. She's wrong. She has indeed been converting her fat into muscle tissue and is unquestionably "skinnier" in terms of having less fat inside her body; but muscle tissue weighs more than adipose tissue, so she does indeed weigh more on the scales. If she had one measuring cup full of her muscle tissue and one cup of her fat tissue, she could put them on the scales and see that the cup of muscle weighs almost two and a half times as much as the cup of fat. Thus, a physically fit adolescent like Samantha can weigh more than her flabby, out-of-shape classmates who have more fat but less muscle than she does. Generally the most athletic and well-conditioned adolescents will weigh more than unathletic youngsters of similar stature. Moreover, the stomach holds two or three pounds of food, so everyone weighs slightly more at the end of a full day of eating than in the morning (Bailey, 1978).

Given these limitations of assessing fat, how do researchers decide when youngsters are too fat for their own well-being? One way is to employ the *skinfold* test. By grabbing the flesh on the abdomen, underneath the upper arm, or at the waist with a pair of calipers, the researcher measures the inches of flesh. If the calipers can pinch more than an inch or so of flesh, the body is probably carrying more adipose tissue than neccessary for good health.

A more amusing way to measure adipose tissue is the "sink or swim" technique. Because fat floats, people who are lean and muscular will sink more quickly than their fat friends. If several adolescents hold their breath after filling their lungs with air, then let all of the air out of their lungs once they are in a pool of water, everyone will begin to sink. The one who hits the bottom of the pool first has the least fat tissue. The one who stays afloat the longest has the most fat. Remember that the youngsters who weigh the most will not necessarily hit bottom first. A 200-pound boy with 25 percent fat and very little muscle will sink more slowly than his 160-pound classmate whose lighter body may nevertheless contain 8 percent fat and a large percentage of muscle (Bailey, 1978).

Losing Fat Although adolescent girls need to maintain their adipose tissue at about 12 percent, boys can reduce their adipose tissue to 6 percent without any ill effects (Edelstein, 1980). Reducing the body's supply of fat below these limits can pose health hazards. The body converts all food into sugar or glucose. This converted sugar, as well as raw sugar contained in foods like candies and cake, provides the energy for breathing, pumping blood, digesting food, and all other

2.6 A Closer Look

Fat Chance, Frank Shorter

America's great Olympic marathon runner, Frank Shorter, reportedly has a body containing only 2 percent fat. He weighs 135 pounds, which means his body contains about 3 pounds of fat tissue. You would think this might be a problem for him since he needs huge quantities of calories to run those 26 miles. But one pound of fat amounts to 3,500 calories of stored energy, so his fat can be converted by his body into 10,500 calories' worth of energy. In a 2½ hour run his muscles use about 800 calories an hour at his speed. In other words, his body burns up less than one third of a pound of fat during his dramatic marathon run!

SOURCE: C. Bailey, *Fit or fat?* New York: Houghton Mifflin, 1978, p. 72.

bodily functions. Sugar also enables a body to move. Thus, if an adolescent eats a sandwich containing 800 calories' worth of carbohydrates and then goes out to play basketball for two hours, everything is fine, because playing ball requires only about 350 calories of energy each hour. If, however, that youngster wants to play basketball for four hours, the body relies on the body's supply of fat for the necessary sugar. Conversely, if youngsters consume more calories than their bodies need to complete their daily activities, the extra calories are converted to fat.

Each pound of fat can be converted into 3,500 calories worth of energy (Bailey, 1978). Hence, youngsters who want to eliminate one pound of fat from their bodies have to exercise rigorously enough to burn up 3,500 calories more than the calories contained in the food they have eaten. Put another way, to lose one pound of adipose tissue in one week, an adolescent must be physically active enough to burn 500 more calories each day than he or she eats (see Box 2.5). Since most of us don't exercise enough to burn up more calories than we consume, losing fat tissue is a slow process. Unfortunately, as the data in Box 2.7 demonstrate, the evidence suggests that most U.S. youngsters are less physically fit today than in previous decades (Carey & Hager, 1985).

In order to have enough adipose tissue for energy, without becoming too fat, adolescents have two alternatives: exercise and proper diet. Having too much adipose tissue is like strapping heavy weights around the ankles and waist and then commanding the body to move at its normal pace. The extra fat creates stress on the adolescent's heart, lungs, muscles, and other internal organs, as well as depositing cholesterol inside the arteries. Adolescents need to understand that healthy bodies require both fat and muscle tissues, which depend on a proper diet and exercise.

Food and Fat How should an adolescent eat and exercise for the healthiest balance of adipose and muscle tissues? Consider this situation: Agatha is aggravated because she is fatter and less muscular than her friend Rosie, despite her

A Closer Look 2.7 

The Younger Generation: Failing in Fitness?

Despite the growing concern over physical fitness among their elders during the 1980s, the younger generation appears less physically fit than their peers in previous decades. In 1956 President Eisenhower was concerned enough over the poor physical fitness of the youth of the United States to create the President's Council of Youth Fitness, which reached its zenith of populartity during President Kennedy's administration. Since that time, it apears that the fitness of U.S. youth has been on the decline.

Since traditional fitness tests like the standing long jump have been replaced with more sophisticated, modern tests of cardiovascular endurance and measurements of factors such as cholesterol levels, comparison from decade to decade are somewhat confounded. Nevertheless, in a three-year National Child and Youth Fitness Study released in 1985, measures like the skin-fold test revealed that representative samples of children and adolescents in the 1980s are fatter than those in the 1960s. Similarly, 10-year-old boys averaged only 2.7 chin-ups and on average took more than ten minutes to run one mile. Other tests conducted in various parts of the country confirm the study's results: Contemporary youths are losing ground in terms of physical fitness.

Although some may trivialize the unfit physical condition of today's youth as an issue related to vanity or limited to "health nuts," the ramifications of physical fitness go far beyond the bounds of physical appearance. Kinesiologist Guy Reiff of the University of Michigan espouses the view of other health-care professionals by saying that "cardiovascular disease starts by the first grade." Poor eating habits and the lack of physical exercise contribute to high cholesterol levels, high blood pressure, and poor cardiorespiratory functioning. In addition, evidence suggests that students who exercise regularly improve their academic skills and their self-concepts.

Several hypotheses have been offered to explain the poor condition of today's young people. First, budget cuts have forced many school districts to dismantle or to drastically reduce their physical education programs. Second, the demands on working parents often result in poorer eating habits, when children come home from school unsupervised and spend hours snacking in front of the television set, prepare their own makeshift dinners, or rely on fast-food industries to provide their meals.

Projects like "Shapedown" in San Francisco are designed to help overweight adolescents learn new eating and exercising habits. Initiated in 1980 by the University of California, Shapedown is available at 400 medical centers throughout the country. During the 12-week programs, which cost from $80 to $200, adolescents discuss their reasons for overeating, keep records of their eating and exercise habits, and learn to institute daily changes in their behavior. Parents are required to attend two sessions, in which they examine their own weight problems and discuss bad habits to which they are contributing, such as buying sweet foods and forcing their children to eat everything on the plate. Data collected months after a program's completion suggest that Shapedown is successful in helping adolescents change their eating and exercising habits on a permanent basis.

SOURCE: J. Carey & M. Hager. *Failing in fitness. Newsweek,* April 1, 1985, 84–87.

2.8 Are You Sure?

Fictions about Fat and Food

How accurately could you advise adolescents who want to lose or gain weight? Which of the following statements would you endorse?

1. Eating grapefruit helps the body burn calories quickly.
2. Dieting is a better way to lose fat than exercising.
3. Younger adolescents are generally not as fat as older adolescents.
4. Most overweight people have thyroid problems.
5. People on diets should avoid as many carbohydrates as possible.
6. Amphetamines decrease appetite.
7. Diet pills deplete the body of water, not of fat.
8. The best way to measure the loss of fat is on the bathroom scales.
9. You can eat as much as you want of certain kinds of food, such as fruit, and never gain weight.
10. A person will lose about one or two pounds of fat tissue per week on a good diet and exercise program.
11. Most adolescents can lose weight by consuming about 1,200 calories a day.
12. Eating a big breakfast, a medium-sized lunch, and a small supper is the best pattern for weight loss.
13. Fruit-flavored yogurt is a low-calorie food.
14. Dill pickles and other sour foods tend to decrease the desire for sweet foods.
15. A plain baked potato is a nutritious, low-calorie food.
16. If you get a headache after eating chocolate or drinking a cola, it's probably the caffeine that's bothering you.
17. Milk is the food that is most likely to cause allergies.
18. Food eaten before you go to bed is more likely to make you gain weight than food eaten at other times of the day.
19. Cellulite is just plain old fat tissue.
20. Exercising reduces appetite.

Answers: 1, 2, 4, 5, 8, 9, 13, and 18 are false.

SOURCES: C. Bailey, *Fit or fat?* Boston: Houghton Mifflin, 1978; B. Edelstein, *The woman doctor's diet for teen-age girls.* New York: Ballantine, 1980.

best efforts to lose weight and build muscles. Agatha cannot understand why this is so, when she bowls six hours a week, never eats breakfast, eats only a bag of potato chips and a coke for lunch, and includes plenty of protein-packed red meat in her dinners, as a way of building muscle tissue. In contrast, lean, muscular Rosie eats three hearty meals a day and jogs only 20 minutes each afternoon.

In assessing her physical fitness, Agatha has failed to consider four essential physiological facts. First, even though Rosie eats more food than Agatha, she may be consuming fewer calories. Second, 20 minutes of daily jogging consumes far more calories than six hours a week bowling. As Table 2.2 illustrates, the

Table 2.2

Scorecard on 14 Sports for Adolescents

Below is a summary of how seven experts rated 14 sports. A score of 21 indicates maximum benefit. Ratings were based on exercising four times a week for 30 minutes to one hour.

	Stamina	*Muscular Endurance*	*Muscular Strength*	*Flexibility*	*Balance*	*Weight Control*	*Muscle Definition*	*Digestion*	*Sleep*	*Total Score*
Jogging	21	20	17	9	17	21	14	13	16	148
Bicycling	19	18	16	9	18	20	15	12	15	142
Swimming	21	20	14	15	12	15	14	13	16	140
Skating	18	17	15	13	20	17	14	11	15	140
Handball Squash	19	18	15	16	17	19	11	13	12	140
Skiing	19	19	15	14	16	17	12	12	15	139
Basketball	19	17	15	13	16	19	13	10	12	134
Tennis	16	16	14	14	16	16	13	12	11	128
Calisthenics	10	13	16	19	15	12	18	11	12	126
Walking	13	14	11	7	8	13	11	11	14	102
Golf	8	8	9	8	8	6	6	7	6	66*
Softball	6	8	7	9	7	7	5	8	7	64
Bowling	5	5	5	7	6	5	5	7	6	51

*Ratings for golf are based on the fact that most people use a golf cart or caddy. If walking, the fitness value increases.

SOURCE: U.S. Department of Health and Human Services. *Children and youth in action: Physical activities and sports.* Washington, D.C.: Department of Health and Human Services, 1980, p. 29.

physiological value of various activities differs considerably. Third, Agatha is confused about the impact of protein on muscles. Muscle tissue is only 22 percent protein; the remainder is water. Hence, the idea of **"protein loading"** as a way of building muscles has limited value. While protein is neccessary for maintaining muscles, exercise is the vital ingredient for building muscles (Bailey, 1978; Heuneman, 1974). Fourth, and most important, Agatha has overlooked the fact that the most efficient way to lose weight and to build muscle is through exercising, not through dieting.

In assessing their caloric needs, adolescents should first determine whether they are inactive, moderately active, or extremely active physically. Those who are inactive should multiply their ideal weight by 12 to determine their daily caloric needs, the moderately active by 15, and the extremely active by 18 (Edelstein, 1980). For example, if Roy wants to weigh 140 pounds and he presently categorizes himself as inactive, he needs only about 1,680 calories a day to maintain a weight of 140 pounds. If Roy presently weighs 150 pounds, he has two options for losing his extra 10 pounds: exercise more to burn more calories every day without dieting, or reduce his calories to 1,680 a day without becomeing more physically active.

Exercise and Fat Despite the importance of physical exercise in maintaining the proper balance of fat and muscle tissue, most adolescents exercise very little and presume that dieting is the most efficient way to lose weight. Even more unfortunately, recent data suggest that adolescents in the 1980s are less physically active than their counterparts in the 1960s and 1970s (Carey & Hager, 1985).

Contrary to most adolescents' notions, the most effective way to lose weight is by exercising, not by dieting. The major difference between fat and thin people is that the overweight people engage in considerably less physical exercise and activity. Indeed, overweight adolescents often consume fewer calories than their thinner peers (Edelstein, 1980; Thompson et al., 1982). For example, in one experiment with obese adolescents, the group that performed exercises before lunch lost more weight than the group that restricted their calories at lunch. The youths who were exercising reduced their intake at lunch voluntarily to about the level that their nonexercising friends were forced to accept (Thompson et al., 1982). Moreover, fat youngsters are more likely than their thin peers to skip meals, underestimate their caloric intake, overestimate their level of physical activity, snack between meals, eat their food hurriedly, and choose the least nutritional and most caloric foods (Carey & Hager, 1985; Edelstein, 1980; Heuneman, 1974). In brief, overweight adolescents should be encouraged to increase their daily exercise rather than focus on dieting.

Although all of us are born with about 25 billion fat cells, overweight people can increase their fat cells by as much as five times the normal amount. When adolescents eat too much and exercise too little, the existing fat cells expand until the body is forced to produce new fat cells to accommodate the excess calories. Although shrunken in size, these new fat cells remain, even after the person loses his or her extra weight (Schowalter & Anyan, 1981). More sadly still, the odds are about 28 to 1 that an overweight adolescent will become an overweight adult (Zakus, 1979).

Basal Metabolism Rate

In addition to the new proportions of fat to muscle tissue, the body's **basal metabolism rate** changes during adolescence. An inherited feature, the metabolic rate is the speed at which a body converts calories into energy. Because their bodies burn calories faster, people with a high basal metabolism can eat more food without creating fat tissue than people with a low rate. Since the basal metabolism rate declines between the ages of 11 and 20, adolescents must either eat less or exercise more in order to maintain a normal weight. Moreover, since the basal metabolism rate continues to decline as we age, many adults find themselves getting fatter, even though their exercise and diet habits are no different from those they practiced as adolescents. Since, however, a male's metabolic rate is usually higher than a female's, boys can consume more calories than girls without gaining weight. Similarly, athletic people of either sex can consume more calories than their nonathletic peers, because muscles have a higher metabolic rate than adipose tissue and because exercise lowers the metabolic rate (Bailey, 1978; Katchadorian, 1977).

Breast Development

Why don't males develop breasts like females, since their bodies produce estrogen? How can a girl increase the size of her breasts? Can a girl who isn't pregnant still produce milk? What's wrong with a boy whose breasts start to swell? Questions like these reflect the concern that many youngsters have about their breasts during adolescence.

Although the male body produces estrogen, its levels are too low to augment breast tissue substantially. In contrast, the female body produces enough estrogen to stimulate the growth of adipose tissue on the chest, hips, thighs, and upper arms (see Box 2.9). Because breasts are primarily composed of adipose tissue, their size diminishes or increases in accord with the amount of overall fat in the girl's body. In other words, a girl who loses 30 pounds will have smaller breasts as well as smaller hips, thighs, and abdomen. Boys' breasts fail to grow like girls' also because they lack mammary glands. The *mammary glands* are milk-producing glands with ducts through which the milk travels to the nipple. Milk is produced only during pregnancy and during the period of time the mother decides to nurse her child. Although some adolescent girls may occasionally produce a milky substance, this is merely a cleansing liquid to keep the nipples' ducts open.

A Closer Look 2.9 

Eating Poultry and Breast Development: A Link?

For the last few years an epidemic of premature *"telarche,"* the medical term for breast enlargement in girls between six months and eight years old, has been spreading in Puerto Rico. According to Dr. Haddock, an endocrinologist at the University of Puerto Rico, 2,000 to 3,000 girls are now afflicted with telarche. Some of the experts suspect that the epidemic on the island is caused by the estrogen that farmers feed chickens to fatten them. Poultry is a staple of the Puerto Rican diet. In 1977 a similar problem arose in Milan, Italy, where boys developed enlarged breasts. The Italian researchers suspected poultry and veal as the culprits. Although premature telarche usually goes away in a year or two, some young Puerto Rican girls have developed more hazardous conditions—ovarian cysts and signs of premature puberty, such as menstruation and rapid bone development. Some researchers suspect that the estrogen in poultry is also causing these abnormalities.

SOURCE: A. Bongiovani, An epidemic of premature thelarche in Puerto Rico. *Journal of Pediatrics,* 1983, *103,* 245–246.

During adolescence the breasts develop in stages. First the *areola,* the area around the nipple, becomes thicker and darker. Depending on the amount of pigment in the skin, the areola can range from light pink to very dark brown. Because the nipples grow before the breast tissue, many girls feel embarrassed by their prominence. Furthermore, once the breast tissue does start growing, it may develop at different rates in the two breasts, leaving girls with anxiety about their unbalanced appearance. Breast size is genetically determined and—contrary to advertisers' claims—cannot be augmented by physical exercise. Certain exercises may increase the size of the pectoral muscles, which underlie the breast tissues, thereby giving the breasts a more uplifted appearance. But the amount of adipose tissue in a breast can be altered only through gaining or losing weight.

Because adipose tissue retains water, the breasts can become swollen and tender just before or during menstruation, when the body tends to retain fluids. This tenderness and swelling diminish naturally at the end of each menstrual period. Although normal breast tissue is somewhat lumpy, adolescents should be taught to examine their breasts for unusual lumps, which may be early signs of malignant growths. When a girl becomes familiar with her own breast tissue, she can more easily detect new lumps that are not part of her natural tissue. Although lumps sometimes disappear on their own and although most are merely benign cysts, one that remains for more than several weeks should be examined by a physician.

In a society that has traditionally placed great emphasis on the size of the female breast, many adolescent girls still worry about being too big or too flat chested (see Box 2.12). Although the size of the breast has no relationship to her ability to nurse children or to any health hazards, the dissatisfied girl who can afford the fees sometimes opts to have cosmetic surgery to decrease or increase breast tissue. Like an adolescent boy who may worry about his penis being too small, an adolescent girl may experience considerable distress over the size of her breasts.

During adolescence some boys' breasts become fleshy and have a somewhat "feminine" appearance. Boys' breasts may also ache and become sensitive to friction from clothing. Despite the anxieties this can evoke, these conditions are temporary and diminish as testosterone levels increase.

Male Reproductive System

The first sign of reproductive maturation for young men is usually the growth of the penis and testicles. Although it is not invariant, the most common sequence is enlargement of the penis and testicles, appearance of pubic hair, and ability to produce active sperm (Katchadorian, 1977; Peterson & Taylor, 1980; Tanner, 1962).

Basic Components The two parts of the penis are the *glans* or rounded head, which is the most sensitive area, and the *shaft,* which becomes engorged with blood during an erection (see Figure 2.1). If a boy has been circumcised as an infant, his glans is exposed. If he is uncircumcised, the glans remains covered by a hood of skin similar to the prepuce that covers a female's clitoris. **Circumcision** is the surgical procedure usually performed within a few days after birth, in

Figure 2.1

Male pelvic organs

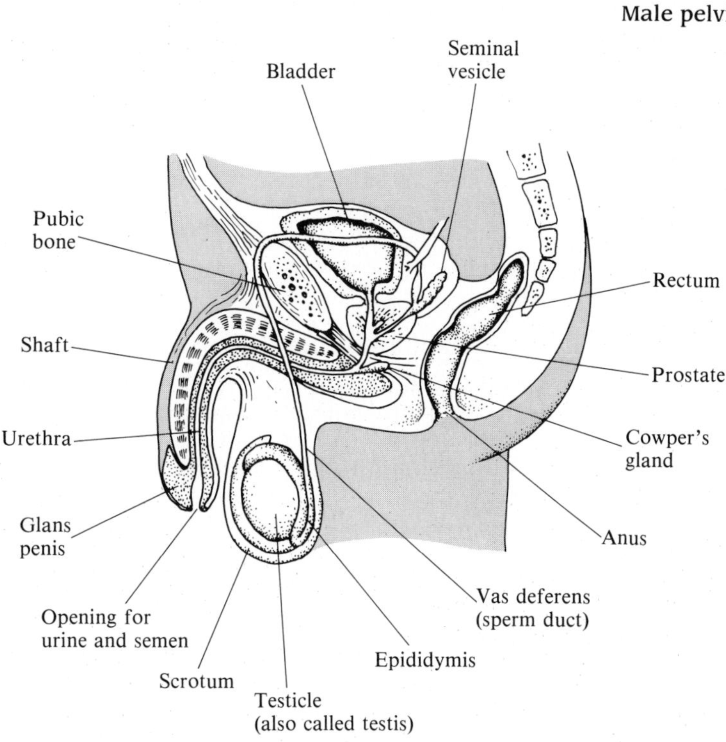

which the skin covering the glans, called the *foreskin,* is cut back. Circumcision has historically been performed as a measure for preventing infections that might develop from bacteria trapped underneath the foreskin. Given the convenience of baths and showers in modern society, however, some physicians are now opposing circumcision as unneccessary surgery that might be depriving the penis of the foreskin's protection against disease (Goldstein, 1976). Nevertheless, because circumcision is still the prevailing practice in our society, many parents have their sons circumcised to prevent the possibility of social embarrassment that accompanies looking different from most other boys.

At the onset of adolescence the young male's reproductive glands, the *testicles,* grow, causing the skin sack that houses them, the *scrotum,* to enlarge. The left testicle generally hangs slightly lower than the right, creating the false impression that one gland is larger than the other. In fact both testicles are the same size. The scrotum's primary functions are to maintain the proper temperature for sperm production and to offer protection against injury to the testicles. In cold weather or in situations of impending physical danger, the scrotum contracts, pulling the testicles nearer to the body for additional warmth and protection. In warmer weather or after hot showers the scrotum relaxes, causing the testicles to descend further from the body, thereby maintaining a cool enough temperature for sperm production.

Inside the testicles the **vas deferens** tubes transport sperm from the testicles to the seminal vesicles for storage. If the vas deferens tubes were unwound, they would stretch the length of several football fields. The seminal vesicles and the **prostate gland** produce **semen,** the fluid ejaculated during orgasm. The semen, also called *seminal fluid,* is primarily composed of protective fluids that insure the sperm's survival in the acidic environment of the vagina. During a *vasectomy* the vas deferens is surgically severed, rendering it impossible for sperm to be added to the seminal fluids that will be ejaculated. The diverted sperm are then absorbed by the male's body, although his testicles continue to produce new sperm and he continues to ejaculate seminal fluids during orgasms. Semen is ejaculated through the **urethra,** the tube that also transports urine from the bladder. Popular beliefs notwithstanding, it is physiologically possible for a male to have an orgasm without ejaculating and conversely to ejaculate without having had an orgasm.

Impregnation A single ejaculation of semen contains about 400 million sperm, which during intercourse propel themselves rapidly through the cervical opening, past the uterus and into the Fallopian tubes. Sperm swim more slowly and are few in number during the early years of puberty, thereby decreasing the chances of a boy's impregnating a girl during this time. Nevertheless, live sperm are present in young adolescents' semen as well as in the drops of fluid that escape from the penis before ejaculation. The pragmatic significance of this physiological fact is that a female can become pregnant even though ejaculation never occurs, if these sperm reach her Fallopian tubes as a consequence of sexual foreplay.

Emotional Reactions As the information in Box 2.10 indicates, the experiences that accompany the reproductive system's maturation create anxiety and confusion in most boys at one time or another during adolescence (Bell, 1980). Among boys' concerns are worries about exhausting their supply of sperm by ejaculating too often. This worry is unfounded, since the male body continually produces fresh supplies of seminal fluid and sperm, although there are fewer sperm in the fluid after several successive ejaculations. Boys may also be embarrassed by erections that occur at inopportune moments. Sometimes just having to urinate or feeling the friction of clothes against the penis can produce an erection. Others worry that becoming aroused but being prevented from ejaculating can cause physical problems. Although the testicles may ache slightly from the blood that is draining away from the aroused penis (a condition that boys sometimes refer to as "blue balls"), the discomfort dissipates without physiological damage of any sort. Ejaculating while asleep, called "wet dreams" or *nocturnal emissions,* can also be a source of embarrassment, despite the fact that these are a normal, unpreventable aspect of a boy's adolescence.

Still another source of numerous jokes, good-natured teasing, and occasional cruelty, the size of his penis can cause a boy considerable consternation and alarm. Falling prey to locker-room comparisons and numerous myths about penis size, a boy may ashamedly feel that his penis is "too small." Despite the fact that almost every male's penis expands to five or six inches when aroused, the differences in size of the flaccid penis (as it most often appears in locker rooms and showers) can lead adolescent males to believe that they are poorly endowed in comparison to other males. Furthermore, most adolescent males know too little about female sexuality or anatomy to appreciate the fact that the length of the penis is almost totally irrelevant to a woman's sexual pleasure.

Adolescent Voices 2.10

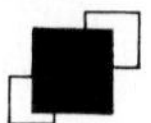

Boys' Feelings about Puberty

"My dad is always bugging me to go on a diet. I think it's because he was fat and unpopular as a kid. I'm heavy, but not that heavy. But when he looks at me with that look in his eyes, I feel like I weigh 300 pounds."

"Where I go to school, I'd say 80 percent of the boys work out with weights. It's pointless, because what happens is the standards just go up. If no one worked out, then the people who had less manly chests would be just as unhappy as they are now. It escalates. Now everybody spends an hour a day working out, when they could be doing something far more enjoyable and useful."

"Well, for me it was weird, because I didn't even start growing until last year. Everybody thought there was something wrong with me, because I still looked like a 10-year-old up until I was 15 or sixteen. That has been really a bad experience for me, because everybody was changing around me and I was standing still. I was changing in my head but not in my body. My parents were even going to take me to the doctor to see if I was deformed or something like that, but they didn't, and finally last year I started to grow. My voice started changing and everything, so I guess I'm normal after all. But I think it's going to be a while before I stop feeling like I'm different from everybody else."

"I had to shave a lot earlier than most of my friends. I was already shaving every day by the time I was 15, and even though I felt macho about it, it really was a pain in the neck. My dad's the same way—he has to shave twice a day to look good."

"When I was 14 I went around for about two weeks with this dirty smudge on my upper lip. I kept trying to wash it off, but it wouldn't wash. Then I really looked at it and saw it was a mustache. So I shaved! For the first time."

"You feel self-conscious, especially talking to a girl. I hear my brother talking on the phone with his girlfriend and he seems to be controlling his voice. He doesn't let himself sound angry or really happy or surprised. Your voice usually goes high when you get emotional or angry. So you try not to get too emotional. That way your voice will keep steady and low."

"All of a sudden I realized my voice was low. On the telephone people started thinking I was my father, not my mother!"

SOURCE: R. Bell, *Changing bodies, changing lives.* New York: Random House, 1980.

Many boys are concerned with the physical appearance of their genitals, but very few have been instructed to examine this part of the body for disease. Although cancer rarely afflicts adolescents, cancer of the testicles can occur during puberty. Just as medical practitioners urge girls to examine their breasts regularly, they urge boys to examine their testicles for unusual lumps. The best time to examine the testes is after a hot bath or shower, when the scrotum is most relaxed and the testicles are suspended farthest from the body. Each testicle should be examined gently with the fingers of both hands. If a boy discovers any lumps, he should contact a doctor for a more thorough examination ("Testes Test", 1981).

Female Reproductive System

Although the sequence is not universally predictable, female maturation generally proceeds in distinct phases: the appearance of pubic hair, the addition of adipose tissue on the breasts, thighs, hips, and abdomen, and finally the onset of menstruation (Katchadorian, 1977; Peterson & Taylor, 1980).

Basic Components During adolescence many girls discover their primary sexual organ—the *clitoris* (see Figure 2.2). Like the penis, the clitoris has a glans and a shaft containing the same type of spongy tissue responsible for a male's erection. The glans is covered by a protective hood of skin, the *prepuce,* while the shaft is buried beneath the skin, rather than exposed above the surface like the shaft of the penis. During sexual arousal, blood rushes into the genital tissues, causing the clitoris and surrounding area to swell. In the event an orgasm does not ensue, a sexually aroused girl sometimes experiences the same physical discomfort as boys whose testicles ache until the extra blood in these tissues is reabsorbed by the body. Unlike the penis, which serves urinary and sexual purposes, the clitoris serves exclusively to provide sexual pleasure. Although researchers have argued since Freud's time about whether females can experience two kinds of orgasm, clitoral and vaginal, most empirical data show that female orgasms are caused by direct or indirect clitoral stimulation. The debate

Figure 2.2

Female pelvic organs

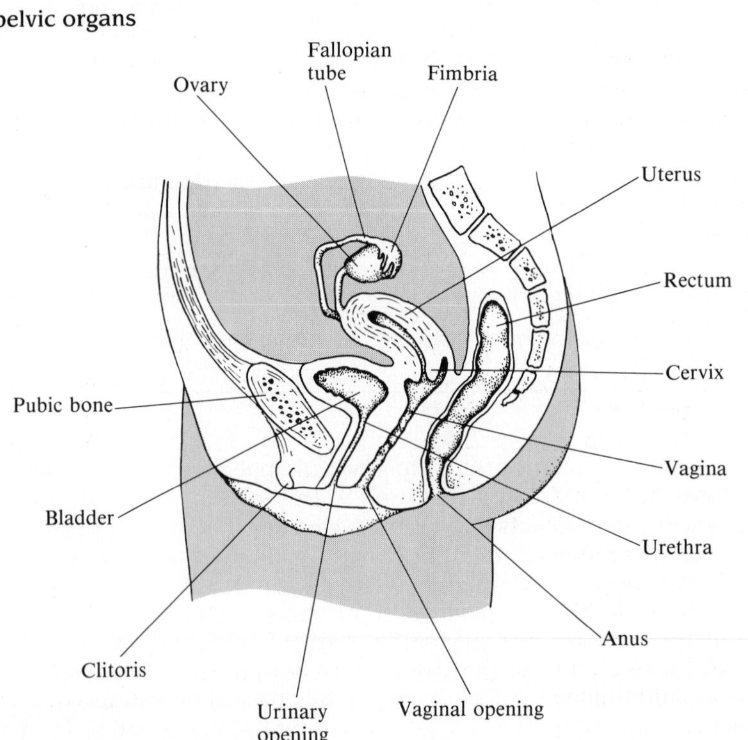

continues, however, since reports during the early 1980s indicated that some women experience an orgasm from stimulation of an area inside the vagina, referred to as the *"G spot."* Despite the continuing controversy, the physiological fact remains that the area near the entrance to the vagina is more abundantly supplied with nerves than the deeper vaginal areas.

Next to the clitoris is the urethra, the tube that carries urine from the bladder. The extremely small urethral opening is almost invisible, because it is surrounded by the *labia,* the folds of skin that protect the genital area. The more noticeable opening is the vaginal entrance. Contrary to many adolescents' beliefs, the vagina is not where the baby is housed. The *vagina* is the passageway through which the baby passes as the uterus contracts and through which the menstrual blood flows after being shed from the uterine walls. It is also the area that accommodates the penis during intercourse. To the surprise of ill-informed adolescents, the vagina is not an endless "open space." On the contrary, the walls of the vagina are touching one another unless an object like a penis, a tampon, a finger, or a baby is separating them. In this sense the vagina is more like an envelope than like the open space inside an inflated balloon. Misunderstanding their own anatomy, many girls believe that a tampon can "get lost" inside the vagina if pushed too far. The vagina, however, is a clearly limited space, whose contours can be explored by touching the walls with the fingers. Even the end of the cervix is clearly discernable by touching it with the end of a finger.

Other myths surround the part of the vagina called the *hymen.* The hymen, also called the "cherry" or the "maidenhead," is a thin membrane that partially blocks the vaginal opening. The crucial word here is "partially." Except in the case of a physical abnormality, the hymen never entirely covers the vaginal opening, since an unobstructed opening is neccessary for the flow of menstrual blood and vaginal secretions. Although often heralded as the sign of a girl's virginity, the hymen is often stretched unknowingly during childhood play or by inserting tampons. Furthermore, some girls are born without hymens. Its stretching is seldom accompanied by any bleeding or discomfort, contrary to stories about a girl's first sexual experiences to which many naive adolescents are subjected.

Near the farthest end of the vagina is the bottom portion of the uterus, the *cervix.* The cervical opening, also called the **os,** is the passageway between the vagina and the uterus. The position of the os within the vagina changes throughout the menstrual cycle, as the uterus changes its position. Early and late in the monthly cycle the os is easy to touch from outside the body because it is slanted toward the vaginal opening rather than toward the back of the vagina. During midcycle, when the egg has been released, the opening of the os is widest and is positioned far back in the vagina. During childbirth the os expands to a width of ten centimeters to allow the passage of the baby's head.

The walls of the vagina produce a liquid, called *mucus,* on most days throughout a girl's monthly cycle. This mucus changes both in quantity and in appearance, depending on the phase of the monthly cycle. Immediately after menstruation there is almost no mucus. As ovulation approaches, the mucus becomes more profuse and assumes a stretchy quality similar in appearance to egg whites. After ovulation has occurred, the mucus loses its stretchy texture, turns white, and diminishes in quantity until the onset of menstruation. The vaginal walls also produce a lubricating mucus in preparation for intercourse, which adolescent girls may notice during sexual arousal. Because vaginal infections and venereal diseases often cause a mucuslike discharge, girls need to learn to distinguish their body's normal mucus cycle from atypical secretions.

The reproductive organs beyond the cervix extend too far up inside the body for a girl to touch or see them. Only the size of a walnut and located low in the abdominal area (not some large empty cavity in the intestinal area that extends up to the belly button, as some girls erroneously imagine!), the *uterus* or womb is an organ whose walls are composed of thick muscles. During pregnancy the womb houses the infant until the uterine muscles contract, forcing the child out through the os and the vagina. It is these same uterine muscles whose contractions are responsible for the sensations referred to as menstrual "cramps." At the top of the uterus a *Fallopian tube* leads to each ovary, where eggs have been stored since the girl's birth. In a *tubal ligation* these tubes are surgically cauterized or clamped, thereby making pregnancy impossible, since the sperm and egg cannot unite once their bridge has been severed. Unlike sperm, which are freshly produced on a continual basis, each female egg is "old" in the sense that it has been inside the ovaries since the girl's birth.

Menstruation Occurring between the ages of 11 and 16, menstruation is the shedding of the uterine lining when no fertilized egg has implanted itself in the uterine wall. Although the menstrual fluid is referred to as blood, it is in fact the mixture of tissue, mucus, and blood that lined the uterus during the previous month. If fertilization occurs, the zygote (fertilized egg) implants itself in the uterine lining, which then becomes the *placenta* that nourishes the infant for nine months. Some adolescent girls erroneously believe they are "losing a lot of blood" during menstruation, which may somehow contribute to anemia. However, the two or three tablespoons of menstrual fluid are not extracted from the body's supply of circulating blood, and unless some physiological disorder is causing excessive bleeding, menstruation does not create anemia.

Most females' menstrual cycles are approximately 28 days long, with menstruation lasting three to four days. During the first year or two of menstruation, the adolescent's cycles are often irregular. She may occasionally skip a period altogether, a condition referred to as **amenorrhea,** which can be caused by tension, illness, dietary changes, certain medications, or excessive weight loss (Gunn & Peterson, 1984). Similarly, some athletes temporarily stop menstruating if their adipose tissue falls to excessively low levels (Frisch, 1984). Some adolescents experience the opposite condition, **menorrhagia,** in which an excessively heavy, prolonged menstrual flow can cause a temporary state of anemia. Avoiding aspirin and taking vitamin K have alleviated this condition in many cases (Wollman & Lotner, 1983).

Particularly during the first few years of menstruation, adolescent girls may be less likely to become pregnant because their ovaries occasionally fail to release an egg into the Fallopian tubes. An **anovulatory** period means that the ovaries have not released an egg during that menstrual cycle, although menstruation still occurs. During adolescence, when the reproductive system is approaching maturity, neither amenorrhea nor anovulatory periods are causes for alarm (Gunn & Peterson, 1984).

Menstrual "cramps" occur when the uterine muscles contract to expel the uterine lining from the body. Recent evidence suggests that the decrease in the body's calcium level prior to menstruation may contribute to the headaches, swollen tissues, or cramps that some girls experience. Taking calcium tablets sometimes alleviates these discomforts. Myths to the contrary notwithstanding, the majority of adolescent and adult females report minimal or no discomfort during menstruation. Fewer that 10 percent of all females report that their menstrual discomfort is severe enough to interefere with their daily activities. **Dysmenorrhea,** or painful menstruation, is the exception—not the rule (Gunn & Peterson, 1984). For those who do experience moderate or severe pain while menstruating, a number of options are now available to reduce their discomfort (see Box 2.11).

Emotional Reactions to Menstruation Why do some girls experience physical pain, irritability, or depression during their periods, while others don't? The controversy surrounding this question is derived from evidence supporting two contradictory perspectives.

Several converging lines of evidence suggest that a girl's physical and emotional reactions to menstruation are primarily determined by the attitudes she has adopted about the experience. Numerous research studies and reports have demonstrated that girls who believe menstruation causes pain, weariness, depression and irritability fulfill this prophecy when they start to menstruate

A Closer Look 2.11 

Relieving Menstrual Cramps

1. Eat more wisely. Cut down on salty foods the week before and during the menstrual period. Also eat less red meat.
2. Avoid certain liquids. Beer, caffeine, and wine can increase cramping and headaches.
3. Take additional vitamins the week before and during menstruation. Some girls find that supplements of dolomite, calcium, vitamin C, vitamin B, and magnesium reduce menstrual cramping.
4. Apply heat. A hot water bottle or heating pad on the stomach or lower back may help. Sometimes curling up in a knee-to-chest position with a hot water bottle against the back relaxes the muscles.
5. Use aspirin. Many girls find that aspirin brings fast and complete relief from cramping. Other pain relivers are also available for menstrual discomfort.
6. Exercise! An extremely effective way to relax muscles is regular, vigorous aerobic exercise, like running or swimming. There is no exercise that is dangerous for girls during their periods.
7. Take birth-control pills. In cases of extereme menstrual pain, some doctors will prescribe birth-control pills, although this poses several dangers for adolescent girls.

(Clark & Ruble, 1978; Dan, Graham, & Beecher, 1980; Gunn & Peterson, 1984). For example, girls with the most liberal attitudes about sex roles and sexuality have been found to experience less menstrual pain than those with more conservative attitudes (Paige, 1973). Further demonstrating the power of self-fulfilling prophecies, researchers in another study convinced one group of girls that they would soon begin their periods and persuaded another group that their periods would not begin for several weeks. The girls' beliefs about when their periods would begin influenced their moods and physical symptoms more than the actual timing of their periods (Ruble, 1977). Evidence also suggests that girls who start their periods before the age of 12 feel the most "abnormal" and uncomfortable about menstruation (Kaplan, 1975).

According to researchers who contend that self-fulfilling prophecies are the primary determinants of reactions to menstruation, girls who have been persuaded that menstruation is an unpleasant, unclean, painful ordeal will experience the most depression and discomfort. Unfortunately, the fact remains that many adolescent girls are still learning that menstruation is a shameful, "dirty" experience. For example, boys who have no knowledge of the experience and young girls who have not yet started menstruating often describe menstruation exclusively in negative terms (Gunn & Peterson, 1984). Furthermore, many adults emphasize only the hygienic aspects of menstruation in their discussions with girls, thereby perpetuating the attitude that menstruation is an unclean experience that needs to be concealed from others in an ashamed fashion (Bell, 1980; Gunn & Peterson, 1984; Whisnant & Zegans, 1975).

In addition to creating feelings of shame and embarrassment, conveying the attitude that menstruation is "unclean" can contribute to an adolescent girl's health problems (Bell, 1980). Believing the body's natural odors and menstrual fluid are repugnant, many girls subject their bodies to vaginal deodorants, deodorized tampons or sanitary napkins, and douches. These products often irritate the genital tissues and create vaginal infections. Douching can interfere with the vagina's natural secretions that cleanse the body and maintain the proper balance between protective yeasts and bacteria. Douching can also exacerbate infections by flushing harmful bacteria from the vagina into the uterus.

Although the research generally acknowledges that a girl's attitudes have a persuasive impact on her physical and emotional reactions to menstruation, the physiological bases of menstrual discomfort cannot be ignored. The physiological perspective is partially undermined by the fact that researchers have been unable to establish any consistent relationship between the levels of estrogen in a female's body and her behavior or moods (Dan, Graham, & Beecher, 1980; Gunn & Peterson, 1984). Nevertheless, the physiological argument is strengthened by recent evidence showing that some females undergo dramatic physiological changes prior to the menstrual period, which contribute to a condition known as **premenstrual syndrome** or **PMS** (Wollman & Lotner, 1983). According to this research, females afflicted with PMS undergo dramatic, unavoidable shifts in mood and behavior during the premenstrual phase of their monthly cycle. Although the debate over the extent or power of PMS presently remains unresolved, the data do suggest a physiological basis for the psychological and physical distress that some females experience during the premenstrual phase.

Other data also reinforce the perspective that the physical discomfort accompanying menstruation for some girls is physiologically—not psychologically—based. For example, some researchers attribute irritability, depression, cramps, headaches, and swollen tissues to the dramatic decline in calcium that occurs in the ten days preceding menstruation. The success of vitamin supplements in alleviating these symptoms suggests that physiological factors are at least partially responsible for the adverse mental and physical reactions reported by some girls just prior to and during menstruation (Wollman & Lotner, 1983).

Impregnation Despite the fact that girls' reactions to menstruation may differ, their bodies all undergo similar hormonal changes during a monthly cycle. Approximately five days after menstruation begins, the pituitary gland signals the ovaries to prepare for ovulation. The ovaries' increased production of estrogen causes the uterine lining to thicken with blood vessels and tissue in preparation for the possible implantation of a zygote. Near the fourteenth day of a 28-day cycle *ovulation* occurs, releasing one or more mature eggs into one of the Fallopian tubes. Some girls feel a slight twinge or lower-back pain when they ovulate. As the egg moves down the Fallopian tube toward the uterus, the ovaries release *progesterone,* causing the uterine lining to become more receptive to implantation. When no fertilization occurs, the egg disintegrates inside the uterus, the supplies of estrogen and progesterone dwindle, and the uterine lining detaches itself and is expelled from the body.

Because the egg survives only from 24 to 48 hours, a girl is fertile for only a maximum of two days per month. Given this amazingly short period of fertility, how do so may thousands of adolescent girls (and adult women) become accidentally pregnant? The answer resides in the amazing tenacity and long lives of sperm. In the three or four days preceding ovulation, the vaginal mucus becomes less acidic and extremely stretchy in texture. These two changes ensure the survival of any sperm deposited into the vagina during the preovulatory days. Yet even under these receptive conditions, sperm can survive only five or six hours in the vagina. If the couple has placed a spermicide within the vagina before sperm are released, many of these sperm will die on contact with the chemicals. And if a spermicide is being used along with a diaphragm, cervical cap, or cervical sponge, additional protection is afforded, since the os is covered and sperm cannot travel into the uterus. (Note the warning on all barrier methods of contraception that these devices must *not* be removed from the girl's body for at least six hours after intercourse.) Unfortunately, most adolescents do not understand that without spermicide the sperm rapidly propel themselves through the os, past the uterus, and into the Fallopian tubes, where they can patiently survive for almost a week. Consequently a couple who has intercourse any time during the week prior to ovulation is introducing millions of sperm to the Fallopian tubes, where only one is needed to penetrate the egg during the brief fertile period.

A second reason many adolescent girls become pregnant is the erroneous assumption that pregnancy is impossible unless a girl has already started having menstrual periods. Because ovulation occurs two weeks before menstruation, a girl is unknowingly fertile before she has her first period. Intercourse or foreplay can thus result in pregnancy. (Remember there are live sperm in the preejaculatory fluids on the penis.) Misguided by uninformed adults or their friends' advice regarding sex, too many adolescents discover these physiological facts through the trauma of unplanned pregnancies.

ABNORMAL DEVELOPMENT OF THE REPRODUCTIVE SYSTEM

Although in most cases physical development proceeds normally, some adolescents undergo ordeals created by their chromosomal abnormalities. Two conditions that affect the adolescent's sexual development are Klinefelter's and Turner's syndromes. Both are caused by an abnormal division of X and Y chromosomes on the twenty-third chromosomal pair at the time of conception (Higham, 1980).

In **Klinefelter's syndrome** a male is born with an extra X chromosome in the twenty-third pair. Although the boy has a penis and testicles, he develops female characteristics as well. His genitals may be quite small and his body less muscular than those of normal boys. Most boys with the extra X chromosome are sterile. The opposite condition, being born with an extra Y chromosome, creates other kinds of problems for the adolescent male. The XYY pattern tends to make boys mature sooner, to be slightly taller, and to suffer from more acne than boys with the normal XY pattern. The extra Y chromosome causes the adrenal glands to secrete too much androgen, causing earlier puberty and additional acne. However, evidence has failed to support the hypothesis that the extra Y chromosome causes boys to be more aggressive (Hamburg & Trudeau, 1981; McConnell, 1983).

A similar condition in females, **Turner's syndrome,** causes the child to be born with female genitals but without ovaries. Consequently, her body cannot produce the estrogen necessary for the development of her secondary sex characteristics during adolescence. Through hormone injections, estrogen is introduced into her body to enhance the development of female characteristics.

ISSUES RELATED TO ADOLESCENT PHYSICAL DEVELOPMENT

Early and Late Maturation

What impact does the age at which puberty begins have on an individual's behavior during adolescence and in later life? Is early physical maturation advantageous or disadvantageous?

In approaching these questions, most researchers have found that early maturation is advantageous for boys (Clausen, 1975; Livson & Peskin, 1980; Peterson & Taylor, 1980). Those who mature early often have an athletic advantage over less physically mature boys in our society, a culture where popularity is often predicated upon success in sports. The studies acknowledge that early maturers usually have higher self-esteem and more sophisticated social skills than boys who mature later. In addition, adults often rate them as more masculine, more relaxed, and more attractive, and afford them more freedom and responsibility than less physically mature boys. Some research also suggests that these advantages continue into adulthood. Men who matured early in adolescence have been found to be more poised, more successful vocationally, and more socially active than men who matured late in adolescence.

In contrast, other studies indicate that whatever advantages might accrue to boys who mature early do not extend beyond adolescence. Accordingly, these data have failed to find a significant relationship between a male's adult personality and the timing of his physical maturation during adolescence (Peterson & Taylor, 1980). Furthermore, some evidence suggests that early maturation can be disadvantageous to the adolescent boy. Because adults tend to treat the boy who matures early like an older adolescent and to base their expectations on his physical maturity, they may deny him the time to develop his social and mental skills at a normal rate. Adults may also inadvertently force him into adopting a vocational and personal identity before he has had adequate time to explore and to experiment with his options (Livson & Peskin, 1980). Despite these possible disadvantages, most boys say they would prefer to mature earlier than their male peers, if given the chance (Bell, 1980; Peterson & Taylor, 1980).

In contrast, the research generally acknowledges that the impact of early maturation is less favorable for girls than for boys (Clausen, 1975; Gunn & Peterson, 1984; Livson & Peskin, 1980; Peterson & Taylor, 1980; Peterson, Richards, & Boxer, 1983; Simmons, 1979; Simmons, Blythe, & McKinney, 1983). Girls who mature early usually date more often, express more dissatisfaction with their bodies, make lower grades, and express less self-confidence than girls who mature at an older age. Moreover, their physical maturity imposes sexual responsibilities that most are ill-equipped to handle, given their mental, social, and emotional immaturity. With these disadvantages, it is perhaps not surprising that, unlike boys, most girls say they do not want to mature earlier than their peers (see Box 2.12).

The disadvantages of early maturation, however, appear to depend, at least in part, on the kind of communication that exists between the adolescent girl and her parents. In support of this hypothesis, middle-class girls in one study were found to have adjusted more successfully to their early maturation than girls from working-class families. According to the researcher, this finding suggests that the working-class parents may have had less time to invest in helping their daughters adjust to early physical maturity, while the middle-class parents may have appreciably diminished their daughters' concerns as a consequence of having discussed the emotional and social ramifications of early maturity with them (Clausen, 1975).

Physical Appearance and Personality

While it might be heartening to believe that "beauty is only skin deep," most empirical data fail to support the maxim. Physical appearance affects not only how adolescents feel about themselves but also how adults and peers respond to them.

Investigations of the relationship between physical appearance and personality are hardly recent. Decades ago Harvard scientist W. H. Sheldon (1940) presented his theories regarding the relationship between body types and personality. According to Sheldon, an individual's personality is related to his or her body type: endomorphic, ectomorphic, or mesomorphic. **Endomorphs** are stocky, short, overweight people who are generally outgoing, sociable, and good-natured, in contrast to the tall, skinny **ectomorphs** who tend to be introverted, intellectual, and inhibited. Most desirable in this typology are the **mesomorphs**—athletic, muscular individuals who are presumably assertive, energetic, extroverted, and courageous.

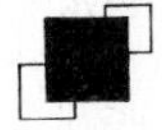

2.12 Adolescent Voices

Girls' Feelings about Puberty

"Every morning when I was in eighth grade my mother would meet me at the door and ask if I was going to put on lipstick that day. Couldn't she see I didn't want to? Why was she so attached to my looking a certain way?"

"Sometimes when I'm all alone I stand in front of the mirror and stare at myself. I stare at all the things I can't stand about myself, like I absolutely can't stand my legs. They're so short and my thighs are huge. And the worst part is my chest. I'm so flat-chested I look like a boy."

"There were some days in high school when I'd shave under my arms and then cover my armpits with adhesive tape. It wasn't much good for my skin, but on those days I knew for sure I wouldn't perspire on my blouse!"

"How about guys whistling at you and bugging you on the street? I hate that. And it's pretty scary, too, people whistling at you when you're walking home at night."

"My mom and I are really close and when I first started getting breasts she took me out to celebrate. It was around my tenth birthday, and I remember feeling very grown-up about it."

"I started maturing physically when I was very young and I never wanted to. When I was about 9 I already started having breasts and I hated it. I was still a tomboy and I used to do anything to hide my chest, like wear baggy shirts and overalls all the time. Now that I'm older I realize that I just didn't feel ready to grow up then. My body was leading the way and my feelings about changing were about a mile behind."

"There's a difference between what you want and what you think other people want. I don't think hairy legs are that bad. It doesn't bother me on me, and it doesn't bother me on other girls. But still I do it at times."

"I'm glad I haven't gotten my period yet. I'm still a kid. No way do I want to worry about that every month."

"I got my period early, when I was in fourth grade, and all my friends were jealous. They wanted to get theirs too."

SOURCE: R. Bell, *Changing bodies, changing lives.* New York: Random House, 1980.

Although Sheldon's theories about body type and personality have generally been discounted by contemporary research, his assumptions regarding the desirability of a mesomorphic body are not wholly unfounded. In this regard, the extant research confirms three hypotheses that are consistent with Sheldon's predictions. First, adolescents generally consider males with a mesomorphic build more attractive than males with endomorphic or ectomorphic bodies. Similarly, most adolescents agree that slender, relatively tall females are more attractive than those with mesomorphic or ectomorphic physiques. Second, most adolescents agree that having a "nice body" is essential both to popularity and to an individual's own self-esteem. In other words, adolescents are convinced that the characteristics associated with physique affect the way individuals interact with one another and the way people feel about themselves. Third, adolescents with endomorphic bodies do tend to be less popular than their mesomorphic and ectomorphic peers (Brenner & Hinsdale, 1978; Clausen, 1975; Hendry & Gullies, 1978; Pomerantz, 1979).

Although research has disproved Sheldon's assertion that body build causes personalities to develop in a predictable fashion, the data have upheld the hypothesis that physique and appearance influence human interactions. Cultural stereotypes associated with different physiques have been well documented by social psychologists (Mischel, 1981). Mesomorphs are generally deemed more influential, more popular, and more self-disciplined than endomorphs. Similarly ectomorphs are often prejudged as being more nervous and less talkative than endomorphs. For example, high-school teachers in one recent study perceived their skinny students as less poised, less extroverted, and less self-confident than mesomorphs and endomorphs (Hendry & Gullies, 1978). Such findings suggest that self-fulfilling prophecies can contribute to adolescents' developing particular traits in accord with other people's expectations based on an individual's physique.

Given the potential impact of an adolescent's physical appearance on other people and on self-esteem, it is worth noting the ephemeral, temporary nature of a society's standards of beauty. Cross-cultural data and the changing standards within a society verify that "beauty is in the eyes of the beholder." For example, in the 1960s many black youths emulated Caucasians' notions of beauty by straightening their curly hair and applying lighter makeup to the skin. By the 1970s, however, this trend had reversed itself, as ethnic pride manifested itself in a new standard of beauty in which afro hairstyles and African clothing and jewelry were prominantly featured.

In this same regard, in central Africa adolescent girls are segregated from the community, fed sweet and fatty foods, rubbed with oils, and returned to the tribe once they are obese and "beautiful" enough. In other tribes both boys and girls are "beautified" by knocking the front teeth loose and bending them forward so the lip will protrude (Klineberg, 1954). Similarly, in our own society adolescent girls learn to apply color to their hair, paint their faces, pluck out portions of their eyebrows, pierce holes in their earlobes, and rub chemicals on their bodies to remove body hair. Thus, each society conveys its own idiosyncratic notions of beauty to the young—notions that influence their self-esteem as well as their judgments of others.

Not surprisingly, social psychologists' data confirm adolescents' conclusions about the importance of physical beauty. For example, attractive people of all ages are perceived as more friendly, intelligent, dependable, influential, independent, and competent than their less attractive peers, even when these notions are unfounded in terms of actual behavior. Attractive people also tend to receive the benefit of the doubt in academic and social situations. For instance, high-school teachers are more apt to overlook the misconduct and the academic mistakes of attractive than of unattractive students (Kash & Borich, 1978). Given our society's emphasis on physical beauty, it is not surprising that attractive adolescents usually express greater self-confidence than their unattractive peers. (For reviews of this literature consult Gergen & Gergen, 1981; Mischel, 1981; McConnell, 1983.)

In our society, where physical beauty is highly valued, it comes as no great surprise that most adolescents (and adults) express dissatisfaction with some aspect of their appearance (Bell, 1980; Brenner & Hindsdale, 1978; Gunn & Peterson, 1984). Contrary to the assumptions of many adults, however, most adolescents are not distressed by the physical changes accompanying puberty. For example, in their extensive cross-cultural studies during the 1960s and 1970s, Offer and his colleagues (1981) found that 70 percent of the adolescents liked their bodies. Consistent with other researchers' findings, however, adolescent girls expressed more dissatisfaction with their physical appearance than boys. Given the consistency of this observed sex difference in the reported research, it appears that unattractive females have more to lose socially than unattractive males, since males can generally compensate for their physical shortcomings through academic, athletic, or financial success (Gergen & Gergen, 1981; Gunn & Peterson, 1984; McConnell, 1983).

Food, Nutrition, and Dieting

At one time or another most adolescents want either to lose or to gain weight in order to appear more attractive to other people. Unaware of a diet's possible impact on physical and emotional well-being, many adolescents also find themselves engaged in battles with their parents over dietary matters: Why do I have to eat breakfast? Why won't you let me go on that high-protein diet? Why are you always nagging me about what I eat? Why won't you let me use your diet pills?

Although the body's metabolic rate and need for calories lowers as we age, an adolescent requires more calories than either adults who are doing heavy physical labor or nursing mothers (Katchadorian, 1977). The average boy needs from 2,500 to 3,000 calories a day between the ages of 14 and 17, while girls need from 2,000 to 2,500 calories daily between the ages of 12 and 15. After these years of most rapid growth, adolescents need fewer calories, because their basal metabolism rate is lower and physical development has ended. Youngsters with smaller bodies and those who exercise very little need fewer calories than larger or more active youths. Although most adolescents eat enough to meet their bodies' caloric demands, many eat foods that create physical, academic, and social problems (see Table 2.3).

The average individual in the United States consumes about 130 pounds of sugar, 295 cans of soda, 125 pounds of fat, and 250 pounds of meat and poultry a year. Only about 20 percent of the average diet is fresh fruits, vegetables, or whole grains (Edelstein, 1980). As a consequence of these cultural habits, most adolescents consume far too many high-cholesterol foods, which contribute to atherosclerosis in later life. **Atherosclerosis** occurs when the inner walls of the blood vessels become coated with the fat, *cholesterol,* thereby causing the heart to work harder to push blood through the narrowed vessels. In cases where the cholesterol completely blocks the vessel, strokes or heart attacks occur. The amount of cholesterol in a person's body can be measured during any time of life by a simple blood test. Ideally, adolescents should eat as little cholesterol as possible and should consume about 12 percent protein, 58 percent carbohydrates, and 30 percent fats in their diets (Edelstein, 1980).

Another unhealthy adolescent habit is the excessive consumption of sugar—a habit that can undermine academic performance and physical energy (Duffy, 1975; Miller & Miller, 1979; Williams, 1973; White, 1977). Because the body converts raw sugar into energy more quickly than it does protein or carbohydrates, an adolescent who eats a candy bar will feel a more sudden surge

How well did you treat your own body as an adolescent in regard to food, sleep, and exercise?

of energy than one who eats an egg or a cup of yogurt. The body, however, burns the raw sugar much more quickly than protein or carbohydrates, causing the blood-sugar level to fall dramatically a short time after the sugar is ingested. This sudden drop in blood sugar can cause irritability, loss of concentration, headaches, and lethargy. Consequently, the adolescent who eats the egg will have longer-lasting energy than the one who eats the candy. High-carbohydrate meals provide energy for about three hours, and high-protein meals provide energy for about six hours (Bailey, 1978).

Foods to which certain adolescents are allergic can also alter a young person's behavior. An *allergen* is any substance in food, in the air, or in the envi-

Table 2.3

Fast-Food Nutrition: How It Adds Up

	Calories	*Protein*	*Fat*	*Carbohydrates (in grams)*
Quarter pounder	420	25	19	37
Hamburger	260	14	9	30
French fries	180	3	10	20
Chocolate shake	315	9	8	51
10-inch pizza	1,200	72	35	152
2-piece fish and chips dinner	900	25	45	99
4 ounces of ice cream	180	5	6	27

ronment that causes an allergic reaction, such as hives, headaches, sneezing, skin rashes, or upset stomachs. In its most extreme forms, allergic reactions can be fatal. For example, a severe attack of asthma causes swelling in the lung tissues that can choke its victim to death. Researchers are exploring the possiblity that certain food allergens cause youngsters to become nervous, lethargic, anxious, or depressed (Miller & Miller, 1979; White, 1977).

A final problem in regard to food and nutrition is dieting. Ill-informed adolescents often opt for diets that are both dangerous and ineffective (Edelstein, 1980). Among these are the popular liquid-protein diets, grapefruit diets, starvation diets, *macrobiotic diets,* high-fiber diets, and low-carbohydrate diets. As the information in Boxes 2.13 and 2.14 demonstrate, these dangerous diets can be replaced with safe, effective methods for losing weight.

The Advantages and Disadvantages of Sports

Since adolescence is the time during which males' and females' muscular development and size enable them to perform physical feats impossible during childhood, sports become an increasingly dominant activity. Although sports have long been a traditional component of a boy's upbringing in our society, recent changes regarding sex roles and recent evidence about the psychological and physical impact of interscholastic sports have elevated athletics to an even more prominent and controversial level.

The potential for physical exercise to reduce depression and elevate the spirits is well documented in contemporary research (Carr, 1981; Driscoll, 1975; Harper, 1978; Kaplan, 1979). These studies have garnered empirical support for the assumption that exercise can improve an individual's mood and self-confidence. According to some researchers, endorphins are responsible for the psychological benefits accompanying rigorous exercise. *Endorphins* are chemicals released by the brain as a natural anesthetic. When the body is severely injured, for example, the brain releases endorphins as a way of diminishing pain. Some evidence suggests that endorphins are released during rigorous exercise, thereby creating an antidepressant effect that improves attitudes and reduces

A Closer Look 2.13 

Dangerous Diets for Adolescents

Fasting: Fasting is a poor method for losing weight, since the body can last only a few days without weakening. Fasting causes dizziness, lethargy, and headaches. Once a fast ends, people are still left with the problem of how to control their fattening habits.

Macrobiotic Diets: The macrobiotic diet progresses through six increasingly severe stages that limit the kinds of foods you can eat. In the final stage the diet consists only of brown rice and tea. Some physicians consider this diet the most dangerous, because it lacks most vitamins and the critically important mineral, iron.

Liquid-Protein Diets: The fad started as a beauty-shop diet marketed as NaturSlim, a powder added to skim milk for breakfast and lunch. When you add a sparse dinner, you consume about 750 calories a day. These protein products are now sold in drug and grocery stores under many brand names. While they do take weight off, they are nutritionally unbalanced and fail to provide the kind of calories necessary for adolescent growth.

Low-Carbohydrate Diets: Low-carbohydrate diets permit one to eat as much protein and fat as desired, but no carbohydrates. These high-protein diets put the body into a state that can be dangerous to diabetics and hard on the kidneys. The initial weight loss is mostly a loss of the body's fluids, not fat. Without carbohydrates most people feel listless.

High-Fiber Diets: According to the advocates of the high-fiber diet, you should load your diet with high-fiber foods like bran, fruits, and vegetables. The fiber supposedly "speeds" food through your intestines and minimizes the chances for the body to absorb the calories. Nonsense! These diets do make you feel "full" and they aren't harmful to the body, but they do not cause weight loss unless the feeling of fullness causes people to eat less.

Diet Pills: Most nonprescription diet pills are a combination of chemicals that cause the body to lose fluids, not fat. Because some bodies may contain as much as ten pounds of water, these pills do cause immediate weight loss and do make people feel thinner. These diets, however, are the equivalent of squeezing out a big sponge, since all the body loses is water. The danger is that the body needs water to keep itself cool, get rid of waste products, lubricate the joints, digest food, and carry nutrients to the cells. To accomplish these tasks the body needs about three quarts of water a day. Most of us "eat" one or two quarts of water in fruits and vegetables. Using diet pills to rid the body of water is potentially dangerous and doesn't cause us to lose fat.

Another kind of diet pill is prescribed by physicians. These contain amphetamines. Amphetamines were originally created to control mental depression, but people soon discovered that the drug also diminished their appetites. While this is true, amphetamines also raise blood pressure, cause headaches, and create restlessness, and they are also addictive. Amphetamines are hazardous enough for the federal government to regulate their sale and put warning labels on the bottles.

SOURCE: B. Edelstein, *The woman doctor's diet for teen-age girls.* New York: Ballantine, 1980.

2.14 A Closer Look

Safe Methods for Adolescents to Lose Weight

1. While eating, get in the habit of putting your utensils down between bites and eating slowly.
2. Drink several glasses of liquid before each meal to give you the feeling of fullness before the food arrives.
3. Eat a large breakfast, a medium lunch, and a small dinner.
4. Cut out snacking between meals.
5. If you can't resist a dessert, eat it before the meal, so that you will eat less food afterward.
6. Record the number of calories you eat every day and be sure to include every snack in your daily record.
7. Eat boiled or baked foods, rather than fried ones.
8. Post photographs of yourself in a bathing suit on the refrigerator door alongside pictures of how you would like to look.
9. Keep a journal for two weeks in which you record the time of day, the place, and the people present when you eat. Use this information to design a behavior-modification plan for dieting.
10. Reward yourself every day for changing your eating habits, rather than for the actual amount of weight you are losing.
11. Leave the table as soon as you are full and do not finish the leftovers on your plate or anyone else's.
12. Eat on a smaller plate and spread the food out so the portions look larger than they really are.
13. Prepare low-calorie snacks ahead of time, so that when you have the urge to eat you won't reach for a prepackaged high-calorie food.
14. Since boredom is the primary reason most people snack, make a list of activities that you can enjoy when you get bored. Keep this list handy, so that whenever you are tempted to eat a snack, you can consult your list. If nothing else, go out for a walk and burn up some calories!
15. Put a bowl full of fat in the refrigerator and go look at it whenever you are tempted to eat.
16. Put tempting foods out of sight, rather than leaving them visible around the house.
17. Avoid fast-food restaurants. Meet your friends some place else.
18. In restaurants order salad dressings and other high-calorie additions "on the side," so you can control how much is added.

anxieties (Carr, 1981). Although hypotheses about endorphins are still disputable, there is general agreement that regular exercise often helps build adolescents' self-confidence and decreases depression.

Although few would argue against the assumption that physical exercise is valuable for adolescents, there is considerable dispute regarding the issue of

How did being athletic or nonathletic affect you in high school?

organized sports: Should adolescents participate in competitive, contact sports? How do sports affect a youngster's academic and social development? What benefits accrue to female athletes? The proponents of interscholastic sports and their critics present convincing arguments on both sides of the debate surrounding questions like these.

Males and Sports According to the research supporting interscholastic athletic activities for adolescent boys, sports generally enhance a boy's academic and vocational success (Snyder, 1972). Representing this point of view, a national survey of high-school seniors showed that both black and white male athletes had better grades, higher academic self-esteem, and higher vocational aspirations than nonathletes. Unlike black males, whites, however, became less interested in sports as they aged—a difference that may reflect the black community's belief that athletic success is a quicker way to achieve upward mobility than academic success (Blythe, 1982). In a similar vein, another study with adolescents found athletes less likely to be delinquent than nonathletes from similar family backgrounds (Schafer, 1969).

Proponents of interscholastic sports offer numerous arguments in support of their view (Sabo & Runfola, 1980). Among the most common are that sports teach boys to overcome obstacles that they will encounter in other areas of their lives and that competition teaches leadership and survival skills. In addition to reinforcing traits like good sportsmanship, self-discipline, and competition, sports supposedly teach social skills and develop a sense of comradeship. Furthermore, athletic success can underwrite the cost of a college education for the fortunate few who excel in high-school athletics.

In contrast to the view that interscholastic sports contribute to an adolescent boy's development, many individuals and professional organizations argue against them—particularly in middle and junior high schools (Freishlag & Schmidke, 1979; Sabo & Runfola, 1980). Most of the opponents of interscholastic sports are supportive of athletic opportunities for adolescents, but oppose our current practice of limiting these opportunities to so few boys. Since only a handful of male students make the team, the majority of young boys and traditionally all of the girls sit inactively on the sidelines, cheering the few who play. Rather than limiting sports to the few outstanding male athletes, why not disperse the school's athletic funds and facilities among all students?

Furthermore, the opponents argue that interscholastic sports encourage a social hierarchy in which "jocks" are separated from the rest of the students and in which most students are denied the social benefits of playing sports. In contrast to the assumption that sports build character, evidence shows that male athletes are often less sensitive to other people and overly concerned with proving their masculinity (Sabo & Runfola, 1980). At least one commentator contends that boys rely on sports to make themselves feel more masculine in a society where automation and legislation have threatened their status vis à vis females (Freishlag & Schmidke, 1979). The emphasis on competition and winning often creates a violent, aggressive attitude among both fans and players. Many sports events resemble battles, with angry coaches leading their troops in front of impassioned parents whose own egos are at stake in their children's performance.

As Box 2.15 indicates, another concern is that too many athletes abuse their bodies with drugs in an effort to improve their performance. Although drug abuse is most prevalent among college athletes, high-school athletes also resort to chemicals to improve their endurance and to diminish pain ("Substances Athletes Use," 1982). Moreover, in their efforts to appear masculine by concealing physical pain and playing despite their injuries, many boys suffer unnecessary physical injury (Sabo & Runfola, 1980).

It is reported that 12 million children suffer permanent physical impairment from sports before the age of 18 and that these injuries are disproportionately high among the youngest adolescents. Additionally, the director of the Division of Sports Medicine at Children's Hospital in Boston reports that, since 1968, sports injuries have surpassed congenital and infectious disease as the leading cause of death and hospitalization in children younger than 14 (Jennes, 1980). Adolescents whose bone and muscle development is not yet complete risk per-

A Closer Look 2.15 

The Substances Athletes Use

The following are some of the substances used by athletes to improve their performance, change their weight, diminish physical pain, or reduce psychological stress:

Alcohol: Alcohol is used by some wrestlers to lose weight through water lose, by marksmen to steady their aim, and by distance runners to replace carbohydrates after long runs. Some athletes also use alcohol to relieve pain, increase self-esteem, and relax their muscles. Alcohol decreases coordination, reaction time, depth perception, and muscle strength.

Amphetamines: Amphetamines, or "speed," cocaine, and benzophetamine, reduce pain and delay exhaustion. Some athletes believe these drugs make them more aggressive and allow them to perform at higher levels for longer periods of time. They can be addictive and cause hypertension, loss of appetite, intracranial hemorrhage, and death.

Steroids and Androgenic Hormones: Steroids are used mainly by weight lifters, body builders, swimmers, and football players to increase strength and muscle mass. The American College of Sports Medicine says that steroids neither help nor hinder performance. The side effects include liver problems, acne, decrease in sperm production, infertility in girls, and decrease in size of the testicles.

Aspirin: Aspirin and other anti-inflammatory drugs reduce pain and make it possible for athletes to perform when injured. These drugs can cause stomach problems, confusion, and lethargy.

Caffeine: Caffeine is a stimulant that some athletes believe increases muscle efficiency and decreases fatigue. The drug causes rapid heartbeat, insomnia, and nervousness.

Nicotine: Nicotine is used by some athletes as a stimulant—for instance, by those who chew tobacco while playing ball. In fact, nicotine decreases athletic performance.

Tranquilizers and Barbiturates: Sedatives counteract nervousness before a game and insure a good night's sleep beforehand. By slowing response and reaction time, they increase the risk of injury. They are also addictive and can cause death.

Protein Supplements and Vitamins: Some athletes believe that protein supplements and large doses of vitamins B, C, and E improve their performance and build muscles. The body does not store protein, however, and more energy is used to digest it than it produces. Massive doses of vitamins do not improve endurance, muscle efficiency, or performance.

SOURCE: Substances athletes use, *Chronicle of Higher Education*, September 1, 1982, p. 26.

manent bone and joint damage, as well as damage to immature hearts, kidneys, and muscles.

Critics continue to argue that too many adults have lost their perspective on competitive sports and place their own needs for athletic entertainment or advancement as coaches ahead of the well-being of adolescent athletes. Yet, in spite of physicians' warnings and evidence that high-pressure competition causes emotional and social problems for some young athletes, competitive athletics for boys continue to be supported by most adolescents, their parents, and their teachers (Braddock, 1979; Coleman, 1980; Sinan, 1979).

Females and Sports Like their male counterparts, female athletes derive a number of benefits besides physical conditioning from their participation in sports. Female athletes tend to be more self-confident, less depressed, more academically successful, and more satisifed with their physical appearance than

How do you feel about females competing in contact sports such as wrestling, football, and basketball?

nonathletes (Harper, 1978; Mayer, 1968; Nielsen, 1983; Ogelsby, 1978; Snyder & Kivlin, 1975). Impressed by the empirical evidence, some counselors argue that physical exercise should be an essential requirement for girls in therapy, since exercise so often improves self-esteem and decreases depression (Harmon, 1978). In regard to academic gains, female athletes consistently outperform unathletic boys on spatial-skills tests, which are reportedly related to mathematical success. Given this apparent relationship between sports and spatial skills, the renowned researcher in the field of math anxiety Sheila Tobias (1978), suggests that participating in sports may help girls perform better mathematically.

Others assert that competitive team sports could give girls more self-confidence and convey skills necessary for vocational success (Harragan, 1978; Hennig & Jardin, 1977; Neal & Tutko, 1976). Most girls engage in individual exercise, like jumping rope, skating, gymnastics, or dancing, in contrast to boys who are typically involved in competitive team sports from an early age. As a consequence, girls are often deprived of opportunities in team sports that teach competitiveness, cooperation, assertiveness, and self-discipline. Team sports also teach participants how to accept criticism, how to relate to authority figures, how to sacrifice personal glory for a team, and how to express opinions and emotions without resorting to tears. Sports also teach athletes to interpret the lingo often encountered later in the workplace: "seventh-inning stretch," "Monday morning quarterback," "playing hardball," and "being a team player." According to this perspective, women's vocational disadvantage can be partially attributed to their deprivation as adolescents in not having acquired these attitudes from playing team sports.

Considering these potential benefits, why don't more adolescent girls participate in competitive team sports? Even though the number of high-school girls playing a sport increased 600 percent from 1970 to 1980, only a third of high-school athletes are girls. Similarly, while the number of girls playing soccer increased from virtually zero in 1970 to almost one million in 1980, female tennis players increased from three to eleven million in the same period (Wood, 1980). In a 1981 survey of 18,000 high schools, girls' participation in sports had increased only 6 percent since 1979 ("Girls Boost Numbers", 1981). Data like these suggest that although girls are becoming more athletic, many are still restricting themselves athletically.

As the information in Box 2.16 demonstrates, girls' willingness to participate in sports has traditionally been undermined, in part, by society's misconceptions and attitudes. Believing that it is unladylike and unfeminine to participate in rigorous, competitive, or contact sports like soccer, long-distance running, basketball, or football, many girls refuse to test or develop their athletic abilities (Neal & Tutko 1976; Parkhouse & Lapin, 1980; Twin, 1979). Society is still more inclined to consider tennis, swimming, gymnastics, and skating more appropriate for girls than basketball, track, soccer, or football. In one study exemplifying these attitudes, both male and female adolescents stated that the female athlete who succeeded in a "masculine" sport would be sadder, less popular, more aggressive, and uglier than a girl playing a "feminine" sport (Methany, 1974). Afraid of being perceived as unfeminine or aggressive, most girls either avoid sports altogether, choose only "ladylike" sports like gymnastics or tennis, or take extra precautions while competing to emphasize their femininity by wearing frilly outfits, jewelry, and makeup (Ogelsby, 1978).

In a survey of 600 female athletes, most agreed that males' opinions influ-

2.16 Are You Sure?

Infamous Moments: Females and Physical Exercise

Which of the following statements are false?

1. The Greeks banned girls from watching or participating in the Olympics, but the Spartans trained girls in wrestling, javelin throwing, running, and jumping to enhance their future roles as procreators.
2. During the 1850s, females were chastised for daring to wear "bloomers," that enabled them to ride the newly invented bicyles without entangling their long skirts in the spokes and pedals. Bloomers, named after Amelia Bloomer, who advocated the costume, were long, loose pants gathered at the ankles, worn underneath a slightly shortened skirt.
3. In 1907 the sociologist William Thomas announced that girls should not participate in sports because they "resemble the child and the lower races."
4. In 1928 a female basketball team caused a stir by abandoning their woolen bloomers, long stockings, and flapping blouses and wearing long shorts and jerseys onto the court.
5. In 1923 many educators joined psychologists and civic leaders in protesting women's participation in the 1928 Olympics.
6. In 1973 the East German female swimmers created a ruckus in international competition when they refused to wear bathing suits with ruffled skirts, and chose instead sleek lycra suits that facilitated their movement through the water.
7. In 1975 one coach, in protest against the new legislation that girls be permitted to play on Little League baseball teams, forced the girls to wear athletic supporters in compliance with the league's regulations.
8. In 1974 the National Collegiate Athletic Association spent almost $300,000 lobbying against Title IX legislation, which advocated athletic equity for males and females.
9. Female runners were not allowed to enter the Boston Marathon until 1973.

Answers: All of the above statements are true.

SOURCES: J. Kaplan, *Women and sports.* New York: Viking, 1979; S. Twin. *Out of the bleachers.* New York: McGraw-Hill, 1979; E. Gerber. *The American woman in sport.* Reading, Mass.: Addison-Wesley, 1974.

enced their athletic decisions during their adolescence more than did females' opinions. Receiving approval from a male was a critical factor in their decisions to continue playing (Greendorfer, 1975). Realizing that many girls are discouraged from participating in sports, some secondary schools are offering classes that dispel myths about girls' physical limitations, while touting the benefits of vigorous exercise and competitive sports (Twin, 1979).

Girls' participation in sports is also discouraged by an unequal distribution of money, facilities, publicity, scholarships, and coaching (Dunkle, 1976; Parkhouse & Lapin 1980). In 1975 the federal government approved **Title IX,** a law intended to insure that male and female citizens would be treated more equitably. In regard to school athletic programs, Title IX states: "No person in the United States shall, on the basis of sex, be excluded from participation in, be denied the benefits of, or be subjected to discrimination under any education program or activity receiving federal financial assistance" (*Title IX*, 1978).

Despite this legislation, resistance to athletic equity has been prevalent at both high-school and college levels. For instance, the National Collegiate Athletic Association spent as much money lobbying against the passage of Title IX as the American Intercollegiate Association of Women spent on their 17 national championships (Kaplan, 1979). Furthermore, in many communities, coaches and parents have publicly defied the law by refusing to let girls participate in Little League, soccer leagues, and other "boys' sports" supported by taxpayers' funds (Twin, 1979). The National Federation of State High School Associations reported that girls' participation in sports actually declined after the passage of Title IX (Parkhouse & Lapin, 1980).

Another deterrent to girls' athletic participation is the amount of money invested in boys' sports. Male teams receive significantly more money for equipment, coaching, travel expenses, uniforms, awards, publicity, facilities, academic tutoring, medical and training services, recruiting, and college scholarships (Dunkle, 1976; Neal & Tutko, 1976; Parkhouse & Lapin, 1980). Most schools accord boys first preference in terms of athletic schedules, scheduling girls' teams before boys' as pregame entertainment, rather than as serious athletic competition. Male teams are usually supported by drill squads, bands, cheerleaders, team sweaters and jackets, community fund-raising drives, pep rallies, booster clubs, and special services like academic tutoring. Girls' teams seldom receive equivalent benefits. The boys' coaches are almost always paid more than girls' and have not generally received any training in female physiology or the needs of female athletes.

Even at the college level some people are worried about the commitment to female athletic programs. For instance, in a 1982 survey of 900 colleges, the number of female coaches had decreased from 58 to 52 since 1977. In 30 percent of these colleges there were no females in the athletic department's administration. In 80 percent of the colleges the females' programs were under the supervision of a male athletic director (Carpenter & Acosta, 1982). Although athletic equity is undeniably more prevalent today than prior to the passage of Title IX, the existing inequities still worry individuals who are dedicated to the athletic development of adolescent girls.

Air Pollution

Another factor affecting the physical fitness of adolescents is air pollution. Youngsters living in inner cities or in heavily trafficked communities may be inhaling dangerous amounts of lead from truck and automobile exhaust fumes. Small daily doses of these fumes can impair an adolescent's hand-eye coordination and reasoning skills. In one representative study, inner-city black students who had the most lead in their blood scored lower on intelligence tests than students with less contaminated blood. Male students were more seriously affected by the lead poisoning than the females, suggesting that there may be genetic differences that cause boys' bodies to absorb lead more easily. In other studies, students who were administered medicine that lowered their lead levels became less hyperactive and better behaved in school. According to these researchers, many youngsters are growing up with a hidden legacy of mental impairment caused by the polluted air in their communities (Fogel, 1980).

Similarly, it appears that air pollution can impair the health of those adolescents who inhale toxic fumes while exercising outdoors. For example, large amounts of carbon monoxide have been found in the blood of runners who jog along city streets. Carbon monoxide binds to the red blood cells and prevents them from carrying oxygen to the body's tissues. The long-term effects can damage the heart and impair breathing and circulation. Insofar as they have any control over the situation, adolescents should try to avoid exercising in polluted air.

While this research might lead us to believe that adolescents would be healthier if they stayed inside and avoided the polluted air outdoors, even indoor air can be contaminated with toxins (Brody, 1981). Modern, air-tight schools sometimes contain air that is more dangerous than the polluted air outside. Because the ventilating systems in some schools recirculate the air, toxic chemicals accumulate from products like floor polish, pesticides, air fresheners, and cleansers. Students breathing this air can become sleepy, lethargic, and prone to headaches. The solution? Keep fresh air circulating through buildings in order to diminish toxic buildups.

ADOLESCENT DISEASES

Although adolescents are generally blessed with good health, thousands are affected by disease during this period of their lives. Contemporary adolescents are afforded protection by vaccines against many potentially lethal diseases that plagued their predecessors: diphtheria, measles, polio, mumps, pneumonia, rabies, tetanus, whooping cough, and small-pox. At present researchers are also experimenting with vaccines against chicken-pox, certain forms of mental retardation, herpes, gonorrhea, malaria, cancer, and hepatitis. Yet many adolescents continue to experience the shame, depression, confusion, and social ostracism caused by their particular illness.

Acne

Although we may be unaccustomed to classifying acne as a disease, in its severest form this skin condition can be disfiguring and emotionally debilitating for adolescents (Katchadorian, 1977). The most serious consequence of acne is probably the social embarrassment it creates for its victims. Many adolescents with acne believe they are less popular or have less fun on dates than their friends with clear complexions (Bell, 1980). In their efforts to cure or conceal the disease, adolescents spend nearly $110 million a year on acne medications (Schowalter & Anyan, 1981). Although girls contract acne at an earlier age than boys, their cases are usually less severe. As testosterone levels rise, the frequency and severity of acne increases among the male population. Yet despite the severity of their acne, boys are less likely than girls to seek a dermatologist's counsel (Schowalter & Anyan, 1981).

While the drug industry is undoubtedly profiting from the sales of acne medications, adolescents are not. There is no convincing evidence that these non-

A joyful dive from an ocean pier into dangerously shallow water paralyzed this young woman for life on the evening of her graduation from high school. Imagine yourself in her place. What are you feeling? What are your visions of the future? Whom would you most rely on to help you adjust to your new circumstances?

prescription drugs help cure acne, although they do help dry the infected areas (Katchadorian, 1977). Dermatologists advise that adolescents with acne keep the skin clean, avoid all creams, and expose the skin to dry air and sunlight. Suntan oils, many makeup products, and hot, humid weather aggravate acne. Foods that contain lots of fat, like whole milk, chocolate, French fries, nuts, and pork also irritate the skin. Although acne diminishes on its own by the end of adolescence, it can permanently scar the skin.

Diabetes

Although not as obvious an affliction as acne, diabetes plagues thousands of adolescents in our society (Court, 1975). The isles of insular in the pancreas produce *insulin,* which carries sugar to the cells for their survival. The diabetic's *isles of insular* produce too little insulin to transport adequate supplies of sugar to the cells. The diabetic's appetite increases, since the body demands more food to compensate for the fact that too little sugar is being delivered to the cells. Simultaneously, the sugar that is supposed to be delivered to the cells is drawn off into the body's urine. This discarded sugar draws water out of the body, leaving the diabetic feeling thirsty and literally dehydrated. Other reactions include drowsiness, abdominal pains, labored breathing, and weight loss. Without treatment, severe cases of diabetes can be fatal.

Daily insulin injections enable diabetic adolescents to live a healthy, reasonably normal life. Ineffective when administrered orally, insulin must be injected with a needle, which most diabetic adolescents can do themselves. Although a youngster's isles of insular may intermittently produce adequate supplies of insulin, this improvement is generally only temporary. There is no medical reason why diabetics can not participate in vigorous physical exercise as long as they are controlling their insulin. Yet many diabetic adolescents are fearful of physical exercise and may need counseling to help overcome their anxieties (Court, 1975).

Epilepsy

Unlike diabetes, the word "epilepsy" often conjures up visions of violent seizures, during which the epileptic convulses violently, gags on the tongue, and thrashes uncontrollably. Given the mystery and misinformation surrounding this disease, it is little wonder that adolescents with epilepsy are embarrassed to mention their disorder to anyone. Yet most epileptic adolescents have never experienced a major or *grand mal* seizure and never will (Katchadorian, 1977).

Epileptic seizures are activated by abnormal electrial surges in the brain waves, called "spikes." During a minor or *petit mal* seizure, the epileptic may simply appear dazed, inattentive, confused, or disoriented, as if a temporary lapse of memory had occurred. Petit mal seizures render the epileptic adolescent temporarily unconscious, although he or she may remain sitting or standing. An attack can be triggered by stress, hormonal imbalances, or a physical accident, such as a blow to the head. Although most epileptic seizures can be prevented through daily administrations of prescribed drugs, the medications are not absolute guarantees that an attack will never recur during the person's lifetime. Consequently, epileptics are instructed to abstain from certain potentially dangerous activities like driving a car or swimming alone, since even a brief petit mal seizure under these circumstances could cause a fatal accident.

Particularly during adolescence, when peer approval and sexual appeal acquire a special prominence, epilepsy poses a threat to self-esteem. Given the social stigma attached to the disease, many epileptic adolescents and adults conceal their illness from their friends. In one study underscoring the stress that epilepsy can create for the young, people who contract the disease as adults have fewer social and academic problems than those who are afflicted as children or adolescents (Golden, 1971). Epileptic youngsters often have poorer social skills and academic abilities than their peers (Green & Hartladge, 1971). Findings like these indicate that epilepsy affects the young most deeply, because they have not yet developed their social and academic skills before the onset of the disease. The young are also more vulnerable than adult epileptics to the social stigma attached to their disease. In a society where epilepsy is generally feared and misunderstood, the epileptic youngster is too often treated in ways that undermine social and academic competence.

Cancer

Although cancer is becoming an increasingly rare cause of death during adolescence, thousands of young people are combating the disease or are in a state of remission from childhood cancer. Two of the most common kinds of cancer during adolescence are leukemia and lymphatic cancer.

Leukemia destroys the normal red cells of the bone marrow and replaces them with immature white cells that invade other parts of the body. With an inadequate supply of red cells, the adolescent becomes anemic. Simultaneously, the shortage of mature white cells renders the body less capable of fighting infections or of controlling blood clotting. As a consequence, youngsters with leukemia must guard against any circumstances that might cause uncontrollable bleeding or expose them to a disease that might prove fatal, given their inadequate supply of mature white cells. An adolescent with leukemia may look pale, tire easily, develop fevers, and have nosebleeds. Through early diagnosis by blood tests and bone-marrow analysis, many adolescents and children recover from leukemia after extensive chemotherapy.

Less prevalent than leukemia among the young, **Hodgkin's disease** is a cancer of the lymphatic system. This disease causes swelling of the lymph nodes as the cancer grows. As the lymphatic system becomes more infected, the body succumbs to the cancer. Although an adolescent with Hodgkin's disease can usually continue to attend school and participate in a number of activities, the fatigue and weight loss eventually become debilitating.

Anemia

In referring to an adolescent as "anemic," a person can be implying one of two conditions: too few red cells in the blood or too little blood in the body (Schowalter & Anyan, 1981). Anemia can result from losing too much blood or from an insufficient production of red blood cells by the bone marrow. If an adolescent's diet is deficient in iron or if a serious infection persists, the bone marrow may decrease its production of red cells. Adolescents can also destroy red cells by consuming too many such medications as sulfa drugs or aspirin. Although a red cell usually continues to circulate in the blood for three months, these cells can eventually be depleted to a level that causes anemia.

Because anemic adolescents have too few red cells to carry adequate oxygen to the body's tissues, symptoms of the disease manifest themselves: tiredness, light-headedness, and shortness of breath after moderate exercise. Anemic adolescents may also feel their hearts beating more rapidly than usual in an attempt to compensate for the anemia. Some anemic youngsters become noticeably paler. During periods of most rapid growth, some adolescents become anemic because they are not ingesting enough iron to meet the needs of their greater volume of blood. Iron tablets and iron-rich foods can eliminate this temporary anemia. Blood tests once or twice a year can easily detect this type of iron deficiency (Schowalter & Anyan, 1981).

Sickle-Cell Anemia

A far less commonly acknowledged and less publicized anemia affecting thousands of black adolescents is *sickle-cell* anemia (Schowalter & Anyan, 1981). Although this form of anemia was first reported in 1910, only recently has it received widespread attention as a disease that affects thousands of black Americans. The body's red cells are normally shaped like doughnuts, but in victims of sickle-cell anemia, these red cells are shaped like bananas or sickles. This sickle shape prevents the cells from delivering an adequate supply of oxygen to the body's organs and tissues. As a consequence, adolescents with this disease periodically have "crises," during which their joints ache, they tire easily, and their eyes may turn yellow. In rare cases the sickle cells can cause death by depriving vital organs, such as the heart, of oxygen. It has been estimated that approximately one in every 500 black Americans has this form of anemia. People of Greek, Italian, Arabic, Turkish, or Asiatic Indian descent are also particularly susceptible to this inherited disease.

A youngster with sickle-cell anemia often undergoes considerable stress, even though the attacks usually become less frequent and less severe after adolescence (Scholwalter & Anyan, 1981). The disease is most active during childhood and whenever the person contracts a cold or other viral infection. During periods of severe attack the youngster's life is disrupted by the blood transfusions and hospitalization often necessitated by the oxygen deprivation. Although the adolescent's mental abilities are unaffected, the disease can nonetheless create considerable embarrassment or shame for its young victims. When the disease is in its dormant stage, there is no reason why these youngsters should refrain from the normal athletic, academic, and social activities of adolescence. Some individuals with sickle cells are almost completely free of serious attacks and lead long, productive lives. The less fortunate have their lives shortened by the disease and suffer frequent attacks.

CONCLUSION

In this chapter we have examined the physical changes that occur during adolescence. We have also considered the impact that many of these changes have on a youngster's personality, moods, and self-esteem. While no two adolescents react to their physical growth in exactly the same manner, all emerge from the years of puberty with the awareness that their child's body is gone forever. The body that will house them for the rest of their lives has completely matured by the age of 20. Many adolescents enjoy their bodies, care well for them, and undergo the physical changes of puberty with relatively little trauma. The less fortunate suffer the humiliation or anxiety that accompany illness, unattractiveness, premature development, or genetic disabilities. As adolescents live through these years of rapid growth, one of our primary responsibilities is helping them accept, understand, and care for their physical selves in ways that will bring them the greatest pleasure and least pain.

Questions for Discussion and Review

Basic Concepts and Terminology

Cite specific statistics, research studies or physiological data to support each of your answers.

1. Which factors influence an adolescent's rate of physical maturity?
2. How do male and female adipose and muscle tissues differ?
3. What impact do estrogen and testosterone have on male and female development?
4. What methods have proven successful in helping overweight adolescents lose fat and build muscle tissue?
5. What changes during adolescence account for the transformation of the face from that of child to that of adult?
6. What misconceptions about impregnation, fertility, and menstruation can result in unwanted pregnancies?
7. Describe the typical pattern of growth during adolescence for males and females. Take into consideration the reproductive system, height, weight, voice, muscles, adipose tissue, and secondary sex characteristics.
8. Which factors determine how much fat or muscle tissue an adolescent develops?
9. What advantages and disadvantages accompany early maturation for males and for females?
10. How much influence do hormones exert over adolescent behavior?
11. How can adolescents' diets affect their behavior?
12. Why don't more adolescent girls participate in sports?
13. How should male and female adolescents examine themselves for cancer?
14. What are sickle-cell anemia and diabetes? How can each alter the course of an individual's life?
15. In what ways are sports and physical exercise advantageous and disadvantageous to adolescent male and female development?

Questions for Discussion and Debate

1. What arguments might people offer against adolescent girls participating in sports?
2. How did your own physical development affect your personality during adolescence?
3. How might your own adolescent and adult life have been different if you had epilepsy? diabetes? sickle-cell anemia? leukemia?
4. What were the wisest and most foolish habits you developed during your adolescence in terms of your own physical fitness and health?
5. What information presented within this chapter might have an impact on the way you are presently caring for yourself physically?
6. How does your own appearance differ from what you consider "the ideal" and how has this affected your social, athletic, academic, and personal development?

7. How do you feel secondary school athletic programs should be designed?
8. What are your happiest and unhappiest memories associated with your physical development during adolescence? In regard to your physical development, how might an adult have helped alleviate some of your anxiety or disappointment?

REFERENCES

Beau, C., Baker, P., & Haas, J. The effects of high altitude on adolescent growth. *Human Biology,* 1977, *49,* 109–124.

Bailey, C. *Fit or fat?* New YorK: Houghton Mifflin, 1978.

Bardin, C., & Paulsen, C. The testes. In R. Williams (ed.), *Textbook of endocrinology.* Philadelphia: Saunders, 1981, 293–334.

Bell, R. *Changing bodies, changing lives.* New York: Random House, 1980.

Blythe, D. *The impact of puberty on adolescents: A longitudinal study.* Rockville, Md.: National Institutes of Mental Health, November 1982.

Bongiovani, A. An epidemic of premature telarche in Puerto Rico. *Journal of Pediatrics,* 1983, *103,* 245–246.

Braddock, J. *Academics and athletics in American high schools.* Washington, D.C.: National Institute of Education, December 1979.

Braddock, J. Race, athletics and educational attainment: Dispelling the myths. *Youth and Society,* March 1981, *12,* 335–350.

Brenner, D., & Hinsdale, G. Body build stereotypes in three age groups of females. *Adolescence,* Winter 1978, *13,* 551–561.

Brody, J. So now its perilous to breathe indoors. *International Herald Tribune,* February 5, 1981, p. 1.

Bruch, H. *The golden cage: The enigma of anorexia nervosa.* Cambridge, Mass.: Harvard University Press, 1978.

Carey, J. & Hager, M. Failing in fitness. *Newsweek,* April 1, 1985, pp. 84–87.

Carpenter, L., & Acosta, R. College athletes. *Chronicle of Higher Education,* 1982, *26,* p. 4.

Carr, D. Physical conditioning facilitates the exercise induced secretion of beta endorphin and beta lipotropin. *New England Journal of Medicine,* September 3, 1981, *305,* 560–563.

Clark, A., & Ruble, D. Young adolescents' beliefs concerning menstruation. *Child Development,* March 1978, *49,* 231–234.

Clausen, J. The social meaning of differential physical and sexual maturation. In S. Dragastin and G. Elder (eds.), *Adolescence in the life cycle.* Washington, D.C.: Hemisphere Press, 1975. Pp. 25–47.

Coleman, J. Friendship and peer group in adolescence. In J. Adelson (ed.), *Handbook of adolescent psychology.* New York: Wiley, 1980. Pp. 408–431.

Court, J. *Helping your diabetic child.* New York: Taplinger, 1975.

Dan, A., Graham, E., & Beecher, C. (eds.). *The menstrual cycle: A synthesis of interdisciplinary research.* New York: Springer, 1980.

Dozier, J. Sports groups: an alternative treatment modality for emotionally disturbed adolescents. *Adolescence,* 1978, *13,* 483–493.

Driscoll, R. Exertion therapy. *Behavior Today,* 1975, *6,* 10–16.

Duffy, W. *Sugar blues.* New York: Warner Books, 1975.

Dunkle, M. *Competitive athletics: In search of equal opportunity.* Washington, D.C.: U.S. Department of Health, Education and Welfare, 1976.

Edelstein, B. *The woman doctor's diet for teen-age girls.* New York: Ballantine, 1980.

Faust, M. Somatic development of adolescent girls. *Monographs of the Society for Research in Child Development,* 1977, *42,* No. 169.

Fogel, M. Auto fumes may lower your kid's IQ. *Psychology Today,* January 1980, 108.

Freishlag, J., & Schmidke, C. Violence in sports: Its causes and solutions. *Physical Education,* 1979, *26,* 182–185.

Frisch, R. Fatness, puberty and fertility. In J. Gunn and A. Peterson (eds.), *Girls at puberty.* New York: Plenum, 1984.

Gallagher, J. *Medical care of the adolescent.* New York: Appleton-Century-Crofts, 1960.

Gergen, K., & Gergen, M. *Social psychology.* New York: Harcourt Brace Jovonovich, 1981, 89–95.

Girls boost numbers of school athletes. *Education Week,* December 1981, p. 3.

Golden, G. Rehabilitation of the young epileptic. *Northeastern University Studies in Vocational Rehabilitation,* 1971, *12,* 130–142.

Goldstein, B. *Human sexuality,* New York: McGraw-Hill, 1976.

Green, J., & Hartladge, L. Comparative performance of epileptic and nonepileptic adolescents. *Diseases of the Nervous System,* 1971, *32,* 418–421.

Greendorfer, S. *Female sport involvement.* Paper presented at the National Convention of American Alliance for Health, Physical Education and Recreation. Atlantic City, N.J., March 1975.

Gunn, J., & Peterson, A. (eds.). *Girls at puberty: Biological, psychological and social perspectives.* New York: Plenum, 1984.

Hamburg, D., & Trudeau, M. (eds.). *Biobehavioral aspects of aggression.* New York: Alan Liss, 1981.

Hammill, P. *Growth curves for children: Birth to eighteen years.* Vital and Health Statistics. Washington, D.C.: National Center for Health Statistics, 1977.

Harmon, L. And soma. In L. Harmon (ed.), *Counseling women.* Monterey, Cal.: Brooks Cole, 1978. Pp. 123–126.

Harper, F. Outcomes of jogging: Implications for counseling. *Personnel and Guidance Journal,* October 1978, *57,* 72–78.

Harragan, B. *Games mother never taught you.* New York: Warner Books, 1978.

Hendry, L., & Gullies, P. Body type, body esteem, school and leisure. *Journal of Youth and Adolescence.* June 1978, *8,* 181–195.

Hennig, M., & Jardin, A. *The managerial woman.* New York: Simon and Schuster, 1977.

Higham, E. Variations in adolescent psychohormonal development. In J. Adelson (ed.), *Handbook of adolescent psychology.* New York: Wiley, 1980. Pp. 472–495.

Hueneman, R. *Teenage nutrition and physique.* Springfield, Ill.: Charles Thomas, 1974.

Jennes, G. Sports competition should not be child's play. *People* magazine, March 17, 1980, pp. 54–57.

Kaplan, J. Retarded sexual development in adolescence. *Medical Aspects of Human Sexuality,* 1975, *9,* 47–55.

Kaplan, J. *Women and sports.* New York: Viking, 1979.

Kash, M., & Borich, G. *Teacher behavior and pupil self-concept.* Reading, Mass.: Addison-Wesley, 1978, 63–99.

Katchadorian, H. *The biology of adolescence.* San Francisco: Freeman, 1977.

Kinsey, A., Pomeroy, W., & Martin, C. *Sexual behavior in the human male,* New York: Saunders, 1948.

Klineberg, O. *Social psychology.* New York: Holt, Rinehart and Winston, 1954.

Livson, N. & Peskin, H. Perspectives on adolescence from longitudinal research. In J. Adelson (ed.), *Handbook of adolescent psychology.* New York: Wiley, 1980. Pp. 47–98.

Macdonald, L. Overweight adolescent girls: Programs that work. *Journal of American Dietetic Association,* March 1983, 16–24.

Malina, R. Secular changes in size and maturity. *Monographs of Society of Research in Child Development,* 1979, *44,* serial 179.

Marshall, J. *The sports doctors fitness book for women.* New York: Delacorte, 1981.

Mayer, J. *Overweight: Causes, cost and control.* Englewood Cliffs, N.J.: Prentice-Hall, 1968.

McConnell, J. *Understanding human behavior.* New York: Holt, Rinehart and Winston, 1983. Pp. 418–422.

McEwin, K. Interscholastic sports and the early adolescent. *Journal of early adolescence,* 1981, *2,* 123–133.

Methany, E. The feminine image in sports. In G. Sage (ed.), *Sport and American society.* Reading, Mass.: Addison-Wesley, 1974. Pp. 289–301.

Miller, S., & Miller, J. *Food for Thought.* Englewood Cliffs, N.J.: 1979.

Mischel, W. *Introduction to personality.* New York: Holt, Rinehart and Winston, 1987.

Neal, P., & Tutko, T. *Coaching girls and women: Psychological perspectives.* Boston: Allyn and Bacon, 1976.

Nielsen, L. Putting away the pom poms: A psychologist's view of females and sports. In B. Postow (ed.), *Women, philosophy and sports.* Metuchen, N.J.: Scarecrow Press, 1983. Pp. 115–130.

Nottelmann, E., et al. Gonadal and adrenal hormone correlates of adjustments in early adolescence. In R. Lerner and T. Foch (eds.), *Biological–psychosocial interactions in early adolescence.* Hillsdale, N.J.: Erlbaum, 1986.

Offer, D., Ostrov, E., & Howard, K. *The adolescent: A psychological self-portrait.* New York: Basic Books, 1981.

Ogelsby, C., (ed.). *Women and sport: From myth to reality.* Philadelphia: Lea and Febiger, 1978.

Paige, K. Beyond the raging hormones: Women learn to sing the menstrual blues. *Psychology Today,* 1973, *7,* 41–46.

Parkhouse, B., & Lapin, J. *Women who win: Exercising your rights in sports.* Englewood Cliffs, N.J.: Prentice-Hall, 1980.

Petersen, A., Richards, M., & Boxer, A. Puberty: Its measurement and its meaning. *Journal of Early Adolescence,* 1983, *3,* 47–62.

Peterson, A., & Taylor, B. The biological approach to adolescence. In J. Adelson (ed.), *Handbook of adolescent psychology.* New York: Wiley, 1980. Pp. 117–158.

Pomerantz, S. Sex differences in relative importance of self-esteem, physical self-satisfaction and identity. *Journal of Youth and Adolescence,* March 1979, *8,* 51–61.

Ruble, D. Premenstrual symptoms. *Science,* 1977, *197,* 291–292.

Sabo, D., and Runfola, R. (eds.). *Jocks: Sports and male identity.* Englewood Cliffs, N.J.: Prentice-Hall, 1980.

Schafer, W. Participation in interscholastic athletics and delinquency. *Social Problems,* 1969, *17,* 40–47.

Schowalter, J., & Anyan, W. *Family handbook of adolescence.* New York: Knopf, 1981.

Sheldon, W. *Varieties of human physique.* New York: Harper & Row, 1940.

Simmons, R. Entry into early adolescence. *American Sociological Review,* 1979, *44,* 948–967.

Simmons, R., Blythe, D., & McKinney, L. The social and psychological effects of puberty on white females. In J. Brooks-Gunn and A. Peterson (eds.), *Girls at puberty: Biological and psychological perspectives.* New York: Plenum, 1983, Pp. 229–272.

Sinan, J. America's attitudes toward youth sports. *Physical Educator,* 1979, *36,* 186–190.

Snyder, E. High school athletes and their coaches: Educational plans and advice. *Sociology of Education,* 1972, *45,* 313–325.

Snyder, E., & Kivlin, J. Women athletes and aspects of psychological well-being. *Research Quarterly AAHPER,* May 1975, 191–193.

Substances athletes use. *Chronicle of Higher Education,* 1982, 26.

Tanner, J. *Growth at adolescence.* Oxford: Blackwell, 1962.

Testes test. *Time,* September 21, 1981, p. 69.

Thomas, J., & French, K. Gender differences across age in motor performance: A meta-analysis. *Psychological Bulletin,* 1985, *98,* 260–282.

Thompson, J., Jarvie, G., Lahey, B., & Cureton, K. Exercise and obesity: Etiology, physiology and intervention. *Psychological Bulletin,* 1982, *91,* 55–79.

Title IX and intercollegiate athletics. Nondiscrimination on the basis of sex in education programs. Washington, D.C.: Office of Civil Rights, December 1978.

Tobias, S. *Overcoming math anxiety.* New York: Norton, 1978.

Twin, S. *Out of the bleachers: Writings on women and sport.* New York: McGraw-Hill, 1979.

Whisnant, L., & Zegans, L. A study of attitudes toward menarche in white middle class American girls. *American Journal of Psychiatry,* 1975, *132,* 809–814.

White, M. Effects of nutrition on educational development. In S. Ball (ed.), *Motivation in education.* New York: Academic Press, 1977. Pp. 173–188.

Williams, R. *Nutrition against disease: Environmental prevention.* New York: Bantam Books, 1973.

Wollman, L., & Lotner, L. *The complete guide to sexual nutrition.* New York: Pinnacle Books, 1983.

Wood, P. Sex differences in sports. *New York TImes Magazine,* May 18, 1980, p. 31.

Zacharias, L., Rand, W., & Wintman, R. The statistics of menarche. *Obstetrical and Gynecological Survey,* 1976, *31,* 325–337.

Zakus, G. A group behavior modification approach to adolescent obesity. *Adolescence,* Fall 1979, *14,* 481–490.

Chapter Outline

Goals and Objectives

This chapter is intended to enable you to:

- *Describe the psychometric, developmental, and information-processing approaches to cognitive development*
- *Identify the differences between male and female adolescents' cognitive skills*
- *Enumerate the strengths and weaknesses of traditional IQ tests*
- *Examine researchers' recommendations for increasing IQ and creativity*
- *Identify the distinguishing characteristics of creative adolescents*
- *Differentiate between the memory and problem-solving skills of adolescents and children*

Concepts and Terminology

stage theories
information-processing theories
Wechsler Scales
SOMPA
standard error of measurement
culturally fair tests
fluid intelligence
sensorimotor stage
concrete operational stage
rule of equivalence
conservation
assimilation
branch model of development
field dependence
metacognition
Piagetian approach
psychometric theories
the Stanford-Binet
WAIS, WISC
validity
nature/nurture debate
crystallized intelligence
preoperational stage
formal operational thinking
rule of reversibility
disequilibrium
schema accommodation
encoding
state-dependent memory
object permanence
convergent and divergent thinking
serialization
class inclusion
eidetic memory
flashbulb memory
brain lateralization

3 Adolescent Cognitive Development

THEORIES OF COGNITIVE DEVELOPMENT

Accompanying the dramatic changes in physical development during adolescence are some equally impressive cognitive gains. Although the brain's size changes relatively little after the age of 10, its abilities expand rapidly during the decade between 10 and 20. These cognitive changes between childhood and adulthood have generated many intriguing, complex questions: How can we measure an adolescent's mental abilities? What enables older adolescents to solve abstract problems that befuddle younger adolescents? How is intelligence related to creativity? Can we increase adolescents' cognitive abilities through education, or are their abilities determined genetically? Questions like these are the basis for the study of human cognition, which can be approached from three different perspectives: the developmental or stage approach, the psychometric approach, and the information-processing approach (Siegler, Liebert, & Liebert, 1973).

The **psychometric approach** focuses on measuring and comparing individuals' intelligence through standardized IQ tests. Researchers using this approach pose such questions as: How can intelligence be measured and defined? How can we predict a child's future mental potential? How are IQ scores related to vocational and academic success? What accounts for the changes in a person's IQ score over a lifetime? This approach quantifies intelligence by converting an individual's performance on mental tasks into IQ test scores. The psychometric approach does not address issues related to the processes by which cognition develops as the individual matures.

In contrast, the **developmental** or **stage theories** test hypotheses related to the development of cognitive skills throughout the life-span. The theories of the most renowned developmental psychologist, Jean Piaget, have dominated the study of cognitive development. Hence the term "Piagetian" has become almost synonymous with developmental theories. The developmental or *Piagetian approach* attempts to delineate the distinctions between the reasoning abilities of children and adolescents and pursues questions related to cognitive growth: What impact do cultural differences exert on an individual's cognitive skills? Does cognitive growth occur in predictable, invariant stages or in a more random, idiosyncratic fashion? The developmental approach relies on data from observations of children's performance on prescribed cognitive tasks in a laboratory setting and from listening to children's explanations of the methods by which they derived their answers.

Although the developmental perspective has dominated the field of cognitive development, the **information-processing approach** has recently been directed toward questions of cognition (Siegler, Liebert, & Liebert, 1973). Intended to uncover the cognitive strategies by which the human brain processes information, this theoretical perspective addresses itself to questions of a more physiological nature: By what chemical or electrical means does the brain encode, decode, and retrieve information? What physiological changes account for the different cognitive abilities of children, adolescents, and adults? Collecting data often involves observations of such physiological processes as the measurement of students' eye movements as they read or recording the repeated patterns they employ in problem-solving situations.

Each of these three theoretical perspectives offers its own unique information about adolescents' cognitive skills and cognitive development. Pursuing its own particular questions about cognition and using its own specialized terminology and methodology, each theoretical approach is limited by particular shortcomings. For example, information processing may contribute to our understanding of how the brain retrieves information from long-term and short-term memory banks, but it contributes virtually nothing to our understanding of the processes by which the more sophisticated mental skills of adults develop throughout childhood and adolescence. Likewise, the developmental approach provides no assistance in measuring an individual's intellectual abilities or potential. Adolescents' cognitive development and abilities are probably best understood through an integrative approach that appreciates the contributions and the limitations of each theoretical perspective.

The Psychometric Approach to Cognition

Defining Intelligence Which adolescent is the most intelligent—Sarah, who can quickly compute quadratic equations? Larry, who adapts quickly to new situations and displays an acute understanding of peoples' feelings and motives? James, who perceives pitch patterns perfectly and composes music? Susan, who can navigate a boat at night among treacherous rocks, relying only on the stars and the feeling of the waves? Or Sam, who writes sonnets and speaks with a vocabulary far beyond his years? When trying to choose the most "intelligent" of these youngsters, we are confronting two of the fundamental dilemmas of the psychometric approach: How should intelligence be defined? Who should be responsible for creating the definitions by which we judge other people and ourselves as "gifted," "normal," "below average," or "retarded"?

Attempts to define intelligence have spurred much controversy (Sternberg & Powell, 1982). In a famous study conducted in 1921, nationally renowned experts provided definitions of intelligence that included: the ability to carry on abstract thinking, the ability to learn to adjust oneself to the environment, the capacity to profit from experience, and the capacity to acquire data. In a more recent version of this study, researchers asked citizens to define intelligence and compared their definitions to those of the experts. The two groups basically agreed that three types of behavior demonstrate "intelligence": verbal abilities, such as having a large vocabulary and talking easily on a variety of subjects; problem-solving skills, such as making good decisions and applying previous knowledge to new problems; and practical intelligence, such as displaying interest in the world and sizing up situations well.

Nevertheless, many psychologists contend that the existing definitions are inadequate to permit accurate assessments of an individual's intelligence. Some, like Robert Williams, contend that intelligence has been inaccurately defined by people whose own perceptions are limited by their racial and cultural biases (Dove, 1968; Williams, 1975). As the information in Box 3.1 demonstrates, Williams questions whether one culture's definitions of intelligence can fairly be applied to another culture. Those who advocate the point of view endorsed by Williams view IQ tests as culturally biased measures that support the assumption that IQ scores represent inherited mental abilities.

Reinforcing this point of view, Howard Gardner contends that our conceptions of intelligence are too narrowly limited to linguistic and logical-mathematical skills (Gardner, 1983). Breaking with psychometric traditions, Gardner argues that intelligence can be defined as seven distinct skills of equal importance: linguistic, mathematical, spatial, musical, interpersonal (understanding others), intrapersonal (ability to know oneself and develop a sense of identity), and bodily-kinesthetic (fine motor movement).

Despite the fact that experts disagree about which skills truly demonstrate intelligence, a youngster's inductive reasoning, verbal comprehension, spatial visualization, and problem-solving skills do reflect certain cognitive abilities. In this regard, traditional IQ tests are at least partially correct in considering these skills indicative of an adolescent's intelligence (Steinberg et. al., 1982). The psychometric approach can, therefore, contribute to an understanding of certain dimensions of adolescent cognition.

Measuring Adolescents' Intelligence The psychometric approach is predicated upon the assumption that intelligence can be defined and measured. Consequently, the problems associated with developing reliable measures of intelligence fall within its domain. To date, the two most popular instruments for assessing the intelligence of children and adolescents are the Stanford-Binet and the Wechsler intelligence tests.

Designed by the French psychologist, Alfred Binet, the **Stanford-Binet** was initially developed to identify the children whose mental retardation would prevent them from benefiting from public schools. U.S. psychologists produced numerous revisions of Binet's original test, the most famous of which was designed by L. M. Terman at Stanford University in 1916. The latest revision of the Stanford-Binet IQ test, in 1972, was the first to include minority children in its sampling (Terman & Merrill, 1960, 1973). The test primarily examines an individual's verbal skills, such as defining words, understanding analogies, completing sentences, interpreting proverbs, and defining abstract terms. Even questions whose content is not predominantly verbal require the youngster to under-

A Closer Look 3.1 

Scientific Racism and Intelligence Testing

When Robert Williams was 15, his school counselor suggested that he become a bricklayer, because he was "good with his hands" and he had scored only 82 on an IQ test (three points above the track for the special education class). Ignoring this advice, Williams earned a doctorate in psychology, became one of the founders of the American Association of Black Psychologists, and established a successful career as a college professor and researcher in the area of intelligence testing. According to Williams, "scientific racism is part of silent racial war and the practitioners of it use intelligence tests as their hired guns. Intelligence and achievement tests are nothing but updated versions of the old signs down South that read 'For Whites Only.'" Williams believes that the testing industry refuses to admit the truth about tests for fear of going bankrupt. The economic survival of the industry depends on defending their tests and convincing public schools and colleges that the tests are necessary.

Williams feels that we need to examine our beliefs about intelligence. First, Williams contends that intelligence cannot be inherited. Second, IQ test scores do not measure a person's ability to succeed in the world. The tests are simply designed to predict school success, and only children who attend good schools will be prepared to do well on the test. Third, the IQ test measures literacy and cultural background—not intellect. IQ tests do not measure a person's capacity to learn. Finally, the questions on IQ tests do not reflect the skills or mental potential of individuals who have grown up in ghetto environments.

Concerned about the placement in special education classes of minority students, Williams urges whites to be equally worried about the educational uses of IQ scores with white youngsters from impoverished environments. "As with every other manifestation of racism, the scientific variety threatens to destroy us all."

SOURCE: R. Williams, The silent mugging of the black community. *Psychology Today,* 1974, *12,* 32–42.

stand fairly complex verbal instructions. As a consequence, adolescents with a language handicap and those with the fewest verbal skills score relatively low on this test (Anastasi, 1982).

Believing that the Stanford-Binet relied too heavily on verbal skills and was poorly adapted to testing adults, David Wechsler developed his *Wechsler Intelligence Scales* for children and adults in 1939 (Wechsler, 1952, Wechsler, 1975). The Wechsler Adult Intelligence Scale (the **WAIS**) is usually administered to older adolescents, while the **WISC** (Wechsler Intelligence Scale for Children) is administered to younger adolescents. Unlike the Stanford-Binet, which provides only one total score, the Wechsler Scales provide a verbal IQ score, a performance IQ score, and an overall IQ score. The verbal IQ subtest score comes from questions about arithmetic, definitions of words, similarities between objects and concepts, the meaning of proverbs, and information on general topics. The performance IQ subtest score comes from such exercises as arranging pictures in the proper sequence to tell a logical story, reproducing designs with colored blocks, assembling cutouts into whole pictures, and identifiying missing parts of pictures. Educators and counselors often prefer the Wechsler, because school personnel can consult these subtest scores to identify an adolescent's specific academic strengths and weaknesses.

Both the Stanford-Binet and the Wechsler employ the same scale for classifying youngsters on the basis of their scores (see Table 3.1). Nevertheless, scores on the two tests should not be similarly interpreted, because their standard error of measurement differs. The *standard error of measurement* on any test is the range within which a person's true score is expected to fall or the range within which we would expect that person to score if he or she is retested. The standard error of measurement on the Stanford-Binet is ten points and on the Wechsler is three points. This means that a boy who scores 104 on the Stanford-Binet has a score somewhere between 94 and 114, but his classmate who scores 104 on the Wechsler has a score somewhere between 101 and 107. Another way to understand the standard error of measurement is to realize that a score of 104 points on the Wechsler is really equivalent to a score between 101 and 107. Understanding the significance of the standard error of measurement will prevent us from concluding that a boy with a score of 90 should be classified as having "normal" intelligence, while one with a score of 88 has "below average" intelligence.

When interpreting an adolescent's score on the Wechsler or the Stanford-Binet, several other factors need consideration (Anastasi, 1982). Individuals with higher IQ scores tend to score better on the Stanford-Binet than on the Wechsler, while those with lower IQ scores tend to score better on the Wechsler. Younger people tend to obtain higher scores on the Stanford-Binet than on the Wechsler, while the reverse is true for older people. Given these tendencies, who is the more disadvantaged in terms of her score—a mother who earns 85 on the Stanford-Binet or her adolescent daughter who earns 145 on the Wechsler? (Answer: The mother is more disadvantaged because, given her age and lower ability, she would probably have scored higher on the Wechsler. The daughter has the advantage because, given her age and high ability, she is earning her best score on the Stanford-Binet.)

Table 3.1

IQ Ranges and Classification Labels

IQ Range	*Label*	*Percent in Population*
130 and above	Very superior	2.2
120–129	Superior	6.7
110–119	Bright-normal	16.1
90–109	Average	50.0
80–89	Dull-normal	16.1
70–79	Borderline	6.7
69 or below	Mental defective	2.2

SOURCE: D. Wechsler, *Manual of the Wechsler Adult Intelligence Scale.* New York: Psychological Corporation, 1955. Reprinted by permission.

Criticisms of IQ Tests One of the major criticisms leveled against IQ tests is that these measures lack **validity** (Anastasi, 1982). To be considered valid a test must measure only the characteristic it proposes to measure and not other characteristics. For example, a French test is an invalid measure of a youngster's mathematical abilities. According to some critics, IQ tests measure aptitude but not innate intelligence. Consequently, if a teenaged girl has been raised in an environment that has not taught her the specific skills being measured on the IQ test, she will score poorly; but the score is no measure of her potential to learn the material or of some quantifiable amount of intelligence.

The practical significance of the arguments related to an IQ test's validity can be demonstrated by its effect on students. Almost all schools rely heavily on IQ scores in assigning students to a curriculum for the retarded, the gifted, or the average learner. As Chapter 7 will explain, once placed in these academic tracks, few students ever change, even if they do possess the abilities to succeed in a more advanced curriculum (Rosenbaum, 1976). Academic tracking is defensible to those who assume that IQ tests are valid measures of a student's mental capacities. If, however, the IQ tests' validity is questionable, then relegating students to a curriculum for the retarded, gifted, or average is both an indefensible and unethical practice.

Questions regarding the validity of IQ tests assume particular significance in relation to the testing of individuals from minority cultures (Anastasi, 1982; Samuda, 1975). If IQ tests are assessing a youngster's aptitudes in academic skills and values espoused by the white middle class, then individuals raised in minority cultures will be handicapped on the test. As a way of underscoring the impact that a minority person's culture often has on IQ scores, Adrian Dove developed the Chitling Test (Dove, 1968). The Chitling Test is intended to highlight the fact that IQ tests assess a person's knowledge of white, middle-class education and experience, while ignoring the language and experiences of minorities (see Box 3.2).

Adrian Dove is not alone in his concern that minority adolescents are handicapped by the cultural biases upon which IQ tests are designed and scored. The psychologist Robert Samuda, who first directed the Institute for the Assessment of Minorities at the Educational Testing Service, presents a thorough analysis of the issues involved in testing U.S. minorities (Samuda, 1975). One of the strongest objections voiced against IQ tests is that their questions are based on the ethnocentric assumption that white, middle-class standards, attitudes, and experiences are superior to all others. The tests thereby deny many minority and poor white youngsters an opportunity to demonstrate their intelligence according to the standards and experiences of their own cultures.

Other criticisms of IQ tests revolve around the methods by which they are administered (Anastasi, 1982). The examiner may inadvertently fail to adhere to the test's detailed instructions or make errors in scoring. Unknowingly, the examiner may also contribute to a person's success on the test by prompting or by eliciting nonverbal cues about the correctness or incorrectness of an answer. Extraneous variables like the noise level in the room where the test is being conducted, or the rapport that is established between the examiner and the student, can also affect test scores. Similarly, some youngsters are more relaxed about taking standardized tests than others—a factor that may enhance their scores. In fact, some students who score poorly on IQ tests have improved their scores through training in basic test-taking skills, such as reading instructions slowly and dividing problems into subproblems (Whimbey & Whimbey, 1975).

3.2 Are You Sure?

The Chitling Test of Intelligence

Adrian Dove, a black sociologist, has devised an intelligence test that emphasizes the impact of a person's culture on intelligence-test scores. Dove believes his test is "culturally biased," like standard intelligence tests used to assess minority children's abilities. Dove's Chitling Test is culturally biased in favor of individuals raised in a black ghetto, rather than those from white, middle-class environments. See how you score on a few of the questions from the Chitling Test:

1. A "handkerchief head" is (a) a cool cat (b) a porter (c) an Uncle Tom (d) a hoddi (e) a preacher.
2. Which word is most out of place here? (a) splib (b) blood (c) gray (d) spook (e) black.
3. A "gas head" is a person who has (a) a fast-moving car (b) a stable of "lace" (c) a "process" (d) a habit of stealing cars (e) a long jail record for arson.
4. If you throw the dice and seven is showing on the top, what is facing down? (a) 7 (b) snake eyes (c) boxcars (d) little Joes (e) 11.
5. "Jet" is (a) an East Oakland motorcycle club (b) one of the gangs in "West Side Story" (c) a news and gossip magazine (d) a way of life for the very rich.
6. T-Bone Walker got famous for playing (a) trombone (b) piano (c) "T-flute" (d) guitar (e) "Hambone."
7. If a pimp is uptight with a woman who gets state aid, what does he mean when he talks about "Mother's Day"? (a) second Sunday in May (b) third Sunday in June (c) first of every month (d) none of these (e) first and fifteenth of every month.

Answers: 1.c 2.c 3.c 4.a 5.c 6.d 7.e

SOURCE: A. Dove, Taking the Chitling Test. *Newsweek*, July 15, 1968, pp. 51–52.

Alternatives to Traditional IQ Tests In response to the criticisms leveled against IQ tests, attempts have been made to develop more valid, culturally fair instruments for assessing intelligence. These tests attempt to avoid questions that reflect one culture's values over another's. Consequently, all individuals should have an equal chance of scoring well on the test. Other researchers are pursuing the option of developing tests that will measure an individual's intelligence by asking questions that reflect the skills being taught in his or her particular culture. For instance, Dove's Chitling Test is *culturally fair* to black youngsters from ghetto neighborhoods, but not to Mexican Americans from rural communities. Like conventional IQ tests, culture-free and culture-fair tests assume that native intelligence can be measured by a well-designed test.

Reflecting this contemporary approach to IQ testing is the SOMPA—System of Multicultural Pluralistic Assessment (Mercer & Lewis, 1978). **SOMPA** was designed to prevent minority children from being misclassified as mentally retarded on the basis of traditional IQ tests. Although the SOMPA is suitable only for children under 11, adolescents' school records may contain SOMPA scores. The SOMPA evaluates a child's intelligence by comparing individuals from the same ethnic group and by measuring other variables that may affect an IQ test score. For example, the test includes an interview with the child's parents, an examination for neurological problems, and assessments of the child's behavior at home and at school. The final score, called the Estimated Learning Potential, is obtained by adjusting the child's actual score on the Weschler IQ test, on the basis of the information from the SOMPA. According to one of the nation's leading experts on psychological testing, Anne Anastasi, the SOMPA "offers a powerful corrective for the routine, superficial misuse of test scores in isolation" (Anastasi, 1982).

Despite the controversy surrounding IQ tests, a number of arguments have been offered on their behalf (Anastasi, 1982). As has been repeatedly demonstrated, IQ tests are highly reliable predictors of an individual's academic performance and can serve a useful diagnostic purpose in identifying those students who need assistance in specific skills. Although IQ test scores become less reliable predictors as children age, the relationship between IQ scores and academic success is .60 to .70 in elementary school, .50 to .60 in high school, .40 to .50 in college, and .30 to .40 in graduate school (Jensen, 1973). Some research also suggests that the effectiveness of certain teaching methods depends on a student's IQ score (Snow, 1982). Hence, IQ scores could help schools individualize instruction by matching specific pedagogical techniques with the student's particular skills and deficits.

The tests' defenders also argue that IQ scores can protect minority youth from subjective or discriminatory assessments of their intellectual abilities. In response to the criticism that IQ tests are culturally biased, their supporters contend that since success in our society is predicated upon mastery of white, middle-class skills and values, minority youths need to know how they function in regard to these criteria. Armed with this knowledge, youths who score poorly on the tests could seek remedial assistance to equip themselves with the skills necessary for success in our society.

Improving Adolescents' IQ Scores: The Nature/Nurture Debate Another problem to be addressed is whether an adolescent's IQ score can be substantially improved by manipulating such environmental factors as education, diet, and interactions with parents. Those who support the view that an individual's intelligence is primarily determined by genetics or by "nature" might hold to the maxim, "You can't make a silk purse out of a sow's ear." In contrast, those who endorse the view that environmental variables or "nurture" primarily determine a person's intellectual abilities might be aligned on the side of the maxim, "As the wind blows, so will the tree grow."

According to the theory that nature limits an individual's intellectual abilities, providing an enriched environment or special education programs for students with low IQ scores will not significantly improve their abilities. One of the most publicized proponents of this view, Arthur Jensen, created a ruckus by asserting that racial differences in IQ scores are primarily the consequence of genetic, not environmental, differences (Jensen, 1969). In addition to the studies cited in Box 3.3, other research corroborating Jensen's view of the importance of heredity shows that identical twins' IQ scores are more similar than fraternal twins' scores (twins developed from two eggs, therefore genetically more different than identical twins); that IQ scores of children raised in foster homes are more similar to their natural parents' scores than to their foster parents' scores;

3.3 A Closer Look

IQ: The Genetic Differences Are Real

In 1969 Arthur Jensen created an uproar with his article on racial differences and IQ. According to Jensen's analysis of the research, genetic factors are about twice as important as environmental factors in determining a person's intelligence. Differences such as education, income, or nutrition are inadequate explanations for the fact that blacks score lower on IQ tests than whites. Amidst the controversy and criticism, Jensen says "The civil rights movement that gained momentum in the 1950's required liberal academic adherence to the theory that the environment was responsible for any individual or racial behavior differences. Thus when I questioned such beliefs I, and my theories, quickly acquired the label 'racist.' I resent this label and consider it unfair and unaccurate" (p. 80).

Jensen is one of the researchers who defend several "unpopular" conclusions: (1) American blacks score an average of 15 points lower than whites on intelligence tests, but this can not be blamed on "culturally biased" tests. If the tests were culturally biased, blacks would not be performing relatively better on the more culture-loaded questions than on the culture-fair ones. Neither would people, regardless of their race, tend to miss the same questions on IQ tests. If the tests favor people raised in the white, Anglo society, Chinese children who have recently immigrated to the United States would not be scoring higher than whites. And if environmental factors controlled IQ scores, then American Indians, who are the most economically and educationally disadvantaged citizens, would not be scoring higher than blacks. (2) IQ tests are valid predictors of academic and vocational performance and of the ability to compete in many aspects of American life. Aptitude, IQ, and vocational tests predict whites' and minorities' abilities equally well. IQ scores reliably indicate that whites have about seven times as many talented people (those with IQs over 115) and seven times as few mentally retarded people as blacks. (3) Since each race's physical characteristics are

that educational programs like Head Start for children from disadvantaged families fail to improve their IQ scores substantially; and that twins raised in different families still have similar IQ scores (Anastasi, 1982; Samuda, 1975; Scarr & Saltzman, 1982; Scarr, Scarf, & Weinber, 1980).

While acknowledging genetic contributions to an individual's intellect, other researchers argue that environmental factors are primarily responsible for the cognitive abilities reflected in adolescents' IQ scores (Anastasi, 1982; Hunt, 1961, 1979; Samuda, 1975; Scarr, Scarf, & Weinber, 1980; Scarr & Saltzman, 1982). A number of empirical findings challenge the assumption that inherited abilities outweigh environmental factors: (1) the IQ scores of poor, minority children who are adopted and raised in upper-middle-class, white homes improve significantly, especially when the children are adopted at an early age; (2) family income, parents' interactions with children, sex-role attitudes, and physical illness can increase or decrease a youngster's IQ score; (3) blacks who inherited, there is a logical reason to presume that mental abilities are also inherited and that races differ. (4) The race and language of the examiner do not inhibit the performance of black youngsters on IQ tests. When the tests are given by black examiners who translate the questions into ghetto dialect, black youngsters' scores remain unchanged. (5) Even though minorities and whites in the same socioeconomic class score more similarly than those with dissimilar incomes, this does not demonstrate that IQ is primarily controlled by environmental factors. These studies fail to consider that blacks in the upper income brackets usually have lighter skin than those in the lower economic classes, indictating that genetic traits are influencing the IQ scores of people in the same economic groups. (6) Malnutrition has little if any impact on an individual's IQ score. Even the victims of severe famine in the Netherlands during World War II had IQ scores similar to their fellow citizens who had not been exposed to the famine.

The conclusions of researchers like Arthur Jensen inevitably fuel impassioned debate. Jensen, however, adheres to his theories and fends off his critics with steadfast confidence:

> The orthodox environmental theories have been accepted, not because they have stood up under proper scientific investigation, but because they harmonize so well with our democratic belief in human equality. . . .
> True liberals and humanists, on the other hand, want to learn the facts. They do not wish to expend their energies sustaining myths and illusions. They wish to face reality, whatever it may be, because only on the level of reality can real problems be effectively confronted (p. 86).

SOURCE: A. Jensen, The differences are real. *Psychology Today,* December 1973, *7,* pp. 80–86.

moved north from the South and those earning high incomes score better on IQ tests than blacks in rural southern communities and those earning low incomes; (4) the mother's health and diet during pregnancy and subsequent malnutrition in the child's first few years of life have a negative impact on the child's academic performance and IQ score; (5) the amount of African ancestry bears no relation to how well a black person scores on IQ tests.

Other findings support the environmentalists' perspective by demonstrating the relationship between certain family variables and a child's IQ score. The first-born child and children from small families usually have higher IQ scores than later-born siblings and children with many siblings. These findings suggest that the economic benefits and extended contact with parents that occur in smaller families increase the likelihood of a child's earning a higher IQ score. It has also been hypothesized that parents have greater intellectual expectations for their first-born or only child, which thereby encourage cognitive growth and higher IQ scores (Zajonc, & Markus, 1975). Both hypotheses have been helpful in predicting adolescents' IQ scores (Witt & Sunningham, 1980).

More support for the environmental view comes from data like Thomas Sowell's comparisons of contemporary black Americans and white immigrants in the early 1900s (Sowell, 1977). After immigrating to the United States, white ethnic groups scored most poorly on abstract sections of intelligence tests, just as black Americans score poorly on these questions today. Like today's black children, the newly immigrated white children tended to score more poorly on IQ tests as they aged. According to Sowell, these similarities demonstrate that the degree to which a group has been assimilated into the culture is more powerful than racial ancestry in determining IQ scores. For this reason, minorities who assimilate most slowly, like Mexican-Americans and black Americans, have a more gradual increase in IQ scores than white minorities like Americans of Polish or Scandinavian descent, who are more quickly assimilated into a predominantly white society.

Given the data supporting each side of the **nature/nurture debate,** which perspective are we to endorse? Can an adolescent's intellectual skills be modified, or are they irreversibly determined by heredity? An award-winning psychologist and researcher in the field of intelligence, Sandra Scarr summarizes the research by concluding that both heredity and environment contribute to a youngster's intellectual abilities; that the overall level of intelligence in our society can be raised by improving the environment; that individual differences determined by heredity can not be entirely eliminated; and that children from extremely disadvantaged backgrounds often develop normal intellectual abilities when given better socioeconomic and educational opportunities (Scarr, Scarf, & Weinber, 1980).

Among other psychologists, J. McVicker Hunt, who believed for the first 30 years of his career that intelligence was essentially fixed by heredity, is convinced that we can raise children's IQ scores (Anastasi, 1982; Hobbs & Robinson, 1982; Hunt, 1961, 1979). According to Hunt, a child's IQ score can be improved by as much as 35 points through education and parenting programs during early childhood and infancy. Given his convictions, Hunt suggests that schools train both male and female high-school students to operate day-care centers in their schools in order to learn the kinds of parenting skills that boost a young child's IQ.

Even among those who support the notion that environmental alterations can improve a child's intellectual abilities, there is dispute over whether adolescents are too old to benefit from such intervention. The traditional assumption that early childhood is the critical period for intellectual development has contributed to a well-entrenched policy of investing the most time and money in programs for young children, rather than for adolescents (Friedrick, 1974). Most educational decisions have been predicated on the belief that experiences during the first few years of a child's life have an irreversible impact on intelligence. Yet recent data are disputing this popular notion by demonstrating that adolescents can overcome early environmental deprivation (Anastasi, 1982; Feuerstein, 1979; Hunt, 1979). After reviewing the recent research, Brim and Kagan voice this more contemporary perspective on cognitive development: "The view that emerges from this work is that humans have a capacity for change across the entire life span. It [the new research] questions the traditional idea that the experiences of the earlier years, which have a demonstrated contemporaneous effect, necessarily constrain the character of adolescence and adulthood" (Brim & Kagan, 1980, p. 128). Similarly, another recent review of the literature by Hobbs and Robinson reinforces the optimistic view that secondary schools do have the potential to improve adolescents' IQ scores and cognitive abilities, despite early childhood deprivation (Hobbs & Robinson, 1982).

Exemplifying this newer perspective, Feuerstein's work testifies to the success of programs designed to improve the cognitive skills of adolescents and young adults (Feuerstein, 1979). Used with Israeli adolescents and young adults in the military, whose poor performance on IQ and achievement tests was attributed to environmental factors, Feuerstein's Instrumental Enrichment Program is designed to alter cognitive structures through specific pedagogical and curriculum strategies. Using his methods, Israeli schools and the military have raised IQ and achievement scores of adolescents and young adults. Preliminary results from studies in the United States and Canada suggest that the Instrumental Enrichment Program can help adolescents overcome many of the cognitive deficits associated with early childhood deprivation (Arbitman-Smith & Haywood, 1980).

Stability of IQ Scores Even without the influence of programs like Feuerstein's, an adolescent's IQ score can change quite dramatically. Most individuals' IQ scores remain relatively stable from elementary school through college, but change less during adolescence than during childhood. In other words, if we were trying to predict a young person's future IQ score, our prediction would be more accurate if based on his or her high-school IQ score than on a fifth-grade score. Nevertheless, extreme caution must be exercised in trying to predict any youngster's future IQ, since large upward and downward shifts in these scores can and do occur. In some cases youngster's scores have been reported to change by as much as 50 points (Anastasi, 1982; Horn, 1976, 1979; Siegler & Richards, 1982).

One explanation for these fluctuations is change in the individual's environment (Anastasi, 1982; Siegler & Richards, 1982). Divorce, adoption, prolonged illness, and educational experiences have all been associated with gains and losses in a child's IQ score. Children whose parents encourage their independence, curiosity, and academic achievement tend to gain IQ points as they age. In this regard it has been suggested that the reason girls' IQ scores tend to decline more than boys' during adolescence is the lack of encouragement many girls receive for independence and intellectual development (Campbell, 1976; McCall, Appelbaum, & Hogarty, 1973). As the data in Chapter 5 will demonstrate, the IQ and achievement scores of girls who are oriented toward traditionally masculine roles increase more than those of girls oriented toward the feminine roles. Furthermore, children from poor families tend to lose IQ points as they age, in contrast to children from richer homes whose scores typically improve. Educational experiences also appear to have more impact on poor youngsters' scores than on richer youngsters'. For example, Jencks's analysis of data from the Census Bureau and the Equality of Educational Opportunity Survey showed that poor children are the most likely to lose their IQ and achievement gains during school vacations (Jencks et al., 1972).

Another possible explanation for the fluctuations in an individual's IQ score is related to the existence of two distinct kinds of intelligence, each of which develops differently during childhood and adolescence (Cattell, 1963; Horn,

1976, 1979). *Crystallized intelligence* is thought to be largely the consequence of educational experiences and societal influences. In contrast, the reasoning and problem-solving skills referred to as *fluid intelligence* are assumed to be less affected by environmental factors. According to this hypothesis, these two forms of intelligence are relatively indistinct from one another prior to adolescence. During adolescence, however, crystallized intelligence increases and continues to grow throughout our lives, while fluid intelligence reaches its peak and steadily declines as we age. Supporting this view, data do show that people in fields like mathematics and science, which require more fluid intelligence, tend to make significant contributions earlier in their careers than those in fields like history and philospohy, which rely more on crystallized intelligence. Supposedly the scientists and mathematicians are handicapped as they age by their declining fluid intelligence, while philosophers and historians benefit from their enhanced crystallized intelligence, which increases with the additional education and experience that age bestows (Guilford, 1967; Horn, 1976, 1979).

Although these hypotheses may be particularly appealing or distasteful, depending on one's age and chosen profession, the data won't permit us to jump to the conclusion that adolescents can boast about their superior fluid intelligence in our presence! Neither do the data permit us to urge young mathematicians and scientists to make their professional contributions before their fluid intelligence dries up. Several authorities argue that the reported declines in fluid intelligence are based on methodologically unsound studies (Keating, 1980; Schaie, 1974). Furthermore, recent research suggests that elderly people have greater intellectual abilities than traditionally supposed, and that their mental performance can be improved through training and practice (Baltes et al., 1980; Carroll & Maxwell, 1979). Until more research is available, theories regarding fluid and crystallized intelligence must be viewed tentatively (Keating, 1980).

The Developmental Approach to Adolescent Cognition

In contrast to the psychometric approach, the developmental perspective addresses itself to questions regarding the specific cognitive skills accompanying physical maturation. Dominating the field of cognitive development, the developmental perspective is predicated on the theories of the Swiss psychologist Jean Piaget. Assuming that cognitive skills develop in predictable, invariant, sequential stages as an individual matures physically, Piaget's theories exemplify the stage theories of adolescence described in Chapter 1. In keeping with other stage theorists, psychologists who endorse Piaget's developmental perspective attribute adolescents' more advanced mental skills to their maturational stage, rather than to environmental variables. Despite the fact that Piaget's theories are being disputed by many contemporary researchers, an understanding of his model is imperative in order to appreciate the developmental viewpoint that has dominated the study of adolescents' cognition throughout recent decades.

The Cognitive Stages between Birth and Adolescence According to Piaget, children advance through three cognitive stages between birth and adolescence: the sensorimotor stage from birth to 18 months, the preoperational stage from 18 months to 7 years, and the concrete operations stage from 7 to 12 years (Inhelder & Piaget, 1958).

During the *sensorimotor stage* children develop simple generalized responses to objects and people. A major advance during this stage is the child's acquisition of the concept of *object permanence.* Initially confused by the relationship between what they see and what exists beyond their vision, young children fail to understand that objects or people still exist, even when they are out of immediate sight. Without the capacity to form mental symbols to represent that which is not immediately visible, young children are greatly amused by games like hide-and-seek, which older children quickly understand as just a game. Once children develop the ability to represent the external world with symbols, however, they can hold an object in mind and realize it still exists, even though it is no longer in sight. Acquiring this skill is, according to Piaget, a mental landmark that signifies the end of the child's sensorimotor period of cognitive development.

During the second or *preoperational stage,* children's cognitive skills advance rapidly because they have acquired language, which permits the mental manipulation of meanings as well as objects. Children also develop the capacity to use objects as symbols for other objects. For example, the child can pretend a doll is a real baby. Preoperational children, however, interpret reality exclusively on the basis of their own perceptions and experiences, without being able to consider anyone else's point of view. Their understanding is based on their own experiences and intuitions in an egocentric fashion that prevents objectivity.

As they advance to the third stage of **concrete operations,** children become capable of perceiving relationships between objects and ideas and of recognizing general rules that apply to these relationships. For instance, the child is able to understand the *rule of equivalence:* If A is equal to B in some way (length or weight), and if B is equal to C, then A and C are also equal. The child also realizes that objects can belong to several categories simultaneously and that categories can be ranked in relation to one other. In other words, a 7-year-old can understand that a puppy belongs to the categories "dog" and "pet" and that "dog" is a part of a larger category called "animals." The child also masters the concept of *reversibility.* This mental skill permits the young child to see that if we take four apples out of a bowl of six apples, divide these four into two equal groups, and then put all the apples back into the bowl again, we still have six apples, despite the divisions.

In a related skill, children learn to reason simultaneously about parts of a whole and the whole itself. This competency enables them to solve problems of *class inclusion.* If we show children in the preoperational stage a box containing eight white buttons and two green ones, they are likely to tell us that "there are more white buttons than there are buttons"; but children in the concrete operations stage are able to discern that there are more buttons than there are white buttons.

In the concrete operations stage youngsters also master the principles of *conservation* and *serialization.* Conservation is the idea that liquids and solids can be changed in shape without changing their volume or mass. Not until about the age of 7 can a child understand that when we pour liquid from a large glass into two smaller glasses, we still have the same amount of water. Serialization is the ability to arrange objects in proper order according to some abstract dimension. For instance, the child can arrange objects in correct order from shortest to longest. When individuals are thinking at the concrete operational stage, they are reasoning in terms of concrete realities and direct personal experiences. They do not yet have the ability to think about abstract ideas.

The Cognitive Stage of Adolescence According to Piaget's theories, most youngsters advance to the stage of **formal operations** near the age of 12 (Elkind, 1968, 1970; Elkind & Weiner, 1978; Flavell, 1971; Inhelder & Piaget, 1958). During this stage, thinking becomes more logical, more abstract, and less egocentric than in childhood. Without having to rely solely on concrete objects or personal experiences, the adolescent is able to think about abstract concepts and to discuss hypothetical situations and problems. Although youngsters in the stage of concrete operations can create hypotheses, they are limited in terms of being able to generate only one possible explanation for a problem and are often ready to accept a hypothesis as true without examining its premises. Formal operational thinking also enables a young person to discard an initial hypothesis more quickly than younger children, when the evidence proves his or her initial reasoning to be incorrect. Furthermore, adolescents become more adept at solving verbal problems that are beyond the limits of younger children's concrete thinking: "If Alan is taller than Bear, but Alan is shorter than Paul, who is the tallest of the three?"

A conversation with a 10-year-old boy and his 15-year-old brother exemplifies several distinctions between concrete and formal operational thinking. The 15-year-old is more apt than his younger brother to consider other people's opinions, to modify his initial hypotheses, to comprehend abstractions, and to generate alternatives. As the research in Chapters 4 and 12 will demonstrate, 15-year-olds are also more apt to empathize with others, to reason morally from a less egocentric view, and to become engaged in religious and political issues formerly beyond their interest or comprehension.

Developing New Cognitive Stages According to Piaget, children develop more advanced reasoning as a consequence of alteration in mental structures, called schemas. A *schema* is a collection of data organized in a way that helps a person interpret the environment and new experiences. Upon encountering new experiences and new data, Piaget argued that we rely on our existing schema to determine our course of action and our interpretations of a situation. When this process, referred to as **assimilation,** fails to help us in a new situation, however, we experience *disequilibrium.* Disequilibrium is eliminated by allowing the new information to alter our old schema in a process Piaget labels *accommodation.* By repeating this process of assimilation and accommodation from infancy through adolescence, we advance from the sensorimotor stage to the formal operational stage of thinking.

As a way of exemplifying these processes, let's assume Howard goes to his girlfriend's house for dinner. Using his existing schema, as soon as he sits down at the table he lunges for the nearest bowl of food, just as he does at home. With red-faced embarrassment he notices that everyone is staring at him and that they all have their heads bowed. Howard quickly withdraws his hand and bows his head. Accommodating this new information into his old schema, when he joins another friend's family for dinner, Howard reaches for the pork chops only after having glanced around the table and seeing his pal lurching for the sweet potatoes.

In a modification of Piaget's original theories, Michael Berzonsky posits that formal thinking develops more gradually than Piaget proposes (Berzonsky, 1978). Furthermore, he suggests that an adolescent's personal experiences will determine the situations in which he or she will rely on formal or concrete thinking. For example, Sally may use formal operational thinking for resolving algebra problems, but rely on concrete thinking for solving verbal problems. Although Berzonsky agrees with Piaget that the sensorimotor, preoperational, and concrete stages are universal and invariant, he contends that adolescence offers a number of different cognitive tracks or "branches," only one of which is formal operational thought. Hence, this theory, first proposed by Dulik, is called the *branch model of cognitive development* (Dulik, 1972). According to this model, all adolescents have the ability to develop formal operational thinking, but environmental influences will determine whether or not a youngster pursues that particular cognitive branch.

Since even Piaget admitted that the age at which adolescents reach the stage of formal operations cannot be precisely predicted, how are we to know which young people have not yet arrived at the stage of formal operations? The empirical evidence in support of Piaget's theories is derived from laboratory observations of children's performance on specific mental problems. The experiment described in Box 3.4 exemplifies a typical Piagetian task for distinguishing adolescents who have arrived at the stage of formal operations from those who are still operating in the concrete stage of reasoning (Kuhn & Brannock, 1977).

Criticisms of Piaget's Theories Although most research on adolescent cognition has been conducted from the developmental perspective, many of the most carefully designed recent studies cast serious doubt on Piaget's theories (Keating, 1980; Siegler & Richards, 1982). These studies have undermined Piaget's position by demonstrating that neither the majority of adolescents nor of adults employ formal operations in any consistent manner. For example, numerous studies show that adults use concrete thinking to solve problems and that even very bright, well-educated adults do best when thinking about real, concrete problems rather than about abstractions (Dulik, 1972; Kuhn & Brannock, 1977; Kuhn et al., 1977; Neimark, 1975). Investigators have also found that young children employ certain aspects of formal thinking well in advance of the age predicted by Piaget (Keating, 1980). Data like these suggest that even if everyone has the potential to develop formal thinking during adolescence, concrete thinking is still the preferred choice in many situations throughout our lives. Furthermore, recent experiments like those described in Box 3.5 undermine Piaget's contention that formal reasoning is superior to concrete reasoning.

Other studies challenging Piaget's theories have failed to find any consistent pattern of cognitive development during adolescence. For example, 37 percent of the eleventh-graders in one study failed to demonstrate formal operational thought, and only 2.4 percent of the 600 adolescents in another study of 25 secondary schools had fully attained formal thinking (Keating & Clark, 1980; Renner & Stafford, 1976). In yet another investigation of girls with above-average IQ scores, most twelfth-graders passed only six of the ten problems that required formal thinking (Mortorano, 1977). Focusing only on college students, one investigator found that one-fourth of them failed to use formal reasoning, while another assessment showed that only 50 percent of college freshmen exhibited formal thought (McKinnon, 1976; Murray & Armstrong, 1978).

By the end of his illustrious career, even Piaget was revising certain aspects

3.4 A Closer Look

A Piagetian Experiment: Formal or Concrete Reasoning?

In order to assess the development of logical thinking, Deanna Kuhn and her associates designed an experiment somewhat more relevant for modern adolescents than Piaget's original tests. In Kuhn's experiment, researchers showed students four plants, two that looked healthy and two that looked sick. Next to each plant were either a large or a small glass of water and a container of light or dark plant food. A bottle of leaf lotion was beside one of the healthy plants and one of the sick plants. In order to answer the problem correctly, students had to consider all three variables.

The researcher then told the students, "I've been raising some plants. I'd like to show them to you and ask what you think. Let's look at this plant first. It seems quite healthy, doesn't it? Every week I gave this plant a large glass of water, some of this dark-colored plant food, and a little of the leaf lotion in this bottle. Now I have another plant like this at home that I've just started working on. My plant at home I'm giving a small glass of water each week, some of the light-colored plant food and I'm not giving it any of the leaf lotion. How do you think my plant at home is going to turn out? How do you know?"

Very young children could not perform this task, which requires the skills of formal operational thinking. Children in the concrete operations stage were aware that they were supposed to separate the variables, but were still unable to differentiate between the important and unimportant factors. Adolescents and college students were more likely to isolate the correct variables and answer correctly. What's your answer?

SOURCE: D. Kuhn and J. Brannock, Development of the isolation of variables scheme in an experimental and "natural experiment" context. *Developmental Psychology,* 1977, *13,* 9–14.

of his initial hypotheses (Piaget, 1972). Although the data are contradictory and inconsistent in many respects, several converging lines of evidence now lead to the conclusion that most people are capable of developing formal thought during their adolescence. Most adults and adolescents, however, apply formal reasoning inconsistently and only in regard to specific types of situations or problems. Among other potential environmental influences, recent evidence implies that cultural differences and educational experiences do advance or retard the development of formal operational thinking. For example, U.S. adolescents aged 13 to 15 were found to be more advanced in formal thought than the same-aged youth in Hong Kong (Douglas & Wong, 1977).

Contrary to Piaget's initial hypothesis that cognitive advances are primarily reliant on physiological maturation, some educational programs have succeeded in enchancing adolescents' formal reasoning abilities. By encouraging independent thinking, using inquiry methods of teaching, and emphasizing individual problem solving, these programs have improved students' formal reasoning abilities (Keating, 1980; McKinnon, 1976; Siegler & Richards, 1982).

In his analysis of the empirical data, Daniel Keating cautions us not to attribute poor academic achievement to a student's presumed level of cognitive development. According to the viewpoint espoused by Keating, IQ scores and Piaget's hypotheses about cognitive stages are inadequate explanations for adolescents'

3.5 A Closer Look

Intuitions about Physics Die Hard

If a person strolling along drops a ball from shoulder height, what path will the ball follow as it falls, if the person keeps walking (dotted line)?

When researchers at Johns Hopkins University asked students to answer questions like this, surprising results occurred. Half of the college students guessed incorrectly that the ball dropped by the walking person would fall straight down and hit the ground directly beneath where it was released. In fact the ball continues moving forward and then slightly downward as gravity exerts pressure. The ball then hits the ground in front of where it was dropped, following a parabolic arc. Why do so many of the students, even those who have had a physics course, misunderstand the laws of physics? And why do young children answer the physics questions more accurately than older children?

academic performance. Like other critics of Piaget, Keating contends that almost all aspects of mental performance improve as children age, but that these improvements do not constitute empirical proof that a new "stage" of cognitive development has emerged. For example, although it seems logical to assume that adolescents with high IQ scores will be more advanced in formal operations than those with low scores, no clear pattern has emerged. After an extensive review of the research, Keating echoes the view of other critics: "I am led to conclude by the evidence above, first, that we know very little about how adolescents' thinking differs from children's thinking beyond the obvious (but important) performance descriptions; and, second, that Inhelder and Piaget's general theoretical model is not an accurate account of the change" (Keating, 1980, p. 238). Another specialist in the area of adolescent cognition, John Flavell goes so far as to assert that the concept of stages will not figure significantly in future work on cognitive development (Flavell, 1971).

The researchers believe that visual illusions and the ability to think at the abstract level contribute to our misperceptions about the laws of motion. For example, when we see a walking person drop a ball, we may concentrate on the person as the frame of reference against which we view the falling ball. Since the ball does fall straight down relative to the moving person who dropped it, we may think that it has fallen straight down relative to the floor. A similar illusion occurs when clouds that are moving to the right across the moon make us believe that the moon is moving to the left.

A second explanation for people's success or failure at these problems may be their level of cognitive development. The youngest children probably deal with the problems on a concrete level by thinking about other identical situations in which they have seen the object move in exactly the same way. Older children, however, have developed the ability to think abstractly and to generalize from previous situations to new ones that are somewhat similar. For instance, noticing that a toy car continues rolling in the direction in which it was pushed, the child may create the abstract hypothesis that "every object set in motion keeps moving in the direction it was set going."

And the consequence of these misperceptions and abstract reasoning? Consider the person who steps from the roof 20 feet above ground to the ladder. Unfortunately the ladder slips. The person tries to push away from the roof to avoid landing in the bushes directly below. Basing her shove on her faulty assumptions about physics, she ends up on the cement sidewalk nine feet away from the side of the house!

SOURCE: M. McCloskey, Intuitive physics. *Scientific American,* 1983, *248,* 122–130.

The Information-Processing Approach to Adolescent Cognition

One of the greatest weaknesses of both the psychometric and the Piagetian approaches to cognition is that neither explains the specific processes involved in thinking (Siegler & Richards, 1982). The information-processing approach attempts to identify the means by which the young and the old process information received from the environment. Information-processing psychologists have concentrated their research efforts in two domains: memory and problem solving.

The Computer Model of Cognition In our technological, computerized age perhaps it comes as no surprise that a computerlike model of cognition exists. Using this approach to understanding adolescent cognition, researchers compare certain aspects of human thinking to the processing of information by computers. Both a person and a computer receive information from outside themselves, process the data internally, and transmit a response back to the environment. The computer's "hardware" is composed of its physical equipment: the central processing unit (CPU), which contains the memory boards and the components for processing data, the keyboard through which data are relayed to the CPU, and the printer through which the CPU conveys its responses. A computer's "software" is any program that has been written onto a disc, thereby providing the CPU with information necessary to perform its operations. For example, one piece of software may provide the CPU with formulas for computing algebraic problems, while another program provides information about French vocabulary and grammar. According to this model, the adolescent's brain and central nervous system are analagous to the computer's hardware, and all plans and mental strategies are analagous to software (Flavell, 1977).

According to the information-processing approach, the computer and the adolescent function in similar fashions (Klahr & Wallace, 1975). For example, the fact that a 15-year-old can remember more items on a list than an 8-year-old is a function of the adolescent's more advanced hardware and software (Eichorn, 1970). With a more physically mature brain and nervous system and more memory and problem-solving strategies, the adolescent can compute information more efficiently than the younger child. In the computer industry, software changes more rapidly than hardware. Researchers who carry this analogy into the domain of human development contend that physiological changes in the brain and nervous system are less dramatic than changes in a child's mental strategies between childhood and adolescence (Sigel & Cocking, 1977). Our ability to process larger quantities of information, to compute data faster, and to store greater amounts of material in our memory banks supposedly increase with age (Richards, 1976).

It's important to note that although the computer provides an interesting and valid analogy regarding human mental processes, this model of cognition oversimplifies the relationship between the brain and the computer. Nevertheless, the information-processing approach does yield information about memory and problem solving that is relevant to our study of adolescents.

Characteristics of Adolescents' Memory Rather than conceiving of human memory as a single concept, researchers are in agreement that two distinct types of memory exist: short-term memory and long-term memory (Loftus, 1980). Information that is not transferred to long-term memory will be forgotten. For example, we relay data to short-term memory when we intend to remember someone's address only long enough to write it on the envelope. Presumably, information retained for more than 15 seconds has been transferred to long-term memory. Unlike long-term memory, whose storage capacity appears limitless, short-term memory can retain only a restricted amount of data. The process of transferring data from short-term to long-term memory is called *encoding*. According to many researchers, data filed in long-term memory never disappear. In other words, no data are ever truly forgotten. When humans forget, they have simply failed to locate or retrieve data that are safely stored in their long-term memory banks. For example, an adolescent who can't remember the state capitals on her geography test is either failing to retrieve the answer from her memory banks or failed to properly transfer the information from her short-term to her long-term bank. Scanning is the act of searching through the stored data (like a computer sifting through its memory banks) until the sought-after information is recognized and retrieved.

The information-processing approach explores the different ways in which children, adolescents, and adults encode and decode information (Keating & Bobbitt, 1978). Although adolescents have better long-term memory than younger children, people of all ages and abilities apparently employ identical strategies for scanning their short-term memory. Adolescents scan and retrieve data faster than younger children. Moreover, during childhood and adolescence an individual's intelligence and scanning abilities are more closely related than during adulthood. In other words, adults depend less on their intelligence for scanning and retrieving data than children or adolescents. It appears that age increases our strategies for data processing, thereby making intelligence a less influential factor in retrieving data. It has also been suggested that what appear as differences in people's mental abilities may actually be differences in how efficiently they process data. For instance, one brother may appear "smarter" than the other, when in fact he simply has better strategies for storing and retrieving information.

The pattern emerging from a number of studies is that adolescents have developed more efficient strategies for encoding and decoding data than children (see Box 3.6). The ability to retrieve data from short-term memory increases with age, which explains why adolescents can immediately recall more words from a list than 10-year-olds and why 10-year-olds recall more than 7-year-olds. Although 7-year-olds employ some of the same strategies as adolescents for remembering the words, they use the strategies far less often (Friedrick, 1974). Furthermore, young children rarely "rehearse" the data they are attempting to encode, in contrast to adolescents. For example, an 8-year-old who is trying to memorize a list of words typically rehearses each word in isolation. After reading the word "cat," the young child will say "cat, cat, cat" to herself and then go on to read and rehearse the next word on the list. Fourteen-year-olds, however, will combine several words while trying to memorize the list. After reading the word "cat," they will rehearse it along with several of the preceding words: "tree," "girl," "boat," "cat" (Ornstein, 1978).

One review of the empirical research offers several practical suggestions in regard to the memory skills of children and adolescents (Siegler, Liebert, & Liebert, 1973). First, although young children have been taught to use more efficient strategies for encoding data in a particular situation, they revert to their less efficient methods when a new task comes along. This implies that physical maturation is a necessary component in developing better encoding and decoding skills. Second, adolescents make better use of mnemonic devices and rehearsal methods than children. Consequently, our efforts to teach adolescents these particular strategies should yield relatively permanent improvements in their encoding and decoding skills. Third, the relationship between age and memory skills is more complex than often acknowledged. For example, some children can remember more information than adults, showing that encoding and decoding skills cannot always be linearly related to chronological age.

Adolescents' Problem-Solving Strategies According to the information-processing view, adolescents have developed problem-solving strategies that are different from those they used as younger children (Flavell, 1971). This can be exemplified by the way in which children and adolescents play the game "Twenty

3.6 A Closer Look

If an Elephant Never Forgets, Why Do Adolescents?

What determines whether or not adolescents will remember what they see or hear? In answering this question, researchers suggest that state-dependent memory and flashbulb memory may be partially responsible for remembering and forgetting. In *state-dependent memory,* information that the individual memorizes in one mood is difficult to retrieve unless the individual is in a similar mood. For example, students who memorized a list of words while smoking marijuana recalled more of the words when they were using the drug again than when they were undrugged. The reverse was also true: Those who had memorized the words while undrugged could not recall them very well when they smoked grass. In another study, college students in happy or sad moods memorized lists of words. The students recalled the words best when they were in the same kind of mood as they had been when they first memorized the words.

The impact of emotions on memory is also demonstrated in research about events like President Kennedy's assassination. Almost all adolescents and adults remember exactly where they were and what they were doing when they heard about the assassination. Many even remember minute details like what objects they were holding or the taste of the food they were eating when they heard the news. The memory of brief, highly emotional moments from the past is called *eidetic* or *flashbulb memory,* because it seems like a photograph taken with a flashbulb. Flashbulb memories are usually incomplete, and more experiments are needed to determine their accuracy. Flashbulb memories occur when a person undergoes an emotionally shocking experience, like hearing about a friend's death. According to some researchers, the shock releases a substance, perhaps a neurotransmitter, into the central nervous system at the same moment that the substance crosses the brain's cortex, causing it to store the highly vivid memory for later use.

SOURCES: J. Eich et al., State-dependent accessibility of retrieval clues in the retention of a categorized list. *Journal of Verbal Learning and Behavior,* 1975, *14,* 408–417; G. Bower, Mood and memory. *American Psychologist,* 1981, *36,* 129–148; R. Brown and J. Kulik, Flashbulb memories. *Cognition,* 1977, *5,* 73–99.

Questions.'' The young child's approach is to ask a series of unrelated, isolated questions, without a premeditated strategy: Is it a cat? Is it a banana? Is it a cake? The adolescent's questions reflect a more careful strategy based on developing categories: Is it an animal? Is it larger than a person? Is it edible?

Another more advanced aspect of adolescents' problem solving is their ability to consider the future. Unlike children, adolescents have developed a perspective of future time and an understanding that formulating strategies ahead of time can sometimes prevent problems from developing in the future. For instance, an adolescent can resolve the immediate problem of ''being broke'' by developing strategies in the present for saving money for the future. Adolescents are also more willing than children to adopt new rules and strategies, when old ones are not helping resolve a dilemma (Siegler & Richards, 1982).

Why are adolescents' strategies for memorization and problem solving superior to children's? According to some, the answer is metacognition (Siegler & Richards, 1982). *Metacognition* is the ability to observe and to evaluate one's own reasoning strategies. It is the act of "thinking about your own thinking." For example, adolescents are more realistic than children about how much information they can remember at a time. A 5-year-old boy is likely to tell us he can remember all ten pictures that we have just shown him and that he "never forgets" anything. An adolescent boy is more realistic, however, and admits beforehand that he can't remember all ten pictures. Adolescents are increasingly efficient at observing their own reasoning and recognizing its limitations.

Sex Differences in Cognitive Skills

The research in subsequent chapters will demonstrate the ways in which sex roles influence adolescents' behavior and attitudes in regard to social, sexual, political, religious, and vocational issues. The controversies and theories related to sex-role development will be presented, along with the empirical data on sex differences in these domains. Later chapters will also explore the arguments regarding the source of these differences between male and female adolescents. In regard to cognitive skills, the relationship between gender and mental performance is more complex than is generally acknowledged either by those who argue that no significant differences exist or by those who argue that the differences are substantial.

Mathematical and Spatial Skills Although jokes about females' lack of mathematical skills are legion, there is some justification for the stereotypes of female ineptness in this domain. In 1974 Eleanor Maccoby and Carol Jacklin reviewed all of the research to date on sex differences (Maccoby & Jacklin, 1974). After reviewing 1,200 studies, they both dispelled and confirmed a number of hypotheses about male and female cognitive and social development. Thus the data revealed that until about the age of 11, boys and girls have similar mathematical abilities; but from the onset of adolescence through the adult years, males retain a lead in mathematical competence.

A recent example of this sex difference is reflected in the SAT scores of college students. Of the 65,000 students who have taken the SAT since 1971, four times as many males as females scored above 600 and thirteen times as many scored above 700 on the math questions. This difference may be partially accounted for by the fact that the SAT measures mathematical reasoning, rather than computation or application of skills, and that several studies have shown girls performing better than boys at computation (Benbow & Stanley, 1983). Nevertheless, most research since Maccoby and Jacklin's famous review continues to support the hypothesis that males generally have better math skills than females (Peterson & Gitelson, 1984; Peterson & Wittig, 1979).

Although the differences are quite small, most research also shows some advantage for males in performing spatial skills (Hyde, 1981; Maccoby & Jacklin, 1974; Scarr & Saltzman, 1982; Schweinhart & Weikart, 1980). Spatial skills are measured by performance on mazes and tests that require mental manipulation of objects or remembering a visual figure in order to locate it later within a more complex figure. For instance, an adolescent might be asked to identify an object viewed from several different angles. Spatial-reasoning skills are often required in engineering, geometry, graphic arts, and architecture. An important caveat is that the differences between males' and females' spatial skills is slight. In no study does gender account for more than 5 percent of the variability.

Two mitigating factors are challenging the traditional notion that the differences in males' and females' mathematical or spatial skills are innate. The first is that although the research generally finds males' skills superior to females' in these two domains, the differences are far slighter than generally presumed. The second is that recent research shows fewer differences in math skills when the educational experiences and social expectations of males and females are similar. For example, the Educational Testing Service, which publishes the SAT, concludes that mathematical differences between males and females are primarily due to the fact that boys complete more math courses than girls (Ekstrom, 1979). Although girls' scores are still lower than boys, their SAT math scores did improve between 1972 and 1979, a period during which more girls were being

3.7 A Closer Look

The Two Sides of the Brain

How does an adolescent's brain affect his or her abilities in mathematics and language? Is the female adolescent's brain different from the male's? What happens to an adolescent's cognitive skills if the brain is damaged? What relationship is there between being left-handed and being mathematically talented?

Researchers who study the brain have discovered fascinating answers to questions like these. The human brain is divided into two cerebral hemispheres each of which controls different mental and physical functions. Brain *lateralization* is the separation of mental and physical functions into one side of the brain or the other. The left half of the brain receives messages from and controls the right side of the body. The right side of the brain does the same for the left side of the body. In most people the left hemisphere is the site of language ability and the right hemisphere is the site of spatial skills, visual imagery, and musical abilities. So if the left hemisphere of an adolescent's brain is damaged, the youngster may be paralyzed on the right side of the body or may develop speech disorders. Likewise, youngsters with damage to the right hemisphere may find it difficult to draw, to find their way from one place to another, or to build a model from a plan. They may also respond inappropriately in social situations, because they misinterpret other people's emotions. For instance, they often mistake another person's joking for hostility.

The two hemispheres process information differently. The left hemisphere uses logical strategies, while the right uses intuitive strategies. This doesn't mean, however, that each half of the brain can process only certain kinds of information. It simply means that each half is more efficient than the other in processing certain kinds of information. The left hemisphere's proficiency in language skills is probably due to the fact that it processes information faster than the right hemisphere, but the right hemisphere can also process language. The two halves of the brain also seem to store different kinds of information. Because they are connected by a cable of neural tissue, encouraged to take math courses than in previous decades (Benbow & Stanley, 1983). Similarly, math scores of high-school juniors are more nearly equivalent, when males and females have taken the same number of math courses (Dewolfe, 1977). Most researchers concur that girls could become as proficient in math as boys, if encouraged to master the subject and if convinced that being mathematically competent was no threat to their femininity (Brush, 1980; Dewolfe, 1977; Ernest, 1976; Fennema, 1974; Hyde, 1981; Peterson & Gitelson, 1984; Siegler & Richards, 1982; Tobias, 1978).

Despite the impressive amount of empirical evidence supporting the view that boys' better performance is a consequence of sex-role stereotypes that discourage girls from developing their mathematical potential, the possibility of physiological differences cannot be entirely dismissed. Relevant data can be found in studies related to brain hemisphericity. As Box 3.7 explains, the brain is divided into two hemispheres, each of which has primary responsiblity for des-

however, the information is passed back and forth between the two sides. If this cable is surgically cut (as surgeons sometimes do to control a patient's epileptic seizures), each half of the brain functions independently. For example, after this kind of surgery, a patient who is shown an object only in front of the left eye (the message is sent to the right brain), reports having seen nothing.

The relationship between the sides of the brain and left- or right-handedness is unclear, but we do know that right-handed people tend to do better on language tasks and left-handed people do better on spatial tasks. For example, Benbow and Stanley found that 20 percent of the students who scored above 700 on the math portion of the SAT exam were left-handed, which is twice the national average.

There also seems to be a relationship between brain lateralization and certain cognitive differences between males and females. Females tend to be more proficient in language tasks and less proficient in mathematical tasks than males. When portions of the left hemisphere are surgically removed, males often develop language disturbances; when portions of the right hemisphere are removed, they often develop problems in spatial skills. This doesn't happen with females. Findings like these suggest that lateralization may be greater in males than in females. Females may use both hemispheres in language and mathematical skills, while males may rely more on just one hemisphere to perform these tasks. These differences between male and female brains are relatively unimportant for practical purposes, because the average differences in mathematical and language skills are so small. The sex differences may eventually be extremely useful, however, in helping us understand more about how the human brain functions.

SOURCES: E. Hall, The brain and behavior. In *Psychology today: An introduction*. New York: Random House, 1983. Pp. 59–61; C. Benbow, and J. Stanley, Sex differences in mathematical reasoning ability: More facts. *Science*, 1983, *222*, 1029–1031.

ignated cognitive skills. Some researchers are exploring the possibility that certain gender differences in cognitive skills are related to differences in the brain's hemispheres. For example, one neurologist at the Harvard Medical School hypothesizes that testosterone may be indirectly responsible for males' better mathematical skills by causing the fetus to develop right-brain-hemisphere dominance. As a consequence of receiving more testosterone than girls in the mother's womb, male children may be born with greater mathematical tendencies (Benbow & Stanley, 1983). Other research suggests that males may develop better spatial abilities than females during adolescence, because the right hemisphere undergoes shifts during puberty (McGee, 1979).

As researchers compile additional data on the relationships between physiological differences and cognitive skills, our understanding of gender differences will inevitably expand.

Verbal Abilities Maccoby and Jackson's review of the literature also showed that girls outperform boys on verbal abilities during adolescence (Maccoby & Jacklin, 1974). Verbal abilities include comprehending written passages, defining words, understanding logical relations, writing creatively, and verbal fluency. During the first few years of life, girls outperform boys in these areas, but during elementary school the two sexes' verbal skills become relatively equivalent. As adolescence begins, the pattern reverses itself and girls regain the lead. As in the case of mathematical abilities, however, these discrepancies between the sexes are far smaller than often imagined. For example, although females generally scored higher than males on the vocabulary subtest of the most recent revision of the Wechsler Adult Intelligence Scale, gender accounted for less than 1 percent of the variance between male and female scores (Schweinhart & Weikart, 1980).

Creativity During Adolescence

Defining and Measuring Creativity

Like the term "intelligence," creativity is a concept that provokes considerable debate in regard to its definitions and measurement. Despite their disagreements, however, the experts on adolescent creativity generally agree that creativity and intelligence involve different abilities (Getzels, 1975; Guilford, 1967; Richards, 1976).

According to experts like Guilford and Torrance, intelligence depends on convergent thinking, while creativity depends on divergent thinking (Guilford, 1967; Torrance, 1966). **Convergent thinking** leads to the discovery of a single, correct answer to the problem. For example, an adolescent uses convergent thinking in solving a math problem for which there is only one correct answer. In contrast, **divergent thinking** is the act of producing a variety of solutions for problems that have no single correct answer. For example, an adolescent is using divergent thinking when offering suggestions for ways to use paper clips and rubber bands, other than for holding things together.

Divergent thinking has three aspects, which are measured on standardized tests: fluency, flexibility, and originality. Fluency is the youngster's ability to produce a large number of responses; flexibility is the ability to create many differ-

Who is the most creative person you know personally, and how would you account for his or her creativity?

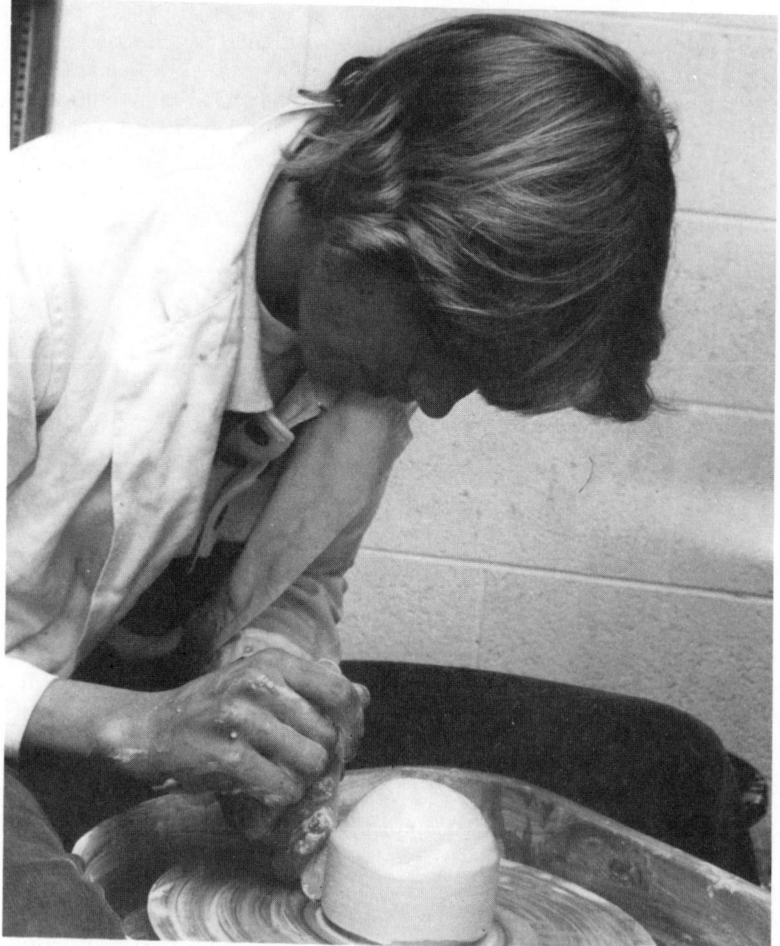

ent categories of responses; and originality is the ability to create unique answers. Three of the most popular tests for measuring adolescents' creativity are Guilford's Creativity Tests for Children, Torrance Tests for Creative Thinking, and the Khatena-Torrance Creative Perception Inventory (Guilford, 1967; Khatena & Torrance, 1976; Torrance, 1966).

Creativity and Intelligence

The relationship between an adolescent's creativity and intelligence is more complicated than many experts initially hypothesized. The well-known studies of Getzels and Jackson attempted to identify the differences between extremely intelligent and extremely creative adolescents (Getzels, 1975). These researchers selected students who scored in the top 20 percent on IQ tests and those who scored in the top 20 percent on creativity tests, excluding those who scored in the top 20 percent on both IQ and creativity. Although the creative students scored an average of 23 points lower on their IQ tests, their achievement test scores were similar to those of the students with the higher IQs. This suggests that creativity is just as much an asset as a high IQ score for academic success. After replicating Getzels and Jackson's work, Torrance also arrived at the conclusion that the relationship between intelligence and creativity is minimal and that creativity is a better predictor of academic success than IQ scores (Torrance, 1966).

While some experts considered these studies a breakthrough in understanding the differences between intelligence and creativity, others have disagreed (Khatena, 1982). Getzels's critics have pointed out several methodological flaws in his studies. For example, the "high creativity-low intelligence" students in his study had a well above average IQ score of 123. In addition, a number of researchers have found positive correlations between creativity and intelligence (Anastasi, 1982; Khatena, 1982; Wallach & Kogan, 1965; Welsh, 1977). Although these researchers do not assert that students with high IQs will necessarily be creative, they do contend that the likelihood of students with low IQs being creative is very slight.

Characteristics of Creative Adolescents

According to some researchers, adolescents have less creativity than younger children, because of their need to conform and to acquiesce to peer pressure (Wolf & Larsen, 1981). On the other hand, Dudek feels that young adolescents are only temporarily less creative, because they are mastering the skills of the formal stage of operations (Dudek, 1974). After acquiring these skills, adolescent creativity should increase.

How does creativity influence an adolescent's personality and interactions with other people? In one exemplary study by Wallach and Kogan (1965), the impact of intelligence and creativity on adolescents was explored. According to these data, adolescents who are both very intelligent and very creative are popular, confident, and insightful. Those who are very intelligent but uncreative are generally conformists with a strong fear of failure. In contrast, very creative students with low IQ scores tend to be disruptive and to lack self-confidence, while those who lack both creativity and intelligence dislike school intensely.

In another study of 100 gifted high-school students, Welsh found similar but not identical patterns (Welsh, 1977). The students who were most creative and intelligent tended to be introverted and self-sufficient, in contrast to Wallach and Kogan's findings of popularity. Those who were very intelligent but not creative were sociable but rather conforming; and those whose creativity surpassed their IQ scores were impulsive, sociable, and inclined toward the performing arts and sales occupations.

An expert in the field of human creativity, Paul Torrance describes creative youngsters as nonconformists who dislike too much authority or structure (see Box 3.8). Creative youngsters generally dislike rules, prefer working alone, and may be rebellious about constraints. They tend to me more tolerant of ambiguity and more socially poised, mature, ambitious, and self-confident than their peers.

A Closer Look 3.8 

Description of the Creative Person

Paul Torrance, one of the leading authorities in the field, developed the following checklist for identifying creative people from his survey of over 50 studies on creativity. How creative are you according to Torrance's criteria?

- Adventurous, risk-taking, testing limits
- Idealistic, sincere, earnest
- Attempting and preferring difficult tasks
- Becoming preoccupied with tasks
- Courageous in convictions
- Curious, searching
- Determined, unflinching
- Feeling and expressing emotions
- Striving for distant goals
- Energetic, virtuous
- Guessing, hypothesizing
- Independent in judgment and thinking
- Industrious, busy
- Intuitive, insightful
- Liking to work alone
- Truthful even when it hurts
- Regressing occasionally to childlike, playful conduct
- Remembers well
- Assertive, self-confident, and self-sufficient
- Sense of humor and beauty

SOURCE: P. Torrance, Assessing children, teachers and parents against the ideal child criterion. *Gifted Child Qurterly,* 1975, *19,* 130–139.

Neither the boys nor the girls have stereotypically masculine or feminine personalities. Instead, their personalities tend to be androgynous—a concept that will be described in more detail in Chapter 5. Given Torrance's descriptions of creative adolescents, perhaps it's not too surprising that when forced to choose between working with highly intelligent or highly creative students, many teachers opt for the most intelligent (Getzels & Jackson, 1962).

The relationship between adolescent and adult creativity is curious in some respects. Creative adolescents will typically grow up to be creative adults, who often pursue the unusual careers they envisioned during their youth (Torrance, 1972). Self-control, however, seems to be more important for enhancing creativity during adolescence than during the adult years. Creative adolescents have more self-control in comparison to their peers than do creative adults, suggesting that being creative during adolescence requires the self-discipline to convert creative urges into a product (Parloff et al., 1968). For example, writing a poem requires self-discipline to convert creative ideas into the appropriate words. Furthermore, a study showing that creative writers score lower in self-control than creative scientists implies that the degree of self-control that enhances creativity may depend somewhat on the person's field (Parloff et al., 1968).

Increasing Adolescents' Creativity

Those who value creativity will inevitably pose the most practical question related to its continuance: What can parents and teachers do to enhance an adolescent's creativity?

The families of creative adolescents tend to differ from other parents in several respects (Getzels & Jackson, 1962; Khatena, 1982; Miller & Gerard, 1979; Wallach & Kogan, 1965). Parents of creative children actively encourage independence, curiosity, and unusual talents. Themselves relatively indifferent to social status and conformity, these parents tend not to have an overly symbiotic relationship either with one another or with their children. These parents tend to be intellectually and socially competent and to deemphasize authoritarian control over their children. Rather than stressing high grades, these parents

3.9 A Closer Look

Increasing Adolescents' Creativity

Teachers and parents can increase adolescents' creativity by:

- Encouraging spontaneous expression and accepting novel ideas
- Relying less on memory activities and asking provocative questions
- Providing a stimulating, nonthreatening environment
- Reducing anxiety and rewarding nonconformity
- Emphasizing the value of working alone rather than in groups
- Discouraging sex-role stereotypes
- Encouraging controversy and disagreement without hostility
- Discouraging the need to "be perfect" and to "never make mistakes"
- Granting responsibility and independence
- Respecting fantasies, daydreaming, and other imaginative activities
- Encouraging disagreements and discussions of controversial ideas
- Providing opportunities for hypothesizing, exploring, and experimenting
- Deferring judgment and evaluation of the adolescent's ideas and work
- Helping the youngster learn to trust his or her own senses and intuitions
- Showing respect for emotion, ambiguity, and imperfections
- Providing games and books that demand creative responses and playfulness

SOURCE: B. Clark, *Growing up gifted.* Columbus, Ohio.: Charles E. Merrill, 1979.

encourage their children to experiment and to learn through making mistakes. By treating their children with respect and providing enough distance and aloofness to foster self-reliance, these adults help their offspring become adventuresome and nonconforming. Researchers have provided a number of specific suggestions for enhancing childrens' creativity at home and at school (listed in Box 3.9).

By studying famous creative people from history, Simonton (1978) has identified several societal factors that influence creativity: formal education, warfare, political unrest, role models, and civil disobedience. While civil disobedience and political disagreement encourage creativity, constant warfare and extremely unpredictable governments cause too much insecurity for creativity to thrive. Societies also need to provide children with role models of creative people who are respected and financially rewarded by their fellow citizens. According to Simonton's analysis, however, too much formal education detracts from an individual's creativity in discouraging nonconformity and inundating students

Of which of your own skills are you proudest? How much do you feel your family's environment and your genetic endowment contributed to your skill?

with traditional perspectives. In the views of social critics like Simonton, contemporary U.S. adolescents would be more creative if our society provided them with more models of successful creativity and deemphasized formal education (Simonton, 1978).

Conclusion

Intelligence was defined by F. Scott Fitzgerald as "the ability to hold two opposed ideas in mind at the same time and still retain the ability to function." Given the disagreements among researchers and the different approaches to studying cognition examined in this chapter, you may be wondering whether you can live up to Fitzgerald's definition of intelligence! Although each theoretical approach to cognitive development is beset by its own particular limitations, each is, at least in part, accurate in its descriptions of children's and adolescents' thought. Assuming an eclectic perspective will permit us to appreciate the theoretical assumptions upon which each approach is predicated and to utilize the pragmatic recommendations that each offers for our interactions with adolescents.

The next chapter will expound upon the ways in which cognitive growth affects adolescents' personalities and Chapter 7 will examine the impact of cognitive abilities on adolescents' academic performance. The data in several later chapters will allude to Piaget's model when presenting other theorists' views on adolescents' political, social, sexual, religious, moral, and vocational development. Similarly, much of the empirical data cited in subsequent chapters is interpreted or disputed in relation to adolescents' IQ scores. For these reasons, clearly understanding the concepts listed for you in this chapter's overview will enhance your ability to critique the data in following chapters with more wisdom and scrutiny.

Questions for Discussion and Review

Basic Concepts and Terminology

Cite specific research studies and statistics to support your answers to each of the following:

1. How do the psychometric, developmental, and information-processing approaches to adolescent cognition differ?
2. Describe each of Piaget's stages of cognitive development by providing specific examples of children's behavior that demonstrate the major advances within each stage.
3. What are the major criticisms leveled against traditional IQ tests?
4. Explain each side of the nature/nurture argument, as it relates to the IQ controversy, by describing the research supporting each perspective.
5. How reliable a measure of intelligence is an adolescent's IQ score?

6. Why must standard error of measurement, validity, chronological age, race, and ability all be considered before interpreting a youngster's IQ score?
7. According to Piaget's theories, how do youngsters advance from one stage of cognitive development to another?
8. According to information-processing theories, how are adolescents' cognitive processes similar to computer processes?
9. In what ways do the functions of the left and right hemispheres of the brain differ?
10. How do males' and females' verbal and mathematical skills differ during childhood and adolescence?
11. How do the problem-solving strategies and memory of adolescents differ from those of younger children?
12. How do creative adolescents tend to differ from their less creative peers?

Questions for Discussion and Debate

1. How would you go about helping young adolescents develop formal operational thinking?
2. What do you consider the major strengths and weaknesses of each approach to the study of adolescent cognition?
3. How do you feel about using IQ tests to measure an individual's intellectual potential?
4. Considering the experts' suggestions for improving IQ tests, how would you determine an adolescent's intelligence?
5. How can we increase adolescents' creativity at home and in school?
6. If given the choice between being extremely creative or extremely intelligent during your adolescence, which would you choose and why?
7. What experiences contributed most to the development or diminishment of your own creativity and intelligence during childhood and adolescence?
8. In regard to an individual's intellectual skills, how would you defend or refute the maxim, "You can't make a silk purse out of a sow's ear"?

REFERENCES

Arbitman-Smith, R., & Haywood, H. Cognitive education for learning disabled adolescents. *Journal of Abnormal Child Psychology,* 1980, *8,* 51–64.

Anastasi, A. *Psychological testing.* New York: Macmillan, 1982.

Baltes, P., Reese, H., & Lipsitt, L. Life-span developmental psychology. *Annual Review of Psychology,* 1980, *31,* 65–110.

Benbow, C., & Stanley, J. Sex differences in mathematical reasoning abilities, *Science,* 1983, *222,* 1029–1031.

Berzonsky, M. Formal reasoning in adolescence: An alternate view. *Adolescence,* 1978, *13,* 280–290.

Bower, G. Mood and memory. *American Psychologist,* 1981, *36,* 129–148.

Brim, O., & Kagan, J. *Continuity and change in human development.* Cambridge, Mass.: Harvard University Press, 1980.

Brown, R., & Kulik, J. Flashbulb memories. *Cognition,* 1977, *5,* 73–99.

Brush, L. *Encouraging girls in mathematics: The problem and the solution.* Cambridge, Mass.: Abt Books, 1980.

Campbell, P. Adolescent intellectual decline. *Adolescence,* 1976, *11,* 629–635.

Carroll, J., & Maxwell, S. Individual differences in cognitive abilities. *Annual Review of Psychology,* 1979, *30,* 603–640.

Cattell, R. Theory of fluid and crystallized intelligence. *Journal of Educational Psychology,* 1963, *54,* 1–22.

Clark, B. *Growing up gifted.* Columbus, Ohio: Merrill, 1979.

Dewolfe, V. High school math preparation and sex differences in quantitative abilities. Unpublished thesis. Seattle: University of Washington, June 1977.

Douglas, J., & Wong, A. Formal operations: Age and sex differences in Chinese and American children. *Child Development,* 1977, *48,* 689–692.

Dove, A. Taking the "Chitling Test." *Newsweek,* July 15, 1968, pp. 51–52.

Dudek, S. Creativity in young children—attitude or ability? *Journal of Creative Behavior,* 1974, *8,* 282–292.

Dulik, E. Adolescent thinking a la Piaget: The formal stage. *Journal of Youth and Adolescence,* 1972, *1,* 281–291.

Eich, J. State-dependent accessibility to retrieval clues in the retention of a categorized list. *Journal of Verbal Learning and Behavior,* 1975, *14,* 408–417.

Eichorn, D. Physiological development. In P. Mussen (ed.), *Carmichael's manual of child psychology, (Vol. 1).* New York: Wiley, 1970 (3d ed.).

Ekstrom, R. *Issues of test bias and validity.* New York: American Psychological Association, September 1979.

Elkind, D. Cognitive development in adolescence. In J. Adams (ed.), *Understanding adolescence.* Boston: Allyn and Bacon, 1968. Pp. 128–158.

Elkind, D. *Children and adolescents: Interpretive essays on Jean Piaget.* New York: Oxford University Press, 1970.

Elkind, D., & Weiner, I. *Development of the child.* New York: Wiley, 1978.

Enright, R., Lapsley, D., & Shukla, D. Adolescent egocentrism in early and late adolescence. *Adolescence,* 1979, *14,* 687–696.

Ernest, J. *Mathematics and sex.* Santa Barbara: University of California Press, 1976.

Fennema, E. Mathematics learning and the sexes: A review. *Journal for Research in Mathematics Education,* 1974, *5,* 126–139.

Feuerstein, R. *The dynamic assessment of retarded performers.* Baltimore, Md.: University Park Press, 1979.

Flavell, J. Stage-related properties of cognitive development. *Cognitive Psychology,* 1971, *2,* 421–453.

Flavell, J. *Cognitive development.* Englewood Cliffs, N.J.: Prentice-Hall, 1977.

Friedrick, D. Developmental analysis of memory capacity and information encoding strategy. *Developmental Psychology,* 1974, *10,* 559–563.

Gardner, H. *Frames of mind: Theory of multiple intelligence.* New York: Basic Books, 1983.

Getzels, J. Problem finding and inventiveness of solutions. *Journal of Creative Behavior,* 1975, *9,* 12–18.

Getzels, J., & Jackson, P. *Creativity and intelligence.* New York: Wiley, 1962.

Guilford, J. *The nature of human intelligence.* New York: McGraw-Hill, 1967.

Guilford, J. Theories of intelligence. In I. B. Wolman (ed.), *Handbook of general psychology.* Englewood Cliffs, N.J.: Prentice-Hall, 1973. Pp. 630–643.

Hobbs, N., & Robinson, S. Adolescent development and public policy. *American Psychologist,* February 1982, *37,* 212–223.

Horn, J. On the myth of intellectual decline in adulthood. *American Psychologist,* 1976, *31,* 701–719.

Horn, J. The rise and fall of human abilities. *Journal of Research and Development in Education,* 1979, *12,* 59–78.

Hunt, J. *Intelligence and experience.* New York: Basic Books, 1961.

Hunt, J. Psychological development: Early experience. *Annual Review of Psychology,* 1979, *30,* 103–143.

Hyde, J. How large are cognitive gender differences? *American Psychologist,* 1981, *36,* 892–901.

Inhelder, B., & Piaget, J. *The growth of logical thinking from childhood through adolescence.* New York: Basic Books, 1958.

Jencks, C., et al. Inequality: *A reassessment of the effect of family and schooling in America.* New York: Basic Books, 1972.

Jensen, A. How much can we boost IQ and scholastic achievement? *Harvard Educational Review,* 1969, *39,* 273–356.

Jensen, A. The differences are real. *Psychology Today,* December 1973, *7,* 80–86.

Jensen, A. *Bias in mental testing.* New York: Free Press, 1980.

Keating, D. Thinking processes in adolescence. In J. Adelson (ed.), *Handbook of adolescent psychology.* New York: Wiley, 1980. Pp. 211–246.

Keating, D., & Bobbitt, B. Differences in cognitive processing components of mental ability. *Child Development,* 1978, *49,* 155–167.

Keating, D., & Clark, L. Development of physical and social reasoning in adolescence. *Developmental Psychology,* 1980, *16,* 23–30.

Khatena, J. *Educational psychology of the gifted.* New York: Wiley, 1982.

Khatena, J., & Torrance, E. *Khatena-Torrance creative perceptions inventory.* Chicago: Stoelting, 1976.

Klahr, D., & Wallace, J. *Cognitive development: An information-processing view.* Hillsdale, N.J.: Erlbaum, 1975.

Kuhn, D., & Brannock, J. Development of the isolation of variables scheme in an experimental and a natural experiment context. *Developmental Psychology,* 1977, *13,* 9–14.

Kuhn, D., Langer, J., Johlber, L., & Haan, N. The development of formal operations in logical and moral judgment. *Genetic Psychology Monograph,* 1977, *95,* 97–188.

Liben, L. Performance of Piagetian spatial tasks as a function of sex, field dependence and training. *Merrill Palmer Quarterly,* 1978, *24,* 97–110.

Loftus, E. *Memory.* Reading, Mass.: Addison-Wesley, 1980.

Maccoby, E., & Jacklin, C. *The psychology of sex differences.* Stanford, Cal.: Stanford University Press, 1974.

McCall, R., Appelbaum, M., & Hogarty, P. Developmental changes in mental performance. *Monographs of the Society for Research in Child Development,* 1973, *38,* serial No. 150.

McCloskey, M. Intuitive physics. *Scientific American,* 1983, *248,* 122–130.

McGee, M. *Human spatial abilities.* New York: Praeger, 1979.

McKinnon, J. The college student and formal operation. In J. Renner (ed.), *Research, teaching and learning with the Piaget model.* Norman: University of Oklahoma Press, 1976.

Mercer, J., & Lewis, J. *System of multicultural pluralistic assessment (SOMPA).* New York: Psychological Corporation, 1978.

Miller, B., & Gerard, D. Family influence on the development of creativity in children. *Family Coordinator,* 1979, *28,* 295–311.

Mortorano, S. A developmental analysis of performance on Piaget's formal operations tasks. *Developmental Psychology,* 1977, *13,* 66–72.

Murray, F., & Armstrong, R. Adult nonconservation of numerical equivalence. *Merrill Palmer Quarterly,* 1978, *24,* 255–263.

Neimark, E. Intellectual development during adolescence. In F. Horowitz (ed.), *Review of child development research (Vol. 4).* Chicago: University of Chicago Press, 1975.

Ornstein, P. (ed.). *Memory development in children.* Hillsdale, N.J.: Erlbaum, 1978.

Parloff, M., Datta, L., Leman, M., & Handlon, J. Personality characteristics which differentiate creative male adolescents and adults. *Journal of Personality,* 1968, *36,* 91–106.

Peterson, A., & Gitelson, I. *Toward understanding sex-related differences in cognitive performance.* New York: Academic Press, 1984.

Peterson, A., & Wittig, M. Sex-related differences in cognitive functioning: An overview. In M. Wittig and A. Peterson (eds.), *Sex-related differences in cognitive functioning: Developmental issues.* New York: Academic Press, 1979.

Piaget, J. Intellectual evolution from adolescence to adulthood. *Human Development,* 1972, *15,* 1–12.

Renner, J., & Stafford, D. The operational levels of secondary school students. In J. Renner (ed.), *Research, teaching and learning with the Piaget model.* Norman: University of Oklahoma Press, 1976.

Richards, R. A comparison of selected Guilford and Wallach/Kogan creativity thinking tests in conjunction with measure of intelligence. *Journal of Creative Behavior,* 1976, *10,* 141–164.

Rosenbaum, J. *Making inequality: The hidden curriculum of high school tracking.* New York: Wiley, 1976.

Samuda, R. *Psychological testing of American minorities.* New York: Dodd, Mead, 1975.

Scarr, S., & Saltzman, L. Genetics and intelligence. In R. Sternberg (ed.), *Handbook of human intelligence.* New York: Cambridge University Press, 1982. Pp. 792–896.

Scarr, S., Scarf, E., & Weinber, R. Perceived and actual similarities in biological and adoptive families. *Behavior Genetics,* 1980, *10,* 145–158.

Schaie, K. Transactions in gerontology—from lab to life. *American Psychologist,* 1974, *29,* 802–807.

Schweinhart, L., & Weikart, D. *Young children grow up: The effects of the Perry preschool program on youths through age 15.* High Scope Educational Research Foundation, 1980, *7,* #4.

Siegler, R., Liebert, D., & Liebert, R. Inhelder and Piaget's pendulum problem: Teaching preadolescents to act as scientists. *Developmental Psychology,* 1973, *9,* 97–101.

Siegler, R., & Richards, D. The development of intelligence. In R. Sternberg (ed.), *Handbook of human intelligence.* New York: Cambridge University Press, 1982. Pp. 493–559.

Sigel, I., & Cocking, R. *Cognitive development from childhood to adolescence: A constructivist perspective.* New York: Holt, Rinehart and Winston, 1977.

Simmons, R., Rosenberg, R., & Rosenberg, M. Disturbance in the self-image at adolescence. *American Sociological Review,* 1973, *38,* 553–568.

Simonton, D. The eminent genius in history. *Gifted Child Quarterly,* 1978, *22,* 187–195.

Snow, R. Education and intelligence. In R. Sternberg (ed.), *Handbook of human intelligence.* New York: Cambridge University Press. 1982. Pp. 493–559.

Sowell, T. New light on IQ. *New York Times,* March *27,* 1977, p. 23.

Steinberg, L., et al. Early work experience: A partial antidote for adolescent egocentrism. *Journal of Youth and Adolescence,* 1982, *10,* 141–158.

Sternberg, R., & Powell, J. Theories of intelligence. In R. Sternberg (ed.), *Handbook of human intelligence.* New York: Cambridge University Press, 1982. Pp. 975–1005.

Terman, L., & Merrill, M. *Stanford-Binet Intelligence Scale.* Boston: Houghton Mifflin, 1960.

Terman, L., & Merrill, M. *Stanford-Binet Intelligence Scale: Manual for the third revision.* Boston: Houghton Mifflin, 1973.

Tobias, S. *Overcoming math anxiety.* New York: Norton, 1978.

Torrance, P. *Torrance tests of creative thinking.* Princeton, N.J.: Personnel Press, 1966.

Torrance P. Career patterns and peak creative achievements of creative high school students twelve years later. The *Gifted Child Quarterly,* 1972, *16,* 78–88.

Wallach, M., & Kogan, N. *Modes of thinking in young children.* New York: Holt, Rinehart and Winston, 1965.

Wechsler, D. *Wechsler Intelligence Scale for Children.* New York: The Psychological Corporation, 1952.

Wechsler, D. Intelligence defined and undefined. *American Psychologist* 1975, *30,* 135–139.

Welsh, G. Personality correlates of intelligence and creativity in gifted adolescents. In J. Stanley, W. George, and C. Solano (eds.), *The gifted and the creative.* Baltimore, Md.: Johns Hopkins University Press, 1977.

Whimbey, A., & Whimbey, L. *Intelligence can be taught.* New York: Dutton, 1975.

Williams, R. The silent mugging of the black community. *Psychology Today,* May 1974, *12,* 32–42.

Williams, R. The BITCH 100: A culture-specific test. *Journal of Afro-American Issues,* 1975, *3,* 103–116.

Witt, S., & Sunningham, W. Family configuration and fluid crystallized intelligence. *Adolescence,* 1980, *15,* 105–121.

Wolf, F., & Larsen, G. On why adolescents' formal operators may not be creative thinkers. *Adolescence,* 1981, *16,* 345–348.

Zajonc, R., & Markus, G. Birth order and intellectual development, *Psychological Review,* 1975, *82,* 74–88.

Zigler, E., & Valentine, J. (eds.). *Project Head Start: A legacy of the war on poverty.* New York: Free Press, 1979.

Chapter Outline

Traditional Freudian Theories of Personality
The Personality's Structure
Psychosexual Stages of Development
Applications to Adolescents
Criticisms of Psychoanalytic Theories
Neo-Freudian Theories of Personality
Erikson's Theory of Psychosocial Development
Marcia's Theory of Identity Statuses
Loevinger's Theory of Ego Stages
Individuation during Adolescence
Criticisms of Neo-Freudian Theories
Cognitive Stage Theories of Personality
Hypocrisy and Idealism
Egocentrism
Pseudostupidity
Trait Theories of Personality
Assessing Personality Traits
Applications to Adolescents
Criticisms of Trait Theories
Phenomenological Theories of Personality
The Theories of Rogers and Maslow
Field Theories
Measuring Adolescents' Self-Concepts
Applications to Adolescents
The Foundations of Adolescents' Self-Esteem
Criticisms of Phenomenological Theories
Behavioristic Theories of Personality
Traditional Behavioral Theories
Social Learning Theories
Applications to Adolescents
Criticisms of Behavioristic Theories
Conclusion

Goals and Objectives

This chapter is designed to enable you to:

- *Describe five different theoretical approaches for studying the adolescent's personality*
- *Review the different methods for assessing adolescents' personalities and evaluate the techniques for modifying adolescents' behavior*
- *Consider the advantages and disadvantages of each theoretical approach to the study of personality*
- *Examine the meanings of "self," "identity," "personality," and "self-concept"*
- *Explore the new aspects of personality that appear during adolescence*

Concepts and Terminology

id, ego, and superego — *Eros and Thanatos*
pleasure principle — *reality principle*
Oedipal complex — *Electra complex*
neo-Freudians — *ego psychologists*
Rorschach test — *TAT*
MMPI — *projective techniques*
locus of control — *cognitive dissonance*
imaginary audience — *personal fable*
primary and secondary reinforcers
classical conditioning — *attribution theories*
desensitization — *behavior modification*
extinction — *psychosexual stages*
psychosocial stages — *defense mechanisms*
homeostasis — *operant conditioning*
individuation — *egocentrism*
pseudostupidity — *personal construct theory*
Rogerian counseling — *self-actualization*
Q-sort technique — *client-centered therapy*
semantic differential — *encounter-group therapy*
role playing — *Gestalt psychology*
contingency management — *Maslow's hierarchy of needs*
looking-glass self — *fixated*
negative identity — *identity status*
free association — *observational learning*
generativity — *contracting*
modeling — *libido*
oral stage — *repression*
anal stage — *denial*
anal aggressive — *regression*
anal retentive — *reaction formation*
phallic stage — *projection*
latency stage — *displacement*
genital stage — *rationalization*
humanistic psychology — *field theory*
life space

4 Adolescent Identity and Personality

As Chapter 3 has pointed out, adolescent cognition can be approached from a developmental, an information-processing, or a psychometric perspective. Similarly, researchers, who have committed themselves to the study of human personality have aligned themselves with specific theoretical viewpoints: traditional Freudian theories, neo-Freudian theories, developmental theories, behavioristic theories, phenomenological theories, or trait theories. Each theoretical perspective offers its own unique conceptualizations of personality, and each is beset by its own particular limitations. Moreover, the empirical evidence supporting the different views is often too scanty or too contradictory to justify excluding any one model and wholeheartedly endorsing another. As this chapter will demonstrate, each theoretical perspective expands our understanding of adolescence, as much by the unanswered questions it provokes as by the empirical studies it can muster on its behalf.

Given the current state of uncertainty regarding one theory's superiority over another, we might well ask ourselves: Why waste our time examining these theories when we could be studying more practical information, such as how to prevent adolescents from abusing drugs or how to prevent parents from sexually abusing their adolescent children?

One reason for studying the various personality theories is that, despite their disagreements and their limitations, each addresses two essential questions of relevance to anyone interested in adolescence: Why do different people behave differently when confronted with the same situation? What accounts for the relative consistency of a person's behavior from one situation to another? Whichever theoretical model practitioners or researchers endorse, these two essential questions generate innumerable recommendations and controversies in regard to our interactions with adolescents.

For example, although wading through the descriptions of such Freudian concepts as the id, the ego, the superego, and individuation may at first seem a wasteful and tortuous exercise, an understanding of these theoretical concepts is essential in order to appreciate more apparently relevant questions, such as: Are an adolescent's behavior and attitudes primarily determined by psychological forces from within or by environmental influences? Does it really matter whether adolescents resolve certain issues related to their parents in terms of their happiness during their adult lives?

Likewise, without first understanding the theoretical concepts and controversies related to behaviorism and social learning theory, we are handicapped in regard to such practical questions as: By permitting adolescents to watch movies and television programs whose content is very sexual and violent, are we contributing to their sexual or violent conduct? Should we attempt to cure a nervous adolescent's stuttering by means of a behavior-modification program, or will the adolescent's nervousness then be manifest in some other form? Why might it be more effective to use sports heroes in an advertising campaign against adolescent smoking than to base the campaign on warnings from the Surgeon General?

A second reason for examining the various theories of personality is that they are inseparable from most issues related to adolescent development. As the remaining chapters in this text will demonstrate, the disputes among personality theorists are intricately related to disputes regarding such contemporary topics as adolescents' sexual behavior, moral development, peer relations, relationships with parents and siblings, and drug abuse.

One hypothetical illustration of the relationship between theories of personality and issues of immediate social interest is drug abuse. Since there is little disagreement over the fact that both society and adolescents would benefit from less abuse of drugs, a question being argued by personality theorists and practitioners is: How should we invest the taxpayers' money in order to most effectively reduce drug abuse? From the perspective of behavioristic and social learning theories of personality, we might be best advised to invest the taxpayers' money in programs that reinforce adolescents for appropriate behavior, punish them for inappropriate behavior, and provide role models who will influence their conduct. In contrast, the phenomenological theorists might urge us to combat drug abuse through programs aimed at raising adolescents' self-esteem. Meanwhile, the cognitive stage theorists might argue that we should design programs aimed primarily at altering adolescents' "personal fable," "imaginary audience," and "egocentricity." Finally, the Freudians could contend that the taxpayers' money will be wasted unless programs are designed to resolve the unconscious motives and psychodynamic conflicts that underlie an adolescent's drug abuse.

Although the preceding is an oversimplification of the possible applications of various theories of personality, it nonetheless serves to underscore the fact that personality theories have a practical relevance to many issues regarding adolescents in our society. This chapter provides further examples of the ways in which the concepts are presently being applied to adolescents within the context of each theoretical perspective. Not to be misconstrued as exhaustive or detailed accounts of therapies or strategies emanating from the theoretical viewpoint, these examples are intended to underscore the relationship between theoretical concepts and their practical applications to adolescents.

TRADITIONAL FREUDIAN THEORIES OF PERSONALITY

Indisputably, the most influential theorist in the field of personality is Sigmund Freud (1856–1939), whose work has provided the basis around which most controversies regarding adolescent and adult development revolve (Adelson & Doehrman 1980; Mischel 1981). To date, some of the most comprehensive explanations of how the psychoanalytic approach applies to adolescents have been written by Freud's daughter, Anna. Despite the fact that both Anna Freud and contemporary adolescent psychologists like Joseph Adelson admit that psychoanalytic theorists have devoted too little attention to the period of adolescence, classical Freudian theories continue to exert a significant influence over our views of the adolescent personality (Adelson & Doehrman, 1980; A. Freud, 1946, 1977).

The Personality's Structure

According to the Freudian perspective, the adolescent's personality is determined by interactions among the id, the ego, and the superego. Oversimplifications of Freudian theories too often result in anthropomorphizing these concepts into agents with independent wills who wage war against one another. From such personifications, we might be led to envision the rational, self-controlled ego as some sort of entity that vigilantly tries to exert its control over both the irrational, impulsive id and the harsh, moralistic superego. In fact, however, Freudians use these terms to refer to motivational forces underlying an individual's behavior, not to suggest three separate entities or any type of physical structure residing somewhere within the brain.

As conceived by Freudians, the **id** (which means "it" in German) represents our unconscious biological drives and instincts. The id supplies the ego and superego with the psychic energy, referred to as the *libido*, that propels the entire personality throughout life. The id's two main instincts are *Eros* (Greek for "love") and *Thanatos* (Greek for "death"). Eros motivates us to fulfill our basic survival needs, such as our desires for food and sex, and is also responsible for artistic and productive work. In contrast, Thanatos is the motivating force that underlies our aggressive and self-destructive behavior.

Since Freudians presume that the id operates on the basis of the *pleasure principle*, the **ego** is necessary to counter the id's impulses with the *reality principle.* The ego (meaning "I" in German) is the part of the personality that a person consciously acknowledges as the "self." Using memory, logic, preplanning, education, discrimination, and judgment, the ego tries to satisfy the id's needs without jeopardizing the individual. For example, a girl's sexual impulses may be motivating her to have sex spontaneously with her boyfriend, although neither of them is protected by a contraceptive. Simultaneously her ego may be intervening with the realistic appraisal that gratifying her immediate need under the present circumstances could have very costly consequences.

The **superego** (meaning "over the I" in German) refers to the part of the personality that imposes society's moral codes—in other words, the "conscience." Like the id, the superego ignores certain objective realities and functions on the basis of values and abstract moral ideals instilled by society—above all, by the individual's parents. For instance, although the adolescent girl may have successfully applied the ego's reality principle by taking contraceptive precautions, her superego may still control her sexual behavior by warning her not to go any further with her boyfriend, because this would be against the principles of her church and her parents.

Within the Freudian context, most human behavior is an attempt to reduce anxieties created by the contradictory needs of the id, ego, and superego. Our behavior is an attempt to maintain and to restore *homeostasis*—a relaxed condition without conflict among id, ego, and superego. When anxiety becomes so acute that there is no readily available way to reduce it, the individual may resort to defense mechanisms. **Defense mechanisms** are strategies by which a person attempts to reduce his or her anxiety by denying or distorting reality. The ways in which adolescents might employ defense mechanisms are explained in Box 4.1.

4.1 A Closer Look

Adolescents' Defense Mechanisms

Repression is a defense mechanism that involves forgetting unpleasant incidents or information by pushing them into the recesses of the unconscious. For example, an adolescent boy may be unable to cope with the fact that he was sexually molested as a child. Consequently, he may repress these memories and be unable to recall the sexual incidents. Youngsters may also temporarily repress information, such as the name of a teacher they dislike.

Denial is refusing to believe that an event is true. A young girl may pretend that her hostile, unloving father is actually friendly and supportive, or a boy whose mother dies can refuse to believe she is dead for months following the funeral. Daydreaming is sometimes a form of denying an unpleasant circumstance from which the individual cannot escape.

Regression is a return to an earlier stage of development in response to a threatening or frustrating situation. When adolescents are failing to illicit the response they want from other people, they may regress to more infantile behavior that was once effective in controlling other people's reactions. When a calm, rational discussion is failing to change her mother's opinion, a daughter may throw a temper tantrum like a 3-year-old child. According to contemporary theorist Peter Blos, occasional regression is a normal part of developing new coping strategies during adolescence.

Reaction formation is the process of replacing an anxiety-producing feeling or impulse with its opposite feeling or impulse. Generally, the stronger the impulse to behave in ways that society designates as inappropriate, the stronger the reaction formation. For instance, an extremely religious girl, who vehemently crusades against all literature, movies, or jokes with sexual overtones, may be concealing her genuine

Psychosexual Stages of Development

According to Freudian perspectives, an individual's personality is primarily determined by the ways in which he or she resolves the psychological conflicts encountered during various *psychosexual stages* of childhood and adolescence. It is further presumed that in cases where these conflicts are not resolved during childhood or adolescence, the individual may either become *fixated* on the unresolved issues or ignore them altogether—either option contributing to problems in the adult personality. As demonstrated in Chapters 1 and 3, the transitions between these psychosexual stages are presumed to occur at approximately the same age in our lives as the transitions between Piaget's stages of cognitive development, Erikson's stages of ego development, and Hall's stages of biological development. (You may want to review Table 1.2 to refresh your memory on the chronological similarities of these four stage theories.)

The *oral stage*, occurring during the first year of life, is so named because desire to look at or read these materials. Or a boy who hates his younger sister may shower her with gifts and affection, since society would condemn him for expressing his hatred.

Projection is attributing one's own feelings to other people, rather than claiming responsibility for these impulses or sentiments. When using this defense mechanism, adolescents reject or ignore the objective evidence in favor of their own projected wishes. According to Freudian psychologists, a boy who accuses his classmates of cheating without any evidence to support his accusation, when in fact he is wanting to cheat, is projecting his dishonest desires onto others.

Displacement is similar to projection in that the adolescent attributes feelings to the wrong source. A youngster who accurately recognizes his or her feelings may inaccurately identify the source from which these feelings emanate. Hence, a boy who has been bawled out by his track coach comes home and starts yelling at his younger brother for "messing with" his stereo. Because the older brother cannot express his anger or defend himself to the coach, he displaces his frustration by getting angry at his defenseless younger brother.

Rationalization is the act of creating reasons that are not indicative of true motives in order to justify behavior. According to the Freudian perspective, rationalizing is a device by which the superego or conscience is overridden in order to satisfy some of an individual's less-than-admirable desires. The boy who breaks up with his girlfriend against her protestations, because he is bored with her and wants to date the cute new girl on his block, is rationalizing if he tells himself "it's for my ex-girlfriend's own good, since she shouldn't be getting tied down to just one boy anyway."

the child's mouth is presumed to be the primary source of pleasure. During this stage the personality is immature, dependent, and in need of nurturance. Consequently, weaning is the crucial conflict to be resolved at this stage. According to Freudians, adolescents who are fixated at the oral stage are likely to develop overly dependent relationships and to expect people to "mother" them.

During the second and third years of life, a child's libido supposedly shifts from the oral to the anal region. In this *anal stage* the child is expected to develop self-control, particularly with respect to bowel and bladder functions. From the Freudian perspective, toilet training becomes a metaphorical act of society's triumph over the child's undisciplined self. Consequently, if a child willingly becomes toilet trained, he or she has supposedly developed the basis for future self-control. In contrast, children who try to counterattack society's wishes by protesting against toilet training may develop an anal aggressive personality as they age. When frustrated, people with anal aggressive personalities resort to anger or hostility. Similarly, children who refuse to urinate or defecate are presumed to develop anal retentive personalities, characterized by stinginess and stubbornness.

During the fourth and fifth years of life, most children do become interested in exploring their genitals, masturbating, and asking sexual questions. According to Freudian views, such behavior is indicative of the *phallic stage,* during which the child's essential conflict is between the unconscious sexual desires toward the opposite-sexed parent and jealousies directed toward the same-sexed parent. This dilemma, referred to as the **Oedipus complex** in relation to the mother-son relationship, causes the son unconsciously to perceive his father as a rival for his mother's sexual attentions. Secretly harboring the jealous desire to eliminate his father, the son fears his father's retaliation—specifically, castration. Once the son represses his incestuous desires by identifying with his father and thereby vicariously possessing his mother by becoming "just like Daddy," the Oedipus complex is presumably resolved.

In regard to the father-daughter relationship, Freudians contend that, like sons, daughters must resolve their incestuous desires for their fathers by overcoming their **Electra complex.** Like sons, daughters first fall in love with their mothers. Upset, however, by her discovery that she lacks a penis, the daughter assumes she must have been castrated and unconsciously blames her mother. Simultaneously, the daughter harbors sexual desires for her father and jealousy toward her mother as a supposed sexual rival. According to Sigmund Freud, once the daughter unconsciously comes to terms with the fact that her incestuous desires cannot be fulfilled, she represses them by identifying with her mother. In disagreement with her father's theory on this point, Anna Freud argues that daughters identify with their mothers out of fear of losing their love.

The resolution of the Electra complex was problematic for Freud. Although he contended that its resolution does not occur until later in a girl's life, he also believed it is never completely resolved. As we will see later in this chapter and in Chapter 5, Freudian theories share a limitation in common with many other theories of personality in that they fail to account as well for female development as for male development. Parenthetically, in case you have now been provoked to wonder why you do not remember your own sexual desires for your opposite-sexed parent, Freudians contend that we suppress our memories of the Oedipus or Electra complex as part of resolving the conflict.

Once beyond the phallic stage, children enter the *latency stage,* which spans the years from 6 to 11. In the Freudian context, this is the stage for strenghening one's identifications with the same-sexed parent through interacting almost exclusively with members of one's own sex. Neither sex has much interest in sexual issues during this stage, and the superego supposedly exerts increasing influence over the child's behavior.

Freudians perceive adolescence as the final phase of psychosexual development, the *genital stage.* The individual's libido is once again focused on the genital area as during the phallic stage. The emphasis during adolescence, however, is on heterosexual pleasure rather than on self-stimulation. Furthermore, the superego becomes somewhat more flexible, as adolescents examine and modify the rules and mores that they learned as children. As we shall see later in this chapter, this process—called individuation—is an essential component of adolescence, according to Freudian and neo-Freudian theories. Freudians maintain that adolescents who successfully resolve the conflicts associated with each psychosexual stage can develop adult personalities that are free of neuroses.

Applications to Adolescents

As we have seen in the preceding section, Freudian theories can be applied in explaining the psychological conflicts that underlie young children's behavior. For example, the clutching, adoring behavior of a 5-year-old daughter toward her father and her snippy, aggressive tone of voice when interacting with her mother could be interpreted as evidence of her Electra complex. As mentioned earlier in this chapter, Freudian theories have most often been applied to periods of development before adolescence. Nevertheless, the following illustrations will serve to demonstrate the continued popularity of Freudian principles among psychoanalytically oriented therapists working with adolescents.

In regard to explaining an adolescent's behavior with his or her parents, the influential contemporary Freudian scholar, Peter Blos, offers a modification of classical psychoanalytic theories (Blos, 1979). According to Blos, the Oedipal and Electra conflicts recur during early and middle adolescence, and their resolution occurs in several phases throughout adolescence. For example, Blos perceives the young adolescent's withdrawal from family activities as a strategy for coping with his or her unconscious sexual desires toward the opposite-sexed parent. Blos contends that as the superego creates stronger barriers against the child's incestuous urges, the older adolescent "falls out of love" with the opposite-sexed parent. During this period of abandoning their incestuous desires, adolescents may develop temporary crushes on other adults like movie stars or teachers. In the classical psychoanalytic tradition, Blos believes that most children successfully transfer their sexual desires from adults to peers by the end of adolescence. Other applications of Blos's theories will be described in subsequent chapters in regard to adolescents' relationships with their families and friends.

Beyond the realm of the family, Freudian principles are often applied by therapists in their work with adolescents. Guided by classical Freudian concepts, psychotherapists try to uncover an adolescent client's unconscious motives and conflicts, which are presumed to be frequently disguised by the youngster's defense mechanisms (review Box 4.1). Within the Freudian context, the therapist's task is to help the adolescent achieve insights into the motives underlying his or her behavior and attitudes. Only when such insights have been achieved is the young person presumed capable of permanently changing his or her behavior. In contrast to social learning and behavioral theories of personality, psychoanalytic counseling is predicated on the assumption that merely modifying the adolescent's problematic behavior will result in other inappropriate acts, since the underlying motives are still unresolved. For instance, Freudian therapists presume that if a behavioral psychologist helps an adolescent overcome his stuttering solely through behavior-modification strategies, the boy may then develop a facial tick, since the boy will have failed to gain an understanding of the unconscious motives that underlay the stuttering.

According to the Freudian perspective, a unified, systematic view of an adolescent's behavior can be attained through effective psychotherapy and the administration of appropriate tests. Because psychodynamic theories assume that an individual's unconscious motives and conflicts are manifested indirectly rather than through overt behavior, **projective techniques** are frequently employed. These techniques are administered and interpreted by therapists whose own subjective judgments of their clients will be combined with the results of the projective strategies in order to identify the unconscious motives responsible for the adolescent's conduct.

Two of the most popular projective tests are the Rorschach and the Thematic Apperception Test. The **Rorschach** consists of a series of complex inkblots similar to the one illustrated in Figure 4.1. As the subject explains what each inkblot resembles, the examiner poses questions and interprets the responses. On the basis of the information gleaned in this manner, the therapist arrives at his or her judgment of the adolescent's unconscious motives and personality.

In a similar fashion, the **Thematic Apperception Test (TAT)** is administered by showing adolescents a series of pictures about which they are then asked to create a story. Subjects are told to create as dramatic and as interesting a story as they can, including an explanation of what preceded the event in the picture, what the characters feel, and what the outcome of the pictured event will be. On the basis of the adolescent's responses, the examiner diagnoses specified aspects of the youngster's personality. As with the Rorschach, the TAT is presumed to reflect the youngsters' own unconscious motives and unresolved conflicts without interference from defense mechanisms.

In addition, two other projective strategies were popularized by Freud—dream analysis and free association. **Free association** is the process whereby the therapist presents a list of words or phrases and interprets the youngster's answers in accord with Freudian assumptions about the personality. For example, an adolescent girl might complete the phrase "my mother" by saying, "My

Figure 4.1

An inkblot of the type employed in the Rorschach technique

What do you see in this configuration? From the psychoanalytic perspective how might your response be interpreted as a reflection of your personality?

mother reminds me of a vampire I saw once in a movie.'' Upon further questioning from the therapist, she might add, ''Just like the vampire, she sneaks up on you, making you believe she's your friend until she sucks the life out of you.'' From a Freudian perspective, hostile responses of this sort might be interpreted as manifestations of an unresolved Electra complex.

The use of projective techniques and the continued existence of psychoanalytic counseling testify to the fact that applications of Freudian theories of personality still maintain their importance in the realm of adolescent psychology. The remaining chapters of this book will introduce you to many contemporary theorists like Peter Blos whose research on adolescence is predicated on Freudian notions of personality development.

Criticisms of Psychoanalytic Theories

Regardless of what the ultimate judgments of Freud's hypotheses regarding the role of adolescence in personality development prove to be, many of his assertions have been challenged. To begin with, research has consistently failed to uphold the Freudian hypothesis that adolescence is a period of considerable turmoil and tension between parents and children (Adelson, 1980; Douvan & Adelson, 1966; Josselson, 1980; Marcia, 1980; Offer & Offer, 1975; Offer, Ostrov, & Howard, 1981). Since this research will be discussed in detail in Chapters 8 and 9, suffice it to say at this point that the comments of Ruth Josselson represent the consensus among even those scholars who are psychoanalytically oriented:

> Identity is a result of minute, seemingly inconsequential choices: whom one chooses for friends, what school one attends, what courses one takes, what one reads or does not read, whether one learns to play tennis or fly airplanes, whether one takes drugs or robs a store. This ''turmoil'' theory of ego development was so widespread that it misled a generation of adolescent researchers (Josselson, 1980, p. 202).

Another criticism leveled against traditional Freudian theories is their inaccuracy and incompleteness in regard to female development. Such criticisms are by no means recent, as evidenced by the fact that in the 1920s the renowned psychoanalyst Karen Horney was criticizing many Freudian hypotheses about females (Homme, 1976). According to neo-Freudian critics like Karen Horney, the traditional psychoanalytic model fails to consider the fact that our society, as well as Freud's, accords greater status, privileges, and power to males. Therefore, the female tendency to develop nurturant, dependent personalities, which are often not individuated from other people during adolescence, is a response to societal influences, rather than an outgrowth of psychosexual phenomena such as ''penis envy'' (Josselson, 1980; Muslin, 1979; Spruill, 1979). From this perspective, both males' and females' personalities are more powerfully affected by societal influences than classical Freudian theories acknowledge.

Moreover, the psychoanalytic approach is criticized for its subjectivity and for the lack of empirical data in support of its hypotheses (Adelson & Doehrman, 1980; Mischel, 1981). According to critics, projective techniques and personal judgments based on the psychotherapist's sessions with the client are too sub-

jective for a reliable appraisal of an individual's personality or for an appraisal of the motives underlying his or her behavior. In the absence of empirical data to substantiate abstract concepts such as fixation or the Electra complex, Freudian theories are also criticized for their reliance on untestable hypotheses. For example, what behavior would allow us to conclude with some assurance that a particular adolescent is fixated at the anal stage? Or what evidence do we look for to substantiate the hypothesis that an adolescent girl has finally resolved her Electra complex?

In regard to the criticism that Freudians incorrectly ascribe psychosexual motives to all behavior, one is reminded of the story of the 5-year-old who asks her well-educated mother, "Mommy, where did I come from?" Having long prepared herself for the sexual questions and jealous, incestuous feelings that she has been forewarned accompany a 5-year-old's Oedipal stage, the mother recounts the stories of conception and birth in great detail, trying simultaneously to take account of her child's Oedipal feelings. In exasperation, her impatient daughter finally interrupts, "No, Mommy! Susie told me she's from New York and I want to know where I come from."

In addition, it has been argued that psychoanalytic therapies have generally failed to demonstrate their effectiveness and their practicality. According to such experts in the field of personality research as Walter Mischel, most of the extant research fails to support traditional psychotherapy (Mischel, 1981). Furthermore, given the financial cost and time required for psychoanalytic therapy, the method is restricted to a very small, select group in our society. Within the psychoanalytic context, clients must work with a psychotherapist both to rationally recognize their unconscious motives and to emotionally accept these insights in a way that extends beyond an abstract, rational understanding. In contrast, intervention strategies emanating from other theories of personality require far less intensive forms of therapy and have been successfully employed in settings like high schools and half-way homes for delinquents, where large groups of adolescents can benefit.

Finally, but perhaps most important from the standpoint of the methodological problems associated with research on adolescence, almost all Freudian theories are predicated upon therapists' individual judgments based on psychotherapy with upper-middle-class, white, adult males, many of whom have voluntarily sought counseling (Adelson & Doehrman, 1980). In terms of clients' socioeconomic status, race, gender, age, and self-selection, the absence of random sampling remains one of the most serious challenges to psychoanalytic hypotheses. As discussed in Chapter 1, without data derived from random samples, generalizing theories to the adolescent population is unwarranted.

NEO-FREUDIAN THEORIES OF PERSONALITY

Although still within the Freudian tradition, a number of psychoanalytic theorists referred to as **neo-Freudians** have modified certain aspects of Freud's original theories. While endorsing Freud's basic principles, neo-Freudians emphasize the importance of environmental factors in affecting adults' and adolescents' personalities. In this regard, neo-Freudians are less likely than classical Freudians to emphasize the overriding importance of early childhood experiences or to perceive adolescence as the final stage of personality development. Rather than perceiving the personality as unalterably determined by the psychosexual conflicts of childhood, neo-Freudians perceive the development of the personality as a lifelong process of which adolescence is a significant phase. In regard to their impact on adolescent psychology, two of the most notable neo-Freudians, whose theories will be examined more thoroughly in subsequent chapters, are Erik Erikson and James Marcia.

Erikson's Theory of Psychosocial Development

Like Freud, Erik Erikson's theories are predicated on the hypothesis that individuals pass through clearly delineated stages in which specific types of conflicts are to be resolved. Also in accord with Freud's model, Erikson contends that the way in which children and adolescents resolve these conflicts will influence their adult personalities. Erikson departs, however, from the classical Freudian model that emphasizes early childhood experiences, in that he views personality as developing throughout the life-span, with adolescence being a particularly decisive period for forming an identity.

As Table 4.1 illustrates, Erikson's eight *psychosocial stages* can be compared with Freud's psychosexual and Piaget's cognitive stages (Erikson, 1968). During the first year of life the child's major task is learning to trust other people and developing a sense of security. According to Erikson, trust enables the child to feel secure enough to explore the environment and to feel comfortable with the unfamiliar. Once having achieved this trust, children need to establish a sense of autonomy, which, in combination with the development of self-control, will enhance their independence.

Erikson maintains that between the ages of 3 and 5, children enter the stage of "initiative versus guilt," which parallels Freud's Oedipal stage in several respects. While in this stage, children must overcome their feelings of rivalry for their mother's attention by assuming the initiative in establishing relationships with their peers. Moreover, children must overcome the feelings of guilt and shame that often accompany the frustration and incompetence encountered in new situations and in peer interactions.

According to Erikson, at about the age when children start school, they enter the stage of "industry versus inferiority." Wanting to be accepted by their peers, children between the ages of 6 and 12 are motivated to acquire new skills in order to overcome their feelings of inferiority and to gain peer status. Although mastering new skills helps diminish feelings of inferiority, children must nonetheless also learn to appraise their strengths and weaknesses more realistically and to accept their own limitations.

Table 4.1

Stages of Personality Development

	Psychoanalytic	*Neo-Freudian*	*Cognitive Developmental*	
	Freud	*Erikson*	*Piaget*	*Loevinger*
Birth–1 year	Oral	Trust versus mistrust	Sensorimotor	Presocial
1–3 years	Anal	Autonomy versus shame	Preoperational	Impulsive
3–5 years	Oedipal	Initiative versus guilt	Preoperational	Self-Protective
5–puberty	Latency	Industry versus inferiority	Concrete operations	Conformist
Puberty	Genital	Identity versus confusion	Formal operations	Conscientious
Adulthood		Intimacy versus isolation	Formal operations	Integrated wholeness
		Generativity versus stagnation		
		Integrity versus despair		

Although these first four psychosocial stages are completed before adolescence, Erikson contends that the adolescent's personality is, nevertheless, influenced by these childhood stages. For example, adolescents who fail to establish a sense of trust during the first psychosocial stage of early childhood may continue to exhibit distrusting attitudes toward people. Moreover, adolescents who never resolved the conflict of "trust versus mistrust" as young children will feel too insecure and dependent upon other people's approval to develop an autonomous personality—a task that Erikson perceives as crucial to adolescent development. Similarly, individuals who fail to develop a sense of initiative during their childhood years may lack the confidence and venturesome spirit necessary to experiment with different identities or to become individuated from other people during adolescence.

According to Erikson, adolescence is the stage of "identity versus role diffusion." Ideally, adolescence should be a period reserved for experimentation with various identities and ideologies—a period during which society encourages the young to experiment before committing themselves to an identity for the future.

Like Havighurst, whose model of adolescent development was described in Chapter 1, Erikson perceives adolescence as a period for acquiring a variety of new developmental skills. (Refer to Box 1.1 for a review of Havighurst's model.) Among these new skills is the development of a more sophisticated, realistic perspective on time. A primary task of adolescence is to overcome "time diffusion," which is the childish notion that one has "all the time in the world" or that one can "just let time take care of things." Erikson argues that young people must come to realize that time is limited and that society expects them to adopt an identity by the end of adolescence.

Erikson's model also supports Havighurst's assertions that two of the primary tasks of adolescence are the development of a vocational identity and the adoption of the masculine or feminine sex role. In creating a vocational identity, adolescents must learn to endorse the "work ethic" in order to enhance their future vocational success in our society. Furthermore, both males and females must resolve their sexual identity crises by examining society's sex roles and adopting appropriate identities of their own. Since this particular aspect of Erikson's model has been the focus of much controversy in recent years, it will be discussed in detail in Chapter 5 in relation to the differences between male and female development (McGuire, et al., 1978). Suffice it to say at this point that Erikson predicates his theories on two questionable assumptions: First, that adolescent males and females must develop a vocational and sexual identity before they can establish intimate relationships as young adults: Second, that males and females differ psychologically in accord with certain physiologically determined differences between the sexes.

In accord with traditional Freudian theories of forming an ego that is independent of one's parents and other people, Erikson believes adolescents should eventually commit themselves to their own values and beliefs. In the midst of a society rife with ideological conflicts and diversity, adolescents will often find the search for their own values a difficult task. As Chapter 12 will illustrate, the difficulty of formulating one's own ideologies makes some young people vulnerable to the influence of authority figures, like gurus and other religious leaders, whose ideologies entice seekers of clear-cut values and answers to complex philosophical issues. Erikson points out that some young people, unfortunately, assume *negative identities* that involve delinquent or antisocial activities as part of their adolescent experimentation with various roles.

Finally, Erikson states that only when individuals have developed identities are they capable of establishing truly intimate relationships with other people. Since Erikson considers adolescence the appropriate time for forming an identity, he perceives "intimacy versus isolation" as the young adult's stage for selecting a mate and establishing close friendships with members of both sexes.

In the context of Erikson's model, older adults' personalities are shaped by the way they come to terms with *generativity*—guiding the younger generation and leaving something of value behind in life. An individual who has failed to master the conflicts in each of life's eight psychosocial stages will experience feelings of despair in these later years of adult life. Erikson's hope is that we develop "integrity" during later life, as a consequence of our having successfully resolved the crises in each of our earlier psychosocial stages.

Marcia's Theory of Identity Statuses

Elaborating on Erikson's model, James Marcia describes four different types of identities that adolescents may adopt: identity diffusion, foreclosure, moratorium, and identity achievement. Marcia refers to each of these options as an **identity status** (Bourne, 1978; Marcia, 1980).

According to Marcia, young people with **diffused identities** have not yet chosen any vocational or ideological direction, even though they may have experimented with various roles and ideologies. For example, a male with a diffused identity might say he has "no idea what to do after graduation," or "one political view is just about as good as any other, I guess." Some research suggests that identity-diffused youngsters frequently resort to defense mechanisms as ways of coping with the anxieties associated with not having developed an identity. From this view, continually being consumed by the latest fad or continually seeking immediate pleasure can be manifestations of an identity-diffused adolescent's sense of meaninglessness (Logan, 1978). Without clear identities or values, these youngsters are the least likely of the four identity-status groups to have close relationships with friends of either sex. Identity diffusion has often been found characteristic of adolescents who feel rejected and detached from their parents (Marcia, 1980).

Similar to identity-diffused youth in that they have not yet adopted an identity, adolescents in the **moratorium** identity status are currently struggling with their identities. In Marcia's model, the moratorium youth's lack of defined goals or clear values contributes to feelings of anxiety. Nevertheless, these young people tend to be characterized by sophisticated levels of moral reasoning, self-esteem, self-directiveness, curiosity, social activity, and emotional expressiveness. The evidence reviewed by Marcia also suggests that these children have an ambivalent relationship with their parents in that, while struggling to liberate themselves from their mothers, they are having some difficulties resolving their Oedipal conflicts. Furthermore, the parents of moratorium youths tend to have encouraged their children's autonomy, expressiveness, and independence (Marcia, 1980).

In contrast to identity-diffused or moratorium youths, an individual with a **foreclosed identity** has adopted an identity and a system of clearly defined

values. Unfortunately, from Marcia's and Erikson's perspectives, these adolescents have prematurely endorsed the viewpoints of their parents and society's other authorities in lieu of examining alternative roles and values. For example, a boy with a foreclosed identity may acquiesce to his parents expectations that he become a physician, without ever exploring any other vocational option. Or a girl whose identity is foreclosed may embrace the religious and political policies of her family without ever discussing or reading about different perspectives.

The pattern that has emerged from most of the existing research associates foreclosed identities with conformity, conservatism, and submissiveness (Marcia, 1980). These adolescents seldom defy the wishes of authorities by engaging in such activities as smoking pot or having premarital sex. Yet because young people with foreclosed identities tend to have a greater need for social approval than youths in the other identity statuses, they are often the most susceptible to persuasion by others—especially by those whom they perceive as authority figures, such as religious leaders, teachers, or parents. Given this proclivity to submit to authority, youths with foreclosed identities appear to have lower levels of moral reasoning than those with achieved or moratorium identities (Marcia, 1980).

Given these characteristics, it is perhaps not too surprising that adolescents with foreclosed identities generally perceive their parents as having exerted considerable pressure on them to conform to the family's values and to society's more conventional mores. Nevertheless, most children with foreclosed identities view their parents as nurturant, protective, and supportive. In sum, these parents tend to assume a position of dominance and protectiveness toward their children, while simultaneously encouraging them to be industrious and obedient (Marcia, 1980).

The fourth type of identity status that Marcia perceives for adolescents is **achieved identity.** Individuals with an achieved identity have experienced the confusion and uncertainties that accompany experimentation with different identities and ideologies during adolescence. As a consequence of their struggles and experimentation, however, these individuals emerge from adolescence with an independently formulated identity in regard to vocational, personal, and ideological issues.

According to the data supporting Marcia's view, identity achievers are the people most likely to be ethical, empathetic, resistant to authorities' unreasonable demands, reflective, self-confident, and academically successful (Marcia, 1980). In accord with Erikson's prediction that an identity must be achieved before true intimacy can be established with another person, identity achievers often have more intimate relationships than adolescents in the other identity statuses. In high school, however, identity achievers are more concerned with preparing for their future vocations and formulating their values and beliefs than in sexual and social experiences.

Adolescents who become identity achievers generally describe their parents as people who have encouraged them to explore a variety of ideologies and to experiment with different social and vocational roles (Marcia, 1980). Correlational studies suggest that adolescents are most likely to develop mature identity statuses when their parents employ a democratic parenting style, demonstrate affection, and support their children's independence (Adams, 1985; Adams & Jones, 1983; Cooper, Grotevant, & Condon, 1984).

Although research generally supports Marcia's and Erikson's theories of identity statuses with regard to male development, female development defies many of their predictions (Adams & Jones, 1983; Matteson, in press). Since the hypotheses regarding identity statuses appear to be related to male and female sex roles, a more thorough examination of male and female identity statuses is reserved for the next chapter.

Loevinger's Theory of Ego Stages

The concepts proposed by contemporary psychoanalytic theorists like Marcia and Erikson emphasize the importance of the ego's role in the formation of the adolescent's personality. According to Freud, the ego is that part of the personality that copes with the real world in a rational manner. As a consequence, those who emphasize the role of the ego in the development of an individual's personality are sometimes referred to as *ego psychologists.* In this context, Jane

Loevinger has described seven stages of ego development that c
cia's and Erikson's theoretical models (Loevinger, 1976). Fr
viewpoint, some adolescents' personalities reflect more advanced
development than do some adults'. As Tables 4.1 and 1.2 demonstr
ger's model has much in common with the stage theories of Freud, Pi
son, and Hall. Unlike most other stage theorists, however, Loevinger
from assigning specific chronological ages to each stage in her proposed

On the basis of her data, Loevinger concludes that the least sophistic
level of ego development is the "presocial or symbiotic" stage. In this sta
young children respond primarily on the basis of their own selfish needs, exhib-
iting dependence on their mothers to meet these needs. Once having begun to acquire language and reasoning skills, however, the child's ego enters the "impulsive stage." During this period the child expresses sexual and aggressive impulses freely, ignores rules, and is governed by reward and punishment rather than by the superego or the conscience.

As individuals age, their personalities advance to the stage in which behavior is primarily motivated by the "self-protective" ego. People whose ego development remains at this third stage tend to be exploitative and manipulative in order to achieve their own protective goals. Furthermore, they obey rules only when doing so is to their advantage, rather than out of social concern or empathy for others. In contrast, people who advance to the fourth stage of ego development manifest a "conformist character." The personality of such an individual is characterized by obedience to rules and the maintainence of an acceptable public image.

According to Loevinger's model, adolescents and adults who have arrived at the fifth stage of ego development, known as the "conscientious character," are introspective, self-critical, and sensitive to the motives that guide their behavior and that of others. These people operate on the basis of their own internalized standards of excellence, while also fulfilling their obligations to others and pursuing their own ideals. Those who eventually arrive at the sixth stage, the "autonomous character," are motivated by their desire to balance personal needs and realities against personal ideals, through tolerance and individualism. In the most sophisticated stage of ego development, "integrated wholeness," the person has renounced unattainable goals, reconciled his or her inner conflicts, and developed a regard for individuality.

In support of Loevinger's hypotheses, some longitudinal studies suggest that children do advance from one ego stage to another during adolescence. In these studies, higher IQ scores were usually, but not consistently, correlated with the more advanced ego stages. Youngsters from impoverished families were the least likely to reach the advanced ego stages, although the researchers contend that these youths could attain high ego functioning through appropriate experiences (Redmore & Loevinger, 1979). In regard to the correlation between intelligence and ego stages, another study showed only slightly more advanced ego stages among college than among noncollege youths (Holt, 1980).

In accord with Loevinger's hypotheses, adolescents functioning at the less sophisticated ego levels have been found to think more simplistically and emotionally about political matters than those functioning at the higher ego levels (Candee, 1974). Furthermore, adolescent girls in the conformist and preconformist stages were found to be less responsive and friendly toward others than those in the postconformist stage (Hauser, 1978). Extrapolating from these data,

ıges, IQ scores, and educational achievement
'd. These studies lend tentative support, how-
'ents' ego stages are related to their attitudes

'he ego's role in the adolescent's person-
ee that ego development is intricately
ıdividuation is the process whereby a
'om parents and forms an autonomous
dy of adolescence by Peter Blos, indi-
e the boundaries between their own
(Blos, 1979). As individuation pro-
sponsibility for their own behavior,
sibilities onto their parents.

at an accelerated pace during adolescence, individua-
by many psychoanalytic scholars as a lifelong process (Blos,
). As the ego gradually becomes individuated from other people, an individual becomes more autonomous and develops new aspects of his or her identity. Contrary to many popular notions about adolescents, however, those who endorse Blos's position do not contend that rebellion and rejection of parental beliefs are necessary components of individuation. In fact, adolescents whose egos are becoming individuated may get along quite well with their parents throughout adolescence. Individuation requires adolescents to organize and to evaluate experiences and values independently, but this process does not necessarily have to entail rejection of their parents' values or overt rebellion against their elders (Blos, 1979; Josselson, 1980).

This view of individuation is not meant to imply that adolescents never rebel against or disregard their parents' values (Josselson, 1980). Indeed, individuation sometimes manifests itself through temporary defiance of adult authority, particularly among young adolescents in their initial, fledgling efforts to become more autonomous. From this perspective, finding ways to irritate parents and other adults can be respected as a young person's attempt to be taken seriously as an individual. Yet despite adolescents' increasing needs for independence and individuation, they continue to recognize their need for parental control and guidance. Although typically unwilling to share these feelings with their own parents, most adolescents consistently express gratitude for their parents' limits, rules, and values during interviews with researchers (Josselson, 1980). Furthermore, being less afraid of losing their identities to other people, older adolescents often reestablish extremely close relationships with their parents (Josselson, 1980).

According to the psychoanalytic perspective, individuation also transforms adolescents' peer relationships (Josselson, 1980). Conforming to the peer group and seeking peer approval are ways of rallying support for newly individuated parts of the ego. In the early stages of adolescents' individuation, the ego is too insecure and separation from parents is still too frightening to permit the individual to reject peer pressure. As adolescents age, however, and the ego becomes more individuated, more secure, and more confident of its own boundaries, conformity to peer pressure seems increasingly oppressive and unnecessary. At this juncture, asserting one's distinctiveness and individuality may actually outweigh the desire to conform to peer standards.

Another function of individuation, from the psychoanalytic view, is to establish a less dominant, more realistic superego (Blos, 1979; Josselson, 1980). Prior to adolescence, the superego reflects the values and rules of the child's parents. Also, children base much of their self-esteem on how well they abide by the superego's ideals and rules. In contrast, an important aspect of adolescents' individuation is establishing personal standards for the superego through independent examination—standards that are more realistic and less idealistic than those adopted during childhood. According to some scholars, young people who turn to gurus or religious cults are seeking ready-made codes that will allow them to skirt this responsibility (Blos, 1979; Josselson, 1980). Unfortunately, failure to examine the superego's values and to replace them, when necessary, with realistic standards may result in the lifelong feeling of "not being good enough." In such cases, the individual's self-esteem resembles a young child's in that it is forever predicated on trying to be "good" in terms of the superego's unrealistic expectations.

Criticisms of Neo-Freudian Theories

Despite the fact that neo-Freudian theories have contributed to our understanding of ego development and identity statuses during adolescence, they are not without their limitations. Even James Marcia himself has enumerated many of these limitations (Marcia, 1980). To begin with, most of the research on identity status has been limited to college students and is thus not generalizable to younger adolescents or to individuals who do not attend college. The importance of more random sampling is illustrated by the few existing studies in which adolescents who start working after high school are more likely to have "achieved identities" than those who go to college (Marcia, 1980). Likewise, while these theories seem to account for the development of identity in most white males, they have been less convincing empirically in regard to minority and female adolescents (McGuire et al., 1978). For example, several studies showed that black high-school students were more likely to have foreclosed identities than whites, a finding that suggests that race may be an important independent variable in identity-status research (Marcia, 1980).

Moreover, critics have challenged the assumption that identity achievement is superior to foreclosure, moratorium, and diffusion (Marcia, 1980). Even Marcia admits that people with foreclosed identities have the appealing attributes of being steadfast, committed, and cooperative; and moratorium people can be described positively as sensitive, ethical, and flexible. Likewise, identity-diffused individuals are generally considered to be quite charming and carefree. Given our rapidly changing society, it's possible that moratorium and identity diffusion may be adaptive roles for some youngsters and adults.

Still another criticism levied against the data on identity status is Marcia's method of collecting data about ego development. Several experts on adolescent development and personality criticize Erikson's personal interviews and Marcia's self-descriptive questionnaires as poor methods for assessing concepts as complicated as identity and ego development (see Box 4.2). In these experts' views,

4.2 A Closer Look

Marcia's Identity-Status Interview

The following are samples of the types of responses representing the various identity statuses proposed by James Marcia. Which type of identity status characterized your adolescence? Which identity status characterizes your present personality?

Occupational Area

"How willing do you think you'd be to give up going into _____ if something better came along?"

- *Achievement:* "Well, I might, but I doubt it. I can't see what something better would be for me."
- *Moratorium:* "I guess if I knew for sure, I could answer that better. It would have to be something in the general area—something related."
- *Foreclosure:* "Not very willing. It's what I've always wanted to do. The folks are happy with it and so am I."
- *Diffusion:* "Oh, sure. If something better came along, I'd change just like that."

Religious Area

"Have you ever had any doubts about your religious beliefs?"

- *Achievement:* "Yeah, I even started wondering whether or not there was a God. I've pretty much resolved that now, though. The way it seems to me . . ."
- *Moratorium:* "Yes, I guess I'm going through that now. I just don't see how there can be a God and yet so much evil in the world or . . ."
- *Foreclosure:* "No, not really. Our family is pretty much in agreement on these things."
- *Diffusion:* "Oh, I don't know. I guess so. Everyone goes through some sort of stage like that. But it really doesn't bother me much. I figure one's about as good as the other."

SOURCE: J. Marcia, Development and validation of ego-identity status. *Journal of Personality and Social Psychology*, 1966, *3*, 551–558.

assessments about adolescents' identities should be based on information from people other than just the youngsters themselves (Ausubel, Sullivan, & Ives, 1979; Mischel, 1981).

Given the current data, definitive statements about the stability of identity status or ego development or the types of experiences that might contribute to higher identity status or more advanced ego stages would be premature. For example, the outcome of studies now under way to determine the correlation between stages of cognitive development, identity status, and ego development could be particularly instructive: Can adolescents become identity achievers or function at the higher levels of Loevinger's ego model without first reaching the formal operations level of thinking? Similarly, the existing literature provides only limited information regarding the stability or consistency of identity statuses and ego development: Can youngsters who are identity achievers revert to diffused or moratorium identities? Is a person's identity status or stage of ego development consistent in all situations? Can individuals who are functioning at the higher ego stages in Loevinger's theoretical model revert to lower stages in specific types of situations? Given that some research already indicates that college students do sometimes regress to an earlier identity status, such questions seem warranted (Adams & Fitch, 1982).

Until more data are available, we can appreciate the possible importance of adolescent stages of ego development, identity status, and individuation. Simultaneously, we must exercise caution by not assuming that an adolescent's identity status or ego stage is a permanent aspect of his or her personality that can be reliably measured or predicted on the basis of certain correlates such as race, IQ scores, or family income.

COGNITIVE STAGE THEORIES OF PERSONALITY

As already shown in Chapter 3, cognitive stage theorists assume that adolescents' more advanced mental skills are primarily the consequence of their entering the formal operations stage of reasoning. Guided by these concepts, cognitive psychologists contend that formal operational thinking is responsible for many of the changes that personalities undergo during adolescence. The theories of David Elkind, a renowned psychologist in the field of adolescent cognition, illustrate the applicability of the cognitive stage perspective to adolescents' personalities.

Hypocrisy and Idealism

In the Piagetian tradition, Elkind contends that adolescents' newly acquired ability to differentiate between reality and ideals permits them to perceive hypocrisy for the first time in their lives (Elkind, 1970, 1978; Elkind & Bowen, 1979). This cognitive awareness often means that parents who previously appeared totally "good" and marvelously "knowledgeable" suddenly fall from grace and appear disappointingly "human," much to the dismay of their adolescent children. Disappointed by the contrasts between ideals and reality, young people may react to criticizing both "the system" and their parents. Others may rebel against the institutions they view as responsible for the hypocrisy in our society.

Elkind believes that this disillusionment also motivates some adolescents to construct their own idealistic, theoretical visions of how society ought to function. Hence, adults often witness the phase in which younger adolescents appear overly optimistic and idealistic. Yet, in the midst of condemning the hypocrisy surrounding them, adolescents are typically unable to recognize the hypocrisy in much of their own behavior. Although able to think abstractly, most adolescents lack the experience necessary to practice their own principles. Furthermore, the egocentricity of the concrete operational stage of reasoning often interferes with adolescents' objectivity in judging their own behavior and their generosity in judging the behavior of others.

Elkind also reminds us that as their new cognitive capacities develop, adolescents become wittier and more satirical. They learn to use irony to mock or tease other people and delight in using *doubles entendres* to demonstrate their new cognitive skills and to flirt with "forbidden" topics.

Egocentrism

As described in Chapter 3, children's personalities are characterized by an **egocentrism,** which Piaget attributed to their relatively low-level stage of cognitive development. In contrast, Piagetian psychologists like Elkind contend that adolescents become capable of empathizing with other people and of assuming the perspectives of someone other than themselves (Elkind, 1970, 1978; Elkind & Bowen, 1979). The ramifications of these new attitudes on adolescents' peer relationships will be carefully examined in Chapter 9.

Elkind argues, however, that adolescents remain "egotistical" in the sense that they assume everyone is as preoccupied with their own thoughts and behavior as they are. This form of egotistical reasoning contributes to adolescents' feelings of being on stage, performing for an imaginary audience. According to Elkind, this feeling about an **imaginary audience** underlies the excessive self-consciousness that characterizes the personalities of many young adolescents. Fearing the judgment of the imaginary audience, many young adolescents may be reluctant to reveal their thoughts or may prefer being alone to interacting with others. Assuming that everyone else is as critical or as approving of them as they are of themselves, adolescents permit their imaginary audience to inflate or deflate their self-confidence almost instantaneously.

For example, an adolescent boy may refuse to go to the grocery store for his mother, arguing vehemently that he simply cannot go out in public unless she buys him new jeans, because "everyone will notice that these jeans are too short, Mom!" The mother's reassurance and counterarguments are generally to no avail in dispelling her son's conviction that every person he encounters will be snickering about his short jeans. According to Elkind, it is beyond the son's comprehension that most people in the grocery store couldn't care less about his presence there, let alone about the length of his jeans.

Furthermore, Elkind perceives adolescence as a time when our personalities are heavily influenced by our beliefs in the **personal fable.** The personal fable is a belief in one's own uniqueness and specialness that distorts or ignores reality. The attitude is manifested in such comments as "I'm the only person who has ever been in love like this!"; "Dad, you couldn't possibly understand how I feel!"; "You mean you've been through something like this too?!" Another dimension of the personal fable is the conviction that no ill or misfortune can befall certain people—above all, not oneself. In this regard, Elkind believes the personal fable is literally detrimental to some adolescents' physical well-being. For example, ignoring the realities and clinging to the personal fable can contribute to adolescents' lax attitudes toward contraception—"I won't get pregnant—that only happens to other people"; or their attitudes toward driving while intoxicated—"Don't worry, get into the car. Nothing can happen to us. We're young. Come on!"

The personal fable also makes adolescents feel that nobody else can possibly understand their feelings or experiences because they're so unique. Hence, the frequent refrain of adolescents: "Oh, you just don't understand me!" The personal fable may thereby prevent youngsters from recognizing the similarities between their feelings and problems and those of other people, including their own parents! Indeed, might the personal fable be partially responsible for the surprised expression on the young adolescent's face who remarks, while thumbing through the family's old photograph album, "Gosh, Mom, you and Dad look so young and so in love! Is this really you guys?"

In accord with Elkind's predictions, researchers have found that the imaginary audience and the personal fable generally decline from early to late adolescence (Elkind & Bowen, 1979; Enright, Lapsley, & Shukla, 1979; Simmons, Rosenberg, & Rosenberg, 1973). Moreover, these studies support Elkind's position that self-consciousnsess and egocentrism tend to be at their zenith in early adolescence. Most older adolescents are more aware of other people's perspectives and of the similarities among people's feelings and experiences. It has been suggested that egocentrism declines partially as a result of older adolescents' experiences in the work force, which engender empathy toward other people (Steinberg et al., 1981). Although this hypothesis has some initial appeal, it is at the center of several controversies regarding adolescents' employment, a topic which will be discussed in Chapter 11.

Pseudostupidity

Why do some youngsters examine so many aspects of a particular problem that they become incapable of making any decision at all? Why do adolescents so often attribute complicated motives to other people's behavior, when none exist? According to Elkind, these dimensions of the adolescent personality are forms of **pseudostupidity.** Because reaching the formal operational stage enables them to consider many possibilities simultaneously, adolescents tend to reason in overly complicated ways about relatively simple problems. Elkind contends that young people often fail to make decisions or solve problems because they complicate the situation by literally thinking too much. Lacking the experience to evaluate alternatives, young adolescents may behave very indecisively or simply not act at all. Similarly, youths often attribute complicated motives to other people as a consequence of thinking too much. For instance, an adolescent might misconstrue a simple request from her father as a manifestation of his intentionally trying to infringe on her freedom and independence.

Elkind reminds us that these forms of seemingly stupid behavior are only pseudostupidity, meaning that the behavior is not indicative of any mental inadequacy. Elkind suggests that we view the young person's seemingly stupid behavior as the natural consequence of his or her cognitive changes and lack of experience—neither of which the adolescent can control. In other words, adults should refrain from judging the youngster as stupid or as intentionally irritating. Instead, we should perceive the youth's personality as being affected by cognitive abilities that have temporarily advanced beyond his or her experiences.

TRAIT THEORIES OF PERSONALITY

A third approach to the study of personality, trait theory, is predicated upon the assumption that humans behave relatively consistently in accord with certain traits that direct their personalities (Mischel, 1981). Maintaining that a person's behavior is primarily influenced by his or her personality traits, trait theorists' primary objective is to identify the characteristics that underlie the individual's personality. Moreover, trait theorists assume that these traits remain relatively constant, thereby permitting some certainty in predicting an individual's future behavior, once his or her traits have been correctly identified. While some trait theorists contend that there are only two or three basic traits, like introversion and extroversion or dominance and submissiveness, others argue that a number of traits direct an individual's behavior. Despite this disagreement, trait theorists share the common contention that an adolescent's personality traits can be ascertained through standardized psychometric tests and therapists' observations.

Research supporting trait theories suggests that certain traits are relatively stable in similar situations over long periods of time; however, an individual's behavior changes across situations (Mischel, 1981). In other words, an adolescent is likely to behave in a relatively similar way across a period of months or years only in situations that are similar to one another. Given the trait theorists' empirical data, we would not be justified in assuming that an adolescent male who behaves aggressively with other boys at school will also behave aggressively at home or with females or with young children. We would be justified, however, in assuming that he probably will continue to behave aggressively with other males in situations similar to the ones at school (Mischel, 1981).

In addition to attempting to identify individuals' traits, trait theorists explore the relationships between personalities and genetic or biochemical variables (Mischel, 1981). Illustratively, some recent studies suggest that severe personality disorders—like schizophrenia, which affects both adolescents and adults—have a biochemical or genetic basis. Similarly, other studies provide tentative support for the hypothesis that such traits as emotional expressiveness, sociability, anxiety, and introversion may have a genetic basis (Dworkin, 1979; Wilson & O'Leary, 1980). Although studies like these should not be interpreted to mean that an adolescent's personality is irrevocably determined by a genetic blueprint, the data provide limited support for the possibility that genetic factors may predispose some individuals to develop certain traits.

Assessing Personality Traits

From the trait theorist's viewpoint, quantitative data from standardized tests are invaluable for identifying traits that characterize an individual's personality. One of trait theory's most renowned proponents, Raymond Cattell, contends that assessments of any personality should be determined on the basis of data from three different sources: records describing the person's daily behavior, self-ratings, and standardized tests (Cattell, 1965).

A description of the many standardized tests that might be employed by trait theorists to identify an adolescent's personality traits is beyond the scope of this text, but a cursory description of one such test, the **Minnesota Multiphasic Personality Inventory** (**MMPI**), can serve to exemplify the trait theorists' psychometric approach (Hathaway & McKinley, 1943). Composed of 550 statements to which the individual responds "true," "false," or "undecided," the MMPI was initially devised to classify mental patients into various categories of psychiatric disorders. The scale is frequently used, however, with people who have no apparent psychiatric problems, in an attempt to compare their traits with those of other people from similar backgrounds or circumstances. For example, the traits on the MMPI that characterize most college students differ considerably from those that typify hospitalized psychiatric patients of the same age.

Like a number of other personality tests, the MMPI combines the adolescent's responses into categories, permitting an overall "profile" of the personality to emerge. For instance, if a statement on the MMPI, such as "I cry easily," is typically affirmed by adolescents who have been hospitalized for psychiatric problems, but rarely affirmed by high-school students who have never been treated for psychiatric problems, the statement could be used as part of the test scale for identifying certain kinds of adolescent maladjustment. The individual's overall profile is then coded in a way that permits a general description of his or her personality or specific dimensions of personality. For example, a young person's MMPI score might yield this description: "This person avoids close relationships with other people, tends to be resentful, often feels tense, manifests anger through somatic illnesses, is very dependent on other people's opinions, and aspires to unrealistic goals for self and others."

Research on the validity and reliability of personality inventories such as the MMPI is extensive. Just for the MMPI alone, almost 100 studies are conducted each year (Mischel, 1981). Although the MMPI is only one among dozens of popular personality scales, it serves as the model for many others, such as the California Psychological Inventory (CPI), the Taylor Manifest Anxiety Scale (MAS), and the Hackson Personality Inventory. In addition, tests to measure specific traits have been designed, such as the California F Scale, which assesses authoritarian attitudes, or the Gough Feminity Scale, which assesses "masculinity" and "femininity."

Applications to Adolescents

In many respects we unkowingly operate in accord with trait theorists' assumptions in most of our interactions with adolescents and with other adults. For example, we frequently ascribe the traits "shy," "introverted," or "reserved" to an adolescent who refuses to go to parties, quivers at the thought of public speaking, stutters on the telephone in conversations with the opposite sex, and always chooses to stay home and read instead of interacting with other young people. Moreover, when giving or receiving descriptions of another person that rely on such labels as "extroverted," "aggressive," or "sociable," we are implying or inferring that the individual will manifest those characteristics in his or her behavior across a number of situations—both in the present and in the future. Consider one simple illustration of the practical significance of trait theory: Once having heard that a particular adolescent girl is "timid," "high-strung," and "restrained," we are not apt to envision her contributing much verbally to a class we might be teaching or to imagine ourselves asking her to babysit for two rambunctious 5-year-old boys.

Since we often behave toward adolescents in accord with the traits that we—correctly or incorrectly—have ascribed to them, it becomes incumbent upon us to reexamine our own behavior and attitudes in terms of the questions that trait theorists explore: Are we correct in expecting an adolescent to behave according to traits that have been ascribed to him or her? Do personality traits determine an adolescent's behavior or attitudes across different situations? Do idiosyncratic situational factors influence the youngster's behavior more than personality traits? Can we modify an adolescent's behavior, or is it fundamentally controlled by his or her intrinsic traits? Do tests or descriptions from other people reliably identify an adolescent's traits or permit us to predict his or her behavior? Such questions reflect the quest of trait theorists.

Unlike cognitive, Freudian, or neo-Freudian theorists, trait theorists approach adolescents' problems without much attention to concepts such as ego stages, identity statuses, formal operational thought, or individuation. As an illustration, if two adolescent boys are suspended from school for fighting, a trait theorist might approach the situation by administering a personaltiy inventory in order to identify the traits that seem to characterize each boy's personality. Once having established a personality profile for each boy on the basis of the test data, the trait theorist might pursue other questions in an attempt to resolve the problem: Was the fight atypical or typical behavior, given each boy's personality profile? Is there behavioral evidence other than the fight to corroborate the test results? Do the descriptions of each boy from friends, family, and teachers confirm or dispute the test results? Given the test results and behavioral reports, do specific traits appear to be influencing each boy's behavior across a number of situations? If the test results contradict the descriptions of these boys' personalities from other people, which source is correct?

Criticisms of Trait Theories

Despite the fact that our own interactions with adolescents and those of teachers, parents, and therapists often embody the concepts of trait theories, this perspective is not without its critics (Mischel, 1981). Critics point out that self-report inventories like the MMPI are unreliable assessments of people's behavior or attitudes, since they rely on the individual's own candor and objectivity. In addition, research has shown that a person's performance on personality tests can be affected by temporary environmental conditions or circumstances that alter their perceptions of themselves. More important, however, are the numerous studies showing that most people's behavior is too inconsistent to attribute their conduct to stable personality traits. In short, critics argue that trait theorists have been relatively unsuccessful in predicting a person's behavior.

According to many experts, characterizations of individuals' personalities or generalizations about their future behavior that are based exclusively on scales such as the MMPI must be viewed tentatively (Mischel, 1981). A renowned scholar in the field of personality, Walter Mischel, cautions us not to attribute other people's conduct and attitudes to unalterable personality traits. Instead,

Mischel urges us to search for the relationship between an individual's behavior and the particular aspects of conditions under which the behavior occurs.

In applying Mischel's suggestions to our interactions with adolescents, we might utilize information from a personality inventory as the basis for constructive discussions, when a particular problem arises in an adolescent's life. A parent or counselor might present the profile to the adolescent and ask for his or her opinions: "Do you feel this accurately describes your behavior here at school?" "How do you think we might use this information to help you resolve your problems at school or at home?" Information from personality scales might also motivate us to explore questions related to the situational variables that affect behavior: When does Herbert become more or less distant from other people? Under what conditions does he feel threatened and aggressive? How am I behaving toward Herbert when he acts withdrawn?

Familiarity with both the advantages and the limitations of trait theories can hopefully diminish the chances of our misusing information regarding an adolescent's supposed traits. Furthermore, trait theorists can advance our understanding of the relationship between traits that may predispose adolescents to behave in certain ways and the situational conditions under which a trait is most likely to manifest itself.

PHENOMENOLOGICAL THEORIES OF PERSONALITY

In contrast to trait theories, phenomenological theories maintain that adolescents play many different roles, rather than behaving in accord with an identifiable set of personality traits.

The various theories within the phenomenological model share several common assumptions about personality (Mischel, 1981). Phenomenological psychologists reject the notion that a youngster's personality is controlled by psychosexual or psychosocial conflicts, cognitive stages, or internal traits. From their viewpoint, the adolescent's personality is directed by the "self," which interprets experiences on the basis of its own private, idiosyncratic concepts and the self-image. Hence, adolescents' personalities depend on the way they perceive the self and the way the self perceives other people and experiences. Phenomenologists contend that we can never completely understand another person's behavior, because his or her "internal frame of reference" in any particular situation is never completely known to us. Adolescents' interpretations of the phenomena in the world—including their interpretation of the self—are too private and too complex for other people to comprehend or to predict.

The Theories of Rogers and Maslow

Two of the best-known advocates of the phenomenological view are Carl Rogers and Abraham Maslow, who refer to their collective theories as *humanistic psychology.* According to Carl Rogers and his advocates, the adolescent's personality is determined by conceptualizations he or she has of the self—the self-concept (Rogers, 1969). Rogers defines the self or self-concept as an organized, consistent, conceptual gestalt composed of perceptions of the characteristics of the "I" or "me" and the perceptions of the relationships of the "I" or "me" to others and to various aspects of life.

The client-centered interview, sometimes referred to as **Rogerian counseling,** was developed by Carl Rogers as a way of helping individuals examine the self-concepts on which their personalities are predicated. The Rogerian counselor must be empathetic, friendly, honest, trustworthy, nonthreatening, nonjudgmental, and unconditionally accepting of the client's feelings and behavior—an attitude Rogers refers to as *unconditional positive regard.* Under these conditions, clients will supposedly disclose their self-concepts, feelings, and perceptions. Unlike psychoanalytic counseling, Rogerian counseling refrains from interpreting a client's motives and from advising the client to adopt any particular course of action. Client-centered therapists assume that clients—even adolescent clients—possess the abilities necessary for resolving their own problems, if helped to disclose and to accept the self.

According to Rogerian theories, "reflective listening" is a crucial component of effective counseling and effective communication. Reflective listening is repeating or reflecting the client's comments without judgment or interpretation. For example, Leon might say, "I feel like adults are ganging up against me and that nothing I do is right." The counselor might then respond, "So you feel that no matter what you do, you can't make adults happy." The Rogerian counselor must trust that clients are intrinsically good and can resolve their own problems through increased awareness of the self.

In a similar vein, Abraham Maslow believes that human beings are motivated by an intrinsic tendency called **self-actualization** (Maslow, 1968; Rogers, 1969). According to Maslow, people want to "actualize" themselves and behave in ways that make self-actualization possible. Before, however, an individual can develop the traits of a self-actualized personality, he or she must fulfill other more basic needs. As Figure 4.2 demonstrates, Maslow presumes that all personalities are motivated by the same needs and, further, that these needs are arranged in a hierarchal order: physiological needs, safety needs, needs for love and belongingness, need for self-esteem, and need for self-actualization.

From Maslow's viewpoint, for example, adolescents who are tired, hungry, or cold will behave in ways that lead toward fulfilling these basic physiological needs. Until these needs are satisfied, the adolescents will not be motivated to behave in ways to meet their needs for self-esteem or other higher-order needs in the hierarchy. Similarly, adolescents who feel inferior to their peers and rejected by their parents cannot develop self-actualized personalities, because their needs for safety and self-esteem are unmet. In regard to our interactions with adolescents, therefore, Maslow would recommend our arranging experiences and environments that assure the fulfillment of their needs as designated in his hierarchy. After so doing, we must then trust that youngsters' intrinsic desires to become self-actualized will direct their personalities in ways that are beneficial to themselves and to others.

As you look at the pyramid in Figure 4.2, which of the needs do you feel most influenced your adolescence? Which are presently exerting the most influence over your personality?

How do we know when adolescents are becoming or have become self-actualized? From Maslow's perspective, specific behaviors and attitudes characterize the self-actualized personality. On the basis of his observations of adults

Figure 4.2

Maslow's hierarchy of needs

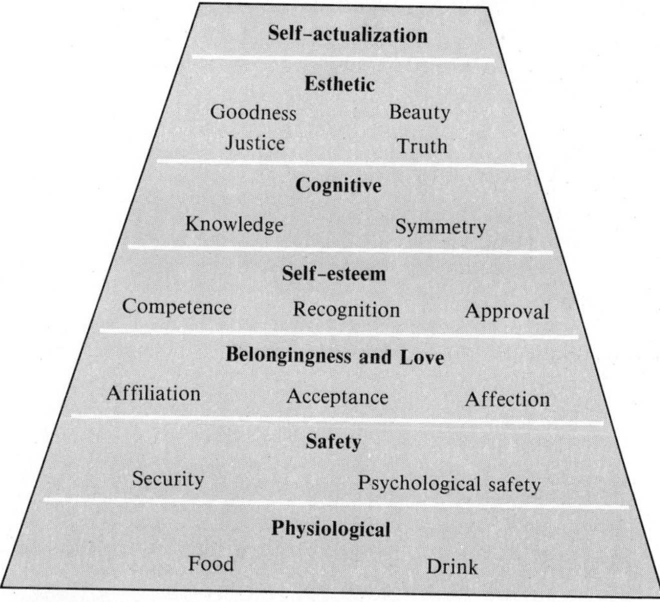

SOURCE: A. Maslow, *Toward a psychology of being*. New York: Van Nostrand, 1968.

whom he considered self-actualized, Maslow compiled the profile presented in Table 4.2. In Maslow's opinion, self-actualized people periodically have "peak" experiences—joyous, contented feelings, sometimes described as feelings of ecstasy, wholeness, or effortlessness.

Field Theories

The phenomenological approach also includes psychologists like Kurt Lewin, who developed many aspects of **field theory.** According to field theorists, the adolescent has a "life space" that determines behavior (Lewin, 1935). The **life space** includes the youngster's self-concept, his or her ways of perceiving the world, and the experiences occurring in the environment at the moment. Within this life space are many "fields of force," as there are in physics, which interact with one another to influence behavior. Altering one part of the force field causes the entire field to change. In other words, an adolescent's interpretation of reality can change dramatically from moment to moment, since some dimensions of his or her life space are inevitably changing.

According to field theorists, the adolescent's perceptions may or may not coincide with objective data or with another person's interpretation of reality. This principle is demonstrated by people's different reactions to "gestalts" like the one in Figure 4.3. Literally translated from German, a gestalt means "shape or outward form"—hence the term **Gestalt psychology.** As used by phenomenological psychologists, the gestalt demonstrates the principle of people's idio-

syncratic interpretations of all phenomena. Looking at Figure 4.3, some of us will see a black vase against a white background, and others will see two white silhouettes against a black background, depending upon which part of the picture we attend to first. Similarly, Gestalt theorists contend that adolescents' personalities and their behavior in any given situation depend on their unique interpretations of a phenomenon—interpretations that will not necessarily reflect any other person's conceptualization of that phenomenon.

Like the gestalt in Figure 4.3, experiences in the adolescent's life are perceived according to the observer's unique and private frame of reference. As a consequence, Gestalt psychologists believe that most human behavior is idiosyncratic and unpredictable. For instance, one adolescent may perceive her

Table 4.2

Qualities of Maslow's Self-Actualized Person

How many of the following qualities of the self-actualized person did you embody as an adolescent? How many of these traits characterize your present personality?

1. Creative and inventive
2. Aware of the need for change and improvement
3. Ethical, unprejudiced, and respectful of others
4. Independent and spontaneous
5. Appreciative of solitude and privacy
6. Accepting of self, others, and the world
7. Realistic in perceiving experiences and people
8. Concerned with problems of others
9. Aware of simple, commonplace experiences, like sunsets and flowers
10. Thoughtful, good-humored, and philosophical
11. Emotionally bonded to relatively few people in profound ways
12. Democratic and broad-minded
13. Capable of "mystical" feelings or "peak experiences," in which one feels separate from ordinary reality and part of nature

SOURCE: A. Maslow, *Toward a psychology of being.* New York: Van Nostrand, 1968.

Figure 4.3

A "gestalt"

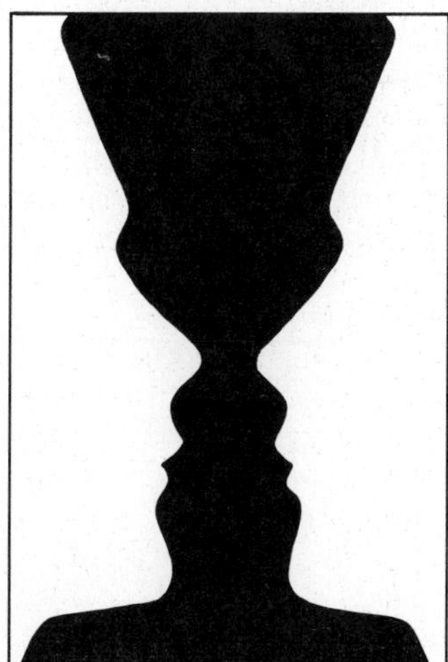

What do you perceive in this gestalt—two white silhouettes or a black vase?

father's bad mood as a problem having nothing to do with her. Her self-concept is not diminished nor her behavior altered by her dad's sultry, unpleasant mood. Another youngster, however, may perceive the identical behavior as a sure sign that her father dislikes her. Her self-concept and behavior may change for the worse as a consequence of her interpretations of this event in her life space.

According to phenomenologists, an individual's interpretations of gestalts and all other phenomona in the world are partially predicated upon the kinds of internal constructs he or she has created. A construct is a belief that determines how the individual interprets experiences and the self. According to psychologists like George Kelly, who originated the *personal construct theory,* adolescents and adults create constructs in order to make the world appear more orderly, controllable, and predictable (Kelly, 1955). Unfortunately, the constructs that some youngsters carry around inside them are either debilitating or unrealistic. For example, a youth's constructs may include beliefs like "There is nothing I can ever do to become more successful or to make more people like me"; "There is absolutely no goodness in the world." The task of the phenomenological psychologist is to help adolescents examine the validity of their constructs, test their constructs against reality, and if necessary, develop new constructs on which to base their personalities.

Measuring Adolescents' Self-Concepts

Since phenomenologists assume that self-concepts and internal constructs directly shape the adolescent's personality, they rely on standardized tests for assessing an individual's perceptions of the self and others. In addition to Carl Rogers's client-centered interviews, tests like the Q-sort technique and the semantic differential can be used to assess adolescents' perceptions of themselves and of other people.

The **Q-sort technique** consists of cards on which are inscribed statements such as "I am likable," "I am a thoughtful person." Adolescents are told to sort the cards into stacks according to which statements are most and least descriptive of themselves. Another way of using the Q-sort is to have a youngster sort the cards into two stacks—one containing the cards that describe the "ideal" self and the other the cards that describe the "real" self. The Q-sort is also sometimes used to determine whether certain kinds of therapy have improved youngsters' self-concepts or have brought their ideal and real self-concepts closer together.

The **semantic differential** is another technique for assessing adolescents' perceptions of others and of themselves. The test consists of phrases like "my father" or "my ideal self." Next to each phrase is a seven-point scale between two opposite words, like "strong-weak" or "pleasant-unpleasant." Respondents assign a numerical rating to each phrase according to how they feel about the concepts being evaluated.

Applications to Adolescents

Assume that Leon is in trouble for setting several fires at school and robbing local merchants. His hostile behavior toward authorities—teachers, parents, and employers—has earned him a reputation as a troublemaker. As a first step, the phenomenological psychologist might assess Leon's self-concept, using techniques like the semantic differential or the Q-sort. On the tests Leon describes himself and other people in very uncomplimentary terms, a finding that indicates that his self-concept and internal constructs are affecting his personality unfavorably. Furthermore, the counselor finds a considerable discrepancy between the way Leon describes his real self and his ideal self on the Q-sort. On the basis of these data, the counselor might pursue one of several options that reflect the phenomenological perspective, such as client-centered therapy, encounter-group therapy, and role playing.

Encounter-group therapy is intended to help participants become more aware of the self through structured activities directed by a trained leader. Sometimes called "T-groups," "personal growth groups," or "sensitivity training groups," these meetings are similar to Rogerian counseling in that they supposedly heighten members' awareness of their internal constructs and self-concepts. Each member is then encouraged to replace inadequate or debilitating constructs with more beneficial alternatives. A number of experimental studies support the hypothesis that participating in encounter groups increases a member's self-confidence and empathy for others (Mischel, 1981). Other studies, however, raise serious doubts about attributing individuals' changes to the encounter-group activities rather than to self-fulfilling prophecies (Mischel, 1981).

Phenomenologists might also ask adolescents like Leon to participate in such therapeutic activities as "the empty chair" in the hope of creating new concepts of the self and new perceptions of other people. In the empty-chair activity, the youth is asked to imagine that a person with whom he or she is in conflict is seated in the empty chair. The youth is then asked to converse out loud with this imaginary person, playing both the role of the other person and of one's self by moving back and forth between the two chairs. The youth might be instructed to create the imaginary conversation along any number of lines: "Create an 'ideal' conversation between yourself and your mother"; "Create a 'typical' conversation between you and your mother"; "Create a conversation in which you tell your mother everything you are presently afraid to express to her and in which she responds as you most fear she will."

The empty-chair exercise can also be used to have an adolescent client create imaginary conversations with the self: "Pretend that you are sitting in that empty chair and talk to yourself as if you were the counselor." The phenomenological counselor's purpose in such an exercise is to help clients gain insights into their relationships with other people and to acquire a better understanding of their own self-concepts.

The Foundations of Adolescents' Self-Esteem

Since the adolescent's self-concept is an essential construct in most phenomenological theories of personality, thousands of studies have been devoted to the question: Why do some adolescents have positive self-concepts, while others maintain negative views of themselves? In attempts to answer this question, researchers have examined adolescents' self-concepts in relation to such variables as family relationships, school grades, gender, and age. The results have been both contradictory and, in many cases, surprising.

How does an adolescent's family influence his or her self-esteem? An expert in the field of self-concept formation, Wylie contends that empirical studies to date have failed to demonstrate clear or consistent relationships between a child's self-esteem and family variables (Wylie, 1979). According to Wylie's review of the literature, researchers still have no reliable way of designing studies that establish the relative impact of the family on children's self-concepts.

Likewise, studies have failed to consistently support the hypothesis that poor grades lower an adolescent's self-esteem (Bachman, Green, & Wirtanen, 1971; Bachman & O'Malley, 1978; Hamachek, 1978; Kash & Borich, 1978; Purkey, 1978). Although succeeding in school often does enhance self-esteem, many students with high self-esteem nonetheless earn low grades. Conversely, a number of students with low self-esteem scores on personality tests do well academically. Given the current state of uncertainty regarding the impact of grades on an adolescent's self-esteem, the soundest conclusion appears to be that a positive self-concept does not guarantee academic success, nor does academic success guarantee a positive self-concept. As Chapter 7 will illustrate, the contradictions in the research suggest that self-esteem is just one among many variables that affect an adolescent's grades. Similarly, grades are just one among many variables that affect an adolescent's self-esteem.

It has been argued by some scholars that age affects an adolescent's self-concept. According to this view, younger adolescents have more negative views of themselves than older adolescents, and therefore an individual's self-esteem scores would be higher at the end than at the beginning of adolescence. One illustrative study in support of this view is Rosenberg's survey of 1,500 adolescents in Baltimore, which showed that black students' self-concepts generally improved during adolescence. Interestingly, however, most white students' self-concepts remained stable throughout adolescence, a finding which suggests that race may be a confounding variable in self-esteem studies (Rosenberg, 1979). Lending further support to the contention that self-esteem is age-related, several studies have shown that the transition from elementary to junior high school undermines the self-confidence of many young adolescents (Blyth, Simmons, & Bush, 1978; Rosenberg, 1979).

On the other hand, many researchers have found no significant relationship between self-esteem and an adolescent's age. For example reports from more than 20,000 adolescents over an 18-year period have led Daniel Offer and his colleagues to conclude that young adolescents have no poorer self-concepts than older ones (Offer, Ostrov, & Howard, 1981). Moreover, Wylie's extensive reviews of the research show self-esteem relatively unchanged between early and late adolescence (Wylie, 1979). In sum, it appears that although some youths do undoubtedly undergo dramatic improvements in self-esteem between early and late adolescence, the self-concepts of the majority remain relatively unchanged throughout their adolescence.

Some of the most surprising information about self-esteem has been derived from studies of minority and impoverished youths. As the extensive research cited in Chapter 6 will demonstrate, it has traditionally been argued by many scholars that members of racial minorities tend to have lower self-esteem than whites. Similarly, part of the mythology surrounding poverty is that children from indigent families have more negative self-concepts than children from richer families—a myth that will be refuted by the empirical data discussed in Chapter 8. In contradiction to these presumptions about the impact of race and poverty, a number of studies show that impoverished and minority youths often have self-images that are equivalent to or better than those of their richer white peers (Jones, 1979; Jenkins, 1982; Petersen, Offer, & Kaplan, 1979; Soares & Soares, 1971; Wells, 1978).

These findings should not be misconstrued to imply that all poor and minority children have positive images of themselves or that poverty and racial prejudice can never undermine self-esteem. Such an assertion would be both fatuous and empirically unfounded. For example, some research indicates that merely living in a neighborhood not of one's own religious faith lowers self-esteem (Rosenberg, 1979).

Searching for the causes of self-esteem yields one consistent outcome—inconclusive results. Most reviews of the research show mixed results regarding the impact on adolescents' self-esteem of race, sex, income, urban or rural environments, family interaction, and school experiences (Wylie, 1979). Since the relationship between self-esteem and environmental or demographic influences is clearly more complicated than traditionally acknowledged, we must avoid the pitfall of stereotyping adolescents on the basis of such popular but empirically unfounded notions as "Well, since he comes from such an indigent family, I can understand why he doesn't have the self-confidence to do better here in school"; "If only her parents had more education, I'm sure her self-concept wouldn't be so negative."

Why do these confusing, contradictory results occur when researchers try to discover the correlates and sources of adolescents' self-esteem? Why is it so difficult to predict which experiences will enhance or detract from a youngster's self-concept? A partial answer resides in our misunderstandings regarding the formation of self-concepts. Among these misunderstandings, perhaps the concept of the "looking-glass self" best illustrates recent changes in researchers' hypotheses about self-concept formation.

According to many traditional theorists, a person's self-image is based solely on feedback from other people. This concept, called the *looking-glass self,* assumes that our self-concepts are reflections of others' reactions to us—analogous to the physical reflections of ourselves in a looking glass. Contemporary theorists discount the looking-glass concept as an overly simplistic model of self-concept formation (Mischel, 1981). Although adolescents' interactions with and feedback from other people undeniably affect their self-concepts to varying degrees, self-concepts are also affected by the individual's cognitive decisions and attitudes.

"What type of information will I choose to attend to about myself?" and "How will I interpret the information to which I decide to attend?" are two of the most important decisions affecting an adolescent's self-concept. An examination of the many factors involved in these two cognitive decisions is beyond the scope of this chapter, but by briefly examining locus-of-control attitudes and cognitive dissonance, we can gain some appreciation of the myriad ways in which an adolescent's cognitive decisions affect his or her self-concept.

In formulating a self-image, adolescents can attribute their behavior either to factors within their control or to factors external to themselves (Phares, 1973). Attributing behavior and outcomes to sources outside of one's own control is referred to as an **external locus-of-control** attitude. For instance, if Samantha is too nervous to speak in class, she might attribute her shyness to her teacher's conduct or to distractions from her classmates. Such attributions are examples of an external locus-of-control attitude. Conversely, adolescents with an **internal locus-of-control** attribute their behavior and outcomes to factors within their control. In Samantha's case, this means that she might attribute her nervousness to her own shyness or to the fact that she never studies and is, therefore, ill-prepared to speak up in class.

As Table 4.3 demonstrates, researchers attempt to assess adolescents' locus-of-control attitudes with a written questionnaire. Through such assessments, adolescents' locus-of-control attitudes have been correlated with a number of attitudes and behaviors that we will be examining in future chapters, such as sexual conduct, academic achievement, delinquency, and drug use. In addition, Chapter 6 will demonstrate that adolescents' locus-of-control attitudes are often affected by the ethnic or racial environment in which they live. Since the ramifications of locus-of-control attitudes on the adolescent's personality will be examined in subsequent chapters, for the moment this discussion serves only to demonstrate a perspective that both phenomenological and cognitive psychologists share in common: The adolescent's self-concept is not merely a reflection of other people's opinions and environmental feedback; it is affected by cognitive concepts such as locus-of-control attitudes.

A second concept affecting adolescents' perceptions of data on which their self-concepts are predicated is cognitive dissonance. **Cognitive dissonance** is the feeling that occurs when we encounter data that contradict our locus-of-control attitude, our existing self-image, and our existing assumptions about other people. According to Festinger's theory of cognitive dissonance, people feel tense and uncomfortable when their beliefs and experiences fail to coincide. In order to reduce these unpleasant feelings, the cognitive dissonance must somehow be diminished (Festinger, 1957).

How does Festinger's theory of cognitive dissonance affect the adolescent's personality? Let's examine the hypothetical example of John, whose self-concept is predicated on his private conviction (remember Kelly's theory about internal constructs?) that he is shy and stupid. According to the theory of cognitive dissonance, John will tend to overlook behavior that contradicts that self-image. When John's friend reminds him that on several occasions he has behaved in ways that are not at all shy or stupid, John experiences cognitive dissonance. His friend's feedback, although quite flattering, is inconsistent with John's cognitions of himself. In order to reduce his cognitive dissonance, John sends himself messages such as "The fact that I did well on the test and impressed people with my comments in class today was just a fluke—it's not the 'real me'."

According to Festinger's theory, cognitive dissonance can also work to enhance a person's self-esteem. For example, John's friend who perceives herself as intelligent and talented tends to disregard information and experiences that create cognitive dissonance by contradicting her positive self-image. If she fails a test, for example, she might dissipate the dissonance by telling herself, "This is just a temporary mishap and implies nothing about my intelligence. Besides, I think the teacher did a crummy job teaching us this material."

In sum, phenomenologists are similar to cognitive theorists in that both discount the looking-glass-self theory of personality. In forming their self-concepts, adolescents do more than passively accept reflections of themselves from other people. According to phenomenological and cognitive theories, cognitive operations within the adolescent are screening and interpreting information about the self. Consequently, adolescents' personalities are ultimately determined by their own private, unpredictable interpretations of the phenomena around them.

Table 4.3

Nowicki's Locus-of-Control Inventory for Adolescents

Answer the following questions and then score yourself to assess your locus-of-control attitude:

1. Do you believe that most problems will solve themselves if you just don't fool with them?
2. Are you often blamed for things that just aren't your fault?
3. Do you feel that most of the time it doesn't pay to try hard because things never turn out right anyway?
4. Do you feel that most of the time parents listen to what their children have to say?
5. When you get punished, does it usually seem it's for no good reason at all?
6. Most of the time do you find it hard to change a friend's opinions?
7. Do you feel that it's nearly impossible to change your parent's mind about anything?
8. Do you feel that when you do something wrong there's very little you can do to make it right?
9. Do you believe that most students are just born good at sports?
10. Do you feel that one of the best ways to handle most problems is just not to think about them?
11. Do you feel that when a student your age decides to hit you, there's little you can do to stop him or her?
12. Have you felt that when people were mean to you it was usually for no reason at all?
13. Most of the time do you feel that you can change what might happen tomorrow by what you do today?
14. Do you believe that when bad things are going to happen they are just going to happen, no matter what you try to do to stop them?
15. Most of the time do you find it useless to try to get your own way at home?
16. Do you feel that when somebody your age wants to be your enemy there's little you can do to change matters?
17. Do you usually feel that you have little to say about what you get to eat at home?
18. Do you feel that when someone doesn't like you there's little you can do about it?
19. Do you usually feel that it's almost useless to try in school because most other children are just plain smarter than you?
20. Are you the kind of person who believes that planning ahead makes things turn out better?
21. Most of the time do you feel that you have little to say about what your family decides to do?

Directions for scoring: Give yourself one point for answering "no" to questions 4, 13, and 20 and one point for answering "yes" to all other questions. A score of 21 reflects the highest possible external locus-of-control attitude, while a score of 1 indicates the highest possible internal locus-of-control attitude.

SOURCE: S. Nowicki and B. Strickland, Locus-of-control scale for children. *Journal of Consulting and Clinical Psychology,* 1973, *40,* 148–154. Copyright 1973 by the American Psychological Association. Reprinted by permission of the authors.

Criticisms of Phenomenological Theories

Critics have raised numerous objections to phenomenological theories of personality (Mischel, 1981; Weiner, 1980). First, relatively little evidence supports the notion that raising an individual's self-concept score appreciably alters his or her behavior. Second, as has already been demonstrated earlier in this chapter, self-concept studies are too contradictory and inconsistent to lend credence to the contention that we know how to improve an individual's self-concept or that we know what contributes to negative self-images.

In further opposition to the phenomenological view, social learning theorists and behaviorists present ample evidence that self-concepts often improve as a consequence of behavioral changes, rather than being prerequisites for behavioral change (Mischel, 1981; Skinner, 1974; Weiner, 1980). These findings and the pursuant controversies are particularly noteworthy in regard to our interactions with adolescents. For example, if we want to help an overweight teenager with a low self-concept improve her self-image, which approach should be adopted—the social learning theorists' view, according to which we should first change her eating and exercising behavior, thereby assuming that her self-concept will improve as a consequence of her losing weight? Or the phenomenologists' view, according to which we should first try to improve her self-concept so that she will become motivated enough to lose weight?

Phenomenological theories are also criticized for failing to adequately explain how personal constructs are created (Mischel, 1981; Weiner, 1980). Like psychoanalytic theorists, phenomenological theorists have been criticized for failing to provide operational definitions and for relying on abstract concepts that cannot be empirically tested. For example, how can it be empirically demonstrated that "José has a hostile, uncooperative personality because his self-concept is poor and his needs for self-esteem and love have not been met"? How are abstractions like self-actualization and the self to be measured and tested?

Finally, many psychologists disagree with phenomenologists like Rogers and Maslow, who maintain that the self is an entity that can evaluate and alter itself through altering its own internal constructs. Furthermore, the belief in an innate drive for self-actualization overlooks the fact that many people behave in destructive, unproductive ways, even when their basic needs have been met. For these reasons, many critics feel that while Rogers's and Maslow's hypotheses may introduce ideals for human behavior, their views fail to offer a heuristic model or empirical data about the human personality. Representing this view, an expert on human motivation, Bernard Weiner, asserts that "although worthy of discussion, in my opinion humanistic theory has not greatly advanced our knowledge of human motivation" (Weiner, 1980, p. 408).

BEHAVIORISTIC THEORIES OF PERSONALITY

In recent years two theoretical approaches have formed the basis for much of the research on adolescent and child development. Referred to collectively as "behavioristic" theories, the traditional behavioral theories and social learning theories share several assumptions that distinguish them from organismic theories of personality.

As Chapter 1 explained (refer to Table 1.1.), social learning and behavioral theories emphasize the importance of environmental influences in the adolescent's cognitive and social development. Behavioristic theories maintain that the adolescent's personality is primarily fashioned by reinforcement, punishment, and modeling. Unlike the organismic theories discussed so far in this chapter, behavioristic theories employ operational definitions and empirical methods for testing their hypotheses. Moreover, behavioral theories reject the notion of distinct stages of development in which children and adolescents must resolve certain psychosocial conflicts or achieve specific skills during a "critical period."

Thanks to the contributions of B. F. Skinner (1974), the terms **behavioral psychology** and **Skinnerian psychology** are often used interchangeably.

Within the context of the present discussion on theories of personality, the term "traditional" is intended to distinguish Skinner's behavioral theories from those of the social learning theorists, whose views, while still behavioristic, represent a departure from several aspects of Skinner's heuristic model.

Traditional Behavioral Theories

According to behavioral psychologists, the entity referred to as the personality is actually a collection of attitudes and acts learned as a consequence of punishment and reinforcement. In other words, adolescents' personalities—just like children's and adults'—are primarily determined by the positive or negative consequences that follow their behavior in particular types of situations. Behavior that is followed by rewarding consequences is likely to be repeated, thereby appearing as part of the youth's personality. In contrast, behavior followed by negative consequences is unlikely to be repeated, and therefore it cannot be construed as part of the youth's personality.

From the behavioral perspective, understanding an adolescent's conduct and attitudes is primarily a matter of observing his or her behavior and its consequences. The behaviorist's goal is to identify the pleasurable consequences that maintain particular behaviors and attitudes, as well as to identify the types of punishment that will diminish undesirable behaviors. This process of eliminating or creating behavior through reinforcement and punishment is called **operant conditioning.**

For example, rather than attributing a boy's fighting to his aggressive personality or to an unresolved Oedipal complex, behaviorists would record data about the circumstances under which this boy fights. Through careful observation, the observer may find that this boy's inappropriate behavior is being maintained by several positive reinforcers: peer approval, the status associated with being "masculine," attention from adults who otherwise ignore him, and freedom from being bullied by other boys.

According to the behavioral model, anything that the adolescent considers pleasurable enough to change or maintain a particular behavior is a **reinforcer.** For example, an adolescent male may consider watching the World Series reinforcing enough to agree to do his homework every night for the privilege of watching the games. An adolescent girl, however, will probably not consider the ballgames reinforcing by her criteria, and therefore her behavior will be unaffected by her parents' offer to let her watch the World Series if she completes her homework. The criticism that behaviorists can manipulate other people through surreptitious reinforcement is undermined by the fact that reinforcers are subjectively determined by each individual's idiosyncratic, ever-changing preferences, thereby rendering surreptitious control over another person highly unlikely.

In regard to deciding what might be reinforcing to a particular adolescent, behaviorists draw distinctions between primary and secondary reinforcers. Experiences or things that are innately pleasurable to human beings, such as food or sex, are referred to as **primary reinforcers.** In contrast, **secondary reinforcers** are experiences or items that are reinforcing only as a consequence of their being paired with primary reinforcers or as a consequence of our having been taught by our society to value them. For example, dollar bills are secondary reinforcers in our society, because their power comes from the fact that they can be exchanged for primary reinforcers like medical aid, food, and clothes. Our currency has no intrinsic value as a primary reinforcer in and of itself, as demonstrated by the fact that a 2-year-old would just as soon tear it up or try to eat it, while a 5-year old has learned from society to put it in a piggy bank for future purchases.

According to behaviorists, aspects of an adolescent's behavior that do not appear to be the consequence of punishment or reinforcement may be the result of prior **classical conditioning.** In classical conditioning a neutral stimulus is paired with a pleasant or unpleasant stimulus. After repeated presentations of the two stimuli together, individuals react to the neutral stimulus just as they do to the one with which it has been paired. This principle can be illustrated by fears that have been conditioned during childhood. For instance, a teenage girl whose mother repeatedly hit her as a young child in the presence of bearded men may develop an excessive fear of all bearded men. Her fear is then a classically conditioned response, which resulted from pairing a neutral stimulus—bearded men—with an aversive stimulus—being hit.

As examples later in this chapter and in subsequent chapters will illustrate, behavioral theories are applied to adolescents by using the principles of reinforcement and punishment to shape new behaviors and attitudes.

Social Learning Theories

In recent years, the principles of Skinnerian psychology have increasingly been subsumed by social learning theories (Mischel, 1981). Expanding on Skinner's behavioristic principles, **social learning theorists** have incorporated observational learning and cognitive processes into their theoretical model (Bandura, 1977; Mischel, 1981). In many respects social learning theories and cognitive developmental theories have grown closer over time. Social learning theorists assume, as do cognitive developmentalists, that adolescents employ constructs that represent their internal mental processes to mediate their responses to reinforcement and punishment. These cognitive processes are presumed to help adolescents organize information and to guide their behavior. Nevertheless, social learning theorists still maintain the behavioristic view that the origins of these mental processes and the means of changing an individual's conduct are primarily environmental. Operant conditioning and observational learning form the core of virtually all social learning theories.

Although concurring with the Skinnerian principles of reinforcement and punishment, social learning theorists like Albert Bandura and Walter Mischel emphasize the importance of **observational learning** in shaping adolescents' personalities (Bandura, 1977; Mischel, 1981). Observational learning, sometimes called "vicarious" learning or "modeling," refers to learning that occurs by observing other people, rather than through direct reinforcement or punishment.

According to social learning theories, adolescents and children are most likely to emulate the behavior of people they value, people with whom they can identify, or people whom they observe receiving rewards. Conversely, the young are least likely to adopt the values or behavior of people who are mocked or punished. For instance, a boy may have extremely bigoted attitudes in regard to race and religion, as a consequence of repeatedly observing and overhearing his parents' critical reactions to "those people." Or a girl may behave in an outgoing, independent manner because she has observed on television and in the world around her that autonomous, gregarious people are more popular than the meek and dependent.

In their departure from traditional Skinnerian views, social learning theorists also maintain that cognitive processes such as locus-of-control attitudes can mediate adolescents' responses to reinforcement and punishment. In this vein, J. B. Rotter's *attribution theories* demonstrate that the values adolescents assign to any potential reinforcer depend on their attribution and expectations of achieveing the reward (Rotter, Chance, & Phares, 1972). On the basis of their own childhood experiences, adolescents attach different values to the same objects or experiences, thereby affecting their potential value as reinforcers. What is reinforcing to one young person may be considered punitive or neutral by another.

According to attribution theories, adolescents, before responding to new situations, ask themselves questions related to the probable consequences of their impending response: "Given what's happened to me in similar situations in the past, what's the outcome probably going to be if I behave in a similar way right now?" "In this situation, what are the odds that I'm going to get rewarded for behaving in one way rather than in another?" In forming their expectations, youngsters also glean information from people's nonverbal cues within the context of the new situation. Raised eyebrows, squinted eyes, scowls, and smiles help youngsters form expectations about what the consequences for various types of responses will probably be.

From this perspective, an adolescent's personality in any particular situation is a consequence of his or her expectations for reward or punishment. For example, whether or not students will be honest during an exam depends on their expectations about what will probably happen to cheaters if they get caught. For this reason a student may cheat on one exam at ten o'clock but not cheat on another at two o'clock. The question is not whether the student has an "honest personality," since honesty depends on the expectations for reward or punishment in particular circumstances.

Most of us have observed instances in which an adolescent's personality seems to have mysteriously changed from one situation to another. According to social learning theorists and Skinnerian behaviorists, the adolescent's conduct has changed because the reinforcement contingencies and the individual's personal expectations about rewards differ from one situation to another. Within the social learning and Skinnerian context, consistencies in an adolescent's behavior, which might seem suggestive of some stable personality trait, are attributed to the similarities in contingencies and expectations of reward.

Applications to Adolescents

Descriptions of the various ways in which social learning and Skinnerian theories are applied to adolescents are reserved for Chapter 15 in order to enhance your appreciation of their relevance to the problems discussed throughout this text. Because programs and strategies predicated upon behavioristic theories have succeeded in alleviating many of the problems adolescents encounter, their applications are also interwoven into subsequent chapters on drugs, sexual conduct, peer relationships, schools, and the family. The information that follows, therefore, is intended as only an introductory overview of the many ways in which behavioristic theories are being utilized to benefit adolescents.

As the methods described in Box 4.3 demonstrate, behavioristic counselors and teachers have had considerable success in diminishing adolescents' defeatist attitudes and feelings of powerlessness by improving their locus-of-control attitudes. In numerous experimental studies, many kinds of adolescent

A Closer Look 4.3 

Changing Adolescents' Locus-of-Control Attitudes

"I only passed that test because it was given on my lucky day"; "I lost that track meet because the coach doesn't like me." An external locus-of-control attitude often underlies expressions like these. Feeling powerless to control the good or the bad in their lives, some adolescents believe "there's no use trying because nothing I do makes any difference." This pessimistic attitude, known as *external* locus of control, often undermines adolescents' academic success as well as their self-confidence. The attitude causes many youngsters to behave "helplessly," when in fact they could have an impact on what is happening to them. In order to increase *internal* locus-of-control attitudes, researchers have implemented a number of strategies for helping adolescents recognize the relationship between their own conduct and the consequences that follow.

Reading or hearing stories about people who have "taken control of their lives" by changing their own behavior lessens some adolescents' feelings of external control. Contingency-management programs, where youngsters are systematically rewarded or punished for their behavior, also diminish feelings of helplessness. In contrast, unstructured classes, an "open" curriculum, and peer competition tend to increase feelings of external control and helplessness. Programs that have helped externally oriented adolescents teach them how to set reasonable goals and how to measure their own behavior and its consequences. For example, when a youngster succeeds, an adult might ask, "What do you think you did differently this past week that caused that improvement on your math test grade and a change in the way your mother is responding to you?" Questions like this can help adolescents learn how to perceive the relationships between their conduct and outcomes.

Of course, all people are sometimes at the mercy of circumstances that are truly beyond their control. There are times when it's surely appropriate for an adolescent to feel that external sources are in control of the outcomes. The ideal attitude is neither to constantly blame other people for the outcomes nor to constantly blame the self. In other words, "Grant me the serenity to accept the things I cannot change, the courage to change the things I can, and the wisdom to know the difference."

SOURCE: L. Nielsen, *Motivating adolescents: A guide for parents, teachers and counselors.* Englewood Cliffs, N.J.: Prentice-Hall, 1982 behavior have been modified by increasing the young person's feelings of personal control over the outcomes, which once seemed beyond his or her influence. According to these data, helping adolescents attain a more internal locus of control has resulted in better academic performance, more appropriate social behavior, and better relationships with parents (Phares, 1973).

Other applications of behavioral principles for adolescents are categorized under the rubric of *behavior modification*. Behavior modification refers to strategies that employ Skinnerian and social learning principles to modify human behavior. Among the most popular and successful of these strategies in working with adolescents are: desensitization, modeling, and contingency management.

Desensitization or **counterconditioning** is a procedure in which a counselor helps the client overcome fears or anxieties through relaxation exercises. First, the client ranks his or her emotional responses to the fear-producing event. For example, an adolescent who is terrified of math exams might rank her nervousness like this: thinking about the exam, hearing people talk about exams, walking to class, going into the classroom, seeing the teacher with the test booklets, taking the exam. The counselor then teaches the youngster how to use relaxation techniques, such as deep breathing or muscle relaxation exercises. Once the client learns to relax, the counselor begins to describe each fear-producing stimulus on the client's list, beginning with the least threatening. When the client is able to remain calm while hearing a particular description, the counselor moves on to describe the next most fearful situation on the list. Detailed descriptions of desensitization are available in the writings of Joseph Wolpe, whose pioneering work popularized these procedures in the 1950s (Wolpe & Lazarus, 1966).

Desensitization techniques are often combined with *modeling* as a way of increasing their effectiveness. To illustrate, a number of experimenters have demonstrated the success of this method in teaching people to overcome their fear of snakes (Mischel, 1981). In these experiments individuals are shown films and live demonstrations of people becoming progressively more friendly with snakes. Models of people interacting with snakes are also presented. Gradually the fearful subjects are encouraged to touch a snake and, eventually, to hold a snake. Through this combination of modeling and desensitization, most subjects completely overcome their snake phobias. Similar procedures have been employed to help adolescents and adults overcome their fears of taking tests, speaking out in class, speaking to large audiences, flying in planes, and dating (Mischel, 1981).

Behavior modification programs often apply the principles of *contingency management* in modifying adolescents' inappropriate behavior. By reinforcing desirable conduct and ignoring or punishing undesirable conduct, contingencies are arranged in ways that increase the likelihood that an adolescent's behavior will change. One method typically used in contingency-management programs is a **contingency contract**—an agreement between the adolescent and another person, which specifies the rewards and punishments for particular behaviors. For example, a father and son might agree verbally that every grade above a C will be rewarded by a weekly allowance increase of two dollars. Similarly, halfway houses for delinquents often use contracts to shape desirable behavior, such as making beds, attending school, completing homework, and talking civilly. Even more impressive, adolescents have been taught to modify their own behavior, as well as the behavior of other people like their parents and teachers, by designing their own contingency-management strategies.

In addition to modifying behavior through the use of rewards and punishment, contingency-management programs can try to eliminate undesirable conduct through extinction. **Extinction** is withholding all forms of reinforcement by completely ignoring the undesirable behavior. This principle can be demonstrated in the hypothetical case of an institutionalized boy throwing a temper tantrum. If his psychiatric nurse totally ignores his tantrum by leaving the room until he calms down, rather than approaching him with comfort or counsel, she would be attempting to eliminate his tantrums through extinction rather than through reinforcement or punishment.

Experimental studies with adolescents in recent years have repeatedly demonstrated the success of behavior modification in a variety of situations, including public schools, psychiatric hospitals, low-income families, and programs for the learning disabled, retarded, delinquent, and psychologically disturbed (Blackham & Silberman, 1975; Homme, 1976; Kanfer & Goldstein, 1980; Mischel, 1981; Nielsen, 1982; Wilson & O'Leary, 1980).

Criticisms of Behavioristic Theories

Despite their success and popularity, behavioristic theories are not without their critics (Mischel, 1981; Weiner, 1980). Reflecting the psychoanalytic position, one criticism is that behavior modification fails to resolve the underlying psychological causes of a person's inappropriate or destructive conduct. As a consequence, argue the critics, the adolescent may temporarily appear "cured" in regard to one particular type of behavior, only to have the problem reappear at a later date in the guise of a supposedly new behavioral problem. Psychoanalytically oriented critics argue that personalities cannot be altered without an understanding of the unconscious psychological roots of behavior.

Another concern is that adolescents may get "hooked" on external reinforcement, rather than developing intrinsic motivation. Behaviorists' critics argue that young people may be particularly prone to becoming dependent on reinforcement from other people, which will undermine their own initiative, independence, will power, and self-discipline. Behaviorists counter this criticism by pointing out that the ultimate goal of any behavior-modification program is to wean people from reliance on external rewards by gradually moving them toward more internal forms of reinforcement. For example, a math teacher's initial objective might be to get her reluctant student to complete his math homework each night for the "reward" of points that will be added to his final grade. Her ultimate goal, however, is to gradually withdraw the points *if* he begins to derive other forms of pleasure from completing his homework or from feeling more masterful in the real world as a consequence of his newly acquired math skills. The behaviorists maintain that using external reinforcement in situations where adolescents are not intrinsically motivated is more humane than permitting these youngsters to fail to develop certain essential skills or to engage in behavior that may be detrimental to their physical or mental well-being.

In a similar vein, behaviorists have been criticized for "manipulating" and "bribing" people through the use of reinforcement and punishment. One counterargument is that bribery involves rewarding illegal or immoral conduct, whereas reinforcement means offering incentives for desirable conduct, when an individual is having difficulty maintaining desirable behavior. Furthermore, behavioral psychologists do not insist that adolescents be secretively manipulated. To the contrary, many behavior-modification strategies require the active participation of the adolescent in designing the program and designating the objectives. Moreover, behavioral psychologists contend that they are teaching people, including children and adolescents, to master the skills of behavior modification in order to gain more control over their own lives and to improve their relationships with other people—acts that accord people more personal power and independence.

Finally, critics contend that behavioral principles have limited power over the individual's personality, when compared to cognitive process and phenomenological aspects of human behavior. From the perspective of cognitive and phenomenological theorists, a number of questions regarding behavioristic strategies remain unanswered: Will behaviors modified through behavioristic techniques transfer to new situations? Are behavioral methods effective for changing complex behaviors and attitudes? Are behavioral changes permanent, or will people eventually revert to their former behavioral patterns? Will behavior that has been eliminated through behavior modification reappear in another form, since the underlying psychological causes have not changed? As social learning theorists and Skinnerians continue to conduct their experimental studies, answers to questions like these will become less tentative.

Conclusion

Considering the contradictory data and the support that each theoretical perspective can muster on its behalf, which theory of personality should we endorse in our quest for a better understanding of adolescents? Given the current state of uncertainty, any definitive statement about the "best" theory of personality would be unwarranted. Hence, it seems wisest to adopt the position of Walter Mischel, a leading authority in the field of personality (Mischel, 1981). According to Mischel, current research suggests that our personalities are determined by both external and internal factors. Although some people do behave rather consistently on certain traits, nobody's behavior is consistent all the time on any trait. As Mischel points out, researchers had hoped to discover which was more important in determining our personalities—the environment or the processes within the person. The answer to this question will always depend, however, on what particular kind of behavior, situation, and person is sampled. As a consequence, the more important question confronting contemporary scholars should be: Under what circumstances are external factors and under what circumstances are internal factors most likely to effect an individual's behavior?

While researchers are pursuing the answer to this question, we can apply Mischel's advice to our own interactions with and perceptions of adolescents. First, we can qualify our descriptions of adolescents by specifying the circumstances under which they behave in particular ways, rather than labeling them as having consistent traits or an unalterable personality. Second, we can appreciate the complexity of the human personality by refusing to adopt any theory that proposes to have identified the single cause of adolescent behavior. Third, we can perceive the adolescent as someone whose behavior is composed of many facets that may sometimes appear contradictory. For example, in the chapters that follow, you may be surprised to discover that adolescents' behavior in regard to sexual issues differs considerably from their behavior in regard to politics or religion.

Throughout this text, recommendations for relating to adolescents will be described in terms of their relationship to a particular theory of personality or a theory of cognitive development. In this regard, a useful exercise at this point would be to review Tables 1.1, 1.2, and 4.1. A thorough understanding of the concepts presented in Chapters 3 and 4 will enable you to critique the suggestions and research in future chapters with more sophistication and care.

Questions for Discussion and Review

Basic Concepts and Terminology

1. In what respects do Freudian and neo-Freudian views of the adolescent's personality differ?
2. How do Freudian, neo-Freudian, cognitive, and behavioristic theories account for the changes in an individual's personality during adolescence?
3. By providing specific examples of adolescent behavior, explain each of the defense mechanisms according to the Freudian view.
4. How are each of the following used in the assessment of adolescents' personalities: the MMPI, TAT, Rorscharch test, Q-sort, locus-of-control inventories, and the semantic differential?
5. How do Rogerian, behavioristic, and psychoanalytic counseling differ in regard to their goals, methods, and assumptions about changing adolescents' attitudes and conduct?
6. How are Erikson's psychosocial stages, Piaget's cognitive stages, Freud's psychosexual stages, and Loevinger's ego stages interrelated?
7. Citing specific examples of adolescent behavior as illustrations, explain the phenomenological perspective of personality in regard to locus of control, attribution theory, self-concepts, and gestalts.
8. In what respects do social learning theories differ from more traditional behavioral theories in regard to adolescents' behavior?
9. What are the strengths and limitations of behavioral, psychoanalytic, cognitive, and phenomenological theories?
10. According to cognitive psychologists, in what specific ways do cognitive changes affect adolescents' personalities?

Questions for Discussion and Debate

1. How do Marcia's identity statuses apply to your own adolescence and to your present life?
2. What evidence do you see of the following in adolescents' behavior: locus-of-control attitudes, cognitive dissonance, the imaginary audience, and the personal fable?
3. Using the principles of behavioristic theories, how would you design a program to change these aspects of an adolescent's personality: fear of going to school, shyness, test-taking anxiety, poor communication with a parent, temper tantrums, and alcoholism.

4. If forced to choose only one of the five theoretical approaches to the study of adolescents' personalities, which would you choose and why?
5. Which of the criticisms levied against each theoretical approach to personality do you consider most significant? What additional criticisms would you add to those presented in this chapter?
6. How have you inadvertently used trait theories in describing and interacting with adolescents and with you own friends? In what ways has this been advantageous and disadvantageous for you?
7. How have the Freudian concepts of individuation and the Oedipal complex affected your development or the development of any adolescent with whom you are acquainted?
8. How does your score on the locus-of-control inventory in Box 4.3 coincide with your present behavior and your feelings of personal powerlessness or control?
9. How closely aligned is Maslow's description of a self-actualized person with your own views of the ideal or mature personality? How did you measure up to Maslow's description in Table 4.2?
10. How do you presently employ defense mechanisms in comparison to the ways you employed them during your adolescence?

REFERENCES

Adams, G. Family correlates of female adolescents' ego identity development. *Journal of Adolescence*, 1985, *8*, 69–82.

Adams G., & Fitch, S. Ego stage and identity status development: A cross-sequential analysis. *Journal of Personality and Social Psychology*, 1982, *43*, 574–583.

Adams, G., & Jones, R. Female adolescents' identity development: Age comparisons and perceived childbearing experiences. *Developmental Psychology*, 1983, *19*, 249–256.

Adelson, J., & Doehrman, M. The psychodynamic approach to adolescence. In J. Adelson (ed.), *Handbook of adolescent psychology*. New York: Wiley, 1980. Pp. 99–116.

Ausubel, D., Sullivan, E., & Ives, S. *Theory and problems of child development*. New York: Grune and Stratton, 1979.

Bachman, J., Green, S., & Wirtanen, I. *Youth in transition: Dropping out—problem or symptom?* Ann Arbor: University of Michigan Press, 1971.

Bachman, J., & O'Malley, P. *The search for school effects: New findings and perspectives*. Ann Arbor: University of Michigan Press, 1978.

Bandura, A. *Social learning theory*. Englewood Cliffs, N.J.,: Prentice-Hall, 1977.

Blackham, G., & Silberman, A. *Modification of child and adolescent behavior*. Belmont, Cal.: Wadsworth, 1975.

Blos, P. *The adolescent passage: Developmental issues*. New York: International Universities Press, 1979.

Blyth, D., Simmons, R., & Bush, D. The transition into early adolescence: A longitudinal comparison of youth in two educational contexts. *Sociology of Education*, 1978, *51*, 149–162.

Bourne, E. The state of research on ego identity: A review and appraisal. *Journal of Youth and Adolescence*, 1978, *7*, 223–251, 371–392.

Candee, D. Ego developmental aspects of New Left ideology. *Journal of Personality and Social Psychology*, 1974, *30*, 620–630.

Cattell, R. *The scientific analysis of personality*. Baltimore, Md.: Penguin Books, 1965.

Cooper, C., Grotevant, H., & Condon, S. Individuality and connectedness. In H. Grotevant and C. Cooper (eds.), *Adolescent development in the family.* San Franciso: Jossey Bass, 1984.

Douvan, E., & Adelson, J. *The adolescent experience.* New York: Wiley, 1966.

Dworkin, R. Genetic and environmental influences on person-situation interactions. *Journal of Research in Personality,* 1979, *13,* 279–293.

Elkind, D. *Children and adolescents: Interpretive essays on Jean Piaget.* New York: Oxford University Press, 1970.

Elkind, D. *The child's reality: Three developmental themes.* Hillsdale, N.J.: Erlbaum, 1978.

Elkind, D., & Bowen, R. Imaginary audience behavior in children and adolescents. *Developmental Psychology,* 1979, *15,* 38–44.

Enright, R., Lapsley, D., & Shukla, D. Adolescent egocentrism in early and late adolescence. *Adolescence,* 1979, *14,* 687–695.

Erikson, E. *Identity: Youth and crisis.* New York: Norton, 1968.

Festinger, L. *Theory of cognitive dissonance.* Stanford, Cal.: Stanford Univ. Press, 1957.

Fisher, S., & Greenberg, R. *The scientific credibility of Freud's theories and therapy.* New York: Basic Books, 1977.

Freud, A. *The ego and the mechanisms of defense.* New York: International Universities press, 1946.

Freud, A. *Normality and pathology in childhood: Assessment of development.* New York: International Universities Press, 1977.

Freud, S. *The ego and the id.* London: Hogarth, 1927.

Freud, S. *Group psychology and the analysis of the ego.* London: Hogarth, 1949.

Gilligan, C. *In a different voice: Psychological theory and women's development.* Cambridge, Mass.: Harvard University Press, 1982.

Hamachek, D. *Encounters with the self.* New York: Holt, Rinehart and Winston, 1978.

Hathaway, S., & McKinley, J. *MMPI manual.* New York: Psychological Corporation, 1943.

Hauser, S. Ego development and interpersonal styles in adolescence. *Journal of Youth and Adolescence,* 1978, *7,* 333–352.

Holt, R. Loevinger's measure of ego development: Reliability and national norms for male and female short forms. *Journal of Personality and Social Psychology,* 1980, *39,* 909–920.

Homme, L. *How to use contingency contracting in the classroom.* Champaign, Ill.: Research Press, 1976.

Horney, K. *Feminine psychology.* New York: Norton, 1967.

Jenkins, A. *Psychology of the Afro-American.* New York: Pergamon, 1982.

Jones, E. Personality characteristics of black youth. *Journal of Youth and Adolescence,* 1979, *8,* 149–159.

Josselson, R. Ego development in adolescence. In J. Adelson (ed.), *Handbook of adolescent psychology.* New York: Wiley, 1980. Pp. 188–211.

Kanfer, F., & Goldstein, A. (eds.). *Helping people change: A testbook of methods.* Elmsford, N.Y.: Pergamon Press, 1980.

Kash, M., & Borich, G. *Teacher behavior and pupil self-concept.* Reading, Mass.: Addison-Wesley, 1978.

Kelly, G. *The psychology of personal constructs.* New York: Norton, 1955.

Lewin K. *A dynamic theory of personality.* New York: McGraw-Hill, 1935.

Loevinger, J. *Ego development.* San Francisco: Jossey-Bass, 1976.

Logan, R. Identity diffusion and psychosocial defense mechanisms. *Adolescence,* 1978, *13,* 503–508.

Marcia, J. Identity in adolescence. In J. Adelson (ed.), *Handbook of adolescent psychology.* New York: Wiley, 1980. Pp. 159–188.

Maslow, A. *Toward a psychology of being*. New York: Van Nostrand, 1968.

Matteson, D. Sex differences in identity formation: A Challenge to the theory. In J Marcia, S. Waterman, and D. Matteson, *Ego identity: A handbook for psychosocial research*. Hillsdale, N.J.: Erlbaum, in press.

McGuire, W., McGuire, C., Child, P., & Fujioka, T. Salience of ethnicity in self-concept as a function of one's ethnic distinctiveness in the social environment. *Journal of Personality and Social Psychology*, 1978, *36*, 511–520.

Mischel, W. *Introduction to personality*. New York: Holt, Rinehart and Winston, 1981.

Muslin, H. The superego in the adolescent female. In M. Sugar (ed.), *Female adolescent development*. New York: Brunner Mazel, 1979. Pp. 296–308.

Nielsen, L. *Motivating adolescents: A guide for parents, teachers and counselors*. Englewood Cliffs, N.J.: Prentice-Hall, 1982.

Nisbet, R., & Ross, L. *Human inference: Strategies and shortcomings of social judgment*. Englewood Cliffs, N.J.: Prentice-Hall, 1980.

Offer, D., & Offer, J. *From teenage to young manhood*. New York: Basic Books, 1975.

Offer, D., Ostrov, E., & Howard, K. *The adolescent: A psychological self-portrait*. New York: Basic Books, 1981.

Petersen, A., Offer, D., & Kaplan, E. The self-image of rural adolescent girls. In M. Sugar (ed.), *Female adolescent development*. New York: Brunner Mazel, 1979. Pp. 141–155.

Phares, E. *Locus of control: A personality determinant of behavior*. Morristown, N.J.: General Learning Press, 1973.

Purkey, W. *Inviting school success*. Belmont, Cal.: Wadsworth, 1978.

Redmore, C., & Loevinger, J. Ego development in adolescence: Longitudinal studies. *Journal of Youth and Adolescence*, 1979, *8*, 1–20.

Rogers, C. *Client centered therapy* (2d ed.). Boston: Houghton Mifflin, 1969.

Rosenberg, M. *Conceiving the self*. New York: Basic Books, 1979.

Rotter, J., Chance, J., & Phares, E. *Applications of a social learning theory of personality*. New York: Holt, Rinehart and Winston, 1972.

Simmons, R., Rosenberg, F., & Rosenberg, M. Disturbance in the self-image at adolescence. *American Sociological Review*, 1973, *38*, 553–568.

Skinner, B. F., *About behaviorism*. New York: Knopf, 1974.

Soares, A., & Soares, L. Comparative differences in self-perception of disadvantaged and advantaged students. *Journal of School Psychology*, 1971, *9*, 924–929.

Spruill, V. Alterations in the ego ideal in girls in mid-adolescence. In M. Sugar (ed.), *Female adolescent development*. New York: Brunner Mazel, 1979. Pp. 310–330.

Steinberg, L., Greenberger, E., Jacobi, M., & Garduque, L. Early work experience: A partial antidote for adolescent egocentrism. *Journal of Youth and Adolescence*, 1981, *10*, 141–158.

Waterman, A. Identity development from adolescence to adulthood: An extension of theory and a review of research. *Developmental Psychology*, 1982, *18*, 341–358.

Weiner, B. *Human motivation*. New York: Holt, Rinehart and Winston, 1980.

Wells, E. *The mythical negative black self-concept*. San Francisco: R and E Research Associates, 1978.

Wilson, G., & O'Leary, K. *Principles of behavior therapy*. Englewood Cliffs, N.J.: Prentice-Hall, 1980.

Wolpe, J., & Lazarus, A. *Behavior therapy techniques: A guide to the treatment of neurosis*. Oxford: Pergamon, 1966.

Wylie, R. *The self-concept: Theory and research*. Lincoln: University of Nebraska Press, 1979.

Chapter Outline

Goals and Objectives

This chapter is designed to enable you to:

- *Define sex roles and sex-role stereotypes*
- *Explain the major theories of sex-role development*
- *Demonstrate the impact of sex roles on the vocational, academic, and personal conduct and attitudes of adolescents*
- *Consider the controversies surrounding sex-role stereotypes*
- *Identify methods for eliminating sex-role stereotypes*
- *Enumerate differences between male and female behavior*
- *Examine the importance of sex-role development during adolescence*

Concepts and Terminology

sex role	*agency*
sexism	*communion*
hermaphrodite	*schema*
Title IX	*locus of control*
symbolic models	*identity achievers*
androgyny	*identity foreclosure*

5 Sex Roles and Adolescent Development

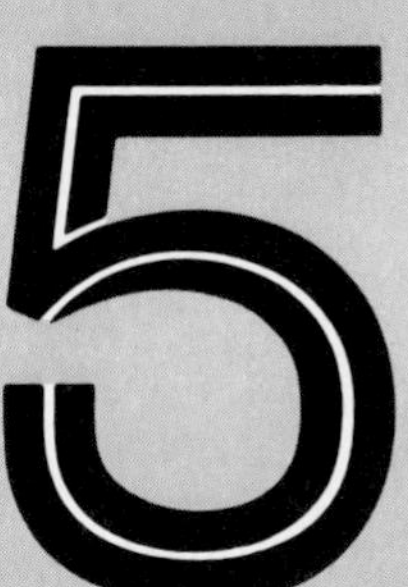

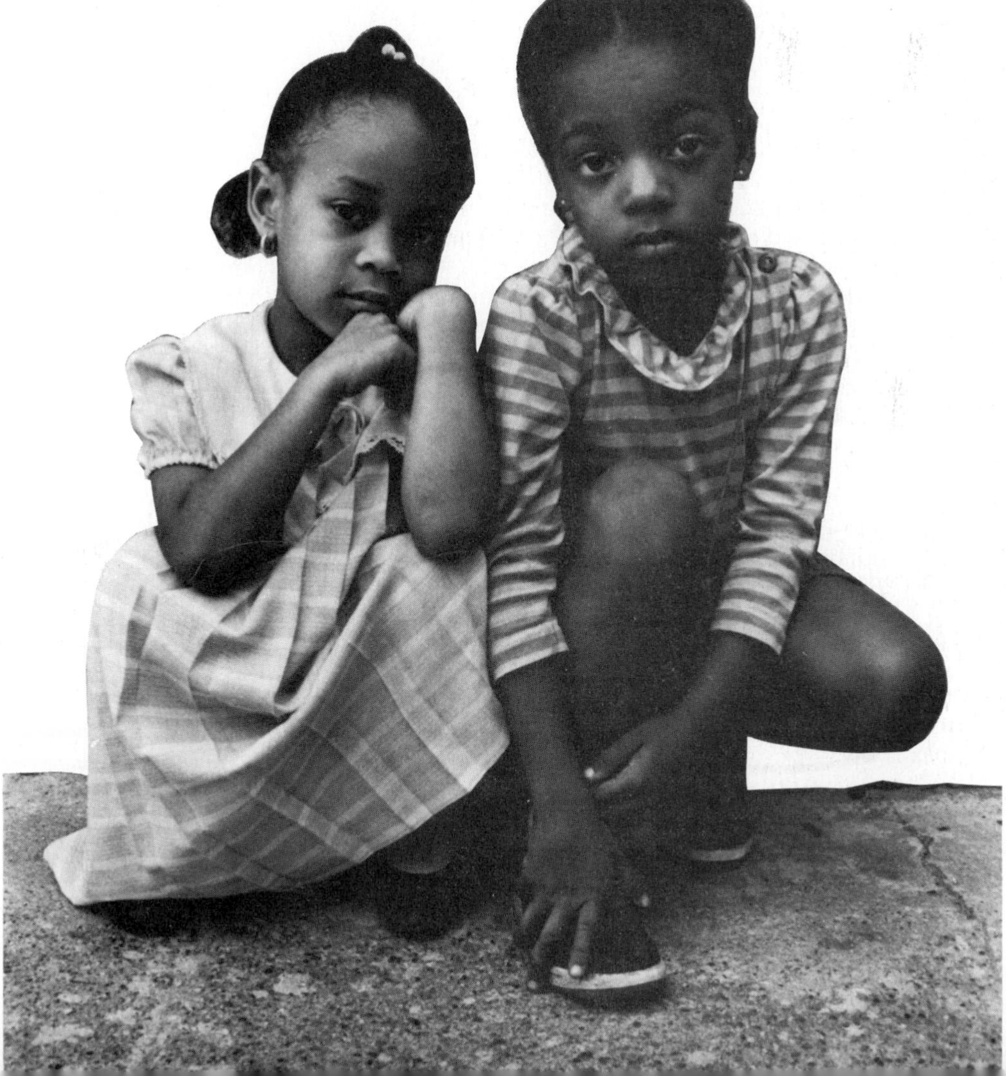

DEFINING SEX ROLES AND ANDROGYNY

In nursery rhymes and aphorisms boys have been described as "Snips and snails and puppy dogs' tails"; "Someone who wants to grow up fast and be a fireman and eat candy for a living"; "A noise with dirt on it"; "An appetite with a skin pulled over it"; "Someone more troublesome than a dozen girls." In like manner, females have been described as "Sugar and spice and everything nice"; "A person who has devised more defensive plays than football coaches"; "A species that cannot love an automobile"; "A person who would rather have a caress than a career"; "A person who will look in a mirror any time—except when pulling out of a parking space" (Brussell, 1970).

In a more serious vein, these characterizations serve as reminders of one of the most dramatic changes in adolescent and child psychology in the past decade—the views regarding sex typing and sex-role development. For example, a comparison of the 1974 and 1984 literature reviews in the *Child Development Handbook* demonstrates that in the early 1970s most psychologists, parents, and educators endorsed the idea of socializing children to adopt our society's prespecified gender roles. In contrast, by 1984 most psychologists deemed sex typing an undesirable aspect of socialization for both male and female human beings (Huston, 1984).

Sex typing and **sex roles** are terms referring to those characteristics, interests, and activities defined by a society as appropriate for members of each sex. Tables 5.1 and 5.2 illustrate the traits that researchers have identified as representative of male and female gender roles in our contemporary U.S. society. It's important to note, however, that sex typing and sex roles are not to be confused with sexuality, sexual preferences, or physiological differences between the two sexes. For example, an adolescent male may have a sexual preference for members of his own sex, although he adheres to our society's male sex role in terms of his activities, values, and characteristics. Similarly, a heterosexual female, with a very petite build and an extremely feminine voice and appearance, may nonetheless adhere most closely to the male gender role by engaging in activities and manifesting personality traits that coincide with our society's notions for the male sex role.

Margaret Mead's classic study of three preliterate societies underscores the importance of our making this semantic distinction between the terms "sex," "gender," "sex role," and "sex typing" (Mead, 1935). In her anthropological studies Mead observed that both male and female members of the Arapesh tribe exhibited feminine conduct, according to U.S. standards of the female sex role. Both males and females were socialized to be cooperative, nurturant, and non-aggressive. In contrast, the nearby Mundugunore tribe socialized both sexes to exhibit traits that reflected U.S. notions of the male gender role—ruthlessness, aggressiveness, and a non-nurturant attitude toward their young. In still further contrast to U.S. notions of gender roles, the Tchambuli society socialized its males to be passive, dependent, and emotional, and socialized females to be aggressive, independent, and rational. In perfect accord with their society's gender roles, Tchambuli males spent considerable time creating new dances, coiffing their hair, creating art, and applying cosmetics to their faces and bodies.

In regard to our study of contemporary adolescents, cross-cultural data like Mead's demonstrate that societies have their own idiosyncratic notions of masculinity and femininity. Although "sex" and "gender" refer to the universal physiological differences between males and females, "sex-typed" behavior, "sex roles," or "gender roles" refer to a society's own particular ideas regarding appropriate masculine and feminine conduct. Behavior deemed masculine in one culture may be considered feminine in another.

Furthermore, in a society as large and as culturally diverse as the United States, sex roles can differ as a consequence of an individual's geographic location, chronological age, or ethnic affiliations. For example, in 1954 a 16-year-old boy who wore a gold necklace, long hair, and a pastel floral shirt would have been considered effeminate and in total violation of his generation's male gender role. By the sex-typed standards of the 1980s, however, this same young man is within the bounds of his sex role and can even permanent or color his hair, pierce his ear and wear an earring, and apply certain cosmetics without threatening his masculinity. Even so, the earring and cosmetics are more likely to violate the limits of masculinity in the rural areas of Arkansas than in Los Angeles. Indeed, the ever-changing sex-role standards by which adolescents and adults are dubbed "masculine" or "feminine" underlie the apocryphal remarks of one adolescent's father to his fishing buddy: "George, I just can't bring myself to have a 'man to man' talk with a boy who's wearing an earring!"

Although society has traditionally socialized males and females into either masculine or feminine sex roles, most psychologists are now endorsing the concept of androgyny as a better model for human development (Bem, 1974; Block 1973; Spence, Helmreich, & Stapp, 1975). Derived from the Greek words denoting man, *andro,* and woman, *gynē,* **androgyny** denotes a combination of stereotypically masculine and feminine characteristics. During the 1970s the literature on sex typing typically viewed masculinity and femininity as opposite traits on a single continuum, rather than as two independent traits that an individual might possess simultaneously. In these early conceptions of sex roles, interests or activities associated with one sex role were assumed to preclude interests and activities associated with the other sex role. For example, an adolescent girl who enjoyed athletics and competition would not have been assumed to have equivalent interests in such domains as child care and cooking. Recent research, however, has challenged this bipolar viewpoint by demonstrating that children and adults can embody the traits that characterize both the male and female sex-role stereotypes (Huston, 1984).

Adhering strictly to neither the masculine nor the feminine gender role, androgynous people embody characteristics once ascribed to the other gender. For example, an androgynous male might have the sex-typed feminine traits of being nurturant, sentimental, and emotionally expressive, as well as the masculine characteristics of being competitive, ambitious, and independent. As research reported later in this chapter will demonstrate, a number of scholars and educators endorse the concept of androgyny by maintaining that characteristics deemed valuable by a society should be encouraged in all individuals, regardless of gender. In other words, if traits such as competitiveness, nurturance, and emotional expressiveness are desirable human attributes, then society should socialize both males and females to adopt these traits, rather than encouraging their development in members of only one sex. This perspective, however, is not without its critics. As the discussion of sex-role theories will demonstrate, not all scholars agree that androgyny can be fostered through environmental means. Moreover, not all parents, adolescents, or educators believe androgyny is an ideal toward which our society should strive.

LIMITATIONS OF THE RESEARCH

Types of Research Available

The research on sex typing during the past decade has included five different areas of investigation (Huston, 1984). The first is the study of relationships between certain physiological sex differences and male and female behavior. This type of research is exemplified by studies, cited later in this chapter, on the relationship between male adolescents' aggressive behavior and their testosterone levels. A second area of research examines the differences between male and female activities and interests. These studies might, for example, compare male and female adolescents' vocational and academic achievements.

A third approach is to compare the sexes in regard to their personal and social characteristics, such as aggression, dependence, and nurturance. A fourth comparison focuses on male and female social relationships. These studies will be discussed in Chapters 9 and 10 rather than here, because their focus is on male and female friendships, dating choices, and sexual behavior. Finally, studies have contrasted male and female communication styles. This research includes the study of nonverbal behavior, speech patterns, and patterns of fantasy.

The existing research on sex typing can be further divided into categories on the basis of the types of dependent variables the researchers have chosen to employ (Huston, 1984). One approach is to study the adolescent's identity or self-perception. This strategy is exemplified by studies in which adolescents are asked to describe themselves in terms that are assessed as masculine or feminine by present sex-role standards. Another approach is to study the adolescent's sex-role beliefs. For example, the researcher might measure adolescents' understanding of our society's sex-role stereotypes. A third strategy has been to measure adolescents' preferences and attitudes—for example, by investigating whether the traits associated with the male sex role are considered more desirable than those associated with the female sex role. Finally, researchers have examined the actual behavior of males and females, including some rather ingenious criteria of behavior, such as "limp-wristedness" in young boys and voice intonations in girls.

Two of the most popular instruments for measuring adolescents' sex-role attitudes and self-perceptions of masculinity and femininity are the Bem Sex Role Inventory (Bem, 1974) and the Personal Attributes Questionnaire (Spence, Helmreich, & Stapp, 1975). A modification of the Bem Sex Role Inventory, designed for children between the ages of 10 and 14, has also recently become available (Thomas & Robinson, 1981).

Methodological Limitations

Despite the fact that researchers have devoted far more attention to the study of sex differences and gender roles in the past decade, the available research is limited in several respects (Huston, 1984; Matteson, 1986).

First, since so few longitudinal studies exist, our present knowledge regarding the impact of sex roles or the actual differences between the sexes is severely limited. This shortcoming is particularly important because studies have already demonstrated that certain sex-typed attitudes and behaviors emerge only beyond a certain age in the individual's life. For example, sex differences in recreational activities and in vocational interests are apparent by middle childhood, whereas sex differences in social, moral, and personal domains tend not to be manifest until later in adolescence (Huston, 1984). Similarly, the research on identity statuses has shown that the relationship between low masculinity and intuitive thinking does not appear until adolescents are at least seniors in high school (Matteson, 1986). Only cross-sectional, longitudinal studies can detect these sex differences and the impact of sex typing during childhood and adolescents. It is unfortunate that so few such studies presently exist.

Another problem to be addressed is the failure to differentiate between well-designed and poorly designed studies before making generalizations about gender roles or sex differences. For example, Maccoby and Jacklin's (1974) frequently cited conclusions about sex differences have been criticized for their failure to take account of the methodological differences among the 1,600 studies in their review and for their focus on research with preschool children (J. Block, 1976). Similarly, it has been argued that the contradictory findings in the research on sex differences are due to variations in the subjects' social class, cultural backgrounds, and age (Unger, 1979).

Furthermore, most of the extant research has focused exclusively on the differences between males and females and has ignored the behavioral and attitudinal differences that exist within each sex. This oversight contributes to exaggerated notions about the differences between males and females, since the wide range of masculine or feminine behavior in both the male and the female population remains unnoticed.

The most serious limitation of the research, however, is that so few data exist on female adolescents, therefore making valid comparisons between male and female adolescents both difficult and, in some cases, unjustifiable. Former president of the American Society for Adolescent Psychiatry, Max Sugar, prefaces his recent text on adolescent female development by stating that the book is hampered by the paucity of data on adolescent girls (Sugar, 1979). Likewise, the renowned adolescent scholar and psychologist, Joseph Adelson (1980), asserts that adolescent psychology is, more accurately, "the psychology of adolescent boys." Adelson acknowledges that our notions about adolescents have generally been derived from male subjects and then, erroneously, generalized to females—a serious methodological flaw noted by numerous scholars and psychologists (Denmark & Goodfield, 1978; Gilligan, 1982; Lipsitz, 1978; Murty, 1978; Offer & Offer, 1975). Consequently, highly popularized adolescence theories, such as Kohlberg's model of moral development and Erikson's hypotheses about identity achievement, have often failed to explain female adolescents' development, as subsequent chapters in this text will demonstrate (Gilligan, 1982).

Given these limitations, many generalizations about the supposed differences between males and females and about gender roles must be viewed tentatively. As the remainder of this chapter will demonstrate, many of our former assumptions about gender roles and sex differences have recently been revised on the basis of more carefully designed studies and more cautious comparisons of data whose samples were drawn from different populations of adolescents.

THEORIES OF SEX-ROLE DEVELOPMENT

Most research on sex roles and sex differences conducted during the past decade has been predicated upon social learning theory and cognitive developmental theory. Nevertheless, physiological, psychoanalytic, and information-processing theories continue to exert their influence and, therefore, merit a brief examination.

Physiological Theories

In regard to sex roles, the adage "anatomy is destiny" assumes that physiological differences between the sexes are the primary determinants of male and female behavior and attitudes. The advocates of the physiological perspective contend that contemporary gender roles emanate from genetically determined sex differences, which society cannot alter. For example, in former times some psychologists relied on cranioscopy—the practice of measuring the size of a person's head to determine his or her intelligence—to substantiate their claim that males were innately more intelligent than females (Shields, 1975). With our contemporary standards of measuring sex differences, cranioscopy now appears amusing. Nevertheless, the assumption underlying the practice of cranioscopy still remains intact. Because the sexes are genetically and biochemically different, many contemporary theorists still maintain that these physiological distinctions are at least partially responsible for behavioral differences between males and females.

Two important caveats are in order before discussing the physiological perspective on sex differences. First, neither social learning, psychoanalytic, nor cognitive theorists would discount the fact that males and females differ genetically and hormonally. This fact is particularly important in regard to our study of adolescents, since puberty is the time when testosterone and estrogen levels in both sexes depart radically from their childhood levels. Perceiving the argument simply as "nature versus nurture," however, fails to aknowledge the complexity of human behavior and would be an insult to advocates of both the environmental and physiological theories. For example, since testosterone does cause males to develop larger muscles than females, and since larger muscles cause us to respond to their owner as if he were more aggressive or more athletic than less muscular people, how can we state definitely whether or not testosterone "causes" males to be more aggressive and athletic? In other words, the essential bone of contention between the biological and environmental theorists is the degree to which they feel male and female behavior is physiologically determined.

A second caveat is that most of the data supporting the physiological viewpoint on sex differences have been derived from animal studies, since comparable experimentation with human subjects would require unethical practices. Generalizing these animal results to humans, however, is problematic, since it is generally acknowledged that human behavior is more heavily influenced by environmental factors than animal behavior. Furthermore, evidence now suggests that hormone levels may increase or decrease as a consequence of behavior. For instance, although a male's testosterone level may be elevated after a fistfight, the fighting itself may have caused the increase (Hoyenga & Hoyenga, 1979).

With these cautions in mind, the physiological perspective can be illustrated by examining several of its hypotheses—for example, that an adolescent's levels of estrogen and testosterone influence her or his sex-typed behavior. Accordingly, then, extremely feminine behavior in males or females should be associated with higher levels of estrogen, and extremely masculine behavior in males or females should be accompanied by higher levels of testosterone. It has also been hypothesized that being born with an extra X or Y chromosome or being exposed to high levels of testosterone *in utero* might affect an adolescent's performance on certain sex-typed skills, such as mathematical and spatial problem solving. Similarly, as described in Chapter 3, recent research on brain hemisphericity is searching for the physiological bases of cognitive differences between the sexes (review Box 3.7 for details).

While such studies have produced many intriguing hypotheses, reviews of the available literature conclude that the data presently fail to support the hypothesis that differences in male and female behavior are genetically or hormonally determined. As the data in Chapter 10 will demonstrate, even the most extreme variations from gender roles, in terms of males and females behaving in ways characteristic of the opposite sex, have not been linked to genetic or hormonal factors (Hoyenga & Hoyenga, 1979; Huston, 1984; Money & Ehrhardt, 1972).

Despite the fact that empirical research has not established a relationship between physiological and behavioral differences between males and females, one of the most influential psychologists in recent decades predicated his theories of adolescence on the physiological model. Erik Erikson, whose personality theories were described in Chapter 4, initially argued that a child's reproductive organs are indirectly responsible for certain aspects of his or her personality. Arguing against the environmentalists' position, Erikson maintained that a girl's reproductive structure results in her becoming dependent, passive, compliant, nurturant, and personable, while a boy's results in his becoming dominant, assertive, independent, task oriented, and nonconforming (Erikson, 1968).

Erikson based his theory on observations of 11- to 13-year-olds who were given blocks and dolls and then instructed to construct scenes of whatever type they wished. Erikson observed that boys built more houses with elaborate walls and protrusions, such as towers, while girls built enclosures with low walls and peaceful interiors. According to Erikson, these constructions metaphorically represented the youngsters' sexual organs, because a boy's penis is erectable and intrusive and a girl's vagina is enclosed and receptive. Given their reproductive differences, males will develop personalities that conform to their "outer space," while girls will be inclined to develop traits oriented to their "inner space."

Not surprisingly, Erikson's theories have provoked criticism from behavioristic theorists. First, Erikson's hypotheses ignore the research that substantiates the impact of socialization on human behavior. Second, criticisms have been directed at Erikson's methodology (Caplan, 1978). Only 8 percent of the boys in Erikson's experiments constructed towerlike structures, and overall, the boys built three times as many enclosed structures as towers. Moreover, Erikson is anatomically incorrect in assuming that the female reproductive organs are similar to "hollow inner space" and that only the penis is "erectable." As Chapter 2 indicated, the vagina and uterus are not hollow spaces and the clitoris is as "erectable" as a penis. Despite the fact that Erikson eventually modified certain aspects of his theories regarding male and female behavior, his model serves as an illustration of the ways in which adolescent psychology is influenced by physiological theories of development.

Psychoanalytic Theories

In the tradition of the psychoanalytic perspective described in Chapter 4, classical Freudian theory contradicts the physiological model's assumptions about sex differences. From the traditional Freudian view, male and female children assume their respective sex-typed characteristics through the process of identification with the same-sexed parent. According to early psychoanalytic theories, "penis envy" motivates little girls to identify with their mothers out of a sense of inferiority to males. Furthermore, females are presumed to want children and to want a submissive role vis-à-vis males as a way of compensating for their feelings of inadequacy.

Within the psychoanalytic framework, however, feminist scholars have challenged these classical Freudian notions of male and female development (Horney, 1932; Lerner, 1978). According to these reformulations, male children may envy the female's ability to bear and feed children. Moreover, since children are psychologically and physically dependent on their mothers, they may become fearful and resentful of her power. It has been suggested that males generalize these feelings about their own mothers to all females, thereby becoming fearful of females and attempting to undermine female power by creating a partriarchal society. Establishing a society whose sex roles assure males a dominant financial and social position over females gives males control over their childhood fears of female power.

According to this feminist viewpoint, sex roles in our society could be modified by encouraging men to assume more child-care responsibilities. In this way, children's fears of dependency on the mother and fears of her power would be partially transferred to the father. Hence, males would have less vested interest in maintaining sex roles and societal policies that assure male dominance, since they would have fewer fears of females. Although a departure from some aspects of traditional Freudian theories, these views still perceive the differences in male and female behavior as rooted in early childhood psychosexual conflicts with parents.

Cognitive Developmental Theories

As previous chapters have demonstrated, cognitive developmental theories are prominent in the field of research on adolescents' cognition and personality. In regard to the study of sex roles and behavioral differences between the sexes, the theories of Kohlberg, Gilligan, and Block are among the best-known representatives of the cognitive developmental perspective.

According to Kohlberg (1966), children develop their distinct male and female behaviors through processes that parallel their stages of cognitive development. In Kohlberg's scheme, children have the cognitive abilities to label themselves correctly as male or female by the age of 3. Between the ages of 3 and 7, however, children's cognitive stage prohibits them from understanding that gender remains constant despite changes in outward appearance. For example, a child will have difficulty understanding that a woman with short hair, dressed in overalls, driving heavy farm equipment, is still a female. As concrete operational thinking becomes more established, however, the child can understand that gender is unaffected by such variables as hairstyles, body size, and clothing. Hence, unlike a 5-year-old, a 10-year-old recognizes that a male dressed like a ballerina is still a male.

According to Kohlberg, male and female children will adhere most rigidly to society's sex-role stereotypes between the ages of 3 and 7. As concrete operational thought develops, children will be more willing to deviate from these prescribed sex roles. With the onset of formal operational thinking, moreover, adolescents are likely to become even more androgynous, because they are cognitively capable of realizing that deviations from a sex role are not threats to identity.

Sharing Kohlberg's assumption that cognitive structures affect an individual's sex-typed behavior, Jeanne Block (1976) proposes that a youth's stage of ego development is related to his or her willingness to adopt society's gender roles. Based on Jane Loevinger's model of ego development, Block's theory maintains that young children behave in ways that are individualistic, self-assertive, and expansive—a tendency referred to as *agency*. During this period, both males and females tend to disregard society's sex roles in order to fulfill their ego's own tendency toward agency. As children age, their behavior is guided by a need for *communion*, the tendency to conform to the group and to seek group approval. Consequently, children will adhere more strictly to the gender role prescribed by society. To this point, Block's model coincides with Loevinger's descriptions of the child's ego in the "presocial," "impulsive," "self-protective," and "conformist" stages (1976). (Refer to Table 4.1 for a review of Loevinger's stages.)

In this context, the ego stages of childhood give way to two more autonomous ego stages during adolescence: the "conscientious character" and "integrated wholeness." As a consequence, the adolescent's perceptions of sex roles are altered. Having been unwilling to risk nonconformity during childhood, adolescents begin to deviate from sex-typed behavior. According to Block, the final outcome of an adolescent ego's maturation in regard to sex-role development is androgyny.

Social Learning Theories

As explained in Chapter 4, social learning and behavioral theorists contend that adolescents' behavior is primarily a consequence of reinforcement, punishment, and modeling. From this perspective, the differences between male and female behavior result from each sex having been rewarded and punished for specific kinds of sex-typed behavior (Bandura, 1977; Mischel, 1970). For example, while the Arapesh in Margaret Mead's (1935) study rewarded boys for dancing and primping, most people in our society have punished this type of male behavior.

According to social learning theorists, adolescents also learn their sex roles by imitating live or symbolic models. *Symbolic models* are people with whom the adolescent does not personally interact, like characters in books or people on radio and television programs. In support of this position, studies have demonstrated the impact of symbolic models on adolescents' sex-typed behavior or attitudes. For example, youngsters who were shown television programs in which women portrayed nontraditional roles were more willing to approve of nontraditional behaviors afterwards than youngsters who did not watch the programs (Miller & Reeves, 1976).

In a similar study, junior-high-school students viewed slides depicting adults as computer-software designers and systems analysts. Some students saw slides in which only females were the systems analysts, while others saw slides in which only males were the analysts. Afterwards the students stated a preference for the occupation depicted in the slides by adults of their own sex (Plost & Rosen, 1974). Reviews of the literature conclude that symbolic models on television do have the power to influence adolescents' attitudes about sex roles (Miller, Brown, & Perloff, 1978).

In regard to the social learning theorists' contention that symbolic models in the media influence adolescents' sex-role attitudes, several considerations deserve attention. First, there is little disagreement that females are still underrepresented or presented primarily in traditional roles in today's television programs, magazine and television ads, and textbooks (Goffman, 1979; Welch et al., 1979; Huston, 1984). Second, although some contemporary publishers and producers are exerting efforts to present males and females in more androgynous, less stereotypic roles, many popular books and TV programs for children and adolescents were created years ago, when awareness about sex stereotypes was virtually nonexistent.

Despite the fact, however, that it seems logical to conclude that the media's presentations of males and females will influence adolescents' gender-role attitudes, the correlational studies show only modest association between the amount of television children watch and their sex-typed beliefs (Huston, 1984). Furthermore, such correlations do not prove causation and do not preclude the possibility that adolescents' sex-role attitudes determine whch programs they watch. For example, one recent study showed that androgynous adolescent girls had favorable reactions toward a popular assertive female TV character, in contrast to more "feminine" girls, who disapproved of the character's behavior (Friedrich et al., 1978). Given the suggestive yet contradictory nature of the present data, the social learning theorists' concern for the impact of the media on adolescents' sex-typed behavior certainly warrants public attention. Yet, construing the data as an argument against all books or media that present males and females in sex-typed roles would be an unwarranted, hasty assumption.

In further support of social learning theories, the research of John Money and his associates is especially noteworthy (Money & Ehrhardt, 1972). As previously noted, biological theories of sex differences suffer the disadvantage of being unable to empirically verify their hypotheses by manipulating the genes and hormones of human subjects. The opportunity to empirically compare biological and social learning theories was, however, available to Money and his colleagues through their investigations of **hermaphrodites**—children born with genetic and hormonal abnormalities that precluded their being classified biologically as either male or female. Some male hermaphrodites had rudimentary testes but an undeveloped penis and well-developed breasts, while female hermaphrodites had ovaries and a penis. Through surgical procedures, these children were altered to appear either male or female. Their appearance did not, however, necessarily reflect their genetic or hormonal constitutions. For example, an infant's penis may have been removed in order to surgically fashion a clitoris and vagina, although the infant was still lacking ovaries to produce the necessary supplies of estrogen that would technically classify the child as female.

Having followed the development of these children from birth through adolescence, Money and his colleagues concluded that as long as society treats a child consistently as either a male or a female, before the age of three, the anatomical organs and hormones of the child are insignificant. Furthermore, there appear to be two critical periods in our lives during which physiological and environmental factors interact to determine sex-typed behavior. The first critical period is between the ages of 1 and 3, and the second is adolescence. In other words, hermaphrodites behave like males throughout their lives if they are treated like boys during these two critical periods, despite the fact that their hormones and secondary sex characteristics may actually be most like a female's. The same is true for female hermaphrodites. In cases where hermaphrodites' parents changed their minds about which sex to ascribe to their children after the age of 3, the children remained confused about how to behave in regard to their masculine or feminine roles.

As explained in Chapters 3 and 4, social learning theorists are incorporating elements of cognitive developmental theories into their model of human behavior. Prominent social learning theorists like Mischel and Bandura admit that adolescents' internal mental processes affect the ways in which observational learning and operant conditioning influence their sex-typed behavior (Bandura, 1977; Mischel, 1981). According to these formulations, cognitive processes influence adolescents' attentiveness to certain people as models, as well as influencing their motivation to emulate a particular person's behavior at any given time. A youth's level of cognitive development, expectations regarding reinforcement, and preexisting concepts affect his or her willingness to imitate another person's masculine or feminine behavior.

As you remember from the previous presentations of Piaget's model and of information-processing theories, the schema is a cognitive structure composed of expectations and associations from prior experiences that help the adolescent organize and interpret new information. Adolescents will tend to discount, ignore, or modify new data that contradict their existing schema's ideas and expectations. Furthermore, in accord with attribution theories discussed in the last chapter, an adolescent is likely to repeat behavior for which he or she has been reinforced in the past, since this raises expectations for reinforcement in the present situation. Cognitive social learning theorists contend that both the adolescent's schema and his or her expectancies regarding reinforcement affect sex-typed behavior.

A hypothetical examination of an adolescent's behavior might illustrate this recent marriage between social learning theory and cognitive developmental theory. Assume that 13-year-old Seymour is not yet functioning at the formal operational stage of reasoning and that his schema has not yet incorporated concepts of behavior that deviates from traditional sex roles. His schema consists of expectations and ideas that adhere rigidly to stereotypic notions of masculinity and femininity. Furthermore, he has not been reinforced in the past for behaving in ways that are characteristic of the female gender role. In fact, Seymour's father mocks him mercilessly whenever he exhibits any "sissy" behavior. Hence, if he observes male athletes participating in a ballet, or if he reads about men who crochet and knit, or if he views television programs in which men play roles submissive to women, Seymour will probably not imitate any of this new male behavior.

Likewise, when he reads books about males and females in other cultures who deviate from our society's notions of appropriate sex-typed behavior, Seymour discounts the information as evidence that "those people are really odd and don't know what's 'normal' like we do." Also, his concrete stage of reasoning may prevent him from formulating abstract principles such as, "Given this new evidence about men and masculinity, I see that males can behave in a number of ways that I once considered 'sissy.' I guess behaving 'like a man' all depends on who's doing the judging!"

In sum, cognitive developmentalists and behavioristic psychologists are in agreement that the differences in male and female behavior are primarily the consequences of socialization. While social learning theorists suggest, however, that mental concepts and sex-typed behavior occur concomitantly, cognitive theorists hold firm to the notion that mental structures such as schemas, ego stages, and cognitive stages precede behavioral change. Furthermore, most cognitive developmentalists assume that the mental structures that affect the adolescent's sex-role behavior develop in distinct, invariant stages—a principle that social learning theorists are less willing to endorse.

Finally, as Huston (1984) notes in her comprehensive review of the literature on sex differences and sex roles, most contemporary scholars no longer emphasize the importance of parental identification in the child's acquisition of sex-typed behavior. Although theories of identification with the same-sexed parent were popular as recently as ten years ago, most modern scholars now consider parents as only one among many socializing influences affecting an adolescent's adoption or rejection of sex-typed behavior. The impact that fathers and mothers have on particular aspects of their sons' and daughters' behavior will be discussed in Chapter 8.

ADOLESCENTS' ATTITUDES TOWARD SEX ROLES

The Popularity of Gender Roles

Despite the fact that androgyny has become an increasingly popular concept among scholars, surveys still show that male and female gender roles are well entrenched in industrialized societies like the United States. For example, according to a recent 30-nation study, industrialized nations' attitudes toward sex-role stereotypes have remained remarkably unchanged during the past decade (Williams & Best, 1982). (See Table 5.1.)

Despite society's growing awareness of the disadvantages associated with sex-role stereotypes, many adolescents still endorse sex-typed beliefs about masculinity and femininity. For example, a comparison of eleventh-graders' attitudes in 1973 and in 1978 showed no change in their contention that a man's career is more important than a woman's and that competing with males decreases a girl's femininity (Ditkoff, 1979). Similarly, in several studies conducted during the 1970s, teenaged girls who were not preparing themselves for any adult vocation said such preparation was unnecessary because they intended to get married. Many of the male and female adolescents in these surveys were unaware of the statistical fact that most married women have to earn incomes for the family's survival. Moreover, many of the girls stated that males disapprove of intelligent females (*Expanding Adolescent Sex Roles,* 1978).

As the research in Chapter 11 will demonstrate, more recent data from the 1980s continue to confirm that male and female adolescents restrict their vocational options on the basis of sex-role stereotypes. Although more adolescent girls are preparing themselves for traditionally masculine vocations than in previous decades, the majority are still restricting their vocational choices to "feminine" jobs in social services, teaching, and nursing. In this regard, Monitoring the Future's data are particularly noteworthy. These data, gathered yearly between 1976 and 1980 from a nationally representative sample of 3,000 high-school seniors, demonstrate the tenacity of sex-typed attitudes. First, marked differences were found between the kinds of jobs males and female seniors envisioned themselves performing at the age of 30. Second, the males' and females' vocational choices and attitudes remained relatively unchanged between 1976 and 1980, with the vast majority of high-school seniors continuing to restrict themselves to traditionally sex-typed jobs. For instance, of the 3,000 seniors, most stated that a wife should be "allowed" to work outside the home, but 85 percent opposed a wife being the breadwinner while the husband cares for their children. Moreover, 70 percent of the seniors opposed a mother's employment if her children were preschoolers (Herzog, 1982; Herzog, Bachman, & Johnston, 1983).

Similarly, although females' educational and occupational opportunities expanded dramatically between 1965 and 1975, the sex-typed attitudes and

Table 5.1

Adjectives Highly Associated with Males or Females

Which of the following characteristics do you associate with each gender?

Adjectives Associated with Males	*Adjectives Associated with Females*
Active	Affectionate
Adventurous	Appreciative
Aggressive	Attractive
Assertive	Changeable
Autocratic	Dreamy
Boastful	Emotional
Coarse	Excitable
Confident	Feminine
Courageous	Frivolous
Cruel	Fussy
Daring	Gentle
Dominant	High-strung
Enterprising	Mild
Forceful	Nagging
Handsome	Poised
Humorous	Inventive
Sentimental	Sensitive
Lazy	Softhearted
Logical	Sophisticated
Masculine	Submissive
Rational	Sympathetic
Reckless	Talkative
Robust	Timid
Rude	Warm
Severe	Weak
Stern	Whiny
Strong	Worrying
Tough	
Unemotional	
Unexcitable	

SOURCE: J. Williams & D. Best, *Measuring sex stereotypes: A 30-nation study.* Beverly Hills, Cal.: Sage Publications, 1982, p. 28.

vocational choices of the young did not necessarily reflect these unprecedented events. One large-scale survey, comparing 2,773 high-school seniors in 1964 and 2,827 seniors in 1975, showed very few changes in traditional sex-typed attitudes in regard to family roles, interpersonal relations, or dimensions of personality such as agency and communion (Lueptow, 1984). Furthermore, there is evidence that the more liberalized attitudes regarding male and female gender roles, which appeared to be occurring in the late 1960s and early 1970s, stabilized in the latter half of the 1970s and are, perhaps, in the process of becoming

What would you find most agreeable and most disagreeable about being a member of the other sex?

even more traditional among the youth of the 1980s (Ruble, 1983; Williams & Best, 1982). For example, a 1981 survey of nearly 900 Florida students in grades 7 through 12 showed that the majority held traditional attitudes toward the division of household tasks and child-care responsibilities, even though most of the respondents came from homes in which both parents were employed (Hansen & Darling, 1985).

On the basis of most recent research, it now appears that the changes in adolescents' sex-role attitudes and behavior are less extensive and less profound than was anticipated during the 1970s. Although today's adolescent girls and their mothers are more likely than any former generation to be employed and to be divorced at some time during their lives, the beliefs about male and female roles appear to be remarkably unaffected. While the contemporary U.S. family has been transformed by such factors as women's employment, the roles of males and females within the family remain fundamentally unaltered—an anomaly that will be explored in Chapter 8.

More Conservative—Males or Females?

Whether adolescent males are more conservative than females in regard to adhering to sex-role stereotypes is an unresolved question. Data from a number of recent studies show that adolescent boys express more opposition to modifying gender roles than girls (Chandler, Sawicki, & Stryffeler, 1981; Fein, 1977; Guttentag & Bray, 1976; Spence & Helmreich, 1979a, 1979b). Some researchers have found that younger adolescent boys admit that sex stereotyping is unfair, but that these egalitarian beliefs are usually replaced with more sexist conduct and attitudes as boys age (Emerich, 1979). Moreover, some educators' attempts to change adolescent boys' attitudes about gender roles actually increased the boys' commitment to traditional sex roles (Guttentag & Bray, 1976).

While most data suggest that adolescent males are more likely to endorse traditional gender roles than are females, several considerations are worthy of note. One comparison of adolescents' attitudes showed that boys' attitudes about women's vocational roles changed more than girls' between 1973 and 1978 (Ditkoff, 1979). This finding suggests that since boys' attitudes about sex roles are more conservative than girls' at the onset of adolescence, male attitudes might need to be measured at a later age in order to make more reliable assessments about the attitudes males carry with them into adulthood. Furthermore, investigations of males' sex-role attitudes may be confounded by the age and socioeconomic class of the boys in the researchers' sample. Evidence supporting this possibility comes from research showing that male adolescents become less sexist as they age (Doyle, 1978). In addition, boys from middle-class families surveyed in several studies were more disapproving of female employment than boys from lower socioeconomic classes (*Expanding Roles,* 1978).

Confounding variables, such as the subjects' age, may be of special importance in trying to make accurate comparisons of male and female attitudes, since gender-role attitudes appear to be particularly volatile during the adolescent years. One study underscoring the potential impact of extraneous variables on sex-typed attitudes found that adolescent girls with siblings had more conservative sex-role attitudes than those who were only children. Although age had no significant effect on the sex-role attitudes of these 450 seventh-, eighth-, or ninth-grade girls, those from rural areas were most likely to believe that women with young children should not have jobs (Hertsgaard & Light, 1984). This finding suggests that assessments of adolescents' sex-role attitudes need to consider variables other than the subject's gender before making comparisons between the sexes or between different age groups.

Androgyny—Gaining Popularity?

Although most of the extant research concludes that sex stereotypes and gender roles are alive and well among the adolescent and adult populations, there is also evidence of a gradual modification of our notions of masculinity and femininity. For example, one recent study of 330 high-school students showed that neither males nor females rated women whom they believed were in masculine professions or those whom they believed had taken masculine courses in high school as less physically attractive than women presumed to have followed the more feminine options. In fact, the students associated the woman's attractiveness with a professional career orientation. When contrasted with research from previous decades, this finding suggests that adolescents may slowly be casting aside the stereotype of the "homely, bright, career-oriented female"(Lanier & Byrne, 1981).

In another study, 200 junior-high-school students deemed traits associated with the female sex role, such as friendliness, neatness, and gentleness, desirable qualities in either sex. In contrast, these young adolescents rated aspects of the male sex role, such as stubbornness, physical aggressiveness, and bragging as undesirable for either sex (Rust & Lloyd, 1982). (See Table 5.2.)

Such findings suggest that adolescents may be becoming more willing to appreciate feminine qualities in both males and females. Nonetheless, it appears that many male and female adolescents consider traits associated with the male gender role more desirable than traits associated with the female gender role. Indeed, girls' preferences for male activities and male values tend to increase as they age, while boys increasingly disassociate themselves from female values and activities (Hanes & Prawatt, 1979; Helmreich, Spence, & Wilhelm, 1981; Huston, 1984; Williams & Best, 1982).

Despite the apparent unpopularity of incorporating feminine traits into one's personality, several recent studies are particularly noteworthy in highlighting adolescents' positive attitudes toward masculine traits. In a survey of 665 students in grades 8 through 10 in a suburban Houston school, masculine and androgynous youths rated themselves more physically attractive than feminine or undifferentiated youths (Downs & Abshier, 1982). This finding is consistent with earlier research showing that androgynous and masculine people have more self-esteem than feminine people (Spence & Helmreich, 1979a).

Table 5.2

Positive and Negative Attributes of Male and Female Gender Roles

Positive Traits	*Negative Traits*
Masculine	
Independent	Egotistical
Active	Arrogant
Competitive	Boastful
Makes decisions easily	Greedy
Never gives up easily	Dictatorial
Self-confident	Hostile
Feels superior	Cynical
Stands up well under pressure	Unprincipled
Feminine	
Emotional	Servile
Able to devote self to others	Spineless
Gentle	Gullible
Helpful	Subordinates self to others
Kind	Whiny
Aware of others' feelings	Nagging
Understanding of others	Complaining
Warm to others	Fussy

SOURCE: R. Helmreich, J. Spence, & J. Wilhelm, A psychometric analysis of the Personal Attributes Questionnaire. *Sex Roles,* 1981, *7,* 1097–1108.

Interestingly, incorporating certain masculine traits appears to enhance both a girl's popularity and her success academically and vocationally, whereas incorporating feminine traits diminishes a boy's status. In support of this position, a study of 305 high-school students from primarily white, upper-middle-class homes showed that boys with the highest masculinity scores on the Personal Attributes Questionnaire were the most accepted by girls and had the most self-esteem. In contrast, girls whose scores reflected a balance between masculinity and femininity were the most accepted by both their male and female peers and had the most self-esteem. Furthermore, girls who scored low on both the masculine and feminine scales were less popular than girls who scored high on both scales (Massad, 1981).

Of special interest in this study is that boys who scored high on both the masculine and feminine scales received higher friendship ratings from other boys than those who scored high on masculinity and low on femininity. This finding suggests that such feminine traits as nurturance, sensitivity, and empathy benefit boys in their male friendships just as they benefit girls' friendships. Unfortunately, the data suggest that a boy is caught in a double bind: In order to be popular with girls, he mustn't appear too feminine; yet, in order to have close male friendships, he needs a balance between masculine and feminine traits.

The data from Massad's study corroborate the finding of other researchers who contend that since males occupy the powerful, dominant positions in our society, both sexes accord more power and prestige to traits associated with the male sex role. Reviews of the research indicate that females are more likely to be praised for succeeding at "masculine" tasks than males are for succeeding at "feminine" tasks (Deaux, 1976). Consequently, a girl who adopts certain masculine traits, thereby becoming more androgynous, gains status and self-esteem. In contrast, a male who becomes more androgynous often loses status and self-esteem, because he is incorporating feminine characteristics and values, which are less esteemed in our society (Antill & Cunningham, 1979; Burke & Weir, 1976, Jones, Chernovetz, & Hanson, 1978; Nicholson & Antill, 1981).

Interestingly, one of the few longitudinal studies available, from several decades ago, also found that the most stereotypically masculine boys were the most popular and best adjusted during their adolescence. Twenty years later, however, these masculine boys were less well-adjusted than their androgynous male peers (Mussen, 1962). In conjunction with recent findings, this longitudinal study suggests that androgynous males may become increasingly appreciated by members of both sexes, once everyone moves beyond adolescence.

In summary, as Tables 5.1 and 5.2 illustrate, although androgyny appears to be somewhat more acceptable among contemporary adolescents, gender roles remain well entrenched. Moreover, the attributes associated with the male gender role continue to be more highly esteemed by both adolescents and adults than the attributes associated with the female role. As Huston's exhaustive review of the literature on sex typing lamentably concludes:

> In the aura of optimism created by these new approaches and the social visions that accompany them, however, one is somewhat sobered by the repeated evidence that masculine attributes are more often socially valued and more often associated with self-esteem and adaptive functioning for both males and females than are feminine traits (Huston, 1984, p. 450).

THE SCHOOL'S IMPACT ON SEX ROLES

There is general agreement among researchers and psychologists that most elementary and secondary schools perpetuate sex-typed behavior and sex-role stereotypes. Messages regarding appropriate and inappropriate behavior for each sex are delivered to students overtly and covertly through the curriculum, pedagogical strategies, counseling, allocation of money, and general school policies. Despite teachers' admirable intentions and their claims of treating male and female students equally, most research demonstrates that teachers' interactions with adolescents are significantly influenced by sex-role stereotypes and by the students' gender (Deem, 1978; Frazier & Sadker, 1973; Good & Brophy, 1984; Guttentag & Bray, 1976).

In an effort to sensitize school counselors and teachers to their behavior and attitudes regarding sex stereotypes, many professional organizations are encouraging adults to examine their own conduct (see Table 5.3). The National Education Association, National Federation of Teachers, American Personnel and Guidance Association, and American Psychological Association are among those who have published guidelines for eliminating sexism in secondary education. Given the efforts of school personnel and of professional organizations for teachers and counselors, some schools appear to be endorsing somewhat more androgynous and less stereotypic behavior among students. For example, in one recent study some high-school teachers stated a preference for students whose abilities and attitudes were more androgynous than stereotypically masculine or

Table 5.3

Sexist and Nonsexist Counseling Strategies

1. Do you encourage males and females to explore the same jobs?
2. Do you inquire about boys' future marriage and parenting plans as often as you do girls'?
3. Do you use sexist language or writing?
4. Do the materials in your office depict men and women with nontraditional jobs, personalities, and lifestyles?
5. Have you read about nonsexist counseling methods?
6. Do you use career or personality inventories that are biased?
7. Have you discussed stereotypes with adolescents, their parents and teachers?
8. Do you consider certain traits "abnormal" for one sex but "acceptable" for the other (sexual activity, physical aggression, ambition, mannerisms)?
9. Do you advocate different punishment for boys and girls?
10. Do you actively encourage students to engage in activities that are traditionally considered appropriate only for the opposite sex?
11. Do you help textbook committees choose nonsexist materials?

A nonsexist counselor would answer "no" to questions 3, 6, 8, and 9.

SOURCES: W. Fetters, *Nonsexist counseling: Helping men and women redefine their roles.* Dubuque, Iowa: Kendall Hunt, 1979; B. Gutik, *Enhancing women's career development.* San Francisco: Jossey-Bass, 1979; L. Hansen & R. Rapoza, *Career development and counseling women.* Springfield, Ill.: Charles Thomas, 1978.

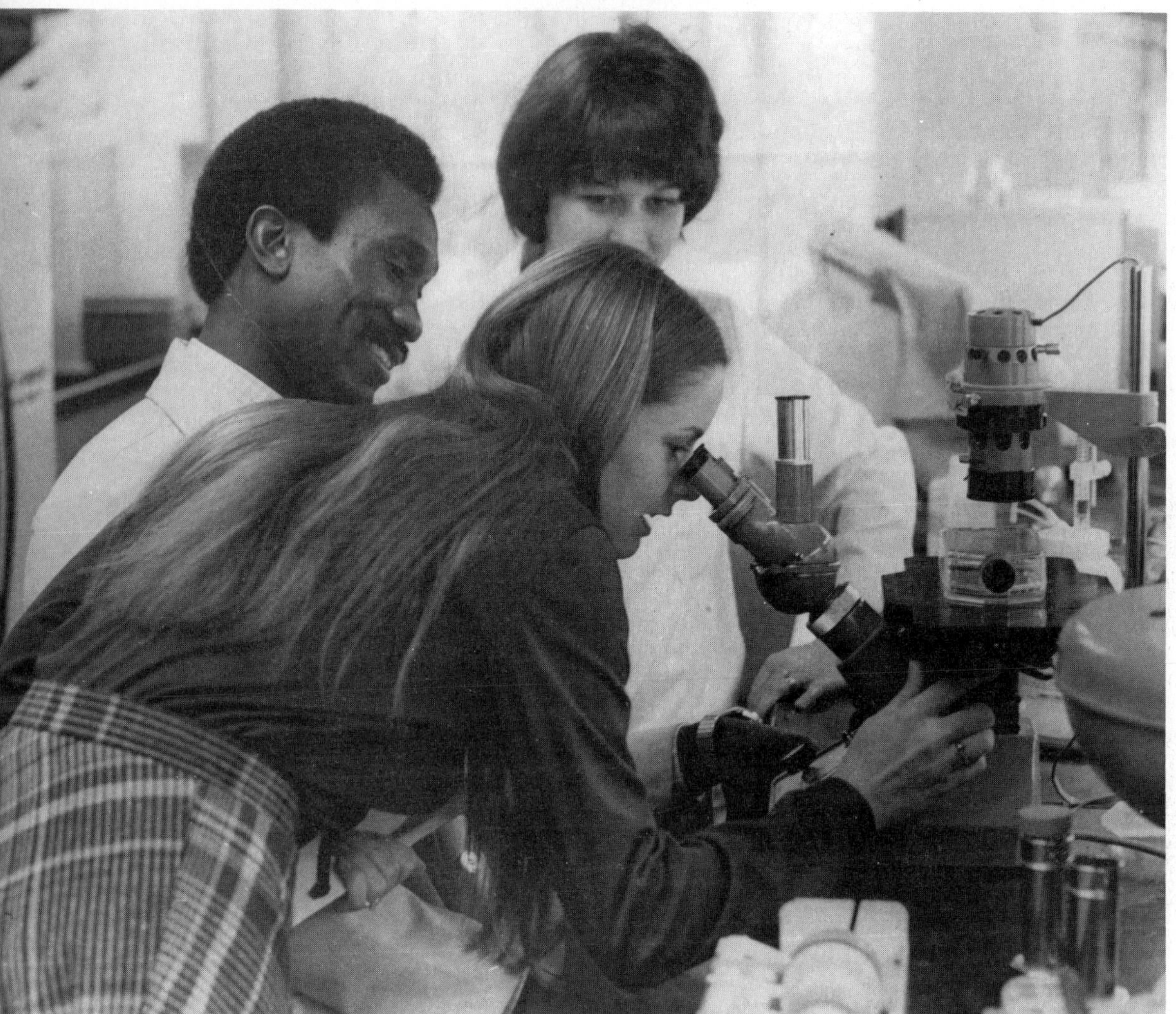

If you could have chosen both your race and your gender before your birth, which would you have chosen? Why?

feminine (Bernard, 1979). Also, as Box 5.1 shows, some adolescents are receiving adult support and international recognition for excelling in domains once reserved exclusively for members of the other sex.

In addition to the nonsexist efforts of many teachers and counselors, the federal government has attempted to correct some of the vocational and educational inequities between males and females through the **Title IX** legislation adopted in 1972. Title IX mandates that "no person in the United States shall, on the basis of sex, be excluded from participation in, be denied the benefits of, or be subject to discrimination under any educational program or activity receiving federal financial assistance" (*Enforcing Title IX,* 1980). As Table 5.4 illus-

A Closer Look 5.1 

The "Mad" Scientist Is a Girl?

Who could save America four billion dollars a year in fertilizer costs without exhausting any of the country's supply of petroleum or natural gas? Eighteen-year-old Elisabeth Bryenton! While working in her home-made laboratory two hours a night and most weekends during her high-school years, Elisabeth Bryenton invented a natural fertilizing agent that could some day save all the energy, natural gas, and petroleum now used for synthetic fertilizer production—an estimated savings of eighteen billion dollars worldwide and four billion in the United States alone. In addition to the interest expressed by several foreign governments in her scientific discovery, Ms. Bryenton was awarded prizes from the U.S. Department of Agriculture, the U.S. Air Force, General Motors, and the 1979 International Science and Engineering Fair.

SOURCE: M. Fisher, Teenage scientist. *Ms.* magazine, July 1980, p. 23.

trates, Title IX legislation affects the lives of millions of adolescents through its legal mandates against sex discrimination.

Between 1972 and 1976, 871 complaints of sex discrimination in public schools were filed under Title IX, 7 percent of which were resolved (*Stalled at the Start,* 1978). Despite the fact that federal money is supposed to be withheld from noncomplying schools, critics have complained that this legal sanction is too seldom invoked (*Enforcing Title IX,* 1980). Although many are disappointed by the government's apparent unwillingness to punish schools for violating the law, Title IX has nonetheless raised the public's awareness of sex discrimination and sex stereotyping in public schools.

MALE AND FEMALE ATTITUDES TOWARD ACHIEVEMENT

Males and Academic Achievement

While it is generally acknowledged that boys receive benefits through the athletic and academic curricula, sex stereotypes nonetheless work to the male adolescents disadvantaged in certain academic areas. Although boys generally receive more praise than girls from their teachers, they also receive more criticism (Good & Brophy, 1984; Parsons, Kaczala, & Meece, 1981). Further, it appears that male students are more reluctant than females to ask their teachers or counselors for assistance or to express their anxiety about academic pressures, for fear that these acts are "unmanly" (Glidewell, 1978). Moreover, because low grades have been found to be more highly correlated with delinquency for boys than for girls, some researchers suggest that male self-esteem is more intricately bound to academic success than a female's (Gold & Petronio,

Table 5.4

Title IX Regulations

Which of the following are true statements based on the federal regulations legislated by Title IX in 1972?

1. All schools receiving federal money must keep records of plans to rectify sexual inequities.
2. Victims of discrimination may file complaints directly to the Department of Health, Education and Welfare.
3. Recipients of federal money must provide grievance procedures for any student or employee who wants to file a complaint.
4. In publicly supported schools students may not be denied admission to any course on the basis of their sex.
5. Limited enrollment percentages for males or females may not be set for entrance to schools or programs.
6. You may not ask students or employees questions about their marital status, pregnancy, termination of pregnancy, or their sex in order to discriminate against then in any way.
7. Residential schools must have the same dormitory rules for both sexes.
8. Separate toilets, locker rooms, and shower facilities for males and females are illegal.
9. Classes on human sexuality may not be taught separately to males and females.
10. Males and females must be admitted to the same teams for contact sports (football, hockey, basketball, rugby, wrestling).
11. Single-sex physical education classes must end.
12. If a course is disproportionately of one sex, the school is obliged to determine whether this is the consequence of biased counseling or testing.
13. Schools that provide full-coverage health services must offer gynecological care.
14. If a student leaves school because of pregnancy, she must be reinstated to her former status when she returns.
15. Both sexes must be allowed on the same teams for noncontact sports.
16. Athletic expenditures must be equal for males and females.
17. Title IX prohibits discrimination in employment, recruitment, and promotion, as well as education.

Statements 8, 9, 10, and 16 are false.

SOURCE: *Title IX of the Education Admendments of 1972,* Washington, D.C.: Resource Center on Sex Roles in Education, 1976.

1980). On the basis of such findings, it can be argued that school is a more stressful, punitive environment for adolescent males than for their female classmates.

In a similar vein, it has been argued that boys have special difficulties at school because the schools' demands for conformity, passivity, obedience, and physical inactivity are inconsistent with male sex-role expectations (Gordon, 1980). In support of this view, it is noted that boys have more difficulty learning to read than girls and that learning disabilities are more frequent among boys than girls. Since most elementary-school teachers are women and since reading is often perceived by young boys as a feminine activity, it has been suggested that sex-role stereotypes are an impediment to certain aspects of young boys' academic progress.

Despite these potential disadvantages of being a male student, however, the benefits of being male outweigh the deficits in terms of academic and vocational achievement. As a multitude of studies cited in Chapters 7, 8, and 11 will demonstrate, parents, educators, and counselors generally provide more encouragement to boys than to girls in regard to developing their intellectual, academic, and vocational skills during adolescence.

Females and Academic Achievement

Teachers' and parents' gender-role expectations and consequent behavior have been implicated in the decline of girls' academic achievements and their lower intellectual self-confidence during adolescence. According to this criticism, most educators, parents, and counselors fail to encourage adolescent girls to develop their intellectual abilities to the fullest or to explore courses or vocations in masculine domains (Ahlum & Howe, 1976; Bernard, 1979; Deem, 1978; Frazier & Sadker, 1973; Frieze, 1978; Guttentag & Bray, 1976).

Unfortunately, most of the evidence supports the hypothesis that adolescence is a time during which many girls' academic achievements and vocational motivation decline. For example, some researchers have found that girls with the highest IQ test scores are the most likely to lose IQ points during their adolescent years (Baruch, 1979; Maccoby & Jacklin, 1974; Sherman, 1979). In this regard, two studies comparing the age at which underachievement begins for the brightest children are of particular note. In the first study, boys with high IQ scores, who began to underachieve, started to do so in about the third grade, in contrast to girls with high IQ scores, whose underachievement did not begin until nearly the ninth grade (Shaw & McCuen, 1960). In a more recent study, male underachievers were found to have had a consistent pattern of underachievement since the first grade, whereas female underachievers did not begin to underachieve until about the sixth grade (Fitzpatrick, 1978). Data like these support the contention that female underachievement is related to the lack of adult encouragement for intellectual development as adolescence approaches and to girls' own perceptions of intelligence as being unfeminine.

In a similar vein, studies repeatedly show that boys' mathematical skills do not exceed girls' until adolescence and that, thereafter, most girls remain more anxious about math than boys (Maccoby & Jacklin, 1974; Tobias, 1978). Girls with more androgynous attitudes, however, tend to perform better in math and science than those who endorse more traditional notions of femininity (Casserly, 1979; Fitzpatrick, 1978; Rodenstein & Hughes; 1979). Consistent in their findings, these researchers have repeatedly urged parents and teachers to foster more androgynous attitudes in female children, especially during the adolescent years, when sex-typed behavior and sex stereotypes exert much influence over a girl's academic and vocational achievement.

Unfortunately, even when girls excel academically, they tend to feel less self-confident about their intellectual abilities than their male classmates who earn similarly high grades (Baruch, 1979; Crandell, 1975; Sherman, 1979). While high-school boys who perform well academically express greater self-esteem than boys who earn poor grades, academically successful girls often feel as anxious and depressed as their less successful female classmates. Throughout the past several decades, research has generally upheld the unfortunate fact that adolescence is often accompanied by a decline in a girl's academic achievements, intellectual self-confidence, and vocational aspirations (Brackney, 1979; Crandell, 1975; Douvan, 1970; Rosenberg & Simms, 1975; Sugar, 1979).

Sex Differences in Locus-of-Control Attitudes

This decline in females' academic achievement, vocational aspirations, and intellectual self-confidence during adolescence may be partially related to the differences in male and female **locus-of-control** attitudes. As explained in Chapter 4, adolescents with internal locus-of-control attitudes feel personally responsible for and in control of most of the events in their lives. In contrast, youths with external locus-of-control attitudes generally feel powerless in terms of controlling their successes or failures.

Girls generally have lower expectancies of success than do boys, and attribute their failures to shortcomings within themselves: lack of skill or lack of intelligence. In contrast, when boys fail, they tend to attribute their failures to lack of effort or to external circumstances. In addition, girls tend to attribute their successes to unstable variables, such as effort or assistance from other people, rather than to permanent qualities such as intelligence or natural ability, whereas boys usually attribute their successes to their ability. In sum, girls have a greater tendency than boys to avoid risking failure and to accept personal responsibility for failure (Dweck, 1984; Mokros, Taylor, & O'Neill, 1977; Parsons, 1982).

Given these research findings, it is perhaps not too surprising that reviews of the literature show female students to be least confident when attempting tasks associated with the male gender role (Dweck, 1984; Schmuck & Schmuck, 1979). According to this research, however, teachers' behavior is of critical importance in determining female students' behavior and attitudes in these situations. When teachers assured girls that they could succeed at masculine tasks, the girls' confidence in their intellectual abilities and their expectations for success became similar to the boys' self-perceptions. That female students, unlike males, were the most self-confident and least tense in situations where they did not have to compete with classmates is of particular interest in these studies.

These male-female differences in regard to competition are further corroborated in Chapters 8 and 12 by research showing that females are generally more cooperative, empathetic, and sensitive toward other people than males. Hence, girls generally prefer cooperative rather than competitive situations. Studies showing that girls in coeducational schools feel more anxious about competition and success than girls in all-female schools suggest that competition against boys may be particularly debilitating for girls (Baruch, 1979). Given these data, it is perhaps not too surprising that the most academically ambitious girls are usually those who have been exposed to successful, bright, female role models and whose parents and teachers have encouraged them to reject the notion that femininity is incompatible with independence, intelligence, and assertiveness (Farmer, 1978; Frieze, 1978).

Most research supports the hypothesis that many adolescent girls define achievement in terms of popularity, physical beauty, social skills, and preparation for roles as future wives and mothers (Baruch, 1979; Brackney, 1979; Douvan, 1970; Farmer, 1978; Marini, 1978). Without having learned to base her self-esteem on her own academic, vocational, or athletic achievements, the adolescent girl often learns to become a "vicarious achiever." Thus, rather than deriving pride and pleasure from her own accomplishments, she learns to base her status and gratification on the achievements of the males in her life (Lipman & Leavitt, 1976).

Sex Differences in Fear-of-Success Attitudes

During the 1970s many researchers hypothesized that a lack of achievement motivation was a consequence of a female's fear of success. The concept of fear of success was derived from Matina Horner's studies, in which high-school and college students were presented with hypothetical stories about females who were succeeding in masculine endeavors. When asked to elaborate upon these stories, the majority of female students imagined negative consequences befalling the successful female. Specifically, the females reported that the successful woman in the story would be socially rejected by males or would lose her femininity (Horner, 1972).

Although subsequent studies on fear of success received considerable attention in the literature of the 1970s, Horner's original hypotheses have been modified on the basis of new data. To begin with, further studies revealed that females' fear-of-success scores diminished when the hypothetical stories placed the successful female student in a class that contained other female students. In addition, the relationship between fear of success and the individual's academic or vocational success has not been consistently established. For example, some high-school girls who excel academically still report fear of success, a finding that suggests that some girls succeed despite their fears of male disapproval (Golden & Cherry, 1982).

In further contradiction of Horner's original hypothesis, male subjects have also expressed anxiety when presented with hypothetical situations in which a male character was succeeding in a traditionally feminine activity. For example, in one study 63 percent of the males imagined negative consequences for a male student who was graduating at the head of his nursing class (Hoffman, 1974). In other words, boys—like girls—fear succeeding in activities that have traditionally been reserved for members of the other sex (Olsen & Williamsen, 1978; Romero, 1975; *Sex Roles,* 1976, 1979).

The modifications in Horner's original hypotheses should not be misconstrued to mean that fear of success cannot undermine an adolescent girl's academic and vocational motivation. As Chapters 7 and 11 will demonstrate, adolescent girls are not fulfilling their intellectual and vocational potential to the same extent as adolescent boys. This suggests that even though both girls and boys may be nervous about success in nontraditional domains, these fears are ultimately more debilitating for girls than for boys in terms of their adult incomes and vocational options. Furthermore, girls and women have reported avoiding certain vocations because of boyfriends' or spouses' disapproval, and fear of success seems to increase for many adolescent girls as they age (Golden & Cherry, 1982; *Sex Roles,* 1976; Topol & Reznikoff, 1979).

Given current uncertainties about the impact of fear of success, our best guess is that fears associated with violating sex-role stereotypes may be discouraging some male and female adolescents from developing particular interests and talents. By encouraging adolescents' adventures into a variety of educational and vocational experiences, without regard for sex stereotypes, we will be diminishing the chances that such fears will impede academic or vocational development.

More Anxiety for Males or Females?

The debate over which sex undergoes the most stress during adolescence, as a consequence of sex stereotypes and gender roles, remains unsettled. It is argued by many psychologists and sociologists that males experience more stress related to sex stereotypes than do females, since our society condones a limited degree of masculine behavior in females, while it sternly disapproves of almost any form of feminine behavior in males (Farrell, 1975; Fasteau, 1976; Gerzon, 1982; Goldberg, 1979; Pleck, 1981; Rubin, 1980; Staples, 1982). From this perspective, adolescent males are under almost continuous pressure to conceal their expressions of emotion, nurturance, dependence, acquiescence, passivity, fear, physical affection, and self-doubt. Moreover, it is also incumbent

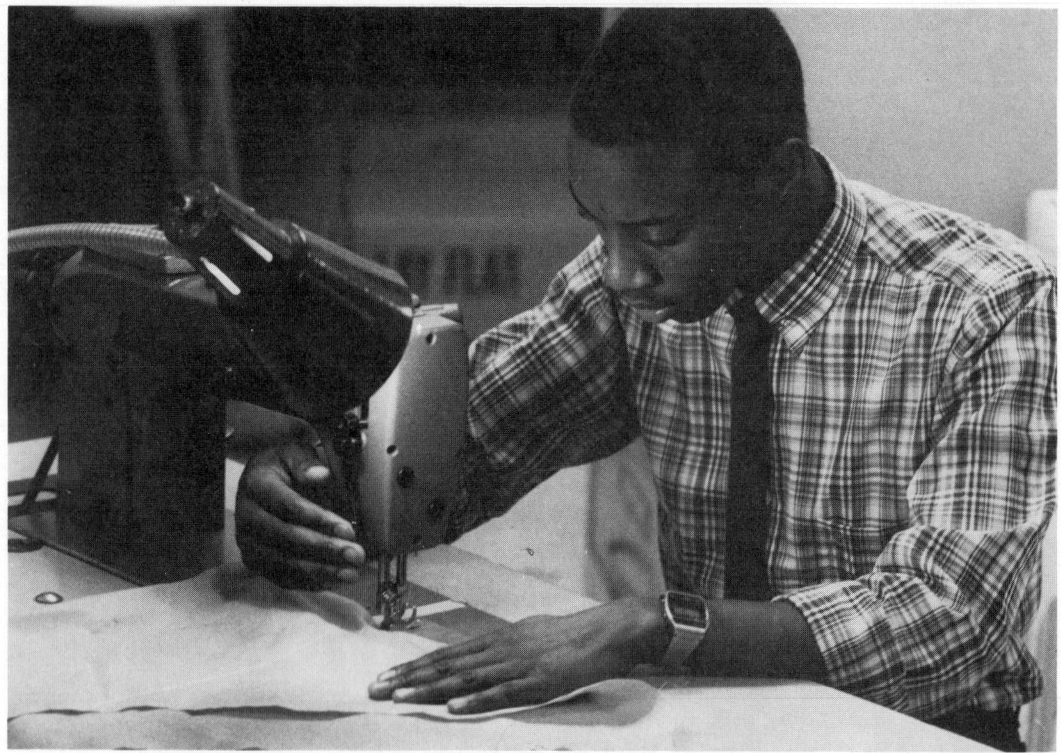

How do you feel about a male's crying publicly, remaining unemployed while his wife works, or choosing a vocation as a seamstress?

upon adolescent males to measure up to their gender role's expectations by being aggressive, competitive, athletic, calm, rational, self-confident, and self-reliant. Going to extraordinary lengths to avoid being compared to females by being called "effeminate," "queers," or "fags," adolescent boys seldom admit their fears publicly or express their emotions with tears—a form of physical restraint that may produce both stress and aggression in males, as Box 5.2 illustrates (Goodman, 1984).

One illustrative study that disputes the notion that boys experience the most anxiety related to gender roles is Offer's investigation of several thousand adolescents from five different countries in the 1960s and 1970s (Offer, Ostrov, & Howard, 1981). According to these cross-cultural data, boys have better feelings about their bodies, are more self-confident, and are less passive and less dependent on others' approval than girls. Boys also reported better feelings about themselves than girls, with respect to vocational achievement and academic success. Moreover, the boys described themselves more confidently than girls in terms of their abilities to solve problems that might arise. While most boys were self-confident about their appearance throughout adolescence, over 40 percent of the younger adolescent girls said they frequently felt ugly or unattractive.

A Closer Look 5.2 

Big Boys Should Cry!

"Act like a man! Don't cry! Only sissies and girls cry!" Such enjoinders to young boys and adolescent males notwithstanding, David Goodman at the Newport Neuroscience Center in California has shown that weeping may be therapeutic for males of any age. Convulsive weeping is a rare experience for most American males, given our society's sex-role stereotypes of masculinity. Yet Dr. Goodman encouraged a group of men to weep intensively and uncontrollably whenever they needed to release tension during the course of the experiment. Goodman found that men with initially high levels of testosterone, who cried regularly, as instructed, lowered their testosterone levels. More surprisingly, men whose testosterone levels had been below the male average prior to the experiment experienced a rise in testosterone level after several weeks of intensive weeping. In some cases, testosterone levels rose or fell by as much as 30 percent during the 4-week period, bringing these men's hormonal levels closer to the male population's average. In addition, the men whose testosterone levels fell as a consequence of their crying reportedly felt less "driven." Conversely, those whose testosterone levels had risen reportedly felt more "assertive." Goodman notes that he asked the men to cry in intense ways that resembled the crying of newborns and young children, because he was "looking for an extraordinarily stressful way of releasing tension." According to Goodman, as boys enter adolescence, their testosterone levels rise to levels that might make crying more difficult than in their childhood years.

SOURCE: D. Goodman, *Biochemical changes during a dacrystic regimen*. Paper presented at the Society of Neuroscience. Anaheim, California, October 1984.

Adolescent girls also described themselves as physically sicker, sadder, and lonelier than boys. Offer and his colleagues maintain that these differences between adolescent girls and boys reflect girls' awareness of their having less economic and social status in their futures and of feeling less capable than boys of controlling their own destinies.

While the contention that males experience more sex-role anxiety than females is debatable, the impact of gender roles on coping with frustration is more certain. Given our society's gender-role definitions, it is not surprising that adolescent males are more likely to express their tensions through verbal or physical aggression, while females are more likely to conceal their frustrations and anger, thereby creating internal stress. In general, adolescent girls report more guilt, tension, depression, and psychosomatic illness than boys (Locksley & Douvan, 1980; Scarf, 1980).

While a boy's sex role permits him to express his frustration through physical or verbal aggression, the traditional female sex role condemns outward displays of anger as "unladylike." Interestingly, however, in studies where girls know that their identities have been concealed from observers, they behave just as aggressively as boys in similar situations, a finding that suggests that girls are reluctant to express aggression for fear of violating our society's notions of femininity (Frieze, 1978). Moreover, unlike most boys, most girls feel guilty or anxious when they choose to put their own needs and desires on a par with the wishes of other people (Gilligan, 1982; Scarf, 1980).

SEX ROLES AND IDENTITY STATUSES

Given the discrepancies between the male and female gender roles in our society, it is perhaps not surprising that the formation of an identity during adolescence takes somewhat different paths for boys than for girls. According to neo-Freudians like James Marcia and Erik Erikson, whose theories were discussed in Chapter 4, one of the desirable outcomes of adolescence is the development of an independent identity—an identity that has become individuated from parents and peers (Erikson, 1968; Marcia, 1980). By examining the research on the four identity statuses in males and females, we can achieve a fuller appreciation of the impact that gender roles appear to have on this aspect of adolescent development. The following data and hypotheses are derived from the most recent reviews of the extant literature by experts in the field of identity statuses, James Marcia and David Matteson (Matteson, 1986).

As you recall from Chapter 4, adolescents with **foreclosed identities** make premature decisions regarding their vocational goals, their personal needs, and their religious, political, and philosophical ideologies. Without questioning the expectations or values of their parents or other adults, youths with foreclosed identities conform to the wishes of others without ever developing their own standards and independent identities through the process of individuation. Those adolescents who reject the foreclosed identity status and pursue the development of an autonomous identity may periodically defy authorities, question the values of the status quo, and experiment with different vocational and social roles as part of the **moratorium identity status.** Through this process of experimentation, adolescents can develop a more individuated ego on which to base their own goals and standards. Youths who fashion an autonomous, individuated identity thereby become *identity achievers*.

Gender Differences in Identity Formation

In studying the identity statuses of adolescents and adults, researchers have found several distinctions between males and females (Matteson, 1986). First, females are more likely than males to form foreclosed identities during adolescence. Most adolescent boys undergo a period of reexamining their parents' values and experimenting with a variety of roles and ideologies that assist them in creating independent identities. Considering the sex-typed characteristics described in Tables 5.1 and 5.2, the relationship between an adolescent's gender role and his or her identity status becomes readily apparent.

For example, traits associated with the male gender role, such as assertive, enterprising, self-reliant, daring, and adventurous, enhance the likelihood of becoming individuated from one's parents, experimenting with various roles, and eventually fashioning an independent identity. In contrast, the traits that represent the traditional female gender role are the antithesis of the adventuresome, self-reliant, self-confident, assertive, independent attitudes that underlie the pursuit of an independent identity. According to the data, not all boys reach the identity achievement status by the end of adolescence. More adolescent males achieve an autonomous identity, however, than females, a finding that is not particularly surprising, given the degree to which most adolescents still conform to our society's current sex-role stereotypes.

Another finding that emerges from the research is that adolescent girls who do create independent identities for themselves tend to experience more anxiety than do boys who create independent identities. In contrast to their male counterparts, females who have achieved independent identities are often more anxious and less confident than girls with foreclosed identities. These findings have led scholars like Marcia and Matteson to conclude that females often receive less support and more disapproval than males when trying to form independent identities. Unlike boys, girls are violating certain aspects of the female sex role by developing an individuated, autonomous sense of self.

After his exhaustive review of the literature on identity statuses, Matteson (1986) concludes that most adolescents girls receive support for developing their own identities only after they have developed their skills in the areas of intimacy and interpersonal relationships. Unlike boys, in late adolescence most girls are pressured either to postpone the development of their own identities or to adopt foreclosed identities. Most girls must either arrive at achieved identities early in their adolescence—which is highly unlikely, given the time and experimentation necessary for identity achievement; or they must divert their energy in late adolescence from the pursuit of an identity to the establishment of intimate relationships. In contrast, adolescent boys inhibit the development of intimacy and interpersonal concerns for the sake of developing their vocational and ideological identities. As a consequence, it is often not until mid-life that females catch up with males in terms of establishing an identity, or that males develop their identities in regard to intimacy and interpersonal concerns.

In this regard, parents' attitudes about gender roles appear to be of critical importance in contributing to the development of more foreclosed identities in daughters than in sons. The data in Chapter 8 show that most parents treat their male and female offspring differently. For example, many parents might approve of a son's using one summer to travel across the country, or associating with friends from a variety of backgrounds, or accepting a summer job in another city. These experiences would be perceived by most boys and their parents as a normal part of "becoming a man," "growing up," and "cutting the apron strings." In contrast, many parents would consider similar experiences for a daughter "unladylike," "dangerous," "foolhardy," or "unnecessary." In accordance with sex-role stereotypes, many adolescent girls are encouraged to remain "Daddy's little girl," while very few adolescent boys are permitted to remain a "Mommy's boy."

According to Erikson's hypothesis, from which Marcia's identity statuses originally emanated, both males and females must establish independent identities before being capable of forming truly intimate relationships with other people in early adulthood (Erikson, 1968). In this context, it is assumed that adolescents have to emerge from either the moratorium or diffused identity status with a clear sense of self, in order to eventually achieve genuine closeness with another person. Furthermore, Erikson maintains that the formation of an autonomous identity generally occurs by the end of adolescence. In each of these respects, however, Erikson's hypotheses are being undermined by recent research.

According to current data, but in opposition to Erikson's theory, females are more likely than males to develop independent identities at mid-life, when their responsibilities as mothers and wives tend to diminish. As Erikson predicts, most males who reach the achieved identity status do so by their mid-twenties. Impressionistic research suggests, however, that both men and women reappraise their notions of masculinity and femininity in mid-life and may, as a consequence, refashion certain aspects of their identities. In further contrast to earlier assumptions, some recent data from adolescent and young adult samples suggest that the sex differences are narrowing somewhat, in that females' vocational identities are developing at an earlier age (Matteson, 1986).

Another deviation from Erikson's model is becoming increasingly clear from the empirical data: Females develop their capacities for intimacy before males, and they do so without first having had to achieve an autonomous identity. Indeed, most females develop the capacities for intimate relationships in late adolescence, irrespective of which identity status they have adopted. Unlike vocational identities, in which the difference between male and female patterns appears to be diminishing, girls and women continue to surpass boys and men in terms of maturity and intimacy in interpersonal relationships. Although some recent studies provide tentative support for the notion that intimacy and interpersonal issues are becoming more important to the young male's identity, occupation is still the most advanced area in a male's identity and intimacy is the most advanced in a female's. Unlike females, most males develop high levels of intimacy only if they have first adopted an identity, as Erikson's theory predicts. Significantly, unlike females, males tend to perceive friendship as a form of mastery and competition through which to further their achievement goals. Even in their interpersonal relationships, males maintain a separateness and autonomy considered essential to their definition of self (Matteson, 1986).

These differences between male and female intimacy are so consistently documented in the research and are so intricately bound to other aspects of adolescent development that careful discussion of the data is reserved for Chapters 9 and 12. By way of brief introduction to these data, the research on friendships and Carol Gilligan's theory of female moral development reinforce the conclusion of identity status researchers: Intimacy has a higher priority than identity in female, but not in male, development (Gilligan, 1982).

Once again, these distinctions between the sexes and the deviations from traditional models of identity formation can be accounted for, in large part, by our society's particular gender roles. Traditionally males have been encouraged to devote their twenties to honing their professional skills through education and job experience, while females are encouraged to devote this first decade of adulthood to relationships with other people—primarily through the roles of wife and mother.

Similarities between Male and Female Identity Statuses

Numerous studies have described the impact of identity statuses on young men and women after adolescence (Marcia, Waterman, & Matteson, 1986). Males and females who do become identity achievers are distinct in several respects from individuals in the other three identity statuses. As might be expected from Marcia's descriptions of adolescent identity statuses, females with achieved identities take account of their own educational and vocational needs in planning for marriage or motherhood. Female identity achievers tend to be androgynous and to have felt "pushed out of the nest" by their parents during adolescence. Like their male counterparts, females with achieved identities focus more on developing their own abilities than on seeking the approval of others or on choosing companions who will "protect" them. Interestingly, the female identity achievers seem more sure of their mothers' affection than girls with foreclosed or diffused identities, a finding that suggests that their mothers encouraged their daughters' independence without withdrawing nurturance, love, or security.

In contrast, males and females who have adopted the moratorium identity status are attempting to become more individuated and are still exploring various roles and ideologies. Both moratorium males and females tend to be critical of authority and somewhat anxious, since they have not yet committed themselves to an identity. Using Loevinger's test of ego development, it appears that females in the moratorium stage and those with achieved identities have reached more advanced stages of ego development than foreclosure or diffusion females. Unfortunately, data suggest that females in the moratorium status who become wives and mothers tend to feel ambivalent about these female roles. Nevertheless, their guilt and fear prevent these ambivalent young women from launching themselves into the course of experimentation and individuation, which are necessary for achieving an independent identity.

Unlike their peers with achieved or moratorium statuses, males and females who leave adolescence with diffused identities tend to fear confrontation, to avoid difficult situations, to make few plans for the future, and to engage in considerable fantasizing as a way of boosting self-esteem. Young women with diffused identities often doubt their femininity and tend to fantasize about the Prince Charming who has not yet come into their lives, but who will inevitably make them happier than their present boyfriend or spouse. Interestingly, however, the female with a diffused identity often perceives her mother as a discouraging and disapproving person, while idealizing her father. These findings are of interest in that, as you may recall from Chapter 2, many psychoanalytic psychologists maintain that the female adolescent who fails to resolve her Oedipal feelings toward her father will be unable to establish satisfactory relationships with men during her adult years. This psychoanalytic perspective will be explored further in Chapter 8, though it is noteworthy at this point in view of the data on the diffused identity status.

Males and females who leave adolescence with foreclosed identities also share several characteristics in common. Not surprisingly, females with foreclosed identities usually become wives and mothers in their early adult years and tend to dismiss any unhappiness as part of the experience of being a woman. These young women perceive themselves as nurturant and devoted, but not as especially competent in vocational terms. Unlike women with achieved identities or those in the moratorium status, women with foreclosed identities tend to be deferential toward their husbands or boyfriends. Similarly, young men with foreclosed identities tend to be well behaved, respectful of authority, diligent, and family oriented. Both males and females with foreclosed identities also tend to score lower on moral reasoning and on Piagetian cognitive tasks than those with achieved identities. Given these characteristics, it is perhaps not too surprising that the families in which individuals with foreclosed identities are raised tend to be dominated by the father and to be characterized by sex-typed notions of masculinity and femininity.

In summarizing the research on sex differences and identity statuses, Matteson (1986) underscores the point that androgynous adolescents appear most advantaged in terms of being able to develop both intimacy and a vocational identity. Expressive traits traditionally associated with the female gender role are beneficial in establishing the intimacy, while traits traditionally associated with the male gender role are beneficial in establishing a vocational and ideological identity.

SEX ROLES AND PHYSICAL HEALTH

As discussed in Chapter 2, gender roles also have an indirect impact on the physical health of male and female adolescents. By behaving in a "manly" fashion through drunk driving, speeding, and showing off behind the wheel, the adolescent boy is more likely than the adolescent girl to be killed or injured in automobile accidents. Boys are also more prone than girls to smoke, abuse drugs, and accept dares that are hazardous. Trying to impress friends with their bravado, many males die needlessly in accidents and homicides—the leading causes of death for males between the ages of 14 and 30. As boys become men, the male gender role further imposes its toll by way of the ulcers, heart attacks, and other stress-related diseases associated with masculine behavior in our society (Goldberg, 1979; Levinson, 1978; Pleck, 1981).

The health hazards associated with our traditional notions of masculinity are both humorously and painfully described in *Real Men Don't Eat Quiche:* "Real men" don't smoke low-tar cigarettes or drink light beer. They still pass in the no-passing zone. They don't settle with words what can be settled with a

How would you describe yourself, your father, and your mother in terms of masculinity and femininity?

flamethrower. They don't floss their teeth; and they don't eat quiche, salads, yogurt, broccoli, or tofu (Feirstein, 1982).

In comparison with the traditional male role, however, the traditional female role fares little better in terms of enhancing an adolescent's health (Bell, 1980; Boston Women, 1984). Femininity has historically excluded physical fitness and emphasized unhealthy practices such as wearing girdles, high-heeled shoes, and excessively tight clothing. In an attempt to live up to the stereotypic feminine role, many adolescent girls injure their bodies with crash diets and with chemical irritants from vaginal deodorant sprays, perfumed soaps, and creams for removing hair. Chapter 14 will explain how these feminine principles, when carried to excess, contribute to the life-threatening female disorder, anorexia nervosa. Further, as Chapter 10 will demonstrate, too many young girls have learned to associate motherhood with femininity, thereby permitting themselves to become mothers during their teenaged years, when physical risks to mother and child are greatest.

In sum, girls would benefit from adopting certain habits traditionally associated with the male role, such as regular physical exercise and muscle development; and boys would benefit from adopting certain "feminine" habits, such as refusing to accept dangerous dares from other males and consuming fewer "masculine" foods rich in carbohydrates and fat. The data leave little doubt that both male and female adolescents (and adults) would benefit from assuming a more androgynous perspective on health-related issues.

Conclusion

Despite the methodological limitations of the extant research, this chapter has demonstrated a number of relatively consistent findings that have emerged in regard to gender roles and sex differences.

The impact of sex roles and sex differences will be discussed in greater detail and repeatedly alluded to in future chapters. In the next chapter, for example, we will examine the differences among various racial groups' definitions of masculinity and femininity—differences that have a considerable impact on the behavior of adolescents who are members of U.S. minority cultures. Chapter 7 will then examine the relationship between gender roles and adolescents' academic achievements. Data regarding the family's role in adolescents' sex-role development was intentionally excluded from the present chapter in order to permit a careful examination in Chapter 8 of such questions as: How important is the father in the development of his daughter's androgynous or stereotypically feminine behavior? What influence does a mother's employment have on her son's and daughter's gender-role attitudes?

The information in this chapter also provides a foundation for later discussions of the differences between adolescent males' and females' moral development, vocational choices, sexual behavior, and peer relationships. In addition, the topics of drug use, suicide, anorexia nervosa, and delinquency cannot be explored without serious reconsideration of gender roles. You will continually be called upon in future chapters to consider the four theoretical positions on sex-typed behavior that have been presented in this chapter. Indeed, the essential questions imbedded in these four theoretical perspectives on sex differences will reappear throughout the next ten chapters: Why do male and female adolescents differ in regard to a particular behavior or attitude? Considering the differences that presently exist between male and female roles and behavior, how are practitioners to approach a particular problem with adolescents of both sexes? How applicable to adolescent females are theories and recommendations predicated predominately or exclusively on studies with male subjects?

As new data continue to be generated, our views regarding the benefits of traditional gender roles and androgyny will inevitably be transformed. Given the current contradictions in the empirical literature and given the fact that gender has only recently been considered an important variable in creating theories of adolescent (male?) psychology, our conclusions about sex differences and sex roles can only be tentative and speculative. The decade of the 1970s heralded a new approach to the study of adolescence—an approach that insists upon considering both an adolescent's gender and race before creating theories or formulating recommendations for practitioners.

Although definitive statements about many aspects of gender roles and sex differences are presently impossible, several conclusions seem well warranted. First, the available research should cause many of us to question our own behavior vis-à-vis adolescents—behavior that inadvertently inhibits adolescents from developing their full human potential by endorsing an adherence to our society's idiosyncratic definitions of masculinity and femininity. Second, the research should dissuade us from assuming that we are presently capable of determining which attitudes or behaviors of males and females are genetically or hormonally determined, rather than environmentally fashioned. Third, the present data and controversies should overwhelmingly convince us that gender cannot be discounted as a confounding variable in studies of adolescents. That is, it is crucially important to note whether theories and practices are based upon studies that included female adolescents. This point will be reiterated in the next chapter, in which we examine the importance of race and ethnicity in the lives of adolescents.

Questions for Discussion and Review

Concepts and Terminology

1. Which traits typically associated with the male and the female gender roles in our society have positive or negative connotations according to recent research?
2. What methodological limitations affect much of the research on sex roles and sex differences?
3. What accounts for the differences between male and female behavior according to each of the four theoretical views offered by contemporary psychologists?
4. In what regards are social learning theories and cognitive theories similar and dissimilar in their views of sex-typed behavior?
5. How androgynous are adolescent males and females in terms of their attitudes and behavior?
6. How are gender roles advantageous and disadvantageous to male and female adolescents in regard to academic achievement, physical health, self-esteem, and identity status?
7. What factors appear to influence males' and females' attitudes toward academic achievement and vocational success?
8. How do secondary schools influence adolescents' gender-role attitudes and sex-typed behavior?
9. How do each of the four theoretical perspectives discussed in this chapter account for androgynous behavior?

10. Considering Erikson's and Marcia's theories regarding identity formation, how and why do male and female development differ during adolescence and early adulthood?

Questions for Discussion and Debate

1. How would your own adolescence and present life be different if you were still your present sex but had been raised in accord with the other sex's gender role?
2. How would you describe your adolescent years and your present self in terms of Marcia's identity statuses? In what ways has your identity status been affected by your gender role?
3. In what ways have your gender-role attitudes been advantageous and disadvantageous to your academic, vocational, physical, social, sexual, and athletic development?
4. How adequately do each of the four theoretical perspectives on sex-typed behavior explain your own adolescent attitudes and behavior?
5. What advantages and disadvantages do you believe accrue to androgynous males and to androgynous females?
6. Given society's current gender roles and attitudes toward sex-typed behavior, would you choose to be a member of the other sex if you could be born again? Why or why not?
7. What specific advice would you give to adolescents' parents and teachers in regard to sex typing and androgyny?
8. If you were having a private conversation with a 13-year-old girl, how would you advise her to live her adolescent years in regard to society's expectations for the female role? How would your advice to a 13-year-old boy differ?
9. In terms of the adjectives in Tables 5.1 and 5.2, how would you describe yourself at the age of 15? How does the description differ from the way you would describe yourself now? Using these same tables, how would you have described your "ideal" date at the age of 15 and at your present age? What do you think accounts for the similarities and differences in your answers to these questions?
10. Considering your answers to the quizzes in Tables 5.3 and 5.4 and your behavior during the past two years, to what degree are your behavior and attitudes influenced by sex-role stereotypes?

REFERENCES

Adelson, J. (ed.). *Handbook of adolescent psychology.* New York: Wiley, 1980.

Ahlum, A., & Howe, F. (eds.). *High school feminist studies.* Old Westbury, N.Y.: Feminist Press, 1976.

Antill, J., & Cunningham, J. Self-esteem as a function of masculinity in both sexes. *Journal of Consulting and Clinical Psychology,* 1979, *7,* 782–785.

Bandura, A. *Social learning theories.* Englewood Cliffs, N.J.: Prentice-Hall, 1977.

Baruch, G. Implications and applications of recent research on female development. In J. Williams (ed.), *Psychology of women.* New York: Norton, 1979. Pp. 188–199.

Bell, R. *Changing bodies, changing lives.* New York: Random House, 1980.

Bem, S. The measurement of psychological androgyny. *Journal of Consulting and Clinical Psychology,* 1974, *42,* 155–162.

Bernard, M. Does sex role behavior influence the way teachers evaluate students? *Journal of Educational Psychology,* 1979, *71,* 553–562.

Block, J. Issues, problems and pitfalls in assessing sex differences: A review. *Merrill Palmer Quarterly,* 1976, *22,* 283–308.

Block, M. Conception of sex roles: Some cross-cultural, longitudinal perspectives. *American Psychologist,* 1973, *28,* 512–525.

Boston Women's Health Collective. *Our bodies, ourselves.* New York: Simon & Schuster, 1984.

Brackney, B. The psychology of female adolescents. In M. Abbot (ed.), *American women.* New York: Holt, Rinehart and Winston, 1979. Pp. 133–160.

Brussell, E. *Dictionary of quotable definitions.* Englewood Cliffs, N.J.: Prentice-Hall, 1970.

Burke, R. & Weir, T. *Sex differences in adolescent life stress, social support, and well-being.* ERIC ED 147 661, 1976.

Caplan, *P. Erikson's concept of inner space.* Paper presented at the American Psychological Association, Toronto, 1978.

Casserly, P. Helping able young women take math and science seriously in school. In N. Colangelo and R. Zaffrann (eds.), *New voices in counseling the gifted.* Dubuque, Iowa: Kendall Hunt, 1979. Pp. 346–369.

Chandler, T., Sawicki, R., & Stryffeler, J. Relationship between adolescent sexual stereotypes and working mothers. *Journal of Early Adolescence,* 1981, *1,* 72–83.

Crandell, V. Sex differences in expectancy of intellectual ànd academic reinforcement. In R. Unger (ed.), *Women: Dependent or independent variable.* New York: Psychological Dimensions, 1975. Pp. 650–685.

Deaux, K. *The behavior of men and women.* Monterey, Cal.: Brooks Cole, 1976.

Deem, R. *Women and schooling.* London: Routledge and Kegan Paul, 1978.

Denmark, F., & Goodfield, H. Second look at adolescence theories. *Sex Roles,* 1978, *4,* 375–381.

Ditkoff, G. Stereotypes of adolescents towards working women. *Adolescence,* 1979, *14,* 277–282.

Douvan, E. New source of conflict in females at adolescence. In J. Bardwick (ed.), *Feminine personality and conflict.* Belmont, Cal.: Wadsworth, 1970. Pp. 35–65.

Downs, C., & Abshier, G. Conceptions of physical appearance among young adolescents. *Journal of Early Adolescence,* 1982, *2,* 255–265.

Doyle, J. Attitude toward the male's role. *Catalogue of Selected Documents in Psychology,* 1978, *2,* 35.

Dubbert, J. *A man's place: Masculinity in transition.* Englewood Cliffs, N.J.: Prentice-Hall, 1980.

Dweck, C. Attribution theory. In P. Mussen and M. Hetherington (eds.), *Child development handbook.* New York: Wiley, 1984. Pp. 210–286.

Emerich, W. *Women in search of equality.* Princeton, N.J.: Educational Testing Service, 1979.

Enforcing Title IX. Washington, D.C.: U.S. Civil Rights Commission, 1980.

Erikson, E. *Identity: Youth in crisis.* New York: Norton, 1968.

Expanding adolescent sex roles. Ithaca, N.Y.: Cornell University, 1978.

Farmer, H. What inhibits achievement and career motivation in women. In L. Harmon (ed.), *Counseling women.* Monterey, Cal.: Brooks Cole, 1978. Pp. 159–172.

Farrell, W. *The liberated man.* New York: Bantam Books, 1975.

Fasteau, M. *The male machine.* New York: McGraw-Hill, 1976.

Fein, R. Examining the nature of masculinity. In A. Sargent (ed.), *Beyond sex roles.* New York: West Publishers, 1977. Pp. 188–200.

Feirstein, B. *Real men don't eat quiche: A guidebook to all that is truly masculine.* New York, Simon & Schuster, 1982.

Fisher, M. Teenage scientist. *Ms.* July 1980, p. 23.

Fitzpatrick, J. Academic underachievement, other direction and attitudes towards women's roles in bright adolescent females. *Journal of Educational Psychology.* 1978, *70,* 645–650.

Frazier, N., & Sadker, M. *Sexism in school and society.* New York: Harper & Row, 1973.

Friedrich, L., Tucker, C., Norris, C., Farnsworth, J., Fisher, D., Hannington, D., & Hoxie, K. Perceptions by adolescents of television heroines. Southeastern Psychological Association, New Orleans, 1978.

Frieze, I. *Women and sex roles.* New York: Norton, 1978.

Gates, B. *Changing learning, changing lives.* Old Westbury, N.Y.: Feminist Press, 1978.

Gerzon, M. *A choice of heroes: The changing faces of American manhood.* Boston: Houghton Mifflin, 1982.

Gilligan, C. *In a different voice: Psychological theory and women's development.* Cambridge, Mass.: Harvard University Press, 1982.

Glidewell, J. The psychological context of distress in school. In D. Bartal and L. Saxe (eds.), *Social psychology of education.* New York: Halsted, 1978. Pp. 167–188.

Goffman, E. *Gender advertisements.* New York: Harper & Row, 1979.

Gold, M., & Petronio, R. Delinquent behavior in adolescence. In J. Adelson (ed.), *Handbook of adolescent psychology.* New York: Wiley, 1980.

Goldberg, H. *The new male: From self-destruction to self-care.* New York: Morrow, 1979.

Golden, G., & Cherry, F. Test performance and social comparison choices of high school men and women. *Sex Roles,* 1982, *7,* 761–771.

Good, T., & Brophy, J. *Looking in classrooms.* New York: Harper & Row, 1984.

Goodman, D. *Biochemical changes during a dacrystic regimen.* Paper presented at Society for Neuroscience. Anaheim, California, October 1984.

Gordon, R. *The ties that bind: The price of pursuing the male mystique.* Washington, D.C.: Peer Project, July 1980.

Gutik, B. *Enhancing women's career development.* San Francisco: Jossey-Bass, 1979.

Guttentag, M., & Bray, H. *Undoing sex stereotypes.* New York: McGraw-Hill, 1976.

Hansen, L. & Rapoza, R. *Career development and counseling women.* Springfield, Ill.: Charles Thomas, 1978.

Hansen, S., & Darling, C. Attitudes of adolescents toward division of labor in the home. *Adolescence,* 1985, *77,* 61–71.

Hanes, B., & Prawatt, R. Sex role perceptions during adolescence. *Journal of Educational Psychology,* 1979, *71,* 850–855.

Helmreich, R., Spence, J., & Wilhelm, J. A psychometric analysis of the Personal Attributes Questionnaire. *Sex Roles,* 1981, *7,* 1097–1108.

Hertsgaard, D., & Light, H. Junior high girls' attitudes toward the rights and roles of women. *Adolescence,* 1984, *19,* 847–853.

Herzog, R. High school seniors occupational plans and values: Trends in sex differences, 1976 through 1980. *Sociology of Education,* 1982, 55, 1–13.

Herzog, R., Bachman, J., & Johnston, L. Paid work, child care and housework: A national survey of high school seniors' preferences for sharing responsibilities between husband and wife. *Sex Roles,* 1983, *9,* 109–135.

Hoffman, L. Fear of success in males and females. *Journal of Consulting and Clinical Psychology,* 1974, *42,* 353–358.

Horner, M. Toward an understanding of achievement related conflicts in women. *Journal of Social Issues,* 1972, *28,* 157–175.

Horney, K. The dread of women. *International Journal of Psychoanalysis,* 1932, *13,* 348–360.

Hoyenga, G., & Hoyenga, K. *The question of sex differences.* Boston: Little Brown, 1979.

Huston, A. Sex-typing. In P. Mussen and M. Hetherington (eds.), *Child development handbook.* New York: Wiley, 1984. Pp. 388–467.

Jones, W., Chernovetz, E., & Hanson, R. The enigma of androgyny. *Journal of Consulting and Clinical Psychology,* 1978, *46,* 298–313.

Kagan, J., & Moss, H. *From birth to maturity.* New York: Wiley, 1962.

Kohlberg, L. A cognitive development analysis of children's sex role concepts and attitudes. In E. Maccoby (ed.), *The development of sex differences.* Stanford, Cal.: Stanford University Press, 1966. Pp. 82–133.

Lanier, H., & Byrne, J. How high school students view women. *Sex Roles,* 1981, *7,* 145–158.

Lerner, H. Adaptive and pathogenic aspects of sex role stereotypes: Implications for parenting and psychotherapy. *American Journal of Psychiatry,* 1978, *135,* 48–52.

Levinson, D. *The seasons of a man's life.* New York: Knopf, 1978.

Lipman, J., & Leavitt, H. Vicarious and direct achievement patterns. *Counseling Psychologist,* 1976, *6,* 26–32.

Lipsitz, J. *Early adolescence.* Lexington, Mass.: Lexington Books, 1978.

Locksley, A., & Douvan, E. Stress on male and female high school students. In R. Moss (ed.), *Adolescent behavior and society.* New York: Random House, 1980. Pp. 275-291.

Loevinger, J. *Ego development: Conceptions and theory.* San Francisco: Jossey-Bass, 1976.

Lueptow, L. *Adolescent sex roles and social change.* New York: Columbia University Press, 1984.

Maccoby, E., & Jacklin, C. *The psychology of sex differences.* Stanford, Cal.: Stanford University Press, 1974.

Marcia, J. Identity in adolescence. In J. Adelson (ed.), *Handbook of adolescent psychology.* New York: Wiley, 1981. Pp. 197–243.

Marcia, J., Waterman, A., & Matteson, D. (eds.). *A handbook for ego identity: Psychosocial research.* New York: Erlbaum, 1986.

Marini, M. Sex differences in the determination of adolescent aspirations: A review of research. *Sex Roles,* 1978, *5,* 723–726.

Massad, C. Sex role identity and adjustment during adolescence. *Child Development,* 1981, *52,* 1290–1298.

Matteson, D. Sex differences in identity formation. In J. Marcia, A. Waterman, & D. Matteson (eds.), *A handbook for ego identity: Psychosocial research.* New York: Erlbaum, 1986.

Mead, M. *Sex and temperament in three primitive societies.* New York, American Library, 1935.

Miller, C., & Swift, K. *The handbook of nonsexist writing for writers, editors and speakers.* New York: Lippincott and Crowell, 1980.

Miller, M., Brown, J., & Perloff, R. Mass media and sex typing. Toronto: American Psychological Association, 1978.

Miller, M., & Reeves, B. Children's occupational sex role stereotypes. *Journal of Broadcasting,* 1976, *20,* 35–50.

Mischel, W. Sex typing and socialization. In P. Mussen (ed.), *Carmichael's manual of child psychology*. New York: Wiley, 1970. Pp. 3–72.

Mischel, W. *Introduction to personality*. New York: Holt, Rinehart and Winston, 1981.

Money, J., & Ehrhardt, A. *Man woman: Boy girl*. Baltimore, Md.: Johns Hopkins University Press, 1972.

Mokros, J., Taylor, R., and O'Neill, M. Adolescents' perceptions of the cause and consequences of success. *Sex Roles*, 1977, *3*, 353–365.

Mussen, P. Long term consequences of masculinity of interests in adolescence. *Journal of Consulting Psychology*, 1962, *26*, 435–440.

Murty, L. Adolescent theories with androcentric bias. *Sex Roles*. 1978, *4*, 369–374.

Nicholson, S., & Antill, J. Personal problems of adolescents and their relationship to peer acceptance and sex role identity. *Journal of Youth and Adolescence*, 1981, *10*, 309–325.

Offer, D., & Offer, J. *From teenage to young manhood*. New York: Basic Books, 1975.

Offer, D., Ostrov, E., & Howard, K. *The adolescent: A psychological self-portrait*. New York: Basic Books, 1981.

Olsen, N., & Williamsen, E. Fear of success: Fact or artifact? *Journal of Psychology*, 1978, *98*, 65–70.

Parsons, J. Attribution, learned helplessness and sex differences in achievement. In S. Yussen (ed.), *The development of reflection*. New York: Academic Press, 1982.

Parsons, J., Kaczala, C., and Meece, J. Socialization of achievement attitudes and beliefs. *Educational Researcher*, 1981, *10*, 7–17.

Pleck, J. *The myth of masculinity*. Cambridge, Mass.: MIT Press, 1981.

Plost, M., and Rosen, M. Effects of sex of career models on adolescents' occupational preferences. *AV Communication*, 1974, *22*, 41–50.

Prager, K. Identity status, sex role orientation and self-esteem in late adolescent females. *Journal of Genetic Psychology*, 1983, *143*, 159–167.

Rodenstein, J., and Hughes, C. Career and lifestyle determinants of gifted women. In N. Colangelo and R. Zaffran (eds.), *New voices in counseling the gifted*. Dubuque, Iowa: Kendall Hunt, 1979. Pp. 370–381.

Romero, N. Motive to avoid success and its effect on performance in school age males and females. *Developmental Psychology*, 1975, *11*, 689–699.

Rosenberg, F., & Simms, R. Sex differences in the self-concept in adolescence. *Sex Roles*, 1975, *1*, 147–159.

Rubin, M. *Men without masks: Writings from the journals of modern men*. Reading, Mass.: Addison-Wesley, 1980.

Ruble, T. Sex stereotypes: Issues of change in the 1970's. *Sex Roles*, 1983, *9*, 397–402.

Rust, J., & Lloyd, M. Sex role attitudes and preferences of junior high school age adolescents. *Adolescence*, 1982, *17*, 34–44.

Sabo, D., & Ross, R. *Jocks: Sports and male identity*. Englewood Cliffs, N.J.: Prentice-Hall, 1980.

Sadker, D. *Being a man: Activities on male sex role stereotyping*. Washington, D.C.: U.S. Office of Education, 1978.

Scarf, M. *Unfinished business: Pressure points in the lives of women*. New York: Ballantine Books, 1980.

Sex Roles, 1976, *2*, 211–320.

Sex Roles, 1979, *5*, 703–859.

Schmuck, R., & Schmuck, P. *Group processes in the classroom*. Dubuque, Iowa: W. C. Brown, 1979.

Shaw, M., & McCuen, J. The onset of academic underachievement. *Journal of Educational Psychology,* 1960, *51,* 103–107.

Sherman, J. Social values, femininity and the development of female competence. In J. Williams (ed.), *Psychology of women.* New York: Norton, 1979. Pp. 200-211.

Shields, S. Functional Darwinism and the psychology of women. *American Psychologist,* 1975, *30,* 739–754.

Spence, J., & Helmreich, R. Comparison of masculine and feminine personality attributes and sex role attitudes across age groups. *Developmental Psychology,* 1979, *15,* 583–584. (a)

Spence, J., & Helmreich, R. On assessing androgyny. *Sex Roles,* 1979, *5,* 721–738. (b)

Spence, J., Helmreich, R., & Stapp, J. Ratings of self and peers on sex role attributes and their relation to self-esteem and conceptions of masculinity and femininity. *Journal of Personality and Social Psychology,* 1975, *32,* 29–39.

Stalled at the start: Government action on sex bias in the schools. Washington, D.C.: Project on Equal Rights, 1978.

Staples, R. *Black masculinity: The black male's role in American society.* New York: Black Scholar Press, 1982.

Sugar, M. (ed.) *Female adolescent development.* New York: Brunner Mazel, 1979.

Thomas, S., & Robinson, M. Development of a measure of androgyny for young adolescents. *Journal of Early Adolescence,* 1981, *1,* 195–209.

Thompson, D. *As boys become men: Class activities for learning new male roles.* Denver: University of Colorado Press, 1980.

Title IX of the education amendments of 1972. Washington, D.C.: Resource Center on Sex Roles in Education, 1976.

Tobias, S. *Overcoming math anxiety.* New York: Norton, 1978.

Topol, P., & Reznikoff, M. Achievers and nonachievers: A comparative study among high school senior girls. *Sex Roles,* 1979, *5,* 85–92.

Unger, R. Toward a redefinition of sex and gender. *American Psychologist,* 1979, *34,* 1085–1094.

Welch, R., Huston, A., Wright, J., & Plehal, R. Subtle sex role cues in children's commercials. *Journal of Communication,* 1979, *29,* 202–209.

Williams, J., & Best, D. *Measuring sex stereotypes: A 30-nation study.* Beverly Hills, Cal.: Sage, 1982.

Wolleat, P. Guiding the career development of gifted females. In N. Colangelo and R. Zaffran (eds.), *New voices in counseling the gifted.* Dubuque, Iowa: Brown, 1979.

Chapter Outline

Goals and Objectives

This chapter is designed to enable you to:

- *Describe the problems that confront many adolescents from minority cultures in contemporary U.S. society*
- *Explain several approaches for ameliorating the problems of minority youth*
- *Discuss the research and statistics that refute the traditional stereotypes of U.S. minorities*
- *Examine the different philosophical views about assimilation and cultural pluralism*

Concepts and Terminology

bicultural
biethnicity
bilingualism
BIA
extended family
haole
machismo
matriarchy
banana syndrome
Project Excel
multicultural
Moynihan report
Nisei
zoot-suit riots
Sansei
Chicano
Third World
ethnocentric
black dialect

6 Adolescents from Minority Cultures

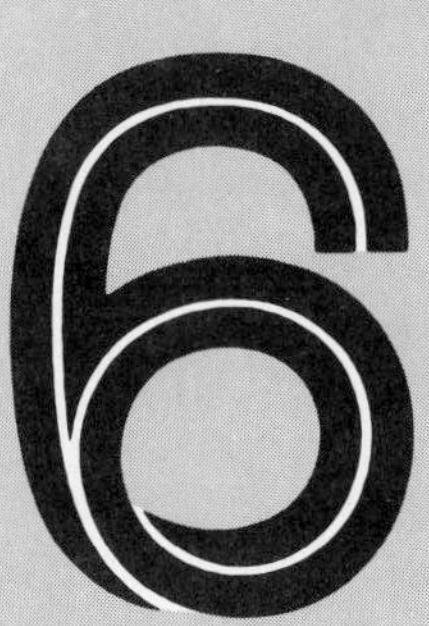

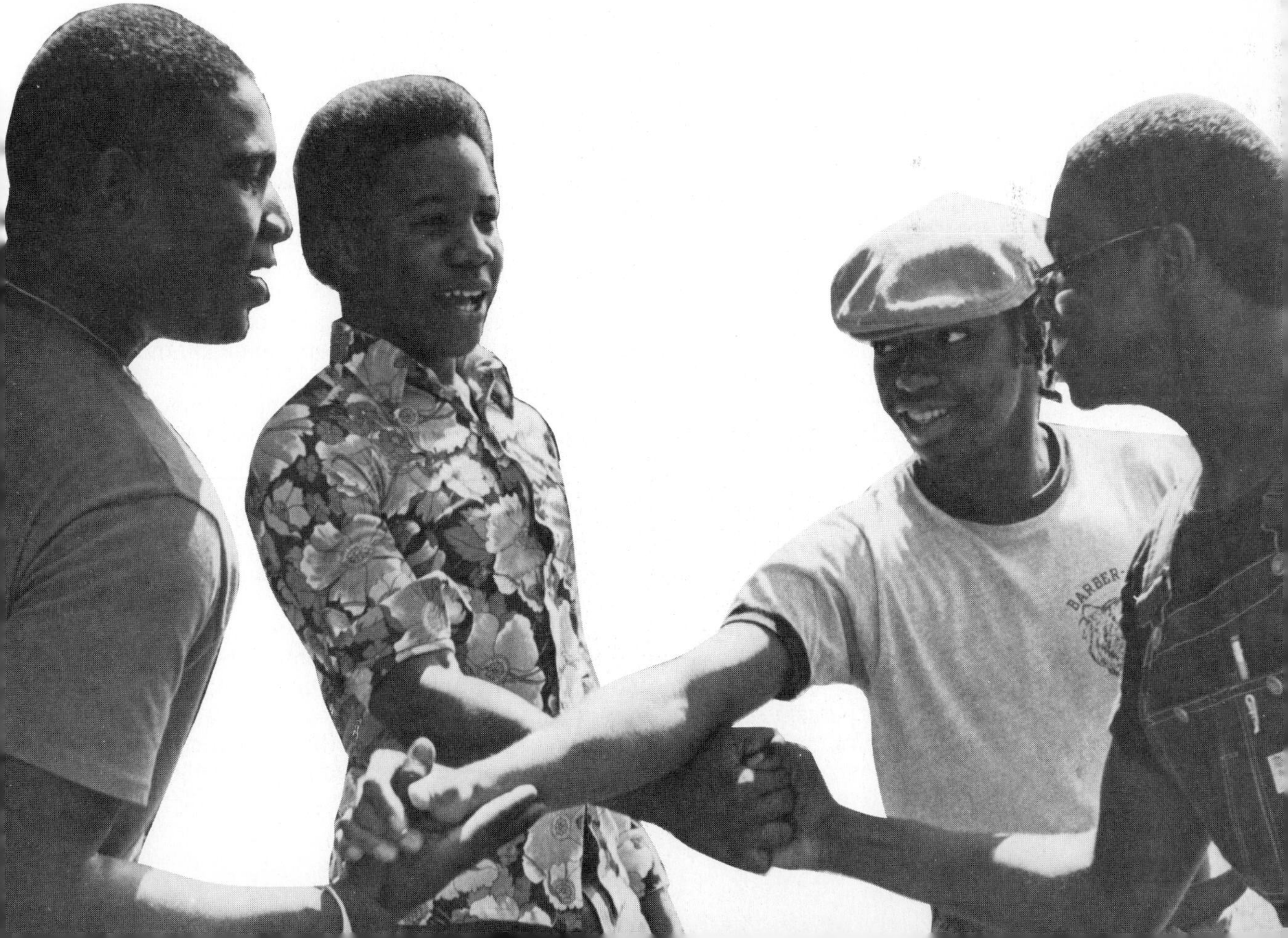

MINORITIES IN THE UNITED STATES

What percentage of adolescents in the U.S. are white, black, yellow, or red? Which minority will be largest by the year 2000? How many adolescents live on Indian reservations? In terms of racial-group membership, which adolescents are the most financially, physically, and educationally disadvantaged? Questions such as these serve to remind us that today's adolescents cannot be conceived of as a monocultural group who share a similar world view or who share a similar middle-class, white background. In the terminology of the 1980s, adolescents have increasingly become a "rainbow" population of varied colors, cultures, and concerns. It is the intent of this chapter to explore some of the variations in that rainbow.

According to the 1980 Census, about 10 percent of all Americans are black, 8 percent are Hispanic, 0.5 percent are Native American, and 1 percent are Asian American (*U.S. Children and Their Families,* 1983). According to some demographers' estimates, by the year 2000 Hispanic Americans will outnumber all other minority groups. In fact, according to some researchers, Hispanics may already account for about 9 percent of our population, although the Census underestimates the count because migrant and illegal aliens are excluded (U.S. Bureau of the Census, 1982).

The significance of these demographic statistics becomes more readily apparent when we examine the minority youth enrollment in public schools. In several cities Hispanic and black students already outnumber whites. For example, in 1970 22 percent of the high-school students in Milwaukee were black, 21 percent in Miami, and 30 percent in New York; but by 1980 these proportions had risen to 39 percent, 25 percent, and 40 percent, respectively. Similarly, between 1970 and 1980 the percentage of Hispanic high-school students increased from 18 percent to 38 percent in Miami and from 21 percent to 26 percent in New York (*Education Week*, 1981). Of the approximately 40 million students presently enrolled in U.S. public schools, 73 percent are white, 16 percent are black, 8 percent are Hispanic, 2 percent are Asian American, and .8 percent are Indian American (Stubbs & Harrison, 1982).

These statistics make it clear that working with adolescents cannot be assumed to mean working with white, middle-class youths. Indeed, white youths represent the minority of those with whom adults are interacting in certain types of jobs in particular areas of the country. As a consequence, acquiring a more thorough understanding of our minority cultures assumes a particular relevance in our contemporary society.

DEFINING MINORITIES AND ETHNIC GROUPS

In regard to the materials that will be discussed in this chapter, a distinction is necessary between the term "ethnic group" and "minority." According to the *Harvard Dictionary of American Ethnic Groups*, an ethnic group is composed of individuals who share several or all of the following features: common geographic origin; migratory status; race; language or dialect; religious faith; ties that transcend kinship, neighborhood, and community boundaries; traditions, values, and symbols; literature, folklore, and music; food preferences; settlement and employment patterns; special interests in regard to politics in the homeland and in the United States; institutions that specifically serve and maintain the group; an internal sense of distinctiveness; and an external perception of distinctiveness.

According to this definition, the *Harvard Dictionary* (1981) lists 106 U.S. ethnic groups. Obviously, therefore, this chapter is not intended to explore ethnic differences among our society's adolescents. The purpose is to provide a brief introduction to some of the distinctive features of the largest minority groups in our society. Moreover, the chapter is limited to those aspects of minority cultures that are most relevant to our study of adolescence. In this regard, the term "minority" is being used to denote a group who, because of physical or cultural traits, is singled out from others in society for differential, unequal treatment and who, therefore, regard themselves as objects of collective discrimination (Atkinson, Morten, & Wing Sue, 1983).

A term sometimes used interchangeably with "minority"—**Third World groups**—is derived from the French term *tier monde*, which originally referred to the world's nonindustrialized nations that were not socialistic or communistic ("second world") or capitalistic ("first world") societies. In recent decades, some minorities in the U.S. have adopted the term and revised its original meaning to connote the comradeship among all oppressed people throughout the world. Hence, the term "Third World" has come to represent the oppression, segregation, political and economic powerlessness, and deprivation that minorities in the U.S. share in common with people in underdeveloped countries. Adolescents who are members of a minority might refer to themselves as Third World citizens, to underscore the similarities among all impoverished people who live in a discriminatory society.

LIMITATIONS OF THE RESEARCH ON MINORITY YOUTHS

The primary limitation of the existing research on minorities is that there is so precious little of it. Among others, the renowned adolescent psychologist Joseph Adelson (1980) maintains that adolescent psychology might more accurately be described as the psychology of white adolescent males, since most of the valuable research was conducted with only white, male samples. The paucity of research on minority youths is exemplified by the fact that 210 of the 250 articles written about Mexican American children were published after 1970 (*Hispanic Mental Health Bibliography,* 1978). Similarly, a survey of the articles published between 1930 and 1979 in *Child Development* showed virtually no studies conducted with children who were not members of the white, middle class until the 1960s, when a few studies conducted with nonwhite children began to appear in print (Super, 1982).

Moreover, much of the available research on which our notions of minority adolescents are predicated has been criticized for its inadequate methodology and biased misinterpretation. Among those who have criticized the extant research on these grounds are Derald Wing Sue, former president of the American Personnel and Guidance Association; Robert Williams, former president of the American Association of Black Psychologists; and the renowned sociologists Robert Staples and Joyce Ladner (Lamfromboise, Dauphinais, & Rowe, 1978; Ladner, 1971; Staples, 1976; Wing Sue, 1981). In a similar regard, Robert Guthrie has critiqued the research employed within the discipline of psychology (1976). According to these critics, researchers have too often misinterpreted data and misconducted experiments in ways that maintain racial stereotypes and that inadvertently support the status quo in regard to discriminatory practices in our society.

While not all scholars agree, there is ample evidence to substantiate these criticisms of the existing research on minorities. For example, poor methodology is exemplified by the fact that most research on Mexican Americans has included only rural populations, even though the majority now live in urban areas. Consequently, many of our present generalizations about Mexican Americans are based on nonrepresentative samples (Melville, 1980). Moreover, the distinct characteristics of minority families have too often been interpreted as "deficits" by white, middle-class standards. For instance, children raised by one parent or by extended families are frequently described by researchers as deprived or culturally disadvantaged because their families differ from the white family's nuclear structure. The term "culturally deprived" became particularly popular in the research of the 1960s as a way of describing youngsters whose cultures did not resemble that of the white middle class. Rather than perceiving these youths as culturally different, most researchers characterized their cultural distinctness as deviance or deficits (Ladner, 1971).

One of the most frequently cited examples of biased research is the 1965 *Moynihan report.* The stereotypes created by this research continue to linger and to influence many of our perceptions of black adolescents and their families. Headed by Senator Daniel Moynihan, a Senate committee studied black incomes, marital status, and family structure. Having gathered its data, the committee publicly announced that unlike white families, black families were **matriarchal** in that women ran the households and dominated the men. In addition, the Moynihan report accused black women of emasculating their men and undermining the progress of the entire family: "The weakness of the family structure is the principle source of most of the aberrant, inadequate and anti-social behavior that perpetuates poverty and deprivation. The matriarchal structure retards progress of the group as a whole and imposes a crushing burden on the negro male" (Moynihan et al., 1965). According to the report, black families were "broken down" and "unstable" because females headed so many of the households. In sum, the report maintained that if black women were not so domineering, black males would be able to make greater economic advances. The study's essential recommendation was that black families should emulate the white nuclear family. Two further assumptions were that strong black women precluded the existence of strong black men and that families must have two parents present in order to be "stable" and "normal."

In the decade that followed this highly publicized report, numerous research studies refuted the committee's conclusions, criticized its ethnocentric interpretations of the data, and lambasted its faulty methodology (Billingsley, 1968; L. Johnson, 1981; Ladner, 1971; Staples, 1976; P. Wallace, 1978). Indeed, as part of the backlash to the Moynihan report, during the 1960s and 1970s nearly 500 articles about black families appeared—five times more than in the entire century that preceded the Senate committee's report. The report's opponents argued that while many black families were indeed different from the white nuclear family, the difference was not "dysfunctional," "pathological," or "deviant." Many scholars attacked Moynihan's report as an example of ethnocentric research that "blames the victims" for their problems and refuses to acknowledge that discrimination contributes in any significant way to the plight of black Americans. The critics pointed out that in 1965 more than 75 percent of all black children were raised by both parents and that the report had classified widows and common-law marriages as "broken homes."

Moynihan's researchers also ignored the fact that when incomes are equivalent, female-headed households are nearly as frequent among whites as blacks, a finding that shows that the essential reason for the different family structures between whites and blacks is poverty, not matriarchy. Black women headed only 7 percent of the families that earned more than $3,000, but 36 percent of the families that earned less than $3,000. The committee also failed to mention that factors other than a woman's "domineering" personality can determine a family's structure. Among these factors was a welfare system that paid larger benefits when the husband was absent, the shortage of marriageable black men due to early death, incarceration, low rate of male births, and the marital strains created by poverty and discrimination. The committee also perceived females who were employed, assertive, and independent as "domineering" and "emasculating," since black female behavior contrasted so sharply with the white culture's definition of femininity and normality in 1965.

Furthermore, scholars who opposed the Moynihan report emphasized that the committee viewed differences as deficits, instead of recognizing the strengths of poor, black families. Why, they argued, should the committee conclude that families could not be "stable" or supportive without a man present? And why should the committee accuse black women of dominating their men, when white women have traditionally made all the decisions related to child rearing and household expenditures without being accused of being domineering? Why were Moynihan's researchers so quick to see the domination of black men by black women, but not to see this same phenomenon in their own culture? Since the statistics showed that in 85 percent of poor families the black women earned less money than men, how could the committee accuse black women of being more "powerful" than black men? According to the researchers who refuted Moynihan, black women wielded no more economic, sexual, or social power over men than did white women.

The Moynihan report remains an excellent example of the kind of research cited by scholars who maintain that too many of our present generalizations about minority adolescents are predicated on faulty data. Further, it remains an example of a second accusation leveled against much of the available research—the accusation of ethnocentrism. **Ethnocentrism** is an attitude that regards one's own race or group as the center of culture and knowledge and regards another group's customs, literature, religion, clothing, or standards of beauty and intelligence as inferior. Exemplary ethnocentric comments include such remarks as: "How disgusting that they eat something as filthy as that!" "What an absurd, primitive religion they have!" "What a pity they haven't learned to appreciate good art and music like ours!"

Ethnocentric attitudes in research on minority adolescents can be manifested by such judgmental words as "deviant" and "culturally deprived" in describing customs that deviate from the white, middle-class norm. For example, instead of describing black dialect as "unique" or "a creative modification of standard English," ethnocentric research may consistently label this speech "substandard" or "deficient." It is argued that because the vast majority of writers and researchers are from the white middle class, few are capable of recognizing the ethnocentrism in their own scholarship (Atkinson, Morten, & Wing Sue, 1983; Guthrie, 1976; Ladner, 1971; Staples, 1976; Wing Sue, 1981). As readers of the research, we might limit our inadvertent participation in ethnocentric judgments by asking ourselves: Is this researcher assuming that one culture's conduct is superior to another's? Do I see evidence of negative judgments against another culture because it differs from the white norm? Could the evidence cited by this researcher be interpreted more favorably if someone from that culture had written this report?

SPECIAL CONCERNS OF MINORITY ADOLESCENTS

In attempting to delineate the special problems or the special characteristics of minority youth, one confounding variable of major importance looms—socioeconomic class. As you recall from the Chapter 1 discussion of research methods, confounding variables such as the income of an adolescent's parents can interfere with accurate generalizations and correct appraisals of the data. In regard to our study of minority adolescents, the confounding variable of family income becomes particularly important, because such an inordinately high percentage of minority youths live below the poverty level in comparison to white youths. For example, how do we know whether the difference between white and Indian academic achievement is caused primarily by the fact that white children generally come from richer families or by the fact that Indian values often differ from those of the white middle class? Although many studies have tried to take into account potentially confounding variables, such as socioeconomic status, in comparing white and minority children, most have not. This shortcoming of the research on minority children will become particularly clear to you in Chapter 8, when we examine the data on single-parent and two-parent families.

Furthermore, as subsequent chapters will demonstrate, the relative influence of parents, peers, genetic endowment, or socioeconomic class are difficult to determine, given the methodological limitations of the extant research. In sum, with these limitations, the research presently offers only one indisputable fact: Most minority adolescents have to contend with a unique set of problems that most white adolescents never confront. These unique aspects of many a minority child's adolescence can be separated into several categories: identity, self-esteem, education, incomes and employment, physical health, and juvenile delinquency.

Skin Color and Self-Esteem

As Chapter 2 demonstrated, an adolescent's self-confidence and self-image are often intricately related to his or her physical attractiveness. Given this relationship between physical appearance and self-esteem, it is of little surprise that researchers have investigated the impact of an adolescent's race on his or her self-image. In a society where attractiveness is defined in terms of Caucasian features and physiques, how do adolescents with thick lips, or slanted eyes, or dark-colored skin, or a wide nose, or large hips feel about themselves? How do the white standards of beauty touted by advertisers and movie makers and fashion magazines affect the self-confidence of minority youth?

In one of the earliest studies to examine the self-concepts of minority children, black preschoolers were shown white dolls and black dolls and asked to answer a series of questions (Clark & Clark, 1947). In this highly publicized study, most of the black children preferred playing with white dolls, perceived the black doll as "bad," and thought the white doll was prettier. Given this finding, which suggested that black children have a negative concept of their own race, a number of other studies were conducted with older children and adolescents. Although the data have been inconsistent, some recent studies do confirm the hypothesis that some Mexican American, black, and Asian American adolescents dislike their skin color and prefer Caucasian features to their own (Howard, 1971; Lerner, 1980; Pinkney, 1975; A. Ruiz, 1975; R. Ruiz, 1977).

For example, some Chicanos powder their necks to look lighter skinned, and others admit a preference for light-skinned members of their race (Maldonado & Cross, 1977). Similarly, some Asian American males have mocked females of their own racial group for being flat chested and short-legged in comparison to white girls. In addition, some Asian American girls have plastic surgery in order to make their eyes less slanted and more "American" (Wing Sue, 1981). Even within a minority family, skin color can create difficulties. For instance, tensions and jealousies can arise in a Puerto Rican family when society treats light-skinned family members as whites, while treating darker-skinned siblings as blacks (Fitzpatrick, 1971; Thomas, 1967).

In contrast to these data, however, other researchers have failed to confirm the hypothesis that racial features diminish minority adolescents' self-esteem (Baldwin, 1979). In support of this position, a 1976 survey of 350 black high-school students showed that 80 percent preferred either dark brown or light brown skin to very white skin (Anderson & Cromwell, 1977). Moreover, several studies have shown that the darkest-skinned Mexican American males were assimilated into white society faster than their lighter-skinned peers, a finding that contradicts most other predictions about assimilation and dark skin color (Mendoza & Martinez, 1981).

In sum, it appears that the relationship between an adolescent's racial features and his or her self-esteem is more complicated than often acknowledged in earlier research. Current data suggest that some minority adolescents may indeed prefer Caucasian features and lighter skin, an assumption that may be most true for those whose physical appearance deviates most from the white cultural norms. Nevertheless, current data do not warrant our assuming that minority youths inevitably experience feelings of shame or inferiority related to their physical distinctiveness.

Education and Minority Youth

Of far greater concern in the current literature is the issue of minority youths' educational deficiencies. Undeniably, minority youths and their parents have made tremendous educational gains in the U.S. in recent decades, as evidenced by the fact that in 1870, 84 percent of black Americans were illiterate in comparison to only 40 percent in 1970 (Goff, 1976). Similarly, between 1974 and 1978 college enrollment for nonwhite students increased by nearly 23 percent (Stubbs & Harrison, 1982).

Despite these impressive gains, however, substantial educational disparities still exist between white and nonwhite students in the 1980s, a fact well documented by the National Center for Education Statistics (Stubbs & Harrison, 1982). For example, only 32 percent of the black, 26 percent of the Hispanic, and 23 percent of the Indian high-school seniors were enrolled in the academic track of their school's curriculum in 1980, compared to 52 percent of their Asian and 40 percent of their white peers. Moreover, although an impressive 62 percent of Asian Americans and 38 percent of whites and blacks enrolled in colleges in 1980, only 27 percent of the Hispanic and 19 percent of the Indian high-school graduates continued their education in college.

These discrepancies in college enrollment and in curriculum choices explain why only about 9 percent of all black and Hispanic males complete four or more years of college, in comparison with nearly one-fourth of all white males. More discouraging still, between 1978 and 1980 college enrollment increased overall, but not among minority males. Among females, recent statistics are even less encouraging: Only 17 percent of the whites, 12 percent of the blacks, and 7 percent of the Hispanics finished four or more years in college in 1981 (Stubbs & Harrison, 1982).

In addition to being less likely to finish high school or college, minority youths achieve less academically than whites while enrolled in public school. For example, nearly one-third of all students who speak Spanish as their native language are at least two years behind their other classmates academically (*The Educational Disadvantages of Language Minority Persons,* 1978). Similarly, national surveys spanning the decade of the 1970s document that black, Indian, and Hispanic adolescents earned lower achievement scores than whites in reading, art, social studies, math, citizenship, and occupational development

(*Changes in Mathematical Achievement,* 1979; *Three National Assessments of Reading,* 1981).

Moreover, a number of studies conclude that in recent years minority students appear to be losing the academic gains made in the 1960s and early 1970s. For example, comparisons of national achievement scores between 1970 and 1979 showed that about one-fifth of the white students were reading at the lowest level. In contrast, the number of black adolescents reading in this lowest category rose from 50 percent to 62 percent over the same period of time (*Three National Assessments of Reading,* 1981). Black 17-year-olds also appeared to have lost their academic gains in mathematics during the same three-year-period (*Changes in Mathematical Achievement,* 1979). Other studies also support the hypothesis that many minority students fall further behind academically as they age. These academic losses have been found in samples of Puerto Rican, Mexican American, and Native American students (Fitzpatrick, 1971; Moore, 1976; Rodriguez, 1979; Wax, 1971).

As Chapter 7 will demonstrate, an adolescent's academic performance is related to variables other than race or income. For example, interviews with 68 academically successful black adolescents from impoverished, rural families showed that their parents' encouragement, the comments of famous black athletes who stress the value of education, and positive educational experiences at school contributed to their academic success. Although most of the youths indicated that their parents were unable to offer academic help, due to their own limited formal education, the parents had nonetheless instilled values and habits that enhanced their children's academic success (Lee, 1985). (In Contrast, see Box 6.1.)

Although poverty and minority status do not necessarily prevent an adolescent from succeeding academically, the fact remains that minority youths receive proportionately more corporal punishment and more suspensions from school than whites—a phenomenon that inevitably contributes to academic underachievement. In addition, data from various parts of the country indicate that minority students, especially males, are the most likely to be suspended for minor offenses, such as being "disrespectful" to teachers (*Children out of School,* 1974; *Corporal Punishment,* 1977; Demarest & Jordan, 1975; Killalea, 1980; *The Student Pushout,* 1978). Furthermore, these data show that minority suspensions in some school districts increased dramatically after court-ordered integration, suggesting that suspensions are sometimes related to racial prejudice. The superintendent of one of Florida's largest school systems has stated that the more a school's population becomes poor, black, or Hispanic, the more often teachers focus on disciplinary methods, rather than on methods for improving academic achievement (J. Jones, 1978).

In conclusion, many researchers maintain that minority students suffer more than whites in terms of unfair punishment, poorly designed educational programs, unresponsive educators, and prejudiced teachers. Despite the continuing debate regarding the causes of academic underachievement, there is little dispute that adolescents from minority cultures are besieged by more than their proportionate share of academic problems in our nation's schools. Consequently, as Box 6.2 illustrates, numerous reforms have been proposed for the education of minority students. Since such commissions are of paramount importance to the education of minority youths, further details of their findings and recommendations are reserved for our examination of secondary schools in Chapter 7.

6.1 A Closer Look

Black Parents Bemoan Too Much Assimilation

Are black adolecents growing up without an adequate awareness of their parents' struggles against racism and without an awareness of the racism that still exists in our society? Have middle-class black youths become too assimilated into white culture, thereby losing all sense of racial identity? According to some black professionals and parents, the answers to these questions are a resounding—and disappointing—yes. In the words of one black 15-year-old from Bethesda, Maryland, whose parents are both lawyers, "Look, I know I didn't come here on the Love Boat, but racist thought is disappearing."

Such attitudes among black youngsters, however, have aroused concern among a number of parents whose hard-fought, firsthand battles against racism in the 1950s and 1960s seem like irrelevant, ancient history to their upper-middle-class offspring. These parents fear that in the process of becoming assimilated into white culture, their children have learned too little about black history and culture and have had too few experiences with racism to understand how to handle discrimination when it occurs. Further, in seeking to protect their children from the hardships and prejudice that they themselves endured, these well-educated, financially successful parents now worry that their children will be unable to cope with the racism they will eventually encounter in their adult years—being denied promotions in leading corporations, being called "niggers," being disapproved of for marrying whites. Without an awareness of racism in the world at large or of the stereotypes of black people that still prevail, young blacks may not have the resources to understand or to cope with discrimination when it arises.

Some older adolescents have begun to share their parents' perspectives, as evidenced by the comments of black students in several universities. A young man at Harvard comments that although he himself had no problems dating white girls in high school, his relationships seldom prevailed in the face of objections from girls' parents. On the basis of his high-school experiences, this young man chose to attend Harvard, where he felt there would be a large enough black student population, and where he now dates only black girls who, he says, "are even prettier than white girls." Similarly, a black female student maintains that, despite having been raised in a predominantly white suburban environment, her self-confidence has improved as a consequence of having chosen to attend an all-black college.

In sum, it appears that a certain segment of the black middle class is seeking to reaffirm its racial heritage and to recapture a lost sense of racial identity that distinguishes it from the white middle class.

SOURCE: Roots III: Souls on ice: A post-civil-rights generation struggles for identity, *Newsweek,* June 10, 1985, pp. 82–84.

A Closer Look 6.2 

Make Something Happen: Secondary Education for Hispanic Youths

During 1984, the National Commission on Secondary Schooling for Hispanics visited schools with high concentrations of Hispanic students in five major cities. After interviewing legislators, teachers, parents, and students, and after assessing more than a dozen reports on the status of U.S. education, the commission presented its findings in a two-volume report of statistics and commentary. Included are:

- Of all Hispanic students who quit school, 40 percent do so before the tenth grade.
- Of Hispanics in high school, 25 percent are over age.
- Over two-thirds of all Hispanics attend schools whose minority enrollment accounts for more than 50 percent of the students.
- Hispanic males are more likely than Anglo or black males to hold full-time jobs while attending school.
- Thirty-five percent of Hispanic students are enrolled in the vocational track, 40 percent in the general education track, and only 25 percent in the academic track.
- Only 4 percent of Hispanic high-school students complete three or more years of Spanish.
- Forty-five percent of Mexican American and Puerto Rican students never earn a high-school diploma.
- Twenty-three percent of the Puerto Rican students, 21 percent of the Mexican American, and 19 percent of the Cuban American quit school before graduating.
- Among Hispanic students, 80 percent drop out of school in New York City, 70 percent in Chicago, 50 percent in Los Angeles, and 32 percent in Miami.
- The percentage of Hispanic high-school graduates who enrolled in college decreased from 46 percent in 1972 to 43 percent in 1982, in contrast to 52 percent of white high-school graduates who enrolled in college in 1982. (Remember that the white students' high-school graduation rate is far higher than that of Hispanics.)

According to the commission's report, Hispanic students' academic deficits could be alleviated through a variety of educational reforms. Among the commission's suggestions are (1) that schools eliminate tracking in favor of a core curriculum that would include two years of foreign language study, computer skills, and four years of English; (2) that vocational skills not be substituted for the required core curriculum; (3) that a personalized education contract be devised for each student; (4) that educators stop focusing on the argument over bilingual education to the exclusion of other educational issues affecting Hispanic students; (5) that all Hispanic students who fail an English proficiency test before beginning high school should be enrolled in a special summer language program; (6) that more social and recreational programs be held on school grounds to bring Hispanic adults from the community into contact with Hispanic youths; and (7) that Hispanic students be kept literate in Spanish as a way of enhancing their marketability as bilingual employees.

SOURCE: *Make something happen: A report on secondary schooling for Hispanics.* Washington, D.C.: National Commission on Secondary Schooling for Hispanics, 1984.

6.3 A Closer Look

The Widening Gap between White and Black Children's Well-Being

Despite hopes of lessening the inequities in U.S. society, the advances made by black Americans during the 1960s appear to be abating. According to national statistics gathered in 1984, the Children's Defense Fund researchers conclude that the gap between white and black children's well-being is widening. Supporting many findings of 1984 reports from the Congressional Research Service and the Congressional Budget Office, the CDF analysis shows the following:

- In 1983, 13.8 million children were living in poverty—the highest level since the mid-1960s.
- Half of all black children and one-third of all Hispanic children are poor, compared with one-sixth of all white children.
- Eight out of every 10 white children live in two-parent families, compared with 4 out of every 10 black children.
- About 67 percent of all black children have an employed parent, compared with 86 percent of white children.
- Approximately 2 out of every 5 black children are living in a household headed by an adult without a high-school diploma—a rate twice that of white children.
- Each month in 1982, 3,000 girls under the age of 15 had babies—60 percent of whom were born to black females.
- White children are four times as likely as black children to grow up in families headed by college graduates.
- Black students are twice as likely as white students to be suspended from school and to be subjected to corporal punishment.
- The unemployment rate of black college graduates is almost as high as that of white high-school dropouts.
- Black children are three to four times as likely as white children to be murdered.

The Children's Defense Fund researchers offer three recommendations for improving the lives of black children in our society. First, Congress should make no further budget cuts in programs serving the poor, and should restore many of the successful programs that have been dismantled since 1980. Second, Congress should enact the "Children's Survival Bill," which includes among its provisions programs to reduce school dropout rates and teenage pregnancy. Third, communities and policy makers should make a more concerted effort to reduce the adolescent pregnancy rate and to provide prenatal care for the infants of indigent mothers.

SOURCE: *Black and white children in America: Key facts.* Washington, D.C.: Children's Defense Fund. 1984.

MINORITY INCOMES AND EMPLOYMENT

In addition to their problems in school, many minority youths suffer the direct consequences of their parents' financial deprivation and lack of education. As the national statistics in Box 6.3 illustrate, the gap between white and black youths' well-being appears to be widening, not narrowing (*Black and White Children*, 1984). For example, in 1982 the median family income was $24,603 for whites, $13,599 for blacks, and $16,228 for Hispanics. As Figure 6.1 illustrates, in 1981 only 11 percent of white Americans were living below the poverty level, in contrast to 34 percent of all blacks and 28 percent of all Hispanics (*Population Profile*, 1984).

These financial discrepancies are relatively easy to understand, considering the vast inequities in white and nonwhite parents' educational levels. The impact of a parent's education on the family's income is self-evident: In 1980, families whose chief wage earner had fewer than eight years of education lived on $10,836, while chief wage earners with more than five years of college had family incomes of $34,740 (*Money, Income and Poverty Status*, 1981). Looking ahead at Table 8.2 will help you appreciate the impact of a parent's education upon the family's income. Consequently, many adolescents continue to be hand-

Figure 6.1

Percentage of persons below the poverty level, by race and Spanish origin: 1969, 1979, and 1981

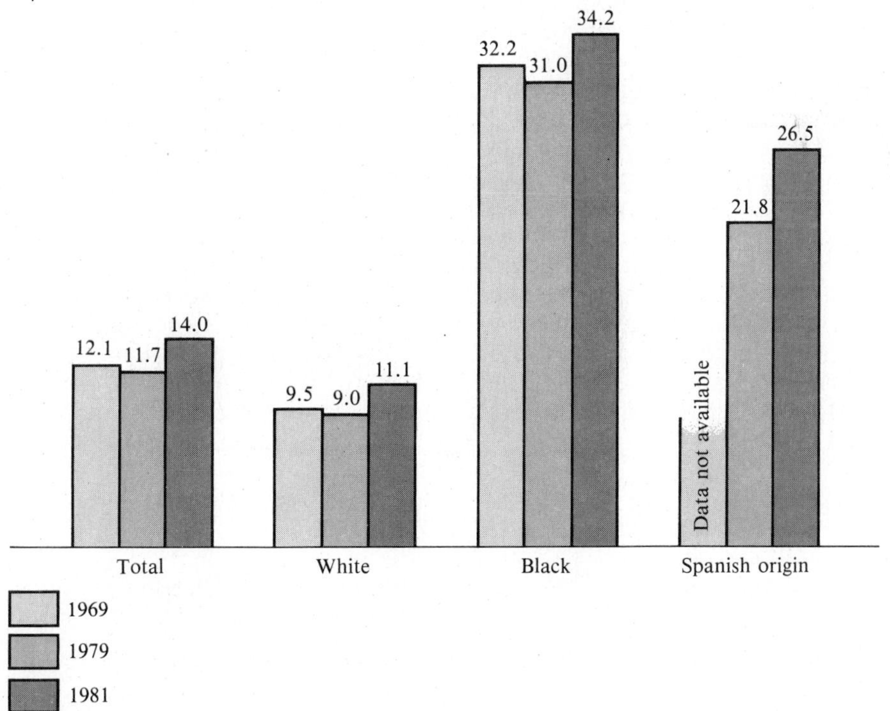

SOURCE: *Population profile of the United States: 1982.* Washington, D.C.: U.S. Bureau of the Census. Current population reports, P-23, no. 130, 1984.

icapped by the fact that their parents grew up in a society that legally deprived minorities of the educational skills and job opportunities to insure their future children a financially enriched environment.

Unfortunately, in an attempt to compensate for their own parents' lack of financial resources, minority youths have a more difficult time than whites in finding part-time or full-time employment of their own. These data and recommendations for alleviating youth unemployment will be examined carefully in Chapter 11. Although teenage unemployment may at first seem too trivial a matter to worry over, the Vice-President's 1980 task force thinks otherwise. According to the task force, jobless adolescents are more likely than the employed to earn money illegally by gambling, prostitution, theft, and drug dealing. Furthermore, as unemployment rises, adolescents commit more rape, assault, murder, and theft. The task force concluded that minority youths' unemployment is related to racial discrimination; therefore, a reduction in unemployment cannot occur until we somehow reduce racial discrimination (*Review of Youth Employment Problems,* 1980).

Researchers for the Ford Foundation reached similar conclusions in 1978 (Mangrim & Seninger, 1978). On the basis of their analyses of inner-city youth unemployment, the Ford Foundation researchers concluded that discrimination and the inferior quality of urban schools make ghetto youths undesirable in the eyes of potential employers. Furthermore, the ghetto environment undermines adolescents' vocational motivation by demonstrating that hard work and education yield less income than illegal business and "hustling" on the streets. Why finish school when chances for a legitimate job are so slim? Why try to earn a minimum wage in a boring job when street skills can be quickly converted into high profits? As we will see in Chapter 11, the forecast for unemployed minority youths is not encouraging, given current trends in federal budget cuts for job-training programs, the move of industries away from the central cities, and the overall state of the economy, which has created fiercer competition for jobs.

According to some analysts, unemployment and educational deficiencies have encouraged an increasing number of minority males to enlist in the armed services. For example, in 1980 blacks comprised about 11 percent of the civilian population, but 18 percent of the armed forces (Staples, 1982). Although the military provides a secure income, vocational training, and opportunities for travel, the overrepresentation of minority males is of concern to some in regard to the obvious physical hazards associated with military occupations. For example, while Hispanic Americans comprised only 7 percent of the U.S. population in 1973, they accounted for 20 percent of the casualties that year in the Vietnam war (Litsinger, 1973).

THE PHYSICAL HEALTH OF MINORITY YOUTH

A national study conducted in 1976 by the Children's Defense Fund identified many of the medical problems undermining the physical well-being of minority youngsters (*Doctors and Dollars,* 1976). According to the CDF report, about 400 ghetto children die each year and 6,000 more suffer irreversible brain damage from lead poisoning in their ghetto communities. In addition, low hemoglobin levels from malnutrition occur twice as often in black children as in white, affecting nearly a third of all black youngsters. Black children also face nearly three times the risk of dying from syphilis or tuberculosis as do whites. Moreover, statistics from the National Center for Disease Control reveal that only half of all black children are inoculated against measles, 40 percent never see a doctor during the course of any given year, and 16 percent have no insurance whatsoever to help defray medical expenses (*National Center for Health Statistics Report,* 1979).

Due to poor prenatal care, malnutrition, unsanitary plumbing, lack of immunization, inadequate medical services, and lack of health insurance, nonwhite youths are physically disadvantaged (*National Center for Health Statistics Report,* 1979). For example, twice as many American Indian children die from heart disease, influenza, and pneumonia as do other American children. Similarly, Chicano youths have four times as much amoebic dysentery and twice as many cases of measles, mumps, tuberculosis, and hepatitis as other youngsters. Moreover, Hispanic adolescents from migrant families often develop diseases related to a scarcity of fresh dairy products, unsanitary toilets, contaminated water, and parasitic diseases transmitted through playing and working in the soil (Cheyney, 1976; Taylor, 1973). Considering these medical problems, it is not surprising that nonwhite youngsters die from illness at a 25 percent higher rate than white children (*National Center for Health Statistics Report,* 1979).

Given these distressing statistics on the health of minority children, the Children's Defense Fund researchers have recommended a number of specific changes in medical practices for the benefit of minority youngsters. To begin with, impoverished and rural communities have few doctors, because physicians prefer to live in higher-income suburban areas. Therefore, programs could be established that would offer financial incentives to doctors to practice in those locales where minority groups are most in need of medical assistance. Likewise, children would receive more immediate medical attention if their parents had convenient mass transportation, nearby medical facilities, and more efficient scheduling of appointments in order not to lose a day's pay for hours of travel and waiting in clinic lobbies. Doctors could also provide office hours that take into account parents' work schedules, rather than assuming one parent can leave work to attend to a child's medical needs.

In addition, the Children's Defense Fund recommends that health-care professionals be trained to understand the cultural differences within our multicultural society. For example, traditional Navajos believe that illness is caused by transgressions committed by the patient or a family member. From this viewpoint, the transgression causes a disharmony between the patient and the supernatural powers, thereby causing physical illness. As a consequence, the traditionally oriented Navajos expect a doctor to treat symptoms, but expect a medicine man to rid the patient of the true cause of the illness. It is taboo among Indian tribes to give direct advice to others. Knowing this, one doctor used storytelling as a way to convey medical advice to her Navajo patients. As a consequence, this doctor's patients heeded her advice instead of ignoring directions, as they had done when she tried to communicate with them through Anglo methods. Moreover, health-care agencies could improve their services to Hispanic patients by providing bilingual literature and bilingual consultation.

The Children's Defense Fund researchers also suggest that we include more minorities in the medical profession. Nurse practitioners, paraprofessionals, and physicians who are from their patients' own cultures are often more effective in administering medical care than those from the outside. Relying on nurses who visit homes and radio and television ads, we can disseminate medical information more effectively to poor communities. Self-help clinics can teach families how to treat some of the less complicated maladies at home, so that the parents can conserve money and time. Medical help for minorities could also include preventive medicine. For example, doctors could act against slum landlords and housing codes that permit conditions like lead-based paint and unsanitary plumbing. The Children's Defense researchers feel that minority parents are concerned about their children's health, but are intimidated by medical agencies unsuited to their needs and culture.

In conclusion, a health hazard of particular relevance during adolescence is the use and abuse of drugs. By way of introduction to the data that will be presented in Chapter 13, the National Institute of Drug Abuse asserts that adolescent drug abuse is related to poverty and that poverty and racism in America are intrinsically linked (*Drug Abuse Prevention,* 1980). Hence, the institute's conclusion supports the view corroborated by numerous studies cited in Chapter 13 that minority youngsters are in more physical jeopardy from drug abuse than white adolescents.

Juvenile Delinquency

Although Chapter 14 will demonstrate that adolescents of every racial and socioeconomic background commit delinquent acts, minority youths are disproportionately represented in the official statistics. It has been argued by some that minority youths are at the greatest risk of becoming delinquent because they are the most likely to live in impoverished environments. Further, it is maintained by a number of critics that white delinquents are treated less harshly than minorities by the juvenile justice system (*Children in Adult Jails,* 1976; H. Myers et al., 1982; Staples, 1976; Wax, 1971). According to the statistics gathered by these researchers, white youths are generally subjected to less police harassment and to less severe penalties than adolescents from minority cultures.

From the viewpoint of these critics, society often defines crime and punishment in ways that protect the interests of white middle-class citizens and ignores the interests of adolescents and adults from minority cultures. In support of this position, a national survey of incarcerated adolescents during the 1970s revealed that 32 percent were members of minority cultures, although they comprised only 20 percent of the adolescent population. These researchers also observed discrimination against Hispanic, Indian, and black children in many local jails (*Children in Adult Jails,* 1976).

Court counselors and probation officers who are unaware of the differences between white and nonwhite cultures can also contribute to the unfair treatment of minority youths. Demonstrating the importance of cultural awareness is the incident of an Indian boy who, when placed on probation by the court, was instructed to spend every night with members of his own family. In a matter of days, the white probation officer reported the boy to the officials for violating the court's rules by staying overnight with several different young women in his community. Before revoking the boy's probation, however, another counselor investigated the case and discovered that the boy had, in fact, been staying with "members of his family," as defined by his Indian community. The young women were his first cousins and, therefore, were considered like sisters, according to tribal mores (Red Horse, 1979).

UNIQUE CHARACTERISTICS OF MINORITY CULTURES

Before examining the characteristics of minority cultures that tend to distinguish them from the white middle-class culture, an important caveat is in order. As stated earlier, one purpose of this chapter is to dispel racial stereotypes that adversely affect the lives of adolescents from minority cultures. It is also important, however, to avoid another error—the error of assuming that racial or ethnic distinctions are totally irrelevant to our interactions with minority youths. As Derald Wing Sue, the former president of the American Personnel and Guidance Association, states, "The failure to recognize the true differences in thought among groups of people leads us to a well-meaning but false sense of humanism and brotherhood. We cannot make all people the same simply by stating so or by treating them alike" (Wing Sue, 1981). In other words, we want to avoid stereotyping minorities, while simultaneously not overlooking the genuine distinctions that often exist between the white middle class and members of minority groups.

In this context, we want to avoid assuming that the distinctions among various racial groups are merely the consequence of their different financial or educational circumstances. For example, a black and a Hispanic adolescent, whose parents earn similar incomes and have similar educations, may nonetheless have distinctly different values, which emanate from their membership in two distinct cultures.

As you will see on the following pages, researchers have determined that adolescents from the same cultural group share certain values with one another, despite differences in their incomes and educations. Nevertheless, researchers have also found that similar incomes and educations create certain shared values, despite individuals' racial and ethnic differences. Thus, the present state of research leaves questions unanswered, such as: Should we expect adolescents from the same socioeconomic background to have more in common than those from the same racial or ethnic group? Could we eradicate the racial differences in juvenile delinquency and academic achievement through educational and financial equity? In sum, at present the data do not permit us to determine how much influence money or education exerts over adolescents' values and behavior in comparison to race or ethnicity.

BLACK ADOLESCENTS

As a consequence of demographic changes during the past century, today's black adolescent is more likely to be an urban resident in a northern state than to be a rural resident of a southern, agricultural community. At the end of the Civil War, 92 percent of all black Americans lived in southern states, whereas only about half remained there by 1980. Among those still living in the South,

60 percent live in urban, not rural, areas. At present, black Americans comprise approximately 20 percent of the population in the southern states, 9 percent in the northern states, 8 percent in the central states, and 5 percent in the western states (U.S. Bureau of the Census, 1982).

Black Families

The steady migration of black Americans from rural to urban areas during recent decades has had a profound impact on the families of today's black youth (Martin & Martin, 1978; Pinkney, 1975; Stack, 1974). To begin with, the migration to urban areas has posed a threat to the extended family system, which has historically provided emotional and economic support for black youths and adults alike. In general, members of extended families are more interdependent on one another financially than members of the white nuclear family. For example, there is less stigma attached to borrowing money from relatives and more likelihood of developing communal attitudes toward sharing one another's possessions. Within an extended-family network, those who offer financial aid to their relatives are often highly esteemed. In further contrast to the nuclear family, the extended family's household often includes relatives from several generations—from great-grandmothers to great great-granddaughters. Furthermore, because black men are likely to die earlier than white men, the head of the extended family is often a woman in her seventies or eighties, who coordinates the household's activities, arbitrates conflicts among family members, oversees the family's children, and acts as the family historian.

Another function of the extended family is to care for children whose mothers are too young, too poor, or too overworked to raise their children alone. In this respect, the extended family has a more communal attitude toward child rearing than the nuclear family. For example, black adolescents who live with or are raised by a relative other than a parent are not stigmatized in their communities. Moreover, the extended family network traditionally provided emotional support and advice for young and old in times of stress or crisis. The family often served as an enclave and provided respite from the vicissitudes of living in a racist society.

The exodus to urban areas, however, has weakened the power of the extended family—above all, its power to influence black adolescents. Initially having migrated to the cities for better jobs and a better education for their children, many impoverished urban parents now worry that street gangs, drugs, high unemployment, and poverty have destroyed the influence of the extended family over its young. While some urban black parents may now talk nostalgically about "going home" to the rural communities of former generations, economic realities insure that by the year 2000, virtually all black adolescents will be growing up in urban areas (*U.S. Children and Their Families,* 1983).

Although black youngsters are still more likely than whites to be raised in extended families, the nuclear family has become an increasingly popular option. As is the case with whites, blacks earning the lowest incomes rely more on extended families than those in high socioeconomic brackets. Moreover, some black parents who have escaped from poverty into the middle class choose to break their ties with the extended family in order to reserve money for their own nuclear family (Martin & Martin, 1978; Staples, 1976; Willie, 1981). Not surprisingly, most middle-class black families endorse the same values as their white middle-class counterparts: thrift, conformity, education, upward mobility, small families, home ownership, and two-parent households. Viewing education as the primary way to insure upward mobility, these parents invest heavily in their children's educations.

As the statistics in Box 6.3 illustrate, the fact that most often distinguishes black families from white families is income. Given the existence of racial prejudice and the educational discrepancies between blacks and whites, black parents are least able to procure the kinds of jobs necessary to become part of the middle class. For example, 30 percent of all black families fell below the poverty level in 1980, in contrast to only 10 percent of all white families. Even more

If you had to live in our present society as a member of a racial group other than the one to which you now belong, which would you choose and why?

significant, by 1984 this figure had risen, and half of all black children were living in families classified as poor by government indexes, in comparison with only one-sixth of all white children (*Black and White Children,* 1984).

In addition to the obvious limitations placed on adolescents whose families are struggling financially, other problems are also associated with low incomes and poverty. First, most indigent black families have an average of five children to support, and most have no father present in the home. Second, the rate of out-of-wedlock births is highest among lower-socioeconomic-class families. Females with the least education and, consequently, with the least potential earning power are less likely than better-educated females to terminate an unplanned pregnancy. Third, the financial burdens of poorly educated parents often require them to seek the assistance of relatives or of foster homes in raising their children (*Black and White Children,* 1984; *U.S. Children and Their Families,* 1983).

Underscoring poverty's impact on the black family, statistics show that only 40 percent of the black children in the United States were living with both parents in 1984, in stark contrast to 80 percent of the white children. More discouraging still is the fact that these 1984 statistics indicate a worsening situation, since in 1960, 75 percent of the black children and 92 percent of the white children lived with both parents. Moreover, while only one in every 38 white children lives with neither parent, one in eight black children lives with neither. Finally, although divorce rates are similar for people in the same socioeconomic bracket, black parents are seven times more likely than whites to be separated or divorced (*Black and White Children,* 1984; *Children without Homes,* 1978; McAdoo, 1981).

Male and Female Roles

On the basis of poorly interpreted data, such as the Moynihan report, several unsubstantiated assumptions about the roles of black males and females have been popularized: first, that black females dominate black males; second, that most black males have few positive role models; third, that black females are vocationally and financially more advantaged in our society than black males. A number of studies, however, indicate that these assumptions are both misleading and exaggerated.

According to some critics, stereotypes of the black female as a domineering matriarch are still perpetuated by programs like "The Jeffersons" and "Sanford and Son," in which black males are often portrayed as less powerful and less forceful than assertive black females. Contrary to the stereotype of the domineering black matriarch, however, studies have generally failed to find significant differences in the sex roles of blacks and whites from similar socioeconomic backgrounds. According to this research, socioeconomic status has a greater impact than race on the sex-typed behavior of males and females (McAdoo, 1981; L. Myers, 1980; Rose, 1980; P. Wallace, 1978; Willie, 1981).

Although black females are no more likely than white females of the same socioeconomic class to dominate males, it has been demonstrated that black and white female sex roles tend to differ along other dimensions. Historically, the financial realities of slavery and racial discrimination have forced black females to be less economically and socially dependent on males, in comparison with white females (Myers, 1980; Rose, 1980; Staples, 1978). This heritage, coupled with the fact that the financial status of many black men in our society is still precarious, contributes to the self-reliant, realistic attitudes that many black adolescent females have toward their own education and employment. Unlike white females, who have traditionally been socialized to depend on males for financial support and social status, black females seldom view their own employment or their self-reliant attitudes as threats to their femininity.

These distinctions between female roles in black and in white cultures can be illustrated by several representative studies. In regard to employment, some researchers have found that young black females believe that their own vocational success would improve their future prospects for social and personal happiness, in contrast to white girls who believe that a future career would threaten males and undermine personal happiness (Weston & Mednick, 1975). Similarly, black females are more likely than black males to earn high grades and to attend college (*Conference on the Educational and Occupational Needs of Black Women*, 1975; Fetters, 1977; *Minority Women*, 1976). These findings, which suggest that most adolescent black girls do not fear being socially rebuffed as a consequence of developing their intellectual talents, contrast rather dramatically with the data in Chapter 5 demonstrating a decline in many white girls' achievement during adolescence. Finally, in relation to the black female role, it is of interest to note that college-educated black women have fewer children than white women with similar schooling (McAdoo, 1981).

Another important factor that shapes the roles of black girls is the shortage of black males. In contrast to white girls, black girls cannot assume there will be an eligible male in her future who can live with her until old age. To begin with, there are 15 percent fewer black males than females, whereas the ratio of white males to females is nearly equal (U.S. Bureau of the Census, 1981). In addition, black males' chances of dying young from disease, murder, military injuries, suicide, and drug abuse are greater than whites'. Also, the welfare laws in some states provide more assistance for indigent women and children when no husband is living in the household, a situation that tends to discourage legal marriage and two-parent households. Given these circumstances, the black female has statistically sound reasons to suppose that her future may very well not include a full-time male partner (Staples, 1978). In testimony to the self-reliance and self-esteem that black girls tend to develop, despite these economic and social hardships, interviews with over 400 black women showed that their self-confidence and pride were not generally determined by whether or not a husband was present in the household. Moreover, most of these women, whose educations ranged from third grade through graduate school, equated being a good mother with being a good provider (Myers, 1980).

In the past decade, legislation intended to diminish the educational and financial discrepancies between the races has been accompanied by the protest that "black females have it made" and that white males are being discriminated against. The statistics, however, do not support the assertion that black females are advantaged in comparison with white males, white females, or black males. For instance, although black females are somewhat more likely to finish college than black males, the majority continue to prepare themselves, unlike black males and white males, for the lowest-paid professions, such as teaching and nursing (Rose, 1980).

It has been suggested that the difference in black females' and males' educational accomplishments can be partially explained by the fact that educators and employers are likely to perceive educated black females as less "threatening" than educated black males. As a consequence, the black female receives more educational encouragement than the black male. Further, it has been argued that the black female's education typically prepares her for a vocation in which racial discrimination is less prevalent than in the jobs pursued by black males. Thus, her employment in professions such as teaching and nursing is not a threat to the status quo or to the vocational status of white males (Gump & Rivers, 1975). Supporting this viewpoint, a national report by black female scientists showed that few of their high-school teachers or counselors encouraged them to pursue their interests in science—a domain typically reserved for white males (Malcolm, Hall, & Brown, 1976). In sum, the black girl's vocational and financial situation, while undeniably an advancement over her grandmother's and her mother's, is still not "advantaged" in comparison with other segments of the population (Wallace, 1980).

In contrast to the black female, it has been argued that black males are deprived of strong male role models. According to Gary's recent review of the research, however, black males have problems similar to those of other males from the same socioeconomic class. Further, Gary is among those who contend that, contrary to the stereotype, positive male role models are available in black communities. Although it is true that black fathers are less likely than white fathers to be living with their sons, male relatives in the extended-family network and male friends are present to socialize black male children. The evidence does suggest, however, that impoverished black males often attempt to establish their masculinity by flouting authority, rejecting society's standards, committing crimes, and abusing drugs. These aspects of the male role, however, are related to poverty, not to race (Gary, 1982).

According to several scholars who have studied the roles of black males in our society, black adolescent males are too often encouraged to pursue only three types of roles: the conformist, the athlete, and the entertainer. The conformist is the quiet, intellectual, nonathletic black male who gains approval from middle-class society by acquiescing to the norms that maintain the status quo. The second socially approved alternative is to become an athlete—a black male presumed to be all brawn and no brains. It is also presumed, however, that the black athlete will express no interest in involving himself in political issues that might threaten the status quo. On this point, the black athletes who wore armbands in the 1968 Summer Olympics to protest racism in our society were considered to have violated their role as "good" athletes. The third role traditionally offered to a black male is that of entertainer—a man who performs as a musician, comic, or actor, without creating controversy. According to these scholars, the black male is perceived as a threat or a danger if he behaves as autonomously, confidently, assertively, or ambitiously as the white male. Moreover, behavior that is acceptable when manifested by white males is too often considered "uppity" or "aggressive" when manifested by black males (Gary, 1982; Staples, 1982).

Black Athletes

An important part of adolescence for many black males is their participation in and dedication to sports. Although most white males also participate in sports, athletic participation has provoked special controversy in relation to black males. Because blacks are more likely than whites to perceive professional sports as their future vocation, a number of parents and educators are questioning the emphasis placed on athletics within the black community: Given the discrepancies between the educational skills of black and white Americans, shouldn't young black males be persuaded to devote more time to academics and less time to preparing themselves for possible success in a professional sports career? Is it fair to encourage black youths' fantasies about becoming professional athletes, when such a small percentage of young athletes can actually be accepted into the pros? Are young black athletes being exploited by adults who have too little regard for their intellectual and vocational development? Such questions have demanded a more thorough examination in recent years of the value of athletics for young black males.

Undoubtedly a number of black males have benefited financially and educationally from their athletic prowess. The most outstanding male athletes are usually awarded college scholarships, which have afforded them educational opportunities far beyond their families' financial means. Such scholarships not only further a boy's athletic skills but attempt to advance his academic skills by providing him with special tutors, counselors, and advisors. Moreover, a lucky and talented few have established lucrative careers in professional sports. Given these potential benefits, it is little wonder that so many black youths are motivated to spend thousands of hours during their high-school years preparing for a chance to become college or professional athletes. In one recent study, for example, black males from both urban and rural high schools overwhelmingly named professional athletes as their most influential role models (Oberle, Stowers, & Falk, 1978).

Recognizing the potential benefits associated with athletic success for minority youths whose parents cannot afford college tuitions, it has been argued that our society should offer more athletic encouragement to black females. Although a number of black females have excelled in sports, particularly in track and field events, college scholarships and Olympic coaching have traditionally been limited to males (Gren, 1981; *Importance of Athletic Opportunity for Women,* 1978; Neal & Tutko, 1976).

Convinced that black girls, like black boys, should have an opportunity to benefit from their athletic talents, a number of coaches formed "The Atoms" in New York City's Bedford Stuyvesant ghetto. These coaches are encouraging black girls between the ages of 6 and 20 to develop their skills in track and field events. The program is predicated upon the philosophy that athletic success can indirectly teach girls from a ghetto environment that hard work can pay off in areas besides sports. For example, one Olympic silver-medal winner comes by with her briefcase after work, changes clothes, and works out in the Atoms' gym as a model for younger girls. A primary aim of the program is to build each girl's self-esteem and to encourage her educational achievements. For example, one 14-year-old runner, who was readying herself for the Olympic tryouts, became pregnant. With the encouragement of her coaches and fellow Atoms, she resumed her running career after her child's birth and eventually earned a college degree. By 1979, 17,000 girls had participated in the Atoms program and had competed in the program's annual Colgate Games in Madison Square Garden (Kaplan, 1979).

Despite the advantages that may accrue to young black athletes, there are disadvantages that, according to the critics, are too often overlooked. First, too few adolescent athletes realize the odds against their being accepted as college or professional athletes. For the thousands of black youths who invest their time honing their athletic talents at the expense of their academic skills, only a handful are accepted on professional or college teams. For this reason, black leaders like Jesse Jackson are urging black youths and their parents to stress academic success instead of athletic prowess (Jackson, 1978). Black psychologists are also among those encouraging black parents to remind their athletic offspring that educational achievements usually yield more financial benefits than athletic talents, despite the media attention devoted weekly to professional and college athletes (Comer & Poussaint, 1975).

Furthermore, some commentators maintain that black athletes encounter racial discrimination and stereotyping that can undermine self-esteem. Sociologist Robert Staples and Georgetown University's basketball coach, John Thompson, are among those contending that black athletes are often stereotyped by coaches and by audiences as less disciplined and less intelligent than their white teammates. In discussing audience responses to his black college basketball players, Thompson says, "Do you know what they say next, after they say we're disciplined? That we play 'like a white team'. Undisciplined, that means nigger. They're all big and fast and can leap like kangaroos and eat watermelon in the locker room, but they can't play as a team and they choke under pressure" (Gilbert, 1980).

In addition, Coach Thompson is among those who maintain that many black athletes' talents are underdeveloped because coaches tend to stereotype blacks as undisciplined players who have more muscle than intelligence (Gren, 1981; Staples, 1976). According to this viewpoint, stereotypes regarding black athletes are further perpetuated, because adolescent athletes observe their older role models in the stereotyped positions and, as a consequence, emulate their style and limit their own athletic expectations. For example, why are there so few black quarterbacks, golfers, or tennis players? And why are black girls encouraged to compete in basketball or track and field instead of tennis or swimming? Are we not stereotyping athletic black youths by channeling them into certain sports and certain positions on a team without encouraging them to consider roles or positions in sports traditionally played by whites?

In conclusion, the media have been criticized for presenting too few examples of black Americans who have achieved financial success and who have won the national esteem of their fellow citizens in areas other than sports and entertainment (Berry, 1979). Hence, it is argued, too many black adolescent males become erroneously convinced that their athletic excellence offers them the best chance for financial success and social status in our society. Unfortunately, given the statistical odds of becoming rich and famous through athletic stardom, it is difficult to refute the argument that most young black athletes have wasted their time and their energy, at least in financial terms, by investing their adolescence in pursuit of their athletic dreams.

HISPANIC AMERICAN ADOLESCENTS

Which city on the face of the earth has the third largest population of Mexican American people? Surprisingly few Americans would guess the correct answer: Los Angeles. As previously mentioned, demographers predict that by the year 2000, Hispanic Americans will be the largest minority group in the United States. The parents or grandparents of most Hispanic American adolescents immigrated from Mexico, Puerto Rico, or Cuba. Contrary to stereotypes of Hispanic Americans as agricultural people, most Hispanic youths, like black adolescents, live in urban communities. In fact, nearly three-quarters of Hispanic youths' employed parents are blue-collar, not agricultural, workers. In regard to geographic dispersement, 87 percent of Mexican Americans live in the Southwest, while almost all Puerto Rican Americans live in New York City, New Jersey, and Connecticut, and almost all Cuban families reside in Florida (U.S. Bureau of the Census, 1982).

Unfortunately, ignorance regarding Hispanic adolescents' cultural origins is more widespread than might be hoped, given the fact that this is the fastest growing minority group in the U.S. For example, many Americans are unable to answer the simple question, Where is Puerto Rico?—despite the fact that this country may become the next U.S. state. Furthermore, many Americans are unaware that residents of Puerto Rico are citizens of the United States. Although Puerto Ricans elect their own governor, pay no U.S. federal taxes, and cannot vote in U.S. elections, they need no passport to travel between the United States and the island of Puerto Rico, which lies about 1,000 miles from Miami and 1,500 miles from New York City. As a further demonstration of our ignorance regarding Hispanic American adolescents, many of us are surprised to learn that the skin color of Puerto Rican adolescents can range from white to deep brown to black (Fitzpatrick, 1971).

These geographic and demographic facts are presented to illustrate that we are often less knowledgeable about Hispanic American adolescents than about far less populous groups, such as Native Americans and Asian Americans. Indeed, the false assumption that black Americans will continue to constitute our largest minority group, and the fact that Hispanic Americans are not widely dispersed throughout many areas of the country, have contributed to our ignorance of Hispanic-American adolescents and their families. Since Mexican Americans constitute the largest percentage of the Hispanic population, most of the available data have been gathered from these populations. Hence, the following discussion of Hispanic adolescents concentrates primarily on Mexican American youths, or Chicanos.

Old and New Images of Hispanic Youth

Since the 1940s, Mexican American adolescents have had a reputation in many regions of the Southwest as hoodlums or *pachuchos*. This stereotype blossomed during the 1940s, when gangs of young Mexican Americans in California, wearing duck-tail haircuts and "zoot suits," gained national notoriety. The zoot suits were full-cut, billowy trousers tightened at the ankle, with a waistband that extended up over the chest, and a long jacket with exaggerated broad shoulders. In the eyes of most white citizens, the zoot suits came to symbolize the young Mexican Americans' defiance of authority and their "moral degradation."

Tensions between Hispanics and whites mounted in many California communities, as a highly publicized murder trial of a gang member contributed further to the public's image of Mexican American youths as depraved delinquents.

Finally, in 1943 a group of police and servicemen tried to teach the young pachuchos a lesson by accosting them on public streets. The ensuing *zoot-suit riots* between Hispanics and whites rose to serious enough proportions to attract the attention of the Mexican government, many of whose officials were less than satisfied with the U.S. government's official reassurance that the riots were totally unrelated to racial prejudice. Leaving aside the property damage and the physical abuse to Mexican American youths, the zoot-suit riots further reinforced many whites' stereotype of Hispanic adolescents as the tough, unruly, immoral offspring of a culture that endorsed aggression and disregarded "American" values (McLemore, 1980).

In contrast to the image of the pachucho, increasing numbers of Mexican American youths have rejected derogatory stereotypes and refer to themselves as **Chicanos.** Similarly, some Chicanos use the term *"La Raza"* (literally "the sacred race") in reference to their group. These linguistic transitions resemble those of black Americans who, during the 1960s, rejected the terms "colored people" and "negro" and adopted "black" as a word with more favorable connotations.

Despite attempts to create a more favorable self-image for Hispanic youths, it has nonetheless been argued that the sociopolitical changes of recent decades have not benefited Hispanic Americans as significantly as they have benefited blacks (Baron, 1981). For example, in contrast to a trend of enhanced self-esteem among black youths in recent years, a survey of 328 eighth- and ninth-graders in Texas showed Chicanos to have lower self-esteem than Anglos (Grossman, Wirt, & Davids, 1985). Such findings suggest that many Hispanic youths still need assistance to combat feelings of unworthiness.

Hispanic American Families

Despite their different origins, individuals of Mexican, Puerto Rican, and Cuban descent share much in common in regard to the structure and values of the family. Once again, as is the case with black families, Hispanic American families should not be stereotyped, since they will differ in the degree to which they have incorporated white-middle-class values. Nevertheless, by increasing our awareness of the Hispanic family's traditions, we can more easily recognize those aspects of contemporary Hispanic American families that represent modifications of or adherence to the traditional.

In contrast to the white-middle-class emphasis on competition and independence, Hispanic families have traditionally emphasized cooperation and interdependence. In this context, striving for individual gain is considered selfish, since achievements should be motivated by a desire to help all members of the family, rather than to enhance one's own self-esteem. This attitude toward competition is frequently demonstrated by studies showing Hispanic students to be less competitive and more cooperative than their white peers. In many studies, even when socioeconomic status is equal, Hispanic students have been found to prefer cooperative activities in school, in contrast to white students who generally maintain competitive attitudes, which increase as they grow older (Baron, 1981; Fitzpatrick, 1971; Hernandez, Hang, & Wagner, 1976; Johnson & Johnson, 1975; Mindel, 1981; Moore, 1976).

Moreover, the Hispanic family has traditionally placed greater emphasis than the white middle-class family on familial loyalty, respect for one's elders, and obedience to one's parents. Despite the fact that Hispanic American parents tend to be less willing than white parents to grant certain social freedoms and independence to their offspring, their teenaged children are nonetheless more likely than white youths to conform to their parents' wishes. To behave ungratefully, to be disobedient, or to show disrespect is considered a way of bringing shame upon one's family.

As is the case with black adolescents, Hispanic American youths are more likely than white youths to come from impoverished families and to live in households headed only by their mothers. Further, Hispanic adolescents are more likely than white youngsters to be living in a household with members of the extended family and to come from a large family. It's important to note, however, that young couples and adults with educations that permit them to move into the middle or upper socioeconomic classes usually adopt the nuclear-family structure and limit the size of their families. Despite the accusatory assertion that the Catholic Church's stance against contraception is responsible for the many children in Hispanic families, the empirical research shows that family size and contraceptive practices are primarily determined by the individual's educational level and income—not by religious affiliation with the Catholic Church (Andrade, 1980).

The Concept of Machismo

In regard to gender roles within Hispanic American cultures, it is often assumed that the ethic of **machismo** creates a system quite dissimilar to the norms of Anglo society. According to many of our popularized notions of this aspect of Hispanic American culture, machismo results in the total domination of females by males and in manifestations of "manhood," such as siring many children and being physically aggressive. Despite this image of Hispanic males and females, a number of psychologists and members of the Hispanic American culture contend that the outsiders' conception of machismo is more an exaggerated stereotype than a social reality (Baron, 1981; Hernandez, Hang, & Wagner, 1976; Trejo, 1980).

According to Hispanic American researchers, the popularized notions regarding machismo generally overlook the fact that, in Hispanic cultures, machismo includes assuming responsibility for the family's support, being trustworthy without the need for written contracts, and revering one's wife and mother. In these regards, the Hispanic culture endorses male behavior that manifests respect, sensitivity, and concern for females and children. Moreover, critics of the machismo ethic tend to ignore the data, which consistently show that male and female gender roles are primarily determined by socioeconomic variables, not by racial or cultural differences. As Chapter 5 demonstrated, studies have failed to confirm the hypothesis that certain racial or ethnic groups unilaterally condone restrictive gender roles for males and females. Finally, those who criticize the supposed effects of machismo often fail to examine the behavior of males within their own culture who dominate women, try to "prove their manhood" through acts of daring, and condone physical violence among males.

By way of illustration, several recent surveys of adolescents have failed to find significant differences in the sex-role attitudes of Hispanic Americans and Anglos (Long & Vigil, 1980). In these comparisons of Anglo and Chicano high-school students, students from both cultures generally agreed that husbands and wives should manage household money together and that working for a female boss is okay. Most of these adolescents approved of girls working on cars and agreed that unhappily married couples should divorce rather than stay married. In these surveys, Chicano males were somewhat more opposed than white males to a father's diapering babies and somewhat more opposed to a husband's adultery being grounds for a divorce than to a wife's. Chicanas were also somewhat less likely than white girls to want to be unemployed as adults.

Data like these are not meant to suggest, however, that the gender roles of Hispanic and Anglo Americans in the same socioeconomic class are identical or that the Hispanic culture exerts no influence over sex-typed behavior. For example, on the basis of the empirical data, it does appear that Hispanic American girls generally have a more traditional, less androgynous gender role than Anglo girls. Of special significance in regard to her educational and vocational plans, the Chicana often believes that her personal progress will hinder the advancement of Chicano males. As Chicanas become more acculturated, however, their beliefs regarding androgyny increasingly resemble those of white females from similar socioeconomic backgrounds. Moreover, some researchers have found that Chicanas with the highest IQ scores are the most likely to modify the traditional female role and to adopt more androgynous forms of behavior (*Educational and Occupational Needs,* 1976; Long & Vigil, 1980; Mirande & Enriquez, 1979; Seynour, 1977).

Adolescents from Migrant Families

Although only a small percentage of the entire Hispanic American population is involved in agricultural work, it has nonetheless been estimated that as many as 800,000 Hispanic children under the age of 18 work on farms as migrant laborers (Cheyney, 1972). Although half of all migrant workers in Florida are black, almost all migrant workers in the Southwest are Chicanos. Hence, the problems associated with migrant labor afflict Hispanic Americans more frequently than other Americans. Considering the poverty associated with migrant labor, it is not surprising that researchers have documented many hardships that adolescents from these families must endure (Cheyney, 1972; Litsinger, 1973; Shannon & Shannon, 1973; Taylor, 1973).

As a consequence of disease, malnutrition, and the strains of stoop labor, adolescents who become migrant workers will die 20 years sooner than the average white American. In addition, these adolescents are usually years below the national achievement norms for their age group, as a result of their sporadic school attendance, frequent moves to new schools, incomplete academic records, language barriers, and forms of deprivation associated with poverty. Furthermore, since migrant families are often forced to rely on adolescents' incomes for economic survival, the adolescents' social and educational needs are often of secondary importance. Indeed, some parents must eventually encourage their oldest children to drop out of school to become full-time wage earners. Given their own academic deficiencies and inadequate skills in the

English language, most migrant parents are unable to offer academic tutoring to their children, and many are embarrassed to seek assistance from social service agencies.

Adults who have worked with migrant children offer advice to educators and medical workers (Cheyney, 1972; Litsinger, 1973; Taylor, 1973). Among their suggestions are that schools should provide vocational guidance that would equip migrant students with skills that could liberate them from farm labor. In addition, the curriculum should stress topics directly affecting the lives of migrants: consumer education, vocational skills, English language training, and health care. By arranging internships with adults in the community, schools could also give migrant students experience in nonagricultural jobs. Teachers might also advise migrant camps' supervisors on issues of relevance to the children's educational well-being. For example, one teacher persuaded a camp's boss to stop at several historical sites for the children's education and amusement, while the workers were traveling from site to site.

Unfortunately, since migrants constitute such a small segment of the Hispanic and black populations, the plight of adolescents from migrant families is often ignored. Yet because migrant labor is relatively common in areas of the country like Florida and the Southwest, it would behoove local politicians and educators in these communities to attend more carefully to the needs of migrant children and adolescents.

INDIAN AMERICAN ADOLESCENTS

In the 1980 Census, 1,418,195 people classified themselves as Native Americans (U.S. Bureau of the Census, 1982). Although Indian Americans live in almost every state, nearly half of the total live in Arizona, New Mexico, California, and Oklahoma, whose Indian population is the largest of any state. Most members of the largest tribe, the Navajo, live on their own reservation, as do the Pueblo Indians in New Mexico. Most Native Americans, however, live among the general population in urban areas.

Since there are 173 separate American tribes, most Indian adolescents identify themselves by their tribal affiliation. Tribes are often distinct from one another in regard to their political organization, vocational skills, and personal values. For instance, Pueblo Indians are known to be among the most peaceful cultures in the world and are world renowned for their skills in designing jewelry and pottery. In contrast, the Navajo have established a reputation for their expert skills as weavers. Moreover, smaller groups exist within some tribes, each of which is culturally distinct in some regard from the others. For example, the Hopi, the Zuni, and the Santo Domingo are all Pueblo Indians, although they live in separate areas of New Mexico and have created their own unique styles and designs in their craft as jewelers.

Although referring to all Native American adolescents as Indians overlooks their tribal distinctiveness, a discussion of adolescents that considers tribal differences is beyond the scope of this chapter. Furthermore, most research on Native American youths fails to make comparisons on the basis of tribal differences. Thus, the term "Indian," as used in this chapter and in most research articles, should be interpreted with at least one caveat in mind: Most of the existing studies and statistics do not permit us to determine how the findings might have differed if the results had been analyzed according to the adolescents' tribal differences.

Native American Families

In comparison to the data on black and Hispanic adolescents, few studies have been conducted with Indian youths. Unfortunately, our understanding of Indian adolescents is severely limited by the fact that most of the extant research focuses on alcoholism, rather than on psychological or sociological variables (Dinges, 1979; Thornton, 1980, 1982).

Despite this shortcoming, available demographic data permit accurate descriptions of many aspects of the Native American family in today's society (Sorkin, 1978; Thornton, 1982). Contrary to the notion that Indians are an agricultural people, most Indian adolescents are growing up in urban areas. For example, in 1980 more than half of all Native Americans were city dwellers, in dramatic contrast to only 7 percent in 1940. As a consequence of this steady migration from reservations to the cities, Los Angeles now has a larger Indian population than any other U.S. city. Having left their reservations in search of better jobs, only 20 percent of the Indians who presently reside in urban areas are living below the poverty level, in comparison with 50 percent of those still living on reservations. Not surprisingly, the most financially successful urban Indians are the best-educated young people, who speak English proficiently and who are trained in specific vocational skills.

Unfortunately, the move to urban areas has had a negative impact on the traditional Indian family in several respects (Thornton, 1982). Although the extended-family system exerts considerable influence over adolescents on the reservation, the family's power over the young has diminished in the cities. As previously mentioned in regard to black families who moved to the cities for better jobs, urbanization has weakened the influence of tribal customs and of the extended family. Furthermore, the move to urban areas has also been accompanied by a rise in alcohol abuse among young Indian males. More so than any other minority group, Indian adolescents are arrested for crimes and public disturbances committed under the influence of alcohol. Although some young Indians who leave their reservations attempt to live biculturally by maintaining contact with their tribes, most become assimilated into the white culture after moving to the city.

Despite the emigration of the young from their reservations, Native American families have traditionally shared certain customs and values that distinguish them from other American families (Bryde, 1971; Pepper, 1976; Price, 1981; Richardson, 1981). The family has been primarily responsible for instilling a sense of respect for and obedience to one's elders. In contrast to the white, middle-class emphasis on youthfulness, Indian communities have historically revered and esteemed the tribe's oldest members. In addition, Indian communities are not likely to socialize the young to be as assertive, as verbal, or as boastful as white children. To allude to one's own accomplishments, to ask too many questions, or to talk too much is considered rude, while to listen and to observe are considered signs of wisdom and respect.

Indian cultures also tend to emphasize humility and community service in lieu of personal advancement or public recognition. For example, it has been noted that many Indian adolescents who pursue a postsecondary education choose vocations like medicine, agriculture, and engineering, with the intent of returning to their communities to offer these needed services. In this context, Indians are less likely than whites to emphasize the importance of accumulating private possessions, consistently delaying pleasure in order to pursue long-term goals, or adhering rigidly to schedules and clocks. Furthermore, unless the entire group can benefit, competition against one's peers is considered a vain, egotistical, attention-seeking activity (Mahan, 1979).

One recent study exemplifying these aspects of Native American culture compared the attitudes of 150 Indian students with 50 non-Indian students. The survey included eleventh- and twelfth-graders in government-run boarding schools and in rural Indian village schools. Indian and non-Indian students named their parents and peers as their top two choices for people with whom they prefer to discuss their problems. In contrast to white students, however, the Indian students chose a relative, not a teacher or a counselor, as their third choice. Moreover, the Indian students attending rural schools in their own tribal village named their parents as more significant individuals than their peers. White students were more likely than Indian youths to want to discuss the topics of drugs and sex with a trained counselor. These findings corroborate the research literature in that they underscore the more family-oriented attitudes of Indian youths in contrast to the more peer-oriented attitudes of white adolescents (Lamfromboise, Dauphinais, & Rowe, 1978).

With regard to religion, Indian families have traditionally tried to instill a respect for tribal religious values in their children. Among the values that characterize many tribes' religious values are a respect for nature, which encourages an attitude of cooperating with, rather than conquering and reshaping, the natural elements. One manifestation of this respect for nature is the attitude that to try to insult someone by comparing him or her to an animal (for example, "You stupid jackass!" "You're a dirty pig!") is inappropriate, because animals are not disdainfully perceived as unworthy creatures in comparison to humans. Indeed, some animals are so revered that they are not to be touched or observed, and many foods are to be treated with a special reverence or ritual in regard to their growth, preparation, and use. For instance, planting seeds as part of a school science project is considered taboo in some tribes (Mahan, 1979).

Some rituals and ideologies involved in Indian religions continue to thrive on reservations, despite the rapid assimilation of young Indians into the white culture. Among the distinguishing characteristics of many tribal religions are the belief in reincarnation, the belief that physical illnesses are caused by a person's moral transgressions, and taboos of specific activities, such as children playing with strings during certain seasons of the year. Some tribes also conduct special religious ceremonies at the onset of a young person's adolescence. Marking the transition from childhood to adulthood, as does the Jewish bar mitzvah, these Indian ceremonies accord adolescents certain adult rights, such as participation in tribal ceremonies and a social status that distinguishes them from children.

Indian Education

Although the educational needs of minority youths were mentioned earlier in this chapter, one distinguishing feature sets Indian students apart from other minority youths—approximately 10,000 Indian students enrolled in grades 9 through 12 live in boarding schools run by the federal government's Bureau of Indian Affairs, more commonly referred to as the **BIA** (Stubbs & Harrison, 1982). Given the fact that many Indian villages had too few children to maintain schools of their own, but were too geographically isolated to make busing students daily to regional schools feasible, the government opted to create the BIA boarding schools. Although these were intended to provide better educations for rural Indian students, critics have expressed their displeasure with the educational and social results.

According to the critics' surveys, most teachers in these boarding schools are too unaware of Indian culture and tribal languages to relate effectively to their Indian students. For example, most of the teachers relied almost exclusively on competitive classroom activities, despite the consistent research finding that competitive practices violate the Indian student's cultural mores. Similarly, in failing to take account of their Indian students' tribal attitudes regarding humility, boastfulness, assertiveness, and verbosity, many of the BIA teachers were erroneously interpreting many students' behavior as manifestations of stupidity and apathy (Fuchs & Havighurst, 1972; Kleinfield, 1973; McDiarmid & Kleinfield, 1982; Wax, 1971).

In addition to the obvious educational handicaps that these forms of unawareness and ethnocentricity can create for Indian students, the critics believe that boarding schools exacerbate certain social problems. From this perspective, being separated from their parents and their community accounts, at least in large part, for the high rates of drug abuse and delinquency among boarding-school students. It is also argued that the BIA schools have such low academic standards and such an outdated curriculum that Indian youths are ill-prepared for the rigorous vocational demands of our technologically advanced society. For these reasons, the critics maintain that local schools would be more beneficial to Indian students than the BIA boarding-school system.

In response to such concerns as the treatment of students in BIA schools, Indian youths joined the civil rights protests against academic and social discrimination during the 1960s and 1970s (Deloria, 1973). For example, in 1969 Indians occupied the deserted federal prison, Alcatraz, located on an island in the San Francisco Bay. Although the plan ultimately failed, Indian adolescents and adults occupied the prison with the avowed purpose of converting the island into a headquarters where all tribes could gather for educational, vocational, physical, and spiritual training. Similarly, in 1972 Indian demonstrators took over the Bureau of Indian Affairs in Washington, D.C. to protest the bureau's ethnocentric policies. While some Indians advocate abolishing the bureau altogether, others argue that its existence protects tribal rights and symbolizes the government's commitment to Indians.

In summary, although only .5 percent of all Americans classified themselves as Native Americans in the 1980 Census, the problems of Indian adolescents are more severe than those of youths from any other U.S. minority. Given that half of all Native Americans still live in geographically isolated areas and that their population is comparatively small, their problems are more easily overlooked by the general public and politicians than those of the larger, more visible, more politically powerful minorities in the United States. Sadly, in comparison to the national averages for Americans of every race, the Indian adolescent continues to have the greatest chances for the shortest life-span, the least education, and the lowest income (U.S. Bureau of the Census, 1982).

ASIAN AMERICAN ADOLESCENTS

Two variables that Asian American and Native American adolescents share in common are the size of their minority group and their geographic location. Like Native American youths, Asian Americans comprise only a small portion of the population—approximately 1 percent (U.S. Bureau of the Census, 1982). Most Asian Americans live in California and Hawaii. In contrast to other minority groups, however, most Asian Americans have achieved vocational, financial, educational, and social success in U.S. society. For this reason, Asian Americans are often considered an "ideal" example of assimilation into our culture against which other minorities are frequently compared. This assertion and its underlying implications, however, warrant our careful examination. To begin with, Asian Americans historically have more in common with other minorities than is generally acknowledged (Kitano, 1976; Levine & Rhodes, 1981; Phillips, 1981). As the numbers of Japanese and Chinese immigrants grew in California during the early part of this century, animosity and suspicion increased among many whites. For example, at one time the Japanese were legally barred from California's white schools and swimming pools. Japanese immigrants were ineligible for citizenship until 1954, and in 1924 the Federal Immigration Act denied entry to Asians. Furthermore, Japanese Americans were disliked for their "heathen" religions and their private schools, where children maintained their Japanese language and culture. By 1942, following Japan's victories in the Pacific, anti-Japanese sentiments were rampant on the West Coast. A historical fact that many Americans would prefer to forget is that during the Second World War nearly 110,000 Japanese Americans were forced to leave their homes and businesses in the western states and interned in the government's "relocation centers"—isolated communities in which barracks were constructed to house Asian Americans—despite protests of racism from some politicians and despite the fact that Americans of Italian and German descent were not similarly treated.

Not surprisingly, the internment resulted in financial ruin for many Japanese American families. Yet, ironically and retrospectively, the relocation camps were a disguised blessing for many families (Kitano, 1976; Levine & Rhodes, 1981; Phillips, 1981). In the relocation camps, the traditional attitudes of deference to the family diminished and a new generation emerged, who assimilated more quickly into U.S. culture. This new generation, called the *Nisei,* were tremendously motivated to achieve upward mobility in U.S. society through educational and occupational achievements. Abandoning many of their parents' customs and attitudes, the Nisei—who became the grandparents of today's Japanese American adolescents, adopted attitudes about competition and independence that shocked their predecessors. Nevertheless, by 1960, the Niseis' children, the *Sansei,* had surpassed both Chinese and white Americans in terms of education and income. Still, until the 1960s, intermarriage between white and Asian Americans was relatively rare, indicating the reluctance to permit social assimilation (Phillips, 1981).

In addition to the fact that Asian Americans have a history of discrimination shared with other minorities, many social scientists disagree with the assertion that Asian Americans are the ideal minority who demonstrate that any minority group can achieve success in the United States if it has enough desire and talent (Henderson, 1979; McLemore, 1980; Wing Sue, 1981). From the viewpoint of these analysts, three factors account for the more rapid assimilation of Asian

Americans into white U.S. society. First, the fact that Asian Americans constitute only 1 percent of the population makes them appear less threatening to the status quo than more populous minority groups. Second, the fact that Asians are lighter skinned than blacks and Hispanics makes them more socially acceptable by white standards. Third, most Asian values were considered compatible with white Americans' values, thereby necessitating less accommodation on the part of white Americans. Hard work, education, conformity, deference to authority, emotional restraint, and politeness were appealing characteristics from the white culture's perspective. Finally, these researchers maintain that we tend to ignore the unpleasant realities still affecting Asian Americans, such as the ghettos in New York and San Francisco, job discrimination, rising delinquency, and psychological stress associated with prejudice and bicultural living.

Asian American Families

Researchers have identified a number of distinctive aspects of Asian American families that appear to have a considerable impact on the personalities of the young (Kitano, 1976; Levine & Rhodes, 1981; Wing Sue, 1981). In the opinion of many Asian American parents, white parents are too indulgent and permissive with their children. In this regard, Asian American children are expected to be quiet, self-disciplined, and respectful toward their elders, rather than to interact, as many white children do, on the basis of a presumed equal status. Since the extended family has traditionally exerted a major influence over the young, Asian American adolescents may seem more attached to their adult relatives than white children. Researchers have noted that Asian American parents tend to include their children in events like funerals, business trips, and evening parties, which in white society are experiences usually reserved exclusively for adults. In this same vein, the data also suggest that Asian American parents are more willing than Caucasians to share the realities and hardships of life with their children, rather than being overly protective about such topics as death.

Moreover, Asian American parents typically discourage their children from publicly expressing emotions, from being too assertive, or from being too self-disclosing (Phillips, 1981). In contrast to white standards of socially appropriate behavior, self-disclosure is considered rude and boastful, rather than a mark of intimacy or esteem. Similarly, the unrestrained, informal, physically demonstrative conduct of whites is perceived as insincere and socially inappropriate. For example, one Asian American college student explained that she did not hug and kiss her parents publicly, as she did her white college friends, in order not to offend them (Phillips, 1981). In addition, expressing hostility through physical aggression is considered inappropriate behavior, even for males, since these forms of behavior indicate both a loss of self-control and an unnecessary impulsiveness. Not surprisingly, most Asian American adolescents have been found to be more cooperative, more deferential, more dependent, and more introverted than their white counterparts.

In his exhaustive review of the research on Orientals in the United States, Vernon Phillips (1981) underscores the relationship between family expectations and the behavior of Asian American youths. According to the research, Asian American youngsters are generally less assertive, less competitive, less self-disclosing, and less impulsive than their white peers. Their behavior is characterized by a reflective, cautious, self-disciplined approach. Similarly, Asian American youths tend to refrain from assertively offering their opinions, to lower their voices when speaking to elders or to those in positions of authority, and to accept the blame in certain situations in order to permit another person to save face. Interestingly, Asian American toddlers have been observed to be more placid, more compliant, and more group oriented than white babies, which indicates that many of these cultural differences emerge early in the child's life.

In relation to academic skills and vocational choices, many researchers have suggested that Asian American youths' achievements are related to their parents' attitudes toward verbal interaction and assertiveness. According to this view, the children are socialized to prefer activities that do not rely heavily on verbal interaction or verbal assertiveness. In support of this position, the data consistently show that Asian American students' verbal and language skills are less well developed than their skills in mathematics and science. Although the family instills a high regard for educational and financial success, the offspring tend to avoid courses in psychology, education, arts, and humanities in favor of courses in the sciences and mathematics. For instance, Chinese Americans are most frequently employed in engineering, the natural sciences, and medicine, while Japanese Americans are most frequently employed in architecture, art, the natural sciences, and technology (Phillips, 1981).

Although these aspects of Asian American families tend to create distinctive characteristics in their children, assimilation is creating certain conflicts between Asian American adolescents and their elders (Levine & Rhodes, 1981; Mindel, 1981). For instance, during the 1970s many Asian American youths defied their parents' sanctions against public displays of emotion and against assertiveness by participating in civil rights protests alongside other minority youths. Still having to answer questions like "How long have you been in America?", Asian American youths are increasingly more vocal and assertive as a minority group. Noted for their academic and vocational achievements, some Asian youths are causing their elders concern by questioning our society's emphasis on money, social status, and competition.

Moreover, some Asian youths are rebelling against what they perceive to be their parents' endorsement of the *banana syndrome*—to be "yellow on the outside," but to behave as if "white on the inside" by rejecting all standards that do not conform to the white status quo. Distraught because society and parents expect them to endorse white values and to behave like "bananas," many of these youths have joined organizations like the Asian American Society in an effort to promote public awareness of their problems as a minority. The differences between some Asian American adolescents and their elders might best be summarized by one frustrated parent who lamented: "I don't worry whether my children feel "banana" or not as long as they are top banana in this rat race!" (Mindel, 1981, p. 120).

In addition to the conflict between children and their parents, certain unfortunate social consequences seem to have befallen Asian American youths who have adopted white-middle-class standards. It has been reported that both male and female adolescents of Asian descent sometimes criticize one another for not "measuring up to" the physical and behavioral characteristics of white youths. For example, some females mock the males for being too sexually passive, too dependent on their parents, and too unassertive in comparison to white boys. Similarly, some males express a preference for dating white girls because, in their view, girls of Asian descent are not as pretty because they are more flat-chested or short-legged or slant-eyed. Perhaps more serious, however, is that as many adolescents have replaced Asian values with those of their white friends, the Asian American rates of delinquency and academic failure have risen dramatically in recent years (Phillips, 1981).

In summary, it appears that the commitment to certain Asian values that have enhanced the group's academic and financial success in U.S. society may be diminishing among Asian American youths. If research a decade hence proves

Is this young woman beautiful? Why or why not? To what degree are your personal standards of beauty ethnocentric?

this to be the case, it will surely demonstrate one of the more unfortunate losses that accompany the assimilation of minorities into our larger society.

Hawaiian Adolescents

As far as the percentage of minorities in each state is concerned, Hawaii has the largest minority population, with only 38 percent of its population being white in comparison with 30 percent of Japanese descent, 7 percent of Chinese descent, 13 percent of Hawaiian descent, and 12 percent of African descent (U.S. Bureau of the Census, 1982). (The remainder are a mixture of several races.) Indeed, in Hawaii, Caucasian residents are often considered the outsiders and called **haoles,** which originally meant "foreigners." In many respects, the Asian American residents of Hawaii are more advantaged than their counterparts in any other state. In terms of past discrimination, for example, these Japanese Americans were not interned in the U.S. government's relocation camps during World War II. Also, they obtained voting rights sooner and intermarried with whites more frequently than their stateside compatriots. Whether a consequence of historical events such as these or of Hawaiians' more liberal racial attitudes, a higher percentage of Asian Americans are employed in professional jobs in Hawaii than anywhere else in the United States. In sum, Hawaii's Asian American adolescents are members of a well-assimilated group, most of whose members enjoy the benefits that accompany high social and economic status (Kitano, 1976; Levine & Rhodes, 1981; Phillips, 1981).

Vietnamese Adolescents

The most recently immigrated Asian Americans, the Vietnamese and the Cambodians, have yet to attract the kind of research attention that more settled minorities have garnered. Nevertheless, data have been collected that describe the problems characteristically encountered by these newly arrived Asian Americans (Monter, 1981). As a consequence of the political upheavals and wars in Vietnam, thousands of Vietnamese fled their homeland for refuge in the United States during the 1960s and 1970s. Many of those who fled were educated people who aided the U.S. government during the war, so it is perhaps not surprising that two-thirds of all Vietnamese immigrants are from the upper-middle classes in Vietnam. Having chosen to support the United States, most of these families were forced to leave their homeland in order to save their lives.

In some respects the resettlement programs and U.S. sponsors have made the Vietnamese transition easier than that of earlier Asian-American immigrants. Moreover, the long-standing French and American influences in Vietnam had familiarized many immigrants with Western customs and with the English language. Nevertheless, most Vietnamese families suffered heavy losses in terms of financial and social status, as well as the emotional stress of leaving relatives in a war-torn country. In addition, many Vietnamese adolescents' parents have had unrealistically optimistic expectations about life in the United States and have had to confront unforeseen hardships in an economy besieged by inflation and high unemployment. As a consequence of these financial and emotional strains for many of the newly immigrated families, many Vietnamese American adolescents are having to cope with difficulties both within their families and in the society at large.

RESOLVING THE PROBLEMS OF MINORITY ADOLESCENTS

While the difficulties confronting many adolescents from minority cultures may seem overwhelming, dedicated adults have created many successful programs for assisting these youngsters. Although some projects demand considerable financial investments, many are inexpensive and relatively easy to implement.

Bilingual Education and Black Dialect

In 1973 the U.S. Supreme Court ruled that a school's failure to provide special programs for students who could not speak English was a violation of the 1964 Civil Rights Act (*Better Chance to Learn,* 1975). According to the ruling, any school system accepting federal money had to provide programs to help immigrant students learn English. Hispanic adolescents are the largest group affected by this legislation, but it's important to note that bilingual education also applied to such groups as the French in New England, the Creoles in Louisiana, and the Native Americans—all of whom have their own languages. Although the 1968 Bilingual Education Act allocated money for bilingual programs, many schools have been slow to implement these services for minority students.

There has been little disagreement among educators that improving the language skills of non-English speakers would benefit thousands of minority students (*Make Something Happen,* 1984). Indeed, it has been pointed out that while public schools spend billions of dollars trying to teach white students minimal skills in a foreign language, virtually no money is invested to maintain the native languages of immigrant students. This irony aside, the arguments surrounding bilingual education have centered around several key questions: Should schools teach courses to these minority students in both their native language and in English? How far do the school's bilingual services have to extend? For example, some advocates of bilingual education contend that counselors and teachers should be required to have facility in speaking some language other than English in order to communicate with their students' parents. In contrast, others argue that taxpayers' money should not be invested in special language programs for students whose native language is not English (Maltitz, 1975; Gaardner, 1977).

An issue related to bilingual education is how to deal with the nonstandard dialect spoken by many black adolescents. Although based on standard English, *black dialect*, also known as black English, has a vocabulary, grammar, pronunciation, and intonation unique unto itself. As the excerpts in Box 6.4 illustrate, black dialect, while often innovative and entertaining, is usually incomprehensible to outsiders. Labov's linguistic studies of inner-city youths have examined the unique characteristics of this English dialect. Although the dialect may appear unstructured and haphazard to outsiders, Labov finds it governed by specific rules. For example, the verb "to be" is rarely conjugated. Thus, youngsters using black dialect are abiding by a consistent rule when saying "she *be* late sometimes," instead of "she *is* late sometimes" (Labov, 1972).

Two of the arguments against permitting children to use black dialect are, first, that it interferes with the development of their standard English skills and,

Adolescent Voices 6.4

Black Dialect

The Three Little Pigs

The wolf came to the big house. And the wolf say, "let me in!" And the pig say, "no, no, no my shinny shin shin!" He huff, and he puff, and he tough, and he rough, but he couldn't knock the house down. And ol wolf say, "I'm a jump down you chimney!" And that ol pig put some water on the fire till when you could jump in it, and the lil pig had cook greens. Yeah, he fool him! He jump in the hot water, and the pig, he had greens and wolf! Greens and wolf!

SOURCE: S. Houston, Black English. *Psychology Today,* March 1974, p. 45.

Dialogue

"Aw, man, you trying to show you grandma how to milk ducks. Best you can do is to confidence some kitchen mechanic out of a dime or two. Me, I knocks de pad with them cack broads up on Sugar Hill and fills 'em full of melody. Man, I'm quick death and easy judgment. Youse just a home boy. Jelly, don't try to follow me."

SOURCE: H. Foster, *Ribbin and jivin and playin the dozens: The unresolved dilemma of inner city schools.* Cambridge, Mass.: Ballinger, 1974, p. 220.

second, that it is a handicap in most educational and vocational situations. From this perspective, adults are doing a disservice to black adolescents by permitting them to use this dialect instead of insisting that they use the standard English dialect. According to Labov, most data indicate that black dialect does not seriously impede a child's skills in reading, writing, or speaking standard English. Thus, it has been suggested that the two dialects be simultaneously maintained in schools, rather than permitting teachers to embarrass black students into abandoning their own dialect. Further, it has been argued that if schools showed more respect for black dialect, students who have deficiencies in standard English might be less embarrassed to ask for help in all academic areas. Moreover, the schools would be assigned the task of helping students identify the types of social and vocational situations in which black dialect is inappropriate, without condescending toward the dialect. Amidst the continuing debate, not even black educators and black parents can reach a consensus on the proper stance vis-à-vis black English dialect.

Multicultural Education

As mentioned at the outset of this chapter, those who endorse an assimilationist philosophy favor the establishment of a multicultural curriculum that instills a respect for minority cultures and aims to preserve the differences among people. In 1972 the first commission on multicultural education recommended that schools actively promote an appreciation of cultural differences, rather than merely teach students to "tolerate" minorities. As a further step toward multicultural education, in 1976 the national association for accrediting teacher-training programs requested that all colleges include information about sexism, racism, prejudice, inequality, and ethnic cultures in their teacher-preparation courses (Gollnick & Chinn, 1983; Klassen & Gollnick, 1977; *Multicultural Teacher Education*, 1980).

Moreover, the association of teacher education has asked colleges to actively recruit more teacher candidates from minority cultures and to equip future teachers with specific skills for combating racism and sexism in U.S. schools. According to the association's national report, many public schools and colleges prohibit the use of discriminatory materials, but very few actually include information about minorities or racism in the curriculum. As a consequence, most public schools' curricula still reflect white American values, perspectives, and achievements, to the exclusion of minorities' views and accomplishments. Finally, the association urges colleges to train teachers in the use of pedagogical methods that are more appropriate for minority youth than traditional techniques based on competition and verbal assertiveness.

Those who advocate multicultural education urge parents and teachers to discuss prejudice and discrimination with adolescents and to explore the discrepancies between U.S. creeds and the social and economic realities. For instance, it has been suggested that, rather than perpetuating historical myths, teachers present history candidly and discuss ways to build a more equitable, tolerant society. With this aim, a number of teachers and parents are already training themselves to detect ethnocentric bias against minority cultures in textbooks, as the quiz in Box 6.5 illustrates. Similarly, a multicultural perspective demands an examination of our own knowledge in regard to racism and minority cultures, in order that we can redress our lack of awareness through remedial instruction. The quiz in Box 6.6 serves to illustrate the areas in which many of us may be deficient as a consequence of our having been deprived of a multicultural education.

Programs Involving Parents

Of particular relevance to a discussion of improving the problems of minority adolescents is a 1979 study showing that white teachers were more likely than Hispanic or black teachers to blame minority parents for their children's academic problems. Moreover, the white teachers were more likely to blame minority parents than to blame white parents whose children had similar academic deficits (Lorton, 1979). This finding, among others, indicates that minority students would benefit if their parents and teachers worked with, rather than against, one another.

In this regard, the Reverend Jesse Jackson's "Project Excel" is an important gesture toward bringing the parents and teachers of minority students closer together (Jackson, 1978). Jesse Jackson, civil rights leader from the 1960s and candidate for the U.S. presidency in 1984, organized Project Excel to motivate poor, black adolescents academically. The project requires participating adolescents and their parents to sign pledges, promising to assume personal responsibility for academic success or failure. In signing the pledge, parents are agreeing to provide a quiet environment in the home for studying every night without

Are You Sure? 6.5 

Recognizing Racism in Books

1. Does the author assume all readers are white and Christian?
2. Are facts romanticized to glorify the white culture's perspective and to gloss over cruelty and inequity toward minorities?
3. Are minorities mentioned as social problems rather than as contributors to society?
4. Are minorities described in degrading terms (the "roaming, ferocious, primitive Indians")?
5. Are words used to support a Caucasian perspective without presenting other views (Indians "massacred," but whites "fought battles," white leaders are "assertive and outspoken," but minority leaders are "aggressive and rebellious")?
6. Are the contributions of other cultures ignored? (Is Africa mentioned only in relation to slavery, but not in relation to its rich civilizations?)
7. Do evolutionary charts end with a white man, as if he were somehow more truly "evolved" than anyone else?
8. Are oversimplified generalizations perpetuated (fat, eye-rolling Chicano; sombrero-wearing, fiesta-loving bandito; inscrutable slant-eyed Oriental; switchblade-toting Puerto Rican)?
9. Does the minority person progress by adapting to white standards? Is success defined only by white-male values?
10. Is the oppression of minorities accurately and candidly represented?
11. Does a white person consistently resolve the problems for the minority group member?
12. Are the only nonwhite heroes and heroines people who avoided serious conflict with or contributed to white society?
13. Does the book encourage the passive, patient acceptance of injustice?
14. Do portrayals of nonwhite cultures create a genuine respect or perpetuate the "quaint natives in costume" syndrome?
15. If authors and illustrators are not members of the groups being written about, is there anything in their background that specifically qualifies them to write this book?

SOURCE: *How fair are your children's textbooks?* Hyattsville, Md.: National Education Association, 1975.

any interruptions for phone calls, television, or radio. The pledge also entails a promise to visit their children's teachers at least four times a year for information and suggestions.

The adolescents themselves pledge to study two hours every night, to attend school regularly, and to apply the same principles in school that they apply in sports: daily practice, repetition, discipline, sacrifice, and high standards. Project Excel also asks local merchants and disc jockeys to reinforce the importance of education by distributing information about school meetings and publicizing the importance of education. According to Jackson's philosophy, black parents should discuss past civil rights violations and should describe the personal struggles of their own relatives, as a way of inspiring the young to maximize their hard-won educational opportunities. Furthermore, Jackson argues that black parents need to convince their children that in today's conservative, competitive society, their only chance for economic or social advancement is through education. Thus, in his speeches to adolescents, Jackson states, "The sickness of racism forces us to be superior so that we may be considered average." "You are not the woman you want to be with a half-developed brain and a full-developed bottom; it doesn't make you a man to make a baby but to care for one" (*Project Excel,* 1980). Jackson's inspirational speeches and tapes for adolescents have motivated many parents and adolescents to sign Project Excel's pledge for academic excellence (see Box 6.7).

Black psychologists have advised parents to provide their children with

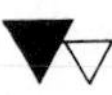

6.6 Are You Sure?

Historical Events Affecting Minority Adolescents

Can you order these events chronologically or affix a date to any of them? Being unable to complete this task successfully may reflect your own high school's lack of a multicultural curriculum:

1. Legalization of interracial marriage in all states
2. Legalization of voting rights for black Americans
3. Legalization of voting rights for female Americans
4. Assassination of Martin Luther King
5. Supreme Court mandate for desegregation of public schools
6. Imprisonment of Japanese Americans in "relocation" camps in the United States
7. Zoot-suit riots in which Mexican American adolescents and police died
8. Supreme Court order that Alabama integrate its public bus system
9. The march of 250,000 people to Washington to hear Martin Luther King's famous "I Have a Dream" speech
10. Voting Rights Act passed to protect black Americans who want to register to vote in the South
11. Nonwhite Americans allowed to eat in restaurants and to enter public facilities
12. The first U.S. sit-ins protesting racial segregation, conducted by black college students in Greensboro, N.C.
13. Black American riots in 56 cities
14. The armed services desegregated
15. The Bureau of Indian Affairs in Washington D.C. taken over by Indian Americans in protest over the treatment of Native Americans.

Answers: 1. 1967; 2. 1870; 3. 1920; 4. 1968; 5. 1954; 6. 1942; 7. 1943; 8. 1956; 9. 1963; 10. 1965; 11. 1964; 12. 1960; 13. 1963–1967; 14. 1948; 15. 1972.

A Closer Look 6.7 

Jesse Jackson's Project Excel

Locke High School in Los Angeles is an inner-city school, almost a ghetto school. Very few of the parents show up for PTA meetings, open house, or back-to-school nights.

When we became involved in PUSH, we in the school administration decided that we would undertake a project for getting our parents into school to hear the story of PUSH. We didn't want the usual 10 or 15 parents to show up. We didn't want the parents of just the goody-good students. We wanted everybody. And we wanted them to come and hear the story of our EXCEL program, ask questions, and get answers. We didn't want to wait until the annual Public Schools Week.

Some of our families are on public assistance and some of our students are parents themselves. We said, "Some of these people listen to music on the radio." So we sent news releases about our proposed program in the school to the radio station. We sent news releases to the community newspapers. We placed a bunch of fliers in the grocery stores so that when the clerk bagged the groceries she stuck a flier in the bag telling about Back-to-School Night.

Well, we had over 600 people in attendance that night, standing room only. We prepared an enjoyable program for them, using our band, dance group, and drama equipment. We did a skit called "I Am Somebody," and we had the audience on their feet saying, "I'm somebody."

After the program many parents picked up their children's report cards. Others had conferences with teachers. Never in the history of our high school have we had so many parents in attendance on one occasion.—Cardriner Bowden, EXCEL Coordinator, Locke High School, Los Angeles.

SOURCE: J. Jackson, In pursuit of equity, ethics and excellence. *Phi. Delta Kappan*, November 1978, pp. 193–198.

information about their cultural history and about the realities of racism in our present society (Comer & Poussant, 1975). Simultaneously, however, these psychologists advise that parents not let their children blame poor academic performance exclusively on racial discrimination. Particularly in cases where the parents have indisputable evidence that their child is not doing his or her part in striving toward academic excellence, the parent must be willing to confront the child's accusations that "society" or "prejudice" is responsible for his or her personal failures. Also, some parents may need to remind their children that every individual from a minority culture who succeeds financially and educationally is not necessarily an "Uncle Tom" or a "banana." It is both important and ironic to note, however, that black parents in the 1980s seem to have fewer worries than black parents of the 1960s or 1970s in terms of convincing their offspring to succeed by the white world's standards ("Roots III," 1985; refer to Box 6.1).

Psychology for Adolescents

Although almost all strategies for improving the academic performance of minority students have attempted to teach psychological strategies to either parents or teachers, several have turned the tables by teaching adolescents to apply psychological principles to their teachers. One program exemplifying this strategy provided weekly instruction for a small group of minority students with academic problems. Each week's instruction explained the principles and practices of a particular psychological strategy, such as transactional analysis or behavior modification. In addition, participants were required to complete an assigned activity aimed at improving their relationships with teachers before the next group meeting. For instance, one assignment was to compliment chosen teachers on one of their behaviors at any time during the week, to greet them each day when entering class, and to ask them for help with an activity or assignment. Each of these assignments was obviously a behavioristic strategy for reinforcing the teachers in such a way that they would feel more positive toward the minority students. Among the results of this study were a decrease in the participants' truancy, an improvement in grades, and a reduction in their referrals to the principal for disciplinary problems (Maldonado & Cross, 1977).

In a project with similar goals, white, black, and Chicano adolescents from a special education class learned to apply the principles of behavior modification to their teachers. The researchers taught these students to reinforce teachers by smiling, nodding, sitting attentively, maintaining eye contact, and asking for the teachers' assistance with class assignments. By first rehearsing their newly acquired skills with a counselor and then viewing these rehearsals on a videotape, the adolescents learned new ways of behaving toward their teachers, which elicited more positive feedback. For instance, one student had a habit of leering at his teachers in a disapproving, aggressive manner whenever they spoke to him. By practicing more hospitable expressions with an assigned "coach" and by viewing his various facial expressions on the videotape, he was able to assume a less surly expression, which, in turn, elicited more positive reactions from his teachers (Grandbard, Rosenberg, & Martin, 1977).

Of particular significance in this study is that these minority students had become so accustomed to negative feedback from teachers that they were virtually unable to recognize compliments from their teachers when they did occur. The researchers found that teaching these students to recognize positive feedback from a teacher was their most difficult task. Fortunately, through the use of discussion and videotapes that demonstrated positive and negative feedback from teachers to students, the program's participants vastly improved their own skills in recognizing compliments from and positive interactions with their teachers.

Among the researchers' most interesting findings were that teachers' negative comments to these students did indeed decrease after the students began displaying new behaviors toward their teachers. In this regard, it's noteworthy that the teachers were most responsive to the students' new habit of exclaiming aloud in class, "Ah ha! Now I understand this material since you've explained it so carefully for me." Moreover, the students reported feeling more self-confident, powerful, and self-controlled. An essential component of the program's success, however, was that the students had to keep written records of their conduct and of their teachers' responses. When this activity was omitted in order to assess its impact, the adolescents' behavior generally failed to improve. Even more impressive, when the program was applied to adolescents' relationships with their parents, siblings, and peers, the results were equally favorable (Grandbard, Rosenberg, & Martin, 1977).

Teaching Adolescents from Minority Cultures

In *The Great School Legend,* Colin Green argues that the failure of U.S. schools to educate minority students as effectively as they educate whites is no recent development, but a shortcoming that has existed since the earliest days of European immigration (Green, 1972). Although Green's perspective is disquieting, there is ample research evidence to support his assertion that most children from minority cultures are less well-prepared academically than their white classmates. Thus, psychologists have continually urged teachers to adopt pedagogical strategies and curricula that are better suited to the needs of minority students, rather than revising the traditional methods that succeed with white students (Cheyney, 1972; Grossman, 1984; Jones, 1976; Litsinger, 1973; Nielsen, 1982; Silberman, 1970).

Among the many strategies being suggested by these researchers is that teachers deemphasize competition between students and rely more on cooperative strategies. In addition, given the charge of cultural bias against IQ tests, it is argued that teachers should rely on diagnostic tests that specify the minority student's academic deficits and learning style, rather than making a diagnosis on the basis of the student's IQ test score. Moreover, instead of segregating minorities into separate classes on the basis of their IQ scores, schools should integrate students of different abilities in the same classes, so that peer tutoring and positive modeling can occur. This is not to suggest, however, that teachers should behave in a condescending manner toward their minority students. On the contrary, teachers who insist on self-discipline, goal setting, and hard work and who refuse to pass those who "try hard," but who nonetheless fail to meet the criteria, are rendering their students an invaluable service. As Chapter 7 will illustrate, methods such as these have succeeded, even in the most impoverished ghetto schools, in raising the academic skills of minority students.

Reaching the Academically Gifted

Scholars have also expressed their concern for the academic welfare of minority youngsters who are intellectually gifted (Colangelo & Zaffrann, 1979; Torrance, 1977). In support of their concern, these scholars cite the research showing that gifted minority students are less likely than whites to be placed in advanced classes or special after-school programs. Moreover, they are concerned that the most precocious students may be the most aware of and sensitive to racial discrimination, and therefore may need special counseling to help them cope with prejudice. Furthermore, when these youngsters come from impoverished families, they must often cope with their own parents' anxieties and insecurities regarding their offspring's intellectual giftedness. In short, the adolescent's precocity will probably threaten adults who are themselves uneducated and insecure about their intellectual abilities. In this regard it is interesting to note that one research study found teachers to be more critical of the gifted minority student than of white students with average or above average academic skills (Rubovits & Maehr, 1973).

According to Paul Torrance, a renowned researcher in the field of creativity, minority youngsters are generally more creative than whites in terms of their abilities to improvise, to express themselves verbally and artistically, and to respond kinesthetically to their environment (Torrance, 1977). This kinesthetic talent involves the skillful use and interpretation of nonverbal messages. In Torrance's studies, most minority students are more persistent and more original in solving problems than whites. Torrance contends that educators are making a mistake by not capitalizing on the creativity that minority cultures have instilled in many children and, further, by trying to replace these creative abilities with skills that are irrelevant to the minority culture.

Counseling Minority Adolescents

According to the former president of the American Personnel and Guidance Association, Derald Wing Sue, most counselors and therapists are trained to work only with verbal, self-disclosing, introspective, white, middle-class clients. Indeed, at the 1973 convention of the Americal Psychological Association, some psychologists recommended that counseling people from a minority culture without having had specific professional training in minority counseling should be deemed unethical (Pederson, 1977). Although this proposal was never adopted, a number of therapists do agree with the accusation that mental-health workers have been ill-prepared to communicate effectively with or to understand the perspectives of individuals from minority cultures or individuals from lower socioeconomic classes (Atkinson, Morten, & Wing Sue, 1983; Baron, 1981; Henderson, 1979; Wing Sue, 1981).

From the perspective of these professionals, counseling minorities more effectively involves both the learning of new skills and the adoption of less ethnocentric attitudes. Among the recommendations is that counselors should rely on behavioral psychology rather than on psychoanalytic approaches in order to resolve the problems of minority clients. The counselor's goal should be to provide concrete remedies for immediate problems confronting minorities and to help them learn the necessary skills for functioning in both the white and the minority cultures. For example, the counselor might explain to a Native American student that, although averting her eyes when speaking to her elders is a manifestation of respect within the tribal community, this gesture will probably be interpreted by white adults as shyness, guilt, shame, or embarrassment. Hence, the counselor would work toward helping the student alter this particular nonverbal gesture or, at the very least, help her understand the negative impact of her gesture on white adults with whom she interacts.

Another recommendation is that counselors assume the role of educating school personnel in regard to the importance of understanding their students' cultural differences. Teaching the faculty how to interpret nonverbal communication and behavior from students' cultural perspectives will prevent miscommunication and misinterpretation. For example, the tendency of Asian Americans to be less publicly expressive and to be less verbal than whites is often misinterpreted as aloofness, disinterest, or rudeness. Similarly, Navajo students' hesitancy to ask their elders too many questions, to initiate intimate conversations, or to disclose personal information to anyone outside the family can be perceived as hostile, repressed, passive, or antisocial. Lest we assume that the differences in nonverbal communication beween cultures are few, it is important to note that many studies have demonstrated cultural difference in regard to the physical distance between speakers, the volume and speed of speech, verbal assertiveness, the use of silence during a conversation, and the amount of self-disclosure in conversations (Wing Sue, 1981).

Although some have argued that counselors and teachers who are themselves from minority groups are the most qualified to work with minority youths, the research data have failed to support this assertion (Atkinson, Morten, & Wing Sue, 1983; Henderson, 1979; Wing Sue, 1981). The data indicate that professionals of any race who can interpret cross-cultural differences accurately and who can put aside their own ethnocentric values can be effective counselors and teachers for minority adolescents. This implies, however, that counselors and teachers will honestly recognize their own cultural biases and will actively work to overcome their prejudices and ethnocentrism in terms of behavior and attitudes, as the case study in Box 6.8 illustrates. Moreover, abandoning one's ethnocentric perspective includes learning to define normal and abnormal behavior within each culture's context. For instance, such a counselor would not judge a Hispanic student's disdain for competition as an abnormal or unhealthy attitude. Although studies have not yet offered convincing evidence that sex, race, or ethnicity prevent anyone from being a fine counselor or teacher, working with adolescents from minority cultures does require special training, sensitivity to cultural differences, and awareness of the prejudices and ethnocentricity within oneself.

Conclusion

In any discussion of prejudice and inequality in a society, there is a fine line between the bleeding-heart posture of some well-intentioned reformers and the hard-hearted posture of some well-intentioned conservatives. In terms of the statistical data, the indisputable fact is that many adolescents from minority cultures are still confronted with a host of educational, vocational, social, psychological, and physical problems, which are related both to their lower socioeconomic status and to racism in our society. Nevertheless, it is also statistically true that adolescents from minority cultures have benefited from legislative and social changes that have ensued since the Civil Rights Act of 1964. Moreover, the data indicate that racism in certain domains is slowly diminishing in our society.

As subsequent chapters in this text will demonstrate, an adolescent's race is only one among many variables affecting his or her development. For example, in regard to problems like delinquency and academic underachievement, any explanation that focuses solely on adolescents' racial or cultural differences has oversimplified the matter by overlooking the impact of such influences as socioeconomic class. The debate regarding the relative influence of an adolescent's race in relation to these other variables will undoubtedly continue for many decades. In the meantime, the statistical fact remains that a dispropor-

6.8 A Closer Look

Counseling an Adolescent from a Minority Culture

John C. is a 21-year-old student majoring in electrical engineering. He first sought counseling because he was failing courses. These academic difficulties became apparent during the first quarter of his senior year and were accompanied by headaches, indigestion, and insomnia. Since he had been an excellent student in the past, John felt that his lowered academic performance was caused by illness. However, a medical examination failed to reveal any organic disorder. He was difficult to counsel because he would respond to inquiries with short but polite statements and would seldom volunteer information about himself. He avoided any statements that involved feelings and presented his problem as a strictly educational one.

As the sessions progressed, John became less anxious and more trusting of the counselor. Much of his earlier difficulty in opening up were caused by his feelings of shame and guilt at having to come to a counselor. He was concerned that his family might discover this help and that it would disgrace them. He was also embarrassed by his academic failures. However, when the counselor informed him that many Chinese students experienced similar problems and that these sessions were completely confidential, John seemed relieved. As he became increasingly able to open up, he revealed problems typical of Chinese students who have strong traditional cultural values and whose self-worth and identity are defined within the family.

John's parents had always had high expectations of him and constantly pressured him to do well in school. They seemed to equate his personal worth with his ability to obtain good grades. This pressure caused him to spend endless hours studying, and generally he remained isolated from social activities. This isolation did not help him to learn the social skills required in peer relationships. His background was in sharp contrast to the informality and spontaneity demanded in Caucasian relationships. Therefore, his circle of friends was small, and he was never really able to enjoy himself with others.

John experienced a lot of conflict, because he was beginning to resent the pressure his parents put on him. He had always harbored secret wishes about becoming an artist, but was pressured into engineering by his parents. His deep-seated feelings of anger toward his parents resulted in failure in school and in his physical symptoms.

The case of John C. illustrates some of the following conflicts encountered by many Chinese students attempting to maintain traditional Chinese values: (a) there is often a conflict beween loyalty to the family and personal desires for independence; (b) the self-restraint and formality in interpersonal relationships often result in a lack of social experience and subsequent feelings of loneliness; (c) the family pressure to achieve academically accentuates feelings of shame and depression when the student fails.

SOURCE: D. Wing Sue (ed.), *Counseling the culturally different*. New York: Wiley Interscience, 1981. Reprinted by permisison.

tionate number of adolescents from minority cultures are plagued by problems that most white youngsters never have to wrestle with. Consequently, rather than allowing ourselves to get bogged down in arguments over which factors are most influential or over who is ultimately responsible for the present condition of minority youths, it seems both wise and pragmatic to employ the techniques that research has already demonstrated to be effective in alleviating many problems of adolescents from minority cultures.

Questions for Discussion and Review

Concepts and Terminology

1. In what ways are many adolescents from minority cultures financially or socially disadvantaged?
2. In what ways are many youths from minority cultures academically, vocationally, and socially handicapped?
3. How do family structures and family values differentially affect adolescents from various minority cultures?
4. In what ways do some scholars contend that the research regarding minorities has been biased, and how is the Moynihan report relevant in this regard?
5. How can sports be disadvantageous or advantageous to minority youths?
6. How do the sex roles of Hispanic, black, and Asian youths compare?
7. In what ways are adolescents from migrant families unique?
8. In what ways are Asian Americans more similar to other minorities than is often acknowledged?
9. How does multicultural education distinguish itself from traditional U.S. education?
10. How can an ethnocentric textbook be indentified?
11. How can the parents of minority youths enhance their children's academic and vocational achievements?
12. Through what methods have counselors helped minority adolescents improve their relationships with teachers?

Questions for Discussion and Debate

1. Assume, if need be, that you are a member of a minority group. What do you perceive as the benefits and losses associated with acculturation?
2. If you had to choose to be a member of a racial group other than your own, which would you choose and why?
3. In what ways are your attitudes and behavior ethnocentric? prejudiced? bicultural?
4. What aspects of the traditional black, Hispanic, Asian American, and Native American families do you most respect? How might your own adolescence have been different if you had been raised in each of these families?
5. How might your adolescence and present life be different if your facial featues, physique, and skin color had been vastly different from the majority of your fellow citizens?

6. What information in this chapter did you find most personally disturbing? Why?
7. How did you fare on the quiz in Box 6.6, and what, if any, implications does your score have for the adolescents with whom you may be relating?
8. In regard to the information in Box 6.1, how would you feel as the upper-middle-class parent of a black adolescent who was well assimilated into white U.S. culture and who seemed to care very little about the history of black Americans?
9. How do you feel about the recommendations and the findings of the Hispanic Secondary Education Association reported in Box 6.2?
10. How have your own experiences with members of minority cultures affected your racial attitudes and your behavior?

REFERENCES

Adelson, J. (ed.) *Handbook of adolescent psychology.* New York: Wiley, 1980.

Allport, G. *The nature of prejudice.* Garden City, N.Y.: Doubleday, 1958.

America's children and their families. Washington, D.C.: Children's Defense Fund, 1979.

Anderson, C., & Cromwell, R. Black is beautiful and the color preferences of Afro-American youth. *Journal of Negro Education,* 1977, *46,* 76–88.

Andrade, S. Family planning practices of Mexican Americans. In M. Melville (ed.), *Twice a minority.* St. Louis: Mosby, 1980. Pp. 17–32.

Atkinson, D., Morten, G., & Wing Sue, D. *Counseling American minorities.* Dubuque, Iowa: Brown, 1983.

Baldwin, J. Theory and research concerning the notion of black self-hatred. *Journal of Black Psychology,* February 1979, pp. 51–77.

Banks, J. The implications of multicultural education. In Frank Glassen (ed.), *Pluralism and the American teacher.* Washington, D.C.: American Association of Colleges for Teacher Education, 1977. Pp. 18–27.

Baron, A. (ed.). *Chicano psychology.* New York: Praeger, 1981.

Berry, G. Television and the black child. In W. Smith (ed.), *Reflections on black psychology.* Washington, D.C.: University Press of America, 1979. Pp. 109–116.

Better chance to learn: Bilingual, bicultural education. Washington, D.C.: Commission on Civil Rights, 1975.

Billingsley, A. *Black families in white America.* Englewood Cliffs, N.J.: Prentice-Hall, 1968.

Black and white children in America: Key facts. Washington, D.C.: Children's Defense Fund, 1984.

Bryde, J. *Modern Indian psychology.* Vermillion: University of South Dakota, 1971.

Casarantes, E. Pride and prejudice. In C. Hernandez (ed.), *Chicanos: Social and psychological perspectives.* St. Louis: Mosby, 1976. Pp. 9–15.

Changes in mathematical achievement 1973–78. Denver: National Assessment of Educational Progress, 1979.

Cheyney, A. *The ripe harvest: Educating migrant children.* Coral Gables, Fla.: University of Miami, 1972.

Cheyney, A. *Teaching children of different cultures.* Columbus, Oh.: Merrill, 1976.

Children in adult jails. Washington, D.C.: Children's Defense Fund, 1976.

Children out of school in America. Washington, D.C.: Children's Defense Fund, 1974.

Children without homes. Washington, D.C.: Children's Defense Fund, 1978.

Clark, K., & Clark, M. Skin color as a factor in racial identification of Negro children. *Journal of Social Psychology,* 1947, *11,* 140.

Colangelo, N., & Zaffrann, R. (eds.). *New voices in counseling the gifted.* Dubuque, Iowa: Kendall-Hunt, 1979.

Comer, J., & Poussaint, A. *Black child care.* New York: Simon & Schuster, 1975.

Conference on the educational and occupational needs of black women. Washington, D.C.: National Institute of Education, 1975.

Corporal punishment. Philadelphia: National Center for the Study of Corporal Punishment, Temple University, 1977.

Day, B. *Sexual life between blacks and whites.* New York: Crowell, 1972.

Deloria, V. *God is red.* New York: Grosset and Dunlop, 1973.

Demarest, S., & Jordan, J. Discriminatory suspensions and the effect of institutional racism on school discipline. *Inequality in Education,* July 1975, pp. 25–41.

Dinges, N. American Indian adolescent socialization: A review of literature. *Journal of Adolescence,* 1979, *2,* 259–96.

Doctors and dollars are not enough. Washington, D.C.: Children's Defense Fund, 1976.

Dougherty, M. *Becoming a woman in rural black culture.* New York: Holt, Rinehart and Winston, 1978.

Drug abuse prevention for low income communities. Washington, D.C.: National Institute on Drug Abuse, 1980.

Education Week, October, 1981, p. 4.

Educational and occupational needs of Hispanic women. Washington, D.C.: National Institute of Education, 1976.

The educational disadvantages of language minority persons. Washington, D.C.: U.S. Department of Health, Education and Welfare, July 1978, Bulletin 78.

Fetters, W. *National longitudinal study of the high school class of 1972.* Washington, D.C.: U.S. Department of Health, Education and Welfare, 1977.

Fitzpatrick, J. *Puerto Rican Americans.* Englewood Cliffs, N.J.: Prentice-Hall, 1971.

Fuchs, R., & Havighurst, R. *To live on this earth: An Indian education.* New York: Doubleday, 1972.

Gaardner, B. *Bilingual schooling.* Rowley, Mass.: Newbury House, 1977.

Gary, L. *Black men.* Beverly Hills, Cal.: Sage, 1982.

Gilbert, B. The gospel according to John. *Sports Illustrated,* December 15, 1980, pp. 89–102.

Goff, R. Educating black Americans. In M. Smyth (ed.), *The black American reference book.* Englewood Cliffs, N.J.: Prentice-Hall, 1976. Pp. 410–452.

Gollnick, D., & Chinn, P. *Multicultural education in a pluralistic society.* St. Louis: Mosby, 1983.

Grandbard, P., Rosenberg, H., & Martin, M. Student applications of behavior modification to teachers and other environments. In D. O'Leary (ed.), *Classroom management.* New York: Pergamon Press, 1977. Pp. 235–249.

Green, C. *The great school legend.* New York: Basic Books, 1972.

Gren, T. *Black women in sport.* Reston, Va.: AAHPERP Publications, 1981.

Grossman, B., Wirt, R., & Davids, A. Self-esteem, ethnic identity and behavioral adjustment among Anglo and Chicano adolescents in West Texas. *Journal of Adolescence,* 1985, *8,* 57–68.

Grossman, H. *Educating Hispanic students: Cultural implications for instruction, classroom management, counseling and assessment.* Springfield, Ill.: Charles Thomas, 1984.

Gump, J., & Rivers, L. A consideration of race in efforts to end sex bias. In E. Diamon (ed.), *Issues of sex bias and sex fairness in career interest measurement.* Washington, D.C.: U.S. Department of Health, Education and Welfare, 1975. Pp. 123–139.

Guthrie, R. *Even the rat was white: A historical view of psychology.* New York: Harper & Row, 1976.

Harvard dictionary of American minorities. Cambridge, Mass.: Harvard University Press, 1981.

Henderson, G. (ed.). *Counseling minorities.* Springfield, Ill.: Charles Thomas, 1979.

Hernandez, C., Hang, M., & Wagner, N. *Chicanos: Sociological and psychological perspectives.* St. Louis: Mosby, 1976.

Hispanic mental health bibliography. Los Angeles: UCLA, 1978.

Howard, J. Toward a social psychology of colonialism. In P. L. Jones (ed.), *Black psychology.* New York: Harper & Row, 1971. P. 327.

Importance of athletic opportunity for women. Washington, D.C.: Project on the Status of Women, March 1978.

Jackson, J. In pursuit of equity, ethics and excellence. *Phi Delta Kappan,* November 1978, pp. 193–198.

Johnson, D., & Johnson, R. *Learning together and alone.* Englewood Cliffs, N.J.: Prentice-Hall, 1975.

Johnson, L. Perspectives on black families: Review of research. In H. McAdoo (ed.), *Black families.* Beverly Hills, Cal.: Sage, 1981. Pp. 87–106.

Jones, J. What superintendents and boards can do. *Phi Delta Kappan,* November 1978, pp. 221–223.

Jones, R. (ed.). *Mainstreaming and the minority child.* Reston, Va.: Council for Exceptional Children, 1976.

Kackley, J. *Helping students survive at home and at school.* St. Petersberg, Fla.: Pinellas School System, 1975.

Kaplan, J. *Women and sports.* New York: Viking, 1979.

Killalea and Associates. State, regional and national summaries of suspensions. Washington, D.C.: U.S. Department of Health, Education and Welfare, Office of Civil Rights, 1980.

Kitano, H. *Japanese Americans: Evolution of a subculture.* Englewood Cliffs, N.J.: Prentice-Hall, 1976.

Klassen, F., & Gollnick, D. (eds.). *Pluralism and the American teacher.* Washington, D.C.: Association of Colleges for Teacher Education, 1977.

Kleinfield, J. *A long way from home: Effects of public high schools on village children.* Fairbanks: University of Alaska Press, 1973.

Labov, W. *Language in the inner city.* Philadelphia: University of Pennsylvania, 1972.

Ladner, J. *Tomorrow's tomorrow: The black woman in America.* New York: Anchor Books, 1971.

Lamfromboise, T., Dauphinais, P., & Rowe, W. *A survey of Indian students' perceptions of the counseling experience.* Toronto: American Educational Reasearch Association, 1978.

Laws, J. The psychology of tokenism. *Sex Roles,* 1975, *1,* 51–67.

Lee, C. Successful rural black adolescents: A psychosocial profile. *Adolescence,* 1985, *77,* 131–141.

Lerner, R. Self-concept, self-esteem and body attitudes among Japanese male and female adolescents. *Child Development,* 1980, *51,* 847–855.

Levine, G., & Rhodes, C. *The Japanese American community: A three generational study.* New York: Praeger, 1981.

Litsinger, D. *The challenge of teaching Mexican American students.* New York: American Book Co., 1973.

Long, J., & Vigil, D. Cultural styles and adolescent sex role perceptions. In M. Melville (ed.), *Twice a minority.* St. Louis: Mosby, 1980. Pp. 164–172.

Lorton, E. *The teacher's world.* Washington, D.C.: Education Research Clearinghouse, 1979.

Mahan, J. Culturally oriented instruction for Native American students. In G. Henderson (ed.), *Counseling minorities.* Springfield, Ill.: Charles Thomas, 1979. Pp. 318–344.

Make something happen: A report on secondary schooling for Hispanics. New York: National Commission on Secondary Schooling for Hispanics, 1984.

Malcolm, S., Hall, P., & Brown, J. *The double bind: The price of being a minority woman in science.* Washington, D.C.: American Association for the Advancement of Science, 1976.

Maldonado, B., & Cross, W. Today's Chicano refutes the stereotype. *College Student Journal,* 1977, *11,* 146–152.

Maltitz, F. *Living and learning in two languages.* New York: McGraw-Hill, 1975.

Mangrim, G., & Seninger, S. *Coming of age in the ghetto: Report to the Ford Foundation.* Baltimore, Md.: Johns Hopkins University Press, 1978.

Martin, E., & Martin, J. *The black extended family.* Chicago: University of Chicago Press, 1978.

McAdoo, H., (ed.). *Black families.* Beverly Hills, Cal.: Sage, 1981.

McDiarmid, W., & Kleinfield, J. *Doctor, lawyer and Indian chief: Aspirations of Eskimo students.* Anchorage: University of Alaska, 1982.

McLemore, D. *RAial and ethnic relations in America.* St. Louis: Mosby, 1980.

Melville, M. *Twice a minority: Mexican American women.* St. Louis: Mosby, 1980.

Mendoza, R., & Martinez, J. Measurement of acculturation. In A. Baron (ed.), *Chicano psychology.* New York: Praeger, 1981. P. 71.

Mindel, C. (ed.). *Ethnic families in America.* New York: Elsevier, 1981.

Minority women and higher education. Washington, D.C.: Project on the status of women, Association of American Colleges, 1976.

Mirande, A., & Enriquez, E. *La Chicana.* Chicago: University of Chicago Press, 1979.

Money, income and poverty status of families and persons in the U.S.: 1980. Washington, D.C.: U.S. Bureau of the Census, March 1981.

Monter, D. Vietnamese assimilation in American society. In D. Claerbaut (ed.), *New directions in ethnic studies.* Saratoga, Cal., Century Twenty One, 1981. Pp. 119–130.

Moore, J. *Mexican Americans.* Englewood Cliffs, N.J.: Prentice-Hall, 1976.

Moynihan, D., et al. *The negro family: Case of national action.* Washington, D.C.: U.S. Department of Labor, 1965.

Multicultural teacher education. Washington, D.C.: American Association for Colleges of Teacher Education, 1980.

Myers, H., et al. (eds.). *Research in black child development: Abstracts 1927–79.* Westport, Conn.: Greenwood Press, 1982.

Myers, L. *Black women: Do they cope better?* Englewood Cliffs, N.J.: Prentice-Hall, 1980.

National Center for Health Statistics report. Washington, D.C., 1979.

Neal, P., & Tutko, T. *Coaching girls and women: Psychological perspectives.* Boston, Mass.: Allyn & Bacon, 1976.

Nielsen, L. *How to motivate adolescents: Guide for parents, teachers and counselors.* Englewood Cliffs, N.J.: Prentice-Hall, 1982.

Oberle, W., Stowers, K., & Falk, W. Place of residence and the role model preference of black boys and girls. *Adolescence,* 1978, *13,* 13–20.

Padila, E., et al. *Inhalant, marijuana and alcohol abuse among barrio children and adolescents.* Los Angeles: UCLA Hispanic Mental Health Center, 1977.

Pederson, P. The trial model of cross cultural counselor training. *Personnel and Guidance Journal,* 1977, *56,* 94–100.

Pepper, F. Teaching the Indian child. In R. Jones (ed.), *Mainstreaming and the minority child.* Reston, Va.: Council for Exceptional Children, 1976. Pp. 133–159.

Phillips, V. *The abilities and achievements of Orientals in North America.* Beverly Hills, Cal.: Sage, 1981.

Pinkney, A. *Black Americans.* Englewood Cliffs, N.J.: Prentice-Hall, 1975.

Population profile of the U.S.: 1982. Washington, D.C.: Bureau of the Census. Current population reports, P-23, no. 130, 1984.

Price, J. An Indian family. In C. Mindel (ed.), *Ethnic families in America.* New York: Elsevier, 1981. Pp. 245–268.

Project Excel. Chicago: Project Push, 1980.

Red Horse. Family behavior of urban American Indians. In G. Henderson (ed.), *Counseling minorities.* Springfield, Ill.: Charles Thomas, 1979. Pp. 307–318.

Review of youth employment problems, programs and problems. Washington, D.C.: Vice-Presidential Task Force, U.S. Department of Labor, 1980.

Richardson, S. Counseling American Indians. In D. Wing Sue (ed.), *Counseling the culturally different.* New York, Wiley Interscience, 1981. Pp. 216–259.

Rodriguez, C. The structure of failure. In G. Henderson (ed.), *Counseling minorities.* Springfield, Ill.: Charles Thomas, 1979. Pp. 251–268.

Roots III: Souls on ice. *Newsweek,* June 10, 1985, pp. 82–84.

Rose, F. (ed.). *The black woman.* Beverly HIlls, Cal.: Sage, 1980.

Rubovits, P., & Maehr, M. Pygmalion black and white. *Journal of Social Psychology,* 1973, *25,* 210–218.

Ruiz, A. Chicano groups catalysts, *Personnel and Guidance Journal,* 1975, *53,* 462–466.

Ruiz, R. The delivery of mental health and social change services for Chicanos. In J. Martinez (ed.), *Chicano psychology.* New York: Academic Press, 1977. Pp. 233–248.

Ruiz, R. Cultural and historical perspectives in counseling Hispanics. In D. Wing Sue, *Counseling the culturally different.* New York: Wiley Interscience, 1981. Pp. 186–216.

Seynour, M. Psychology for the Chicano. In J. Martinez (ed.), *Chicano psychology.* New York: Academic Press, 1977. Pp. 329–354.

Shannon, L., & Shannon, M. *Minority migrants in the urban community.* Beverly Hills, Cal.: Sage, 1973.

Silberman, D. *Crisis in the classroom.* New York: Random House, 1970.

Sorkin, A. *The urban American Indian.* Lexington, Mass.: Lexington Books, 1978.

Stack, C. *All our kin: Strategies for survival in a black community.* New York: Harper & Row, 1974.

Staples, R. To be young, black and oppressed. *The Black Scholar,* 1975, *7,* 2–5.

Staples, R. *Black sociology.* New York: McGraw-Hill, 1976.

Staples, R. *The black woman in America.* Chicago, Ill.: Nelson Hall, 1978.

Staples, R. *Black masculinity.* San Francisco: Black Scholars Press, 1982.

Stubbs, N., & Harrison, J. F. *Digest of education statistics 1982.* Washington, D.C.: National Center for Education Statistics, 1982. Pp. 4, 38.

The student pushout. Atlanta, Ga.: Southern Regional Council, 1978.

Super, C. Secular trends in child development and the institutionalization of professional disciplines. *Newsletter of the Society for Research in Child Development,* Spring 1982, Pp. 10–11.

Taylor, R. *Sweatshops in the sun.* Boston: Beacon Press, 1973.

Thomas, P. *Down these mean streets.* New York: Knopf, 1967.

Thornton, R. *Sociology of American Indians: A critical bibliography.* Bloomington: Indiana University, 1980.

Thornton, R. *The urbanization of American Indians: A critical bibliography.* Bloomington: Indiana University, 1982.

Three national assessments of reading: Changes in performance 1970–1980. Denver, Col.: National Assessment of Educational Progress, 1981.

Torrance, P. *Discovery and nurturance of giftedness in the culturally different.* Reston, Va.: Council for Exceptional Children, 1977.

Trejo, A. *The Chicanos.* Tucson: University of Arizona Press, 1980.

U.S. Bureau of the Census. *Statistical reports of 1980 supplement.* July 1982.

U.S. children and their families. Washington, D.C.: House Committee on Children and Families, May 1983.

Wallace, M. *Black women in the labor force.* Cambridge, Mass.: MIT Press, 1980.

Wallace, P. *Black macho and the myth of superwoman.* New York: Dial Press, 1978.

Wax, M. *Indian Americans: Unity and diversity.* Englewood Cliffs, N.J.: Prentice-Hall, 1971.

Weston, P., & Mednick, M. Race, social class and motive to avoid success in women. In M. Mednick (ed.), *Women and achievement.* New York: Wiley, 1975. Pp. 114–129.

Willie, C. *A new look at black families.* New York: General Hall, 1981.

Wing Sue, D. (ed.). *Counseling the culturally different.* New York: Wiley Interscience, 1981.

Chapter Outline

Goals and Objectives

This chapter is designed to enable you to:

- *Describe the characteristics of the average U.S. high school that distinguish it from schools of the past*
- *Describe adolescents' attitudes toward school*
- *Examine the researchers' recommendations for improving adolescents' education*
- *Describe the academic skills of adolescents from different racial and economic groups*
- *Analyze the major problems confronting adolescents in school*
- *Examine the factors that influence adolescents' academic performance*

Concepts and Terminology

Coleman report	*meritocracy*
self-fulfilling prophecies	*mainstreaming*
field dependent	*contingency contracting*
field independent	*shaping*
criterion-referenced grading	*mastery learning*
mixed ability grouping	*tracking*
baseline behavior	*extrinsic reinforcement*
intrinsic reinforcement	*minimum competency testing*

7 Adolescents and the Schools

THE CHANGING RELATIONSHIP BETWEEN SCHOOLS AND ADOLESCENTS

In contrast to earlier periods in U.S. history, secondary education today has assumed an unprecedented importance in the lives of adolescents. Indeed, among the many images associated with the word "adolescent," the role of student is foremost in the minds of most of the young and their elders. There is little argument that the activities associated with school have a tremendous impact on the lives of adolescents—an impact that reaches beyond learning specific academic skills. Moreover, the role that formal education has assumed and the character of the U.S. high school have changed dramatically over recent decades, often leaving those of us who are no longer high-school students with an outdated image of the relationship between adolescents and their schools. Adolescents spend more of their waking hours in school than in any other single environment, which lends even greater importance to an examination of the characteristics that distinguish today's secondary schools from the schools of yesteryear.

The Importance of Formal Education

To begin with, in 1900 only 11 percent of U.S. adolescents were enrolled in school. In the early decades of this century, almost all adolescents were already engaged in their adult vocational roles—males employed and females working in the home. In contrast to contemporary mores, no social or financial stigma was attached to being a "high-school dropout," since attending secondary school was a pastime reserved primarily for rich, white males. By 1914, however,

40 percent of U.S. adolescents were enrolled in school and nearly one-fourth were earning high-school diplomas (Hampel, 1984).

Of further significance to today's adolescents is that the high-school diploma has become a prerequisite for economic and social status in our society. Thus, it is not surprising that almost 95 percent of today's adolescents are enrolled in school and that nearly 75 percent earn high-school diplomas. Moreover, of the 75 percent who graduate from high school, 60 percent enroll in college. If the present emphasis on formal education continues, almost one-fourth of all Americans will eventually be earning bachelor's degrees, 7 percent master's degrees, and 1 percent doctoral degrees (Grant & Snyder, 1984).

Characteristics of Schools and Teachers

In addition to the fact that adolescence has come to imply full-time student status, the schools themselves have changed dramatically in the past few decades. In contrast to the small numbers of students enrolled in private schools in the past, almost 11 percent of the 14.3 million adolescents in grades 9 through 12 now attend private schools (Plisko, 1984). Some analysts, disturbed by this increase, attribute the trend to parents' loss of faith in public education and to whites' objections to racial integration. Although the reasons underlying the trend are debatable, the fact remains that the popularity of private education is not abating.

Moreover, today's adolescents are more likely than their counterparts in former years to be attending large schools with racially and economically diverse populations. Although almost half of all high-school populations are fewer than 600, some enroll as many as 5,000 students—an almost unheard-of phenomenon prior to the "Baby Boom" generation's reaching adolescence in the 1960s. Significantly, there is both more racial integration and a greater percentage of minority students in public high schools than at any time in the nation's history. In 1980, racial minorities comprised 27 percent of the total enrollment in public elementary and secondary schools—an increase of 6 percent over 1970 (Plisko, 1984).

In stark contrast to the past, high-school students in several states are more likely to be members of minority cultures than to be Caucasian, as Figure 7.1 illustrates. For example, 57 percent of New Mexico's public-school students are from minority cultures, as are 52 percent of Mississippi's, 75 percent of Hawaii's, and 93 percent of the District of Columbia's. Further highlighting the ethnic diversity of adolescents' schools is the fact that more than one-third of the public-school students in New Mexico are from homes in which a language other than English is spoken. In fact, the number of 5- to 14-year-olds who speak a language other than English at home grew by 27 percent between 1976 and 1982 (Plisko, 1984). As Box 7.1 illustrates through the story of Hollywood High School, most U.S. high-school students are more exposed than ever before to the cultural diversity in our society.

In addition, today's adolescents are interacting with a type of teacher very different from the "school marm" who typically headed the one-room schoolhouse at the turn of the century. Adolescents are now interacting with highly educated teachers, nearly half of whom have bachelor's degrees and another 49 percent of whom have master's degrees. Like their predecessors, however,

Figure 7.1

Minority enrollment as a percent of public elementary secondary school enrollment, by state

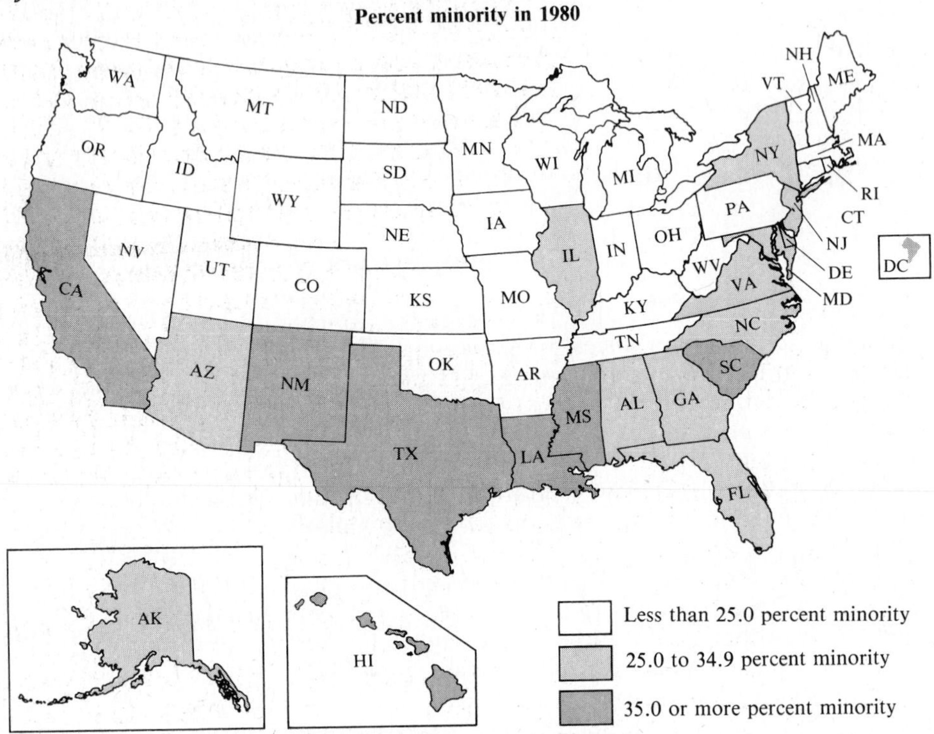

SOURCE: V. Plisko (ed.). *The condition of education.* Washington, D.C.: National Center for Education Statistics, 1984, p. 19.

today's adolescents are still taught primarily by women, since there are approximately 35 percent more female than male secondary-school teachers. Few adolescents will ever encounter a secondary-school principal who is not a white man, since only 7 percent are women and fewer than 5 percent are members of minority cultures. On the average, adolescents' teachers are 37 years old, have 13 years of teaching experience, and earn about $23,000 a year (Grant & Snyder, 1984; National Education Association, 1982).

Discrepancies in the Quality of Adolescents' Education

Although all adolescents share certain school experiences in common, such as being required to take at least one course in English, math, history, and science, the quality of their schools can differ dramatically. Among other factors, the disparities in local taxpayers' commitments to their schools prevent the quality of adolescents' education from being equitably distributed across the nation. For example, in 1982 the average state expenditure per pupil was $2,724, but the state allotments ranged from $1,800 per student in Mississippi to $4,000

A Closer Look  

Hollywood High School: A New Script

A few decades ago many children of the rich and famous attended the prestigious Hollywood High School. The school had a classical college-preparatory curriculum. Many students drove their sporty cars to campus—but this is not the Hollywood High School of 1984.

Today 70 percent of the 2,300 students are immigrants and 36 percent cannot comprehend English. Thirty-two different languages are spoken in the student body. Los Angeles has become a city to which thousands of immigrants flock in search of the comfortable life so often depicted on television shows made in Hollywood. The reality for most immigrants, however, is tenement living in crime-infested ghettos. José Garcia came to Hollywood High School knowing no English and planning to "be an electronic," but his aunt insists that he work all day loading trucks if he expects to keep living at her home. So he has missed many days of school in the past two years. He dreams of someday, on his future wages as an electrician, bringing his relatives to the United States from El Salvador.

The coach of Hollywood High School's football team looks forward to developing the athletic talents of his Asian players, but a disgruntled and disillusioned English teacher compares himself to "the Pope teaching atheists." Meanwhile the old billboard still displays the school's motto: "Achieve the Honorable." The first "o" in Honorable is missing.

Source: Adapted from "Hollywood High's New World." *Newsweek*, April 2, 1984, pp. 15–16.

in New York (Plisko, 1984). Similarly, in Forest City, Iowa, local industrialists have created the most computerized school system in the United States through their contributions of computers for classroom use. Consequently, Forest City's 1,317 students spend nearly one-third of their academic time using computers, in contrast to thousands of adolescents in less-affluent school systems who have yet to work with a computer ("Access without Success," 1984). In sum, the quality of adolescents' education can vary widely as a consequence of their taxpaying neighbors' varying amounts of good will toward public education or discrepancies in communities' financial resources.

In regard to the apparent unwillingness of many taxpayers to invest more money in adolescents' education, it is argued that too many of the most affluent Americans are enrolling their own children in private schools and voting against tax increases for the support of public education. For instance, in a 1974 national survey, two-thirds of the adults rated public schools as good or excellent, but by 1981 this approval had dropped to 47 percent (Williams, 1981a, 1981b). According to critics of this attitude, it is myopic to assume that withholding money for public education will save tax dollars. To the contrary, it has been pointed out that more tax money is invested in trying to correct the problems created by inadequate education than in trying to prevent the problems from developing through investments in better public education. For example, providing a college education to an impoverished adolescent would cost taxpayers about $20,000, while incarcerating a criminal youth for four years costs taxpayers about $50,000 (Southern Regional Council, 1973).

In the midst of recent debates surrounding school finances, adolescents' teachers are becoming increasingly frustrated. As the president of the American Federation of Teachers stated in 1981, "Teachers are getting fed up with parents who expect schools to raise their kids and who complain about teachers while they're out making more money" (Williams, 1981a, 1981b). While the controversy between educators and taxpayers continues, the crucial question affecting the development of the millions of adolescents whose parents cannot afford private schools remains: How are we to improve adolescents' education unless we are willing to invest more money in salaries and supplies for our public schools?

ADOLESCENTS' ATTITUDES TOWARD SCHOOL

How do adolescents feel about their schools? Do they dread each new school year or anticipate it as a welcome relief from summer vacation? Because students' experiences in school can be so vastly different, it is not surprising that their attitudes about the institution are also vastly different. For example, a youngster who has encountered years of academic failure, social rejection by classmates, or personal problems with teachers, will not express the same enthusiasm about school as the honor-roll student or the school's star quarterback. These differences notwithstanding, certain shared reactions to school often emerge from surveys conducted with adolescents.

The research indicates that most adolescents consider school neither an exhilarating nor an excruciating experience. Not surprisingly, these data also show that young people who make the worst grades are the most dissatisfied with their schools (Bachman, Johnston, & O'Malley, 1981; Godlad, 1983; Good & Brophy, 1984; Larkin, 1979). In contrast, however, to the assumption that most adolescents are disinterested in academic standards, a number have expressed dissatisfaction with their teachers' lax academic standards and their schools' emphasis on athletics (Carnegie Foundation, 1980; Johnston & Bachman, 1976). Moreover, high-school students often willingly admit that their own poor study habits are the primary reason for their poor grades and express a desire for more assistance from their teachers (Fetters, 1977). In general, however, it appears that adolescents' most frequent complaint about their school is that the classes are boring.

The most comprehensive recent survey of adolescents' opinions of their schools is the "High School and Beyond" project, whose data were derived from 28,000 high-school seniors and 30,000 sophomores enrolled in 1,015 public and private schools across the nation in 1980. As Table 7.1 indicates, the high-school seniors in the academic curriculum track are more satisfied with their schools and with the quality of their classroom instruction than their counterparts in the general and vocational tracks. Disappointingly, only half of the public-school

Table 7.1

Adolescents' Views of School

School Characteristic	28,000 Seniors	Curriculum: Academic	Curriculum: General	Curriculum: Vocational	Type of School: Public	Type of School: Private
	(percent of seniors giving "good" rating)					
Reputation in the community	68	77	64	64	73	90
Library facilities	67	66	67	71	68	60
Quality of academic instruction	63	75	55	60	73	85
Condition of buildings	62	69	60	60	67	76
School spirit	60	60	59	61	59	64
Teacher interest in students	56	66	48	50	62	82

SOURCE: S. Peng, W. Fetters, & A. Kolstad, *High school and beyond: A national longitudinal study for the 1980s*. Washington, D.C.: National Center for Education Statistics, 1981, p. 13.

seniors in the general or vocational track believed that their teachers were interested in them. Moreover, in 1980, 70 percent of the high-school seniors agreed that their schools should have placed more emphasis on academic subjects, in contrast to only half of the seniors surveyed in 1972 (Peng, Fetters, & Kolstad, 1981).

Adolescents' expressions of boredom and their feelings of teacher disinterest are both sad and ironic, given that high-school teachers consistently cite demoralization over students' apathy as one of their primary reasons for having left or wanting to leave the profession (Boyer, 1983; Godlad, 1983; Lorton, 1979). Affirming the teachers' perspective, the dean of Harvard's School of Education, Thomas Sizer, concludes that today's high-school students are disappointingly docile, unrebellious, and apathetic. In that Sizer and his colleagues derived their data from on-site observations in several hundred high schools in 15 states over a five-year period, their judgment is particularly noteworthy and unsettling (Sizer, 1984).

Aware of adolescents' complaints and apathy, teachers continue to urge taxpayers and policy makers to provide the financial support to enable high schools to better meet adolescents' needs (Boyer, 1983; Sizer, 1984). Teachers are asking taxpayers how schools can be expected to provide a relevant, stimulating, or individualized education to adolescents, given the number of students in each class, the lack of modern equipment, the outdated texts, and the low salaries that encourage the most talented teachers to leave the profession in order to support their families. Furthermore, while adolescents complain of being bored, many creative teachers complain of being constrained by conservative school boards and principals, who deprive them of the power to use in their classes the innovative methods that they know will motivate their apathetic students.

7.2 A Closer Look

Recommendations for Improving Adolescents' Education

Which of the following recommendations from the national surveys and commissions for improving secondary education do you endorse? Why? Which have your community's schools adopted and for what reasons are they unwilling or unable to adopt the other recommendations? How do these recommendations compare with the suggestions in Box 6.2 for improving the education of Hispanic adolescents?

Factors Influencing Teachers

1. Give teachers more money, public recognition, and promotions as rewards for excellent teaching.
2. Raise the college requirements for students who want to become teachers and require higher scores on tests for teacher competencies.
3. Give teachers more control over which books they use in class.

School Policies

4. Involve the business community in public education by having businesses provide money for school equipment, teacher retraining, cash rewards for excellent teaching, and vocational training for students.
5. Promote students to the next grade only if they pass competency tests, not on the basis of their age.
6. Establish more programs for gifted students, such as special schools supported by state taxes.

Unfortunately, adolescents may already be suffering the consequences of their teachers' dissatisfaction with the profession. Since 1965 the number of teachers with more than 20 years of experience has dropped by almost half. College students are less likely now than at any time in the past 30 years to choose the teaching profession, and 40 percent of those now teaching plan to quit before retirement (*Time*, 1980). Burnout after three or four years has become a common occupational hazard.

In summary, the data indicate that two of the most prominent problems confronting adolescents at school are their own boredom and their teachers' frustrations with being unable, either financially or politically, to use methods that would motivate more students. Although very few adolescents express serious complaints about their schools, the majority appear bored and apathetic. Not suprisingly, students in lower-income, neighborhood schools are less satisfied with their educational experiences than those in middle-class suburban or private schools. As Box 7.2 illustrates, a number of recommendations have been made by national commissions for enhancing students' motivation.

7. Require more math, foreign-language, science, and computer courses.
8. Establish more alternative schools and remedial programs for adolescents, including courses on college campuses for gifted and for students needing remedial help.
9. Avoid segregating students in tracks that separate them on the basis of academic abilities.
10. Lengthen the school year and teach reading and mathematics at an earlier age.
11. Provide more vocational education and award students academic credit for community service.
12. Assign teachers fewer classes, fewer nonacademic duties—like monitoring the hallways—fewer students per class, and more time during the day to prepare their lessons and tutor students.

Classroom Instructional Strategies

13. Use more computers and television in classroom instruction.
14. Require more homework and design more difficult textbooks.
15. Rely more on cooperation, student participation, and discussion in the classroom, rather than on competition, lecturing, silence, conformity, written exercises, and mere regurgitation of facts.

SOURCES: E. Boyer, *High school.* New York: Harper & Row, 1983; J. Godlad, *A place called school.* New York: McGraw-Hill, 1983; National Task Force on Excellence in Education, *A nation at risk.* Washington, D.C.: U.S. Government Printing Office, 1983; Task Force on Education for Economic Growth, *Action for excellence.* Washington, D.C.: Education Commission for the States, June 1983.

ADOLESCENTS' PROBLEMS AT SCHOOL

Decline in Academic Achievement

In examining the relationship between adolescents and their schools, researchers have directed considerable attention to the apparent decline in adolescents' academic achievement in recent years. The concern generated by this academic decline warrants our care and examination.

Cross-Cultural Data One way of assessing adolescents' academic skills has been through cross-cultural comparisons with other industrialized countries. Using this method, one of the most impressive studies conducted between 1973 and 1977 compared adolescents' achievement scores from 12 industrialized nations. According to this survey, U.S. high-school students scored in the lowest third on reading, mathematics, and civic education. Critics of the report have argued, however, that the conclusions were confounded by the fact that the least

What was your most embarrassing and your most profitable experience in high school?

capable students were more likely to have dropped out of school in the foreign countries than in the United States, thereby making the samples on which the conclusions were based unequivalent. For example, in Sweden only 45 percent of students remain in school through the twelfth grade, in comparison with 75 percent in the United States. With this consideration in mind, the data were reanalyzed, using only the top 9 percent of the students from each country. This analysis showed that the best U.S. adolescents scored as well as the best students from other industrialized countries like France, Germany, England, and Sweden (Husen, 1979).

SAT Scores Another method of assessing contemporary adolescents' academic skills has been to compare their scores on college entrance examinations with students' scores from previous years. Unfortunately, such comparisons have generated considerable distress and controversy in recent years. Between 1960 and 1980 the average scores on the Scholastic Aptitude Test (SAT) declined from 477 to 424 on mathematical skills and from 498 to 466 on verbal skills (College Entrance Exam Board, 1981). The concern aroused by these declines is predicated on the assumption that lower SAT scores reflect a deterioration in the academic skills or the motivation of U.S. youth. Yet, before adopting this discouraging assumption about today's young people, several considerations and caveats demand our careful attention.

To begin with, analysts have rightly pointed out that comparisons of SAT scores from the 1960s, 1970s, and 1980s are derived from groups of students that differ significantly from one another (Wertz et al., 1977). These differences in the samples present an important confounding variable for those who contend, on the basis of declining SAT scores, that today's young people are less motivated or less academically skilled than their predecessors. First, more minority and lower-income students are taking the SAT than in previous decades. In 1984, for example, 20 percent of those taking the SAT identified themselves as minorities, which was the highest percentage of minority participants to date (Ranbom, 1984). This greater diversity in the ethnic and economic backgrounds of students taking the SAT might account for the declining scores, since it has been noted in several studies that the tests are biased toward white, upper-income students (Owen, 1984; Rincon, 1981).

The fact that larger numbers of high-school seniors are taking the SAT than in former years appears to be correlated with a decline in scores. This assumption is supported by comparisons on average SAT scores in 1984, which showed that the higher the percentage of seniors taking the test, the lower the average score for the state. For example, only 3 percent of Iowa's high-school seniors took the SAT in 1984, earning the highest average score of students from any state—1,089 points. In contrast, 49 percent of South Carolina's high-school graduates took the SAT and earned the lowest average score for all states—803 points (Ranbom, 1984). Such statistics underscore the point that lower SAT scores do not necessarily mean that today's adolescents are any less educated or less motivated than their predecessors, but that there is greater diversity in the large numbers of high-school seniors now taking SATs in comparison to the smaller, more homogeneous group of test takers in the 1960s and 1970s.

Other analysts maintain that adolescents are just as motivated and as intellectually capable as ever, but that secondary schools have negated students' academic skills through grade inflation, low academic standards, and less emphasis on academic courses (National Science Foundation, 1980). It has also been suggested that the increase in adolescents' television viewing and the decrease in their reading and homework have contributed to the lower SAT scores. As Table 7.2's data from a 1980 national survey illustrate, the time that many adolescents devote to reading and doing homework is quite disappointing (Grant & Snyder, 1984). More disappointing still, as Figure 7.2 illustrates, the most extensive national surveys show that adolescents were investing less time in doing their homework in 1980 than their counterparts in 1972. Although female and Asian American students spend more time on their homework than other adolescents, only 35 percent of high-school seniors in 1980 spent more than five hours per week on homework (Peng, Fetters, & Kolstad, 1981).

On a more optimistic note, however, a slight increase in SAT scores occurred between 1983 and 1984 (Ranbom, 1984). The average mathematics score increased to 471 out of a possible 800, the highest level since 1975; and the verbal scores increased to 426, which was two points higher than the 1979 all-time low. The 1984 SAT scores represented the largest increase since 1962, at which time the average score was 83 points higher than the average score of college-bound seniors in 1984.

Table 7.2

How Students Invest Their Time (Percent of Students Surveyed)

Hours Spent Daily	*Age 13*	*Age 17*
Homework		
None	36.5	43.7
Less than 1	32.6	23.8
1–2	23.5	22.3
2 or more	7.2	9.3
Reading		
None	42.5	43.6
Less than 1	29.8	32.3
1–2	20.6	19.5
2 or more	5.8	4.2
Television		
None or some	22.8	38.8
1–2	28.2	30.4
3 or more	47.9	30.3

SOURCE: National Assessment of Educational Progress, *Reading, thinking and writing: Results from the 1979–80 national assessment of reading and literature.* Princeton, N.J.: Educational Testing Service, 1981.

In accounting for this slight improvement in scores, it has been noted that students who took the 1984 SAT reported taking more academic courses than their predecessors in all areas except biological sciences (Ranbom, 1984). The largest enrollment increases occurred in high-school mathematics and physical science courses. This finding suggests that educators and parents are partially responsible for the trends in adolescents' SAT scores, since these adults have the ultimate power to dictate a student's high-school curriculum. In addition, several researchers have found correlations between national SAT scores and the average size of the family—the more siblings in a family, the lower the SAT scores (refer to Box 8.7 in Chapter 8). Thus, since today's adolescents have fewer siblings than their cohorts in the 1960s and 1970s, these researchers contend that the recent increases in SAT scores are understandable (Zajonc, 1986).

National Surveys In addition to SAT scores and cross-cultural comparisons, adolescents' academic abilities and progress can be assessed through yearly comparisons of national achievement scores. As Tables 7.3 and 7.4 indicate, these national surveys have yielded some disappointing results. In 1978 and 1982 the National Assessment of Educational Progress (NAEP) conducted mathematics assessments of 9-, 13-, and 17-year-old students. Unfortunately, of the three age groups, only the 13-year-olds improved significantly in overall mathematics performance. Fortunately, however, the 13-year-olds' gains were made across all racial groups, community types, and achievement quartiles, and in both predominantly white and predominantly minority schools. Although minority and urban adolescents are still below the national norms in math achieve-

Figure 7.2

Percentage of 1980 high-school seniors reporting varying amounts of time spent on homework per week, for 1972 and 1980

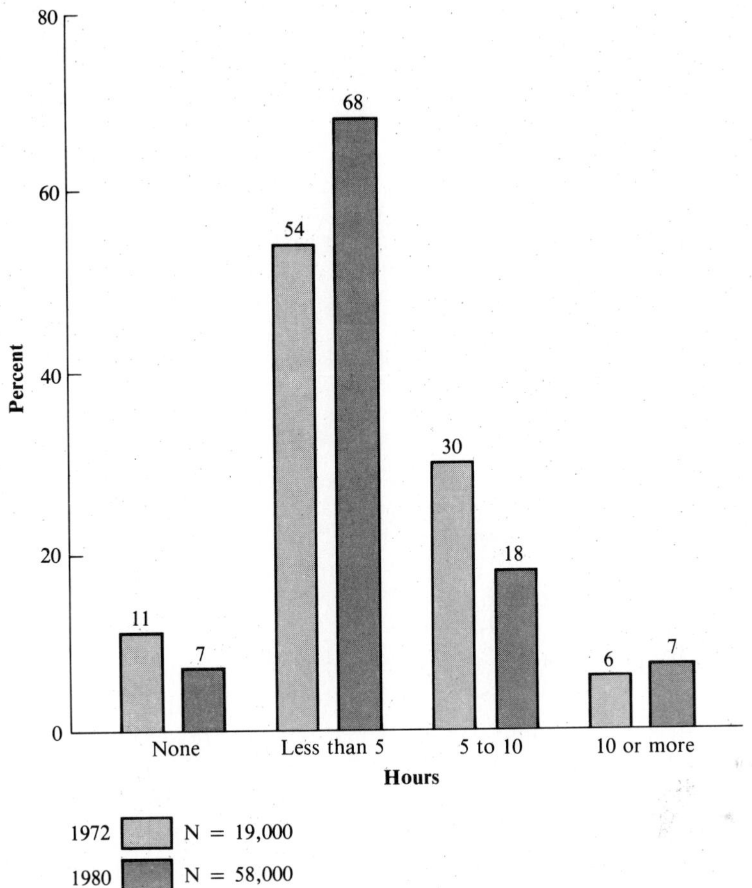

SOURCE: S. Peng, W. Fetters, & A. Kolstad (eds.), *High school and beyond: A national longitudinal study for the 1980s.* Washington, D.C.: National Center for Education Statistics, 1981, p. 7.

ment, the greatest improvements were noted among 13-year-old blacks, Hispanics, low achievers, and students in heavily minority schools in urban areas (NAEP, 1983).

Adolescents' progress in science has been measured by both the NAEP and the Science Assessment and Research Project (SARP). According to these data, across all age groups, only 9-year-olds made any significant gains between 1977 and 1982 in the areas of science, technology, and society. Among these 9-year-olds, white boys registered the greatest gains. Unfortunately, during this five-year period, the science scores of 17-year-olds declined among both males and females, both blacks and whites. In contrast, the science scores of 13-year-olds remained unchanged (NAEP, 1978; SARP, 1983).

Regrettably, adolescents' skills in reading and language seem to be diminishing. According to NAEP surveys, adolescents' abilities in literal comprehen-

Table 7.3

National Assessment of Educational Progress for Age 17, by Subject and by Selected Characteristics of Participants: United States, 1975–1982

Selected Characteristics of Participants	*Reading/ Literature Comprehension*	*Music*	*Art*	*Citizenship*	*Social Studies*	*Science*	*Mathematics*
National mean p[1]	79.1	50.0	50.6	67.4	67.6	53.5	60.2
Mean delta p[1] (difference from national means):							
Region							
Northeast	0.2	−0.2	0.9	0.8	0.9	2.2	2.6
Southeast	−2.0	−1.9	−2.0	−2.2	−2.4	−4.1	−3.5
Central	0.5	0.9	0.2	0.9	0.9	1.2	1.9
West	1.1	0.9	1.0	0.1	0.2	−0.8	−1.8
Sex							
Male	−1.4	−1.8	−1.3	0.0	0.2	2.6	1.4
Female	1.4	1.7	1.2	0.0	−0.2	−2.5	−1.3
Race							
Black	−16.6	−6.6	−4.6	−8.6	−9.4	−15.7	−15.2
White	2.9	1.2	0.8	1.6	1.6	2.6	2.9
Hispanic	−8.0	−6.2	−3.4	−8.2	−8.3	−10.8	−10.8
Parental education							
Not high-school graduate	−8.6	−5.6	−4.6	−6.4	−6.6	−8.0	−9.9
Graduated high school	−2.2	−2.1	−2.4	−1.5	−1.5	−1.8	−2.0
Post high school	3.4	3.4	3.1	4.6	4.6	5.1	2.9
Size and type of community							
Low metropolitan	−10.4	−4.9	−2.3	−5.8	−6.1	−12.3	−12.5
Extreme rural	−0.7	−2.4	−5.0	−0.1	−0.3	0.0	−3.2
Small place	0.5	0.1	−1.0	0.2	0.2	0.5	−1.0
Medium city	0.7	0.2	0.6	−0.2	−0.2	1.7	1.8
Main big city	−3.3	−0.6	0.2	−1.2	−1.2	−5.8	−2.8
Urban fringe	1.1	0.1	1.4	0.8	0.8	2.8	2.1
High metropolitan	5.9	3.2	3.6	4.2	4.2	4.4	9.5

[1]Data are for the following years: 1975–76—Citizenship, social studies; 1976–77—Science; 1978–79—Music, art; 1979–80—Reading/literature comprehension; 1981–82—Mathematics.

SOURCE: V. Grant & T. Snyder (eds.), *Digest of education statistics: 1983–84.* Washington, D.C.: National Center for Education Statistics, 1984, p. 19.

Table 7.4

National Assessment of Educational Progress for Age 13, by Subject and by Selected Characteristics of Participants: United States, 1975–1982

Selected Characteristics of Participants	*Reading/ Literature Comprehension*	*Music*	*Art*	*Citizenship*	*Social Studies*	*Science*	*Mathematics*
National mean p[1]	74.0	52.3	47.0	63.2	62.9	49.1	60.5
Mean delta p[1] (difference from national means):							
Region:							
Northeast	1.4	−0.2	1.5	1.8	1.7	2.1	3.9
Southeast	−2.7	−1.3	−1.2	−2.0	−2.2	−3.0	−4.3
Central	2.3	1.3	−0.4	1.2	1.5	1.6	1.4
West	−0.9	0.3	0.1	−1.3	−1.3	−1.5	−1.5
Sex							
Male	−2.1	−1.2	−0.9	−0.1	0.0	1.8	−0.1
Female	2.0	1.2	0.9	0.1	0.0	−1.7	0.1
Race							
Black	−14.3	−6.0	−3.5	−7.6	−8.2	−11.7	−12.3
White	3.3	1.3	0.7	1.4	1.6	2.9	2.6
Hispanic	−11.4	−5.9	−0.8	−7.6	−7.9	−10.3	−8.6
Parental education							
Not high-school graduate	−10.5	−4.2	−2.5	−5.9	−6.1	−6.9	−8.1
Graduated high school	−0.9	−0.4	−1.0	−1.0	−0.9	−0.9	−1.7
Post high school	4.5	3.0	3.0	5.1	5.1	5.7	3.2
Size and type of community							
Low metropolitan	−9.8	−5.6	−1.9	−5.5	−6.1	−11.1	−11.2
Extreme rural	−3.9	−2.2	−0.7	−0.7	−0.8	−0.2	−4.2
Small place	0.1	0.0	0.1	−0.4	−0.3	0.0	−1.7
Medium city	−0.4	−0.8	−0.2	−0.8	−0.8	0.6	2.5
Main big city	−3.7	−0.9	−0.1	−1.0	−1.5	−2.2	−3.1
Urban fringe	2.0	1.3	−0.6	2.9	3.0	1.9	3.9
High metropolitan	8.5	3.3	1.7	6.6	6.6	6.3	10.2

[1]Data are for the following years: 1975–76—Citizenship, social studies; 1976–77—Science; 1978–79—Music, art; 1979–80—Reading/ literature comprehension; 1981–82—Mathematics.

SOURCE: V. Grant & T. Snyder (eds.), *Digest of education statistics 1983–84*. Washington, D.C.: National Center for Education Statistics, 1984, p. 18.

7.3 A Closer Look

Adolescents Sue School Systems for Educational Malpractice

Edward Donahue graduated from a Long Island high school in a blue-collar neighborhood of New York, after failing 7 of his 23 courses. Edward read at the lower elementary-school level when he graduated. His parents sued the school system because they felt that their son had not been properly educated. At about the same time Daniel Hoffman's parents also sued. Daniel had been assigned to classes for the mentally retarded soon after he began kindergarten and remained there throughout his education. When he was 18, the school system's error was discovered: Daniel was not retarded. The lower courts awarded the parents of Daniel Hoffman $750,000. But in 1979 New York State's appeals court rejected both suits on the grounds that courts cannot judge the validity of educational policies.

SOURCE: G. Maeroff, *Don't blame the kids.* New York: McGraw-Hill, 1982, pp. 63–64.

sion, spelling, and punctuation remained virtually unchanged between 1970 and 1980. The quality and coherence of adolescents' writing had declined, however, as had their comprehension of written materials in which they were asked to infer the meanings of the passages. Even the most talented 17-year-olds in 1980 were reading more poorly than their counterparts in 1970. On a more optimistic note, the reading skills of blacks, males, and students from the southeastern states improved from 1970 to 1980, although their scores were still below those of female adolescents and wealthy white students (NAEP, 1981). For example, some recent surveys show that 20 percent of black male adolescents are unable to read at the fourth-grade level (Gibbs, 1984).

In response to these national statistics on adolescents' declining academic performance, a number of states have instituted the policy of *minimum competency* testing. Passing the minimum competency test has become a prerequisite for a diploma in about one-fifth of the nation's high schools. The requirement varies significantly by geographic region. For example, in 1981, 37 percent of the high schools in the Northeast, but only 3 percent of the schools in North Carolina, required the tests for a high-school diploma (Peng, Fetters, & Kolstad, 1981). The hesitancy of many states to adopt the policy of competency testing, however, has not prevented some adolescents' parents from suing their local school systems for educational "malpractice" in cases where high-school graduates have been found to be illiterate (Maeroff, 1982). (See Box 7.3.)

Vandalism, Violence, and Misbehavior

Are today's adolescents pillaging and plundering their way through our nations' schools? Are youngsters less well-behaved than their parents were as students? How much should high-school teachers fear their students? Why do some schools have so much more vandalism than others?

Extent of the Problem Questions like these reflect the growing concern over crime and misbehavior in secondary schools during the past decade. During the late 1970s, several highly publicized national surveys directed the public's attention to adolescents' misbehavior in the schools (National School Board Association, 1977). Among the most publicized was the congressional "Safe School Study" of 1977 (National Institute of Education, 1977). According to this congressional survey of 4,000 schools, about 10 percent of them had problems with trespassing, breaking and entering, and theft. Another 4 percent reported problems with arsonists, and nearly a third reported losses from vandalism. Corroborating these findings, others who have reviewed statistics from the 1970s estimate that adolescents inflict about $200 million worth of damage on their schools each year and that 8 percent of all schools have a "serious problem" with crime (Casserly, Bass, & Garrett, 1980).

These data gathered during the 1970s have resulted in a clearer understanding of adolescents' misconduct in school. It now appears that adolescents who are at greatest risk of being robbed or attacked at school are junior-high-school students, since misconduct tends to diminish as adolescents age. Moreover, schools in the Northeast and those in large urban areas throughout the country are the most likely to be vandalized. Surprisingly, although the rates of breaking and entering, trespassing, and theft are highest in large urban schools, the rates of property destruction are greatest in small cities and in the suburbs. More significantly, youths who are part of their school's minority population, regardless of their race, are more likely to become involved in fights than those who are part of the school's majority racial group (Casserly, Bass, & Garrett, 1980; McPartland, 1977; National Institute of Education, 1977).

Despite the publicity surrounding the topics of students' misconduct and school violence and vandalism, most data fail to support the notion that secondary schools are dangerous, lawless environments. First, it is noteworthy that adolescents, administrators, and teachers in many surveys have agreed that fights, theft, and vandalism are only minor problems in their school, compared to tardiness, truancy, apathy, discourtesy, or drug abuse (Boyer, 1983; Duke, 1978). Second, although the rates of violence and vandalism did rise during the early 1970s, neither appears to have increased since 1975 (Casserly, Bass, & Garrett, 1980; McPartland, 1977; National Institute of Education, 1978). Third, recent research has helped educators and counselors become more astute at designing programs that prevent violence and vandalism from occurring (Nielsen, 1982). Finally, an accurate view of adolescents' school conduct has too often been obscured by the respondents' confusion over the researchers' terms. For example, in the absence of operational definitions, "misconduct" or "disrespect" can range from cutting class and being tardy to physical fighting and cursing teachers.

Factors Affecting Adolescents' Misconduct The most comprehensive investigation of students' misconduct to date, the "High School and Beyond" (HS & B) project, is involving a nationally representative sample of 58,000 sophomores and seniors from 1,015 private and public high schools. Data will be collected every two years throughout the 1980s as part of this ongoing longitudinal study. In addition to its impressive sample size, the HS & B study has operationally defined "misconduct" as specific types of behavior, such as tardiness, truancy,

Table 7.5

Percentage Distribution of 988 Schools According to School Administrators' Reports of the Seriousness of School Problems: Spring 1980

	Seriousness of School Problems			
School Problem	*Serious*	*Moderate*	*Minor*	*Not at All*
Absenteeism	8.1	39.7	43.5	8.7
Student use of drugs or alcohol	5.6	36.5	50.5	7.4
Class cutting	4.7	25.6	51.6	18.1
Vandalism of school property	2.4	19.6	68.5	9.5
Robbery or theft	1.7	16.1	69.1	13.1
Verbal abuse of teachers	0.1	8.3	62.8	28.8
Physical conflicts among students	0.1	5.8	62.6	31.5
Conflicts between students and teachers	0.0	5.2	69.5	25.3
Student possession of weapons	0.0	0.5	21.1	78.4
Rape or attempted rape	0.0	0.2	3.9	95.9

SOURCE: T. DiPrete, *Discipline and order in American high schools.* Washington, D.C.: National Center for Education Statistics, 1981.

refusal to do homework, cutting class, robbery, vandalism, and disobedience to teachers' instructions (DiPrete, 1981).

The HS & B data collected thus far corroborate many of the findings from studies conducted during the 1970s. In accord with earlier findings, the 1980 data show that male students are more likely than females to vandalize their schools, to fight with other students, and to refuse to do their homework. Males are no more likely than females, however, to cut class, to be tardy, or to be truant. Most important, the principals and students agreed that the most serious forms of misbehavior in their schools are absenteeism, class cutting, and use of drugs or alcohol. As Table 7.5 shows, serious misconduct such as vandalism, theft, and physical conflict are not as widespread as might commonly be presumed.

In further agreement with the major studies from the 1970s, the HS & B study has failed to find any significant relationship between an adolescent's socioeconomic class and his or her misconduct in school. Some data did suggest, however, that students from middle-income families had slightly lower rates of misbehavior than students from extremely low- or from extremely high-income families. For example, sophomores who came from families with incomes below $7,000 had the highest rates of absenteeism, class cutting, and tardiness, and sophomores from families with incomes above $38,000 had the highest rates of tardiness. Thus, it appears that if there is any association whatsoever between family income and adolescents' school misconduct, the relationship may be curvilinear.

A tentative hypothesis offered by the researchers for this puzzling finding is that high-income parents are less intimidated by the authority of the school and that they pass this attitude on to their children. In contrast, working-class parents, whose own high-school grades and experiences may have left them with a certain awe or fear of school and of authorities, might convey to their offspring a more respectful, obedient attitude. If working-class parents deem academic success important, though somewhat mysterious and difficult, they might be more insistent about their children's obeying school rules. Further, working-class parents might perceive small violations, such as tardiness, as more serious than upper-income parents (DiPrete, 1981).

Given the extensive sampling in the HS & B study, several other findings from this investigation are worthy of careful attention. Consistent with the research on delinquency which will be discussed in Chapter 14, the data show that high-school sophomores are more likely than seniors to be in serious trouble with the police, to refuse to do their homework, and to vandalize their schools. Seniors, however, are more likely than sophomores to cut class, to be truant, and to be tardy. Not surprisingly, adolescents who have both parents present in the home and whose parents monitor their schoolwork and their whereabouts are better behaved at school than those whose parents are uninvolved in their academic or social conduct. In fact, the level of parents' involvement is a more powerful predictor of an adolescent's misbehavior than the family's socioeconomic position. In contradiction, however, to the popular notion that large schools somehow encourage more lawless, aggressive behavior than small schools, a school's size was unrelated to students' misconduct.

In regard to race, the HS & B data show that Hispanic males and females are more likely than members of other ethnic groups to cut class, to refuse to do homework, and to be in serious trouble with the police. Conversely, black seniors had the lowest rates of absenteeism, cutting class, legal trouble, and not doing homework. Furthermore, a school's racial composition was not found to have any appreciable effect on students' misbehavior. Since minority enrollments are usually highest in urban schools, it is also important to note that the differences in misbehavior between suburban, rural, and urban schools were found to be statistically insignificant when other variables, such as students' grades, were considered.

Perhaps the single most consistent finding from the High School and Beyond project and from previous research is that poor grades are strongly associated with vandalism, classroom misconduct, and truancy. Indeed, the earliest harbingers of future vandalism, and misconduct in school are a child's truancy and poor grades during elementary school. In brief, students who are making poor grades are the most likely to vandalize their schools and to behave aggressively and disrespectfully toward their teachers and classmates (Casserley, Bass, & Garrett, 1980; DiPrete, 1981; McPartland, 1977; National Institute of Education, 1977).

This relationship between poor grades and misconduct is further corroborated by the data cited in Chapter 14, which show high correlations between academic failure and juvenile delinquency (Gold & Petronio, 1980). An important caveat, however, is that these correlational studies do not permit us to conclude that academic failure "causes" adolescents to become vandals or delinquents. Although poor grades and misconduct are highly correlated, causality cannot be determined on the basis of correlational data. Given this limitation of correlational research, the relationship between delinquency and poor grades will be discussed more thoroughly in Chapter 14.

Although adolescents' poor grades are highly correlated with their vandalism rates, so, too, are their school's disciplinary policies and teachers' behavior. According to several reviews of the literature, schools with the lowest rates of vandalism and misconduct endorse several common philosophies and practices (Casserly, Bass, & Garrett, 1980; McPartland, 1977; National Institute of Education, 1978). First, these schools allow students to participate in making the rules and in designating punishments according to their own conceptions of fairness. The data suggest that adolescents who participate in designing the school's policies are more willing to obey the rules than students who have rules imposed on them by the school's staff, even when the students' self-made rules are stricter than those of the staff. Second, at the outset of the year these schools publicize the rules and penalties for violations, thereby reassuring students that nobody has to fear a "subjective" system of justice based on a particular teacher's or principal's momentary whims. Third, the rules are consistently enforced without resorting to dictatorial behavior. Fourth, lowering a student's grades is not used as a punishment for misbehavior. And fifth, instead of resorting to threats and punishment, the least-vandalized schools provide many kinds of opportunities through which students can earn praise from adults.

Evidence also suggests that vandalism and misconduct in the classroom are exacerbated by the fact that adolescents and school personnel often perceive the causes of misbehavior differently. Many teachers blame students' misbehavior and vandalism on sources beyond the school's control, such as the adolescent's family or emotional problems within the youngster (Lorton, 1979; McPartland, 1977; Medway, 1979). In contrast, high-school students themselves often blame misbehavior and vandalism on poor communication with teachers, boring classes, unfair rules, and the school's authoritarian methods of policy making (Medway, 1979). For instance, in one survey of 8,500 junior- and senior-high-school students, 91 percent of the youngsters felt that teachers' ways of dealing with classroom conflicts failed to resolve the problem or lower the tension level (Johnson, 1978).

Although the "Students' Bill of Rights," in Box 7.4, written by high-school students, lampoons school rules, it is also a serious representation of many adolescents' dissatisfaction with their school's policies. Researchers at the Center for Early Adolescent Development at the University of North Carolina contend that too many schools stereotype young adolescents as unruly and unreasonable. As a consequence, junior high schools typically impose more-authoritarian, less-democratic discipline than elementary or senior high schools (Lipsitz, 1977; 1983). Interestingly, among the 30,000 sophomores surveyed in the HS & B study, students from higher-income families were more likely than those from lower-income families to feel that discipline and policies in their schools were unfair and ineffective. Furthermore, the sophomores' feelings about unfair discipline were strongly related to their schools' policies on leaving campus for lunch. This finding suggests that school policies that appear relatively insignificant from an adult's viewpoint, such as where students are permitted to eat lunch, can create a general feeling of unfairness and ill-will among the students. It might be noted, in this regard, that 40 percent of the 1,014 high schools in the HS & B study refused to let students leave campus during lunch (DiPrete, 1981).

Adolescent Voices 7.4

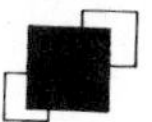

The Student Bill of Rights

Although teachers drew up the Constitution for their pupils, students found certain inalienable rights that are not guaranteed in the original document. To protect these rights, students have developed the Student Bill of Rights.

Amendment I. Students shall have the right to escape cruel and unusual punishment, such as pop quizzes and oral reports.

Amendment II. Students shall have the right to sleep during study hall.

Amendment III. Students shall have the right to miss important tests or term paper deadlines by "becoming ill" unexpectedly (five times per semester) or by "attending funerals" of relatives (three times per semester).

Amendment IV. Students shall have the right to seek refuge in the nurse's office to avoid going to gym class when they have forgotten their gym suits.

Amendment V. Students shall have the right to intercept report cards in the mail, thus sparing their parents the risk of cardiac arrest and themselves the risk of losing car privileges.

Amendment VI. Students shall have the right to PDA (public display of affection) in the hallways providing they do not block doorways, stairs, or other passageways.

Amendment VII. Students shall have the right to refuse search and seizure by hall monitors and to refuse to carry "petty passes" when going to the washrooms.

Amendment VIII. Students shall have the right to edible and inexpensive food in the cafeteria.

Amendment IX. Students shall have the right to towels after showering in gym class; these towels must meet size specifications bigger than 3″ × 5″.

Amendment X. Students shall have the right to procrastinate daily, provided they do one thing on time—graduate.

SOURCE: Glenbard East "Echo," *Teenagers themselves.* New York: Adama Books, 1984, p. 66.

Truancy

Although truancy may at first appear to be a rather innocuous habit, school absenteeism more than doubled in some urban areas during the 1970s, and 7 percent of all 12- to 15-year-olds are absent without excuse—a figure totaling nearly one-half million students (Sommer, 1985). More important, chronic absenteeism can undermine the academic progress of young people with the fewest academic skills. Not surprisingly, truancy is often correlated with delinquency, academic failure, and drug abuse (Hersov & Berg, 1980; Sommer, 1985). It is worth noting, however, that absenteeism appears questionable insofar as its connection with dropping out of school is concerned. This point is underscored in a study of 1,000 high-school students, in which truants who graduated from high school were not significantly different from nontruant high-school graduates in regard to employment, health, and arrest records during early adulthood (Kandel, Raveis, & Kandel, 1984).

With the concern over the rising truancy rates, considerable attention has been devoted to discovering the underlying causes of truancy (Hersov & Berg, 1980; Kahn, Nursten, & Carroll, 1981; Sommer, 1985). According to some speculations, truancy is related to variables in the adolescent's family. For example, it has been hypothesized that some truants have overly protective mothers who oppose their child's independence. Consequently, in an effort to escape this maternal overprotectiveness, the adolescent tries to establish his or her independence by defying the school's attendance laws. Others support the view that truancy is a manifestation of anger and depression arising from poor relationships between children and their parents. In this context, truancy has also been attributed to such variables as parents' unemployment, alcoholism, and divorce. The relationship between socioeconomic class and truancy, however, has not generally been upheld by the correlational data.

It has also been maintained that truancy is caused by school-related factors. For example, some truants appear to have a fear of attending school, based upon unpleasant experiences with peers or teachers. From this perspective, adolescents who have experienced academic failure or those who have alienated their

7.5 A Closer Look

Reducing School Violence, Vandalism, and Academic Failure

Each of the following techniques has succeeded in improving adolescents' conduct or academic performance in schools. Which of these strategies are being used in your community's school system? Why do you believe these methods would or would not be successful in your hometown community?

Schedule Changes. Discipline problems are recorded to determine how often and when they occur. Class periods are then rotated so that the same course does not always occupy the least or most desirable time of the day.

Teacher Release Time. Teachers who are the least effective in motivating and managing their classes are released from teaching for a day or two. They are assigned to accompany some of their most disruptive students throughout the day so they can see school from the student's viewpoint.

Smoking Clinic. Students who would otherwise be suspended from school for violating nonsmoking policies are assigned to evening seminars. A parent must accompany the student to each seminar. During these classes health professionals present the hazards of smoking and methods for quitting. One school district reduced its suspensions from 45 percent to 13 percent after four years with this method.

Students' Handbooks. A handbook stating the school's policies is given to all students. This must be signed by the parents at the beginning of the school year to insure that they, too, know the rules and the penalties for infractions. The book is written at a fifth-grade level so that all parents and students can comprehend it.

School Survival Training. Disruptive students learn to use behavior modification for relating more effectively to their teachers. Students learn to record their behavior and to reinforce teachers with smiles, eye contact, verbal praise, and attentive posture.

Photography Project. Several dozen of the most disruptive, unmotivated students are photographed when they are "caught" studying or behaving appropriately. These teachers or peers are the most likely to become truant. Moreover, the most successful students may avoid school in reaction to a fear of disappointing their parents by a future failure to maintain their high grades. Unfortunately, the scarcity of empirical data has resulted in much speculation regarding the etiology of truancy.

Fortunately, problems such as truancy can often be controlled through relatively inexpensive methods, as Box 7.5 illustrates. An especially noteworthy method, **contingency contracting** has frequently succeeded in improving adolescents' behavior (Nielsen, 1982). As Box 7.6 shows, contingency contracts have the added attraction of being inexpensive and relatively simple to design and to institute. Even in communities with soaring crime rates, schools have reduced violence and vandalism by using such methods as contingency contracting, academic tutoring, peer counselors, classes for students in criminal law, student-made films about vandalism, and walls for students' murals, where graf-

photos are enlarged to poster size and hung in the main corridors. Contrary to teachers' expectations, the students did not destroy the posters. In fact, 75 percent of the photographed misfits improved their conduct in school. Apparently they received peer approval and self-satisfaction from "being caught being good."

Community Cards and Stroke Notes. The school gives students business cards that read: "You have just been served by ______, a student at Jefferson High School." A student who performs a service for a fellow citizen leaves a card. Many principals receive complimentary phone calls and letters from citizens, which they share with the students. "Stroke notes" follow this same principle. When teachers or principals observe good conduct in school, they send a flattering note home to the adolescent's parents.

Telephone Services. The teacher tape-records a two-minute telephone message each day that gives the homework assignment and summarizes the day's class activities. The recording also provides daily attendance figures and information about special school events. As a result of this project, many students' homework and grades improved.

Money in Escrow. The school system creates a special fund for students at the beginning of the school year. Whatever money is left at the end of the year, after paying to repair the damage created by vandals, is returned to that school's government. The students then use the money for entertainment or other items they want to buy for their own pleasure at school. Using this method, Oakland, California reduced its 1977 vandalism bill from $433,205 to $133,306 in 1978.

SOURCES: L. Nielsen, *How to motivate adolescents: Guide for parents, teachers, and counselors.* Englewood Cliffs, N.J.: Prentice-Hall, 1982; M. Casserly, S. Bass, & J. Garrett, *School vandalism.* Lexington, Mass.: Lexington Books, 1980.

7.6 A Closer Look

Contingency Contracting with Adolescent Students

Let's assume that Homer is a sophomore in high school who must learn to read at an eighth-grade level if he wants a diploma. Because he is presently reading at only a fifth-grade level, Homer is short-tempered or bored when asked to do the classwork necessary to improve his reading skills. His temperament is making life pretty difficult for his English teacher, Mr. Snodgrass. If Homer could ever improve his reading skills, he would probably begin to find reading **intrinsically reinforcing.** He might eventually be motivated to read because of the intrinsic pleasure that comes from the activity of reading. Until that happens, Mr. Snodgrass and Homer's parents can use **extrinsic** or **external reinforcement** to motivate him to do the tedious assignments that will eventually improve his reading skills.

Mr. Snodgrass decides to set up a **contingency contract** with Homer for each small improvement in his classwork. This process of rewarding each small step is called **shaping.** Many adults make the mistake of expecting too much from the adolescent too soon and of being too stingy with external rewards. So Homer's teacher uses a **continuous schedule** of reinforcement, so that the youngster will receive rewards for each day's improvement. In order to design the contract, Mr. Snodgrass and Homer make a written record of the **baseline behavior.** Baseline is the period of time before any external incentives are introduced to motivate Homer. Homer's baseline charts show that for the last two weeks he has worked only 10 minutes of each class period on his assigned work. The ultimate goal is for him to work 50 of the 60 minutes. Mr. Snodgrass proposes to Homer that he try to accomplish this goal within six weeks from the time that the contingency contract begins.

fiti once reigned. Given the many alternatives now available to schools for reducing vandalism and misbehavior, it is particularly distressing that most schools are not employing these practices with their adolescent students (Casserly, Bass, & Garrett, 1980).

High-School Dropouts

In addition to the decline in certain areas of academic achievement and the continuance of certain forms of misbehavior at school, high-school dropout rates have aroused considerable concern among educators, parents, and educational psychologists. Of the approximately 14 million adolescents enrolled in grades 9 through 12, nearly one-third quit school before graduation. Particularly disturbing, however, are the excessively high dropout rates for minority youths. Forty percent of American Indians and 20 percent of blacks and Hispanics quit school, in contrast to only 3 percent of Asian American and 12 percent of white students (Grant & Snyder, 1984; Plisko, 1984). The high dropout rate among

The teacher allows Homer to choose his own reward for each day's progress. The teacher also provides **social reinforcement** by complimenting him for any improvement. Whenever Homer is not doing his work, the teacher avoids and ignores him, so that Homer will not learn to gain the teacher's attention by misbehaving. Both Homer and his teacher keep daily records of the time he works in class. On the days when he fails to reach his goal, he loses 4 points on his contract. His contract specifies that for every five additional minutes that he works in class, over his previous day's record, he will receive 4 points. At the end of each week these points can be "cashed in" for the following:

- 20 points—use of the family's car on Saturday night
- 15 points—15 minutes of free time in class on Friday
- 10 points—a complimentary letter that will be sent home to his parents describing his progress that week
- 5 points—permission to continue sitting next to whomever he chooses in class

Many adults would say that Homer is not truly motivated unless he gives up his reliance on this contract and completes his classwork without any external incentives. Another interpretation, however, is that external incentives motivate many of us to complete tasks that are not inherently pleasurable. Why else do employers offer us money to show up for a boring day's work, when we would rather be out on the tennis courts or home watching television?

SOURCE: L. Nielsen, *How to motivate adolescents: A guide for parents, teachers, and counselors.* Englewood Cliffs, N.J.: Prentice-Hall, 1982.

minorities is particularly evident in state-by-state comparisons. For example, in 1982, 37 percent of the adolescents in Mississippi quit school, 34 percent in New York, and 31 percent in California (National Institute of Education, 1984).

These disappointing statistics are not meant to imply that no educational progress for minority youths has occurred during recent decades. To the contrary, between 1970 and 1980 the dropout rate for black youths fell from almost 22 percent to 16 percent (U.S. Bureau of the Census, 1981). Nevertheless, the statistics continue to uphold the notion that black, Hispanic, and Native American youths are far more apt to quit school than white or Asian American adolescents. Moreover, despite improvements in the overall dropout rate during the 1960s, the rate increased from 23 percent in 1972 to 27 percent in 1982 (National Institute of Education, 1984). Thus, as Figure 7.3 illustrates, vast educational discrepancies still exist among Americans from different racial groups.

In regard to the reasons adolescents quit school, data from national surveys conducted during both the 1970s and the 1980s have yielded remarkably similar results (Bachman, Green, & Wirtanen, 1971; Howard & Anderson, 1978; Plisko, 1984). Adolescents most frequently cite poor grades and pregnancy as their rea-

Figure 7.3

Percentage of persons 25 to 34, by educational attainment, race, and Spanish origin: March 1970 and 1982

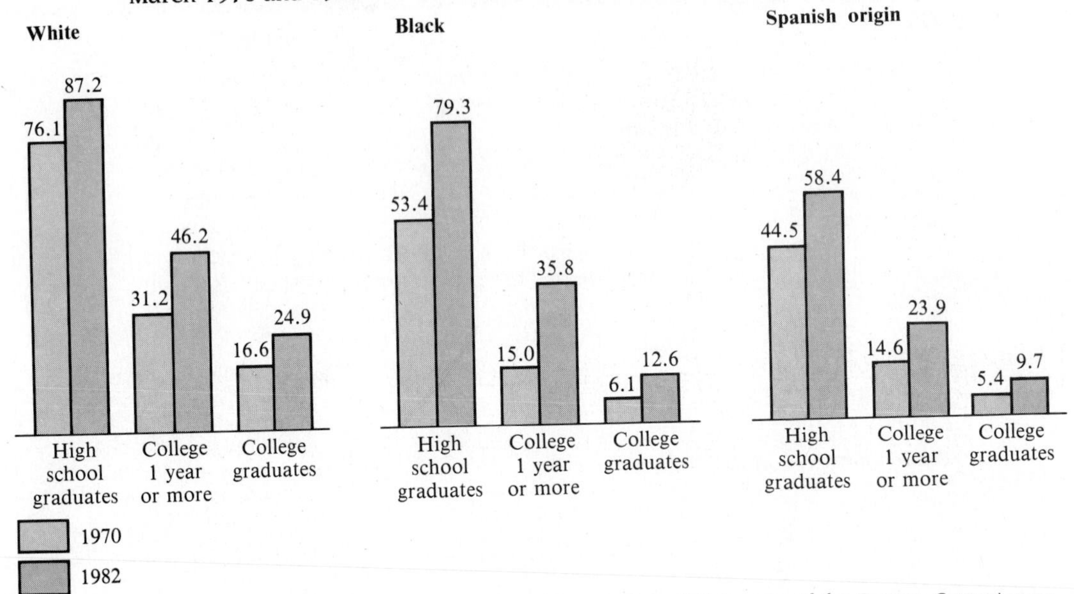

SOURCE: *Population profile of the United States: 1982.* Washington, D.C.: U.S. Bureau of the Census. Current population reports, P-23, no. 130. 1984.

sons for quitting school. The third most frequently cited reason is a desire to earn an immediate income through full-time employment. The importance of academic success is underscored by research showing that most high-school dropouts were already making poorer grades than other students as early as the third grade (Lloyd, 1978). Dropout rates are highest among adolescents from low-income families and among those whose friends have dropped out of school. The finding that dropouts report having more headaches, more insomnia, and more illnesses than high-school graduates suggests that these youngsters are undergoing excessive stress in their lives (Bachman, Green, & Wirtanen, 1971; Combs & Cooley, 1968).

Although high-school dropout rates are distressing, it's worth noting that some researchers contend that the financial benefits of a high-school diploma have been grossly exaggerated. According to these analysts, high-school graduates earn only slightly more money over their lifetimes than high-school dropouts (Bachman, Green, & Wirtanen, 1971; Yankelovich, 1979). The significant financial gains accrue to those individuals who earn a college degree. These analysts concede that dropouts encounter more difficulties in getting hired than high-school graduates. Nevertheless, their data indicate that dropouts who do find employment earn as much money, have as much vocational status, and feel as satisfied with their work as high-school graduates. Moreover, dropping out of school does not appear to contribute to a youth's delinquent behavior or to

What were your hopes and aspirations on the day of your graduation from high school? What was most memorable about your high-school graduation?

undermine his or her self-esteem. Although dropouts do tend to have lower self-esteem and to be more delinquent than other students, these problems appear to precede their decision to quit school (Bachman, Green & Wirtanen, 1971).

Studies like these suggest that staying in school for 12 years may not be the best option for all adolescents. This is not to imply that a high-school diploma has no value, but rather to suggest that quitting school can be less tragic and less catastrophic than is generally acknowledged. The data also indicate that some youths might benefit more from quitting school after the tenth grade and starting to work. From this perspective, the greatest disadvantage of quitting school might be the social stigma that our society attaches to not having a high-school diploma.

Suspensions and Expulsions

In an effort to cope with truancy, vandalism, and misbehavior, schools often resort to suspending or expelling students. Although students of every race are suspended and expelled, a number of researchers are worried that minority students are bearing the brunt of this disciplinary policy (Children's Defense Fund, 1975, 1985; Edelman, 1980). According to these researchers, black, Hispanic, and Indian youths are disciplined more harshly and more frequently than white and Asian American students. For example, although black students constitute only 16 percent of the school population, they account for nearly 30 percent of those suspended, expelled, and physically punished. Moreover, minority students appear to be in greatest jeopardy of being suspended when they are from low-income families. For example, a survey conducted by the National Urban League showed that one-third of black families with incomes below $6,000 have had at least one child suspended from school, in contrast with only 18 percent of black families with incomes above $20,000 (Williams, 1982).

Although the statistics indisputably establish the fact that minority youths are suspended, expelled, and corporally punished more often than whites and Asian Americans, the reasons underlying these differences continue to be contested. Some educators, like the superintendent of one of Florida's largest school systems, conclude that white teachers become overly concerned with disciplining and controlling students when the school's enrollment is primarily minority (Jones, 1976). Other commentators contend that—intentionally or unintentionally—educators suspend minority students for offenses that are usually overlooked when committed by white students.

It has been argued that minority students who do not conform to white, middle-class standards of dress and social conduct attract attention to themselves for subjective offenses, such as being "disrespectful" by wearing hats to class or talking too boisterously. Finally, the fact that suspensions of minority students rose dramatically after court-ordered desegregation in the early 1970s suggests that minority students are sometimes being pushed out of schools where integration is unwanted. Indeed, some contend that the brightest, most articulate, and most politically sophisticated minority students are most likely to be perceived as potentially "threatening" to the status quo and are, therefore, the most prone to being suspended for minor offenses (Children's Defense Fund, 1975, 1985).

Corporal Punishment

In 1975 the assistant principal of an Atlanta high school was critically wounded and paralyzed by a 15-year-old boy with a gun, who was shouting "You are not going to whip me anymore" (Welsh, 1978, p. 341). Despite such incidents, in 1977 the Supreme Court upheld the schools' right to discipline students by using corporal punishment (Flygare, 1978). The advocates of corporal punishment argue that hitting disobedient adolescents is both an effective and an efficient method for improving their behavior.

Among the arguments against corporal punishment, on the basis of empirical studies, is that hitting is an outdated, harmful, ineffective method for improving behavior (National Center for the Study of Corporal Punishment, 1977; Rutter et al., 1979; Vargas, 1977). Since data indicate that the parents of physically aggressive students resort to corporal punishment at home more often than the parents of nonaggressive children, it appears that "violence begets violence." Thus, in hitting students, it can be cogently argued that schools are encouraging the young to resolve their problems through the infliction of physical pain. Moreover, the data show that although corporal punishment often puts a temporary halt to unacceptable behavior, most youngsters thereafter become more hostile, more resentful, and more anxious. Worse still, the inappropriate behavior almost always returns.

Many teachers are opposed to using this method for disciplining students except as a last resort (Levine, 1978); yet recent studies of secondary schools show that the practice remains widespread, especially in schools with many poor and minority students (Sizer, 1984). Fortunately, as an alternative to suspensions and corporal punishment, some schools have instigated in-school suspension programs to keep misbehaving students on the school's campus and off the streets. In these programs, students continue to receive daily academic instruction, as well as to receive counseling for the problems that caused their suspensions (Nielsen, 1979a, 1979b, 1982).

In summarizing the problems today's adolescents encounter in their schools, it becomes clear that decline in academic achievement and minor misdemeanors, such as cutting class, affect large numbers of students. In contrast, more serious problems, such as dropping out of school before graduation, being suspended, being physically punished, or participating in school violence and vandalism, mainly afflict adolescents from lower-income families and those with the most academic failure. Given that low incomes and academic failure are both closely associated with minority-group membership in our society, it is self-evident that black, Hispanic, and Indian students are presently bearing more of the brunt of these school-related problems than white and Asian American youngsters.

FACTORS INFLUENCING ADOLESCENTS' ACADEMIC ACHIEVEMENT

A question that often plagues educators, counselors, and parents is: Specifically, what can I do to improve adolescents' academic performance? Given the number of variables that researchers have identified as correlates of adolescents' academic success, it would be impossible to enumerate all possible reasons underlying a particular young person's poor academic performance. Moreover, most of the research in educational psychology has been correlational rather than experimental, thereby limiting our understanding of the actual causes of poor academic performance. With these caveats in mind, the sections that follow are to be read as brief introductions to the major areas of research regarding adolescents' academic development. Although some of the research is experimental rather than correlational, it is beyond the scope of this chapter to delineate or to expound upon the differences. The cited references, however, will provide this detailed information for anyone interested in the aspects of educational psychology relevant to the education of adolescents.

Variables Related to Teachers' Behavior

Self-Fulfilling Prophecies You are a tenth-grade math teacher. As you look around your new class of 36 students, you notice seven Asian American students sitting quietly. Behind them, ten black males, wearing high-fashion clothing and afro hairstyles are speaking rather loudly in black street vernacular. The males are tall and muscular, some sporting one earring. Back in the corner is an overweight girl who speaks with a distinct, slow, southern drawl, and beside her are three pretty girls in cheerleading uniforms, who are obviously flirting with the two white boys in football jerseys. You also recognize the son of the professor who taught your statistics course and the daughter of the wealthiest family in the community. The question is: What do you expect academically and socially from each of these adolescents?

According to some research, our preconceived expectations about other people, derived from such factors as socioeconomic class, sex, race, and dialect, unconsciously alter our behavior in ways that encourage them to "fulfill our prophecies" (Insel & Jacobsen, 1975; Rosenthal & Jacobson, 1968). From this viewpoint, for example, even if two adolescents' intellectual abilities are equivalent, we tend to attribute more intelligence to the one who is light-skinned, affluent, obedient, and attractive. Moreover, it is argued, preconceived prophecies often undermine our ability to perceive an adolescent's behavior accurately. In support of the importance of teachers' prophecies, Theodore Sizer and his colleagues concluded, on the basis of their recent extensive study of secondary schools, that teachers' expectations are primarily determined by students' socioeconomic backgrounds. In Sizer's words, "Most of this is realism that many Americans prefer to keep under the rug: it is no easy task for the poor in America to break out, if they choose to, of their economic condition" (Sizer, 1984, p. 36).

According to the empirical data supporting the notion of *self-fulfilling prophecies*, educators convey their preconceived prophecies to students through both covert and overt methods (Good & Brophy, 1984). The classroom observations in this research have shown that, when interacting with students whom they presume to be bright, teachers give more cues, repeat their questions more often, offer more praise, and interact more frequently. In addition, teachers have been observed to pay more attention to the academic work and verbal responses of richer students and to wait less time for poor or minority youths to answer a question. It is also argued that counselors and teachers encourage enrollment in either the academic or the vocational curriculum on the basis of a student's race and socioeconomic class.

In contrast to the data supporting the power of self-fulfilling prophecies, researchers maintain that adolescents' intellectual abilities are recognized by their teachers, regardless of factors like race and socioeconomic class. Moreover, they contend that the power of self-fulfilling prophecies to influence students' academic achievements has been exaggerated. Exemplifying this perspective, one relatively recent longitudinal study of family incomes and adolescent achievement showed equal treatment of poor and rich students when intellectual abilities were equal. In this investigation, high-school students' decisions to enroll in either the college-preparatory or the vocational curriculum were attributed to their academic skills and their parents' values, not to the school's preconceived prophecies for rich and poor students (Rehberg & Rosenthal, 1978).

Given the contradictory research on the power of self-fulling prophecies, the best tactic is to accept the possibility that our preconceptions and stereotypes may, indeed, influence our behavior toward adolescents. In this light, we might well ask ourselves, as a matter of course in interacting with adolescents: What are my preconceived expectations for this adolescent? On what information am I basing my prophecies? Is this information relevant and is it colored by my own stereotypes or prejudices? How am I inadvertently conveying my expectations to this youngster? Such self-monitoring can at least reduce the likelihood that we are contributing to negative self-fulfilling prophecies for the adolescents in our lives.

The Teacher's Sex and Race Researchers have also explored the possibility that a teacher's or a counselor's race or sex influence adolescents' academic performance. Thus, it has been argued that teachers and counselors who are themselves members of minority cultures might be better able to empathize with and to design effective teaching or counseling strategies for minority youths. In a similar vein, researchers have wondered whether subjects such as English and mathematics, in which male and female performance are most discrepant, might be more effectively taught by members of the student's own sex. According to these hypotheses, females' math skills might improve, if math were more frequently taught by female teachers and if the subject were recast as a feminine activity. Likewise, males' reading skills might improve, if the subject were introduced by male teachers in elementary school and if English were recast as a masculine activity in high school.

Intriguing as these possibilities may be, the empirical data have yielded contradictory, inconsistent results. Although, in particular instances, some adolescents have fared better with teachers or counselors of their own sex and race, the data are neither consistent nor significant enough to warrant the matching of adolescents and adults on the basis of sex or race. Overall, the research has failed to substantiate the assumption that adults' race and sex are the critical variables in determining their effectiveness as adolescents' teachers or counselors (Atkinson, Morten, & Wing Sue, 1983; Brophy, 1979; Good & Brophy, 1984; Wing Sue, 1981).

Moreover, the empirical data regarding adolescents' preferences cannot necessarily be translated into educational policies. For instance, in one recent study, adolescents clearly expressed their preferences for attractive, young teachers in lieu of older or unattractive teachers (Goebel & Cashen, 1979). Yet this finding cannot ethically or reasonably be employed for establishing criteria by which to hire adolescents' teachers or counselors. In sum, the data indicate that although such variables as age, sex, race, and attractiveness may sometimes add or detract from an adult's effectiveness as an adolescent's counselor or teacher, the more crucial variables are the ability to communicate effectively, to listen nonjudgmentally, and to interact without prejudice regarding race, socioeconomic class, or gender.

Variables Related to School Structure and Policies

Competition and Cooperation Many adolescents perceive their schools as competitive environments where being "number one" means having to beat their friends at the academic game (Johnson & Johnson, 1975; Kirschenbaum,

Simon, & Napier, 1971). Of particular interest are the findings that, as white youths age, they tend to become more academically competitive. Moreover, white, middle-class students have often been found willing to reduce their own rewards in order to prevent friends from winning in the process (Johnson & Johnson, 1975). Unfortunately, such competitive attitudes have frequently been found to create sufficient anxiety to interfere with adolescents' academic learning (Hansen, 1977).

On the basis of the empirical findings, many psychologists and educators have concluded that most adolescents would fare better academically if their schools encouraged more cooperation and less competition (Covington & Omelich, 1979; Glasser, 1969; Hansen, 1977; Johnson & Johnson, 1975; Pepitone, 1980). According to these investigators' data, adolescents in cooperative classes are more likely than those in competitive situations to interact socially with one another, to offer one another academic help, to feel relaxed and self-confident, to be intellectually adventuresome, and to share contoversial ideas. Perhaps most important, cooperation has not been found to diminish students' motivation or to undermine their academic progress. To the contrary, competition often appears to detract from the kinds of skills and attitudes that enhance academic achievement.

For example, an eight-year study of 1,500 high-school students found that those who had learned to study without the pressure of competitive grading performed as well in college as those who graduated from very competitive high schools. Indeed, the college professors perceived the 1,500 students from the noncompetitive schools as more intellectually curious and more resourceful than students from the schools where competitive grading was considered a motivating strategy (Chamberlain, Drought, & Scott, 1972).

Critics of the traditional competitive grading system argue that more effective methods are available for teaching, motivating, and evaluating today's adolescents (Nielsen, 1982). At present the grading system employed most often rewards students who work quickly, who respond without hesitation and who thrive on competition. The present system also benefits adolescents who are verbally responsive in class and who perform well on written tests. A less competitive alternative, *criterion-referenced* grading or *mastery learning,* assesses each student in terms of his or her success at achieving certain prescribed skills, rather than in terms of relative standing in class performance. Under criterion-referenced grading systems, all students who master certain skills receive the predesignated grade, regardless of other students' achievements. For example, if the coach decides that anyone who can run a mile in six minutes deserves an A, then all students who achieve this level of mastery receive As. Likewise, if nobody achieves the criterion, nobody receives an A.

Many adults are opposed to deemphasizing competition in adolescents' academic lives. Arguing that the United States is a dog-eat-dog society, where adolescents must learn how to survive amidst rugged competition, it is argued that competing against peers motivates adolescents to work harder. From this perspective, competition is an invaluable means for building character in adolescents. Although most research refutes these beliefs, the myths about teaching adolescents the value of competition die hard.

Curriculum Tracking One of the most vehemently debated and long-standing arguments regarding the academic well-being of adolescents is the practice of

tracking students into a particular curriculum throughout their years in school. Almost all secondary schools track students into either the academic, the general, the vocational, or the "special education" curriculum on the basis of such criteria as IQ tests and teachers' recommendations. Historically, U.S. schools have also tracked adolescents on the basis of their physical handicaps. For example, deaf and blind students with perfectly normal intellectual skills have traditionally been tracked into special education classes, segregated from nonhandicapped students throughout their academic careers. Assigning adolescents to separate curriculum tracks has been predicated on the assumption that such segregation provides students with an education especially tailored to their intellectual and vocational needs.

Although many people who endorse tracking and special education are undoubtedly well intentioned, a number of educators, legislators, and parents see this form of segregation as disadvantageous to most adolescents. First, the data have convinced many educators and researchers that low-income and minority youths are the most likely to be assigned to lower-track classes, even when their abilities are similar to white and higher-income students. Second, the data indicate that, in comparison to white or upper-income students with equivalent intellectual skills, youngsters from impoverished homes and members of racial minorities are the least likely to be transferred to a more advanced track when their skills improve (Edelman, 1980; Godlad, 1983; Good & Brophy, 1984; Rosenbaum, 1976).

In addition to the evidence that tracking discriminates against adolescents on the basis of race and income, the empirical data from the most intensive and extensive studies refute the widespread belief that tracking benefits students academically (Boyer, 1983; Godlad, 1983; Good & Brophy, 1984; Rosenbaum, 1976; Rutter et al., 1979; Sizer, 1984). As the information in Box 7.2 illustrated, the major commissions and surveys of secondary education in the 1980s have agreed that curriculum tracking should be abolished. Moreover, the National Education Association (NEA) itself conceded nearly two decades ago that on the basis of empirical studies of the impact of tracking on the academic achievement of students from various income and ability levels, tracking was an indefensible policy (NEA, 1968).

Yet, despite the overwhelming evidence against the academic benefits of tracking, the suggestion of creating one academic track for all adolescents evokes fear and condemnation from many upper-income parents and educators. The proponents of tracking typically raise three arguments on its behalf. First, they fear that educating college-bound students alongside students from the general or vocational tracks will impede the academic progress of the fastest learners. In other words, they perceive the abolishment of tracking as a "sacrifice" on the part of college-bound students for the academic advancement of less-able students. Second, it is feared that faster learners will shun or mock their classmates who learn the material more slowly, thereby undermining the self-confidence and academic progress of slower learners. Third, it is presumed that, if adolescents with a wider diversity of skills and with different learning rates are permitted to attend the same classes, their educational needs will not be as well met by their teachers as in academically segregated classes.

Despite the tenacity of these convictions about the academic benefits of tracking, the data formerly cited have failed to support these fears. Among the numerous findings from this vast body of research are that the least-talented

How do you feel in the presence of physically or mentally handicapped people? How did your adolescent or childhood experiences influence your present feelings?

students make the most progress and tend to have higher self-concepts, when permitted to attend classes with college-bound students. Moreover, in contrast to expectations, the fastest learners often tutor their other classmates, thereby learning the material more thoroughly themselves than in tracked classes. Further, teachers tend to offer students more, not less, individualized instruction in heterogeneous classes, thereby providing more academic benefits for both the fastest and the slowest learners. Many teachers have been observed to instruct their heterogeneous classes more like advanced classes than like lower-track classes. In summary, educating college-bound students in classes with the noncollege-bound has not been found to undermine the academic progress or the self-confidence of either group.

These data should not be construed to mean, however, that the opponents of tracking object to all forms of grouping students. To the contrary, the concept of **mainstreaming** means that students who need special services for their physical or mental handicaps will spend part of each school day receiving special instruction. Conversely, youths with special talents should be afforded opportunities to develop their skills. For example, mathematically brilliant students might enroll in college-sponsored summer programs or might attend seminars conducted by college instructors on the high-school campus during the school year. Similarly, a blind student might spend several hours each week receiving instruction from a special education teacher who, in conjunction with regular classroom teachers, designs pedagogical modifications that permit the student to be educated in classes with sighted classmates (Jones, 1976). It's important to note, however, that the vast majority of students do not fall within the extremes at either end of the continuum in regard to their intellectual abilities or their academic skills.

In his intensive study of a high school and his review of the relevant literature, Rosenbaum (1976) delineates the damaging consequences of curriculum tracking. Like other opponents of tracking, Rosenbaum points out that U.S. education is predicated on the concept of *meritocracy*—the belief that a young person's eventual social and financial position is almost wholly dependent upon his or her intellectual abilities and academic skills. Thus, in a meritocracy, one of the school's primary responsibilities is to assess each child's intellectual and academic potential and to assign him or her to the appropriate curriculum track as early as possible.

Unfortunately, according to those who share Rosenbaum's view against tracking, most schools pass judgment on a child's intellectual potential and assign students to tracks on the basis of invalid criteria such as IQ tests, sex, race, socioeconomic class, and teachers' subjective opinions. More distressing still, once assigned to a track, the data consistently show that there is virtually no chance of a student's being transferred to a higher level. Moreover, most adolescents and their parents defer to the opinions of teachers and counselors without questioning the future financial and social consequences of assignment to the vocational or the general track. For example, in opting not to enroll in a foreign-language elective, many junior-high- and elementary-school students are unknowingly signalling educators to their disinterest in a "college prep" curriculum. In this regard, the data show a remarkably high correlation between adolescents' curriculum choices in the seventh grade and their future college attendance (Rosenbaum, 1976).

According to Rosenbaum's high-school study and his review of the literature, students' curriculum choices are primarily determined by their teachers' and counselors' advice, despite the school's assertions that students are free to pursue their own educational and vocational desires. From this perspective, the most insidious part of tracking is the deception of adolescents, their parents, and perhaps even of educators, into believing that the student's curriculum and vocational plans are freely chosen.

Among others, Rosenbaum's investigation demonstrates the social and intellectual ramifications that typically accompany tracking. In regard to intellectual development, the IQ test scores of adolescents in the vocational and general tracks generally decreased during their high-school years, in contrast to the scores of students in the academic track. Not surprisingly, in regard to social development, most students limit their friendships to members of their own track, thereby creating a castelike social system within the school. Since tracking generally results in the segregation of students along racial and socioeconomic lines, it perpetuates the segregation that characterizes the society outside the school. The social segregation that accompanies tracking manifests itself, for example, in adolescents' extracurricular activities. Students in noncollege tracks are most apt to join such activities as the band or an athletic team, while the college-track students typically run the student council, the school publications, and class offices. Perhaps more important, youngsters in noncollege tracks often describe themselves as less intelligent than their academic track peers and express negative stereotypes associated with a vocational curriculum track (Rosenbaum, 1976).

Researchers and educators who oppose curriculum tracking contend that high schools should enroll all students in the same curriculum, with the exception of the small minority whose serious physical handicaps, mental retardation, or intellectual brilliance necessitate their segregation from other students. According to these proposals, although all adolescents would receive some vocational education, the curriculum's primary focus would be the acquisition of academic skills. In contrast to the present educational system, high schools would no longer be charged with the responsibility of teaching specific vocational skills, since job training would be the responsibility of well-equipped, post-secondary schools. Moreover, a single-track system would protect students' options to prepare themselves for a college education, since they would not be forced to make irreversible vocational and curriculum decisions at an early age. In a similar vein, "late bloomers" would have a better chance of developing their academic talents, since they would not have been prematurely placed in a lower-track curriculum.

Even if one personally chooses to endorse the policy of curriculum tracking by ignoring the empirical data, a number of disturbing questions, relevant to adolescents' intellectual and social development, remain: How do adolescents benefit from the social hierarchy of curriculum tracking, which separates the "haves" from the "have nots"? Should adolescents base their own self-esteem and their esteem for others on people's physical, academic, or intellectual differences? Who profits from maintaining the present system of curriculum tracking? Such questions lend a special complexity to the empirical findings that have consistently challenged the benefits of tracking for adolescents in both former and present times.

Racial Integration In 1954, the Supreme Court of the United States ordered the nation's public schools to end racial segregation and discrimination "with all deliberate speed." Today, more than three decades after the Supreme Court's decision, social scientists continue to investigate two of the central assumptions underlying the court's momentous ruling: first, that school desegregation will enhance the academic and intellectual development of the nation's minority students; and second, that school integration will ameliorate racial hostilities and prejudice by establishing social bonds among the young. Thus, federally mandated desegregation has generated more than two decades of research aimed at uncovering the academic and social benefits of integrated education. Since Chapter 9 discusses the ramifications of school integration on adolescents' social relationships, the present discussion will focus primarily on the impact of integration on adolescents' academic development.

Despite optimistic expectations, some data indicate that the relationship between integration and academic achievement is more complicated than generally acknowledged. For example, St. Johns's careful analysis of the data, derived from 41 studies in elementary and secondary school during a 35-year period, found both positive and negative academic consequences from desegregation. According to St. Johns's analyses of the research available in the mid-1970s, although desegregation generally improved minority students' academic achievement and self-confidence, sometimes the reverse occurred. In other words, integration sometimes appeared to impede the academic progress and undermine the academic self-confidence of minority students (St. Johns, 1975).

In a similar vein, an extensive recent study based on data from several thousand black and white seniors in 11 high schools challenges the contention that interacting with white classmates will improve the academic skills of minority youths. In an attempt to unravel the discrepancies in the previous research, the confounding variables of gender, socioeconomic class, academic track, IQ scores, and previous experiences with integration were considered before assessing the relationship between integration and academic achievement. Contrary to expectations, as the percentage of white students in a class rose, black students' grades generally declined. On the positive side, however, as the proportion of white students increased, the academic efforts of black students increased. Surprisingly, having attended an integrated elementary school was not significantly correlated with better high-school grades for black students. In a similar regard, having white classmates from well-educated, upper-income families was no more correlated with higher grades for black students than having white classmates from lower-income families (Patchen, Hoffman, & Brown, 1980).

On the basis of their correlational findings, these investigators conclude that minority students' academic skills are affected more by their teachers' behavior than by the race or the socioeconomic status of their friends and classmates. In other words, the benefits that accrue to minority students in integrated schools are primarily attributable to their teachers' behavior, rather than to the interactions between black and white classmates. Although such research demonstrates the complexity of the relationship between integration and academic achievement, this particular study clearly undermines the validity of the suggestion that schools for each race can be "separate but equal," since teachers' behavior presumably varies in both segregated and desegrated classes.

More optimistically, however, data from a number of studies conducted during the 1970s and 1980s support the hypothesis that school integration enhances the academic and intellectual development of minority youths. For example, black and white students in integrated schools have been found to have equivalent dropout rates, in contrast to the higher dropout rates of blacks in segregated schools (Bachman, Green, & Wirtanen, 1971). It is interesting that when black students were forcefully and violently integrated into South Boston High School in 1975, the school's white, predominantly Irish students from working-class families protested the court-ordered integration on the grounds that their academic achievement would be impeded. Ironically, by 1980, the white students' scores on national reading tests and their college enrollment had reached the highest level in the school's history, a finding that suggests that integration can have unforeseen benefits for even its most vociferous opponents (Kozberg, 1980).

Given the contradictions that exist in the extant research and the enormous significance of the findings for educational policy makers and for minority students, the 15-year study recently concluded at Johns Hopkins University's Center for Social Organization of Schools is of critical importance (Braddock, Crain, & McPartland, 1984). The most extensive and most recent longitudinal study to date, the Project Concern experiment is the first thorough, long-term study of the broad effects of school desegregation in our society. Begun in 1966, the investigation traced the educational, economic, and social development of 661 black pupils from a predominantly lower-income black community with a high crime rate, from the time they entered elementary school until they were working or attending college. At the outset of the study, half of the students were bused to predominantly white suburban schools and the remaining control group was educated in their local, predominantly black city schools.

In regard to academic achievement, Project Concern reached several heartening conclusions. Black students who attended the integrated schools were more likely to graduate from high school, to attend predominantly white colleges, and to earn higher achievement test scores than their black counterparts in the predominantly black city schools. In addition, the black students who had attended the integrated schools tended to receive the higher grades in college, to complete the most years of college, and to feel less victimized in white-run institutions. It is especially noteworthy, considering the data on sex roles and race discussed in Chapter 5 and 6, that—in contrast to black males—the black females who attended the suburban schools did not complete more years of college than females who remained in the predominantly black schools. According to the investigators, this finding indicates that the social structure and the counseling that exists in suburban high schools may be more beneficial to black males than to black females. Further, the investigators suggest that high schools use these findings to examine their teaching and counseling practices with black females.

While these academic achievements are in and of themselves impressive, Project Concern's data also demonstrate the positive impact of school desegregation on adolescents' social development. Black students who attended the desegregated suburban schools were more likely than those from the segregated schools to have closer and more frequent social contact with whites and to live in desegregated neighborhoods after their high-school graduation. They also had fewer incidents with the police and were involved in fewer fights than black students who had attended the segregated schools. Not surprisingly, given their educational achievements and commitments, the females from the integrated schools were also less likely to have children before the age of eighteen. Of special significance, the relationships that blacks established with their white classmates in desegregated schools later appeared to help them break into the traditionally impenetrable "old-boy network" in whites' social and professional groups.

In summary, Project Concern offers the most compelling data to date in support of the academic and social benefits of school desegregation. Project Concern's data clearly undermine the argument of desegregation's critics that simply educating minorities and whites together in the same classes does not produce academic, financial, or social equity.

On the basis of such data as Project Concern's and of the research that refutes claims of integration's academic benefits, several implications emerge. First, it appears that the benefits of school desegregation can be undermined by certain variables, such as academic tracking or an atmosphere within the school which—whether intended or unintended—makes minority adolescents feel inferior and unwelcome. Understandably, under such subversive circumstances, integration is likely to be more disadvantageous than beneficial to both minority and white adolescents. In this regard, a survey of 10,000 students in 200 high schools showed the most successfully integrated schools to be those in which race relations were intentionally emphasized in the curriculum and in which teachers consciously tried to treat white and minority students alike (Crain, Mahard, & Narot, 1980). Second, the academic and social benefits that often accrue from desegregation are not limited to minority students, as the data from South Boston High School exemplify. Thus, the presumption that integration is an academic sacrifice on the part of white students is generally unsupported by the data. Third, most data do indicate that school desegregation can, in and of itself, benefit minority students academically and socially. Although the reasons underlying these benefits are disputable, at present most data acknowledge the wisdom of the Supreme Court's decision in 1954 in terms of adolescents' academic gains.

Class Size Another factor that researchers have considered influential in regard to adolescents' academic achievement is class size. It has generally been assumed that students learn best in small classes where their teachers supposedly offer the most individual attention. Following this logic, it has also been expected that adolescents engage in more class discussions and interact more frequently with their classmates in small classes.

The empirical data, however, only partially support these assumptions about the relationship between class size and adolescents' achievements or classroom behavior. For example, some data do indicate that when classes have fewer than 25 students, teachers tend to use a greater variety of teaching methods, to encounter fewer disciplinary problems, and to encourage more student participation. Reducing the size of a class from 40 to 30 students appears, however, to have no appreciable impact on pedagogical strategies or student-teacher interactions. Moreover, contrary to expectations, most literature reviews and correlational studies, including Coleman's national investigation of students in black and in white schools, have not found significant correlations between the number of students in a class and students' academic achievement (Averch, 1974; Coleman et al., 1966; Cahen & Filby, 1979).

On the basis of their data, these researchers contend that the least-skilled adolescents probably benefit more academically from small classes than the most skilled, but this premise has not been tested in most studies. In addition, the researchers concede that smaller classes are probably more pleasurable for teachers and students, even if academic gains are unrelated to class size. Finally, the researchers have noted that many teachers, regardless of the small number of students in their classes, rely solely on lecturing and on assigning written work to be completed silently at one's desk. Thus, it has been argued that if teachers would experiment with new pedagogical strategies, smaller classes would indeed yield greater academic gains for adolescents than large classes. At present, however, the empirical data make it difficult to support the claim that smaller classes do, in and of themselves, improve adolescents' academic skills.

School Size In a similar line of reasoning, researchers have explored the ways in which a school's size affects adolescents academically and socially (Alexander & George, 1981; Boyer, 1983; Garbarino, 1980; Grabe, 1981; Gross & Osterman, 1971; Gump, 1966; Schmiecheck, 1979). In smaller schools, more students participate in extracurricular activities than in large schools. Feeling alienated is easiest in large schools where a young person can remain virtually anonymous in the huge crowd year after year. Many adolescents also experience greater difficulty forming social attachments and feeling part of the school's community in large schools. Academically, young people with the weakest academic skills seem to benefit most from small schools. It has been suggested that these academic benefits are the consequence of students in small schools having more opportunities outside the classroom to gain esteem and social status, which subsequently contribute to their academic success. For these reasons, it is argued that smaller schools should be created for adolescents.

Despite these findings in support of small schools, some reviewers conclude that a school's enrollment has less impact on students than such factors as friendly teachers or a cooperative attitude among students (ERIC, 1982). Moreover, some data suggest that youngsters who lack ability or who lack interest in extracurricular events feel worst about themselves in small schools where there is generally greater pressure to participate (Grabe, 1981). Others have suggested that large high schools should be subdivided into units, which would enhance adolescents' sense of belonging to a smaller community within a huge institution. This option would preserve the benefits of large schools, such as the diversity of course offerings and exposure to a greater variety of teachers and classmates, while offering the benefits of a small community (Boyer, 1983).

Variables Related to the Adolescent

Although the research does substantiate that the school's policies, teachers' behavior, and such variables as school size can influence adolescents' academic performance and social behavior, ascribing total responsibility to the school and to teachers would be both naive and empirically unwarranted. Variables related to the adolescent and to his or her family are also acknowledged as crucial to academic success and appropriate social conduct. The variables correlated with academic performance that relate to adolescents or to their families are too numerous to delineate within the context of this chapter. Three variables, however, can be presented as representative of the fact that academic performance is not solely related to circumstances within the control of the schools or of individual teachers.

The Adolescent's Cognitive Style The effectiveness of any teacher's particular personality and teaching style often depends on the student's cognitive style (Brophy, 1979; Moursund, 1976). For instance, adolescents with a **field dependent** cognitive style have been found to prefer more structured classroom environments and more authoritarian teachers than their classmates who have a

field independent cognitive style. Thus, a teacher who offers students opportunities to exercise their independent judgments may confuse, rather than stimulate, students with a field dependent style. Similarly, as Chapter 6 explained, adolescents' cultural differences often result in different locus-of-control attitudes and different attitudes toward competition and public speaking. As a consequence of these cultural differences in learning styles, classroom strategies that motivate some students, such as competing publicly with classmates, will debilitate others. Not even the most sensitive and most talented teachers can be expected to anticipate or to correctly identify the various learning styles in a class of 20 or 30 students. Thus, learning styles continue to exert an influence over each adolescent's academic performance, which is only partially within a teacher's control.

Anxiety Another variable beyond a teacher's immediate control, which often affects academic performance, is the adolescent's anxiety. Researchers who have investigated the relationship between anxiety and academic performance have described a number of findings relevant to our understanding of adolescents (Hansen, 1977; Phillips, 1978; Sarason, 1980; Tobias, 1979). First, anxiety interferes more with academic performance during adolescence than during childhood. In a culture that typically judges an individual's intellectual abilities and ascribes status on the basis of academic performance, it is perhaps not surprising that the data show students becoming more anxious over their academic successes and failures as they age. Second, the data show that the relationship between an adolescent's academic success and anxiety is curvilinear—a minimal amount of anxiety tends to enhance academic performance, but excessive anxiety undermines academic performance. For instance, when taking tests, excessively anxious youngsters worry so much about their performance in comparison to everyone else's that their concentration falters; whereas adolescents with absolutely no anxiety seem to develop a self-confidence that undermines their motivation to study adequately. Moreover, anxiety interferes more with an adolescent's short-term memory than with long-term memory.

Fortunately, researchers have made a number of creative suggestions for alleviating adolescents' anxieties. Some counselors teach students deep breathing exercises that relax the muscles in tense situations. Contingency contracts and criterion-referenced grading have also been used to reduce adolescents' anxieties that are associated with peer competition and with grading. Teachers have diminished students' anxieties by deemphasizing competition and speed as criteria for verbal answers or test taking. Other teachers have desensitized test-anxious students by allowing them to use their books during the first few exams and then gradually requiring students to rely solely on memory for test answers. Counselors have also successfully reduced adolescents' test anxieties by showing videotapes of other students taking tests and then discussing test-taking techniques. Although such methods do not always improve adolescents' grades, they almost always decrease students' anxieties about school.

A type of anxiety that has received considerable attention in recent years is math anxiety. Given the sex-role stereotype that "girls don't have mathematical minds like boys," it is not surprising that adolescent females experience math anxiety more often than their male classmates (Ernest, 1976; Kogelman & Waren, 1979; Tobias, 1978). Thus, it has been argued that reducing female adolescents' math anxiety would result in their taking more math courses, which would subsequently prepare them for a wider variety of careers. For example, in 1972 only 8 percent of the girls entering the University of Califronia at Berkeley had four years of high school math, compared to 57 percent of the boys. This deficit limited the girls to 22 of the university's 44 majors and to two of the 12 colleges (Sells, 1978). Furthermore, math anxiety has been implicated in the fact that only 7 percent of the doctorates in mathematics in the last four decades have been earned by females (Ernest, 1976). In an effort to reduce male and female adolescents' math anxieties, researchers have designed programs for high-school and college students, in which participants are helped to recognize their math anxieties and to understand the vocational consequences of avoiding math courses.

Family Income Finally, the family's income has been found to be one of the variables most highly correlated with an adolescent's academic performance. The strong positive correlation between family income and academic achievement is highlighted by a number of educational statistics. For example, only 14 percent of 1980 college freshmen came from families with yearly incomes under $10,000, in contrast to nearly 60 percent with family incomes above $20,000 (Grant & Snyder, 1984). Similarly, only 38 percent of 1980 high-school graduates from low-income families participated in any form of postsecondary education, in contrast to nearly 80 percent of graduates from high-income families (Plisko, 1984).

A family's income is associated not only with adolescents' actual academic performance but also with expectations for the future. For example, 37 percent of 1980 high-school seniors from high-income families expected to earn college degrees, and a startling 40 percent expected to earn graduate degrees. In contrast, only one-fourth of middle-income students and 16 percent of low-income students had any expectations of earning college degrees. Considering the vast discrepancies in the average education and income of minority and white parents, it is understandable that only one-third of the Indian adolescents who were committed enough to stay in school until graduation in 1980 believed they would earn college degrees, in contrast to 80 percent of the Asian American and 50 percent of the white graduates (Peng, Fetters, & Kolstad, 1981).

Since adults' incomes and educational levels are closely aligned, it is not surprising that adolescents' parents who earn the least money also have achieved the least formal education. For instance, 53 percent of 1980 college freshmen had fathers with more than a high-school education, and only 17 percent had fathers without a high-school diploma (Grant & Snyder, 1984). In general, these correlational data mean that adolescents with the poorest academic skills have parents who are handicapped both by having the least formal education and by having the least access to the kinds of opportunities for their children that money can buy.

Conclusion

Considering the number of hours students spend in school and the social and academic impact that educational institutions exert on the young, it is little wonder that researchers have directed so much attention to adolescents and their schools. At a time when formal education has assumed a paramount role in the future social and financial status of the young, the characteristics of and interactions within the U.S. high school assume a particular relevance to the study of adolescence. In our roles as professionals who interact with adolescents or in our roles as adolescents' parents or friends, we cannot escape a multitude of issues related to the education of the young. Moreover, many of the problems that so often plague adolescents are intricately bound up with their roles as students. As subsequent chapters will continue to demonstrate, the schools affect adolescents' peer relationships, vocational development, and attitudes in regard to sex, drugs, religion, and moral values. Thus, without an understanding of the social and academic experiences that adolescents typically encounter in today's schools, we are handicapped in respect to our abilities to empathize with the young or to suggest constructive alternatives for their school-related problems.

Questions for Discussion and Review

Basic Concepts and Terminology

1. In what regards has the relationship between adolescents and schools changed since the turn of the century?
2. How do the academic skills of adolescents from various minority groups and socioeconomic levels compare?
3. Which factors have been correlated with adolescents' academic achievements? In what ways might each of these variables have an influence on academic performance?
4. How have researchers recommended that the education of adolescents be improved? On what data are each of their recommendations based?
5. How extensive is school violence and vandalism among the adolescent population?
6. Considering data from the past decade, how well are today's adolescents faring in terms of their academic skills and educational accomplishments?
7. How effective is school desegregation in terms of adolescents' academic achievements? What variables might account for integration's success or failure?

Questions for Discussion and Debate

1. What four problems in U.S. schools do you consider most detrimental to adolescents' academic and social development? Which were most detrimental to your own development as an adolescent?
2. If you had total control of a school system for two years, what changes would you implement in adolescents' schools? Rank your priorities and defend them to an imaginary school board.
3. How could you defend the practice of enrolling adolescents in private schools and still endorse the principle of "equal opportunity" for different

socioeconomic groups? If you attended a private school, what benefits do you believe accrued to you that a public school could not have provided?

4. Which of the recommendations for improving adolescents' education do you endorse and why? (Refer to Boxes 7.2 and 6.2.)
5. Assume you are the principal in a high school plagued with vandalism, violence, and truancy. How would you attempt to improve the situation? How would you persuade parents and your staff to implement your recommendations?
6. If you were a high-school teacher and most of your students were apathetic, unruly, and uncooperative, how would you improve their behavior? How did your own high-school teachers combat your apathy or antipathy toward their subjects?
7. Given the current controversies regarding the ideal high-school curriculum, which courses would you require for adolescents in grades 7 through 12? Why? In retrospect, how would you modify your own high-school curriculum? Why?
8. On what empirical or statistical grounds can you refute or defend the practice of curriculum tracking? How was curriculum tracking beneficial or disadvantageous to your own adolescent development?
9. How has school integration affected your own social and academic development? How might your experiences with integration have been improved?
10. What factors do you believe are most critical in determining an adolescent's academic performance? Which factors most affected your grades and future educational plans?

REFERENCES

Access without success. *Newsweek,* March 19, 1984, pp. 96–97.

Alexander, W., & George, P. *The exemplary middle school.* New York: Holt, Rinehart and Winston, 1981.

Atkinson, D., Morten, C., & Wing Sue, D. *Counseling American minorities.* Dubuque, Iowa: W. C. Brown, 1983.

Averch, H. *How effective is schooling: A critical review of research.* Englewood Cliffs, N.J.: Prentice-Hall, 1974.

Bachman, J., Green, S., & Wirtanen, I. *Youth in transition: Dropping out—problem or symptom?* (Vol. 3). Ann Arbor: University of Michigan Press, 1971.

Bachman, J., Johnston, J., & O'Malley, P. *Monitoring the future: Questionnaire responses from the nation's high school seniors.* Ann Arbor: University of Michigan Press, 1981.

Bachman, J. & O'Malley, P. *The search for school effects: New findings and perspectives.* Ann Arbor: University of Michigan Press, 1978.

Blyth, D., Simmons, R., & Bush, D. The transition into early adolescence. *Sociology of Education,* 1978, *51,* 149–62.

Bowles, S., & Gintis, H. *Schooling in capitalist America.* New York: Basic Books, 1976.

Boyer, E. *High school.* New York: Harper & Row, 1983.

Braddock, J., Crain, R., & McPartland, J. A long-term view of schools' desegregation. *Phi Delta Kappan,* December 1984, pp. 259–265.

Brophy, J. Teacher behavior and its effect. *Journal of Educational Psychology,* 1979, *71,* 733–750.

Cahen, L., & Filby, N. The class size–achievement issue. *Phi Delta Kappan*, 1979, *60*, 492–495.

Carnegie Foundation. *Survey of high school and beyond*. New York: Carnegie Foundation, 1980.

Casserly, M., Bass, S., & Garrett, J. *School vandalism*. Lexington, Mass.: Lexington Books, 1980.

Chamberlain, D., Drought, N., & Scott, W. *Adventures in American education: Did they succeed in college?* New York: Harper & Row, 1972.

Children's Defense Fund (CDF). *School suspensions: Are they helping children?* Washington, D.C.: Children's Defense Fund, 1975.

Children's Defense Fund (CDF). *Black and white children in America: Key facts*. Washington, D.C.: Children's Defense Fund, 1985.

Coleman, J., et al. *Equality of educational opportunity*. Washington, D.C.: U.S. Government Printing Office, 1966.

College Entrance Exam Board. *National college bound seniors*. New York: College Entrance Exam Board, 1981.

Combs, J. & Cooley, W. Dropouts: In high school and after school. *American Educational Research Journal*, 1968, *5*, 343–363.

Covington, M., & Omelich, C. It's best to be able and virtuous too. *Journal of Educational Psychology*, 1979, *71*, 688–700.

Crain, R., Mahard, R., & Narot, R. *Making desegregation work: How schools create social climates*. Baltimore, Md.: Johns Hopkins University, Center for Social Organization of the Schools, 1980.

DiPrete, T. *Discipline and order in American high schools*. Washington, D.C.: National Center for Education Statistics, 1981.

Duke, D. How administrators view the crisis in school discipline. *Phi Delta Kappan*, January 1978, pp. 325–330.

Edelman, M. *Portrait of inequality: Black and white children in America*. Washington, D.C.: Children's Defense Fund, 1980.

Epstein, J. *Secondary school environments and students' outcomes*. Baltimore, Md.: Johns Hopkins University Press, 1981a.

Epstein, J. (ed.). *The quality of school life*. Lexington, Mass.: Lexington Books, 1981b.

ERIC Clearinghouse on Educational Management. *School size: A reassessment of the small school*. Research brief # 2. February 1982.

Ernest, J. *Math and sex*. Santa Barbara: University of California Press, 1976.

Fetters, W. *National longitudinal study of high school class of 1972*. Washington, D.C.: Department of Health, Education and Welfare, 1977.

Feuerstein, R. *Instrumental enrichment*. Baltimore, Md.: University Park Press, 1977.

Feuerstein, R. Cognitive modifiability in adolescence. *Journal of Special Education*, 1981, *15*, 269–287.

Flygare, T. The Supreme Court approves corporal punishment. *Phi Delta Kappan*, 1978, *59*, 347–348.

Garbarino, J. Some thoughts on school size and its effects on adolescent development. *Journal of Youth and Adolescence*, 1980, *9*, 19–31.

Gibbs, J., Black adolescents and youth: An endangered species. *American Orthopsychiatric Journal*, 1984, *54*, 6–21.

Glasser, W. *Schools without failure*. New York: Harper & Row, 1969.

Glenbard East "Echo". *Teenagers themselves*. New York: Adama Books, 1984.

Godlad, J. *A place called school: Prospects for the future*. New York: McGraw-Hill, 1983.

Goebel, B., & Cashen, V. Age, sex and attractiveness as factors in student ratings of teachers. *Journal of Educational Psychology,* 1979, *71,* 646–653.

Gold, M., & Petronio, R. Delinquent behavior in adolescence. In J. Adelson (ed.), *Handbook of adolescent psychology.* New York: Wiley, 1980.

Good, T., & Brophy, J. *Looking in classrooms.* New York: Harper & Row, 1984.

Grabe, M. School size and importance of school activities. *Adolescence,* 1981, *16,* 21–31.

Grant, V., & Snyder, T. (eds.). *Digest of education statistics.* Washington, D.C.: National Center for Education Statistics, 1984.

Gross, R., & Osterman, P. *High School.* New York: Simon & Schuster, 1971.

Gump, P. *Big schools, small schools.* Moravia, N.Y.: Chronical Guidance Publications, 1966.

Hacker, A. The schools flunk out. *New York Review of Books.* April 12, 1984, pp. 35–40.

Hampel, R. *American high schools since 1940.* Boston: Houghton Mifflin, 1984.

Hansen, R. Anxiety. In S. Ball (ed.), *Motivation in education.* New York: Academic Press, 1977.

Hersov, L., & Berg, I. (eds.). *Out of school: Modern perspectives on truancy and school refusal.* New York: Wiley, 1980.

Howard, M., & Anderson, R. Early identification of potential school dropouts: A literature review. *Child Welfare,* 1978, *57,* 221–231.

Husen, T. *The school in question: A comparative study of the school and its future in Western society.* Oxford: Oxford University Press, 1979.

Insel, P., & Jacobsen, L. (eds.). *What do you expect?: An inquiry into self-fulfilling prophecies.* Menlo Park, Cal.: Cummings Publishers, 1975.

Jencks, C., & Brown, M. Effects of high schools on their students. *Harvard Educational Review.* 1975, *45,* 273–324.

Johnson, D. Conflict management in the school and classroom. In D. Bar-Tel and L. Saxe (eds.), *Social psychology in education.* New York: Halsted, 1978.

Johnson, D., & Johnson, R. *Learning together and alone.* Englewood Cliffs, N.J.: Prentice-Hall, 1975.

Johnston, L., & Bachman, J. Educational institutions. In J. Adams, (ed.), *Understanding adolescence.* New York: Allyn and Bacon, 1976.

Jones, J. What superintendents and schools boards can do. *Phi Delta Kappan.* November 1978, pp. 221–223.

Jones, R. (ed.). *Mainstreaming and the minority child.* Reston, Va.: Council for Exceptional Children, 1976.

Kahn, J., Nursten, J., & Carroll, H. *Unwillingly to school: School phobia or school refusal.* New York: Pergamon, 1981.

Kandel, D., Raveis, V., & Kandel, P. Continuity in discontinuities: Adjustment in young adulthood of former school absentees. *Youth and Society.* 1984, *15,* 325–352.

Kirschenbaum, H., Simon, S., & Napier, R. *Wad-ja-get: The grading game in American education.* New York: Hart, 1971.

Kogelman, S., & Waren, J. *Mind over math.* New York: McGraw-Hill, 1979.

Kozberg, G. Left out kids in a left out school. *Harvard Graduate School of Education Association Bulletin,* 1980, *25,* 24–26.

Larkin, R. *Suburban youth in cultural crisis.* New York: Oxford University Press, 1979.

Levine, M. Are teachers becoming more humane? *Phi Delta Kappan.* January 1978, p. 353.

Lipsitz, J. *Successful Schools for Young Adolescents.* Carrboro, N.C.: Center for the Study of Early Adolescence, 1983.

Lloyd, D. Prediction of school failure from third grade data. *Educational and Psychological Measurement,* 1978, *38,* 1193–1200.

Lorton, E. *The teachers' world.* Washington, D.C.: ERIC Clearinghouse on Teacher Education, 1979.

Maeroff, G. *Don't blame the kids: The trouble with America's public schools.* New York: McGraw-Hill, 1982.

Make something happen: A report on secondary schooling for Hispanics. National Commission on Secondary Schooling for Hispanics. New York, 1984.

McPartland, J. *Violence in schools: Prospectives and programs.* Lexington, Mass.: Lexington Books, 1977.

Medway, F. Causal attributions for school-related problems. *Journal of Educational Psychology,* 1979, *71,* 809–818.

Moursund, J. *Learning and the learner.* Monterey, Cal.: Brooks-Cole, 1976.

National Assessment of Educational Progress (NAEP). *National science assessment.* Denver, Col.: Education Commission of the States, 1978.

National Assessment of Educational Progress (NAEP). *Reading, thinking, and writing: Results from the 1979–80 national assessment of reading and literature.* Denver, Col.: Education Commission of the States, 1981.

National Assessment of Educational Progress (NAEP). *The third national mathematics assessment: Results, trends and issues.* Denver, Col.: Education Commission of the States, 1983.

National Center for Education Statistics (NCES). *High school and beyond study: 1980 sophomore cohort.* Washington, D.C.: NCES 1983.

National Center for the Study of Corporal Punishment. *Corporal punishment in schools.* Philadelphia, Pa.: Temple University, 1977.

National Education Association (NEA). *Ability grouping: A research summary.* Washington, D.C.: National Education Association, 1968.

National Education Association (NEA). *Status of the American public school teacher.* West Haven, Conn.: NEA, 1982.

National Institute of Education (NIE). *Compensatory education study.* Washington, D.C.: Department of Health, Education and Welfare, 1977.

National Institute of Education (NIE) *Violent schools—safe schools. The safe school study report to the Congress.* Washington, D.C.: National Institute of Education, 1978.

National Institute of Education (NIE). *State education statistics.* Washington, D.C.: National Institute of Education, January 1984.

National School Board Association (NSBA). *Discipline in our big city schools.* Washington, D.C.: National School Board Association, 1977.

National School Public Relations Association (NSPRA) *Suspensions and expulsions: Current trends in schools' policies and programs.* Arlington, Va.: National School Public Relations Association, 1976.

National Science Foundation. *What are the needs in precollege science, math and social science education?* Washington, D.C.: U.S. Government Printing Office, 1980.

National Task Force on Excellence in Education. *A nation at risk: The imperative for educational reform.* Washington, D.C.: U.S. Government Printing Office, April 1983.

Nielsen, L. Creating in-school suspension programs. *The School Counselor.* May 1979, 325–331. (a)

Nielsen, L. Let's suspend suspensions. *American Personnel and Guidance Journal.* May 1979, 442–446. (b)

Nielsen, L. *How to motivate adolescents: A guide for parents, teachers and counselors.* Englewood, Cliffs, N.J.: Prentice-Hall, 1982.

Owen, D. *None of the above.* Boston: Houghton Mifflin, 1984.

Patchen, M., Hoffman, G., & Brown, W. Academic performance of black high school students under different conditions of contact with white peers. *Sociology of Education,* 1980, *53,* 33–51.

Peng, S., Fetters, W., & Kolstad, A. *High school and beyond: A national longitudinal study for the 1980s.* Washington, D.C.: National Center for Education Statistics, 1981.

Pepitone, E. (ed). *Children in cooperation and competition.* Lexington, Mass.: Lexington Books, 1980.

Phillips, B. *School, stress and anxiety.* New York: Human Science Press, 1978.

Plisko, V. (ed.). *The condition of education: 1982–1983.* Washington, D.C.: National Center for Education Statistics, U.S. Department of Education, 1984.

Ranbom, S. S.A.T. scores up 4 points, biggest jump in 21 years. *Education Week.* September 26, 1984, p. 1.

Rehberg, R., & Rosenthal, E. *Class and merit in the American high school.* New York: Longman, 1978.

Rincon, E. Aptitude testing, higher education and minority groups: A review of research. In A. Baron (ed.), *Chicano psychology.* New York: Praeger, 1981.

Rosenbaum, J. *Making inequality: The hidden curriculum of high school tracking.* New York: Wiley, 1976.

Rosenthal, R., & Jacobson, E. *Pygmalion in the classroom.* New York: Holt, Rinehart and Winston, 1968.

Rutter, M., Maughan, B., Mortimore, P., & Ouston, J. *Fifteen thousand hours: Secondary schools and their effects on children.* Cambridge, Mass.: Harvard University Press, 1979.

Sarason, I. The test anxiety scale. In C. Speilberger and I. Sarason (eds.), *Stress and anxiety.* Washington, D.C.: Hemisphere Press, 1980. pp. 220–241.

Science Assessment Research Project. *National assessment of science achievement:* Minneapolis: University of Minnesota, 1983.

Schmiecheck, R. Adolescent identity formation and the organizational structure of high schools. *Adolescence,* 1979, *14,* 191–196.

Sells, L. Mathematics—a critical filter. *The Science Teacher,* 1978, *45,* 2.

Sizer, T. *Horace's compromise: The dilemma of the American high school.* Boston: Houghton Mifflin, 1984.

Sommer, B. Truancy in early adolescence. *Journal of early adolescence,* 1985, *5,* 145–160.

Southern Regional Council. *The student pushout.* Atlanta, Ga.: Southern Regional Council of Education, 1973.

St. Johns, N. *School desegregation outcomes for children.* New York: Wiley, 1975.

Task Force on Education for Economic Growth. *Action for excellence.* Washington, D.C.: Education Commission for the States, June 1983.

Time. June 16, 1980, pp. 54–63.

Tobias, S. *Overcoming math anxiety.* New York: Norton, 1978.

Tobias, S. Anxiety research in educational psychology. *Journal of Educational Psychology,* 1979, *71,* 573–582.

Trickett, E., & Moos, R. Personal correlates of contrasting environments: Student satisfaction in high school classrooms. *American Journal of Community Psychology,* 1974, *2,* 1–12.

U.S. Bureau of the Census. *School enrollment: Social and economic characteristics of students, 1980.* Washington, D.C.: U.S. Government Printing Office, 1981.

Vargas, J. *Behavioral psychology for teachers.* New York: Harper & Row, 1977, pp. 163–183.

Welsh, R. Delinquency, corporal punishment and the schools. *Crime and Delinquency,* 1978, *24,* 336–354.

Wertz, W., et al. *Report of the advisory panel on SAT score decline.* Princeton, N.J.: College Entrance Exam Board, 1977.

Williams, D. Teachers are in trouble. *Newsweek,* April 27, 1981, pp. 78–84. (a)

Williams, D. Why public schools fail. *Newsweek,* April 21, 1981, pp. 62–65. (b)

Williams, J. (ed.), *The state of black America.* New York: National Urban League, 1982.

Wing Sue, D. (ed.). *Counseling the culturally different.* New York: Wiley, 1981.

Yankelovich, D. Who gets ahead in America? *Psychology Today,* 1979, *13,* 28–34.

Zajonc, R. The decline and rise of scholastic aptitude scores. *American Psychologist,* August 1986, *41,* 862–867.

Chapter Outline

Goals and Objectives

This chapter will enable you to:

- *Debunk myths about the ''typical'' U. S. family of the 1980s*
- *Describe the impact of single-parent families, divorce, poverty, and mothers' employment on adolescents*
- *Examine the validity of the ''generation gap'' and explore the transformations in a family during adolescence*
- *Explore the father's role in adolescents' intellectual, emotional, and social development*
- *Consider the ramifications for adolescents of their parents' homosexual relationships and exogamous marriages*
- *Present the limitations of the research on family interactions and parental influence*
- *Explore the etiology and the consequences of child abuse and incest*
- *Compare the effects of various styles of parenting*

Concepts and Terminology

AFDC	*dual-career families*
blaming the victim	*Cinderella complex*
exogamy	*individuated*
authoritarian style	*authoritative style*
confluence theory	*permissive style*

8 Adolescents and Their Families

Changes in the Family: Impact on Adolescents

The poet Ogden Nash described the family as "a unit composed not only of children, but of men, women, an occasional animal and the common cold" (Brussell, 1970). Unfortunately, Nash's definition does not bring us any closer to answering some of the serious questions confronting sociologists and psychologists who study U. S. families: What constitutes a "good" family? How do family members influence each other's behavior and development? When people complain about the "deterioration of the family," to what dimensions of the family are they referring?

Although authorities disagree over how families affect adolescents' development, there is little disagreement that today's families differ considerably from those of former generations. Examining recent trends, such as single-parent and interracial families, expands our understanding of the kinds of families in which today's adolescents are growing up. Completing the quiz in Box 8.1 may underscore the point that many of our images of the family are statistically unwarranted. Since we are apt to base our visions of the "typical" adolescent's family on our own lives or on stereotypes from the media and folklore, we too often develop ideas that are far from the realities.

Single-Parent Families

The rising rates of out-of-wedlock birth and of divorce have placed U. S. adolescents in a new kind of family. Divorce, an option virtually nonexistent in earlier decades, has literally transformed the family unit. For example, in 1880 only about 5 percent of married couples ever divorced, whereas today more than one-third of all first marriages end in divorce (Paddock & Thomas, 1981). Demographers are now predicting that half of all marriages begun in the 1980s will fail to last a lifetime, and that 40–50 percent of the children born during the 1970s will experience either the death of a parent or a parent's divorce before the age of 18 (Glick & Norton, 1979). More dramatic still, experts predict that between 30 percent and 50 percent of all U. S. families will be headed by a single parent in 1990 ("Playing both Mother and Father," 1985).

As the statistics in Chapter 10 will demonstrate, the rising illegitimacy rate is also contributing to the phenomenon of single-parent families. Births to unmarried women have increased more than fourfold since 1950 and have doubled since 1965 (U. S. Bureau of the Census, 1982). As a consequence of these high rates of illegitimacy and divorce, the two-parent household has become almost an anomaly. For example, by 1982 only 63 percent of U. S. children were living with both biological parents, and almost 23 million young people are living in a family other than one in which both biological parents are present. About 20 percent of U. S. children are being raised by their mothers, 2 percent by their fathers, 10 percent by one parent and a stepparent, and 10 percent by adoptive parents. In addition to these figures, another 1.1 million children live alone with their mothers because their fathers are dead (see Table 8.1 and Figure 8.1).

Even though the problems associated with being a single parent extend far beyond financial worries, the relationship between poverty and single parenthood is staggering. According to a U. S. Commission on Civil Rights study, 54 percent of single-parent families were living below the poverty line in 1983. Combined with the fact that 90 percent of the nation's one-parent households are headed by the mother, these statistics explain why some analysts have referred to a "new class of poor" and to "the feminization of poverty" ("Playing both Mother and Father," 1985).

Divorce and Adolescent Development

Since divorce has become such a common phenomenon in our society, researchers have devoted increasing attention to the impact of parents' separations on adolescents. Although divorce does not affect all adolescents in a similar fashion, certain reactions appear to be fairly common (Allers, 1982; Francke, 1980; Kulka & Weingarten, 1979; Wallerstein & Kelly, 1980).

To begin with, most adolescents report wanting more information about the divorce than their parents have provided. Moreover, some youths initially feel responsible for the divorce and want their parents to reunite, even in cases where children are aware that the marriage was an unhappy one. Adolescents, however, are far less likely than younger children in the family to feel personally responsible for their parents' marital difficulties. Interestingly, most siblings spend more time together after their parents' divorce, offering each other solace and exchanging information about the custody agreements and their parents' new lifestyles. It is not surprising that adolescents often resent the additional household and child-care responsibilities that they must assume after a divorce. Unfortunately, some young people are also expected to become counselors and confidants to their parents whose unhappiness, loneliness, and stress cause them to turn to the eldest children for comfort.

8.1 Are You Sure?

The U. S. Family: Facts and Fictions

How accurate is your vision of the U. S. family? When envisioning the typical adolescent's family, do you permit your own personal history to obscure the statistical realities of the 1980s? After answering the following questions, study the correct answers that follow and note the discrepancies between your own family experiences and the national statistics on families in our society.

1. How old are the children in most families?
2. What percentage of the children born in 1980 had unmarried mothers?
3. What proportion of children are being raised in female-headed households?
4. Do most children under the age of 14 grow up in central cities, suburbs, or nonmetropolitan areas?
5. What percentage of the children in the United States are living in a situation other than a family where both biological parents are present?
6. How typical is it for children to be raised only by the father?
7. How many children live with adoptive parents, foster parents, or grandparents?
8. How many children are being raised by one biological parent and a stepparent?
9. How common is it for children to be living with both their biological parents?
10. What percentage of children are living with mothers who are widowed?
11. How large is the average U. S. family?
12. How common are only children?
13. How educated are the heads of households for white and black adolescents?
14. How much money do black, white, and Hispanic families earn?
15. How many married and divorced mothers are employed?
16. When mothers are employed, who takes care of the children?
17. How financially well-off are today's children, compared to those who grew up in the 1960s and 1970s?
18. What proportion of U. S. children receive some assistance from the federal welfare program, Aid to Families with Dependent Children?

According to psychologists like David Elkind (1981), too many parents hurry their teenage children into adulthood after a divorce by disclosing too much information about their marital problems. From the perspective of those who share Elkind's view, parents should not treat their adolescent children like adult peers by seeking their counsel on sexual or marital issues. After interviewing homosexual parents and their children, Joe Gantz (1983) criticizes divorced parents for disclosing too much intimate information to their adolescent children:

> There was a time many years ago, when I thought such honesty with children was terrific. I now have misgivings about this tendency to censor nothing in our conversations with them. What we end up with are children, having the same capabilities and needs that children have always had, pretending to be adults, using words they can't possibly really understand, mimicking our insights, our excuses for not acting like parents (p. xii).

19. How much welfare money do families with children receive?
20. After separating from their families, how much financial support do U. S. fathers give their children?

Answers:

1. In 1982 there were 62.7 million children under the age of 18 in the United States. Of these, 20.6 million were between the ages of 0 and 5, 19.8 million between 6 and 11, and 22.3 million between 12 and 17.

2, 3. See Table 8.1.

4. In 1980 about 27 percent of all children under the age of 14 were living in central cities, 39 percent in the suburbs of metropolitan areas, and 34 percent in nonmetropolitan areas. Black children are more than twice as likely as whites to grow up in central-city neighborhoods.

5–9. See Table 8.1.

10. In 1982, 1.1 million children were living with widowed mothers.

11, 12. In 1981, 48 percent of adult couples had no children living with them. They either had not yet had children or their children were no longer living at home. About 21 percent of all couples had one child, 19 percent had two children, 8 percent had three children, and 4 percent had four or more children.

13. In 1979, 75 percent of all white high-school students came from families in which the head of the household had 12 or more years of education. In contrast, only 45 percent of black high-school students came from homes where the head of the household had 12 or more years of education.

14. See Table 8.2 and Figure 8.2.

15–20. Read the paragraphs under "Women's Employment" and "Poverty and the Family."

SOURCE: Based on data from Select Committee on Children, Youth and Families, *U. S. children and their families: Current conditions and recent trends.* Washington, D. C.: Foundation for Child Development, 1983

Besides having to assume new roles with their parents and siblings, most adolescents must also confront new economic and sexual issues after their parents' divorce. Because the family's income almost always declines after two households are established, many adolescents resent their parents for depriving them of the material possessions they could once afford. Vacations, clothes, records, and expensive gifts may suddenly become luxuries that parents can no longer provide. In addition, many adolescents feel resentful, jealous, or embarrassed when their divorced parents begin to date. Some try to sabotage their parents' new romances by making unkind comments or by behaving badly in the presence of their parents' dates. Since almost all divorced parents eventually remarry, adolescents' hostilities can create special distress for parents who want their children to approve of their dates as potential stepparents.

Unfortunately, the social and financial changes that usually accompany a divorce generally cause disruption in the adolescent's academic or personal life

Table 8.1

The U.S. Family, 1981–1982

	Percent of All Families
Illegitimate births to white females	10
Illegitimate births to black females	55
White children living with mothers only	15
Black children living with mothers only	46
Children living with fathers only	2
Children living with both biological parents	63
Children living with parent and a stepparent	10
Children living with adoptive parents	10
Children living with relatives other than parents	2
Children living in foster homes or institutions	1
Children living in families below the poverty level	20
Whites	20
Hispanics	45
Blacks	53
Children receiving AFDC assistance*	11

* Aid to Families with Dependent Children is a federally funded welfare program for impoverished families with children.

SOURCE: Select Committee on Children, Youth and Families, *U.S. children and their families: Current conditions and recent trends.* Washington, D.C.: Foundation for Child Development, 1983.

Figure 8.1

Living arrangements of children under 18: 1982

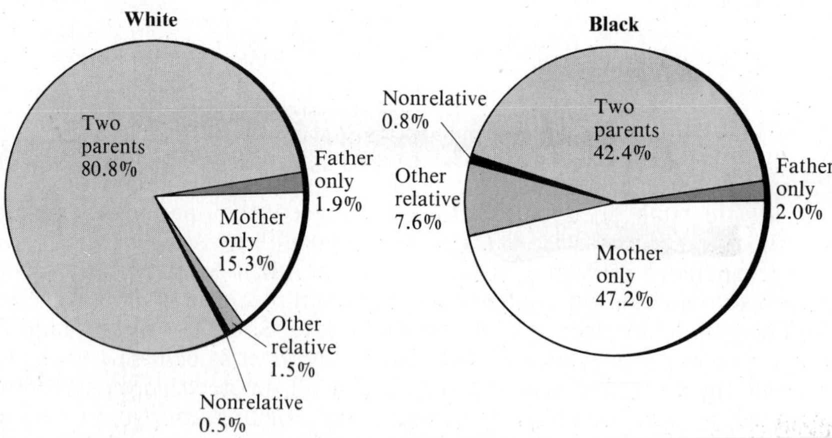

SOURCE: *Population profile of the United States: 1982.* Washington, D. C.: U. S. Bureau of the Census. Current population reports, P-23, no. 130, 1984.

outside the family setting. If an adolescent is going to develop academic or social problems, these generally manifest themselves before the actual divorce occurs, since most older children are aware of the tensions in their parents' marriage. Among the manifestations of an adolescent's distress over the divorce are lethargy, moodiness, withdrawal, a decline in grades, and the development of physical ailments like headaches, tics, or stuttering.

It has been argued that, during their parents' divorce, children undergo stages similar to those of patients who know they are dying, as described by Elizabeth Kübler-Ross (Allers, 1982). First is the denial of reality: "No, my parents are fine. They aren't really getting divorced. This is just a bad dream." Next is anger, "Why is this happening to my family? What did I do to deserve parents who are doing this to me?" This stage is often followed by a period of bargaining: "Dear God, if only you will make my parents happy with each other, I'll get along better with my brother." "Dad, if only you won't divorce Mom, I'll get along better with my brother." When the bargaining fails, depression begins: "It doesn't matter what I do, they're going through with this divorce. How am I ever going to be happy again?" Finally, comes acceptance: "Okay, Mom and Dad are divorced and there's nothing I can do about it. Lots of other kids are in this situation and somehow I'm going to adapt to this mess."

In observing adolescents' reactions to their parents' divorce, some researchers contend that the child's behavior may be influenced as much by society's expectations as by the actual dynamics within the family. Illustrating this hypothesis, a study was conducted with 30 teachers who viewed a videotape of a boy interacting with his friends. Half of the teachers were told that the boy's parents were divorced, and the other half were told his parents were married. After viewing the videotape, the teachers rated the boy's personality and predicted how he would behave in five hypothetical situations. Teachers who believed the boy's parents were divorced described him as less content, less able to cope with stress, and less well-adjusted emotionally than those who believed he was living with both parents. Despite the fact that all these teachers had viewed identical behavior in the videotape, they interpreted the boy's conduct differently on the basis of the information they were given about his parents' marital status (Santrock & Tracy, 1978).

Findings such as this suggest that adults who interact with adolescents from divorced families need to avoid creating self-fulfilling prophecies that may exacerbate problems. Such findings should not be construed to mean, however, that adolescents would suffer no negative consequences whatsoever after their parents' divorce if it weren't for other people's negative expectations and self-fulfilling prophecies. To the contrary, there is ample evidence that a father's absence from the family affects his children's social and academic development, as we shall see in subsequent sections of this chapter.

The extent to which divorce interferes with an adolescent's development is understandably debatable, given the idiosyncratic nature of each family's circumstances and of its members' personalities. Nevertheless, data such as Hetherington's (1972, 1979) studies indicate that the impact of a parent's divorce may extend far beyond childhood or adolescence. According to her, adolescent girls with divorced parents more often seek boys' attention, act socially uninhibited around boys, and date and have sex earlier than girls living with both parents. In contrast, girls whose fathers have died tend to be withdrawn and shy around boys. Daughters of divorced parents expressed the most negative attitudes toward men, tended to marry younger, and more often chose husbands with drug or employment problems. Their husbands expressed more negative feelings toward them and their children and were more impulsive emotionally than husbands of the women from widowed or two-parent families. Widows' daughters were more likely to marry men who were vocationally successful and ambitious but socially inhibited.

Moreover, Hetherington's data show that girls from two-parent families appear to make wiser marital choices and to be more sexually satisfied with their husbands. They reported having fewer sexual problems than girls raised in homes without fathers. It is important to note that Hetherington's research was limited in that she studied only girls from lower- and lower-middle-class families in one city. Despite this methodological shortcoming, Hetherington's research suggests that divorce or a father's death can have considerable influence over a daughter's relationships with men.

Further corroborating Hetherington's findings, Rutter's review of the literature shows that loss of a parent through death is not associated with subsequent development of antisocial behavior in children, while loss of a parent through abandonment or divorce is correlated with delinquency. It is noteworthy that parental discord and disharmony are correlated with children's subsequent antisocial behavior, even when the parents remain married, which suggests that preserving an unhappy marriage can do as much if not more harm to children than obtaining a divorce (Rutter, 1981). Furthermore, when divorced parents continue to expose their children to their quarrels, the children's behavior is disrupted over a longer period of time than when parents resolve their conflicts in private (Hetherington, Cox, & Cox, 1982).

At present the most comprehensive study regarding the impact of divorce is based on data collected between 1966 and 1970 from a nationally representative sample of 7,514 adolescents (Dornbusch et al., 1985). Although more current data might yield different results, given the changes in social norms since the 1960s, the study is nonetheless noteworthy for its large, representative sample and for the number of variables examined. Moreover, socioeconomic class was factored out before making comparisons between one-parent and two-parent households, thus eliminating an important confounding variable, since most one-parent households are from lower-income brackets.

Analyses of these data revealed that divorce has certain negative ramifications for adolescents from all income brackets. First, adolescents from one-parent families exhibited more deviant behavior than those living with both biological parents. The measures of deviance included being truant, smoking regularly, running away from home, being disciplined at school, and being arrested for delinquent acts. Even though females were less deviant than males, the differences between coming from a single-parent or a two-parent family were of almost as great a magnitude as among males. Of particular interest, however, is that male adolescents with stepfathers had rates of deviance almost as high as males being raised by their mothers alone. In contrast, females with stepfathers were engaged in less deviant behavior than girls living only with their mother. This finding suggests that male adolescents may in some ways be better off being raised alone by their mothers than having to interact with a stepfather.

As might be expected, adolescents living only with their mothers tended to have more input into decisions and to be granted more independence than their peers in two-parent households. And on the basis of our society's gender roles, single mothers granted their adolescent sons autonomy and decision-making powers at an earlier age than their daughters. The presence of another adult in a mother-only household, however, brings the level of control exerted over adolescents closer to the control exerted over children in two-parent families. Similarly, having another adult in the household was associated with lower rates of adolescent deviance. When the level of the parent's education and the family's income were considered, these results remained unchanged.

In sum, such data lend considerable support to the contention that adolescents living with both biological parents are generally in a more advantageous position than those living with only their mothers. Nevertheless, other data indicate that divorce is not always as permanently or as profoundly disturbing to adolescents as is often assumed (Allers, 1982; Wallerstein & Kelly, 1980). In situations where parents quarrel frequently and create stress within the family, children are often better off socially, emotionally, and academically after their parents separate. In assessing the effects of divorce, it must be noted that youngsters who react most negatively to their parents' separation often had serious difficulties within their families preceding the divorce. Moreover, the impact of divorce is generally greater on young children than on adolescents, who are often able to resume a normal pattern of life a year or so after their parents' separation. Teenagers subjected to the most distress are those whose parents pressure them to take sides in marital disputes or custody settlements. In general, the older children are at the time of the divorce, the more easily they adjust to their family's new situation.

Contrary to expectations, some investigations have found few differences between adolescents who live with both parents and those whose parents are separated (Biller, 1981a). These investigations do suggest, however, that in many families children interact with their fathers so infrequently that their development is not as dramatically affected by his absence as might be anticipated. This point is corroborated by data in subsequent sections of this chapter, showing that the father's mere presence in the household is no guarantee that meaningful interactions are occurring between him and his children.

Although almost all adolescents are inevitably unsettled and disturbed by their parents' divorce, the extent of the disturbance can vary widely, depending on the circumstances surrounding the divorce and the adolescent's own level of cognitive and emotional development (Wallerstein & Kelly, 1980). Although unsettled by the change in the family's structure, adolescents who are socially sophisticated and cognitively mature often endorse their parents' decision to divorce and adapt relatively quickly to the new circumstances. In contrast, early adolescence appears to be a more emotionally turbulent time, during which the effects of divorce tend to be more upsetting. Nevertheless, the data do not warrant our assuming that all children will inevitably respond to their parents' divorce with maladaptive behavior, depression, or hostility, especially in cases where the divorce occurs during the child's adolescence and under circumstances that offer support and an absence of hostility between the parents. It has been hypothesized that since divorce has become such a common phenomenon in our society, children today feel less ostracized and less stigmatized by the experience than their counterparts during the 1950s and 1960s.

One recent investigation tested these hypotheses with 234 eighth-graders from divorced and intact families. In contrast to research conducted during the early 1970s, the 1980 study found that neither the adolescents from intact homes nor those from divorced families attached a stigma to having divorced parents. Only about one-tenth of the children said they tried to keep their friends from finding out about their parents' divorce. As a further reflection of changing social mores, 60 percent of all the adolescents disagreed with or were undecided about the statement, "Marriage means living happily ever after," and 85 percent agreed that divorce is sometimes necessary. Interestingly, these attitudes were not significantly affected by whether or not the adolescent's own parents were divorced (Paddock & Thomas, 1981).

This same study, however, serves as a demonstration that several findings from earlier research are still valid in the 1980s. According to this research, 98 percent of the adolescents from intact homes agreed that their friends acted differently after their parent's divorce. Moreover, children from intact homes had somewhat more positive self-images than those from divorced homes. Almost all the adolescents viewed divorce as a "big deal," and those from intact families clearly expressed the wish that their own parents remain married. Neither the children of divorce nor those from intact homes saw many positive aspects to divorce in their own families.

Although the research generally acknowledges that divorce causes most children to suffer considerable short-term trauma, relatively little is known about how divorce affects a child's adult life. One fact that seems fairly well documented is that young people whose parents divorce tend to have more divorces themselves than those whose parents remain married, although they are no more unhappy, more depressed, or more anxious during their adult years than people raised by both parents (Kulka & Weingarten, 1979). Interestingly, data from the 1972 through 1977 General Social Surveys found that adults whose parents had divorced were more trustful and confident and less estranged and anomic than those from intact families (Nock, 1982).

Data deemphasizing the negative consequences of divorce, however, are not unchallenged. Representing the long-term negative consequences of divorce is one recent study based on data from 703 white adults in eight national surveys between 1973 and 1982. The adults from divorced families fared less well in terms of most of the researchers' measures of psychological well-being, happiness, health, and satisfaction than those whose parents had died or those from intact families. In addition, the age of the adults did not seem to affect the differences between adults from divorced and intact families, a finding that suggests that the impact of a parent's divorce may not diminish with age, as has often been hypothesized. Despite their findings, Glenn argues that the data should not be interpreted to mean that the effects of divorce are negative for all children or that divorce cannot have positive effects. Glenn points out that today's adolescents generally experience less stigma associated with their parents' divorce, which may, therefore, limit the negative ramifications of their parents' divorce on their future adult lives (Glenn & Kramer, 1985).

Adding still another complexity to the research on divorce are the recent changes regarding child custody. Until the very recent past, the question of child custody was relatively simple: Mothers were awarded custody of all the children, unless the father chose to establish her mental or physical incompetence. Between 1970 and 1978, however, the number of single-parent families headed by men doubled, meaning that 2 percent of the children in today's single-parent homes are living with their fathers (*U. S. Children and Their Families*, 1983). As social mores have changed, the courts, social scientists, and parents are beginning to question the assumption that living with the mother is always in a child's or an adolescent's best interest. Some recent research indicates that children who live with the same-sex parent are more mature, more sociable, and more independent than those who live with the opposite-sex parent (Santrock & Warshak, 1979). As divorced men assume more responsibility for the primary custody of their children, and as single men become more willing to adopt children, researchers will be able to more clearly delineate the advantages and disadvantages of being raised by a father.

In summary, although definitive statements about the immediate effects of divorce on any particular adolescent must be tentative, most data suggest that adolescents respond to their parents' separation with a mixture of sadness, anger, confusion, and regret, as Box 8.2 indicates. The long-range effects, however, are far less certain, given the scarcity of data and the contradictions that exist in the extant research. Arguments supporting or refuting the permanent effects of parents' divorce on a child's adult life can be viewed only tentatively until more data become available. Since there is no evidence of present divorce rates abating, questions related to the impact of divorce on adolescents will inevitably continue to attract the attention of contemporary researchers.

Women's Employment

In addition to divorce, many families are undergoing dramatic transformations as a consequence of women's employment. Society's more tolerant attitudes about educating and employing women have enabled more females to develop their vocational talents. More important, changes in the U. S. economy and the rising rates of illegitimacy and divorce have necessitated the entry of women into the workforce. In short, most mothers have become employed out of economic necessity. For example, in 1980 only 7 percent of all married couples with children were classified as "poor," in contrast to 44 percent of the families maintained by women (Grossman, 1983). Thus, the assertion that most mothers do not "have" to work is financially inaccurate. To reiterate this point, national statistics show that the lower the husband's salary, the more likely it is that his wife will be employed (U.S. Bureau of the Census, 1980).

Since most adolescents' families are headed by two employed parents, it may seem surprising that median family incomes are still relatively modest: $21,904 for white families, $12,674 for blacks, and $14,717 for Hispanics (see Table 8.2). Moreover, as the statistics in Figure 8.1 demonstrate, increasingly few children have unemployed mothers. Underscoring this relatively rapid change in the U.S. family, in 1950 only one-third of all women were employed, but by 1981, 45 percent of all preschoolers had working mothers, and 60 percent of all married couples with children under 18 had two wage earners (Grossman, 1983). Demographers estimate that before the end of the 1980s, 55 percent of mothers with preschool children and 70 percent with children in school will be employed (Smith, 1979). In sum, within the decade, very few adolescents' mothers will remain unemployed (see Figure 8.2).

With the dramatic rise in women's employment, the question of interest to adolescent psychologists has become: How does a mother's employment affect her adolescent children? To begin with, today's adolescents are more likely than

8.2 Adolescent Voices

The Kids' Book of Divorce

Twenty students between the ages of 11 and 14 at the Fayerweather Street School in Cambridge, Massachusetts have written a book about divorce for other young people. Describing their fears and experiences, these adolescents are trying to help others cope with the confusion and sadness surrounding divorce. The following excerpts are from their book.

> I came home from school one day last fall and found that my mother wasn't home. This was unusual. My father was sitting at the kitchen table, talking to my older brother and when I entered the room they fell silent and looked at me with long, serious faces. I made a couple of jokes, but it was obvious it was no joking matter. Then they hit me with it: My parents were getting divorced. "Are you kidding? What the hell do you and mom think you're doing just deciding to get divorced, huh?" I said in a high pitched voice to my father. "Shut up, Katie, and listen," my older brother Tom replied. My father took over from there and explained that mom and he had decided to get divorced about two months ago, and a fight they had had earlier today set off the separation and "bye-bye mom." My stomach churned as it always does when I'm upset and I bit my nails feverishly. I was furious with resentment and anger that they hadn't told me earlier. I felt as though I had been denied the information that formed my future. Though I still resent my parents for not telling me, I now see their reasons for their actions. That makes it a little easier.
>
> It was very hard for me to remember what went on around the time they signed the legal papers saying they weren't married anymore, though it was only one year ago. I can remember only one thing: asking my mother approximately one week after it was over exactly what day it happened so I could put it on my calendar. It as a very trying and confusing time for me and I think that I have mentally blocked out all of it.
>
> Before we started writing this book, we had a lot of discussions about the myths about divorce and about kids of divorced families. We got together as a large group and we brainstormed the ideas of "experts" who supported the nuclear family and hated divorce. We wanted to think of all the bad things that people say might happen to the kids when their parents get a divorce. These myths say that kids of divorce: would become mentally disturbed, would commit suicide, could get a rare disease, would be on drugs, would become alcoholics, would become thieves and rob banks, and steal cars, would get divorced themselves, would murder their siblings, would talk back to teachers, would become violent, would smoke pot in class, would be angry all the time, would be lonely all the time, would have no friends, and would think something's wrong with them. We think these things are not true. Some people still think that a divorce will ruin a kid's life. While we disagree with this, we are aware that having divorced parents can change us in some important ways.

SOURCE: Fayerweather Street School, *The kids' book of divorce: By, for, and about kids.* New York: Vintage Books, 1982.

Table 8.2

Family Income, 1982

	Median Income ($)
White	
All white families	24,603
Completed 4 years high school	24,617
Completed 4 years or more college	38,980
Black	
All black families	13,599
Completed 4 years high school	16,425
Completed 4 years or more college	30,412
Hispanic	
All Hispanic families	16,228
Completed 4 years high school	20,358
Completed 4 years or more college	34,193
Total number of families 61,393,000	23,433

SOURCE: U.S. Bureau of the Census, *Current Population Reports.* Series P-60, No. 142, 1984.

their cohorts in earlier decades to have been cared for during the day, as young children, by adults other than their parents. Adolescents with younger siblings are often familiar with their parents' concerns regarding day-care services. At present, most day-care services are expensive and very few child-care services are provided by employers. In addition, recent administrations have been less than enthusiastic about funding day-care centers for employed parents, viewing such services as contributing to the "deterioration of the American family." Thus, only about 15 percent of all preschoolers are enrolled in day-care centers. Understandably, lower-income families are the most dependent on federally funded day-care. For example, of those children who were enrolled in day-care programs in 1980, 61 percent of the blacks were in publicly funded programs, in contrast to 30 percent of the whites (U.S. Bureau of the Census, 1982).

In addition to witnessing or to personally experiencing the phenomenon of child care by adults outside the family, adolescents are more likely than ever before to be members of dual-career families (Rappaport & Rappaport, 1977). In dual-career families, both the husband and wife have professional careers, earn similar salaries, and share equivalent vocational status in society. Interestingly, however, adolescents growing up in dual-career families will observe their mothers doing most of the child rearing and most of the housework. Even when their mothers are as professionally successful and as well educated as their fathers, most data indicate that adolescents will seldom witness an equal sharing of household or child-care responsibilities between their parents (Ericksen, Yancey, & Ericksen, 1979; Ferber & Huber, 1979; Rappaport & Rappaport, 1977; Smith, 1979).

Despite the fact that most of their own mothers are employed, many adolescents still endorse the traditional perspective that women with preschool chil-

Figure 8.2

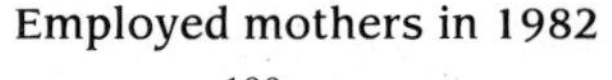

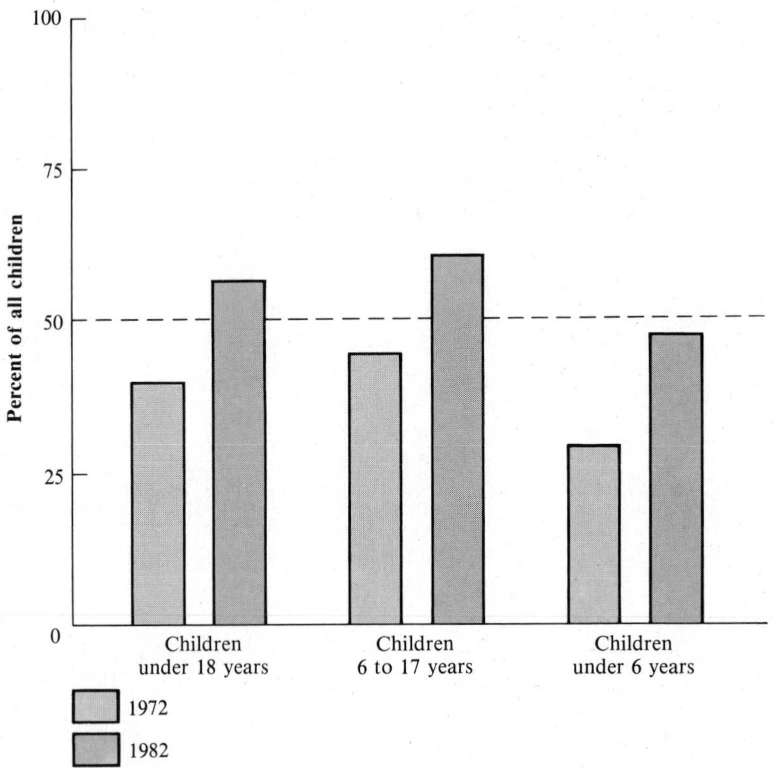

SOURCE: *Women at work,* Washington, D.C.: Bureau of Labor Statistics, Bulletin 2168, April 1983, p. 21.

dren should be full-time homemakers and that fathers should never relinquish their jobs to raise the children while the mother works. For example, in *Monitoring the Future*'s national samples of several thousand high-school seniors from across the country, in 1980 only 6 percent of them approved of both the husband and wife working if they had preschool children (Bachman, Johnston, & O'Malley, 1981). As the data cited in Chapter 5 demonstrated, despite the economic reality that most families need both parents' incomes, a number of adolescents and their elders continue to believe that fathers should bring home the bacon while mothers rock the cradle.

The attitudes of adolescents who oppose a mother's employment are predicated upon notions that were especially popular during the 1950s. At that time many researchers reinforced the popular notion that a mother's employment deprived her children of emotional and psychological support. Thus, the employed mother was accused of contributing to her child's juvenile delinquency, emotional disturbances, and poor academic performance (Glueck & Glueck, 1957). Despite the fact that recent research disputes these assertions, updated versions of these fears are still voiced: "If we let day-care centers assume a mother's responsibilities, children will be deprived of intellectual and emotional experiences that only their own mothers can provide." "If you're going to let someone else take care of your children during the day, why be a parent in the first place?" "The family is deteriorating because nobody wants to stay home and raise their own kids anymore." "I would feel guilty letting other adults stay with my young child while I worked."

According to the well-known psychologist Sandra Scarr (1983), society is still tyrannized by the belief that any option other than a mother's care will adversely affect a child's development. While most Americans feel comfortable with the idea of adolescents' mothers working, many are still ill at ease with the idea of a preschooler's mother working. Yet, according to Scarr's analyses of the research, carefully designed day-care programs can provide certain advantages for children that do not accrue from full-time care in the home by the mother. Unfortunately, given the poor quality of most day-care centers and babysitting services, most preschoolers do not find themselves in enriching environments. Thus, the concern about the quality of children's lives while their parents work remains both valid and widespread.

Would today's adolescents be better off if their mothers could devote themselves to full-time mothering and homemaking? According to most recent studies, no. Indeed, it appears that children with employed mothers derive certain benefits denied to those whose mothers are full-time homemakers. According to the data, adolescents whose mothers work tend to be more independent and to describe their mothers as more intelligent and competent than housewives' children. In contrast to earlier predictions, adolescents with working mothers have not been found to be more delinquent or more academically handicapped than children with unemployed mothers. Moreover, the data suggest that daughters tend to benefit more than sons from their mother's employment, in terms of their academic and vocational achievements (Dellas, Gaier, & Emihovich, 1979; Gold & Andres, 1978; Hoffman, 1979; Hoffman & Nye, 1974).

In this regard, it is noteworthy that one study found daughters of working-class and managerial-class families more approving than sons of their mothers' employment, while no such differences existed in professional families (Dellas, Gaier, & Emihovich, 1979). This finding suggests that the mother's employment may be particularly important to girls in lower-income families. In sum, current evidence suggests that most adolescents are not emotionally, academically, or psychologicaly deprived as a consequence of their mothers' employment, although the impact of her employment may vary as a function of such variables as the family's socioeconomic status or the child's age.

Several hypotheses have been offered to explain why a mother's employment usually benefits her children (Hoffman, 1979). First, employed mothers generally have more self-esteem and are more satisfied with their lives than housewives. Thus, it has been argued that employed mothers are able to create more-satisfying relationships with their children than full-time housewives who feel personally or vocationally frustrated with their lives. Evidence also suggests that in homes where mothers are employed, fathers are more involved in child rearing, and the parental disciplinary style is less authoritarian (Gold & Andres, 1978). In addition, a woman's own attitudes and behavior in regard to vocational success may be critical to her children's academic and vocational development. From this perspective, employed mothers might be better able to model the types of attitudes and behavior that enhance their children's academic and vocational success. Indeed, it has been suggested that a mother's influence over her children's academic and vocational achievements may be more significant than the father's. In support of this position, a recent study of several thousand sixth- through twelfth-graders found higher correlations between the mother's attitudes toward education and children's academic goals and achievements than between the father's attitudes and his children's achievements (Smith, 1981).

Poverty and the Family

Despite the fact that more mothers are working than ever before, U.S. young people are more likely to be living in poverty than they were in the 1960s and 1970s. In 1981 about 20 percent of all white children, 45 percent of all Hispanic children, and 53 percent of all black children were living in families whose incomes fell below the poverty level (see Figure 8.3). As a consequence of family poverty, about 11 percent of all children receive federal or state welfare assistance from the *Aid to Families with Dependent Children (AFDC)*, 15 percent receive free or reduced-price school lunches, food stamps, or medicaid, and 4

Figure 8.3

Number of related children under 18 living in families below the poverty level, by type of family: 1969, 1979, and 1981

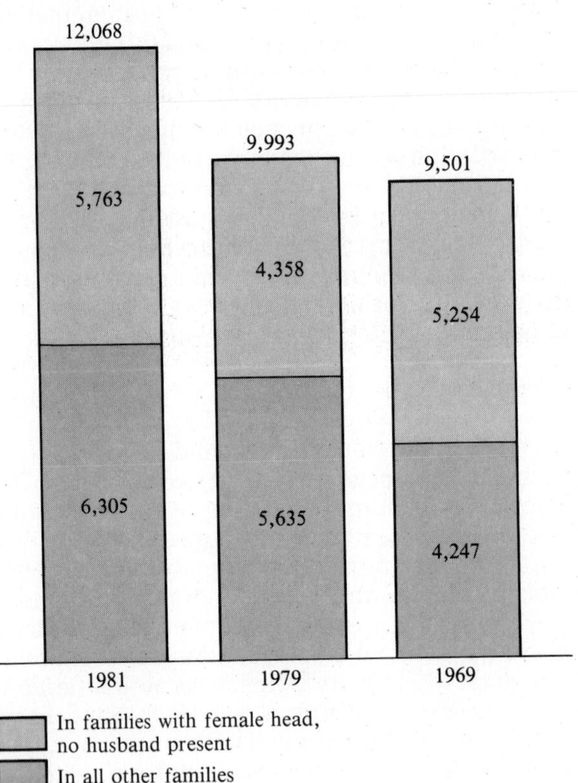

SOURCE: *Population profile of the United States: 1982*, Washington, D.C.: Bureau of the Census. Current population reports, P-23, no. 130, 1984.

percent receive some federal assistance for their family's housing (U.S. Bureau of the Census, 1981).

AFDC payments vary widely among the states. In 1981, for example, the highest state monthly payment per family was $573 and the lowest was $92. An adolescent living in a single-parent family usually receives very little financial aid from his or her father through child-support payments. Even though adolescents whose mothers are white, college graduates are most likely to receive financial support from their fathers after a divorce, the average child-support payment from these fathers is still only about $2,574 annually. In families where the mother has only a high-school education, the child-support payment from an absent father drops to $1,503 (*U.S. Children,* 1983).

As the national poverty rate continues to escalate, the impact of poverty on adolescents becomes even more far-reaching. As we have seen in previous chapters, adolescents living in poor families are less likely to succeed in school, to fully develop their mental abilities, to limit the size of their future families, and to postpone marriage until they become adults. As we will see in future chapters, financially impoverished adolescents are also more likely than youngsters from wealthier families to abuse drugs, to have illegitimate children, to resort to illegal money-making activities, and to be unemployed.

In addition to these disadvantages, adolescents from impoverished families are more likely to be separated from their parents than adolescents from higher socioeconomic classes. According to researchers at the Children's Defense Fund (CDF) (1978, 1984) and the National Black Child Development Institute (1981), too many social workers remove children from indigent families without considering ways to keep the family together. These researchers contend that because many social service workers disapprove of minority or poor children's cultures, they are too ready to remove these children from their homes rather than provide temporary assistance to the family during periods of crisis. Minority and poor children, therefore, are at high risk of being unnecessarily placed in foster homes or institutions. In addition, children sent to live in another state are too often left without opportunities to voice their complaints against foster parents or to work toward becoming reunited with their own parents. In short, these researchers feel that too many social service agencies have an "anti-family" bias against the indigent.

In addition to the problems confronting adolescents living in poverty, their parents are often blamed for the family's predicament. Whether blatantly stated or discreetly implied, an accusation often leveled against the adolescent's parents is that "if only low-income parents would instill the right attitudes in their children, those youngsters could escape from poverty and pull themselves up by their own bootstraps." This line of reasoning, however, ignores a number of empirical studies and statistics. Although parental attitudes can indeed undermine an adolescent's academic success, there is considerable evidence that most impoverished parents do instill in their children a respect for school, for the work ethic, and for academic success (CDF, 1979; Edelman, 1981; Jones, 1984; Staples, 1975). According to the data, most low-income parents have high educational and occupational aspirations for their children. Moreover, in regard to the question of racial differences, data from the national longitudinal study of high-school seniors of 1972 showed that black adolescents had higher vocational and academic goals than whites in the same socioeconomic class (Fetters, 1977).

In sum, much of the existing research indicates that most low-income parents are instilling achievement-oriented attitudes in their children. An important distinction between low- and middle-income parents, however, is that most economically deprived parents must eventually come to terms with the reality that their offspring will not reach their desired academic or vocational goals. Sadly, low-income parents tend to overestimate their children's academic potential and to maintain their high expectations in spite of their children's poor grades (Jones, 1984).

If economically disadvantaged parents are instilling the proper values in their children, then why are they often blamed for their children's academic, social, or vocational problems? According to a number of social critics, part of the answer resides in the fact that society often chooses to blame impoverished people for problems that actually arise from the attitudes and institutions that uphold the status quo. Psychologist and social analyst William Ryan (1976) labels this phenomenon *blaming the victim*. According to Ryan, many of us blame the victims of poverty and prejudice for their disadvantaged circumstances without assigning any blame to the inequalities of U.S. society from which we ourselves benefit. Thus, all problems of the underpriveledged are ascribed to supposed "defects" within the victims themselves, rather than to any

What changes would you most like to see in American families?

deficiencies in middle-class society's attitudes and institutions. In the context of blaming the victim, the sole emphasis is upon changing some characteristic of the victimized people, rather than upon changing any aspects of the status quo.

In Ryan's view, blaming the victim serves the financial and social interests of those who practice it. Thus, the norms of the majority are applied to the problems of the disadvantaged without questioning whether the norms themselves may be contributing to the problem. The typical victim blamer is a middle-class person who is benefiting from the social, political, and financial system in its present form. Although aware of injustices, this person rejects proposals for social changes that would benefit the victims, since such changes would threaten the victim blamer's own well-being.

Instead of altering the institutions or laws that benefit themselves, victim blamers search for characteristics within the victims that "explain" their poor circumstances and that liberate victim blamers from personal guilt or responsibility. Thus, for example, rather than support school policies and reforms that would benefit poor children, those employing a victim-blaming strategy would insist that poor parents change the way they relate to their children. By blaming poor children's problems solely on their own parents, the middle class and wealthy can avoid thinking about personally costly and unpalatable options like school busing, increasing taxes, racially mixed neighborhoods, or an untracked school curriculum. Other social critics who support Ryan's notion of victim blaming believe we have devised myths about the poor in order to avoid confronting the fact that our society's institutions, such as public schools, are mainly designed to meet the needs of the middle and upper classes (Bowles & Gintis, 1976; Ginsberg, 1972). While we may feel uncomfortable with the assertions of Ryan and other researchers who share his perspective, the ideas are relevant in any discussion of who is to blame for the plight of adolescents from economically disadvantaged families.

Interracial and Homosexual Families

In addition to the impact of poverty on U.S. families, thousands of adolescents are experiencing changes related to their parents' interracial or homosexual relationships. Although both interracial marriage and homosexuality have continued to receive the disapproval of most Americans, neither appears to be diminishing.

"Children of the rainbow"—those whose parents are of two different races—now number well over a million ("Children of the Rainbow," 1984). Among the dilemmas facing these youngsters are how to relate to each parent's culture and how to cope with social situations related to race. For example, a black male from a biracial family might discover that white girls who were his friends at a younger age no longer return his friendly hugs and now shun his invitations to dance at a party. How does he reconcile this with the fact that his own white mother and black father have been relating to each other sexually for 20 years? How do the rebuffs from his friends make him feel about his own parents, whom he may now perceive as having cast him into a morass of unpleasant social situations? As Box 8.3 illustrates, questions like these are receiving the attention of researchers and psychologists as the number of rainbow children in our society continues to increase.

8.3 A Closer Look

Children of the Rainbow: Interracial Families

Between 1970 and 1980 the number of mixed racial marriages in the United States rose from 310,000 to 613,000. Today the one million offspring of these marriages—sometimes referred to as "rainbow children"—must often confront difficulties that extend beyond mere racial discrimination: What should youngsters do if they prefer one parent's racial heritage over the other's? How do parents show respect for one another's culture during times when they may feel that the children are rejecting one heritage in favor of the other? How are the rainbow children to relate to relatives who may disapprove of the interracial family network?

Among the difficulties frequently encountered by rainbow children, interracial dating becomes a particularly prominent problem during adolescence. In trying to explain an adolescent's confusion, one male clinical psychologist with a black father and a white mother recalls feeling that his family was perfectly normal until he reached adolescence: "It didn't hit me until I was 13 and approached a white girl for a date. Then one of my black buddies pulled me aside and told me the facts of life."

With the high divorce rate in U.S. society today, interracial youths are often left in a particularly volatile situation after their parents separate. Since one parent must assume the primary responsibility for raising the children, how is he or she to acculturate them into a racial heritage that is now foreign and perhaps even hostile, without the other spouse? As one white mother whose child's father is black admits, "I'm not a black person, and I'm not going to indulge my daughter in something that's not natural to me." Yet are such decisions fair to the racially mixed child?

Moreover, some of the discrimination that rainbow children encounter depends

Research on the offspring of mixed marriages is scant, despite the fact that investigators who have studied *exogamy* have seldom been hesitant to express their concern for the emotional and psychological well-being of these children. It has been argued that children of exogamous couples will experience conflicts related to their self-concepts, their biethnic identity, their social networks, and their adjustment to two different cultures, although such concerns have not been empirically confirmed (Cleveland & Longaker, 1972; Murguia, 1982; Ramirez, 1969).

In order to explore such concerns, researchers recently administered a questionnaire to 63 children between the ages of 12 and 18, with one Mexican American parent and one white parent. Nearly all of the 70 percent who identified themselves as of Mexican origin instead of as American said they were proud of their Mexican heritage. Rather than disassociating themselves from their heritage, approximately 40 percent of these adolescents spoke some Spanish and listened to Spanish radio or television programs. Over 90 percent of the respondents perceived intermarriage to be as successful as in-group marriage. Moreover, only 15 percent reported disadvantages in mixed parentage, such as differ-on the shade of their parents' skin color. Adolescents with white-Hispanic or white-Oriental backgrounds generally assimilate more easily into U.S. society than do those with a black parent. Despite the lightness of their skin, youngsters with black heritage are generally perceived and treated as members of the black community. For example, psychiatrist Alvin Poussaint of the Harvard Medical School completed a study of 37 interracial people between the ages of 17 and 35. All of the individuals with a black heritage reported feeling more accepted by the black community than by the white.

The largest conference ever to focus on the subject of interracial children was held in New York City in the summer of 1984. According to experts at the conference, books need to be written for and about interracial children in order to allay some of the difficulties encountered by these young people. In addition, the experts argued against the practice of asking children to identify their racial heritage on school forms and other institutional records, contending that such classification is often misused for ranking one racial group above another.

Despite the experts' concerns, not all adolescents from racially mixed marriages agree that their parents' races have complicated their lives. For example, Aminta Steinback, 15, and her 13-year old sister, Tirien, whose father is white and whose mother is black, claim that being interracial is "no big deal." Aminta says she doesn't prefer other interracial kids any more than someone with red hair would prefer other redheads. "It's not like we cling together," she explains, "though we might say, 'Oh, we're both mixed—that's neat'." As for Tirien, she says her white friends don't comment on her mixed heritage "except to say that I'm lucky I've got a year-round tan."

Adapted from "Children of the rainbow," *Newsweek*, November 19, 1984, pp. 120–122.

ences in child-rearing practices or identity conflicts. The majority reported advantages of having parents from two cultures, such as being able to speak two languages and growing up with no prejudices. Counter to many of the hypotheses regarding exogamous marriages, the overall findings revealed that children of Mexican interethnic marriages were not experiencing conflict as a consequence of their mixed ethnic backgrounds (Snyder, Lopez, & Padilla, 1982).

In addition to the rise in interracial marriages, society has witnessed an increase in the number of homosexual parents who, in contrast to their counterparts in earlier decades, have been willing to disclose their sexual orientation to their children and to friends. Joe Gantz (1983), one of those directing their research toward this alternative family structure, has interviewed homosexual parents and their children in an effort to better understand the special dynamics within these families. According to his data, adolescents with gay parents must not only accept their parents' sexual orientation but must often keep their discovery a secret from anyone outside the family. Although keeping their parents' homosexuality a secret protects the family from the community's hostility, the secrecy also places extra responsibilities and stress on the young. Afraid of ridicule from their friends or afraid that the courts might revoke their parents' custody, many of these children live in constant tension.

The children of gay parents must also resolve the dilemma of how to form a loving, respectful relationship with their parents while in a society where homosexuality is seldom condoned. On the basis of his interviews with gay parents and their teenage children, Gantz is reluctant to offer any generalizations other than that all the children reported feeling distant from their peers. Even when the family lifestyle had been publicly acknowledged in supposedly tolerant communities, the children felt that their parents' homosexuality had created social handicaps for them with their young friends. Such findings suggest that, given society's prevailing attitudes about homosexuality, adolescents with gay parents will continue to be beset by problems related to social acceptance by their heterosexual friends.

Inevitably, as gay parents become more open about their sexual orientation, with their children and with their fellow citizens, more empirical studies related to this family lifestyle will become available. Given the present lack of data, any speculations, hypotheses, or definitive statements about the impact of this family lifestyle on adolescents can only be, at best, tentative.

ADOLESCENCE AS A FAMILY CRISIS: FACT AND FICTION

The titles of many popular books for parents suggest that adolescence is to be feared like a plague. For example, in the nationally famous "Tough Love" approach, parents are trained to discipline their teenaged children and preserve the family by controlling adolescent unruliness with the help of other parents (York, York, & Wachtel, 1982). Amidst discussions on television and radio about programs like Tough Love and jokes about adolescence, it's little wonder that many parents dread their children's teenage years. "You just wait a few more years until they're teenagers and then you'll see!" is a familiar refrain repeated by many older parents to their younger friends. How justified are such warnings and fears about adolescence? Just how much strife is there between most adolescents and their parents? Despite the fact that many talk about the generation gap as if it were as predictable and as real as the sunrise, to what extent does such a phenomenon exist? In short, how much of a family crisis does adolescence present?

The Generation Gap

While very much alive and well, Mark Twain once wrote, "reports of my death have been grossly exaggerated." The same can be said of the generation gap. Contrary to popular belief, research repeatedly shows that the generation gap is grossly exaggerated. Undoubtedly young people during the 1960s were more publicly outspoken on issues like the Vietnam war than their predecessors in the "silent generation" of the 1950s. Yet even at the height of the counterculture movement of the 1960s, when youthful protestors opposed their elders on issues like the Vietnam war, only about a fourth of the young people and their parents felt that there was a large gap between them (Yankelovich, 1969, 1974). Moreover, during the 1960s and early 1970s, people tended to attribute the highly publicized behavior of a minority of young people who were openly critical of the older generation and "the establishment" to all adolescents. As a consequence of such inappropriate generalizations, many stereotypes about the generation gap became well established, although the actual relationships between the majority of young people and their parents had been ignored. Furthermore, as adults themselves became more and more critical of society after events like the Vietnam war and the Watergate scandal, disagreements between the young and their parents were even less common (Conger, 1981; Yankelovich, 1974, 1981).

Although many adolescents disagree with their parents on issues like curfews, manner of dress, and playing loud music, the majority accept their parents' religious, political, educational, and social values. The data from the 1970s and 1980s have been remarkably consistent on this point (Bachman, Johnston, & O'Malley, 1981; Berndt, 1979; Douvan & Adelson, 1966; Gallatin, 1980; Hamid & Wyllie, 1980; Offer & Offer, 1975; Offer, Ostrov, & Howard, 1981; Offer, Maroh & Ostrov, 1979; Yankelovich, 1969, 1981). As Chapter 9 will demonstrate, the influence that peers exert over each other during adolescence is generally limited to social matters, such as how to dress, what kind of lingo to use, what music to listen to, and what hours constitute a fair curfew. Given this repeated message from the research, it becomes almost a wonder in itself that the myths about the generation gap have clung so tenaciously in public opinion.

More important, factors other than age play an important role in determining the values of the young and the old. Because individuals' education, income, and race also affect their opinions, the young cannot automatically be presumed more liberal than their elders on controversial issues like abortion, premarital sex, or legalizing marijuana. In general, people with the most education, highest incomes, and weakest religious affiliations are more liberal in regard to social and political issues, regardless of their age. To categorize the young and the old into two groups without regard to their socioeconomic and educational differences is to contribute to the myth that there are two separate generations of people who have very little in common.

While it goes without saying that adolescents spend more time with their peers than younger children, it is also true that parents continue to exert a strong influence over their children throughout adolescence (Youniss & Smollar, 1985). In a representative study involving 180 adolescents, the frequency of discussions with parents remained relatively unchanged between the ages of 12 and 20. Not surprisingly, however, discussions with friends increased with age, and issues related to peer relationships were discussed more often with peers than with parents (Hunter, 1985). It is also important to remember that parents' choices of neighborhoods, schools, churches, and adult friends influence the pool from which their children select friends (Hartup, 1983; Rubin & Sloman, 1984). Consequently, adolescents' friends typically manifest values, behavior, and opinions of which their parents approve.

As might be expected, the extent of a parent's influence appears to depend on several extraneous factors. For instance, some research shows that boys between 13 and 16 interact more with their parents than girls do, while the reverse is true between the ages of 16 and 19 (Montemayor & VanKomen, 1980). This finding suggests that a parent's influence over an adolescent may vary according to the youngster's age and sex. Other research suggests that regardless of the adolescent's sex or age, he or she will be most likely to imitate the values and behavior of whichever parent is perceived as the most powerful in the family (McDonald, 1980). While it has traditionally been hypothesized that the same-sex parent has the most influence over a youngster's behavior, McDonald's research suggests that a parent's power may rest on the child's perception of the parent's social and financial power. For example, if a son perceives his mother as having most of the power in the family, he is more likely to be influenced by her behavior and values than by those of his father.

In summary, perceiving adolescence as a perpetual struggle between parents and their child's peers is an exaggerated view that ignores the research demonstrating parental influence on important issues and values. Peer influence notwithstanding, the old adage still holds true for most of today's adolescents: The acorn doesn't fall far from the tree.

8.4 Adolescent Voices

The Kids' Book about Parents

In addition to their book on divorce, the adolescents at Fayerweather Street School have written a book for other young people about relationships with their parents. The following excerpts from *The Kids' Book about Parents* represent the central theme underlying the text: "In the world we live in, we know that kids are no longer happy, simple little people who play in the park all day and do whatever their parents tell them to do."

> Here are some of the flaws that we've noted in our parents: being impatient, yelling too easily, being a health nut, embarrassing you in public, having a closed mind, changing their minds a lot, being obnoxious in public, nagging, using old-fashioned words, being a bad cook, forgetting birthdays, acting too sweet, talking loudly, pretending to listen to you, letting people push them around, picking fights over nothing, making arrangements with kids and then breaking them, being stubborn, driving too slowly, never being home, being lazy. (p. 23)

> Sometimes you'll find that parents will surprise you with their generosity, even when you think they might give you a hard time about it. Calbe said, "Recently I asked my father if I could have a raise in my allowance which had been at about $1 for the past three years. Sometimes it's pretty hard to talk to my father about things like this, and I was all ready to compromise at around $3, but I was surprised when he offered $5. Afterward although I definitely like the raise I got, I felt a little guilty because of the size of the allowance." (p. 36)

> It's important to be ready with a good excuse when you want to stay up later. Here's a list of excuses we've used: "I'm not tired." "I have homework to do." "I went to bed early last night." "John gets to stay up as late

Feelings between Adolescents and Parents

Not only is the generation gap an exaggerated notion, but most adolescents and their parents like each other and have relatively few conflicts during adolescence. As the students' comments in Box 8.4 illustrate, adolescents can be surprisingly sensitive and insightful in regard to their parents' moods and needs (Fayerweather Street School, 1984). While there's no doubt that skirmishes about loud music or hairstyles and clothing create tension and disruption in the family, most teenagers and their parents say they like and enjoy one another (Norman & Harris, 1981; Offer & Offer, 1975; Offer, Ostrov, & Howard, 1981; Speizer, 1978).

Daniel Offer's extensive study of adolescents exemplifies the consistency and positive nature of young people's feelings about their families. Offer and his colleagues (1981) studied adolescents during the 1960s and 1970s in an effort

as he wants." "I have to watch this TV show for my social studies class." But you should be prepared for your parents to give you one of these answers: "You'll be grouchy in the morning." "I let you stay up later than most kids. The least you can do is go to bed when I ask you to." "Because I said so." "Go to bed as a present to me." (p. 43)

We made a list of all the gross and disgusting foods we could think of that parents like kids to eat: artichokes, beets, broccoli, brussel sprouts, cabbage, cauliflower, clams, eggplant, kale, kidney beans, kiwi fruit, lamb, lentil soup, lima beans, liver, mushrooms, oatmeal, pea soup, poached eggs, quiche, salmon, spinach, squash, succotash, tofu, turnips, yogurt, zucchini. If your parents start to tell you that you only eat lousy food and you should eat more okra, you can tell them that you like some of these foods: apple juice, baked potatoes, bread, carrots, chicken, corn, grape juice, hamburger, hot dogs, milk, orange juice, pies, rice, salad, spaghetti, steak, turkey, veal. (p. 54)

Not all situations turn out with parents and kids feeling good about the pet. Last year Jake's grandpa came for a visit from New York and took Jake to a pet store. Jake told us, "He bought me two lizards. My mom was not thrilled with this, so we made a deal. If either of the lizards ever escaped, my mom would check into an expensive hotel at my grandpa's expense." (p. 75).

We all have different ways of knowing when our parents are unhappy. Here is a list of common warning signals for kids to watch out for: eating a lot, not talking, going to sleep early, not saying hi when they come home from work, chain smoking, arguing with cashiers, constantly cleaning things, snapping at everyone, ignoring your questions, making fun of your friends, beating up on the pets, driving too fast, yelling at other drivers and beeping the horn unnecessarily, slamming doors, staring blankly at the TV. (p. 93)

SOURCE: Fayerweather Street School, *The kids' book about parents.* Boston: Houghton Mifflin, 1984

8.5 Adolescent Voices

An Adolescent Male's View on the Elderly

He stares for a moment at the magazine that lies open before him on the table. "Now take this ol' cat, will you," he says, as he leans forward and points to a large color photograph of an elderly Navajo shepherd. "Would you look at his hands. Now those are some man's hands, all right. They've got wisdom in 'em. You can see his whole accumulated life experience right there, in all them craggly ol' wrinkles." He places a finger on the photographed hand. His young hands, like his feet, seem disproportionately large for his small but solid frame.

"Old people, man. You know, we've gotta stop trashing them. They've got a lot they can teach us. Now, I know that probably sounds real crazy comin' from a teen such as myself, but it's really true. Straight up. Older people is real important for young dudes like myself, and even for the young women. They're the ones who can show us how to do things, and when and where to do 'em at. They're the ones who should be models for us to show us what's good and bad, desirable and undesirable in life. I bet this old Indian here had someone to show him how to do things so he could feel like somebody. Bet he didn't have no deep blue funks. I remember in school this teacher tellin' us how the Indians really prepared their kids for manhood and womanhood. It was hard work, probably, you know, goin' through all them rituals and all, but at least those kids always knew there was a place for 'em and that there was somebody who was gonna help them get there. I tell ya, man, guidance. That's what it's all about, guidance. Having people around who've been there and can help you through whatever you're contendin' with. Just this morning as I was walking over here I saw this old lady. Man, it just gave me such a good feelin' to see her. I didn't talk to her or nothin', I haven't in years. But she recognized me, too, and we waved to each other." He is smiling. "She used to baby-sit me when I was real little. Just knowin' she's around and that she still remembers lets me know I still have a place in her mind.

to understand more about young people's perceptions of themselves and their families. More than 80 percent of the adolescents sampled during these two decades said they felt close to their parents and believed their parents were proud of them. They perceived their parents as dependable, patient, and democratic. Very few harbored any ill-feelings toward their parents or experienced a generation gap. Males and females viewed their parents similarly, as did younger and older adolescents. Physically ill and healthy adolescents also described their parents in comparable terms. No dramatic shifts had occurred in teenagers' perceptions of their parents between the 1960s and the 1970s.

In contrast, delinquent and psychiatrically disturbed youngsters described their families negatively on almost all items on Offer's Family Relationships scale. Only half of the delinquents and 60 percent of the disturbed youths wanted to have families similar to their own someday, as compared to 76 percent of the other adolescents. Likewise, 90 percent of the normal adolescents felt their parents were satisfied with them, compared to only 60 percent of the delinquent and disturbed youths. Disturbed and delinquent youngsters disagreed more often

"Now most of my partners don't know what I'm talkin' about when I feel these things. They're always jivin' old people and making fun of 'em behind their backs. Maybe it's cause I'm changin', man. I don't know. Maybe it's cause they ain't. But it just seems to me that if you just look at life straight on and up front, you'd see, like I see, that being fifteen and being old, like in your fifties, or sixties, or seventies or eighties, is all pretty much the same, man.

"We're all outsiders; just outsiders lookin' for our place in this damn world of ours. For us young people it's like we've been cast out on to the sea of life, the Lake Michigan of living, all on our own, havin' to survive and find our way. And with old people, it's like they've been cast out, too, but in a different way. It's like they've been tossed out or kicked out, with the rest of the world sayin' to 'em, 'you're just too old, old man, we got no use for your tired old ways or your haggard old bones!'

"What I want to know," he says, raising his voice and pointing a finger at me, "is where do we get this idea? I mean, who gives who the almighty right to go and tell somebody he's no good, he's all washed up, he's not needed or wanted around anymore? I mean, really, man. This is down 'n out sick. Straight up cold blooded.

"And besides, like I was sayin' before, young people and old people got a lot in common. Far as I see it, we need each other. Young people need some solid and together guidance and old folks, well, they need to be needed, too. Seems to me we ought to find some way to help each other. You know, young and old banding together." He pauses and shakes his head. "And you know why we got to band together, don't you? It's got to do with trust. Seems like all them adults in the middle don't trust either of us, the young or the old. Now how are we gonna get it together, like Ed says, if we don't trust each other and work together for all of us, all black people? No wonder the white man, no offense or nothin', Dan, is keepin' his jump on us. It's 'cause of this generational thing. Young versus adults and adults versus the old."

SOURCE: D. Frank, *Deep blue funk: Portraits of teenage parents.* Chicago: The Ounce of Prevention Fund, 1983, pp. 152–153. Reprinted by permission.

with their parents' standards and said they could not understand their parents. Believing that their parents consider them a bother, the delinquents spent less time at home than other children. In summary, delinquents and the psychologically disturbed viewed their families negatively, while other youngsters viewed them positively.

Two factors that can contribute to tensions in an adolescent's family are the isolation of the nuclear family and the nation's mobility. The nuclear family tends to isolate parents from other relatives and adults who can offer advice, support, and assistance in matters related to child rearing. Some evidence suggests that the smaller the family, the more intense the relationships among its members and the more difficult it is to change their interactions at critical periods like adolescence (Biller, 1981a). In contrast, an extended family can provide parents with other adults' opinions and assistance in child rearing. As Box 8.5 poignantly illustrates, adolescents and elderly adults often have much to share that the parent-child relationship cannot offer.

Furthermore, almost half of all families move every five years and the average American can expect to move 13 or 14 times during a lifetime. Between March 1975 and March 1980 half of the people between the ages of 5 and 24 changed their residence at least once (U.S. Bureau of the Census, 1982). Consequently, most parents have little time to establish bonds with such neighborhood organizations as schools and churches, which might help to alleviate problems with their children.

Despite the fact that most adolescents and their parents enjoy and love one another, two less pleasant facets of the parent-child relationship cannot be dismissed. First, many parents and adolescents characterize the early adolescent years as more stressful and more demanding than the preceding or following years. Given the physical and cognitive transformations that accompany the years between 12 and 14, it is not surprising that both the child and the parents find this transitional period between childhood and adolescence the most taxing to their relationship (Elkind, 1981; Offer & Offer, 1975; Steinberg, 1981).

Second, it cannot be denied that some parents and adolescents are unable to establish harmonious relationships with one another. For example, on the basis of his years of psychotherapy with young adults, Halpern (1981) suggests that if adults are unable to improve a debilitating relationship with their parents after adolescence, they should seriously consider the possibility of terminating the relationship altogether:

> If we are aware of the songs and dances and the terrible cost involved, and we have struggled to change our end of it but our parents won't budge, we must confront the possibility of ending the relationship. The act of terminating the tie may be taken by us, if we have reached the limit of our ability to tolerate their insistence on the old pattern, or it may be initiated by the parent if he or she no longer can accept the person we now are (p. 221).

RESEARCH ON THE FAMILY'S INFLUENCE

Before examining the available data about the family's impact on adolescents, the known limitations of the existing research studies need to be directly confronted. In an extensive review and critique of the family's influence on children's cognitive development and academic achievement, Diane Scott Jones (1984) dispels many myths by enumerating the methodological shortcomings in the research and by identifying many factors that must be considered before generalizing from the existing data. To begin with, even studies demonstrating a relationship between a specific kind of parental behavior and a particular response from a child are not "proving" that the parent's conduct is causing the child's behavior. For instance, it's as logical to assume that children's innate intelligence and natural assertiveness are causing their parents to treat them in a democratic, independent way as to assume that their parents' democratic, independent style is causing them to be intelligent and self-reliant. Because a parent's child-rearing style is influenced by the child's own characteristics, we cannot automatically interpret parents' actions as the cause of their offsprings' conduct. The parent's and the child's mutual influence on one another makes it virtually impossible for researchers to prove whose behavior is exerting the most power over whom.

A second shortcoming encountered in studying adolescents and their families is the overemphasis on interactions between the mother and her children. Researchers have traditionally limited their attention to mothers' interactions with their children and ignored the influence of fathers, siblings, and other relatives. Also, most researchers have ignored the child's developmental stage in analyzing the family's influence. For example, the kinds of family interactions that may be critically important to the cognitive or social development of a 5-year-old may be irrelevant to the development of an adolescent. Future studies of the family need to consider children's developmental stage in trying to determine how the family is influencing their development.

Another methodological difficulty is tied to the complexities associated with attempting to measure the family environment and interaction (Jones, 1984). How can a researcher reliably determine how much intimate conversation, paternal affection, or sibling aggression exists in a family? How can an investigator assess how much tutoring older siblings give to younger ones? How do we compare the interactions between parents and sons to those between parents and daughters in the same family? As they try to answer complicated questions like these, most researchers have had to piece together a picture of the family by relying on estimates, indirect measures, or retrospective recollections. Measuring what actually transpires between family members is problematic yet significant, if we are to determine the kinds of behavior that are advantageous or disadvantageous to a child's development at a particular age. Given the methodological problems involved, interactions within a family have not yet received much attention from researchers. Unfortunately this deficiency leaves unresolved such fundamental questions as why siblings grow up with such different personalities and mental abilities, even when they are twins.

In order to appreciate the intricacies involved in studying adolescents and their families, let us examine the problems surrounding one popular research question: How are adolescents and children affected by being raised in a single-parent family? In attempting to answer this question, researchers are confronted with a barrage of problems. After their exhaustive analyses of the research, Henry Biller (1981a) and Diane Scott Jones (1984) remind us that methodological problems have contributed to many misinterpretations and oversimplifications about the effects of growing up in one-parent or two-parent families. Although the research consistently shows that children benefit most from being raised by two parents, we can not automatically infer that the millions of adolescents who are being raised by only one parent are less well-off cognitively or emotionally than those being raised by both parents. For example, one confounding variable that contributes to misinterpretations about single-parent families is income. About 25 percent of white divorced women and 41 percent of black divorced women are raising their children on incomes below the poverty level (U.S. Bureau of the Census, 1981). Since so many single parents are women living in poverty, many researchers have erred in not taking account of socioeconomic factors before drawing conclusions about one- or two-parent families.

Indeed, some researchers are already finding that when socioeconomic status is equal, single- and two-parent families have a similar impact on their children's academic achievement and intelligence (Jones, 1984). Since, however, most single-parent families fall into the lower income brackets, it is not particularly surprising to find adolescents from two-parent families advantaged in regard to variables, such as academic success, that are highly correlated with adequate incomes in the family. In sum, it is reasonable to conclude from the data that adolescents growing up in two-parent families are generally more advantaged academically and socially than those in one-parent families.

Among the many questions to be considered when examining the differences between one-parent and two-parent families are: How old was the child when the father and mother were separated? Is the father's absence due to death, abandonment, or divorce? Is the child a son or a daughter? How is the mother reacting to the father's absence? Are other males available to act as surrogate fathers? How happy was the marriage before the father and mother separated? How much interaction exists between the parent or other relatives and the youngster? Does the youngster's racial or ethnic culture have views of the family that differ from those of the white middle class? Questions like these have traditionally been overlooked in the research. Very rarely, for instance, have researchers compared two-parent families where fathers are unavailable to their children against those where fathers frequently interact with their children. And seldom have researchers investigated the support available to adolescents and their single parents from the extended family or the community (Biller, 1981a; Jones, 1984).

When researchers do ask such traditionally overlooked questions, the results often provide us with new images of the family. For example, some researchers have discovered that single mothers in housing projects near middle-class neighborhoods and schools support their children's educational goals more than mothers in similar housing surrounded by other low-income neighborhoods and schools (Jones, 1984). Others have found that lower-income black adolescents from mother-grandmother families do as well as those from mother-father families in regard to academic achievement, mental-health status, and successful social adjustment (Kellam, Engsminger, & Turner, 1977). Recently, researchers have also reported that Mexican American girls from one-parent families do not differ from those in two-parent families in terms of egocentrism and antisocial behavior, a finding that is incompatible with most of the research investigating the characteristics of white girls from single-parent homes (Castellano & Dembo, 1981). Moreover, the literature suggests that a father's absence is generally more damaging to boys than to girls and that his absence is more highly correlated with his children's mathematical abilities than with their verbal skills (Radin, 1981).

In sum, much of the research presently available on the family's influence on adolescent development is limited by methodological problems and by the investigation of narrow questions. As researchers refine their methods for measuring interactions within families and as they explore nontraditional questions, our understanding about the family's impact on adolescents will expand.

THE FATHER'S ROLE IN ADOLESCENT DEVELOPMENT

According to a Jewish proverb, "God could not be everywhere so he therefore made mothers." Another aphorism describes a mother as "she who can take the place of all others, but whose place no one else can take." And fathers? Aphorisms have described them as "the quietest member of the family unit," "A man who can't get on the phone, into the bathroom, or out of the house," and "a banker provided by nature" (Brussell, 1970).

Although traditionally ignored in the research on adolescent and child development, the role and influence of the father within the family structure is slowly gaining a fairer share of researchers' attention. For example, while researchers have historically focused their attention on the negative effects of "maternal deprivation," few have investigated the negative effects of "paternal deprivation." Most of the existing literature has focused on the father's physical presence or absence in the home, rather than upon his emotional absence from his children. Indeed, it is only within the past decade that researchers have attended seriously to the father's role in a child's development (Lamb, 1983).

Among the more prominent questions now being addressed are: What advantages accrue to children when fathers participate in their upbringing? Why do so few fathers share in the responsibilities of raising their own children, even in families where both the husband and wife are employed? What benefits accrue to adolescents whose fathers have spent time interacting with them during their infancy and childhood?

Fathers' Involvement with Children

Some critics are chastizing men for not assuming more responsibilities as fathers, as Letty Pogrebin (1983) observes:

> Have you ever wondered why there are so many men in the "right to life" movement and so few in child care? Or why a man who testifies so passionately about "unborn babies" is usually mute about babies already born and living in sickness? I attribute these contradictions to the fact that on public issues men act as men and not as fathers. They are protecting their power, not expressing their love of children. I wish that groups of men and women cared as much about each man's fathering and considered it as crucial a measure of his character and his humanity as motherhood is for a woman (pp. 193–194).

While we may disagree with Pogrebin's interpretation of men's conduct as fathers, the research does support her assertion that very few men are willing to participate in the responsibilities of raising their own children, despite the more relaxed sex roles in our contemporary society. Pogrebin reminds us that many children consider their fathers almost expendable to the family, aside from their wage-earning contributions. Illustratively, Pogrebin (1983, p. 196) offers the following scenario: Two little girls are playing house. Karen is the mother, Kathy is the grandmother. "And who can be the father?" asks Karen. "No one," answers Kathy. "You don't need a father."

Because most adolescents are growing up in families where traditional sex roles prevail, their fathers have delegated the responsibility for establishing intimate relationship with the children to the mothers. As a consequence, most adolescents spend relatively little time with their fathers, in comparison to time

8.6 A Closer Look

Do Fathers Want to Spend Time with Their Children?

Sweden is the only country in the world where the government has made an official commitment to involve fathers in raising their own children. Recognizing that traditional employment practices prevented men from participating in child care, the government devised a policy that permitted both parents to care for their children.

The present policy entitles each couple to six months of paid leave, which may be taken any time within the first nine months of each child's birth. The parents are free to decide for themselves how to divide the leave. The parent who is on leave receives 90 percent of his or her regular salary out of a national insurance fund. Each parent is then entitled to another six weeks' leave any time in the first seven years of the child's life, which can be used to reduce an employed parent's workday from eight to six hours. Both parents are also entitled to 12 days of paid leave per year to take care of sick children. In addition, employers are required to give parents their former jobs and their former salaries when they return to work.

When the paid parental leave was first introduced in 1974, its advocates expected fathers to respond favorably to the idea of spending time with their children without financial penalties. Instead, only 2 percent of the fathers took parental leaves. A nationwide advertising campaign was then launched, picturing wrestlers, soccer players, and other "masculine" men who were walking, feeding, or holding their babies. Booklets describing the policy were widely distributed. Despite the advertising campaign, in 1979 only 11 percent of the fathers took any leave in families where both adults were employed full time. Of those men who did take a child-care leave, half left their jobs for only one month. Fathers with the most education and the highest salaries were the most likely to take a child-care leave.

Why haven't Swedish fathers taken advantage of the chance to take care of their own children? According to researchers who interviewed the Swedish fathers, many men refused to leave their jobs for fear of losing future advancement opportunities, fear of diminishing their professional reputation, or fear of displeasing their employers. Men in lower-status jobs were particularly worried about losing their status or chances for advancement by taking time away from work to care for their children. Moreover, the researchers found that sex-role stereotypes also discouraged Swedish men from taking care of their children. Like U.S. men, most Swedish males are still socialized to perceive child care as "women's work."

In Sweden's case, the government's financial incentives and publicity campaigns have failed to entice most fathers to take time away from work in order to care for their own children. Most Swedish men have chosen to ignore their government's "pro-family" policy and to leave the child-rearing responsibilities to women. How do you think U.S. fathers would respond to a policy like Sweden's? How might U. S. children benefit from more time with their fathers during infancy, childhood, and adolescence?

SOURCE: M. Lamb and J. Levine, The Swedish parental insurance policy: An experiment in social engineering. In M. Lamb and A. Sagi (eds.), *Fatherhood and family policy.* Hillsdale, N. J.: Erlbaum, 1983. PP. 39–48.

spent with their mothers. Like young people in former generations, most young people today are still deprived of intimate, nurturant interactions with their fathers (Lamb, 1983, Pogrebin, 1983; Salk, 1982). Not surprisingly, adolescents have reported that their mothers are more communicative, more empathetic, and more interested in their day-to-day problems than their fathers (Youniss & Smollar, 1985).

Why don't men participate more often in raising their own children? The most obvious answer would be that most fathers are too busy earning the family's income to have time for interacting with their children. This explanation, however, is oversimplistic. For example, as Box 8.6 illustrates, in Sweden, where government policies enable fathers to spend extensive time with their children without financial penalties, few fathers choose to do so (Lamb & Levine, 1983). Even though movies like "Kramer versus Kramer" are popularizing the notion that men want to assume the responsibilities of child care, only 2 percent of all U.S. children live with their fathers, while 20 percent live with their mothers (*U.S. Children,* 1983).

An expert on the male sex role and male development, Joseph Pleck, (1981) asserts that men will remain uninvolved with their children until women are given more equity in the workplace. In his view, as long as women are less well-educated and less well-paid than men, the family will continue to confine men to the role of breadwinner and women to the role of parent. Sweden's failure to involve fathers in child care suggests, however, that many men need other incentives besides financial reassurance to entice them to assume more responsibility for raising their children (Lamb & Levine, 1983).

Despite our more liberal attitudes about masculinity and fatherhood, most U.S. children and adolescents still interact primarily with their mothers. For example, in 1972 only 27 percent of fathers were present in the delivery room when their babies were born, and even when mothers are employed, fathers spend far less time than mothers caring for their infants or interacting with their older children. It has been estimated that most U.S. fathers devote somewhere between 1.7 and 2.8 hours per week caring for their infant children. As children age, their fathers spend about eight hours a weeks playing with them, compared to 14 to 20 hours a week for mothers. As these statistics indicate, the major responsibility for child care still rests with the mother, even when the husband and wife work equal numbers of hours outside the home each week (Russell & Radin, 1983).

In an effort to understand why fathers aren't more involved with their children and to encourage men's participation in child rearing, several researchers have founded the Fatherhood Project (Levine & Pleck, 1983). The project is gathering information about programs that encourage men and boys to become more active in assuming responsibilities for child care. Some schools, for example, are offering child-care classes for teenage boys, in which boys learn to diaper and to feed babies, to express affection publicly for children, and to perceive the father's role as more than that of breadwinner. Although the Fatherhood Project has just begun, its eventual goal is to increase men's involvement with their children by disseminating relevant information to employers, policy makers, and the public. Some research suggests that adolescent males are already anticipating more interaction with their future children than their own fathers, which indicates that school-sponsored child-care classes for boys may be particularly relevant for today's adolescent boys (Eversoll, 1979).

How comfortable are you with infants and what accounts for your feelings?

Fathers and Sons

Dr. Lee Salk, child psychologist and author of several texts on child development, is among those who urge fathers to reexamine the ways in which they relate to their sons (Salk, 1982; Yablonsky, 1982). According to Salk, Freudian theories regarding the Oedipus complex have contributed to the erroneous assumption that the relationship between most fathers and sons will be tinged with jealousy, hostility, and competitiveness. Moreover, men's nurturant qualities have been ignored or ridiculed for so long that most fathers are reluctant to bestow affection on their sons through kissing, hugging, or verbal affirmations, such as "I love you." Consequently, Salk argues, while many boys express a desire to have more intimate relationships with their fathers, our notions of masculinity prevent either from forming an intimate, communicative relationship.

After interviewing fathers and sons from different generations, different socioeconomic classes, and different ethnic groups, Salk concludes that most father-son relationships are not conflict ridden, a finding that contradicts the

Freudian position. In further opposition to the Freudian view, the men interviewed by Salk consistently expressed regret over not having received more affection, more physical contact, and more time with their fathers during their childhood and adolescence. Despite their educational, racial, age, and socioeconomic differences, not one of the interviewed males wished his father had been less affectionate or less demonstrative (Salk, 1982).

On the basis of his experiences and data, Salk also contends that boys whose fathers are living at home, but who are unresponsive to and uncommunicative with their sons, often become juvenile delinquents or criminals. Indeed, Salk goes so far as to maintain that having an emotionally distant father at home can be more damaging to a son's psychological well-being than having no father in the home at all. Salk also asserts that fathers who are actively involved in their children's birth and who invest time in caring for their young infants will interact more with their children throughout their lives than fathers who separate themselves from their children's birth and infancy. Endorsing such policies as four-day workweeks, shorter workdays, paternity leaves, and househusbandry, Salk is among those psychologists who hope men will choose to participate more fully in the lives of their children from childbirth through adolescence.

The Son's Social Development Although still scant in comparison to the research on mother-child relationships, the data that have been collected on fathers and sons demonstrate both the social and cognitive ramifications of the father-son relationship. Biller's (1981b) exhaustive review of the relevant literature shows that fathers have a considerable impact on their sons' heterosexual development. A father who is secure in regard to his own masculinity and who establishes a warm relationship with his son thereby contributes to his son's social self-esteem. In this regard, a positive relationship between father and son has been found to be correlated with both the son's marital success and with his confidence in relating to females.

In contrast, the data indicate that fathers who are punitive, rejecting, or passive tend to undermine their sons' sexual and social self-confidence. Further, boys whose fathers are emotionally distant and uncommunicative are likely either to reject the male role altogether or to adopt excessively masculine behavior and values. Moreover, boys whose fathers are nurturant are more likely to adopt their father's values and to emulate their behavior than boys whose fathers are distant and unresponsive. In other words, boys do not perceive their fathers' nurturance either as effete or as unrespectable in ways that would diminish their desire to emulate their behavior (Biller, 1981b).

In regard to the adoption of the identity statuses described by James Marcia, a boy's relationship with his father also appears to be significant. Boys who achieve independent identities during their adolescence are the most likely to have fathers who exert moderate control over them, who support and praise their efforts, and who interact with them frequently. In contrast boys with foreclosed identities generally have fathers who are tolerant and protective, but who pressure their sons to conform to the family's values. These fathers often discourage the expression of emotions and dominate their sons (Marcia, 1980).

Moreover, a father's ralationship to his son seems to assume a particular importance during adolescence. According to several studies, both a father's and a mother's behavior are partially determined by their son's physical maturity, irrespective of his actual cognitive or social maturity (Steinberg, 1981). That is, the more physically mature their son appears, the more likely his parents are to treat him like an older adolescent.

Conversely, if the son is slow to mature and appears younger than his actual chronological age, his parents tend to treat him like a younger child. Interestingly, however, these studies indicate that during adolescence the son becomes increasingly more dominant and more powerful in his relationship with his mother. Thus, conflicts between mothers and sons tend to arise during adolescence as the mother's influence tends to decline. In contrast, the son's respect and deference toward his father generally remain constant during childhood and adolescence. Studies such as these suggest that the father's influence may be especially important to his son during adolescence, when the mother's power seems to diminish.

The Son's Cognitive Development In addition to these areas of social development, an adolescent boy's cognitive development is significantly influenced by his father. In general, the research demonstrates that fathers have a greater influence on their sons' intellectual growth than on their daughters'. It has been suggested that the father's influence is greatest over his son because boys tend to identify with and to imitate their fathers more than girls. The data also show that fathers generally invest more time and express more interest in their sons' than in their daughters' intellectual development. Even recent studies continue to demonstrate that fathers are most concerned about their sons' intellectual development and about their daughters' development of interpersonal skills (Biller, 1981a, 1981b; Radin, 1981).

Most studies acknowledge that a father who is punitive, distant, or hostile undermines his son's intellectual and academic abilities. In contrast, fathers who support their sons' attempts at problem solving without much interference or criticism, contribute to the independence, curiosity, and self-confidence that enhance academic success and intellectual growth. Moreover, sons appear to develop cognitive styles similar to their fathers'. It appears that the father conveys his cognitive style to his son through modeling, reinforcement, and direct instruction during problem-solving situations. As a consequence, a son's spatial ability skills, analytical approaches, and field independence or field dependence are usually highly correlated with his father's. The impact of the father's interactions with his children is supported by several studies showing a higher correlation between a father's behavior with his child and the child's IQ score than between the father's level of education and the youngster's IQ. In sum, a father's nurturance and frequent interaction with his son seem to enhance the son's cognitive skills (Radin, 1981).

Fathers and Daughters

> I have been surprised at how rare it is in this Freudian age that any of these troubled daughters identify their fathers as a contributing factor in their adult unhappiness. Through my research I have learned that it takes a woman until the age of thirty to completely understand her relationship to her father. By this time he is sixty, fully evolved and revealed. If a woman understands her development with respect to her father, she will have enough information to help her in all facets of her life (Appleton, 1981, pp. ix, xii).

While the foregoing Freudian perspective on the father-daughter relationship continues to provoke controversy among contemporary psychologists, few would disagree that fathers have an influence on their daughters that extends beyond her adolescence. As contemporary researchers have begun to redirect some of their attention from mothers toward fathers and from male adolescents toward females, the father's impact on female development is becoming clearer. The available research is already recasting many former assumptions about the father's role in a daughter's development by addressing such questions as: How do fathers relate differently to sons and daughters? How does a father influence his daughter differently than a mother? How can a father enhance his daughter's academic achievement, vocational success, self-esteem, and sexual relationships?

Although fathers generally interact more with their sons than with their daughters, the research suggests that daughters are more likely than sons to emulate their parents' values (Feather, 1980; Lynn, 1979). Since these data indicate that daughters may be more impressionable than sons in regard to their parents' values, fathers may have an opportunity to instill values and attitudes in female children that their sons may resist. Unfortunately, many fathers remain unaware of their impact on their daughters' intellectual, vocational, and social development.

During the nineteenth century the family's role was to encourage submission and dependence in female children, while also training them to be the more moral of the two sexes (Wynne & Frader, 1979). In contrast, the twentieth century's challenge to parents has been that of helping their daughters adapt to new economic and social realities, such as the necessity of acquiring vocational skills for adult employment. Interestingly, in this regard, girls in the 1960s tended to view their parents' restrictions as fair, while their counterparts in the 1970s and 1980s tend to want more autonomy and equality from their parents (Douvan & Adelson, 1966; Lerner, Sorrell, & Brackney, 1981; Offer, Ostrov, & Howard, 1981). Given these trends, the father-daughter relationship has increasingly captured the interest of contemporary researchers.

The Daughter's Cognitive Development Several implications emerge from the current research in regard to the impact of fathers on their daughters' cognitive development (Radin, 1981). Although a father's nurturance and affection are positively correlated with his son's academic and cognitive development, too much paternal nurturance and affection appear to interfere with his daughter's cognitive development and academic achievements. Girls generally become more autonomous, more self-confident, and more intellectually curious, when their fathers are not providing constant support, nurturance, and assistance. In order to foster his daughter's autonomy and cognitive development, a father is best advised to discourage her dependence upon him for constant approval or guidance.

From the social learning and behavioral perspectives, a father influences his daughter's intellectual and vocational development by the types of behavior he chooses to reward or to punish. In this regard, it is noteworthy that several studies have found that black fathers reinforce their daughters' independence and encourage their intellectual curiosity at an earlier age than white fathers (McAdoo, 1981). As you may recall from Chapters 5 and 6, black adolescent girls tend to be more independent and more motivated to gain vocational skills than their white counterparts. Taken together, these data suggest that black and Caucasian fathers' different styles of interacting with their daughters in early childhood may be partially responsible for these later differences in their daughters during adolescence.

In a similar vein, given the combined effects of modeling and reinforcement, the prediction is often made that girls who spend considerable time with their fathers ought to perform better mathematically than girls who spend very little time with their fathers. As predicted, several studies of college women have shown that those whose fathers were often present when their daughters were between the ages of 1 and 9 had higher math achievement scores than daughters whose fathers were absent in their early childhood years. Similarly, researchers have found positive correlations between fathers' and daughters' field-independent cognitive styles in families where fathers took time to interact with their daughters. In combination, these findings suggest that girls model their fathers' analytical style and mathematical skills, if given the opportunity to interact frequently with them (Radin, 1981).

Unfortunately, the data show that daughters are less likely than sons to have the kind of relationship with their fathers that engenders vocational, intellectual, and academic competence. This difference between sons and daughters appears to occur for two reasons. First, studies consistently show that fathers interact less frequently with their daughters than with their sons. Thus, a daughter is less likely to derive the positive intellectual benefits that can accrue from interacting with her father (Biller, 1981a, 1981b; Lamb, 1983; Polikoff, 1983; Radin, 1981).

Second, these studies demonstrate that most fathers interact with their daughters in ways that interfere with her cognitive and vocational development. Because many fathers still consider academic achievement, vocational commitment, and intellectual growth to be masculine endeavors, they fail to reinforce these values in their daughters as they do in their sons. Most fathers encourage more risk taking, nonconformity, assertiveness, independence, and vocational commitment in their sons than in their daughters, despite the fact that daughters also need these attitudes to develop independent identities and to insure financial security in the future. To further underscore the distinctions between sons and daughters, it is noteworthy that girls who have brothers are less likely to attend college or to develop their academic talents than girls without brothers.

The Daughter's Sexual and Social Development In addition to cognitive development, most research acknowledges the father's influence over his daughter's attitudes about males and her own sexuality (Biller, 1981(a)(b); Lynn, 1979). A father who has been nurturant, while still discouraging his daughter from becoming overly dependent on male approval for her sense of self-esteem, enhances his daughter's chances of developing an independent identity vis-à-vis males. By encouraging her to develop her own identity, the father prepares his daughter for the criticism and occassional rejection she will encounter from males in her life. Likewise, the father who accepts his daughter's sexuality, rather than mocking her relationships with boys or making her feel ashamed of her body, contributes to her sexual self-esteem. As discussed earlier in this chapter, Hetherington's (1972) research exemplifies the potential power of fathers to influence the kinds of men their daughters choose to marry and the degree to which their daughters enjoy their sexual experiences as adults.

Unfortunately, fathers too often discourage their daughters' independence and individuation (Appleton, 1981). They become angry or try to evoke guilt whenever their daughters choose not to behave as "Daddy" thinks his "little girl" should. Feeling threatened by their adolescent daughters' increasing independence and by their sexual interest in boys, many fathers behave in ways that undermine autonomy. Unfortuantely, if the adolescent daughter does not learn to overcome her dependence on her father's approval, she can inadvertently retard her own development in a never-ending struggle to maintain her father's approval.

It has been argued, from a psychoanalytic viewpoint, that the adolescent daughter should eventually relinquish her childhood visions of her father as a Prince Charming (Appleton, 1981). In the process of perceiving her father more realistically, an adolescent girl often feels angry or disappointed when she discovers her father's human frailties: He drinks too much; or he is unkind to his wife; or his sense of humor suddenly appears foolish. Moreover, some fathers refuse to relinquish their image as heroes or princes by denying their shortcomings in the presence of their daughters. In such cases, the daughter may continue to idealize her father, thereafter expecting the men in her life to "measure up to Daddy" by fulfilling her unrealistic expectations and her fantasies for the male gender.

These daughters have become victims of what has been alluded to as the *Cinderella complex*—the expectation that an infallible Prince Charming should be there to rescue them from all troubles and to create perpetual bliss in their lives. Predictably, these young women are repeatedly disappointed in their relationships with males, since human foibles disqualify males from remaining princes for very long. Moreover, it has been argued that a daughter whose father has not helped her dispel the Cinderella complex generally fails to assume responsibility for her own happiness and fails to prepare herself for coping with the vicissitudes of adult life (Appleton, 1981).

Undoubtedly, the amount of influence a father exerts over his daughter's sexual and social development varies according to such factors as the amount of time they spend together and their idiosyncratic traits as separate individuals. Nevertheless, the father-daughter relationship clearly influences some of the ways in which adolescent girls perceive themselves intellectually, vocationally, and socially. As research like Hetherington's demonstrates, even the father's absence as a consequence of his death or a divorce appears to influence a daughter's social relationships both during and after adolescence. Moreover, a father cannot help but influence his daughter's attitudes toward males, if in no other way than by manifesting his own attitudes about men and women through his own behavior toward his wife.

ADOLESCENTS AND THEIR SIBLINGS

In comparison with the number of studies devoted to the mother-child relationship, research regarding adolescents and their siblings is relatively scarce. Demographic data, however, do underscore several distinctions between today's adolescents and those of yesteryear in regard to their sibling relationships.

How would you change your sibling relationships if given the power to do so?

In contrast to their peers in former generations, today's youths generally have only one or two siblings. This trend toward smaller families is demonstrated by the fact that in 1979 only 45 percent of the women between the ages of 18 and 24 expected to have more than two children, whereas only ten years prior, 64 percent of the women in the same age bracket expected to have more than two children (U.S. Bureau of the Census, 1981). As a consequence of women's more active participation in the job market, the growing financial demands of raising a child, and more effective birth-control methods, the size of the typical U.S. family is still shrinking. Nevertheless, since having two children in the family is still the most popular option, an adolescent's being an only child is still relatively rare. Thus, adolescents' sibling relationships continue to attract the attention of researchers who are trying to unravel such questions as: How is an adolescent's development affected by being the first- or last-born child? In what ways is being an only child an advantage and in what ways a handicap? How do brothers and sisters affect one another's cognitive and social development?

The Influence of Birth Order

There are two views on whether family size and birth order have any significant advantages for an individual's cognitive development. Researchers who support the **confluence theory** contend that an individual's intellectual development is influenced by his or her birth order, number of siblings, and number of years' difference between children. According to studies supporting the confluence theory, first-born children are intellectually advantaged in comparison to their brothers and sisters. The first child supposedly receives more parental attention, more mental stimulation from adults, and more pressure to live up to parents' high expectations than later-born children. In addition, older children supposedly tutor younger brothers and sisters, and thereby provide intellectual stimulation for themselves, which the younger siblings and only children miss (Cicirelli, 1977; Zajonc, 1983; Zajonc & Markus, 1975).

The importance of being the youngest or eldest child decreases, however, when the children are far apart in age. When siblings are close together in age, the impact of birth order is greater than when they are several years apart. In other words, an adolescent boy whose only sibling is ten years older is more likely to have received parental attention and to have been treated as if he were a first-born than someone whose only sibling is two years older. Siblings close in age supposedly detract from one another's cognitive development, because they are not as intellectually challenging to one another as either adults or as much older siblings would be. According to confluence theory, having too many siblings or having too little interaction with adults detracts from an adolescent's intellectual abilities and academic achievement. For this reason, youngsters from single-parent families or those with two employed parents are supposedly less advantaged than those in two-parent homes where one adult is unemployed.

In support of the confluence theory, researchers cite studies showing a relationship between birth order and academic or professional achievements (Zajonc, 1983; Zajonc & Markus, 1975). First-born children have attained a disproportionate percentage of merit scholarships, Ph.D.s, and fame in their chosen professions in comparison to later-born children. A study of high-school students, for example, showed that first-borns earned high scores on National Merit Scholarship qualifying exams. Test scores declined as the student's birth order and family size increased (Breland, 1982). Supporters of the confluence theory also assert that the recent rise in adolescents' college-board scores is attributable to smaller families, as Box 8.7 illustrates (Zajonc, 1986).

As might be expected, however, the confluence theory is not without its critics, especially since research has not consistently supported its predictions (Jones, 1984). One criticism is that variables other than birth order confound the results of some studies that supposedly support the confluence model. For example, the confluence model contends that only children score more poorly on IQ tests than the eldest child with siblings, because only children have no opportunities to teach younger siblings. Yet this explanation overlooks the fact that only children are more likely to live in single-parent families than children with siblings. Therefore, some researchers feel it is just as reasonable to assume that their lower IQ scores are partially accounted for by their parent's marital situation, rather than by having no younger siblings to tutor (Falbo, 1982). Fur-

8.7 A Closer Look

Family Size and SAT Scores: A Connection?

Between 1963 and 1980, adolescents' scores on the College Board's Scholastic Aptitude Tests steadily declined, leaving both researchers and educators perplexed, and generating a host of hypotheses to explain the declines. According to some analysts, like Hunter Breland of the Educational Testing Service, about 44 percent of the decline is a consequence of the fact that so many more adolescents apply for college than in previous decades, especially students from minority groups. Others have argued, however, that the declines since 1971 cannot be wholly attributed to the greater heterogeneity of the students taking the SAT. Thus, some researchers have blamed the public schools, claiming that teachers have lowered their standards so dramatically that students' performance on the college boards has suffered. Still others are criticizing parents for not instilling the proper motivation and values in their children.

In contrast to these hypotheses, however, Richard Franke, a professor of management at Loyola College, and Hunter Breland are placing the blame on another phenomenon: bigger families. According to Franke and Breland's analysis of the data, birth order and the number of children in a family account for 87 percent of the decrease in SAT scores with these scores dropping 20 points for each additional child after the first.

Moreover, Franke and Breland contend that the high divorce rate and women's employment have detracted from SAT scores by limiting the intellectual stimulation that preschool children receive from their parents. On the basis of their analyses of data from 1965 to 1984, which take divorce rates and mothers' employment into consideration, Franke and Breland estimate that 97 percent of the SAT decline can be

thermore, while it seems reasonable to assume that older siblings tutor younger ones, this has not yet been empirically demonstrated in natural family settings outside the laboratory.

The relationship between achievement and birth order is not altogether clear. For example, some researchers have found no relationship between high-school achievement-test scores, family size, and spacing between children (Melican & Feldt, 1980). Furthermore, the prediction that youngsters from one-parent families should score lower on IQ and achievement tests than those with two parents has not always been borne out (Brackbill & Nichols, 1982). Finally, the confluence model loses more ground when the family's socioeconomic status is taken into account. Because the upper socioeconomic classes generally have fewer children than the poor, differences among brothers and sisters can be mistakenly attributed to the family's size or birth order, when the primary influence may actually be money. Opposition to the confluence theory has been summed up quite concisely by Smith (1982): "Given that birth order effects with a few notable exceptions have relatively little power in accounting for psychological outcomes, it remains a puzzle that so many thousands of studies have been devoted to such minimal ends" (p. 153). In sum, the degree to which family explained. According to their analyses, SAT scores have decreased 1.4 points for each 1 percent increase in the divorce or employment rate for mothers with preschool children.

In support of their theory, Franke and Breland point out that SAT scores declined during the 1960s and 1970s, when families were larger than in the two preceding decades. They attribute recent increases in SAT scores to the fact that adolescents in the 1980s come from smaller families than their cohorts in the 1960s and 1970s. Robert Zajonc, whose research on children without siblings is well known, also predicts that SAT scores will rise as children from smaller families reach college age. According to Zajonc's research, first-born children develop more intellectual skills and are likely to have higher achievement scores as a consequence of being intellectually stimulated through their early childhood interactions with adults rather than with siblings. From this perspective, the only child and children with the fewest siblings are the most intellectually advantaged.

As predicted by these theorists, the SAT scores for 1983's high-school seniors did increase one point on the verbal scores and three points on the math scores. Since neither the divorce rates nor the rates of female employment are declining, however, the outcomes of the SAT and other achievement tests may come increasingly to depend on the quality of preschool children's day-care centers. Thus, the question arises: Will the day-care experiences of today's preschoolers have any significant impact on the SAT scores of adolescents in the year 2000?

SOURCE: R. Zajonc, The decline and rise of scholastic aptitude scores. *American Psychologist*, 1986, *41*, 862–867.

size and birth order influence an adolescent's intellectual or psychological development still remains to be determined.

Sibling Rivalries and Loyalties

In addition to examining the relationship between birth order and adolescents' behavior, researchers have pursued questions related to the quality of the relationships between siblings: How much rivalry exists? Do these rivalries last a lifetime? Are sisters more likely to be rivals than brothers? Can parents prevent sibling jealousies, or is it an inevitable part of growing up?

Contrary to some popular notions, most research confirms that siblings usually relate without much rivalry during childhood and adolescence. Brothers, however, tend to engage in more conflict and more competition than sisters or than brothers and sisters. Moreover, brothers are the most likely to continue competing with one another beyond adolescence in terms of their financial, professional, and social accomplishments. In contrast, as sisters age, they tend to become less rivalrous. Data also suggests that olders sisters are better tutors than older brothers for the younger siblings. Although the research may be tainted by the fact that some people are more reluctant than others to admit their sibling rivalries, most research refutes the notion that siblings are arch rivals or intimate friends (Cicirelli, 1977, 1982).

The Only Child

In regard to the adolescent who is the only child in the family, the literature both refutes and confirms several popular notions (Falbo, 1982). Like first-born children, only children tend to achieve more academically and professionally than other youngsters. Also like first-borns, the only child often has more internal locus of control than later-born children. It is hypothesized that having received the most pressure and the most attention from his or her parents, the only child generally becomes achievement oriented at an early age and develops a sense of personal responsibility. The only child tends to join fewer school or social organizations, to spend less time with other people, and to have a smaller circle of acquaintances than children with siblings. On the other hand, the only child generally has as many close friends and holds as many leadership positions in clubs as children with siblings.

While some clinicians once argued that only children had less-satisfactory marriages than children with siblings, the research has failed to bear this out (Falbo, 1982). Moreover, divorce rates and age of first marriage seem unrelated to whether or not a person has a sibling. In regard to self-esteem, the research has been too inconsistent to argue cogently either for or against the assertion that the only child has a better self-concept than children with siblings.

In summary, it appears that the adolescent who has no brothers or sisters usually benefits in terms of his or her academic and vocational development. In addition, assumptions that the only child will inevitably become spoiled, lonely, or socially handicapped now appear to be misrepresentations more often than they are valid.

Similarities among Siblings

Since the majority of adolescents have at least one sibling, researchers have continued to pursue questions related to siblings' similarities: How similar are the intellectual abilities of siblings? How much of the difference among siblings is genetic and how much is within the parent's control? What accounts for the differences between the children in a family?

An expert on the development of human intelligence, psychologist Sandra Scarr has analyzed the research on siblings' similarities in an attempt to answer such questions. At the outset of her analysis, Scarr reminds us that siblings are far more dissimilar than professionals and the public generally assume. For example, although siblings are most similar to each other on IQ test scores, the correlations are typically only .35 to .50. These low correlations mean that approximately 75 percent of the variability in siblings' IQ scores is not accounted for by their being siblings. Moreover, the average difference between siblings IQ test scores is 13 points, in comparison with an average difference between any two strangers of 18 points. These IQ statistics mean that siblings raised in the same home have IQ scores that differ by two-thirds of the number of random pairs of individuals in the population (Scarr & Grajek, 1982).

Furthermore, Scarr notes even greater dissimilarities between siblings on measures of personality, attitudes, and psychological disturbances. Surprisingly, correlations between siblings' scores on such measures are typically only .15 to .20, which are exceedingly low correlations. As Scarr states succinctly,

> Upper middle class brothers who attend the same school and whose parents take them to the same plays, sporting events, music lessons and therapists, and use similar child rearing practices on them are little more similar in personality measures than they are to working-class or farm boys whose lives are totally different. Now perhaps this is an exaggeration of the known facts, but not by much. Given the low correlations of biological siblings and the near zero correlations of adopted siblings, it is evident that most of the variance in personality arises in the environmental differences among siblings, not in the differences among families (Scarr, 1983, p. 361).

How can it be that most siblings have so little in common (Scarr & Grajek, 1982)? First, each child in a family receives only half of each parent's genes; therefore, the number of different genetic combinations between siblings is greater than is generally presumed. Second, the impact of genetic endowment on an individual's behavior has not yet been established. Given the methodological problems involved, how is a researcher to verify whether a particular type of behavior is genetically or environmentally determined? Moreover, since a parent's behavior is partially determined by the child's innate characteristics, how can researchers confidently separate the two? For example, is one sister more aggressive than the other because her parents treated her differently from the outset, or did her own genetic makeup cause her to behave in ways that, in turn, elicited different responses from her parents? Third, merely being raised in the same family does not mean that siblings have experienced the same environmental influences. For example, a study of 348 families with two adolescent children found that siblings in the same family had different experiences with their parents, as reported by both parents and children (Daniels & Plomin, 1985).

Scarr and her associates have developed a theory that credits both the genotypes and the environment for similarities and dissimilarities among siblings. According to their theory, a child's genetic makeup is primarily responsible for sibling differences, because the genotype determines the unique manner in which each sibling will respond to common experiences. In other words, two sisters may be exposed to exactly the same family interactions and experiences, but each will respond uniquely on the basis of her genetic makeup. In addition, each sister's genetic uniqueness will elicit different reactions from other people. In some situations, however, siblings will respond similarly to an experience because of their genetic likeness to one another. In these situations other people will respond to both siblings similarly, thereby reinforcing that particular behavior for each of them. In this fashion parents learn to interact differently with each child in the family, thereby magnifying whatever initial distinctions existed between siblings.

According to Scarr and her colleagues, siblings with similar genotypes are more likely to evoke the same responses from their parents than two siblings with extremely different genotypes. Thus, understanding the differences between siblings' personalities and abilities becomes a matter of exploring the ways in which genotypes interact with parents' and other siblings' behavior, rather than a matter of deciding whether a child's genetic endowment has a greater or lesser influence than the environment. In summary, Sandra Scarr and her associates recommend that psychologists be less reluctant to admit the importance of genetics in sibling differences, while still understanding that this admission does not discount the environment's role in shaping each individual's personality.

PHYSICAL ABUSE AND INCEST

While the United States views itself as a child-loving, pro-family society, statistics testify to the reality that thousands of parents are physically abusing and sexually molesting their children. Each year about 10 percent of all U.S. children are reported as having been abused by a parent, though authorities feel these figures are grossly underestimated (Helfer & Kempe, 1982). Other figures suggest that parental violence and lack of parental concern for one's own children are domestic realities in millions of households. For example, in June of 1982, 50,000 children were missing and 1,000 dead children remained unnamed and unclaimed. Further, in the United States today, one-third of all murdered children are killed by their own parents or stepparents (Pogrebin, 1983).

Some social commentators, such as Letty Pogrebin, contend that child abuse is related to some adults' fundamental fear and dislike of children. As Pogrebin states her position, "In our own era pedophobia is more subtle. It is also more pernicious because it exists within the lie that Americans are a child-loving people" (Pogrebin, 1983, p. 46). While we may disagree with Pogrebin's radical assessment of U.S. attitudes toward children, the statistics do support her contention that child abuse is more widespread than is commonly acknowledged by our society. At the very least, the disturbing statistics on child abuse and incest call into question the assumption that all adults should become parents in order to have a "fulfilling life."

As well as alerting us to the fact that some adults should not become parents, the statistics on abuse also provoke researchers into examining complex questions about U.S. families: What factors contribute to the physical and sexual abuse of children? What psychological consequences befall adolescents who have been victims of physical abuse or incest? How should abusive parents be rehabilitated? Investigations of such questions have uncovered a number of disturbing realities regarding U.S. family life.

Physically Abused Children

Although researchers have no single or definitive explanation for child abuse, several theories prevail (Helfer & Kempe, 1982). According to one perspective, families in which the power is unequal between husband and wife are more likely to abuse children than those in which the two adults have a more egalitarian, democratic relationship with one another. For example, if the family's financial and social power is concentrated too exclusively in the father's hands, the mother is often subjected to psychological or physical abuse from her husband. She, in turn, vents her anger and her powerlessness through physically abusing her children. The root of the child abuse, however, is the parents' personal or marital unhappiness.

Second, it is argued that parents abuse their children because they themselves were raised by abusive parents. According to this viewpoint, abusive parents never learned from their own parents the appropriate methods for resolving conflicts or for communicating with family members. As a consequence, the children of abusive parents learn to resolve their conflicts and to express their emotions through physical violence. Thus, the cycle of family violence is transmitted from generation to generation.

Third, some analysts perceive the source of child abuse as a parent's low self-esteem and his or her own desperate need for love and security—human needs that the parent never had gratified as a child. From this viewpoint, marital stress, financial crises, or the countless other vicissitudes of adult living cause parents with low self-esteem to vent their frustrations on their children in sudden outbursts of temper and physical violence. The fact that most reported cases of child abuse are committed by indigent mothers lends credibiity to this perspective. It is important to note, however, that the high correlation between poverty and child abuse may be based on inflated statistics, since middle-class and wealthy parents are better able to conceal their abusive behavior by reporting their children's injuries to their private physicians as "accidents." In contrast, indigent parents who depend upon public clinics are more likely than the more well-to-do to be reported for child abuse (Helfer & Kempe, 1982).

While these explanations regarding the etiology of child abuse are well documented in the literature, some researchers have recently challenged certain aspects of these traditional assumptions. According to several studies presented at the 1984 national convention of the American Psychological Association, child abuse cannot be explained simply by the assumption that abusive parents were themselves abused as children. On their behalf, these researchers cite several studies showing that women who were abused as children were no more abusive than other mothers. In further contradiction to traditional theories, the abusive mothers reported feeling no more depressed or no more unhappy than the nonabusive mothers. Although contradicting the vast majority of extant studies, these recent studies offer tentative support for the assertion that the etiology of child abuse may be more complex than has formerly been acknowledged (Fisher, 1984).

Although adolescents' may respond differently to physical abuse, experts have identified a number of relatively common reactions (Helfer & Kempe, 1982; Hjorth, 1982; Kratcoski, 1982). Aside from developing a distrust of adults, physically abused youths often find it difficult to establish trusting relationships with their peers. Sadly, in their attempts to find the love and support that are missing at home, physically abused youngsters often make unrealistic demands on their peers and are overly sensitive to even the most minor rebuffs. Moreover, these children not only harbor an intense anger toward the abusive parent, they often come to dislike the parent who appears to be allowing the abuse to continue. Unfortunately, a number of abused children also adopt the posture that they themselves are responsible for their parents' physical violence. Thus, their self-image suffers as they convince themselves that if only they were somehow "better," their parents would stop beating them.

Not surprisingly though, given their feelings of anger, rejection, and self-deprecation, abused adolescents often resort to running away from home or committing delinquent acts (Helfer & Kempe, 1982). Anger that cannot be expressed at home is vented against others outside the family.

Incest

Although child abuse has gained an increasing amount of publicity and national attention, sexual offenses against the young and incest are still considered taboo topics for discussion. In general, the television networks and other media have shied away from the topics. For example, it was not until 1983 that a national television network was willing to air a movie on the topic of father-daughter incest, entitled "The Trouble with Amelia." In 1984 and 1985, however, headlines proclaimed a "national epidemic of child sexual abuse," as stories about pornography and sexual abuse in preschools and elementary schools came to the nation's attention. As a consequence, some school systems are now instructing preschoolers, as well as adolescents, on topics such as rape, incest, and child molestation (Collins, 1985).

In terms of its psychological impact on adolescents, one of the most serious sexual offenses is incest between parent and child. Although our attention is typically directed to the female victims of incest, adolescent males are by no means immune from incestuous experiences. Incest involving male children can be equally as upsetting to family members as acts involving female children (Bass & Thornton, 1983). Moreover, it has been argued that boys who are victims of incest remain silent, in part because the male sex role discourages expressions of helplessness and vulnerability (Nasjleti, 1980). Fortunately, despite the shame and secrecy that have traditionally surrounded the topic, both researchers and victims have become increasingly willing to explore and to publicize, "the best kept family secret"—incest (Armstrong, 1978; Bass & Thornton, 1983; Rush, 1980). Nevertheless, according to some estimates, sexual abuse may be more common than physical abuse in the contemporary U.S. family (Anderson, 1981).

The Etiology of Incest Why do some families violate the cultural taboos against sex within the family? According to older theories, the etiology of incest was explained primarily from a sociological perspective (Mrazek, 1981; Slovenko, 1980). From this viewpoint, geographically isolated families, like those in the remote areas of the Appalachian Mountains, and indigent families were considered the most-likely candidates for incestuous relationships. More recent research, however, generally disputes sociological explanations. For example, incestuous relationships exist in middle- and upper-income families, where external sociological factors do not appear to be creating stress within the family.

Thus, the sociological position yielded to the view that an individual's sexual self-restraint could be diminished by means of external influences. First, this perspective presumed that drugs could trigger incestuous acts by lessening the sexual inhibitions of the family members. For instance, a father and daughter who are drinking heavily together might become intoxicated enough to temporarily suspend the incest taboo. Second, it has been argued that individuals with the least intelligence are more likely to be involved in incest than those with higher levels of intelligence. Although positive correlations between low IQ scores and reported incidents of incest have been found in several studies, it may simply be the case that people with the least intelligence are less able than their more intelligent counterparts to keep their incestuous acts secret. More important, correlational studies do not warrant statements regarding causality (Mrazek, 1981; Slovenko, 1980).

In contrast to former theories, the most prevalent views today regard incest as the consequence of psychodynamics both in the individual and in the family. In attempting to explain why incest occurs in a particular family, the psychodynamic viewpoint considers the characteristics of all family members, rather than directing attention exclusively to the offender's personality or history. In this context, the family is perceived as a system in which each member exerts an influence on the behavior of the others. For example, marital unhappiness between the husband and wife might motivate the husband to become sexually involved with his daughter; or a son's feelings of emotional deprivation from his father might underlie his sexual interests in his sister.

Although most incest occurs between fathers and daughters, these acts occur far more often between stepfathers and stepdaughters than between natural fathers and daughters (Mrazek, 1981; Slovenko, 1980). Often, but not always, the father feels abandoned emotionally by his own mother or by his wife. Clearly distinguishable patterns of psychological or sexual disturbance have not, however, emerged from most studies of incestuous fathers. For example, some have sex often with their wives as well as with their daughters, while others have no sexual relationship with their wives whatsoever. Some men have sex with their daughters only during periods of intense stress or marital disharmony. For others, the incest is continuous and seems to serve as an outlet for reducing family tensions.

Researchers still disagree about the extent of the mother's involvement in father-daughter incest. Thus, a number of disturbing questions remain unanswered: Can a mother truly be unaware of the incestuous relationship within her own household? Does she herself collude in the incest by refusing to establish a satisfying relationship with her husband? Does the mother intentionally let her daughter take her place as a surrogate wife?

Although some adults who engage in incest with younger family members are brutal and violent, the majority are described as nonviolent men, seeking nurturance and approval through sexual encounters with their sons, daughters, nieces, or nephews. Indeed, these adults are often able to persuade the young people at an early age that their sexual experiences are expressions of love and affection, which are not to be feared or to be shunned. Given a child's sexual naivete and natural affection for a relative, he or she may feel too intimidated or too confused to resist or to report the relative's sexual advances. By adolescence, however, a young person's discomfort with the situation and the awareness of society's sexual mores typically exacerbate the problems associated with the incestuous relationship. Distressingly, as with many physically abused children, the adolescent victims of incest often blame themselves for their relatives' sexual aberrance.

Although psychodynamic explanations are presently the most promising, the research is still too contradictory to permit such complicated questions to be answered with confidence. In sum, the critical factors explaining why incest occurs in some families but not in others have not yet been isolated.

The Impact on Victims Although the etiology of incest remains obscure, the effects of incest on adolescents are more discernable. Once adolescence begins, a child who formerly overlooked the implications of the incestuous relationship can no longer avoid the sexual and emotional issues involved. Understandably, adolescents are reluctant to admit that they have been or are involved in an incestuous relationship, particularly if the sex has involved force or violence. In reaction to the incestuous relationship, adolescents have been known to attempt suicide, resort to prostitution, quit school, run away from home, become sexually promiscuous, and fail their academic work at school (Anderson, 1981; Mrazek & Mrazek, 1981; Steele & Alexander, 1981).

More sadly, because many adults refuse to believe an adolescent's stories about incest, the youth can come to doubt his or her own perceptions and feelings. Moreover, when a parent refuses to believe or to protect the child from the incestuous relative, feelings of anger and betrayal are almost inevitable. Unable to escape from the situation, many youngsters have developed attitudes of powerlessness associated with an external locus of control. Not surprisingly, nervous symptoms such as overeating, nail biting, psychosomatic illnesses, and impulsive or self-damaging behavior are among adolescents' reactions to incest.

Penalties and Rehabilitation Incest is a crime punishable in all states by penalties ranging from 1 to 50 years' imprisonment. In many states, sex between adoptive or stepparents and their children is not punishable under the law as "incest." In these states, however, an adult can be prosecuted under the "indecent liberties with a minor" statutes (Slovenko, 1980).

The current controversy revolves not around the legal sanctions against incest but around the question: How should incestuous families be helped? Historically, both in cases of incest and of child abuse, the adolescent and the offending family member have been separated for the child's physical and psychological well-being. This traditional strategy, however, is now being reexamined by many psychologists and social service agencies (Rittenberg, 1980; Slovenko, 1980; Krieger & Robbins, 1985). Among the questions now being raised are: Should a family undergo the ordeal of courtroom procedures and the financial difficulties associated with removing the husband from the home, when less drastic alternatives might be devised for helping the incestuous family? Would the adolescent victim and other family members benefit most from therapy, with the eventual goal being the reestablishment of one household? Should the adolescent be assigned to a foster home until the offending relative is supposedly "cured," or is it best that the youngster be permanently removed from the family?

According to critics of the traditional approach, social service agencies and counselors should attempt to keep families together, rather than to remove the victimized child to an institutional setting or to a foster home. For example, new approaches have required intensive counseling for the offender, the victim, and all other family members, while both the offender and the victim continue to live in the same household. Other programs temporarily remove the offender from the family, while maintaining the goal of returning him if he and the victim can reestablish a trusting relationship.

Given the persistent and often covert nature of incest, it appears that the behavior may indeed be serving a function for the entire family. For example, one family met with a therapist only one week after the father had been discovered committing an incestuous act with his 14-year old daughter. While the father expressed his regret and the mother expressed her anger, both admitted their unhappiness in the marriage. Nevertheless, the couple refused further counseling, protesting that their troubles were now over and downplaying the significance of the incest. Meanwhile, their daughter remained silent in both her individual and family counseling sessions (Will, 1983).

In sum, our understanding of the etiology and treatment of incest needs to be predicated upon a far more extensive data base than is presently available. Sociological and psychological data on family dynamics and on the idiosyncratic characteristics of the victims and the offenders appear vital to our future understanding of this problem that besets thousands of adolescents.

STYLES OF PARENTING: THEIR IMPACT ON ADOLESCENTS

In addressing the question, How permissive or authoritarian should today's parents be with their adolescent children?, a crucial methodological problem arises—the confusion over operational definitons. In attempting to assess the desirability of one style of parenting in relation to another, parents and researchers would have to consistently agree on the kinds of behavior that characterize concepts such as "authoritarian." For instance, behavior that is deemed "permissive" by one father may be perceived as quite ordinary by the father next door. Likewise, some adolescents describe their parents as authoritarian because they consistently administer punishment when their children violate certain prescribed rules. In contrast, most researchers would classify such parental behavior as "authoritative," rather than authoritarian. Thus, the research on parenting styles must be viewed with at least this one caveat in mind: A particular type of parental behavior has not necessarily been classifed similarly in every study.

Moreover, it is worth noting that the terms "authoritarian" and "permissive" may be colored by our personal views about the issues to which these terms are being applied. As the true story in Box 8.8 illustrates, some U.S. observers would consider it dictatorial and authoritarian to force adolescent children to return to their Communist homeland with their parents who have chosen to leave the United States. These same onlookers, however, may consider it permissive to permit an American adolescent to remain in a Communist country against the will of her American parents. In a similar fashion, parents who permit their sons to smoke marijuana under their supervison at home may be deemed permissive, while those who permit their sons to get drunk away from home may be described as understanding.

8.8 A Closer Look

Obey Thy Parents?

In 1980, 17-year-old Natalie Polovchak and her 12-year-old brother, Walter, refused to leave Chicago and return to the Soviet Union with their parents who had become disillusioned with life in the United States. The parents insisted that Walter be forced legally to return with them to their homeland, since he was still a minor. Walter, however, who was living with an American cousin, asked the U.S. government for political asylum, claiming he had a right to remain in a democratic society rather than be forced to return to a Communist country.

A Chicago judge first decided to honor Walter's request; however, his ruling was overturned by the Illinois Appellate Court. In the interim, the U.S. Immigration and Naturalization Service granted Walter asylum and provided him with armed bodyguards. The Reagan administration issued an executive order preventing him from leaving the States, and the Justice Department granted him permanent-residency status. In an unprecedented decision, the president of the United States had sided with a 12-year-old child against his parents. Moreover, the Soviet Union protested that the United States was violating human rights by interfering with the parents' wishes and by separating the child from his family.

The incident provokes a number of questions related to pro-family attitudes and the role of family and state: Should children have the right to leave home against their parents' wishes? If so, at what age? Should a court or a government side with a minor against his or her parents? Are 12-year-olds mature enough to decide when to leave their parents and whether to establish citizenship in a new country? Would Americans who supported Walter's request have endorsed his viewpoint if he had been an American-born youth who wanted to leave his American parents to live in a Communist country?

On their own behalf, both Walter and his sister, Natalie, provided several powerful arguments underlying their wishes to remain in the United States. In Natalie's words, "I never had love for my parents. I was always a slave in their house." Walter added, "I have never been close to my parents. I was raised by my grandmother until I was 12 years old. My father was coming home once a week and sometimes never."

Nevertheless, in defending Walter and Natalie's parents, the American Civil Liberties Union argued that neither the children's antipathy for their parents nor their request for political asylum were in question. According to the ACLU, the legal issue was simply whether children under the legal age should be allowed to decide for themselves where they want to live. Similarly, a *New York Times* editorial agreed that "this case isn't about freedom from political oppression but the freedom of a boy to defy his parents."

In your opinion, how should the U.S. government have responded to Walter's request for asylum? How would you feel if you were Walter's parents? How would you feel about an American 12-year-old who refused to return to Chicago with her parents because she wanted to live in the Soviet Union? What do you think about the ACLU's position in this case?

SOURCES: *New York Times,* December 31, 1981; January 6, February 16, April 19, 17, and 28, and October 7, 1982. *National Review,* March 18, 1983, p. 314.

In an effort to provide operational definitions for the various parenting styles, Diana Baumrind has categorized parents' behavior into three basic styles: authoritarian, permissive or laissez faire, and authoritative (Baumrind, 1978). In Baumrind's most recent conceptualization, each parenting style is composed of two dimensions: Parental demandingness and parental responsiveness. Using Baumrind's classification system, researchers have generated invaluable information relevant to adolescents and their parents (Elder, 1980; Maccoby & Martin, 1983).

Authoritarian Parents

According to Baumrind's typology, parents who are **authoritarian** or autocratic place demands on their children without establishing a reciprocal relationship in which children may also make certain demands of the parents. In these families, children are expected to suppress their needs and, in extreme

How did you feel about family gatherings when you were an adolescent? What experiences do you remember most fondly?

cases, are denied the right to speak before being spoken to by an adult. Rules are not discussed in advance or agreed to by consensus or by compromise. Authoritarian parents attach the greatest value to maintaining their authority and to punishing deviations from a set of standards that are both absolute and inflexible. Valuing obedience, respect for authority, work, tradition, and the preservation of order, these parents discourage verbal exchange between themselves and their children. In terms of Baumrind's two dimensions of parenting, these parents score high on "demandingness" and low on "responsiveness."

Not surprisingly, authoritarian parents experience considerable difficulty when their children reach adolescence, since an adolescent is intellectually capable of assessing the shortcomings in a parent's logic. Furthermore, authoritarian parents generally discourage young people's independence and individuality, therby creating restrictions that most adolescents resent. As might be expected, children with authoritarian parents tend to be academically successful, but to have less social ease with their peers, less spontaneity, and less self-confidence than children with more democratic parents (Maccoby & Martin, 1983).

Studies that have attempted to assess the impact of authoritarian parenting on a child's resistance to temptation in contrived laboratory situations have been too inconsistent to permit conclusions (Maccoby & Martin, 1983). Authoritarian parenting does, however, appear to have a slight impact on a child's willingness to confess a transgression and to feel guilty. For example, in one of the few analyses of the available data, children with authoritarian parents scored low on measures of conscience in four of eight studies (Hoffman, 1970). Although these findings suggest only a slight relationship between parenting styles and a child's conscience or guilt, it is noteworthy that the authoritarian style does not appear to instill an internal locus-of-control attitude or high levels of conscience that control one's behavior through guilt (Maccoby & Martin, 1983).

As you may recall from Chapter 4's discussion of Marcia's identity statuses, adolescents with authoritarian parents are the most likely to adopt a foreclosed identity (1980). Discouraged by their parents from experimenting with various ideologies, vocational options or social roles, these adolescents generally adopt their parents' values, acquiesce to the wishes of authorities, and maintain the status quo. Remaining dependent on their authoritarian parents, these youths seldom become individuated enough from others to create their own independent identities.

Finally, researchers have explored the relationship between authoritarian parenting and children's aggressive behavior. At present most of the evidence has failed to demonstrate a strong or consistent correlation between a youth's aggressiveness and authoritarian parenting. Since authoritarian parents tend to use more physical punishment than other parents, it seems reasonable to suppose that their children might, in turn, behave more aggressively toward other people. In other words, "violence begets violence." However, although there is generally a positive relationship between punishment for aggression and children's aggressiveness at home, the findings are too inconsistent to conclude that a child's aggressive behavior generalizes to situations away from home. More important, longitudinal studies have failed to substantiate the hypothesis that frequent physical punishment during an individual's childhood results in aggressive behavior later in life (Maccoby & Martin, 1983).

Permissive Parents

In direct contrast to authoritarian parents, **permissive** parents permit their adolescent children to regulate much of their own behavior (Baumrind, 1977). According to Baumrind, these parents place very few demands on their children, seldom use punishment, and whenever possible, avoid asserting their authority or imposing restrictions. Further, permissive parents are generally tolerant of their children's impulsive behavior, including sexual and aggressive impulses. In many ways permissive parents appear to be uninvolved in their children's lives, since they abdicate most of the responsibility that society typically expects parents to assume.

Although most permissive parents are relatively nurturant toward their children, many have been described as detached and uninvolved with their offspring. Moreover, the motivations underlying the permissive style of parenting are not altogether clear. It has been suggested that some indulgent parents are intimidated by their children and are, therefore, too afraid to impose any restrictions whatsoever. Other parents seem to be overindulging their children as a way of compensating for their own childhood deprivation or an overly strict upbringing. Still other adults in this category seem to be unattached emotionally to their adolescent children and, consequently, choose not to invest time interacting with their older children in any fashion. Whatever its etiology, the permissive parenting style sometimes results in an adolescent's not feeling loved.

According to Baumrind, permissive parents make few demands for mature behavior from their children, but are generally responsive toward their offspring. Not surprisingly, children with indulgent parents have been characterized as impulsive, immature, aggressive, and lacking in independence. Furthermore, these children tend not to assume responsibility or to discipline themselves. In sum, the negative consequences of permissive parenting generally outweigh the positive (Baumrind, 1978; Elder, 1980; Maccoby & Martin, 1983).

Authoritative Parents

In contrast to the permissive and authoritarian sytles, parents can adopt what Baumrind and others refer to as a **democratic** or **authoritative** perspective on child rearing. While assuming the ultimate responsibility for their children's decision, these parents allow adolescents to participate in the decision making and to assume responsibility gradually for their own behavior. While imposing rules and administering punishment when necessary, these parents explain the rationale underlying their regulations. Moreover, these adults encourage their children to discuss disagreements that arise from their different perspectives on issues like curfews, dating, household chores, and homework. Adolescents with authoritative parents are expected to behave maturely, to communicate openly with their parents, to express their individuality, and to recognize the rights of their parents and other siblings.

According to Baumrind's research, adolescents with authoritative parents generally develop more self-confidence, more self-direction, and more social and academic competence than their peers from permissive or authoritarian homes. Having been accorded the right to disagree with their parents, these youngsters develop a respect for their parents without feeling that adults' rules are unfairly imposed on them without rhyme or reason. Furthermore, children with authoritative parents are typically concerned with the impact of their misbehavior on other people, rather than merely concerned with conforming to rules for the sake of deference to authority (Hoffman, 1970).

Perhaps more important, adolescents overwhelmingly prefer authoritative parents over the authoritarian or permissive counterparts. For instance, in a study of several thousand Danish and U.S. youths, the authoritative parents were the most popular in both countries (Kandel & Lesser, 1972). As might be expected, young people appreciate parents who allow them to participate in designing the family's rules and regulations. In particular, adolescents express appreciation for parents who explain the rationale underlying their rules. Although adolescents with democratic parents admit feeling independent from their parents, they also express their respect and their willingness to obey their parents' rules (Baumrind, 1978; Elder, 1980).

Although authoritative parents and their adolescent children are more likely to become engaged in arguments with one another than are members of authoritarian families, some conflict appears to enhance adolescents' development. First, conflict between adolescents and their parents contributes to individuation, which, as you may recall from Chapter 4, is essential for the development of an independent identity status (Marcia, 1980). For example, longitudinal research from the Fels Institute studies acknowledged that adolescent girls who eventually developed independence had experienced conflicts with their parents, which enabled them to overcome their dependence and, thereby, to establish an independent life (Kagan & Moss, 1962).

Finally, in contrast to permissive or authoritarian parents, authoritative parents behave in ways that are least likely to result in psychological, academic, or social problems for their children. Research generally demonstrates that ineffective communication and lack of nurturance within a family are correlated with certain psychological and physical disorders in children. For example, the parents of schizophrenics tend to send contradictory, critical, hostile messages to their children. While it might be argued that the child's psychological disorder caused the parents to respond critically, recent evidence suggests that poor communication and hostility characterized these families before the adolescent manifested any symptoms of schizophrenia (Goldstein, 1978). In addition to psychological disorders such as schizophrenia, adolescents' academic problems, delinquency, and physical disorders have been correlated with their parents' rejection, hostility, or apathy (Offer, Ostrov, & Howard, 1981; Weiner, 1970; West, 1981; Rutter, 1980; Rutter & Giller, 1983).

In conclusion, the strategies used by authoritative parents have been identified as central to the well-being of adolescents and their parents. For example, after ten years of working with the families of aggressive and maladapted children, Patterson and his colleagues devised a training program for parents in order to teach them the skills of authoritative parenting. In the Patterson program, parents learn to state clear guidelines for acceptable and unacceptable behavior in their children and to establish contingencies beforehand in regard to the penalties for infractions of the rules. In addition, parents are taught to monitor their children's behavior in ways that permit immediate and consistent rewards and punishments. Most important, however, the parents learn not to respond to their children's unacceptable conduct with bickering, whining, or yelling. Instead, parents are urged to employ external rewards and punishments, such as giving or withdrawing privileges. Special emphasis is placed on rewarding children for desirable behavior, rather than on using punitive discipline (Patterson, 1982).

Conclusion

The data presented in this chapter make it clear that Ogden Nash's definition of the family fails to convey the myriad complexities of the families in which today's adolescents are being raised! Indeed, the interactions within any particular adolescent's family are too complex to categorize, either from the perspective of the curious onlooker or of the trained researcher. With the advent of video recorders and sensitive tape recorders, the methodology for observing family interactions outside contrived laboratory situations is becoming increasingly sophisticated. Indeed, researchers are now beginning to videotape families at the dinner table to reveal their patterns of bickering (Vuchinich, 1985). Undoubtedly such sophisticated technology will produce far more accurate information in the future about the aspects of family life that enhance or detract from an adolescent's development. Until more data are available, however, particularly data that are gathered as unobtrusively as possible within the adolescent's own home, a number of questions about the family's impact on children must remain unanswered.

Nevertheless, the research presently available permits us to make a number of assertions regarding adolescents and their families with confidence. First, today's adolescents are being raised in families that differ dramatically from families of the past in regard to income, mother's employment, divorce, and interracial and homosexual relationships. Thus, in relating to adolescents, we must expand our visions of the term "family" in order to encompass the changes of recent decades—changes that may not have affected our own upbringing but that are affecting the lives of most young Americans today.

Second, whatever generation gap exists has been grossly exaggerated and has, unfortunately, exacerbated parents' fears regarding their children's adolescence. In this regard, we might render parents a service by disseminating more of the empirical data that would allay many of their anxieties about their children's adolescent years. Moreover, we can provide parents and teachers with the specific skills that researchers have found effective in working with adolescents, many of which are examined in Chapter 15 of this text.

Third, the data acknowledge that the father's influence over his children's development during childhood and adolescence has been too often ignored and underestimated. Thus, in the future, practitioners, educators, and family members should focus more attention on ways of involving fathers in their children's lives. Given the disappointing results of the Swedish government's profatherhood policies, increasing U.S. fathers' involvement with their children present an intriguing challenge to our society.

Finally, the statistics on the physical and sexual abuse of children within their own families are ample testimony to the fact that many adults are ill-equipped to cope with the responsibilities of parenting. Although the etiology of these parents' abusive behavior remains unclear, thousands of adolescents and their younger siblings live in jeopardy of physical or sexual abuse. In response, educators, the courts, and social service agencies must continue to focus the public's attention on these two family problems, despite the shame and embarrassment that often accompany such publicity.

The remaining chapters of this text will underscore the family's influence over specific matters, such as adolescents' peer relationships, sexual behavior, drug use, delinquency, religious values, and vocational choices.

Questions for Discussion and Review

Basic Concepts and Terminology

1. In what ways are adolescents' families different from those of previous decades? Cite statistics to support your answers.
2. How can you defend or refute the assertion that "youngsters from divorced or single-parent families are cognitively and emotionally disadvantaged in comparison to children from families with two parents"?
3. How does a mother's employment appear to be related to an adolescent's development?
4. What special concerns might be encountered by adolescents whose parents are of different races?
5. How deep is the generation gap? Defend your answer with specific studies and statistics.
6. In what regards might adolescence and middle age be considered similar?
7. What methodological problems do researchers encounter in trying to understand adolescents' interactions with other family members and to determine the family's influence on a child's development?
8. How involved are most fathers in raising their children and how might their involvement be increased?
9. What types of interactions between fathers and sons seem to enhance a boy's cognitive, social, and sexual development?
10. How do fathers' interactions with their daughters generally compare with interactions with their sons?
11. How can a father's relationship with his daughter affect her relationships with other men and her cognitive development?
12. According to confluence theory, how does the family influence an adolescent's intellectual development and academic achievement?
13. How disadvantaged is the only child in a family?
14. What are the different theoretical perspectives offered as explanations for child abuse and incest?
15. In what ways can being a victim of child abuse or incest affect an adolescent?
16. What kinds of parental discipline and communication generally enhance an adolescent's self-esteem and cognitive growth?

Questions for Discussion and Debate

1. Recall several television programs, children's stories, nursery rhymes, popular songs, and movies about marriage, children, and happy families. What do you envision? How closely does your vision match the statistical facts presented in this chapter?
2. What benefits might accrue to adolescents being raised by their fathers rather than by their mothers? How has divorce affected your own life and the lives of your friends? In what ways have your views of divorce changed since you were a child? If you were a divorced parent, what family arrangements do you feel would be most beneficial for your adolescent son and daughter?
3. How do you feel about women working outside the home while their children are infants and preschoolers? How might their mothers' employment detract from adolescents' social or intellectual development? In what ways do you view women's employment as detracting from the quality of family life? How do you intend to reconcile your future family's financial needs with your child-rearing and vocational responsibilities?
4. How would your own adolescence have differed if your family's income had been below the poverty level? In what ways might impoverished adolescents be considered advantaged in comparison to the very wealthy?
5. How do you think you or your acquaintances have participated in "blaming the victim"?
6. What are your opinions of interracial marriage? In what ways do you think interracial families detract from and add to an adolescent's development?
7. Should adolescents be legally permitted to live in a family where one or both parents are gay? How would you have reacted as an adolescent to the knowledge that your parents were gay? How have your sentiments about interracial and homosexual couples being parents changed during the past decade?
8. What were the most serious conflicts between you and your parents during your adolescence? In what ways have your conflicts with your parents changed since adolescence? What methods were most and least effective for resolving the differences between you and your parents as a child and as an adolescent?
9. Why do you think so few fathers are willing to accept the responsiblities of caring for infants and interacting with their children? What programs would you design to encourage adolescent boys to adopt more positive attitudes toward child rearing? What duties do you feel are reasonable for a father to assume in a household where both parents are employed? How involved was your father in your upbringing before, during, and after your adolescence?
10. How has your father enhanced or detracted from your cognitive and social development? What differences have you observed in the way your father relates to male and female children and adolescents? What aspects of your relationship with your father would you have changed during your childhood and adolescence? How would your relationship with your father have differed if you had been the opposite sex from what you are? Whose relationship with his or her father do you most envy and why?
11. What is unique about your sibling relationships? How might your adolescence have differed if you had been an only child? How do you feel your

birth order and your family's size affected your cognitive development and personality? If you could change anything about your sibling relationships, what would it be? How would you account for the differences between you and your siblings?

12. From both the legal and the psychological perspectives, what do you think should be done for families in which child abuse or incest is occurring?
13. In terms of Baumrind's parenting styles, how would you categorize your own parents? How accurately does Baumrind's typology describe the parent-child interactions you have personally observed?
14. When you envision having a family in the future, in what ways would it be similar to and different from the family in which you were raised?
15. Which of your conceptions about U.S. families have the research and statistics in this chapter called into question?

REFERENCES

Allers, R. *Divorce, children and the school.* Princeton, N.J.: Princeton Books, 1982.

Anderson, L. Linkage between sexually abused children and suicidal adolescents. *Journal of Adolescence.* 1981, *2,* 157–163.

Appleton, W. *Fathers and daughters.* Garden City, N.Y.: Doubleday, 1981.

Armstrong, L. *Kiss daddy goodnight: A speak-out on incest.* New York: Hawthorn Books, 1978.

Bachman, J., Johnston, L., & O'Malley, P. *Monitoring the future: Questionnaire responses from the nation's high school seniors 1980.* Ann Arbor: Institute of Social Research, University of Michigan, 1981.

Bass, E., & Thornton, L. (eds.). *I never told anyone: Writings by women survivors of child sexual abuse.* New York: Harper & Row, 1983.

Baumrind, D. Parental disciplinary patterns and social competence in children. *Youth and Society,* 1978, *9,* 239–276.

Berndt, T. Developmental changes in conformity to peers and parents. *Developmental Psychology,* 1979, *15,* 608–616.

Biller, H. Father absence, divorce, and personality development. In M. Lamb (ed.), *The role of the father in child development.* New York: Wiley, 1981. Pp. 489–552. (a)

Biller, H. The father and sex role development. In M. Lamb (ed.), *The role of the father in child development.* New York: Wiley, 1981. Pp. 319–359. (b)

Bowles, S., & Gintis, H. *Schooling in capitalist America: Educational reform and contradictions of economic life.* New York: Basic Books, 1976.

Brackbill, Y., & Nichols, P. A test of the confluence model of intellectual development. *Developmental Psychology,* 1982, 18, 192–198.

Breland, H. Birth order, family configuration, and verbal achievement. In M. Smart & R. Smart (eds.). *Adolescents.* New York: Macmillan, 1978.

Brussell, E. (ed.). *Dictionary of quotable quotes.* Englewood Cliffs, N.J.: Prentice-Hall, 1970, p. 192.

Castellano, V., & Dembo, M. The relationship of father absence and antisocial behavior to social egocentrism in adolescent Mexican American females. *Journal of Youth and Adolescence,* 1981, *10,* 77–84.

Children of the rainbow. *Newsweek,* November 19, 1984, pp. 120–122.

Children's Defense Fund. *Children without homes.* Washington, D.C.: Children's Defense Fund, 1978.

Children's Defense Fund. *America's children and their families.* Washington, D.C.: Children's Defense Fund, 1979.

Children's Defense Fund. *Black and white children in America: Statistical facts.* Washington, D.C.: Children's Defense Fund, 1984.

Cicirelli, V. Family structure and interaction: Sibling effects on socialization. In M. McMillen & M. Segio (eds.), *Child psychiatry: Treatment and research.* New York: Brunner Mazel, 1977.

Circirelli. V. Sibling influence throughout the lifespan. In M. Lamb and B. Smith (eds.), *Sibling relationships.* Hillsdale, N.J.: Erlbaum, 1982.

Cleveland, E., & Longaker, W. Neurotic patterns in the family. In G. Handel (ed.), *The psychosocial interior of the family.* Chicago: Aldine, 1972. Pp. 159–185.

Collins, G. Everybody works in city program to fight child abuse. *Winston Salem Journal,* Winston Salem, N.C., April 13, 1985, p. 13.

Conger, J. Freedom and commitment: Families, youth and social change. *American Psychologist,* 1981, *36,* 1475–1484.

Daniels, D. & Plomin, R. Differential experience of siblings in the same family. *Developmental Psychology,* 1985, *21,* 747–760.

Dellas, M., Gaier, E., & Emihovich, C. Maternal employment and selected behaviors and attitudes of preadolescents and adolescents. *Adolescence,* 1979, *14,* 579–589.

Dornbusch, S., Carlsmith, M., Bushwall, S., Ritter, P., Leiderman, H., Hastorf, A., & Gross, R. Single parents, extended households and the control of adolescents. *Child Development,* 1985, *56,* 326–341.

Douvan, E., & Adelson, J. *The adolescent experience.* New York: Wiley, 1966.

Edelman, M. *Portrait of inequality: Black and white children in America.* Washington, D.C.: Children's Defense Fund, 1981.

Elder, G. *Family structure and socialization.* New York: Arno Press, 1980.

Elkind, D. *The hurried child: Growing up too fast too soon.* Reading, Mass.: Addison-Wesley, 1981.

Ericksen, J., Yancey, W., & Ericksen, E. The division of family roles. *Journal of Marriage and the Family,* 1979, *41,* 301–313.

Eversoll, D. A two generational view of fathering, *Family Coordinator,* 1979, *28,* 503–508.

Falbo, T. Only children in America. In M. Lamb and B. Smith (eds.), *Sibling relationships.* Hillsdale, N.J.: Erlbaum, 1982. Pp. 285–305.

Fayerweather Street School. *The kids' book of divorce: By, for, and about kids.* New York: Vintage Books, 1982.

Fayerweather Street School. *The kids' book about parents.* Boston: Houghton Mifflin, 1984.

Feather, N. Values in adolescence. In J. Adelson (ed.), *Handbook of adolescent psychology.* New York: Wiley, 1980. Pp. 247–295.

Ferber, M., & Huber, J. Husbands, wives and careers. *Journal of Marriage and the Family,* 1979, *41,* 315–325.

Fetters, W. *National longitudinal study of the high school class of 1972.* Washington, D.C.: U.S. Department of Health, Education and Welfare, 1977.

Fisher, K. Family violence cycle questioned. *American Psychological Associaton Monitor,* December 1984, p. 30.

Francke, L. Children of divorce. *Newsweek,* February 11, 1980, pp. 58–66.

Frank, D. (ed.), *Deep blue funk: Portraits of teenage parents.* Chicago: The Ounce of Prevention Fund, 1983, pp. 150–154.

Furstenberg, R. Recycling the family: Perspectives for a new family form. *Marriage and Family Review,* 1980, *2,* 1–22.

Galbo, J. Adolescents' perceptions of significant adults: A review of the literature. *Adolescence.* 1984, *16,* 951–970.

Gallatin, J. Political thinking in adolescence. In J. Adelson (ed.), *Handbook of adolescent psychology.* New York: Wiley, 1980. Pp. 344–382.

Gantz, J. *Whose child cries: Children of gay parents talk about their lives.* Rolling Hills Estates, Cal.: Jalmar Press, 1983.

Ginsberg, H. *The myth of the deprived child.* Englewood Cliffs, N.J.: Prentice-Hall, 1972.

Glenbard East "Echo". *Teenagers themselves.* New York: Adama, 1984.

Glenn, N., & Kramer, K. The psychological well-being of adult children of divorce. *Journal of Marriage and the Family,* 1985, *47,* 905–913.

Glick, P., & Norton, A. Marrying, divorcing and living together in the U.S. today. *Population Bulletin,* 1979, *32,* 1–40.

Glueck, S., & Glueck, E. Working mothers and delinquency. *Mental Hygiene,* 1957, *41,* 327–352.

Gold, D., & Andres, D. Comparison of adolescent children with employed and nonemployed mothers. *Merrill-Palmer Quarterly,* 1978, *24,* 242–254.

Goldstein, M. Familial precursors of schizophrenia spectrum disorders. In L. Wynne, R. Cromwell, and S. Matthysse (eds.), *The nature of schizophrenia.* New York: Wiley, 1978. Pp. 180–192.

Gove, W., & Peterson, C. An update of the literature on personal and marital satisfaction. *Marriage and Family Review,* 1980, *3,* 63–96.

Grossman, A. *Children of working mothers.* Washington, D.C.: Bureau of Labor Statistics, Bulletin 2158. March 1983.

Halpern, H. *Cutting loose: An adult guide to coming to terms with your parents.* New York: Bantam Books, 1981.

Hamid, P., & Wyllie, A. What generation gap? *Adolescence,* 1980, *15,* 385–391.

Hartup, W. The peer system. In E. Hetherington (ed.), *Socialization, personality and social development: Handbook of child psychology.* New York: Wiley, 1983.

Helfer, R., & Kempe, C. (eds.). *Child abuse and neglect: The family and the community.* Cambridge, Mass.: Ballinger, 1982.

Hetherington, E. Effects of father absence on personality development in adolescent daughters. *Developmental Psychology,* 1972, *7,* 313–326.

Hetherington, E. Divorce: A child's perspective. *American Psychologist,* 1979, *34,* 851–855.

Hetherington, E., Cox, M., & Cox, R. Effects of divorce on parents and children. In M. Lamb (ed.), *Nontraditional families.* Hillsdale, N.J.: Erlbaum, 1982.

Hill, J., Hommbeck, G., Marlow, L., Green, T., & Lynch, M. Pubertal status and parent-child relations in families of seventh-grade boys. *Journal of Early Adolescence,* 1985, *5,* 31–44.

Hjorth, C. The self-image of the physically abused adolescent. *Journal of Youth and Adolescence.* 1982, *11,* 71–76.

Hoffman, L. Maternal employment: 1979. *American Psychologist,* 1979, *34,* 859–865.

Hoffman, L., & Nye, F. *Working mothers.* San Francisco: Jossey-Bass, 1974.

Hoffman, M. Moral development. In P. Mussen (ed.), *Carmichael's manual of child psychology.* New York: Wiley, 1970.

Hunter, F. Adolescents' percepton of discussions with parents and friends. *Developmental Psychology,* 1985, *21,* 433–440.

Jones, D. Family influences on cognitive development and school achievement. In E. Gordon (ed.), *Review of research education.* Washington, D.C.: American Educational Research Association, 1984. Pp. 259–304.

Kagan, J., & Moss, H. *Birth to maturity: The Fels study of psychological development.* New York: Wiley, 1962.

Kandel, D., & Lesser, G. *Youth in two worlds.* San Francisco: Jossey-Bass, 1972.

Kellam, S., Engsminger, M., & Turner, R. Family structure and the mental health of children. *Archives of General Psychiatry,* 1977, *34,* 1012–1022.

Kratcoski, P. Child abuse and violence against the family. *Child Welfare.* 1982, *61,* 435–444.

Kreiger, M., & Robbins, J. The adolescent incest victim and the judicial system. *American Journal of Orthopsychiatry,* 1985, *55,* 419–425.

Kulka, R., & Weingarten, H. The long-term effects of parental divorce in childhood on adult adjustment. *Journal of Social Issues,* 1979, *33,* 50–78.

Lamb, M. Fatherhood and social policy in international perspective. In M. Lamb and A. Sagi (eds.), *Fatherhood and family policy.* Hillsdale, N.J.: Erlbaum, 1983. Pp. 1–13.

Lamb, M., & Levine, J. The Swedish parental insurance policy: An experiment in social engineering. In M. Lamb and A. Sagi (eds.), *Fatherhood and family policy.* Hillsdale, N.J.: Erlbaum, 1983. Pp. 39–48.

Lerner, R., Sorrell, A., & Brackney, B. Sex differences in self-concept and self-esteem in late adolescents: A time lag analysis. *Sex Roles,* 1981, *7,* 1237–1247.

Levine, J., & Pleck, J. The fatherhood project. In M. Lamb and A. Sagi (eds.), *Fatherhood and family policy.* Hillsdale, N.J.: Erlbaum, 1983. Pp. 101–113.

Lynn, D. *Daughters and parents: Past, present, and future.* Monterey, Cal.: Brooks-Cole, 1979.

Maccoby, E., & Martin, J. Socialization in the context of the family: Parent-child interaction. In P. Mussen (ed.), *Handbook of child psychology.* New York: Wiley, 1983. Pp. 37–101.

Marcia, J. Identity in adolescence. In J. Adelson (ed.), *Handbook of adolescent psychology.* New York: Wiley, 1980. Pp. 159–187.

McAdoo, H. Involvement of fathers in the socialization of black children. In H. McAdoo (ed.), *Black families.* Beverly Hills, Cal.: Sage, 1981. Pp. 225-237.

McDonald, G. Parental power and adolescents' parental identification: A reexamination. *Journal of Marriage and the Family,* 1980, *42,* 289–296.

Melican, G., & Feldt, L. An empirical study of the Zajonc-Markus hypothesis for achievement test score declines. *American Educational Research Journal,* 1980, 17, 5–19.

Montemayor, R. The relationship between parent-adolescent conflict and the amount of time adolescents spend alone and with parents and peers. *Child Development,* 1982, *53,* 1511–1519.

Montemayor, R. Parents and adolescents in conflict: All families some of the time and some families most of the time. *Journal of Early Adolescence,* 1983, *3,* 83–103.

Montemayor, R. and Hanson, E. A naturalistic view of conflict between adolescents and their parents and siblings. *Journal of Early Adolescence,* 1985, *5,* 23–30.

Montemayor, R., & VanKomen, R. Age segregation of adolescents in and out of school. *Journal of Youth and Adolescence,* 1980, *9,* 371–381.

Mrazek, P. The nature of incest: A review of contributing factors. In P. Mrazek and H. Kempe (eds.), *Sexually abused children and their families.* New York: Pergamon Press, 1981. Pp. 97–108.

Mrazek, P., & Mrazek, D. The effects of child sexual abuse: Methodological considerations. In P. Mrazek and H. Kempe (eds.), *Sexually abused children and their families.* New York: Pergamon Press, 1981. Pp. 235–247.

Murguia, E. *Chicano intermarriage: A theoretical and empirical study.* San Antonio, Tex.: Trinity University Press, 1982.

Nasjleti, M. Suffering in silence: The male incest victim. *Child Welfare,* 1980, *59,* 269–276.

National Black Child Development Institute. The status of black children in 1980. Washington, D.C.: Black Child Development Institute, 1981.

Norman, J., & Harris, M. *The private life of an American teenager.* New York: Rawson Wade, 1981.

Nock, S. Enduring effects of marital disruption and subsequent living arrangements. *Journal of Family Issues,* 1982, *42,* 25–40.

Offer, D., & Offer, J. *From teenage to young manhood.* New York: Basic Books, 1975.

Offer, D., Maroh, R., & Ostrov, E. *The psychological world of the juvenile delinquent.* New York: Basic Books, 1979.

Offer, D., Ostrov, E., & Howard, K. *The adolescent: A psychological self-portrait.* New York: Basic Books, 1981.

Olweus, D. Familial and tempermental determinants of aggression behavior in adolescents: A causal analysis. *Developmental Psychology,* 1980, *16,* 644–660.

Paddock, K., & Thomas, S. Attitudes of young adolescents toward marriage, divorce and children of divorce. *Journal of Early Adolescence,* 1981, *3,* 303–310.

Patterson, G. *Coercive family process.* Eugene, Or.: Castalia Press, 1982.

Playing both mother and father. *Newsweek,* July 15, 1985, pp. 42–50.

Pleck, J. *The myth of masculinity.* Cambridge, Mass.: MIT Press, 1981.

Pogrebin, L. *Family politics: Love and power on an intimate frontier.* New York: McGraw-Hill, 1983.

Polikoff, N. Gender and child custody determinations: Exploding the myths. In I. Diamond (ed.), *Families, politics and public policy.* New York: Longman, 1983.

Radin, N. The role of the father in cognitive, academic and intellectual development. In M. Lamb (ed)., *The role of the father in child development.* New York: Wiley, 1981. Pp. 379–428.

Ramirez, M. Identification with Mexican American values and psychological adjustment in Mexican American adolescents. *International Journal of Social Psychiatry,* 1969, *15,* 151–156.

Rappaport, R., & Rappaport, J. *Dual career families reexamined.* New York: Harper & Row, 1977.

Rittenberg, W. Parens patriae—The state as parent: A case of child abuse and neglect. In M. Sugar (ed.), *Responding to adolescent needs.* Jamaica, N.Y.: Spectrum Publications, 1980. Pp. 35–49.

Rubin, Z., & Sloman, J. How parents influence their children's friendships. In M. Lewis (ed.), *Beyond the dyad.* New York: Plenum, 1984. Pp. 115–140.

Rush, F. *The best kept secret: Sexual abuse of children.* Englewood Cliffs, N.J.: Prentice-Hall, 1980.

Russell, G., & Radin, J. Increased paternal participation. In M. Lamb and A. Sagi (eds.), *Fatherhood and family policy.* Hillsdale, N.J.: Erlbaum, 1983. Pp. 139–166.

Rutter, M. *Changing youth in a changing society: Patterns of adolescent development and disorder.* Cambridge, Mass.: Harvard University Press, 1980.

Rutter, M. *Maternal deprivation reassessed.* New York: Penguin Books, 1981.

Rutter, M., & Giller, H. *Juvenile delinquency: Trends and perspectives.* Baltimore: Penguin Books, 1983.

Ryan, W. *Blaming the victim.* New York: Random House, 1976.

Salk, L. *My father, my son.* New York: Putnam, 1982.

Santrock, J., & Tracy, R. The effects of children's family structure status on the development of stereotypes by teachers. *Journal of Educational Psychology,* 1978, *70,* 754–757.

Santrock, J., & Warshak, R. Father custody and social development in boys and girls. *Journal of Social Issues,* 1979, *35,* 112–115.

Scarr, S. *Mother care/other care.* New York: Basic Books, 1983.

Scarr S., & Grajek, S. Similarities and differences among siblings. In M. Lamb and B. Smith (eds.), *Sibling relationships.* Hillsdale, N.J.: Erlbaum, 1982. Pp. 357–383.

Sebald, H., & White, B. Teenagers' divided reference groups: Uneven alignment with parents and peers. *Adolescence,* 1980, *15,* 979–984.

Slovenko, R. Criminal laws setting boundaries on sexual exploitation. In M. Sugar (ed.), *Responding to adolescent needs.* Jamaica, N.Y.: Spectrum Publications, 1980. Pp. 181–198.

Smith, B. Birth order and sibling status effects. In M. Lamb and B. Smith (eds.), *Sibling relationships.* Hillsdale, N.J.: Erlbaum, 1982. Pp. 153–166.

Smith, R. (ed.). *The subtle revolution: Women at work.* Washington, D.C.: The Urban Institute, 1979.

Smith, T. Adolescent agreement with perceived maternal and paternal educational goals. *Journal of Marriage and the Family,* 1981, *43,* 85–93.

Snyder, N., Lopez, C., & Padilla, A. Ethnic identity and cultural awareness among the offspring of Mexican interethnic marriages. *Journal of early adolescence,* 1982, *2,* 277–282.

Speizer, J. The teenage years. In Boston Women's Health Collective, *Ourselves and our children.* New York: Random House, 1978. Pp. 87–109.

Staples, R. *Introduciton to black sociology.* New York: McGraw-Hill, 1975.

Steele, B., & Alexander, H. Long-term effects of sexual abuse in childhood. In P. Mrazek and H. Kempe (eds.), *Sexually abused children and their families.* New York: Pergamon Press, 1981. Pp. 223–235.

Steinberg, L. Transformations on family relations at puberty. *Developmental Psychology,* 1981, *17,* 833–840.

U.S. Bureau of the Census, *Geographic mobility: March 1975 to March 1979.* Washington, D.C.: U.S. Government Printing Office, Current Population Reports, P-20, No. 353, 1980.

U.S. Bureau of the Census. *Money income and poverty status of families and persons in the United States: 1980.* Washington, D.C.: U.S. Government Printing Office, 1981.

U.S. Bureau of the Census. *Characteristics of American Children and Youth: 1980.* Washington, D.C.: U.S. Government Printing Office, Current population reports, P-23, No. 114, 1982.

U.S. children and their families: Current conditions and recent trends. Washington, D.C.: Select Committee on Children, Youth and Families, 1983.

Vuchinich, S. Arguments, family style. *Psychology Today,* 1985, *19,* 40–46.

Wallerstein, J., & Kelly, J. *Surviving the break-up: How children and parents cope with divorce.* New York: Basic Books, 1980.

Weiner, I. *Psychological disturbance in adolescence.* New York: Wiley, 1970.

West, K. Assessment and treatment of disturbed adolescents and their families. In M. Lansky (ed.), *Major psychopathology and the family.* New York: Grune and Stratton, 1981. Pp. 26–59.

Will, D. Approaching the incestuous and sexually abusive family. *Journal of Adolescence.* 1983, *6,* 229–246.

Wynne, L., & Frader, L. Female adolescence and the family: A historical view. In M. Sugar (ed.), *Female adolescent development.* New York: Brunner Mazel, 1979. Pp. 63–82.

Yablonsky, L. *Fathers and sons.* New York: Simon & Schuster, 1982.

Yankelovich, D. *Generations apart.* New York: Columbia Broadcasting System, 1969.

Yankelovich, D. *The new morality: A profile of American youth in the 70's.* New York: McGraw-Hill, 1974.

Yankelovich, D. *New rules: Searching for self-fulfillment in a world turned upside down.* New York: Random House, 1981.

Youniss, J., & Smollar, J. *Adolescent relations with mothers, fathers and friends.* Chicago: University of Chicago Press, 1985.

York, P., York, D., & Wachtel, T. *Tough love.* Garden City, N.Y.: Doubleday, 1982.

Zajonc, R. Validating the confluence model. *Psychological Bulletin,* 1983, *93,* 457–480.

Zajonc, R. The decline and rise of scholastic aptitude scores. *American Psychologist,* August 1986, *41,* 862–867.

Zajonc, R. & Markus, G. Birth order and intellectual development. *Psychological Review,* 1975, *82,* 74–78.

Zuckerman, D. Too many sibs put our nation at risk? *Psychology Today,* January 1985, p. 5.

Chapter Outline

Limitations of the Research
The Parent-Peer Conflict?
Factors Affecting Peer Conformity
Domains of Influence
Quality of the Parent-Child Relationship
Parents' Status
Adolescent's Age
Self-Esteem and Identity Status
Adolescent's Gender
Factors Affecting Choice of Friends
Factors Affecting Popularity
Personality
Scholar or Athlete?
Physical Attractiveness
Changes in Friendship during Adolescence
Definitions of Friendship
Intimacy and Trust
Empathy and Reciprocity
Opposite-Sex Friendships
Differences in Male and Female Friendships
Interracial Friendships
The Impact of School Desegregation
The Bases for Interracial Friendships
Enhancing Interracial Friendships
Loneliness and Shyness
Characteristics of Adolescent Loneliness
Shyness during Adolescence
Overcoming Loneliness and Shyness
Adolescent Dating
Who, What, When, and Where?
Dating Expectations
Interracial Dating
Conclusion

Goals and Objectives

This chapter is designed to enable you to:

- *Discuss the limitations of the research on adolescents' peer relationships*
- *Explain the factors influencing an adolescent's popularity*
- *Explore the relative influence of parents and peers during adolescence*
- *Delineate the differences between childhood and adolescent friendships*
- *Examine the distinctions between male and female friendships*
- *Consider the ways in which schools influence adolescents' friendships*
- *Explore ways of encouraging interracial friendships*
- *Examine ways of helping adolescents overcome shyness and loneliness*

Basic Concepts and Terminology

identity statuses
revisionist view
assertiveness training
behavior rehearsals
Teams Games Tournament
jigsaw teaching
peer counseling
systematic desensitization

9 Adolescents and Their Peers

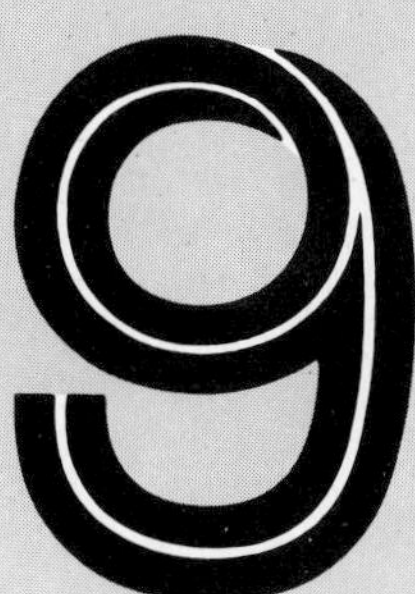

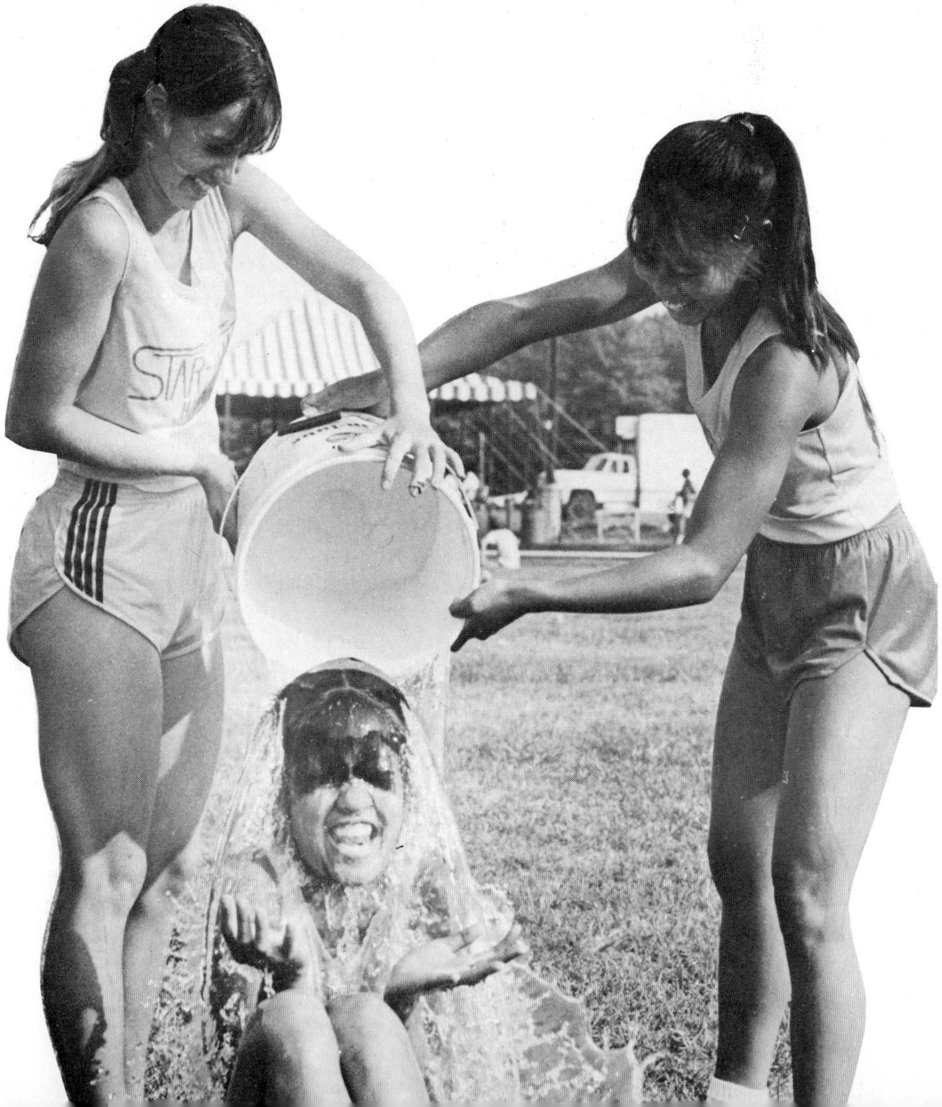

Perhaps no aspect of adolescence, other than sexuality, provokes as much anxiety and commands as much attention among adults as the peer group. While parents worry about the possible impact that peers might have on their adolescent child's behavior and attitudes, researchers are exploring a multitude of questions involving adolescents' peer interactions: In comparison to parents, how much influence do peers exert over an adolescent's behavior? On what bases do adolescents choose their close friends, acquaintances, and dates? How do friendships and peer interactions change from childhood through adolescence? How do males' and females' friendships differ? Such questions are the bases for much of the research that will be presented in this chapter.

Although parents continue to exert their influence over adolescents' attitudes and behavior, the importance of peers is unrivaled in terms of helping young people hone their social skills and experience the myriad dimensions of friendship. Even the most nurturant and empathetic parents cannot provide the type of interactions that eventually enhance adolescents' self-confidence with their peers. Moreover, it is through experiences with peers that adolescents have opportunities to cultivate the intimacy, reciprocity, and trust that distinguish mature friendships from the peer interactions of childhood years. The self-disclosure and trust that characterize adolescents' deepening friendships are indeed distinct from the types of sharing and intimacy appropriate with one's own parents.

Finally, interacting with peers permits adolescents to fashion and refashion their own values and identities. Through observing others' behavior, through discussing discrepant ideologies, and through good-hearted and not so good-hearted teasing, adolescents examine their own behavior and attitudes—casting aside certain dimensions of "self" and reaffirming others. In the process, the young learn the relative gains and losses of conforming to the wishes of others, rather than manifesting one's individuality. Furthermore, peers introduce one another to a number of painful social realities: that popularity is generally associated with physical beauty and athletic prowess, or that interracial friendships are often frowned upon by the "in-crowd." Such lessons, both poignant and painful, cannot be conveyed nearly as effectively by one's parents as by one's peers.

In sum, although adolescents' parents often express their anxieties about their children's friends, peer interactions are a prerequisite for normal adult development. Indeed, older people may need to be reminded that without peer experiences adolescents in many regards would remain, to everyone's great misfortune, forever children.

LIMITATIONS OF THE RESEARCH

Before examining the data on adolescent friendships and peer influence, it's important to note the methodological flaws that several prominent scholars have identified in the existing adolescent research. Hallinan underscores a number of these in his analysis of the literature on peer influence (Hallinan, 1983). To begin with, most studies attribute the similar behavior of adolescents and their friends to peer influence. Most adolescents (and adults), however, choose only people who are already similar to themselves to be their friends. Consequently the research tends to overestimate the significance of peer influence by ignoring or underestimating the initial degree of similarity that was present between friends. Second, many studies fail to distinguish among an adolescents' close friends, their acquaintances, and strangers who happen to be of the same age attending the same school. Nevertheless, the degree to which one individual may influence another may be a function of the level of intimacy they share. In this context, a close friend's influence may be much stronger than that of a stranger who happens to attend the same school.

Researchers have been inconsistent in their definitions of peers, thereby confounding the distinctions which may exist between the influence of close friends and other peers. Most research has suggested that friends and the larger reference group in a school or in society exert equal influence over an adolescent's attitudes and behavior. Such a position, however, seems untenable, since the term "peer" lacks a precise operational definition. A more specific operational definition would help us distinguish between the influence of adolescents' close friends and their more distant acquaintances.

Furthermore, many studies have failed to distinguish among the types and degrees of peer influence that may be exerted in academic, vocational, or social spheres. Traditionally, it has been assumed that if peers are influencing each other in one domain such as drug use, they must also be influencing each other in other domains such as academic aspirations. Yet recent research suggests that the degree of peer influence differs according to the type of issue involved. Historically, many researchers presumed that adolescents belong to a single peer group that influences their behavior. Studies challenging this assumption, however, demonstrate that young people can belong to several distinct peer groups simultaneously and that each may endorse different values. In addition, researchers have often failed to consider the importance of parents' and teachers' values in their scholarly assessments of the power of peer influence. It is quite possible that adults' opinions mitigate peer influence. Given the multiple sources of influence operating upon an adolescent, complex interactive effects are highly likely. Taken together, these methodological shortcomings leave a number of crucial questions unattended: How do close friends protect one another from the influence of more distant peers? Why are some adolescents better able to resist peer pressure than others? How do students react to contradictory expectations from different peer groups?

Cohen's commentary on the research provides several specific examples of the shortcomings addressed by Hallinan (1983). For example, further analyses of Coleman's renowned study on peer influence in the 1960s revealed that although high-school students valued athletes and scholars, they made few efforts to emulate them. In other words, those in the leading crowd were exerting no real influence over other students' behavior, even though they had been identified as the most popular people in the school. Recent research is also suggesting that behavior once attributed to the broad category of peer influence is often attributable only to an adolescent's closest friends (Cohen, 1983). Cohen also documents the importance of the fact that certain behaviors tend to cluster together. For instance, drinking, smoking, being a poor student, and dating a lot tend to be correlated. Consequently, when adolescents choose a friend on the basis of one such trait, they will usually be selecting someone who resembles them in many ways. This phenomenon may then create the false illusion that friends are exerting peer influence over one another, when in fact their similarities existed from the outset.

Analyses like Cohen's demand that we reconsider many traditional assumptions about peer relationships. For example, some research shows that peers are most likely to conform in regard to issues of the least importance to them (Cohen, 1983). In other words, friends are least willing to conform to each other's demands on matters of greatest importance. Moreover, Cohen found that new friends have as much influence as old friends on youngsters' educational aspirations. Furthermore, the research has not consistently demonstrated that the stronger the bond between friends, the more influence they exert on one another. In sum, Cohen suggests—as others have—that we reexamine many of our assumptions about adolescents' friendships and peer influence.

Further methodological problems that need to be addressed are identified by Coates (1984) in her analysis of the research on early adolescence. Coates critiqued 26 studies conducted between 1976 and 1983 on peer influence during early adolescence. Virtually all the studies were limited to white, middle-class youngsters and only 20 percent used random samples. While four of the studies were conducted on adolescents from other countries, none explored peer relations for U.S. minorities. While most of the studies did examine sex differences in peer relations, the youngsters' family status was generally ignored. Consequently, we are unable to distinguish between the degree of peer influence over young people from intact homes and over those whose parents have recently divorced. Such confounding is particularly unfortunate, since the period following parents divorce may be one during which children are particularly susceptible to peer influence or during which friends may temporarily assume special importance.

Coates points out that most of the studies merely asked adolescents for their own perceptions of their peer relationships, rather than actually observing adolescent behavior when interacting with their peers. About 75 percent of the stud-

SOURCE: Glenbard East *Echo, Teenagers themselves.* New York: Adama, 1984.

ies used only self-report measures, which introduce a potential source of psychometric bias. The possibility of such bias inevitably undermines the reliability and validity of the data, as does the fact that the studies seldom retested youngsters' responses to determine whether their opinions remained stable over any length of time. Especially during the period of early adolescence, when definitions of friendships are undergoing rapid change and when students are being moved from elementary to secondary schools, measures of test-retest reliability are particularly relevant. Establishing the correlations between adolescents' self-reports and their actual behavior would be of definite benefit in future research (Coates, 1984).

The Parent-Peer Conflict?

As discussed in Chapter 8, there is little doubt that a dramatic shift occurs between childhood and adolescence in terms of the amount of time a child spends with his or her peers. This point is underscored by a study that electronically monitored 25 adolescents to determine how they invested their time with peers and adults during a typical week. Beepers were used to remind students several times a day to record their activities and feelings. Nearly 40 percent of their time was spent talking to other people, and most of their conversations with adults were with their parents (61 percent), which itself is an interesting commentary, considering the number of hours adolescents spend in the presence of teachers during a week. Adolescents felt most relaxed when interacting with peers, although they felt their interactions with adults were the most exciting (Csikszentmihalyi, Larson, & Prescott, 1977).

Since adolescents spend much of their time with friends, and since the peer group provides a refuge where adolescents can experiment with different ideologies and behavior, there's a natural inclination for parents to worry about losing their influence. Yet, as the research cited in Chapter 8 demonstrated, adolescents' political, religious, educational, and vocational values generally reflect their parents' views. In the vast majority of families there is no generation gap that isolates adolescents from their parents or pits them and their peers against the older generation. After his expert review of the research, Coleman (1980, p. 425) concludes that "it has commonly been assumed that an inevitable consequence of increased involvement with the peer group is a rejection of parental values. Clearly, however, this is not an either/or phenomenon."

Several studies can be cited to demonstrate that adolescents' spending more time with their peers does not undermine their parents' influential positions. A study of white, middle-class tenth-graders showed that these 64 youngsters spent equal time with parents and peers. Surprisingly, even those who had disagreeable relationships with their mothers invested time with their fathers, instead of turning away from both parents to their peers (Montemayor, 1982). Similarly, a study of 213 high-school juniors and seniors showed that most adolescents seek counsel from their parents even when they perceive the relationship as generally unsatisfactory. Peers did not assume increasing influence as

these adolscents aged (Greenberg, Siegel, & Leitch, 1983). The 2,800 adolescents surveyed in still another study almost always listed parents among the most significant, influential people in their lives. In fact, over 40 percent of those named as "significant others" were adults (Blyth, Hill, & Thiel, 1982).

One of the most impressive demonstrations of the significance that adults maintain in adolescents' lives is Galbo's recent review of the literature (Galbo, 1984). The studies included rural and urban youth, minorities, delinquents, younger and older adolescents, and both low- and high-income families. Despite their differences, most adolescents named a parent or the relative who had raised them as the most significant adult in their lives. Emotional support from an adult, particularly from a parent, was significantly related to adolescents' feelings of self-esteem and well-being. Adult relatives or neighbors were more significant to young people than their teachers, ministers, or recreation leaders. Most adolescents named from six to nine adults among the most influential people in their lives. Influential adults were almost always the same sex as the adolescent and were almost always older than 24. Although adolescents appreciated qualities like honesty, accessibility, and empathy in their favorite adults, no characteristics that distinguished the influential adults from others were consistently identified.

Although already detailed in Chapter 8, Montemayor's conclusions, based on the research from 1929 through 1982, bear repeating: While parents tend to

SOURCE: Glenbard East *Echo, Teenagers themselves.* New York: Adama, 1985.

have more conflicts with young adolescents than with older ones, these disagreements typically involve the same issues that have plagued families since the 1920s—curfews, doing homework, sibling quarrels, personal hygiene, and household chores. Montemayor also reminds us that conflict is part of almost all human relationships and that most parent-adolescent arguments reflect parents' efforts to teach their children to delay gratification and to conform to rules. Montemayor concludes that serious conflicts between parents and adolescents occur in only 15 or 20 percent of all U.S. families (Montemayor, 1982).

Undoubtedly some young people perceive adolescence as "that period in life when a boy refuses to believe that someday he'll be as stupid as his parents" or "that period when the young feel their parents should be told the facts of life." Such feelings notwithstanding, the research repeatedly demonstrates that most adolescents and their parents share similar values and interact quite harmoniously (refer to Chapter 8 for specific studies).

FACTORS AFFECTING PEER CONFORMITY

Why are so many parents apprehensive about losing their influence when their children become adolescents? Are parents' anxieties totally unfounded? The answer to these questions is both yes and no. Yes, many parents are unduly worried about the adolescent peer group in terms of its potential to sever relationships between the young and old and its power to overrule adults' influence. Parents do have legitimate reasons, however, to worry about peer influence over specific kinds of adolescent behavior and during particular periods of adolescence. We currently know that a number of factors affect an adolescent's susceptibility to peer pressure. Examining each of these factors and considering the interactions among them can assist practitioners and parents in evaluating the magnitude and the limitation of peer power.

Domains of Influence

One factor determining how much influence parents will have vis-à-vis their children's peers is the type of decision confronting the adolescent. Parents' views generally outweigh peers' in regard to educational goals, vocational aspirations, religious views, use of hard drugs, and political or moral issues. On social issues, however, the situation is reversed. Thus, with regard to such interpersonal issues as engaging in premarital sex, using marijuana, tobacco, or alcohol, clothing, hairstyles, and musical taste, adolescents generally rely on their peers' opinions. Nevertheless, young people tend to continue to seek their parents' counsel on matters involving school, careers, money, politics, or religion (Coleman, 1980; Marcia, 1980).

Differential parental and peer influence is underscored in a number of recent studies. Junior- and senior-high-school students have been found to rely more on their peers for advice on social matters as they age, while continuing to depend on adults' counsel on moral issues (Young & Ferguson, 1979). Moreover, a comparison of 100 white, middle-class adolescents in 1960 and 1976 showed similar divisions between the domains influenced by parents and peers. More of

How have your tastes in music, clothing, decor, and personal appearance changed since your adolescence?

the youngsters in 1976, however, relied on their friends' advice than did adolescents in 1960, suggesting a possible decline in parents' influence. Of note, perhaps, is the self-reported data that 17 percent of the young people in the 1976 survey said they would rely neither on parents' or peers' advice, but on their own opinions (Sebald & White, 1980).

Quality of the Parent-Child Relationship

A parent's influence relative to the peer group also depends on the quality of the parent-child relationship. As evidenced by Baumrind's (1978) research described in the previous chapter, parents who employ authoritarian or permissive styles usually exert less influence over their children than those who exhibit either a democratic or an authoritative style. This is the case, it appears, because adolescents whose parents are overly strict and authoritarian are likely to rebel by conforming to peer values that defy their parents' views. Children are more likely to be influenced by democratic parents who explain the reasons underlying their rules and who respect their children's ideas by encouraging honest, reciprocal communication, than they are by autocratic parents who discourage discussion, dictate without providing their rationale, and espouse the principle that adults "always know best."

In sum, the quality of the relationship between adolescents and their parents often determines whether teenaged children will continue to seek the counsel of their parents and conform to the family values. There is some truth to the notion that adolescents may turn to peers for advice with greater frequency when communications with their own parents have been blocked or temporarily disrupted.

Parents' Status

Parents' influence also seems to be partially dependent upon how much esteem they have established in the eyes of their children. As children age, this esteem may often be based on such standards as financial success or educational accomplishments. In a study of 9,000 students in grades 7 through 12, adolescents expressed more trust in their parents' advice than in their friends' counsel. The value placed on their parents' opinions, however, varied according to the parents' income, particularly in the case of the fathers's influence. Adolescents from lower-income homes often perceived their parents as being less competent and having fewer resources than those from middle-class families. The middle-class adolescents tended to value their parents' opinions more highly than their classmates from lower-income families (Crain & Weisman, 1972).

As you may also remember from the last chapter, employed mothers are generally held in higher esteem by their adolescent children than mothers who are full-time housewives. Studies such as these suggest that a parent's influence over an adolescent child may be partially contingent upon the respect he or she commands outside the family in terms of professional status and income.

Adolescent's Age

An adolescent's willingness to reject parents' values by conforming to peer pressure is also partially contingent upon the youngster's age. According to the literature, younger adolescents are more likely to acquiesce to peer pressure than older adolescents (Coleman, 1980). For example, Berndt (1979a, 1979b) asked more than 500 third- through twelfth-graders how they would react in hypothetical situations involving conformity to peers or adherence to parental values. Sixth-graders were the most likely to conform to peer expectations in socially acceptable situations like helping a classmate with an academic project. Ninth-graders were the most willing to conform to peers in a neutral situation, such as agreeing to participate in activities that really didn't interest them. Ninth-graders were also the most willing to acquiesce to peer pressure in situations involving delinquent forms of behavior. Such willingness to conform to peer pressure and engage in delinquent acts peaked, however, at the ninth grade and declined steadily thereafter. By the eleventh and twelfth grades, adolescents were frequently making decisions that relied on neither parents' nor peers' opinions.

Some adults fear that younger adolescents are particularly vulnerable to pressure from older teenagers to engage in socially undesirable behavior. Many parents worry that contact with older adolescents may inadvertently encourage younger children to become sexually active or to experiment with alcohol, tobacco, or marijuana. In this regard, a recent study of almost 3,000 seventh- through ninth-grade students in a white suburban school district provides data that underscore the possibility of older adolescents inappropriately influencing younger adolescents. The influence of older students was strongest for ninth-graders educated in schools with tenth-graders, in contrast to being kept in schools with seventh-grade students. Specifically, the presence of the tenth-graders seemed to increase the ninth-graders' use of drugs. Similarly, more eighth-grade males tended to use marijuana and tobacco when ninth-graders were present in their school. Going to school with older students also seemed to make younger students more sophisticated in regard to dating and sexual behavior (Blyth, Hill, & Thiel, 1982).

Although studies like Blyth's do not substantiate the claim that older adolescents will negatively influence their younger peers, they help create a rationale for investigating the advantages and disadvantages of age segregation. A number of questions worthy of further investigation become apparent: At what age should young adolescents be placed in school with older peers? What academic or social advantages might accrue to younger students educated in the same schools as older adolescents? How might older adolescents serve as positive models for their younger friends?

While these questions remain unanswered, the research nonetheless demonstrates that older adolescents are generally less susceptible to peer pressure than young adolescents. Why? From a Piagetian perspective, the stage of formal thought is more likely to have developed in older adolescents than in younger cohorts (Piaget & Inhelder, 1969). Hence, older adolescents are more capable cognitively of making their own decisions without needing approval or input from their peers. In this regard, it might be speculated that conforming to the peer group loses much of its appeal as the adolescent develops more advanced cognitive capacities. In addition, the psychoanalytic view proposes that as the adolescent's ego becomes increasingly individuated from the identities of other people, he or she is more willing to make independent decisions. Since individuation supposedly advances with age, older adolescents are in a better position to reject demands for peer conformity on which younger adolescents tend to rely (Josselson, 1980).

Self-Esteem and Identity Status

According to most studies, people with higher self-esteem and social status are less susceptible to peer pressure than those with low self-esteem and low status (Coleman, 1980). Since older adolescents have usually acquired more status and esteem than younger ones in terms of their ability to earn money, drive a car, compete in varsity athletics, and master social skills with the opposite sex, they would tend to feel less need to conform to peers' expectations.

Along similar lines, an individual's susceptibility to peer influence depends on how much he or she needs information from another person (Hallinan, 1983). How much we need particular information from someone else depends on the newness of a situation, the immediacy of the decision, and the visibility of the act in question. Thus, for example, a new student in school, who is unfamiliar with the prevailing social standards, is likely to be easily influenced by a popular girl who can offer her information about how to dress for Friday night's dance—especially if the newcomer is already halfway through the doorway to the dance hall and must quickly decide whether or not to remove the earrings that were considered so "cool" by classmates in her former school. On the other hand, even though a newcomer in school, she will be less susceptible to her girlfriend's influence on the matter of whether or not to start eating tofu for breakfast—a decision that need not be made quickly, nor that is visible to her new classmates. In this regard, older adolescents are less likely than younger ones to be susceptible to peer influence, because they are generally more knowledgeable about issues that might publicly embarrass them. Younger adolescents, however, must often make spur-of-the-moment decisions in regard to their public acts. But once having become more knowledgeable about such matters, they too will be less susceptible to peer influence, like their older counterparts.

Marcia's theories on identity statuses suggest that older adolescents have had more time to develop an independent or achieved identity, an accomplishment that lessens their need for constant peer approval. In contrast, younger adolescents tend to have diffused or foreclosed identities, definitions of self that rely on the peer group for direction and reinforcement. In summary, from this perspective, the further the adolescent has advanced toward an independent identity, the more easily he or she can withstand pressures to conform. Consequently older adolescents are more likely than the young to be nonconformists (Marcia, 1980).

Adolescent's Gender

Finally, some researchers propose that an adolescent's sex influences his or her susceptibility to peer pressure. One view is that females conform more than males to the desires of their peers (Coleman, 1980). According to this perspective, girls are committed to pleasing other people and winning their approval through conformity, because society has traditionally endorsed this behavior as feminine. Boys, however, are taught to demonstrate masculinity by behaving independently and by overcoming too much sensitivity to others' opinions. Yet not all researchers are in accord on this point. For example, after their extensive review of the literature on sex differences, Maccoby and Jacklin (1974) conclude that although girls tend to conform more to adults' wishes than boys, neither sex conforms more than the other to peer influence.

Examining the results of several studies demonstrates the contradictory data on the relationship between an adolescent's sex and his or her responsiveness to peer or parental values. Some adolescent boys have been found to spend more time with their parents between the ages of 13 and 16 than girls, while the situation reverses itself between the ages of 16 and 19 (Montemayor & Von-Komen, 1980). These data tentatively suggest that the age at which parents exert the most influence may differ for males and females. For example, ninth-grade boys in one study chose the parent-approved alternative in a hypothetical situation more often than girls (Emmerich, 1978). In contrast, two surveys of 100 adolescents in 1960 and 1976 showed the girls to be more influenced by their parents' opinions than boys (Sebald & White, 1980). Girls have been reported spending more time actually talking with their parents, while boys spend most of the time with their parents playing sports or watching television (Larson, 1983).

To confuse matters further, others have found no relationship between an adolescent's sex and the relative power of parents or peers. The adolescent's race, not his or her sex, was the strongest predictor of parent or peer influence. White adolescents were generally more peer-oriented than blacks (DiCindio, 1983). Moreover, data collected from 4,163 students in grades 5 through 12 showed that peer influence on academic and social issues was similar for males and females (Epstein, 1983c).

On the basis of these contradictory data, it is clear that the effects of gender on the relative power of parents and peers are more complex than often acknowledged. To determine an adolescent's susceptibility to peer pressure or the likelihood of his or her rejecting a parent's influence, we must avoid oversimplification and consider a number of relevant questions: How mature is the youngster in terms of ego development and individuation? At what stage of cognitive development is he or she functioning? What type of decision is involved? What kind of relationship exists between the parent and child? In sum, adults need help in understanding that the young will not automatically side with their peers in rebellion against their elders' values.

FACTORS AFFECTING CHOICE OF FRIENDS

On what basis do adolescents choose their friends? Across all developmental stages, one of the essential qualities of friendship is the freedom to share without fear of being betrayed (Parlee, 1979). But what factors determine whom adolescents will choose as their most trustworthy companions? Perhaps not surprisingly, when adolescents dream about their friends, their recurrent fear is of separation and abandonment (Roll & Millen, 1979). Given this concern regarding a friend's reliability, how do young people decide who is potentially a friend, foe, or mere acquantance?

As might be expected, most research demonstrates that "birds of a feather flock together" in regard to friendships. Even though adolescents sometimes choose friends whose personalities complement rather than replicate their own, friends are almost always similar in terms of their backgrounds and values. The literature consistently underscores the point that most adolescent friendships are founded upon similarities in socioeconomic class, sex, race, intellectual abilities, values, and interests (Berndt, 1982b; Duck, 1983; Duck & Gilmour, 1981; Epstein, 1983b; James & Jongeward, 1975; Kandel, 1978).

Given the methodological shortcomings mentioned at the outset of this chapter, however, these findings must be interpreted with one important caveat in mind: Almost all research studies on adolescent and adult friendships have been conducted in settings such as school, where people are not given free rein to choose their friends. For example, curriculum tracking typically precludes students from interacting with people from different socioeconomic or racial backgrounds. A review of over 250 references confirms that a school's organization can considerably alter students' cross-sex, cross-race, and mixed-age choices in friends (Epstein, 1983b). Thus, before making hasty judgments about adolescents' unwillingness to select friends who differ from themselves, we need more data about adolescents' choices in settings where they are allowed to interact with peers from diverse backgrounds. In sum, "birds of a feather flock together" may hold less true in situations where the birds are permitted more frequent and more extended contact with creatures unlike themselves.

This caveat notwithstanding, it is nonetheless true that friends tend to reflect one another's social, political, and educational ideologies. In other words, young people who drink, smoke, use marijuana, or have premarital sex usually have friends who also engage in these activities. In the same vein, youngsters who are religious converts or athletes or beauty queens tend to have friends with these same values. So, for example, a study of nearly 1,000 New York state students in five different high schools showed that drug use by peers was one of the strongest predictors of an adolescent's initiation into drugs. If friends disagreed on drug use, the friendship usually either ended or one of the friends modified his or her stance on drugs (Kandel, 1978; Kandel & Kessler, 1978).

We would be mistaken, however, to assume that only adolescent friendships are based on individuals' similarities. Like adolescents, adults usually become friends with people of their own race and sex who share the same religious views, socioeconomic class, educational level, and recreational interests. The more alike two people's attitudes, the more likely they are to become friends—particularly if they share an unusual perspective that sets them apart from other people. For example, two people who both believe the end of the world will take place before the year's end are likely to find fertile ground for developing a friendship (Berscheid & Walter, 1978; Duck, 1983).

Not only do adults and adolescents choose friends with attitudes similar to their own, but their judgments of other people are affected by these similarities. For example, researchers have found that bank managers give bigger loans to customers whose attitudes reflect their own than to those who differ appreciably. Likewise teachers, therapists, and physicians tend to prefer and to attend more to students or clients whose views are similar to their own. In short, both adolescents and adults generally befriend and judge most favorably people similar to themselves (Berscheid & Walter, 1978; Duck, 1983).

Factors Affecting Popularity

Personality

Although adolescents tend to choose friends on the basis of similarity to themselves, popularity is negotiated on other terms. Researchers have devoted considerable attention to the reasons underlying an individual's popularity with surprisingly few inconsistencies in their results. Studies assess popularity by administering sociometric tests on which individuals indicate whom they would like to sit next to in class, play with, work with, or date. These studies also compare the personality traits of popular and unpopular individuals as a way of delineating the characteristics that distinguish them from one another. In general, these studies agree that despite a young person's age or sex, popularity seems to depend on friendliness, cheerfulness, a good sense of humor, initiative in talking to or playing with others, and enthusiasm (Coleman, 1980; Hartup, 1983; Hill & Lynch, 1983; Sebald, 1981).

Studies have also tried to identify other correlates of adolescents' popularity. For example, some have found that adolescents who have older brothers and sisters are more popular than first-borns, suggesting that the later-born children developed more social skills than their first-born siblings (Miller & Maruyama, 1976). Yet young people who spend up to 30 percent of their time by themselves tend to be better liked than those who spend no time by themselves, implying that popularity depends on a certain amount of independence and privacy (Larson & Csikszentmihalyi, 1978). Surprisingly, however, Coopersmith (1967) found that some of the most popular adolescents have extremely low self-esteem. Therefore, Coopersmith hypothesized that a poor self-image can sometimes motivate youngsters to behave in ways that please other people and increase popularity. Whatever their underlying motive, youngsters who behave in a friendly, enthusiastic manner toward others generally enhance their popularity.

The importance of conformity and social class in becoming popular has become recognized through additional research. Sebald (1981) found that 94 percent of the 100 adolescents he surveyed in 1960 and 86 percent in 1976 named conformity as the most necessary ingredient for social success. Upper-middle-class youngsters expressed more concerns about being popular than those from lower-income families. In a similar vein, some data suggest that middle-class adolescents are generally more popular than those from lower socioeconomic groups because they are more apt to control the means for setting social standards (Hollingshead, 1975). It also appears that popularity is linked to how effectively an adolescent empathizes with others and recognizes their emotions and motives (Adams, 1983). Results like these imply that being somewhat of a conformist, empathizing with others, and adhering to middle-class social standards tend to advance an adolescent's social status.

Scholar or Athlete?

How important is athletic or academic success in determining popularity? Is the "jock" generally more popular than the scholar? In the early 1960s James Coleman focused on this issue by trying to identify the characteristics that distinguish members of a high school's leading crowd from those in less powerful, less popular crowds (Coleman, 1961). Across a number of different high schools, Coleman posed some insightful questions to young people: What does it take to get into the leading crowd? How would you most like to be remembered in school—as an athletic star, a brilliant student, or the most popular? Students who participated in the Coleman research asserted that athletic ability, personality, and good looks were the most important traits determining a male's popularity. They also reported that for girls physical beauty, personality, and pretty clothes topped the list. Across both sexes, being a good student ranked relatively low, although boys ranked academic success higher than girls. On the basis of his data, Coleman concluded that a boy's popularity primarily rests with his athletic prowess and a girl's with her success in social relationships. Furthermore, Coleman concluded that adolescents generally disregard academic success as a criterion for popularity.

It has been argued that Coleman's studies overemphasized the importance of athletics and underemphasized the role of academic success in generalizing about adolescents' criteria for popularity. Even in Coleman's own data, there were vast differences among schools in terms of the importance of academics and athletics. The male athletes in Coleman's study were usually chosen as more popular than the male scholars, but the most popular boys were successful in both academics and athletics. In other words, although a girl's social skills and a boy's athletic talents helped to ensure their popularity, adolescents did not disparage their peers' academic success.

More recent studies have brought Coleman's hypotheses about the relationship between athletics and a male's popularity into clearer perspective. In a 1975 replication of Coleman's study, 47 percent of the high-school boys said they wanted to be remembered as athletic stars, in comparison to 44 percent of the boys in Coleman's 1960 study. Being an athlete was more important in determining a boy's popularity in small schools, rural communities, and less-educated areas than in larger urban or suburban schools, where academic success is more highly valued (Eitzen, 1975). In support of these results, a more recent 1980 survey of nearly 2,000 junior- and senior-high-school students and 850 college students showed that 57 percent of the boys in junior high, 43 percent in high school, and 46 percent in college wanted to be remembered as athletic stars. Not unexpectedly, perhaps, boys in schools with winning athletic teams considered athletic success more important than boys in schools with losing teams (Williams & White, 1983). Contrasting these percentages with those associated with a desire for scholastic eminence, only 28 percent of the boys in Williams's 1980 survey, 23 percent in Eitzen's 1975 survey, and 31 percent in Coleman's 1960 survey wanted to be remembered as brilliant students. Other surveys in the 1980s have also shown that a boy's athletic abilities are consistently related to his popularity among male and female peers (Savin-Williams, 1980; Weisfeld, Bloch, & Ivers, 1983).

The formula for female popularity, however, is quite different. In Coleman's 1960 study, girls were not given the option of "star athlete," since interscholastic sports for girls were nonexistent at that time. In a 1978 survey, however, 20 percent of the girls wanted to be remembered as athletes, 24 percent as brilliant students, 28 percent as most popular, and 26 percent as leaders in school activities (Feltz, 1978). Similarly, 22 percent of the girls in a recent survey of girls from junior high through college wanted to be remembered as athletic stars, 28 percent as brilliant students, 16 percent as most popular, and 30 percent as leaders in school activities (Williams & White, 1983).

In sum, adolescent males today, like their counterparts in earlier decades, still perceive athletic success as the path to popularity. Unfortunately, however, some evidence suggests that schools that overemphasize competition in either sports or academics decrease adolescents' abilities to empathize with one another (Adams, Schvaneveldt, & Jenson, 1979). Moreover, despite the expanding opportunities in athletics that have accompanied Title IX legislation, it still does not appear that most girls perceive athletics as a way of achieving popularity.

Physical Attractiveness

How important is an adolescent's physical attractiveness to his or her peers? Can unattractive youngsters nonetheless become popular by dazzling their peers with their personalities or intelligence? Unfortunately, it appears that neither adolescents nor adults behave as though "beauty is only skin deep." Most research suggests that the majority of us—adolescents and adults—tend to disregard the maxim, "Don't judge a book by its cover." Although society tries to reassure young and old that it values brains before beauty, the research generally fails to confirm this notion (Berscheid & Walter, 1978; Duck, 1983; Duck & Gilmour, 1981).

The importance of physical attractiveness in regard to adolescents' feelings about themselves and about their peers has already been discussed in Chapter 2. As you may recall, the research demonstrated that attractive youngsters are generally perceived as more friendly, intelligent, dependable, influential, and competent than their less attractive peers, even though their actual behavior may be identical. Particularly in the case of girls, physical attractiveness is an important criterion in determining popularity, since, as Chapter 5 documented, adolescent boys are more able than girls to acquire social status through athletic, academic, or vocational success. Moreover, judgments of physical attractiveness can be influenced by other personality characteristics. For example, in a study with sixth- and eighth-graders, students with athletic and academic abilities were also perceived as "good looking" by their classmates (Felson & Bohrnsted, 1979).

Another consideration already addressed by the studies in Chapter 2 is the relationship between popularity, physical maturity, and body build. Both boys and girls who mature physically earlier than their peers are initially more popular than those who mature later, although these differences tend to diminish with age. Early maturation seems to give young people the physical attributes considered beautiful by their peers—muscles and height for boys, developed breasts and fleshier hips for girls. Furthermore, adolescents with endomorphic builds are generally considered less attractive by their peers than those with mesomorphic or ectomorphic bodies. Although beauty is determined by "the eyes of the beholder," in our culture people who are somewhat slim, not too short and relatively muscular have the social edge in the eyes of their peers. In addition, boys who mature early and have mesomorphic builds are in a better position to reap the social advantages of becoming athletes. For these reasons, it's not surprising that many adolescents (and adults) contend that "having a nice body" is extremely important for sexual and social reasons (see Chapter 2 for references).

The importance of physical attractiveness is underscored in one particularly interesting comparison of third- and eighth-graders' criteria for choosing friends (Zakin, 1983). While viewing photographs of attractive and unattractive children, the students were told whether each photographed child was shy or outgoing, athletic or unathletic. Then the 120 white suburban students were asked whom they would choose as friends from among the photographs. Both the third- and eighth-grade students preferred the attractive child as a friend, even when he or she had been described as shy and nonathletic. Surprisingly, both the third- and eighth-grade boys preferred the attractive peer over the athletic peer. More suprising still, the third-grade students preferred the athletic child over the sociable child, while the eighth-grade students showed no preference. Thus, the findings contradict the notion that athletic prowess assumes a more influential role than physical attractiveness in males' or adolescents' friendship selections.

CHANGES IN FRIENDSHIPS DURING ADOLESCENCE

Definitions of Friendship

In regard to the ways in which adolescent friendships differ from the friendships of younger children, the data are remarkably consistent (Asher & Gottman, 1981; Coleman, 1980; Duck, 1983; Rubin & Ross, 1982; Seltzer, 1982). Between the ages of 2 and 4, children define their friends in terms of simplistic, concrete characteristics. Hence, the 4-year-old may tell us she likes Suzie because "she has lots of nice toys." At this stage the child expects little reciprocity or cooperation from friends, while in later childhood the child describes his or her friends in more personalized terms: "I like her because she is nice."

Further, the research shows that as children age they come to value their friends primarily on the basis of the benefits that accrue from the friendship: "I like her because we play together." Within this context, friends are perceived as people who provide support against enemies, offer assistance, and share in joint activities. After the age of 9, children start shifting toward a less self-centered view of friendship and begin appreciating the importance of collaboration, cooperation, and unselfishness. During adolescence, however, youngsters extend their conceptualization of friendship and begin perceiving friends as those people with whom they can share their feelings, resolve personal problems, and reveal their innermost thoughts.

Smollar's studies with children, adolescents, and young adults are representative of the research describing our changing perspectives of friendship as we age (Smollar & Youniss, 1982). Smollar's research reveals that 6- to 10-year-olds believe two strangers will become friends if they help each other or share an activity. As one 10-year-old said, "Friends are easy to make. All you have to do is go up to a guy, say hello, and ask him if he wants to play ball; then he's a friend. If he don't want to play ball, then he's not a friend, unless you decide to play something else." As this example illustrates, for this age group becoming best friends primarily depends on spending time together in mutually enjoyable activities. In contrast, by the age of 12 or 13 most children feel that becoming friends is predicated upon "getting to know each other." Close friendships are expected to develop only if the two people are similar enough to one another. Given this perspective, a 12-year-old says, "If they don't have anything in common, one of them is kind of shy but the other is popular, then they won't be friends."

By mid-adolescence, however, Smollar found that most young people express more sophisticated expectations and definitions of a friend. Nearly 70 percent of the females and 53 percent of the males felt a friend's foremost obligation was to provide emotional support. Although the 13- and 14-year-olds also mentioned the importance of a friend's providing emotional support, they were more concerned about a friend's being "protective"—keeping one another out of trouble and standing up for one another. Furthermore, in comparison to children between the ages of 6 and 12, the adolescents and the 22- to 24-years-olds emphasized the mutual acceptance and nonjudgmental nature of their friendships. In addition, the adolescents and young adults mentioned being open, honest, and spontaneous as important dimensions of their friendships (Smollar & Youniss, 1982).

Consistent with the findings from other researcher's studies, Smollar's studies demonstrate that children perceive friends as those with whom they share activities and interests, while adolescents and young adults perceive friends as those with whom they can share personal problems and feelings.

Intimacy and Trust

Only when children become adolescents do they begin to define a friend in terms of someone with whom they can share secrets, divulge private information, or develop trust and loyalty. Unlike children, adolescents become concerned with a friend's reliability, trustworthiness, and ability to provide emotional support and advice. Consequently adolescents start attending to the psychological makeup of their peers. Factors that played no role in determining childhood friendships become of paramount concern: Is this person going to divulge my secrets? Is she honest? Is he unselfish? Can this person accept my faults and shortcomings or will I have to wear masks? Significantly, in this regard, whereas only 20 percent of the sixth-graders in one study mentioned loyalty as an important quality in a friend, 40 percent in the seventh grade valued this quality highly (Bigelow & LaGaipa, 1975).

Empathy and Reciprocity

Unlike younger children, adolescents develop the capacities to empathize with their friends and to establish reciprocal relationships. Both males and females become more aware of the motives underlying others' behavior and more capable of recognizing others' emotional states. Instead of focusing exclusively on what friends can offer them, adolescents awaken to the fact that friendships are reciprocal arrangements in which each partner must contribute and compromise if the relationship is to continue. In order to maintain friendships, adolescents must learn how to decipher and how to fulfill the needs of others. While this process often generates considerable self-doubt, it's an important skill that prepares young people for adult friendships that demand reciprocity and empathy.

Why are adolescents' friendships more intimate and more reciprocal than children's? Why do adolescents generally become more empathic and more adept at social interactions as they age? According to the theories of Jean Piaget and David Elkind, the cognitive abilities that enhance social interactions become more sophisticated as adolescents age (Elkind, 1980; Piaget & Inhelder, 1969). As the research in Chapters 3 and 4 demonstrated, younger adolescents are generally more worried about their "imaginary audience" and are more egocentric than older adolescents. Fearing the judgments of peers and assuming that everyone is noticing their conduct and appearance, young adolescents are often incapable of empathizing with or attending to the needs of other people. According to the Piagetian perspective, however, aging is accompanied by the increased capacity to assume other people's perspectives and to behave less egocentrically. Hence, older adolescents are better equipped to create intimate friendships and to value such qualities in a friend as loyalty, empathy, and trustworthiness.

● 9.1 A Closer Look

Adolescents' Perceptions of Aggressive and Retarded Peers

What do adolescents think of their mildly retarded classmates? How do they perceive their obstreperous, aggressive peers? Would adolescents be more critical of a retarded, a hyperactive, or an antisocial classmate? To answer these questions, several researchers presented 654 students in grades 4 through 10 with a description of four hypothetical classmates: The first is a normal, well-adjusted boy who succeeds academically and interacts with his classmates in a cooperative, enjoyable manner. The second is a mildly retarded boy who has trouble remembering things and needs help in class. He often acts younger than his age and behaves in an odd manner, but nonetheless enjoys being with other people. The third is a hyperactive male—impatient, easily frustrated, inattentive, impulsive, and moody. The fourth boy is antisocial and aggressive—showing off, dominating others, being argumentative, occasionally stealing and picking on his classmates. How do adolescents feel about these four boys?

Of the four, adolescents described the antisocial, not the retarded boy, as the one most likely to have problems in his future life. Not surprisingly, adolescents expected the normal boy to become the wealthiest, the most famous, and the most acceptable to others. The mildly retarded boy, however, was seen as more likely than the antisocial one to become rich and to become like other people as an adult. In addition, adolescents said they would be more willing to befriend the retarded boy than the antisocial one. In terms of treating the boys with leniency, the ratings for the mildly retarded and the normal boy were similar. In other words, most adolescents did not recommend that the retarded boy be treated more strictly by adults, in contrast to their recommendations for dealing with the hyperactive and antisocial boys.

Even more surprisingly, most adolescents described the antisocial boy as they did the retarded boy on the categories of "brain damaged" and "mentally retarded." They did, however, recommend that both the retarded and the aggressive boys be provided with professional help. Adolescents were less likely than younger children to use labels like "mentally ill" or "bad" to describe any of the atypical boys. Likewise, adolescents were less likely to view the solutions to the boys' problems as adults being more strict or seeking professional help for the boys. Males and females generally agreed in their descriptions of the four boys, although girls were somewhat less likely to recommend that parents be stricter and to label any of the boys as "mentally retarded."

SOURCE: C. Whalen, B. Henker, S. Dotemoto, & S. Hinshaw, Child and adolescent perceptions of normal and atypical peers. *Child Development,* 1983, *54,* 1588–1598.

Research generally supports Elkind and Piaget's developmental explanations for the changes in adolescents' friendships (Asher & Gottman, 1981; Berndt, 1982b). For example, only 13 percent of the 10-year-olds sampled in one study described their friends in psychological terms, as compared to 90 percent of the 16-year-olds (Barenboin, 1981). As Box 9.1 indicates, such studies support the cognitive view that age enables a person to make better inferences about other people.

Another perspective concerning developmental changes in the quality of friendships is provided by Marcia's and Erikson's theories of identity statuses discussed at length in Chapters 4 and 5. As you recall, Erikson and Marcia hypothesized that adolescents with achieved identities would be more capable of establishing intimacy in their relationships than their peers with foreclosed or diffused identities. Moreover, Erikson, whose theories Marcia has attempted to operationalize, presumed that the ability to establish intimate relationships developed only after adolescents had mastered the stage of "identity and role confusion." Thus, from Erikson's perspective, young adolescents are less capable of developing intimate friendships because they are grappling and experimenting with different identities. According to Erikson, most young people will weather the storm of identity confusion and will establish identities of their own by the end of adolescence. Accomplishing this developmental milestone then enables them to focus their attention on establishing intimacy with other people (Erikson, 1968).

As the data previously examined have shown, however, Marcia's and Erikson's views have been challenged by recent research. Thus, it now appears that while males with achieved identities have more intimate relationships than males in other identity statuses, most females develop the capacity for intimate relationships during adolescence, regardless of which identity status they adopt (Matteson, in press). Moreover, as you recall, Carol Gilligan's (1982) research confirms that females are more intricately bound than males by their empathy for and intimacy with other human beings.

Opposite-Sex Friendships

As adolescents' expectations of friendship differ from those of younger children, so too do their attitudes about friendships with the opposite sex. During the early years of adolescence, friendships are particularly segregated along the gender line: Girls and boys generally avoid one another. Beyond the age of 12 or 13, however, young people become more willing to befriend members of the opposite sex. Yet despite this more accepting attitude, friendships with the opposite sex remain a rarity throughout most individuals' lives (Hartup, 1983; Karweit & Hansell, 1983b; Schofield, 1981).

Furthermore, while race and sex both assume major importance in the selection of friends, being members of the opposite sex is a far stronger deterrent than being members of different races. It is noteworthy that, after reviewing the literature, Schofield concludes that sex accounts for nearly 20 times as much variance as race in children's choices of friends. For example, in her own study of sixth- and seventh-graders, half of whom were black, fewer than 10 of the 200 students in the cafeteria at one time would be eating with someone of another race, and fewer still with someone of the opposite sex. Similarly the boys and girls segregated themselves from one another in classroom activities (Schofield, 1981).

Studies with older adolescents confirm the fact that most males and females limit their friendships to members of their own sex (Hartup, 1983). While unwillingness to have friends of the opposite sex is most pronounced in early adolescence, even in high school 80 to 90 percent of adolescents' friends are still members of the same sex (Karweit & Hansell, 1983b). It is striking, although perhaps of little-appreciated significance, that adolescents are far more likely to form friendships with people of another race than with members of the opposite sex.

DIFFERENCES IN MALE AND FEMALE FRIENDSHIPS

One of the most intriguing facts about the friendships of adolescents and adults is that so few males and females have friends of the opposite sex. Aside from the interactions required for dating, very few individuals select someone of the opposite sex as a friend. With society's attitudes about sex-role stereotypes slowly changing and recent legislation that is trying to equalize opportunities for males and females, why do the sexes continue excluding each other as friends? What differences between males and females might account for this phenomenon?

Perhaps the most obvious reason is that the sexes tend to have different definitions of friendship. Consequently, males and females typically behave differently with their friends. According to the available data, females are more empathetic, more nurturant, and more self-disclosing with their friends than males. In addition, female friends rely more on one another for emotional support in times of confusion or crisis and share more intimate information than males. In contrast, most male friendships are often predicated on their mutual participation in common activities such as sports. Males typically maintain more autonomy and place more emphasis on becoming independent than on honing their interpersonal skills and building close friendships. These differences between male and female friendships are consistently documented in the research (Berndt, 1982b; Coleman, 1980; Hill & Lynch, 1983; Karweit & Hansell, 1983b; Smollar & Youniss, 1982).

Douvan and Adelson's (1966) extensive study of adolescents in the 1960s demonstrates that male and female friendships differed then much as they do today. In their interviews with more than 2,000 adolescents, boys seldom mentioned sensitivity or empathy as important characteristics of a friend. They cared less than girls about being understood by or sharing emotions with their friends. Instead, most boys wanted friends who could share activities like sports with them or who could "help me out of a jam." Adolescent girls invested more emotionally in their friendships and were more dependent upon their friends for a sense of security and self-worth than were boys.

Recent research continues to support the conclusions reached by Joseph Adelson and Elizabeth Douvan. For example, Offer's comparison of adolescents in the 1960s and 1970s demonstrates that girls are more attached to their friends than boys (Offer, Ostrov, & Howard, 1981). Girls invest more time and energy in interpersonal relationships and are more worried about rejection from their friends. In contrast, boys are more autonomous and less affected by their friends' disapproval. Girls also report being more concerned about "hurting other people" than boys and feel more upset if other people disapprove of them. Researchers are generally in accord that most girls are more emotionally involved with and dependent upon their friends than most boys (Adams, 1983; Berg & Mussen, 1978; Gilligan, 1982; Zedlin, Small, & Savin-Williams, 1982).

Girls also disclose more personal information to their friends than do boys. This distinction typically emerges during adolescence, rather than in childhood. In lieu of sharing their intimate thoughts or expressing their emotions, male friends prefer to share activities together. For example, in a recent survey of seventh- through tenth-graders, girls at every grade level named more friends as important to them than boys did. Although both boys and girls shared more of their feelings with their friends as they aged, tenth-grade boys reported feeling intimate with fewer friends than seventh-grade girls (Hill & Lynch, 1983). A seventh-grade boy in Shofield's study of early adolescent friendship succinctly expressed the conclusions reached by many researchers: "The boys talk about football and sports and the girls talk about whatever they talk about" (Schofield, 1981).

Smollar and Youniss's (1982) studies with people between the ages of 6 and 22 underscore these differences between male and female development. At all age levels, females are more likely than males to consider their friends' feelings in determining their own behavior. Sharing personal problems appears in early adolescence between female friends, but not until late adolescence between males. Most male friendships are characterized by sharing similar interests, while female friendships are typified by sharing personal problems and intimate feelings.

Why are most males reluctant to share intimate feelings and discuss personal problems with their friends? Researchers like Smollar contend that most males refuse to exchange any information that involves admitting weakness, fear, or confusion. They avoid discussing personal problems for fear of compromising their masculinity. Another hypothesis is that most male friendships involve group activities—primarily sports—that are not conducive to intimate conversation. Then, too, males often prefer to discuss personal issues or feelings with a female, whom they perceive as more understanding than other males. Regardless of the underlying reasons, most male friends disclose less intimate information and seek less help in resolving personal problems than female friends.

There also appear to be differences in males' and females' cliques. Some data suggest that boys are more likely than girls to join crowds or form gangs early in adolescence (Kon, 1981). Another study found that boys who are rejected by existing cliques more typically rally together and form a group of their own, while rejected girls tend to remain isolated (Damico, 1975). This finding is consistent with reviews of the research showing that girls seem less willing than boys to make new friends, an observation suggesting that female friendships are more intimate and more exclusive than those of boys. Girls also express greater concern about the faithfulness of their friends and worry more about the possibility of being rejected (Berndt, 1982b). Some developmental psychologists have suggested that girls prefer dyadic relationships and tend to avoid group activities, because dyads provide more opportunities for intimacy and self-disclosure. In contrast, boys' participation in sports and their preference for group activities diminish their opportunities for intimate conversations (Karweit & Hansell, 1983a).

Having reviewed the literature on adolescents' and childrens' friendships, Karweit and Hansell (1983b) offer several explanations for the fact that males and females prefer friends of the same sex from early childhood through adulthood. In preschool years girls are generally more willing to obey rules, more oriented toward adults, and less individualistic in their peer interactions than boys. Hence, neither sex finds the other's behavior compatible with their own. Given a natural inclination to interact with people who behave similarly to themselves, young children play with members of their own sex. As sex segregation continues and is reinforced by school, the interests and activities of males and females become increasingly more discrepant. Differences between the sexes that initially were relatively minor thus become prominent, and interactions between the sexes become increasingly rare. In classes where teachers have intentionally encouraged boys and girls to work together, more cross-sex friendships do develop, but the norm in school and in society is to continue encouraging sex segregation as children age.

Another distinction between male and female friendships lies in the criteria employed to select friends. Teenage males seem less willing than females to select friends of lower status in terms of income, academic achievement, curricular track, or father's education and income (Karweit & Hansell, 1983a). Karweit and Hansell examined data from 20 high schools with 20,345 students and compared male and female adolescents' college plans, curricular track, father's education, and peer status rating with their best friends' status in each of these categories. Consistent with previous researchers' conclusions, they found that males were less likely than females to befriend people of lower status than themselves. This suggests that males, more so than females, may perceive friends as a means of acquiring or maintaining status.

The fact that most males and females do not befriend members of the other sex is, while disappointing, understandable. First, their expectations for and behaviors with friends are too discrepant to make friendship between them very likely. Second, most of our experiences as adolescents and as adults reinforce sex segregation in athletic, social, and academic endeavors. Consequently, the differences between male and female friendships are emphasized rather than diminished.

INTERRACIAL FRIENDSHIPS

As you can surmise from the adolescents' comments in Box 9.2, racial prejudice still interferes with friendships between many white and nonwhite youths. Although interracial friendships are more common than friendships between males and females, most adolescents still choose friends from within their own racial group (Asher & Gottman, 1981; Epstein, 1983a, 1983b).

The Impact of School Desegregation

Although one of the intentions underlying the Supreme Court's decision to desegregate U.S. schools was to improve the academic achievement of minority students, another hope was that desegregation would enhance interracial friendships and diminish racism among the young. As well as ruling against segregation, the Supreme Court ruled that offering minorities the "freedom of choice" to attend either segregated or desegregated schools was unconstitutional. In making this decision, the Court recognized that minorities who had always lived in a segregated society would not feel comfortable sending their children to integrated schools or to place themselves in desegregated neighborhoods or social settings. As social psychology predicts, people naturally avoid interracial situations in which they might be humiliated or rejected. Not surprisingly, since the Court's historic decision in *Brown* v. *Board of Education* (1954), researchers have been measuring the impact of integration on students' interracial relationships and on their racial attitudes.

Unfortunately, data from the 1970s and 1980s acknowledge that most students in integrated schools still segregate themselves socially along racial lines (Miller, 1983; Slavin & Hansell, 1983). For example, in recent observations of sixth- and seventh-graders whose school enrollment was 50 percent black, only 5 percent of the students were likely to be eating lunch with someone of another race on any given day (Schofield, 1981). Similarly, in St. John's analysis of 120 studies on the impact of integration, interracial friendships were found to be extremely rare. In fact, racist attitudes and behavior were sometimes exacerbated rather than diminished by school integration. Not surprisingly, interracial friendships were most likely to develop when students had attended integrated schools from an early age rather than beginning in secondary school. Moreover, several of the studies reviewed by St. John showed that minority students had lower self-esteem scores after desegregation (St. John, 1975).

Although discouraging, these data must be regarded as evidence that school integration does not always automatically result in more interracial friendships or in less racist attitudes. A number of recent investigations have found, however, that school desegration does create positive social outcomes for both white and minority students. Among these studies, the most impressive in terms of their sample size, random sampling, longitudinal data, and control of confounding variables, such as socioeconomic status, are the investigations that have been conducted throughout the past decade at the Center for Social Organization of Schools at Johns Hopkins University.

The Center's findings have repeatedly demonstrated that school desegregation does increase social and vocational desegregation in adolescents' present and future interactions. To begin with, minority students who attend desegregated schools are more likely to attend predominantly white colleges and to work in desegregated firms than those from segregated schools (Braddock, 1980; Braddock, McPartland, & Trent, 1984). In addition, graduates of desegregated schools express less discomfort in working under a white supervisor than graduates of segregated schools (Braddock, 1983; Braddock & McPartland, 1983; Braddock, McPartland, & Trent, 1984). As might be expected, a survey of 4,080 employers showed that hiring preference is given to blacks who attended desegregated suburban schools (Crain, 1984).

Furthermore, the social gains of integrated schooling are not limited to minority youths. Data derived from national surveys show that attending integrated schools improves the attitudes of both whites and blacks toward future interracial contacts. From these surveys, it appears that desegregated schooling reduces white students' racial stereotypes and diminishes their fear of hostile reactions from minorities (Scott & McPartland, 1982). For example, in a smaller yet similar study involving 100 high-school students, the whites from desegregated schools had more tolerant racial attitudes toward blacks than white students from segregated schools. More specifically, the whites from segregated schools were the least willing to perceive the contradictions between their racist beliefs and their endorsement of principles such as equality and justice (Merritt, 1983).

Finally, one other frequently overlooked, yet socially significant, fact

9.2 Adolescent Voices

Adolescents Talk about Prejudice

The only reason that my special friend and I stopped dating each other is because I am a Mexican-American, and her parents are very prejudiced. They demanded her to stop talking to me and never to see me again. Well, as it turned out, we had no other choice. . . . We had to hide to just talk to each other. Whenever I would call her, I would have to use another name so that her parents wouldn't know that it was me.

Well, this went on for one whole year. Finally, we realized that we would have to see each other a different way. As it turns out now, we're the best of friends, just like two loving brothers and sisters.

Her parents don't mind. I think they're finally getting to like me. There might still be hope. (Ricky Mendez, 17, Lubbock, Texas)

In my family, there is prejudice everywhere. My dad just doesn't like blacks. Even if they are nice to him, he swears at them and still hates them. When someone murders some blacks, he's happy. I think that is just sick to wish someone dead. . . .

I grew up hating blacks. That's all anyone ever told me—that they were bad people and to hate them always. But as I grew older, I grew smarter. Now I don't judge people by color.

I really wish there was no prejudice in the world. It would be a happier place to live. (14-year-old female, Illinois)

An example of being prejudiced against a black person found inside the high school would be letting a fellow black borrow a personal item such as a comb, hat, or lip balm, then later, after it is returned, treating it with disinfectant or even throwing the borrowed item away for fear of catching germs. If one feels this way about blacks causing germs, then maybe they would be better off not lending anthing out.

A common example of prejudice against the Trainable Mentally Retarded students would be not eating lunch in the lunch room because the only table left is the one which is for the TMRs. . . .

Not everyone in McMinnville High shows prejudice against others. In fact, some even try to live without it. An example of where it might not exist in McMinnville High would be volunteering to become a peer tutor to let someone "special" know that they are cared for. Another example might be choosing a partner for sports who is unaccepted by society in P.E. (Kimberly Ault, 18, McMinnville, Oregon) emerges from the Johns Hopkins' data on school integration: Cities with desegregated schools have more desegregated housing than do cities with segregated schools (Pearce, Crain, & Farley, 1984). Because the price of housing is affected by where a city decides to draw its school district lines, cities that choose to assign students to a particular school in ways that promote segregation are thereby segregating their neighborhoods. In many communities the school district's lines are gerrymandered so that children from racially segregated neighborhoods continue to be assigned to segregated schools. In contrast, if school-

I think a lot of people are prejudiced even though they think they're not. If you ask a white girl if she is prejudiced against blacks, she will probably say "no," but then she will never go out with a black guy. (Laurel MacLaren, 15, Kirkwood, Missouri)

I feel that prejudice is discriminating against a particular group or its beliefs. Prejudice happens all the time, all around us. In our beautiful state of Hawaii, there is a wide assortment of different racial groups and beliefs. At my school of Kamehameha, students must have Hawaiian blood in order to attend. This was part of the will of the school's founder, a Hawaiian princess.

In the past, many opposed Kamehameha's requirements of claiming Hawaiian ancestry to attend, saying it was racial prejudice. However, Kamehameha was founded solely to benefit children of Hawaiian and part-Hawaiian ancestry.

Racial groups in Hawaii must learn to interact to survive. The Chinese, the Filipinos, the Japanese, the Samoans, the Hawaiians, the Caucasians—although all have the ability to interact, many do not. Business in Hawaii thrives when all groups cooperate with each other to survive. In Hawaii many different groups have learned long ago to do just that. There are many different religions in Hawaii also. Roman Catholics worship next door to Buddhists in some parts of our islands. By interacting to help each other, all are happy. (Amy Soares, 16, Honolulu, Hawaii)

An example of prejudiced people is the use of one of our gas stations around the corner from my house. This gas station is owned by a Chinese family so only Chinese men work there. The people that live in my neighborhood would rather drive an extra mile or two just so they won't have to be served by Chinese gas attendants.

I feel that this is very wrong. A Chinese gas attendant can serve gas just as well as any other nationality gas attendant. (Sandy Scalise, 15, Chicago, Illinois)

I know plenty of people who claim that they aren't prejudiced "because they have a black friend or a Jewish friend." But when they are in downtown Boston, they don't hesitate to yell racial remarks out of their car window at them. It doesn't say much for those people. They must feel so threatened by those different people in order to say things like that.

I think anyone that allows a public showing of prejudice should wake up to today's society. Why anyone ever lets the KKK march is still confusing to me and stirs up an unquenchable anger inside me. (Kathleen McKie, 17, Newton, Massachusetts)

SOURCE: Glenbard East *Echo, Teenagers themselves.* New York: Adama Books, 1984.

district lines are drawn in such a way that students from racially segregated neighborhoods are assigned to the same school, the real-estate values of the neighborhoods become more equivalent, since parents usually choose their residence on the basis of school-district assignments. In this way, school desegregation can indirectly enhance interracial friendships by increasing the likelihood that adolescents will be growing up in racially mixed neighborhoods.

The most recent and perhaps most impressive data from the Johns Hopkins' research center is the 15-year longitudinal study referred to as "Project Concern" (Crain & Strauss, 1984). Having compared lower-income blacks who attended either segregated or desegregated schools from 1966 until the year after their high-school graduation in 1981, the researchers found that black students do reap social benefits from school integration. The black students from the integrated schools had more white friends and were more likely to live in integrated neighborhoods after their high-school graduation. In addition, they felt less hostile toward and more socially at ease with whites than their black counterparts who were educated in predominantly black schools. Moreover, blacks educated with whites perceived less discrimination in their interactions with white employers and were more likely to attend predominantly white colleges than those who had been educated in black schools. Also noteworthy is the finding that blacks from the integrated schools had lower delinquency rates, fewer pregnancies, and fewer contacts with the police than those from segregated schools.

Interestingly, these 1981 findings corroborate the results of research conducted in earlier decades. A 1966 survey of 1,074 black adults found that blacks from desegregated schools were more likely to have white social contacts and to live in integrated neighborhoods (Crain & Weisman, 1972). Similarly, a ten-year follow-up of 1,971 black college freshmen showed that black adults who graduated from predominantly white colleges and who grew up in primarily white neighborhoods were more likely to have white coworkers and friends (Green, 1982).

In summary, school desegregation does not always, in and of itself, enhance interracial friendships or lessen racial prejudice. The Johns Hopkins studies, however, are so compelling, both in terms of the consistency of their findings and in terms of Project Concern's rigorous methodological design, that their conclusions merit special attention in the ongoing debate over the impact of school desegregation on adolescents' interracial attitudes and friendships. Recognizing that the Johns Hopkins findings are not corroborated by all other existing research, the most pertinent question now appears to be: What distinguishes integrated schools that do have a positive impact on adolescents' racial attitudes and interracial friendships from schools that have a less favorable impact? Or, to rephrase the question: If we want adolescents to befriend more people from other races and to develop less racist attitudes, specifically what must we do as teachers, counselors, recreation directors, coaches, parents, or administrators to bring our hope to fruition?

The Bases for Interracial Friendships

In addressing the problem of promoting interracial friendships, many researchers have predicated their work on the hypotheses proposed by Gordon

Allport in his highly acclaimed text, *The Nature of Prejudice* (1958). According to Allport, interactions between people from different races do not necessarily reduce prejudice. Indeed, such interactions often intensify racism. Thus, in regard to adolescents' racial attitudes, it is crucial to attend to the conditions under which Allport notes prejudice is most likely to decrease: The first is when people are having to work together cooperatively toward a mutually beneficial goal—as in athletic competition where all players on a racially integrated team are united in their efforts to beat their opponents; second, when people of each race have equivalent status in terms of their abilities, incomes, or other measures of social stature—as in a class for the intellectually gifted in which students from different races have similar academic skills; third, when people in positions of authority within the status quo actively promote racial tolerance and denounce racism—as in President Kennedy's decision to send federal troops to Alabama so that a black adolescent, James Meredith, could enroll in a white college.

Schofield's (1981) research is representative of the many studies that have subjected Allport's hypotheses to empirical verification with adolescents. Schofield's study was conducted with 1,400 sixth-, seventh-, and eighth-graders in a school whose enrollment was half white and half black. Most white students came from middle- or upper-middle-class families and most blacks from poor or working-class families. By examining interactions among the students in the first three years of the school's opening (1975–1978), Schofield found that both whites and blacks perceived whites as the most academically talented and compliant and perceived blacks as the most assertive, physically tough, and domineering. The fact that most white students were actually more academically skilled and were more financially advantaged had created a disequilibrium in status between blacks and whites that discouraged interracial friendships, just as Allport predicted. Indeed, Schofield found that adolescents viewed the academic differences between whites and blacks as "proof" of innate racial differences, rather than as the consequence of the socioeconomic discrepancies between the two races.

Of particular note, white students who offered academic help to blacks were often perceived as condescending or haughty. In turn, those whites whose help was rejected felt offended and hurt. Feeling that whites were conceited and prejudiced, many of the black students were easily offended by words or actions not intended as offenses. For example, one black girl expressed her sensitivity to rejection this way: "Some white kids act conceited. They don't want to talk to you. You be talking to them and they'll talk to you for about a minute or so and then they'll go over to their other friends and act like they don't know you" (Schofield, 1981, p. 77).

In further accord with Allport's hypotheses, white students tended to stereotype all blacks on the basis of observing the behavior of the minority of blacks who were boisterous and domineering. In contrast, black youths usually distinguished between the blacks who were "bad" and those who were "normal." As one black male explained: "Some blacks is friendly. The friendly blacks get along with whites. But the black people that think they're bad, they just don't like people that much. They pick fights with whites and then with blacks. They fight with everybody" (Schofield, 1981, p. 76). Unfortunately, many whites with the preconceived notion that all blacks were tough and bad became passive and subservient around blacks, thereby soliciting harrassment and domination. Other whites misinterpreted black classmates' harmless teasing or mild hassling as forms of personal threat and aggression. Although the majority of the black students were just as offended by aggressive blacks as were white students, most whites focused on the behavior of the few and generalized to all blacks in ways that undermined friendly relations.

In addition, some black students exerted pressure on other blacks to avoid friendships with white classmates, perceiving such friendships as an alliance with whites and a rejection of blacks. Black girls were especially prone to feel jealous of interracial friendships and to express feelings of isolation and discrimination. Moreover, although most white students claimed to have no prejudice, most blacks disagreed. Ironically and sadly, each race perceived the other as being the more conceited and as expecting special treatment. Although Schofield's conclusions are based on data from young adolescents, studies conducted with other adolescents have corroborated her findings (Miller, 1983; Savin-Williams, 1980; St. John, 1975). In sum, contemporary studies generally support Allport's assertions regarding the circumstances under which interracial contacts are most likely to reduce an adolescent's racist attitudes and behavior.

Enhancing Interracial Friendships

Subjecting Allport's hypotheses about prejudice to further empirical examination, researchers have found that integrated schools that meet Allport's criteria foster more interracial friendships than schools that merely educate the different races together in the same buildings. One representative study tracked 1,800 children for five years after they had been bused from ghettos to integrated schools. Most interracial friendships developed in classes where teachers provided opportunities for positive interactions between the races, gave minority students duties through which to achieve status, modeled nonracist attitudes and behavior for their students, and used class discussions to foster interracial communication. Finding their results consistent with most of the extant literature, these investigators are among those who conclude that integrated schools must actively promote more positive racial attitudes if interracial friendships are to thrive (Miller, 1983).

Given such findings, researchers at the Center for Social Organization of Schools at Johns Hopkins University have developed two specific techniques that have proven successful in increasing adolescents' interracial and cross-sex friendships (Slavin & Hansell, 1983). The *Teams Games Tournament* (TGT) and *Student Teams-Achievement Divisions* (STAD) have been extensively researched and are presently being used in many secondary schools.

In STAD, the teacher first presents lectures on the academic material and then assigns students to teams that must complete worksheets together. Each team is interracial and is composed of four or five classmates with different academic abilities. After working together on their written assignments, each student takes a quiz over the material. These quiz scores are then converted into a team score, which takes account of each student's improvement over his or her previous performance. Teams' rankings are then publicized in a newsletter or on the bulletin board. In TGT the same method is used, except that teams compete in academic tournaments against one another. Similarly in the "Learning

Together" methods, team members work together on common worksheets and are praised and rewarded as a group.

Also being used in schools to enhance interracial friendships are methods known as *jigsaw teaching*. In jigsaw teaching, each student in a six-member team is assigned a particular portion of the material to teach his or her teammates. For example, one person might be in charge of teaching the principles of cell division while another is responsible for teaching the concept of osmosis. Those from the teams who have the same assignment meet together to discuss the material, then return to their own teams to teach the information. Everyone is then quizzed over all the material and receives an individual grade.

The empirical data from these approaches generally support Allport's hypotheses about reducing prejudice. Students participating in these classroom activities for periods of 10–12 weeks generally form more friendships with classmates of other races and of the opposite sex than those in traditional classes. In some schools, teachers have reported fewer interracial fights after implementing the new classroom procedures. It is also noteworthy that these results have been found in studies with black, Asian American, Mexican American, white, and Anglo-Canadian students. Interestingly, however, several studies found that while white students' attitudes toward minorities improved after participating in the cooperative groups, minorities' racial attitudes remained unchanged. These findings may indicate that students whose racial attitudes are the most negative at the outset will undergo the greatest change (Slavin & Hansell, 1983).

In sum, the data acknowledge that schools can promote interracial friendships by providing opportunities for students to interact in situations of equal status. Since minority students often do have fewer academic skills and lower socioeconomic status than their white classmates, it is critical that schools not exacerbate these differences by inadvertently relegating minority youths to being recipients of peer tutoring from white classmates. By according every student the status associated with having to teach classmates the new material, techniques such as jigsaw teaching are striving to minimize such status differences. Fortunately, the strategies developed at Johns Hopkins have helped minority youths narrow the gap between their academic skills and those of their white classmates, thus making everyone's academic status more equivalent (Slavin & Hansell, 1983).

LONELINESS AND SHYNESS

Characteristics of Adolescent Loneliness

Although extensive, systematic studies of loneliness throughout childhood and adolescence have not been conducted, most of the available research suggest that adolescence may be one of the loneliest periods of life (Brennan, 1982). In a survey of 9,000 adolescents, 10 to 15 percent were categorized as seriously lonely and another 45 percent as suffering from less severe levels of chronic loneliness. Nearly 55 percent of these young people agreed with the statement "I often feel lonely" (Brennan & Auslander, 1979). In another survey of 5,000 youths from America, Australia, and Ireland, 22 percent of the boys and 20 percent of the girls aged 12 to 16 said they felt very lonely. While aging seemed to diminish their feelings of loneliness, in the period between 16 and 20, 14 percent of the boys and 12 percent of the girls still said they felt extremely lonely (Ostrov & Offer, 1978).

Because adolescents are just developing the needs for intimacy with their friends, loneliness may become a problem not experienced during the earlier years of childhood, when little more was expected of a friend than sharing an activity together. Unfortunately, with adolescents' heightened awareness of the value of a friend both for intimate conversation, validation of the self, and solace comes the increased likelihood of feeling lonely. Some theorists argue that both the adolescent's more advanced cognitive abilities and the emergent process of individuation contribute to feelings of loneliness. Becoming aware of their separateness from parents and their independent identity, adolescents sense a loneliness unknown in their childhood years. Further, it has often been suggested that our highly competitive, industrialized society increases feelings of loneliness and isolation (Brennan, 1982; Ostrov & Offer, 1978).

A recent review of the few available studies on adolescent loneliness serves to identify its attributes and correlates during the teenage years (Brennan, 1982). Not surprisingly, feelings of loneliness shift rather dramatically during adolescence, depending on the person's particular circumstance at any given time. Adolescents report feeling loneliest on Friday and Saturday nights, if they are sitting home alone. Being alone on weekends tends to provoke feelings of isolation and rejection. There's no evidence that an adolescent's race, number of siblings, parents' marital status, or social class affect his or her feelings of loneliness. In general, adolescents with an external locus of control and those who behave passively around their peers report feeling lonelier than internally oriented and assertive youngsters.

The literature also shows that adolescents cope with their loneliness in different ways (Brennan, 1982). Some become overly attached to a romantic relationship and try to compensate for their loneliness by clinging to one other person. Others devote themselves to fantasies about famous athletes, rock stars, television heroes, or other unreachable idols. Then there are those who diminish the pain of their loneliness by redirecting their energy into nonsocial activities like vocational training, sports, or academic endeavors. Some researchers even contend that loneliness is the motivating factors that underlies adolescents' creative writing, art, and music. In their view, these creative activities typically cease at the end of adolescence, because loneliness diminishes (Ostrov & Offer, 1978). Unfortunately, some young people attempt to overcome their loneliness by resorting to drugs, alcohol, rebellious behavior, or sexual promiscuity.

These general characteristics of loneliness are typified in a recent study with 100 adolescent males and females. Loneliness was positively correlated with anxiety, external locus of control, depression, and self-consciousness. Not surprisingly, the loneliest young people felt physically unattractive, unlikable, and unhappy. The lonely youngsters were also the least willing to take social risks, such as assuming the initiative to start a conversation, going to a party alone, introducing themselves to a stranger, or asking a friend to introduce them to someone they found attractive. In contrast to other research findings, age was unrelated to loneliness. Moreover, although girls reported feeling lonely for longer periods of time than boys, this difference may reflect girls' greater willingness to admit their loneliness, rather than an actual difference in males' and females' experiences. Most of these adolescents coped with their loneliness by becoming engaged in some activity—typically by watching television (Moore & Schultz, 1983).

Unfortunately, there are no longitudinal studies that identify the childhood precursors of adolescent loneliness. In a society where sex roles are being challenged, one might well wonder whether a masculine, feminine, or androgynous orientation has any appreciable impact on an adolescent's popularity, which, in turn, might affect his or her feelings of loneliness. At least one attempt has been made to assess the relationship between loneliness and an adolescent's sex-role orientation (Avery, 1982). Results compiled from a survey of 225 high-school students indicate that boys with feminine scores on the Bem Sex-Role Inventory are lonelier than boys with masculine or androgynous scores. Further, boys with masculine and androgynous scores reported similar feelings of loneliness. These conclusions must be viewed tentatively, however, since boys who score high on the femininity scale may be more willing to admit their loneliness than boys with the masculine attitude of not disclosing such feelings. No significant differences in loneliness existed for girls with feminine, masculine, or androgynous scores.

Although the empirical research is scant, it appears that adolescent loneliness is a commonly shared experience. Indeed, as some have argued, longitudinal studies may someday demonstrate that adolescence is one of the loneliest periods in life, since peer relationships and social acceptance loom particularly large during the teenage years.

Shyness during Adolescence

As might be expected, the research indicates that loneliness is frequently related to an adolescent's shyness—a trait that naturally interferes with the ability to make friends (Peplau & Perlman, 1982). For example, Zimbardo's research with high-school and college students shows that 80 percent of these young people regarded themselves as shy at some time in their lives. While most of these students felt they had outgrown their shyness, almost 40 percent continued to feel embarrassed by their shyness (Zimbardo, 1981). Unfortunately, an adolescent's shyness is often misperceived by his or her peers as aloofness, apathy, boredom, or hostility. Thus, shy people's loneliness is compounded, since other people avoid them as a way of protecting themselves from what they have misperceived as rejection or condescension.

According to Zimbardo, an adolescent's shyness can range from mild discomfort in social situations to an almost neurotic phobia of other people (Zimbardo, 1981). There are shy adolescents who are comfortable with others, but simply prefer to spend most of their time engaged in activities by themselves. Then there are those youngsters who are easily embarrassed and lack self-confidence and social skills in the presence of their peers. At the most extreme end of the spectrum are those whose shyness is so intense as to be debilitating in almost every social encounter. They become imprisoned by their own self-criticism and excessive fears of interacting with other people.

Given your own experiences with male and with female friendships, do you prefer a male or female as a friend? Why?

Overcoming Loneliness and Shyness

If the research has not yet enabled us to identify the precursors of adolescent loneliness, has it provided us with methods whereby we can help the afflicted overcome their loneliness? If we are unable as yet to identify which children will be at highest risk of becoming chronically lonely during their adolescence, can the empirical research direct us toward remedying loneliness? Fortunately, yes. Among the ways of diminishing adolescents' loneliness and shyness are *assertiveness training* programs, *peer counseling,* and classroom discussions.

Assertiveness Training One of the common problems that beset lonely adolescents is their inability to assert themselves (Peplau & Perlman, 1982). These young people are too timid to express their opinions, their objections, or their desires. The unassertive adolescent is afraid to ask someone for a date, to speak up against aggressors, or to defend a rational position in the presence of any objection. The lonely adolescent is often too unassertive to ask questions, to state a preference, or to express ideas and emotions. Hence, these youngsters can and have profited from assertiveness training (Galassi & Galassi, 1978).

While the term "assertive" is often used synonymously with the term "aggressive," those who train adolescents to become more assertive clearly distinguish between the two concepts. Being assertive means expressing oneself in an honest, straightforward manner without resorting to angry, obscene, or manipulative methods. In contrast, being aggressive means disregarding the feelings and opinions of others by dominating through angry, hostile, or coercive measures. For example, an assertive adolescent might calmly but firmly assert, "Yes, I do mind if you smoke because I'm very allergic to it and I'd really have a much better time this evening if you didn't smoke." An aggressive adolescent might say in an angry, sarcastic tone, "If you don't put out that disgusting cigarette, I'm going to leave this damn restaurant right now!"

Several recent studies demonstrate the utility of assertiveness training for shy and lonely adolescents. For example, after a month-long assertiveness training program conducted by their school counselor, 23 13-year-olds developed more internal locus-of-control attitudes and earned higher self-concept scores (Waksman, 1984a). Their four-week treatment included role playing, group compliment sessions, modeling of assertive behavior, observation of their assertive peers, and homework assignments on assertive and passive behavior. Activities were designed to teach the difference between assertive, aggressive, and passive behavior and to demonstrate the social and emotional benefits of behaving assertively. These adolescents learned to use eye contact, body posture, voice, and self-praise in ways that enhanced their assertiveness. Seven weeks after the original posttesting, the students were retested to determine whether the positive effects of the assertiveness training persisted. A third of the students had even higher self-concept scores in the second testing, a finding that suggests that the benefits of assertion training may become most apparent as time passes.

In a similar study, 13-year-olds underwent a two-week assertiveness training program (Waksman, 1984b). Activities came from resources such as *The People Book: Transactional Analysis for Students* (James & Jongeward, 1975) and *Making Sense of Our Lives* (Harmin, 1974). After eight sessions of 45 minutes each with the school's counselor, the students' self-concept scores improved. Locus-of-control and anxiety scores, however, remained unchanged. The investigator concluded that the two-week program was too brief to affect changes in locus-of-control attitudes. Nevertheless, the students in the two-week training group maintained their improved self-concept scores four weeks after the program's completion.

Several investigators contend that females might find assertiveness training particularly beneficial, since the stereotypic feminine role encourages passivity and discourages agentic skills and self-efficacy. Although this hypothesis had been validated by studies with adult females, until recently it had not been tested with adolescent girls (Galassi & Galassi, 1978). Thus, in a recent study, 148 white, middle-class, senior-high-school girls received 12 hours of assertiveness training. In addition to experiencing the traditional elements of the training, such as modeling, behavior rehearsals, and group feedback, the girls kept journals in which they recorded the consequences of their assertive behavior. The journal entries were then used as the basis for group discussions and rehearsals. At the end of their training the girls' self-esteem scores had improved significantly; moreover, those initially having the least self-esteem benefited most (Stake, Deville, & Pennell, 1983).

In addition, self-esteem scores had improved still further when the girls were retested three months after their assertiveness training. It appears that the three months provided additional opportunities for the girls to practice their newly acquired assertiveness skills, a set of experiences that heightened their self-esteem. The girls reported feeling a greater sense of personal control in interpersonal situations and generally positive responses to their assertive behavior. According to the girls' own reports, the most dramatic improvements occurred in relationships with their teachers—not with their peers. The researchers suggest that because girls tend to be more dependent on adult approval than boys, boys who receive assertiveness training might experience the greatest changes in their relationships with peers rather than with adults (Stake, Deville, & Pennell, 1983).

Peer Counseling A second option for helping adolescents overcome loneliness and shyness is *peer counseling*. Young people with few friends might be coached by those who are popular in ways to initiate conversations, to ask for dates, to introduce themselves to strangers, or to ask others to participate in an activity. Through modeling, rehearsals, and peer reinforcement the shy and lonely can gradually learn to behave in ways that elicit friendly responses from others. Adolescents have repeatedly demonstrated their talents in tutoring one another academically. In these studies both the youngster doing the tutoring and the one being tutored profit academically (Nielsen, 1982). Why not apply the same principles to teaching social skills? Why presume that all adolescents will learn their social skills as a natural consequence of aging?

In support of the position that social skills may be taught by peers, one study with tenth-graders exemplified adolescents' talents in counseling one another (Dooley, Whalen, & Flowers, 1978). Having viewed videotapes of peers with personal problems, most tenth-graders were able to give very specific advice for solving others' problems. In response to the question, "What is the best thing you can do when a friend comes to you to talk about a problem?", adolescents most frequently responded, "Try to help the person understand the problem" and "try to find out more about the problem." In contrast, elementary-school children responded most frequently, "Try to solve it." Data such as these suggest that by the age of 15 or 16 adolescents have developed the cognitive capacities to approach their peers' problems with empathy, care, and maturity.

Classroom Techniques The research has also shown that schools can help shy, lonely, or isolated adolescents develop social skills and build friendships (Epstein, 1983c, 1983d). As explained earlier in this chapter, classes can be arranged in ways that encourage cooperation and interaction, thereby decreasing the likelihood that shy students will remain isolated. The Teams Games Tournament, jigsaw teaching, and cooperative learning methods all serve to exemplify this approach.

In addition, school personnel can help adolescents to examine their expectations about friendship and to learn new patterns of behaving toward their peers. For example, many unpopular youngsters were observed to be very bossy and demanding, as well as egocentric, in their conversations and behavior with classmates or playmates. Programs designed for these youngsters focused on teaching them ways of giving more reinforcement to others and of being more compromising with their peers. Researchers' observations also revealed that popular children usually offer their friends several alternatives during work or play activities. In contrast, the unpopular students tended to give specific orders to their peers, without providing alternatives or allowing for discussion. With this observational information, adults have been able to help unpopular youths master the specific behaviors that enhance their popularity with their peers. While behaviors like these may seem relatively inconsequential, they have nonetheless been found to affect a young person's ability to make friends and have given adults specific techniques for helping the unpopular child (Duck, 1983; LaGaipa, 1981; LaGaipa & Wood, 1981).

Adults can also note atypical patterns in adolescents' social development. For instance, it is atypical for adolescents to associate only with younger children, rather than with same age or older peers. Adults who recognize this pattern in youngsters might work with them to insure that they do not remain at a younger level of social development than their peers.

Unfortunately, the data suggest that young people who are unable to make friends experience problems that extend beyond loneliness itself (Duck, 1983; Duck & Gilmour, 1981; LaGaipa & Wood, 1981). Unpopular, friendless youngsters experience more than their statistical share of academic problems, delinquency, physical illness, and mental problems in adulthood. Consequently researchers are trying to determine whether a child's inability to make friends has consequences for later life. While this issue has not yet been resolved, it has created enough attention to warrant our being concerned for those youngsters who have a chronic problem making friends.

ADOLESCENT DATING

Who, What, When, and Where?

Adolescence has been described as "the time when Humpty-Dumpty is replaced by hanky-panky"; and love—"a beautiful dream with glandular activity," or "the exchange of two momentary desires and the contact of two skins" (Brussell, 1970). While adolescents may not concur with these adult descriptions of their sexual or dating experiences, the young nonetheless agree with the premise that sex, love, and dating constitute a new and important dimension of life during the teenage years.

Although most adolescents start dating near the age of 15, the "right" age for a first date depends more on the standards of the clique to which an adolescent belongs than on chronological age or sexual maturity (Dornbusch et al., 1981; Place, 1975). Although the age for dating may vary somewhat from community to community, most young people have been involved in at least one serious romantic relationship before the end of adolescence (Bell, 1980; Glenbard East *Echo,* 1984).

Not surprisingly, those who are the most achievement oriented and academically successful usually date less frequently than those with lower vocational aspirations and poorer grades. For example, in a survey of 1,700 high-school seniors, those from blue-collar families were more likely to be going steady than those from white-collar families. Likewise, black males were more likely to go steady than white males. There was also an inverse correlation between the number of hours adolescents studied each week and their commitment to a steady relationship—the most studious were the least prone to invest their time going steady (Larson, Spreitzer, & Snyder, 1976). Moreover, it appears that the amount of time adolescents actually spend dating may be overestimated by many adults. For example, only one-third of the several thousand high-school seniors in "Monitoring the Future" 1980 national survey dated more than once a week, and half dated only once a week (Bachman, Johnston, & O'Malley, 1980).

Where do most adolescents go on a first date? In a national survey of young people aged 16 to 21, the majority wanted to go either to a movie or to a party on a first date. Going out to dinner, dancing, studying together, or "parking" ranked far behind. On a second date, however, nearly one-fifth of those surveyed wanted to spend a quiet evening with their date in order to get to know one another better (Gaylin, 1978, 1979).

Perhaps what is most evident from adolescents' own comments about their social lives, however, is the diversity in their preferences—a diversity that serves as a caveat in regard to stereotyping today's youth. For example, one adolescent girl says, "My favorite way to have a good time is going to church or to Bible study and praising the Lord." In contrast, a 16-year-old boy says, "My favorite way to have a good time is to go out with some friends and get wasted. My parents hate it when I come home stoned or drunk or when I party at my house." On the other hand, another 17-year-old male responds, "One of my favorite ways to have a good time is to go out to eat with my fiancée, stop at the store to get a couple of beers, and go back to my house and make sweet, beautiful love when nobody is there" (Glenbard East *Echo,* 1984, pp. 90–91).

Dating Expectations

As the research in Box 9.3 demonstrates, our conceptions of love and friendship differ rather dramatically (Davis, 1985). We tend to be more critical of, have higher expectations for, and be more jealous of people we date than people we categorize as friends. Adolescents' expectations about dating and romance can be influenced by a number of factors. For example, it is argued by some that adolescents' expectations about dating and romance are being negatively influenced by the unrealistic notions perpetuated in teenage literature. Some analysts have criticized the authors of adolescents' books for contributing to youths' unrealistic notions regarding sex and romance (Hauck, 1982; Parish & Atwood, 1984).

In addition to external influences such as the literature an adolescent chooses to read, some data indicate that an adolescent's sex-role orientation influences his or her dating expectations. In a comparison of adolescents with masculine, feminine, and androgynous attitudes, both males and females with feminine orientations expressed less interest in sexual activities with their dates than their peers with masculine or androgynous views. Regardless of their sex-role orientation, however, the young adolescent males were more interested in

A Closer Look 9.3 

A Comparison of Friends and Lovers

What distinguishes a friendship from a sexual relationship, other than the sex itself? Psychologists like Keith Davis and Michael Todd are attempting to find out. In their surveys with college students and young adults these researchers developed a profile of the characteristics that distinguish friends from lovers. Friends and lovers are very much alike in terms of their mutual respect and trust, confiding in each other, offering mutual assistance, and enjoying one another's company. People also tend to feel as much freedom to be themselves with their lovers as they do with friends. Friends, however, are much less fascinated with one another and view their relationship as more stable than that of lovers. Surprisingly, almost one-third of the people in these studies named a person of the opposite sex as their "best friend," and nearly 60 percent of the men and 45 percent of the women named a person of the opposite sex as one of their close friends. Friends of the same sex, however, were more likely than those of the opposite sex to reveal personal information, offer practical assistance, and perceive their relationship as stable. A third of the people in Todd and Davis's studies said their friends had not lived up to their expectations. For example, some best friends had violated a confidence or tried to seduce a friend's lover. Despite these problems, sexual relationships have the greater potential for conflict, insecurity, and ambivalence. Relationships between lovers demand more problem-solving discussions and include more conflict than friendships. Lovers also seem to be less willing than friends to accept one another as they are and to refrain from criticizing each other. Like Dorothy Tennov, who defines the differences between love and "limerence" in her research, Davis and Todd agree that people who are "in love" often have an acute longing for reciprocal passion and let their moods depend on their lover's conduct toward them.

Research like Tennov's, Davis's, and Todd's provokes a number of questions about adolescents' friendships and sexual relationships: Is being "in love" less likely to enhance a youngster's happiness than "loving" someone? Can friendships with members of the same sex provide benefits that those with the opposite sex can not? Do adolescents need to learn to have less idealistic expectations of their lovers in order to have more realistic and more satisfactory relationships as adults? Is our society encouraging adolescents to confuse the feelings associated with "falling in love" with the realities of maintaining loving relationships, once the newness wears off?

SOURCES: K. Davis, Near and dear: Friendship and love compared. *Psychology Today,* 1985, *19,* 22–28; D. Tennov, *Love and limerence.* New York: Stein and Day, 1978.

having sexual experiences with their dates than females of any age and than older males. Both males and females expressed more desire for affection from a date as the couple becomes more emotionally involved. Indeed, even the youngest adolescent boys wanted girls to whom they felt committed to express affection on their dates, rather than just engage in sexual activities (McCabe & Collins, 1979).

9.4 A Closer Look

Adolescent Romance Novels and Judy Blume Books

What role do books play in adolescents' understanding about romance and the problems of adolescence? At the 1984 meeting of the International Reading Association, researchers reported that publishers are doing a brisk trade selling teenage romance novels to adolescent girls. Yet not everyone is happy about the situation. Many teachers and librarians question the content of these books and wonder whether they ought to be incorporated into a school's reading program. Most of the teenage romance books follow a predictable plot: Female character meets older, handsome, sensitive boy in school or at the beach or a fast-food restaurant and falls in love. The sentences are typically quite short and uncomplicated, with lots of dialogue and a simple story line. Critics feel that these romance novels are presenting male-female relationships in sexist, stereotypical terms, as well as distracting girls from reading more challenging books. Nevertheless, the authors of the paper at the I.R.A. meeting concluded that junior- and senior-high-school girls who read these romances also read other kinds of literature and that teachers need not be concerned about including them in the curriculum.

A similar criticism has been directed against the popular books for adolescents written by Judy Blume. An English instructor who examined nine of the Judy Blume books disapproves of the way in which the books represent the world to adolescents. The teacher's analysis of the books showed that they dealt with adolescents' problems in a superficial way and avoided serious problems like drugs and alcohol. The stories also focused on affluent families where only the father was employed outside the home. School was portrayed as a negative experience, where teenagers encounter boring, apathetic adults. The novels afforded few opportunities for the adolescent reader to encounter ethical or moral issues and parents played a minimal role in the stories. The teacher also felt that the characters were usually very self-centered teenagers who were looking out for their own interests and were extremely competitive. They did, however, offer insights for teenagers on their behavior and their problems. Despite this teacher's negative statements about Judy Blume's stories, the 12 young adolescents she interviewed liked the books. They enjoyed the light, humorous style, the use of the first-person narration, and the easy reading level. The adolescents also said they liked feeling that other youngsters shared their worries and problems.

Disagreements over books like Judy Blume's and the romance novels for teenage girls provoke a number of debatable questions: How realistic should adolescents' books be? How useful can they be in helping youngsters resolve problems in their friendships or romances? Which kinds of problems should they tackle and which should they avoid?

SOURCES: B. Parish and K. Atwood, *Enticing readers: The teen romance craze.* International Reading Association annual meeting. Atlanta, Georgia, May 1984; P. Hauck, *Judy Blume and beyond.* Canadian Council of Teachers of English. Saskatoon, Canada, August 1982.

Despite the supposed sexual sophistication of contemporary adolescents, many feel shy about asking someone for a date, an anxiety-producing responsibility that continues to fall primarily on boys (Bell, 1980; Glenbard East *Echo*, 1984). As an example of the tenacity of "old-fashioned" ideas about initiating dates, only one-third of the girls in a recent survey said they had ever asked a boy out for a date. Furthermore, half the males and females in these surveys still believed that boys should shoulder all of the expenses on a date (Gaylin, 1978, 1979). As one young man explains, "I'm already in the tenth grade and I've never even gone out with a girl and that bugs me. I'm shy to an extent, but I think I could overcome it if I knew there were some girls who liked me. Then I could probably ask them out or something, but I haven't been able to be friends enough with a girl to give her a reason to like me" (Bell, 1980, p. 65). And as one adolescent girl laments, "It always blows me away when I run into a guy who says, 'I can't go out with you because you asked me, I didn't ask you.'" (Bell, 1980, p. 67).

How can we help alleviate adolescents' intial difficulties in asking one another out and having an enjoyable date? Two strategies successfully employed by some researchers with adolescent males are **systematic desensitization** and **behavior rehearsal.** In these programs adolescent males are given a manual on dating skills and opportunities to rehearse their social skills with girls who work for the counselor. During the behavior rehearsals, the males practice and receive feedback on their conversational skills, abilities to initiate contacts with females, and listening skills. Using systematic desensitization techniques, boys with specific fears are gradually helped to master the situations that once made them most anxious with girls (McGovern, Arkowitz, & Gilmore, 1975).

Interracial Dating

Another issue relevant to adolescents' social life is interracial dating. How comfortable are today's adolescents with the idea of dating someone of another race? Obviously adolescents' attitudes about interracial dating are influenced by the social mores in their local community and among their friends. Moreover, it appears that the adolescent's age may be important in terms of the sources that influence his or her racial attitudes. Underscoring this possibility, a survey of 5,800 Georgia adolescents found that eighth-graders' racial attitudes correlate more highly than twelfth-graders' with their parents' attitudes. As students matured, their racial attitudes also conformed more to the attitudes they perceived among their friends and in their community (Bullock, 1977). Findings such as this suggest that friends' racial attitudes become increasingly important to adolescents' as they grow older. Thus, on topics such as interracial dating, a younger adolescent's decisions may be more influenced by his or her parents' racial views, while an older adolescent's attitudes may be more influenced by peers.

Young people who have grown up in metropolitan areas, where schools have been desegregated for many years and where minorities have achieved positions of economic and social prominence, are more likely to endorse interracial dating than those who have grown up in racially segregated, rural areas, where minorities seldom achieve equal social or economic status with whites. Moreover, prejudice against a particular race that is prevalent in some areas of the country can be virtually nonexistent in other regions. For example, white and Native American adolescents in the Southwest may have acquired certain prejudices toward one another that would be considered bizarre by adolescents raised in the Southeast, where interracial experiences are primarily limited to blacks and whites.

Despite such regional differences, however, black adolescents still experience more discrimination in regard to interracial dating and marriage than Asian, Indian, or Mexican American youths (Bass, 1982). As might be supposed, interracial dating is still an incendiary issue for many of today's adolescents and their parents. Considering that only in 1967 was interracial marriage ruled legal in all states by the Supreme Court and that, only as recently as 1976, 30 percent of the adults in one national survey wanted to outlaw marriage between whites and blacks, the attitudinal differences between many adolescents and people their parents' age is understandable (McLemore, 1980).

Racial barriers seem to be diminishing somewhat in social domains. For example, marriages between blacks and whites doubled during the 1960s, so that by 1977, there were 350,000 marriages of blacks and whites (Glick, 1981). It appears from adolescents' own comments, such as those in Box 9.2, that interracial dating is becoming more acceptable among the young (Bell, 1980; Glenbard East *Echo,* 1984). Having recently conducted their national study of U. S. high schools, Sizer (1984) and his colleagues conclude that interracial dating is "an accepted exception" among today's adolescents.

Unfortunately, most studies on interracial dating have been conducted with college students. Therefore the data must be interpreted with this limitation in mind. Since college students are generally more liberal in their social attitudes than their peers who choose other options after high school, the generalizability of the data to adolescents in secondary schools is limited. There appears to be a general tolerance toward interracial dating on predominantly white campuses. Black males tend to be more willing to date and marry someone of another race than black females. Black females are more apt to express anxiety over peer rejection for interracial dating. There has been little support for the stereotypic assumption that minority males would rather date white females than females from their own race. In fact, in several studies, minorities have expressed biases against dating whites. White females have been described as more materialistic, sneakier, and more masculine than black females, and white males have been described as more effeminate, self-centered, and complacent than black males (Clark, 1985; Clark & Pearson, 1984; Lampe, 1981; Stimpson et al., 1979).

One reason some black females may oppose interracial dating is demographic: There simply aren't enough black males to go around. Among blacks, females outnumber males by 11 percent at age 18 and by 20 percent at age 30. In contrast, white females do not have to confront the problem of outnumbering white men until after the age of 30. To complicate matters further, black males are twice as likely as black females to marry outside their race. In 1975 only 4.4 percent of black males and 2.4 percent of black females had a spouse of a diferent race—almost always white. In contrast, only .7 of 1 percent of the whites married outside their race, with less than half of these interracial marriages involving blacks. In short, interracial dating and marriage are presently working against the black female by detracting more than adding to her pool of marriageable candidates (Spanier & Glick, 1980).

What ramifications might these demographic facts have on black adolescent girls? Given the shortage of black males, do black girls feel more pressured than whites to form a committed relationship during their adolescence or to marry young? Are they readier than white females to marry males with less education and those who are divorced? Are they more willing than white girls to engage in premarital intercourse, perceiving it as a means to build bonds that will lead to matrimony? Using data from the 1975 Census, researchers have confirmed these hypotheses. Black females marry younger and are more likely to marry a less educated man than white females. Among whites, the husband is more educated in 31 percent of the couples and less educated in 24 percent; but among blacks, the husband is more educated in only 18 percent of the couples and is less educated in 36 percent. In addition, black women are more than twice as likely as whites to marry a divorced man (Spanier & Glick, 1980).

As the research cited in the next chapter will demonstrate, there are racial differences in adolescents' sexual behavior. Blacks are more likely than whites to have intercourse during their adolescent years. Some investigators report that 63 percent of the black females between 15 and 19 are sexually experienced, compared to 31 percent of white females (Zelnick & Kantner, 1977). While we will be exploring in Chapter 10 a number of reasons that might account for these differences, one possibility is the indirect connection between the shortage of black males and black females' sexual behavior. It has been hypothesized that, faced with the reality that there are too few eligible males, black girls may indeed feel pressured into becoming sexually active sooner than their white peers (Spanier & Glick, 1980).

While the shortage of black males is one possible factor influencing interracial dating, there are others. Many white adolescents are still being socialized to adopt unfounded sexual stereotypes about members of other races. For example, blacks are often stereotyped as being more sexual and more desirous of intermarriage or interracial dating than whites. In a similar vein, reactions to a white girl who dates a black male are often still laced with remnants of the old assumption that minority males are in pursuit of white females. As a consequence of such attitudes, the white girl with a black boyfriend is not immune from racist comments and innuendos: "What's wrong with her that she would want to date him? I understand why he wants to be seen with her but why would she want to date him?" (Bass, 1982).

In sum, strong prejudices and stereotypes still come to the fore when adolescents date, have sex with, or plan to marry someone of another race. White and minority parents who endorse school integration and avidly support high schools' integrated athletic teams often feel uncomfortable when their adolescent son or daughter dates a member of another race. While many adults may have encouraged children to treat all races equally in childhood play and academic activities, the situation often changes once sex or marriage is introduced into the situation. That children of different colors play together in a sandbox or on a basketball court is often cited as evidence that the United States has overcome its racial prejudices, but this is a misrepresentation of the realities confronting many adolescents who choose to interact socially or sexually with young people of other races.

Conclusion

Clearly, as children become adolescents, peers become increasingly important to their sense of self-esteem and contentment. At their worse, peer relationships can create sadness and anxiety. Worrying about popularity and acceptance, the young too often develop a self-consciousness and a conformity that create as much anxiety as they dissipate. Friendships that go awry often leave adolescents with intense feelings of loneliness, worthlessness, and rejection. Perhaps more sadly, the failure to form a close relationship with a peer can con-

On what occasions did you experience the most disapproval from your peers as an adolescent? When were you proudest of yourself for resisting peer pressure?

tribute to profound self-incrimination, withdrawal, and envy. For both the shy and the lonely, there is the sorrow of being surrounded each day by others whose friendships seem to fill their days with joy and security. In one 17-year-old girl's words, "I'm afraid that if people really knew the way I was, they would hate me" (Glenbard East *Echo,* 1984, p. 108).

Yet, at their best, peers can offer one another the security, the self-esteem, and the pleasure that an adolescent's family and older acquaintances cannot replace. As demonstrated by the data, adolescent friendships can provide the empathy, intimacy, reciprocity, and trust that children's friendships lack. Through their friendships and peer activities, adolescents are gradually formulating their own values and fashioning unique aspects of their own personalities. Thus, adolescents have opportunities to discover the joys of friendship that accompany growing up—"We then travel back silently and keep our wonderful thoughts of the day to ourselves" (Glenbard East *Echo,* 1984, p. 93).

Without having to examine the empirical data, we are well aware that most adolescent friendships also develop a sexual or romantic dimension—the consequences of which will be explored in the next chapter. While sex and romance can surely evoke the most profound sentiments and pleasures, they are, for many adolescents, unfortunately accompanied by unwanted babies, abortions, sexually transmitted diseases, and early marriages.

Finally, as subsequent chapters of this text will demonstrate, adolescents' peer relationships influence their religious, political, and moral development. Thus, in many regards, from adolescence through old age, our development remains intertwined with our peer relationships.

Questions for Discussion and Review

Basic Concepts and Terminology

1. What shortcomings have scholars identified in the research on peer interactions and friendships?
2. How much influence do adolescents' peers exert over their attidues and behavior in comparison to parents? Which adolescents are most likely to conform to the pressures of the peer group?
3. Why do older adolescents generally conform less to their peers than younger adolescents?
4. What distinguishes cliques from crowds in the adolescent's peer culture?
5. In what ways do the school's organization, curriculum, and pedagogical techniques influence adolescents' friendships?
6. On what basis do adolescents select their friends?
7. How important are athletic success and physical attractiveness to an adolescent's popularity?
8. On the basis of the research, what advice would you offer an adolescent who was trying to become more popular?
9. What distinguishes adolescents' friendships from those of younger children?
10. In what respects are the friendships of adolescents and adults similar?
11. Why do adolescents' capacities for empathy and intimacy generally increase as they mature?

12. What distinguishes male from female friendships?
13. How are interracial friendships generally affected by desegregated schools?

Questions for Discussion and Debate

1. Given your own experiences with interracial friendships, how do you believe society could encourage more social interaction between adolescents of different races?
2. In what regards are your present friends similar and dissimilar to the friends you had as a young adolescent? How have your own views of friendship changed as you have aged?
3. Considering your own shyness in the past or in the present, how could teachers, counselors, parents, or friends help shy adolescents feel more at ease?
4. When did you feel loneliest during your adolescence and what might have helped alleviate your feelings? How do your present feelings of loneliness differ from the feelings of loneliness you experienced as an adolescent?
5. Given the research on the differences between male and female friendship, how do you perceive each sex as advantaged or disadvantaged? How have your own relationships with males and females corroborated or failed to corroborate the researchers' empirical findings?
6. How do your own experiences with peer pressure confirm or refute the data cited in this chapter? What factors influenced your own susceptibility to peer pressure and parental influence as a young adolescent? How do your peers and your parents influence your present behavior?
7. Recalling some of the foolhardy decisions you made as an adolescent in response to peer pressure, how do you believe adolescents could be more liberated from peer pressure? How would your answer differ in regard to peer pressure on high-school students and on college students?
8. Since your first date, in what ways have your dating experiences changed and in what ways have they remained the same? How have your criteria for a "good date" and your own behavior and feelings during a date changed as you have matured? In retrospect, what advice would you offer today's young adolescents about dating?
9. How do you feel about interracial dating and interracial marriage? How do your present feelings compare with those you had ten years ago? Who or what has influenced your attitudes on interracial dating?
10. Given your own experiences and the research cited in this chapter, how could you have made yourself more "popular" during your adolescence? What advantages or disadvantages might have accrued to you if you had been more popular? How do the standards for popularity on this college campus compare with those at your high school?

REFERENCES

Adams, G. Social competence during adolescence: Social sensitivity. *Journal of Youth and Adolescence,* 1983, *12,* 203–211.

Adams, G., Schvaneveldt, J., Jenson, G. Sex, age and perceived competency as correlates to empathic ability in adolescence. *Adolescence,* 1979, *14,* 811–818.

Allport, G. *The nature of prejudice.* Garden City, N.Y.: Doubleday, 1958.

Asher, R., & Gottman, J. (eds.). *The development of children's friendships.* New York: Cambridge University Press, 1981.

Avery, A. Escaping loneliness in adolescence: The case for androgyny. *Journal of Youth and Adolescence,* 1982, *11,* 451–459.

Bachman, J., Johnston, L., & O'Malley, P. *Monitoring the future: Questionnaire responses from the nation's high school seniors, 1980.* Ann Arbor, Mich.: Institute for Social Research, 1981.

Barenboin, C. The development of person perception in childhood and adolescence. *Child Development,* 1981, *52,* 129–144.

Bass, B. Interracial dating and marital relationships. In B. Bass (ed.), *The Afro-American family.* New York: Grune and Stratton, 1982. Pp. 347–356.

Baumrind, D. Parental disciplinary patterns and social competence in children. *Youth and Society,* 1978, *9,* 239–276.

Bell, R. *Changing bodies changing lives: A book for teens on sex and relationships.* New York: Random House, 1980.

Berg, N., & Mussen, P. Empathy and moral development in adolescence. *Developmental Psychology,* 1978, *14,* 185–187.

Berndt, T. Developmental changes in conformity to peers and parents. *Developmental Psychology,* 1979, *15,* 606–616.

Berndt, T. Fairness and friendship. In K. Rubin and H. Ross, *Peer relationships and social skills in childhood.* New York: Springer Verlag, 1982. Pp. 251–278. (a)

Berndt, T. The features and effects of friendship in early adolescence. *Child Development,* 1982, *53,* 1447–1460. (b)

Berscheid, E., & Walter, E. *Interpersonal attraction.* Reading, Mass.: Addison-Wesley, 1978.

Bigelow, B., & LaGaipa, J. Children's written description of friendship. *Developmental Psychology,* 1975, *11,* 857–858.

Blyth, D. Hill, J., & Thiel, K. Early adolescents' significant others. *Journal of Youth and Adolescence,* 1982, *II,* 425–450.

Bowles, S., & Gintis, H. *Schooling in capitalist America.* New York: Basic Books, 1976.

Braddock, J. The perpetuation of segregation across level of education. *Sociology of Education,* 1980, *53,* 178–186.

Braddock, J. College race and black occupational attainment. Baltimore, Md.: Johns Hopkins University, Center for Social Organization of Schools, 1983.

Braddock, J., Crain, R., & McPartland, J. A long term view of school desegregation: Some recent studies of graduates as adults. *Phi Delta Kappan,* 1984, *65,* 259–265.

Braddock, J., & McPartland, J. More evidence on social psychological process that perpetuate minority segregation. Baltimore, Md.: Johns Hopkins University, Center for Social Organization of Schools, 1983.

Braddock, J., McPartland, J., & Trent, W. *Desegregated schools and desegregated work environments.* Baltimore, Md.: Johns Hopkins University, Center for Social Organization of Schools, 1984.

Brennan, R., & Auslander, N. *Adolescent loneliness: An exploratory study of social and psychological predispositions and theory* (Vol. 1). Washington, D.C.: National Institutes of Mental Health, Ro1MH 2891201, Behavioral Research Institute, 1979.

Brennan, T. Loneliness at adolescence. In L. Peplau and D. Perlman (eds.). *Loneliness: A sourcebook of current theory, research and therapy.* New York: Wiley Interscience, 1982. Pp. 269–290.

Brown v. *Board of Education,* 347 U.S. 483 (1954).

Brussell, E. (ed.). *Dictionary of quotable quotes.* Englewood Cliffs, N.J.: Prentice-Hall, 1970.

Bullock, C. Maturation and change in the correlates of racial attitudes. *Urban Education,* 1977, *12,* 229–238.

Cavior, N., & Dokecki, P. Physical attractiveness, perceived atttitude similarity and academic achievement as contributors to interpersonal attraction among adolescents. *Developmental Psychology,* 1973, *9,* 44–54.

Clark, M. Dating preferences and patterns of black students on predominantly white southern campuses. Unpublished ms. Winston Salem, N.C.: Wake Forest University, 1985.

Clark, M., & Pearson, W. Racial stereotypes revisited. *International Journal of Intercultural Relations,* 1984, *6,* 381–393.

Coates, D. *Methodological issues in the study of peer relations in early adolescence.* Paper presented at American Educational Research Association, New Orleans, 1984.

Cohen, J. The relationship between friendship selection and peer influence. In J. Epstein and N. Karweit (eds.), *Friends in school.* New York: Academic Press, 1983. Pp. 163–174.

Coleman, J. *The adolescent society.* New York: Free Press, 1961.

Coleman, J. Friendship and the peer group in adolescence. In J. Adelson (ed.), *Handbook of adolescent psychology.* New York: Wiley, 1980. Pp. 408–432.

Coopersmith, S. *The antecedents of self-esteem.* San Francisco: Freeman, 1967.

Crain, R. The quality of American high school graduates: What personnel officers say and do about it. Baltimore, Md.: Johns Hopkins University, Center for Social Organization of Schools, 1984.

Crain, R., & Strauss, J. *School desegregation and black occupational attainments: Results from a long term experiment.* Baltimore, Md.: Johns Hopkins University, Center for Social Organization of Schools, 1984.

Crain, R., & Weisman, C. *Discrimination, personality and achievement.* New York: Seminar Press, 1972.

Csikszentmihalyi, M., Larson, R., & Prescott, S. The ecology of adolescent activity and experience. *Journal of Youth and Adolescence,* 1977, *6,* 281–294.

Damico, S. The effects of clique membership upon academic achievement, *Adolescence,* 1975, *10,* 93–100.

Davis, K. Near and dear: Friendship and love compared. *Psychology Today,* 1985, *19,* 22–28.

DiCindio, L. Race effects in a model of parent-peer orientation. *Adolescence,* 1983, *70,* 369–381.

Dooley, D., Whalen, C., & Flowers, J. Verbal response styles of children and adolescents in a counseling analog setting. *Journal of Counseling Psychology,* 1978, *25,* 85–95.

Dornbusch, S., Carlsmith, L., Gross, R., Martin, J., Jenning, D., Rosenberg, P., & Duke, D. Sexual development, age and dating. *Child Development,* 1981, *52,* 179–185.

Douvan, E., & Adelson, J. *The adolescent experience.* New York: Wiley, 1966.

Duck, S. *Friends for life: The psychology of close relationships.* New York: St. Martin's Press, 1983.

Duck, S., & Gilmour, R. (eds). *Personal relationships.* London: Academic Press, 1981.

Dunphy, D. The social structure of urban adolescent peer groups. *Sociometry,* 1963, *26,* 230–246.

Eitzen, D. Athletics in the status system of male adolescents: A replication of Coleman's *The adolescent society. Adolescence,* 1975, *10,* 267–276.

Elder, G. *Adolescent socialization and personality development.* Skokie, Ill.: Rand McNally, 1971.

Elkind, D. Strategic interactions in early adolescence. In J. Adelson (ed.), *Handbook of adolescent psychology.* New York: Wiley, 1980.

Emmerich, J. The influence of parents or peers on choices made by adolescents. *Journal of Youth and Adolescence,* 1978, *7,* 175–180.

Epstein, J. *Choice of friends over the life span: Developmental and environmental influence.* Baltimore, Md.: Johns Hopkins University, Center for Social Organization of the Schools, 1983. (a)

Epstein, J. Examining theories of adolescent friendships. In J. Epstein and N. Karweit (eds), *Friends in school.* New York: Academic Press, 1983. Pp. 39–62. (b)

Epstein, J. School environment and student friendships. In J. Epstein and N. Karweit (eds.), *Friends in school.* New York: Academic Press, 1983. Pp. 235–245. (c)

Epstein, J. Selection of friends in differently organized schools and classrooms. In J. Epstein and N. Karweit (eds.) *Friends in school.* New York: Academic Press, 1983. Pp. 73–92. (d)

Epstein J. The influence of friends on achievement and affective outcomes. In J. Epstein and N. Karweit (eds.), *Friends in school.* New York: Academic Press, 1983. Pp. 177–200. (e)

Erikson, E. *Identity: Youth and crisis.* London: Faber, 1968.

Felson, R. and Bohrnsted, G. Are the good beautiful or the beautiful good? *Social Psychology Quarterly,* 1979, *42,* 386–392.

Feltz, D. Athletics in the status system of female adolescents. *Review of Sport and Leisure,* 1978, 98–108.

Galassi, M., & Galassi, J. Assertion: A critical review. *Psychotherapy, Theory and Research Practice,* 1978, *15,* 16–29.

Galbo, J. Adolescents' perceptions of significant adults: A review of the literature. *Adolescence,* 1984, *16,* 951–970.

Gaylin, J. What boys look for in girls. *Seventeen,* March 1978, 107–113.

Gaylin, J. What girls really look for in boys. *Seventeen,* March 1979, 131–137.

Gilligan, C. *In a different voice: Psychological theory and women's development.* Cambridge, Mass.: Harvard University Press, 1982.

Glenbard East *Echo. Teenagers themselves.* New York: Adama Books, 1984.

Glick, P. Demographic picture of black families. In H. McAdoo (ed.), *Black families.* Beverly Hills: Sage, 1981. P. 119.

Green, K. Integration and attainment: Results from a national longitudinal study of the impact of school desegregation. American Educational Research Association, Los Angeles, 1982.

Greenberg, M., Siegel, J., & Leitch, C. Nature and importance of attachment relationships to parents and peers. *Youth and Adolescence,* 1983, *12,* 373–386.

Hallinan, M. New directions for research on peer influence. In J. Epstein and N. Karweit (eds.), *Friends in school.* New York: Academic Press, 1983. Pp. 219–234.

Harmin, M. *Making sense of our lives.* Niles, Ill: Argus Communications, 1974.

Hartup, W. Peer relations. In P. Mussen and E. Hetherington (eds.) *Handbook of child psychology* (4th ed.). New York: Wiley, 1983. Pp. 103–196.

Hauck, P. *Judy Blume and beyond.* Saskatoon, Canada: Canadian Council of Teachers of English, 1982.

Hill, J., & Lynch, M. The intensification of gender related role expectations during early adolescence. In J. Gunn and A. Petersen (eds.), *Girls at puberty.* New York: Plenum Press, 1983. Pp. 87–120.

Hollingshead, A. *Elmtown's youth and Elmtown revisited.* New York: Wiley, 1975.

James, M., & Jongeward, D. *The people book: Transactional analysis for students.* Reading, Mass.: Addison-Wesley, 1975.

Johnson, F., & Aries, E. Conversational patterns among same sex pairs or late adolescent close friends. *Journal of Genetic Psychology,* 1983, *142,* 225–238.

Josselson, R. Ego development in adolescence. In J. Adelson (ed.), *Handbook of adolescent psychology.* New York: Wiley Interscience, 1980. Pp. 188–210.

Kandel, D. Homophily, selection and socialization in adolescent friendships. *American Journal of Sociology,* 1978, *84,* 427–437.

Kandel, D., & Kessler, R. Adolescent initiation into stages of drug use: A developmental analysis. In D. Kandel (ed.), *Longitudinal research on drug use.* Washington D.C.: Hemisphere, 1978.

Karweit, N. Extracurricular activities and friendship selection. In J. Epstein and N. Karweit (eds.), *Friends in school.* New York: Academic Press, 1983. Pp. 131–141.

Karweit, N., & Hansell, S. School organization and friendship selection. In J. Epstein and N. Karweit (eds.), *Friends in school.* New York: Academic Press, 1983. Pp. 29–39. (a)

Karweit, N., & Hansell, S. Sex differences in adolescent relationships: Friendship and status. In J. Epstein and N. Karweit (eds.) *Friends in school.* New York: Academic Press, 1983. (b).

Kon, I. Adolescent friendship: Some unanswered questions for future research. In S. Duck and R. Gilmour (eds.) *Personal Relationships.* London: Academic Press, 1981. Pp. 187–204.

LaGaipa, J. Children's friendships. In S. Duck and R. Gilmour, (eds.), *Developing personal relationships.* London: Academic Press, 1981.

LaGaipa, J., & Wood, H. Friendship in disturbed adolescents. In S. Duck and R. Gilmour (eds.), *Personal relationships.* London: Academic Press, 1981.

Lampe, P. Interethnic dating. *International Journal of Intercultural Relations,* 1981, *6,* 116–126.

Larson, D., Spreitzer, E., & Snyder, E. Social factors in the frequency of romantic involvement among adolescents. *Adolescence,* 1976, *11,* 7–12.

Larson, R., Adolescents' daily experience with family and friends. *Journal of Marriage and the Family,* 1983, *45,* 739–750.

Larson, R., & Csikszentmihalyi, M. Experiential correlates of time alone in adolescence. *Journal of Personality,* 1978, *46,* 677–693.

Maccoby, E., & Jacklin, C. *The psychology of sex differences.* Stanford, Cal.: Stanford University Press, 1974.

Marcia, J. Identity in adolescence. In J. Adelson (ed.), *Handbook of adolescent psychology.* New York: Wiley, 1980.

Matteson, D. Sex differences in identity information. In J. Marcia, A. Waterman, and D. Matteson (eds.), *A handbook for ego identity.* New York: Erlbaum, in press.

McCabe, M., & Collins, J. Sex role and dating orientation. *Journal of Youth and Adolescence,* 1979, *8,* 407–425.

McGovern, K., Arkowitz, H., & Gilmore, S. Evaluation of social skill training programs for college dating inhibitions. *Journal of Counseling Psychology,* 1975, *22,* 505–512.

McLemore, D. *Racial and ethnic relations.* Boston: Allyn and Bacon, 1980.

Merritt, R. Comparison of tolerance of white graduates of racially integrated and segregated schools. *Adolescence.* 1983, *18,* 67–70.

Miller, N. Peer relations in desegregated schools. In J. Epstein and N. Karweit (eds.), *Friends in school.* New York: Academic Press, 1983. Pp. 201–218.

Miller, N., & Maruyama, G. Ordinal position and peer popularity. *Journal of Personality and Social Psychology,* 1976, *33,* 123–131.

Montemayor, R. Relationship between parent-adolescent conflict and amount of time adolescents spent alone and with parents and peers. *Child Development,* 1982, *53,* 1512–1518.

Montemayor, R. Parents and adolescent in conflict: All families some of the time and some families most of the time. *Journal of Early Adolescence,* 1983, *3,* 83–103.

Montemayor, R., & VonKomen, R. Age segregation of adolescents in and out of school. *Journal of Youth and Adolescence,* 1980, *9,* 371–381.

Moore, D., & Schultz, N. Loneliness at adolescence: Correlates, attributions and coping. *Journal of Youth and Adolescence,* 1983, *12,* 95–100.

Nielsen, L. *How to motivate adolescents: A guide for parents, teachers and counselors.* Englewood Cliffs, N.J.: Prentice-Hall, 1982.

Offer, D., Ostrov, E., & Howard, K. *The adolescent: A psychological self-portrait.* New York: Basic Books, 1981.

Ostrov, E., & Offer, D. Loneliness and the adolescent. In G. Feinstein and R. Giovacchio (eds.), *Adolescent psychiatry.* Chicago: University of Chicago Press, 1978. Pp. 34–50.

Parlee, M. The friendship bond. *Psychology Today,* 1979, *15,* 43–45.

Parish, B., & Atwood, K. *Enticing readers: The teen romance craze.* International Reading Association. Atlanta, Georgia, May 1984.

Pearce, D., Crain, R., & Farley, R. Lessons not lost: The effect of school desegregation of residential desegregation in large central cities. American Educational Research Association, New Orleans, Louisiana, 1984.

Peplau, L., & Perlman, D. (eds.). *Loneliness: A sourcebook of current theory, research and therapy.* New York: Wiley Interscience, 1982.

Piaget, J., & Inhelder, B. *The psychology of the child.* New York: Basic Books, 1969.

Place, D. The dating experience for adolescent girls. *Adolescence,* 1975, *10,* 157–174.

Roll, S., Millen, L. The friend as represented in the dreams of late adolescents. *Adolescence,* 1979, *11,* 689–699.

Rubin, K., & Ross, H. Some reflections on the state of the art: The study of peer relationships and social skills. In K. Rubin and H. Ross (eds.), *Peer relationships and social skills in childhood.* New York: Springer Verlag, 1982.

Rubin, Z., & Sloman, J. How parents influence their children's friendships. In M. Lewis (ed.), *Beyond the dyad.* New York: Plenum, 1984.

Savin-Williams, R. Dominance hierarchies in groups of middle to late adolescent males. *Journal of Youth and Adolescence.* 1980, *9,* 75–85.

Schofield, J. Complementary and conflicting identities: Images and interaction in an interracial school. In S. Asher and J.Gottman (eds.), *The development of children's friendships.* New York: Cambridge University Press, 1981.

Scott, R., & McPartland, M. Desegregation as national policy: Correlates of racial attitudes. *American Educational Research Journal,* 1982, *19,* 397–414.

Sebald, H., & White, B. Teenagers' divided reference groups: Uneven alignment with parents and peers. *Adolescence,* 1980, *15,* 979–984.

Sebald, J. Adolescents' concept of popularity and unpopularity comparing 1960 with 1976. *Adolescence,* 1981, *16,* 187–192.

Seltzer, V. *Adolescent social development: Dynamic functional interaction.* Lexington, Mass.: Lexington Books, 1982.

Sizer, T. *Horace's compromise: The dilemma of the American high school.* Boston: Houghton Mifflin, 1984.

Slavin, R., & Hansell, S. Cooperative learning and intergroup relations: Contact theory in the classroom. In J. Epstein and J. Karweit (eds.), *Friends in school.* New York: Academic Press, 1983. Pp. 93–114.

Smollar, J., & Youniss, J. Social development through friendship. In K. Rubin and H. Ross (eds.), *Peer relationships and social skills in childhood.* New York: Springer Verlag, 1982. Pp. 279–298.

Spanier, G., & Glick, P. Mate selection differentials between whites and blacks in the United States. *Social Forces,* 1980, *58,* 707–725.

St. John, N. *School desegregation outcomes for children.* New York: Wiley, 1975.

Stake, J., Deville, C., & Pennell, C. The effects of assertive training on the performance and self-esteem of adolescent girls. *Journal of Youth and Adolescence.* 1983, *12,* 435–443.

Stimpson, S., Stimson, J., Kelton, T., & Carmon, B. Interracial dating: Willingness to violate a changing norm. *Journal of Social and Behavioral Sciences,* 1979, *25,* 36–45.

Tennov, D. *Love and limerence.* New York: Stein & Day, 1978.

U.S. Bureau of the Census. *Current population reports.* Washington, D.C.: U.S. Government Printing Office, Series P-20, No. 287, 1981.

Waksman, S. A controlled evaluation of assertion training with adolescents. *Adolescence,* 1984, *19,* 277–282. (a)

Waksman, S. Assertion training with adolescents. *Adolescence,* 1984, *19,* 123–130. (b)

Weisfeld, G., Bloch, S., & Ivers, J. A factor analytic study of peer perceived dominance in adolescent boys. *Adolescence,* 1983, *18,* 229–243.

Whalen, C., Henker, B., Dotemoto, S., & Hinshaw, S. Child and adolescent perceptions of normal and atypical peers. *Child Development,* 1983, *54,* 1588–1598.

Williams, J., & White, K. Adolescent status systems for males and females at three age levels. *Adolescence,* 1983, *18,* 381–389.

Young, J., & Ferguson, L. Developmental changes through adolescence in the spontaneous nomination of reference groups as a function of decision content. *Journal of Youth and Adolescence,* 1979, *8,* 239–252.

Youniss, J. *Adolescents: Their mothers, fathers and friends.* Chicago: University of Chicago Press, in press.

Zedlin, R., Small, S., & Savin-Williams, R. Prosocial interaction in two mixed sex adolescent groups. *Child Development,* 1982, *53,* 1478–1484.

Zelnick, M., & Kantner, D. Sexual and contraceptive experience of young unmarried women in the United States. *Family Planning Perspective,* 1977, *5,* 55–71.

Zakin, D. Physical attractiveness, sociability, athletic ability and children's preferences for their peers. *Journal of Psychology,* 1983, *115,* 117–122.

Zimbardo, P. *The shy child.* New York: McGraw-Hill, 1981.

Chapter Outline

Differences between Male and Female Attitudes
Masturbation
Petting and Intercourse
Homosexuality
The Etiology of Homosexuality
Problems Confronting Homosexual Adolescents
The Process of "Coming Out"
Limitations of the Research
A New Morality?
Sexually Transmitted Diseases
AIDS: Acquired Immune Deficiency Syndrome
Herpes Simplex
Gonorrhea
Syphilis
Yeast Infections
Pregnancy during Adolescence
A Pregnancy Epidemic?
Abortion
Motherhood's Impact on Adolescent Girls
Adolescents' Offspring
The Adolescent Father
The Etiology of Pregnancy
Personality and Attitudes
Knowledge of Conception and Contraception
Cultural Influences
Sex Education
U.S. Attitudes toward Sex Education
Adolescents' Sources of Sex Information
Kinds of Sex Education for Adolescents
Sexual Responsibility and Adolescent Boys
Conclusion

Goals and Objectives

This chapter is designed to enable you to:

- *Describe the limitations of the research on adolescent sexuality*
- *Examine the sexual attitudes and behavior of adolescents in the past and present*
- *Explore adolescent homosexuality*
- *Identify the major sexual issues confronting heterosexual and homosexual adolescents*
- *Describe the symptoms, cures, and ramifications of venereal diseases*
- *Analyze the possible causes of unplanned pregnancies*
- *Debunk some of the popular misconceptions about adolescents' sexual conduct and attitudes*
- *Explain the consequences of adolescent pregnancy and parenthood*
- *Consider the various methods for providing adolescents with accurate sexual information*
- *Present the legal aspects involved in adolescent sexuality*
- *Identify the kinds of contraceptives available to adolescents*
- *Explore the causes and consequences of abortion decisions*

Concepts and Terminology

cloacal theory
Type I and Type II herpes
bisexuality
chlamydia
homophobia
gonococcus bacteria
asymptomatic carriers
AIDS

10 Adolescent Sexuality

Are today's adolescents participating in a sexual revolution that sets them apart from former generations? Are they more sexually active and more permissive than adolescents of the 1960s and 1970s? What impact are bisexuality and homosexuality having on contemporary youth? How have legal abortions and more advanced methods of birth control affected adolescents? Are adolescents victims of a VD epidemic?

Questions such as these indicate our society's concern regarding adolescent sexuality. Perhaps no other topic related to adolescence generates more questions and discussion among adults. Bombarded with visual images of adolescents in tight skimpy clothing, who are provocatively posed in order to advertise products and adorn magazine covers, we are encouraged to equate youth with sexuality. Moreover, the media direct our attention to sensational topics such as the herpes epidemic, illegitimacy and abortion rates, and bisexuality among the young.

Undeniably, generational differences exist in regard to sexual attitudes and behavior. Unfortunately, however, many adults too readily embrace sexual myths about today's adolescents that are not substantiated by the empirical data. Given the sensational information depicting the young to the general public, it is little wonder that many adults perceive adolescents as a sexually wanton group whose behavior has little in common with their elders' values or conduct. An examination of the empirical data in this chapter may create a more accurate image of adolescents, since, as the comments in Box 10.1 illustrate, adolescents' sexual experiences and attitudes are more varied than is frequently acknowledged.

Adolescent Voices

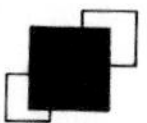

Adolescents' Sexual Experiences

When I was in junior high school I found that my fantasies were a lot more pleasurable than the reality. In my imagination I could make things work perfectly and be with just who I wanted to be with but the reality of it at the time wasn't anywhere near as great. In fact I was really awkward with girls and had trouble getting it on with them—but in my fantasy world it was really smooth.

I've never been in an experience where I might have to compromise my morals, because most of the people I hang out with feel the same way I do. I know I want to be a virgin when I get married, and that's all there is to it.

In sixth grade my friends and I made a pact that we would never ever French-kiss anyone because it was such a gross thing to do. Needless to say, we all broke the pact sooner or later.

When I was 16 I learned about sex all the wrong ways. I never knew what I was doing and I never got any pleasure out of it. And I was always so afraid everyone would see I didn't know what I was doing, so I had to get drunk and stoned to get me through.

It's like a game. My friends told me that when a girl says no she doesn't really mean it. So if a girl tells me quietly to stop, and doesn't yell out loud about it and hit me over the head with it, I'm not supposed to listen. It's a game to find out if she really means it.

Can you imagine making out with a guy and being able to say, "Oh, I don't like that. Oh, I wish you would do this." I think that's ridiculous. I'm not comfortable enough with my own body to be able to tell some other person about it.

The first time I had intercourse I was lying there thinking, You mean this is IT? Am I supposed to be thrilled by this? It wasn't that it hurt me or anything because it didn't. It just didn't feel like anything to me. I figured there must be something wrong with me so I didn't say a word to him.

Everyone's going around wondering why they aren't having the greatest sexual experiences in the world and nobody's saying anything about it.

SOURCE: R. Bell, *Changing bodies, changing lives: A book for teens on sex and relationships.* New York: Random House, 1980. For college students' recollections of their sexual experiences, you may want to read *Growing up sexual* by E. Morrison, K. Starks, C. Hyndman, and N. Ronzio. New York: Van Nostrand, 1980.

With a goal of arriving at an empirically defensible description of adolescent sexuality, we must be cognizant of several caveats in regard to the existing data. First, collecting reliable data about adolescents' sexual conduct is fraught with methodological difficulties. Though gathering accurate information about human sexual behavior is a challenge with subjects of any age, the problems become even more complex with teenage subjects. For example, an often-cited survey by Sorensen (1973) was expected to be a major analysis of adolescent sexual attitudes and behavior; but only 47 percent of the original sample of 839 adolescents agreed to respond to the 40-page questionnaire because of the need for parental consent. In addition, parents who do grant permission for their children to answer sexual surveys may be more liberal than most, and this may create an unrepresentative sample. Thus, a variable that frequently confounds the data on adolescent sexuality is the difficulty of random sampling.

Moreover, the data can be confounded by adolescents' misconceptions about sexual terminology and by a desire to appear sexually sophisticated. Believing there is a "sexual revolution" of which they are supposedly a significant part, adolescents who agree to be questioned may exaggerate their sexual experiences and may overstate their liberal attitudes for fear of appearing unpopular or old-fashioned. Adolescents may also be reluctant to ask for explanations of the sexual terminology before answering the researchers' questions. For instance, some youngsters have reported that "sexual intercourse" was the equivalent of "socializing with the opposite sex." Even college students have disagreed about what constitutes "loss of virginity." Some believe that a girl who has not acutally had a boy ejaculate in her vagina is still a "virgin," despite any other sexual experiences a couple may have shared, while others believe a girl is no longer a virgin if she has had an orgasm while being masturbated by her boyfriend.

In addition to these difficulties, much of the research has relied exclusively on college students' responses. Since college students do not need parental permission to participate in research, and since they are generally more literate and more willing to answer sexual questions than are younger adolescents, their popularity with researchers is understandable. Nevertheless, college youth are not a representative sample from which to generalize about adolescent sexuality. Furthermore, much of the data on which our present generalizations are predicated were derived from small, white, middle-class samples more than a decade ago (Jorgensen, 1983).

Finally, most of the available literature has focused on premarital intercourse and teenage pregnancy, leaving us with little information about other forms of adolescent sexuality (Jorgensen, 1983). For example, little is known about the development of sexual attitudes in early adolescence or about the relationship between physiological maturation and sexual conduct. Perhaps even more important, researchers have asked adolescents very few questions about how they themselves interpret their sexual experiences. For example, how much significance do today's adolescents attach to the size of a male's genitals or a female's breasts, and what impact does sexual status have on overall self-esteem? Or under what conditions do adolescents feel guilty about their sexual conduct? Unfortunately, since researchers' interests are aligned with the topics for which funding is available, the study of adolescent sexuality during the 1980s will most likely remain focused on teenage pregnancy.

DIFFERENCES BETWEEN MALE AND FEMALE ATTITUDES

Despite the fact that the sexual attitudes of males and females are becoming more similar, discrepancies between the sexes are still prevalent. As in former generations, today's adolescent girls tend to be more sexually conservative than boys, both in terms of their behavior and their interpretations of sex. Boys are still more likely than girls to perceive intercourse as a sign of maturity and social status, to have a number of sexual partners, to have sex with relative strangers, and to disassociate sex from love (Astin, 1981; Bell, 1980; Hamburg & Trudeau, 1981; Miller & Simon, 1980; Sorensen, 1973). For example, boys' fantasies are more likely to involve having sex with a stranger, while girls' fantasies are more likely to include emotional attachments with a loved one (Miller & Simon, 1980). Similarly, in a sample of 120 black, white, and Hispanic adolescent girls, 40 percent cited "love" as the reason they had engaged in intercourse with their boyfriend, and another 20 percent cited "pressure from their boyfriend" (Scott, 1983). Given these differences, it is not particularly surprising that some girls still acquiesce to their boyfriends' requests for intercourse as a way of demonstrating their affection and of hoping to deepen the emotional commitment between them.

These data, however, should not be interpreted to mean that every adolescent boy is a sexually unrestrained being whose sexual experiences are devoid of affection and commitment. Nor do these data imply that all girls are more sexually conservative than boys. Either conclusion would be a gross exaggeration. For example, in some recent surveys of 15- to 18-year-olds, 41 percent of the boys believed an emotional commitment should exist before having intercourse with a girl (Haas, 1979). In the words of one 17-year-old male, "As well as teaching youngsters to eat their spinach and make beds, mothers and fathers should teach their youngsters strong moral and ethical values. Maybe if the training started in the homes, then Americans could cut down this enormous and popular sin of premarital sex" (Glenbard East *Echo,* 1984, p. 128).

Given today's less restrictive sex roles, why do male and female adolescents still tend to perceive sex differently? According to some hypotheses, girls are less preoccupied with sex than boys because a boy's more visible sexual organs focus his attention on sexuality (Masters & Johnson, 1966). In other words, "out of sight, out of mind." This argument, however, fails to explain the changes in females' sexual attitudes and behavior in recent decades. We may presume that the visibility of people's sexual organs has remained unchanged, since the memory of humanity runneth not to the contrary.

It has been argued that girls are generally less interested in sex than boys, because they are so poorly informed about their own sexuality. For example, the female child has traditionally been kept ignorant of the names, locations, and functions of her own vagina, vulva, clitoris, and urethra. With such lack of information, many female children believe that urination, defecation, reproduction, and menstruation occur through one orifice—like the cloaca in amphibians and reptiles. Thus, some researchers refer to our ignorance of female physiology as the *cloacal theory* of female sexuality (Rosenbaum, 1979; Shopper, 1979).

Unfortunately, during adolescence a girl's ignorance regarding her own body is often perpetuated by adults who fear that any discussion related to the female reproductive organs will somehow encourage promiscuity. For example, many girls learn about tampons or visit a gynecologist only after they have left home or after they have been educated about these matters by someone other than their mothers. Further highlighting these negative feelings about their own bodies, it is interesting to note that American girls have been found to be more reluctant than their European counterparts to use tampons that are inserted

10.2 A Closer Look

Sexual Morality: According to Whom?

Should society condone sexual intercourse during adolescence or should this form of sexual expression be reserved exclusively for married adults? Is masturbation an act of which adolescents should be made to feel ashamed? As might be expected, the answers to such questions vary throughout the world.

By contemporary U.S. standards, adolescents in some societies are being socialized to adopt excessively conservative sexual mores. For example, among the Cuna of Panama, people remain sexually ignorant until the last stage of the marriage ceremony. Cuna children and adolescents are even forbidden to watch animals give birth. In the Ashanti tribe of Africa, premarital intercourse is punishable by death. In still further contrast to U.S. views, New Guinea's Kwoma boys are constantly warned not to handle their genitals, not even while urinating. If a Kwoman woman sees a boy with an erection, she will beat his penis with a stick.

In regard to female sexuality, many African countries still subject female children to genital mutilation as part of their society's sexual standards. These rituals include cutting away the clitoris, the inner labia, and parts of the outer labia, and then stitching the vulva together, leaving only a small opening for urination. At the time of marriage, the stitches are removed for intercourse and childbirth. The operations are often performed with broken glass or sharp stones, without the aid of anesthetics or antiseptics. Some societies perform these operations on female infants several weeks after birth, while others perform the clitorectomies as part of the rites of passage at the onset of adolescence. Not surprisingly, thousands of African girls continue to die from these operations each year.

While most U.S. adolescents would be taken aback by such conservative sexual practices, our own society's sexual mores might also be construed as conservative from a cross-cultural perspective. For example, the Chewa of Africa encourage sexual activity from childhood throughout adolescence. With their elders' approval, Chewa boys and girls pretend to be husband and wife and have intercourse with several different partners before their actual marriage. Likewise, the Alorese of Oceania encourage their children's sexuality by fondling their children's genitals and condoning masturbation.

SOURCES: C. Ford and F. Beach, *Patterns of sexual behavior*. New York: Harper & Row, 1951; M. Daly, *Gyn/Ecology*. Boston: Beacon Press, 1978, pp. 153–177.

manually rather than with cardboard applicators (Shopper, 1979). More detrimentally, many adolescent and adult females refuse to use contraceptives like the diaphragm, the sponge, or the cervical cap because they feel ill at ease touching the inside of their own vaginas (Bell, 1980; Boston Women's Health Collective, 1982). Thus, it is argued that adolescent girls' sexual attitudes are intimately linked with the feelings they have adopted during childhood toward their own genitals.

It has also been argued that the differences in male and female sexual conduct are consequences of males being more easily aroused than females by sexual stimuli such as pornographic books and erotic art (Masters & Johnson, 1966; Miller & Simon, 1980). The validity of this argument is undermined, however, by recent evidence showing that females become as sexually aroused as males when the material is designed to meet females' standards of erotica. For instance, when erotic materials include romance and emotional involvement, girls become more sexually aroused than when the themes involve sex with strangers, forcible sex, and explicit sexual scenes (Miller & Simon, 1980; Wing Sue, 1979; *Report of the Commission on Obscenity and Pornography,* 1970). Thus, it now appears that males and females are equally responsive to sexual stimuli when females' values are included.

Some researchers have maintained that testosterone is responsible for the distinctions in male and female sexual conduct (Hamburg & Trudeau, 1981). According to this perspective, males' higher testosterone levels predispose them to have a greater interest in sexual activity and a lesser interest in associating sex with love. As demonstrated in Chapter 2, however, the data have failed to substantiate a cause-and-effect relationship between hormones and behavior. More important, as Box 10.2 illustrates, the role hormones might play in determining any individual's sexual behavior is difficult to assess, given the impact that a society's sexual mores exert over its members' behavior.

Indeed, given the cross-cultural and cross-generational data now available, environmental theory remains one of the most convincing explanations for the differences between male and female sexual conduct and attitudes. As you recall from Chapters 4 and 5, the environmentalists or social learning theorists maintain that human behavior is primarily determined by the contingencies of reward and punishment established by the society and by modeling other people's behavior. Thus, since our society has historically arranged contingencies that support the "double standard" of sexual ethics, it is not surprising that the sexual behavior and attitudes of males and females have differed. Until very recent years, both males and females have been socialized to believe that "good girls" shouldn't have intercourse before marriage, since no husband wants "spoiled goods." In contrast, "good boys" were expected to sow their wild oats by becoming sexually experienced—but only with "bad girls." In regard to this double standard of ethics, it is interesting to note the contention of some theorists that patriarchal societies impose sexual restrictions on females because males fear females' sexual appetities and their unlimited potential for multiple orgasms (Sherfey, 1972).

Although the etiology of the double standard is debatable, its popularity in our society appears to be diminishing in certain respects. For example, girls who choose to have intercourse before marriage are generally not condemned by the public or by their boyfriends, as once was the norm in our society. Nevertheless, many adolescents still endorse updated versions of the traditional double standard. For instance, a girl can engage in some sexual activity before marriage, but her experiences should not rival those of males. A girl whose sexual experiences equal or surpass those of her male companions, in terms of number of partners, type of activities, or frequency of contacts, is still more likely to be characterized as "promiscuous" than is a male with similar experiences, whose behavior qualifies him as a "stud" or an "experienced" lover. Many "liberated" males still feel uncomfortable about their girlfriends' being the more sexually experienced or sexually assertive.

MASTURBATION

Among the distinctions between male and female sexual behavior is the frequency of engaging in sexual self-stimulation. Like males of their fathers' generation, today about 90 percent of all boys have masturbated before the age of 19. In contrast, only about 60 percent of all girls have masturbated before the age of 20, although this percentage is twice as large as that of young women in their mothers' generation (Haas, 1979; Kinsey, Pomeroy, & Martin, 1948; Kinsey et al., 1953; Sorensen, 1973).

Fortunately, unlike young people in former generations, most adolescents no longer believe that masturbation is immoral, harmful, or unnatural (Bell, 1980; Haas, 1979). Nevertheless, "Don't do that, it's dirty!" is still an admonition that many of today's young people have received from their own parents. Because the power and impact of such statements can be far-reaching, the beliefs on which they are predicated demand careful examination. Having examined the impact of masturbation on the physical and emotional development of adolescents, contemporary researchers concur that sexual self-stimulation can provide harmless sexual pleasure as well as self-knowledge, which can later be shared with a sexual partner (Barbach, 1976; Comfort & Comfort, 1979; Masters & Johnson, 1970). Yet, while our society's attitudes toward masturbation have grown more lenient, most adolescents still feel embarrassed or guilty about masturbating. Indeed, both adolescents and adults seem to have more difficulty discussing masturbation with researchers than any other sexual topic (Haas, 1979; Sorensen, 1973).

PETTING AND INTERCOURSE

In addition to giving sexual pleasure to oneself, receiving and giving sexual pleasure with someone else without "going all the way" is an appealing alternative for adolescents who have decided to refrain from intercourse. Among the most obvious advantages of "petting" (referred to as "foreplay" in adult lingo) are the greatly diminished risks of pregnancy, venereal disease, and guilt. Given these advantages, many adolescents and adults consider foreplay morally more acceptable than intercourse before marriage—a somewhat ironic attitude considering that females are more likely to have orgasms through clitoral stimulation than through vaginal penetration. Moreover, the nudity, creativity, intimacy, and physical pleasure involved in foreplay often leave few distinctions between petting and intercourse.

As might be expected, most young people have engaged in sexual foreplay by the end of adolescence. For example, several surveys show that about 60 percent of all adolescents have engaged in petting and about 30 percent have had genital stimulation without intercourse before age 15 (Diepold & Young, 1979). Other data suggest that today's adolescents engage in more intimate forms of foreplay and begin such experiences at a slightly younger age than young people in previous generations (Center for Population Options, 1980a; Diepold & Young, 1979; Haas, 1979; Sorensen, 1973). As Box 10.1 illustrates, these petting experiences range from oral-genital sex to touching one another's bodies through a layer of clothing.

Despite the popularity of petting, stories of the "sexual revolution" among the young are based on assumptions about premarital intercourse, not on assumptions about the prevalence of foreplay. Thus, two questions of interest to most U.S. adults are: How prevalent is premarital intercourse among today's adolescents? Has a sexual revolution occurred? Despite the foregone conclusion in the 1960s and 1970s that a sexual revolution was definitely under way, few data were available regarding youths' sexual behavior until Sorenson's 1973 survey of 450 adolescents (Sorensen, 1973).

Given the differences in the ages, geographic locations, race, and socioeconomic backgrounds of the adolescents in the various surveys, it is not surprising that the prevalence of premarital intercourse varies from study to study. For example, in Sorensen's survey of 450 youths during the early 1970s, almost half of the 16-year-old boys and a third of the girls had had intercourse. Yet among 19-year-olds, only one-fourth of the boys were still virgins, in contrast to 40 percent of the girls. Other surveys from the 1970s, however, arrive at somewhat lower estimates for girls, with only about half of the girls surveyed having had intercourse by the age of 18 (Norman & Harris, 1981). Despite these variations in data collected during the 1970s, two facts consistently emerged. First, boys engaged in premarital intercourse more often than girls. Second, girls' rates of premarital intercourse, unlike boys', were rising.

More recent data from the 1980s continue to confirm both of these earlier findings. According to the Alan Guttmacher Institute's national data, about 80 percent of all males and 70 percent of all females have sexual intercourse before the end of adolescence. Stated differently, about 22 of the 29 million young people between 13 and 19 have experienced sexual intercourse. Further highlighting the changing sexual mores in our society, as Figure 10.1 illustrates, adolescents become more sexually active in regard to intercourse as they age (Alan Guttmacher Institute, 1981a, 1981b).

On the basis of the data, can we conclude that premarital sex is more prevalent among today's adolescents than among youths in their parents' generation? The answer seems to be yes for girls and no for boys. For example, in stark contrast to recent data, only 20 percent of the 19-year-old girls in Kinsey's samples from the 1940s had engaged in intercourse. Approximately 75 percent, however, of all males in the present generation and in their father's generation have intercourse before the age of 19 (Kinsey, Pomeroy, & Martin, 1948; Kinsey et al., 1953; Zelnick, Kantner, & Ford, 1981). Indeed some recent evidence even suggests that fewer boys are having intercourse today than in the 1940s and 1950s

Figure 10.1

Adolescents' sexual behavior

Number of males aged 13–21, and number of females aged 13–19, who are sexually active, by age and marital status, United States, 1978

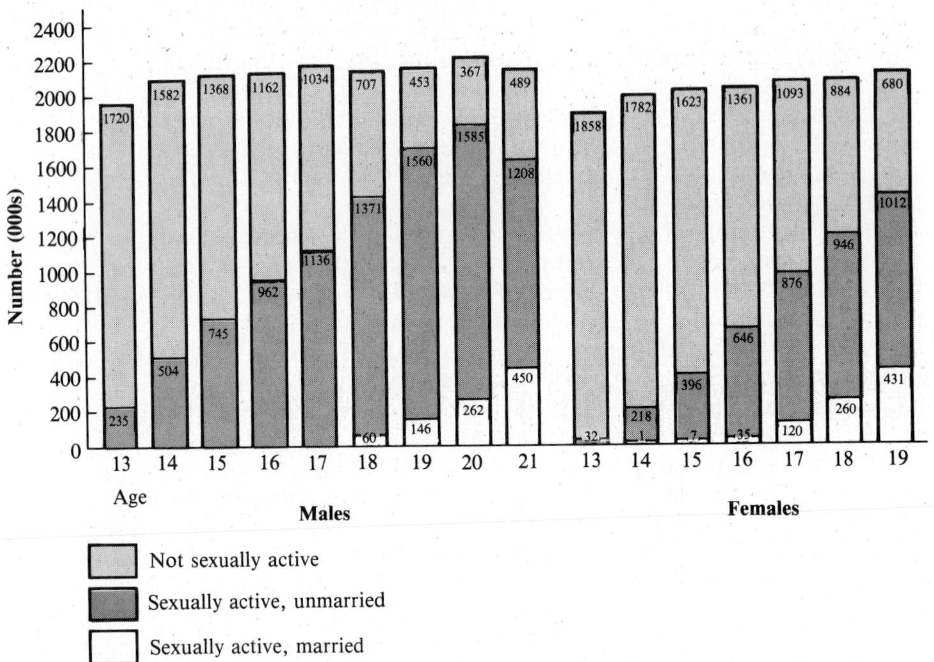

SOURCE: Alan Guttmacher Institute, *Teenage pregnancy: The problem that hasn't gone away.* New York: Alan Guttmacher Institute, 1981, p. 7.

(Miller & Simon, 1980). In sum, if there has been a "sexual revolution," it has been limited to females.

In addition to dispelling the myth that today's adolescent males have been forerunners in a sexual revolution, the data fail to substantiate other popular assumptions about adolescent promiscuity. First, the majority of adolescents have had intercourse with only one person—someone with whom they share an important, emotional relationship. Although some adolescents undoubtedly participate in "one-night stands" with strangers, most do not roam in a devil-may-care fashion from one sexual partner to another. Moreover, contrary to the popular image of sex in the back seat of a car, many adolescents have their sexual experiences in the privacy of someone's home. Finally, most young people are not having intercourse on a regular basis during any given period of time (Bell, 1980; Furstenberg, 1980; Miller & Simon, 1980; Sorensen, 1973; Zelnick, Kantner, & Ford, 1981).

Since a person's initial experiences with sexual intercourse at any age can be less fulfilling than he or she might have imagined, it is not particularly surprising that some adolescents regret their decision to have engaged in this form of sexual expression. As do adults, some youngsters report feeling guilty, exploited, rejected, or disappointed after intercourse. Given worries about pregnancy and the feelings about the sexual double standard, girls generally express more disappointment, guilt, and anxiety than boys after having intercourse (Bell, 1980; Haas, 1979; Norman & Harris, 1981). Unlike older people who engage in premarital intercourse, however, many adolescents experience the guilt of having violated the guidelines of their parents or church. Since most segments of our society still ostensibly disapprove of premarital sex for adolescents, a young person's decision to engage in this forbidden sexual activity can be accompanied by considerable psychological turmoil. Thus, according to some theorists, resolving the issue of premarital intercourse becomes an important component of an adolescent's moral development (Mitchel, 1976).

Although the pattern emerging from the research demonstrates more lenient sexual attitudes among the young, characterizing all adolescents as sexual liberals would be fatuous. For example, one 16-year-old laments, "I know that there are a lot of people who would rather marry a virgin. If everyone goes around having sex, there won't be any left to marry!" (Glenbard East *Echo,* 1984, p. 130). As the data throughout the remainder of this chapter will demonstrate, the sexual attitudes and behavior of any particular young person are intricately bound up with his or her own history of experiences, as well as with demographic and socioeconomic factors.

Homosexuality

The Etiology of Homosexuality

According to recent estimates, approximately 20–25 percent of all males and 6 percent of all females have at least one homosexual experience before the age of 20. Stated differently, between seven and ten million adolescents have had a sexual experience with someone of their own sex. After adolescence, it is estimated that between 2 percent and 6 percent of the population remain exclusively homosexual, while a larger percentage continue to engage in occasional sexual activity with members of the same sex as part of a bisexual orientation (Bell, Weinberg, & Hammersmith, 1981; Sorensen, 1973).

It is often proclaimed that homosexuality is rapidly increasing as a consequence of our society's more tolerant sexual attitudes, but this contention is faulty on two counts. First, the empirical data suggest that the percentage of the population that claims to be homosexual has remained surprisingly constant during recent decades. For example, from Kinsey's statistics in the 1940s, it was estimated that 6 percent of the males and 4 percent of the females had homosexual experiences beyond adolescence (Kinsey, Pomeroy, & Martin, 1948; Kinsey et al., 1953). Recent legislation offering people protection against being evicted from their residences, being fired, being expelled from school, or being discharged from the armed services for their sexual orientations have undeniably made gay citizens more relaxed about disclosing their sexual preferences publicly, as do heterosexuals. Statistics do not, however, substantiate the claim that the gay community is burgeoning at a rapid pace.

How do you feel about homosexuality? Should gay people be legally excluded from professions such as teaching, the ministry, or medicine?

Second, and most important, the assertion that society's more tolerant attitudes are generating an increase in homosexuality is predicated upon the notion that an individual's sexual orientation is determined by social sanctions and external contingencies. From this perspective, it is assumed that gay adolescents could arbitrarily reverse their sexual orientation if society would impose harsher sanctions against homosexuality. Applying the same line of reasoning, those who assume that homosexuality is "caused" by a society's tolerance of sexual diversity would logically have to endorse the corollary hypothesis: Heterosexuals could arbitrarily become homosexuals if the proper contingencies and social approval were available. However logical, espousing the sentiment that "heterosexuals could become homosexuals if they really wanted to" tends to arouse considerable consternation and confusion.

Nevertheless, many of these who declaim against homosexuality have adopted the position that the etiology of an individual's sexual orientation has been irrefutably determined by the empirical data. In reality, however, the etiology of heterosexuality and homosexuality remains clouded by contradictory findings and correlational data. Thus the search continues for the causes of human sexual orientation—a search that approaches the question primarily from three perspectives: biological, societal, and familial.

The Biological Perspective According to the biological viewpoint, physiological variables are primarily responsible for an individual's sexual orientation (Bell, Weinberg, & Hammersmith, 1981; Masters & Johnson, 1979). In support of this hypothesis, for example, some evidence suggests that male homosexuals mature earlier physically than male heterosexuals. Such a finding might indicate that genetic or hormonal differences somehow set homosexual and heterosexual children apart (Higham, 1980).

Pursuing hypotheses related to genetic and hormonal bases for homosexuality, researchers have conducted numerous studies comparing testosterone levels and the chromosomal makeup of homosexuals and heterosexuals. For example, several studies found that girls whose mothers received excessive doses of testosterone during pregnancy tended to exhibit more masculine behavior than other girls. None of the daughters in these studies, however, exhibited homosexual tendencies during adolescence (Green, 1980). Similarly, researchers have been unable to establish significant differences between testosterone levels of homosexuals and heterosexuals, thereby undermining the hypothesis that hormones are a decisive factor in determining sexual preferences (Higham, 1980; Weinrich, Gonsorick, & Holred, 1982). Although researchers continue to investigate the possibility that prenatal hormones may influence an individual's sexual orientation, the research presently available is too scanty and too contradictory either to reject or to accept the hypothesis that prenatal or adolescent hormones determine an individual's sexual preferences.

The Environmental Perspective In juxtaposition to the biological approach to the etiology of sexual preferences, the environmental approach has yielded somewhat more convincing data (Masters & Johnson, 1979; Weinrich, Gonsorick, & Holred, 1982). According to the environmental viewpoint, an individual's orientation toward heterosexuality or homosexuality is more significantly influenced by external experiences than by genetic or hormonal variables.

Exemplifying the environmental research perspective are the studies conducted at Johns Hopkins University Medical School by John Money and his associates (Money & Ehrhardt, 1972). The investigations were conducted with children who, due to physical abnormalities at birth, were reared as the sex that did not correspond to their actual genetic structure. For example, some male infants were born with a vagina and with testes that had failed to descend, due to an enzyme deficiency. Despite the fact that these infants were male in terms of their chromosomes, they were reared as females, on the basis of their genital structure. The researchers' longitudinal observations, found that a child's masculine or feminine behavior depended on which gender society believed the child to be, rather than on his or her actual chromosomal sex. Although Money's research was not directly addressing the etiology of homosexuality, his findings highlight the importance of environmental factors and undermine the significance of genes in determining behavior.

Within the environmental context, it is not surprising that attempts have been made to identify the characteristics that distinguish the families of homosexuals and heterosexuals. As might be expected, the empirical findings have been contradictory. For example, some researchers have found that homosexual males perceived their fathers as somewhat more detached, hostile, unfair, or rejecting, and their mothers as more dominant and overprotective than did heterosexual males. In these studies, gay males generally identified more closely with their mothers than with their fathers. Contrary, however, to the hypothesis that gay males learn to dislike women as a consequence of a maladaptive relationship with their own mothers, the gay males liked their mothers as much as did heterosexual males (Bell, Weinberg, & Hammersmith, 1981).

Similarly, some researchers have found distinctions between gay and heterosexual females' perceptions of their families. In these studies, lesbians remembered their fathers as emotionally detached, hostile, or exploitative more often than did heterosexual women. Gay females also viewed their mothers as more uncommunicative, frustrated, distant, tense, unloving, and bitter. Unlike gay males, gay females expressed more negative feelings about their mothers than did heterosexual females. For example, fewer homosexual than heterosexual girls said they had identified with their mothers as they were growing up or wanted to be like their mothers as adults (Bell, Weinberg, & Hammersmith, 1981; Green, 1980).

Although such research might be construed as support for the hypothesis that an adolescent's homosexuality is significantly influenced by interactions with his or her parents, such a conclusion would be empirically indefensible on the basis of the available studies. First, although homosexuals in some studies report having more problems with their parents than do heterosexuals, many homosexuals are also found to have very satisfying relationships with their parents. Similarly, many heterosexuals admit having had terrible relationships with their parents, yet their sexual orientation remains unaffected. Second, the research relies on homosexuals' and heterosexuals' memories of their childhood experiences, rather than on actual observations of family interactions. Thus, the reliability of studies based on retrospective recollections is highly questionable.

More important, however, the data regarding the etiology of homosexuality are derived from correlational studies. Thus, statements about causality are methodologically unwarranted. For example, despite the fact that this has not yet been accomplished, assume for a moment that the research consistently demonstrated a difference between gay and heterosexual adolescents' interactions with their parents. Although noteworthy, such correlational findings could well be explained by the possibility that homosexual children behave differently from a very early age and that their distinctive behavior shapes their parents' reactions toward them. Indeed, in support of this position, some studies do suggest that gay males and females who exhibit behavior that is extremely characteristic of the other gender manifest this behavior very early in their lives at a time when their parents could be profoundly influenced by their children's unusual behavior (Bell, Weinberg, & Hammersmith, 1981). Such behavior from the child, one might cogently argue, may have had a greater impact upon the parents than the parents' behavior had on the child. Stated differently, in correlational studies the impact of a gay child's behavior on parents and on other people cannot be discounted as a valid explanation for the creation or the maintenance of homosexuality.

In sum, the relationship between an adolescent's sexual orientation and his or her parents' behavior remains unclear. Moreover, the relative influence of prenatal hormones, chromosomal factors, and environmental influences has yet to be determined. Until such issues regarding the etiology of heterosexuality and homosexuality are empirically resolved, those who declaim against homosexual youths would be well advised to reexamine the premise that sexual orientations can be donned or cast aside as one might change political parties or religious affiliations.

Problems Confronting Homosexual Adolescents

Aside from their sexual preferences, how do homosexual adolescents differ from their heterosexual peers? Traditionally, our society has portrayed homosexuals as sick, disturbed, and sometimes dangerous people who need psychiatric help in order to become healthy, normal human beings. Despite the former popularity of such assumptions, the empirical data have not borne them out. As many gay adolescents are now aware, homosexuality does not preclude a person from making significant professional and cultural contributions or from living a fulfilling life—a fact witnessed by the lives of homosexuals such as Walt Whitman, Gertrude Stein, and Oscar Wilde. Reflecting this newer, more accurate perspective, the American Psychiatric Association (1980) no longer lists homosexuality as a mental disorder.

Despite society's increasing tolerance and knowledge, however, gay adolescents still encounter difficulties that their heterosexual peers escape, as Box 10.3 poignantly illustrates (Bell, 1980). First, gay youths must confront the fact that many of their closest friends, future employers, teachers, and fellow citizens hold steadfastly to unfounded myths about homosexuals—myths that underlie the cruel jokes, the snickering, and the name calling to which gay adolescents are often exposed (Price, 1982).

For example, many heterosexual adolescents erroneously believe that in all gay couples one partner always assumes a masculine role and the other a feminine role. Others are convinced that gays have sex more often and are more preoccupied with sex than heterosexuals. There are also the unfounded accusations that most homosexuals molest children and that most can be identified by their exaggerated manner of speaking, moving, or dressing—hence, terms such as "fag," "Dyke," "femmes," or "butch" become synonymous with homosexual. Moreover, many heterosexual youths have adopted as foregone the conclusion that gay people cannot be fit parents to their own children, an assumption often coupled with the accusation that gay parents will naturally "brainwash" their children into being gay. Although these myths have not been borne out by the research, they continue to create pain for gay adolescents, as the commentaries in Box 10.3 illustrate (Bell, 1980; Smoot, 1984).

Regardless of the similarities between heterosexual and homosexual human beings, most gay adolescents have special problems to overcome as a consequence of their sexual orientation. Many experience the confusion, guilt, and loneliness that accompany "being different." Moreover, gay youngsters have the additional burden of coming to terms with their sexuality and establishing self-esteem in a society where homosexuality often creates fear, hostility, and discrimination. For example, even among the most-educated members of today's young generation, college freshmen, support has been expressed for legislation outlawing homosexuality (Astin, 1981). Similarly, high-school students in several surveys oppose the employment of homosexuals as teachers, ministers, or doctors (Fact "File," 1981; Gallup, 1979). Interestingly, male students in these surveys generally express more sentiments against homosexuality than females,

10.3 Adolescent Voices

Homosexuality: Experiences and Reactions

How do you feel about these adolescents' experiences and reactions to homosexuality?

When Ed first said he was gay, I thought, "Let me out of here!" But I knew the guy. We were friends already. I knew what he did in his spare time, what kinds of fights he had with his mother, what kind of movies he dug. I mean, he's a person. So by now his being gay is just something else I know about him. I never thought I'd hear myself saying that.

In a straight person's mind, getting a homosexual guy in bed with a girl is going to be all he needs to make a miraculous change into being a heterosexual. It's funny. Some people think that the only reason you're gay is because you had a bad experience with a woman. Like a woman laughed at you or something. So they think all you need is a good experience to turn you straight.

I had more enjoyment with guys than I did with girls and it just confirmed what I had already been thinking. I cried about it a lot. I said to myself, you're a homosexual. And I didn't want to be, not then anyhow. I called myself all sorts of names: "You're a fag, you're a freak." Where was my belief in God? Where was my future with a wife and kids? All this was going through my mind at that time.

After people at school found out that I was gay, a lot of them kind of kept a distance from me. I think they were scared that I was going to do something to them. You know, the old fears about gay people attacking you and that junk. I guess that was one of the reasons why I didn't come out sooner, because I was afraid that they would be scared of me.

For me, it was a real lonely experience. I could never show the real me, especially that part of me, to anyone, because I felt that would mean no one would want to be with me. I was sure that if I told them about my

a finding that suggests that males in our society are particularly threatened or offended by homosexuality.

Not surprisingly, gay adolescents are often made to feel ashamed of themselves and engage in self-reproach for being unable to fit in with the majority's way of life. As a consequence, homosexual youths in some communities have attempted to create environments in which they can feel socially and sexually at ease—discos, restaurants, social clubs, and youth organizations where gays can interact without being taunted or physically threatened by heterosexuals. In 1984 the New York City Board of Education established a special high-school program for gay students who were being harrassed into chronic truancy and homosexual feelings, no one would care about me. The loneliness was awful.

Finally, just about when I was graduating from high school, I looked at myself and just accepted the fact that I was gay. I looked in the mirror and said, not "You're a homosexual," but "I'm a homosexual." And from that point on I could admit to myself who I was, and that made me a man in my own feelings. It's funny, because a lot of people think that being a homosexual robs a guy of his manhood. But for me, admitting my own homosexuality gave me my manhood.

The only other gay guys I knew in my high school were both jocks—real macho, on the football team and all that. I was clearly not as masculine as they were. In fact, I look more like the stereotype many people have of homosexuals. It's one thing to be gay and macho, and another to be gay and effeminate. I felt really isolated.

My mother said, "You didn't need to tell me. I knew it all the time." But I wanted to tell her, because it was coming from me. I needed to tell her, even if she already knew.

I've always been proud that I wasn't embarrassed about being a lesbian. I always enjoyed being able to open up other people's minds about it. Being different for me was a way of teaching people to respect others and to open their minds.

SOURCE: R. Bell, *Changing bodies, changing lives: A book for teens on sex and relationships.* New York: Random House, 1980, pp. 112–123. For more commentaries from adolescent homosexuals you may want to read S. Alyson's *Young, gay and proud;* A Heron's *One teenager in ten: Writings by gay and lesbian youth;* and A. Fricke's *Reflections of a rock lobster: A story about growing up gay* (Boston: Alyson Publications); or S. Wolfe and J. Stanley's *The coming out stories* (Watertown, Mass.: Persephone Press, 1980).

dropping out of school by their heterosexual classmates in their former schools (Bridgman, 1985). (See Box 10.4.)

The Process of "Coming Out"

Given the prevailing attitudes against homosexuality in many communities, the reluctance of gay or bisexual adolescents to "come out of the closet" is understandable. Fearing rejection, humiliation, and physical harm, many youngsters live with the tensions, confusion, and loneliness of having to hide their

10.4 A Closer Look

N.Y.C. Schools Fund Program for Homosexuals

Off-Site Service for Victims of Harassment

by Anne Bridgman

The New York City Board of Education has contracted with a private, nonprofit homosexual-rights institute to offer a special academic high-school program geared to homosexual students who, because of harassment in school, have become chronic truants and dropouts.

The program, informally called the Harvey Milk School, is one of 39 "off-site educational services" provided by the New York City public schools in conjunction with community-based organizations to serve youths who have problems in conventional schools, according to Joseph Mancini, a spokesman for the school board.

Named after the San Francisco city supervisor and homosexual activist who was murdered in 1978, the six-week-old program operates in a Greenwich Village church, enrolling 14 boys and 6 girls.

The program, believed to be the first of its kind in the nation, has the backing of Mayor Edward I. Koch. "As far as the educational component is concerned, the mayor said he's supportive of it because it is helping kids stay in school instead of dropping out," said Larry Simonberg, a spokesman for Mr. Koch.

"Driven Out of Schools"

The Institute for the Protection of Lesbian and Gay Youth, a four-year-old social-service agency, first approached the school board with a request that it supply a teacher for the program last June, according to A. Damien Martin, the institute's executive director.

"The special problem is not the homosexuality, but the harassment the kids have experienced," Mr. Martin explained. "These kids were already separated; they were driven out of the schools."

The board's professional staff approved the program and appropriated $50,000 to cover the costs of a teacher, curriculum materials, and supervisory assistance, according to Mr. Mancini. Because the board established the off-site-services program several years ago, it was not necessary for all board members to ratify the establishment of the Harvey Milk School.

The institute, which is supported through private donations and through contracts with the New York City Youth Bureau and the New York State Division for Youth, will supply approximately $15,000 to $20,000 for rent and other materials, Mr. Martin said.

"School-Phobic"

The 20 students who are enrolled in the program are dropouts or truants who have received counseling at the institute, which annually offers social services to 800 gay and lesbian youths, their families, and others, according to Mr. Martin.

The institute counsels students who are often "school-phobic" and concerned about the harassment they have experienced at school, according to Mr. Martin. Many of the youths, he said, are "terrified about going to school" and do not perform well academically because they are afraid to draw attention to themselves. Some have been the victims of violence, he said.

The students who are enrolled in the program are "tremendously relieved," Mr. Martin said. "We have kids who haven't been to school for two years, who go every day now, who want to learn."

Students who are interested in enrolling in the program are screened by its teacher and program director, according to Mr. Martin, to ascertain their problems, experiences, and academic needs.

Specific Problems

"We don't want them to come to the school just because they're gay or lesbian," Mr. Martin said. "They have to have specific problems. We're not trying to set up some sort of ghetto."

Mr. Martin also noted that the program would accept students who are not homosexual but who are having problems in other areas and are referred to the program by city social-service agencies. "We do not discriminate against anybody on any grounds," he said.

Mr. Martin said the institute plans to spend the summer searching for new quarters, so the program can enroll more students, and contacting high-school guidance counselors who might know of students who could benefit from it. There are already about 60 names on a waiting list for fall enrollment, the board of education estimates.

Program's Legality

Leonard Graff, legal director of National Gay Rights Advocates, a nonprofit public-interest law firm in San Francisco, said the program "probably is legal because every child is entitled to a proper public-school education."

"It's a shame in one sense that the school administration is incapable of providing that kind of education within a mixed setting of the ordinary public-school system," he continued. "On the other hand, at least they've recognized that there is a problem, that there is a great number of such students with special needs."

SOURCE: *Education Week,* June 12, 1985, p. 7. Reprinted by permission.

homosexuality from friends and family, as well as from strangers. Nevertheless, with society's increasing tolerance for sexual diversity, adolescents are more likely than in former decades to disclose their homosexuality or bisexuality.

"Coming out" has been described as a process that occurs in stages (Weinrich, Gonsorick, & Holred, 1982). In the first stage people usually develop a poor self-concept as a consequence of their awareness of being gay in a predominantly heterosexual society. Adopting society's derogatory images of homosexuals as depressed, immoral, confused, or sick, these youngsters often do feel depressed by their situation. While some try to resolve the conflicts at this stage by seeking professional help, the less fortunate may attempt suicide or may succumb to chronic depression, which can continue into their adult lives.

In contrast, those who decide to disclose their sexual orientation have moved into the stage referred to as "coming out." People's reactions to an adolescent at this point are critical in determining his or her self-concept. Unfortunately, the gay adolescent's family and friends may react with recrimination, withdrawal, and shock, which can exacerbate the youth's feeling of self-hatred and shame. Even in cases where close friends and family suspected the truth long before it was announced, the adolescent may encounter distance, shock, or anger. Fearing negative reactions, some homosexuals choose to share the information with supportive friends before telling their families.

Following the initial disclosure, the young person typically enters a period of sexual exploration and experimentation which, to heterosexuals, may appear either irresponsible or promiscuous. Having been denied the opportunities to express themselves sexually, homosexuals need to undergo the same kinds of sexual experimenting that heterosexual youths experience. This stage is characterized by the awkwardness, intensity, confusion, and sexual experimentation that accompany almost everyone's entry into the world of dating and sexual activity. Thereafter, more stable, committed relationships with one partner are likely to be established between homosexuals.

Limitations of the Research

Although more reliable information about homosexual and bisexual adolescents has become available in recent years, many generalizations about homosexual youths are still predicated upon methodologically flawed data. First, many of the data have historically been collected from therapists working with gay clients. Information based on individual case studies, however, cannot legitimately be generalized to the gay population. To do so would be to ignore the fact that most people in therapy are either financially well-to-do or have exhibited forms of maladjustment that necessitated their referral to a therapist. Most gay adolescents would fit neither category. Furthermore, many individual therapists have failed to examine their own assumptions about homosexuality and have interpreted their gay clients' behavior from a strictly heterosexual perspective. Consequently, many of our assumptions regarding homosexuality are predicated on therapists' personal constructions of reality, derived from personal observations rather than based on carefully documented theories or empirical research.

Second, since strong sentiments against homosexuality still prevail in our society, it is likely that many of those who collect and interpret the data will inadvertently reflect a heterosexual bias. In this regard, it is noteworthy that most research has focused exclusively on trying to unearth the causes of homosexuality—a focus that, in and of itself, presupposes that homosexuality must be eliminated and prevented. In contrast, very few investigators have directed their attention to questions that might better serve the needs of gay adolescents: How do gay people develop strategies for coping with discrimination? How might society help gay adolescents function successfully in a heterosexual society? How can high schools discourage discrimination against gay students and foster a more accurate understanding of homosexuality?

Finally, our generalizations about the impact homosexuality may have on an adolescent's life are limited by the skewed samples from which the data are derived. Most studies have either relied on samples of adult homosexuals experiencing legal or psychological problems or adults who are politically active and outspoken about their homosexuality. Similarly, many studies have relied on white, middle-class, well-educated males who are willing to discuss their homosexuality with researchers. Such sampling leaves us with little information about homosexuals who are female, less well-educated, poor, nonwhite, or young.

Given these limitations, definitive statements about homosexual and bisexual adolescents would be both hasty and empirically indefensible. Until more data are available from random samples of young males and females who are either exclusively or primarily homosexual, we are best advised to limit our generalizations to the realm of tentative hypotheses.

A NEW MORALITY?

Have the majority of adolescents adopted a "new morality" by rejecting many of the sexual mores of the preceding generation? According to most data, yes. Adopting a new morality, however, is not a phenomenon limited to the young. Indeed, most adults have also modified the sexual beliefs that were prevalent during their youth, a fact evidenced by voters' support on issues like legalizing abortion and permitting homosexuals to hold public office. Likewise, most adults have accepted expressions of sexuality in movies, television, and popular song lyrics that would have shocked their own peers a decade ago. For example, an analysis of 64 prime-time television programs in 1977 revealed four times more flirtatious or seductive behavior than was aired in 1975. Moreover, topics like homosexuality, incest, prostitution, and sexual aggression appeared once every 1½ to 2 hours during prime-time hours (Silverman, Sprafkin, & Rubinstein, 1978).

Similarly, most U.S. adults have become more tolerant of premarital sex and of couples living together without being legally married. For example, in national surveys conducted during 1969 only one-fifth of the adult population approved of premarital sex. By 1979, 55 percent said it was acceptable (Reinhold, 1979). Given the new sexual mores of the older generation, it is hardly surprising that today's adolescents are more sexually liberal than adolescents in their parents' generation.

This is not to imply that no differences exist between the sexual attitudes of adolescents and their parents. Although the differences have narrowed in recent years, the fact that several decades may separate adolescents from their parents is bound to have some impact on their respective views of the world. For example, adolescents and young adults are still more approving than older Americans of premarital sex, of contraceptives for minors, and of cohabitation without marriage (Conger, 1980). In several recent polls, approximately half of the adults surveyed disapproved of premarital sex and cohabitation (Gallup, 1979; Glenn & Weaver, 1979; Singh, 1980). In contrast, about 75 percent of the adolescent population condones premarital sex and cohabitation without marriage (Astin, 1981; Norman & Harris, 1981; Sorensen, 1973). It is worth noting that both adults and adolescents with the least education, the lower income, and the strongest religious affiliations tend to express similar sexual values. Thus, variables other than age can exert a strong influence on any particular individual's sexual attitudes.

In constrast to their elders, adolescents are generally more honest and self-disclosing about sexual issues and more apt to base sexual decisions on personal judgments than on institutionalized social codes (Bell, 1980; Center for Population Options, 1980; Conger, 1980; Yankelovich, 1974). Nevertheless, these differences between young and old should not be misconstrued to mean that adolescents are unprincipled or amoral in regard to their sexual conduct. To the contrary, most young people disapprove of having premarital intercourse when no love exists between the two people. Moreover, most adolescents do not name sex as the most important dimension of their relationships with the opposite sex (Allgeier & Allgeier, 1983; Conger, 1980; Haas, 1979; Norman & Harris, 1981; Sorensen, 1973). Given the greater sexual openness and freedom available to today's adolescents, it might even be argued that the young are less preoccupied with sex and more interested in other dimensions of a relationship than young people were in their parents' generation.

A caveat worth repeating is that adolescents cannot be perceived as a monolithic group in terms of their sexual attitudes and behavior. It must always be kept in mind that age cannot be the sole criterion for predicting an individual's sexual attitudes. Some young people are more conservative than their elders. Similarly, although some young people conduct themselves sexually in purely selfish terms, others, despite their age, are capable of considering the emotional well-being of their partners and of restraining their own needs.

In this regard, it has been suggested that adolescents adopt one of three kinds of moral reasoning when making sexual decisions (D'Augelli & D'Augelli, 1977). In the first, referred to as "egoistic reasoning," individuals perceive sexual relationships solely in terms of their own gains and losses. Accordingly, a relationship offering immediate sexual benefits is better than one that requires self-sacrifice. In the second level of moral judgment, referred to as "dyadic reasoning," the young person relinquishes his or her own needs in light of the other's expectations. Thus, in contrast to his own values, a boy might agree to have intercourse in order to meet his girlfriend's expectations. In the most sophisticated level of sexual reasoning, however, "interactive reasoning," both partners express their own needs and reach a mutual decision about their sexual behavior. Neither forces the other to disregard his or her own feelings, and both share in the sexual decision making.

Sexually transmitted diseases

Even adults who condone premarital sex worry about two serious threats to the sexually active adolescent's well-being: pregnancy and disease. Undeniably, many sexually active adults also find themselves the victims of these two unwelcomed events. The rates of unplanned pregnancy and venereal disease are escalating, however, far more dramatically among the young. At present, venereal disease is most common among 20- to 24-year-olds, with 15- to 19-year-olds having the next highest rates. Although venereal diseases occur least frequently among those under age 14, the rates are increasing at the fastest rate among this age group. It has been estimated that half of all young people will contract either gonorrhea or syphilis by the time they are 25 (NIAID Study Group, 1981).

In spite of the fact that most adolescents are aware of the dangers of sexually transmitted diseases, they are often uninformed about the symptoms, treatments, or methods of prevention. As Box 10.5 illustrates, many of today's supposedly sophisticated adolescents are dangerously misinformed. The most common sexually transmitted diseases can be classified in three categories: the viruses, such as herpes and AIDS; the bacteria, such as gonorrhea, syphilis, and chlamydia; and the yeast infections, such as monilia.

AIDS: Acquired Immune Deficiency Syndrome

Although far more rare than any other sexually transmitted disease in the adolescent or adult population, the AIDS virus is unrivaled in terms of the terror and publicity it has generated in the U.S. public. Having first come to the general public's attention in the early 1980s as a disease confined to homosexuals and intravenous drug users, AIDS created alarm among heterosexuals, as it became apparent that the virus could definitely be contracted through contaminated blood and hypodermic needles, through anal, oral, or genital sex with bisexuals, and possibly through tears and saliva. By the summer of 1985 when actor Rock Hudson—emaciated and sunken-eyed—publicly announced that he was dying from AIDS, heterosexual adolescents and their elders could no longer dismiss the virus as a malady confined to homosexuals. For example, in Africa, AIDS strikes males and females in equal proportions. Moreover, nearly 30 percent of all AIDS cases in the United States in 1985 involved heterosexuals, although it is important to note that many of these individuals were intravenous drug users ("AIDS," 1985).

Of special relevance to adolescents is the controversy surrounding young people who have contracted the virus. For example, one 13-year-old hemophiliac contracted AIDS while receiving injections of a clotting agent and was barred from resuming his seventh-grade classes ("AIDS," 1985). Yet in a small Massachusetts town, the superintendent, doctors, and school officials met with 700 parents to defend their decision to admit a 13-year-old AIDS patient to school ("AIDS Conflict," 1985). While some parents have refused to let their children attend schools where someone with AIDS is known to be enrolled, others contend that children with the disease should not be ostracized from society on the basis of present knowledge regarding how the virus is spread.

10.5 Are You Sure?

Adolescents' Misconceptions about Venereal Diseases

Which of the following are true?

1. If the symptoms of the venereal disease go away, it means I'm cured.
2. Wearing a prophylactic is a fail-safe way to protect against herpes.
3. Diaphragms and contraceptive jellies offer no protection against sexually transmitted diseases.
4. If someone has herpes, gonorrhea, or syphilis, I could see the sores or a discharge or some other visible sign that he or she is infected.
5. Once people have had a venereal disease and have been cured, they cannot contract it again, because they are immune.
6. The only sexually transmitted diseases are gonorrhea, herpes, and syphilis.
7. I cannot contract or transmit a venereal disease through oral sex.
8. Homosexuals do not have to worry about catching venereal diseases.
9. If a person catches a venereal disease, he or she will definitely know about the infection from their symptoms.
10. Penicillin and other modern drugs can cure all venereal diseases.
11. Urinating before and after sex will protect me from catching VD.
12. If a female has a vaginal discharge, this means she has VD.
13. You can't infect other people with herpes unless you have visible sores.
14. Symptoms of a venereal disease will always show up within a month or so of contracting the infection.
15. You can't catch genital herpes from kissing someone who has cold sores on the lips.
16. You can easily catch venereal disease from toilet seats, towels, swimming pools, or door knobs.
17. There's no permanent damage that can be done from any venereal disease except herpes.
18. Douching immediately after intercourse prevents girls from catching venereal diseases.
19. Birth-control pills and the I.U.D. reduce a girl's chances of catching venereal diseases.
20. Once you've finished taking the medicine prescribed by a doctor for VD, you can be sure it's gone and it's safe to have sex again.

Answers: All 20 statements are false.

SOURCE: R. Bell, *Changing bodies, changing lives: A book for teens on sex and relationships.* New York: Random House, 1980.

Initially heralded by some as "God's revenge" on homosexuals, it was argued by homosexuals that the public's outrage over AIDS was just another form of persecution against gay people (Cahill, 1983). Such political and social controversies notwithstanding, the AIDS virus poses a lethal threat to adolescents whose sexual activities put them at greatest risk for contracting this disease. Since the disease was first recognized in 1979, the number of AIDS victims has at least doubled every year, with more than 12,067 cases recorded in the United States alone and with 6,000 deaths attributed to the disease by 1985 ("AIDS," 1985). The symptoms include swollen glands, fatigue, profuse sweating at night, and weight loss. Most of the victims are homosexual males under age 50 who live in large cities on the east and west coasts. While much still remains unknown, it presently appears that AIDS is spread primarily through contact with the semen or blood of an infected person. Thus, heterosexual youths can contract the virus through blood transfusions or through skin punctures that might occur in ear piercing, tattooing, or sharing hypodermic needles.

Evidence that AIDS might be transmitted through saliva has stirred up a new controversy and fright: If an infected person sneezes on your food or gives you a welcoming kiss at a party, can you contract AIDS? Although there is no documentation of AIDS being spread by saliva, some researchers are concerned because the virus has shown up in saliva samples of AIDS victims. Though most experts concur that the AIDS virus is unlikely to be spread through saliva, some warn that intimate kissing might spread AIDS, since the virus is thought to enter the body through broken skin and mucous membranes—both of which are common inside the mouth ("New AIDS Saliva Scare," 1984).

Whatever theory eventually proves correct, the indisputable fact is that AIDS kills its victims by destroying the immune system. Because the victim's body can no longer produce antibodies to fight ordinary infections, the person eventually dies of diseases that are ordinarily not fatal, like pneumonia, herpes, or some forms of cancer.

Sexually active adolescents, either homosexual or heterosexual, can reduce the likelihood of their contracting the AIDS virus by taking certain precautionary measures. First, sex with strangers or sex with people living in metropolitan areas where AIDS is most prevalent should be entered into with great caution, if not avoided altogether. Second, condoms might offer some protection against the virus, although the data are inconclusive and contradictory on this point. Third, a test is now available that permits a person to determine if he or she has been exposed to the AIDS virus. Although not everyone who is exposed to the virus will contract AIDS, adolescents who receive positive results from the test should refrain from further sexual contacts until their physician advises otherwise.

Herpes Simplex

Although AIDS has undoubtedly become the nation's most frightening sexually transmitted disease, herpes remains the more distressing illness in terms of its prevalence in the adolescent population. It appears that about one fifth of the U.S. population is currently infected with genital herpes, with over half a million new cases being reported each year (NIAID Study Group, 1981). Among the officially reported cases, the typical herpes victim is white, well educated, and finacially well-off. About 51 percent of herpes victims are female, 95 percent are white, 53 percent have at least a college degree, 80 percent are between 20 and 39 years old, and 56 percent earn at least $21,000 a year. As health specialists have noted, however, the incidence of herpes is undoubtedly higher than officially reported among minorities and the poor who cannot afford medical services. Nevertheless, on the basis of the official medical data, herpes is often referred to as "the venereal disease of the Ivy League" ("*Time*'s New Scarlet Letter," 1982).

Although not identified until 1940 as a virus, herpes is not a new disease ("*Time*'s New Scarlet Letter," 1982). The Roman Emperor Tiberius supposedly banned kissing because of the epidemic of lip sores created by herpes. Not until the late 1960s, however, did researchers discover that there were two types of herpes virus. One strain, called Type I herpes virus, causes chicken pox, shingles (a painful skin disease), and common cold sores that appear around the mouth.

The strain responsible for genital herpes is the Type II herpes virus—a virus that continues to mystify researchers in terms of both prevention and cure. Only recently has it been discovered that Type I herpes can be transferred from cold sores to the genitals by finger or mouth, thereby causing genital herpes. Thus, while hoping to avoid herpes by refraining from intercourse, adolescents may contract the virus through oral-genital sex and other intimate forms of foreplay. Researchers are still debating whether young people can protect themselves from herpes by using condoms, since the virus may be small enough to penetrate a prophylactic. Sadly, some evidence suggests that herpes can be spread by contaminated towels and toilet seats, since live viruses have been found on some objects up to 72 hours after contact with a herpes victim. Although the data are still inconclusive on this point, some doctors warn herpes victims and their friends not to share towels or bathroom facilities ("*Time*'s New Scarlet Letter," 1982).

Ironically, some data indicate that adolescents from lower socioeconomic classes may have less chance of contracting the herpes II virus than children from higher-income families. According to this hypothesis, the lower rates of genital herpes among the poor might be related to their higher incidence of cold sores as children. Since richer parents tend to emphasize excessive cleanliness, their children seldom contract Type I herpes and therefore don't form the type of antibodies that seem to offer some protection against genital herpes later in life.

Whether or not the hypothesis about socioeconomic class is ultimately confirmed, one uncontested fact remains: Once an adolescent contracts Type II herpes, he or she is infected for life. Although researchers have made considerable progress in developing medication for the treatment of the herpes blisters, neither a vaccine nor a cure is presently avialable. While not every adolescent who is exposed to the herpes virus will contract the disease, those who do first experience an itching or tingling sensation around their genitals. These initial symptoms may also be accompanied by a slight fever, headache, swollen glands, and general achiness—all of which are easily ignored by naive young people who may mistake the symptoms for a simple case of the flu. Although the incubation period may last up to a year, most adolescents develop the small, painful, red blisters around the genital area within 2 to 20 days after contact.

The initial outbreak of blisters can endure as long as two weeks, after which they may never reappear or may return periodically throughout the individual's lifetime. Unfortunately, many adolescents deceive themselves into believing they are "cured" after the blisters disappear, as they inevitably do, even without any medical treatment. The virus, however, is alive and well, traveling up the nerves to the base of the skull, the spinal column, or the ganglia to live in a dormant state until the next outbreak.

Although the first attack is usually the most severe and most painful for both male and female adolescents, the virus poses far more serious threats to the female (Bell, 1980). For unknown reasons, females tend to have more painful and more frequent attacks than males. More seriously, girls with herpes are eight times more likely than uninfected females to develop cervical cancer (*Harvard Medical School Health Letter,* 1981). For this reason, females with herpes should have a PAP test for the early detection of cancer twice a year for the rest of their lives. More sadly still, a baby can contract the herpes virus as it passes through the birth canal of an infected mother. Consequently, a female whose herpes virus is in its active state near the time of delivery is advised to have a Caesarean section. Herpes can also cause miscarriages, birth defects, and brain damage to the unborn infant.

Some people are asymptomatic carriers, meaning that they show no external symptoms of having the disease. Because girls' sores may appear only inside the vagina, the virus is often harbored unknowingly and transmitted innocently to others. Similarly, boys may carry the virus without symptoms.

Although we cannot presently offer adolescents a cure for herpes, we can offer them advice for diminishing the severity and the frequency of their attacks (Bell, 1980; "*Time*'s New Scarlet Letter," 1982). When an adolescent is under stress, sick, upset, run-down, tired, or exposed to too much sun, the herpes virus tends to be reactivated. Thus, avoiding junk foods, staying out of the sun as much as possible, and getting enough sleep and exercise are advised as prophylactics against further attacks. Furthermore, friction from clothing can also trigger an attack, so herpes victims are well advised to dispose of their skin-tight jeans, snug-fitting underwear, and pantyhose. Prescribed drugs are also available to reduce the blisters' pain during an attack, although it has been argued that topical creams can spread the infection, and some physicians refuse to prescribe them. Some doctors recommend applying ice and keeping the sores as clean and dry as possible.

Unknown to themselves, infected adolescents can spread the virus to their friends in the days prior to the actual appearance of the sores. Therefore, it is of utmost importance that young people learn to recognize their preattack symptoms, which may include tingling or tenderness around the mouth or genital area, a dry or red spot on the skin, fever, swollen glands, or flulike aches and depression. Although condoms cannot be considered absolute safeguards against the virus, adolescents who have had a herpes attack or who are having intercourse with someone who has herpes are advised to use prophylactics. Adolescents must be made to understand, however, that using condoms is no substitute for honesty with their sexual partners. Since it appears that the virus is sometimes contracted even when no sores are visible, and since condoms are not an absolute assurance of protection, only by telling one's lover the truth can fairness be assured.

Understandably, adolescents with herpes often experience considerable remorse, guilt, anger, sadness, and stress. Some become seriously depressed and impotent, while others feel "dirty" and become obsessed with constant bathing. Living in shame and social isolation, many fear that nobody except another herpes victim would want to have sex with or marry them. Although it is legitimate to argue that adolescents with herpes should apprise their dates and perhaps even their closest friends of the situation, their hesitancy to disclose this information is surely understandable. By way of empathizing, we might ask ourselves: Would I have sex with someone who was honorable enough to tell me that he or she had herpes? Would I accept a date with someone who I knew had herpes? Would I feel comfortable sharing a bathroom with a roommate who had herpes?

Fortunately, many young people with herpes have found professional counselors who help them cope with the psychological, social, and physical aspects of their disease. Indeed, some of the most effective counselors are themselves herpes victims. Sharing this fact with their clients, these therapists are often the best qualified to empathize with the young victim's physical and psychological pain ("*Time*'s New Scarlet Letter," 1982).

Gonorrhea

Less worrisome than herpes, because it can be cured with antibiotics, gonorrhea nevertheless continues to effect thousands of adolescents. Also known as "the clap," "dose," "drip," "morning dew," "gleet," and "the whites," gonorrhea is caused by the gonococcus bacteria. Since these bacteria die on contact with air, there is no truth to the myths that gonorrhea can be contracted from swimming pools, clothing, door knobs, or toilet seats. Adolescents contract this disease in two ways: through anal or vaginal intercourse and oral-genital sex. Even though gonorrhea is less frightening than herpes because it can be cured, it's consequences are far more serious if left untreated. The gonococcus bacteria are twice as prevalent as the herpes virus among both young and old, with approximately one million new cases of gonorrhea reported each year in the entire population (NIAID Study Group, 1981).

Since the gonococcus bacteria grow well in the vagina, penis, mouth, throat, and anus, adolescents who perform fellatio or cunnilingus can contract gonorrhea of the throat. The bacteria can also be spread through anal sex. Though most symptoms show up within two weeks after contact, almost 80 percent of all infected females and 10 to 20 percent of infected males are asymptomatic. Since its symptoms are less likely to be recognized by its young carriers, gonorrhea is more easily spread than herpes. If symptoms do occur, the infected girl will experience frequent urination, lower abdominal pain, swollen glands, sore throat, or a discharge from the anus or vagina. The most common symptoms among males are a discharge from the penis (sometimes noticed as a drip before urinating in the morning), burning, itching, or pain when urinating, sore throat or swollen glands, and discharge from the anus. An adolescent's doctor must diagnose the disease by taking cultures from the affected area or by conducting a gram-stain test on the male's discharge.

Fortunately for adolescents who detect the disease, it is curable with antibiotics. Unfortunately, too many fearful youngsters borrow inappropriate antibiotics or divide their own prescription with a friend without realizing that the medicine is effective only if taken in its full dose for the full period of time prescribed. Even after taking the medicine correctly, adolescents should return to their doctors for another test, to be certain that all the bacteria have been destroyed. Since, like herpes, gonorrhea's symptoms will disappear on their own without medical treatment, many adolescents never seek a doctor's counsel and continue to spread the bacteria to other sexual partners. Unlike herpes, untreated gonorrhea can inflict permanent, irreversible damage to the reproductive organs, rendering both males and females infertile. If the gonococcus bacteria infect the eyes, blindness can result.

Unlike the herpes and AIDS viruses, the gonococcus bacteria can be barricaded by condoms and spermicides. Using a diaphragm in conjunction with a spermicide or using the vaginal sponge (which is already presaturated with spermicide) affords adolescents additional protection. In addition, gargling with salt water immediately after oral sex acts as a deterrent to gonorrhea of the throat, and squeezing the penis for signs of any suspicious discharge provides some assurance regarding the absence or presence of an infection (Bell, 1980; Boston Women's Health Collective, 1984).

Syphilis

If an adolescent catches a venereal disease, it is unlikely to be syphilis. Only about 100,000 new cases are reported annually (NIAID Study Group, 1981). Caused by spiral-shaped bacteria, syphilis can be cured with antiobiotics. Sometimes called "siff," "the pox," "lues," "bad blood," "Old Joe," or "haircut," syphilis first appears as sores, called chancres, around the genitals or mouth. Unlike herpes sores, syphilis sores are painless. A rash may also appear on the body, especially on the hands and feet. The sores usually appear within 10 to 90 days after oral sex, anal sex, or vaginal intercourse with an infected person. The sores gradually disappear without any medication, while the bacteria continue to thrive inside the victim's body. Several months after the sores disappear, some people notice other symptoms: fever, aches, sore throat, mouth sores, swollen glands, rash, loss of hair. These symptoms also disappear without any treatment. During these first two stages of the disease the infected adolescent is highly contagious.

Unfortunately, as with herpes and gonorrhea, many victims are asymptomatic. Consequently, no matter how carefully an adolescent visually inspects a sexual partner, there is no way to be absolutely certain whether he or she has syphilis, gonorrhea, or herpes. More distressing, some young people never consult a doctor because the symptoms gradually disappear without medical treatment. The same kinds of prophylactic measures, however, that diminish adolescents' chances of catching the gonococcus bacteria appear to offer some protection against syphilis. On the basis of a blood test or an examination of the rash or chancres, doctors can reliably diagnose and treat the bacteria. Unfortunately, too many young victims stop taking their medicine as soon as they start feeling better and never return for a second examination to determine whether all the bacteria have been destroyed. If not completely destroyed, the syphilis bacteria can cause heart disease, blindness, deafness, insanity, paralysis, and death.

Yeast Infections

Although many adolescents assume that any form of discharge or genital irritation indicates the presence of a venereal disease, this is not the case. A number of infections in both males and females can be caused by an overproduction of yeast in the reproductive or urinary tracts. Yeast and bacteria are always present in the healthy vagina and around the male's penis and anus. Sometimes, however, due to changes in diet, excessively hot weather, nylon underwear, or deodorant soaps and douches, these microorganisms get out of balance and multiply beyond their natural limits. Although these infections can be extremely uncomfortable, often accompanied by painful urination, itching, and burning, they cause no permanent damage even when untreated. Nevertheless, these infections seldom disappear without treatment and are easily communicated to sexual partners. Thus, adolescents should seek medical advice for these genital or urinary-tract infections.

Depending on the type of infection, the adolescent may be treated with oral medicines, vaginal suppositories, or topical creams applied to the penis. Nonprescription treatments like douches and anti-itching creams only mask the symptoms temporarily and may even spread the infection. Moreover, unless both sexual partners are treated, these annoying infections continue to recur as the untreated partner continues to reinfect the other.

In sum, adults must somehow convince more adolescents to seek medical advice whenever signs of a genital infection appear or whenever they suspect they have been exposed to a sexually communicable disease. Given the understandable embarrassment that surrounds sexually transmitted diseases, the most crucial task is to help the young overcome their shyness in regard to protecting their own health and the health of their sexual partners. Only by being helped to overcome their timidity and their discomfort can young people learn to ask their dates the appropriate questions before having sex, to seek medical advice when necessary, and to notify their sexual partners of any signs of disease. Medical handbooks written especially for young people, such as *Changing Bodies, Changing Lives,* should be made visibly available in every school library and at home in order to keep adolescents apprised of the most recent information regarding sexually transmitted diseases (Bell, 1980).

PREGNANCY DURING ADOLESCENCE

Although sexually transmitted diseases frequently capture the public's attention, another less publicized ramification of adolescent sexuality is statistically far more rampant—pregnancy. Each year in the United States more than one million girls between the ages of 13 and 19 become pregnant (Alan Guttmacher Institute, 1984). As might not be fully realized, the ramifications of teenage pregnancy extend far beyond the $8.3 billion that supporting adolescents' children costs taxpayers each year (Center for Population Options, 1980). Given the enormous financial, educational, and psychological burdens that accompany unplanned teenaged pregnancies, it is little wonder that researchers continue to pursue the question. Given the availability of contraception, why do one million adolescent girls become pregnant each year?

A Pregnancy Epidemic?

The statistics on adolescent pregnancy are starkly sobering: More than one-tenth of all adolescent girls become pregnant each year. In 1982 alone, almost

10,000 girls under the age of 15 and 514,000 girls between the ages of 15 and 19 gave birth to children, while nearly another 500,000 terminated their unplanned pregnancies ("Natality Statistics," 1984). If current trends continue, approximately 780,000 (40 percent) of the two million girls who turned 14 in 1981 will have at least one pregnancy, 420,000 will have at least one baby, and 300,000 will undergo at least one abortion before the age of 20. Moreover, nearly one-fifth of the girls who become pregnant will have a second pregnancy before their adolescence ends. Given such statistics, it is not surprising that U.S. teenagers have one of the highest birthrates in the industrialized nations of the world. For example, in Japan only 3 out of every thousand births are to teenagers, compared to 52 out of every thousand in the United States (Alan Guttmacher Institute, 1981a, 1981b).

Although these statistics seem to suggest that today's adolescents are responsible for an unprecedented "epidemic" of pregnancies, the data need to be examined more thoroughly before casting such aspersions on the young. First, adolescent girls have no more than their statistical fair share of children, when compared to older females. For example, in 1978, adolescents accounted for about 17 percent of the fertile female population and for 18 percent of the births (Alan Guttmacher Institute, 1984). More important, a smaller percentage of the adolescent population is giving birth than in previous decades. By way of comparison, in the "conservative" year of 1957, a higher percentage of teenagers gave birth than in the "liberal" 1960s, 1970s, and 1980s. Unfortunately, however, the decreases in birthrate have occurred primarily among older adolescents, with the birthrate for girls under age 15 remaining constant (Alan Guttmacher Institute, 1984). It is also noteworthy that females with the least education are having fewer children than in previous decades (Scott, 1982).

In view of the decline in the overall percentage of adolescents giving birth, why are adolescents often accused of being responsible for an unprecedented increase in birthrates? One reason is that teenage pregnancy and illegitimacy are less apt to be hidden from public view than previously. In the "good old days," pregnant girls were not allowed to attend school, to continue working, or to socialize with "decent" girls. Significantly, "shotgun weddings" made most unplanned pregnancies appear legitimate. Furthermore, since today's adolescents account for a larger percentage of the nation's population than before, the actual number of teenage pregnancies has increased in comparison to the past. There has also been more publicity about the costs that indirectly fall upon taxpayers as a consequence of teenagers' illegitimate births. Finally, as the number of teenage pregnancies among the white middle class has increased, parents have become more aware that their higher socioeconomic class provides no immunity against unplanned pregnancies (Zelnick, Kantner, & Ford, 1981).

Although the birthrates among adolescents are not burgeoning, as is often presumed, the illegitimacy rates among adolescents are far higher than among older parents—a trend that has increased steadily in the past decade. Teenaged mothers gave birth to approximately 40 percent of the nation's illegitimate children in 1982, a total of 269,346 babies ("Natality Statistics," 1984). Illustrating the rapidity with which out-of-wedlock births have grown, between 1950 and 1978 illegitimate births tripled among girls under the age of 15. Similarly, illegitimate births among all adolescents increased by 34 percent during the 1960s and by 13 percent during the 1970s (U.S. Bureau of the Census, 1980). As a consequence, there are now 1.3 million children living with 1.1 million adolescent mothers, only about half of whom are married (Alan Guttmacher Institute, 1981a, 1981b).

In regard to racial differences, it is noteworthy that the 13 percent rise in illegitimacy during the 1970s was almost totally a consequence of births to white females. As the popularity of "shotgun" weddings has declined, white illegitimacy rates have risen. For example, between 1963 and 1966, 77 percent of all pregnant white girls married, in comparison with only 58 percent between 1975 and 1978. In contrast, illegitimate births decreased by 7 percent among black adolescents during the 1970s (Zelnick, Kantner, & Ford, 1981). Despite the rapid rise in white illegitimacy rates, however, girls from minority groups are still more likely than white females to have children out of wedlock—a difference partially accounted for by the fact that white girls are the most likely to abort their unplanned pregnancies. For example, as Table 10.1 illustrates, in 1980, of the births to black adolescents 85 percent were illegitimate, in contrast to 33 percent of the births to whites (Ventura, 1983).

Table 10.1

Percentage of Births to Unmarried Adolescent Girls: 1980

Age	All Races (Percent)	Hispanic (Percent)						White (Percent)	Black (Percent)
		Total	Mexican	Puerto Rican	Cuban	Other			
Under 20	48.3	42.5	37.6	66.8	24.0	47.3		33.4	85.6
Under 15	88.7	73.6	68.8	88.5	—	83.8		75.4	98.5
15–17	61.5	50.7	45.4	73.4	33.8	50.2		45.2	92.8
18–19	39.8	36.5	31.9	61.1	19.8	40.8		27.0	79.2

SOURCE: S. Ventura, Births of Hispanic percentage: 1980. *Monthly Vital Statistics Reports*, 1983, *32*, p. 4.

Abortion

Incidence The Supreme Court's 1973 *Wade* v. *Rowe* decision has dramatically altered the lives of millions of U.S. adolescents. The number of teenage abortions more than doubled in the five years following the Court's ruling, until by 1978 more adolescents were terminating their unplanned pregnancies than were choosing to carry the pregnancy to term. Indeed, the pregnancy rate among adolescents has declined by nearly 25 percent in the ten years since abortion has been legalized, as Figure 10.2 illustrates ("Natality Statistics," 1984).

National data from 1981 provide the most recent demographic profile of females who choose to terminate unplanned pregnancies (Alan Guttmacher Institute, 1984). Approximately 70 percent of all abortions are performed on white females, although the percentage of nonwhite females who obtain abortions is almost twice that of whites. Specifically, 2 percent of all white women aged 15 to 44 have abortions, compared with 6 percent of nonwhite women. In regard to age, females under the age of 19 account for nearly 30 percent of all abortions and women in their twenties account for another 35 percent. Contrary to what some opponents of legalized abortion predicted, however, legal abortion has not made adolescents less responsible about using contraceptives. In fact, Figure 10.3 demonstrates that contraceptive use has increased by 35 percent since 1973 (Alan Guttmacher Institute, 1984).

Nationwide, about 40 percent of all medical clinics require parental consent before terminating pregnancies of girls under 16. Yet more than half of the girls under 18 who terminate a pregnancy tell their parents. It has been estimated that if all clinics required parental consent, 19,000 girls each year would resort to self-induced or illegal abortions and another 18,000 would continue an unplanned pregnancy to term. Thus, the experts are in general agreement that making abortions illegal or more difficult to obtain would not reduce adolescents' sexual activity, but would increase the number of illegitimate births (Alan Guttmacher Institute, 1981a, 1981b; Zelnick, Kantner, & Ford, 1981).

Factors Influencing Abortion Decisions The adolescents most likely to terminate an unwanted pregnancy are the rich, the white, and the well educated

Figure 10.2

Adolescent pregnancy rate and outcomes, 1970–1982[a]

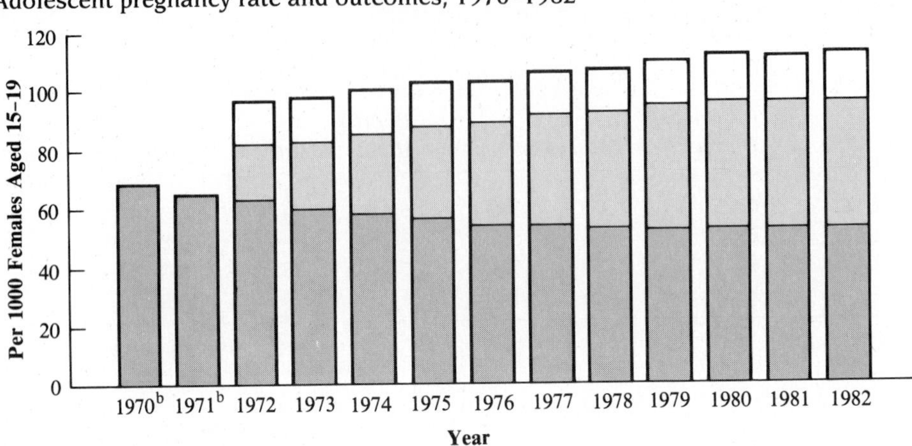

[a]The pregnancy rate is the sum of the birth rate, abortion rate, and miscarriage rate.
[b]Pregnancy, abortion, and miscarriage data are not available before 1972 because abortion was not legal in many areas at that time.

Miscarriage rate
Abortion rate
Birth rate

SOURCE: Alan Guttmacher Institute, *Birth data from National Center for Health Statistics,* 1982 (Vol. 33). September 1984, p. 16.

(Alan Guttmacher Institute, 1981; Zelnick, Kantner, & Ford, 1981). Since most girls eventually ask their mothers, boyfriends, or female friends for advice, these people's values inevitably play some role in many abortion decisions. The significance of other people's opinions, however, does not appear to be a constant or predictable variable. For example, in one recent study, the mother's advice was most important for white girls who gave their babies up for adoption and for black girls who chose abortion. White girls who decided to continue their pregnancies were persuaded to do so primarily by their boyfriends. Similarly, unmarried girls who continued their pregnancies had often heeded the advice of their mothers or other female relatives who were themselves unmarried mothers (Klerman et al., 1982).

A girl's decision is also partially determined by the amount of accurate and inaccurate information at her disposal (Dryfoos, 1982). For example, adolescents girls sometimes rule out the possibility of an abortion when operating under the false impression that the procedures endanger her future pregnancies. The more knowledgeable a girl is about the lifelong consequences of becoming an adolescent mother, the more likely she is to perceive abortion as a viable alternative. It is perhaps not surprising that girls who use contraceptives regularly are more likely to terminate an accidental pregnancy than girls who never or seldom used birth control (Bolton, 1980; Chilman, 1978).

One of the most compelling studies regarding adolescents' abortion decisions is Carol Gilligan's (1982) recent research at Harvard University. Both

Figure 10.3

Adolescents' contraceptive habits

Percentage of never-married sexually active women aged 15–19 from metropolitan areas, by whether they practiced contraception at last intercourse, according to type of method used, 1971, 1976, and 1979

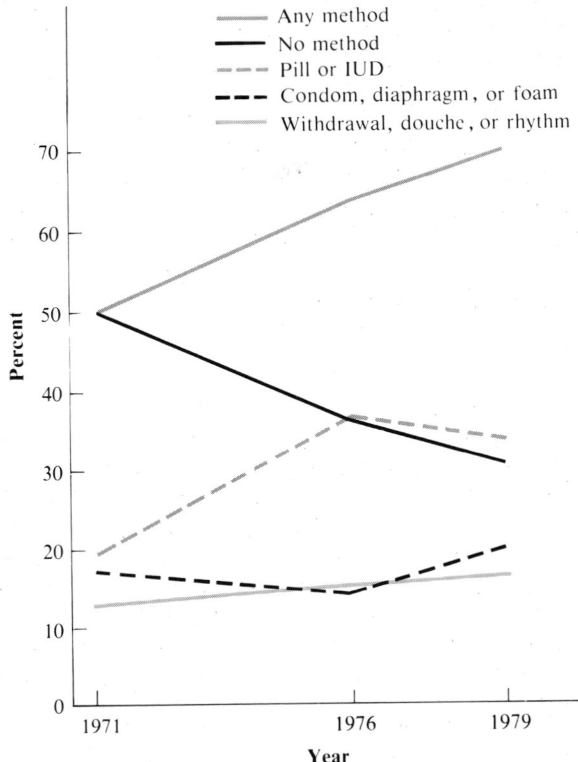

SOURCE: *Teenage pregnancy: The problem that hasn't gone away,* Alan Guttmacher Institute. New York, 1981, p. 11.

before and after their decisions, Gilligan interviewed 29 pregnant women between the ages of 15 and 33, who were contemplating abortions. Gilligan's primary purpose was to study the type of reasoning employed by females of different ages and socioeconomic and racial backgrounds in resolving moral dilemmas. Gilligan's research will be examined in Chapter 13 as it relates to the development of moral reasoning in females.

Although Gilligan was not investigating the issue of abortion per se, her results have a special significance to a discussion of adolescents' abortion decisions. To begin with, the females perceived their dilemma as being one of how to care for oneself while silmultaneously caring for other people. Stated differently, being "moral" was perceived to mean making a choice that hurt the fewest people, while making a decision in order to fulfill one's own desires was perceived as selfish. Unlike males, females were found to go through several distinct stages in resolving their moral dilemma of the unplanned pregnancy.

In the first phase, the females tended to focus exclusively on their own well-being and to make decisions regarding the pregnancy that fulfilled their own needs. For example, one woman may decide at this stage to have an abortion because she "selfishly" wants to continue her education and to have a child when she feels more mature. In contrast, another woman might "selfishly" decide not to abort the pregnancy because she wants an excuse to quit school and because having a baby would make her "feel like a real woman." The second stage of moral reasoning involves self-criticism: "I'm selfish and bad for only thinking about my own needs in this situation." At this point, one woman might reverse her decision to terminate the pregnancy because her boyfriend has expressed an ardent desire to have a child. Similarly, a woman who had first decided to continue the pregnancy might opt for an abortion because she has considered it "selfish" to disregard the child's financial and emotional needs, which she cannot meet. In the final phase of moral reasoning, a woman attempts to weigh her feelings for self-sacrifice against her concerns for other people.

Although Gilligan's research does not allow us to predict a pregnant girl's decisions, her findings reveal the types of reasoning that females seem to employ in moral dilemmas. Thus, in counseling a pregnant adolescent, we might help her to better understand the conflict she is undergoing between the needs of the self and the needs of others.

Ramifications of Abortion Given the moral difficulties involved in deciding to terminate an unplanned pregnancy, one might well wonder how adolescents respond to their decisions afterward (Bolton, 1980; Klerman et al., 1982). Most girls report feeling relieved after an abortion, with residual feelings of guilt or sadness usually being short-lived. The literature presently available suggests that most girls who terminate an unplanned pregnancy have fewer psychological problems thereafter than those who become mothers (Olson, 1980).

The medical procedures involved in abortions conducted by trained medical personnel during the first trimester of the pregnancy pose no threats to the female's physical well-being (Chilman, 1978). First-trimester abortions are not associated with birth defects, miscarriages, or difficult labor in later pregnancies. Moreover, for an adolescent whose own body is not yet mature, bearing a child can literally pose more dangers to her health than terminating the pregnancy. Unfortunately, however, teenagers are more likely than older women to postpone the abortion to the later, more dangerous weeks of pregnancy. Out of fear, embarrassment, or ignorance about the early symptoms of pregnancy, nearly 60 percent of the abortions among 15- to 19-year-olds take place after the eighth week of pregnancy. Indeed, and the younger the teenager, the more likely she is to delay an abortion (Alan Guttmacher Institute, 1981a, 1981b).

Motherhood's Impact on Adolescent Girls

Although the demands of motherhood require considerable energy and stamina at any age, adolescents who continue their unplanned pregnancies add a host of problems to their lives, which are not typically associated with motherhood at a later age (Simkins, 1984).

Perhaps the most serious consequence of adolescent motherhood is a lifetime of financial loss. Even when girls come from similar economic, social, and racial backgrounds, those who become mothers are only half as likely as others to complete their high-school education and one-fifth as likely to finish college (Alan Guttmacher Institute, 1981a, 1981b). It has been argued that early child-bearing has a more detrimental effect on a girl's education than her race, her parents' socioeconomic status, or her academic abilities (Zelnick, Kantner, & Ford, 1981). Not surprisingly, young mothers are seldom able to acquire the vocational skills needed to earn decent incomes as adults. To complicate the financial situation even further, an adolescent mother is likely to have more children than other girls (Alan Guttmacher Institute, 1984). Among women 35 to 52 years of age, those who had their first child before age 18 have an average of more than five children each (Moore, 1981). It has been suggested that lacking vocational skills or academic credentials, the adolescent mother loses her incentive to avoid another pregnancy. In endorsing this possibility, helping teenaged mothers finish their education and obtain jobs can be construed as one of society's most effective methods for discouraging second pregnancies during adolescence.

As might be expected, given adolescents' lack of educational and vocational training, many teenage parents and their offspring must rely on financial aid from state or federal governments. In fact, half of the money spent on Aid to Families with Dependent Children is given to adult women who first became mothers as teenagers (Alan Guttmacher Institute, 1984). There is no empirical evidence, however, to support the accusation that adolescent girls intentionally become pregnant in order to collect money from the government (Bolton, 1980; Chilman, 1978; Furstenberg, 1980; Zelnick, Kantner, & Ford, 1981).

Given the financial and psychological demands of raising a child, it might seem that an adolescent mother would fare best when the child's father married her; but this has not been verified by the empirical data. To begin with, whether or not the wife is pregnant, adolescent marriages seldom last. Thus, whatever benefits might initially accrue from a "shot gun" wedding are usually short-lived. For example, approximately 45 percent of all adolescent mothers are separated or divorced within 15 years of their marriage—a divorce rate three times that of couples who waited to have children until their twenties (Alan Guttmacher Institute, 1984).

In addition, teenaged mothers who stay single are more likely than those who marry to finish school and to avoid another pregnancy. While 25 percent of the adolescent mothers who stay single drop out of school, nearly 80 percent of the girls who get married quit school (Moore, 1981). This phenomenon may be partially accounted for by the fact that single mothers will receive child-care assitance and emotional encouragement from their own parents to finish school. In contrast, an adolescent husband is less likely to help his wife cope with the burdens of motherhood or encourage her to complete the education necessary to support herself. In support of this hypothesis, black adolescent mothers generally suffer fewer educational losses than white teenage mothers (Moore, 1981). This finding has been attributed to the black family's and the community's willingness to offer financial and psychological support to unmarried mothers. Nonetheless, irrespective of the girl's race, the data indicate that teenaged mothers are generally better off educationally if they remain single (Alan Guttmacher Institute, 1981a, 1981b; Furstenberg, 1980; Presser, 1980; Russell, 1980; Zelnick, Kantner, & Ford, 1981).

Despite the disadvantages of being an adolescent parent, it is important to note that the negative consequences of teenage parenthood might not be a direct consequence of parenthood itself. In this regard, the follow-up surveys conducted with over 22,000 high-school seniors from the class of 1972 are particularly noteworthy (Haggstrom et al., 1981). First, adolescents who became parents generally had lower vocational and educational ambitions initially than their peers who postponed parenthood. Second, adolescents who married but remained childless were comparable in many ways educationally and vocationally in their early adulthood to those who had been teenage parents. Both findings suggest that the lower educational and vocational outcomes in early adulthood that are often attributed to being a teenage parent or to early marriage might be due to lower aspirations that predated the adolescent marriage or the pregnancy.

Nevertheless, the analyses did reveal that married females clearly lowered their career aspirations when they became mothers and that their educational aspirations suffered. In contrast, the effects of adolescent parenthood for males were barely distinguishable from the effects of early marriage. Although these samples did not include high-school dropouts and did not include young adolescents, the findings call into question the prevalent notion that early parenthood, in and of itself, is responsible for the lowered ambitions and lower achievements of adolescents in early adulthood.

Adolescents' Offspring

In addition to the disadvantages that accrue to adolescent girls as a consequence of motherhood, the offspring of adolescent parents also pay penalities related to their parents' youth. In relation to their physiological development, babies born to adolescent mothers are much more likely than those of older mothers to have low birth weights and more childhood illnesses, birth injuries, neurological defects, and mental retardation (Alan Guttmacher Institute, 1981a, 1981b; "Natality Statistics," 1984). Such problems have primarily been attributed to the fact that teenaged mothers generally receive poor prenatal care during the first trimester of pregnancy, the period most critical to fetal development. Unfortunately, only 30 percent of all pregnant girls under age 15 and 50 percent of those between 15 and 17 receive any prenatal care. An astounding 15 percent of the mothers under age 15 received absolutely no medical care until the last three months of their pregnancy (Alan Guttmacher Institute, 1981a, 1981b).

Moreover, it appears that the negative consequences of having adolescent parents extend even farther (Alan Guttmacher Institute, 1981a, 1981b). First, the children of adolescent parents are themselves more likely to have children during their teenage years. Second, having adolescent parents is correlated with lower IQ and achievement scores. Third, some evidence suggests that children with adolescent mothers are more often the victims of child abuse than those with older mothers (Kinard & Klerman, 1980; Sahler, 1980).

These findings have been accounted for by several variables. First, teenage mothers tend to have less education than older mothers and to come from lower socioeconomic backgrounds. Thus, it has been hypothesized that many adolescent mothers are unable to provide the kinds of experiences that foster a child's intellectual development. In this regard, adolescent mothers have been characterized as impatient and intolerant with their children, as well as developmen-

Adolescent Voices 10.6

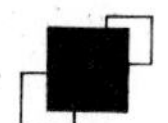

Comments from Adolescent Mothers

Thirteen-year-old mother: "You know, sometimes I look at him and he don't seem like he's mine. I guess I'm not used to him yet. Even in the hospital, right after he was born he didn't seem like he was mine. It's hard to think he's what I had in me for nine months. After he came out of me, the doctor put him on my stomach. 'Get that messy thing off me!' I yelled at that doctor. Maybe he don't seem like he's mine 'cause he can't talk yet. Now, my little cousin, he's different. He's three years old and he seems like he's mine, but he ain't. It's funny, I know he ain't a baby doll, but he don't yet seem like he's a real baby, like my cousin. He's sorta in between." (Frank, 1983, p. 54).

Fifteen-year-old mother: "Here's to all those doctors and teachers who said I couldn't raise a baby at my age, let alone graduate from school early. I had to prove to all of them, my grandmother, other teens that not all teens are dumb and ignorant about makin' good choices for themselves. I love proving people wrong, I was gonna be a good example. I knew all about raising children. I had stored up in me all this knowledge about babies and with my own baby I felt I could apply it to my own instead of always telling others what I know. When I was seven, my cousins were having babies. I've been around babies all my life. I'm still the same person I was before I was a parent. Only thing that's changed is that I have a baby. Same ol' me, though." (Frank, 1983, p. 76)

Eighteen-year-old mother: "But one thing I'll never do is get married. No way. Too much divorce in my family. My mother's been divorced twice, my uncle twice, my grandmother twice. I've learned that marriage just doesn't work. I'll have plenty of boyfriends, but no husbands. Women got to be careful of men. The reason I don't let my baby's father see our son is because he's not helpin' support him financially. If the father wants rights, he's got to live up to his responsibilities. No responsibilites, no rights. I won't let no man just barge in here and start ordering me around whenever he damn pleases. Not with me. I'm not one of those girls! No man's gonna beat me or push me around. My girl friend couldn't say no to her boyfriend and I found her all bloody and beat up with her blouse torn off. Any man who raises a hand to me is gone, and I mean fast!" (Frank, 1983, p. 96)

Fifteen-year-old mother: "I was lucky in that the labor was short in duration, only five and a half hours, because I don't think I could have stood any more. And then sharing a room. My roommate's husband was a minister and he was awful to me. He embarrassed me, he said wise comments, which just made me lie there and cry—made me feel even more awful." (McGuire, 1983, p. 90).

SOURCES: D. Frank, *Deep blue funk and other stories: Portraits of teenage parents.* Chicago: University of Chicago Press, 1983; P. McGuire, *It won't happen to me: Teenagers talk about pregnancy.* New York: Delacorte, 1983.

tally unprepared for their new roles as parents. For example, in observations of rural teenage mothers interacting with their 6-month-old infants, most of the mothers were constricting, nonverbal, and nonstimulating. Moveover, the nonverbal style of interaction was more characteristic of the younger than the older adolescents and of those who had the least knowledge of normal child development and child-rearing practices (Epstein, 1980).

In addition, given the high illegitimacy rates, most children with adolescent mothers are deprived of having two parents to attend to their intellectual, educational, and emotional needs. Finally, as the stories in Box 10.6 illustrate, many adolescent fathers and mothers are barely beyond their own childhood when they are encumbered with the adult responsibilities of raising a child. Accordingly, the higher incidence of child abuse among teenage mothers has been attributed to the economic stress, the upheaval created by factors such as dropping out of school and losing a youthful figure, the feeling of suddenly being set apart from one's peers, and the constant demands that infants and toddlers make upon a parent.

Having thus characterized teenage mothers, however, one important caveat is in order: The behavior of these mothers may be as much a function of such variables as poverty and lack of education as of age. Highlighting this point, a comparison of children born to adolescent mothers and children born to mothers in their twenties found no differences in their behavioral or emotional functioning during kindergarten or third grade. The variable that did relate to the child's functioning, however, was the mother's level of education (Kinard & Reinherz, 1984). In yet another study that highlights the contradictory nature of the existing research, 60 black, white, and Hispanic mothers between 14 and 19 years old were similar to older mothers on a Knowledge of Child Development Scale. Contrary to predictions, socioeconomic status was unrelated to the mothers' scores, although minorities tended to score lower on the scales of maternal involvement and organization of the infant's environment. Nevertheless, the teenage mothers in the study were not as deficient in their knowledge as might have been hypothesized from other research (King & Fullard, 1982).

In sum, although most of the data indicate that both the parents and the children benefit when the parents themselves are beyond adolescence, sweeping condemnations of adolescent parents should be avoided, since variables such as income, race, and education may influence an adolescent's effectiveness as a parent. Moreover, as Box 10.7 illustrates, the time has come to re-examine some of our views regarding the legal rights of adolescent parents.

The Adolescent Father

Understandably, the research on adolescent pregnancies has historically been focused on the adolescent girl and her child. More recently, however, researchers have attempted to gather information regarding the impact of unplanned pregnancies or parenthood on adolescent males.

One of the first research studies on adolescent fathers, conducted in the early 1970s, included only middle-class boys and, therefore, is restricted in the generalizability of its findings (Pannor, Massarik, & Evans, 1971). Although these young fathers were found to be clever and verbally skilled, they also tended to have low self-esteem. Moreover, the young fathers were characterized as impul-

Closer Look 10.7 

Adolescents' Sexual Rights

Selection Criteria for Girls' Program Illegal, Judge Rules

A state judge in Montana has ruled that the American Legion Auxiliary's regulations prohibiting girls who are married or who have had children from participating in its Girls State programs are illegal.

But the judge declined to order the organization to allow the teen-age mother who brought the suit to attend the program this year.

Judge C. B. McNeil's ruling followed a hearing on a civil suit filed by Raecille Ann Vaughan, a 17-year-old student in the Charlo school district, and her mother. In the suit, Ms. Vaughan claimed that her equal-protection and due-process rights were denied when she was bypassed for consideration by Girls State because she was pregnant when she applied for the program, according to Girls State officials.

Girls State, an annual American Legion program in which students learn about state government, prohibits girls who are married, have been married, or are single parents from participating in the program, according to Elsie Daniels, director of Montana Girls State.

Judge McNeil, while ruling that the organization's selection policies are illegal, declined to order that the group admit Ms. Vaughan to this year's program, which began on June 9, according to Ms. Daniels.

Ms. Daniels added that the organization plans to eliminate the restriction on married teen-agers or youths who have children and will consider such students for future Montana programs. "The way it stands right now," she said, "we don't have much choice."

Attempts to reach Ms. Vaughan's lawyer were unsuccessful.

SOURCE: *Education Week,* June 19, 1985, p. 3. Reprinted by permission.

Suspension of Player Who Fathered Child Is Held Legal

A county judge upheld a Pottsville, Pa., Catholic school's suspension of a varsity football player who fathered the child of another student, on the grounds that "due process does not apply to private and parochial schools" and that the suspension did not cause him any immediate or irreperable harm.

Judge John E. Lavelle of Schuylkill County refused last month to issue a preliminary injunction allowing the Nativity Catholic High School junior, Robert Doyle Jr., to continue to play.

The parents decided not to appeal the injunction or pursue the case, according to their lawyer, Richard Smolens.

The school's principal, the Rev. Steven Maco, said at the hearing last month that the suspension resulted from the student's failure to "reflect the values and moral principles of the Catholic Church," according to a press account.

Judge Lavelle ruled that the student's suspension from the football team was a legitimate disciplinary action.

The Doyles had sued the school and the diocese after Reverend Maco told them on Sept. 4 that their son could no longer publicly represent the high school.

SOURCE: *Education Week,* October 17, 1984, p. 3. Reprinted by permission.

sive, socially immature, and unable to postpone immediate gratification. Contrary to expectations, however, the boys had not intentionally impregnated their girlfriends, nor were they cavalier in their attitudes about the pregnancy. In fact, some of these young fathers expressed more sorrow and guilt about the pregnancy than the girls themselves.

More recent research shows that many adolescent boys are distressed by an unplanned pregnancy and that some young fathers want to be involved in caring for their child (Connally, 1978; Frank, 1983; Walters & Walters, 1980). In addition, it appears that, even in cases where no marriage occurs, some adolescent fathers play a meaningful role in the lives of the mother and the child. Others have expressed considerable sadness when excluded from the pregnancy and child rearing. Finally, recent studies generally show that adolescent fathers are psychologically similar to males who do not become fathers (Barret & Robinson, 1982; Earls & Siegel, 1980).

Understandably, young unwed mothers and their families may attempt to isolate the teenage father from his child. Whether warranted or not, the unwed father may serve as the scapegoat upon whom some families vent their wrath. The young father's situation is further complicated in situations where he is discouraged from seeing his child, while simultaneously being criticized for abandoning the mother and child. It is worth noting that when the adolescent father shares child-care responsibilities with the unwed mother, the child's cognitive development is superior to that of children raised solely by their mother (Furstenberg, 1980; Parke, Power, & Fisher, 1980). Thus, aside from disappointing the father, separating him permanently from his child may have certain deleterious effects on the child.

The few available investigations of young males' feelings about abortions dispel some stereotypic notions regarding male insensitivity and irresponsibility (Scales & Beckstein, 1982). Young males have expressed confusion, worry, and regret after the termination of an unplanned pregnancy. Others complain of having been completely excluded from the decision. According to the National Abortion Federation, 40 percent of those who call their abortion hotline are males. Of these callers, most are concerned for the woman's physical safety, but others are troubled by the fact they have no legal rights over the abortion decision.

The Etiology of Pregnancy

Given the emotional, financial, and physical distress that accompany unplanned pregnancies, sociologists and psychologists have understandably devoted considerable attention to the etiology of adolescent pregnancy. In pursuit of the answer, researchers have typically focused their attention on particular attributes of the girl's personality and on the couple's attitudes toward contraception and early parenthood, their socioeconomic and cultural backgrounds, and their knowledge of conception and contraception.

Personality and Attitudes

It was once commonly argued that girls who became pregnant were motivated to do so by psychological problems. The empirical evidence has generally failed to support this contention, and most experts today have rejected the psychoanalytic explanation for teenage pregnancy (Black & DeBlassie, 1985; Bolton, 1980; Furstenberg, 1980; Mindick & Oskamp, 1982; Quay, 1981). It now appears that very few girls intentionally become pregnant in order to fulfill needs for affection, to gain adult status, to resolve an Oedipal conflict, or to escape parental control. While a few girls undoubtedly get pregnant intentionally for such reasons, the vast majority become pregnant by accident and are extremely distressed by news of their pregnancy.

There is ample evidence, however, to support the contention that girls with low self-esteem are more likely to become pregnant than those with high self-esteem (Bolton, 1980; Chilman, 1978; Herold, Goodwin, & Lero, 1979). A girl who esteems herself generally has educational and vocational aspirations that motivate her to postpone motherhood by using contraceptives or by terminating an accidental pregnancy. In contrast, the girl without such goals or self-regard has fewer incentives to avoid pregnancy. Moreover, it has been hypothesized that girls with low self-esteen are more easily motivated to engage in frequent sexual activity by their desire to gain males' approval. In a similar vein, girls who become pregnant may be operating at a lower level of ego development, and therefore are more willing to acquiesce to the requests of males.

In one representative study that characterizes the research, sexually active girls who became pregnant more often had foreclosed identities than the nonpregnant, sexually active girls (Protinsky, Sporakowski, & Atkins, 1982). Rather than experimenting with various roles and ideologies in order to create an independent identity, the pregnant girls were less inclined than nonpregnant girls to believe that working hard and delaying immediate gratification would eventually bring them satisfaction.

Adolescents' lax attitudes about using contraceptives have also been attributed to their belief in the personal fable and the imaginary audience (Cvetkovich, 1975). Acting in accord with their belief that "nothing bad can happen to me," a number of adolescent couples fail to use contraceptives. Thus, as David Elkind (1979) proposes, at an early stage in their cognitive development, adolescents' "personal fable" exacerbates foolish decisions such as failing to use birth control. Moreover, as Elkind contends, young adolescents tend to believe that everyone is as preoccupied with them as they are with themselves—the imaginary audience. As a consequence, many adolescents may refuse to use contraceptives because they erroneously assume that everyone will notice their visit to the family planning center or their trip to a drug store for contraceptives.

The research also indicates that adolescents with an external locus-of-control attitude are less likely to use contraceptives than those with an internal locus-of-control attitude (Bolton, 1980; Herold, Goodwin, & Lero, 1979). Believing that they are virtually powerless to control the outcomes in their lives, adolescents with an external orientation reliquish responsibility for the consequences of their sexual activities.

In sum, attitudes such as locus of control and the personal fable may partially explain why some adolescent couples use contraceptives more responsibly than others. The evidence does not, however, support the contention that underlying psychological forces motivate most adolescent couples to intentionally plan a pregnancy. Even among married teenagers, half of all pregnancies are accidental (Alan Guttmacher Institute, 1981a, 1981b).

Knowledge of Conception and Contraception

A second viewpoint on the etiology of accidental pregnancies is that adolescents are too poorly educated about conception and contraception to behave responsibly. In support of this view, young people with the least amount of sexual knowledge are more likely to become pregnant than their more knowledgeable peers (Byrne, 1983). Nevertheless, most couples involved in an accidental pregnancy do have enough knowledge of contraception to have prevented the pregnancy. For example, as Figure 10.3 illustrates, in 1979 nearly 70 percent of the sexually active teenagers were using contraceptives (Alan Guttmacher Institute, 1981a, 1981b).

The problem appears to be not so much adolescents' ignorance regarding birth control, but their inconsistent use of contraceptives. For example, only one-third of the adolescents who used contraceptives said they did so every time they had intercourse. Moreover, adolescents are relying on less reliable methods of birth control than their predecessors in the 1970s. For instance, the number of teenage girls using the pill and the IUD almost doubled between 1971 and 1976, but declined by 8 percent in 1979. While it is no doubt true that the pill and the IUD pose more threats to the female's health than the diaphragm, condoms, or cervical sponge, teenage girls are five times more likely to die of causes related to a pregnancy than of causes related to the pill. Distressingly, the teenagers questioned in 1979 were more than twice as likely to have used the "withdrawal technique" as their method of preventing conception than teenagers surveyed in 1976 (Alan Guttmacher Institute, 1981a, 1981b).

What do you remember about your first date? How does your present concept of an "ideal" date differ from the concept you had at the age of 14?

Given the inconsistency with which adolescents use contraceptives, their reasons for not using them on certain occasions assume special significance (Alan Guttmacher Institute, 1981a, 1981b; Bolton, 1980; Byrne, 1983; Zelnick, Kantner, & Ford, 1981). The two most popular responses are: "We thought it was the safe time in the month so we didn't think we needed birth control"; and, "We didn't plan to have intercourse, so we didn't have anything with us." Other reasons include: "We don't have sex very often, so we didn't think there was much chance of getting pregnant"; "We were too embarrassed to go into a store or to a clinic for birth control"; "My friends told me you couldn't get pregnant the first time you did it"; "It's unromantic to use contraceptives"; "If a boy wears a rubber, he can't enjoy sex"; "I'm just not the kind of girl who purposely plans to have sex and gets contraceptives beforehand"; "It's the girl's responsibility to take care of birth control, so I just assumed she was using something."

As Table 10.2 demonstrates, adolescents' inaccurate knowledge might help explain why more than half of all teenage pregnancies occur within six months of first having intercourse (Alan Guttmacher Institute, 1981a, 1981b). Moreover, even when well informed about contraceptives, most adolescents fail to discuss birth control with their partners before having intercourse (Cogswell et al., 1982; Cvetkovich & Grote, 1981; O'Hara & Kahn, 1985)

It is tempting to assume that only the youngest or the least educated adolescents are irresponsible in regard to their contraceptive habits, but studies of college students undermine such an assumption. For example, students attending the university that houses the internationally known Kinsey Institute for Sex Research have easy access to contraceptives through the university's health service. While almost all the sexually active undergraduates in the survey said they were aware of the easy availability of birth-control services, only one-third said they used contraceptives regularly. Over two-thirds said they used contraceptives on an irregular basis or not at all (Byrne, 1983). More interestingly, on the subject of age and sexual responsibility, nearly 40 percent of married adult women say their pregnancies were accidental (Thornburg, 1981). Finally, other surveys show that although adolescents from higher socioeconomic backgrounds are more likely to use contraceptives, they use them as inconsistently as do youngsters from less wealthy families (Zelnick, Kantner, & Ford, 1981).

Cultural Influences

As might be expected, given the high rates of pregnancy among adolescents from minorities and from lower socioeconomic backgrounds, researchers have hypothesized that cultural factors might influence adolescents' contraceptive practices and attitudes about early parenthood. Table 10.1 highlights these racial differences between white, black, and Hispanic adolescents' birthrates.

Given these racial discrepancies, it has been hypothesized that minority cultures are more accepting of early parenthood and of illegitimacy than the white culture. According to this view, some minorities encourage teenage pregnancies by endorsing the philosophy that having children at an early age proves you're a "real man" or a "real woman." In addition, some researchers suggest that the hardships experienced by black Americans have nurtured a stronger belief in the value of the family as a source of strength and satisfaction.

Table 10.2

Adolescents' Knowledge of Birth Control

Questionnaire Item (N = 1190)	*Percent, by Type of Response* Correct	Incorrect	Don't Know
The pill must be stopped every year (F)	32	4	64
The pill is generally dangerous (F)	65	5	30
The pill can be taken with other drugs without decreasing its effectiveness (T)	31	8	61
The pill may not be taken if the woman has a history of certain illnesses (T)	39	4	57
The pill is the most effective method of birth control (T)	72	6	22
An IUD is inserted before each act of intercourse (F)	39	14	47
An IUD cannot be felt by the man or woman during intercourse (T)	37	7	56
The IUD is the second most effective method of birth control (T)	29	6	65
The IUD works best if the uterus has been stretched by pregnancy (T)	20	7	73
A diaphragm must be worn at all times (F)	40	14	47
The diaphragm should be used only after being fitted by a doctor (T)	55	5	40
The effectiveness of a diaphragm is increased when used with cream or jelly (T)	34	6	61
A diaphragm cannot be felt by the man or the woman when properly in place (T)	44	3	53
A condom should be tested before use (T)	55	14	47
Rubbers break easily (F)	19	48	33
A rubber should be held around the base of the penis when withdrawn (T)	48	5	48
Spermicides should be inserted just before each act of intercourse (T)	68	6	26
They work by killing sperm (T)	63	5	32
They can be bought without prescription (T)	67	5	27
When used with a rubber, they are a highly effective birth control method (T)	41	11	48
They should be washed out with a douche after intercourse (F)	16	26	58
Rhythm is a highly effective method of birth control (F)	49	6	45
Withdrawal is a highly effective method of birth control (F)	61	11	28
Douching after intercourse is a highly effective birth control method (F)	58	7	35

Table 10.2 *(cont.)*

Adolescents' Knowledge of Birth Control

Questionnaire Item (N = 1190)	*Percent, by Type of Response* Correct	Incorrect	Don't Know
Menstruation is a cleaning of the uterus to prepare again for possible pregnancy (T)	74	9	16
A woman's fertile time covers the middle interval between her periods (T)	64	10	27
A girl can get pregnant the first time she has intercourse (T)	76	12	12
Sperm can live in the female's system for about 72 hours (T)	43	17	40
If a woman does not have an orgasm, she can't get pregnant (F)	70	6	24
An abortion can be done safely by a doctor during the first 12 weeks (T)	81	5	14
An abortion makes a woman sterile (F)	87	3	10
Anyone can tell if a girl has had an abortion (F)	85	1	14

Percents may not add to 100 because of rounding.
SOURCE: P. Reichelt and H. Werley, Contraception, abortion and venereal disease: Teenagers' knowledge and the effects of education. In F. Furstenburg et al. (eds.), *Teenage sexuality, pregnancy and childbearing*. Philadelphia: University of Pennsylvania Press, 1981, 305–317.

A study conducted with 150 black and 150 white high-school students from upper-lower- and lower-middle-class families serves as a demonstration of this hypothesis about cultural differences (Thompson, 1980). To reduce the confounding variables, the researchers included only students from two-parent homes where both parents had at least a high-school education, and they matched the two samples in terms of their age, general living conditions, and religious faith. Despite these similarities, the black adolescents were more convinced than whites that "having children promotes marital success, personal security and approval from others"; that "the most intimate and satisfying of interpersonal relations between a man and a woman is defined by the conception of a child"; that "married couples should have as many children as they wish"; and that "the father who is able to announce the birth of his child is the proudest of men."

Other evidence, however, suggests that what are often labeled as racial differences are actually differences related to socioeconomic status. For example, although the black youths in Thompson's study considered children to be more important, they planned to have the same number of children in their families as their white counterparts. Likewise, despite their different attitudes about children, the youths from similar socioeconomic backgrounds had similar plans for their future families. In another study representing the importance of economic class, black adolescents from lower-income families did not see marriage as a prerequisite for motherhood. Also in contrast to the middle-class whites, the blacks did not view economic independence from their parents as a phase of development that should precede parenthood (Gabriel & McAnarey, 1983).

It is also worth noting that the fact that black or Hispanic families are willing to help adolescents care for their illegitimate children does not "prove" that these adults are encouraging their teenaged children to become pregnant. Nor does it prove they are any more overjoyed than white parents when their 14-year-old daughter announces, "I'm pregnant." In fact, even mothers who helped their daughters through a pregnancy report being angry at being given the responsibility for an infant's primary care after its birth (Smith, 1975).

Thus, it is argued that income, not race, is the most influential factor in determining adolescents' feelings about early parenthood. According to this hypothesis, adolescents of any race who come from low-income families will bear more babies than those from richer homes, where there is greater emphasis on postponing parenthood until educational and vocational aspirations have been achieved. From this viewpoint, better education, job training, and employment for impoverished youths should serve as an indirect incentive to postpone parenthood.

In regard to racial differences, it has also been suggested that pregnancies and illegitimacy among the white population have been underestimated (Bolton, 1980). Since white youths are more likely than minorities to come from middle-class and affluent families, they can avail themselves of legal and medical services that keep their pregnancies more hidden from view. For example, with enough money adolescent girls can live away from home until their children are born and arrange for adoptions through private lawyers. In addition, many white births are not classified as illegitimate, because the couple weds—an option that is condoned more often among whites than among blacks.

Finally, it has been suggested that early maturation plays a part in black adolescents' higher pregnancy rates (Bolton, 1980). According to this hypothesis, the fact that black adolescents mature physically somewhat sooner than whites contributes to their engaging in sexual activities at an earlier age. As a consequence, it is then more likely that black adolescents will become pregnant, since they have more years to experiment with sex.

Given the complexities involved in the etiology of teenage pregnancy, it is unlikely that researchers will discover a single cause through which we can eliminate unplanned pregnancies. Thus, the wisest approach on the basis of the present research is to consider with equal regard all possible avenues for reducing unplanned pregnancies.

SEX EDUCATION

U.S. Attitudes toward Sex Education

Given the rates of venereal disease and unplanned pregnancy, it has long been argued that public schools should be allowed to assume more responsibility for sex education. In contrast to previous decades, when many adolescents' parents disapproved of sex education in the schools, particularly of dispensing information about contraception, most adolescents' parents now support these programs (Alan Guttmacher Institute, 1981a, 1981b).

Nevertheless, a small but vocal segment of the population, referring to themselves as "the moral majority," oppose sex education in the schools. A religiously conservative group that tends to have less education and lower incomes than those who favor sex education, this "moral majority" has protested assertively enough in many communities to control school boards' decisions on sex education (Mahoney, 1979). Central to their position is the view that if schools remove fear by teaching adolescents how to prevent VD and pregnancy, the young will have no incentive to remain virgins. Unfortunately, this position ignores the finding that ignorance about contraception does not prevent young people from having intercourse, and sex-education courses do not cause adolescents to abandon their sexual principles (Alan Guttmacher Institute, 1981a, 1981b; Bolton, 1980; Kilman et al., 1981; Kornfield, 1985; Spanier, 1978; Zelnick, Kantner, & Ford, 1981). More sadly still, the charactersitc most commonly shared by the parents of pregnant girls is their fear of the adolescent's sexuality (Bolton, 1980).

Adolescents' Sources of Sexual Information

Despite most parents' favoring sex education in school, at present many adolescents are not receiving such programs. Moreover, many courses referred to as "sex education" avoid any information about birth control, homosexuality, or abortion. Furthermore, most states permit local school systems to make the decisions about sex education. Consequently, it is estimated that of the 21 million students in secondary schools, only 9 million receive some sex education in school and only 6.5 million of these students receive information about birth control (Alan Guttmacher Institute, 1981a, 1981b).

Despite the fact that many parents express a willingness to discuss sex with their own children, most never do (Bennett & Dickinson, 1980; Norman & Harris, 1981). For example, in one 1980 poll of 1,400 parents in Cleveland, Ohio, only 60 percent of the mothers had explained menstruation to their teenage daughters, and 92 percent had never discussed sex (Langway, 1980). Even more surprisingly, many well-intentioned parents are poorly informed about reproduction, contraception, and VD. In one study only 45 percent of the mothers knew the time of month when a woman is most likely to get pregnant; only 41 percent knew how long sperm can live inside a woman after intercourse (five days); and only 18 percent knew that a woman can get pregnant up to two days after ovulation. In a recent national survey, 98 percent of the parents said they needed help in talking to their children about sex (Alan Guttmacher Institute, 1981a, 1981b).

If parents and schools are not providing adolescents with adequate information, where are they going for sexual advice and information? More are turning to family planning clinics. For example, one-third of the patients at clinics in 1978 were adolescents, which represented a tripling of adolescent patients since 1972. Unfortunately, almost 80 percent of the girls have had intercourse before they come to the clinic for contraceptive advice. Most have been sexually active for at least nine months and nearly half come to the clinic only because they think they are already pregnant. Why the long delay? Girls say, "Because I was afraid my family would find out if I came"; "Because I was afraid to be examined and thought birth control was dangerous"; "Because I wanted to wait until my boyfriend and I had a closer relationship.'' About half the girls tell their parents about their visit to the clinic, but one-fourth say they would not go to a clinic for advice if their parents had to be informed (Alan Guttmacher Institute, 1981a, 1981b).

Where else do adolescents get their sexual ''facts''? Just like their parents and grandparents, most are educated by their friends (Cohen & Rose, 1984; Fox, 1983). Unfortunately, much of what they learn from their peers is untrue or dangerously incomplete. One example comes from a 1973 survey of 1,200 adolescents attending rap sessions required by Planned Parenthood prior to receiving contraceptive services (Reichelt & Werley, 1981). As you can see from Table 10.2, these youngsters were woefully lacking in accurate information about contraceptives. Although this study was conducted in 1972, adolescents' comments from the 1980s are strikingly similar (Bell, 1980).

Kinds of Sex Education for Adolescents

According to some experts, the government has assumed too little responsibility for alleviating the problem of teenage pregnancies. In 1978 Congress passed the first legislation specifically aimed at reducing the consequences of teenage pregnancy. The Adolescent, Health, Services, Pregnancy Prevention and Care Act, however, addressed only one aspect of the problem—supportive services to pregnant girls and their children. Although the legislation passed, very little money has been appropriated to set up services for adolescents. The debate over abortion, the Hyde Amendments, and the vocal minority of religious fundamentalists have slowed the expansion of sex-education programs and services for pregnant youths. Funds for developing effective, safe contraceptives have also diminished. In the view of many experts, school boards have let themselves be intimidated by a small number of parents who oppose sex education, and the government has failed to appropriate enough money to combat the adolescent pregnancy problem.

Although sex-education courses make adolescents more knowledgeable, the experts agree that sex education must go beyond formal classes in the schools. Parents should be encouraged to discuss sex and contraception with their children, which may mean providing programs through which parents themselves can receive accurate information about sex and contraception. Merchants could also help by openly displaying nonprescription contraceptives in drugstores and supermarkets and by putting contraceptive vending machines in public rest rooms and other areas, where adolescents can purchase them without embarrassment. As Table 10.3 demonstrates, a number of nonprescription contraceptives are available for adolescents. Through proper advertising, merchants could also serve as educators who teach adolescents that douching after intercourse (whether with vinegar or coca-cola!), withdrawal before ejaculation, and lubricant jellies do not prevent pregnancies or venereal diseases. Likewise, adolescents need to learn that self-administered pregnancy tests are often not reliable until the second month of pregnancy.

The media could also become more involved in sex education. Like antismoking messages, messages about contraception and VD could help adolescents accept the realities and responsibilities of sexuality. Disc jockeys, magazines, public-service messages on television and radio, billboards, and even

How would you try to increase adolescent males' sense of sexual responsibility

match-book covers could convey information about contraception and venereal diseases.

Television could also stop promoting irresponsible sexual behavior through its protrayals of sex as an unpremeditated, spontaneous, care-free activity. For example, the original version of a 1970s television program called "James at Sixteen" showed James preparing for his first sexual experience by getting condoms from a friend beforehand. The NBC censors cut this portion of the script, however, so that the young couple have intercourse without preplanning about contraception. In contrast, when John Travolta and a girl are ready to have intercourse in "Saturday Night Fever," Travolta asks her a series of direct questions about contraception. When she answers no to every question, he zips up his

Table 10.3

Contraceptives for Adolescents

Diaphragm or Cervical Cap

A diaphragm is made of soft rubber in the shape of a shallow cup and is inserted into the vagina so that it covers the cervix. The cervical cap is a smaller covering which fits snugly over the cervix. A spermicide must be applied to the inside of the diaphragm or cup.

Advantages: No side effects other than that a particular brand of spermicide may irritate the vagina or the penis; offers protection against certain sexually transmitted diseases.

Disadvantages: Requires a visit to a physician so that the correct size diaphragm can be prescribed; requires that girls feel comfortable touching their genitals.

Effectiveness: 98 percent effective when properly fitted, when used with a proper amount of spermicide, and when used during every incidence of intercourse.

Condoms (Rubbers, Prophylactics, "Safes")

Worn as long ago as 1350 B.C. by Egyptian men as decorative covers for their penises, the condom is a sheath made of thin, strong rubber or of lamb membrane, which fits over the penis to keep semen from entering the vagina.

Advantages: Offers protection against certain sexually transmitted diseases; requires no visit to a physician; readily available at drug stores; inexpensive.

Disadvantages: Limits the "spontaneity" of intercourse; is perceived as "old-fashioned" by many males.

Effectiveness: 98 percent effective when used as directed.

Spermicides

Spermicidal jelly, cream, or aerosol foams that are inserted into the vagina act as contraceptives by killing sperm.

Advantages: Require no prescription; easily available in drugstores; offer some protection against certain sexually transmitted diseases.

Disadvantages: High rate of pregnancy when used without a diaphragm or a condom; allergic reactions to a particular brand of spermicide; must be inserted immediately before intercourse for maximum effectivness.

Effectiveness: Limited effectiveness unless used in conjunction with a diaphragm or condom.

The Contraceptive Sponge

Functioning on the same principle as the diaphragm and the cervical cap, the recently developed contraceptive sponge is presaturated with spermicide, which is activated by dampening the sponge with water before inserting it into the vagina. While covering the cervix, the sponge releases spermicide into the vagina. Several hours after intercourse, the sponge is removed and thrown away.

Advantages: Requires no prescription; available at drugstores; offers some protection against sexually transmitted diseases; can be disposed of in privacy several hours after intercourse.

Disadvantages: The spermicide may irritate the vagina or the penis; no data are yet available on possible long-term side effects; relatively high failure rate in comparison to other methods.

Effectiveness: Failure rate of nearly 17 percent.

Birth-Control Pills

By releasing synthetic estrogen or progesterone into the female's body, birth-control pills inhibit the development of the egg so that fertilization cannot occur.

Advantages: Provide continual protection without the necessity of preplanning immediately before intercourse; lessen menstrual bleeding, cramping, and acne; regulate irregular periods; offer the most protection against pregnancy of all contraceptives.

Disadvantages: Require a doctor's prescription; side effects associated with the pill include heart attack, strokes, nausea, swelling and weight gain, high blood pressure, cervical cancer, headaches, depression, fatigue, vaginitis, urinary-tract infections, and aggravation of diseases such as epilepsy.

Effectiveness: Almost 100 percent effective for women who remember to use the pill daily.

Intrauterine Device (IUD)

A small device made of plastic or copper, the IUD is inserted into the uterus by a doctor, where its presence prevents pregnancy. Although it is not yet clearly understood how the IUD works, the most widely accepted theory is that the IUD causes an inflammation or chronic low-grade infection in the uterus, thereby causing an elevated number of white cells, which destroy sperm or fertilized egg.

Advantages: Offers continual protection without preplanning immediately before intercourse; no worry about forgetting to take a pill.

Disadvantages: Spontaneous expulsion of the IUD; perforation of the uterus; increased incidence of ectopic pregnancies; vaginal and uterine infections, heavier menstrual bleeding and cramping; high miscarriage rate if pregnancy occurs while IUD is present; irritation to the penis from the plastic string that extends into the vagina; less effective with women who have not yet borne a child.

Effectiveness: 97 percent effective.

The "Morning After" Pill

Within three days of unprotected intercourse, a series of very high doses of synthetic estrogens (DES), progesterones, or combination pills (Ovral) can be injected, which prevent a fertilized egg from implanting itself in the uterine wall.

Advantage: Less expensive than an abortion.

Disadvantages: The long-range effects of DES have not been studied. Side effects of Ovral and DES include nausea and vomiting, high incidence of ectopic pregnancy, and birth defects; if the drugs fail, heart attack or stroke.

Natural Birth Control

By keeping track of her daily temperature, her daily cervical secretions, and the dates of her last menstrual period, a woman can try to estimate the day on which she is fertile. The seven days preceding and the three days following this day of ovulation are the days on which she abstains from intercourse.

Advantage: No immediate or long-term physical side effects.

Disadvantage: High incidence of failure; requires careful daily measurement of bodily functions and great familiarity with one's own body; the irregularity of the menstrual cycle makes predictions by the calendar highly unreliable; particularly impractical for adolescent-age girls whose physiological knowledge of their own bodies is limited; sperm can survive for 5 or 6 days in the uterus, and thus the couple must refrain from intercourse for a week prior to the day of ovulation as well as for days thereafter.

Birth Control Pills for Males

Although not yet available on the market and not a high priority among researchers, gossypol (extracted from cottonseed) has been found effective in stopping sperm production and in changing sperm motility. Pills made from gossypol have been researched in the People's Republic of China, but have not yet been clinically tested in the United States. Given the tradition of allocating the responsibility for birth control to females, there appears little incentive at present for developing pills or shots that would permit males to share in the responsibility of contraception.

SOURCE: Boston Women's Health Collective. *Our bodies, ourselves.* New York: Simon & Schuster, 1984.

pants and leaves the car. This example of responsible sexual behavior, however, was not available to adolescents under age 17, because the movie was R-rated (Byrne, 1983).

The research presently available indicates that television probably exerts a greater influence over adolescents' sexual behavior than sex-education programs, parents, and perhaps even than peers (Darling & Hicks, 1982; Strouse & Fabes, 1985). In this regard it is noteworthy that a recent survey of 1,400 adolescents found that black males', black females', and white males' friends exerted no significant influence over their sexual behavior. Only white females, whose best friends of both sexes were sexually active, were almost certain to have intercourse within the two years of the study (Billy & Udry, 1985).

Sexual Responsibility and Adolescent Boys

Have you ever wondered why all the methods of birth control except two—the condom and vasectomies—are designed for females? Do you feel ill at ease or amused when you hear people discussing male birth-control pills? If so, you are encountering an assumption that many researchers are urging us to reconsider: that it is the girl's responsibility to control a couple's sexual behavior and to take the necessary precautions to prevent pregnancy.

Many experts are now suggesting that sex-education programs would be more successful if males could be convinced to take pregnancy and venereal disease more seriously (Bolton, 1980; Cohen & Rose, 1984; Finkle & Finkel, 1981; Fox, 1983; Philliber & Tatum, 1982; Scales & Beckstein, 1982). One aspect of the problem is that when the adolescent boy acts responsibly by having condoms available, the girl may punish rather than praise him. For example, a 16-year-old from Los Angeles explains that his girlfriend responded to his having a condom by saying "Oh, were you planning this all along?" He responded, "Don't blame me for having a rubber. I thought you'd be glad not to have to worry about getting pregnant" (Bell, 1980, p. 160). A second aspect of the problem is that parents and educators tend to give more contraceptive information to girls than to boys. For example, in one survey 80 percent of the parents were in favor of discussing birth control with their daughters, but only 60 percent said they would discuss birth control with their sons (Alan Guttmacher Institute, 1981a, 1981b).

A recent study with 421 black, Hispanic, and white adolescent males highlights several important points about boys and sexual responsibility (Finkle & Finkel, 1981). Almost 40 percent of these boys learned what they knew about sex and contraception from their male friends. Another 20 percent learned from teachers or doctors, and 20 percent from their female friends. Among the myths that these males believed were that douching is a good way to prevent pregnancy; that sperm lives less than a day inside a woman; that a girl can most easily get pregnant just before her period starts; that withdrawing before ejaculation prevents a girl from getting pregnant. Although most of the boys knew that condoms help prevent pregnancies and VD, only 60 percent agreed that "a male who uses a rubber shows respect for his girlfriend." Almost 40 percent said they would not want their friends to know if they used a condom.

Despite the fact that condoms are still the most reliable way to prevent VD and quite effective in preventing pregnancy, they have steadily lost their popu-

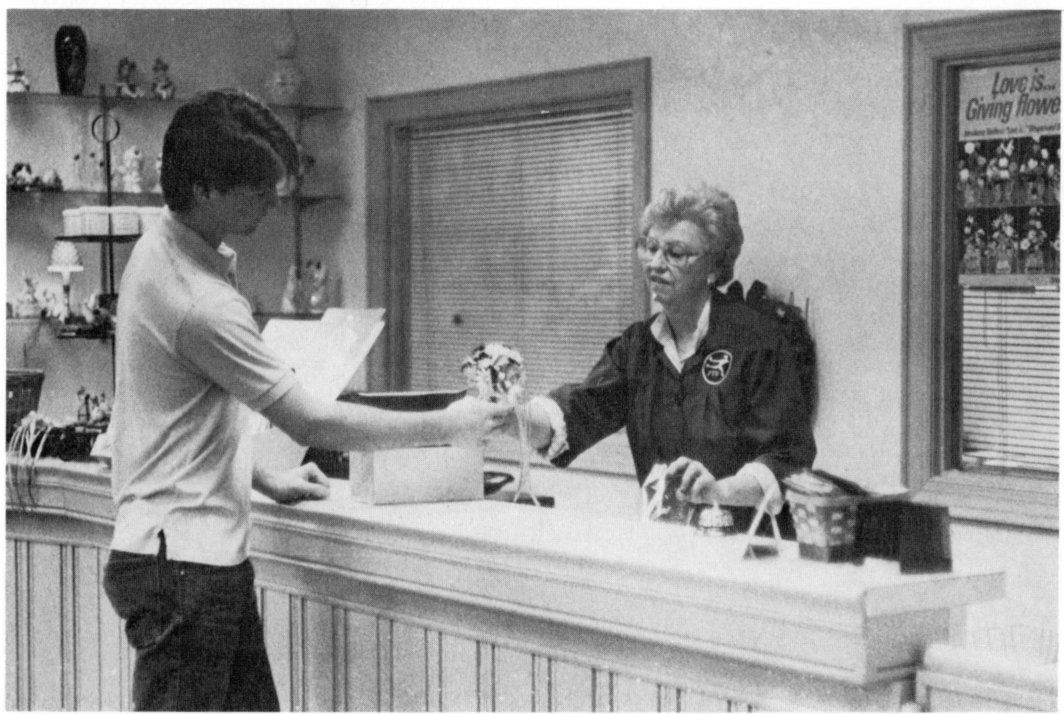

What do high-school and college males have to do in order to please a date? How important is a male's appearance and financial status?

larity since the pill and IUD came onto the market. Until 1965, condoms were the most popular method of birth control in the United States. Unfortunately, most adolescents and adults have come to view the condom as an outdated contraceptive. Many boys are taught that condoms reduce a man's sexual pleasure—a belief adopted without ever having had the experience (Scales & Beckstein, 1982). Boys' negative feelings about condoms are particularly disturbing, since most adolescents use no birth-control device at all during their first act of intercourse, unless they use a condom (Alan Guttmacher Institute, 1981a, 1981b).

It is both sad and ironic that most sex-education programs and information from parents are directed at girls. Considering the fact that boys are more sexually active and have more partners than girls, their sexual attitudes are particularly crucial to decisions regarding birth control. In this vein it is noteworthy that boys who are least likely to use contraceptives are those who are either sexually naive or who have exploitative attitudes about sex (Chilman, 1978; Hornick, Doran, & Crawford, 1979).

Fortunately, many programs have begun to consider the boy's role in preventing pregnancy and venereal disease more seriously. One example is the Condom Couplet Contest, designed to promote the purchase and use of prophylactics (Center for Population Options, 1980). Among the winning couplets written by adolescents have been "At first a condom may seem a bother, but it could prevent an unwanted father!" and "From using a condom you will learn, that no deposit means no return!" Another idea sponsored by some Planned Parenthood

Associations is distributing "condom six-packs" with different varieties of condoms, plus detailed instructions that allow a young person to select a condom that meets his unique needs.

Still other programs are designed to help boys explore traditional sex-role expectations, male sexuality, and relationships with girls by offering the chance to discuss sexual issues in nonthreatening situations where nonmacho attitudes are acceptable (Scales & Beckstein, 1982). Rather than blaming boys for being selfish, irresponsible, and immature, these programs try to teach new sexual attitudes in ways that enhance the male ego. Rather than encouraging boys to use condoms or to refrain from sex merely for the girl's sake, the emphasis is placed on personal benefits of thoughtful sexual decisions: "I have a right to protect myself against disease by wearing a rubber, even if the girl is using birth-control pills." "I have a right to say no to a girl if I'm worried about pregnancy or VD." "I have a right to have a friendship with a girl that doesn't include sex." "I have a right not to make fun of girls and tell insulting sexual jokes about them when I'm with my male friends." "I can be different from my friends in terms of how I treat girls and still be a 'real man' in my own eyes."

Conclusion

Adolescent sexuality is a mixed blessing. Indeed, there are the pleasures and intimacy that so often accompany sexual sharing. Yet there are the awesome responsibilities associated with venereal disease and pregnancy and the feelings of guilt, so often a part of even the most normal sexual activities like masturbation. Given the complexities of human sexuality, it is understandable why both adolescents and their parents express certain anxieties regarding this new aspect of life during the teenage years.

In regard to adults' anxieties, there are those who worry that providing information to adolescents about topics such as contraception and homosexuality will remove the taboos and fears that restrain the young from engaging in forbidden sexual activities. Yet there are also those who fear that, without ways to protect themselves from sexually transmitted diseases and pregnancy, the young will continue to pay unnecessary penalities for their sexual activities—activities that could not have been prevented by withholding information about preventing disease and pregnancy.

Given the profound emotions underlying each viewpoint, a wise course must be one that attends carefully to the empirical data—data that repeatedly demonstrate that adolescents contract venereal diseases and become pregnant most often when they have not been well educated about sexual issues. More important, we must attend to the consistent finding that having accurate information about preventing pregnancy and disease does not seem to be the crucial variable that determines an adolescent's sexual behavior. Thus, for adults who want adolescents to refrain from certain sexual experiences, it would appear a wise investment of time and energy to present the rationale underlying such restraint without demanding that the facts about contraception or disease be withheld. In so doing, a sense of sexual ethics can be developed that arises not out of fear founded on ignorance, but out of a concern for the emotional well-being of oneself and others.

Questions for Discussion and Review

Concepts and Terminology

1. What are the limitations of the research regarding adolescents' sexual attitudes and behavior?
2. How do the sexual attitudes and behavior of male and female adolescents generally differ?
3. What factors are researchers investigating as the possible causes of homosexuality?
4. In what ways is there or is there not a "new morality" that sets adolescents apart from their parents?
5. Has there been a sexual "revolution"?
6. How are the symptoms of AIDS, herpes, syphilis, and gonorrhea similar and dissimilar? How do these diseases differ in terms of prevention, cures, and consequences?
7. What factors appear to be contributing to the pregnancy rate among adolescents?
8. What special problems confront homosexual adolescents?
9. In what ways does adolescent parenthood affect the mother, the father, and the child?
10. How serious are the problems of pregnancy and venereal disease among the adolescent population?

Questions for Discussion and Debate

1. Which of your beliefs regarding adolescents' sexual behavior were not supported by the statistics and research in this chapter?
2. Which of the problems confronting homosexual adolescents do you feel would be most difficult to cope with in your own life? Why?
3. If you were in charge of a community program intended to reduce venereal disease and pregnancy among the adolescent population, what strategies would you implement?
4. How have your own feelings about abortion and birth control for adolescents changed during the past five years?
5. What factors do you think should be considered in trying to determine whether a 15-year-old girl should terminate her accidental pregnancy?
6. How do you believe sex-education programs should be designed in grades 6 through 12?
7. What aspects of your own sexual development created the most unhappiness for you as an adolescent? How might your unhappiness have been alleviated by adults?
8. How do you feel about homosexuality during adolescence? Do your feelings differ in regard to adults' homosexual experiences?
9. What factors do you feel were most influential in determining your sexual attitudes as an adolescent? How did these influences change as you aged?
10. What disturbs or pleases you most when comparing adolescents' sexual attitudes and behavior today with those of your friends during early adolescence?

REFERENCES

AIDS. *Newsweek,* August 12, 1985, pp. 20–29.

AIDS conflict. *Newsweek,* September 23, 1985, pp. 18–24.

Alan Guttmacher Institute. *Factbook on teenage pregnancy.* New York: Alan Guttmacher Institute, 1981. (a)

Alan Guttmacher Institute. *Teenage pregnancy: The problem that hasn't gone away.* New York: Alan Guttmacher Institute, 1981. (b)

Alan Guttmacher Institute. *U.S. and crossnational trends in teenage sexuality.* New York: Alan Guttmacher Institute, 1984.

Allgeier, E., & Allgeier, A. *Sexual interactions.* Lexington, Mass.: D. C. Heath, 1983.

American Psychiatric Association. *Diagnostic and statistical manual of mental disorders* (3d ed.). Washington, D.C.: American Psychiatric Association, 1980.

Astin, A. *The American freshmen: National norms for fall 1980.* Los Angeles: American Council on Education and Graduate School of Education, University of California at Los Angeles, 1981.

Barbach, L. *For yourself: The fulfillment of female sexuality.* New York: Simon & Schuster, 1976.

Barret, R., & Robinson, B. Teenage fathers: Neglected too long. *Social Work,* November 1982, *24,* 484–488.

Bell, A., Weinberg, M., & Hammersmith, S. *Sexual preference: Its development in men and women.* Bloomington: Indiana University Press, 1981.

Bell, R. *Changing bodies, changing lives: A book for teens on sex and relationships.* New York: Random House, 1980.

Bennett, S., & Dickinson, W. Student-parent rapport and parent involvement in sex, birth control and venereal disease education. *Journal of Sex Research,* 1980, *16,* 97–113.

Billy, J., & Udry, R. The influence of male and female best friends on adolescent sexual behavior. *Adolescence,* 1985, *20,* 21–32.

Black, C., & DeBlassie, R. Adolescent pregnancy. *Adolescence,* 1985, *20,* 281–290.

Bolton, F. *The pregnant adolescent: Problems of premature parenthood.* Beverly Hills: Sage, 1980.

Boston Women's Health Collective. *Our bodies, ourselves: A book by and for women* (2d ed.). New York: Simon & Schuster, 1984.

Bridgman, A. NYC schools fund program for homosexuals. *Education Week,* June 12, 1985, p. 7.

Byrne, D. Sex without contraception. In D. Byrne and W. Fisher (eds.), *Adolescents, sex and contraception.* Hillsdale, N.J.: Erlbaum, 1983. Pp. 3–33.

Cahill, K. (ed.). *The AIDS epidemic.* New York: St. Martin's Press, 1983.

Center for Population Options. *Options.* Washington, D.C.: Fall 1980, p. 2.(a)

Center for Population Options. *Some heavy facts about teenage sexuality.* Washington, D.C.: 1980.(b)

Chilman, C. Adolescent sexuality in a changing American society: Social and psychological perspectives. Washington, D.C.: U.S. Government Printing Office, 1978.

Cogswell, B., Cohen, J., Mikow, V., Kanoy, K., & Margolin, R. *Adolescents' perspectives on the health care system.* Chapel Hill: University of North Carolina, 1982.

Cohen, D., & Rose, R. Male adolescent birth control behavior. *Journal of Youth and Adolescence,* 1984, *13,* 239–252.

Comfort, A., & Comfort, J. *The facts of love: Living, loving, and growing up.* New York: Crown, 1979.

Conger, J. A new morality: Sexual attitudes and behavior of contemporary adolescents. In P. Mussen, J. Conger, and J. Kagan (eds.), *Readings in child and adolescent psychology*. New York: Harper & Row, 1980.

Connally, L. Boy fathers. *Human Behavior,* 1978, *7,* 40–43.

Cvetkovich, G. On the psychology of adolescent contraceptive use. *Journal of Sex Research,* 1975, *11,* 256–270.

Cvetkovich, G, & Grote, B. Psychosocial maturity and contraceptive use. *Journal of Population and Environment,* 1981, *4,* 211–225.

Darling, C., & Hicks, M. Parental influence on adolescent sexuality. *Journal of Youth and Adolescence,* 1982, *11,* 231–245.

D'Augelli, J., & D'Augelli, A. Moral reasoning and premarital sexual behavior. *Journal of Social Issues,* 1977, *33,* 46–66.

David, S., & Harris, M. Sexual knowledge, sexual interests and sources of sexual information of rural and urban adolescents. *Adolescence,* 1982, *17,* 471–492.

Diepold, J., & Young, R. Empirical studies of adolescent sexual behavior: A critical review. *Adolescence,* 1979, *14,* 45–64.

Dryfoos, J. The epidemiology of adolescent pregnancy. In I. Stuart and C. Wells (eds.), *Pregnancy in adolescence: Needs, problems and management.* New York: Van Nostrand, 1982. Pp. 27–48.

Earls, F., & Siegel, B. Precocious fathers. *American Journal of Orthopsychiatry,* 1980, *50,* 469–480.

Elkind, D. Imaginary audience behavior in children and adolescents. *Developmental Psychology,* 1979, *15,* 38–44.

Epstein, A. *Assessing the child development information needed by adolescent parents with very young children.* Ypsilanti, Mich.: High Scope Educational Foundation, Grant 90 C 1241, 1980.

Fact file. *Chronicle of Higher Education,* 1981, *21,* 7–8.

Finkle, M., & Finkel, D. Sexual and contraceptive knowledge, attitudes and behavior of male adolescents. In F. Furstenberg, R. Lincoln, and J. Menkin, *Teenage sexuality, pregnancy and childbearing.* Philadelphia: University of Pennsylvania Press, 1981. Pp. 327–336.

Forrest, J., & Henshaw, S. What U.S. women think and do about contraception. *Family Planning Perspectives,* 1983, *15,* 157.

Fox, L. Adolescent male reproductive responsibility. *Social Work in Education,* 1983, *6,* 32–43.

Frank, D. (ed.). *Deep blue funk and other stories: Portraits of teenage parents.* Chicago: University of Chicago Press, 1983.

Furstenberg, F. Burdens and benefits: The impact of early child bearing on the family. *Journal of Social Issues,* 1980, *367,* 46–87.

Gabriel, A., & McAnarey, E. Parenthood in two subcultures. *Adolescence,* 1983, *18,* 595–608.

Gallup, G. Gallup youth survey. *Contemporary Denver Post,* June 10, 1979, p. 40.

Gilligan, C. *In a different voice: Psychological theory and women's development.* Cambridge, Mass.: Harvard University Press, 1982.

Glenbard East *Echo; Teenagers themselves.* New York: Adama Books, 1984.

Glenn, N., & Weaver, C. Attitudes toward premarital, extramarital and homosexual relations in the U.S. in the 1970's. *Journal of Sex Research,* 1979, *15,* 108–118.

Green, R. Homosexuality. In H. Kaplan, A. Freedman, and B. Sadock (eds.), *Comprehensive textbook of psychiatry* (vol. 2). Baltimore, Md.: Williams and Wilkins, 1980 (3d ed.). Pp. 1762–1770.

Haas, A. *Teenage sexuality: A survey of teenage sexual behavior.* New York: Macmillan, 1979.

Haggstrom, G., Blaschke, T., Kanouse, D., Lisowski, W., & Morrison, P. *Teenage parents: Their ambitions and attainments.* Santa Monica, Cal.: Rand Corporation, 1981.

Hamburg, D., & Trudeau, M. *Biobehavioral aspects of aggression.* New York: Alan Liss, Inc. 1981.

Harvard Medical School Health Letter. Cambridge, Mass.: Harvard University, Department of Continuing Education, April 1981.

Heiman, J., Lopiccolo, L., & Lopiccolo, J. *Becoming orgasmic: A sexual growth program for women.* Englewood Cliffs, N.J.: Prentice-Hall, 1976.

Herold, E., Goodwin. M., & Lero, D. Self-esteem, locus of control and adolescent contraception. *Journal of Psychology,* 1979, *101,* 313–326.

Higham, E. Variations in adolescent psychohormonal development. In J. Adelson (ed.), *Handbook of adolescent psychology.* New York: Wiley Interscience, 1980. Pp 472–495.

Hornick, J., Doran, L., & Crawford, S. Premarital contraceptives usage among male and female adolescents. *Family Coordinator,* 1979, *28,* 181–190.

Jorgensen, S. Beyond adolescent pregnancy: Research frontiers for early adolescent sexuality. *Journal of Early Adolescence,* 1983, *3,* 141–155.

Kilman, P., Wanlass, R., Sabalis, R., & Sullivan, B. Sex education: A review of its effects. *Archives of Sexual Behavior,* 1981, *10,* 177–205.

Kinard, E., & Klerman, L. Teenage parenting and child abuse: Are they related? *American Journal of Orthopsychiatry,* 1980, *50,* 481–488.

Kinard, W., & Reinherz, H. Behavioral and emotional functioning in children of adolescent mothers. *Journal of Orthopsychiatry,* 1984, *54,* 578–594.

King, T., & Fullard, W. Teenage mothers and their infants: New findings on the home environment. *Journal of Adolescence,* 1982, *5,* 333–346.

Kinsey, A., Pomeroy, W., & Martin, C. *Sexual behavior in the human male.* Philadelphia: Saunders, 1948.

Kinsey, A., Pomeroy, W., Martin, C., & Gebhard, P. *Sexual behavior in the human female,* Philadelphia: Saunders, 1953.

Klerman, L., Bracken, M., Jekel, J., & Bracken, M. The delivery-abortion decision among adolescents. In I. Stuart and C. Wells (eds.), *Pregnancy in adolescence.* New York: Van Nostrand, 1982. Pp. 219–236.

Kornfield, R. Who's to blame: Adolescent sexual activity. *Journal of Adolescence,* 1985, *8,* 17–31.

Langway, L. Sex ed 101 for kids and parents. *Newsweek,* September 1, 1980, p. 50.

Mahoney, E. Sex education in the public schools: A discriminant analysis of characteristics or pro and anti individuals. *Journal of Sex Research,* 1979, *15,* 276–284.

Masters, W., & Johnson, V. *Human sexual inadequacy.* Boston: Little, Brown, 1966.

Masters, W., & Johnson, V. *Human sexual inadequacy.* Boston: Little, Brown, 1970.

Masters, W., & Johnson, V. *Homosexuality in perspective.* Boston: Little, Brown, 1979.

Miller, P., & Simon, W. The development of sexuality in adolescence. In J. Adelson (ed.), *Handbook of adolescent psychology.* New York: Wiley Interscience, 1980. Pp. 383–408.

Mindick, B., & Oskamp, S. Individual differences among adolescent contraceptors. In I. Stuart and C. Wells (eds.), *Pregnancy in adolescence.* New York: Van Nostrand, 1982. Pp. 140–177.

Mitchel, J. Adolescent intimacy. *Adolescence,* 1976, *11,* 275–280.

Money, J., & Ehrhardt, A. *Man and woman, boy and girl.* Baltimore, Md.: Johns Hopkins University Press, 1972.

Moore, K. Teenage childbearing: Consequences for women families and government welfare expenditures. In K. Scott, T. Field, and E. Robertson (eds.), *Teenage parents and their offspring.* New York: Grune and Stratton, 1981. Pp. 35–55.

Nadelson, C., Notman, M., & Gillon, J. Sexual knowledge and attitudes of adolescents: Relationship to contraceptive use. *Obstetrics and Gynecology,* 1980, *55,* 340–345.

Natality statistics. *Monthly Vital Statistics Report.* Washington, D.C.: National Center for Health Statistics, September 1984, 6.

New AIDS saliva scare. *Newsweek,* October 22, 1984, p. 103.

NIAID Study Group. *Sexually transmitted diseases: 1980 status report.* Washington D.C.: U.S. Government Printing Office (NIH Publications No. 812213), 1981.

Norman, J., and Harris, M. *The private life of the American teenager.* New York: Rawson Wade, 1981.

O'Hara, D., & Kahn, J. Communication and contraceptive practices in adolescent couples. *Adolescence,* 1985, *20,* 33–43.

Olson, L. Social and psychological correlates of pregnancy resolution among adolescent women: A review. *American Journal of Orthopsychiatry,* 1980, *50,* 432–445.

Pannor, R., Massarik, R., & Evans, B. *The unmarried father.* New York: Springer, 1971.

Parke, R., Power, R., & Fisher, T. The adolescent father's impact on mother and child. *Journal of Social Issues,* 1980, *36,* 88–106.

Philliber, S., & Tatum, M. Sex education and the double standard in high school. *Adolescence,* 1982, *17,* 273–283.

Presser, H. Sally's corner: Coping with unmarried motherhood. *Journal of Social Issues,* 1980, *36,* 107–129.

Price, J. High school students' attitudes toward homosexuality. *Journal of School Health,* 1982, *52,* 469–474.

Protinsky, J., Sporakowski, M., & Atkins, P. Identity formation: Pregnant and nonpregnant adolescents. *Adolescence,* 1982, *17,* 73–79.

Quay, H. Psychological factors in teenage pregnancy. In K. Scott, T. Field, and E. Robertson (eds.), *Teenage parents and their offspring.* New York: Grune and Stratton, 1981. Pp. 73–91.

Reichelt, P., & Werley, H. Contraception, abortion and venereal disease: Teenagers' knowledge and the effect of education. In F. Furstenberg, R. Lincoln, and J. Menken (eds.), *Teenage sexuality, pregnancy and childbearing.* Philadelphia: University of Pennsylvania Press, 1981. Pp. 305–317.

Reinhold, R. Census finds unmarried couples have doubled from 1970 to 1978. *New York Times,* June 27, 1979, pp. 1; B5.

Report of the Commission on Obscenity and Pornography. New York: Bantam Books, 1970.

Rosenbaum, M. The changing body image of the adolescent girl. In M. Sugar (ed.), *Female adolescent development.* New York: Bruner Mazel, 1979. Pp. 234–252.

Russell, C. Unscheduled parenthood. *Journal of Social Issues,* 1980, *36,* 45–63.

Sahler, O. Adolescent parenting: Potential for child abuse and neglect. *Pediatric Annals,* 1980, *9,* 67-75.

Scales, P., & Beckstein, D. From macho to mutuality: Helping young men make effective decisions about sex, contraception and pregnancy. In I. Stuart and C. Wells (eds.), *Pregnancy in adolescence.* New York: Van Nostrand, 1982. Pp. 264–290.

Scott, J. The sentiments of love and aspirations for marriage and their association with teenage sexual activity and pregnancy. *Adolescence,* 1983, *18,* 898–897.

Scott, K. Epidemiologic aspects of teenage pregnancy. In K. Scott, T. Field, and E. Robertson (eds.), *Teenage parents and their offspring.* New York: Grune and Stratton, 1982. Pp. 3–15.

Sherfey, M. *The nature and evolution of female sexuality.* New York: Random House, 1972.

Shopper, M. The rediscovery of the vagina and the importance of the menstrual tampon. In M. Sugar (ed.), *Female adolescent development.* New York: Brunner Mazel, 1979. Pp. 214–234.

Silverman L., Sprafkin, J., & Rubinstein, E. *Sex on television: A content analysis of the 1977 season.* Paper presented at American Psychological Association, Toronto, Canada, August 1978.

Simkins, L. Consequences of teenage pregnancy and motherhood. *Adolescence,* 1984, *19,* 39–54.

Singh, B. Trends in attitudes toward premarital sexual relations. *Journal of Marriage and the Family,* 1980, *8,* 387–393.

Smoot, C. Bisexuality: Breaking out of the school closet. *New Expression Magazine,* January 1984.

Smith, E. The role of the grandmother in adolescent pregnancy and parenting. *Journal of School Health,* 1975, *45,* 278–283.

Sorensen, R. *Adolescent sexuality in contemporary America: Personal values and sexual behavior ages 13–19.* New York: Abrams, 1973.

Spanier, G. Sex education and premarital sexual behavior among American college students. *Adolescence.* 1978, *13,* 659–675.

Strouse, J., & Fabes, R. Formal versus informal sources of sex education. *Adolescence,* 1985, *78,* 251–262.

Thompson, K. A comparison of black and white adolescents' beliefs about having children. *Journal of Marriage and the Family,* 1980, *42* 133–139.

Thornburg, H. The amount of sex information learning obtained during adolescence. *Journal of Early Adolescence.* 1981, *1,* 171–183.

Time's new scarlet letter: Herpes. *Time,* August 2, 1982, pp. 62–68.

U.S. Bureau of the Census. Statistical abstract of the United States: 1980 (101st ed.). Washington, D.C.: U.S. Government Printing Office, 1980.

Ventura, S. Births of Hispanic percentage: 1980. *Monthly Vital Statistics Reports,* 1983, *32.*

Walters, J., & Walters, L. Trends affecting adolescent views of sexuality, employment, marriage and child rearing. *Family Relations* 1980, *29,* 191–198.

Weinrich, J., Gonsorick, J., & Holred, M. (eds.). *Homosexuality: Social, psychological and biological issues.* Beverly Hills: Sage, 1982.

Wing Sue, D. Erotic fantasies of college students during coitus. *Journal of Sex Research, Wing.* 1979, *15,* 299–305.

Yankelovich, D. *The new morality: A profile of American youth in the 1970's.* New York: McGraw-Hill, 1974.

Zelnick, M., Kantner, J., & Ford, K. *Sex and pregnancy in adolescence.* Beverly Hills, Cal.: Sage, 1981.

Chapter Outline

Adolescents' Vocational Values
Adolescents in the Marketplace
Types of Employment for Adolescents
Advantages of Adolescent Employment
Disadvantages of Adolescent Employment
Adolescent Unemployment
Theories of Vocational Development
The Differentialist Perspective
The Developmental Perspective
A Challenge to Traditional Theories
The Family's Influence on Vocational Development
Females' Vocational Development
Distinctions between Males and Females
Trends in Vocational Attitudes of Males and Females
Modifying Female Vocational Patterns
Vocational Preparation
Job Projections for the Future
The Value of a College Education
High-School Vocational Education: The Pros and Cons
Conclusion

Goals and Objectives

The materials presented in this chapter will enable you to:

- *Compare the vocational values of contemporary adolescents to the values of adolescents in the 1960s and 1970s*
- *Present the advantages and disadvantages of employment during adolescence*
- *Enumerate the differences between the leading theories of vocational development*
- *Explain the differences between male and female vocational development*
- *Identify the means by which families and society influence adolescents' vocational aspirations and achievements*
- *Advise adolescents and their parents in regard to the value of college or technical education for future employment and salaries*
- *Present a statistical profile of employed and unemployed adolescents in today's society*
- *Consider the roles that family, race, gender, and other sociocultural factors play in determining adolescents' vocational aspirations and achievements*
- *Present the arguments against the traditional theories of vocational development and career counseling*
- *Describe several different approaches to vocational training being used in secondary schools today.*

Concepts and Terminology

Holland's occupational types *satellite schools*
federal Fair Labor Standards Act
Strong-Campbell Interest Inventory
Super's stages of vocational maturity
Ginzberg's stages of vocational maturity
Havighurst's stages of development
Women's Educational Equity Act
premature affluence *Foxfire project*
developmental theory of vocational maturity
differentialist theory of vocational maturity

11 Adolescents and Vocations

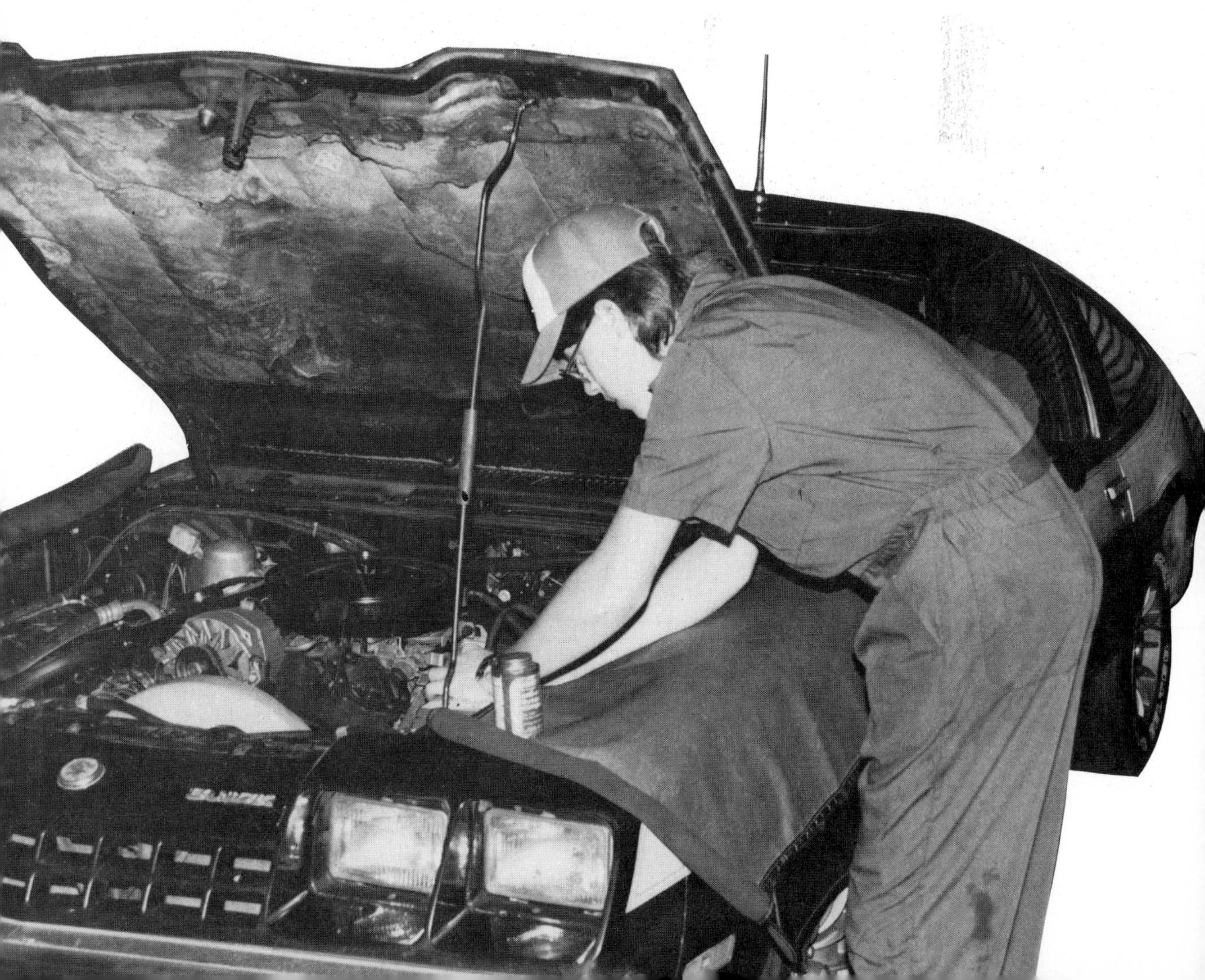

ADOLESCENTS' VOCATIONAL VALUES

If you had all the money you could ever possibly spend in your lifetime, would you still choose to be employed? When confronted with this question in 1980, more than 82 percent of 17,000 high-school seniors answered yes (Bachman, Johnston, & O'Malley, 1985). Unquestionably, as the comments in Box 11.1 will demonstrate, not all adolescents are enamoured with their part-time jobs. Nonetheless, most young people today are deeply concerned about their future vocational roles, and part-time employment is valued by most adolescents for its contributions to self-esteem, financial independence, and social maturity.

Indeed, adolescents in the 1980s have distinguished themselves as a group extremely concerned with vocational and financial issues. Not only are more adolescents employed in the 1980s than at any other time in the past 40 years; they are working more hours each week than their predecessors. For example, in 1940 only 1 in 25 tenth-grade boys and 1 in 100 tenth-grade girls worked part time while attending school (Steinberg, 1981). In contrast, almost half of all juniors and seniors in high school and almost a third of ninth- and tenth-graders are now working part time while attending school. Stated differently, by high-school graduation, almost 80 percent of the adolescent population has been employed (Nilsen, 1984).

Cross-cultural data also suggest that U.S. adolescents are more likely than their counterparts in other industrialized countries to be employed while in school. In 1979 over two-thirds of U.S. adolescent students were employed, in comparison with 37 percent in Canada, 21 percent in Sweden, and less than 2 percent in Japan (Ruebans, Jarrison, & Rupp, 1981). In other cross-cultural comparisons of several thousand adolescents during the 1960s and 1970s, U.S. adolescents expressed more allegiance to work-related values than their Australian, Israeli, and Irish counterparts. Moreover, on the "Self-Image Questionnaire" the

U.S. youngsters endorsed the item, "A job well done gives me pleasure" more frequently than any other item (Offer, Ostrov, & Howard, 1981).

In addition to the changes in high-school students' employment patterns, college students' behavior also acknowledges a shift in vocational emphasis within the past decade. Since the 1960s, college students have increasingly come to perceive a college education primarily as vocational preparation, rather than as an opportunity for self-discovery (Maggarrel, 1981, 1980). Exemplifying this altered attitude, in 1969 fewer than half of the college freshmen espoused a commitment to financial success, and nearly 80 percent stressed the importance of developing a philosophy of life while in college. In contrast, nearly two-thirds of the college freshmen in comparable 1981 surveys viewed financial success as an important objective in life, and fewer than half felt that developing a philosophy of life was an important goal during their college years. Moreover, the 1981 freshmen were more interested in achieving recognition in their professions than their cohorts in the 1960s (Astin, 1981). In accord with the philosophies of the 1980s, college enrollment in the arts, humanities, and social studies has steadily declined, as students have opted to pursue more lucrative jobs in business, computer science, engineering, and preprofessional programs (Yankelovich, 1981).

High-school students also tend to be more concerned with financial and vocational matters than their predecessors. Given the longitudinal nature of the data and the large sample sizes, *Monitoring the Future's* data, gathered from nearly 17,000 high-school seniors yearly throughout the 1970s and 1980s, are particularly instructive (Bachman, Johnston, & O'Malley, 1985). As Table 11.1 indicates, seniors polled in 1984 felt that chances for professional advancement and opportunities for a high salary were more important aspects of their future jobs than did adolescents in comparable polls since 1976. The importance of vocational advancement, job prestige, and income have all increased in recent years. Furthermore, the idea of working for large corporations has become more palatable to high-school seniors in the 1980s than to their predecessors in the 1970s, while interest in employment as teachers or social service workers has declined in popularity. Moreover, the values of males and females are strikingly similar, although females still tend to rate high salaries as less important than males.

Particularly among middle- and upper-middle-class youths, concerns about the vocational and financial realities of our times appear more prevalent than in previous decades (Andrew, 1981). Understanding the vagaries of unemployment and inflation, these youngsters are more inclined than their cohorts in the 1960s to worry about their future vocational success in a competitive, uncertain economy. Recognizing that, in comparison to the past, many more college graduates are unemployed and that many jobs that once seemed secure have been replaced by computers, the young can no longer confidently assume that a good education will insure employment or financial security. Data like these lend credence to the assertion that the majority of young people have enthusiastically adopted the traditional work ethic. As one high-school senior remarks, "It's a real panic mentality. A lot of students are scared of not being as well off as their parents" (Andrew, 1981, p.1.).

Commentators have noted, both facetiously and seriously, that "Yuppie" attitudes of the 1980s seem to have replaced the "Hippie" attitudes of the 1960s. Undoubtedly, some observers regard the vocational and financial attitudes of today's adolescents with dismay, worrying that the young's emphasis on finan-

Table 11.1

Important Things in a Job (percent rating very important, classes of 1976–1983)

	Males									Females								
	1976	*1977*	*1978*	*1979*	*1980*	*1981*	*1982*	*1983*	*1984*	*1976*	*1977*	*1978*	*1979*	*1980*	*1981*	*1982*	*1983*	*1984*
Interesting to do	84	88	87	88	85	85	85	86	86	92	91	91	91	91	91	91	89	89
Uses skills and abilities	65	70	69	71	68	70	68	69	66	76	78	74	73	76	76	76	75	76
Predictable, secure future	62	64	66	65	64	63	66	64	66	62	62	62	64	65	66	66	67	65
Good chances for advancement	59	65	67	64	65	67	66	65	67	54	59	59	65	61	66	65	65	64
See results of what you do	55	55	58	58	54	58	56	54	53	61	63	63	62	64	64	62	61	61
Chance to earn a good deal of money	54	54	56	60	58	59	61	61	61	40	43	44	47	50	52	52	51	54
Chance to make friends	47	50	47	52	47	48	46	44	45	61	63	61	62	59	59	57	57	58
Worthwhile to society	39	40	36	39	36	40	37	39	36	50	51	50	50	51	49	50	51	47
A job most people look up to and respect	32	35	33	35	36	37	36	36	38	36	37	39	38	39	42	43	41	43
High status, prestige	22	24	24	28	26	29	30	29	29	18	21	23	23	24	28	30	27	29

SOURCE: J. Bachman, L, Johnston, & P. O'Malley, *Recent findings from Monitoring the Future.* Ann Arbor: Institute For Social Research, University of Michigan, 1985.

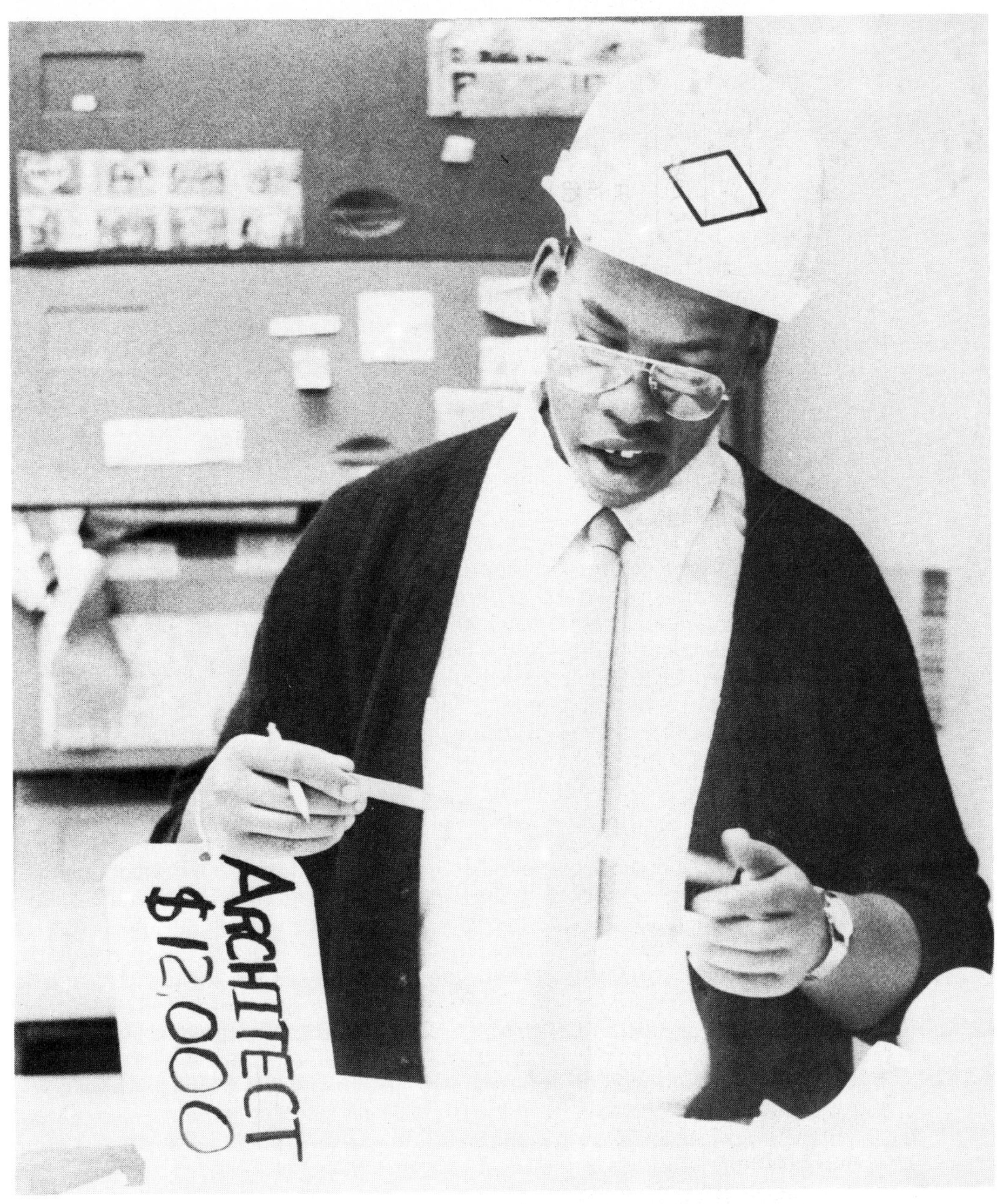

To what extent have your vocational plans been influenced by the salary and social status associated with particular jobs?

cial security and vocational success may override their willingness to be independent, creative, empathetic, or personally fulfilled. From this perspective, one might well ask whether youth's quest for financial security in an unpredictable, inflationary society will result in a more selfish, competitive, insensitive society. Moreover, will "making it" financially exacerbate psychological and physical problems, such as ulcers, heart attacks, alcoholism, and stress-related mental breakdowns? Will the desire for financial security further detract from relationships between children and parents or between spouses whose jobs compete with their family's needs? Given the data presented in Chapter 8 regarding the importance of father-child interactions, will the younger generation of males be willing to devote time to their children in lieu of attending to the rigorous demands of their jobs?

Although such questions worry the critics of the Yuppie generation, others observe, with considerable satisfaction, that the trend toward more conservative vocational and financial values is both admirable and reassuring (Andrew, 1981). From this perspective, the young's emphasis on financial security and vocational success reflects a mature, productive attitude and a lifestyle reminiscent of the 1950s. Why not dedicate oneself to the career-oriented values of the 1950s? Why not place social relationships in a position secondary to financial security and professional success? Whichever perspective one opts to endorse, the empirical data leave little doubt that most adolescents today are dedicated to the work ethic and to their future financial well-being.

Are we then to conclude that contemporary adolescents are replicas of the "silent generation" of young people who typified the 1950s? Did the events of the 1960s and 1970s leave no lasting impact on the vocational and financial values of today's young? While the data indicate that high-school students in the 1980s are more concerned about financial security and vocational success than their counterparts in the 1960s and 1970s, the young nonetheless distinguish themselves in several respects from their cohorts in previous decades.For example, while the 17,000 college-bound seniors surveyed in 1980 viewed jobs with a large corporation as more desirable than their predecessors in the late 1960s, they still considered corporate life less desirable than youths in the 1950s. In contrast to the 1950s endorsement of large corporations, 29 percent of the youths surveyed in 1980 said corporations were not serving society well, and 55 percent wanted corporations to have less influence (Bachman, 1982). Furthermore, although almost half of the high-school seniors surveyed in 1984 agreed that having a chance to make a high salary was an important aspect of a future job, they still maintained that being able to use their skills and being stimulated by the job were more important than prestige or potential income. Also, having a happy family life and finding a purpose and meaning in life were rated as more important than steady work. Convincingly, surveys with college students reinforce these findings (Yankelovich, 1981).

An important caveat, however, is that the shift to more conservative vocational attitudes seems to have occurred primarily among college-bound and wealthier adolescents. Not surprisingly, adolescents who seek employment or attend technical schools after high school have traditionally been more attentive than college-bound youth to issues like unemployment, inflation, vocational training, and job security. Such differences, however, do not imply that the vocational values of noncollege youth have been unaffected by the more liberal, humanitarian values of the 1960s and 1970s. For example, adolescents who were not planning to attend college in 1980 espoused values similar to their college-bound classmates in terms of wanting jobs that offer personal satisfaction and intellectual stimulation (Bachman, Johnston, & O'Malley, 1985). Likewise, young men without college educations have expressed more interest in the nonmonetary aspects of their jobs than older men without college educations (Miller & Simon, 1979). Such findings suggest that, although the shift from liberal to conservative attitudes may be most pronounced among college-bound students, most young people have become more interested in the nonmonetary aspects of jobs than young people before the 1960s.

In sum, college-bound youths of the 1980s seem more willing than students in the 1960s to commit themselves to certain kinds of conformity and "conservatism" in order to secure financial success. In general, however, both college and noncollege-bound adolescents seem less willing to sacrifice their personal happiness for their employers than were the youths of the 1950s.

ADOLESCENTS IN THE MARKETPLACE

Types of Employment for Adolescents

Although most adolescents have been employed before graduating from high school, many are far from satisfied with their employment experiences, as Box 11.1 illustrates (Glenbard East *Echo,* 1984). Given the part-time, temporary nature of their employment, it is not surprising that adolescents are generally performing jobs that require little education and provide little intellectual stimulation. For example, 1983 statistics reveal that one-third of all young people are employed in the food-service industry alone, while another third are equally divided between manual-labor jobs and retail sales. Interestingly, only 10 percent are employed in custodial work and only 10 percent in clerical work (Nilsen, 1984). As Table 11.2 illustrates, among the youngest adolescent workers, most are employed as salespeople or as private household workers. Yet even among older adolescents, one-fourth remain employed in service industries and another fourth as laborers, as Table 11.3 indicates. Considering the nature of the jobs to which most adolescents are consigned, it is argued by some researchers that the benefits of employment for high-school students have been exaggerated (Steinberg, 1981, 1982).

Since a great many adolescents' jobs involve menial, unchallenging labor, it is perhaps surprising that so many young workers continue to be so dedicated to part-time employment. In 1983, 15 percent of all 14- and 15-year-olds, 42 percent of the 16- and 17-year-olds, and 65 percent of the 18- and 19-year-olds were employed. Of special significance is the fact that 15 percent of all adolescents work more than 22 hours a week. Moreover, even in early adolescence, males are employed in a greater variety of jobs than females—a pattern that continues throughout adulthood, as the tables in this chapter illustrate (Nilsen, 1984).

Although the range of jobs available to adolescents is limited in part by their lack of education and experience, legal restrictions also deem young workers ineligible for many types of employment. Initially enacted to protect children from being physically or emotionally abused by their employers, child-labor laws

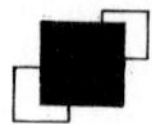

11.1 Adolescent Voices

Adolescents' Views on Working

Charlotte, age 16, from Georgia:
"Well, the job that I had was not like I had expected it to be. I couldn't handle it. It was putting too many pressures on me. I mostly worked on the weekends, and that's when everything happens. I couldn't stand to see other people go out. I am not a lazy person. I just didn't like the job or the employers. They treated me like I was a nobody. I was trained to work on a cash register, but as time passed they had me taking out trash, mopping a large floor, sweeping the floor, and cooking. They embarrassed me many times so I decided to just leave it alone."

Jason, age 17, from Kansas:
"Among my friends maintaining a nice car is the primary reason for having a job. Others have jobs so they can get out of the house and away from mom and dad for a while. Also, having a job provides a form of independence from financial restrictions imposed by parents. My parents never allowed me to have a job during school. They say that they would rather give me an allowance than for me to be distracted from my studies. So far it has worked. My grade point average has been 3.8 to 4.0. In addition I have been able to participate in forensics, debate and the school plays. I feel that parents that allow and even encourage their teens to get an after school job 'for the experience' are doing their children a great disservice. One's education and high school experience are much more important and valuable than the little bit of spending money acquired from minimum wage slave labor."

Kim, age 17, from Illinois:
"Teenage workers' biggest problem is that their employers don't treat them with enough respect. One of my managers is constantly making plays at me. When I stand up for myself, he threatens me with my job."

restrict the number of hours that minors are permitted to work, as well as the types of jobs in which they may be employed. In addition, the legal age at which adolescents may be employed was intended to protect children from the crippling labor in industrial "sweatshops," coal mines, cotton mills, and in agriculture.

The *federal Fair Labor Standards Act,* the major statute in the child-labor field, governs both the quality and quantity of youth employment (Nilsen, 1984). Under the law, children under the age of 14 may be employed only as actors, newspaper deliverers, or in a nonagricultural business owned by their parents. Fourteen- and 15-year-olds may not be employed in any manufacturing, mining, or processing occupations, such as laundering clothes or dressing poultry. Minors are also prohibited from working for a public messenger service, from operating power-driven machinery, and from jobs involving transportation, warehousing, construction, or communications, with the exception of office or sales work. While young adolescents are eligible for jobs such as picking crops,

Martin, age 18, from Nevada:
"I don't know why other teenagers work, but for me it is mainly parent pressure. I want to make them feel I'm good for something. Also I want to relieve them of some financial burden. I am a very materialistic person and very label conscious. I firmly believe you get what you pay for. Thus, I spend lots of money for the things I want."

Kevin, age 18, from Indiana:
"I work for a carpet cleaning company. My pay is good and my co-workers are real nice. I'm treated like an adult and a partner or co-worker. My only problem is when we clean a restaurant. I don't start until ten thirty or twelve at night so I usually get home from one thirty to three in the morning. This is a bit hard since I'll only get three to five hours sleep."

Sunni, age 15, from Indiana:
"I have a job training and showing horses for different farms. I can't imagine not having to go to the farm after school. Getting there on time, making sure all my horses I work are healthy and doing well is my way of being independent. It's not necessarily the money. It's more or less the way I try and earn respect for being responsible."

Brian, age 16, from Illinois
"I think it's great to work. In my case I have to. My mother and father are divorced and I have to help my mom any way I can. So my brother and I got jobs. He works four nights a week at Woolworths and I work for the city of Centralia as a sports director. We both make good money and we never have to ask for money. Sometimes we even give her money out of our checks. Don't get me wrong—my mom works too. We have made it for two years at our jobs and we love to work."

Source: Glenbard East *Echo. Teenagers themselves.* New York: Adama Books, 1984, pp. 77–87.

they are legally barred from agricultural work classified as hazardous, such as operating farm equipment. In most cases, state or federal laws prohibit young adolescents from cooking, working in freezers or boiler rooms, loading and unloading goods, window washing, and engaging in maintenance or repair work.

With regard to working hours and schedules, youths under the age of 16 in nonagricultural jobs are barred from working more than 40 hours a week or more than eight hours a day during school vacations. During the school year, young adolescents are limited to 18 hours of employment per week. Moreover, young adolescents in many states are legally prohibited from working between 7 p.m. and 7 a.m. during the school year and from 9 p.m. to 7 a.m. during the summer. Although beyond the age of 15 the legal restrictions become more relaxed, state and federal laws continue to mandate which jobs are acceptable for young workers.

Current debates focusing on child-labor laws have provoked a number of controversial questions: Should the hours that 14- and 15-year-olds are cur-

Table 11.2

Occupations of 14- and 15-year-old students: October 1982

Occupation	*Total (percent)*	*Boys*	*Girls*
Professional and technical	0.8	0.7	0.9
Managers and administrators	0.2	0.5	< 0.1
Sales	21.5	34.3	8.8
Clerical	4.4	2.5	6.2
Craft and kindred	0.7	0.9	0.5
Operatives, except transport	2.2	3.9	0.5
Transport equipment operatives	0.3	0.7	< 0.1
Nonfarm laborers	17.0	28.9	5.1
Service workers—nonhousehold	13.3	12.0	14.5
Private-household workers	33.3	4.6	61.9
Farm managers	0.6	0.7	0.5
Farm laborers	5.8	10.2	1.4
Total number surveyed, enrolled in school	865,000	432,000	433,000

SOURCE: D. Nilsen, The youngest workers: 14- and 15-year-olds. *Journal of Early Adolescence,* 1984, *4,* 189–197.

rently permitted to work be extended? Should these young adolescents be allowed to work until nine o'clock on school nights? Should the youngest workers be permitted to compete with older adolescents for jobs from which they are now restricted? Should those between the ages of 16 and 20 be paid $2.50 an hour—85 cents less than the current minimum wage—during summer months, in order to reduce youth unemployment? Would such a proposal be fair to older workers who might lose their jobs to adolescents who can work for lower wages? Although the Labor Department and President Reagan proposed legislation favoring such modifications, opposing views from organizations like the AFL-CIO, the National Child Labor Committee, and the PTA have halted reforms until the advantages and disadvantages are more thoroughly considered. Thus, as Box 11.2 illustrates, legislative debates over issues related to adolescent employment continue.

Advantages of Adolescent Employment

Given the controversy regarding adolescent employment, what benefits accrue to employed adolescents? Indeed, should parents encourage their adolescent children to take time away from their academic, recreational, or athletic activities for a part-time job? Among the commonly held assumptions about employment is that jobs help adolescents develop a sense of responsibility and provide them with an understanding of the marketplace that will serve them well

Table 11.3

Major Occupation Group of Employed Persons 16- to 24-Years-Old: 1980 Annual Average (percent of civilian noninstitutional population)

	Male		*Female*	
Occupation Group	*16–19 years*	*20–24 years*	*16–19 years*	*20–24 years*
White-collar workers	16.9	30.5	52.4	67.5
Professional, technical, and kindred workers	2.5	10.8	2.8	14.2
Managers and administrators, except farm	1.4	5.8	1.4	4.7
Sales workers	5.8	5.4	12.2	6.3
Clerical and kindred workers	7.2	8.5	36.0	42.2
Blue-collar workers	52.9	55.8	10.3	13.0
Craft and kindred workers	11.9	21.4	1.2	1.8
Operatives, including transport	18.2	22.8	6.6	9.6
Laborers, except farm	22.8	11.5	2.4	1.6
Service workers	24.0	10.4	35.9	18.8
Private household workers	0.2	(Z)	5.4	1.1
Service workers, except private household	23.8	10.4	30.5	17.7
Farm workers	6.2	3.3	1.5	0.7
Farmers and farm managers	0.5	1.0	(Z)	0.1
Farm laborers and supervisors	5.7	2.3	1.4	0.6
Total employed (thousands)	4,016	7,254	3,587	6,360
Percent	100.0	100.0	100.0	100.0

Note: (z) = 0.0
SOURCE: U.S. Department of Commerce, Bureau of the Census, unpublished 1980 Current Population Survey data.

in their future vocation. Moreover, it has been argued that a job provides diversion, which diminishes the likelihood of delinquent behavior. Yet are these supposed benefits of part-time employment empirically defensible?

Interviews with adolescents, such as those quoted in Box 11.1, testify to the fact that young people can profit from their jobs in ways that go beyond monetary remuneration (Cole, 1983; Glenbard East *Echo,* 1984). In this regard, a job does appear to help some young people develop a sense of pride, responsibility, and independence. For other young workers, a job enhances their skills in managing money, budgeting time, and communicating with adults. In addition, families can benefit when an adolescent's supplemental income provides amenities or even necessities that many parents would like to provide but cannot afford. In these cases, the income from part-time jobs can afford adolescents enriching opportunities, such as participating in summer athletic programs or learning to operate computers. In these respects, the research suggests that many adolescents do indeed benefit from their employment (Cole, 1983; Cook, 1983; Greenberger & Steinberg, 1981; Greenberger, Steinberg, & Vaux, 1981; Steinberg, 1981).

Over and above the benefits that often accrue from part-time employment,

Should adolescents be employed as school bus drivers? How did employment affect your adolescent development?

adolescents whose job experiences are coordinated by the school can derive additional advantages. Some innovative programs coordinated through the schools offer students opportunities for innovative part-time jobs in local government, health services, industry, business, and the arts. Adolescents in these well-designed vocational programs are more apt to be protected against the relatively meaningless sorts of part-time employment to which many young workers are subjected. Moreover, school-supervised programs afford young people the opportunities of apprenticeship to experienced, adult workers who can serve as their vocational mentors. Such apprenticeship opportunities permit young workers to experiment with different vocational interests, test their skills, develop attitudes complementary to future success and learn from adults with superior skills in a supportive environment.

Beyond the advantages that many adolescents derive from their jobs, teenage employment also contributes to local communities by providing the type of part-time or temporary help that older workers can no longer afford to accept because of the low pay or poor fringe benefits. Working in fast-food restaurants, washing cars, delivering newspapers, babysitting, or cutting grass are economically unfeasible options for most adult workers. Indeed, many companies could not survive without the ready supply of part-time labor provided by the young during busy seasons of the year. Furthermore, employed adolescents are an indirect asset to the economy by virtue of their role as consumers. If adolescents were deprived of their discretionary earnings from part-time jobs, businesses like the cosmetic, movie, and record industries would certainly fare less well. As the data in Table 11.4 illustrate, many of today's employed adolescents might be considered "prematurely affluent," given the purchasing power their discretionary salaries have bestowed on them.

Several national commissions have endorsed the value of adolescent employment for the young. Like their counterparts in the 1970s, commissions in the early 1980s have recommended that school curricula and employment continue to be integrated as a means of providing youngsters with a meaningful role in society (Carnegie Council, 1980; National Commission on Youth, 1980). Endorsing this position, during the 1970s the U.S. Department of Labor launched a 3 billion dollar youth employment program, and the National Institute of Education created a model espousing vocational education and work experiences as part of all students' curricula. Data from these programs suggest that work experiences increase adolescents' school attendance, improve their grades, instill positive attitudes toward work, and increase their future wages (Barton & Frazer, 1980).

Disadvantages of Adolescent Employment

Despite the potential advantages that can accrue from part-time jobs, it is argued that the disadvantages of adolescent employment too often override the benefits. Some data acknowledge that our idealistic expectations regarding the benefits of employment during adolescence materialize less often than might be hoped. By way of illustration, a recent study of 3,100 tenth- and eleventh-graders in four California schools showed that adolescents' jobs did not enhance their sense of social responsibility, commitment to the welfare of others, or tolerance of individual and cultural differences. Perhaps not surprisingly, the employed adolescents expressed more negative, cynical attitudes about working than their unemployed peers. In addition to increasing their cynicism about the intrinsic value of work, employment appeared to have increased their use of marijuana and tobacco, a phenomenon that was not accounted for solely by their increased incomes (Greenberger & Steinberg, 1981; Steinberg, 1981, 1982).

According to the opponents of youth employment, most adolescents' jobs fail to engender attitudes or skills relevant to their future employment. The argument is substantiated by the Labor Department's national longitudinal survey of

11.2 A Closer Look

New Wage for Youths Is Pushed

Subminimum Pay for Summer Jobs

WASHINGTON (AP)—The Reagan administration is campaigning hard for support among minorities and other groups for legislation to cut the minimum wage for youths by 25 percent during summer vacation—a move the Labor Department says would create 400,000 jobs.

Identical legislation introduced last May failed to come to a vote in the Senate or House before the 98th Congress expired at year's end. But President Reagan gave the idea prominent notice in his State of the Union address Feb. 6, and the legislation will be introduced within a month, Bruce Navarro, the Labor Department's acting chief of legislative affairs, said yesterday.

The three-year test program would allow a subminimum wage of $2.50 an hour, down from the minimum wage of $3.35 an hour, from May 1 to Sept. 30 for workers 16 to 19 years old.

Efforts to garner support among minorities have had mixed results.

For and Against

The Labor Department obtained an endorsement late last year from the National Association for Equal Opportunity in Education, which represents 114 historically black colleges and universities. Black teenage unemployment was 43.1 percent in February.

The National Conference of Black Mayors endorsed the proposal last April with some stipulations, among them that federal funds for summer youth employment not be cut and that adults not be displaced by youths earning the subminimum wage. At least one conference member, Philadelphia Mayor Wilson Goode, has since withdrawn his support.

the youth labor market between 1979 and 1981, which showed that more than three-fourths of the jobs held by workers between the ages of 14 and 22 require less than a high-school education and that nearly half require no more than a brief explanation to master the necessary job skills (Borus, 1984). From this perspective, working in a fast-food restaurant, typing, or ringing up groceries in a supermarket are not perceived as experiences that instill skills or attitudes that are particularly relevant for vocational success in an adolescent's future.

Critics of youth employment contend that a part-time job diminishes the amount of time that adolescents can invest in their academic work. For instance, in the California study, more than one-fourth of the 3,100 students admitted that their grades declined after they became employed, and only one in nine said their grades had improved (Greenberger & Steinberg, 1981; Greenberger, Steinberg, & Vaux, 1981). Similarly, in the Labor Department's national surveys, employed high-school and college students invested less time studying, attend-

The Rev. Jesse Jackson opposes the proposal, saying society should train youths for more highly skilled jobs. The National Urban League and other civil-rights groups also oppose it, as does organized labor, which says subminimum wage teen-agers would replace higher-paid adults.

The proposal contains criminal penalties against displacing adults with low-paid youths. Mark A. de Bernardo, manager of labor law for the U.S. Chamber of Commerce, said that wouldn't occur anyway.

Panel Reluctant

At a hardware store in Nashville,Tenn., the owner said that he no longer can afford to employ a teen-ager to reorganize the storeroom and do other odd jobs, said de Bernardo. "Now the cleanup either doesn't get done or the hardware store owner does it himself," he added.

The House Subcommittee on Labor Standards, to which a subminimum wage likely would be referred, "would not be eager to consider it," said Tom Lamb, the panel's staff director.

The minimum wage has not been revised in four years, so "inflation has had the effect of producing a subminimum wage anyway," he said.

Lamb said many in the business community would rather have the issue "left where it is. Any effort, they feel, for a subminimum wage might be accompanied by some adjustment in the minimum wage."

There is disagreement over precisely how many jobs a subminimum wage would create. The Labor Department arrived at a figure of 400,000 by adopting a study concluding that historically, each 10 percent increase in the minimum wage produced a decline in youth employment of 1 percent to 3 percent.

SOURCE: *Winston-Salem Journal*, Winston-Salem, N.C., March 16, 1985. Reprinted by permission.

ing class, sleeping, watching television, reading for pleasure, and performing household chores than their unemployed classmates. Moreover, the employed males tended to take more time away from their studies than the employed females (Borus, 1984).

In addition, advocates of adolescent employment are inclined to endorse the aphorism, "Idle hands are the devil's workshop." According to many who support adolescent employment, jobs decrease delinquency by reducing the need to procure money illegally and by providing social and economic status through legitimate activities. It is further assumed by the pro-employment advocates that jobs counteract delinquency by making adolescents feel less alienated from their society and more bonded to the social order.

Although such assumptions initially appear logical, the empirical data demonstrate a more complicated relationship between unemployment and delinquency than is commonly acknowledged. For example, in the California study of

3,100 high-school students, employed adolescents had somewhat more police contacts and were engaged in more serious kinds of misbehavior than their unemployed classmates. Moreover, there were significant increases in the number of police contacts and seriousness of offences for those who started full-time jobs after the age of 17 (Greenberger & Steinberg, 1981). Likewise, the Labor Department's national surveys from 1979 through 1981 showed that employed high-school students were more involved in illegal acts, particularly the use of illegal drugs, than the unemployed. An important finding from these surveys, however, is that the effects of employment seem to depend partially on the adolescents' age. Among 18- to 23-year-olds who were not enrolled in college, the length of unemployment was significantly correlated with illegal activities for earning money (Borus, 1984).

Data such as these have contributed to the hypothesis that employment may actually increase delinquency by providing adolescents with too much privacy, mobility, and distance from adults (Greenberger & Steinberg, 1981; Hirschi, 1983; Steinberg, 1982). From this perspective, adolescents who have an independent source of discretionary income are less reliant on their parents and are more willing to ignore parental advice than their unemployed peers. Thus, income provides a liberation from parental control and separates the young from traditional sources of socialization within the family. Furthermore, the kinds of jobs most youths hold may expose them to stress and isolate them from interaction with adults. Both the California study and the Labor Department statistics lend support to this supposition by showing that employed youths do spend less time with their families than the unemployed.

Other evidence, however, indicates that employment neither increases nor decreases delinquency. A recent Milwaukee study of 406 16- and 17-year-old dropouts failed to establish any relationship between unemployment and delinquency (Cook, 1983). The study included male and female dropouts from Hispanic, black, and white families with low incomes. By testing these youngsters before and after six months of employment, the researchers found that being employed did not affect their psychological health scores, delinquent behavior, or personal characteristics. Returning to school, however, lowered the youths' scores on "interpersonal competency." In contrast, working full time tended to instill feelings of personal competence and independence. Delinquency was associated with being male, being a younger adolescent, and having low scores on interpersonal competence. Thus, the study undermines the hypothesis that employment in and of itself either deters or contributes to delinquency.

In yet another carefully designed study investigating the relationship between employment and delinquency, data were collected in 1980 and 1981 from 11,130 students in grades 6 through 12 (Gottfredson, 1985). The students were enrolled in 169 schools in 17 cities, primarily in economically depressed, inner-city districts. Perhaps the single most important findings from this study is that employed students differed from their unemployed classmates *before* they became employed. Through statistical comparisons of the students both before and after they became employed, the researchers were able to isolate the characteristics distinguishing employed and unemployed adolescents before they began working. For example, employed girls were more interpersonally aggressive and used twice as many drugs before beginning their jobs as did girls who remained unemployed. Similarly, males who obtained jobs were less attached to their parents than boys who chose not to seek employment.

Given the initial differences between young people who were employed and those who were not, the seemingly surprising results of this study become more comprehensible (Gottfredson, 1985). Boys who had jobs used no more drugs and committed no more crimes against property than their unemployed counterparts. The employed males, however, were more likely than their unemployed classmates to commit crimes involving aggression against other people. Contrary to expectaions, employed boys spent more time on homework and were more involved in extracurricular activities than unemployed boys. Contradictions like these can more easily be explained by remembering that the employed boys were more involved in school activities and less attached to their parents at the outset.

In contrast, the older high-school girls who worked were not significantly different from their unemployed classmates in regard to delinquency or drug use. The younger junior-high-school girls who worked were much more likely, however, to use drugs and to commit crimes against persons and property than their unemployed female classmates. Employment did not detract from males' or females' commitment to school, except in the case of Hispanic girls. Only the employed Spanish American girls were more truant than their unemployed classmates, but this was not accompanied by increases in their delinquency. Of special note is the fact that working had no effect for either males or females on their feelings of attachment to their parents (Gottfredson, 1985).

These findings underscore a crucial methodological shortcoming in prior research: Studies that have attempted to relate delinquency to employment are confounded by the fact that unemployed and employed youngsters differ from one another at the outset. Hence, much of what has been attributed to being employed or unemployed may in reality be a consequence of the initial differences between adolescents who seek jobs and those who remain full-time students. Further, Gottfredson's data indicate that the potential effects of adolescent unemployment may vary as a function of the adolescent's age, gender, and race.

Finally, among the other disadvantages of adolescent employment, researchers surveying representative samples of high-school seniors since the mid-1970s suggest that many of today's employed adolescents are being subjected to the vagaries of premature affluence. According to data from *Monitoring the Future,* more than half of all employed high-school seniors have been earning more than $50 a week since 1979. Given these adolescent incomes and the popularity of jobs among the young, the researchers decided to test the assumptions that employment affords adolescents the opportunities to learn money-management skills, to confront the realities of the financial world, and to appreciate the value of money (Bachman, 1983).

Contrary to expectations, very few of the seniors surveyed in 1982 were becoming acquanted with the financial realities of society. Indeed, most employed seniors were contributing nothing to their families for groceries, rent, utilities, or the other expenses they will eventually confront in the adult world. Likewise, half had saved no money whatsoever, and only slightly over one-third of those who were planning to complete four years of college were putting aside any money to help defray their college expenses. As Table 11.4 illustrates, most of the adolescent wage-earners invested their money in owning or operating a car, buying clothes, and entertaining themselves.

Ironically, it also appears that high-school students' part-time jobs might

Table 11.4

High-School Seniors in 1982: Disposition of Earnings (percent responding)

	1,500 Males	*1,520 Females*
1. Savings for your future education?		
None	48	50
A little	23	21
Some	19	19
Most	11	10
2. Savings or payments for a car or car expenses?		
None	35	58
A little	19	16
Some	29	18
Most	17	9
3. Other savings for long-range purposes?		
None	48	48
A little	26	25
Some	18	20
Most	8	8
4. Spending on your own needs and activities?		
None	4	5
A little	21	17
Some	38	34
Most	36	44
5. Helping to pay family living expenses?		
None	56	55
A little	26	25
Some	13	14
Most	5	6

SOURCE: J. Bachman, Premature affluence: Do high school students earn too much? *Economic Outlook USA*, 1983, *10*, 64–67.

subsequently detract from their satisfaction with life. On the basis of follow-up surveys of high-school graduates, the researchers found that adolescents' who had been employed in high school became less satisfied with their standard of living in the years immediately following their graduation. Although most high-school seniors rated their life satisfaction as 5.7 on a 7-point scale, the scores of those who enrolled in college declined by about one point during the next six years. Moreover, those who enrolled in college were the most likely to be dissatisfied with their financial situation in comparison with their financial circumstances as high-school students. In contrast, the life satisfaction ratings of young people who did not continue their education after high-school graduation fell by only half a point. On the basis of these responses, the researchers suggest that employed high-school students become accustomed to an unrealistic standard of living as a consequence of being permitted to treat their earnings purely as discretionary income. Having become prematurely affluent, the employed high-school students subsequently become discontented when confronted with the economic realities and contingencies which operate in adult society (Bachman, 1983).

Moreover, the researchers contend that adolescents who are permitted to spend their incomes on their own immediate desires are not learning to delay gratification. Thus, financial permissiveness contributes to the "Now" generation's assumption that people have an unquestionable right to have every immediate desire satisfied. For example, young people who have become accustomed to spending their money on their own immediate pleasures may find it difficult to deprive themselves in later life in order to save enough money for a home, or retirement, or other long-range benefits.

Worried about the possible ramifications of adolescents' affluence, Jerald Bachman, director of *Monitoring the Future,* suggests that parents impose certain guidelines on their employed children. For instance, parents might require that part of their income be saved for the future or that some contribution be made to the family's household expenses. Having gathered and examined data for almost a decade, Bachman concludes: "I continue to believe that there is much to be gained from youth employment experiences, but I am troubled by the present patterns of earning and spending. Young people's views about money are an important part of their development. I am concerned that premature affluence may be teaching the wrong lessons" (Bachman, 1983).

In sum, generalizations about the relative advantages and disadvantages of employment for adolescents must be tempered by several caveats. First, considering the evidence that initial differences may exist between employed and unemployed youth at the outset, correlational research that compares employed and unemployed youths should be interpreted cautiously. Second, the impact of employment on a particular adolescent is difficult to predict, since variables such as the nature of the job, the youth's age, and the youth's situation at school appear to enhance or detract from the experience. For example, having a part-time job appears to be an instructive experience for many adolescents in terms of enhancing skills such as money management and self-discipline. Yet, for young people with academic problems who could benefit from the additional hours of study or for those with menial jobs that exacerbate negative feelings about employment, even part-time employment can undeniably do more harm than good.

Adolescent Unemployment

Profile of the Unemployed Although unemployment is generally regarded as a problem restricted to adults, adolescents are also affected by the anxiety and frustration that accompany the failure to find work. Unfortunately, although young people between the ages of 16 and 24 constitute one-fourth of the potential labor force, they account for half of the unemployed (Robison, 1980). Moreover, although chronic unemployment affects only about 10 percent of all teenaged Americans, it wreaks its greatest toll on young people who live in inner cities and those who are members of racial minorities. Sadly, minority youths from the inner cities are only half as likely as white youngsters from the suburbs to find employment. For example, almost 30 percent of the youths classified as hard-core unemployed are black, and blacks' overall unemployment rate is increasing at a faster rate than whites' (Borus, 1984). Likewise, youths from lower socioeconomic families, who could most benefit financially from part-time employment, have only half the chance of being hired as adolescents from more financially advantaged families (Rodriguez, 1980).

A more detailed profile of unemployed adolescents emerges from the Labor Department's statistics collected between 1977 and 1981 (Borus, 1984; Nolfi, 1978). From these representative samples of approximately 13,000 young people between the ages of 14 and 22, black youths and youths of all races from families below the poverty level have the highest unemployment rates. As would be expected, high-school dropouts had higher unemployment rates than high-school graduates. In terms of geographic location, the highest unemployment rates for females are in the Northeast and for males are in the North Central states. Given the industrial expansion in the southern states, it is not surprising that the unemployment rates for males were lowest there. Further, as might be anticipated, the youths who were least successful in finding jobs were those who had children and those who lived in the central cities.

In regard to the motivation of both the employed and unemployed youths, only 1 in 13 said they needed to work in order to support themselves or to support their families. Interestingly, however, only one-third of young people read newspaper advertisements when searching for a job, and fewer than 20 percent had ever consulted a public employment service for assistance during periods of unemployment. Moreover, the unemployed youths who were seeking employment invested only about five hours of their time each week in the search for a job.

Contrary to the assumption that jobless youths have an inflated sense of their own vocational worth, one-third of the young people seeking jobs said they would accept any type of employment. In addition, half said they were willing to work for salaries below the minimum wage. Specifically, only 10 percent of the unemployed were looking for salaries of $5.00 an hour, although one-fourth of the employed young people were actually earning this hourly wage. In sum, these national statistics fail to support the notion that unemployed young people have unrealistic or unreasonable aspirations regarding salaries or job status (Borus, 1984).

Unfortunately, the Labor Department data garner only limited support for the assumption that participating in a vocational education program increases a young person's employability or income (Borus, 1984). For example, females who had completed an additional semester of academic or vocational courses in high school earned only 3 percent higher salaries than those without the equivalent semester's training. Similarly, boys' salaries were unaffected by their additional academic or vocational training, although those with more coursework in either academic or vocational areas did have lower unemployment rates. More disappointing still, vocational training had less impact on salaries for blacks and Hispanics than for whites, leading the analysts to conclude that "since members of each of these groups (blacks, Hispanics, and whites) take similar types of high-school courses, vocational training appears to have little impact on racial and ethnic inequality" (Borus, 1984, p. 184). In sum, regardless of the adolescent's race, vocational training had a less beneficial impact on employment and salaries than would have been expected.

Given the discouraging results regarding the value of high-school vocational training, one might well wonder about the value of the high-school diploma itself in terms of reducing unemployment and raising salaries. Encouragingly, high-school graduates' unemployment rates from 1979 to 1981 were less than half those of high-school dropouts. Indeed, dropouts constituted nearly half of the chronically unemployed. The assertion that graduating from high school literally "pays off," therefore, is empirically validated. It is noteworthy, however, that the types of courses a student completes in high school are less strongly correlated with vocational success than are nonacademic factors such as good work habits and vocational or personal attitudes that impress prospective employers (Borus, 1984).

The Consequences of Unemployment While incurring the obvious financial disadvantage of being unemployed, many young people who are seeking jobs also experience feelings of helplessness and cynicism (Nilsen, 1984; Swinton, 1980). Unemployment can simultaneously undermine self-esteem and create feelings of an external locus of control. As you recall from Chapter 3, feeling externally controlled is being convinced that fate, happenstance, or other people determine both the good and the bad in a person's life. Once having adopted this attitude of personal powerlessness as a consequence of their thwarted attempts to find jobs, young people often become convinced that our society will never offer them an opportunity for employment. In a society that tends to confer status and esteem on the basis of financial success, chronically unemployed youths can come to feel disenfranchised and alienated.

Moreover, data indicate that young people pay social and physical penalties as a consequence of chronic unemployment. It has been argued that chronically unemployed youths tend to resort to illegal activities like prostitution and illegal drug traffic (Swinton, 1980). In support of this hypothesis, statistics have shown a high correlation between chronic youth unemployment and automobile fatalities, mental breakdowns, narcotics violations, homicide, rape, assault, robbery, car theft, and prostitution (Brenner, 1980). Nevertheless, as mentioned previously in this chapter, it is noteworthy that a number of studies have failed to uphold the hypothesis that unemployment exacerbates delinquency. Hence, assertions about the relationship between unemployment and antisocial or criminal behavior must take into consideration the initial differences that may have existed between employed and unemployed people—differences that in and of themselves might account for high rates of delinquency, depression, or fatalities.

Proposals for Reducing Youth Unemployment A myriad of proposals have been offered in hopes of increasing youth employment. Some legislators and economists have proposed that the minimum wage be lowered as a way of permitting more employers to hire young workers (Kelly, 1980; Robison, 1980). Since the 1979 minimum-wage increase is estimated to be costing adolescents about 90,000 jobs a year, this proposal initially seems reasonable (Lerman, 1980). Opponents of lowering the minimum wage, however, contend that, even if the 90,000 jobs adolescents lost through the higher minimum wage were reinstated, unemployment would decline by only one percentage point. Furthermore, employers' racial and economic discrimination would continue to deprive many youngsters of jobs, and lowering the minimum wage would do little to compensate for the paucity of jobs in the inner cities where chronic unemployment is worst. For such reasons, legislators, including those who are themselves members of racial minorities, have generally viewed the Reagan administration's campaign to reduce youths' minimum wages to $2.50 an hour with ambivalence (see Box 11.2).

Other mitigating factors associated with youth unemployment are underscored in a recent study of 1,500 adolescents from indigent families in the inner cities (Gottleib & Driscoll, 1982). Interviewing employers who had hired these financially disadvantaged youngsters, the investigators found that most employers were dissatisfied with their young employees' academic skills and attitudes toward work. Despite the fact that most of these inner-city youths had received vocational training before being hired, most employers felt the youngsters needed to improve their work-related attitudes and their behavior on the job. For example, there was displeasure with adolescents' high job turnover rates, absenteeism, and tardiness. Employers cited these deficiencies far more frequently than they requested that adolescents have better training in specific job skills. Interestingly, however, the employers were insisting that adolescents' meet certain entrance criteria, such as academic skills and personal appearance, which were unrelated to the actual requirements of the job. Also noteworthy is the finding that, despite their criticisms, most employers were sympathetic to the fact that the routine, menial nature of the work and the low wages exacerbated their young employees' poor attitudes and behavior.

Unfortunately, the quandary remains: How can inner-city youths be motivated to perform menial, low-paid jobs with enough care or enthusiasm to suit their employers? How is the problem of youth unemployment in inner cities to be resolved? In the midst of ongoing attempts to reduce youth unemployment, it has nonetheless become clear that the ultimate resolutions will require an eclectic approach, rather than a search for one single panacea such as lowering the minimum wage.

THEORIES OF VOCATIONAL DEVELOPMENT

"What do you want to be when you grow up?" is a childhood version of questions often posed to adolescents both by adults and by peers: What are your future plans? Do you want to go to college? Are you going to accept that job offer from your uncle or go back to school? Do you really think the courses you plan to enroll in this fall will help you get a job next year? From the theorists' perspectives, however, the more important questions are of a different nature, such as: What factors are most influential in determining adolescents' vocational choices? How might we identify which vocations a particular adolescent is best suited for in terms of skills and temperment? In this regard, the theoretical perspectives associated with vocational development can be broadly categorized into two distinctive approaches: differentialist views and developmental views.

The Differentialist Perspective

According to the *differentialist perspective,* young people's vocational choices should be based on matching their own abilities, interests, and temperaments to the demands of a particular vocation. For example, an adolescent who is manually inept, disdains the study of science in any form, and becomes restless at indoor activities would be ill-advised to pursue a career as a surgeon, despite her parents' wishes. In like fashion, the shy, retiring, mathematically talented youth should be steered away from jobs that demand assertiveness and public speaking, since he is better suited to jobs requiring mathematical profi-

Do you have a vocational plan? If so, what experiences in your life have influenced your present vocational path? If not, how will you go about devising such a plan?

ciency and privacy. Within the differentialist context, the vocational counselor's primary goal is to assess adolescents' skills and attitudes and to apprise youths of which jobs are best suited to their personalities and talents.

In accord with this view, differentialists have developed a variety of written tests to assess adolescents' talents and attitudes. Items from one of the most popular tests, the *Strong-Campbell Interest Inventory,* are presented in Box 11.3 (Campbell, 1974). Once an adolescent has completed a vocational interest inventory, his or her vocational profile is compared with the characteristics required for success in various types of jobs. One of the better known classifications of jobs is Holland's (1966) six-category scheme of *occupational types* described in Box 11.4.

Although research generally supports the notion that people with similar personalities are often found in similar types of jobs, the differentialist view is not without its critics (Osipow, 1973). To begin with, most adolescents base their vocational decisions on factors other than the congruence between personal interests or skills and a particular job's requirements (Gottfredson & Becker, 1981). Furthermore, congruence between an adolescent's score on a vocational interest inventory and a job's characteristics does not necessarily assure success or happiness in a particular job. For example, a 17-year-old girl could express no interest whatsoever in a medical career simply because she has

11.3 A Closer Look

Excerpts from the Strong-Campbell Interest Inventory

Here are several pairs of activities or occupations. Show which one of each pair you like better: if you prefer the one on the *left,* mark in the space labeled "*L*" on the answer sheet; if you prefer the one on the *right,* mark in the space labeled "*R*"; if you like *both the same,* or if you *can't decide,* mark in the space labeled "=". Work rapidly. Make one mark for each pair.

Airline pilot	282	Airline ticket agent
Taxicab driver	283	Police officer
Headwaiter/Hostess	284	Lighthouse keeper
Selling things house to house	285	Gardening
Developing plans	286	Carrying out plans
Doing a job yourself	287	Telling somebody else to do the job
Dealing with things	288	Dealing with people
Taking a chance	289	Playing safe
Drawing a definite salary	290	Receiving a commission on what is done
Outside work	291	Inside work
Work for yourself	292	Carrying out the program of a superior whom you respect
Superintendent of a hospital	293	Warden of a prison
Vocational counselor	294	Public health officer
Physical activity	295	Mental activity
Dog trainer	296	Juvenile parole officer
Thrilling, dangerous activities	297	Quieter, safer activities

never been exposed to relevant courses or experiences. Similarly, a 20-year-old male may develop interests in working with young children as a consequence of working at a summer camp because no others jobs were available. Yet his newly discovered interests may not have been assessed on a previous written interest inventory. Thus, one limitation of the differentialist view is its underemphasis on the impact of new experiences on an individual's vocational aptitudes and preferences.

Moreover, the differentialists' critics contend that written vocational interest inventories are methodologically questionable means for predicting an individual's future success in any specific job. First, adolescents can lie about or exaggerate their interests and skills on the tests. Motivated by a desire to give socially desirable answers or to please parents, a youngster might not admit, for example, that he or she is completely disinterested in the sciences and prefers to work with handicapped children. In addition, some interest inventories may use language beyond the comprehension of adolescents who read poorly, thus biasing their answers. Finally, since an individual's interests are likely to change

Physical education director	298	Free-lance writer
Statistician	299	Social worker
Technical responsibility (in charge of 25 people doing scientific work)	300	Supervisory responsibility (in charge of 300 people doing business-office work)
Going to a play	301	Going to a dance
Teacher	302	Salesperson
Experimenting with new grooming preparations	303	Experimenting with new office equipment
Being married to a research scientist	304	Being married to a sales executive
Working in a large corporation with little chance of being president before age 55	305	Working for yourself in a small business
Working in an import-export business	306	Working in a research laboratory
Music and art events	307	Athletic events
Reading a book	308	Watching TV or going to a movie
Appraising real estate	309	Repairing and restoring antiques
Having a few close friends	310	Having many acquaintances
Work in which you move from place to place	311	Work where you live in one place

SOURCE: D. Campbell, *The Strong-Campbell Interest Inventory*. Palo Alto, Cal.: Stanford University Press, 1974.

relatively quickly during adolescence, a single test score during this period may yield particularly inaccurate appraisals of his or her adult interests and skills.

Despite such criticisms, methods predicated upon the differentialist perspective continue to garner the support of many high-school counselors. Indeed, assessing adolescents' vocational interests with written tests and attempting to match these results with characteristics of particular jobs has remained popular in both theory and practice (Gottfredson & Becker, 1981).

The Developmental Perspective

In contrast to the differentialists' view, psychologists and practitioners who endorse the developmental perspective contend that an individual's vocational development advances in an invariant sequence of stages from childhood through adulthood. In regard to vocational maturity, the developmental view is congruent with the *developmental-stage theories* of Jean Piaget, Erik Erikson, and

11.4 A Closer Look

Holland's Personality-Occupational Types

Which of the following descriptions are most characteristic of your present and your past vocational orientation?

Realistic

These people are robust, rugged, practical, physically strong, and often athletic. They have excellent motor coordination and skills but are weak in verbal, interpersonal skills. They perceive themselves as mechanically inclined and uncomfortable in social settings. They prefer concrete to abstract problems and are conventional in political or social matters. Rarely do they perform creatively. These realistic types enjoy practical occupations like mechanics, engineering, farming, construction, wildlife specialties, and tool designing.

Investigative or Intellectual

These people are typically task oriented, introspective, asocial, and unconventional. They are strongly inclined toward science and prefer to think through rather than act out problems. They prefer to work independently and they feel confident intellectually. Describing themselves as reserved, curious, and analytical, these people prefer jobs in the sciences, psychology, or technical writing.

Enterprising

These individuals have verbal abilities that enable them to lead others and sell products or ideas. They tend to avoid situations that require long periods of intellectual effort, although they have a high energy level. They are concerned with power, status, and leadership, seeing themselves as assertive, self-confident, and sociable. Vocations for which they are well suited include real estate sales, retail merchandising, political or business management, or television production.

David Havighurst presented in previous chapters. As you may recall, David Havighurst (1972) argues that work-related tasks are one of the primary issues that should be mastered during adolescence. Similarly, Erik Erikson (1968) maintained that during early adolescence one of the primary developmental tasks is to develop a sense of "industry"—an advancement that involves such tasks as organizing time efficiently and delaying gratification. Moreover, Erikson perceived the years between 15 and 25 as the period for acquiring a vocational identity within one's society. Accordingly, developmental theories of vocational preference assume that children's cognitive capacities advance in stages that permit them to make more sophisticated vocational decisions during adolescence.

Among the most renowned researchers endorsing the developmental view are Donald Super (1976) and Eli Ginzberg (1972, 1980). According to Ginzberg, vocational maturity advances through three distinguishable phases: the *fantasy*

Artistic

These people enjoy expressing themselves and are inclined toward impulsive, creative behavior. They prefer unstructured situations that permit introspection and individual expression. They avoid situations that are too structured or that require too much conformity. Perceiving themselves as creative, intuitive, independent, introspective, and expressive, these people's occupational preferences include musician, artist, author, composer, and stage director.

Social

These individuals are sociable, humanistic, verbally skilled, and group oriented. They are often religious, have good interpersonal skills, and like structured activities. They prefer to solve problems through feelings and interpersonal manipulation of others, tend to avoid intellectual problem solving and physical exertion, and enjoy activities that inform, train, or enlighten others. Describing themselves as understanding, idealistic, and helpful, these people's occupational preferences include social worker, missionary, teacher, therapist, and counselor.

Conventional

People of this type are usually conformists who prefer well-structured environments and subordinate rather than leadership roles. They avoid situations involving ambiguity, physical skills, or interpersonal relationships. Describing themselves as conscientious, efficient, obedient, calm, orderly, and practical, these individuals value status and money. Their vocational preferences include bank examiner, bookkeeper, clerical worker, financial analyst, traffic manager, and statistician.

SOURCE: Adapted from D. Campbell and J. Hansen, *Manual for the Strong-Campbell Interest Inventory* (3d ed.), Form T325, pp. 29–30. Stanford, Cal.: Stanford University Press, 1981. Reprinted with permission.

stage, the *tentative stage*, and the *realistic stage*. In early and middle childhood, a child's vocational ideologies are shaped by his or her naive visions regarding the requirements of particular professions. For example, during this stage children may express a desire to be astronauts, or cowboys, or firefighters, because they envision only the romance and excitement that they believe each job entails. Consequently, most children's vocational choices are unrealistic, taking no account of the individual's own talents or the actual requirements of a particular job. Prior to adolescence, however, children begin to evaluate their own talents and to assess the actual demands of different kinds of work. With increasing age, adolescents become more capable of narrowing vocational options through realistic assessment of their own skills and job requirements. Thus, a boy at the age of 10 may cling tenaciously to the idea of becoming a surgeon, while at the age of 17 he willingly discards this option after having realized his ineptness in the physical sciences and his unwillingness to devote ten more years of his life to being a student.

Ginzberg (1980) initially maintained that the "realistic phase" of vocational maturity would be achieved before the age of 25; but his more recently revised theory concedes that appraising one's own vocational skills in relation to various types of work continues throughout the life-span (Ginzberg, 1980). Accordingly, people periodically change jobs after recognizing the discordance between their personal needs, their actual skills, and the demands of a particular job. Furthermore, in contrast to his earlier theory, Ginzberg's recent revisions acknowledge that many adolescents are not in the privileged position of being able to choose a job on the basis of its compatability with their personal talents, temperaments, or desires. Among other researchers, Ginzberg now maintains that many youngsters are forced to restrict their career options on the basis of socioeconomic, racial, and sexual influences over which they have little control or awareness.

In accord with Ginzberg's revised theory regarding adolescents' vocational choices, the developmentalists' assumption that people advance in predictable, invariant stages toward making more realistic vocational decisions has been undermined by the empirical data. For example, longitudinal analyses of data from several thousand high-school graduates in the class of 1972 revealed that approximately 40 percent of the graduates never achieved their vocational or educational goals. Indeed, only half of the high-school graduates who had aspired to continue their education while being simultaneously employed met their goal. Given economic realities of the time, most were forced to lower their educational aspirations by quitting school for full-time jobs. Moreover, even among the high-school graduates who had set a more reasonable goal by limiting themselves to a single option, such as enlisting in the military, working full time, or being a full-time student, only half reached their goal (Nolfi, 1978).

Furthermore, the national longitudinal study of the class of 1972 acknowledges that adolescents' occupational aspirations are frequently related to their race, gender, and socioeconomic background, rather than to their degree of vocational maturity. For example, although many black and female adolescents believed they had the intellectual ability to succeed in postsecondary education, they were less likely than white males to pursue more education. In addition, almost 90 percent of the female high-school graduates who had chosen to seek full-time employment cited marriage or a desire to be a secretary or a salesperson as the reasons for discontinuing their education. In this regard, the findings confirm the data discussed in Chapter 5, which demonstrated that gender exerts a tremendous impact on adolescents' vocational decisions (Nolfi, 1978). Thus it appears that, despite positive self-appraisals, race and gender are extremely influential in determining adolescents' vocational plans.

Given findings such as those from the national longitudinal study of the class of 1972, a second developmental view has been advanced by developmentalists such as Donald Super (1976; Super & Hall, 1978). According to Super's theory, self-concepts established in early childhood are the forerunners of adolescents' vocational choices. These self-concepts are developed in large part through parents' expectations, encouragement, and attitudes. By adolescence, the child's self-concept has become firmly enough entrenched to determine the young person's vocational decisions.

Super's self-concept theory proposes five stages of vocational development, which are said to occur throughout late adolescence and young adulthood. Between the ages of 14 and 18 the *crystallization stage* occurs, during which the individual establishes his or her ideas regarding work. Subsequently, in the *specification stage* between the ages of 18 and 21, the person chooses an occupation and, in the few years that follow, implements these plans by becoming employed or by acquiring the additional education necessary for employment. Following this *implementation stage*, people become established in their chosen careers and the *stabilization stage* is under way—a stage that is presumably completed by the age of 35.

In a representative study supporting Super's theory, a longitudinal investigation conducted between 1966 and 1974 followed the vocational development of 2,213 minority and white males (Bachman, O'Malley, & Johnston, 1978). As Super's theory predicts, the boys' self-concept scores were highly correlated with their academic success and with their vocational choices across all socioeconomic groups. As might be expected, boys with the most self-esteem pursued the most professional jobs and achieved the highest educational levels. In further accord with Super's theory, the quality of the boys' high-school education had an unappreciable impact on the status of their future jobs. Moreover, the researchers found that the boys' occupational aspirations were fairly well established by the tenth grade.

A Challenge to Traditional Theories

While most of the research in vocational psychology has been devoted to either the developmental or the differentialist views, some theorists and researchers are challenging both perspectives. Gottfredson's research at the Center for Social Organization of Schools at Johns Hopkins University is representative of these challenges (Gottfredson & Becker, 1981). After reviewing the empirical literature, Gottfredson questions the assumption that adolescents' aspirations or particular skills play a significant role in determining the type of job they eventually acquire. Instead, the evidence indicates that young people's vocational goals are primarily a reflection of such variables as their childhood concepts regarding the appropriate roles for people of a certain race, sex, or socioeconomic class. Moreover, the nation's economic circumstances and the needs of local employers appear to be more significant determinants of an adolescent's future job than variables such as compatability between an individual and the job or the individual's level of vocational maturity, as proposed by Ginzberg or Super.

In this vein, data from numerous investigations suggest that adolescents' future jobs are determined by factors other than their occupational aspirations, their vocational maturity, or the congruence between their personalities and the demands of a particular job (Gottfredson & Becker, 1981). Not only have many discrepancies been found to exist between young people's aspirations and their jobs, many employees also tend to lower their aspirations to fit the jobs in which they find themselves, rather than to change jobs, as Holland's theory predicts. In other words, if a person's job, personal aspirations, and vocational skills appear to become more congruent with age, the compatibility can be explained by the person's having modified his or her goals to fit the realities of the job, rather than as a consequence of having found a job that better suits personal needs, temperament, or aptitude.

Moreover, Gottfredson is among those who, on the basis of the existing research, questions the predictive value of career interest tests in relation to other predictive variables. Although studies have established the validity of many career interest inventories in predicting people's future vocations, few studies have examined whether or not the tests are any more predictive than other variables, such as socioeconomic class. As a consequence of this methodological shortcoming, it can be argued that an adolescent's socioeconomic class, high-school grades, sex, or mother's occupation may be more valid predictors of future careers than the scores earned on written tests such as the Strong-Campbell Interest Inventory.

Gottfredson's own study of adolescent and adult males is representative of investigations designed to reexamine traditional hypotheses about career aspirations and job outcomes (Gottfredson & Becker, 1981). Interviews were conducted yearly from 1966 through 1971 with a nationally representative sample of 3,730 white males between the ages of 14 and 24. Each male was asked to describe the job he would like to have by age 30, after which their actual jobs and vocational aspirations were coded according to Holland's typology of work (refer to Box 11.4). Consistent with the results of other studies, the males' aspirations became more stable as they aged. Fifty-two percent of the males, however, responded to the discrepancies between their aspirations and their actual jobs by lowering their expectations. The other 35 percent changed jobs to fit their aspirations, and 13 percent changed both their aspirations and jobs. The researchers concluded that even though occupational goals may sometimes be related to a person's future job, these aspirations are not as predictive as developmental theorists have traditionally proposed.

One of the most important aspects of Gottfredson's study and others of its kind is the reassessment of how vocational goals develop and of the ways in which people adjust to discrepancies between their goals and their jobs. According to traditional theories of vocational psychology, people often fail to achieve their goals because they made unrealistic choices as a consequence of their own vocational immaturity. Thus, adolescents with poor decision-making skills will misjudge their own aptitudes, their real interests, and the demands of particular jobs. Critics of this traditional view, however, suggest an alternative theory: People formulate and readjust their vocational goals on the basis of the options available to them in society at the time. In addition, on the basis of sex, social class, and race, young children inadvertently learn to identify the occupations for which they are supposedly well suited, and they formulate their goals accordingly. From the critics' view, vocational goals are not primarily determined by the adolescent's own aptitudes or vocational maturity, but by the social stereotypes and economic realities of the time. Consequently, the occupational goals of children from different social classes and racial groups are generally well established by adolescence.

Those who challenge the traditional developmental and differentialist approaches to vocational psychology offer several recommendations for vocational counselors and researchers (Gottfredson & Becker, 1981). First, recognize that the labor market and sociocultural attitudes limit the opportunities and aspirations of many young people in our society. Although traditional theorists like Holland and Super allude to the role of economic and social factors in restricting adolescents' choices, they continue to emphasize the importance of career interest inventories, vocational maturity, and congruence between the individual's characteristics and the requirements of particular jobs. Hence, most theorists and counselors continue to focus too little attention on the importance of the social attitudes and economic circumstances that determine most people's jobs. For instance, the career opportunities for females, minorities, and the poor are still limited by sociocultural factors beyond the adolescent's control—a fact that tests of vocational maturity and career interests continue to ignore.

Similarly, the critics of traditional vocational approaches suggest that researchers devote more attention to issues heretofore receiving little attention (Gottfredson & Becker, 1981): How useful are the traditional concepts like vocational maturity and individual interests with regard to the task of counseling young people whose occupational futures are primarily controlled by social and economic factors beyond their control? At what age are occupational attitudes actually developed and to what extent might such attitudes be altered? In this context, how might counselors counteract the restrictions and stereotypes that young children may be permanently incorporating into their occupational self-concepts? How can counselors and teachers best serve adolescents whose vocational goals are grossly out of line with the sociocultural and economic realities of our times? Questions like these underline the role that vocational psychology could assume in helping contemporary adolescents cope with the economic uncertainties of the present and future.

THE FAMILY'S INFLUENCE ON VOCATIONAL DEVELOPMENT

Neither differentialists nor developmentalists would dismiss the influence of the family over adolescents' vocational aspirations and achievements. While we might initially presume that young people's vocational decisions are more powerfully influenced by their educational experiences than by their families, the statistics show otherwise. With a candid starkness, the statistical data show that occupational status generally remains relatively constant between generations. In brief, while educational variables are not to be entirely discounted, family variables are more reliable predictors of adolescents' future occupations.

The family's socioeconomic class wields the single most powerful influence over children's vocational attitudes and achievements. According to some reviewers of the literature, "If one were permitted only a single variable with which to predict an individual's occupational status, it would surely be the SES of the indivudial's family of orientation" (Schulenberg, Vondracek, & Crouter, 1984, p.11). Such an observation is not to imply that adolescents can never surpass or never fail to achieve the status of their parents' jobs or incomes. The data do show, however, that if we are trying to predict an adolescent's future occupational status and income, the parents' socioeconomic class is the single most reliable predictor. As the statistics in Chapter 7 repeatedly demonstrated, the higher the family's income the more likely it is that the children will attend college, a step that will qualify these privileged offspring for professional and white-collar jobs.

Among the studies demonstrating the vocational similarities between parents and children and the importance of the family's income is a ten-year investigation of college males' vocations (Mortimer & Kumka, 1982). Most of these young men chose to enter their fathers' occupations. Even those who chose different careers, however, chose occupations with characteristics and status very similar to their fathers'. In addition, the fathers and sons shared similar attitudes about work. Sons from professional families stressed the inherent values of the work itself, while those from white-collar, business families stressed values such as the salaries in their chosen vocation. As might be expected, a son's attitudes were most similar to his father's when the two had a close relationship and when the father held a high-status job. Moreover, even ten years after the son's college graduation, these vocational similarities between fathers and sons persisted.

Studies with high-school boys have also corroborated these findings with college males. Having followed the vocational development of 2,200 minority and white males from the tenth grade through early adulthood, Bachman and his colleagues concluded that "in many ways the most basic predictor variable in the Youth in Transition study is family socioeconomic level" (Bachman, O'Malley, & Johnston, 1978, p. 21). A consistently strong relationship existed between a family's socioeconomic level and the son's academic abilities, college plans, vocational goals, and self-concept. Boys from the wealthier families were the most likely to enter high-prestige, high-income jobs like their fathers, and those from poorer families pursued less prestigious, lower-paid vocations like their fathers.

Although the research shows a clear correlation between family income and male adolescents' vocational aspirations, the literature shows a more ambivalent relationship for female adolescents. Several studies have shown strong relationships between family income and a girl's educational aspirations. A girl's decision about whether or not to seek employment, however, appears unassociated with her family's socioeconomic status. Current data suggest, therefore, that female adolescents' vocational decisions are less influenced by the family's socioeconomic level than are those of her male adolescent counterparts (Marini, 1978).

Although the relationship between a boy's vocational choices and his family's income is quite strong, it might be argued that boys from poorer families have fewer intellectual abilities, which accounts for their not being qualified to pursue higher-prestige vocations. As the data in Chapter 7 demonstrated, however, the relationship between academic success and family income is not simply a matter of indigent children's being less mentally capable than their wealthier classmates. In this regard, you may recall that a number of educational programs have been successful in raising both the IQ scores and the grades of adolescents from lower-socioeconomic-class families. Hence, it would be naive to accept the disclaimer that adolescents from lower-income families achieve less vocationally because they are intellectually incapable of mastering the skills necessary for higher-income jobs.

Several representative studies underscore this point. Young people from wealthier families have been found to attend the most selective, prestigous colleges, even when their academic abilities were similar to those of youths from the lower-income families who were attending less prestigous schools (Karabel & Astin, 1975). Similarly, girls from lower socioeconomic backgrounds tended to enroll in community colleges or technical schools, while girls from richer families with similar academic abilities generally attended four-year colleges

(Mclaughlin, Hunt, & Montgomery, 1977). Such findings suggest that adolescents from the less financially privileged families often lower their educational or vocational aspirations, even when their intellectual and academic abilities are similar to those of their cohorts from wealthier families.

Several hypotheses have been suggested to account for the lower aspirations of adolescents from less financially privileged homes (Bachman, O'Malley, & Johnston, 1978; Schulenberg, Vondracek, & Crouter, 1984). First, lower-income parents are without the economic means to provide opportunities like home computers, travel, private schools, books, and summer workshops, which expand a young person's vocational aspirations and skills. In addition, not having the financial resources to underwrite a college education, these parents may encourage their children to aspire to goals that are congruent with the family's economic situation. Consequently, a youth's academic and intellectual abilities assume an importance secondary to the family's financial restrictions. Given the economic realities of the family, these youths may inadvertently be socialized by their family and friends throughout childhood to limit their vocational and educational aspirations.

In comparison to the family's income, race is less highly correlated with an adolescent's vocational ambitions and achievements. Interestingly, several studies have actually found that black children have higher vocational ambitions than white children when socioeconomic class and academic abilities are similar (Leifer & Lessor, 1976). Other investigators have failed to find significant differences between the career expectations of white, black, and Puerto Rican high-school students with similar socioeconomic backgrounds or between white and black adolescent girls in classes for the academically talented (Dillard & Campbell, 1981; George, 1981).

Finally, although both the mother's and the father's vocational attitudes inevitably affect their children's vocational decisions, it appears that the relative influence of each parent may vary with the child's age. In an investigation comparing students in grades 6, 9, 10, and 12, researchers found that both boys' and girls' vocational values were most similar to the attitudes of their same-sexed parent until the tenth grade. By the twelfth grade, however, both boys and girls reflected more of their fathers' vocational attitudes than their mothers' (Wijting, Arnold, & Conrad, 1978).

FEMALES' VOCATIONAL DEVELOPMENT

Distinctions between Males and Females

In addition to the family's influence, an adolescent's gender is intricately bound to his or her vocational ambitions and achievements. As a consequence of socialization within and beyond the family, male and female children are encouraged to perceive their vocational roles and their vocational aptitudes differently. As a consequence, significant discrepancies persist between the incomes, the vocational accomplishments, and the job status of U.S. males and females. As witnessed by statistics such as those in Tables 11.2 and 11.3, the vast majority of males and females continue to limit their vocational choices to traditionally sex-typed jobs. For instance, 95 percent of dentists, 89 percent of physicians, and 87 percent of lawyers are men. In contrast, 96 percent of nurses, 84 percent of elementary-school teachers, and 78 percent of librarians are women (U.S. Department of Commerce, 1980).

As the statistics in Chapter 8 demonstrated, given the divorce rate, the inflated economy, and the rising rate of illegitimate births, female employment has become an integral part of most U.S. families. Thus, issues related to the vocational development of female adolescents assume paramount importance, as so many young women are moving into the labor force for substantial portions of their adult lives.

The vocational circumstances in which today's adolescent women find themselves can be accounted for primarily by the dramatic social and economic changes that have occurred since the mid-1960s (Waldman, 1970). The recessions in 1969 and in 1973–1974, coupled with the highest inflation rates in several decades, have driven women into the marketplace out of economic necessity. In addition, the passage of such legislation as the *Equal Employment Opportunity Act* of 1972, the *Women's Educational Equity Act* of 1974, the Tax Reform Act of 1976, and Public law 95-555 in 1978 encouraged more women to enter the marketplace. Collectively, these legislative acts established tax credits for child-care services, permitted pregnant women to work without discrimination, and reduced the inequities between male and female salaries and educational opportunities. Society has also supported women's employment by becoming more tolerant of women's deciding to remain child-free, to postpone marriage, to raise a child without being married, and to support "househusbands." Although such vocational changes are perceived as progress by some and as deterioration by others, they have nevertheless profoundly affected adolescent and adult females in today's society.

Although the reasons why adolescent girls have lower vocational aspirations than boys were examined in Chapter 5, a few representative studies underscore the distinctions between the sexes in this domain. For example, it is worth noting that at both the college and high-school levels, girls who aspire to traditionally male-oriented occupations are still in the minority. Even girls who are ambitious and career oriented enough to enroll in college generally pursue traditionally female occupations like nursing, teaching, and social work (Astin, 1980). In addition, many adolescent girls still express concern over the future dilemma of combining motherhood with a vocation (Hoffman, 1979, 1983). As might be expected, recent studies demonstrate that girls with traditional views on marriage and motherhood are the most likely to limit their educational and vocational goals. In contrast, young women with expectations of entering high-prestige, well-paid professions are the least committed to having large families, to marrying young, or to relinquishing their jobs while their children are young (Tittle, 1981).

In this vein, it is worth reflecting upon the similarities between male and female adolescents who are willing to develop their intellectual capacities to the fullest and to pursue careers (Hoffman, 1979; Marini, 1978; Tittle, 1981). As is the case with boys, females who have high educational and vocational aspirations are independent, assertive, and unafraid to demonstrate their intellectual, academic, and vocational competence. Moreover, these young women's vocational aspirations tend to be closely related to their own mothers' attitudes, just as males' attitudes are closely aligned with their fathers' values. As a consequence, girls with the highest vocational and educational aspirations endorse nontraditional views of male and female sex roles, as do their mothers. For example, girls with employed mothers generally have higher vocational goals and pursue more jobs in domains traditionally reserved for men than girls with unemployed mothers. Similarly, as already discussed in Chapter 8, girls whose fathers encourage their independence, assertiveness, and intellectual achievements tend to feel more comfortable with their intellectual and vocational pursuits.

While most girls do plan to work at some time during their adult lives, fewer view their work as on a par with the work of their future husbands. Indeed, many adolescent girls who plan to have jobs in the future perceive their primary roles as those of mother and wife. To emphasize this point, a nationally representative survey of several thousand high-school seniors found that only 40 percent of the girls felt they should continue working if they had preschool children. The other 60 percent said they would be only "somewhat likely" or "not very likely" to work if they had young children (Bachman, 1982).

Male and female adolescents are still not immune from vestiges of the belief that, for females, brains and beauty are mutually exclusive. Illustrating this point, researchers asked high-school students to rate pictures of women in regard to physical attractiveness, probable occupation, and educational background. The majority of male and female adolescents believed that the least attractive women were employed in the most "masculine" professions and had enrolled in the most "masculine" courses in school. In contrast, the most attractive women were assumed to be employed in the female-dominated professions like nursing and teaching (Lanier & Byrne, 1981). Put differently, there are still adolescents who assume that the brilliant female mathematician or scientist will be more masculine and more unattractive than the nursery-school teacher.

Trends in Vocational Attitudes of Males and Females

Recognizing that vocational discrepancies still exist between males and females should not be construed to mean that females' occupational attitudes have remained unchanged over the century. First, the proportion of adolescent girls in the labor force has increased appreciably during recent decades. For instance, twice as many 14- and 15-year-old girls are employed now as 30 years ago, while the rate for boys has declined slightly, making the employment rates for male and female youths almost equivalent (Nilsen, 1984). Second, some recent reports indicate a slight decline in vocational sex differences. For instance, one survey found an increase in female high-school seniors' aspirations toward professional jobs in Virginia between 1970 and 1976 (Garrison, 1979). Similarly, comparisons in Wisconsin between 1964 and 1975 found females aspiring to more male white-collar jobs (Lueptow, 1981).

Nevertheless, the occupational attitudes of contemporary adolescents do not diverge from the past as much as one might expect, given the publicity about the women's movement and "reverse discrimination" against males. Among the most convincing research studies in this regard are the ongoing annual comparisons of high-school seniors across the country being conducted by the *Moni-*

toring the Future project (Herzog, 1982). The data obtained from 3,000 males and females between 1976 and 1980 show significant sex differences in occupational goals, although a slight overall decline in sex differences appears to have occurred during the period. In accord with traditional sex roles, girls more often chose careers that were education or service oriented and avoided jobs of a more independent, competitive nature, such as self-employment.

Unlike males, the female seniors emphasized the nurturant, supportive aspects of a job by expressing a need for work that would benefit other people, rather than expressing a need for jobs with high incomes and high prestige, as did most males. The young women also aspired less often than the men to jobs involving much decision making and problem solving. In general, the females ascribed more importance than males to the interpersonal and altruistic aspects of a job and to stimulating work than to salaries, status, and vacation time. It should be noted, however, that both males' and females' concerns about salaries had increased over the years, a finding that corroborates the data presented at the outset of this chapter. The overall findings, however, reveal that although high-school seniors' attitudes toward employed women have become more liberal, their views regarding the types of jobs that men and women should hold have remained remarkably unchanged throughout recent years.

Modifying Female Vocational Patterns

Since many adolescent males and females continue to restrict their vocational plans on the basis of sex-role stereotypes, researchers and educators have been implementing programs designed to expand adolescents' vocational attitudes. In one such intervention project, 230 eighth- and tenth-grade students from urban, suburban, and rural communities in New York viewed filmstrips and participated in student-parent conferences, class discussions, and individual activities designed to diminish sex-stereotyped attitudes. As a consequence, both male and female participants became more positive in their attitudes toward nontraditional careers for men and women. Interestingly, the activities and discussion had the greatest impact on the male students whose attitudes were the most stereotypic at the outset. It is noteworthy that the parents' involvement was deemed to be particularly important in helping adolescents change their attitudes (Veres & Carmichael, 1982).

As legislation continues to support equal educational and vocational opportunities for females, adolescent girls will hopefully venture forth into vocations heretofore reserved for males. For example, before 1975 girls were not admitted to the nation's military academies. As a consequence, girls were denied access to the kinds of occupational opportunities afforded males who graduated from West Point, Annapolis, the Air Force Academy, and the Coast Guard Academy. As the stories in Box 11.5 demonstrate, the eventual integration of the country's military academies was accompanied by considerable stress and controversy. Nevertheless, subsequent to the 1975 congressional acts, young women have availed themselves of the opportunity to enroll in the U.S. military academies as a way of preparing themselves for careers in the nation's armed services (Stiehm, 1981).

A Closer Look 11.5 

Military Training for Females

"The kind of women we want in the Air Force are the kind who will get married and leave."—A major at the U.S. Air Force Academy

"I disagree with the admittance of women to the academies. This is just another step taken for political reasons that will tend to weaken our combat capability."—An Air Force general stationed in the Midwest

"Maybe you could find one woman in 10,000 who could lead in combat, but she would be a freak, and the Military Academy is not being run for freaks."—General William Westmoreland

Despite such opposition, on May 21, 1975, the House of Representatives mandated by a vote of 303 to 96 that females be admitted to the Department of Defense academies for academic and military training. During the first 16 months of coeducation at West Point, data was collected to examine the transformation that the academy was undergoing in educating female cadets for the first time in its history.

The Department of Physical Education and Athletics was responsible for deciding how the physical training requirements needed to be altered in accord with the physiological differences between males and females. While the program rather consistently emphasized the differences in male and female upper-body strength, it did not bother to incorporate into the program physical tests on which females typically perform better than males. Neither did the department question whether the tests on which females characteristically performed more poorly than males were actually related to skills required by their military jobs. For example, is the requirement to run three miles in 24 minutes related to any military activity, or is it merely one way of testing a cadet's self-discipline and dedication to the academy? If the latter, must females be required to complete the same physical task as males in order to demonstrate their professional commitment or will power?

In a program designed exclusively for male students and faculty, a number of provocative questions arose: How were male cadets going to respond to academic competition and physical combat with females? Since the seminude pictures of "spacemates" in the academy's training manuals were intended to "motivate" the male cadets, how appropriate were these photographs once the academy became coeducational? Would male cadets learn to trust female cadets in situations where they believed their physical differences would somehow jeopardize them? If the role of "warrior" is no longer reserved exclusively for males, will men lose their feelings of masculinity? How would males respond to female leadership in noncombat or combat situations? Would jealousies arise as a consequence of females' presence that would undermine male morale and camaraderie? Focusing their attention on such questions, researchers and authors studied the female cadets and their male classmates carefully during the first few years of the academy's shift to coeducation.

Since the curriculum had been designed by and for males, unexpected dilemmas arose. For instance, in regard to gynecological matters, the Air Force Academy's materials failed to inform the female cadets or their instructors that excessive physical exercise can result in amenorrhea (the cessation of menstrual periods). For those female cadets who had need to worry about pregnancy, this minor "omission" in the curriculum created considerable anxiety until accurate information about amenorrhea and physical exercise was eventually provided. In addition, male officers had to be made comfortable enough with issues related to female physiology, so that saying words like "menstruation" in public did not embarrass them.

Making the military academies coeducational also provoked an interest in how the female cadets differed from other college women: Were they somehow more masculine because of their interest in a military career? How did their family backgrounds, political attitudes, or social interests differ from those of civilian girls? How similar were male and female cadets' personal attitudes and academic qualifications? One survey of West Point's freshman class conducted in 1980 showed that 60 percent of the male and 70 percent of the females did expect to have children in the future, compared to 67 percent of the males and 61 percent of the females in other colleges. However, 41 percent of the West Point males and 37 percent of the males in other colleges felt that married women ought to confine their activities to the home and family, in contrast to 5 percent of the West Point females and 19 percent of the civilian college women. Among other comparisons, the academic and high-school activities, physical skills, and academic skills of the male and female cadets in the class of 1980 were compared:

	Freshman Males	*Freshman Females*
CEEB Mean Scores		
Verbal aptitude	550	587
English composition	539	579
Math aptitude	647	668
Math achievement	647	668

VOCATIONAL PREPARATION

Job Projections for the Future

The Labor Department statistics provide some guidance fór young people who are trying to decide which occupational paths to pursue. For example, as Figure 11.1 illustrates, adolescents would be taking a greater risk of unemployment by preparing themselves for a career in college or high-school teaching than for a career in medicine or computer programming. To the extent that they are indicative of future trends, statistical projections such as these can benefit

	Freshman Males		Freshman Females	
ACT Mean Scores				
English	23.1		24.7	
Social studies	26.6		26.9	
Math	29.5		28.3	
Natural science	29.9		29.6	
Physical Aptitude				
Examination (PAE)	557		595*	
Medical Qualification at Entry				
Pilot	1053	(73.3%)	57	(36.3%)**
Navigator	150	(10.5%)	9	(5.7%)
Air Force Academy—nonflying	233	(16.2%)	91	(58.0%)
All sports—team captains		29.3%		28.7%
All sports—letter winners		78.9%		55.4%
Class presidents		11.2%		4.5%
Editors or business managers		5.3%		14.9%
Boys/Girls State		19.1%		10.8%
Valedictorians		19.1%		12.1%
National Honor Society		56.9%		78.6%
Boy/Girl Scouts		46.0%		27.4%
Civil Air Patrol		6.2%		5.7%
Private pilot's license		3.3%		1.3%

*Males' and females' tests were not identical. Women were "better" physical specimens, as compared to U.S. women, than were the men, as compared to U.S. men.
**Women were not permitted to train as pilots when this selection was made, so no selection was made based on medical qualifications for flying.

SOURCE: J. Stiehm, *Bring me men and women: Mandated change at the U.S. Air Force Academy.* Berkeley: University of California Press, 1981.

students who are trying to increase the odds of their being employed in the future.

Unfortunately, most adolescents are poorly informed regarding the nation's occupational needs and the requirements necessary to succeed in a particular profession (Borus, 1984; Nolfi, 1978). This point is well illustrated by Boyer's recent national study of several hundred high schools across the country, in which most school counselors were too overburdened to provide more than minimal vocational guidance to students. In addition, the counselors were usually most confident about counseling college-bound students, even though this often meant simply providing advice about how to get accepted into the most

Figure 11.1

Actual 1982 and projected 1995 employment and change projected in employment from 1982 to 1995

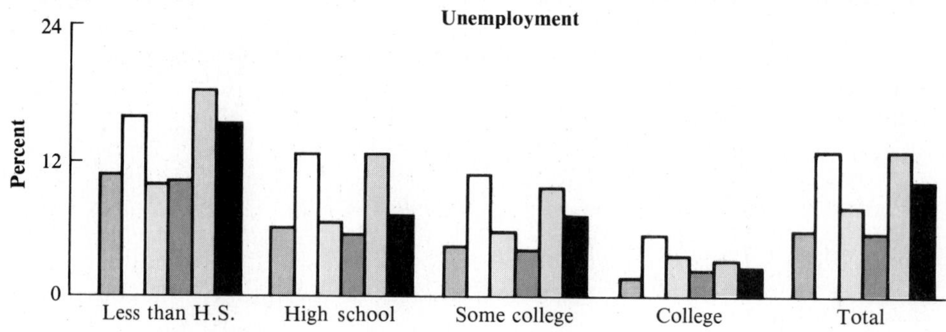

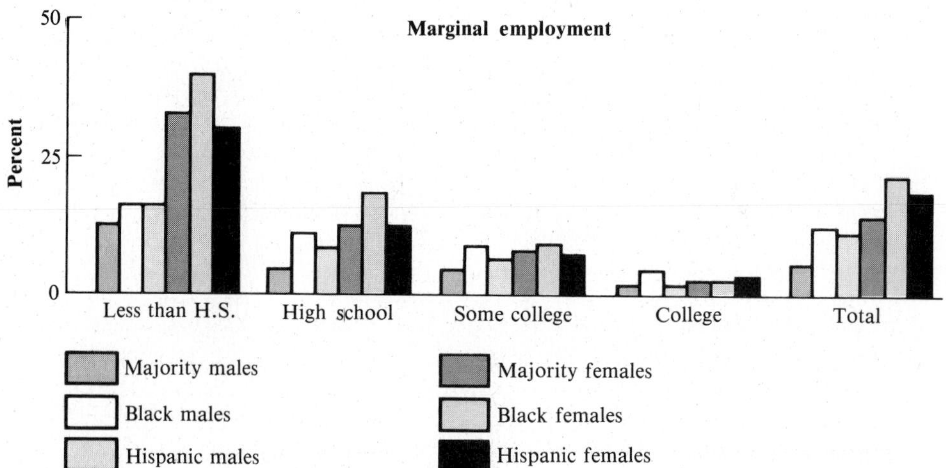

SOURCE: V. Plisko, *The Condition of Education*. Washington, D.C.: National Center for Education Statistics, 1985, p. 111.

competitive colleges. Thus, the researchers involved in this major study of U.S. secondary education concluded that U.S. high-school students were in dire need of a more adequate system of vocational counseling and vocational preparation (Boyer, 1983).

The Value of a College Education

While earning a college diploma was once considered the best insurance against unemployment or low-paying jobs, this assumption is now being questioned by many young people and their parents. As the labor market has shifted toward more technological jobs, computerization, and service industries, the financial value of a college education has decreased. Thus, while in 1970 college graduates earned 40 percent more than high-school graduates, by 1977 they earned only 24 percent more (U.S. Department of Commerce, 1980). Although most college graudates still earn more money during their lifetimes than high-school or vocational-school graudates, the gap is clearly narrowing.

The soaring costs of a college education have also caused many to delay or abort their plans to enroll in college. Furthermore, a greater percentage of students are now attending public colleges instead of the more expensive private institutions. Significantly, enrollment at local, accessible two-year colleges almost doubled between 1967 and 1977. With regard to curriculum choices, more than half of all comunity-college students are enrolled in a vocational program like nursing, computer science, or police science, each of which has been designed to make students more marketable immediately after graduation (Plisko, 1985). Finally, as mentioned earlier in this chapter, even students who are attending four-year colleges are more likely to be preparing themselves for a specific vocation than to be pursuing a general program in the humanities or social sciences.

While college graduates were virtually assured of good jobs during the 1960s, their value in the marketplace changed dramatically during the 1970s. Like their cohorts with high-school and technical diplomas, college graduates are currently being subjected to the vicissitudes of a highly competitive marketplace, in which supply outweighs demand in many professions. Consequently, a number of college graduates are now occupying jobs for which they would have been considered "overeducated" in previous decades—such as public-school teaching and blue-collar labor. To appreciate more fully the recent changes in supply and demand, one must realize that while the number of college graduates rose from 400,000 in 1961 to nearly one million in 1981, the number of jobs requiring a college education diminished. As a consequence, between 1978 and 1980 there were approximately 3.3 million more college graduates looking for work than there were jobs intended for people with a college education (U.S. Department of Labor, 1980).

Data like these, however, do not mean that adolescents who are considering a college education should necessarily abandon their plans. Although unemployment among college graudates tripled during the 1970s, the risks of being unemployed are still greater for high-school graudates (U.S. Department of Commerce, 1980). According to the Labor Department's statistical projections, only one-fourth of college graduates will have to seek employment in jobs that have not traditionally required a college degree. Furthermore, jobs that require a college education are growing at a greater rate than those requiring less education.

Some critics have questioned the value of formal education in preparing young people for their future vocations: Does having more formal education mean that a young person is a better employee? Do the skills involved in most jobs require the amount of formal education that employers typically demand? Do the paper credentials of a high-school or college diploma mean the owner is any more qualified for a job than someone without the diploma? Those who believe that we have overemphasized the relationship between formal education and job performance present several arguments on their behalf. First, most employers admit that employees generally receive their training on the job rather than in school. Second, the skills involved in many jobs are not directly related to the skills taught in school. Third, the research itself offers little evidence of a direct relationship between job performance and formal education (Squires,

1979). According to this perspective, the value of a college or a high-school diploma can be questioned on the grounds that neither is indicative of a prospective employee's potential to succeed at the job. Despite these arguments, the importance of credentials in the job market remains virtually unchallenged.

Irrespective of the increasing ambivalence about the importance of a college degree, almost half of all high-school graduates still attempt to complete a college education. The percentage of high-school graduates enrolling in college reached a peak at 55 percent in 1968 and has now stabilized at about 46 percent for females and 53 percent for males (Plisko, 1985). The greatest decline has occurred among males, whose college enrollment fell sharply between 1968 and 1972 from 63 percent to 52 percent. During the same years, female college enrollment declined from 49 percent to 46 percent and has been increasing since (A. Young, 1979).

Despite these declines in college enrollment, by 1990 nearly half of all high-school graduates will be enrolled in college, and one-third of the workers between 25 and 34 will have earned a college degree (U.S. Department of Commerce, 1980). More impressively, by 1990 four-fifths of the entire population of workers and nine-tenths of the workers between 25 and 34 will have at least a high-school diploma. In short, the average young worker today has more formal education than his or her predecessors, perhaps a reality that itself partially contributes to the decline in the value of a college education.

High-School Vocational Education: The Pros and Cons

As parents and adolescents have become increasingly concerned over economic issues like unemployment and inflation, the debate over vocational education has escalated. Should high schools be providing a vocational curriculum or is this undermining the academic competence that employers say is more important than specific job skills? Given the rapidly changing technology and expensive equipment necessary for vocational training, how are high schools to afford vocational training? Should vocational training be limited to technical schools or offered in regular high schools? Questions like these have provoked controversy and innovation in secondary schools.

Having students work off campus in various occupations has been considered an integral part of vocational education in high schools. These programs offer academic credits for students' supervised vocational experiences off campus. While the high-school supervisor offers advice at the job site, the student is often paid by the employer for part-time work. Part of each school day is typically reserved for traditional coursework on campus, while the remainder of each day is dedicated to off-campus work at a job site. Advocates of vocational education in public schools argue that these work-study experiences teach adolescents specific job skills and attitudes that will impress their prospective employers. A basic premise underlying these programs is that vocational training makes adolescents more employable than does the regular curriculum. While very few vocational training programs have established an international reputation like the *Foxfire project* described in Box 11.6, almost two-thirds of U.S. high schools now offer some type of off-campus work experiences (Plisko, 1985).

A Closer Look 11.6 

Foxfire: An Appalachian High School's International Success

In the 1960s, when Eliot Wigginton went to Rabun Gap, Georgia, in the Appalachian mountains, he expected to use his master's degree to teach the well-worn classics of the traditional high-school curriculum. His students reponded with apathy and unruly behavior, eventually convincing Wigginton to replace the prescribed curriculum with one that captured his students' interest and excited the entire community. "Foxfire" was born. Curious about Appalachian culture, Wigginton convinced his students to preserve their community's oral history by interviewing their elders and writing down their stories. As the students ventured into the community with their tape recorders, notebooks, and cameras, they became increasingly motivated to learn reading and writing skills that would enable them to convey to others what they were learning. Trusting his students, Wigginton gave them the independence to pursue their projects beyond the school's boundaries. He permitted them to learn from the community's elders and to engage in activities that they considered relevant to their own lives. Since its beginning in 1966, adolescents in the Foxfire project have created four best-selling books, a magazine subscribed to in 50 states and a dozen foreign countries, a furniture-building business, and a record album of Appalachian music. This outstanding high-school program has indeed become like "foxfire"—a tiny organism that glows in the dark in shaded mountain coves.

SOURCE: E. Wigginton, *Sometimes a shining moment: 20 years in the high school classroom—The Foxfire experience.* Garden City, N.Y.: Doubleday, 1985.

Despite their popularity with most students and parents, occupational training in public schools is not without its critics. Among others who have criticized vocational training in secondary schools are Ernest Boyer and his colleagues, a team of esteemed higher education professionals, who recently conducted a national study of secondary education in the United States (Boyer, 1983). By visiting secondary schools across the country and by assessing national statistics on education, these researchers provide a uniquely designed investigation that affords a comprehensive view of current practices in U.S. secondary schools.

In making their recommendations for reforming vocational education, Boyer and his colleagues summarize the major criticisms of occupational programs in high school. To begin with, there is little relationship between the kind of vocational training most adolescents receive in school and the actual skills needed for today's jobs. Although most administrators, parents, and students are pleased to have vocational training in their schools, job prospects for graduates of the programs are not significantly better than for students who pursue the regular academic curriculum.

In defense of vocational education, the principal of a high school with 5,000 students told researchers: "I'm convinced if we cut out our vocational program,

How might your present life be different if your English teacher had established a "Foxfire" project in your high school?

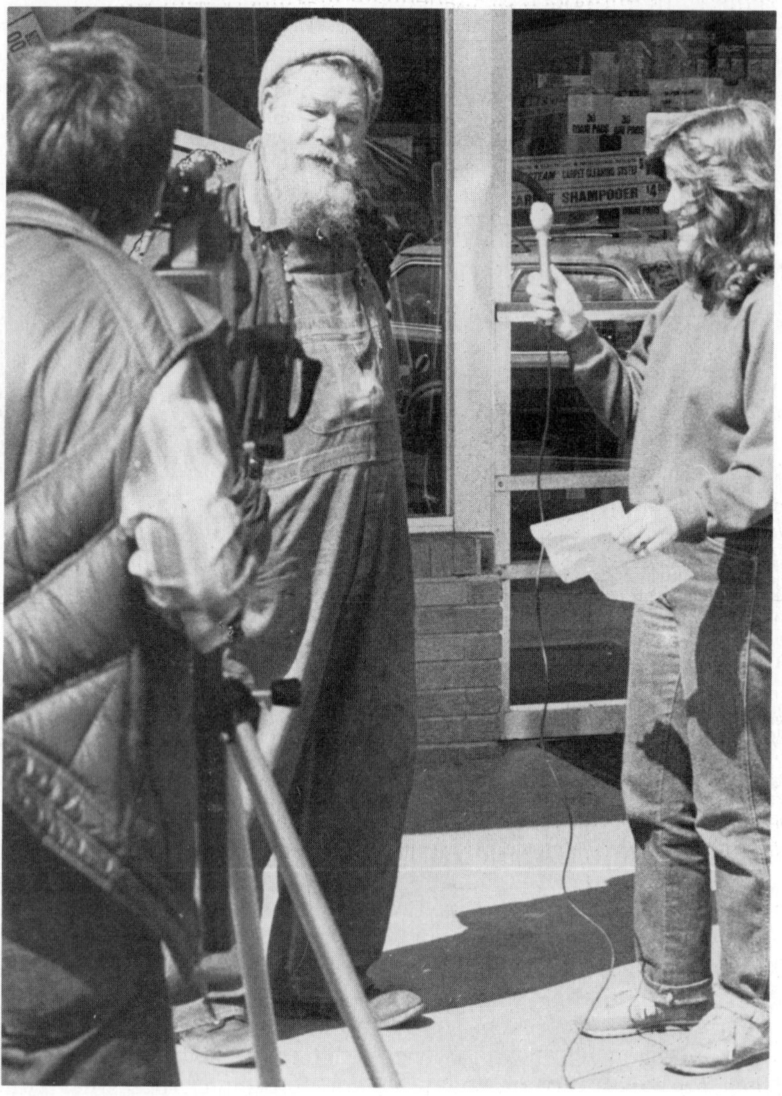

our dropout rate would skyrocket. It would shoot up 25 percent almost overnight" (Boyer, 1983, p. 120). Yet the instructor of an auto mechanics program in a large urban school admitted that only about a third of the students get jobs related to their training: "And then two of those three will probably pump gas more than they will work on cars. But the kids really like the program. They love to tune their engines" (Boyer, 1983, p. 121). The uncomfortable reality appears to be that, with the exception of training for secretarial work, most high schools' occupational programs are not preparing students for their future professions.

One reason for the discrepancy between the hopes and the realities of vocational education lies in the financial restraints within which high schools must design their programs. Given the shortage of funds, most occupational programs are equipped with outmoded or inadequate machinery with which to train students. Auto mechanics students learn to repair engines that are no longer popular in the marketplace, and secretarial students learn to type on manual or electric typewriters rather than to master word processing on computers. Given the rapidly expanding technology in today's society, few schools can afford to keep abreast by investing thousands of dollars for vocational equipment. With rapid expansion projected for the 1990s in areas like computer and medical technology, how can high schools afford to offer relevant vocational education?

A second reason for the gap between hopes and realities in occupational training in public schools is that the skills necessary for most jobs are either of such a specific nature that employers need to provide training to their employees on the job or of such a simplistic nature that no prior training is necessary. Working at fast-food restaurants, for example, requires no former occupational training, while working for a privately owned business requires specific training in the company's own methods. The question then arises: What purpose are vocational classes in high schools serving?

Echoing the concerns of educators and researchers whose opinions we explored in Chapter 7, Boyer and his colleagues are also concerned that the concept of vocational education has become synonymous with academic inferiority. Students in the vocational track are generally perceived by teachers and peers as intellectually inferior to their classmates enrolled in the general or college-preparatory tracks. The stereotype of the "voc ed" student is one that encompasses intellectual inferiority, a lower socioeconomic family background, and unambitious career aspirations. Whether or not such a perception is justified, the stereotype often pervades potential employers' and society's views of vocational track graduates. In sum, the student who has pursued a college track or general curriculum is often perceived as brighter and more marketable than one with training in vocational education.

One vocational teacher interviewed by Boyer and his colleagues summarized the situation succinctly: "The counselors are sending us kids who are not really interested and are failing in school, so they put them in the vocational classes to strengthen their needed credits." Similarly, a new English teacher was advised not to invest much energy preparing for her vocational students' classes: "They don't belong in school. Those kids need boxing gloves, not books." Ignoring this advice, the novice teacher presented the same curriculum to both her college preparatory and her vocational classes and found that her vocational students were "walking in the hall with their Shakespeare turned so that the whole world could see that they were reading *Othello*" (Boyer, 1983, p. 124).

As a consequence of their findings on secondary education, Boyer and his colleagues recommend that all adolescents enroll in a single curricular track—one that is not divided into vocational, academic, or general divisions. The single-track program would provide all young people with academic skills in reading, writing, communication, and mathematics, a preparation that would serve their needs as college students or as employees after high-school graduation. Given employers' conplaints that young workers are poorly educated in basic academic skills, the single-track curriculum would service both adolescents' and future employers' needs. High schools would provide a core curriculum in academics onto which vocational training could be added throughout an individual's lifetime. All students might enroll in a course or two that introduced them to vocational issues such as decision making, career options for future decades, and money management, but training for a specific vocation would be delayed until after high-school graduation.

Requiring all students to enroll in the same track would also expand adolescents' vocational options by permitting them to make decisions about attending college or technical schools later in their high-school careers. In the present system, juniors or seniors in the vocational or general tracks who want to consider attending college are ill-equipped to apply because of their nonacademic coursework. Unfortunately, as you may recall from Chapter 7, most students are currently forced to decide whether or not to pursue a college-preparatory curriculum as early as the seventh or eighth grade. In contrast, the proposed single-track curriculum would permit vocational decisions to be delayed until later in adolescence, when most young people are better prepared to make such weighty decisions.

While the single-track curriculum is their preferred choice for the future, Boyer and his colleagues recognize that this option may not be adopted in our society. Consequently, they argue that if high schools continue to offer the multitrack curriculum, the *satellite concept* of vocational training would be a superior alternative to the traditional practices now supported in most schools (Boyer, 1983). Under this concept, the students attend their own high schools for their basic academic work, but vocational training is offered at other sites within the district. For example, in one urban area visited by Boyer and his colleagues, students from 12 high schools in six different school districts attend the regional vocational school for occupational training. Unlike the more limited resources available to an individual high school within a given district, the regional school is equipped with modern equipment, technical materials, and a well-trained staff. Furthermore, the faculty has been enriched by the inclusion of part-time teachers from local industries and businesses.

A similar concept is currently being employed in some schools through the use of well-equipped, portable classrooms, which travel to high schools on a temporary basis (Boyer, 1983). For example, in some of the most rural areas of North Dakota, portable classrooms with special teachers and equipment offer a program for one semester at each school. In one Massachusetts district, mobile classrooms equipped with materials for computer training, foreign-language instruction, and art instruction move from school to school on a one-semester basis. Similarly, a program in the Bronx, New York, trains students in health care at nearby hospitals rather than on high-school campuses. The principle underlying these ventures is to provide students with technologically relevant state-of-the-art instruction on a temporary, intensive basis, rather than to serve up years of generalized, outdated vocational education within the confines of their own high schools.

Conclusion

In sum, there can be little doubt that most vocational education programs are failing to prepare high-school students for the highly technological jobs the market now demands. Both the prohibitive expense of operating relevant vocational programs and employers' feedback regarding the traits they most desire in young employees lend credence to the argument that high schools should limit their emphasis to academic skills and relinquish responsibility for providing specific job skills to postsecondary schools. Moreover, many adolescents are not receiving the type of vocational counseling at school that will best equip them for the future occupational needs of the United States. Of particular importance, given the financial demands incumbent upon most adult females in modern times, female adolescents need more encouragement and guidance in preparing themselves for a wider array of vocations in fields from which women have historically been excluded.

The differentialist and developmental theories of vocational maturity appear to be in need of considerable revision. Rather than focusing on idealistic visions of adolescents whose socioeconomic background and society could afford them the luxury of freely choosing their vocations, vocational counselors might better serve today's youth by examining the more recent data regarding job choice. Given the ways in which most adolescents appear to make their vocational decisions, counselors might attend as carefully to variables within the family, to sex-role stereotypes, and to economic forecasts as to the results of written tests intended to match adolescents' vocational aptitudes with the characteristics of a particular job.

Questions for Discussion and Review

Basic Concepts and Terminology

1. In what ways are the vocational values of today's adolescents different from and similar to those of their counterparts in the 1960s and 1970s?
2. Considering wages, hours, and type of work, how would you describe the employment situation of most adolescents today? How do the employment situations differ depending on the adolescent's age, sex, and race?
3. What are the relative advantages and disadvantages of part-time employment for today's adolescents?
4. How do unemployment and delinquency appear to be related?
5. In what ways are the differentialist and developmentalist views of adolescents' vocational development alike and different?
6. On what grounds are the developmental and differentialist theories of vocational development being challenged?
7. How do adolescents' families influence their vocational development?
8. How do the vocational aspirations and achievements of male and female youths differ, and what factors seem to contribute to these differences?
9. According to the statistics on employment and salaries, how valuable are a college education, a high-school diploma, and high-school vocational education?
10. Considering the projections for future jobs and the economy, what would adolescents who are now in the seventh grade be best advised to do in regard to their vocational futures?

Questions for Discussion and Debate

1. Are you in agreement with the occupational values of today's adolescents or do you personally endorse the values of the 1960s?
2. What factors at school, at home, and in society influenced your occupational and educational aspirations as an adolescent? How do these factors compare with the present influences on your career plans?
3. How should vocational education be implemented in high schools in order to serve the needs of college- and noncollege-bound students?
4. How would your occupational plans have differed had you been a member of the opposite sex? A lower socioeconomic class? Another race?
5. Which experiences during your adolescence or childhood were most beneficial in helping you readjust your vocational and educational plans?
6. How do you feel about females' enrollment in U.S. military academies and their pursuit of careers in the armed services?
7. How would you attempt to resolve the problem of adolescent unemployment, particularly among minority youth in inner cities?
8. As a prospective employer of an adolescent, what characteristics or credentials would you be seeking?
9. What advice would you offer parents whose adolescent child wanted their permission to get a part-time job during the school year?
10. Do you think today's adolescents are being adversely affected by premature affluence? How did part-time employment affect your adolescence?
11. Which of Holland's personality-vocational types best describes you as you were during your adolescence, and how does this compare with your present self-assessment?
12. Considering the job projections for the future and the factors influencing career aspirations and achievements, how would you advise adolescents in regard to their vocational and educational plans?

REFERENCES

Andrew, J. Getting ahead: In high schools today, youths are absorbed with material goals. *Wall Street Journal,* June 3, 1981 pp. 1; 27.

Astin, A. Characteristics and attitudes of first year college students. *Chronicle of Higher Education,* 1981, *19,* 4–5.

Bachman, J. *The American high school student: A profile based on national survey data.* Ann Arbor: Institute for Social Research, University of Michigan, 1982.

Bachman, J. Premature affluence: Do high school students earn too much? *Economic Outlook,* 1983, *10,* 64–67.

Bachman, J., Johnston, L., & O'Malley, P. *Recent findings from Monitoring the Future.* Ann Arbor: Institute for Social Research, University of Michigan, 1985.

Bachman, J., O'Malley, P., & Johnston, J. *Youth in transition: Change and stability in the lives of young men.* Ann Arbor: University of Michigan Press, 1978.

Barton, P., & Frazer, B. *Youth knowledge development report. Between two worlds: Youth transition from school to work.* Washington, D.C.: U.S. Government Printing Office, 1980.

Borus, M. (ed.). *Youth and the labor market: Analyses of the national longitudinal survey.* Kalamazoo, Mich.: Upjohn Institute for Employment Research, 1984.

Boyer, E. *High school: A report on secondary education in America.* New York: Harper & Row, 1983.

Brenner, M. Estimating the social costs of youth employment problems. *A review of youth employment problems, programs and policies.* The Vice President's Task Force on Youth Employment. Washington, D.C.: U.S. Department of Labor, 1980.

Campbell, D. *The Strong-Campbell Interest Inventory.* Palo Alto, Cal.: Stanford University Press, 1974.

Carnegie Council on Policy Studies in Higher Education. *Giving youth a better chance.* San Francisco: Jossey-Bass, 1980.

Cole, S. *Working kids on working.* New York: Lothrop, Lee and Shepard, 1983.

Cook, M. *Jobs and schooling: Youth employment, personality and delinquency in a sample of dropouts from urban schools.* Baltimore, Md.: Johns Hopkins University, Center for Social Organization of Schools, 1983.

Dillard, J., & Campbell, N. Influences of Puerto Rican, Black and Anglo parents' career behavior on their adolescent children's career development. *Vocational Guidance Quarterly,* 1981, *30,* 139–148.

Erikson, E. *Identity: Youth and crisis.* New York: Norton, 1968.

Garrison, H. Gender differences in the career aspirations of recent cohorts of high school seniors. *Social Problems,* 1979, *27,* 170–185.

George, V. Occupational aspirations of talented black and white adolescent females. *Journal of Nonwhite Concerns in Personnel and Guidance,* 1981, *9,* 137–145.

Ginzberg, E. Toward a theory of occupational choice: A restatement. *Vocational Guidance Quarterly,* 1972, *21,* 169–176.

Ginzberg, E. *The school work nexus.* Bloomington, Ind.: Phi Delta Kappan, 1980.

Glenbard East *Echo. Teenagers themselves.* New York: Adama Books, 1984.

Gottfredson, D. Youth employment, crime and schooling: A longitudinal study of a national sample. *Developmental Psychology,* 1985, *21,* 419–432.

Gottfredson, L., & Becker, H. *A challenge to vocational psychology: How important are aspirations in determining career development?* Baltimore, Md.: Johns Hopkins University, Center for Social Organization of Schools, May 1981.

Gottlieb, D., & Driscoll, E. *Entering the world of work: Young Americans and their employers.* Princeton, N.J.: Educational Testing Service, 1982.

Greenberger, E., & Steinberg, L. The workplace as a context for the socialization of youth. *Journal of Youth and Adolescence.* 1981, *10,* 185–210.

Greenberger, E., Steinberg, L., & Vaux, A. Adolescents who work: Health and behavioral consequences of job stress. *Developmental Psychology,* 1981, *17,* 691–703.

Hamilton, D., & Crouter, A. Work and growth: A review of research on the impact of work experience on adolescent development. *Journal of Youth and Adolescence,* 1980, *9,* 323–338.

Havighurst, R. *Developmental tasks and education.* New York: McKay, 1972.

Herzog, R. High school seniors' occupational plans and values: Trends in sex differences 1976 through 1980. *Sociology of Education,* 1982, *55,* 1–13.

Hirschi, T. Crime and the family. In J. Wilson (ed.), *Crime and public policy.* San Francisco: Institute for Contemporary Studies, 1983. Pp. 53–64.

Hoffman, L. Maternal employment: 1979. *American Psychologist,* 1979, *34,* 859–865.

Hoffman, L. Work, family and socialization of the child. In R. Parket (ed.), *The review of child development research.* Chicago: University of Chicago Press, 1983.

Holland, J. *The psychology of vocational choice: A theory of personality types and model environments.* Waltham, Mass.: Blaisdell, 1966.

Karabel, J., & Astin, A. Social class, academic ability and college quality. *Social Forces,* 1975, *53,* 381–398.

Kelly, T. Youth differentials to the minimum wage: A summary of the arguments. *A review of youth employment problems, programs and policies.* The Vice President's Task Force on Youth Employment. Washington, D.C.: U.S. Department of Labor, 1980.

Lanier, H., & Byrne, J. How high school students view women: The relationship between perceived attractiveness, occupation and education. *Sex Roles,* 1981, *7,* 145–148.

Leifer, A., & Lessor, G. *The development of career awareness in young children.* Washington, D.C.: National Institute of Education, 1976.

Lerman, R. An analysis of youth employment problems. *A review of youth employment problems, programs and policies.* The Vice President's Task Force on Youth Employment. Washington, D.C.: U.S. Department of Labor, 1980.

Lueptow, L. Sex typing and change in the occupational choices of high school seniors. *Sociology of Education.* 1981, *54,* 16–24.

Maggarrel, J. Today's students, especially women, more materialistic. *Journal of Higher Education,* 1980, *19,* 3.

Maggarrel, J. Fewer liberals, more moderates among this year's freshmen. *Chronicle of Higher Education,* 1981, *20,* 5.

Marini, M. Sex differences in the determination of adolescent aspirations: A review. *Sex Roles,* 1978, *4,* 723–753.

Mclaughlin, G., Hunt, W., & Montgomery, J. Socioeconomic status and the career aspirations and perceptions of women seniors in high school. *Vocational Guidance Quarterly,* 1977, *25,* 155–162.

Miller, P., & Simon, W. Do youth really want to work: A comparison of the work values and job perceptions of younger and older men. *Youth and Society,* 1979, *10,* 379–404.

Mortimer, J., & Kumka, D. A further examination of the occupational linkage hypothesis. *Sociological Quarterly,* 1982, *23,* 3–16.

National Commission on Youth. *The transition to adulthood: A bridge too long.* Boulder, Col.: Westview Press, 1980.

New wage for youths is pushed. *Winston-Salem Journal,* March 16, 1985,. p. A-14.

Nilsen, D. The youngest workers: 14 and 15 year olds. *Journal of Early Adolescence,* 1984, *4,* 189–197.

Nolfi, N. *Experiences of recent high school graduates: The transition to work or postsecondary education.* Lexington, Mass.: Lexington Books, 1978.

Offer, D., Ostrov, E., & Howard, K. *The adolescent: A psychological self-portrait.* New York: Basic Books, 1981.

Osipow, S. *Theories of career development.* Englewood Cliffs, N.J.: Prentice-Hall, 1973.

Passmore, D., & Welch, F. Relationship between preferences for part-time work and characteristics of unemployed youths. *Adolescence,* 1983, *18,* 81–92.

Plisko, V. (ed.). *The condition of education.* Washington, D.C.: National Center for Education Statistics, 1985.

Robison, D. The youth unemployment problem: Facts and figures. *A review of youth employment problems, programs, and policies.* The Vice President's Task Force on Youth Employment. Washington, D.C.: U.S. Department of Labor, 1980.

Rodriguez, J. Youth employment: A needs assessment. *A review of youth employment problems, programs and policies.* The Vice President's Task Force on Youth Employment. Washington, D.C.: U.S. Department of Labor, 1980.

Ruebans, B., Jarrison, J., & Rupp, A. *The youth labor force 1945–1995: A cross national analysis.* Totowa, N.J.: Alanheld, Ossman, 1981.

Schulenberg, J., Vondracek, F., & Crouter, A. The influence of the family on vocational development. *Journal of Marriage and the Family,* 1984, *46,* 366–374.

Somers, J. The effect of industrial arts upon the career maturity of selected seventh and eighth grade adolescents. *Journal of Industrial Teacher Education,* 1981, *18,* 46–60.

Squires, G. *Education and jobs.* New Brunswick, N.J.: Transaction, 1979.

Steinberg, L. Jumping off the work experience bandwagon. *Journal of Youth and Adolescence,* 1981, *11,* 183–205.

Steinberg, L. The effects of working on adolescent development. *Developmental Psychology,* 1982, *18,* 385–395.

Stiehm, J. *Bring me men and women: Mandated change at the U.S. Air Force Academy.* Berkeley, Cal.: University of California Press, 1981.

Super, D. *Career education and the meanings of work.* Washington, D.C.: U.S. Office of Education, 1976.

Super, D., & Hall, D. Career development: Exploration and planning. *Annual Review of Psychology,* 1978, *29,* 333–372.

Swinton, D. Towards defining the universe of need for youth employment policy. *A review of youth employment problems, programs and policies.* The Vice President's Task Force on Youth Employment. Washington, D.C.: U.S. Department of Labor, 1980.

Tittle, C. *Careers and family: Sex roles and adolescent life plans.* Beverly Hills, Cal.: Sage, 1981.

U.S. Department of Commerce, Bureau of the Census. *Statistical abstract of the U.S.: 1980,* Washington, D.C.: U.S. Government Printing Office, 1980.

U.S. Department of Labor, Bureau of Labor Statistics. *Occupational outlook for college graduates, 1980–81.* Bulletin 2076. Washington, D.C.: U.S. Government Printing Office, 1980.

Veres, H., & Carmichael, M. *Changing adolescents' attitudes toward nontraditional career choices.* Paper presented at American Educational Research Association, New York, March 1982.

Waldman, E. Working mothers in the 1970s: A look at the statistics. *Monthly Labor Review,* 1970, *102,* 39–48.

Wigginton, E. *Sometimes a shining moment: 20 years in a high school classroom—The Foxfire experience.* Garden City, N.Y.: Doubleday, 1985.

Wijting, J., Arnold C., & Conrad, K. Generational differences in work values between parents and children and between boys and girls across grade levels 6, 9, 10 and 12. *Journal of Vocational Behavior,* 1978, *12,* 245–260.

Yankelovich, D. *New rules: Searching for self-fulfillment in a world turned upside down.* New York: Random House, 1981.

Young, A. The difference a year makes in the nation's youth work force. *Monthly Labor Review,* 1979, *102,* 34–38.

Young, R. Vocational choices and values in adolescent women. *Sex Roles,* 1984, *10,* 485–492.

Chapter Outline

The Development of Moral Reasoning
The Cognitive Perspective
The Psychoanalytic Perspective
The Social Learning Perspective
The Cognitive-Social Learning Perspective
Differences between Male and Female Moral Development
Adolescents and Religion
The Nation's Religious Climate
Adolescents' Religious Attitudes and Behavior
Membership in Religious Cults
Religious Diversity among U.S. Youth
Adolescents' Political Values
The Development of Political Thinking
Shortcomings of the Research
Adolescents' Political Activism
Voting Patterns of the Young
Adolescents' Views of the Military
Conclusion

Goals and Objectives

The information in this chapter should enable you to:

- *Compare and contrast the theories of moral reasoning*
- *Discuss the differences evident in male and female moral reasoning*
- *Describe adolescents' religious attitudes and behavior*
- *Enumerate the factors influencing adolescents' political and religious attitudes*
- *Provide examples of the changes in political and religious reasoning during adolescence*

Terms and Concepts

moral realism
autonomous morality
cognitive disequilibrium
preconventional reasoning
conventional reasoning
existential guilt
superego
individuation
Unification Church
evangelical Christians
Hare Krishna
deprogramming
Latter Day Saints
bar and bat mitzvah
Reform and Orthodox Judaism
Sephardic Jews
pogroms
Moonies

12 Adolescent Moral, Religious, and Political Development

THE DEVELOPMENT OF MORAL REASONING

Adolescents are confronted with a host of situations that demand their making moral decisions without adult intervention. Unlike younger children, adolescents are afforded opportunities to rely on their own moral judgments in decisions concerning issues such as premarital sex, drug use, cheating, and racial prejudice. How young people reach their decisions is of considerable interest not only to their elders but also to members of the research community. Debates over the factors that influence adolescents' moral reasoning and determine their values provoke a number of unresolved questions: Why does one youngster's moral reasoning resemble that of a much younger child, while another's resembles that of an adult? Can youngsters be taught to resolve moral dilemmas more maturely, or is moral reasoning primarily a function of age, mental ability, and peer interactions? Why does an individual's moral reasoning change as a function of age?

In their attempts to answer such questions, psychologists have approached the study of moral reasoning through four theoretical perspectives: cognitive, psychoanalytic, social learning, and cognitive-social learning (or *affective*) (Rich & DeVitis, 1985). In reviewing the literature on moral reasoning, Hoffman (1980) reminds us, however, that each of these four perspectives is limited, for each focuses mainly on young children or college students, rather than on adolescents. Furthermore, very few of the studies that have been conducted with adolescents have included comparable data from other age groups, thereby making developmental patterns difficult to establish. Nevertheless, despite these limitations, each of the four perspectives provides information relevant to the development of moral reasoning from childhood through adolescence.

The Cognitive Perspective

According to cognitive theorists, moral reasoning develops in distinct, invariant stages as individuals age. Each new stage is more comprehensive than its predecessor and embodies the skills learned in earlier stages. As noted in Chapter 3, cognitive theories contend that youngsters at the same stage of cognitive development will reason similarly. Cognitive theorists likewise assume that adolescents in the same stage of moral reasoning will arrive at similar resolutions to moral dilemmas, since they are relying on the same types of mental processes to analyze problems. In addition, cognitive psychologists presume that an individual applies the same type of reasoning to different kinds of moral problems. Stated differently, whether considering the morality of abortion or the morality of cheating on an exam, an adolescent will employ the same type of reasoning to arrive at the decision.

As earlier chapters have demonstrated, cognitive theorists maintain that the environment exerts less control over an adolescent's mental skills than does his or her cognitive stage. The same principle applies with regard to the relative

How would you compare your political views during adolescence with your present ideologies?

influence of environmental variables and cognitive development on adolescents' moral reasoning. Within this context, it is argued that regardless of their cultural or socioeconomic differences, children and adolescents pass through the stages of moral reasoning in an ordered sequence. It is further recognized that the pace and outcomes of this development vary. Some youngsters advance through the stages more quickly than others, and some never arrive at the highest stage. In terms of public and professional recognition, the cognitive perspective on moral development is best exemplified by its two most eminent proponents, Jean Piaget and Lawrence Kohlberg.

Piaget's Theories of Moral Development Piaget derived his theories of moral development from children's responses to hypothetical moral dilemmas. For example, Piagetian researchers ask children to determine whether a boy who accidentally knocks over 15 cups is "naughtier" than the boy who breaks one cup while trying to sneak jam out of the cupboard. In contrast to the prominent theorists of his time, Piaget argued that young children analyze moral situations on the basis of entirely different principles than adolescents or adults (Piaget, 1932).

Accordingly, Piaget proposed two distinct stages of moral development during childhood and adolescence: *moral realism* and *autonomous morality*. Children in the stage of moral realism obey rules out of deference to authority. Rather than evaluating rules in order to determine their fairness or legitimacy, children simplistically equate morality with obedience to authority. Believing that behavior is either totally right or totally wrong, children judge goodness and badness on the basis of how far an act deviates from the prescribed rules and how severely an individual is punished for violating the rule. Thus, in accord with Piaget's theory, most young children state that the boy who accidentally broke the 15 cups is naughtier than the boy who broke one, regardless of the extenuating circumstances, because he broke the most cups.

In contrast to children, adolescents advance toward the stage of autonomous morality or a morality of cooperation and reciprocity. Behavior that previously had been obediently categorized as either right or wrong is now subjected to more personal evaluation and independent scrutiny. Unlike the younger child, adolescents' judgments regarding the morality of a particular act take account of people's intentions as well as of the actual consequences of the act itself. Consequently, the boy who breaks one cup with the intention of stealing is more "immoral" than the one who breaks 15 cups accidentally. Adolescents also come to expect punishment to be commensurate with the transgression, rather than an inflexible penalty imposed by authorities. For example, adolescents would find it more morally reasonable that a vandal be asked to pay for the damage rather than be spanked, as a young child might find appropriate. Furthermore, adolescents in the stage of autonomous morality are less willing to obey rules or to adopt moral codes merely out of deference to authority. With age, an adolescent's willingness to obey rules laid down by authorities without question is tempered by considerations such as the impact of the rules on one's well-being, peer opinions, a sense of reciprocity, and feelings of empathy. Consequently, a high-school student might refuse to report her best friend for cheating, despite the teacher's honor code, because she empathizes with her friend's fear of math and because her friend formerly did her a similar favor.

What causes children to advance from the stage of moral realism to the more sophisticated stage of autonomous morality during adolescence? According to Piaget, both cognitive development and peer interactions are responsible for this maturation in moral reasoning. Adolescents who develop autonomous moral reasoning have outgrown three cognitive limitations that restricted their moral development as children: egocentrism, realism, and heteronomous respect for adults. The first limitation, the egocentric assumption that everyone else shares the same perspective as oneself, prevents children from perceiving themselves as individuals whose moral decisions may differ from other people's. Similarly, the second limitation, children's realism, restricts their moral reasoning by causing them to confuse subjective and objective experiences. Finally, the third limitation, their feelings of inferiority, dependence, fear, and admiration of adults, undermines children's abilities to make moral decisions that contradict adults' wishes.

From the Piagetian perspective, as children mature, their interactions with peers help them overcome these three cognitive limitations. First, interacting with peers permits young people to participate actively in constructing rules, in determining punitive contingencies for those who violate the rules, and in modifying rules when necessary to suit the group's needs. Second, peer interactions afford children opportunities to assume the perspective of other people and to examine the motives underlying others' conduct. Third, peer interactions create *cognitive disequilibrium*. As explained in Chapter 3, cognitive disequilibrium is the experience of being unable to fit new information into existing schema; therefore, the existing schema must be modified to accommodate the new data. These modifications in the schema subsequently result in more advanced forms of moral reasoning. Thus, Piaget maintains, the challenges that peers present to each other's moral viewpoints and to each other's ways of reasoning create the cognitive disequilibrium that is necessary for reorganizing the schema and for subsequently advancing to a higher level of moral reasoning.

Kohlberg's Theories of Moral Development Refining and expanding upon Piaget's theories, Lawrence Kohlberg has formulated a three-level, six-stage theory of moral development, described in Table 12.1 (Kohlberg, 1983, 1984). In the **preconventional stage,** a child's moral decisions are based on conforming to the rules in order to avoid punishment and on reciprocating for the sake of personal gain. For instance, a child might say she would not "snitch" on her classmate who cheats because "someday I may need to cheat and I don't expect her to snitch on me." The basic premise on which moral decisions are predicated is that "it's okay as long as you don't get caught." This first level of moral reasoning ignores the intentions underlying people's behavior and overlooks people's different perspectives.

In further accord with Piaget, Kohlberg contends that, as children age, they begin to base their moral decisions on concepts that extend beyond the fear of punishment or the desire for personal gain. The desire to live up to others' expectations, to uphold society's goals, and to fulfill duties are manifestations of the **conventional stage** of moral reasoning. At this stage, the young person has internalized society's standards without having questioned their premises. Children functioning at this stage, however, have become concerned with concepts like fairness and are able to examine other people's motives. This new capacity creates the ability to empathize with other people and to assume their perspectives before passing judgments about the immorality of any act. Accord-

Table 12.1

Kohlberg's Stages of Moral Development

Level One: Preconventional Reasoning

Stage 1: Heteronomous Morality

Obeying rules out of fear of punishment and respecting authorities without question. Reasoning from an *egocentric point of view,* the perspectives and needs of other people are not recognized as different from one's own, nor are others' needs considered in making moral decisions.

Stage 2: Individualism

Obeying rules in order to obtain immediate rewards. Although making decisions on the basis of meeting one's own needs, the individual also lets the concepts of fairness, equal exchange, and keeping agreements serve as rationale for moral decisions. Reasoning from the *concrete individualistic perspective,* the person recognizes that people have different needs, which create conflicts.

Level Two: Conventional Reasoning

Stage 3: Interpersonal Expectations and Conformity

Living up to what others expect and showing concern for others constitute "being good." The individual tries to abide by rules and make decisions that gain social approval. Abiding by the Golden Rule, mutual agreements and societal expectations take precedence over individual interests.

Stage 4: Social System and Conscience

Fulfilling duties and abiding by laws that maintain a fixed order, whether social or religious. Contributing to society, a group, or an institution are manifestations of "being good." Through obeying the rules one tries to avoid any disruptions in the established order. Reasoning from a societal point of view, the person considers individuals' interests and interpersonal relationships as secondary to maintaining social order.

Level Three: Postconventional Reasoning

Stage 5: Social Contract

Being aware the people's opinions differ and that rules and values are relative to each group's idiosyncratic perspectives. Certain values, however, such as liberty, are presumed to be appropriate for all groups. Emphasis is upon equality and mutual obligation within a democratic order. Reasoning from a rational perspective, the person recognizes moral conflicts and finds it difficult to integrate moral, legal, and societal points of view.

Stage 6: Universal Principles

Principles such as justice and equality take precedence over obedience to particular laws or agreements. When laws violate these principles, the person acts in accordance with the principle. Reasoning from the universal perspective, the person transcends any particular culture's perspective of morality.

SOURCES: L. Kohlberg, *Moral stages: A current formulation and response to critics.* London: Karger, 1983; *The psychology of moral development.* San Francisco: Harper & Row, 1984.

ing to Kohlberg, it is this conventional level of reasoning that is most prevalent among both adolescents and adults. Although conventional reasoning permits an adolescent to consider the welfare of a group instead of focusing exclusively on personal gain, it offers no method for resolving moral dilemmas in which society's laws conflict with other human values. To resolve moral conflicts of this more complex nature, individuals must have advanced to postconventional reasoning.

From Kohlberg's perspective, the **postconventional** level represents the most sophisticated type of moral reasoning an individual can attain. It emanates from the awareness that people's values differ and that rules and moral codes are relative, not universal or inflexible. Applying postconventional reasoning, individuals create their own ethical codes, based on universal principles rather than on allegiance to any particular group or society. Consequently, it is at this highest level of moral reasoning that people are most likely to defy authorities, to question social conventions, and to scrutinize their culture's values. For example, a young person reasoning at the postconventional level might argue that Communists who are starving should be fed through U.S. foreign aid because human life is more important than political ideologies.

On the basis of his research, Kohlberg contends that very few individuals will advance to postconventional reasoning during their adolescence. Indeed, most empirical studies demonstrate that the majority of adults never reach this level of moral reasoning (Colby et al., 1980). In regard to Kohlberg's contention that most people never attain postconventional reasoning, which would enable them to question authorities and to rely on their own moral codes, the results of Stanley Milgram's (1974) famous experiments, presented in Box 12.1, are noteworthy.

In Kohlberg's own investigations of moral development, subjects are presented with hypothetical moral dilemmas and then interviewed to determine the kind of reasoning underlying each decision. For example, the researcher asks adolescents why a druggist should or should not give a life-saving drug to a dying woman when her husband is too poor to buy it. Or a youngster is asked to explain why it is or is not better to save the life of one important person instead of the lives of many unimportant people. An individual's score is based on the kind of reasoning he or she uses to arrive at a decision and not on the specific choice he or she makes. In other words, two young people who both say the druggist should withhold the drug from the dying woman can earn different scores on Kohlberg's test of moral reasoning, if the reasons underlying their decisions differ.

Like Piaget, Kohlberg contends that children advance to higher stages of moral reasoning as a consequence of their more sophisticated cognitive skills and the cognitive disequilibrium fostered by peer interactions. Thus, Kohlberg maintains that it is possible to raise the level of an adolescent's moral reasoning by encouraging him or her to interact with people whose moral reasoning is more advanced. Moreover, Kohlberg argues that parents who encourage their children to consider others' perspectives and who discuss controversial issues at home are promoting more sophisticated moral reasoning. To demonstrate this point, Kohlberg compared the moral reasoning scores of U.S. adolescents in an orphanage with Israeli adolescents living in a kibbutz. Although neither setting afforded much contact between adolescents and adults, the kibbutz provided far more group discussions and group decision making among peers. In accord with

12.1 A Closer Look

Obeying Authorities: Vice or Virtue?

Sigmund Freud defined authority as "the longing for the father that lives in each of us from his childhood days." Whether or not we endorse this psychoanalytic definition, questions related to obeying authorities have intrigued both social scientists and philosophers. The atrocities committed against the Jewish people under Hitler, the mass murders carried out by young U.S. soldiers under orders from their commanding officer at Mai Lai in Vietnam, and the mass suicides of cult members under the direction of their religious leader, Jim Jones, in South America testify to the fact that both young and old are willing to acquiesce to authorities' inhumane demands. While we may try to disassociate our own behavior from these events, the question remains: How willing are we to obey authority even when obedience requires cruel or foolhardy behavior?

The social psychologist, Stanley Milgram, is well known for his attempts to answer this question empirically. Believing that the greatest threat to moral conduct is our readiness to obey authority, Milgram designed experiments in which subjects were asked to test the relationship between electric shocks and a student's rate of learning. Subjects were people who had responded to Milgram's advertisement in a local paper and who were paid for their participation. The experimenter instructed the subjects to administer an electric shock each time the "student" in the adjacent room missed an answer. Subjects were also aware that the shocks ranged from mild to extreme voltages. Unknown to the participants, the student to whom they were administering the shocks was a confederate of Milgram's and the electrical equipment had been disconnected.

At the outset the mildest shock was administered to the subjects so that each personally experienced the physical pain associated with the experiment. The subjects also had the experience of hearing the student's pleas to stop, followed by screams and finally silence, after severe shocks. Milgram and his associates assumed that no more than 1 or 2 percent of the participants would obey the experimenter's instructions to administer the shocks. Yet almost two-thirds of the subjects followed the experimenter's orders, even when requested to administer shocks at the highest voltages. Although many were sweating, crying, and begging the experimenter to end the

Kohlberg's predictions, the Israeli adolescents earned higher scores on the tests of moral reasoning that the U.S. orphans (Baryam, Reimer, & Kohlberg, 1983).

Criticisms of Kohlberg's Theory Although highly acclaimed for its heuristic value, Kohlberg's theory has been the subject of considerable criticism and debate (Bronfenbrenner & Garbarino, 1976; Snarey, 1985; Wallach & Wallach, 1983). First, the stages proposed by Kohlberg have not been found to be universal or invariant. Adolescents in different countries do not invariably pass through these stages in a universal or predictable manner. Second, Kohlberg's notion that certain types of reasoning are superior to others has been criticized as eth-

test, the majority continued to obey authority by administering further shocks. When the experimenter was not in the room, however, the obedient subjects administered the mildest shocks.

According to Milgram, one public dissenter can often be incentive enough for others to defy authority. If one individual will refuse to conform to the authorities' demands, others will often follow. Unfortunately, Milgram is among those who believe that many of us are willing to let people with higher status or those in positions of authority determine our moral conduct. In Milgram's view, "for the man who sits in front of the button that will release Armageddon, depressing it will have about the same emotional force as calling for an elevator. . . . Evolution has not had a chance to build inhibitors against such remote forms of aggression."

How can we encourage adolescents to resist blind obedience to authority in a society that values conformity? How are we to encourage the young to defy the enticing forms of authoritative, mesmerizing leadership that underlay the Jonestown massacres, the Mai Lai incident, and Hitler's youth brigades? According to Kohlberg and his supporters, courses in moral development should be incorporated into the academic curriculum. The experiences and activities in these classes would teach adolescents to dissent, to examine rules before obeying them, and to assume the perspective of other people before reaching moral conclusions. Students would learn to be wary of leaders and authorities who offer easy, simplistic solutions to complicated problems. In short, the classes would be enhancing adolescents' chances of thinking at the postconventional level of moral reasoning.

Should schools become involved in this form of moral training? If so, who should determine the content of the courses and who should decide which forms of moral reasoning are the most "advanced"? If schools should not assume this responsibility, who should? Should moral reasoning be solely the responsibility of parents whose own ethnocentric attitudes and level of moral reasoning would interfere with the development of their children's postconventional thinking?

SOURCES: S. Milgram, *Obedience to authority.* New York: Harper & Row, 1974; S. McCarthy, Why Johnny can't disobey. *The Humanist,* October 1979, pp. 30–34.

nocentric. Significantly, the types of reasoning that Kohlberg considers most advanced—abstract thinking, individualism, and democratic principles—are predicated on Western cultural values. Moreover, cross-cultural studies show that stages 5 and 6 seem to occur mainly in technological, democratic societies, where individual liberties and democratic political concepts prevail. Third, the theory is criticized for its inadequacy in explaining females' moral development. As a later section of this chapter will demonstrate, Kohlberg's theory was formulated on the basis of experiments with male subjects, thereby restricting its generalizability.

Furthermore, with regard to the claim that an individual's level of moral reasoning can intentionally be advanced, the methods suggested by Kohlberg have yielded inconsistent results (Carrol & Rest, 1982; Hoffman, 1980). In contradiction to Kohlberg's predictions, interacting with people with higher moral reasoning scores has generally failed to raise a person's level of moral reasoning. Some studies have shown that adolescents at the lowest levels of moral reasoning tend to move toward higher stages when given exercises requiring them to function at the higher levels. Adolescents with the higher levels of moral reasoning in these studies, however, made no advances after exposure to exercises demanding even higher levels. In addition, the youngsters who made the greatest gains had high scores on social desirability tests, a phenomenon suggesting that social influence rather than cognitive disequilibrium caused the improvements in moral reasoning. Nevertheless, some studies have shown that having adolescents discuss controversial issues with peers does enhance their moral reasoning abilities (Lockwood, 1978). In sum, the question of whether or not moral reasoning can be improved by producing cognitive disequilibrium remains unresolved.

Another problem to be addressed is the reversibility and distinctiveness of the various levels of moral reasoning. According to Kohlberg's theory, individuals advance from one stage to the next and, in so doing, develop modes of moral reasoning that are clearly distinguishable from stage to stage. In contradiction to these predictions, however, data show that an individual's moral reasoning can actually revert to a former stage and that the same type of moral reasoning is not necessarily applied to all moral dilemmas (Kuhn, 1976; Turiel, 1980). Furthermore, the characteristics of reasoning that supposedly distinguish one stage from another have been found to exist in several stages (Seiber, 1980).

According to the 20-year longitudinal study from which Kohlberg's theory was initially derived, most U.S. males advance through the stages of moral reasoning at a gradual but steady pace (Colby et al., 1980). Even in this study, however, about 7 percent of the participants regressed in moral reasoning, and distinct differences between the various levels of reasoning did not always exist. Furthermore, other researchers have found that an individual's stage of cognitive development is not necessarily commensurate with his or her level of moral reasoning, as Kohlberg's theory implies (Rowe & Marcia, 1980). Nevertheless, in support of Kohlberg's theory, most data do indicate that moral reasoning tends to advance with age (Hoffman, 1980).

In addition to the contradictions in the empirical data, Kohlberg's conclusions have been criticized on methodological grounds (Hoffman, 1980). Because the data-generating questions about moral reasoning are open-ended rather than objective, subjects must formulate their own responses orally in front of the experimenter. This procedure may confound the results, if subjects try to provide answers that they feel will gain the investigator's approval or that are deemed desirable by our culture's standards. Moreover, the investigator may also inadvertently prompt the respondent verbally or nonverbally to provide answers that do not reflect his or her real feelings. Since the consistency of individuals' scores from one testing to another has not been well established, the reliability of the test instrument is also in question. Finally, the types of dilemmas presented to adolescents in Kohlberg's interviews have very little in common with the kinds of moral problems young people typically confront. Indeed, when adolescents were asked to describe the kinds of moral dilemmas that were personally meaningful to them, their responses were unlike the types of problems used to assess moral development in Kohlberg's interviews (Yussen, 1977).

Given these criticisms, perhaps it is not surprising that a relationship between an adolescent's score on Kohlberg's interviews and his or her actual behavior has been difficult to establish. For example, in studies with college students, no relationship existed between moral stages and political attitudes. According to Kohlberg's theory, students reasoning at the lower stages should prefer political candidates who express utilitarian views, while advanced moral thinkers should choose candidates with more universal values. In fact, however, most students chose the candidate with the highest level of moral reasoning, regardless of their own level of moral reasoning (Steindorf, 1978). In contrast, other studies have found some relationship between students' stage of moral reasoning and their political attitudes (Rest, 1979). Although variables like age and sex may account for the discrepant research results, a clear relationship between moral reasoning and attitudes on issues like politics has not yet been firmly established.

Similarly, the existing literature shows no clear relationship between an adolescent's level of moral reasoning and his or her antisocial behavior (Blasi, 1980). Some researchers report that nondelinquents have higher levels of moral reasoning than delinquents and that altruistic, honest people have even higher levels of moral reasoning. The hypothesis, however, that people at the postconventional stage are the least likely to yield to social pressure or to behave unethically has not been confirmed. In sum, it does not appear that an individual's moral stage is as closely reflected in his or her behavior as Kohlberg's theory predicts.

Another objection to Kohlberg's theory has been raised by researchers who argue that even young children distinguish between social convention and moral dilemmas (Turiel, 1980). Kohlberg contends that people are capable of distinguishing between moral issues and society's rules only in late adolescence, when postconventional reasoning develops. Yet some investigators have shown that even preschoolers can reason at levels that Kohlberg regards as postconventional. For example, in one study 90 percent of the preschoolers said that moral acts like hurting someone or stealing would be wrong, even if no rule existed to prohibit the act (Nucci & Turiel, 1978).

Kohlberg himself suggests that the lack of empirical support for many aspects of his theory may be attributed to inadequacies in the scoring procedures (Kohlberg, 1983). In fact, Kohlberg's method for assessing moral reasoning has been criticized for its complicated scoring, a task that requires a well-trained interpreter. As an alternative to Kohlberg's methods, James Rest has developed the *Defining Issues Test* (DIT) for assessing stages of moral reasoning (Rest, 1979). Using multiple-choice questions that can be objectively scored, the DIT presents a series of dilemmas and a list defining the major issues involved. Subjects are asked to rate the importance of each issue involved and to identify the most important values governing human interactions.

Despite the criticisms leveled against Kohlberg's theories, they have been invaluable in advancing our understanding of moral development. As the research described in Box 12.2 demonstrates, Piaget's and Kohlberg's work has stimulated a great deal of research and thus has had a heuristic influence on the field of developmental psychology. Moreover, although Kohlberg's theory fails to provide a universal explanation for adolescents' moral reasoning, it does describe the stages through which most U.S. males pass in their moral development. Hence, having analyzed the literature, Hoffman (1980) concludes that "the strength of theories in the Piaget and Kohlberg tradition lies in the elabo-

12.2 A Closer Look

Fairness and Friendship: How the Concept of Justice Develops

Two boys, a little one and a big one, once went for a long walk in the mountains. When lunchtime came, they were very hungry and took their food out of their bags, but they found that there was not enough food for both of them. What should have been done? Give all the food to the big boy or to the little one, or the same to both? (Piaget, 1932)

A class of school children drew pictures to sell at a fair. Some of the children were lazy and didn't draw many pictures. Other children were poorer than their classmates. What should be done with the money collected by the class after the fair? Should everyone get the same portion of the money or should those who worked hardest get more money? Should the poor children receive more than others? (Damon, 1980)

You and your friend have each been given a picture to color, but your friend's is twice as large as yours. The teacher tells you that rewards will depend on how much of the picture each person completes. Although you are told that you may help one another, you are also told that there will be no rewards for helping. What will you do? (Berndt, 1981)

These three hypothetical dilemmas exemplify the types of questions posed to children and adolescents by researchers who study the development of such moral values as justice and fairness. From such research we have learned that the principles that children apply in deciding what is fair or unfair change with age. Testing the theories of Piaget and Kohlberg, contemporary researchers are exploring questions about distributive justice: Does an adolescent treat a friend differently than a stranger when deciding what constitutes fair conduct? How do our concepts of justice change as we age? How are our cognitive abilities related to treating our friends fairly?

Piaget's work on moral judgment represented the first major attempt to explain the development of distributive justice. According to Piaget, young children are egocentric, lacking the cognitive ability to appreciate another person's point of view and to behave with mutual respect. Since they rely solely on authorities for their moral codes, young children will accept unfair treatment as fair, if it is condoned by an authority. As children age and have more experiences with peers, however, they begin to perceive fairness as synonymous with equity. For example, confronted with the hypothetical situation of the two boys and the sandwiches, most 6- and 7-year-olds say the bigger boy should get the most food because he is older, not because he is hungrier. Most 9- and 10-year-olds, however, say that the younger boy should have more food for such reasons as, "He will not be able to finish their walk without a good lunch, because he is little." Older children are more concerned with creating an equitable outcome. During his long and productive career, Piaget did not try to determine the relationship between the amount of time children spent with peers or adults and their dedication to equity. Neither did he try to determine empirically the antecedents of children's changing concepts of fairness. Such empirical questions were left to other researchers, such as Damon.

During the 1970s Damon's investigations of children's moral reasoning focused extensively on the development of distributive justice. In accord with Piaget and Kohlberg, Damon contends that our moral reasoning abilities develop in distinct stages, which are related to our cognitive development. Furthermore, Damon believes that the changes in our childhood notions about distributive justice are primarily related to our abilities to engage in the classification and seriation of physical objects. In other words, our childhood beliefs about distributing rewards fairly depends on our capacity to reason logically about physical objects. Consequently, Damon argues that in order to reason maturely about the concept of fairness, a child must be functioning at least in the stage of concrete operational thinking—the stage that permits him or her to classify and seriate objects without confusion. (Refer to Chapter 3 for a review of Piaget's principles of classification and seriation.)

Damon demonstrates his theory by citing children's responses to the hypothetical dilemma involving the distribution of money after the class art sale. Children reasoning at the lowest level of distributive justice make self-centered decisions without providing any logical rationale: "I should get most of the money because I want it." Children at the next higher level justify their decision by considering some external characteristics of other people, such as age or gender. Nevertheless, the underlying rationale is still self-serving. Hence, a boy says, "The boys should get more money than girls because they're boys." Children then progress to equating fairness with equity: "Everyone should get the same amount of money, no matter how many pictures they drew." Finally, children equate fairness with distributing rewards on the basis of relative performance: "Those who drew the most pictures should get the most money."

According to Damon, children cannot attain the next stage of distributive justice until after the age of 9. In this stage a child can consider several principles simultaneously in making judgments about fairness. A young person in this stage may consider giving the most money to the poorest children in the class, giving the most to those who drew the most pictures, or giving everyone the same amount because it was a class project rather than an individual venture. While capable of considering all these possibilities simultaneously, such a child will nonetheless eventually choose one principle on which to base his or her choice.

Having reviewed the research on adults' and children's concepts of fairness, Hook and Cook (1979) agree that distributive justice is related to an individual's cognitive understanding of physical proportions. Between the ages of 4 and 6, children usually distribute rewards equally or keep most of the rewards for themselves. Between 7 and 12, children typically give more rewards to the person who completes the most work, but the proportion of work to reward is incongruent. Thus, under such a process, doing 70 percent of the work might yield only 40 percent of the rewards. After the age of 13, however, adolescents are able to perceive fairness as distributing the rewards in direct proportion to each person's contribution. With the development of formal operational thinking, adolescents are able to apply the principle of proportions to moral dilemmas, as well as to physical objects.

In contrast to the cognitive views of researchers like Piaget, Kohlberg, Damon, and Hook and Cook, social psychologists offer a different perspective on the development of fairness. According to the social-psychological perspective represented by Lerner's research, an individual's concepts of justice depend on the type of relationship that exists between people. From this viewpoint, adolescents' decisions about fairness depend on what kind of relationship they believe exists between themselves and the other person (Lerner & Whitehead, 1980).

Lerner suggests five relationships: (1) "Coworkers" are members of the same institution, whose relationship is based on their official roles rather than on their individual personalities. In these situations people want rewards distributed on the basis of relative contributions to the organization's goals. (2) "Teammates" are working together in situations where everyone expects rewards to be distributed equally, because all are contributing to a team goal. (3) "Competitors" are expected to compete with each other in official roles and to earn rewards commensurate with their achievements. Fairness in these situations requires that everyone abide by the preestablished rules for the competition. (4) "Enemies" base competition on their personal antipathies, although they, too, establish rules for the acquisition of the rewards. The rule may sometimes be "no holds barred," but it is nonetheless understood by all involved parties. (5) "Close friends" react unselfishly toward one another, thereby extending the concept of fairness beyond equity. Being fair is no longer merely a matter of distributing the goods equally.

Having reviewed the research on fairness and friendship, Thomas Berndt (1982) concludes that adolescents and adults take account of several principles when deciding how to distribute rewards. Like young children, adults consider it fair to attend only to their own self-interests in certain situations involving the distribution of rewards. Although people of all ages sometimes view competition as the fairest way to distribute rewards, competition and lack of equity between friends seem most common during middle childhood. In addition, Berndt contends that "by the time children enter elementary school, if not earlier, they appear to understand all of the principles of fairness that adults use frequently" (p. 273). For Berndt, the changes between childhood, adolescence, and adulthood can primarily be accounted for by our changing perspectives on friendship, rather than as a function of our inability to understand the principles of fairness.

Whichever theoretical perspective we choose to adopt in regard to the development of fairness and distributive justice, the questions confronting researchers are complex. The famous Scopes Trial lawyer, Clarence Darrow, said, "There is no such thing as justice—in or out of court," and George Bernard Shaw quipped, "The golden rule is that there is no golden rule." How adolescents are to formulate their notions of fairness and how these notions change with age will no doubt continue to intrigue both philosophers and social scientists for some time to come.

SOURCES: T. Berndt, Fairness and friendship. In K. Rubin and H. Ross (eds.), *Peer relationships and social skills in childhood.* New York: Springer Verlag, 1982; T. Berndt, Age changes and changes over time in prosocial intentions and behavior between friends. *Developmental Psychology,* 1981, *17,* 408–416; W. Damon, Patterns of change in children's social reasoning: A two year longitudinal study. *Child Development,* 1980, *51,* 1010–1017; J. Hook & T. Cook, Equity theory and the cognitive ability of children. *Psychological Bulletin,* 1979, *86,* 429–445; J. Piaget, *The moral judgment of the child.* New York: Free Press, 1932; M. Lerner & L. Whitehead, Procedural justice viewed in the context of justice motive theory. In G. Mikula (ed.), *Justice and social interaction.* New York: Springer, 1980.

ration of the development and complex nature of moral thought; these theories are limited, however, because they neglect the motivational side of the phenomenon called conscience'' (p. 304).

The Psychoanalytic Perspective

Conscience has been defined as ''a cur that will let you get past it but that you cannot keep from barking''; as ''something that is thoroughly well-bred and soon leaves off talking to those who do not wish to hear it''; and as ''the inner voice that warns us that someone may be looking'' (Brussell, 1970). In a similar vein, the psychoanalytic perspective maintains that it is primarily this ''conscience,'' known in Freudian terminology as the ''superego,'' that determines adolescents' moral reasoning. Thus, without necessarily recognizing our views as such, many of us nonetheless endorse the psychoanalytic viewpoint by attributing people's immoral behavior to their ''lack of conscience.'' Within this psychoanalytic framework, the traditional Freudians and the ego psychologists espouse somewhat different perspectives on the development of moral reasoning during adolescence.

Freudian Perspectives Within the traditionally Freudian model, the **superego** or conscience assumes a special significance during adolescence, as children become individuated from their parents and develop their own moral standards for judging behavior (Freud, 1961; Josselson, 1980). During childhood a child's superego influences his or her behavior by producing guilt over actions that violate the parents' values. During adolescence, however, a change occurs: The superego begins to operate on principles that have been carefully evaluated by the ego, rather than having been automatically accepted on the basis of one's parents' values. Increasingly aware of the duplicity and contradictions in society, adolescents lose the security provided by their childhood superego—a conscience that judged acts simplistically as right or wrong on the basis of parents' values. Consequently, a primary task of adolescense is to reevaluate the superego's standards, a process that may sometimes mean rejecting the values of one's parents. This process, referred to as **individuation,** allows adolescents to formulate a ''conscience'' of their own, after they have carefully examined and judged its childhood contents. For a more thorough explanation and review of the individuation process, refer to Chapter 3.

As may be recalled from Chapter 4, the psychoanalytic view has been criticized on a number of grounds (Hoffman, 1980). In addition to there being little empirical support for this theory, the evidence offered by its advocates is typically derived from male subjects and from personal observations by psychoanalysts. Furthermore, there is no explanation for the process by which the superego (which is presumably unconscious) acquires new values and incorporates them into itself. Other unanswered questions undermine the psychoanalytic explanations of moral development: What motivates a person to utilize the superego's and ego's capacities for moral rather than for immoral purposes? Why does the superego become more able to incorporate values that are antithetical to the child's parents? In sum, the psychoanalytic perspective still lacks the empirical support necessary to explain adolescents' moral development.

Ego Psychologists' Perspectives As described in Chapter 4, psychologists like James Marcia, Jane Loevinger, and Erik Erikson endorse the psychoanalytic assumption that an individual's ego undergoes important transformations during adolescence (Erikson, 1968; Loevinger, 1976; Marcia, 1980). Reexamining Table 4.1 may help you review the importance of these ego changes for the adolescent's personality. Unlike traditional Freudian theorists, however, ego psychologists contend that environmental factors contribute appreciably to an adolescent's ego development. Ego psychologists, therefore, try to identify the socio-cultural factors that influence an adolescent's moral reasoning and to describe the characteristic behavior associated with different stages of ego development. As Table 12.2 illustrates, both ego psychologists and cognitive psychologists describe stages of development that they contend are directly related to an adolescent's moral reasoning abilities.

According to ego psychologist Jane Loevinger, for example, adolescents who advance from the conformist to the conscientious or autonomous levels become increasingly tolerant, individualistic, objective, and introspective in their moral reasoning. Adolescents in the higher stages of ego development make their moral decisions less impulsively, less selfishly, and less ethnocentrically than their peers in lower stages. In contrast, adolescents at the conformist stage base their moral conduct and values on the unexamined rules of authorities, the need for peer approval, and fear of losing status or material possessions (Loevinger, 1976).

Table 12.2

Three Stage Theories Related to Adolescents' Moral Reasoning

Theoretical View	*Stage*	*Moral Characteristics*
Psychoanalytic Theories		
Freud	Oedipal stage	Developing a morality individuated from one's own parents' values
Ego Theories		
Erikson	Identity versus confusion	Developing independent ideologies by experimenting with roles and values
Marcia	Identity achieved	Developed a moral code independently
	Foreclosed identity	Adopts the morals of authorities
	Moratorium or diffused	Uncertain of one's own moral values
Loevinger	Conformist	Adopts the moral values of others
	Conscientious	Moving toward independent morality
	Autonomous	Endorses tolerance and individualism
Cognitive Stage Theories		
Piaget	Formal operations	Developing a less egocentric view
Elkind	Formal operations	Becoming less controlled by the personal fable and imaginary audience
Kohlberg	Conventional reasoning	Becoming more empathetic and aware of society's needs and people's motives

In a similar vein, James Marcia has investigated the relationship between an adolescent's identity status and stages of moral reasoning (Marcia, 1980). Adolescents with foreclosed identities tend to accept the moral values of those in positions of authority, like parents and teachers. Committed to moral values largely defined by other people, these youngsters tend to be authoritarian, conventional, and obedient. Thus, for example, one would predict that adolescents and adults with foreclosed identities would be the most likely to obey the commands of authorities in experiments like Stanley Milgram's, which are described in Box 12.1.

In contrast, young people who are undergoing the confusion and experimentation that eventually lead to an achieved identity are evaluating the moral principles of their parents, society, and friends. Adolescents who arrive at an achieved identity are willing to examine the perspectives of other people before formulating their own moral principles. Moreover, rather than endorsing conventional social standards and authorities' views without question, as do the adolescents currently in the moratorium or diffused stages, they are more willing to defy peer pressure and authority in order to formulate a moral code of their own. As a consequence, these young people, as they undergo the process of moral development, may rebel against their parents and society's most established institutions, demand proof from authorities before accepting anything as fact, and appear impertinent to adults who feel uncomfortable with their questions and skepticism (Marcia, 1980).

The Social Learning Perspective

As you recall from Chapter 3, social learning theorists contend that human behavior is shaped through reinforcement, punishment, and modeling. These same principles, they would argue, apply to the development of an adolescent's moral reasoning and moral values (Bandura, 1977; Mischel & Mischel, 1976; Seiber, 1980). Starting from the position that human behavior is both lawful and predictable, social learning theorists assert that an adolescent's moral behavior depends on the types of rewards and punishments to which he or she is exposed. An adolescent's moral decisions are primarily determined by the contingencies for reward and punishment operating at the time, rather than on a stage of moral reasoning or a well-developed superego. For example, students who cheat on an exam do so when the benefits of cheating—such as passing the course—outweigh the risk of punishment.

In the context of social learning theory, the criteria by which adolescents judge behavior as moral or immoral are derived from their community's particular standards. Consequently, there are differences among adolescents' conceptions of right and wrong. Conduct considered immoral in one culture is sometimes totally ignored or even appreciated in another. Through reinforcement, punishment, and modeling, children learn to distinguish acceptable from unacceptable behavior. Through a similar process they learn which moral principles their community condemns and which it condones. Given these assumptions about human behavior, social learning theorists direct their attention to the conditions under which different moral decisions occur: Under what conditions do students cheat? Under what contingencies do adolescents decide to have premarital intercourse or to abstain? Under what circumstances do the young obey leaders like Hitler?

In agreement with cognitive theorists, social learning theorists attribute the changes in adolescents' moral reasoning to their increased cognitive maturity, as well as to their social experiences. As children age, their expanding cognitive abilities help them better understand the relationships between their behavior and the consequences. Adolescents' cognitive abilities interact with their social experiences to create more refined moral reasoning. For example, young children's limited cognitive abilities prevent them from being able to perceive the intentions or perceptions of other people; therefore, their decisions are based on the pleasurable or unpleasurable consequences of their behavior. They may choose not to hit their playmates because they fear that an adult will punish them, but not because they are cognitively able to empathize with their friends or comprehend the principle of fairness or reciprocity. In contrast, an adolescent has the cognitive abilities to understand abstract principles like reciprocity and to connect the act of hitting someone with undesirable consequences, such as losing popularity.

Watching others receiving rewards or punishment also affects an adolescent's moral decisions (Mischel & Mischel, 1976). Individuals tend to emulate people who are receiving rewards, although particular characteristics enhance a person's appeal as a model to others. For instance, a male adolescent who loves sports is more likely to model himself after a famous athlete than after a female opera star. As you will recall from Chapter 10, campaigns to decrease adolescent pregnancies apply this principle by having famous athletes and movie stars endorse the use of birth-control devices. Adolescents are most likely to base their moral decisions on people whom they personally know and those with high status and prestige in society. Adults who are nurturant and supportive are also more likely to become adolescents' models than those who are critical and distant.

How do social learning theorists explain the fact that adolescents and adults report feeling guilty when they transgress, even though they may escape punishment? Is there no such thing as a conscience that influences adolescents' moral decisions? According to the social learning perspective, guilt feelings arise as a consequence of the conditioning we receive from society in regard to appropriate and inappropriate thoughts and acts. When adolescents appear to be directed by a conscience, they are actually being directed by the sanctions and values that they have internalized from their society (Seiber, 1980).

The Cognitive-Social Learning Perspective

One of the most sophisticated and comprehensive socialization theories is that of Martin Hoffman (1980, 1983, 1984). According to Hoffman, adolescents' moral behavior and style of moral reasoning depend both upon their stage of cognitive development and upon the ways in which they have been socialized.

Within the framework of Hoffman's theory, an individual's moral code and conduct are primarily the consequences of socialization—primarily, the values and style of discipline of one's parents. Thus, children initially learn their moral values and behavior at home. As children age, however, they erroneously come to believe that their moral beliefs are self-produced, rather than determined by their parents or by society. Moreover, the type of reasoning adolescents employ when making moral decisions depends upon their parents' predominant style of discipline. In this regard, Hoffman endorses a belief shared by both the psychoanalytic and the social learning theorists: The type of relationship that exists between adolescents and their parents has a considerable impact on their moral reasoning and conduct.

In order to test this hypothesis, Hoffman (1980, 1981) reviewed the empirical data on the relationship between child-rearing styles and adolescents' moral development. According to Hoffman's analysis of the data, adolescents who base their conduct and moral decisions on the fear of external detection and punishment generally have parents who use "power-assertive" discipline. These power-assertive parents try to control their children through physical force, threats, direct commands, and withdrawal of possessions or privileges. In contrast, young people who experience guilt after having committed a moral transgression and who base their moral decisions on their own internalized principles have parents who use "inductive" methods of discipline. These parents provide the rationale underlying their rules, appeal to a child's compassion for others, and try to instill a cognitive understanding of the consequences of bad behavior. Such an approach appears to encourage internalization of values. Moreover, Hoffman contends that the methodological designs of the studies make it improbable that the outcomes are the consequence of the adolescents' sex, social class, or IQ scores. Rather, the differences in moral reasoning appear to be related to the type of discipline employed by the adolescents' parents.

A particularly noteworthy aspect of Hoffman's analysis is that mothers appear to be more influential than fathers in determining adolescents' moral outlook (Hoffman, 1981). Although some earlier studies had shown that boys from homes without fathers had lower scores on guilt, moral internalization, and conformity to rules, Hoffman suggests that these boys may be responding to conflict in the home or to their mothers' changed behavior, rather than to their fathers' absence. Indeed, it appears that after a father leaves, the mother uses power-assertive rather than inductive discipline with her son. Interestingly, the pattern seems to be reversed for daughters: Mothers become more affectionate and use more inductive discipline with daughters when there is no father living in the home. In contrast to mothers, there seems to be no consistent relationship between either the father's disciplinary techniques or his presence in the home and his children's moral internalization. Fathers do, however, seem to have more influence than mothers on adolescents' achievement values, and they do serve as figures with whom sons can identify in acquiring moral standards. Nevertheless, mothers are generally the ones who teach both sons and daughters to evaluate their own behavior by developing internalized moral standards.

Hoffman also contends, however, that a person's moral development is also dependent upon a cognitive ability to empathize with other people—an ability that is aroused by physical cues, such as witnessing another person's facial expressions. In other words, an adolescent's moral development cannot be explained simply by the socialization process. Specifically, Hoffman argues that children's cognitive limitations permit them to empathize with others only in specific, concrete situations, whereas adolescents' cognitive abilities allow them to empathize with another person's general circumstance. For example, a young child can empathize with a playmate who falls down and cries, but is cognitively incapable of empathizing with people living in another country who are starving. While the young child's ability to empathize is limited by cognitive restraints, the adolescent is able to reason in terms of abstract concepts like poverty, a capacity that makes it possible to imagine the circumstances of other people.

Hoffman maintains that most adolescents have become capable of experiencing distress and guilt on the basis of empathizing with other people's circumstances. Adolescents also become capable of feeling guilt in situations where they have personally committed no wrongdoing. For example, some young people feel guilty over the fact that millions of the world's inhabitants are dying of starvation, while they themselves waste food. Others may feel guilty for having survived an unavoidable car accident in which a friend was killed. Hoffman refers to this feeling as *existential guilt,* in contrast to the type of guilt arising from personal wrongdoing. Existential guilt influences adolescents' moral reasoning by provoking feelings of empathy and compassion for those who are less fortunate or are unjustly treated. For example, many of the student dissenters in the 1960s were affluent, well-educated young people who expressed guilt regarding their advantaged social and economic positions. Empathizing with the less fortunate, these young people developed moral philosophies and behavior intended to redress society's inequities.

In addition to evoking adolescents' compassion, Hoffman believes that guilt contributes to adolescents' altruism by triggering an examination and reevaluation of moral values. For example, studies with college students show that those who believe they have harmed someone are subsequently more willing to behave altruistically toward other people. Motivated by their guilt, these college students were more willing to make charitable donations, to assist strangers, and to volunteer for altruistic projects (Hoffman, 1980). Although much of the research has been limited to college students, Hoffman concludes that guilt is often a powerful incentive underlying adolescents' moral behavior.

Hoffman's assumption that an adolescent's empathy and moral values are closely related receives support from data such as *Monitoring the Future*'s yearly surveys of high-school seniors (Herzog, Bachman, & Johnston, 1978). Questionnaires assessing adolescents' concern for other people were administered to nearly 3,000 high-school seniors from a representative national sample. The questions focused particularly on adolescents' empathy toward the poor, minorities, and people in other regions of the world. The survey found that the empathetic seniors had more positive attitudes toward other races, were more supportive of policies such as integration and equal opportunity, and were more concerned about improving race relations. The empathetic seniors were also the most likely to have a close friend of another race and to be willing to work, live, or be educated in interracial situations.

Moreover, adolescents' levels of empathy were related to their views about women and families. Empathetic males were more likely to endorse equal opportunities for women and to disagree with statements like "A wife making more money than her husband would cause trouble in the marriage." Empathy was not strongly related, however, to boys' feelings about whether or not women should be employed. The empathetic boys were more opposed to premarital sex, however, a finding that might be interpreted as a reflection of their concern for the well-being of people besides themselves. Nevertheless, there were no significant differences in the most and least empathetic adolescents' willingness to limit the size of their future families in order to prevent overpopulation. The researchers suggest that this unexpected finding may be due to society's assumption that choosing not to have children is selfish. Further, it is possible that adolescents are still too young to fully comprehend the relationship between limiting a family's size and insuring the well-being of others.

Empathy was less strongly related to adolescents' feelings and behavior with regard to pollution and energy conservation. Although the most empathetic seniors were more likely to say they would use energy-saving measures like public transportation, paying higher taxes, and changing their diets, their actual behavior did not live up to their stated ideals. In other words, there were few differences in the polluting or energy-conservation activities of the empathetic and nonempathetic youngsters. The researchers suggest this may be due to the fact that adolescents have too little control over pollution and energy conservation to actively adopt countermeasures for combating these problems. On the other hand, students with the highest grades and college aspirations were more concerned with others' well-being than their less gifted classmates. The empathetic youngsters were also more interested in politics, although they were not any more or less politically liberal than their less empathetic peers (Hoffman, 1981).

The researchers suggest that academic success, college aspirations, and a concern for the welfare of others are related, because each requires similar intellectual abilities—above all, the mental capacity to think beyond immediate circumstances and apparent contingencies. In sum, *Monitoring the Future*'s data support Hoffman's contention that an adolescent's ability to empathize with other human beings affects his or her moral values and behavior.

DIFFERENCES BETWEEN MALE AND FEMALE MORAL DEVELOPMENT

Although unrecognized and overlooked for many years, recent studies suggest that gender is an important variable in understanding adolescents' moral development (Gilligan, 1982). Unfortunately, however, one of the major shortcomings of moral development theories has been their failure to account for the course of moral development in females. The most comprehensive analysis of the differences between male and female moral development has been prepared by Carol Gilligan, a developmental psychologist who initially worked with Kohlberg at Harvard University. Having examined the influential theories of Freud, Piaget, Kohlberg, and Erikson, Gilligan (1982, p. 6) asserts that "implicitly adopting the male life as the norm, they [psychological theories] have tried to fashion women out of a masculine cloth."

In her assessment of Freudian theory, Gilligan points out that females' moral reasoning is considered inferior to males' primarily because it deviates from Freud's description of male development. Having formulated his theories on the basis of boys' experiences, Freud assumed that a healthy superego could develop only during adolescence, when castration anxiety motivates boys to resolve their Oedipal complex. Consequently, Freud concluded that females' moral development is inferior to males' because girls lack the impetus to resolve the Oedipal dilemma. Without resolving their Oedipal complex and thereby developing a healthy superego, females supposedly remain dependent on the moral views of other people, while males act independently on the basis of internalized moral principles. In Freud's own words, "For women the level of what is ethically normal is different from what it is in men. Their superego is never so inexorable, so impersonal, so independent of its emotional origins . . . they have less sense of justice, less tendency to submit themselves to the great necessities of life and frequently permit themselves to be guided in their decisions by their affections or enmities" (Gilligan, 1982, pp. 257–258).

One formidable problem with the Freudian perspective is that most empirical data fail to substantiate its predictions about male and female moral conduct. Even more damaging to the Freudian position is that the existing studies suggest that females are more likely than males to act on the basis of internalized moral principles. Several representative studies demonstrate this point. In a study using Stanley Milgram's paradigm, female subjects were more likely than males to defy authorities and to abide by their own moral principles by refusing to inflict pain on other people (Kilham & Mann, 1974). In comparison to males, females were more likely to return valuable items found in the street when no witnesses were present. When there were witnesses, however, males returned the items as often as females, a finding that suggests that the males' moral principles were not as internalized as the females' (Hoffman, 1980). Similarly, a study conducted with fifth- and seventh-graders showed that girls were most apt to feel guilty about their transgressions, while the boys were more apt to feel worried about getting caught and being punished (Hoffman, 1980).

Gilligan also notes a second significant problem with the perspectives of Freud, Piaget, and Kohlberg: the assumption that male development is synonymous with human development and that deviation from the male norm is a reflection of immaturity. For example, Piaget assumed that girls' greater tolerance of those who violate rules and their greater willingness to make exceptions to the rules reflect a less well-developed "legal sense"—a capacity that Piaget deemed essential for moral development. Likewise, Kohlberg assumes that moral decisions that subordinate relationships to rules are superior to moral decisions that are based on pleasing and assisting other people. Consequently, since most females learn to define their "goodness" on the basis of harmonious interpersonal relationships, unselfishness, and empathy toward others, they are judged less "mature" than males on Kohlberg's scale of moral reasoning.

The fact that most girls emerge from adolescence basing their behavior on empathy and intimacy has been well established in the literature, as demonstrated by the studies examined in Chapter 9. For example, studies conducted from kindergarten through eighth grade have shown that girls are more willing than boys to assist classmates and to share rewards with their close friends, whereas boys treat their friends no differently from other classmates in situations that require sharing and assisting (Berndt, 1981, 1982). Similarly, *Monitoring the Future*'s data showed that high-school-senior girls consistently express more concern than boys for the welfare of other people (Herzog, Bachman, & Johnston, 1978). In sum, as Gilligan (1982) contends, the literature shows that girls emerge from adolescence with empathy as part of their self-definition and as part of their moral code in a way that boys do not.

Given these differences between males and females, Gilligan explains that investigators have failed to see the maturity and logic of females' moral responses in experiments such as Kohlberg's. For example, in asking youngsters what people should do when responsibility to themselves and responsibility to others conflict, a young boy in one experiment responded, "You go about one-fourth to the other and three-fourths to yourself. The most important thing in your decision should be yourself; don't let yourself be guided totally by other people, but you have to take them into consideration." In contrast, a young girl answered, "Well, it really depends on the situation. . . . If it's just your responsibility to your job or somebody that you barely know then maybe you go first—but if it's somebody that you really love and love as much or even more than you love yourself, you've got to decide what you really love more, that person or the thing or yourself. You can't just decide, 'Well, I'd rather do this or that'" (Gilligan, 1982, p. 36).

In Gilligan's words, "Beginning with [the boy's] responsibility to himself, a responsibility that he takes for granted, he then considers the extent to which he is responsible to others as well." In contrast, "Proceeding from a premise of connection that 'if you have a responsibility with somebody else, you should keep it,' [the girl] then considers the extent to which she has a responsibility to herself." Rather than adopting Kohlberg's patterns of moral development as the ideal for males and females, Gilligan suggests that each sex has its own moral developmental tasks. She recommends that for a boy "development would entail coming to see the other as equal to the self and the discovery that equality provides a way of making connection safe," while for a girl "development would follow the inclusion of herself in an expanding network of connection and the discovery that separation can be protective and need not entail isolation" (Gilligan, 1982, pp. 37–39).

According to Gilligan's analyses, most females view moral behavior as acts that involve self-sacrifice and that diminish other people's pain. Thus, in contrast to boys, girls must somehow resolve the contradiction between values that are considered to be feminine in the culture's view and the type of moral reasoning that is equated with mature adult behavior. In this regard, Gilligan's research with pregnant females between the ages of 15 and 33, who were considering abortions, demonstrates the unique moral dilemma confronting females. When the woman focused on her own personal needs as she arrived at her moral decision, she thereafter chastised herself for being selfish. Women who were uncertain about their own worth were least able to include their own well-being in their moral decisions without feeling guilty. Fearing that others would judge them unfavorably for considering their own personal needs, and recognizing that there was no way to resolve the unplanned pregnancy without hurting someone, the women were caught in the quintessential female quandary: How can I take account of my own needs and avoid hurting anyone else? As Gilligan came to appreciate, in making decisions about abortion each woman had to decide whether it was acceptable to consider her own needs in making a moral judgment.

Gilligan concludes that, unlike boys, girls must somehow reconcile their notions of self-sacrifice and unselfishness with questions of responsibility, free choice, and self-care. In expanding their conceptions of morality girls will be learning to include new principles: Moral issues cannot always be resolved without someone being hurt; responsible behavior can include a concern for one's own interest; self-sacrifice does not always have to be equated with integrity; and self-serving behavior is not always the antithesis of responsibility. Gilligan contends that as girls learn that asserting one's needs and caring for the self are compatible with empathizing and caring for others, their moral decisions will be based on interdependence rather than dependence.

Adolescents and Religion

One of the domains in which adolescents' moral reasoning affects their values and behavior is religion. With their more sophisticated reasoning abilities come new perspectives on concepts like God, heaven, and hell. Adolescents' religious views, however, are clearly influenced by factors other than just their own reasoning skills. Not surprisingly, factors such as the family's attitudes, the adolescent's age, and peer values can also have a considerable impact on a young person's religious convictions and behavior.

The Nation's Religious Climate

Before examining the religious conduct of adolescents, it behooves us to consider the societal context within which their religious values are being formulated. How religious are the parents and teachers of today's adolescents? What kinds of religious views are we instilling in the young? How is the nation's religious climate in the 1980s different from that of previous decades?

In order to answer such questions, the Princeton Religion Research Center gathers longitudinal data on the religious conduct and attitudes of Americans. Under the auspices of the center, surveys of 1,000 adolescents were conducted biyearly between 1977 and 1983 by the Gallup organization, in order to assess the religious beliefs and practices of the young. During the same period, comparable surveys were conducted on representative nationwide samples of adults. Based on these surveys, the 1984 Gallup report, *Religion in America* (1984), provides a contemporary view of adolescents' and adults' religious attitudes and behavior.

As Table 12.3 illustrates, religious preference varies in accord with variables such as age, income, race, and geographic location (*Religion in America,* 1984). Given that nearly 85 percent of all Americans characterize themselves as Christians, it is perhaps not surprising that Jesus Christ is frequently identified by adolescents as one of the most famous historical figures (see Box 12.3). Among people who label themselves as Protestants within the Christian faith, the largest denomination is Baptist (21 percent), followed by Methodist (10 percent), Lutheran (7 percent), Presbyterian (3 percent), Episcopalian (2 percent), Church of Christ (2 percent), and Disciples of Christ (2 percent). Individuals living in rural areas and those with lower incomes and less education report more religious affiliation than younger, more educated people living in urban or suburban areas. Interestingly, as the data in Box 12.4 demonstrate, among those who believe in the concept of heaven, college graduates are more optimistic about their chances of going to heaven than people with less education (Gallup & Proctor, 1982).

Attendance at churches or synagogues has remained fairly consistent during the past 50 years, with approximately 40 percent of all adults attending either a church or synagogue weekly (*Religion in America,* 1984). The highest rates of attendance, 49 percent, were reached in 1955 and 1958 and the lowest rate, 37 percent, in 1940. Since 1969, the rate has not changed by more than two percentage points. More women attend church than men, and more people living in the East attend church than in other regions, a finding that has been attributed

Table 12.3

Religious Preferences: Major Faiths (percent based on national sample: 1983 surveys)

	Protestants	*Catholics*	*Jewish*	*No Religious Preference*
National	56	29	2	9
Sex				
Men	54	28	2	12
Women	59	29	2	7
Race				
Whites	55	31	3	9
Blacks	77	7	*	12
Education				
College graduates	51	26	6	12
College incomplete	52	30	3	10
High-school graduates	56	32	1	8
Less-than-H.S. graduates	58	26	1	11
Region				
East	39	45	5	7
Midwest	51	26	2	14
South	59	30	*	8
West	73	14	1	8
Age				
Under 50 years	49	31	2	13
18–24 years	47	33	2	14
25–29 years	51	29	2	13
30–49 years	55	29	2	10
50 and older	63	26	2	6
50–64 years	61	28	2	6
65 and older	67	23	2	6
Income				
Under $15,000	60	25	1	10
$15,000 and over	54	31	3	8
Politics				
Republicans	66	24	1	6
Democrats	55	31	3	8
Independents	52	29	2	12

Table 12.3 (*cont.*)

Religious Preferences: Major Faiths (percent based on national sample: 1983 surveys)

	Protestants	*Catholics*	*Jewish*	*No Religious Preference*
Urbanization				
Center cities	46	35	3	11
Suburbs	47	36	3	9
Rural areas	70	18	*	8
Marital Status				
Married	58	29	2	10
Single	46	31	2	16
Widowed	65	25	2	4
Divorced/ separated	57	25	2	12

* Less than 1 percent

SOURCE: *Religion in America: The Gallup Report.* Princeton, N.J.: Princeton Religion Research Center, 1984. Reprinted by permission.

to the large Catholic population in the East. Nearly half of U.S. Catholics attend mass each week, compared to 39 percent of the Protestants, although Catholics' attendance has fallen 23 percent since 1958.

According to Gallup's nationwide polls, "America in 1984 appears to be confronted with a giant paradox: Religion is growing in importance among Americans but morality is losing ground" (*Religion in America,* 1984, p. 1). To support this contention, Gallup provides data on the rates of alcoholism, cheating in big business, government, and education, crime, drug abuse, child abuse, the declining quality of television, political corruption, and high unemployment and poverty. Despite these problems, Gallup is among those who insist that U.S. values are not collapsing. Instead, the surveys show that Americans endorse religious values related to their families, health, and self-respect. For example, according to Gallup's surveys, 90 percent want "more emphasis on family ties" and "more respect for authority," and the majority say they want religion to play a greater role in society. Furthermore, nine in ten people believe in God, the majority believe in heaven and hell, and at least half believe in a devil.

While the vast majority of adults say that religion is important in their lives, very few say it is the most important influence or that they are making a dedicated effort to follow Christ's example. Most Americans rank health, family, love, and friends ahead of religion in terms of its importance to their happiness. Despite these priorities, however, there seems to be an increasing interest in religious matters nationwide. For example, 60 percent of those surveyed said they were more interested today in religious matters than they were five years ago. In contrast, only 36 percent say they are more confident than five years ago that science and technology can resolve the world's most important problems (*Religion in America,* 1984).

A Closer Look  

Jesus Christ Is Fifth on Teens' List of "Greatest Persons in History"

Jesus Christ is fifth on the list of persons in history most admired by U.S. teenagers today. He follows Abraham Lincoln (the top choice), George Washington, John Kennedy, and Martin Luther King, Jr.

The fact that Jesus Christ is not at the top of the list or nearer the top, is probably due in considerable measure to the fact that some survey respondents (who were not given a list) may not think of Jesus Christ in a historical context.

The following table gives the top 10 places on the list, based on responses to these questions:

What one person that you have heard or read about at any time in history do you think was the greatest person in history? And who would be your second choice?

Greatest Person in History

(First two choices of all teenagers)

1. Abraham Lincoln
2. George Washington
3. John Kennedy
4. Martin Luther King, Jr.
5. Jesus Christ
6. Albert Einstein
7. Benjamin Franklin
8. Thomas Jefferson
9. Franklin Roosevelt
10. Elvis Presley

The findings are from a recent Gallup Youth Survey, based on telephone interviews with a representative national cross-section of 506 youths, ages 13 through 18, conducted in December 1982.

SOURCE: *Religion in America: The Gallup report.* Princeton, N.J.: Princeton Religion Research Center, 1984, p. 61. Reprinted by permission.

From a historical frame of reference, U.S. conceptions of religion have changed during recent decades (*Religion in America,* 1984). Although 70 percent believe that God loves them "to a great extent," only about half say they are absolutely sure that Christ was divine. Most believe that Christ's mission on earth was to show people how to love one another selflessly and to forgive others, yet only 10 percent say they "come very close" to following the example of Christ. Furthermore, 40 percent express doubts that Jesus was perfect, and many who consider themselves Christian hold views inconsistent with traditional

12.4 A Closer Look

66% of Americans Describe Their Chances of Going to Heaven as "Excellent" or "Good"

Two Americans in every three (66%) describe their chances of going to Heaven as "excellent" or "good," while 34% say they are "only fair" or "poor."

Persons with a college background are more optimistic (77% see their chances of going to Heaven as excellent or good) than are persons with a high-school background (61%) or with only a grade-school education (66%). Protestants and Catholics hold closely comparable beliefs.

Questions and Detailed Findings

Here is the question asked in the survey and the findings in tabular form:

How would you describe your own chances of going to Heaven—excellent, good, only fair, or poor?

Here are the results, based on the 71% who believe there is a Heaven:

Chances of Going to Heaven

	Excellent, good %	*Only fair, poor* %
National	66	34
College education	77	23
High school	61	39
Grade school	66	34
Protestants	67	33
Catholics	65	35
East	64	36
Midwest	70	30
South	64	36
West	63	37

SOURCE: G. Gallup and W. Proctor, *Adventures in immortality*. New York: McGraw-Hill, 1982. Reprinted by permission.

Christian beliefs. Even among the most religiously committed, few Americans have much actual knowledge of the *Bible*'s contents.

George Gallup also concludes from surveys during the 1980s that "most shocking of all, little difference is found in the ethical views and behavior of the unchurched and the churched (defined in surveys as those who both belong to and have attended a regular service in the last six months). The behavioral items tested in the surveys included those related to lying, cheating, pilferage and non-reporting of theft" (*Religion in America,* 1984, p. 19). In a broader context, it has been argued that information such as this concerning the religious views of adults who are teaching and parenting adolescents may help make the religious views of the young appear less confusing.

Adolescents' Religious Behavior and Attitudes

Differences between Children and Adolescents As adolescents become more proficient at abstract thinking, which accompanies the formal operations stage of cognitive development, their religious views are subsequently affected. Among the changes in religious ideologies are a less literal translation of the Bible and a less anthropomorphized vision of God (Farel, 1982; Fowler, 1981). For example, in one study 74 percent of the fourth-graders but only 49 percent of the eighth-graders believed the Bible was always right or correct. Moreover, the eighth-graders were less willing than the fourth-graders to believe that the Ten Commandments and other religious rules must always be obeyed (Nelson, Potvin, & Shields, 1977). Similarly, Gallup's nationwide surveys report that 13- and 15-year olds are much more likely than 16- or 18-year-olds to believe that God literally observes and punishes their actions (*Religion in America,* 1984).

Investigating the changes that typically occur in religious concepts as children age, a recent survey of 4,800 children from various religious backgrounds asked children to draw a picture of God. Children between the ages of 3 and 6 drew pictures representing a fairy-tale stage of religious thinking, while those between the ages of 13 and 18 portrayed God in individualistic, abstract terms. When a sample of 180 of these children were interviewed, the youngest children were significantly less abstract in their expressions of the concept of God than were older children. In comparing these children according to their different religious affiliations, no significant differences emerged in regard to the ages at which children's religious thinking became more abstract. Children younger than 11 were generally unable to formulate the abstract thoughts necessary for a sophisticated conceptualization of God (Nye & Carlson, 1984).

Further representing the differences between children's and adolescents' religious thinking, only 40 percent of the adolescents in Gallup's nationwide surveys gave answers classified as "authoritarian" when asked why they believed in God. In contrast, younger children typically gave answers that relied on authorities, such as "because the Bible says so" or "because my parents told me there was." Among adolescents, nearly one-fourth said they believed in God for rational reasons, such as "because the laws of the universe show there's a God" or "because nature is too wonderful for there not to be a God." About 13 percent stated empirical reasons related to an experience in their lives, like a close escape from death or a relative's recovery from an illness. The remaining 5 percent gave "utilitarian" responses, reflecting the notion that they needed to have something to anticipate after death. Surprisingly, nearly one-third of the adolescents and one-fifth of the adults in Gallup's surveys said they believed in reincarnation (*Religion in America,* 1984).

Perhaps the most impressive investigations of religious development, in terms of its heuristic value, is James Fowler's (1981) continuing study of the stages of faith. By interviewing people between the ages of 4 and 84 from various socioeconomic, racial, and educational backgrounds, Fowler has delineated six stages of religious faith. The third stage, occurring in early adolescence, depends upon the ability to think abstractly and to reflect on one's own thinking. A principal task of this stage is to adapt to the incongruence of one's own religious views and the views of others. The fourth stage, which Fowler refers to as "individual reflective faith," requires a capacity for critical self-reflection, which involves an objective examination of how one's religious beliefs evolved. Although Fowler's theory has been criticized by those who believe that faith is a gift bestowed by God and by those who object to a stage theory of faith, his work represents one of the few attempts to study the changes in religious thinking that accompany aging.

Differences between Adolescents and Adults In regard to the importance of religion, older people tend to accord it more importance than the young. Among 18- to 24-year-olds, only 14 percent indicate that their religious beliefs are the prominent factor in their lives, in comparison with nearly twice that many people between the ages of 25 and 29. Moreover, among those over 50, nearly 42 percent consider religion to be the dominant factor in life (*Religion in America,* 1984).

These findings suggest several hypotheses. First, it is possible that religion becomes more important as a person ages, although longitudinal data from people of the same cohort group would be necessary in order to test this hypothesis. Second, it is possible that, as people age, they are more willing to express their religious beliefs publicly. Finally, it may have become more popular during recent years for both young and old to profess their religious beliefs. Such professions, however, should not be construed to mean that religion has necessarily become any more influential or more important in adolescents' lives than in former decades.

Some differences also exist between adolescents and their elders in regard to religious affiliation. For example, the proportion of college students who identify themselves as Jewish (5 percent) is twice as high as the proportion in the adult population (2 percent). Nearly 40 percent of young people between the ages of 13 and 18 identify themselves as Catholics, in contrast to only about one-fourth of those over the age of 25. Overall, nearly half of all adolescents identify themselves as Protestants, 38 percent as Catholics, 3 percent as Jewish, 3 percent as "other," and 6 percent as "no preference" (*Religion in America,* 1984).

The Degree of Religiosity among Adolescents Obviously, not all adolescents share the same degree of commitment to organized religions, as Table 12.4 illustrates. The majority of adolescents in Gallup's nationwide surveys describe themselves as "moderately religious," meaning that they attend a religious service at least once a month and consider themselves somewhat religious. The 10 percent who reported themselves as "highly" religious attend services at least once each week and consider themselves very religious people. Nearly a third of the adolescents labeled themselves as "low" in religiosity, since they attend a religious service only on occasion. Black adolescents and youngsters from the South are the most likely to be attached to religious values and to engage in religious activities like reading the Bible and attending church (*Religion in America,* 1984).

Charismatic movements show no signs of abating and more young people

Table 12.4

The Importance of Religion to High-School Sophomores and Seniors in 1980 (percent of total)

	High	*Moderate*	*Low*	*None*
All students	10	46	33	11
Religion in which raised				
Jewish	5	23	50	22
Catholic	8	55	30	7
Main-line Protestant	9	46	36	9
Baptist				
White	14	46	33	7
Black	8	54	34	4
Other Christian	19	42	30	8
Other religion	21	43	29	7
Not raised in any religion	1	9	39	50

Note: "High" religiousness means attending religious services once or more per week and considering oneself a religious person. "Moderate" means attending a service once a month or more and considering oneself somewhat religious. "Low" means attending a service occasionally, while "none" means never attending a service and rating oneself not at all religious.

SOURCE: National Center for Education Statistics, *1980 High Schools and Beyond Survey of High School Sophomores and Seniors*. Washington, D.C.: National Center for Education Statistics, 1981.

are involved in evangelical movements than in previous decades. Moreover, the percentage of college students who state that religion is very important in their lives increased from 39 percent in the 1975 Gallup polls to 50 percent in 1979. On the basis of these data and international surveys, some contend that young people's interest in religion seems to have a worldwide scope (*Religion in America*, 1984). In addition, the longitudinal data from *Monitoring the Future* in Table 12.5 acknowledge that most adolescents are concerned about finding purpose and meaning in life (Bachman, Johnston, & O'Malley, 1985).

Nevertheless, the contention that today's adolescents are more interested in religion than their predecessors can be contested on several grounds. First, young people today may simply be more willing to express their religious interests than their counterparts in earlier decades. Second, given that regional, socioeconomic, and racial differences appear to have a considerable impact on adolescents' religious attitudes, the increased interest in charismatic religions and other religious activities may be less widespread throughout the country than is often acknowledged. For example, in regard to the issue of prayer in the schools, blacks, children from blue-collar families, and children from the South are most in favor of praying at school (*Religion in America*, 1984).

Third, and most important, adolescents' verbal expressions of religious interest appear to have little relationship to their actual behavior. Although the statistics may show that young people profess more interest in religion, the data show a discrepancy between adolescents' professed religious interests and their behavior. For example, only one-fourth of the adolescents in the nationwide Gallup surveys expressed confidence in religious organizations, and only 20 percent believed church attendance was a necessary part of being a "good Christian."

Table 12.5

Important Things in Life (percent rating extremely important, Classes of 1976–1983)

	Males									*Females*								
	1976	*1977*	*1978*	*1979*	*1980*	*1981*	*1982*	*1983*	*1984*	*1976*	*1977*	*1978*	*1979*	*1980*	*1981*	*1982*	*1983*	*1984*
A good marriage and family life	66	69	70	73	70	71	69	69	67	80	78	80	82	82	82	83	82	79
Finding steady work	66	65	67	68	68	69	73	74	73	61	58	62	63	62	65	70	73	71
Being successful in my work	53	55	58	60	55	58	61	60	59	52	58	54	57	55	57	60	61	59
Strong friendships	57	58	63	62	59	60	62	60	61	60	62	65	65	67	65	66	65	64
Finding purpose and meaning in my life	54	53	57	55	54	52	51	52	48	75	72	74	73	68	72	71	72	67

SOURCE: J. Bachman, L. Johnston, & P. O'Malley, *Recent findings from Monitoring the Future.* Institute for Social Research, University of Michigan, Ann Arbor, 1985.

Table 12.6

Worries of High-School Seniors about Problems Facing the Nation (percent of total surveyed, classes of 1975–1984)

Problems Facing the Nation	*Males*										*Females*									
	1975	*1976*	*1977*	*1978*	*1979*	*1980*	*1981*	*1982*	*1983*	*1984*	*1975*	*1976*	*1977*	*1978*	*1979*	*1980*	*1981*	*1982*	*1983*	*1984*
Chance of nuclear war	7	13	18	19	23	30	27	31	28	29	8	8	12	11	18	24	20	30	23	30
Population growth	18	14	12	13	10	8	9	7	6	4	21	24	20	15	14	10	10	8	9	6
Crime and violence	43	43	39	38	35	29	40	37	34	30	63	65	67	61	55	49	67	59	57	52
Pollution	38	35	36	32	26	24	24	19	16	16	36	37	35	29	28	21	21	18	16	13
Energy shortages	39	31	42	32	49	51	40	23	15	12	33	26	38	31	44	47	33	17	12	7
Race relations	15	17	16	16	14	12	15	16	16	14	23	24	25	24	19	17	22	20	20	18
Hunger and poverty	18	16	13	11	9	11	13	11	12	13	36	31	27	29	22	24	28	27	29	26
Economic problems	32	26	20	20	25	36	33	28	31	23	32	24	22	17	23	30	31	29	30	22
Drug abuse	23	24	23	24	22	20	25	26	23	22	38	40	39	37	38	37	42	41	41	40

SOURCE: J. Bachman, L. Johnston, & P. O'Malley, *Recent findings from Monitoring the Future.* Institute for Social Research, University of Michigan, Ann Arbor, 1985.

Similarly, although 95 percent said they believed in God and 80 percent said religion played a "fairly important" part in their lives, only 5 percent were interested in enrolling in a seminary and half did not consider religious faith a very important trait for someone their age. Finally, although 70 percent of the surveyed adolescents were church members, only 40 percent attended services on a regular basis and only 12 percent read the Bible daily, in contrast to 52 percent who reported reading the newspaper daily.

Perhaps most significantly, although almost 90 percent said they pray, and 80 percent said they believe in the Ten Commandments, only 35 percent could actually name five or more of the Commandments. Moreover, the best-remembered Commandment was "Thou shalt not steal," and more adolescents remembered the injunction against adultery than against murder. Interestingly, 30 percent of the surveyed adolescents—20 percent of whom attended church regularly—had no idea why Easter is celebrated. While almost 70 percent say they have felt the presence of God, only 22 percent say their religious beliefs are "the most important" influence in their lives.

These contradictions notwithstanding, some still contend that today's adolescents are more interested in religious matters than their predecessors. From their perspective, it has been suggested that the increasing anxieties over nuclear war may be partially responsible for a renewed interest in religion among the young. Although no relationship between religious interests and nuclear fears has yet been established, it does appear that today's adolescents have become increasingly worried over nuclear war, as Box 12.5 illustrates (Yudkin, 1984). Moreover, the longitudinal surveys of high-school seniors described in Table 12.6 show that, since 1975, worries about nuclear war have increased more than about any other problem adolescents believe to be facing the nation. More than one-third of the high-school seniors in 1984 agreed with the statement that "this country will be caught up in a major world upheaval in the next ten years," and 29 percent agreed that "nuclear or biological annihilation will probably be the fate of all mankind within my lifetime" (Bachman, Johnston, & O'Malley, 1985).

It has been suggested that any increased interest in religion among the young is related to their disenchantment with certain aspects of our modern, technological society. Feeling isolated and lonely, many Americans report feeling that "people just don't seem to care about each other anymore." Substantiating this point, Gallup's 1980s polls show that people believe others are less willing to help one another than they were a decade ago (*Religion in America*, 1984). Given these feelings, young and old may rely on religious organizations for the networks and social gatherings that provide a sense of community and caring. Consequently, it has been argued that churches should devote more attention to the social needs of young adolescents, a time when religious issues seem to assume a special significance, in designing programs to increase church membership (Warren, 1982; Westerhoff, 1980).

Membership in Religious Cults

Reports like Gallup's national surveys suggest that a growing number of adolescents are disenchanted with traditional religious institutions and are seeking other options to meet their spiritual needs. While many adolescents are concerned with spiritual matters, they appear less satisfied than their elders with the

12.5 A Closer Look

Adolescent's and Childrens' Fears of Nuclear War

"I am constantly aware that at any second the world might blow up in my face." "I have now accepted the fact that there quite possibly will be an 'end of time'." Answers like these are representative of the responses from many adolescents in recent surveys on fear and nuclear war. Two child psychiatrists from Harvard University, John Mack and William Beardslee, began studying the impact of the nuclear age on U.S. youth in 1978. Although only a few studies during the 1960s had been conducted to show children's fears of nuclear war, Mack and Beardslee were surprised by adolescents' responses to their surveys. During 1980 they collected responses from 1,151 students in grades 5 through 12 at schools in Los Angeles, Boston, and Baltimore. Nearly 40 percent of the youngsters said they were aware of the nuclear threat by the age of 12. Most students were worried about their future, in view of their fears of nuclear war.

To ascertain whether students in small towns shared similar values with their more urban peers, a psychologist at Bridgewater State College in Massachusetts surveyed high-school and college students. Most of these young respondents from a working-class conservative town said they thought about nuclear war "sometimes," with nearly a third saying they thought about it "often" or "all the time." Most felt there was at least a 50–50 chance of nuclear war and almost two-thirds felt they would die in the event of a nuclear war.

Research being conducted by Jerald Bachman and his colleagues since 1978 at the Institute for Social Research at the University of Michigan suggests that high-school seniors are becoming increasingly worried about nuclear war. These surveys of 130 high schools across the country each year since 1975 show that adolescents' worries about nuclear issues have grown more steadily than have concerns about any other issue addressed by the researchers. In 1975 only 7.2 percent of the males surveyed said they worried about nuclear war, contrasted to 31.2 percent who expressed such a concern in 1982.

Another psychologist, Scott Haas, surveyed 60 high-school juniors in Connecticut and Massachusetts during 1983. Even though half of the questions made no references to war, 80 percent of the students mentioned nuclear war on at least one question.

traditional means through which to develop spiritual interests. In support of this hypothesis, data show that adolescents are more likely than adults to be members of nontraditional religious groups. Moreover, the evangelical movement appears to have gained popularity among the young. Nearly 20 percent of adolescents and adults are *evangelicals*—people who have experienced being "born again" and who are trying to convert others to Christianity (*Religion in America*, 1984).

While joining traditional churches is often influenced by race, sex, and education, other factors seem to motivate young people who join religious sects like *Hare Krishna* or the *Unification Church* of Sun Myung Moon. Several character-

Upper- and middle-class students named nuclear war as their primary concern, while students from lower socioeconomic backgrounds named unemployment and economic issues as their primary concerns.

President of Educators for Social Responsibility, Roberta Snow, determined from her surveys in 1982 and 1983 tht adults are unaware of the extent to which nuclear war worries young people. In these surveys of classes in grades 1 through 9 in the Boston area, students expressed many fears related to nuclear war. One 6-year-old said he worried whenever he heard a plane fly overhead that it might be "the war plane." Older students were quite aware of the devastating powers of nuclear weapons, even though these issues had not been presented in their school's curriculum. The researchers contend that children's worries are further complicated by adults' unwillingness or nervousness in discussing nuclear war.

Echoing this view, some psychologists contend that children lose faith in adults who refuse to discuss nuclear issues with them. The silence and reluctance of adults enhances young people's fear of war. According to these psychologists, parents should admit to their adolescent children that they, too, are afraid of war. Yet the parents should also encourage their adolescent children to actively express their fears to political leaders, rather than passively accept the threat of war. Indeed antinuclear speakers often recount the story of the young child who said he didn't think there would be a nuclear war "because my daddy is out every night trying to prevent it."

In order to overcome their sense of powerlessness in the face of nuclear threats, adolescents can be encouraged to join organizations like the Children's Campaign for Nuclear Disarmament (CCND). The CCND was formed by 15-year-old Hannah Rabin and her younger sister in 1980. The group's purpose is to express young people's feelings about nuclear issues to political leaders. On October 17, 1981, CCND members read nearly 3,000 letters addressed to President Reagan in front of the White House. One year later they repeated this act by reading more than 5,000 letters. CCND has also written a booklet, *The Nuclear Threat: What Kids Can Do,* which explains how other adolescents can form antinuclear organizations in their communities.

SOURCE: M. Yudkin, When kids think the unthinkable. *Psychology Today,* April 1984, *18,* 18–25.

istics seem to distinguish young people who join cults from those who join more traditional churches (Stoner & Parke, 1977; Swope, 1980). Cult members tend to have idealistic attitudes about helping others and improving society. Their well-intended altruism often increases their vulnerability to religious leaders who convince them that their ideals can be realized only within a religious community. These young people have a naiveté that permits them to believe that anyone speaking in the name of God is trustworthy. Their curiosity about world problems like nuclear war and famine incline them to accept invitations from those who promise religious remedies for these problems. New cult members are often away from home for the first time and are feeling somewhat lonely and

How religious are you, and what accounts for your present religious beliefs? What does it mean to be religious?

disoriented. These young people also tend to be examining their values and seeking an identity. The combination of their curiosity and insecurity makes them particularly willing to turn to others for advice.

The process by which adolescents join religious cults has been described as occurring in several distinct phases (Lofland, 1977). First, the candidate is approached by a cult member who makes him or her feel "special" and loved. Next, the candidate is exposed to activities like lectures or weekend retreats, where the sect's doctrines are presented in the midst of an enthusiastic, loving audience. If successful, these efforts convince the young person that the sect offers unique insights that will alleviate his or her personal problems. Finally, at the point of joining the group, candidates may be asked to relinquish all ties with their families as well as their material possessions. Contrary to some adults' fears, young adolescents seldom affiliate themselves with cults. Most people do not join religious cults until after the age of 18, the average age being about 20.

Some researchers and psychologists contend that cults appeal to individuals with emotional or psychological problems (Singer, 1979). According to data supporting this viewpoint, cult members are more likely than other young people to have abused drugs and to have psychological problems. The depression, loneliness, and alienation of these young people consequently make them prime candidates for cults that promise to alleviate their suffering and to provide them with love, security, and freedom from responsibility. Lacking the internal strength to cope with the vicissitudes of adult living, these confused people are relieved to turn their lives over to religious authorities.

Others, however, argue that cult members are no more abnormal in respect to drugs or emotional disturbance than other young people. For example, in a study assessing IQ scores, personality disturbances, and interpersonal skills, cult members scored in the normal ranges (Ungerleider & Wellisch, 1979). A recent book based on interviews with and observations of *Moonies* (members of Sun Myung Moon's Holy Spirit Church for the Unification of World Christianity) shows that the typical Moonie is in many ways above average in comparison to the general population. These cult members usually come from religious homes that endorse traditional values of morality and family life. Most have satisfying relationships with their parents, did well in school, and have independent personalities that are not characterized by being overly susceptible to persuasion. The author concludes that Moonies are not coerced into joining the group by devious methods, but that their backgrounds simply predispose them to endorse the kinds of values that Sun Myung Moon's church represents (Barker, 1984).

Despite the different reasons underlying young people's decisions to join religious cults, their parents often want them divorced from the cult and remarried to society. In a process perceived by parents as a counterattack on the cult's "brainwashing," *deprogramming* is sometimes used to break a young person's ties to a religious community (Stoner & Parke, 1977) During the deprogramming process, cult members are forced to reevaluate their religious ideologies and to examine the methods by which they were encouraged to join the sect. It is the deprogrammer's task to enumerate the religious leader's shortcomings and to underscore contradictions in the sect's ideologies. Since some deprogrammers are themselves former sect members, they are able to speak with an especially personalized zeal against the sect's methods and doctrines. If deprogramming fails, parents generally have no legal right to force their children to leave the cult. Acting in accord with a series of Supreme Court decisions, most state courts uphold an individual's right to remain in a cult against the wishes of friends and family members (Schwartz & Isser, 1979).

An important caveat in any discussion of religious issues is that certain nontraditional alternatives like the Moonies and the Hare Krishnas receive more publicity and more skeptical scrutiny than other nontraditional options. To counter this disproportionate public attention, the information condensed in the following pages is intended to familiarize you with adolescents' religious alternatives in our multicultural society.

Religious Diversity among U.S. Youth

Although most of the families in our society are raising their children in a traditional Christian religion—56 percent in Protestant denominations and 29 percent in the Catholic faith—many adolescents are members of less well-known religions. Although only 2 percent of Americans identify themselves as Jewish and 1 percent as Mormon, these religious groups constitute large portions of the population in some states (*Religion in America,* 1984). It would be virtually impossible, for example, to live in Utah without interacting with Mormon adolescents and their families. yet adolescents raised in the Southeast may have no concept whatsoever of the tenets of the Mormon church. Given the importance of these religious persuasions in particular areas of the country, a cursory description of each is relevant to our understanding of adolescents' religious development. Ideally, even a brief description of the Mormon and the Jewish faiths will broaden our appreciation of the scope of potential religious influence on adolescent development.

The Mormon Faith and Culture Mormons endorse certain practices that set them apart from Protestants and Catholics in the U.S. (Campbell & Campbell, 1981). The official name of the Mormon church, founded in the United States by Joseph Smith in the 1830s, is the *Church of Jesus Christ of Latter-Day Saints.* Due to conflicts arising between Mormons and non-Mormons which ultimately led to Smith's death, the church moved its settlements to Utah's valley of the Great Salt Lake in 1847. Under the leadership of men like Brigham Young, for whom the Mormons' most famous university is now named, the Mormon population grew rapidly in Utah, Idaho, and Arizona. Today nearly 75 percent of Utah's population is Mormon, and the church's membership continues to expand at a rate said to be one of the fastest among the world's religions.

Like the Amish, the Mormons place a great deal of emphasis on the family's role in religious, social, and economic domains (Campbell & Campbell, 1981). The church now opposes polygamy, which it condoned and practiced at one time. The church also opposes divorce, birth control, abortion, and marriage outside the Mormon faith. Contrary to church doctrine, the Mormons' birth rate is falling, even though many express guilt over their decision to use contraceptives. Interestingly, however, while it has been predicted that Mormon and non-Mormon families will be the same size within the next 150 years, Mormons still have more children than other Americans, including Roman Catholics. Unlike the Amish, who are mainly farmers, only about 6 percent of Mormons are still employed in agricultural jobs. Nevertheless, because the church promotes such practices as keeping a garden and having a year's supply of food on hand, Mormons have sometimes been characterized as urban dwellers with rural ideals.

The values of a Mormon adolescent depend on how completely he or she has adopted orthodox church practices (Campbell & Campbell, 1981). Some researchers have found that urban Utah Mormons conform to more church doctrines than do urban Mormons on the west coast. Others have found very few differences between the practices of the most liberal Mormons and other Americans. For example, contraceptive practices and divorce rates of the least orthodox Mormons and non-Mormons are highly similar. Indeed, it may be argued that Mormon youths resemble the stereotyped "white, middle-class U.S. family" in many respects. Their clothing, language, education, and economic status reflect mainstream U.S. values. Most Mormon adolescents grow up in homes that have adopted middle-class norms and have striven for acceptance through assimilation.

Nevertheless, recognition of these commonalities is not to imply that Mormon adolescents have no special issues to resolve in relation to their religious doctrines (Campbell & Campbell, 1981). For example, the church's stand on the roles of males and females has caused considerable controversy among both its young and older members. The church opposes the Women's Liberation Movement and related matters, such as the Equal Rights Amendment. Although Mormon women do work outside the home out of economic necessity in our modern society, the church continues to endorse the roles of wife and mother as the most important functions of women. In 1979 the church's stand on these issues gained national attention, when Sonia Johnson, a church member, was excommunicated for her endorsement of the E.R.A. The question of whether a Mormon can be a feminist and be permitted to remain in the church is still unresolved. Furthermore, the church's strict stance against premarital sex and drugs like marijuana creates dilemmas for young people whose participation in the U.S. mainstream brings them into contact with more liberal social standards.

Other Mormon practices also serve to set Mormon youth apart. During late adolescence and early adulthood a number of Mormon males become missionaries for their church (Campbell & Campbell, 1981). Presently about 25,000 young men between the ages of 19 and 22 dedicate themselves to missionary work in the United States and in other countries. Supported by money from their families, these young men adhere to strict standards of sexual abstinence and cover their bodies in conventional black attire while working for the church.

Currently it appears that although the Mormons have continued to preserve their own religious and social identities in our modern society, maintaining their identity is becoming increasingly difficult. Because of their similarity to non-Mormon Americans in terms of their values and appearance, Mormon youths are more easily assimilated into the general culture than youngsters from more non-traditional religions like the Amish. In all probability, as the church membership becomes more diverse, the bonds that have kept Mormon communities closely knit may become weakened.

The Jewish Faith and Culture Adolescents being raised in the Jewish faith are members of a religion that embraces about 14 million people throughout the world, 43 percent of whom live in the United States (Farber, Mindel, & Lazerwitz, 1981). Even though Jewish population constitutes only 2 percent of the total U.S. population, its six million people have managed to maintain a distinct social and religious culture in contemporary U.S. society.

Jewish immigration to the United States was most clearly marked by the arrival of *Sephardic Jews* from Spain and Portugal in the 1600s, German Jews during the mid-1800s, and eastern European Jews, largely from Poland and Russia, in the early 1900s. The German Jewish immigrants arriving in the 1800s dispersed throughout America. Over time they became important figures in banking and finance during a period of industrialization, when the need for capital investments was great. In contrast, the eastern European Jews tended to isolate themselves in their own communities and to practice *Orthodox* Judaism. Such conservatism contrasted with the more modernized customs practiced by Jews of German descent. Significantly, many of these more conservative eastern European Jewish immigrants, who left eastern Europe as a consequence of the *pogroms* (devastation and destruction) being conducted by the Russian government, are the great-grandparents of today's U.S. adolescents.

Today's Jewish adolescents have several options from which to choose in regard to the type of Judaism they practice (Farber, Mindel, & Lazerwitz, 1981).

The Orthodox denomination practices the strictest social and religious customs. For example, the Orthodox Jews place more emphasis on studying the *Torah*—the religious text containing books from the Old Testament and commentaries on the books of Moses. The Orthodox Jews are also more dedicated to keeping a *kosher* household. "Kosher" refers both to eating only those foods specified as acceptable by old Jewish law and preparing foods in accord with traditional customs. For example, it is not kosher to eat pork or crustaceans or to serve dairy products and meat at the same meal. Orthodox Jews also tend to marry more frequently within the Jewish faith and to have more children than other Jewish denominations.

In contrast, members of *Reform Judaism* are very liberal in regard to religious practices and social customs. Adolescents who affiliate with this Jewish denomination are more likely to marry someone who isn't Jewish, not to attend synagogue services, and ignore the rules of a kosher diet. In between the two extremes is the third alternative, known as the *Conservative* Jewish denomination. In terms of denominational affiliation, only about 11 percent of the adult Jewish population currently consider themselves Orthodox, while 42 percent consider themselves to be Conservative and 33 percent view themselves as practitioners of Reform Judaism.

As might be anticipated, within the Jewish faith certain customs are being modified in accord with changing U.S. social mores. One of the most significant modifications affecting adolescents is the introduction of the *bat mitzvah* for girls (literally, "the daughter of the commandments"). Jewish boys have traditionally been encouraged to participate in the religious ceremony, the *bar mitzvah* ("the son of the commandments") at the time of their thirteenth birthday. In preparation for this ceremony, they must study the Torah and learn to speak some Hebrew under a rabbi's tutelege during the year preceding the ceremony. The official religious ceremony is conducted by the rabbi in a synagogue and is traditionally followed by partying, eating, and dancing in celebration of the young man's entry into adulthood. Reflecting the need to respond to changing times, the option to undergo this initiation ceremony is now available to Jewish girls.

Rather than affiliating with either of these three denominations, Jewish adolescents may opt not to identify themselves in any religious way with the Jewish faith (Farber, Mindel, & Lazerwitz, 1981), which about 15 percent of the Jewish population do. These youngsters consider themselves Jewish only in the sense that their ancestors practiced the Jewish faith and that their family has instilled in them a respect for certain Jewish values. For example, the Jewish culture holds education in high regard and encourages children to excel as students. U.S. Jews are also extremely conscientious in regard to family planning. By limiting the family's size, Jewish parents have traditionally provided the kinds of educational and financial opportunities that insure their children a high socioeconomic status in U.S. society.

As is the case among the Mormons and the Amish, some Jewish people lament the fact that assimilation into U.S. culture is threatening to undermine the bonds between the young and their Jewish faith. For instance, as more young people attend secular colleges, interfaith marriages have become more common. Similarly, as more Jewish women enter the work force, the emphasis on being the quintessential "Jewish mother," whose primary obligation is to her children, tends to diminish. While religious concerns over such changes undeniably have merit, the fact remains that a greater proportion of college students consider themselves Jewish (5 percent) than do adults (2 percent) (*Religion in America*, 1984).

Adolescents' Political Values

Recognizing that adolescents' religious ideologies are different from children's, researchers have also examined the changes in political ideologies between childhood and adolescence. Since moral decisions during adolescence are typically accompanied by more abstract, more altruistic, and more independent reasoning, it seems reasonable to assume that ideas related to political issues might also undergo similar transformations.

The Development of Political Thinking

According to the literature, there are four perspectives explaining the development of political ideas during adolescence (Gallatin, 1980). The most popular, social learning theory, assumes that socializing agents like parents, schools, and churches inculcate specific political ideologies in adolescents. By the time adolescence begins, this political socialization is virtually complete. A related view, the generational or sociological school, argues that individuals' political views

What social, political, or religious issues would be most likely to compel you to protest publicity? What forms should protest take?

are usually formed in the later years of adolescence, when young people are experiencing the need to establish distinct identities. Older adolescents' needs to distinguish themselves from their elders incline them to endorse political views that differ from the older generation's. Sociological theorists try to identify historical and societal factors that influence each generation's political views.

In contrast, the third perspective—the psychodynamic view—argues that individuals align themselves with particular political ideologies on the basis of their personalities. Although most of this research has been limited to adult populations, some studies with adolescents and college students do show relationships between certain aspects of personality and political ideas. For example, some have demonstrated that adolescents with low self-esteem are less interested in politics than those with high self-esteem. Others have shown that youths with external locus-of-control attitudes are less trusting and more dissatisfied with government than those with internal locus-of-control attitudes (Gallatin, 1980).

The fourth perspective, the cognitive-developmental or Piagetian orientation, contends that adolescents' new cognitive abilities are primarily responsible for their political development. Although proponents of this theory agree that socialization affects a young person's political views, they argue that the adolescent is more than just a passive recipient of the socialization process. Equipped with the more advanced mental skills that accompany formal operational thinking, adolescents finally have the potential to comprehend political thoughts and to develop their own ideologies. Cognitive-developmental researchers explore the relationship between capacity for political thinking, moral development,and the most advanced stage of cognitive development—formal operational thinking (Gallatin, 1980).

Whichever perspective we assume most adequately explains adolescents' political development, there is little doubt that youths' political ideas do undergo rather dramatic changes from early to late adolescence (Gallatin, 1980). These transformations have been well documented in the studies of U.S., West German, and English youths conducted by Joseph Adelson and his colleagues (Adelson, 1975, 1982). These researchers posed a hypothetical political question to adolescents: "Imagine that a thousand people venture to an island in the Pacific to form a new society. Once there, they must compose a political order, devise a legal system, and in general confront the myriad problems of government." Adolescents' answers to a number of questions related to government, protest, police, law, and political parties were then analyzed. While there were few differences related to adolescents' sex or race, the answers of younger and older adolescents differed considerably.

Adelson's research shows that, as adolescents age, their political reasoning becomes more abstract. Younger adolescents could not formulate answers related to abstract concepts like equal representation in government or individual liberties. In contrast to older adolescents, the younger ones associated political thoughts with personalized concepts. For example, in discussing government, the younger adolescent refers to people like the mayor, while in discussing law enforcement, he or she refers to a policeman or a judge. Older adolescents were also better than their younger counterparts at devising specific political strategies such as forming unions or electing legislators to protect one's interests. In addition, they were able to think beyond an immediate time frame and to consider the perspectives of other people in formulating political strategies for resolving a society's problems. Unlike their younger peers, 15- and 16-year-olds were adept at developing principles on which to base their judgments. Although some younger adolescents were able to refer to concepts such as "individual freedom," they were generally incapable of demonstrating any understanding of the concept.

In regard to law enforcement, younger adolescents were more inclined than their older peers to recommend harsh punishments like solitary confinement and death for violators. As Adelson states, "perhaps the most unnerving discovery we made upon first reading the interview transcripts was that a substantial minority of our youngest respondents were capable, on occasion, of the moral purview of Attila the Hun" (Adelson, 1982, p. 9). As adolescents age, however, they come to view laws less as punitive measures and more as benevolent measures intended to maintain harmony.

Adelson's investigations suggest that adolescents' political views are somewhat influenced by their nationality. German adolescents were the most likely to make political choices that relied on order and consistency. For example, they opted for leadership by one person, rather than by a representative form of government, more than twice as often as U.S. or British youngsters. German youths perceived government as benevolent and wise, while the British and Americans expressed ambivalence about authorities. In contrast, the British youngsters were the most dedicated to protecting individual liberties, the most tolerant of individual differences, and the least concerned for the welfare of the community as a whole in comparison to the individual. From Adelson's research it appears that adolescents' political reasoning undergoes change consistent with Piaget's descriptions of cognitive development. Aging is accompanied by increased capacities for abstract reasoning, enriched abilities for adopting the perspective of other people, and enhanced capabilities for considering time that extends beyond the present.

The assumption that adolescents' political ideologies are influenced by their abilities to take the perspective of other people gains further support from a recent study exploring youths' conceptions of rich and poor people (Leahy, 1981). If Piaget's and Kohlberg's assumptions about cognitive and moral development are correct, adolescents, as they mature, should become more able to recognize the similarities between people from different economic classes. Testing this hypothesis with 720 children between the ages of 5 and 18, Leahy found that older adolescents were the most able to perceive similarities between rich and poor people, thereby demonstrating their cognitive ability to take another person's perspective. In accord with Piaget's theory concerning the child's limited ability to engage in classification during the preoperational stage, the youngest children had the most difficulty finding common traits between the categories of "rich" and "poor" people. Significantly, however, children from the more impoverished families were more likely than their upper-middle-class peers to refer to the thoughts of poor people, while those from upper-middle-class families were most likely to refer to the traits of the poor.

In sum, the literature on political thinking demonstrates distinct differences in children's and adolescents' reasoning (Gallatin, 1980). In later adolescence, youths are more knowledgeable about politics and have an expanded image of government. In contrast to childhood perceptions of government and the law as agencies whose primary purpose is to coerce and police people, adolescents perceive governments as a more cooperative tool for maintaining harmony in a diverse society. Older adolescents are also more likely than the young to support policies guaranteeing individual liberties. Interestingly, however, older adolescents are still not knowledgeable about certain political issues, like the differences among the political parties. Moreover, when comparing younger and older adolescents, it's also important to note that political views can be influenced by racial and economic factors as well as by chronological age. For example, Appalachian and black children have been found to express more cynical, realistic ideas about government than their white middle-class cohorts (Jaros, Hirsch, & Fleron, 1968). In general, however, younger adolescents do seem less realistic about political issues than their older peers (Gallatin, 1980).

Shortcomings of the Research

An assessment of the available research underscores several methodological shortcomings of each of the four perspectives employed to study adolescents' political thinking (Gallatin, 1980). Confronting these methodological limitations may help to foster a healthy skepticism and to reduce the tendency toward eager endorsement of a singular position.

From the social learning theorists' view it seems reasonable to assume that parents, teachers, peers, and the media have a considerable impact on adolescents' political views. This assumption has not been empirically demonstrated, however. Most studies have merely correlated adolescents' political behavior with factors such as their parents' political affiliation and socioeconomic status, but correlational studies do not permit identification or isolation of the causes of a person's attitudes or behavior. For example, the research generally shows that young people who attend college develop more open-minded, liberal political attitudes than their peers who don't go to college. These correlational data, however, can just as well be the result of differences between the two groups when they graduate from high school as the result of college attendance. Furthermore, correlational studies have not shown high or consistent relationships between adolescents' political views and many of the variables suspected to be highly influential: parents' political attitudes, high schools' courses in civics or politics, and peers' attitudes. For instance, even though adolescents depend more than do adults on television for political information, a recent review of the research concludes that TV's impact on youths' political attitudes has been exaggerated (Chaffee, 1977).

Likewise, the generational theorists have been unable to establish a "generation gap" in the political views of young and old. As the research cited in earlier chapters has demonstrated, the assumptions made concerning large rifts between the young and their parents have been unfounded empirically. Moreover, the psychodynamic researchers have also been unable to establish their assumption of a teenage rebellion that supposedly inclines the young to turn against the politics of their elders. Finally, most cognitive developmentalists have studied only small samples through personal interviews and have failed to collect longitudinal data from early childhood through adolescence. This shortcoming limits the reliability of their assertions about the relationship between cognitive stages and political thinking. Furthermore, the cognitive-developmental researchers have found very weak relationships between intelligence scores and adolescents' political thinking, thereby undermining their argument for the link between cognitive ability and political thought (Gallatin, 1980).

In sum, it appears that all four theoretical perspectives on adolescents' political thinking are limited by certain methodological shortcomings. Thus, a definitive position concerning the relationship between political development and the variables investigated from each of the four theoretical perspectives will not be immediately forthcoming.

Adolescents' Political Activism

Dissatisfied over issues like racial discrimination, nuclear energy, or U.S. involvement in wars throughout the world, some young people involve themselves in political activities. This involvement may take the form of public protests with placards and speeches in front of the White House or of less-public measures such as voter registration drives in black communities or door-to-door campaigning for a candidate. Among the political movements of the 1980s are those advocating civil rights for U.S. minorities, gays, and women, those working for amnesty for political prisoners around the world, those opposing nuclear weapons and biological warfare, and those wanting to protect the environment from pollution and defoliation.

While the issues may vary from country to country, political movements with which youths align themselves tend to share certain similarities (Braumgart, 1980). Most of the movements are organized on college campuses where critical thinking is typically fostered. This environment also provides an interntional medium through which information can be exchanged with relative ease and speed. Since most college youths share similar values despite their national affiliations, their ideological values bind them together.

Certain descriptive facts about the youthful protesters of the 1960s are indisputable (Braumgart, 1980; Hoffman, 1980). First, liberal Protestant and Jewish youths were overrepresented in left-wing protest organizations in comparison to those with conservative Protestant and Catholic backgrounds. Second, youths from Quaker, Unitarian, and Episcopalian faiths were also disproportionately represented in the activist groups. And third, the majority of the student activists were attending the country's most prestigious universities. Nevertheless, these facts don't answer the researchers' essential question: What distinguishes young people who join protest organizations from those who remain silent members of the status quo?

Researchers who have reviewed the data collected during the 1960s, when youths' activism was at its zenith, shed some light on this question (Braumgart, 1980; Gallatin, 1980; Hoffman, 1980; Horn & Knott, 1971). During this period of relatively strong political controversy, young activists were most likely to have been raised by parents who relied on democratic, egalitarian child-rearing practices. In this regard, the literature suggests that not only did protesters' parents rarely resort to physical punishment, they also encouraged both honest expression and personal responsibility, Hence, it appears that politically radical young people were not the offspring of overly permissive parents, as some had initially suggested. In contrast, the debate over whether or not political activism is related to stages of moral development remains unresolved. Some researchers suggest that youthful protesters may be functioning at higher levels of moral reasoning than their peers (Hoffman, 1980). Guided by principles and reasoning that extend their loyalties beyond their own culture, those who speak out against their government's policies in situations like the Vietnam war have sometimes been found to be motivated by existential guilt and nonchauvinistic ideas in regard to humankind. Such a perspective has been disputed, however, by other investigations showing that the politically radical youth of the 1960s had no higher levels of moral reasoning and were no more intelligent than their more conservative peers (Gallatin, 1980).

While some contend that children from affluent homes with well-educated parents were the most likely to protest during the 1960s and 1970s (Hoffman, 1980; Horn & Knott, 1971), others argue that radicals were not from upper-class families (Lewis & Kraut, 1972). Most research does show that the political protesters were seldom rebelling against their own parents. To the contrary, most of the active youths shared values similar to those of their parents. Most activists had even chosen high-school and college courses in areas similar to those of their parents. To reiterate and paraphrase the data presented in Chapters 8 and 9, "The acorn doesn't fall far from the tree."

Perhaps the most noteworthy aspect of students' activism during the 1960s, 1970s, and 1980s is that there is so little of it. Even during the most active decade, the 1960s, only about 15 percent of all college students ever participated in demonstrations (Gallatin, 1980; Hoffman, 1981). Indeed, given such low levels of involvement, it has been suggested that the young's apathy toward politics is so well established that social scientists devoted inordinate amounts of attention to the protesters in the 1960s and 1970s because of their rarity as a social phenomenon (Gallatin, 1980).

Voting Patterns of the Young

There is little disagreement that today's adolescents are less politically radical and less activist than youths in the past two decades (Braumgart, 1980; Hoffman, 1980). Voting patterns of young people during the 1980s demonstrate a general apathy and conservatism toward political matters. Since 1972 the percentage of voters between the ages of 18 and 24 has declined. Similarly, the national longitudinal study of high-school graduates from the class of 1972 shows that between 1976 and 1979 only one-sixth participated in a political activity such as talking about public problems to community leaders, attending a political meeting, or contributing time or money to a campaign (Burkheimer & Novak, 1981).

The political views of today's youngest voters can be examined in the results of the 1984 presidential election ("Every Region," 1984). Although it had been expected that the youngest voters would support the more liberal candidates like Walter Mondale and Geraldine Ferraro, the young voted as conservatively as their elders. Support for the more liberal Mondale-Ferraro ticket came from Jewish people (65 percent), blacks (91 percent), Hispanics (69 percent), and those earning the least money (69 percent with incomes under $5,000 and 53 percent under $10,000). Hoping to attract young voters by their positions on abortion, women's rights, a nuclear freeze, and minority rights, the Democrats' "Rainbow Coalition" fared worse with young people in 1984 than in 1980. Nearly 60 percent of the youngest voters supported Reagan's conservative platform, as did the

Yuppies (67 percent), the born-again Christians (69 percent), and women (55 percent).

According to political analysts, the young voted for the conservative candidate on the basis of economic self-interest and a foreign policy supportive of nuclear arms ("Every Region," 1984). Although 38 percent of the voting population are registered as Democrats and 32 percent as Republicans, the majority of voters under the age of 24 registered as Republicans in 1984. Even the fact that Reagan was 74 years old when he ran again for president did not deter the young from supporting him. In sum, the 1984 election dispelled the myth that young people are more politically liberal than their elders.

Adolescents' Views of the Military

One final method by which we might assess adolescents' political attitudes is to compare their views toward the military with those of their counterparts throughout the past decade. Fortunately, *Monitoring the Future*'s longitudinal data make such comparisons possible. As Table 12.7 illustrates, the attitudes of today's adolescent males are not strikingly different from those of their male predecessors. For example, data show that 55 percent of the male high-school seniors and 24 percent of the females surveyed in 1984 stated that they would volunteer for military service in the event of war, in comparison with 43 percent of the males and 18 percent of the females in 1976. The greatest changes in attitude appear to have occurred among adolescent females. By way of illustration, female seniors in 1982 were much less likely than female seniors in 1976 to believe the military would treat them fairly (Bachman, Johnston, & O'Malley, 1985).

Only one-fourth of the males and one-fifth of the females in 1982 believed the military leadership had many problems with dishonesty or immorality. On the other hand, the young were generally less attracted to careers in the military than in former years. Furthermore, endorsing such issues as lack of fair treatment and discrimination in the armed forces became more common between 1976 and 1980. Similarly, ratings of the military as doing a "good job for the country" declined between 1978 and 1980 to levels comparable to ratings of public schools and only slightly higher than large corporations and labor unions. Adolescents' ratings of the national news media and the nation's universities were higher than their opinions of the military.

In addition, during the late 1970s, the young expressed considerable support for increased military spending and influence. In the high-school class of 1980, for example, most males felt that U.S. military power should be increased. In contrast, only one-sixth felt that government was investing too much money in the military. The analyses show that between 1976 and 1979 high-school seniors' support for increased military spending rose gradually and then experienced a sharp increase in 1980. In spite of certain consistencies, however, sometimes adolescents' responses on political matters were contradictory. For example, although 70 percent agreed that "the only good reason for the U.S. to go to war is to defend against an attack on our own country," 60 percent agreed that "the U.S. should be willing to go to war to protect its own economic interests."

In an attempt to explain the changes in adolescents' attitudes, *Monitoring*

Table 12.7

High-School Seniors View the Military (percent of those surveyed)

	1974		1982	
	Males Agreeing	Females Agreeing	Males Agreeing	Females Agreeing
The military would be a desirable or acceptable place to live	33	29	29	19
I would receive more fair treatment as a civilian than as a member of the military service	29	34	32	19
There is great discrimination against women in the military	13	22	16	25
There is great discrimination against black people in the military	11	11	10	11
The U.S. military is doing a good job for the country as a whole	58	52	50	48
The amount the United States is spending on armed service is too much	25	34	28	36
I often worry about nuclear war	7	31	8	30
I think the country will be caught up in a major world upheaval in the next ten years	35	45	37	46
If college expenses were paid in return for military service I would probably sign up	—	38	—	23

SOURCE: J. Bachman, American High-School Seniors View the Military: 1976–1982. *Armed Forces and Society*, Fall 1983, 86–104.

the Future's analysts conclude that events such as the war in Afghanistan, the SALT II treaty, and the U.S. hostage incidents have gradually increased both adolescents' and adults' support of the military. Yet despite the fact that high-school seniors are increasingly supportive of a strong military, they are less willing to participate actively in the armed services themselves. In fact, the only adolescents whose vocational interests in the military have been rising are those who are not college bound—in other words, those whose job options are most limited in the civilian economy (Bachman, 1983a, 1983b).

Conclusion

In attempting to understand the development of moral reasoning during adolescence, it seems premature on the basis of the research available at present to discount any of the perspectives—the cognitive, psychoanalytic, social learning, or affective. Moreover, the distinctions between male and female moral development seem well documented by the research. What does emerge from

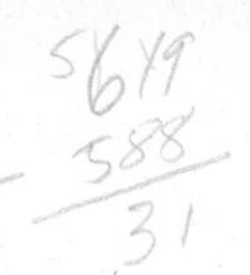

the research, despite gender differences and differences in theoretical perspectives, is that adolescents are more willing than children to base their moral codes on reciprocity, empathy, relative justice, and extenuating circumstances. Thus, it is not surprising that adolescents are apt to question authorities, to ask for the rational underlying rules and moral codes, and to examine the fairness of various forms of punishment.

As would be predicted from their increasing sophistication in moral reasoning, adolescents also become more capable of abstract religious and political thinking. Hence, the political and religious abstractions that evade younger children are no longer as mysterious and perplexing to adolescents. Perceived in this context, adolescents' ventures into various religions, including those that deviate most from mainstream denominations, are neither incomprehensible nor necessarily undesirable. Even considering their explorations into various religious options, however, most young people do not appear to differ considerably from the religious beliefs or religious activities of their elders.

Questions for Discussion and Review

Basic Concepts and Terminology

1. What discrepancies and similarities exist among the four theoretical perspectives on adolescents' moral development?
2. In what ways is the moral reasoning of males and females different?
3. What contradictions exist between adolescents' expressed religious attitudes and their actual religious activities?
4. Which factors appear to influence adolescents' religious and political ideas?
5. How are Kohlberg's stages of moral development supposedly related to adolescents' religious, political, and moral attitudes?
6. In what ways might the lives of Mormon and Jewish youths differ from the lives of youths from the Protestant and Catholic faiths?
7. How do the different theorists explain the development of adolescents' political attitudes and behavior?
8. In what ways do religious and political reasoning typically change during adolescence?
9. What factors appear to influence an adolescent's obedience to authority?

Questions for Discussion and Debate

1. Which theory of moral and political reasoning best describes your own adolescent and adult development? Which aspects of your own moral and political reasoning are not covered by your chosen theory?
2. How do you feel about the social and religious tenets of the Mormon and the Jewish faiths in comparison to your own religion?
3. In what ways do you feel religious cults such as Hare Krishna and religious schools such as Bob Jones University or Brigham Young University are advantageous or disadvantageous to an individual's development? To what extent do you believe adolescents voluntarily choose such environments?
4. How do your religious views and your religious activity compare to those reported by Gallup's surveys on adults and adolescents?

5. To what extent did political and religious issues affect your adolescent development? How has religion or politics affected you differently in recent years?
6. How would you account for people's reactions to Milgram's experiments and what implications, if any, might Milgram's findings have for contemporary adolescents?
7. Where would you place yourself in Kohlberg's stages of moral development? How do you think schools, parents, and churches should utilize Kohlberg's theories?
8. Which aspects of male and female moral reasoning appeal most to you? Why?
9. What are the advantages and disadvantages associated with acquiescing to authority during adolescence?
10. Considering the many perspectives presented by contemporary theorists, how would you explain the development of your present moral values and of your present style of resolving moral dilemmas?

REFERENCES

Adelson, J. The development of ideology in adolescence. In S. Dragastin and G. Elder (eds.), *Adolescence in the life cycle.* New York: Wiley, 1975. Pp. 63–78.

Adelson, J. Rites of passage: How children learn the principles of community. *American Educator,* 1982, *18,* 60–67.

Bachman, J. American high-school seniors view the military: 1976–1982. *Armed Forces and Society,* Fall 1983, 86–104.(a)

Bachman, J. *Trends in high school senior's views of the military.* Ann Arbor: Institute for Social Research, University of Michigan, 1983.(b)

Bachman, J., Johnston, L., & O'Malley, P. *Recent findings from Monitoring the Future: A continuing study of the lifestyles and values of youth.* Ann Arbor: Institute for Social Research, University of Michigan, 1985.

Bandura, A. *Social learning theory.* Englewood Cliffs, N.J.:Prentice-Hall, 1977.

Barker, E. *The making of a Moonie.* New York: Basil Blackwell, 1984.

Baryam, M., Reimer, J., & Kohlberg, L. Development of moral reasoning at the kibbutz. In L. Kohlberg (ed.), *Recent research in moral development.* New York: Holt, Rinehart and Winston, 1983.

Berndt, T. Age changes and changes over time in prosocial intentions and behavior between friends. *Developmental Psychology,* 1981, *17,* 408–416.

Berndt, T. Fairness and friendship. In K. Rubin and H. Ross (eds.), *Peer relationships and social skills in childhood.* New York: Springer Verlag, 1982. Pp. 252–278.

Blasi, A. Bridging moral cognition and moral action: A critical review of the literature. *Psychological Bulletin,* 1980, *88,* 1–45.

Braumgart, R. Youth movements. In J. Adelson (ed.), *Handbook of adolescent psychology.* New York: Wiley, 1980. Pp. 560–599.

Bronfenbrenner, U. & Garbarino, J. The socialization of moral judgment and behavior in cross cultural perspective. In T. Likona (ed.), *Moral development and behavior.* New York: Holt, Rinehart and Winston, 1976.

Brussell, E. (ed.) *Dictionary of quotable quotes.* Englewood Cliffs, N.J.: Prentice-Hall, 1970.

Burkheimer, G. & Novak, T. *A capsule description of young adults seven and a half years after high schools: National longitudinal study.* Washington, D.C.: National Center for Education Statistics, 1981.

Campbell, B., & Campbell, E. The Mormon family. In C. Mindel and R. Habenstein (eds.), *Ethnic families in America.* New York: Elsevier, 1981. Pp. 386–417.

Carrol, J., & Rest, J. Moral development. In B. Wolman (ed.), *Handbook of developmental psychology.* Englewood Cliffs, N.J.: Prentice-Hall, 1982.

Chaffee, S. Mass communication in political socialization. In S. Renshon (ed.), *Handbook of political socialization.* New York: Free Press, 1977.

Colby, A., Kohlberg, L., Gibbs, J., & Lieberman, M. *A longitudinal study of moral development.* Cambridge, Mass.: Center for Moral Education, 1980.

Damon, W. Patterns of change in children's social reasoning: A two year longitudinal study. *Child Development,* 1980, *51,* 1010–1017.

Erikson, E. *Identity: Youth and crisis.* New York: Norton, 1968.

Every region, every age group, almost every voting bloc. *Time,* November 19, 1984, pp. 42–43.

Farber, B., Mindel, C., & Lazerwitz, B. The Jewish American family. In C. Mindel and R. Habenstein (eds.), *Ethnic families in America.* New York: Elsevier, 1981. Pp. 350–386.

Farel, A. *Early adolescence and religion: A status study.* Carrboro, N.C.: Center for Early Adolescence, 1982.

Fowler, J. *The psychology of human development and the quest for meaning.* San Francisco: Harper & Row, 1981.

Freud, S. Some psychical consequences of the anatomical distinction between the sexes. In J. Strachey (ed.), *Standard edition of the complete psychological works of Sigmund Freud,* Vol. 19, London: Hogarth Press, 1961. (Originally published in 1925)

Gallatin, J. Political thinking in adolescence. In J. Adelson (ed.), *Handbook of adolescent psychology.* New York: Wiley, 1980. Pp. 344–383.

Gallup, G., & Proctor, W. *Adventures in immortality.* New York: McGraw-Hill, 1982.

Gilligan, C. *In a different voice: Psychological theory and women's development.* Cambridge, Mass.: Harvard University Press, 1982.

Herzog, A., Bachman, J., & Johnston, L. Concern for others and its relationship to specific attitudes on race relations, sex roles, ecology and population control. Ann Arbor: Institute for Social Research, University of Michigan, 1978.

Hirsh, R., Paolitto, D., & Reimer, J. *Promoting moral growth: From Piaget to Kohlberg.* New York: Longman, 1979.

Hoffman, M. Moral development in adolescence. In J. Adelson (ed.), *Handbook of adolescent psychology.* New York: Wiley, 1980. Pp. 295–344.

Hoffman, M. The role of the father in moral internalization. In M. Lamb (ed.), The role of the father in child development. New York: Wiley, 1981. Pp. 357–377.

Hoffman, M. Affective and cognitive processes in moral internalization. In E. Higgins, D. Ruble, & W. Hartup (eds.), *Social cognition and social development.* Cambridge, England: Cambridge University Press, 1983. Pp. 236–274.

Hoffman, M. Empathy, its limitations and its role in comprehensive moral theory. In W. Kurtines & J. Gewirtz (eds.), *Morality, moral behavior and moral development.* New York: Wiley Interscience, 1984. Pp. 283–302.

Hook, J., & Cook, T. Equity theory and the cognitive ability of children. *Psychological Bulletin,* 1979, *86,* 429–445.

Horn, J., & Knott, P. Activist youth of the 1960s: Summary and prognosis. *Science,* 1971, *171,* 977–985.

Jaros, D., Hirsch, H., & Fleron, F. The malevolent: Political socialization in an American subculture. *American Political Science Review,* 1968, *62,* 564–575.

Johnston, L., Bachman, J., & O'Malley, P. *Monitoring the future: Questionnaire responses from the nation's high school seniors.* Ann Arbor: Institute for Social Research, University of Michigan, 1985.

Josselson, R. Ego development in adolescence. In J. Adelson (ed.), *Handbook of adolescent psychology.* New York: Wiley, 1980. Pp. 188–211.

Kilham, W., & Mann, L. Level of destructive obedience as a function of transmitter and executant roles in the Milgram obedience paradigm. *Journal of Personality and Social Psychology,* 1974, *29,* 696–702.

Kohlberg, L. *Moral stages: A current formulation and a response to critics.* London: Karger, 1983.

Kohlberg, L. *The psychology of moral development: Essays on moral development.* San Francisco: Harper & Row, 1984.

Kuhn, D. Short-term longitudinal evidence for the sequentiality of Kohlberg's early stages of moral development. *Developmental Psychology,* 1976, *12,* 162–166.

Leahy, R. The development of the conception of economic inequality. *Child Development,* 1981, *52,* 523–532.

Lerner, M., & Whitehead, L. Procedural justice viewed in the context of justice motive theory. In G. Mikula (ed.), *Justice and social interaction.* New York: Springer, 1980.

Lewis, S., & Kraut, R. Correlates of student political activism and ideology. *Journal of Social Issues,* 1972, *28,* 151–170.

Lockwood, A. The effects of values clarification and moral development curricula on school age subjects: A critical review of recent research. *Review of Educational Research,* 1978, *48,* 325–364.

Loevinger, J. *Ego development.* San Francisco: Jossey-Bass, 1976.

Lofland, J. Becoming a world saver revisited. *American Behavioral Scientist,* 1977, *20,* 805–818.

Marcia, J. Identity in adolescence. In J. Adelson (ed.), *Handbook of adolescent psychology.* New York: Wiley, 1980. Pp. 159–188.

McCarthy, S. Why Johnny can't disobey. *The Humanist,* October 1979, 30–34.

Milgram, S. *Obedience to authority.* New York: Harper & Row, 1974.

Mischel, W., & Mischel, H. A cognitive social learning approach to morality and self-regulation. In T. Likona (ed.), *Moral development and behavior.* New York: Holt, Rinehart and Winston, 1976. Pp. 84–107.

Nelson, H., Potvin, R., & Shields, J. *The religion of children.* Washington, D.C.: U.S. Catholic Conference, 1977.

Nucci, L., & Turiel, E. Social interactions and the development of social concepts in preschool children. *Child Development,* 1978, *49,* 400–407.

Nye, W., & Carlson, J. The development of the concept of God in children. *Journal of Genetic Psychology,* 1984, *145,* 137–142.

Piaget, J. *The moral judgment of the child.* New York: Free press, 1932.

Religion in America: The Gallup report. Princeton, N.J.: Princeton Religion Research Center, 1984.

Rest, J. *Development of judging moral issues.* Minneapolis: University of Minnesota Press, 1979.

Rich, J., & DeVitis, J. *Theories of moral development.* Springfield, Ill.: Charles Thomas, 1985.

Rowe, I., & Marcia, J. Ego identity status, formal operations and moral development. *Journal of Youth and Adolescence,* 1980, *9,* 87–99.

Schwartz, L. & Isser, N. Psychohistorical perceptions of involuntary conversion. *Adolescence,* 1979, *14,* 351–359.

Seiber, J. A social learning theory approach to morality. In M. Windmiller, N. Lambert, and E. Turiel (eds.), *Moral development and socialization.* Boston: Allyn and Bacon, 1980.

Singer, M. Coming out of the cults. *Psychology Today,* 1979, *13,* 72–82.

Snarey, J. The cross-cultural universality of social-moral development: A critical review of Kohlbergian research. *Psychological Bulletin,* 1985, *97,* 202–232.

Steindorf, J. *Effects of moral perspective on political choice.* Paper presented at American Psychological Association Meetings, Toronto, August 1978.

Stoner, C., & Parke, J. *All God's children.* Radnor, Pa.: Chilton, 1977.

Swope, G. Kids and cults: Who joins and why? *Media and Methods,* 1980, *16,* 18–21.

Turiel, E. The development of social convention and moral concepts. In M. Windmiller, N. Lambert, and E. Turiel (eds.), *Moral development and socialization.* Boston: Allyn and Bacon, 1980.

Ungerleider, J., & Wellisch, D. Coercive persuasion, religious cults and deprogramming. *American Journal of Psychiatry,* 1979, *15,* 90–92.

U.S. Department of Commerce. *Characteristics of American children and youth: 1980.* Washington, D.C.: U.S. Bureau of the Census, 1982.

Wallach, M., & Wallach, L. *Psychology's sanction for selfishness: The error of egoism in theory and therapy.* San Francisco: Freeman, 1983.

Warren, M. *Youth in the future of the church.* New York: Seabury Press, 1982.

Westerhoff, J. *Bringing up children in the Christian faith.* Minneapolis: Winston Press, 1980.

Yudkin, M. When kids think the unthinkable. *Psychology Today,* 1984, *18,* 18–25.

Yussen, S. Characteristics of moral dilemmas written by adolescents. *Developmental Psychology,* 1977, *13,* 162–163.

Chapter Outline

Drug Use and Abuse
Depressants
Alcohol
Barbiturates
Marijuana
Physical Effects
Current Usage
Characteristics of Users and Abstainers
Characteristics of Frequent Users
Legal Controversy
Stimulants
Nicotine
Cocaine
Amphetamines
Narcotics
Heroin
Hallucinogens
LSD
PCP
Mescaline and Psilocybin
Inhalants
Drug Prevention Strategies
Conclusion

Goals and Objectives

This chapter is designed to enable you to:

- *Compare and contrast the various drugs used by contemporary adolescents*
- *Discuss the differences between drug use of adolescents in the 1970s and 1980s*
- *Describe the distinctions between occasional and regular users of marijuana*
- *Identify the physical and social effects of drugs now available to adolescents*
- *Discuss the qualities of effective drug prevention programs*

Concepts and Terminology

barbiturate	*palinopia*
amphetamine	*angel dust*
hashish	*depressant*
PCP	*narcotic*
LSD	*peyote*
THC	*psilocybin*
free basing	*popping, snorting*
opiates	*fetal alcohol syndrome*

13 Adolescents and Drugs

With the highly publicized drug-related deaths of personalities like John Belushi and the tragic deaths of thousands of adolescents in alcohol-related automobile accidents, it is understandable that adults have serious concerns about the drug habits of the young. Moreover, the fact that adolescents of the same age can vary considerably in regard to their social and cognitive maturity exacerbates adults' anxieties regarding a young person's ability to make wise judgments about drug use. While one 14-year-old may be operating at the more sophisticated levels of cognitive and moral reasoning, another may be functioning at more childlike levels that make him or her more apt to yield to immediate gratification without serious regard for the long-range impact of a decision.

While an adolescent's childlike reasoning or temporary lapses into less mature thinking often cause little more than annoyance or inconvenience, such immaturity can literally be lethal in situations involving drugs. Thus, the 16-year-old who fails to apply sound reasoning might agree to get drunk with friends while out driving one evening—a decision that, while not necessarily characteristic of most of that youngster's thinking, can be fatal. Since most of the drugs with which adolescents experiment are illegal—including alcohol—there are legal ramifications for the parents of adolescents who use drugs. Therefore, without wanting to assume an alarmist attitude, it is nonetheless true that drug use is unlike other forms of behavior with which adolescents typically experiment, in that the outcomes can be both legally injurious and lethal.

DRUG USE AND ABUSE

The drugs that adolescents and adults in our society use can be categorized as depressants, hallucinogens, stimulants, narcotics, or euphoriants (see Table 13.1). The drugs in each category differ on the basis of their physiological and

Table 13.1

Facts about Drugs

Name	*Alternative Terms*	*Source*	*Intake Method*
Depressants			
Alcohol	Booze, juice, shot	Fruits, grains	Swallowed
Methaqualone	Quaaludes	Synthetic	Swallowed
Barbiturates	Blue devils, downers, yellow jackets, reds, goofballs, phenies, blue heavens	Synthetic	Swallowed, injected
Tranquilizers	Valium, librium	Synthetic	Swallowed
Narcotics			
Heroin	Horse, smack, scag, stuff, scat	Opium	Injected, sniffed, smoked
Codeine	Cough syrup	Opium	Swallowed
Demerol	——	Synthetic	Swallowed
Morphine	White stuff	Opium	Swallowed
Methadone	Dolly	Synthetic	Swallowed or injected
Hallucinogens			
LSD	Acid, sugar, cubes	Semisynthetic	Swallowed
PCP	Angel dust, tic, tac	Synthetic	Swallowed, injected, smoked
Mescaline	Mesc	Peyote	Swallowed
Psilocybin	Magic mushroom	Psilocybe	Swallowed
Stimulants			
Amphetamines	Speed, uppers, bennies, pep pills, dexies, hearts	Synthetic	Swallowed, injected
Cocaine	Snow, coke, flake, Bernice, star dust, crack	Coca leaves	Injected, swallowed, sniffed
Caffeine	——	Coffee plant	Swallowed
Nicotine	A smoke, a chaw	Tobacco plant	Chewed, smoked
Relaxants, euphoriants			
Marijuana	Mary Jane, grass, pot, hash, tea, dope, reefer, joint	Cannabis plant	Smoked, sniffed, swallowed
Inhalants			
Glue, gasoline, paint thinner, lighter fluid, toluene	——	Synthetic	Sniffed

psychological effects, their costs and availability, the method of introducing them into the body, and their popularity among adolescents of different races, sexes, and social classes. In discussing the impact of drugs on contemporary adolescents, it is important to specify which drug and which adolescents. For example, when some people allude to the "drug epidemic," they are often referring to the perceived popularity of a specific drug that has received particular attention in the media, rather than to the drugs that most adolescents actually use or abuse.

In discussing drugs it is necessary to distinguish between drug use and drug abuse. Perhaps because some adults are reluctant to concede that an adolescent's experimentation with a drug is not always an abuse of the drug, the two terms too often are used synonymously. Thus, in this context, adolescents who are pack-a-day smokers are abusing a drug more than those who have tried marijuana on one or two occasions, irrespective of their parents' sentiments about the relative dangers of each drug. Furthermore, certain drugs have become more socially acceptable than others without regard to their actual physical or psychological effects. For example, although adolescents abuse nicotine and alcohol far more frequently than marijuana, these common abuses generally arouse less concern among either the adolescent or the adult population because of their traditional acceptability in our society. Thus, having chosen to overlook the well-substantiated empirical data, many parents who observe their adolescents smoking and drinking express relief that their children are not "on drugs" like other young people.

Although none of the drugs discussed in this chapter are without hazards and most are illegal, it is worth reminding ourselves that our familiarity with drugs like alcohol and nicotine may make us more tolerant toward adolescents who use them and less tolerant toward young people who opt to try drugs with which we are less familiar. For instance, it may be more tempting to label adolescents who occasionally use cocaine "drug abusers" than to label those who drink beer excessively with similarly disparaging terms. We also risk making false generalizations about adolescents' drug use, without first considering factors like age, race, sex, and socioeconomic class. For example, it would be unwise to make assertions about the abuse of the inhalants listed in Table 13.1 without considering that their use is primarily limited to boys in the early years of adolescence.

In order to avoid false generalizations about the drug use of the young as compared to their elders, we also need to specify at what particular age comparisons are being made between adolescents and adults. Simply categorizing those under the age of 18 as adolescents and those over 18 as adults, in regard to drug use, creates misleading assumptions about the similarities and differences across cohorts. For example, although only 23 percent of adults over the age of 26 have tried marijuana, compared to nearly 65 percent of the people between 18 and 25, it is important to remember that the older the adult, the less likely he or she is to have smoked pot ("Drug Use Levels Off," 1984). Similarly, older adolescents are far more likely to have tried marijuana and alcohol than 13- and 14-year-olds (Bachman, Johnston, & O'Malley, 1986). Data like these remind us that when searching for the differences between the younger generation's and adults' drug use, we need to consider both the age of the adults and the age of the adolescents involved in our comparisons.

Finally, in attempting to formulate conclusions about contemporary adolescents' use and abuse of drugs, comparisons with data from earlier years is imperative. Perhaps the most important source of information about adolescents' drug use during the past decade is the *Monitoring the Future* project discussed in earlier chapters of this text. On the basis of their annual surveys of nearly 17,000 high-school seniors since 1975, the researchers at the University of Michigan are comparing adolescents' drug use, both at the time of graduation and several years thereafter. Data from this project are particularly helpful in allowing us to make comparisons among the graduating classes from 1975 to the present.

DEPRESSANTS

Alcohol

Current Usage and Effects Despite the fact that alcohol receives less condemnation in our culture than many of the illegal drugs like cocaine and marijuana, it remains the substance most frequently abused by adolescents and their elders. Although causing more accidental deaths and injuries in each year than any other known factor, and contributing to a host of financial and psychological problems in families, alcohol nonetheless remains the favorite drug in the United States. The data derived from seven nationwide studies between 1971 and 1982, show that nearly 65 percent of young people between 12 and 17 have consumed alcohol, in comparison to only 27 percent who have tried marijuana and 7 percent who have tried cocaine ("Drug Use Levels Off," 1984).

How has your own behavior in regard to drug use changed since the beginning of your adolescence?

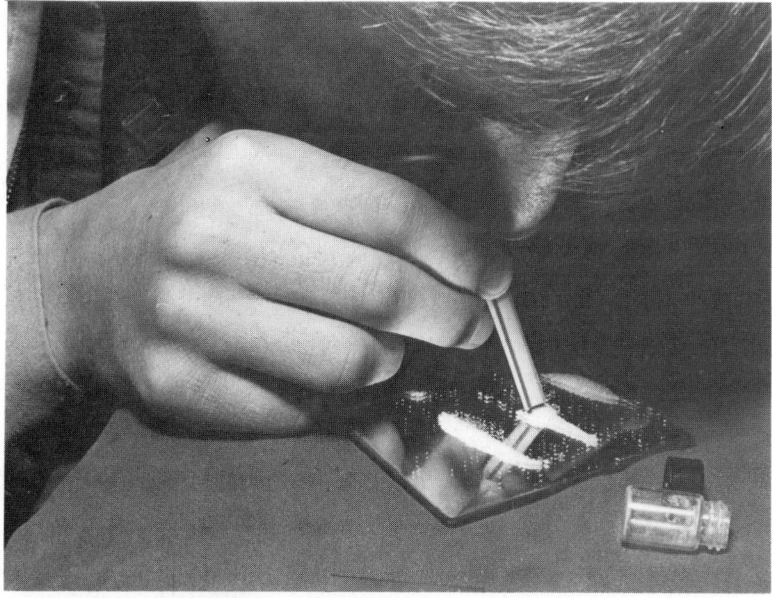

Unlike many other drugs, the use of alcohol by high-school seniors has not declined appreciably since 1975 (Bachman, Johnston, & O'Malley, 1986; O'Malley, Bachman, & Johnston, 1984). As shown by *Monitoring the Future* data in Figure 13.1, daily alcohol use was at its highest peak in 1979 and has now fallen to a level comparable to that of 1975. Only about 7 percent of male high-school seniors and 3 percent of female seniors consume alcohol daily—roughly the same percentage using marijuana daily. Approximately two-thirds of the female seniors and more than three-fourths of the males, however, report having had a drink during the past month. Moreover, about half of the males and a third of the females report having had five or more consecutive drinks during the past two weeks (see Figures 13.1 and 13.2).

A popular drug in ancient and modern cultures around the world, alcohol is made by a distilling or fermenting process that involves any number of fruits and vegetables: Vodka is created from potatoes, wine from grapes, beer from barley,

Figure 13.1

Trends in daily use of marijuana and cigarettes, by sex

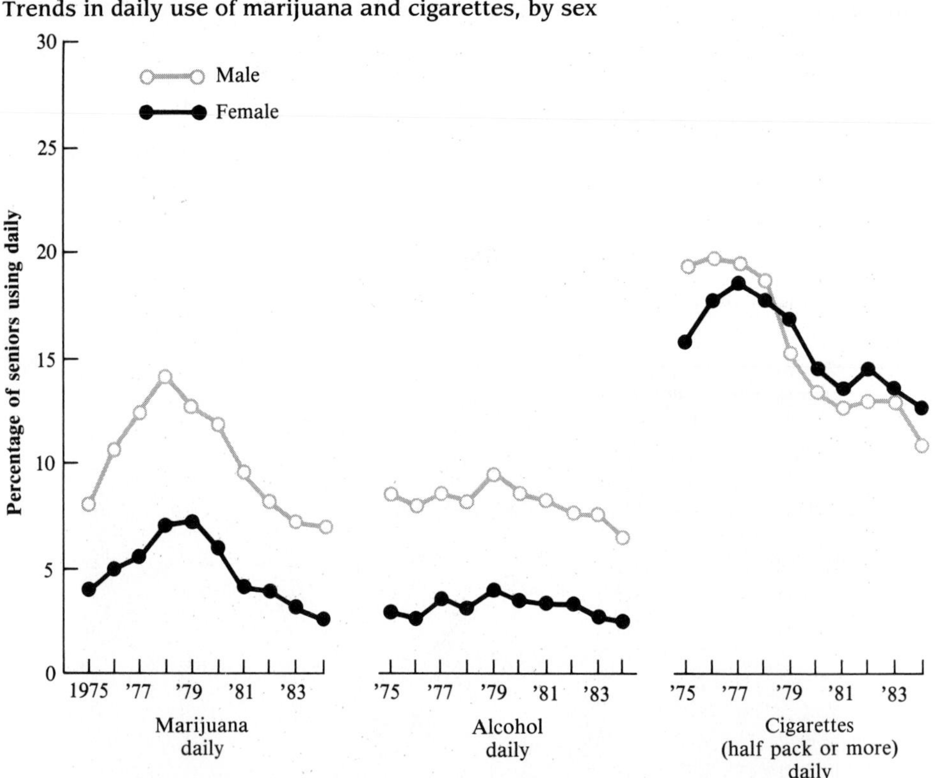

Note: Daily use for alcohol and marijuana is defined as use on 20 or more occasions in the past thirty days. Daily use of cigarettes is defined as smoking a half-pack or more per day in the past thirty days.

SOURCE: J. Bachman, L. Johnston, & P. O'Malley. Recent findings from Monitoring the Future. In F. Andrews (ed.), *Research on the quality of life.* Ann Arbor: University of Michigan, 1986.

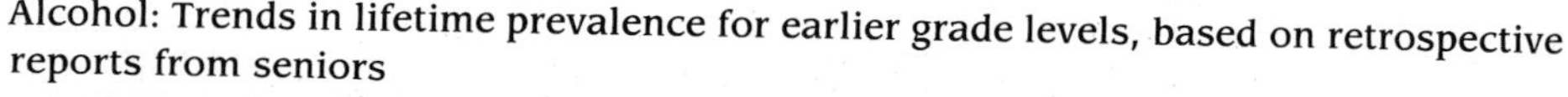

Figure 13.2

Alcohol: Trends in lifetime prevalence for earlier grade levels, based on retrospective reports from seniors

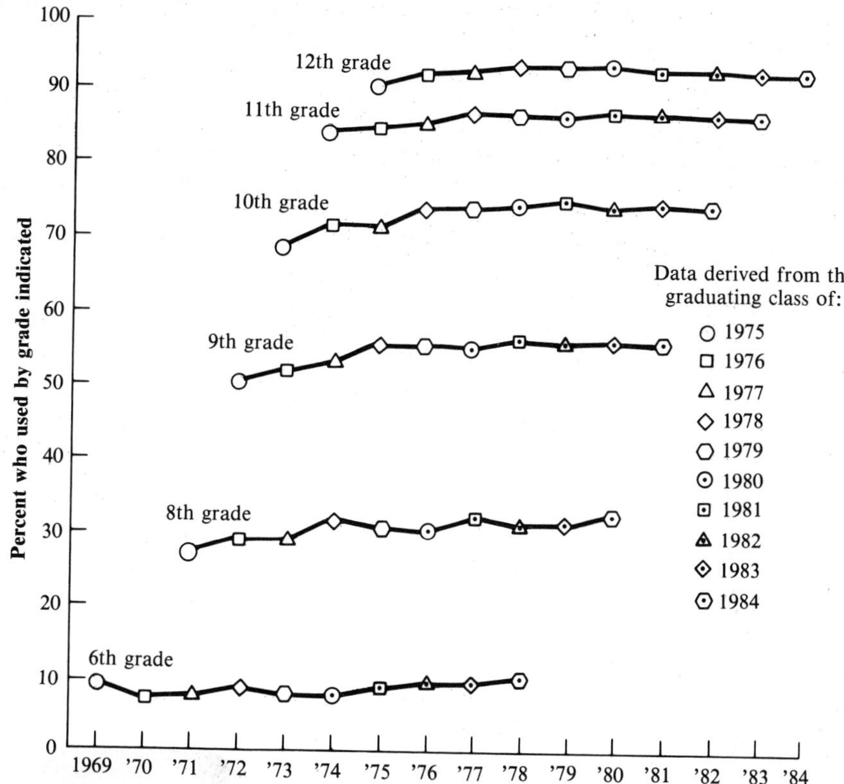

SOURCE: J. Bachman, L. Johnston, & P. O'Malley. Recent findings from Monitoring the Future. In F. Andrews (ed.), *Research on the quality of life.* Ann Arbor: University of Michigan, 1986.

whiskey and "white lightening" from corn, wine from rice. The final product can contain 5 percent or less alcohol, as in some "light" beers, or as much as 50 percent alcohol as in 100 proof whiskey. Alcohol consumed on an empty stomach will enter the bloodstream more quickly than that imbibed on a full stomach. Likewise, the smaller the drinker's body, the more dramatically the alcohol will effect him or her. Limited by their lack of experience and lack of information from adults, many adolescents are unaware of these distinctions until they have discovered the physical consequences first hand. Thus, on the advice of his 200-pound friend, a 130-pound boy may naively feel confident that he can handle four or five beers without any dangerous side effects. Similarly, a girl drinking highly sweetened, fruity "ladies' drinks" may have no understanding of the amount of alcohol in her relatively tasteless tequila, vodka, or rum.

While naive young drinkers often escape with a hangover or a traffic citation for driving under the influence, too many others pay physical or psychological consequences for abusing alcohol. As the story in Box 13.1 illustrates, the com-

13.1 A Closer Look

Minnesota Students Suspended from School Activities

More than 10 percent of the 365 students who attend the Olivia (Minn.) High School have been barred from extracurricular activities following a fatal automobile accident after a party that violated the school's drinking policy.

Thirty-eight students from the high school attended the party, which took place in a public park near Olivia on Sept. 23. Todd Mathiowetz, aged 17, was killed when the car he was driving ran off the road as he left the party that night.

"Not all the students were drinking," said Jerry Bass, superintendent of the high school. "But our rule states that 'a student shall not consume, possess, or be in the presence of others who are consuming or in possession of an alcoholic beverage.'"

The rule covers all circumstances, not just gatherings related to school activities, according to Delbert J. Altmann, principal of Olivia High School.

The students, who were members of the band, the National Honor Society, and school athletic teams, were suspended for four to eight weeks.

The reaction to the suspensions has been generally favorable, Mr. Bass said. "The majority of the people I've been in contact with are supportive of the decision. Some said that it was something that should have been done years ago, that could possibly have averted this tragedy."

SOURCE: *Education Week,* October 27, 1984, p. 3.

bination of alcohol and driving is often lethal. Moreover, alcohol is a physically addictive drug. In other words, alcoholism is not limited to the adult population. Studies show that when adolescents become alcohol dependent, they develop academic problems and tend to abuse other drugs (Burkett, 1980; Chase, Jessor, & Donovan, 1980; Donovan & Jessor, 1978). Even when young drinkers do not become physically addicted, thousands are killed or seriously injured while driving under the influence of alcohol. Between 45 percent and 60 percent of all traffic fatalities involving young drivers are related to drinking. Drinking has also been linked to liver, kidney, brain, and cardiovascular damage and to *fetal alcohol syndrome* in newborn babies. It has been recently postulated that pregnant females who drink as little as three ounces of alcohol a day might retard fetal growth and create physical and mental abnormalities in the unborn child (Delucca, 1981).

Given the legal ages for purchasing alcohol and the social functions at which drinks are served, it is not too surprising that adolescents tend to drink somewhat more frequently during the first few years after high-school graduation (Bachman, Johnston, & O'Malley, 1986). Having legal access to alcohol does not, however, usually increase excessive drinking among young adults or older adolescents. In other words, *Monitoring the Future* data show that young adults who drink to excess are those who drank heavily in high school before it was legally permissible. These encouraging data offer reassurance that adolescents who are moderate or light drinkers seldom become heavy drinkers after graduation, even though they tend to drink more often than in their high-school days.

Characteristics of Users and Abusers Adolescents who drink are motivated by numerous factors (Delucca, 1981; Finn, 1979; Kandel, 1980; Kandel, Kessler, & Margulies, 1978: Kandel, Single, & Kessler, 1976). Some are trying to overcome their anxiety in social situations. Because it reduces inhibitions, alcohol can often decrease the anxieties related to asking someone out for a date, making sexual overtures, or speaking up in a group of strangers. Others drink to diminish their sexual inhibitions—an ironic twist, since alcohol is a sedative that in excess reduces a male's sexual abilities and a female's sensitivities. Young people also drink to cope with the tensions associated with home or school. Fear of failing a course or worrying about a parent's impending divorce might evoke enough anxiety to make a few beers seem particularly appealing. Finally, drinking can serve as a rite of passage demonstrating entry to adulthood. Exposed to advertising that associates alcohol with sexuality, independence, maturity, and good times, adolescents imbibe for the promised pleasures of the adult life. In sum, adolescents drink for many of the same reasons as adults.

Adolescents who drink excessively are distinct from abstainers or light drinkers in several other respects (Delucca, 1981; Donovan & Jessor, 1978; Jessor & Jessor, 1977). Heavy drinkers are the most likely to be impulsive, socially active, tolerant of deviant behavior, and independent. They also tend to be less studious, less trustful, and less optimistic than their peers. Many report feeling bored, unhappy, cynical, and apathetic. They also report more problems with parents and teachers than moderate drinkers. In both the adult and the adolescent population, excessive drinking is more common among males than females, more prevalent among urban dwellers than rural inhabitants, and more frequent among those with no religious affiliations than among those with religious ties.

Barbiturates

Unlike alcohol, which can be legally purchased in all states by the age of 21, *barbiturates* are illegal at any age without a prescription. Nevertheless, most adolescents have little difficulty obtaining them from sources that are sometimes as nearby as their parents' medicine cabinet. Known as "downers," sedatives, or tranquilizers, barbiturates are depressants which operate to lower blood pressure and slow respiration, as they simultaneously create a feeling of relaxation. Especially when ingested together with alcohol, barbiturates can be lethal. Each year in the United States about 5,000 people die from abusing barbiturates (Simmonds, 1977).

Between 1976 and 1982 the use of barbiturates and tranquilizers declined from about 10 percent to 4 percent among the high-school seniors sampled by *Monitoring the Future* researchers (Bachman, Johnston, & O'Malley, 1986; O'Malley, Bachman, & Johnston, 1984). While this trend is encouraging, the easy accessibility of tranquilizers and sedatives still pose a danger to adolescents who are interested in experimenting with illicit drugs. Indeed, the popularity of tranquilizers like valium and librium among adults seeking relief from stress make these prescription drugs easily accessible to many adolescents in their own homes.

In addition to their relatively easy accessibility, barbiturates pose a special threat to those young who are unaware that these drugs are physically addictive. In a culture where medicine is marketed as a speedy cure-all for almost any malady, too many young people grow up assuming that pills are a socially acceptable elixir for coping with daily stress, responding to physical pain, or achieving personal goals. They have seen adults who always respond to a headache by taking pills, rather than by going for a walk or practicing muscle-relaxation exercises. As a consequence, the simple act of swallowing a pill to ease anxieties over an upcoming test may seem perfectly normal in a pill-oriented culture. Unfortunately, these simple acts can also be the beginning of a serious physical addiction for the naive adolescent who is unaware of the addictive potential of barbiturates.

Marijuana

Physical Effects

Perhaps no drug has generated more publicity and research during recent decades than marijuana. Derived from the dried leaves of the Indian hemp plant, *cannabis sativa,* marijuana provides fiber for rope as well as bird seed. When the leaves and flowering tops of the plant are dried and crushed, they can be smoked in pipes, rolled into "joints" with cigarette paper or mixed with foods and eaten. The drug varies in potency, depending on factors such as the particular variety of the plant, the climate in which it is grown, and the part of the plant that is used. *Hashish,* for example, is the most potent form of marijuana, gathered from the dark brown resin at the tops of the high-quality cannabis plants. The basic ingredient responsible for marijuana's effects is *THC,* tetrahydrocannabinol, which varies in concentration, thereby making some marijuana more potent than the rest. In large doses marijuana can create effects similar to hallucinogens. In smaller quantities, it serves as a relaxant or a euphoriant. As a mild hallucinogen or euphoriant, marijuana often heightens the user's sensory awareness, a state of being that supposedly adds pleasure to activities such as listening to music, watching movies, and making love (Committee to Study the Health-Related Effects of Cannabis and Its Derivatives, 1982).

Although marijuana is not addictive, as are the legal drugs alcohol and nicotine, it can nonetheless damage the body (Committee to Study the Health-Related Effects of Cannabis and Its Derivatives, 1982). As is the case for both cigarette smoking and drinking, the most serious consequences arise from frequent or excessive use. Like alcohol, pot alters an individual's mental abilities and physical reactions in ways that impair driving ability. Other reactions include an increase in heart rate, eye and throat irritations, loss of memory, increased appetite, drowsiness, a distorted sense of time, and intensified sensations of sight, sound, and touch. Like regular cigarettes, smoking grass contributes to heart and lung damage, cancer, and damage to unborn babies.

Reseachers are still gathering data regarding the long-term effects of moderate or heavy marijuana use (Committee to Study the Health-Related Effects of Cannabis and Its Derivatives, 1982). The results are not fully consistent. Some

Figure 13.3

Marijuana: Trends in lifetime prevalence for earlier grade levels, based on retrospective reports from seniors

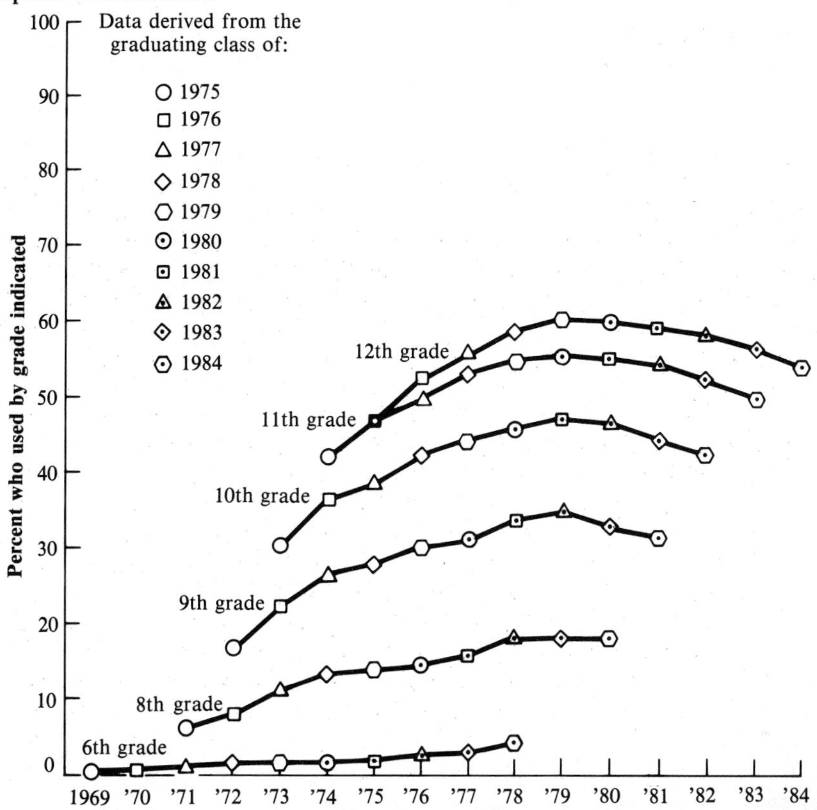

SOURCE: J. Bachman, L. Johnston, & P. O'Malley. Recent findings from Monitoring the Future. In F. Andrews (ed.), *Research on the quality of life*. Ann Arbor: University of Michigan, 1986.

have found that marijuana can produce irreversible changes in brain tissue, genetic abnormalities, damage to a fetus, and diminished production of sperm. Others have failed to confirm these findings. There is concern that heavy users ("potheads") become lethargic, apathetic, and confused in their daily behavior. Because heavy users usually take other drugs like alcohol, and because personality traits such as lethargy may have predated the use of drugs, identifying the effects of heavy marijuana use is difficult.

Contrary to the claims of its opponents, marijuana rarely leads to the use of hard drugs (Committee to Study the Health-Related Effects of Cannabis and Its Derivatives, 1982). Nevertheless, it can not be considered a harmless substance. Some users have died as a result of using marijuana laced with strychnine, and a small percentage become psychologically dependent on the drug. In sum, marijuana is not as innocuous a drug as some of its proponents may have wished nor as dangerous as some of its opponents have contended.

Current Usage

Contrary to some people's assumptions about the younger generation, *Monitoring the Future* data show that contemporary adolescents are using less marijuana than their predecessors in the 1970s (Bachman, Johnston, & O'Malley, 1986; O'Malley, Bachman, & Johnston, 1984). While the number of seniors using grass daily rose from 6 percent in 1975 to 11 percent in 1978, it declined to 5 percent in 1984 (see Figure 13.2). Fewer seniors in the class of 1982 had used marijuana within the previous year than in any year since 1976 (see Figure 13.4). Significantly, this nationally representative sample shows that approximately 45 percent of high-school seniors have tried marijuana before graduation.

As Figure 13.4 demonstrates, one of the primary reasons for the decrease in smoking cigarettes and marijuana is adolescents' growing awareness of the health hazards involved (O'Malley, Bachman, & Johnston, 1984). Among the high-school seniors who had used marijuana more than 40 times, 41 percent cited a fear of physical side effects as their reason for quitting. Similarly, 71 percent who had never tried pot cited fear of physical and psychological consequences as their reason (Johnston, 1981). During the 1970s the damage inflicted on the body by cigarette and marijuana smoke was not nearly as well documented or as well publicized as in the 1980s. Because research is being presented to the public in a less moralistic and more statistically documented fashion, young people are more responsive to evidence about the dangers of marijuana than they were to the exaggerated scare tactics often employed during the 1960s and 1970s.

Figure 13.4

Trends in perceived harmfulness of marijuana and cigarettes

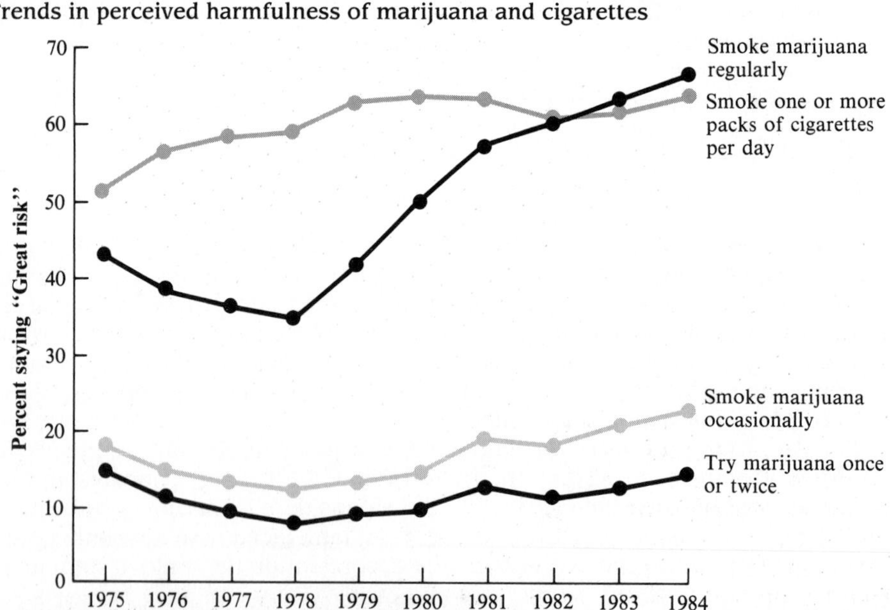

SOURCE: P. O'Malley, J. Bachman, & L. Johnston. Period, age, and cohort effects on substance use among American youth. *American Journal of Public Health,* 1984, 74, 682–688.

Characteristics of Users and Abstainers

Which adolescents are most likely to try marijuana and which ones usually abstain? In attempting to answer this question, researchers have identified a number of characteristics that seem to distinguish occasional users from abstainers (Bachman, Johnston, & O'Malley, 1986; Brook, Lukoff, & Whiteman, 1980; Jessor, 1979; Jessor & Jessor, 1977; Johnston, 1981; Kandel, 1980; Kandel, Kessler, & Margulies, 1978; Kandel, Single, & Kessler, 1976; O'Malley, Bachman, & Johnston, 1984). Students planning to attend college are less likely to try marijuana during high school than their peers who have no college plans—a reversal of the pattern during the 1970s. Males at all ages, however, are still more likely than females to experiment with marijuana. The least likely to try marijuana are those whose parents oppose the use of all drugs and who personally abstain from alcohol, tobacco, and other drugs.

As is the case with the use of alcohol and nicotine, adolescents are usually introduced to marijuana by friends who use the drug themselves. This being the case, many adults worry that peer influence will inevitably outweigh that of parents in regard to adolescents' drug use. The data do not, however, support the notion that parents are powerless in the face of peer pressure to influence their children's drug decisions. One representative study showed that 85 percent of the high-school students who had smoked grass had a best friend who had also tried the drug. Notably, the students whose parents as well as their friends used drugs had the highest rates of marijunana use. Parental ties can mitigate peer influences, however: Adolescents who felt close to their mothers were less influenced by their friends' behavior than those who had distant relationships (Kandel, Single, & Kessler, 1976).

Another study that reinforces the importance of the parent-child relationship found that adolescents who are close to their parents are the least likely to use marijuana. Furthermore, when these adolescents were questioned three or four years after the first interviews, the relationship between their current marijuana use and the behavior of their friends years earlier had diminished (Stone, Miranne, & Ellis, 1979). These data suggest that whatever influence friends have on one another's drug use may be short-lived. As the data in Chapters 8 and 9 demonstrated, the power of a peer group usually depends on the quality of the relationship between the adolescent and his or her parents.

In considering the facts that influence an adolescent to use marijuana, it's important to distinguish between young people who experiment with the drug at a very early age and those who begin later in adolescence. Only about 10 percent of 12- and 13-year-olds have tried grass, in contrast to almost 60 percent of 18-year-olds (Committee to Study the Health-Related Effects of Cannabis and Its Derivatives, 1982). This finding suggests that those who begin using marijuana in early adolescence may be different from those who use the drug later in adolescence. A study of 12,000 students in grades 4 through 12 supports this hypothesis (Smith & Fogg, 1978). Early users tended to be more impulsive, dependent, inconsiderate, emotional, and pessimistic than later users. These students were also perceived as more irresponsible, more untrustworthy, and more interested in social matters than were their peers who began using marijuana at a later age. These results suggest that individuals who begin using marijuana at a very early age may be resorting to the drug for reasons other than the recreation or curiosity that motivate older adolescents.

Young people who experiment with marijuana a few times and then give it up are generally similar to those who never use the drug (Jessor, 1979; Jessor & Jessor, 1977; Kandel, 1980; Kandel, Kessler, & Margulies, 1978). Nevertheless, while moderate marijuana use is not correlated with lower grades for college students, it is correlated with lower grades for high-school students (Jessor, 1979; Kandel, Kessler, & Margulies, 1978; Smith & Fogg, 1978). Several explanations have been offered for this contrast. Since the high-school population is more heterogeneous in terms of students' abilities, these findings may mean that marijuana is an academic impediment only to students with the least ability. It has also been suggested that high-school students with the poorest grades are more likely to use drugs than talented students. In other words, using marijuana may be the consequence of poor grades rather than the cause (Lipton & Marel, 1980).

Characteristics of Frequent Users

Although adolescents who use marijuana on occasion resemble those who abstain, those who use grass regularly can be distinguished from their peers (Jessor, 1979; Jessor & Jessor, 1977; Kandel, 1980; Kandel, Kessler, & Margulies 1978). Regular users tend to be more adventuresome, independent, impulsive, and expressive than experimenters or nonusers. They are also less interested in delayed gratification, authoritarianism, and religion. Their political and religious views tend to make them more tolerant of deviant behavior in themselves and in others.

Although the majority of young people are using pot less fequently and in more moderate quantities than during the 1970s, 3 percent of the females and 7 percent of the males in the 1984 graduating class were using marijuana on a daily basis (Johnston, 1981) (see Figure 13.1). Furthermore, approximately 13 percent of those who discontinue their education after high school, and 8 percent of those who go on to college, use marijuana daily. Almost twice as many high-school seniors without plans to attend college smoke pot daily, as do seniors planning to attend college. Interestingly, socioeconomic factors, parents' marital status, and region of the country have a negligible impact on daily use. As might be expected, those with strong religious commitments and those with the most conservative political attitudes are the least likely to use grass on a regular basis.

Not surprisingly, the high-school seniors who smoke grass daily have lower grades, are truant more often, and stay away from home more often at night than occasional users or abstainers. Nearly 35 percent of these students were out with friends six or seven nights every week. In contrast to only 7 percent of their peers, over one-fourth of daily pot users consume alcohol daily. Similarly, 60 percent smoke cigarettes every day, in contrast to only 25 percent of their peers. They also experiment with other drugs at a rate five to seven times greater than their peers. Most daily users of pot begin using cigarettes, alcohol, and other drugs at an early age. By the eighth grade 40 percent were smoking cigarettes daily and 50 percent had already had their first drink. At this point half had already tried marijuana and an additional 30 percent had started in the ninth grade (Johnston, 1981).

Why do adolescents who use marijuana regularly say they use the drug (Johnston, 1981)? On a list of 13 possible reasons, "to feel good or get high" was checked by 94 percent of the daily users; "to relax" by 67 percent; "to have a good time with my friends" by 79 percent; and "to relieve boredom" by 45 percent. Other reasons named by about one-fourth of the daily users were "to get through the day," "because of anger or frustration," and "to get away from my problems." Only 1 percent said they used pot daily because they felt "hooked" on the drug. Nearly 85 percent of the daily users say that most or all of their friends smoke pot, drink alcohol, and smoke cigarettes. Unlike those who use grass only occasionally, the daily users almost always belong to peer groups that smoke, drink, and use drugs often. In other words, adolescents who use marijuana excessively seldom have friends who abstain from drugs.

It might seem reasonable to assume that adolescents who are abusing marijuana continue their habit because they perceive no negative consequences from their behavior. Data from high-school seniors show, however, that many of these youngsters do perceive the harmful effects of their excessive drug use (Johnston, 1981). Among the daily users, 42 percent claimed that marijuana causes them to have less energy, 32 percent said it causes them to be less interested in other activities, and 34 percent said it hurts their academic and vocational performance. Given that those who use marijuana regularly have friends who also abuse the drug, it's not surprising that only 10 percent thought their habit was detracting from their friendships. Over a third, however, felt their drug use had hurt their relationships with their parents. Unfortunately, only 11 percent of the daily users thought the drug interfered with their driving skills, despite the fact that research shows otherwise.

Do the seniors who use marijuana excessively outgrow their habit after high school? According to *Monitoring the Future* surveys, generally not (Johnston, 1981). Roughly 60 percent of the adolescents who use pot almost daily in their senior year of high school are still using it on a daily basis a year later. Even four years after high school, half of these young people still use pot daily, and another third still use it occasionally.

Legal Controversy

Data regarding the psychological and physiological effects of marijuana continue to provoke controversial questions: Should the drug be legalized in order to protect its consumers from more dangerous substances that might be mixed with it? Why shouldn't marijuana be legalized, when other harmful drugs like nicotine and alcohol are still legal? Is it reasonable to invoke legal penalties against young people who occasionally experiment with small quantities of marijuana? Questions like these have motivated many states to reduce the legal penalties for possession of small quantities of marijuana. In 1983 Spain became the first European country to legalize pot, although punishment for dealers and users of hard drugs remains severe. The Roman Catholic Church virtually ignored the legal status of the drug, and the new law has been generally well received ("Guess Which Country Has Legalized Pot?", 1983). Nevertheless, the issue of legalizing marijuana in the United States remains unresolved.

STIMULANTS

Nicotine

Physiological Effects Despite the fact that stimulants like cocaine have received considerable national attention, the stimulant most frequently used and abused by adolescents is nicotine. Furthermore, unlike marijuana but like alcohol, there is evidence that nicotine may be physically addictive. Some smokers who try to break their habit report physiological withdrawal symptoms, such as headaches, trembling, and drowsiness.

Among the dangers associated with cigarette smoking are heart attacks and strokes, cancer of the larynx, mouth, pancreas, bladder, lungs, and throat, emphysema and chronic bronchitis, and burns from fires started by cigarettes. Because nicotine is a stimulant, it increases the heart rate and constricts the blood vessels, thereby limiting the flow of oxygen to all parts of the body. In addition, females who smoke and take birth-control pills run a much higher risk than nonsmokers of cancer and strokes. Pregnant smokers also run a greater risk than nonsmokers of miscarriage, stillbirths, premature births, and babies who have a greater number of illnesses during the first year of life. The amount a person smokes during his or her lifetime is related to the seriousness of the illnesses he or she may incur. For example, males who start smoking before the age of 15 have a five times higher incidence of death from cigarette-related diseases than males who began smoking after age 25. Some data are now showing that these ill effects of nicotine can affect nonsmokers who are exposed to smoke-filled air. Fortunately, the damage inflicted on the body by nicotine is sometimes reversible, if an incurable disease has not already developed. For instance, former pack-a-day smokers' death rates do decline and approach levels of nonsmokers after a ten-year period of abstinence (*Cigarette Smoking: Take It or Leave It,* 1980; *Danger Cigarettes,* 1978; *Smoking and Health: A Report of the Surgeon General,* 1979).

Aside from serious health hazards caused by nicotine, there are other side effects of particular interest to young people (*Cigarette Smoking,* 1980; *Danger Cigarettes,* 1978; *Smoking and Health,* 1979). In financial terms nicotine is expensive. A person who smokes a pack a day will be about $500 poorer at the end of the year as a consequence of maintaining the nicotine habit. Smoking also dries the skin, exacerbating wrinkles and creating a toughened, leathery look. Nicotine yellows the teeth, diminishes the powers of taste and smell, and fouls the breath. Many programs, directed at young people to deter smoking, stress these unesthetic aspects of smoking. For example, a poster featuring the "sexy" young actress, Brooke Shields, emphasizes the fact that smoking does not enhance sex appeal.

Current Usage Fortunately, as Figure 13.1 illustrates, today's adolescents are less likely than their cohorts in the 1970s to smoke during high school or in the years thereafter (Bachman, Johnston, & O'Malley, 1986). Based on surveys conducted during both the 1970s and the 1980s, it appears that young people are responding to the message that cigarette smoking is dangerous to human health ("Drug Use Levels Off," 1984). Although data like these are encouraging, the tenacity of the nicotine habit among the young cannot be overlooked. Despite the declines, some surveys show that nearly half of the young people between 12 and 17 occasionally smoke ("Drug Use Levels Off," 1984). Similarly, in *Monitoring the Future* surveys, about 12 percent of the 1981 high-school seniors smoked at least half a pack a day, nearly 20 percent smoked at least one cigarette daily, and 30 percent smoked occasionally (Bachman, Johnston, & O'Malley, 1986).

Furthermore, a higher percentage of girls and women are now smoking than ever before (*When a Woman Smokes,* 1978; *Women and Smoking: Report to the Surgeon General,* 1980). Recent data are showing that females exceed males in lifetime smoking and in smoking more than ten cigarettes a day (Gritz, 1982). It has been suggested that teenaged girls are smoking more as a consequence of advertising that associates cigarettes with sex appeal, success, liberation, and independence. Heeding the advice of advertisements like the Virginia Slims quip, "You've come a long way, baby," adolescent girls may perceive smoking as a manifestation of their liberation and sexiness. Although the causes underlying the rise in female smoking are debatable, the physiological consequences are irrefutable: Females' death rates from lung cancer alone almost doubled between 1967 and 1977 (*When a Woman Smokes,* 1978; *Women and Smoking,* 1980).

Prevention Programs Because most smokers develop the habit as adolescents, attempts to prevent smoking are often aimed at the young. If an individual manages to make it through adolescence without smoking, chances of becoming a smoker as an adult are drastically reduced. Questions, however, continue to plague researchers and practitioners who are trying to design effective programs to stop adolescents from smoking: How much of a deterrent is information about cancer and other illnesses, since their effects are delayed rather than immediate? How can social mores be changed so that smoking loses its appeal as a sex or status symbol? What causes some adolescents to begin smoking while others abstain?

The most successful antismoking programs include two essential ingredients: an appeal to abstinence as a manifestation of both sexual and social status; and convincing role models. One representative study compared several smoking-prevention programs for junior-high-school students and found that those taught by students, stressing the immediate social consequences of smoking, were more effective than those taught by teachers (Murray, Luepker, & Mittlemark, 1984). Rather than emphasizing the health hazards of smoking, the effective programs focused on such negative social aspects of smoking as bad breath, yellow teeth, and loss of sex appeal. Moreover, the results of this study emphasize the importance of letting peers direct antismoking programs for their friends. The fact that the programs were ineffective with youngsters who had already started smoking suggests that smoking-prevention programs ought to begin in elementary school, before experimentation with nicotine begins.

A similar approach sponsored by the American Heart Association has instituted an education and behavior-modification campaign in the Milwaukee area (McCormick, 1983). The "Save a SweetHEART" campaign disseminates buttons and posters with antismoking slogans that appeal to the young: "Smoking causes bad breath and yellow teeth"; "I'm kissable. I don't smoke"; "I'm saving a sweetHEART.'' The Heart Association sponsored a one-day no-smoking event on Valentine's Day. The schools' counselors and coaches design behavioral contracts with students who want to quit smoking.

A number of investigations have shown that adolescents' friends and parents are extremely influential in their decisions about smoking (Bachman, Johnston, & O'Malley, 1986; Covington, 1981; Kandel, Kessler, & Margulies, 1978). For example, in a recent study of 300 seventh-graders, the most valid predictors of smoking were the number of the adolescent's friends and siblings who smoked (McCaul, 1982). According to the American Heart Association data, 90 percent of the teenaged smokers say at least one of their best friends smokes. Similarly, those whose parents smoke are more than twice as likely to take up the habit as those with nonsmoking parents. Although almost all of the adolescent smokers believed cigarettes were harmful to their health, two-thirds were able to rationalize their habit by saying that smoking was acceptable as long as it didn't become a habit. Perhaps in an attempt to avoid cognitive dissonance, 85 percent of the smokers said they planned to quit within the next five years (McCormick, 1983). Data like these suggest that antismoking programs need to include the adolescents' parents and friends, whenever possible. Antismoking programs also need to help adolescents recognize the discrepancy between their behavior and their cognitive awareness of the hazards of nicotine.

Even though both the young and the old abuse nicotine, peer approval and social status appear to be more important incentives among the young. Adult smokers usually cite personal rather than social reasons for smoking: to alleviate tension, to lose weight, to accompany an activity like watching television or eating (Sherman et al., 1979). In contrast, adolescent smokers cite reasons associated with independence, peer approval, social status, and personal power. In a recent survey demonstrating this point, several hundred junior-high students from various ethnic and economic backgrounds cited fear of peer rejection and the need to acquire power over others as the most common reasons for smoking. Only 4 percent cited enjoyment of smoking and only 2 percent cited curiosity as reasons why they or their friends smoke (Covington, 1981).

Given this information from adolescents about their motives for smoking, the Risk and Youth Smoking Project at the University of California is among the programs trying to prevent adolescents from smoking, through training in decision making and resistance to peer pressure (Covington, 1981). These researchers base their methods on several facts about smokers' decision-making skills. First, young people who smoke tend to be less realistic than nonsmokers about the consequences of their actions in all social situations. Having exaggerated notions of how their peers will react to them if they dare to make an independent decision, these youngsters are the least likely to resist a friend's offer of a cigarette. Second, the project's researchers found that many young adolescents who smoke refuse to identify themselves as ''smokers.'' While admitting that they do smoke, they nonetheless refuse to accept responsibility for their decision by rejecting the label of ''smoker.'' Third, people with external locus-of-control attitudes are more likely to smoke than those with internal attitudes. This external locus-of-control attitude is manifest in comments like, ''There's nothing I can do to prevent cancer and besides I knew a person who smoked her whole life and lived to be 98.''

Researchers at the Risk and Youth Smoking Project are attempting to teach youngsters to become more independent thinkers, to resist peer pressure, and to develop a more internal locus-of-control attitude (Covington, 1981). One goal is to teach adolescents to perceive that there may be more than one option available in social situations with their peers. Another is to help them recognize the relationship between their present behavior and future consequences.

In sum, the most effective antismoking campaigns begin before junior high school, stress the immediate social disadvantages of smoking, and teach skills for resisting peer pressures. Since peer approval is a primary incentive for adolescents to smoke, programs must be designed to undermine the messages that smoking is a way to establish independence, to gain popularity, or to enhance sex appeal.

Cocaine

Although nicotine is by far the most widely used and abused stimulant in both the adult and adolescent population, cocaine has captured the headlines and national attention in recent years. Although its high price has traditionally made cocaine prohibitive for most adolescents and for the vast majority of adults, the recent glut on the world cocaine market has brought prices down in some places like New York City to $50 a gram—cheaper than an ounce of marijuana. Once hailed as a drug for affluent Yuppies, the drug is becoming more prevalent among lower-income adults and rural residents. According to government estimates, 25 million Americans have tried cocaine and 5 to 10 million use it at least once a month. Some analysts like Arnold Washton, the cofounder of the national cocaine hotline, contend that the estimates are too conservative and that 5,000 Americans try cocaine for the first time every day (Beck, 1985).

Although the drug's lowered price may eventually contribute to an increase in its use, most users are still white males over the age of 30 who earn more than $25,000 a year (Beck, 1985). Approximately 6 percent of high-school seniors in 1976 and 12 percent in 1981 had tried cocaine. Usage increased to between 20 percent and 25 percent in 1982 for people in their twenties. Although twice as many seniors had tried cocaine in 1979 (6 percent) as in 1977 (12 percent), levels seem to have stabilized (O'Malley, Bachman, & Johnston, 1984). Data from several national surveys suggest that cocaine is still among the least frequently used drugs among young and old ("Drug Use Levels Off," 1984).

Derived from the leaves of the South American coca plant, cocaine is a white powdery substance that can be swallowed, sniffed *("snorted")*, or rubbed on the inside of the gums. Although cocaine's recent notoriety suggests that the drug is a newly discovered substance, its history shows otherwise (Brecher, 1972; Grinspoon & Bakalar, 1976). Cocaine has been used throughout the ages in a variety of contexts: among the Incas for religious ceremonies, by the Spanish to increase the productivity of native South American workers, and by the Europeans in the 1850s in patent medicines and wine. Mariani's wine, a product known to contain coca, even received the approval of Pope Leo XIII. In 1886 an Atlanta, Georgia, pharmacist patented a popular medicine containing coca and proclaimed it as a remedy for an assortment of maladies. Capitalizing on the ingredient, he called his marvel medicine Coca-Cola. Long before it was marketed as today's Coca-Cola, however, the coca was replaced by other substances. Cocaine has also been used as an anesthetic and as an antidepressant. As was well known within the psychological community, at one time Sigmund Freud endorsed cocaine as a wonder drug for relieving depression.

Despite its former popularity as a stimulant and antidepressant, cocaine's use declined, as negative side effects were reported. Freud, for example, discontinued the drug for his own personal use and for his patients, when a close friend who had been using cocaine to treat his morphine addiction became psychotic and afflicted by formication—the belief that insects or snakes are crawling on or under the skin. Although moderate doses and occasional use tend to increase alertness and lift the spirits, larger doses or prolonged use can cause hallucinations, convulsions, or death. Contrary to earlier beliefs that cocaine is a safe, nonaddictive stimulant, recent data suggest that cocaine is addictive and that it contributes to cardiac arrests, seizures, and respiratory ailments. According to the National Institute of Drug Abuse, deaths related to cocaine have nearly tripled since 1980. Incidents like Richard Pryor's burning while *free basing* and the deaths of John Belushi and David Kennedy from mixing cocaine with other drugs have made the public increasingly aware of its hazards (Beck, 1985).

Amphetamines

Other stimulants used by adolescents and adults are categorized as *amphetamines.* These pills, popularly known as "uppers," are addictive. Despite their popularity among students who use "speed" and other amphetamines to keep them awake all night for last minute cramming, many young people are aware that "speed kills." When taken in excessive doses or when taken along with alcohol, amphetamines can be lethal.

Unlike most other drugs, the use of amphetamines has been steadily rising, according to *Monitoring the Future* data (O'Malley, Bachman, & Johnston, 1984). Only 15 percent of seniors in 1976 reported using amphetamines during the year, contrasted with 18 percent who so reported in 1982. The researchers point out, however, that some adolescents may incorrectly be identifying pills that contain caffeine and other psychoactive agents as amphetamines. Nonprescription diet pills, for example, contain caffeine and other agents that might be pawned off on unsuspecting adolescent buyers as "speed." This kind of misidentification may be inflating the statistics on amphetamine use among the young. Nevertheless self-reports since 1976 indicate that high-school seniors are using more amphetamines than did seniors in 1976. Those who graduated in 1976 are also using more amphetamines than they used in 1976, a finding that suggests a general trend across all age levels.

Narcotics

Drugs classified as *narcotics* are derived from morphine, a substance that is found in the poppy plant's opium. *Opiates* like heroin and morphine have been used in various cultures throughout the world, both to ease physical pain and to create the pleasurable sensations often compared to orgasms. Opium, heroin, and morphine were easily accessible in the United States until legislation passed in the early 1900s prohibited their use.

Heroin

The most frequently used opiate, heroin, can be sniffed or smoked. Most users, however, inject it directly into a vein ("shooting up") or under the skin's surface *("popping")* for a quicker "rush." The pleasurable rush is eventually followed by lethargy and sleep. In addicted individuals withdrawal symptoms like convulsions and vomiting begin once the drug wears off. Since the percentage of pure heroin differs from "bag" to "bag," users can inadvertently die from an overdose or from mixing the drug with alcohol. Although addiction is not inevitable, most users do become physically dependent on heroin. Because the habit is expensive, addicts often become involved in criminal activities to support their addiction. The addict's lifestyle also increases the likelihood of such diseases as malnutrition, pneumonia, and edema of the lungs (Zinberg, 1979).

Perhaps as a consequence of the adverse publicity, of the fear of addiction, and of the accessibility of less dangerous drugs, adolescents seldom experiment with narcotics. Among middle and upper economic classes, heroin use is rare. Most users come from extremely poor families in large, urban areas, where one or both parents are often drug abusers (Woody & Blaine, 1979). Heroin use by high-school seniors has remained lower than 1 percent since 1976 (Bachman, Johnston, & O'Malley, 1986; O'Malley, Bachman, & Johnston, 1984).

Hallucinogens

LSD

During the 1960s the hallucinogen, *LSD,* received considerable attention in popular music and in the media. LSD was hailed by some—like Timothy Leary, a Harvard psychologist—as a drug that could raise an individual's consciousness and produce profound insights. For others the drug was used simply to intensify sensory experiences and produce pleasurable hallucinations. LSD, lysergic acid diethylamide, may be eaten as a tablet, as a small square of gelatin, or saturated on paper. Taking effect within 30 minutes and lasting for 7 to 12 hours, the results range from pleasurable sensory experiences and enjoyable hallucinations to psychotic behavior and frightening hallucinations—a "bad trip." Some users experience *palinopia* or "flashbacks," a frightening phenomeonon during which they relive their trips without using the drug again. At the present time, the long-term psychological or physical effects of LSD are still unclear, particularly questions regarding its impact on genetic structure and prenatal development. Contrary to earlier beliefs, however, the drug is not physically addictive (Jacobs & Trulson, 1979).

LSD has not gained popularity among the young during the past decade. *Monitoring the Future* data show that fewer high-school seniors were using LSD in 1982 than in 1976 (Bachman, Johnston, & O'Malley, 1986; O'Malley, Bachman, & Johnston, 1984). The percentages using LSD have hovered between 6 percent and 9 percent from 1976 through 1982. Even during the years following high school, the percentage of young people using LSD remains relatively low.

PCP

Among the hallucinogens or psychedelics, phencyclidine has gained some popularity since the 1960s (Cohen, 1979b; Pittel & Oppendahl, 1979). *PCP,* or *angel dust,* is a synthetic drug that can be swallowed, injected, or smoked. Like LSD, the effects of PCP depend on the amount consumed and the kinds of other substances that may have been mixed with it. First used as an anesthetic and still used as an animal tranquilizer, PCP can be classified as both a depressant and a hallucinogen. It simultaneously has the properties of a sedative, a stimulant, a convulsant, and a hallucinogen. The effects range from sensory distortions, euphoria, depression, short-term memory loss, and hallucinations to feelings of detachment, paranoia, and uncontrollably violent behavior. According to some, PCP poses the greatest threat to adolescents, because it can produce psychological disturbances as severe as schizophrenia and sudden fits of violent behavior.

Although PCP was first produced in 1926, its popularity is relatively recent, a fact that restricts our empirical knowledge both of the drug and of the adolescents who use it. Although limited by its small sample size, one available study suggests that adolescents who use PCP begin taking the drug at about the age of 10. These young users were found to be more violent and antisocial than their peers (Simmonds, 1977). In contrast to some reports, however, another study of 70 young PCP users found no long-term effects of violent or emotionally unstable behavior (DeAngelis, Koon, & Goldstein, 1980).

Despite the increase in PCP's use, its popularity seems to be declining among younger age groups. National surveys by the National Institute of Drug Abuse showed an increase among adolescents from 3 percent in 1976 to 6 percent in 1977 (Cohen, 1979a). *Monitoring the Future* data, however, show a decrease from 7 percent in the class of 1979 to 3.2 percent in the class of 1981. As the report written by the adolescent reporter from the newspaper *New Expression* in Box 13.2 illustrates, adolescents are becoming increasingly aware of the dangers of "dust."

Mescaline and Psilocybin

Two other hallucinogens, mescaline and psilocybin, of lesser power than PCP or LSD, are derived from plants indigenous to Mexico and parts of the Southwest (Committee to Study the Health-Related Effects of Cannabis and Its Derivatives, 1982). Mescaline is taken from the mescal bud of the *peyote* cactus and *psilocybin* from the psilocybe mushroom. Both are mild hallucinogens, which have been used in religious ceremonies by some Native American tribes. Once ingested, these drugs cause mild distortions and intensify sensory experiences. Although the experience is usually pleasurable, some users report feeling anxious, depressed, or afraid while under the drugs' influence. The frequency with which adolescents use these drugs would be difficult to determine accurately, since access to them is rather rare in most areas of the country.

INHALANTS

Because of their convenience to young adolescents who can not afford or gain access to other drugs, inhalants (excluding ethyl chloride, amyl nitrite, and butyl nitrite)continue to attract a segment of the adolescent population. The intoxicating effects of inhaling substances like gasoline, model airplane glue, and paint thinner are similar to those of alcohol. The feeling of being "high" is relatively short-lived and makes the youngster feel somewhat "drunk." It is unquestionably true, however, that excessive doses can cause unconsciousness and death. Although the evidence is inconclusive and sometimes contradictory, some researchers contend that inhalants can damage the kidneys, the nervous system, brain tissue, and bone marrow, especially in cases of prolonged use.

Fortunately most of the adolescents who experiment with inhalants are in their early teens and abandon these solvents as they age. Inhaling solvents is most common among males between the ages of 10 and 14 and among Hispanic and Native American youths (Bruno & Doscher, 1979; Cohen, 1979a; Dworkin & Stephens, 1980; Humm-Delgado & Delgado, 1983; Oetting, 1982; Seffrin & Seehafer, 1976). Given these data, programs aimed at reducing the abuse of inhalants should be designed primarily for a male audience and for young adolescents. Programs with a special appeal to Hispanic and Native American cultures would also be most likely to meet the needs of these young males.

DRUG PREVENTION STRATEGIES

The fact that some adolescents are purchasing hemp seeds to smoke for a "high" similar to that of marijuana testifies to the fact that drug prevention programs must keep abreast of the variety of new products with which the young have been known to experiment (refer to Box 13.3). Indeed, drug education and prevention programs based on ignorance of contemporary drugs, misinformation, or false stereotypes are doomed to fail. Not only will adolescents come to distrust adults who provide them with false information, they will come to discard the truth along with the falsehoods. Considering the importance of trusting the source of drug information, it is noteworthy that the U.S. Justice Department is attempting to reduce drug abuse by relying on the influence of school coaches and athletes. As Box 13.4 explains, the program is predicated on the premise that athletes can serve as trustworthy sources of information about the ill effects of drugs and as role models for other students who might abuse drugs.

In this regard, one of the primary reasons adolescent drug use seems to be on the decline is that young people are more willing to accept the data about the negative effects of certain drugs. Unlike the exaggerated scare tactics often used in drug education programs during the 1970s, many contemporary drug pro-

13.2 A Closer Look

Homemade High Trips Out Teens; Playing with Dust May Brush You Off

by Hassan Rosell

Victor Bailey, 16, like many Chicago teens, experiments with drugs. He's tried everything from purple microdots to valiums. But Victor has sworn off PCP, otherwise known as tic or tac or Angel Dust.

"I can't hang with that dust; it was f______ with my head." Victor said. He told of an experience when he and a friend drank some beer and smoked eight dust joints at a park. "My friend went off and started climbing trees and grunting real loud. It kept me so up that I was seeing all kinds of s______. It felt like the stuff was eating at my brains."

Later he witnessed a friend of his brother's under the influence of PCP. "Reno went after his mother, and she had to lock herself into the house because he was hollering about trying to kill her. The police came and took him to the crazy house."

After these experiences Victor refused to use dust any more. "I couldn't take it," he said. "When I came down from my high, my head felt like it was bursting."

At the same time that Victor was withdrawing from PCP, other teens in the Chicago area were increasing their use of the drug. Other than marijuana, it's the most accessible drug on the streets.

Unlike marijuana, which is smuggled in from growers, Angel Dust is illegally manufactured in local laboratories. These labs are usually primitive facilities with amateur chemists. Victor knows some of these amateur dust-makers. "They get drugs from the drugstore or from dealers and mix them with a chemistry kit," he said. Then the pushers sell this dust brewed by amateurs without telling their customers what they're buying into."

A hustler taught Darrell Pearson, 16, how to make a batch for sale. He watched Anacin, Bromo Seltzer, valium (from a forged prescription) being mixed and cooked in bay leaves, evaporated and ground up. "He sold that as tac to snort," he said. "To make Angel Dust he sprinkled it over common marijuana to create a $2 joint." But Darrell didn't try any. Not after watching it being mixed.

According to Dr. James Gearien, Chairman of the Dept. of Medicalogical Chemistry at the University of Illinois, Circle, "It would be very difficult for teens to get the proper elements or to properly prepare the drug. Only hospitals and pharmacies have them," he said.

Gearien also believes that it would be very difficult for an amateur pharmacist to brew the proper formula. "They don't have the proper laboratory facilities. They just mix it up and hope it's Angel Dust."

A pharmacist at the Master Poison Control Center called tac a modern day form of moonshine. "The amateur makes it in the back closets like moonshiners made gin during Prohibition," he said. The results of this incorrect mixing are often deadly.

At the present the only legal manufacturer of PCP is the Bio-Ceutic Laboratories. This lab prepares PCP for veterinarians who occasionally use it as an animal sedative.

Even when PCP is prepared professionally by Bio-Ceutic, it's too strong for humans, according to Dr. Gearien. "PCP is harmful to the entire body, including the blood and the cardiovascular system," he explained. That's why doctors have not used PCP as a human anesthesia since 1965.

Alvin Redding, 16, who tried Angel Dust because a friend told him to check it out, says he couldn't handle it. Alvin says of his first and only encounter with Angel Dust, "After I smoked some, I came out of the house to meet a few friends at the car. As they were getting out of the car, it looked like they were all running at me. I was so scared, I almost ran back into the house. The stuff is too wild."

Curtis Ford, 18, who stopped blowing the dust because it hurts his chest, says he sees his friends "graduating from marijuana to Angel Dust. My friends prefer dust joints," he said. "They smoke every time they get their hands on it and come to class in a daze. I think they're addicted."

This Angel Dust Graduating Class are producing tragic medical stories. The "duster" rarely knows how much he's using whether he smokes, eats, injects or snorts the drug. "This is why it is so dangerous," said a local counselor from a drug rehabilitation center. "It's unpredictable."

Reactions to using PCP in any form could range from minor problems with eyes and coordination to a short circuit of the nervous system and a coma state.

Last March *New Times* reported the case of a man in Baltimore who was arrested with a high level dose of PCP in his system. A jailer found him the next morning with his eyes gouged out. Even when his eyeballs were dripping down his cheeks he showed no sign of pain. He was still unaware of what he had done.

Dr. Gearien believes that any user can suffer these effects from any amount of Angel Dust because of the amateur pharmacists' incorrect technique. "Who knows how strong the stuff is," Gearien said. "Anything could happen to the user."

Angel Dust pusher Barry Crawford, 17, who gets his drugs ready-to-sell from his dealer, says he doesn't know much about the drug's content or its danger. "I don't feel bad about selling it," he said. "If they don't buy it from me, they'll get it from somebody else."

"I don't believe all that stuff about its (PCP's) ingredients anyway," he laughed. "Do you?"

SOURCE: *New Expression*, February 1979, Chicago, Illinois. Reprinted by permission.

13.3 A Closer Look

Hemp Seeds Are for the Birds . . . Or Are They?

In Palm Beach County, Fla., what started out as just another student fad has turned into a murky legal issue that has district officials grappling with how to deal with students who are smoking bird seed to get high.

When Johnny McKenzie, director of security for the Palm Beach County School Board, heard that some youths in his 73,000-student district were mashing, rolling, and smoking hemp seeds—a high-quality bird seed that is sold in local pet stores—he decided to investigate further.

First, labrador retrievers used by the district to sniff out narcotics in the schools successfully detected hemp seeds in the schools. Next, a crime-lab criminal-evaluation test found that the seeds contained three psychoactive ingredients that are found in marijuana, including tetrahydrocannabinol (THC). And the test found that the seeds are capable of germination. "Those seeds that the kids can go out and buy—they can also grow them," Mr. McKenzie said.

The seeds, which sell in West Palm Beach pet stores for $1.25 to $1.40 a pound, are said to give students one-third to one-half the high that marijuana produces, Mr. McKenzie said.

After sharing the test results with Superintendent Thomas J. Mills, Mr. McKenzie last week sent a letter to the district's 102 principals stating that "it is illegal to possess hemp seeds on school grounds." Furthermore, he said, the district intends to treat students who are found to be in possession of hemp seeds in the same way as those who have marijuana—they will suspend them for up to 10 days.

Robert S. Schwartz, assistant state attorney for juvenile justice, said last week that any substance that contains THC or cannibis is covered in the statute that relates to marijuana possession and use.

Under the state, Mr. Schwartz said "if someone is caught with the seeds, it would be violative of the section. We would treat it as possession of marijuana. . . . There is no reason we wouldn't prosecute."

Mr. Schwartz did note that there would be a problem of proving an individual in possession of the hemp seed intended to use it to get high, not to feed his or her birds.

In recent weeks, a number of pet-store operators and veterinarians in the Palm Beach County area have said the only thing the seeds do is make birds fat. And one bird specialist wrote in a newspaper column that it is impossible to get high by smoking the seeds.

"The kids could smoke that and chew it and eat it until they're blue in the face," he said. "You can't get stoned on it."

SOURCE: *Education Week,* October 31, 1984, p. 3. Reprinted by permission.

A Closer Look 13.4 

Drug-Abuse Program Focuses on Athletes

Citing the likelihood that student athletes may become involved in drug or alcohol abuse, the U.S. Justice Department in June announced a drug-abuse-prevention program that it hopes will reach more than 5 million such athletes.

The program stresses the influential role school coaches can have in educating their students about alcohol and drug abuse. Coaches "have loyalty, commitment, and dedication in athletics which may not be present in other areas of the school," a promotional booklet said.

Through training clinics and literature, the department's Drug Enforcement Administration plans to target 48,000 coaches and 5.5 million student athletes in 20,000 high schools.

The program is expected to run for at least three years at an estimated cost of $5 million, said Ronald Trethric, preventive programs coordinator at the D.E.A.

"Our goal is to reach every coach and student ahtlete in the country," Francis M. Mullen Jr., the D.E.A. administrator, said.

Federal officials stress that educating athletes is especially significant since the pressure to succeed and the influence of peers can make drugs and alcohol look more tempting for such students than for others. Printed literature for coaches stresses that they should not ignore evidence of substance abuse, but should instead "open a dialog"with their athletes.

"The bottom line is that the coaches will train their athletes to serve as role models in the area of drug-abuse prevention," said Carey McDonald, a spokesman for the National High School Athletic Coaches Association, which cosponsors the program.

Other organizations sponsoring the program are the International Association of Chiefs of Police, the National Football League Players Association, and the National Football League.

SOURCE: *Education Week,* August 22, 1984. Reprinted by permission.

grams are trying to present the data more objectively. Adults and researchers are also more willing to admit to adolescents that certain drugs like marijuana may prove to be no more hazardous than our culture's favorite drugs—alcohol and nicotine. As the young gain more confidence in their elders' objectivity, they become more willing to alter their behavior on the basis of the empirical evidence about certain drugs (O'Malley, Bachman, & Johnston, 1984). The questions in Box 13.5 are designed to help you assess your own knowledge about drugs.

One issue in need of clarification for the benefit of accurate information during drug education programs is whether using drugs such as alcohol and marijuana will inevitably lead to the use of so-called harder drugs. It has long been argued by some theorists that using marijuana causes adolescents to move on

13.5 Are You Sure?

Quiz: Facts and Fictions about Drugs

In working with adolescents, your knowledge about drugs will contribute to or detract from your credibility as a counselor or confidant. To determine the accuracy of your information, decide which of the following statements are true.

1. Marijuana and cocaine are addictive substances, unlike alcohol and nicotine.
2. Hashish and marijuana are different drugs.
3. Adolescents are using more marijuana today than ever before.
4. The highest number of deaths and injuries to adolescents are caused by abuse of narcotics and hallucinogens.
5. Using "uppers" and "downers" can be lethal.
6. Nicotine is a stimulant like caffeine, which constricts the blood vessels, limits the flow of oxygen to the brain, and increases heart rate.
7. Smokers can cause physical damage to nonsmokers who inhale smoky air.
8. Cocaine is a recently discovered synthetic drug.
9. "Free basing" is a creative method for introducing marijuana into the body.
10. Since 1976 adolescents' use of nicotine, marijuana, cocaine, and amphetamines has increased.
11. PCP and THC are synonyms for the same drug.
12. Nicotine and alcohol are both addictive drugs.
13. Mescaline and psilocybin are synthetic drugs.
14. Smoking marijuana does not have the damaging effects of smoking cigarettes.
15. Heroin is derived from the synthetic drug opium.

Answers: Statements 5, 6, 7, and 12 are true.

to more dangerous drugs. While it is clear that many adolescents have tried marijuana without ever progressing to harder drugs, it is also true that adolescents who use hard drugs almost always had earlier experience with alcohol and marijuana (Johnston, 1981; Kandel, Kessler, & Margulies, 1978). For example, a survey of young adults, conducted nine years after data were first collected during their adolescence, showed that those using illegal drugs had initially used marijuana (Yagamuchi & Kandel, 1984). Similarly, 1982 surveys by the National Institute on Drug Abuse show that people who have tried hallucinogens, cocaine, or heroin are a subset of those who have tried marijuana (Miller, 1983).

Another hotly contested issue is whether adolescents who feel alienated and those with low self-esteem will use drugs most often. Indeed, many theorists and practitioners have simply assumed that such relationships existed. Self-esteem and alienation have not, however, been found to be consistently related to adolescents' drug use (Hays, 1984). Similarly, youths with the lowest educational and vocational aspirations do not necessarily use drugs more often than their peers with higher goals. In one representative study of almost 1,700 Pennsylvania students aged 10 to 19, youngsters' beliefs about access to educational or occupational roles did not predict their use of either alcohol or hard drugs

(Truckenmiller, 1982). Data like these suggest that it is oversimplistic to assume that adolescents with high self-esteem or those who feel part of "the system" are somehow invulnerable to drug use and abuse. The findings also underscore the importance of not creating a stereotype of the drug abuser as a person with low educational and vocational aspirations or with low self-esteem.

An extension of the low-self-esteem/drug-use connection is the assumption that unemployment increases a young person's drug use. Yet this rather popular notion has now been called into question by recent findings. Contrary to their own expectations, *Monitoring the Future* researchers failed to find clear evidence that unemployment after high school increases drug use. To their own surprise, the researchers found that unemployed males used fewer drugs than when they were seniors in high school and that their rates of binge drinking remained virtually unchanged from their senior year. The contradiction with other research may be explained by the fact that others' conclusions were based on cross-sectional data that failed to determine whether unemployment actually leads to increased drug use or whether individuals with high rates of drug use are less likely to find jobs (Bachman, Johnston, & O'Malley, 1986). Since the *Monitoring the Future* project is based upon a longitudinal design, high-school seniors are tracked over time, permitting the unraveling of questions that cross-sectional research cannot address.

Another assumption being challenged by recent research is that adolescents who use drugs in moderation are motivated by psychological factors that distinguish them from other young people. Contemporary research suggests that adolescents who occasionally use alcohol, marijuana, or nicotine are primarily motivated by a desire for social acceptance and by their curiosity (Bachman, Johnston, & O'Malley, 1986; Brook, Lukoff, & Whiteman, 1980; Chase, Jessor, & Donovan, 1980; Covington, 1981; Jessor, 1979; Kandel, 1980; Sherman et al., 1979). For example, the adolescents surveyed by members of the *Monitoring the Future* project most often said they used drugs "to have a good time with my friends" (Bachman, Johnston, & O'Malley, 1986). Such data should not be interpreted to mean that adolescents who use drugs frequently or in excessive doses are in no way unique from other young people. As the findings presented throughout this chapter have already demonstrated, adolescents who abuse drugs are distinct from those who abstain or those who use drugs in moderation. In this regard, it is noteworthy that high correlations are often found between young people who abuse drugs and parental absence, an authoritarian discipline style in the home, divorce, and poor communication with one's parents (Jurich et al., 1985). Research does not, however, support the notion that adolescents who occasionally use drugs like marijuana are motivated by complex or hidden psychological problems that set them apart from their peers who abstain.

Because adolescents often use nicotine, marijuana, and alcohol for social acceptance rather than as an act of rebellion against their parents or as a reaction to psychological problems, programs that include social-skills training have been effective in reducing drug abuse. A recent review of school-based prevention programs shows that those that have social-skills training as a major component have reduced adolescents' use of alcohol, cigarettes, and marijuana (Severson, 1984).

Another successful approach has been to teach adolescents to assert themselves in the presence of peers who are encouraging them to try drugs. One representative program for 500 sixth-, seventh-, and eighth-graders had students role-play situations in which they wanted to say no to an offer of drugs. Students were taught to use verbal and nonverbal communication for asserting themselves and for resisting peer pressure. In comparison to a control group of untrained students, the students in the program had fewer drug-related suspensions and no new drug users during the following school year (Englander, 1984).

Rather than devising programs intended to be applicable to all young people, drug programs could be targeted toward those adolescents who are most vulnerable to particular types of drug problems. For example, the drug use of Native American youths appears to differ from that of other adolescents. One recent study compared data from over 9,000 American Indian students to data from several national and local surveys of drug use (Oetting, 1982). The Indian adolescents in grades 7 through 12 were found to have more exposure to alcohol, marijuana, pills, and inhalants than non-Indians. They also used more inhalants and started using marijuana and inhalants at a younger age than non-Indians. Those most identified with Indian culture were the least likely to become seriously involved with drugs. Another example of the importance of identifying which adolescents are most vulnerable to particular types of drug abuse is a recent investigation of 342 delinquents' alcohol use. Drinking was strongly related to minor offenses for black, white, and Hispanic youths (Dawkins & Dawkins, 1983). These data suggest that delinquents may have a special need for programs designed to combat alcohol abuse.

Conclusion

Given the easy accessibility of drugs in today's society and the myriad reasons for which an individual may choose to experiment with a drug during adolescence, drug use is similar in many respects to sexual experiences. First, it is doubtful that either premarital sex or experimentation with drugs can be eliminated either among adolescents or among adults. Second, many adults feel that our discussions with adolescents on the topics of drugs or sex must be aimed at scaring the young away from experimenting with either. Third, it is often argued that by providing young people with information about how to protect themselves from the negative consequences of these two activities, we are condoning and even promoting their drug use and premarital sex. For example, from this perspective, providing information about birth control or giving the truthful answer that marijuana is not lethal is considered a form of approval of smoking pot and having sex.

Although the proponents of these arguments are undeniably concerned for the well-being of adolescents, their good intentions overlook several indisputable facts. Unlike doing household chores or completing homework, an adolescent's sexual activities and drug use cannot be monitored by adults. Given the nature of the activities, adolescents who are so motivated can engage in either, despite the careful policing of adults. More important, given the inherent pleasures and the immediate gratification that sex and drugs offer, it is unlikely that any amount of information and proselytizing from adults will curtail these activities completely.

In sum, the best tactic appears to be an honest sharing of information with adolescents, in which the pros and the cons of drugs are presented. Moreover, adolescents must be helped to understand the difference between drug use and drug abuse. Perhaps most important, adults must convince young people that when they do make foolish decisions in regard to drugs, they should notify someone who can offer immediate assistance. Whether this means seeking a professional counselor in cases of drug abuse or calling a taxi instead of trying to drive home drunk to sneak in the back door, adolescents must be assured that they need not exacerbate their potential problems with drugs by hiding their mistakes from others. In regard to drug use, this may indeed by the most valuable gift adults can offer the young.

Questions for Discussion and Review

Basic Concepts and Terminology

1. In what ways are nicotine, cocaine, and amphetamines similar?
2. How are hallucinogens distinct from narcotics in terms of their effects on users' behavior and their physiological impact?
3. Which drugs pose the most serious threats to adolescents' physical and psychological well-being?
4. How has adolescent drug use changed since the 1960s and 1970s?
5. Despite the popularity of alcohol and nicotine in our culture, what disadvantages can accrue to adolescents who use or abuse these common drugs?
6. What distinguishes adolescents who abuse alcohol, nicotine, and marijuana from those who use these drugs in moderation?
7. What statistical information and empirical studies should be considered in order to design effective drug-prevention programs?
8. How would you defend or refute the statement that "today's adolescents are a drug-oriented generation"?

Questions for Discussion and Debate

1. On what grounds can you argue for and against the legalization of marijuana and the lowering of the drinking age in all states to 18?
2. If the majority of adolescents and adults insist on using drugs for recreation and relaxation, which should they use? Why?
3. How would you design a program to help adolescents who are abusing nicotine? alcohol? marijuana? hallucinogens? Are there commonalities that all drug-education programs should have?
4. In what ways did experiences with drugs affect your adolescence? What short-range and long-range consequences accrued to you as a function of these experiences? (In answering these questions, remember that alcohol and nicotine are drugs!)
5. Since peer approval and social status are prime motivators for the use of alcohol, nicotine, and marijuana, how should parents, teachers, and counselors help adolescents resist the temptation to abuse or use these drugs?
6. Which of your personal beliefs about drugs did you find least supported by the data cited in this chapter?

7. Given your own experiences and those of your friends, what advice would you offer young adolescents who are considering occasional experimentation with drugs?
8. In what ways could using drugs be beneficial to adolescents? Do the benefits outweigh the liabilities?

REFERENCES

Bachman, J., Johnston, L., & O'Malley, P. Recent findings from Monitoring the Future. In F. Andrews (ed.), *Research on the quality of life.* Ann Arbor: Institute for Social Research, University of Michigan, 1986.

Baizerman, M. Youth and alcohol: Is there really an epidemic? *Journal of Alcohol and Drug Education,* 1982, 43–54.

Beck, M. Feeding America's habit. *Newsweek,* February 25, 1985.

Blum, A., & Singer, M. Substance abuse and social deviance: Youth assessment framework. *Child and Youth Services,* 1983, 7–21.

Brecher, E. *Licit and illicit drugs.* Boston: Little, Brown, 1972.

Brook, J., Lukoff, J., & Whiteman, M. Initiation into adolescent marijuana use. *Journal of Genetic Psychology,* 1980, *137,* 133–142.

Bruno, J., & Doscher, L. Patterns of drug use among Mexican American potential school dropouts. *Journal of Drug Education,* 1979, *9,* 1–10.

Burkett, S. Religiosity, beliefs and normative standards and adolescent drinking. *Journal of Studies on Alcohol,* 1980, *41,* 662–671.

Chase, J., Jessor, R., and Donovan, J. Psychosocial correlates of marijuana use and drinking in a national sample of adolescents. *American Journal of Public Health,* 1980, *70,* 604–612.

Cigarette smoking: take it or leave it. Washington, D.C.: American Cancer Society, 1980.

Cohen, S. Inhalants. In R. Dupong, A. Goldstein, and J. O'Donnell (eds.), *Handbook on drug abuse.* Washington, D.C.: U.S. Government Printing Office, 1979. Pp. 213–220. (a)

Cohen, S. The angel dust states: Phencyclidine toxicity. *Pediatrics in Review,* 1979, *1,* 17–20. (b)

Committee to study the health-related effects of cannabis and its derivatives. National Academy of Science, Institute of Medicine. *Marijuana and health.* Washington, D.C.: National Academy Press, 1982.

Covington, M. Strategies for smoking prevention and resistance among young adolescents. *Journal of Early Adolescence,* 1981, *1,* 349–356.

Danger cigarettes. Washington, D.C.: American Cancer Society, 1978.

Dawkins, R., & Dawkins, M. Alcohol use and delinquency among black, white and Hispanic adolescent offenders. *Adolescence,* 1983, 799–809.

DeAngelis, G., Koon, M., & Goldstein, E. Treatment of adolescent PCP abusers. *Journal of Psychedelic Drugs,* 1980, *12,* 279–286.

Delucca, J. (ed.). *Alcohol and health: Fourth special report to the U.S. Congress.* Rockville, Md.: National Institute on Alcohol and Alcohol Abuse, 1981.

Donovan, J., & Jessor, R. Adolescent problem drinking: Psychosocial correlates in a national sample, *Journal of Studies on Alcohol,* 1978, *38,* 1506–1523.

Drug use levels off. *Psychology Today,* 1984, *18,* 76.

Dworkin, A., & Stephens, R. Mexican American adolescent inhalant abuse. *Youth and Society,* 1980, *11,* 493–506.

Englander, G. *Say it straight: Adolescent substance abuse prevention training.* Ontario, Canada: American Psychological Association, August 1984.

Finn, P. Teenage drunkenness. *Adolescence,* 1979, *14,* 819–834.

Grinspoon, L., & Bakalar, J. *Cocaine: A drug and its social evolution.* New York: Basic Books, 1976.

Gritz, E. *Cigarette smoking by adolescent females: Implications for health and behavior.* Washington, D.C.: American Psychological Association, 1982.

Guess which country has legalized pot? *Newsweek,* August 1, 1983, p. 40.

Hays, R. *Multistage path models of adolescent alcohol and drug use: A reanalysis.* Las Vegas, Nev.: Rocky Mountain Psychological Association, April 1984.

Humm-Delgado, D., & Delgado, M. Hispanic adolescents and substance abuse: Issues for the 1980s. *Child and Youth Services,* 1983, *6,* 71–87.

Jacobs, B., & Trulson, M. Mechanisms of action of LSD. *American Scientist,* 1979, *67,* 396–404.

Jessor, R. Marihuana: A review of recent psychosocial research. In R. Dupont, A. Goldstein, and J. O'Donnell (eds.), *Handbook on drug abuse.* Washington, D.C.: U.S. Government Printing Office, 1979. Pp. 337–356.

Jessor, R., & Jessor, S. *Problem behavior and psychosocial development: A longitudinal study of youth.* New York: Academic Press, 1977.

Johnston, L. *Frequent marijuana use: Correlated, possible effects and reasons for using and quitting.* Ann Arbor: Institute for Social Research, University of Michigan, 1981.

Johnston, L., O'Malley, P., & Sacks, M. *A worldwide survey of seniors in the Department of Defense dependent schools: Drug use and related factors.* Ann Arbor: Institute for Social Research, University of Michigan, 1983.

Jurich, A., Polson, C., Jurich, J., & Bates, R. Family factors in the lives of drug users and abusers. *Adolescence,* 1985, *77,* 143–155.

Kandel, D. Drug and drinking behavior among youth. *Annual Review of Sociology,* 1980, *6,* 235–285.

Kandel, D., Kessler, R., & Margulies, R. Antecedents of adolescent initiation into stages of drug use: A developmental analysis. In D. Kandel (ed.), *Longitudinal research on drug use: Empirical findings and methodological issues.* Washington, D.C.: Hemisphere Publishing, 1978. Pp. 78–99.

Kandel, D., Single, E., & Kessler, R. The epidemiology of drug use among New York State high school students. *American Journal of Public Health,* 1976, *66,* 43–52.

Lipton, D., & Marel, R. The white adolescents' drug odyssey. *Youth and Society,* 1980, *11,* 397–413.

McCaul, K. Predicting adolescent smoking. *Journal of School Health,* 1982, *52,* 342–346.

McCormick, P. Teens get the advertising message: Don't smoke. *Winston-Salem Journal,* Winston-Salem, N.C., June 12, 1983.

Miller, J. *National survey on drug abuse: Main findings 1982.* Rockville, Md.: National Institute on Drug Abuse, 1983.

Murray, D., Luepker, R., & Mittlemark, M. The prevention of smoking in children: A comparison of four strategies. *Journal of Applied Social Psychology,* 1984, *14,* 274–285.

Oetting, E. *Drug use among Native American youth: Summary of findings 1975–1981.* Western Behavioral Studies, Ft. Collins, Col., 1982.

O'Malley, P., Bachman, J., & Johnston, L. Period, age, and cohort effects on substance use among American youth 1976–1982. *American Journal of Public Health,* 1984, *74,* 682–688.

Pittel, S., & Oppedahl, M. The enigma of PCP. In R. Dupont, A. Goldstein, and J. O'Donnell (eds.), *Handbook on drug abuse.* Washington, D.C.: U.S. Government Printing Office, 1979.

Seffrin, J., & Seehafer, R. A survey of drug use beliefs, opinions and behaviors among junior and senior high students. *Journal of School Health,* 1976, *46,* 263–268.

Severson, H. Adolescent social drug use: School prevention program. *School Psychology Review,* Winter 1984, 150–161.

Sherman, S., Chassin, L., Presson, C., & Olshavsky, R. *Social psychological factors of adolescent cigarette smoking.* Toronto, Canada: American Psychological Association, 1979.

Simmonds, R. Conversion or addiction? *American Behavioral Scientist,* 1977, *20,* 909–924.

Smith, G., & Fogg, C. Psychological predictors of early use, late use and no use of marijuana among teenage students. In D. Kendel (ed.), *Longitudinal research on drug use.* Washington, D.C.: Hemisphere Publishers, 1978.

Smoking and health: A report of the Surgeon General. U.S. Department of Health, Education and Welfare. Washington, D.C.: U.S. Government Printing Office, 1979.

Stone, L., Miranne, J., & Ellis, G. Parent peer influence as a predictor of marijuana use. *Adolescence,* 1979, *14,* 115–121.

Truckenmiller, J. *Differential prediction of alcohol vs. hard drug use level in a general youth sample.* Washington, D.C.: American Psychological Association, August 1982.

When a woman smokes. Washington, D.C.: American Cancer Society, 1978.

Women and smoking: Report to the Surgeon General. Washington, D.C.: Department of Health, Education and Welfare, 1980.

Woody, G., & Blaine, J. Depression in narcotics addicts. In R. Dupont, A. Goldstein, and J. O'Donnell (eds.), *Handbook on drug abuse.* Washington, D.C.: U.S. Government Printing Office, 1979.

Yagamuchi, K., & Kandel, D. Patterns of drug use from adolescence to young adulthood. *Journal of Public Health,* 1984, *74,* 673–678.

Zinberg, N. Nonaddictive opiate use. In R. Dupont, A. Goldstein, and J. O'Donnell (eds.), *Handbook on drug abuse.* Washington, D.C.: U.S. Government Printing Office, 1979.

Chapter Outline

Delinquency
Prevalence and Trends
Contributing Factors
Female Delinquency
Rehabilitation
Runaways
Prevalence
Contributing Factors
Suicide
Prevalence and Trends
Contributing Factors
Preventing Adolescent Suicide
Eating Disorders
Anorexia Nervosa
Bulimia
Rehabilitation and Prevention
Coping with Death and Dying
Dimensions of Bereavement
Death Education
Chronically Ill Adolescents
Conclusion

Goals and Objectives

This chapter is designed to enable you to:

- *Discuss the factors contributing to delinquency and running away from home*
- *Compare and contrast male and female delinquency*
- *Distinguish between bulimia and anorexia*
- *Summarize the factors that contribute to adolescents' suicidal thoughts*
- *Explain several approaches for helping delinquent, suicidal, and bulimic or anorexic youths*
- *Compare adolescent problems in terms of their prevalence in the population*
- *Explain the perspectives of those who advocate death education for children and adolescents in our society*

Concepts and Terminology

socialized subcultural delinquents
psychopathic delinquents
disturbed-neurotic delinquents

status offense
bisocial
anomie
bulimarexic

anorexia
bulimic
DSM III
EAT test

14 Atypical Problems during Adolescence

In previous chapters we have examined many of the problems that adolescents often share in common, as well as problems that beset particular groups of adolescents. Although the data throughout this text have demonstrated that no problem is typical of all adolescents, even when such variables as sex and race are similar, certain kinds of problems are more common than others among the adolescent population as a whole. Unfortunately, some of the problems that are relatively rare among adolescents attract the most attention in the media and create the most anxiety for parents. For example, despite the attention directed toward anorexia nervosa, suicide, marijuana, and cocaine, these problems affect far fewer young people than problems like academic underachievement, cigarette smoking, and alcohol abuse, although the former do make more headlines.

This is not to say that the topics that will be discussed in this chapter are unimportant. The fact that delinquency, eating disorders, and suicidal thoughts cause the death of thousands of adolescents clearly demonstrates their significance; but these topics must be placed in proper perspective by considering the small percentage of adolescents experiencing these phenomena, in comparison to those affected by other problems discussed throughout this text. For example, it's worth juxtaposing the number of adolescent suicides against the number of deaths from car accidents. It's also instructive to compare the number of adolescents suffering the physical and emotional strains of being overweight with the number of anorexics. Table 14.1 is intended to help us put adolescents' various problems into perspective and to dispel certain unfounded stereotypes regarding the types of problems confronting most adolescents in our society.

Table 14.1

Adolescents' Problems in Perspective

	Adolescents' Ages	*Yearly Estimates (percent)*
Deaths from suicide	13–19	0.0002 (1983)
Deaths from car accidents	15–24	0.0003 (1983)
Arrests for drunk driving	under 18	0.0008 (1984)
Anorexia nervosa and bulimia	college females	0.0001 (1983)
Girls who become pregnant	14–19	10.0 (1983)
Legal abortions	14–19	5.0 (1983)
Miscarriages	14–19	1.0 (1983)
Victims of child abuse	12–19	10.0 (1984)
Official arrests	under 18	7.0 (1984)
Runaways	10–17	10.0 (1982)
Cigarette smokers	12–17	30.0 (1983)
Alcohol drinkers	12–17	70.0 (1984)
High-school drop-outs		
Indian		40.0 (1983)
Black or Hispanic		20.0
White		12.0
Living below the poverty level		
Hispanic		45.0 (1983)
Black		53.0
White		20.0
Total population of adolescents aged 12–17 = 22.3 million (1985)		

For sources and additional details consult: Tables 8.1, 8.2, 10.1, 14.2; Boxes 6.2, 6.3, and 8.1; Figures 10.2 and 13.1. Since data are gathered in different years and from adolescents of different ages, the percentages above can only approximate the exact figures.

DELINQUENCY

Prevalence and Trends

How common is delinquency among today's adolescent population? According to information from adolescents' self-reports, about 80 percent commit acts that could be officially designated as delinquent if the youngsters were apprehended (Gold & Petronio, 1980). Most of these delinquent acts, however, are **status offenses**—that is, acts that would not be considered illegal if committed by someone above the legal age. Status offenses include drinking alcohol, being truant, running away from home, violating curfews, and having sexual intercourse. These kinds of delinquent acts increase from childhood through middle adolescence, remain relatively constant after the age of 15, and subside during the early twenties. In contrast, serious offenses such as vandalism, robbery, and assault escalate most dramatically from early to middle adolescence and then decline (Gold & Petronio, 1980).

It is currently estimated that about 12 percent of all youngsters will have been placed on record with the juvenile court system for having committed a delinquent act before the age of 20 (U.S. Bureau of the Census, 1984). Those arrested under the age of 18 account for nearly half of the nation's arrests for acts of vandalism, car theft, burglary, and arson. According to FBI official records, however, very few people under the age of 18 are arrested for serious crimes like rape, murder, or aggravated assault, in comparison to the percentage of adults who commit such crimes (see Table 14.2). Nevertheless, since 1960, the rate of adolescents' serious crimes has escalated faster than the overall delinquency rate and twice as fast as similar crimes perpetrated by adults (U.S. Bureau of the Census, 1984).

The 1984 report of the National Advisory Committee for Juvenile Justice and Delinquency Prevention confirms that a very small percentage of adolescents are responsible for most of the serious crimes (National Advisory Committee, 1984). According to the committee's data for the ten years since 1974, very little federal money has been directed at controlling these chronic delinquents. One of the committee's principal recommendations is that the government focus more attention on rehabilitating and controlling these serious juvenile offenders.

Other reports indicate that delinquent gangs still pose a serious threat to the security of many inner-city neighborhoods. As the information gathered from gang members by the teenaged staff of *New Expression* magazine demonstrates, gangs in Chicago have relatively easy access to guns and have used them against rival gang members and innocent victims (see Boxes 14.1 and 14.2). A recent investigation of black gangs in Chicago found that recruiting activities are more prevalent in the poorest communities and are targeted toward veteran delinquents rather than toward nondelinquents. Further, the data reveal that the new recruits are more involved with school and with their parents than those who have been in the gang for some time, suggesting that gang membership encourages further alienation from adults (Johnstone, 1983). Unfortunately, although 45 percent of the police departments recently surveyed in 60 cities said gangs created serious problems for the community, only 15 departments had any specialized units to deal with these gangs (Needle & Stapleton, 1983).

Contributing Factors

The research tends to be inconsistent and incomplete with respect to identifying the factors responsible for a juvenile's delinquency (Farrington, 1985). For example, a 1981 report that has been deemed influential in determining federal funding of delinquency prevention projects in the 1980s argues that the causes of delinquency lie in social institutions, rather than in individuals (Johnson et al., 1981). In contrast, one of the most thorough reviews of delinquency prevention research concludes that interventions need to be directed primarily at changing the home environment and the patterns of parent-child interactions. Moreover, the reviewers contend that delinquents need help learning more effective problem-solving and social competency skills (Rutter & Giller, 1983). In brief, it appears that while we cannot ignore the relationship between delinquency and factors like poverty, academic failure, or poor relationship with par-

Table 14.2
Total Arrests of Adolescents in 1984, by Race

	Arrests under 18					Percent Distribution				
Offense Charged	*Total*	*White*	*Black*	*American Indian or Alaskan Native*	*Asian or Pacific Islander*	*Total*	*White*	*Black*	*American Indian or Alaskan Native*	*Asian or Pacific Islander*
TOTAL	1,543,372	1,153,612	354,038	11,969	14,753	100.0	75.2	23.1	.8	1.0
Murder and nonnegligent manslaughter	1,004	539	454	7	4	100.0	53.7	45.2	.7	.4
Forcible rape	4,394	1,986	2,364	31	13	100.0	45.2	53.8	.7	.3
Robbery	27,788	8,421	19,041	67	259	100.0	30.3	68.5	.2	.9
Aggravated assault	31,126	18,508	12,225	217	176	100.0	59.5	39.3	.7	.6
Burglary	127,521	96,975	28,589	1,010	947	100.0	76.0	22.4	.8	.7
Larceny-theft	338,235	240,949	89,552	3,634	4,100	100.0	71.2	26.5	1.1	1.2
Motor vehicle theft	33,795	24,335	8,769	348	343	100.0	72.0	25.9	1.0	1.0
Arson	6,235	5,285	845	61	44	100.0	84.8	13.6	1.0	.7
Violent crime	64,312	29,454	34,084	322	452	100.0	45.8	53.0	.5	.7
Property crime	505,786	367,544	127,755	5,053	5,434	100.0	72.7	25.3	1.0	1.1
Crime Index total	570,098	396,998	161,839	5,375	5,886	100.0	69.6	28.4	.9	1.0
Other assaults	66,809	44,512	21,008	512	777	100.0	66.6	31.4	.8	1.2
Forgery and counterfeiting	6,172	5,134	971	43	24	100.0	83.2	15.7	.7	.4
Fraud	16,992	8,720	7,936	39	297	100.0	51.3	46.7	.2	1.7
Embezzlement	454	353	94	1	6	100.0	77.8	20.7	.2	1.3
Stolen property; buying, receiving, possessing	22,963	15,367	7,350	121	125	100.0	66.9	32.0	.5	.5
Vandalism	87,040	73,761	12,282	486	511	100.0	84.7	14.1	.6	.6
Weapons; carrying, possessing, etc.	20,644	14,383	5,992	82	187	100.0	69.7	29.0	.4	.9
Prostitution and commercialized vice	2,375	1,363	977	20	15	100.0	57.4	41.1	.8	.6
Sex offenses (except forcible rape and prostitution)	13,385	10,052	3,212	51	70	100.0	75.1	24.0	.4	.5

Table 14.2 (*continued*)
Total Arrests of Adolescents in 1984, by Race

	Arrests under 18					Percent Distribution				
Offense Charged	*Total*	*White*	*Black*	*American Indian or Alaskan Native*	*Asian or Pacific Islander*	*Total*	*White*	*Black*	*American Indian or Alaskan Native*	*Asian or Pacific Islander*
Drug abuse violations	66,484	52,497	13,020	301	666	100.0	79.0	19.6	.5	1.0
Gambling	671	216	372	1	82	100.0	32.2	55.4	.1	12.2
Offenses against family and children	1,564	1,287	261	7	9	100.0	82.3	16.7	.4	.6
Driving under the influence	18,391	17,720	406	194	71	100.0	96.4	2.2	1.1	.4
Liquor laws	101,662	97,529	2,471	1,220	442	100.0	95.9	2.4	1.2	.4
Drunkenness	23,510	21,919	1,158	390	43	100.0	93.2	4.9	1.7	.2
Disorderly conduct	73,478	55,164	17,703	390	221	100.0	75.1	24.1	.5	.3
Vagrancy	2,043	1,779	242	15	7	100.0	87.1	11.8	.7	.3
All other offenses (except traffic)	256,012	188,219	63,323	1,229	3,241	100.0	73.5	24.7	.5	1.3
Suspicion	2,493	1,884	586	2	21	100.0	75.6	23.5	.1	.8
Curfew and loitering law violations	67,073	47,225	18,778	423	647	100.0	70.4	28.0	.6	1.0
Runaways	114,059	97,530	14,057	1,067	1,405	100.0	85.5	12.3	.9	1.2

SOURCE: *Crime in the United States.* Washington, D.C.: U.S. Department of Justice, July 1985, p. 181.

ents, no single factor can be empirically justified as the primary cause of delinquency. Neither can we build a complete theory of delinquency on the basis of the data supporting any one of the factors that will be discussed in this section. At present the data suggest that the relationship between delinquency and any single variable is more complex than was generally acknowledged in earlier decades, when stereotypes about "the juvenile delinquent" often remained unchallenged.

Academic Failure Researchers suggest that delinquency is associated with academic failure. During adolescence students become increasingly aware of the relationship between making good grades and achieving social and economic status in our society. As the data in Chapter 5 revealed, a growing recognition of such a relationship is particularly characteristic of boys, since they are more likely than girls to link self-esteem with future income and vocational status. Consequently, the poorest students are more likely than their successful classmates to feel a sense of despair about their future and a loss of status in the present. Accordingly, delinquent acts may serve to create a sense of self-worth and to gain peer approval. The fact that the highest delinquency rates occur at about age 15 suggest that by this point adolescents have had to come to terms with their success or failure as students (Gold & Petronio, 1980).

In support of the hypothesis about academic success and delinquency, children with low IQs from low-income families who attended Head Start projects were found to perform better academically and behave better at the age of 15 than adolescents from similar backgrounds without the preschool enrichment program (Schweinhart & Weikart, 1980). Up to age 19, 51 percent of the control group had been arrested or charged with delinquency, in comparison with only 31 percent of the experimental preschool enrichment group (Barrueta-Clement et al., 1984). On the basis of such data, it has been cogently argued that preschool enrichment programs can serve as deterrents to future delinquency (Consortium for Longitudinal Studies, 1983).

The contention that delinquency is associated with academic failure is echoed by others who assert that delinquency is related to learning disabilities. One-fourth of the institutionalized delinquents participating in a survey prepared for a congressional report were diagnosed as having learning disabilities. Another 50 percent had learning problems severe enough to have placed them two grades behind their age group (*Learning Disabilities*, 1977). Further data come from parents of learning-disabled adolescents who have rated their children as more delinquent than parents of nondisabled students (Pihl & McLarnon, 1984). Finally, an extensive review of the research shows delinquents to have a disproportionate share of academic problems, particularly in regard to reading (Gagne, 1977). Since some studies show that the longer learning-disabled students stay in school the more likely they are to become involved with the police, it has been argued that school can inadvertently contribute to delinquency (Gagne, 1977).

Since academic problems are sometimes caused by physical maladies, it is not too surprising that some relationship seems to exist between certain kinds of health problems and delinquency. For example, delinquents appear to have a disproportionate number of visual, auditory, and neurological problems (Penner, 1982). It has been argued, therefore, that some physical disabilities might indirectly contribute to delinquency.

14.1 A Closer Look

Gangs with Guns out of Control

The adolescent staff of *New Expression* magazine provides information about gangs in Chicago by interviewing gang members. The following excerpts from their article represent the viewpoints of these teenaged staff reporters and gang members:

During the last two minutes of his life, Santos Martinez was playing "Centipede" in a hot dog stand on the Near North side. Santos was 15-years-old, a good student, and a guy who enjoyed playing video games with his friends.

Perhaps Santos didn't hear the door of the hot dog stand open behind him. Perhaps he didn't see the young gang member walk through the door with a Remington riot gun in his hand.

The killer fumbled with his gun. He tried to fire it but couldn't because he had forgotten to release the safety.

According to police, the teenaged killer had never handled a riot gun before. He may not even have known that the gun had a safety.

Panicked, the gunman ran out of the hot dog stand to check his gun. And then, moments later, he returned to complete his job.

This time the safety was off. He fired the gun. Three times.

One of the three shots bulled its way into Santos Martinez' left side and came out on the right. On the floor of Sammy's Red Hots on Dec. 11 at 7:53 p.m. Santos Martinez lay dying. He was the 89th Chicago teen to die in a gang-related shooting in 1984.

A gang member, Keith Hoddenbach, and two other alleged conspirators have been arrested and indicted for First Degree murder. The rival gang member who was the real target of the shooting, according to police, was only injured.

The person who ended Santos Martinez' life didn't even know how to handle the gun he used to shoot three people. That gun, by the way, had been stolen in a burglary a month before the incident.

New Expression talked to Carlos (not his real name) about the role of guns in street gangs. Carlos, 17, has been involved in gangs since the age of 12. He told us that there is absolutely no training or practical experience that a gang member normally gets when he acquires a gun.

Carlos claims that guns can be gotten anywhere. Many are stolen from parents;

Although the relationship between academic failure and delinquency is rather clearly established, most of the research suffers from the same methodological shortcoming as all correlational studies: Correlation does not establish causation. Several alternative hypotheses challenge the assumption that delinquency is a reaction to academic problems. First, traits that contribute to delinquency, such as impulsiveness, unwillingness to delay gratification, or an external locus of control may be the same traits that contribute to poor school performance. Second, the vast majority of unsucessful students do not resort to some are obtained in robberies, and others are just bought off the street. He said that "the kids sometimes go wild with the guns, especially on New Years Eve."

We talked to Jim (not his real name), a gang member, about his experience with guns. "The gang leaders hold meetings to pay for guns and drugs," he said, "and each member has to pay dues. It's like a P.T.A. meeting."

Jim claims that there are policemen who will go to gun shops and buy guns legally, and then sell them to gang members. Another gang member described an incident in which he was caught by a policeman with a loaded, unlicensed gun. The policeman allegedly removed the bullets from the gun and returned it to the youth. The gang member said he was not arrested or brought into the station.

Tom Krowiac, a Chicago policeman, insists that something like this couldn't happen. He told us that the worst a policeman would do is take the gun for himself; but he would never give it back to the carrier.

New Expression asked Kevin (not his real name), a reliable source within the gang structure, about how large numbers of guns were being obtained and how easy it was for someone to get one. "A lot of guns are brought in over the border, from places like Detroit," he said." Recently, I was inquiring about how to get a gun. Essentially, it'd be no problem as long as I had something like $55. They could get me anything I wanted."

It hasn't always been like this, according to George (not his real name). "When I was in the Stones from 1967 to 1973, only the guy who did the most robbing and stabbing got the gun from the leader. We never knew where he got the gun; and you didn't ask, or you might be considered a spy," he said.

But today the guns are everywhere. Gangs no longer control which members are carrying guns. Amateurs—real amateurs—are handling sophisticated weapons. Members of six major Chicago gangs admitted to us that this is what is happening.

Newspaper, radio and television stories tell us that the gang problem in Chicago is out of control. But talks with the gang members tell us that it's the gangs themselves that are out of control.

SOURCE: *New Expression: The Magazine of Youth Communication.* Chicago, February 1985, p. 3. Reprinted by permission.

delinquency despite their poor grades in school. This in itself creates the problem of explaining why some unsuccessful students become delinquent while others don't. Third, as you recall from Chapter 7, the relationship between poor grades and a poor self-concept has not been clearly established. A number of unsucessful students maintain a positive self-image through resources other than their grades. The major problem, however, with the argument that academic failure promotes delinquency is the research contesting the relationship between self-esteem and delinquency.

14.2 A Closer Look

Legion of Doom: Young Vigilantes?

Two weekends ago, 16-year-old Trey Hill found his blue Datsun heavily damaged by a pipe bomb. Attached to the shattered windshield was a message in blue ballpoint, signed off with a red swastika: "Thieves will not be tolerated." The same weekend, two other students from Ft. Worth's R. L. Paschal High School found their cars vandalized—one smeared with the blood of a mutilated cat left hanging on the steering wheel, the other with a window shot out and a note declaring Paschal "Nazi territory. You are short-lived if you return."

Late last week, Ft. Worth police arrested three members of a Paschal group called the Legion of Doom for questioning in 30 such acts of off-campus violence and intimidation. The legion—all white, all male, predominantly athletes and honor students—purports to be dedicated to ridding the city's oldest high school of thieves and drug users. But police think it has been involved in a vigilante campaign punctuated by arson and other criminal mischief. Cases against nine Paschal students may be presented to a grand jury this week.

What drove the Legion of Doom? One detective said they seemed to be "kids with good intentions who went outside the law," frustrated by campus thefts. Some students, though, citing ugly legion graffiti in nearby parks, argued that minorities at Paschal (which is 60 percent white) often were singled out. "The only thing their victims did is either be black or just suspected of something," argued Trey HIll. "Butchering cats is a funny way to clean up the school."

SOURCE: *Newsweek*, April 8, 1985. Reprinted by permission.

Self-Esteem It has long been assumed that children with poor self-concepts are the most likely to resort to delinquency in order to enhance their self-esteem through peer approval. This hypothesis is based on studies showing correlations between low self-concept and delinquency. Representing this viewpoint are Offer's descriptive surveys comparing delinquent and nondelinquent youth during the 1970s and 1980s (Offer, Marohn, & Ostrov, 1979). On self-report questionnaires the delinquents described themselves as less social, less academically talented, and less pleasing to their parents than nondelinquents. The delinquents also said, more often than nondelinquents, that they felt empty, confused, and anxious. Likewise, a study of 135 white, Mexican American, and black males revealed lower self-esteem scores for the delinquents than for nondelinquents (Calhoun, 1984).

A second type of research supporting the self-esteem hypothesis relies on longitudinal correlations. This approach is represented by the Rosenbergs' analysis of white high-school boys (Rosenberg & Rosenberg, 1978). Beginning during the sophomore year in high school, data were collected five times between 1966 and 1974 on nearly 2,000 boys in 48 states. The correlations between low self-esteem and subsequent delinquency were higher than those between delinquency and subsequent lowered self-esteem. In other words, it is more likely that low self-esteem leads to delinquency than that delinquency reduces self-esteem. According to this investigation, "The low self-esteem person thus engages in delinquency both in order to retaliate against the society which disdains him and in order to gain a much needed feeling of self-esteem" (Rosenberg & Rosenberg, 1978, p. 271).

In yet another longitudinal study of 3,000 boys and girls in 36 junior high schools, students with the lowest initial self-esteem, who subsequently committed delinquent acts, increased their self-esteem more than those who did not become delinquent (Kaplan, 1975). Studies like these support the notion that adolescents who fail to meet society's expectations often ally themselves with peers who endorse delinquency. In this way the alienated, unsuccessful adolescents enhance their self-esteem and status among peers.

The assumption that low self-esteem is related to delinquency is being challenged by more recent research and by reevaluations of prior studies. Using Rosenberg's data, investigators categorized the boys into high and low self-esteem groups (Bynner, O'Malley, & Bachman 1981). Reexamining the data in this way revealed that boys with initially low self-esteem tended to be more delinquent than those with higher self-esteem and that delinquency did restore some self-esteem for them. However, "the most striking result for the total sample and the high self-esteem groups is the weakness of all the paths from self-esteem to delinquency" (Bynner, O'Malley, & Bachman, 1981, p. 420). In short, the evidence did not support the view that low self-esteem is a significant precursor to delinquency. In addition, these researchers found that boys who had been held back a grade had no less self-esteem and were no more delinquent than those who were successful students. Even when socioeconomic status and educational attainment were controlled, the researchers were unable to establish a strong relationship between self-esteem and delinquency.

In another recent longitudinal study involving 1,658 junior- and senior-high-school students over a three-year period, those who started out low in self-esteem were no more delinquent than those who began with high self-esteem (McCarthy & Hoge, 1984). By monitoring the self-images and the incidence of theft, vandalism, serious crime, and classroom misbehavior, the researchers found a slight tendency among students to have lower self-esteem after becoming delinquent than before. The loss of self-esteem was most pronounced for those delinquents who had started out with the highest levels of esteem. Delinquent behavior apparently undermined feelings of self-worth by subjecting the violators to negative feedback from peers and adults. This finding refutes the traditional assumption that adolescents raise low self-esteem through delinquency.

How can these contradictions in the research be explained? Why are some researchers finding correlations between low self-esteem and delinquency, while others aren't? In an effort to understand the inconsistencies in the data, it is important to recognize that, for several reasons, the age of the adolescents in the samples becomes a significant confounding variable. First, grades tend to be a more important source of self-esteem in early adolescence than in later adolescence. Second, self-esteem tends to increase and to be derived from a greater variety of sources as adolescents age. Third, delinquent acts are more likely to receive peer approval among younger than among older adolescents (Bynner, O'Malley, & Bachman, 1981; O,Malley & Bachman, 1979).

As a consequence of these influences on self-esteem, studies using samples of young adolescents would tend to find higher correlations between self-esteem and grades, and would also tend to find lower levels of self-esteem in general than those using samples of older adolescents. Members of young adolescent samples would be more tempted to resort to delinquency as a way to boost self-esteem than would members of older adolescent samples. Finally, the questionable validity and reliability of instruments used to measure self-esteem inevitably result in the misclassification of a certain percentage of the participants in any study.

Unfortunately, these methodological problems and the contradictory data leave practitioners understandably confused. Are we to assume that adolescents with low self-esteem are particularly vulnerable to becoming delinquent, or not? Should we design delinquency prevention programs on the basis of trying to enhance self-esteem, or is this a wasted effort? It appears that low self-esteem may influence some youngsters' decisions to commit delinquent acts, particularly in the earlier years of adolescence. Nevertheless, a poor self-concept is not sufficient in and of itself to cause delinquency, and a strong self-concept is not a foolproof inoculation against delinquency.

Parent-Child Relationships Another logical tactic in the search for the causes of delinquency has been to compare the families of delinquent and nondelinquent youths. What kinds of families do delinquents come from? Can parents prevent their children from becoming delinquent? The data collected through investigations of family characteristics have yielded mixed results. The majority of studies have identified characteristics in families that seem to contribute to delinquency. Others have found no essential differences in delinquents' and nondelinquents' families.

One dimension on which researchers have focused is the relationship between family violence and delinquency. Assuming that "violence begets violence," we might hypothesize that adolescents from homes where the wife or children are physically abused would tend to rely on aggression to resolve their conflicts. The data, however, suggest a more complicated relationship between family violence and delinquency. On the one hand, there is evidence that delinquents come from more violent families than nondelinquents. For example, an Ohio study found that a significant percentage of adolescents arrested for violent crimes had been victims of severe child abuse and often behaved violently toward their family members (Kratovsky, 1982). Similarly, one recent review of the literature confirms the hypothesis that parental rejection and aggression are positively correlated with delinquency (McCord, 1982). In contrast, another review concludes that although much of the literature shows an association between child abuse and delinquency, the data are inconsistent. This review concedes that the data are conflicting enough to warrant further research before generalizing about the relationships between child abuse, family violence, and delinquency (Paperney & Deisher, 1983).

There is more agreement among researchers in regard to other aspects of the family than the display of physical abuse, which appear to be related to delinquency. Most studies have found correlations between delinquency and parents' overly strict standards, rejection, poor communication, excessively lax standards, and indifference or hostility (Patterson, 1981; Rutter & Giller, 1983). As demonstrated by the data in Chapter 8, adolescents whose parents are communicative, supportive, affectionate, and democratic are more swayed by their parents' opinions than those whose parents are critical, authoritarian, hostile, indifferent, and uncommunicative. A close relationship with parents also diminishes the likelihood that adolescents will adopt peer values that contradict those of their parents.

The accumulated empirical data raise serious questions, however, about the assumption that divorce contributes to delinquency. While studies have found correlations between divorce and delinquency, the data are inconsistent (Gold & Petronio, 1980; Rutter & Giller, 1983). As Chapter 8 demonstrated, the father's role in some families after a divorce is similar to his role before the divorce, in terms of the intimacy or frequency of contact with his children (Lamb, 1981). Furthermore, parents who remain unhappily married often create a climate of hostility, apathy, and conflict that is more likely than divorce to contribute to a child's delinquency. Given the methodological problems discussed in Chapter 8,

As a high-school principal or as a city mayor, how would you attempt to reduce the problems that plague many of the young people in your community?

establishing the impact of divorce on a child's behavior remains a difficult task. It appears that divorce, particularly when occurring under adverse conditions, may provide an incentive for some adolescents to become delinquent. Under other circumstances, however, divorce may diminish delinquency by creating a more favorable relationship between children and their parents.

Not all researchers have found differences in the families of delinquent and nondelinquent children. In one analysis of self-reported delinquency for males and females, family factors were generally insignificant (Farnworth, 1984). In a study of 59 lower-class youths classified by their neighbors as being either "problematic" or "promising," no differences emerged on the youths' perceptions of their family relationships (Weller & Luchtarhand, 1983). Although studies like these challenge the assumption that delinquents' families are somehow different from nondelinquents', the majority of studies uphold the view that adolescents' families do have a considerable impact on their delinquent behavior.

Most data also support the view that differences between delinquents and nondelinquents are usually apparent before the onset of adolescence. Teachers perceive children who later become delinquent as more dishonest, antisocial, unpopular, rebellious, aggressive, and quarrelsome than other children (Gold & Reimer, 1974; Rutter & Giller, 1983). In other words, adolescence in itself is not responsible for evoking delinquent behavior.

One particularly unique study demonstrating the early manifestations of delinquency examined the antisocial, aggressive, and criminal behavior of approximately 400 males and females over a 22-year period (Huesmann, 1984). Starting when participants were in the third grade, the researchers collected data from the subjects, their parents, and, subsequently, their spouses. Although the kind and amount of aggressiveness changed dramatically with age, aggressive children generally remained aggressive throughout adolescence and adulthood. In sum, the most aggressive 8-year-old is likely to be the most aggressive 30-year-old. Adult aggressiveness manifested itself in males in criminal behavior, physical aggression, child and wife abuse, and reckless driving. Aggressive behavior appeared to be learned early in a child's life, to create a sensitivity to aggressive cues in the environment, and to be transmitted across generations within a family. According to these investigators, genetic, physiological, and cultural factors may all contribute to aggression. Nevertheless, the most influential factor that contributes to aggressive behavior is learning early in life that aggression is an effective way to solve social problems.

Race and Income Another issue to be addressed is the relationship between delinquency, income, and race. Are adolescents from impoverished homes more delinquent than their middle or upper-income peers? Given the fact that a larger percentage of minority youths are living below the poverty level than are whites, the relationship between delinquency and income also becomes a question of race: Are minority youths more delinquent than whites? In attempting to answer this question, the methodological problems involved in collecting accurate data become of paramount importance. Adolescents' self-reports and national statistics from official records are generally consistent regarding age and sex differences in delinquency, but the data are frequently inconsistent with respect to the questions of race and income.

In contradiction to official reported statistics of arrests, most adolescents' self-reports of delinquent acts fail to discriminate between young people on the basis of socioeconomic class or race (Balk, 1982; Gold & Petronio, 1980). For example, the 1972 National Survey of Youth, which interviewed a nationally representative sample of 1,395 youths in 40 areas throughout the country, found no significant differences in delinquent behavior by race or income (Gold & Reimer, 1974). In addition, some studies that do not rely on adolescents' own reports have failed to find relationships between race, income, and delinquency. For example, a longitudinal study of nearly 2,000 white males between 1966 and 1974 failed to find significant relationships between socioeconomic status and delinquency (Bynner, O'Malley, & Bachman, 1981).

In contrast, arrest records consistently show that adolescents from minority groups and lower-income families are more delinquent in terms of the frequency and the seriousness of their offenses (Gold & Petronio, 1980; Hindelang, Hirschi, & Weis, 1979; Federal Bureau of Investigation, 1984). Even though most studies using adolescents' self-reports refute these data, one of the largest self-report studies confirms that delinquency is most frequent among racial minorities and low-income youngsters. According to this 1977 survey of 1,726 youths between the ages of 11 and 17, lower-income youths reported nearly three times as many crimes against property (burglary, car theft, and vandalism) and nearly twice as many crimes against people (sexual assault, robbery, aggravated assault) as middle-class youths. Similarly, black youths reported almost twice as many crimes against people as whites and almost three times as many crimes against property (Elliot & Ageton, 1980).

The latter finding reinforces data from the Uniform Crime Report compiled by the Federal Bureau of Investigation. According to FBI statistics, blacks account for about 25 percent of all arrests for people under 18 and for about 55 percent of the arrests for violent crimes (Federal Bureau of Investigation, 1984) (see Table 14.2). These observations are corroborated by other studies showing that adolescents from low-income families, particularly those in urban ghettos, commit more crimes than those from wealthier homes (Rutter & Giller, 1983).

Several hypotheses have been advanced to explain the contradictions between self-reports and official statistics (Hindelang, Hirschi, & Weis, 1979). It has been suggested that the police and the juvenile justice system are most likely to catch and to prosecute minority and low-income youths. According to this view, unintentional or intentional economic and racial bias inflates the official statistics on delinquency among the poor and minorities, while underestimating delinquency among richer youths and whites (Children's Defense Fund, 1976; McCord, 1982). A second factor confounding the research is that adolescents may systematically differ in terms of their honesty about delinquent acts. For example, in comparing youths' own reports with police records, one study found that black males failed to report their violations three times as often as whites (Hindelang, Hirschi, & Weis, 1979). Differences like these in researchers' samples would help account for some of the discrepancies in the data.

Analysts have argued that the term "delinquency" is often too nebulous to permit accurate comparisons or generalizations (Gold & Petronio, 1980). Studies using adolescents' own reports tend to ask questions about less serious crimes than studies based on official police records. The self-report studies therefore tend to minimize racial and economic differences, while official reports tend to accentuate them. To exemplify this principle, one study based on nearly 2,000 adolescents' self-reports showed that race and economic class were correlated with crimes against property and people, but were not correlated with the less serious offenses like disorderly conduct, hitchhiking, drunkenness, or drug use (Elliot & Ageton, 1980). Thus, it appears that when serious offenses are the focus of examination and are distinguished from minor violations, the self-reports and official records generally agree that blacks are more delinquent than whites. When minor offenses are examined, however, no significant racial differences based on either self-report or official data are generally observed (Hindelang, Hirschi, & Weis, 1979).

Some analysts contend that the statistics on delinquency are confusing because researchers have typically failed to separate race and income when analyzing the data (Hindelang, Hirschi, & Weis, 1979). According to this criticism, if the data were reanalyzed, there would be few differences between economic classes within the same racial group and significant differences among the races.

The relationship between poverty and delinquency may also be difficult to establish because researchers have limited their comparisons to families' incomes rather than to other aspects of poverty. In other words, a family's income may be less important in predicting crime than the size of the discrepancies between the poor and the middle class. If the size of the income gap between various classes were considered, stronger correlations between crime and poverty might emerge. For example, data from 193 cities over a six-year period showed that crime rates could be predicted on the basis of the size of the income gap between poor and average workers, but not from the actual percentage of the population living below the poverty level (Braithwaite, 1981). Data like these suggest that adolescents from impoverished homes, who see tremendous differences between their lifestyles and the lives of higher-income families, will be more likely to become delinquent than those who see fewer differences between their standard of living and that of other Americans.

In sum, it appears that while we cannot ignore the relationships between race, socioeconomic status, and delinquency, we cannot construct explanations for delinquency solely around the assumption that poverty causes delinquency or that wealth somehow immunizes adolescents against it. The data suggest a more complex relationship than is generally acknowledged by official records or adolescents' self-reports.

Peer Relationships Could a lack of social skills contribute to a youngster's becoming delinquent? Is it possible that adolescents who have few friends and feel lonely and isolated might be more susceptible to delinquency than those who are popular and socially adept? Would it be possible to lower the delinquency rate by teaching adolescents how to cope more effectively with interpersonal problems and how to establish more satisfying relationships with their peers? To explore these possibilities some researchers are comparing the social skills and attitudes of delinquent and nondelinquent youth.

There is evidence to suggest that delinquents have fewer interpersonal skills than nondelinquents. In a study of adolescent girls' responses on the Problem Inventory for Adolescent Girls, delinquent girls' answers reflected less competence in handling interpersonal problems than nondelinquents' answers (Gaffney, 1984). In a more extensive study comparing hundreds of adolescents during the 1960s and 1970s, delinquents described themselves as less friendly and less social than nondelinquents. They also reported feeling "strange" when entering a room of new people more often than nondelinquents (Offer, Marohn, & Ostrov,

1979). In a related study, human relationship variables were found to be the most important predictors of self-reported delinquency in a study involving 1,230 youngsters between the ages of 11 and 19 (Truckenmiller, 1982).

It has been suggested that delinquents may be less able to empathize with other people than nondelinquents. Although the data are inconclusive, further investigation may yield helpful information about the moral development of delinquent youth. For example, in one study of 14- and 15-year-olds, delinquents and nondelinquents had similar abilities in being able to assume other people's perspectives. In responding to hypothetical dilemmas on the Defining Issues Test of moral development, the delinquents were as capable of assuming the perspectives of a teacher and a police officer as the nondelinquents (Mullis & Hanson, 1983).

In contrast, another investigation found delinquents to be significantly less empathetic than nondelinquents. Such a finding implies that antisocial or aggressive behavior may be linked to the capacity to empathize with others (Ellis, 1982). Taken together, the two studies might be interpreted to suggest that the ability to assume the perspective of another person does not guarantee that one can be or chooses to be empathetic.

Another question related to delinquents' social skills and attitudes is whether they feel lonelier than nondelinquents. If delinquents have fewer social skills or less ability to empathize with others, it would stand to reason that they would be handicapped in making friends. Having few friends might then create a greater feeling of loneliness among delinquents than among nondelinquents. In order to test this possibility, researchers asked youngsters in a detention facility about loneliness and interpersonal relations (Williams, 1983). The delinquent adolescents expressed no greater feelings of loneliness than nondelinquents, nor was there a significant correlation between how much loneliness they expressed and the types of crimes they had committed. Delinquents with the highest scores on the "need to control others" were, however, lonelier than those with low scores on this dimension of interpersonal relations. Such a finding suggests that the need to dominate other people may indeed undermine some delinquents' popularity in ways that make them feel particularly lonely.

From the available data it appears that we cannnot ignore the possible relationship between deficient social skills and delinquency. While more data are being accumulated, adults could help adolescents who seem to have difficulty making friends or whose social skills seem less mature than those of their peers. As the data in Chapter 9 made clear, the ability to establish and maintain friendships is an important component of adolescent development and presupposes a set of skills that cannot always be assumed to develop without specific counseling or training. Despite the fact that a link between delinquency and social skills has not yet been clearly established, providing adolescents with the skills to make friends, to resolve interpersonal conflicts, and to empathize with others seems a worthwhile endeavor to enrich the lives of both delinquent and nondelinquent youth.

Genetic and Physiological Factors In addition to the sociological and psychological variables that are correlated with delinquency, some researchers contend that genetic and physiological factors predispose certain children to delinquency (Anolik, 1983; Quay, 1975; Schwarz, 1979). This *biosocial* viewpoint assumes that genetic tendencies related to aggressive or criminal behavior can either be exacerabated or diminished by the child's experiences in the family and society. According to this position, both biological and environmental factors contribute to criminal behavior. It is observed that some children are born with a temperament with which their particular family is unable to cope successfully. For example, excessively active and assertive children may have parents who lack the skills for restraining their behavior. In combination with the parents' disciplinary style, these children's genetic inclinations are more likely to result in delinquent behavior than similar genetic dispositions in children whose parents have the skills to control their behavior from an early age.

Biosocial theories derive support from studies showing a relationship between criminal behavior and the functioning of the autonomic nervous system (Mednick & Christiansen, 1977). According to these data, criminals' autonomic nervous systems recover more slowly from environmental stimulation like rewards and punishment. Consequently, the nervous system is seen to undermine the criminals' abilities to alter their behavior through punishment and reinforcement from the environment. Furthermore, the nervous system's slow responsiveness causes such individuals to be less affected by punishment than people with normally functioning nervous systems. For example, their reactions of feeling afraid after punishment are delayed. These data have also shown a higher incidence of nervous-system malfunctioning in the children of criminals, suggesting that the malfunction may be hereditary. Such findings are cited by supporters of the genetic and physiological explanations for criminal behavior.

Although the biosocial approach fails to account for the fact that many delinquents and adult criminals do not have dysfunctional nervous systems, it does challenge the assumption that delinquency is solely related to sociological and psychological factors (Anolik, 1983). To bridge the gap between social and biological views, Quay has developed a theoretical model that integrates both the biosocial and the psychosocial explanations of criminal behavior. According to his typology, delinquents can be divided into three separate types: *socialized-subcultural, unsocialized-psychopathic,* and *disturbed-neurotic* (Quay, 1975).

Each type differs in the extent to which it is influenced by biological factors. The socialized-subcultural delinquent is primarily influenced by such social factors as a dysfunctional family or delinquent peers. In contrast, unsocialized-psychopathic delinquents are unable to control their behavior, primarily as a consequence of biological deficits, such as a hypoactive nervous system. They continue misbehaving even after punishment, because their nervous systems or other physiological dysfunctions prohibit them from responding to rewards and punishments like other people. The disturbed-neurotic delinquents tend to have a combination of problems, which may include mental retardation, attention deficit disorders, and forms of psychotic or neurotic behavior.

On the basis of his typology, Quay suggests that before effective rehabilitation can be designed for delinquents, we must first understand which type of delinquency the youngster is displaying. For example, those suffering from biological deficits seem to benefit most from programs using tangible rewards and punishment that underscore the consequences of behavior. It has, therefore, been recommended that researchers include a diagnosis of the type of delinquency being displayed, so that more accurate appraisals can be made for effective rehabilitation.

Female Delinquency

During the past several decades the rate of female delinquency has been rising steadily. National statistics for 1960 through 1972 show that arrests for major crimes increased 82 percent for adolescent males and 306 pecent for girls (Adler, 1975). Both the official records and adolescents' self-reports confirm the fact that adolescent girls are committing more delinquent acts than in previous decades (Braithwaite, 1981; Gold & Petronio, 1980; Rutter & Giller, 1983). Although adolescents' self-reports show that male and female delinquency resemble each other more closely than has traditionally been acknowledged, boys still commit nearly four times as many delinquent acts as girls (Federal Bureau of Investigation, 1984).

In the past most female delinquents were apprehended for status offenses. A daughter's running away from home and sexual behavior constituted forms of "incorrigibility," which many parents sought the juvenile court's help in controlling. Recent data, however, show girls engaging in more aggressive crimes like theft, vandalism, and drug use—crimes that have traditionally been considered almost the exclusive domain of males (Miller, 1979; Tugend, 1984). Several hypotheses have been offered to explain this rise in female crime and the change in the types of crime that girls are committing.

One body of theoretical literature contends that recent changes in girls' criminal behavior can be attributed to society's less restrictive sex-role expectations (Adler, 1975; Tugend, 1984). According to this view, stereotypically masculine traits like aggressiveness, assertiveness, and independence are more conducive to delinquency than feminine traits like passivity, dependence, and conformity. Unlike girls, many boys supposedly commit delinquent acts in order to bolster their masculinity, particularly if they have reason to believe their peers perceive them as effeminate. In contrast, girls have traditionally been socialized to behave in a feminine manner and have been more carefully supervised, a life pattern that has afforded them fewer opportunities to engage in illegal activities. From this perspective, society's more relaxed sex-role stereotypes have contributed to the rise in female crime and to the increasing similarities between male and female crime. The fact that girls are now being permitted to exhibit more traditionally masculine traits supposedly results in their behaving more like males in terms of their delinquent behavior.

Although this argument has been offered as an explanation for the changes in females' criminal behavior, some empirical research suggests a more complex explanation. In a study of 617 students in grades 8 through 12, researchers compared the types of self-reported delinquency admitted by males and females with their scores on a gender-traits scale (Thornton, 1982). According to the gender-trait hypothesis, the most violent, aggressive offenses like robbery and fighting should be committed by the males and females with the most masculine self-descriptions, while the social violations like illegal drinking and truancy should be perpetrated by the most feminine youngsters. Those with masculine traits should also commit more delinquent acts than those with feminine traits. Contrary to these predictions, masculine and feminine traits were unrelated to the kinds of offenses adolescents committed or to the frequency of their delinquent acts. A slight relationship existed between boys' scores on feminine traits and their admitted thefts, but the relationship between masculinity and aggressive offenses was insignificant for males and females. The researchers concluded that "in general masculine and feminine gender traits do not significantly relate to frequency of delinquency or types of delinquency for males or females" (Thornton, 1982, p. 764).

Another argument offered to explain the recent changes in girls' delinquent behavior relates to the changing attitudes of police and juvenile justice workers. Operating under sex-stereotyped expectations, police and court officials have traditionally perceived female offenders as less likely than males to commit violent, aggressive crimes. While females have traditionally been prosecuted for offenses overlooked in males, like sexual promiscuity, males have been stereotyped as the perpetrators of the most serious crimes. For instance, in an armed robbery with her boyfriend, a girl was more likely to have been viewed as the accomplice than as an equal partner or as the instigator. These preconceived notions would contribute to an overestimation of females' status offenses and an underestimation. of their involvement in serious delinquency. As society's stereotypic notions of masculine and feminine behavior change, there is a greater willingness to perceive the similarities that exist between male and female delinquents.

Rehabilitation

Although many adolescents commit delinquent acts without being apprehended, those who do become involved with the juvenile justice system are sometimes incarcerated along with adult prisoners, and this has caused considerable concern. Those opposed to this practice argue that even housing adolescents temporarily with adult prisoners can lead to suicide, rape, and psychological trauma (Children's Defense Fund, 1976). Representing this viewpoint, one investigation used a nationally representative sample to compare delinquents in adult jails with those in juvenile detention facilities. The suicide rate for adolescents in adult jails was more than 3.5 times as great as that experienced in the general population, while the number of suicides in juvenile detention facilities was lower (Flaherty, 1983).

Unfortunately, most attempts to rehabilitate delinquents have met with minimal success (Braithwaite, 1981; Elliot & Ageton, 1980). The recidivism rates for delinquents have been estimated to be somewhere between 60 and 80 percent (Rutter & Giller, 1983). The most commonly used approaches include counseling, psychotherapy, recreational programs, educational and vocational training, family counseling, and half-way houses. The limited success of these programs can be explained, in part, by the fact that most are instituted only after adolescents have become seriously involved in delinquency, rather than as preventive measures. In addition, a particular technique may have the potential for helping delinquents, but implementation by poorly trained personnel may undermine its success. Nevertheless, despite the fact that the data are often discouraging, several approaches emerge as more successful than others.

To begin with, the available data raise serious questions about the effectiveness of incarceration for rehabilitating delinquents (Prescott, 1981; Rutter & Giller, 1983; Sechrest, White, & Brown, 1979; Wooden, 1976). Incarceration in traditional facilities usually exacerbates delinquents' problems by exposing them to poor role models and subjecting them to traumatic experiences like rape, physical violence, and humiliation. Some studies indicate that when first offenders are given suspended sentences, probation, or stern warnings from police, they are less likely to repeat their offenses than juveniles who are incarcerated (Rutter & Giller, 1983). Unfortunately, many adolescents are incarcerated for minor status offenses. In one national survey of 722 correctional institutions, nearly two-thirds of the females and one-third of the males had been sentenced to confinement for status offenses (Wooden, 1976).

Among the many approaches to rehabilitation, programs based on behavioral learning theories have the highest rates of success with youthful offenders (Blakely & Davidson, 1984; Rutter & Giller, 1983; Sechrest, White, & Brown, 1979). The Achievement Place program exemplifies these principles (Kirigin, 1979). In accord with the principles of behavioral psychology discussed in previous chapters, the adults who operate these half-way houses use reinforcement, punishment, contingency contracting, and token economies to teach adolescents new ways of behaving. For example, for completing household tasks like making beds and getting to meals on time, youths receive tokens. The tokens, as all understand at the outset, can then be cashed in for privileges like going to movies and watching television. By attending school and earning acceptable grades, the youngsters can earn social praise, social privileges, and the right to return to their own families on weekends. The half-way house creates a nurturant atmosphere, while consistently enforcing the prearranged contingencies. The data convincingly demonstrate that delinquents in this program have lower recidivism rates than those in traditional correctional schools.

Another use of behavioral principles is training the parents of delinquents to use contingency management in their homes (Patterson, 1981). Rather than relying on their traditional patterns of physical punishment, yelling, or threatening, these parents learn to use positive and negative reinforcement to control their children's behavior. The programs often involve showing videotapes of appropriate and inappropriate ways of responding to an adolescent's misbehavior. Counselors may also visit the family and record the behaviors of children and parents during the course of a typical meal or during a family discussion.

Although the success of rehabilitation programs for delinquents has been limited, the idea that these youngsters are unmalleable is challenged by data from programs like Achievement Place. As researchers continue to use carefully trained personnel to implement and to supervise the use of behavioral principles with delinquents and their families, the results may create more optimism among those working with young offenders.

RUNAWAYS

Prevalence

According to the National Network of Runaway and Youth Services, more than two million young people run away from home each year. Although nearly 70 percent return home on their own within a week and only about one-fifth travel more than 50 miles from home, these young people can create serious problems in large cities where they tend to congregate (Rosenbaum, 1983). It has been estimated that nearly 30,000 runaway youths roam the streets of New

York City alone (Children's Defense Fund, 1976). Without housing or money, many of these young runaways resort to illegal acts like prostitution, theft, and drug dealing, and so become easy prey for exploitative adults.

Contributing Factors

Runaways are typically categorized as one of three types: those who leave home because of an intolerable family situation, those who leave in quest of adventure, and those who leave as a consequence of problems at school (Roberts, 1982). One of the most extensive classification systems for runaways, suggested by Brennan and his colleagues, is outlined here (Brennan, Huizinga, & Elliot, 1978). "Class I" runaways are neither highly delinquent nor alienated young people. In this category are "middle-class loners," who have good relationships with family and teachers, but have few friends. In contrast, the "peer-oriented" runaways have problems at school, and "overcontrolled escapists" are leaving an unpleasant situation with their parents.

In contrast to these nondelinquent runaways, most "Class II" runaways are delinquent and alienated from their families and teachers (Brennan, Huizinga, & Elliot, 1978). In this category are the "rejected and constrained peer runaways," youngsters who are failures at school and unhappy at home. Although they have friends, most of their peers are delinquents. A second subgroup consists of the "rebellious and constrained middle-class girls," young females who are trying to escape their parents' rejection, marital conflicts, sibling rivalries, or physical abuse. A third subtype, the "normless, rejected, unrestrained" runaways, are usually boys who have poor relationships with their parents and strong bonds to a few friends who are often delinquent. The last group, "pushouts and socially rejected youths," have few friends, are members of dysfunctional families, and have poor academic records.

A distinction does appear to exist between those who run away only once and those who repeatedly run away (Nye & Edelbrock, 1980; Olson et al., 1980; Thornton, 1982). Repeaters tend to be plagued by more personal and social problems, more academic and vocational deficits, and poorer family relationships than those who run away only once. Many who repeatedly run away from home are protecting themselves from sexual or physical abuse. After returning home, these young people often find their problems getting worse. Unlike those who run away once for adventure or to escape a transitory problem, those who repeatedly run away are in need of counseling and intervention to help rectify their problems in family or academic life.

Once runaways have been returned to their families, only a small portion receive help to alleviate the problems that motivated them to leave home (Brennan, Huizinga, & Elliot, 1978; Chase, Crowley, & Weintraub, 1979). Nevertheless, it is possible to intervene in the lives of such young people. Some programs have succeeded in helping former runaways by teaching family members better methods for communicating with one another and by helping runaways improve their social and academic skills. Furthermore, the growing recognition that not all young people run away from home because of conflicts with their parents, poor grades, or low self-esteem will permit programs to be more effectively designed to meet the particular needs of various types of runaways. For instance, it would be inappropriate to focus all programs on the development of better relationships between runaways and their parents, when the data show that perhaps as many as a third of all runaways are well-adjusted adolescents who are merely enacting Huckleberry Finn's dream of independence and adventure (Jorgensen, Thornburg, & Williams, 1980; Orton & Soll, 1980). On the other hand, the desperation exhibited by many young people who leave home without resources for independent survival suggests that, for many runaway youths, family and personal problems seem insurmountable.

SUICIDE

Prevalence and Trends

While some adolescents react to their problems by running away from home, others choose a more drastic measure—suicide. During the last decade there appears to be a dramatic increase in attempted and completed suicides among the adolescent population (Blaine, 1979; Emery, 1983). Among 15- to 19-year-olds the suicide rate in 1950 was between 2.7 and 3.5 suicides per 100,000. By 1977 this figure had risen to 14.2, the highest increase in the suicide rate of any age group except 20- to 24-year-olds. Further, the tendency not to attribute suicidal motives to young adolescents and the desire to spare families public embarrassment result in a number of suicides being officially recorded as "accidents" (Husain & Vandiver, 1984). As a consequence, some analysts estimate that the actual rates of adolescent suicide may be three times as high as the official government statistics, which show that, in 1983 alone, 6,000 young people killed themselves (Tugend, 1984). Some also contend that for every suicide there are ten unsuccessful attempts—most of which remain unreported. And yet, despite the likelihood of underestimating the actual number of suicides, suicide is still the third leading cause of death among adolescents (see Box 14.3).

According to the national centers for disease control, the increase in youth suicide is primarily due to the dramatic changes in the male suicide rate (Tugend, 1984). From 1970 to 1980 the male suicide rate increased by 50 percent, in comparison to a 2 percent rise for females. Almost 90 percent of male suicide victims are white, although there are no significant racial differences among female suicide victims. Because males choose the most violent methods for killing themselves, like shooting and hanging, their suicide attempts are far more successful than females' attempts. In contrast to males, females typically employ methods that are less lethal and more time-consuming, such as trying to poison themselves with pills.

The increasing concern about suicide has resulted partially from a number of apparent "cluster" suicides during recent years (Tugend, 1984). For example, in three of New York's northern suburbs, 36 adolescents killed themselves in 22 months; in a Houston suburb 6 adolescents took their own lives in three months; and in Plano, Texas, seven adolescents committed suicide in one year. Although in some of these incidents the adolescents did not know one another, in others the friendship between the youths suggest that their suicides may have been related. In response to increasing public concern, the national centers for disease control began extensive research on cluster suicides in 1984, a measure that should provide valuable data about this phenomenon. In the meantime, the

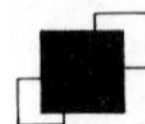

14.3 Adolescent Voices

Mark: An Adolescent's Account of His Attempted Suicide

I was nine years old when I first started drinking, but I didn't get into it seriously till I was twelve. I'm seventeen now. All my troubles started off with my drinking. Things just weren't working out for me, and I'd just take it out on myself with booze. After drinking for a couple of weeks I'd get sick; sometimes I'd end up in the hospital.

I started drinking because both my parents were alcoholics. My mother died when I was six. My father turned into a real alcoholic then. You'd think that seeing such a bad example, I would want to stay away from it; and when I was ten I tried. When I got to be eleven I started back into it, nipping beer off my father and my uncle. Then, when I was twelve, I started getting into trouble. I started fighting and stealing things to drink. That just got me into deeper trouble and it kept on building up.

When I look back I see that I started drinking more or less because I was unhappy, and it was a way to make me feel better. I knew from watching older people that if you were really down, booze could make you feel better. Just before my father passed away he said he didn't want me to drink. I thought about it for a while, then I said that's a bunch of garbage. He went out drinking, why can't I? I just kept repeating to myself, "I'm really alone now," and it got drilled into my skull that I was gonna become a loner. Nobody could tell me what to do. I did my own thing and just kept on going.

When I was about fifteen I made an attempt at suicide by jumping out of a window. I landed in the hospital for that. I remember everything except right after jumping out the window. I split my head open and got twelve stitches across my forehead. I was in the hospital for three weeks, in the psychiatric ward. I really freaked out there. I was kind of mad that I failed. I guess I wanted to be dead with my parents. I thought I'd be happier that way. As an Indian, my view of death or life after death may be different from yours. I really believe that when you die you still live. You come back in a different form. So in suicide I was just ending this life, not all life, so I wasn't afraid to do it.

It wasn't really planned. The night before I was drinking and talking to a friend, and I said I should kill myself because I want to be with my parents. He said that was no way to go about it. So I started to get mad at him and I left. I kept on drinking and I went back to his place that night. I passed out there and started drinking again the next morning. I passed out and got up again and drank some more. That's when I jumped out of the window. It was about nine o'clock I guess. I don't remember getting to the hospital or anything. It's kind of hard to describe what happened in the psychiatric ward. After a couple of days I came back to my mind and wondered why I was there. I was mad because I had failed.

SOURCE: B. Rabkin, *Growing up dead.* Nashville, Tenn.: Abingdon Press, 1979, p. 70.

uncertainty over whether too much publicity contributes to multiple suicides has made researchers proceed cautiously about directing too much public attention to the matter.

Interestingly, the suicidal behavior of adolescents and adults is similar in several respects (Husain & Vandiver, 1984; Weiner, 1980, 1982). Irrespective of age, three times as many males commit suicide as females, but females attempt suicide three times more often than males. There is more suicide among whites than blacks, more in urban than in rural communities, more in higher socioeconomic groups than among the poor, and more among Protestants than among Catholics and Jews. Older adolescents and adults usually kill themselves by hanging or shooting, while younger adolescents and children usually take a drug overdose. Most people who fail in a suicide attempt have taken poisonous drugs, a method that increases the chances that someone will discover them before death occurs.

Although the adolescent suicide rate appears to be rising, it's important to note that official reports show adolescents committing only 6 percent and attempting only 12 percent of the suicides in our society (Weiner, 1980). Despite the apparent rise in adolescent suicides, young people are still far less likely than their elders to opt for this dramatic course.

Contributing Factors

Depression Although many people assume that a clear relationship has been established between suicide and depression, the data suggest otherwise. Many adolescents who kill themselves do manifest symptoms of depression, but this is not always the case, and to assert that depression is the prime cause appears to be overly simplisitic. The preponderance of evidence indicates that a number of other variables seem to have an impact on a person's decision to commit suicide (Emery, 1983; Weiner, 1980, 1982).

Attempts are being made to identify the types of behavior that might be harbingers of a youngster's future suicide attempts (Weiner, 1980, 1982). Some psychologists contend that depression among the young is often overlooked, because we dismiss the symptoms as a normal part of adolescence. For example, in a 1982 survey of 116 adolescent girls from different racial and socioeconomic backgrounds, attending San Francisco's public high schools, 23 percent were moderately to severely depressed as measured by the Beck Depression Inventory; and 39 percent reported occasional thoughts of suicide (Gibbs, 1983). Even among adolescent psychiatric patients, fewer than 20 percent are diagnosed as having problems primarily caused by depression, yet half of these young people manifest symptoms of depression, including behavior such as self-deprecation, crying spells, suicidal thoughts, and experience feelings of sadness, pessimism, and worthlessness (Weiner, 1980). Data like these have led to the suggestion that adults should become more sensitive to adolescents' symptoms of depression.

Yet how are we to recognize the types of depression that might lead to suicide without jumping to false conclusions about youngsters who—like all human beings—occasionally feel sad and disheartened? Indeed, depression can be a perfectly normal yet transitory reaction to negative events in the adolescent's life. To begin with, the type of depression that contributes to suicidal thinking often emanates from a serious loss in the adolescent's life. The loss might be created by incidents like someone's death, parents' divorce, or a breakup with a boyfriend or girlfriend. In addition, feelings of loss can emanate from the loss of self-esteem. Hence, academic failure, social embarrassment, a disfiguring accident, or a serious illness can contribute to suicidal thinking (Husain & Vandiver, 1984; Weiner, 1980). Furthermore, chronic depression during adolescence tends to be characterized by excessive self-criticism, feelings of powerlessness, inexplicable crying spells, and feelings of hopelessness about the future (Chartier & Ranieri, 1984).

Not all adolescents manifest their depression in the same way. Many will be persistently tired, behave like hypochondriacs, or have problems concentrating at school. In their efforts to escape depressing thoughts, depressed youngsters sometimes become engaged in the quest for continual stimulation and entertainment. They appear excessively restless and become easily bored. They tire quickly of new activities and of former friends, searching for more entertaining substitutes. Still others withdraw into solitary activities, where they need not fear human rejection. Older adolescents often express depression through delinquency, drug abuse, sexual promiscuity, and rebellious behavior at home and at school. A few attempt to cope with depression by joining groups that attract attention to themselves for their unconventional values.

In sum, behavior that is symptomatic of depression distinguishes itself in three ways from the aggressive or impetuous behavior that almost all adolescents occasionally manifest (Weiner, 1980). First, the depressed adolescent misbehaves in ways that almost assure being observed and apprehended. Second, the behavior marks a dramatic change from the youngster's former conduct. And third, the behavior can usually be linked to a specific loss in the young person's life.

Unrealistic Conceptions of Death It has also been suggested that adolescents with unrealistic conceptions about death are prone to suicidal thoughts (Husain & Vandiver, 1984; McKenry, Tishler, & Christman, 1980). According to this view, the cognitive limitations of early adolescence can distort young people's understanding of death. In our culture, where death is often presented in euphemistic, vague, or exaggerated terms, the realities of death are too often hidden from the young. The melodramatic or emotionless portrayals of death in the media often sustain the image that suicide is an instructive act that can teach one's enemies and careless loved ones a lesson.

The argument has also been offered that rock stars can create a glamour about death that appeals to the young (Holinger, 1978). Record albums and stage shows sometimes depict mock hangings and suicidal gestures in an effort to entice the audience. Such acts might create genuine confusion among young adolescents, whose views of fantasy and reality may be influenced by the drama of stage lights and illusive images on photo albums. Although the relationship between suicide and our society's portrayals of death in the media or in the entertainment world is still uncertain, the assistant chief of the National Centers for Disease Control states that "there is evidence that possibly people imitate suicides they view on television or through other media sources" (Tugend, 1984, p. 12)

Several studies confirm the hypothesis that suicidal youths tend to engage in wishful, "magical thinking" about death (Husain & Vandiver, 1984; Rabkin, 1979). These unrealistic thoughts about death reflect the limitations of children's cognitive development, which include egocentric thinking, the imaginary audience, and the personal fable, as cogently described by Piaget and Elkind. For example, a disproportionate number of suicidal youths have been found to believe in reincarnation and to believe that they will remain cognitively aware of events on earth after they die. Adolescents whose suicide attempts failed have explained that they imagined how good it would feel to observe the effects of their act on those here on earth. Some imagined that their suicides would radically transform the world or would cause their lovers who rejected them to feel forever guilty. Suicide is sometimes envisioned as a chance to be reunited with a deceased loved one. Conceiving of death as an escape from problems rather than as a permanent end to life, suicidal youths tend to differ from nonsuicidal children in their belief that death is temporary.

Societal Factors Does living in a highly technological, competitive society contribute to adolescent suicide? According to some cross-cultural data, yes (McArnarney, 1979). In societies with a high degree of what has been called "anomie," suicide rates are higher than in countries with low anomie. **Anomie** is a condition that manifests itself as a feeling of alienation and detachment from other individuals and from society. Anomie is said to arise in situations where personal bonds are discouraged. Societies with the most anomie are those that stress such values as competitiveness, mobility, rapid change, and materialism at the expense of family intimacy and dedication to interpersonal relationships. According to cross-cultural comparisons, adolescents in highly industrialized, modern countries like Japan and the United States commit suicide more often than those in more rural, religious, and traditional countries. Such suicides are thought to occur partly in response to adolescents' feelings of culture-induced anomie.

It has also been suggested that modern society creates feelings of anomie and insecurity in adolescents through overemphasizing competition and financial success (Husain & Vandiver, 1984). In a society where self-esteem and social status are often derived through money, many adolescents grow up under the pressure of having to be "number one" in social, athletic, and academic pursuits. Pressured on the homefront to succeed, young people may feel overwhelmed by the economic instability, high mobility, competitiveness, and rapid change operative in our technological society. Feeling powerless and lonely in the midst of these pressures, some youngsters may feel so overwhelmed that they opt for suicide.

In support of this argument, data regarding the suicide rates of American Indian youths are particularly instructive (Berlin, 1984). Reported suicides among Native American youths have increased by almost 1000 percent during the past two decades, becoming the second leading cause of death in the 10- to 20-year-old age group. Environmental factors contributing to the suicide escalation include a breakdown of tribal tradition, the increasing incidence of divorce, and a decline in the importance of religion. As Indian communities have become more acculturated, the factors contributing to the feeling known as anomie have grown. In support of this analysis, it has been noted that the lowest suicide rates exist in tribes with the most traditional customs and in areas where opportunities for employment and education exist within the tribal community.

Sex-Role Stereotypes Because three times as many females of every age attempt suicide than do males and use less lethal methods in their attempts, it has been suggested that gender stereotypes may be influencing suicidal behavior (Husain & Vandiver, 1984). According to this view, society offers males certain outlets for expressing their aggression and frustration that are typically denied to females. For example, disobedience to elders, sexual promiscuity, and physical aggression are generally condemned more severely in females than in males. Girls tend to learn to turn their hostile feelings inward rather than to express them overtly. This anger directed toward the self contributes to suicidal thinking. Although the reasons underlying the higher rate of suicide attempts among the female population are debatable, girls are clearly at a higher risk than boys. Recognizing this, special attention might be directed toward adolescent girls who manifest symptoms of depression.

Family Factors Among the variables associated with adolescent suicide a number are related to the adolescent's family (Husain & Vandiver, 1984; Weiner, 1980). It appears that drug abuse, marital discord, and physical abuse are more common in the families of suicidal than nonsuicidal youths. Suicidal youth often report feeling unloved and unwanted, suggesting that their parents have been unable to create an accepting, loving atmosphere in the home. Many suicidal children also report that their parents are excessively critical and have high expectations in regard to vocational and academic goals.

Preventing Adolescent Suicide

Some states are assuming legislative initiative in suicide prevention programs (Folkenberg, 1984; Tugend, 1984). In 1984 California and Florida enacted state laws requiring suicide prevention programs in high schools. The programs are aimed at teaching students to recognize suicidal tendencies in themselves and in their friends and to seek help when suicidal thoughts occur (see Box 14.4). Given the stigma attached to the word "suicide," some schools are presenting the information under the guise of "student-stress" programs. Brochures are also being provided for parents and teachers. The Florida law further requires that to be eligible for teacher certification, college graduates must receive suicide prevention training in order to recognize the signs of depression and stress in their students: "We have cases where an English teacher would grade an essay by a student on suicide and return it corrected for grammar" (Tugend, 1984, p. 12).

Recognizing the need for more data to aid in suicide prevention and rehabilitation, the National Centers for Disease Control and the National Institutes of Mental Health instituted suicide research programs in the early 1980s (Tugend, 1984). Through these federally funded programs studies are being conducted on the possible genetic, biological, and family causes of suicide. Since children who come from a family where a suicide has been committed are six times as likely to kill themselves than are other young people, researchers are simultaneously examining genetic data and investigating the interpersonal interactions within these families. In addition, researchers are continuing to examine the relationship between suicide and the body's chemicals. For example, low levels of the brain chemical, serotonin, have been correlated with aggressive, impulsive behavior. Since males almost always have less serotonin than females, this finding suggests a possible link between the high attempted-suicide rate of females and chemically related impulsivity. Such data should eventually yield a clearer profile of suicidal youth and provide a sounder basis for prevention and treatment.

A Closer Look 14.4 

Possible Harbingers of Adolescents' Suicidal Behavior

Experts advise that adults be aware of the situations and behavior that often indicate depression leading to adolescent suicide:

- Changes in eating or sleeping habits
- Increasing isolation from friends and family
- Behaving more aggressively or more beligerently
- Giving away valued possessions or making comments about "getting my life in order"
- Talking or asking questions about suicide
- A sudden interest in religion and an afterlife
- Experiencing recent losses: a parent's divorce, breaking up with a boyfriend or girlfriend, the death of a friend or relative, a personal injury or chronic illness, the death of a pet
- Making lower grades at school
- Complaining often about being tired
- Expressing excessive concern over physical health (hypochondria)
- Breakdowns in communication with parents or other important people
- A history of repeated "accidents"
- Truancy, delinquency, drug abuse, or sexual permissiveness
- Appearing excessively bored, restless, and hyperactive
- Verbalizing feelings of helplessness: "It just doesn't matter any more what I do"
- Expressing excessive shame or guilt

SOURCES: G. Blaine, *Is adolescent suicide preventable?* Chicago: American Association of Adolescent Psychiatry, 1979; S. Husain & T. Vandiver, *Suicide in children and adolescents.* New York: SP Medical and Scientific Books, 1984; P. McKenry, C. Tishler, & K. Christman, Adolescent suicide and the classroom teacher. *Journal of School Health,* 1980, *50,* 130–132.

From the available data it appears that depression, misconceptions about death, a sense of anomie, family factors, and sex-role influences contribute to suicidal thoughts, but two important caveats must be issued. First, although crises like losing a job, having a violent fight with a parent, or getting pregnant may appear to account for a suicide, a single incident is seldom the primary motivator. We must take careful note of Weiner's summary of the literature:

> A common myth about adolescent suicide attempts holds that they are shallow, histrionic and impulsive reactions to immediate distress, such as failing an examination or breaking up with a boyfriend or girlfriend. Although current disappointments and frustrations may be the last straw in precipitating a suicide attempt, suicidal behavior has been conclusively demonstrated to have more complex origins than these. Adolescents who attempt suicide have typ-

> ically been wrestling for some time with conflicts and concerns that they cannot resolve. Usually they have experienced increasing family instability and discord during this time, so that they have felt alienated from their parents and unable to turn to them for support (Weiner, 1980, p. 458).

A second caveat is that researchers do not agree that suicides could be prevented if only someone had taken heed of the youngster's cries for help. Some psychologists who have worked with suicidal youths feel that suicide is not clearly enough related to depression to permit us to identify suicide-prone adolescents: "In my experience, most suicides in adolescents come totally out of the blue" (Blaine, 1979). A similar view is echoed by those who have reviewed the research or who have worked with suicidal youths and have concluded either that many adolescents give no warning before their suicide or that their symptoms are too imperceptible to cause adults much alarm (Husain & Vandiver, 1984). Before hastily concluding that all suicides could be avoided if only some adult would notice the adolescent's cues, it's important to attend to the controversy surrounding this issue among the experts.

EATING DISORDERS

Anorexia Nervosa

During the early 1980s incidents like the death of singer Karen Carpenter directed more public attention toward the life-threatening psychological disorder known as **anorexia nervosa.** Researchers, however, had been studying the etiology and examining the characteristics of anorexia nervosa long before that (Bruch, 1978; Bryant & Bates, 1985; Garfinkle & Garner, 1982; Gilbert & Deblassie, 1984). Thus we know that although some males are anorexic, the incidence of anorexia is ten times as great among females. Furthermore, because the disease almost always develops during adolescence, it assumes a particular relevance to those adults working with high-school and college students.

With regard to the characteristic patterns of behavior associated with the disorder, it is well established that girls afflicted with anorexia nervosa are engaged in an endless effort to lose weight, despite their emaciated appearance and the possibility of death by starvation. Anorexics begin dieting for the same reasons as do many other adolescent girls who feel—rightly or wrongly—that they are overweight by our culture's standards of beauty. The anorexic's desire to lose weight, however, becomes secondary to her need to feel a sense of mastery and control over her life by depriving her body of food. As the anorexic's body loses it vital supplies of adipose tissue, the signs of starvation become apparent: loss of hair, amenorrhea, disturbed sleeping patterns, constipation, cold chills, scaly skin, bloating, nausea, irritability, and lethargy.

In its initial stages, anorexia may go unnoticed, since the girl merely appears to be dieting, as are so many females in our society. The anorexic typically begins her regime by limiting her food intake, and often continues to restrict her intake until she is eating as few as 600 calories a day before anyone notices her behavior. By this time she may already have resorted to other forms of restricting her calories: regurgitating or taking laxatives after eating, consuming large quanti-

How do you feel about your own weight? How has society influenced the standards of beauty by which you judge other people and yourself?

ties of appetitie suppressants and amphetamines to maintain energy without food, or drinking large quantities of water to make the stomach feel full and to suppress sensations of hunger. Many anorexics alternate between dieting and binging—the condition known as bulimia—and others become religiously dedicated to strenuous daily exercise.

In spite of protestations from other people and her emaciated appearance, the anorexic continues to insist that she is too fat. Having lost her perspective on reality, she either denies that she has lost too much weight or insists that one particular part of her body is still too fat. She remains in a state of constant dissatisfaction with her appearance. When she submits to her need for food, the anorexic chastises herself for lacking self-discipline.

Among other hypotheses, it has been suggested that anorexia is at least partially a response to our society's notions regarding thinness and beauty. While it may be an exaggeration that in our society "a girl can never be too thin or too rich,'' it is nonetheless true that many females grow up with erroneous images of the ''normal'' amount of fat on women's bodies. As the data in Chapter 2 demonstrated, most adolescent girls perceive themselves as fat even when their weight is well within the normal range for their skeletal structure and age. Basing their self-esteem on the assumption that a thin body is socially desirable, many girls develop the kinds of attitudes that make them susceptible to anorexic behavior. For example, in a study of 100 sixth- and seventh-grade girls, only half correctly estimated their weight. Moreover, both the girls who underestimated and those who overestimated their weight reported more depression and a poorer self-concept (Forehand & Faust, 1985).

Data also suggest that anorexics are most likely to come from upper-middle-class white families, in which parents overemphasize perfection and self-control. Anorexics are typically excellent students who have presented no difficulties for their parents or teachers before the onset of the disorder. Intent on pleasing others, these girls bind their identifies in overly dependent ways to their parents and to other people. The anorexic's parents are often overly protective people who are threatened by the idea of their daughter becoming too independent. Consequently, as a way of coping with their tense relationships at home, anorexics may resort to excessive dieting in order to gain control over what appears to them to be a chaotic existence. For the anorexic, thinness is perceived as the solution to her problems at home or with friends.

Anorexia has also been viewed as a response to depression and to the sexual pressures that increase during adolescence. Symptoms tend to appear with the onset of puberty and to be related to physiological changes that make a girl increasingly aware of the sexual expectations and conflicts now confronting her (Romeo, 1984). Moreover, given the apparent etiology of the disorder, it is not surprising to find that anorexics often manifest symptoms of depression. For example, a study of 42 anorexic patients and four control groups showed a strong positive correlation between the female adolescents' scores on the Beck Depression Inventory and the Anorexia Scale of the State of Mind questionnaire. Whether the depression is present before the onset of anorexia, however, cannot be ascertained from this study (Piazza, 1983).

Bulimia

A disorder closely allied in many instances with anorexia nervosa is **bulimia**—binge eating (Garfinkle & Garner, 1982; Gormally, 1984; Hamilton, Gelwick, & Meade, 1984). Although the literature has typically treated bulimia and anorexia as facets of the same disorder, the American Psychiatric Association officially designated bulimia as a separate psychiatric disorder in the 1980 Diagnostic and Statistical Manual of Mental Disorders, the **DSM III:** ''The essential features are episodic binge eating accompanied by an awareness that the eating pattern is abnormal, fear of not being able to stop eating voluntarily, and depressed mood and self-deprecating thoughts following the eating binges. The bulimic episodes are not due to anorexia nervosa or any known physical disorder'' (American Psychiatric Association, 1980, p. 69). In addition, recent research demonstrates that bulimia is not limited to the college population or to white females. For example, a survey of 1093 high-school girls showed almost 17 percent of the whites and 17 percent of the blacks to be bulimic (VanThorre & Vogel, 1985).

In order to be clinically diagnosed as bulimic, the adolescent must meet three of the following criteria: (1) consumption of high caloric, easily ingested food during a binge; (2) inconspicuous eating during a binge; (3) termination of such eating episodes by abdominal pain, sleep, social interruption, or self-induced vomiting; (4) repeated attempts to lose weight by severely restrictive diets, self-induced vomiting, or use of cathartics or diuretics; (5) frequent weight fluctuations greater than ten pounds due to alternating binges and fasts (American Psychiatric Association, 1980).

Some adolescents with bulimia are overweight, but others are anorexic. To recognize the presence of both sets of symptoms, researchers refer to adolescents with symptoms of both disorders as *bulimarexic*. Characteristically, bulimarexics alternately binge and purge themselves of food through the use of laxatives or self-induced vomiting. To distinguish the bulimic patient from the anorexic, researchers have developed self-report instruments. Consequently, it is possible, using instruments such as the Eating Attitudes Test **(EAT)** and the Binge Scale, to identify the distinctions between adolescent anorexics with and without bulimia (Hamilton, Gelwick, & Meade, 1984). Those who are bulimic as well as anorexic tend to have the most distorted body images, the most bizarre notions about food and bodily processes, and the most complicated illness. Most bulimic anorexics manifest more serious affective disturbances, abuse drugs more often, and have more suicidal thoughts than nonbulimic anorexics. Although not all researchers have found these differences, most studies suggest that bulimic anorexics have a more serious disorder and a poorer prognosis than nonbulimic anorexics.

Little information exists concerning the etiology of bulimia, since it has not traditionally been studied as a separate disorder from anorexia (Hamilton, Gelwick, & Meade, 1984). There is some preliminary evidence that compulsive eating is a neurological disorder that can be treated with anticonvulsant drugs. Furthermore, it appears that bulimia most often affects females whose self-image is poor and whose culture overemphasizes the importance of thinness, and anecdotal and research data suggest that girls in late adolescence and in their early twenties are at the greatest risk of developing bulimia. Estimates are that 1 or 2 percent of college-age women clearly fit the diagnostic criteria for bulimia, although as many as 10 percent on some college campuses express attitudes on questionnaires that are similar to those of anorexics and bulimics. Finally, it is worth noting that although the relationship between bulimia and anorexia is still unclear, it appears that about 25 percent of all anorexics are also bulimics (Hamilton, Gelwick, & Meade, 1984).

Rehabilitation and Prevention

Behavioral scientists have suggested three different approaches to understanding the etiology of both anorexia nervosa and bulimia: the physiological model, the social learning model, and the psychodynamic model. Each offers its own insights into devising preventive and rehabilitative programs for adolescents afflicted with these two eating disorders (Bruch, 1978; Gormally, 1984).

According to the physiological approach, adolescents with anorexia or bulimia might be suffering from certain forms of chemical or physical imbalances. It is believed, moreover, that such imbalances are partially correctible through drug therapy. For example, some bulimics have been helped through treatment with anticonvulsant drugs. Although chemical intervention is ineffective in resolving the psychological problems underlying adolescents' eating disorders, the possible physiological bases for anorexia and bulimia merit careful attention.

The social learning view contends that eating disorders are closely allied with our society's attitudes about beauty and thinness and with a family's methods of resolving problems. Therapy based on social learning theories teaches bulimics and anorexics the principles of behavior modification and applies these principles to control dieting, binging, and purging. Through the use of behavioral techniques such as reinforcement, punishment, and modeling, these programs teach girls to institute healthy patterns of eating and exercising, as well as to modify their views about thinness and beauty.

Although the principles of behavior modification and social learning theory can help anorexic and bulimic girls establish healthier eating habits, these methods do not address the causes underlying the disorder. Consequently, psychodynamic therapy or forms of family therapy that examine the girl's relationships with other people and her self-concept are often critical, if the adolescent and her family are to understand anorexia and bulimia. Therapy with the families of bulimics and anorexics has helped alleviate some of the tensions that may underlie the disorder. By teaching adolescents ways to enhance self-esteem and express anger other than through overeating, purging, or dieting, counselors have helped some young women overcome their eating disorders. Rather than using food to cope with tension and anger, these young women learn to express their feelings, avoid anxiety-producing situations, or seek reinforcement through other media.

In sum, it appears that the most fruitful way to help adolescents with eating disorders is a combination of the physiological, social learning, and psychodynamic approaches (Bruch, 1978; Wilson, 1984).

Coping with Death and Dying

Adolescence is a period associated with liveliness and longevity—a period during which death and dying are not assumed to be spectres on the immediate horizon. Yet, such visions of adolescent bliss do not represent the experiences of thousands of adolescents in our society for whom death or dying have become immediate realities. Whether a consequence of physical illnesses such as cancer, or car accidents, or murder, or suicide, thousands of adolescents die each year, leaving the bereaved to cope with the pain and shock of a young person's death. In addition, thousands of adolescents each year confront death through the loss of a parent, sibling, or friend—deaths sometimes accompanied by a violence and a poignancy as dramatic as the fatal shooting of Benjamin Wilson, described in Box 14.5. Moreover, given the advances in modern medicine that can prolong life in cases of terminal illness, thousands of young people confront the possibility of their own death in their daily battles against diseases like cancer and sickle-cell anemia. Yet despite these realities, a perusal of the table of contents in adolescent psychology texts, an assessment of our television programs, and a cursory review of our daily conversations collectively demonstrate our profound discomfort with the topics of death and dying.

Although we are quick to applaud those who work on oncology wards and to praise parents with terminally ill children, most of us are far from willing to read about or to discuss the realities of death. Our awkwardness around the terminally ill, our unwillingness to candidly answer children's questions about death, and our discomfort with a person whose loved one has recently died attest to our society's tradition of avoiding topics related to death whenever possible. Unfortunately, this attitude too often leaves us unequipped to respond to adolescents and their families who have had to confront the inescapable realities of death.

Dimensions of Bereavement

In her provocative books on death and dying, Dr. Elizabeth Kübler-Ross criticizes our attitudes toward those who are dying and to their survivors (Kübler-Ross, 1969, 1983). On the basis of her work with dying patients and their families, Kübler-Ross has identified stages that both the dying and their loved ones undergo: denial, anger, bargaining, depression, and acceptance. As Box 14.5 illustrates, adolescents' reactions to a parent's death poignantly demonstrate these stages of grieving (Krementz, 1982; Kübler-Ross, 1983).

From her own work with children and adolescents dying of terminal illnesses and those who commit suicide, Kübler-Ross discusses a number of provocative questions:

> How are children different from adults when faced with terminal illness? Do little ones also go through the five stages of dying? Are they aware of their impending death even if parents or hospital staff do not mention the seriousness of the terminal illness? What is their concept of death at different ages, the nature of their unfinished business? How can we best help them and their parents, grandparents and siblings during this time of parting? (Kübler-Ross, 1983, p. xviii).

During the period of bereavement, honest communication can be especially beneficial to members of the family. Although feelings like anger and guilt are often difficult to express, sharing them can prevent more serious depression and greater disruption within the family (Kübler-Ross, 1969, 1983; Turkington, 1984). For example, in some families a deceased sibling is portrayed by parents as the "perfect" child, thereby creating a sense of jealousy, anger, guilt, and confusion in the surviving children. Or if one child has a terminal illness, the other siblings may need help working through their feelings of jealousy and resentment over the inordinate amounts of attention bestowed upon a victim of a long-term illness.

In the case of a parent with a terminal illness, it can sometimes be useful for children to express their anger, fear, or sadness in the presence of the parent before he or she dies, as a way of diminishing the children's future feelings of guilt or anger. Given the upheaval created by death, it is perhaps not surprising that between 70 percent and 90 percent of all couples separate or divorce after the death of a child (Turkington, 1984). Bereaved adolescents and adults also become more susceptible to alcohol and drug abuse in an attempt to cope with their sadness, guilt, and anger (Kübler-Ross, 1983).

14.5 A Closer Look

Chicago High School Star Dies Following Shooting.

Benjamin Wilson, considered to be one of the finest high school basketball prospects in the country, died today after being shot Tuesday in a sidewalk altercation with some teen-agers near his school. He never regained consciousness.

Wilson, a 17-year-old senior at Neal F. Simeon Vocational High School on the city's Southwest side, was a power forward on a team that won the 1984 Illionis state championship last March, and seemed headed for glory again this season.

The 6-foot-8 senior, who was described by Principal Ned L. McCray as "a good student, not a dumb athlete," was a B student and an all-around player already heavily recruited by a number of major colleges. Wilson's death plunged the 1,889-student school into gloom, and hundreds wept, moaned, and shouted with grief during a morning-long memorial service in the gym today. His teammates were not allowed to attend because their coach feared they might become too upset.

The shooting occurred Tuesday afternoon, as Wilson was accompanying his girlfriend and another girl on a walk in the neighborhood during lunch hour. Although not married to her, Wilson had fathered a 2-month-old son by the girl, according to his school friends. School officials refused to comment on his relationship with the young woman.

The Simeon students were confronted on a sidewalk by a trio of teenage boys from another school. According to police, who gathered numerous eyewitness accounts, Wilson reportedly "bumped into" the trio, then apologized.

Instead of accepting his apology, one of the trio pulled a pistol and shot him twice. One bullet struck and destroyed his liver, and the other severed a major abdominal artery. The three fled as Wilson slumped against a fence.

He was taken by ambulance to St. Bernard Hospital nearby, and doctors worked for more than five hours to save his life. As the surgery proceeded, friends and students crowded hospital corridors, holding an impromptu prayer vigil. Others gathered outside and waited through the cold night. Because of massive bleeding, Wilson required two complete full-body transfusions. But hospital officials said the victim had arrived

Although it is often presumed that friends help the bereaved through their grief, the reality often falls short of this expectation. Both adolescents and adults have explained that some friends avoided them during their period of mourning and that others, although well-intentioned, worsened matters considerably (Krementz, 1982; Kübler-Ross, 1969, 1983). Because most of us feel uncomfortable about death, we act in ways that exacerbate the bereaved's feelings of loneliness, anger, or guilt. Not knowing how to behave, we too often avoid any topic even remotely related to the death or take the opposite tack by dwelling incessantly on the topic. In the words of one adolescent whose father had died, "I guess my friends didn't know what to say because they felt kind of embarrassed, so they'd just look at me and no one would say hello. But it got to be a little too much—

with no pulse and their efforts to save him failed. He was pronounced dead at 6 A.M. today.

The shooting captured headlines here and across the country. An aroused and saddened City Council demanded a crackdown against teen-age gangs, which plague many Chicago neighborhoods, including the middle-class residential area around Simeon. McCray, the Simeon principal, described his school as "an oasis, an island in a sea of troubled water. People can be accosted leaving the oasis, as Ben was."

Two youths, one 15, and one 16, were arrested and held without bond in the killing. They were identified as William Moore and Omar Dixon, students at Calumet High School and cousins. They were charged with murder and attempted armed robbery and will be tried as adults. Police have recovered a 22-caliber pistol that they identify as the weapon used in the slaying.

The third youth who was present has not been charged and is said by police to have turned state's evidence and already has testified before a Cook County grand jury.

Under state law, the two suspects cannot get the death penalty because of their age. A grandparent of each suspect contacted today said both were innocent.

Wilson, who shaved his head as a trademark, was rated the nation's No. 1 high school basketball player last summer after showcasing his talents at a summer camp at the Athletes for Better Education Camp at Princeton, N.J. His emergence on the national high school scene propelled Simeon to a top ranking in several national preseason polls. Wilson had the versatility to play guard or center as well as forward. He averaged 20 points a game and shot 75 percent last year.

"I thought he was the best player in the country," said De Paul's Joey Meyer, who had been intensively recruiting Wilson.

The Simeon team tonight was headed for Rockford, Ill., 90 miles west of Chicago, for a tournament. Simeon's opponent tonight was Evanston Township High School on a rematch of last year's Class AA state tournament final. In that game, Simeon beat Evanston, 53–47. Tonight, Simeon won, 71–52.

SOURCE: K. Klose, *Washington Post*, November 22, 1984. Reprinted by permission.

like no one would say the word 'father' in front of me. So I finally transferred to a different school" (Krementz, 1982, p. 92). The most supportive friends somehow manage to achieve a delicate balance between a willingness to discuss the death and an eagnerness not to condescend or to pity.

The grieving process is especially difficult for young people who have witnessed a murder or for those who have known a victim of murder (Turkington, 1984). For youngsters in either of these positions the process of bereavement often includes feelings of revenge and anger toward the murderer or toward police who seem indifferent about apprehending the murderer. Although the data have been relatively scanty on the grief responses of children after witnessing or learning of a murder of a loved one, the existing data show that rage often overshadows expressions of sadness. A child whose loved one or friend has been murdered often regresses to bedwetting, aggression, and other forms of childish behavior. Violent deaths also leave the bereaved with the depressing conviction that society is an orderless, chaotic, and frightening place in which to live.

Although Kübler-Ross is the most renowned researcher on the topic of death and dying, others are beginning to gather empirical data as well. One example is a study of 33 white middle-class adolescents whose siblings had died. The researcher found that 17- and 19-year-olds felt angrier about their siblings' death than the 14- to 16-year-olds. Adolescents from the most cohesive families experienced shock, numbness, loneliness, and fear when their siblings died, while those from less cohesive families tended to feel guilty and angry. Following their siblings' death, almost all the adolescents suffered academically at school (Balk, 1982). Although virtually nonexistent in present research, data like these will hopefully contribute to our quest to help the young and ourselves cope more effectively with death and dying.

The growing concern currently focused on young people who have experienced a death has provoked the attention of a number of psychologists (Turkington, 1984). The existing data about dying and bereavement rely primarily on retrospective reports gathered from the bereaved years after the death of a friend or loved one. While of some value, such retrospective reports are flawed by the methodological problems that plague all retrospective data, such as inaccurate memory. Gathering data from those who are undergoing the process of dying or bereavement will generate a more accurate understanding of these experiences. In addition, data concerning the nature of the relationship between the sex and age of the deceased and the sex and age of survivors will also enhance our knowledge about grieving and help us recognize the forms of pathologic mourning that require assistance from professional counselors.

Death Education

With our society's disquieting discomfort with topics related to death and dying, a number of educators besides Elizabeth Kübler-Ross are urging us to educate children about death and dying from an early age (Turkington, 1984). Authors are now writing books on topics related to death in an effort to help parents explain death to young children (Klas, 1979; Wass & Coor, 1984). Books are also available for adolescents on topics such as a parent's death, funerals, terminal illness, and suicide (Krementz, 1982; Kushner, 1981; Rabkin, 1979; Kübler-Ross, 1983). Some books not only provide information about topics like decomposition but also tackle the kinds of philosophical questions reflected in the title of the best-seller *When Bad Things Happen to Good People* written by a rabbi about his son's death (Kushner, 1981). It has been suggested that high schools implement courses in death education, which will help students ask questions about death and dying in an atmosphere that is both sensitive and objective (Schvaneveldt, 1982).

One of the most impressive and controversial attempts to educate children about death was the 1984–1985 exhibit at the Boston Children's Museum—Endings: An Exhibit about Death and Loss ("Children Learn That Dying Isn't a Vacation," 1984; Weld, 1984). The first of its kind, the exhibit taught children about death through experiences like touching a tombstone, looking into a coffin, hear-

Was the Boston Children's Museum's exhibit, "Endings," an appropriate medium through which to introduce young people to the topics of death and dying? Would you have attended a similar exhibit in your own community? Why or why not?

ing funeral music from around the world, and watching a speeded-up videotape of a dead mouse's body being eaten by insects, with a sign saying "Everything that is alive now will die, decompose and return to life." Also on display were the chemicals used to embalm bodies, burial clothes, and signs asking questions like "Do you remember the death or birth of anyone in your family?" and "Were you named for someone who died?"

One goal of the exhibit was to help children understand the difference between fantasies and realities about death. On one videotape children viewed a director and actor enacting a death scene replete with fake blood and ending with "Ok, cut, that's a take." Another videotape showed live scenes from the fighting in Lebanon and concluded with the narrator's comment "Sometimes it's hard to tell the difference between what's real and what isn't." As a general theme, the exhibit tried to dispel children's myths about death. One puppet in a videotaped show says "Dying isn't a vacation. It's not like going to visit your grandmother. You don't come back again." And in a story about a grandfather's death, the script concludes with the boy's admission, "I still miss him."

The youngest children at the exhibit tended to spend time with their parents mastering the differences between "living" and "dead." Older children and adolescents spent most of their time on the more advanced sections of the exhibit. Janet Kamien, the exhibit's creator, hopes the experience will provide children and their parents with a reference point from which they can discuss death with one another. The exhibit elicited mixed reactions from parents: "How dare you present this topic in a children's museum!" "Thank you so much for being brave and courageous enough to do this." And mixed reactions from children: "I hate thinking about death." "I like this exhibit because I love my grandmother dearly and the doctor said she might die and I don't want her to, so this makes it a littler easier." It is estimated that nearly 450,000 visitors viewed the show before it closed in June 1985 (Weld, 1984).

According to Kübler-Ross and others who share her views, children and adolescents should be allowed to participate in funerals, to relate to dying parents and siblings, and to have the facts about death and dying from which society typically shields us (Kübler-Ross, 1983; Turkington, 1984). After a death each family member, including very young children, should be allowed to say their private farewells to the deceased. This may sometimes mean rocking, singing to, or bathing and dressing the body before it is removed from the home.

Opponents of this view argue that adolescents and children should be shielded from the unpleasantnesses associated with death, because they are incapable of coping with such distress. In response, Kübler Ross and her supporters argue that adolescents and children would be better equipped to cope with their own death and the deaths of loved ones if given honest information and if included in conversations and events related to death and dying. Without information young people are more likely to respond to death by denial, aggression, withdrawal, and other self-destructive means of grieving.

In coming to terms with their own deaths, some terminally ill adolescents have prepared their own wills and have helped make arrangements for their own funerals (Kübler-Ross, 1983). Adolescents seem to be particularly interested in deciding how they are to be dressed, what music will be played and who will be speaking during the service. In some families an older sibling has occasionally asked to help plan the funeral for a younger brother or sister who has died. Conversations and preparations of this sort require an accepting, communicative family, in which parents and children have somehow come to terms with the impending death.

Those who advocate a more open attitude and a more formal system of instruction about death contend that adults who have difficulty facing the reality of death cannot offer much guidance or comfort to grieving children. If we adults were more willing to come to terms with our own dying and the deaths of those we love, we could offer better care and advice to the young. Under such conditions, adolescents would be more willing to share their grief in all its forms—including anger and suicidal thoughts—with adults who could discuss their own feelings about the dead and dying (see Boxes 14.6 and 14.7).

CHRONICALLY ILL ADOLESCENTS

In addition to the legal and emotional problems surrounding adolescents who are terminally ill or critically injured, thousands of families are coping with the difficulties associated with an adolescent's chronic illness. Directing their attention to these adolescents and their families, researchers and physicians have offered suggestions for ameliorating some of the physical and emotional

Adolescent Voices 14.6

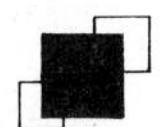

Two Adolescent Boys' Reactions to Their Mothers' Deaths

First Boy:

Shortly after my mother died, I wrote down my feelings and felt much better.

What Am I: I Am My Mother's Spirit

I am my mother's slow-moving footsteps as she walks down to the hospital to get her cancer check-up, her utter despair as she finds the results, and her trouble in finding the words to tell Dad. I am the slow and reluctant boy who takes a couple of Mom's things to the hospital where she will stay before the operation. I am Mother's loneliness in her hospital bed as she patiently awaits Father's next visit. I am her joy to find us with him as he walks near her bed, her curiosity to learn of the day's events, and her sorrow as a very short visiting period ends. I am my mother's frail, ever-weakening body as Mom slips into a coma. I am the sparkling tear that runs down her stiff face as the words of a friend's letter roll out. I am the disbelief of everyone as the news reaches us that Mom has died. I am not the pounds of make-up that hide the painful expression on her cold, still face, nor am I her whole shell that lies in an open casket, but I am her spirit walking somewhere about the room. I am the sorrow of all as the casket is being lowered into the ground. I was my mother, I am her spirit.

Second Boy:

I'm still glad I knew how sick she was because even if it didn't make it that much easier, it did give me a chance to make the most of the time we had left. I got very close to my mother that last year. Before she was sick, she always used to want me to go hiking with her and do things with her and I never did because—I hate to say it, but—who wants to do something with a mother, especially if you're a boy and your friends are saying, "Oh, c'mon Dave, let's go bike-riding or skiing, or whatever"? It's hard to do something with your mother because they're stick-in-the-mud old fogeys. And the sad thing is that I didn't realize what it would be like *not* to be able to do something with her if I wanted to until after she couldn't do things like that. Actually, I did go hiking with her a couple of times before I knew she had cancer. We went across some of the White Mountains and we climbed Mount Madison. I had started doing more things with her because I realized I too would become an old-fogey stick-in-the-mud myself one day. But when she got sick, I guess I got closer to her because I paid more attention to her. I realized she wouldn't be around to be ignored.

SOURCE: J. Krementz, *How it feels when a parent dies.* New York: Knopf, 1982.

traumas that chronic illness can engender (Hobbs & Perrin, 1985; Hobbs, Perrin, & Ireys, 1985).

Research conducted with diabetic adolescents and their families serves to exemplify the difficulties that a chronic illness can impose (Hauser et al., 1985; Powers et al., 1985). In addition to the physical pain, diabetic adolescents must often undergo periodic separations from family and friends and experience a

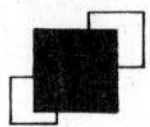

14.7 Adolescent Voices

Adolescents' Views of Death

A young girl of my community was murdered. She was murdered six months ago. The police are having a difficult time figuring out the killer. The feeling that is in the air at school, in town, and even in my own home is unreal. It is a creepy feeling.

Sometimes I wonder if the killer is sitting next to me in class or if he is passing me on the streets. The girl died in a way that I hope no one ever has to again. I hope and pray for her and her family. I know that I cannot bring her back, but maybe my prayers will help others. *(Jeri Parvin, 17, Mannford, Oklahoma)*

I remember the day "Phil" died. November 11, 1980 was a cold and windy day. I felt the coldness running through my blood as I began to realize that he was gone forever.

"'Phil' shot himself last night," I said to one of my friends, only half believing and half hearing the words I said. "He's gone." With those words as my stepping stone, I knew I would make it through, for that was the first time I had admitted what had happened to my best friend several hours earlier.

For weeks my thoughts wandered. I felt as though I was walking through each memory in my mind, seldom being able to return to reality. . . .

"Phil" has been gone for two years now. I still miss him very much. There are times I want him to come back so badly to help me through, but I know he is gone.

Many other people take death in such a way that it is hard for them to ever carry on. Life, of course, will be different without them, but a person never really dies if their memories live on in your heart. *(Michelle Skinner, 17, Lincoln, Nebraska)*

Death is a natural part of life. It is hard to accept sometimes, but I have learned to accept death. I experienced the death of a boyfriend in 1981. I really took it hard.

He was really too young, only 16. It made me a stronger person though. When someone close to you dies, it always takes a part of you. But the best thing to do is always remember the good times you shared with them. *(Cheryl Browder, 17, Winston-Salem, North Carolina)*.

I don't understand death, but I know it affects people when they are involved indirectly or directly. I wrote a poem to a friend of mine that was killed in a car accident. His name was Raschelle. I went to the wake and to the funeral. It was so weird seeing him lie in the coffin up at the front of the room.

I felt like all I had to do was close my eyes and he'd be alive again. I sometimes still go back to a classroom, where I had him in class, hoping he'll be sitting there, laughing and telling jokes.

Over this last Christmas vacation, I knew Raschelle was dead, but I said to myself, aloud, "I'm going to call Raschelle and wish him a very merry Christmas." I only said that to myself, knowing he was dead, because he was a friend I'll never forget. I wanted him to have a very merry Christmas, wherever he was. *(Christi Pennel, 17, Independence, Missouri)*

SOURCE: Glenbard East *Echo, Teenagers themselves.* New York: Adama Books, 1984, pp. 196–198.

feeling of isolation as a consequence of being different from their peers at a time in life when peer approval is particularly important to self-esteem. Not surprisingly, diabetic adolescents have often been found to feel more anxious and to be more dependent on their parents than their nondiabetic peers.

As might be expected, the diabetic adolescent's illness may require modifications in family activities and increased financial burdens. In caring for a diabetic child, parents have less time and energy for their careers, for interacting with their other offspring, and for their own recreational activities. Sadly, the family members may even experience social isolation from friends and neighbors who feel uncomfortable with the adolescent's chronic illness. Moreover, although unwarranted, the parents and siblings may experience strong feelings of guilt about their possible role in the development of the adolescent's disease.

Do you have any personal responsibility to the physically handicapped? Do we as a society?

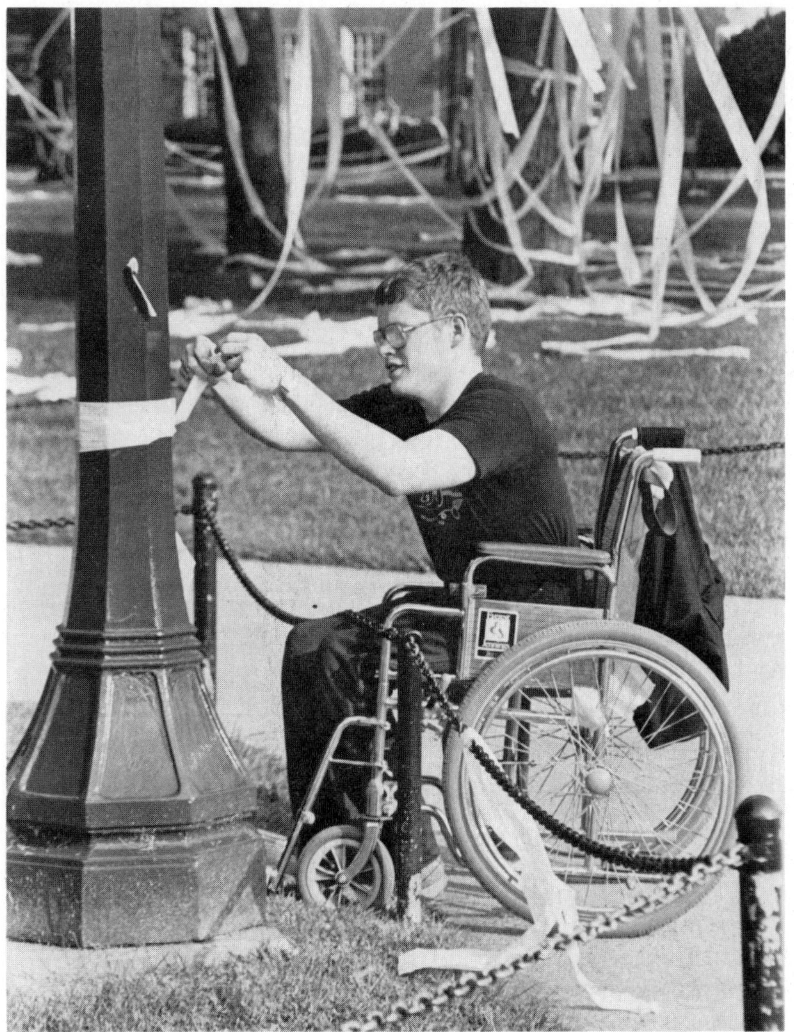

In coping with an adolescent's chronic illness, such as diabetes, a family can inevitably profit from the compassion of their friends and from assistance from teachers and counselors. As the concept of accommodating the special needs of chronically ill and physically handicapped students in society becomes more widely accepted, these adolescents and their families will hopefully be able to share the burdens of their special circumstance with their friends and fellow citizens.

Conclusion

In conjunction with the data presented in previous chapters, the statistics in the present chapter enable us to understand the extent to which specific types of problems affect the adolescents in our society. For example, we have seen that highly publicized problems such as anorexia nervosa and suicide affect a relatively small percentage of the adolescent population, in comparison to less sensational problems like cigarette smoking and teenage pregnancies. As Table 14.1 illustrates, thousands more adolescents lose their lives from traffic accidents caused by drunk driving and from the heart and lung diseases caused by cigarette smoking than from other kinds of drug abuse, which are scintillating enough to the public to make their way more frequently onto the covers of news magazines.

A second consideration in regard to the seriousness of various types of adolescent problems is the extent to which each problem affects the individual's future. In some cases, the long-term consequences of adolescents' problems are readily apparent. For example, irreversible physical injuries from a car accident clearly mar all the remaining years of an individual's life—a permanent price to be paid for the temporary pleasures of one night's careless drinking at the age of 15. Yet, in other cases, the lifelong impact of certain adolescent problems is less apparent. For example, the girl who, at the age of 14, lets her fantasies about motherhood and marriage determine her behavior may continue her unplanned pregnancy and marry her teenage boyfriend. The price that she, the child, and the teenaged husband most often pay includes lifelong educational and financial losses, a higher divorce risk and poorer physical health for mother and child. In sum, before too quickly judging certain teenage problems as unimportant in relation to others, we might assess both the number of adolescents being affected and the less apparent, lifelong consequences, such as a shortened lifespan or permanent financial losses.

Given the limited financial resources that local and federal governments have for preventing or responding to adolescents' problems, it is understandable why controversy continues to surround such questions as: Should the money be allocated to programs for preventing teenage pregnancies? Since teenage suicide rates have risen so dramatically in recent years, should taxpayers' money be rechanneled from antidrug-abuse programs into programs for the prevention of suicide? Unfortunately, no simple solutions exist for deciding how to allocate a society's limited financial and human resources among those in need of such assistance.

Nevertheless, on a more optimistic note, one way to assist adolescents with the types of problems discussed throughout this text is to foster better communication and to employ the kinds of intervention strategies that require little or no money. Hence, the following chapter is designed to introduce you to the types of communication and the kinds of strategies that have often succeeded in alleviating the problems of troubled youths. Fortunately, many of these approaches can be implemented without inordinate amounts of funding and without years of formal psychological training—a motivating and uplifting note for those of us committed to diminishing the problems that many adolescents confront.

Questions for Discussion and Review

Basic Concepts and Terminology

Cite the conclusions from specific research studies or national statistics to support your answers to each of the following:

1. In what ways are male and female delinquents alike and different?
2. In what ways do the methodological difficulties limit our understanding of delinquency and suicide?
3. How do each of the following affect delinquency: gender, age, race, socioeconomic class, family and peer relationships, self-esteem, and academic success?
4. Given the existing data, which adolescents are most likely to attempt suicide?
5. What factors place adolescents at the greatest risk of developing anorexic or bulimic behavior?
6. How are adolescents who run away from home different from those who don't? How do runaways differ from one another and what factors may increase the likelihood of an adolescent's becoming a runaway?
7. In what ways do the issues of death and dying affect adolescents?
8. How do the advocates of Kübler-Ross's beliefs on dying and death education defend their position?
9. What kinds of approaches have been suggested for diminishing the rates of suicide, delinquency, and eating disorders among adolescents?
10. Reexamining the problems of adolescence that have been discussed in the first 14 chapters of this text, how would you compare them quantitatively in terms of the number of young people being affected by each? Which appear to be the most frequent, the most severe, and the most profound in terms of their consequences for an individual's adult development?

Questions for Discussion and Debate

1. How do you believe juvenile delinquents should be dealt with by the juvenile justice system? Should the treatment of male and female delinquents differ? What kinds of training do you think members of the juvenile justice system need to cope most successfully with delinquents?
2. What stereotypes about delinquents and suicidal youth did you previously endorse, which this chapter has dispelled?
3. How has suicide personally affected your life or the life of one of your friends?

4. How do you feel about the legal and moral aspects of euthansia? adolescents' writing their own wills? parental control over adolescents' medical treatment for terminal diseases? the Boston Children's Museum's exhibit on death?
5. What creates the most discomfort for you in reading the section of this chapter on death and dying? Why?
6. How were the topics of death, dying, and suicide treated in your school and in your family during your adolescence? What benefits might accrue to both the adolescent and the society if death education were to become more widespread?
7. If you were in charge of creating a school program to discourage anorexic or bulimic behavior, how would you design it?
8. As a parent or a teacher, how would you try to help an adolescent who had expressed suicidal thoughts?

REFERENCES

Adler, F. *Sisters in crime: The rise of the new female criminal.* New York: McGraw-Hill, 1975.

American Psychiatric Association. *Diagnostic and statistical manual of mental disorders* (3d ed.). Washington, D.C.: American Psychiatric Association, 1980, p. 71.

Anolik, S. Family influences upon delinquency: Biosocial and psychosocial perspectives. *Adolescence,* 1983, *18,* 487–498.

Balk, D. *Sibling death during adolescence: Self-concept and bereavement reactions.* Unpublished manuscript, University of Illinois, Champaign, 1982.

Barrueta-Clement, J., Schweinhart, L., Barnett, W., Epstein, A., & Weikart, D. *Changed lives.* Ypsilanti, Mich.: High Scope, 1984.

Berlin, I. *Suicide among American Indian adolescents.* Washington, D.C.: National American Indian Courts Judges ASsociation, March 1984.

Bernhart, G., & Praeger, S. *After suicides: Meeting the needs of the survivors.* Washington, D.C: American Personnel and Guidance Association, 1983.

Blaine, G. *Is adolescent suicide preventable?* Chicago: American Association of Adolescent Psychiatry, 1979.

Blakely, C., & Davidson, W. Behavioral approaches to delinquency: A review. In P. Karoly and J. Steffen (eds.), *Adolescent behavior disorders.* Lexington, Mass.: Heath, 1984. Pp. 241–283.

Braithwaite, J. The myth of social class and criminality reconsidered. *American Sociological Review,* 1981, *46,* 36–57.

Brennan, T., Huizinga, D., & Elliot, D. *The social psychology of runaways.* Lexington, Mass.: Lexington Books, 1978.

Bruch, H. *The golden cage: The enigma of anorexia nervosa.* Cambridge, Mass.: Harvard University Press, 1978.

Bryant, R., & Bates B. Anorexia nervosa: Aetiological theories and treatment methods. *Journal of Adolescence,* 1985, *8,* 93–103.

Bynner, J., O'Malley, P., & Bachman, J. Self-esteem and delinquency revisited. *Journal of Youth and Adolescence,* 1981, *10,* 407–441.

Calhoun, G. Comparison of delinquents and nondelinquents in ethnicity, ordinal position and self-perception. *Journal of Clinical Psychology,* 1984, *40,* 323–328.

Chartier, G., & Ranieri, D. Adolescent depression: Concepts, treatments, prevention. In

P. Karoly and J. Steffen (eds.), *Adolescent behavior disorders.* Lexington, Mass.: Lexington Books, 1984. Pp. 153–195.

Chase, A., Crowley, C., & Weintraub, M. Treating the throwaway child. *Social Casework,* 1979, *60,* 538–546.

Children's Defense Fund. *Children in adult jails.* Washington D.C.: Children's Defense Fund, 1976.

Children learn that dying isn't a vacation. *New York Times,* August 26, 1984.

Colen, B. *Karen Ann Quinlan: Dying in the age of eternal life.* New York: Nash Publishing, 1976.

Consortium for Longitudinal Studies. *As the twig is bent: Lasting effects of pre-school programs.* Hillsdale, N.J.: Erlbaum, 1983.

Elliot, D., & Ageton, S. Reconciling race and class differences in self-reported and official estimates of delinquency. *American Sociological Review,* 1980, *45,* 95–110.

Elliot, D., Huizinga, D., & Ageton, S. *Explaining delinquency and drug use.* Boulder, Col.: Behavioral Research Institute, 1982.

Ellis, P. Empathy: A factor in antisocial behavior. *Journal of Abnormal Child Psychology,* 1982, *10,* 123–134.

Emery, P. Adolescent depression and suicide. *Adolescence,* 1983, *18,* 245–257.

Farnworth, M. Family structure, family attributes and delinquency in a sample of low income minority males and females. *Journal of Youth and Adolescence,* 1984, *19,* 349–364.

Farrington, D. Delinquency prevention in the 1980s. *Journal of Adolescence,* 1985, *8,* 3–16.

Federal Bureau of Investigation. *Crime in the United States.* Wasington, D.C.: Federal Bureau of Investigation, 1984.

Flaherty, M. The national incidence of juvenile suicide in adult jails and juvenile detention centers. *Suicide and Life Threatening Behavior,* 1983, *16,* 85–94.

Folkenberg, J. Preventative legislation. *Psychology Today,* 1984, *18,* 9.

Forehand, R., & Faust, J. Accuracy of weight perception among young adolescent girls. *Journal of Early Adolescence,* 1985, *5,* 239–245.

Gaffney, L. A multiple choice test to measure social skills in delinquent and nondelinquent adolescent girls. *Journal of Consulting and Clincial Psychology,* 1984, *52,* 911–912.

Gagne, E. Educating delinquents: A review of research. *Journal of Special Education,* 1977, *11,* 13–27.

Garfinkle, P., & Garner, D. *Anorexia nervosa: A multidimensional perspective.* New York: Brunner Mazel, 1982.

Gibbs, J. *Psychosocial factors associated with depression in urban adolescent females.* San Francisco: Western Psychological Association, April 1983.

Gilbert, E., & Deblassie, R. Anorexia nervosa: Adolescent starvation by choice. *Adolescence,* 1984, *19,* 839–846.

Gold, M., & Petronio, R. Delinquent behavior in adolescence. In J. Adelson (ed.), *Handbook of adolescent psychology.* New York: Wiley, 1980. Pp. 495–536.

Gold, M., & Reimer, D. *Changing patterns of delinquent behavior among American 13 to 16 year olds. National Survey of Youth, 1972.* Ann Arbor: Institute for Social Research, University of Michigan, 1974.

Gormally, J. The obese binge eater. In R. Hawkins, W. Fremouw, and P. Clement (eds.), *The binge-purge syndrome.* New York: Springer, 1984. Pp. 47–73.

Hamilton, K., Gelwick, B., & Meade, C. The definition and prevalence of bulimia. In

R. Hawkins, W. Fremouw, and P. Clements (eds.), *The binge-purge syndrome.* New York: Springer, 1984. Pp. 3–27.

Hauser, S., Vieyra, M., Jacobson, A., & Wertlieb, D. Vulnerability and resilience in adolescence. *Journal of Early Adolescence,* 1985, *5,* 81–100.

Hindelang, M., Hirschi, T., & Weis, J. Correlates of delinquency: The illusion of discrepancy between self-reports and official measures. *American Sociological Review,* 1979, *4,* 995–1014.

Hobbs, N., & Perrin, J. (eds.). *Issues in the care of children with chronic illness.* San Francisco: Jossey-Bass, 1985.

Hobbs, N., Perrin, J., & Ireys, H. *Chronically ill children and their families.* San Francisco: Jossey-Bass, 1985.

Holinger, P. Adolescent suicide: An epidemiological study of recent trends. *American Journal of Psychiatry,* 1978, *135,* 754–756.

Huesmann, L. Stability of aggression over time and generations. *Developmental Psychology,* 1984, *20,* 1120–1134.

Husain, S., & Vandiver, T. *Suicide in children and adolescents.* New York: SP Medical and Scientific Books, 1984.

Johnson, G., Bird, T., Little, J., & Beville, S. *Delinquency prevention: Theories and strategies.* Washington, D.C.: Office of Juvenile Justice and Delinquency Prevention, 1981.

Johnstone, J. Recruitment to a youth gang. *Youth and Society,* 1983, *14,* 281–300.

Jorgensen, S., Thornburg, H., & Williams, J. The experience of running away. *High School Journal,* 1980, *64,* 87–96.

Kaplan, H. *Self-attitudes and deviant behavior.* Pacific Palisades, Cal.: Goodyear, 1975.

Kirigin, K. Achievement place. In J. Stumphauzer (ed.), *Progress in behavior therapy with delinquents.* Springfield, Ill.: Thomas, 1979. Pp. 118–145.

Klas, G. *They need to know: How to teach children about death.* Englewood Cliffs, N.J.: Prentice-Hall, 1979.

Kratovsky, P. Child abuse and violence against the family. *Child Welfare,* 1982, *17,* 435–444.

Krementz, J. *How it feels when a parent dies.* New York: Knopf, 1982.

Kübler-Ross, E. *On death and dying.* New York: Macmillan, 1969.

Kübler-Ross, E. *On children and death.* New York: Macmillan, 1983.

Kushner, H. *When bad things happen to good people.* New York: Avon, 1981.

Lamb, M. (ed.). *The role of the father in child development.* New York: Wiley, 1981.

Learning disabilities: The link to deliquency. Washington, D.C.: Health, Education and Welfare Congressional Report, March 1977.

Long twilight comes to an end. *Newsweek,* June 24, 1985, p. 81.

McArnarney, E. Adolescent and young adult suicide in the United States. *Adolescence,* 1979, *14,* 765–774.

McCarthy, J., & Hoge, D. The dynamics of self-esteem and delinquency. *American Journal of Sociology,* 1984, *90,* 396–410.

McCord, J. *Adolescent mental health: Delinquency.* Washington, D.C.: Adminstration for Children, Youth and Families, 1982.

McKenry, P., Tishler, C., & Christman, K. Adolescent suicide and the classroom teacher. *Journal of School Health,* 1980, *50,* 130–132.

Mednick, S., & Christiansen, K. *Biosocial bases of criminal behavior.* New York: Gardner Press, 1977.

Miller, P. Female delinquency: Fact and fiction. In M. Sugar (ed.), *Female adolescent development.* New York: Brunner Mazel, 1979. Pp. 115–141.

Mullis, R., & Hanson, R. Perspective taking among offender and nonoffender youth. *Adolescence,* 1983, *18,* 831–836.

National Advisory Committee for Juvenile Justice and Delinquency Prevention. *Serious juvenile crime: A redirected federal effort.* Washington, D.C.: author, 1984.

Needle, J., & Stapleton, W. *Police handling of youth gangs: Reports of the National Juvenile Justice Assessment centers.* Sacramento, Cal.: American Justice Institute, September 1983.

Nye, F., & Edelbrock, C. Some social characteristics of runaways. *Journal of Family Issues,* 1980, *1,* 165–188.

Offer, D., Marohn, R., & Ostrov, E. *The psychological world of the juvenile delinquent.* New York: Basic Books, 1979.

Olson, L., Liebow, E., Mannino, E., & Shore, M. Runaway children twelve years later. *Journal of Family Issues,* 1980, *1,* 165–188.

O'Malley, P., & Bachman, J. Self-esteem and education. *Journal of Personality and Social Psychology,* 1979, *37,* 1153–1159.

Orton, J., & Soll, S. Runaway children and their families. *Journal of Family Issues,* 1980, *1,* 249–261.

Paperney, D., & Deisher, R. Maltreatment of adolescents: The relationship to a predisposition toward violent behavior and delinquency. *Adolescence,* 1983, *18,* 499–506.

Patterson, G. *Coercive family processes.* Eugene, Ore.: Castala Publishing, 1981.

Penner, M. The role of selected health problems in the causation of juvenile delinquency. *Adolescence,* 1982, *17,* 347–368.

Piazza, E. Measuring severity and change in anorexia nervosa. *Adolescence,* Summer 1983, 293–305.

Pihl, R., & McLarnon, L. Learning disabled children as adolescents. *Journal of Learning Disabilities,* 1984, *17,* 96–100.

Powell, C. *Adolescence and the right to die: Issues of autonomy, competence and paternalism.* Washington, D.C.: American Psychological Association, August 1982.

Powers, S., Dill, D., Hauser, S., Noam, G., & Jacobson, A. Coping strategies of families of seriously ill adolescents. *Journal of Early Adolescence,* 1985, *5,* 101–113.

Prescott, P. *The child savers.* New York: Knopf, 1981.

Quay, H. Classification in the treatment of delinquency and antisocial behavior. In N. Hobbs (ed.), *Issues in the classification of children.* San Francisco: Jossey-Bass, 1975. Pp. 377–392.

Rabkin, B. *Growing up dead: A hard look at why adolescents commit suicide.* Nashville, Tenn.: Abingdon, 1979.

Rich, P. The juvenile justice system and its treatment of the juvenile. *Adolescence,* 1982, *17,* 141–152.

Roberts, A. Adolescent runaways in suburbia: A new typology. *Adolescence,* 1982, *17,* 386–396.

Romeo, F. Adolescence, sexual conflict and anorexia nervosa. *Adolescence,* 1984, *19,* 551–555.

Rosenbaum, A. *The young people's yellow pages: A national sourcebook for youth.* New York: Putnam, 1983.

Rosenberg, R., & Rosenberg, M. Self-esteem and delinquency. *Journal of Youth and Adolescence,* 1978, *7,* 279–291.

Rutter, M., and Giller, H. *Juvenile delinquency: Trends and perspectives.* Baltimore, Md.: Penguin, 1983.

Schvaneveldt, J. Developing and implementing death education in high schools. *High School Journal,* 1982, *65,* 189–197.

Schwarz, J. Childhood origins of psychopathology. *American Psychologist,* 1979, *34,* 879–885.

Schweinhart, L., &. Weikart, D. *Young children grow up.* Ypsilanti, Mich.: High Scope, 1980.

Sechrest, L., White, S., & Brown, E. (eds.). *The rehabilitation of criminal offenders.* National Research Council Report. Washington, D.C.: National Academy of Sciences, 1979.

Thornton, W. Gender traits and delinquency involvement of boys and girls. *Adolescence,* 1982, *17,* 749–768.

Truckenmiller, J. Delinquency, bread and books. *Behavioral Disorders,* 1982, *20,* 82–85.

Tugend, A. Researchers begin to examine youth suicide as a national problem. *Education Today,* October 31, 1984, p. 11–12.

Turkington, C. Support urged for children in mourning. *American Psychological Association Monitor,* December 1984, pp. 16–17.

U.S. Bureau of the Census. *Statistical abstract of the United States.* Washington, D.C.: U.S. Government Printing Office, 1984.

VanThorre, M., & Vogel, F. The presence of bulimia in high school females. *Adolescence,* 1985, *20,* 45–51.

Walker, B., & Mehr, M. Adolescent suicide—a family crisis: A model for effective intervention by family therapist. *Adolescence,* 1983, *8,* 286–292.

Wass, H., & Corr, C. *Helping children cope with death: Guidelines and resources.* New York: Hemisphere, 1984.

Weiner, I. Psychopathology in adolescence. In J. Adelson (ed.), *Handbook of adolescent psychology.* New York: Wiley, 1980.

Weiner, I. *Child and adolescent psychopathology.* New York: Wiley, 1982.

Weld, E. Seeing death as part of life. *Boston Globe,* October 3, 1984.

Weller, L., & Luchtarhand, E. Family relationships of problem and promising youth. *Adolescence,* 1983, *18,* 93–100.

Williams, E. Adolescent loneliness. *Adolescence,* 1983, *18,* 51–65.

Wilson, T. Toward the understanding and treatment of binge eating. In R. Hawkins, W. Fremouw, and P. Clement (eds.), *The binge-purge syndrome.* New York: Springer, 1984. Pp. 264–292.

Wooden, K. *Weeping in the playtime of others.* New York: McGraw-Hill, 1976.

Chapter Outline

Goals and Objectives

When you have finished studying this chapter, you should be able to:

- *Demonstrate verbal skills involved in active listening*
- *Explain the importance of behavioral statements in communicating with adolescents*
- *Interpret a conversation in accord with the principles of transactional analysis*
- *Design a written contingency contract for an adolescent*
- *Describe how rational emotive therapy can be used in communicating with adolescents*

Concepts and Terminology

unconditional positive regard
active listening
contingency contracting
behavioral statements
transactional analysis
TA games
reality therapy
rational emotive therapy
intrinsic rewards
extrinsic rewards

15 Communicating with Adolescents

Throughout this text we have explored many of the problems confronting adolescents in our contemporary society. Although strategies for counseling and for communicating with adolescents have been integrated into each chapter, an extensive explanation of any single approach to counseling, teaching, or parenting is beyond the scope of an introductory text in adolescent psychology. Thus, this final chapter is intended only as a brief introduction to several of the most prevalent strategies for communicating with and for modifying the behavior of adolescents. As this chapter's references demonstrate, there are available a number of books that elaborate upon the general principles introduced in the following pages. Hopefully, after reading this chapter, you will elect to pursue additional information through these bibliographic sources. Collectively, they provide the detailed explanations and the empirical research related to each strategy.

Active Listening

On the basis of the views of the phenomenologists whose concepts of self-actualization were examined in Chapter 4, a number of theorists have developed models for training professional counselors to listen effectively to their clients. Undoubtedly two of the most renowned educators and theorists in this domain are Carl Rogers (1961) and Richard Carkuff (1969). Their suggestions are seen by many to be applicable to any adult trying to communicate with adolescents. The basic premise underlying the Rogers and Carkuff models of communication is that warmth, openness, and genuineness are crucial to establishing rapport with adolescents. According to this viewpoint, the effectiveness of any therapeutic method is undermined without these components of verbal communication.

Fortunately, both Rogers and Carkuff agree that these communication skills can be learned by parents and teachers as well as by professional therapists.

The first step in establishing effective communication is to accept the adolescent with what is referred to by these theorists as **unconditional positive regard.** What this requires is that rather than assuming a critical, judgmental, or authoritarian attitude, we are to converse with the adolescent from a more empathic posture. Indeed, authoritarian behaviors such as advising, directing, urging, forbidding, warning, moralizing, or commanding are seen to impede discourse and to serve as obstacles to effective communication. For example, at 2 a.m. frightened parents may confront their daughter coming in the front door with an accusatory statement about her whereabouts, rather than stating their fears to her and asking her for an explanation. This response represents an authoritarian posture. In contrast to this reaction, Carkuff and Rogers believe we must master the skills of *active listening.*

The first step in active listening is to rephrase or reflect the youngster's statements: "If I understand you correctly, you're feeling that your dad and I are being unfair to you by staying awake until 2 a.m. to talk to you, and this makes you feel both sad and angry." The second step is clarifying: "Do you mean that you feel angry because you don't think we trust you enough to go to bed even though you're not home? I'm not really sure what the source of your anger and sadness is, so can you explain it to me?" The third step is to acknowledge the youngster's perspective even though it may differ from our own: "I can understand that from your viewpoint our staying up until you came home seems foolish and unnecessary." And the final step is an exchange of feelings and perspectives: "Now let me tell you my feelings and my perspective about tonight. Let me start by telling you how afraid I was, because I love you so much, and then let me tell you why I feel angry at you."

According to the Carkuff and Rogers models of effective communication, active listening demands more than simply comprehending the meaning of the speaker's words. Empathetic, active listening involves interpreting the speaker's nonverbal gestures—his or her facial expressions, breathing, eye movements, tone of voice, and posture. When these nonverbal messages contradict the adolescent's verbal statements, the active listener elicits more information before accepting the youngster's verbal comments for their literal meaning. So, for example, if an adolescent is scowling, slumped over in her chair, and taking shallow breaths while saying that she isn't upset about being suspended from school, the counselor might respond: "I sense that there's really a part of you that doesn't agree with what you've just said to me. Would you like to tell me a little more about how you're feeling?"

Another important component of these models of communication is that both the adult and the adolescent "own their feelings." Often a therapist may hear an adolescent's parent and the adolescent expressing their feelings in the guise of aggressive, critical statements leveled against someone else. For example, the parent standing at the door at 2 a.m., when her daughter walks in, may yell, "Where have you been? Why are you so immature and irresponsible? Don't you have any respect for me?" And the adolescent may retort: "You're unreasonable and you treat me like a 2-year-old! Get off my back!" When people are taught to express their sentiments in terms of their feelings by using "I" messages, which avoid blaming the other person, the exchange is altered considerably: "I have been waiting for you since midnight because I was so afraid that something terrible had happened to you, and I could feel my heart sinking into my stomach as the hours passed. I even had a terrible vision of your lying alongside the road in an overturned car. Then I started to get angry at you for not phoning to let me know that you were safe somewhere." These "I" messages avoid putting the other person on the defensive.

The exercise in Box 15.1 exemplifies the types of responses considered appropriate and inappropriate in terms of the principles espoused by phenomenological counselors like Carkuff, Maslow (1968), and Rogers. All three of these theorists believe that we can learn to listen actively and that the development of active listening is a crucial skill in communicating effectively with adolescents.

BEHAVIORAL LANGUAGE

A number of therapeutic models for helping adolescents depend upon our ability to communicate by using behavioral terminology. **Behavioral statements** rely exclusively on words that represent observable, measurable behavior, rather than referring to aspects of the adolescent's character or to vague generalities like "attitudes" and "will power." From this perspective, the most efficient way to bring about behavior changes in adolescents is to state our compliments, our criticisms, and our expectations in behavioral terms (Goldstein, Sprafkin, & Gershaw, 1981; Goodwin & Coates, 1976; Nielsen, 1982; Zastrow, 1979).

The purpose of a behavioral statement is to identify the specific behavior that is being criticized, praised, or desired. For example, instead of saying, "I want you to improve your attitude here around the house, young man," we would specify the particular behavior we want changed: "I want you to empty the garbage at least three times a week without my nagging you." Likewise, if we want to maintain an adolescent's behavior through praise, our compliments should be stated in behavioral terms rather than in vague generalities: "I really feel happy when I see that you have taken the garbage out and cleaned your room three times this week without my having to remind you at all," instead of "I like your new attitude here around the house." Box 15.2 exemplifies the differences between behavioral and nonbehavioral statements.

Behavioral language can also be invaluable in designing strategies for improving unpleasant situations that arise in the adolescent's life. For example, assume we have an adolescent client who is constantly complaining about the "unfair treatment" she's receiving from her math teacher, an interaction that is causing her to feel depressed and frustrated. We could ask our client any number of questions intended to identify the specific behaviors underlying her frustration and the specific behaviors that would remedy the situation: What does your teacher actually do that makes you feel she doesn't like you? Describe her behavior to me in detail during the last incident when you felt unliked. How are you behaving when the teacher does or doesn't seem to like you? How do the students she likes behave in class? How do you think you would have to change your behavior in order to make her like you?

Teaching adolescents to use behavioral statements in their own language facilitates communication and enhances the effectiveness of certain kinds of

A Closer Look 15.1

Active Listening and Empathetic Communication

Which of the following exchanges with an adolescent represent the principles of active, empathetic communication espoused by phenomenological theorists like Carl Rogers, Abraham Maslow, and Richard Carkuff?

1. *Client:* I really don't want to go back into that class because I know that teacher hates me.
   Counselor: You seem really worried about interacting with this teacher and I can understand that must make you reluctant to stay in the class. Can you tell me what the teacher does that makes you feel she doesn't like you?
2. *Daughter:* I had a terrible day at school with that big math test and all.
   Mom: You really shouldn't be so negative about school all the time. Life is hard, you know, and you really have it good.
3. *Son:* I couldn't help it, Dad. I just didn't see the post and I backed the car right into it.
   Dad: Why don't you watch where you're going? Do you have to be so irresponsible?
4. *Student:* I guess I need to talk to you about my grade, Mr. Snodgrass. I don't seem to be doing so hot.
   Teacher: I can tell you're feeling pretty tense about this, and it must have been hard for you to muster the courage to come in to talk.
5. *Father:* I feel angry when you promise to do your household chores without my nagging you and then you go out with your friends all weekend without doing a single chore.
6. *Teacher:* You make me mad when you don't come to class because it shows what an irresponsible person you are.
7. *Client:* My boss is on my back all the time and I want to quit that job before it gets worse.
   Therapist: What I seem to hear you saying is that you're feeling frustrated and confused right now about your relationship with your boss and you're not sure how to make things better without quitting the job.
8. *Adolescent boy:* I'm just not cut out for any sport. I try because I want to be popular and I know I ought to get in better shape, but it just seems too useless.
   Adult friend: Well, give it a while and everything will work out.
9. *Adolescent girl:* You just don't seem to appreciate anything I do for you and I can't seem to do anything right anymore.
   Adult friend: You don't make me feel very good about myself either, as a matter of fact. I've been wondering what's gotten into you lately.

Answers: 1, 4, 5, and 7 represent active, empathetic listening skills. The other statements represent an inattentive, critical, judgmental, or authoritarian attitude toward the adolescent.

15.2 A Closer Look

Behavioral and Nonbehavioral Communication

Which of the following statements is using behavioral terminology to communicate a message?

Statements about Adolescents:

1. Susan has no will power or self-discipline at home or at school.
2. That boy just isn't cooperative.
3. This student demonstrates an attitude that bothers me by wearing a hat in class and by never getting here on time.
4. Why can't my son get along with his brother?
5. I really want the whole team to be able to run eight consecutive laps before the end of the semester.
6. George and I have an argument every time I ask him to babysit for his younger sister.
7. Young people today don't respect their elders.
8. I can't be happy unless he cleans up his room without my nagging.
9. I keep telling him to read at least 30 minutes a night, but he won't.

Statements by Adolescents:

10. I'm just an aggressive person, so what you're asking is almost impossible for me, you see?
11. I have to learn to speak up in class when I don't understand the material, or I'm going to fail. Can you help me?
12. Shyness just runs in my family.
13. I seem to have an attitude problem, don't I?
14. I'm going to have to do something to make myself run laps after school, or I'll never get in shape before the season starts.
15. I want to be able to talk to my sister without our yelling at each other.

Answers: Statements 3, 5, 6, 8, 9, 11, 14, and 15 are using behavioral terminology. The underlined words in each statement indicate either behavioral or nonbehavioral terms. For example, in number 12 the term "shyness" would have to be changed to a phrase indicating specific behaviors in order to qualify as a behavioral statement: "Everybody in my family seems unable to speak up in a group of more than two people."

behavioral therapy. Adolescents who learn to express their frustrations and to identify their needs in behavioral terms can more effectively set goals for themselves, alter their interactions with other people, and avoid catastrophizing events in ways that make them seem impossible to remedy (Glasser, 1965; Mahoney & Thoresen, 1974; Nielsen, 1982; Williams & Long, 1982).

Transactional Analysis

Another approach frequently employed by counselors to enhance communication between adolescents and adults is **transactional analysis** (Ernst, 1972; Freed, 1976; Woolams & Brown, 1979). Transactional Analysis, commonly referred to as "TA", is a model for analyzing verbal communication that categorizes all our statements as representing the perspective of either the "child," the "adult," or the "parent" within us. Statements representing a child's perspective merely impart emotion and are typically impulsive and self-serving. In contrast, statements representing the parent within us are typically reprimanding, restrictive, authoritarian, and judgmental. They are intended to invoke feelings of guilt and shame. According to the TA model, the statements most conducive to productive communication are those that come from the perspective of the adult within us. These statements are rational, nonjudgmental, and nonmanipulative, in the sense that they represent honest feelings and reasonable expectations. The comments in Box 15.3 demonstrate an analysis of conversations according to the principles of transactional analysis.

In addition to providing a scheme by which to analyze conversations, transactional analysis also teaches adults and adolescents to recognize the "games" we play with each other during communication. According to TA, a *game* is an exchange in which one person is verbally manipulating the other into a predictable and inescapable position, rather than communicating in an honest manner about the real problem. A game is an attempt to evade personal responsibility by casting the burden onto another person. For example, in the game entitled "Uproar," the adolescent stockpiles all of the real or imagined insults she believes her teacher has been sending her. When she collects enough of these insults she feels justified in creating an uproar in front of the whole class, during which she enumerates all the injustices perpetrated against her.

Similarly, in the game entitled "Make Me," the student tries to force the adult into an adversary position by complaining, "You just don't like me and that's why I'm making a D in here." The teacher can refuse to play the game by saying, "If you choose to make a passing grade in here, you may do the following things. If you choose to do otherwise, that is totally your right and your responsibility. I'm not here to force you to do things against your will." For those who would appreciate a more complete description, the games that adolescents typically play are comically yet candidly described in the books *Transactional Analysis for Teens* and *Games Students Play* (Freed, 1976; Ernst, 1972).

By combining the suggestions of those who advocate empathetic, active listening, transactional analysis, and behavioral terminology, therapists, parents, and teachers have been able to improve their communications with adolescents. Although effective communication is not a panacea that can replace other forms of therapy, it is certainly an essential beginning in relating to adolescents as we function in both our professional and personal roles.

Behavioral Contracting

In terms of providing specific methods for improving our communication with adolescents, the behavioral and social learning models have been among

15.3 A Closer Look

Transactional Analysis: A Model for More Effective Communication

According to the principles of transactional analysis, all comments in a conversation can be categorized according to one of three perspectives: that of a child, of a parent, or of an adult. How would you classify each of the following statements—As that of the child, the parent, or the adult within the speaker?

1. My parents don't love me because they make me come home so early and don't give me much allowance.
2. I'm your father and as long as I pay the bills, you'll do exactly as I say without needing to know the whys and wherefores!
3. This assignment is frustrating me and is making me feel stupid. Can you show me how to do it?
4. I'm fed up with your behavior and your brother's and I don't intend to discuss any of this with you, so get out of here!
5. You know that your behavior is wrong and you are violating the principles of the school.
6. You ought to feel ashamed of yourself, young man!
7. What you've done makes me very angry, and we need to sit down and discuss the situation to devise some sort of remedy.
8. Nothing ever goes right for me, and I just don't see any need of trying anymore!
9. I can't believe you did that, given all we've done for you all these years.
10. Let's talk about this after we both calm down.

Answers:

Spoken from the perspective of a child who is impulsive, irrational, emotional, and self-centered: 1, 4, 8.

Spoken from the perspective of a parent who is critical, judgmental, threatening, authoritarian, and guilt-producing: 2, 5, 6, 9.

Spoken from the perspective of an adult who is rational, candid, and emotionally expressive, yet nonaccusatory: 3, 7, 10.

the most popular and most empirically successful (Bandura, 1977). These behavioral approaches for improving communication are based on the principles of behavioral and social learning theories discussed in several previous chapters. In brief, this perspective contends that an adolescent's negative self-judgments and emotions, such as depression or anxiety, can best be alleviated through systematically altering the rewards, punishments, setting events, and models in the environment. Hence, the best way to help adolescents in our professional or personal roles is to utilize the principles of behavioral psychology. Furthermore, the behavioral view contends that self-control is a learned skill that involves applying the principles of behavioral psychology to one's own life. This means that we can teach adolescents the principles of behavioral psychology and thereby give them the skills of self-management and self-control.

Reality Therapy

One of the more popular approaches to behavior contracting and to improving communications with adolescents is William Glasser's (1965) *Reality Therapy.* Originally designed during his work with delinquents, Glasser's principles have been successfully used with adolescents in public schools, detention centers, and special education classes. Basically, in **reality therapy** the adult functions as a guide and discusses a series of prescribed questions with the adolescent: (1) What are you doing? This question demands a description in behavioral terms of the problematic behavior. (2) How is your behavior helping you? (3) Since in some cases the adolescent's behavior is harming other people but not the self, the next question is often necessary: How is your behavior helping other people—your family, your classmates, your girlfriend? (4) What plan can you and I devise to remedy this situation? (5) Will you commit yourself to this plan? (6) Will you check back with me in a week to reevaluate this behavioral plan so we can determine whether it is remedying the problem?

The purpose of communicating through reality therapy contracts is to clarify each person's expectations of and promises to the other. In an effort to avoid misunderstanding and to prevent future arguments, the contract serves as an important vehicle in communication between adolescents and adults. The contract agreed to between the adolescent and the adult guide may be either verbal or written; but Glasser recommends written contracts, so that misunderstandings will be minimized. Although the contract may take a variety of forms, the guidelines suggested in Table 15.1 insure that both the adolescent and the adults involved will understand the contingencies clearly from the outset.

Contingency Contracts

Although Glasser's reality therapy represents one form of contracting, another option referred to as **contingency contracts** has repeatedly demonstrated its success in improving adolescents' behavior in both home and school settings. Contingency contracts have improved communication between adolescents and adults and modified adolescents' unacceptable behavior. Moreover, contracting has proven itself successful with delinquents, retarded youths, and learning-disabled students, as well as with normal adolescents (Blackham & Silberman, 1975; Homme, 1976; Jones, 1980; Mahoney & Thoresen, 1974; Nielsen, 1982; Ramp & Semb, 1975; Stumphauzer, 1973; Williams & Long, 1982).

As you recall from Chapter 7, a contingency contract specifies the behavioral goals toward which the adolescent is working, as well as the daily system of rewards and punishments for each day's progress toward the ultimate goal. Thus, contingency contracts are excellent means through which to communicate our expectations to adolescents and to specify each person's commitments, without relying on forms of communication that can later be misconstrued.

Table 15.1 serves as a summary of the recommendations presented in Chapter 7 for designing contingency contracts most effectively. In conjunction with studying Box 15.2, rereading Box 7.6 would provide a thorough review of the concepts and terminology involved in contingency contracting.

Contracts have advantages seldom found in other communication strategies. Because contracting requires people to be specific and candid with each other throughout their discussion, disputes are less likely to arise over issues like discriminatory treatment and truthfulness. Most adults have an unwritten contract of sorts etched inside their heads during their conversations with adolescents. Contingency contracts are methodical ways to transfer these plans into public, written form for the adolescent's benefit. Contracts also oblige adults who are confused about their objectives or who are communicating contradictory messages to adolescents to come to terms with these discrepancies and confusion. As Box 15.4 illustrates, contingency contracts can be designed to communicate with adolescents on academic, social, or familial issues. The contracts can be as elaborate or as simple as seems necessary for the adolescent's particular needs.

Contracting is especially beneficial when communicating with adolescents who are not motivated by internal or **intrinsic rewards.** When an activity is not intrinsically pleasurable, people must rely on external or **extrinsic rewards** to motivate themselves to continue. For example, society gives us external rewards for our work by offering paychecks, promotions, or special awards such as "best salesperson of the month." These external rewards often motivate us to com-

Table 15.1
Self-Management Contracting Checklist

In helping adolescents learn to create their own self-management programs, we can use the following statements as guidelines for writing effective contingency contracts:

1. State your goal in behavioral terms.
2. Choose only one goal at a time to work toward.
3. Allow yourself ample time to achieve your goal.
4. Be certain you possess the skills necessary to achieve your goal.
5. Choose a goal that is within your power to control and not one that is dependent upon changes in other people.
6. Determine your daily rewards and punishments.
7. Record your behavior daily.
8. Reward yourself for accomplishing goals on a daily basis.
9. Arrange the physical environment to help you reach your goal.
10. Increase your goal very gradually at the end of each week.
11. Do not choose the most difficult problem in your life as your first self-management project.
12. Provide role models for yourself, even if these are just characters in a book you can read.
13. Get someone to help you design your self-management contract who knows your skills and can help you set reasonable goals for each day.
14. Arrange to have friends reward you for your progress each day.
15. Talk to others who have succeeded in meeting goals similar to yours.
16. Rehearse your new skill first in the presence of people you trust.

SOURCE: L. Nielsen, *How to motivate adolescents*. Englewood Cliffs, N.J.: Prentice-Hall, 1982.

A Closer Look 15.4 

Contingency Contracts for Adolescents

As a method for enhancing our communications with adolescents, contingency contracts provide candor, structure, and clarity regarding people's expectations and agreements. Contracts diminish the likelihood of misinterpretation, miscommunication, and disharmony that result from verbal agreements between adolescents and adults. Contracts can vary in terms of their goal, their simplicity, or their format. Although some adolescents are capable of communicating responsively through verbal contracts, others need written contracts that specify the expectations and contingencies. In situations where the adolescent's conduct is extremely disruptive or represents a long-standing pattern of behavior, written contracts with detailed explanations and daily recording are particularly useful in diminishing conflict and assuring clear communication. The books by Goldstein, Goodwin, Homme, and Williams, listed in this chapter's references, offer excellent suggestions for designing contracts with adolescents and for teaching adolescents how to design their own self-management contracts. The following contracts are representative of the alternatives available to those who opt to try contracts for improving communication or for altering their own behavior through self-management projects.

Contract between Teacher and Student:

Points I Earned Today					*Maximum Possible*		*Activity*
Mon.	Tues.	Wed.	Th.	Fri	Daily	Weekly	
2	0	2	2	0	2	10	Attending class
5	0	3	3	0	5	25	Completing the assigned work in class
3	0	3	3	0	3	15	Turning in last night's homework assignment
			5			5	Making fewer than two mistakes on the weekly quiz

My weekly total: 31 Total: 55

Weekly totals will be recorded in the teacher's gradebook as follows:
50–55 points = A; 45–50 points = B; 40–45 points = C; 35–40 points = D.

Contract between Parent and Child:

If Susan (1) makes up her bed each morning this week without being reminded, (2) babysits with baby Joey for three hours during the week without complaining, and (3) washes the dishes after two dinners, Mom will (a) let her have the car for four hours on the weekend without complaining, (b) let her have an extra hour on Friday or Saturday night's curfew, and (c) refrain from nagging or reminding her about these three chores.

Signed: ____________ Mom ____________ Susan ____________ Date: 3/21/87 plete tasks that are less pleasurable and less appealing than other alternatives—like sleeping late or watching television instead of getting up on a rainy Monday morning to go to a dreary job. Contracts also expedite the accurate sending and receiving of messages with adolescents who—intentionally or unintentionally—tend to misunderstand or forget what has been communicated to them. In sum, contracts between adolescents and adults are meant to serve the same purposes as contracts between employers and employees in terms of facilitating communication and avoiding misunderstandings.

RATIONAL EMOTIVE THERAPY

Our attempts to communicate with adolescents may reveal that a young person's feelings and judgments are being based on illogical thinking or on data that do not coincide with the actual facts. For example, a student can be convinced that a teacher is singling her out for discriminatory treatment, even though objective observers note that she is being treated just like other students. Another student may be firm in her conviction that nothing in her own behavior could possibly improve any of her grades at school. Trying to communicate with an adolescent who is basing his or her behavior on irrational thinking or erroneous data becomes a frustrating exchange wherein our advice will be dismissed and our perceptions ignored.

One approach that has proven effective in helping people reexamine the data on which they are basing their feelings and judgments is **rational emotive therapy.** Developed by Albert Ellis (1977) during his work as a psychoanalyst, rational emotive therapy is predicated on the assumption that many emotional disturbances result from illogical thinking. Unconsciously some individuals indoctrinate themselves repeatedly with negative, irrational "self-talk" that governs their behavior. The task of rational emotive therapy is to make individuals aware of the covert messages they are sending themselves and to confront them with the irrationality of the messages.

According to Ellis, many neurotic people believe illogical thoughts, such as "It is essential that a person be loved and approved of by everyone"; "There is always a solution to every problem and unless it is found, the results will be catastrophic"; "I must be perfectly adequate and competent at all times or people will not like me." The first task is to identify these internal messages. Once the counselor has helped an adolescent identify his or her particular self-talk, the task of replacing the old messages with new ones begins. The objective is to replace the debilitating, irrational messages with self-talk that is more consistent with reality and reason.

In the cleverly illustrated and witty book, *Talk to Yourself,* the principles of rational emotive therapy are presented to adolescents in comprehensible terms (Zastrow, 1979). Among the book's suggestions for reexamining the logic of one's self-talk is to look for objective evidence that supports or refutes one's beliefs. For example, the adolescent is instructed to write down one of his or her self-talk statements: "Doing homework is a waste of time because it doesn't help me pass the course." Then he or she must write the thought as a testable hypothesis: "My belief that doing homework is a waste of time is true if most people in this class who did their homework still fail tomorrow's test, but false if most people who did their homework pass the test."

Another technique suggested for adolescents by these authors is to write "counter cards." On a small card the adolescent writes the irrational thought, followed by three or four rational statements that counteract it. For example, "The coach hates me and forces me to do things nobody else has to do" might be followed by these countering statements: "The coach did give me a compliment last week, which isn't compatible with my idea that she hates me. The coach does make everyone run laps, not just me, which is inconsistent with the belief that she is singling me out for unkind treatment." The techniques employed in rational emotive therapy can enhance communication between adults and adolescents by requiring that they both reexamine the logic of the covert messages they are sending to themselves. Methods based on rational emotive therapy are being used effectively by teachers, parents, and counselors to help adolescents gain more control over their own irrational feelings and behavior (Bernard, 1984).

ADOLESCENTS' OWN VOICES

In our efforts to establish rapport with and understand adolescents, we too often rely exclusively on empirical research from limited samples of the entire adolescent population. While the empirical approach undoubtedly offers certain advantages, as was discussed in the previous chapter, it nonetheless obscures the value of a different kind of data—information from adolescents about themselves.

In an apocryphal story about the limits of empirical investigations and sophisticated methods for gathering data, a psychology professor asks her class of graduate students, "What is your most reliable and valid method for determining whether or not a woman is homosexual?" The students respond enthusiastically: "With projective tests." "With a psychological profile." "With an intensive investigation of her past." And the grinning professor answers, "No. Just ask her." In a similar vein, a joke on the erroneous assumptions we sometimes make on the basis of seemingly infallible statistics asks, "Did you hear about the six-foot man who couldn't swim and drowned because he confidently tried to cross a stream that a statistician told him had 'an average' depth of four feet?" Both stories are intended to underscore the fact that statistics and sophisticated psychometric techniques can lead to misinterpretations about adolescents.

Without disregarding the information gleaned from descriptive and experimental research, we can expand our understanding of adolescents by venturing into another domain—books written by adolescents and books whose authors recount stories in adolescents' own words. One advantage of this approach is that it permits us more detailed views of the lives of adolescents, whose personal stories are overlooked in empirical research. Both descriptive and experimental research present data on groups of adolescents, rather than detailing the personal experiences of any single individual. The poignancy, humor, and wisdom often revealed through an individual adolescent's own poetry, commentary, or essay is thus lost to us in the process of averaging scores and sampling large groups—much like the six-foot man who drowns in a stream whose average depth is only four feet, but whose deepest water is obviously well above the six-foot mark! A second advantage of studying stories and commentary from adolescents themselves is that the perspective of the adult researcher does not overshadow the young person's language or vision. As a consequence, there is less likelihood that the researcher's self-fulfilling prophecies are confounding our conclusions about adolescents.

The number of books containing writings by adolescents is still rather limited. Although excerpts from several of these books have been included in previous chapters, their titles and topics bear repeating as a reminder of their value to students and practitioners of adolescent psychology. As a continuing source of the current topics most affecting the young, Chicago's *New Expression* magazine provides new stories and information of relevance to both young and old. Written and published by adolescents, the newspaper is the largest teen newspaper in the nation. In addition to the benefits that accrue to the adolescents on the staff, the newspaper's readers profit from the fact that teenage reporters gain access to information from other adolescents, which would otherwise be inaccessible to adults. For example, among *New Expression*'s recent headlines are "Teen Alcoholics Break Out of the Bottle"; "Bisexuality: Breaking Out of the School Closet"; "Will Teens from Divorced Families Self-Destruct?"; and "Tables Turned: Males Expose Their Side of Sex Issues" (*New Expression,* 1986).

Publications such as *New Expression* are testimony to the fact that adolescent writers are willing to tackle issues that are both controversial and emotion

What writings, speeches, or artistic creations of adolescents have most impressed you?

laden. Adolescents at the Fayerweather Street School in Cambridge, Massachusetts, have written two books under the direction of their teacher, Eric Rofes. The first, *The Kids' Book of Divorce,* presents stories of children's and adolescents' reactions to their parents' divorce (Rofes, 1982). The second, *The Kids' Book about Death and Dying,* reflects these adolescents' interviews with parents, children, hospice workers, veterinarians, funeral directors, cemetery workers, religious leaders, and medical personnel (Rofes, 1985). In the process of writing their book, these adolescents visited hospitals, funeral homes, graveyards, and heath-care centers. The result is a text that treats such topics as reincarnation, the death of a pet, funeral customs, and immortality with a poignancy and candor that equal those of many adult books on death and dying.

Also written by adolescents for a teenaged audience, *Teenagers Themselves* offers cartoons, short stories, interviews, and poetry by young people across the nation (Glenbard East *Echo,* 1984). The adolescents on the staff of the *Echo* at Glenbard East High School in Lombard, Illinois, gathered responses to a number of open-ended questions over the period of a year. Choosing the best cartoons and writings from nearly 9,000 responses from every state in the nation, the student writers and editors developed a 20-chapter text that includes such topics as religion, interracial dating, work, honesty, violence, death, prejudice, drinking, and drugs. Written by and for adolescents, it presents an insightful glimpse of the many facets of adolescence in our contemporary society.

In a similar vein, *Changing Bodies, Changing Lives* offers a number of comments and stories from adolescents about their views and experiences regarding relationships with parents and peers (Bell, 1980). In their efforts to create a book for adolescents on sex and relationships, the adult authors interviewed hundreds of young people from various socioeconomic, racial, and religious backgrounds. The stories and commentaries represent the views of homosexuals and heterosexuals, of males and females, of younger and older adolescents, and of those with liberal and conservative perspectives on social and sexual issues. The authors state that their two main goals are to give adolescents accurate information about sex and physical development and to give them the opportunity to learn about other adolescents' experiences and feelings.

Other adult authors have dedicated themselves to interviewing adolescents and transcribing the conversations into texts. Among these are *How It Feels When a Parent Dies* (Krementz, 1983), in which adolescents and children have recounted their feelings about their confrontation with death; and *Growing up Dead,* in which young people who have attempted suicide express their feelings and experiences (Rabkin, 1979). In a different vein, *The Me Nobody Knows* (Joseph, 1969) offers essays and poetry written by young residents of New York's ghettos, and *Whose Child Cries* recounts the concerns of adolescents with gay parents (Gantz, 1983).

In regard to adolescents' vocational experiences, nonfiction books are scarce. One valuable source, however, is *Working Kids on Working,* in which 25 children between the ages of 9 and 15 describe their work experiences (Cole, 1980). Similar in many ways to Studs Terkel's (1972) portraits of adult workers whom he interviewed across the country for his book, *Working,* Cole's book poignantly presents the stories of adolescents working in situations far removed from the suburbs and the fast-food restaurants.

In contrast, nonfiction by adolescents is more available on the topics of teenage pregnancy and parenthood. Representing this category of books are three particularly noteworthy recent works. *Deep Blue Funk* is a collection of stories about black adolescents' experiences as mothers and fathers, which captures both the dialect and the emotional fervor of these young parents. Above all, this book distinguishes itself for its portrayals of teenage fathers, a group that is typically excluded from both the empirical and the nonfictional literature on pregnancy and parenting (Frank, 1983). In a somewhat different vein, *It Won't Happen to Me* recounts the author's interviews with pregnant adolescent girls and with professionals who work with teenage mothers (McGuire, 1983). Perhaps most dramatic, however, is an adolescent girl's own autobiography based on excerpts from her journal during her pregnancy and first year of motherhood—*The Magic Washing Machine* (Slapin, 1983).

These citations are not intended as an exhaustive list of the nonfiction presently available, which either transcribe conversations with adolescents or which rely on adolescents' own writing. They are presented as a representation of the types of recent publications now available, which rely on adolescents' own expressions and subjective viewpoints. By acquainting ourselves with these more personalized sources of information, we expand our views of adolescents and enhance our abilities to communicate and to empathize with a clearer vision. Inevitably such books deepen our insights in ways that statistics alone cannot.

Conclusion

To reiterate, the suggestions offered in this chapter for improving our communication with adolescents and for helping adolescents modify certain dimensions of their behavior are not intended as an exhaustive presentation of contemporary therapies. Nor has the chapter been designed primarily as a presentation of the empirical literature supporting the various therapeutic approaches. Hopefully, however, the chapter has achieved several other independent purposes.

First, the fact that the techniques cited have been demonstrated empirically effective in altering adolescents' behavior undermines the skeptic's assertion that "nothing can be done with today's adolescents." To the contrary, we are in the fortunate position of having myriad techniques at our disposal for alleviating many of the problems that contemporary adolescents most frequently encounter. The problem is not so much that we lack the methods for improving communication or for helping adolescents change certain aspects of their behavior. The greater problem is that we have not disseminated the available information to most parents or to adults who are interacting with adolescents in a professional capacity.

Second, the data in this chapter should not be construed to mean that there is a panacea for every possible problem that an adolescent in today's society might confront. Such a sanguine view would be both spurious and foolhardy. Moreover, to assert unequivocally that "where there's a will, there's a way" is to invoke feelings of guilt in cases where beleaguered parents and professionals are indeed unable to alleviate the problems of an adolescent whom they love. Unquestionably, some adolescents are besieged with problems of such a serious nature that not even the most-skilled professionals or most-loving parents can eliminate their pain or suffering. In addition, the absence of data in regard to the etiology of certain adolescent disturbances, such as schizophrenia, chronic delinquency, and suicide, impedes the development of effective therapeutic approaches or preventive measures.

While recognizing that such extreme situations do exist, it is nonetheless essential to remember that only a minority of adolescents are afflicted by problems of such a serious nature—a message underscored repeatedly by the data cited in Chapter 14. Thus, adults who invest time developing their skills in relatively simple techniques, such as contingency contracting and rational emotive therapy, should take heart in the fact that these techniques do help. In this regard, a third purpose of the present chapter has been to avoid arguing exclusively on behalf of any single type of therapy or communication technique. The empirical data at present simply do not warrant our adopting any single approach to the exclusion of all others. More important, it is doubtful that any formula will ever be applicable to all adolescents regardless of their sex, race, age, socioeconomic background, intelligence, and idiosyncratic personalities.

In concluding a chapter on communication, as well as in concluding a text on adolescence, one final dilemma presents itself: How are we to decide when to offer the young our guidance—perhaps even our dictates and our restrictions—and when are we to respect their own perspectives and judgments? On the one hand, it seems wise to recognize that older people should not impose themselves on the young in ways that preclude youth's fresh, new visions and perspectives. As aptly phrased by the poet, Kahlil Gibran (1968, p. 18):

> Your children are not your children.
> They are the sons and daughters of Life's longing for itself.
> They come through you but not from you,
> And though they are with you, yet they belong not to you.
> You may give them your love but not your thoughts.
> For they have their own thoughts.
> You may house their bodies but not their souls,
> For their souls dwell in the house of tomorrow, which you
> cannot visit, not even in your dreams.

Yet, on the other hand, how are the young to profit from the mistakes of their elders, if not through instruction? Is it not a waste of youth's precious time and energy—perhaps even a risk of putting oneself in physical jeopardy—to be deprived of the advice of elders? Thus, one 16-year-old black male from the ghetto speaks (Frank, 1983, p. 152):

> "Now take this ol' cat, will you," he says, as he leans forward and points to a large color photograph of an elderly Navajo shepherd. "Would you look at his hands. Now those are some man's hands, all right. They've got some wisdom in 'em. You can see his whole accumulated life experience right there, in all them craggly ol' wrinkles." He places a finger on the photographed hands. His young hands, like his feet, seem disproportionately large for his small but solid frame. "Old people, man. You know, we've gotta stop trashing them. They've got a lot they can teach us. I bet this old Indian here had someone to show him how to do things so he could feel like somebody. I remember in school this teacher tellin' us how the Indians really prepared their kids for manhood and womanhood. It was hard work, probably, you know, goin'

> through all them rituals and all, but at least those kids always knew there was a place for 'em and that there was somebody who was gonna help them get there. I tell ya, man, guidance. That's what it's all about, guidance."

How are we to balance our desire to respect the integrity of the young with our desire to offer counsel that we hope will spare them some of our own youthful pain and frustration? Prior to adolescence this question is moot, since children's physical and emotional dependence on us is necessitated by their cognitive and physiological limitations. Consequently, we are spared the doubt that our counsel is of value to young children. In contrast, an adolescent's cognitive and physiological abilities make possible a considerable degree of independence from adults. Thus, during a child's adolescence, we are left in a quandary, wondering when to accede to the young person's own judgments and when to impose restrictions based on our greater experience.

Considering the advice reflected in Gibran's poem and in the 16-year-old male's comments, it seems wisest to embrace both perspectives, in part, rather than to feel forced into choosing between the two. In offering our counsel, can we not also permit adolescents to select their own course in situations where learning to exercise independent judgments is of greater value than making a remediable mistake? And can we not simultaneously consider it an act of respect

If you could ask only one question to people over the age of 60, what would you ask? If you could develop a close friendship with a person at least 30 years older than yourself, whom would you choose and why?

for the young to impose our decisions on them in situations where an error in their judgment would wreak irremediable harm? Hopefully, the answer to both is yes, for in so doing, we will be tendering the protective guidance that the young male desires from the old, wrinkled Indian, while still aknowledging the wisdom and integrity that the young so often harbor within them.

Questions for Discussion and Review

Basic Concepts and Terminology

1. According to the models of Rogers and Carkuff, what specific skills enhance communication with adolescents?
2. In what ways can behavioral language facilitate communication?
3. How do the principles of transactional analysis explain the miscommunication that often occurs in conversation?
4. In helping adolescents design contingency contracts, what criteria can be applied to increase the likelihood of the contract's success?
5. Employing the tenets of rational emotive therapy, how can adolescents be helped to interpret their experiences more rationally and less subjectively?
6. What advantages might accrue to adults who read materials produced by adolescents themselves, rather than those that rely on empirical data?

Questions for Discussion and Debate

1. How could active listening skills and behavioral contracting have facilitated communication between you and your parents during your adolescence? In answering this question, recount a specific incident between you and your parents as it actually occurred, and then as it might have been improved.
2. How could you respond to each of the adolescent's statements in Box 15.1 in a way that demonstrates active listening skills?
3. What do you see as the advantages and disadvantages of reality therapy and transactional analysis in communicating with adolescents?
4. How could you convert each nonbehavioral statement in Box 15.2 into a behavioral comment?
5. If you were given the power and the money to create three new community services for youths, what kinds of organizations would you establish? Why?
6. What writings by adolescents have affected you most profoundly and why? With whom have you shared your feelings concerning these writings?

REFERENCES

Bandura, A. *Social learning theory.* Englewood Cliffs, N.J.: Prentice-Hall, 1977.

Bell, R. *Changing bodies, changing lives: A book for teens on sex and relationships.* New York: Random House, 1980.

Bernard, M. *Rational emotive therapy with children and adolescents.* New York: Wiley, 1984.

Berne, E. *Games people play: Theories of transactional analysis.* New York: Grove Press, 1964.

Blackham, G., & Silberman, A. *Modification of child and adolescent behavior.* Belmont, Cal.: Wadsworth, 1975.

Cole, S. *Working kids on working.* New York: Lothrop, Lee and Shepard Books, 1980.

Carkuff, R. *Helping and human relations.* New York: Holt, Rinehart and Winston, 1969.

Ellis, A. Rational emotive therapy: Research data that support the clinical and personality hypothesis of RET and other methods of cognitive behavior therapy. *Counseling Psychologist,* 1977, *7,* 2–42.

Ernst, K. *Games students play.* Milbrae, Cal.: Celestial Arts, 1972.

Frank, D. *Deep blue funk and other stories: Portraits of teenage parents.* Chicago: Ounce of Prevention Fund, 1983.

Freed, A. *Transactional analysis for teens and other warm important people.* Sacramento, Cal.: Jalmar Press, 1976.

Gantz, J. *Whose child cries: Children of gay parents talk about their lives.* Rolling Hills Estates, Cal.: Jalmar Press, 1983.

Gibran, K. *The prophet.* New York: Knopf, 1968.

Glenbard East *Echo. Teenagers themselves.* New York: Adama Books, 1984.

Glasser, W. *Reality therapy.* New York: Harper & Row, 1965.

Goldstein, A., Sprafkin, R., & Gershaw, J. *I know what's wrong but I don't know what to do about it.* Englewood Cliffs, N.J.: Prentice-Hall, 1981.

Goodwin, D., & Coates, T. *Helping students help themselves: How you can put behavior analysis into action in your classroom.* Englewood Cliffs, N.J.: Prentice-Hall, 1976.

Homme, L. *How to use contingency contracting in the classroom.* Champaign, Ill.: Research Press, 1976.

Jones, V. *Adolescents with behavior problems.* Boston: Allyn and Bacon, 1980.

Joseph, S. (ed.). *The me nobody knows: Children's voices from the ghetto.* New York: Discus Books, 1969.

Krementz, J. (ed.). *How it feels when a parent dies.* New York: Knopf, 1983.

Mahoney, M., & Thoresen, C. (eds.). *Self-control: Power to the person.* Monterey, Cal.: Brooks/Cole, 1974.

Maslow, A. *Toward a psychology of being.* New York: Van Nostrand, 1968.

McGuire, P. *It won't happen to me: Teenagers talk about pregnancy.* New York: Delacorte, 1983.

New Expression: Magazine of Youth Communication. 207 South Wabash, Chicago: 1986.

Nielsen, L. *How to motivate adolescents: A guide for parents, teachers and counselors.* Englewood Cliffs, N.J.: Prentice-Hall, 1982.

Rabkin, B. *Growing up dead: A hard look at why adolescents commit suicide.* Nashville, Tenn.: Abingdon Press, 1979.

Ramp, G., & Semb, G. (eds.). *Behavior analysis: Areas of research and application.* Englewood Cliffs, N.J.: Prentice-Hall, 1975.

Rofes, E. (ed.). *The kids' book of divorce: By and for kids.* Boston: Little, Brown, 1982.

Rofes, E. (ed.). *The kids' book about death and dying: By and for kids.* Boston: Little, Brown, 1985.

Rogers, C. *On becoming a person.* Boston: Houghton Mifflin, 1961.

Slapin, B. *The magic washing machine: A diary of single motherhood.* Mesquite, Tex.: Ide House, 1983.

Stumphauzer, J. (ed.). *Behavior therapy with delinquents.* Springfield, Ill.: Thomas, 1973.

Terkel, S. *Working.* New York: Avon Books, 1972.

Williams, R., & Long, J. *Toward a self-managed lifestyle.* Boston: Houghton Mifflin, 1982.

Woolams, S., & Brown, M. *The total handbook of transactional analysis.* Englewood Cliffs, N.J.: Prentice-Hall, 1979.

Zastrow, C. *Talk to yourself: Using the power of self-talk.* Englewood Cliffs, N.J.: Prentice-Hall, 1979.

Glossary

acculturation The process by which people learn the assumptions, beliefs, and behavior of a culture, either as children growing up in a certain culture or as adults moving from one culture to another.

achieved identity Adopting one's own roles and values after having first experimented with and examined various ideologies and alternatives during adolescence.

adipose tissue The body's fat tissue.

AIDS Acquired Immune Deficiency Syndrome—A sexually transmitted virus that eventually kills its victims by destroying the immune system.

amphetamines Commonly known as "uppers" or "speed"; addictive drugs that can be lethal when consumed with alcohol.

amenorrhea The cessation of the menstrual period.

androgyny The combination of both masculine and feminine characteristics or behavior within an individual.

angel dust *see* PCP

anglicized Adoption by a minority of the norms and values of white, middle-class society.

anomie A societal condition in which people become confused about their role in society and about their personal identity, as a consequence of rapidly changing societal norms.

anorexia nervosa A psychological disorder typically restricted to adolescent girls, in which compulsive dieting becomes a health hazard, sometimes resulting in death by starvation.

anovulatory A menstrual cycle in which the ovaries do not release an egg, therefore making conception impossible.

assimilation Piaget's term for the ways in which children integrate new experiences into their existing cognitive framework and give meaning to the new data.

atherosclerosis The partial or complete blockage of arteries in the body as a result of fat deposits from unhealthy diets.

authoritarian style A style of parenting in which adults dictate to and control their children in a dictatorial rather than a democratic fashion.

authoritative style A style of parenting that combines nurturance, honest communication, and democratic decision making with parental supervision, the enforcement of prescribed rules, and the administration of punishment when necessary.

barbiturates Depressant drugs, known commonly as "downers," which lower blood pressure and slow respiration as they create a feeling of relaxation.

bar mitzvah A Jewish religious ceremony for young adolescent males, which follows a year's training in the Hebrew language and in Jewish teachings under the direction of a rabbi.

bat mitzvah The equivalent of a bar mitzvah for Jewish females.

basal metabolism rate The rate at which the body converts calories from food into sugar for the energy necessary to keep the body alive and mobile.

baseline behavior The measurement of a person's or an animal's behavior in its natural state, before any therapeutic intervention occurs.

behaviorism A school of psychology that examines only observable behavior and that rejects the notion that mental processes can be used to explain human behavior. *See also* Skinnerian psychology *and* operant conditioning.

BIA Bureau of Indian Affairs.

biosocial theories Theories that contend that human behavior is determined by the interaction between biological and environmental influences.

bisexual An individual who is sexually attracted to both sexes.

bulimia A psychological disorder characterized by binging on food and then regurgitating what has been eaten.

cannabis The plant from which marijuana is derived.

cervical sponge A newly developed contraceptive that prevents sperm from entering the uterus by covering the os and by exposing sperm to a spermicide.

chlamydia A sexually transmitted bacterial infection of the urethra and cervix, which can cause sterility and complications during birth and pregnancy in women.

chicano An American of Mexican descent

circumcision The surgical removal of the foreskin from the penis; typically performed several days after a male child's birth.

classical conditioning A form of learning by association, which involves pairing a "conditioned stimulus" (sound of a bell) with an "unconditioned stimulus" (food), thereby eliciting a "conditioned response" (salivation) to the conditioned stimulus, which is similar to the response once elicited by the unconditioned stimulus; developed by Pavlov in the early twentieth century.

cognitive dissonance Leon Festinger's theory, which states that if people try to maintain two inconsistent beliefs at the same time, or if a person's behavior is not in accord with his or her cognitions, an unpleasant feeling of tension arises, which the person is then motivated to eliminate.

cognitive theories Theories of psychology that oppose the behavioristic view that stimulus and response are directly linked, by arguing that human behavior involves the restructuring of knowledge by the brain.

cohort A group of people who have experienced the same event during the same interval of time, generally referring to people born at approximately the same time in history.

concrete operational stage In Piaget's theory, the level of cognitive ability typically occurring between the ages of 7 and 11, which precludes abstract thinking.

confluence theory The view that certain aspects of personality and behavior are determined by one's birth order and the number of children in a family.

confounding variables In experimental studies, factors other than the independent variable (the treatment), which might account for changes in the subjects' attitudes or behaviors as measured by the dependent variable.

contingency contracts Written agreements between individuals, which state goals in behavioral terms and which specify rewards and punishments for specific behaviors.

contracting *see* contingency contracts

convergent thinking Thinking along conventional lines in order to find the best single answer to a problem; in contrast to divergent thinking.

correlation coefficient *see* correlational study

correlational study A study in which two or more variables are compared to determine the strength of the relationship between them. The strength of a relationship is indicated by correlation coefficients, which range from .0 (no correlation) to +1.00 (perfect positive correlation) to −1.00 (perfect negative correlation).

cross-sectional design A research design in which subjects from two or more different age groups are measured at the same point in time.

cultural pluralism The belief that the uniqueness of various cultures within one society should be preserved, in contrast to the "melting pot" theory, which maintains that all cultures should become assimilated into one societal norm.

culture-free tests Psychological tests from which the influences of any particular cultural experiences have been eliminated in order that no racial or ethnic group will be discriminated against on the test.

defense mechanisms Freud's term for the ways in which the ego protects itself from threatening ideas or from external dangers: denial, projection, rationalization, reaction formation, regression, repression, and sublimation.

dependent variable In experimental research studies, the variable that depends upon the "treatment" or independent variable.

desensitization Sometimes referred to as "systematic desensitization"; a form of behavior therapy that helps a person overcome a fear by presenting the threatening stimuli in small doses and simultaneously teaching the client to relax.

diaphragm A rubber contraceptive device shaped like a shallow bowl, which prevents pregnancy by holding spermicide against the cervix.

diffused identity A state during which the adolescent has not adopted an identity and is not experimenting with various roles, values, and alternatives for the future.

divergent thinking Thinking that is creative and original in that it deviates from the obvious and produces several solutions to a particular problem, in contrast to convergent thinking.

Down's syndrome A form of congenital mental retardation due to genetic abnormality, which is typically characterized by certain facial characteristics like those of Asiatic people; hence, also the term "mongolism."

DSM *Diagnostic Manual of Mental Disorders*—The diagnostic reference book produced by the American Psychiatric Association.

dysmenorrhea Excessive physical pain during the menstrual period.

EAT test A written test for diagnosing anorexia and bulimia.

ectopic pregnancy A dangerous condition in which a fertilized egg implants itself in the walls of a Fallopian tube rather than in the uterine wall. If the egg is not surgically removed, a pregnant woman can die when the egg eventually bursts.

ectomorph One having a body structure that is tall and lean.

ego According to Freud, the part of the personality that attempts to balance the id's unconscious drives and the superego's restrictions; most closely aligned with external reality.

egocentrism As used by developmental psychologists, a nonperjorative term that describes a child's inability to adopt the perspective of other people, thereby limiting his or her ability to empathize with others.

Electra complex In Freudian theory, a daughter's unconscious desire to have sexual intercourse with her father.

endomorph One having a body structure that is short and stocky.

estrogen The hormone in male and in female bodies which, when produced in large enough quantities, causes the appearance of female secondary sex characteristics.

ethnocentrism The tendency to consider one's own group, particularly one's own ethnic group, as superior to all others, thereby making it impossible to assume the perspective or to appreciate the values of people from other groups.

external locus of control *see* locus of control

extinction The weakening of a particular behavior either by withholding reinforcement or by presenting the conditioned stimulus without the unconditioned stimulus.

extrinsic reinforcement Rewards that serve to motivate people, which are external to the activity itself.

field dependence The cognitive style in which people require more visual cues from the environment or "field" in order to orient themselves to new situations.

field independence The cognitive style in which people require fewer visual cues from their environment or "field" in order to orient themselves to new situations.

field theory The theory that assumes that human behavior is determined by the interaction of various environmental influences and internal variables, rather than by responses to the obvious stimuli occurring in any given moment.

formal operational stage According to Piaget, the fourth stage of cognitive development occurring during adolescence, in which children become capable of logical reasoning and abstract thinking.

foreclosed identity Prematurely adopting a social and vocational role and set of values without first experimenting with various ideologies and roles during adolescence.

free association A Freudian technique for discovering unconscious motives and conflicts that requires patients to express their thoughts and images without restraint or guidance, when presented with particular words or phrases, such as "my mother."

Gestalt psychology A type of field theory, formed in reaction against behaviorism, that contends that psychological phenomena are like "gestalts," which cannot simply be equated with the elements that appear to compose them. Thus, it is argued that human behavior cannot be understood through mere analysis of the variables that appear to be related to any particular action or attitude.

gonads The ovaries and the testes.

gonadotrophins The hormones released by the pituitary gland that cause the ovaries and the testes to release estrogen and androgen in greater supplies at the onset of puberty.

glans The rounded head of the penis.

haole A term used by native Hawaiians to refer to Hawaiians of white descent.

hashish "Hash," the most potent form of marijuana, gathered from the dark brown resin in high-quality cannabis plants.

hermaphrodite A person or animal with both male and female sex organs.

herpes A sexually transmitted virus that causes painful sores in the genital area or the mouth.

heuristic An idea, method of teaching, or theory that stimulates further thinking and discovery.

Hodgkin's disease A form of cancer affecting the nervous system.

hypothalamus The upper brain stem, which signals the pituitary gland to release the hormones that begin puberty.

id According to Freudian psychologists, the part of the personality that houses those unconscious drives that are most in touch with the biological nature of the body, such as sex and aggression.

identity statuses In Erikson's and Marcia's typology, the four types of identity that adolescents may adopt in the process of creating their adult identities and ideologies. *See* foreclosed, achieved, *and* diffused identity, *and* moratorium.

imaginary audience According to Elkind, the young adolescent's erroneous belief that he or she is continually being surveyed and assessed by other people.

independent variable In experimental studies, the factor (or factors) that remains constant throughout the study, such as the subject's sex or race. The independent variable is also known as the "treatment" that subjects receive in experimental studies.

individuation According to Freudian psychologists, the process of forming a more independent identity by examining and modifying the contents of the superego, particularly the values adopted in childhood from one's parents.

institutional discrimination Prejudiced behavior that results from conforming to the conventions of a society whose institutions discriminate against certain racial groups or against one sex.

instrumental conditioning *see* operant conditioning

internal locus of control *see* locus of control

intermittent reinforcement Rewarding a person or an animal intermittently rather than continuously for making correct responses; produces slower but more strongly established conditioning.

internalization Adopting the ideas or values of other people as one's own without being aware of their external origins.

intrinsic reinforcement Receiving pleasure internally for the completion of an act without having to receive external rewards in order to maintain the behavior.

inverse correlation A relationship between two or more variables in which an increase in one variable is associated with a decrease in the other.

IUD Intrauterine device—An object inserted into the uterus that acts as a contraceptive by preventing a fertilized egg from implanting itself in the uterine wall.

Klinefelter's syndrome A chromosomal abnormality in some males, which results in the failure to develop normal secondary sex characteristics during adolescence.

locus of control A concept first developed by Phares regarding an individual's beliefs about internal or external control. People who believe the events in their lives are controlled by their own behavior or characteristics are said to have an "internal locus of control." In contrast, people who believe that events in their lives are a function of luck, chance, fate, or other people are said to have an "external locus of control."

longitudinal study A study in which people from the same cohort group are measured on the same variables periodically over a period of years.

mainstreaming The federally mandated educational policy requiring that physically and mentally handicapped students be educated in regular classes with nonhandicapped students whenever feasible.

matriarchy A society or social group controlled by women, in contrast to a patriarchy, which is run by men.

mean A statistical term for the arithmetic average found by summing a group of numbers and dividing by the total number of items summed.

median A statistical term for the number that divides a group of scores in half, with half the scores falling above the median score and half below.

menorrhagia Excessively heavy menstrual bleeding.

mesomorph One having a body structure that is muscular, athletic, and neither too heavy nor too lean. Typically considered the most "desirable" structure for males in the United States.

monozygotic twins Identical twins who develop from the same fertilized egg, in contrast to dizygotic twins who develop from two eggs.

moratorium The state during which an adolescent is exploring various ideologies and roles as part of the process of forming an independent identity in the future.

MMPI Minnesota Multiphasic Personality Inventory—A paper-and-pencil test of 550 statements, to which the subject responds as being true or false about himself or herself. From the responses a "personality profile" is determined by the psychometrician.

nature-nurture question The debate over the relative influences of heredity and environment on human behavior.

neo-Freudians Advocates of Freud's theories, who have also adopted more recent modifications of psychoanalytic theory.

observational learning According to social learning theorists, learning that occurs through observing the behavior of others without receiving direct reinforcement.

Oedipus complex According to Freud, the unconscious sexual desire of a son for his mother and his consequent jealousy and hatred of his father.

operant conditioning A form of altering human or animal behavior that uses reinforcement and punishment to shape new behavior; introduced by B. F. Skinner.

operational definitions Concepts defined in terms of specific, observable behavior, operations, or techniques, from which empirically verifiable hypotheses can be constructed.

opiates Drugs derived from the poppy plant's opium, the most common being heroin and morphine.

organismic model Theories that attribute human behavior primarily to environmental influences rather than to biological or psychological forces within the individual.

os The small opening at the end of the uterus through which, unless covered by a diaphragm or cervical sponge, sperm will pass into the uterus, where fertilization can occur.

palinopia "Flashbacks" of a drug "trip," which can occur unexpectedly weeks or months after the actual use of a hallucinogen.

personal fable According to Elkind, the young adolescent's erroneous belief that he or she is immune from harm.

PCP Also called "angel dust"; a hallucinogenic drug that can produce sudden fits of violence and psychological disturbance.

PMS Premenstrual syndrome—An unusually dramatic shift in mood and behavior that in some women accompanies the hormonal changes prior to the onset of each menstrual period.

postconventional morality The third level of Kohlberg's theory of moral development, in which an individual's moral decisions are determined by an independently formulated code of ethical principles.

primary reinforcement According to behaviorists, objects or activities that motivate individuals because they satisfy biological needs, such as food and water, in contrast to secondary reinforcement.

projective techniques Methods for revealing a person's unconscious motivations, anxieties, and conflicts, which involve presenting stimuli onto which the respondent will supposedly project his or her unconscious thoughts. *See, for example,* TAT *and* Rorschach.

prostate gland The male gland that produces semen. Located near the base of the penis, this gland can be manually examined through the anal canal by a male himself or by his physician to check for cancer or other infections.

protein loading A way erroneously presumed to build muscle tissue by consuming foods high in protein.

psychoanalytic theory Theories that emphasize uncovering and understanding the unconscious motivations that underlie a person's behavior and attitudes; predicated upon the beliefs of Freud.

psychometrics Measuring psychological factors through various tests such as IQ tests or a locus-of-control inventory.

pseudostupidity Attributing complex motives to other people or being unable to make decisions; a consequence of the new cognitive abilities that occur during early adolescence.

Pygmalion effect *see* Rosenthal effect

Q-sort A technique for assessing personality traits, in which a person is given written statements on cards which he or she then sorts into stacks that represent characteristics of the "real" or "ideal" self.

random sample A sample of people in an experiment or a survey who possess similar characteristics to those people to whom the results are going to be generalized.

rational emotive therapy A form of therapy developed by Albert Ellis, in which clients are helped to examine the rationality or irrationality of the beliefs that underlie their behavior.

reality therapy A counseling technique devised by William Glasser through his work with adolescents, which is based upon contingency contracting and other principles of operant conditioning.

reinforcement, reinforcers Rewards that increase the likelihood that a person will repeat a particular behavior.

reliability The ability of a measuring device to yield consistent results over time.

Rogerian counseling A form of nondirective therapy developed by Carl Rogers, in which clients are encouraged to resolve their own problems by mobilizing their psychic resources through self-disclosures to a counselor.

Rorschach test A series of inkblots presented to subjects on a card; the most famous of all projective tests. On the basis of the subject's free associations with each inkblot, the therapist creates hypotheses about the subject's unconscious drives and personality.

Rosenthal effect A type of experimental bias or self-fulfilling prophecy in which individuals tend to behave as others expect them to behave, whether or not the expectations actually reflect reality.

schema The mental framework in which new experiences are integrated and digested; extensively used in Piaget's theories.

self-actualization According to Abraham Maslow, a desire that exists in psychologically healthy people to develop their capacities to their fullest.

self-fulfilling prophecy The idea that expectations about one's own or other people's behavior can lead to the expected behavior appearing. *See* Rosenthal effect

semantic differential A technique that asks the individual to rate a list of terms along dimensions like good-bad or active-passive as a way of assessing his or her feelings about particular concepts.

semen The fluid released from the penis during ejaculation, which contains both sperm and seminal fluids; not synonymous with "sperm."

sequential design A research design that permits a comparison of two different cohort groups by comparing data from at least two cross-sections of two longitudinal studies.

sex role The behavior and attitudes a society expects of a male or a female on the basis of gender.

sexism Stereotyping or discriminating on the basis of a person's gender.

Skinnerian psychology A term used synonymously with operant conditioning and behaviorism; named after the founder of radical behaviorism, B. F. Skinner.

social learning theory The view that human behavior is primarily the consequence of reinforcement and modeling, although cognitive variables such as the individual's expectations and selective perceptions influence his or her responses to external reinforcement.

sociobiology The study of the biological bases of human and animal behavior.

SOMPA System of Multicultural Pluralistic Assessment—A test that evaluates a child's intelligence by comparing individuals from the same ethnic groups and by measuring environmental variables that may affect a written IQ test score; developed by Jane Mercer.

stage theories Theories that contend that an individual's development occurs in distinct, progressive, invariant stages, each of which subsumes the preceding stages.

Stanford-Binet An intelligence test first developed by the French psychologist, Alfred Binet, and revised by L. M. Terman at Stanford University in 1916.

status offense A violation for which children can be legally prosecuted, but which would not be considered illegal if committed by an adult.

STD Sexually transmitted disease—A more contemporary term for VD (venereal disease), referring to the viruses, bacteria, yeasts, and lice that can be transmitted through sexual intercourse or foreplay.

superego According to Freud, the part of the personality that has internalized society's values and standards, particularly the attitudes of one's parents, and that is in conflict with the impulses of the id; the equivalent of a conscience.

systematic desensitization *see* desensitization

TA *see* transactional analysis

TAT Thematic Apperception Test—A projective technique containing ambiguous and vague drawings, usually of one or two human figures, about which the subject has to make up a story. The themes emerging from these stories are then used to diagnose the subject's emotional conflicts and unconscious motives.

testosterone The hormone in both males and females which, when released in large enough quantities, produces male secondary sex characteristics.

THC Tetrahydrocannabinol, the ingredient in the cannabis plant that creates the "high" of marijuana.

Third World Originally referring to the nonindustrialized nations of the world, a term that has come to refer to members of minority groups throughout the world who share poverty and discrimination in common; from the French *tier monde.*

Title IX The 1972 federal legislation mandating that no person in the United States shall be discriminated against or excluded from participating in federally funded programs on the basis of his or her sex.

token economy A procedure used in behavioral counseling or teaching, where tokens are used as rewards that can later be exchanged for something the individual desires, such as money, special privileges, or grades.

tokenism Allowing a member of a minority group into one's own group or into an institution as a way of demonstrating, often in response to legal mandates, a lack of prejudice; hence, the terms a "token Jew," a "token woman," or a "token black."

tracking The practice in U.S. schools of segregating students into separate classes on the basis of their placement in a college-preparatory, vocational, general, or special-education curriculum.

transactional analysis A theory of personality developed by Eric Berne, in which the personality is conceived of as an interrelationship between parent, adult, and child "ego-states," each of which has its own system of communicating and behaving.

Turner's syndrome A chromosomal abnormality in females that results in the failure to develop normal secondary sex characteristics during adolescence.

urethra The tube that transports urine and semen to the outside of the male body and that transports urine to the outside of the female body.

validity The ability of a test to measure accurately that which it claims to be measuring.

vas deferens The tubes which transport sperm from the testicles to the seminal vesicles for storage. As a contraceptive measure, these tubes are surgically severed in a vasectomy.

WAIS Wechsler Adult Intelligence Scale.

WISC Wechsler Intelligence Scale for Children—An intelligence test developed by David Wechsler in 1939, which relies less heavily on verbal skills than the Stanford-Binet.

CREDITS *(Continued from p. iv)*

Chapter 1 *pp. 6, 8, 9* The Bettman Archive, Inc. *p. 16* Ken Heymann

Chapter 2 *p. 35* Roy Schraer. *pp. 69, 76* Wake Forest University. *p. 73* Winston Salem Schools. *p. 81* Frank Carmines.

Chapter 3 *p. 91* New Expression Magazine. *p. 119* Wake Forest University.

Chapter 4 *p. 131* Wake Forest University. *pp. 133, 142, 147, 162, 171* © Ruth Anne Clarke, 1985.

Chapter 5 *p. 185* © Ruth Anne Clarke, 1985. *p. 199* Winston Salem Schools. *p. 210* Wake Forest University.

Chapter 6 *p. 262* Winston Salem Schools. *pp. 227, 245* © Ruth Anne Clarke, 1985.

Chapter 7 *p. 283* © Rick Friedman, Boston Public Schools, 1980. *p. 309* Photos courtesy of Paul Ribisi. *p. 292* Winston Salem Schools. *p. 316* Wake Forest University.

Chapter 8 *p. 333* Reprinted by permission of Paul Ribisi. *pp. 366, 385* Robert Beck. *pp. 350, 373* © Ruth Anne Clarke, 1985.

Chapter 9 *pp. 401, 409, 434* Wake Forest University.

Chapter 10 *pp. 455, 498* Wake Forest University. *p. 485* © Ruth Ann Clarke, 1985. *p. 505* Pharmacists' Planning Series.

Chapter 11 *p. 562* Photographs courtesy of the Foxfire Fund, Inc. *p. 523* Youth Communication/Chicago Center. *p. 541* North Carolina Schools of the Arts. *pp. 519, 530* Winston Salem Schools.

Chapter 12 *p. 573* Photograph by Janet Harris. *p. 571* Charles Richman. *p. 607* Bill Anderson from Monkmeyer Press Photo Service. *p. 611* Wake Forest University.

Chapter 13 *pp. 625, 629* © Margaret Thompson.

Chapter 14 *p. 699* Courtesy of Boston Children's Museum. *p. 703* James Allen Garrison. *p. 661* Joel Garden Photography. *p. 691* George S. Zimbel from Monkmeyer Press Photo Service

Chapter 15 *p. 713* Wake Forest University. *p. 730* New Expression Magazine.

Name Index

Subject Index